The Complete
Dictionary
of Sexology

The Complete Dictionary of Sexology

New Expanded Edition

Robert T. Francoeur
Editor-in-Chief

Martha Cornog, Timothy Perper, and
Norman A. Scherzer, Coeditors

CONTINUUM · NEW YORK

2-8-96

1995
The Continuum Publishing Company
370 Lexington Avenue, New York, NY 10017

Copyright © 1991 by Robert T. Francoeur, Timothy Perper, and Norman A. Scherzer
New material Copyright © 1995 by Robert T. Francoeur, Martha Cornog, Timothy Perper, and
Norman A. Scherzer

Printed in the United States of America

Library of Congress Cataloging-in-Publication Data

The complete dictionary of sexology / edited by Robert T. Francoeur
  Martha Cornog, Timothy Perper, and Norman A. Scherzer, coeditors. — New expanded ed.
    p.   cm.
  Enlarged ed. of: A Descriptive dictionary and atlas of sexology.
1991.
  Includes bibliographical references.
  ISBN 0-8264-0672-6 (pbk. : alk. paper)
  1. Sex—Dictionaries.   I. Francoeur, Robert T.   II. Perper, Timothy, 1939–
III. Cornog, Martha.   IV. Descriptive dictionary and atlas of sexology.
HQ9.C64   1995
306.7′03—dc20

94-21305
CIP

Contents

Preface

Robert T. Francoeur

Sexuality has always interested humans. In the era before our ancestors learned to write, their cave paintings and fertility statues, like the voluptuous Venus of Willendorf, testify to an early religious and philosophical fascination with anatomy, sex, and reproduction. The great empires of Babylonia, Sumer, Egypt, India, and China added creation myths that sought to explain the origin of differences between males and females, often with a bias in favor of the male. Egyptian papyruses document a medical interest in contraceptives. The early Hebrew writings reveal a natural approach to sex with a strong interest in sexual behavior and morality. Plato and Aristotle discussed the causes and merits of homosexuality, and Hippocrates, the Father of Medicine, made important discoveries about reproduction. Sappho wrote lesbian poetry on her Aegean island. Soranus, a Roman physician, wrote the first manual on contraception, and Galen developed the first coherent theory of sexuality. Most of this knowledge was lost for centuries after barbarians from the north destroyed the Roman Empire.

During the Dark Ages, Islamic physicians in the Middle East and North Africa preserved much of this knowledge and expanded it before bringing it back to Europe through Spain and Italy in the Middle Ages. While medieval theologians extolled the virtues of sexual abstinence, the troubadors of Provence sang of a new kind of romantic or courtly love. In the Renaissance, artists and scholars rediscovered the Greek interest in the human body. Detailed drawings made from direct observations and dissections replaced the unquestioned authority of Galen and Aristotle. Leonardo da Vinci's workbooks contain explicit and detailed sketches of sexual responses, intercourse, and fetal development based on careful observations. The pioneering dissections of cadavers by Fallopius, Bartholin, de Graaf, and other anatomists resulted in the discovery of internal sexual organs that still bear their names. Spallanzani and Leuvenhoek discovered and studied the sperm. Spallanzani even experimented with artificial insemination.

In the eighteenth century, physicians revived an ancient, devastating fear of sexuality and masturbation as a major cause of disease. At the same time, the voyages of Captain Cook and Captain Bougainville brought news of the sensuous cultures of the South Pacific to challenge the sexual repression then prevalent in Europe. Libertarian philosophers like Voltaire and Diderot brought to the French Revolution demands for legal reforms and greater sexual freedom. The English political economist Thomas Malthus warned of overpopulation and called for sexual restraint in 1798. The obvious failure of preaching "Just say no" to the peasants soon led courageous physicians like the American Charles Knowlton in 1832 to produce the first comprehensive manual of contraception since the days of Soranus. In the late 1800s, after Russian, German, and Austrian doctors developed a concept of sexual psychopathology, the Viennese psychiatrist Richard von Krafft-Ebing classified all the sexual deviations known at the time.

Finally, in the past century, the scientific study of sexuality blossomed. Early feminists launched campaigns to fight prostitution and at the same time discussed the separation of sexual relations and pleasure from reproduction. Sigmund Freud rejected the idea of sexual psychopathology and degeneracy, arguing instead that traumatic sexual experiences in childhood led to abnormal sexual behavior. He also raised the issue of children's and women's sexual interest. The practical research of Havelock Ellis, Iwan Block, and Magnus Hirshfeld laid the groundwork for a new discipline of *Sexualwissenschaft*, sexual science, or sexology. In 1906, Wasserman announced a test for syphilis; in 1910 Ehrlich and Hata discovered a cure for the disease. Marie Stopes and Margaret Sanger brought "birth control" to poor women in England and America. In 1926, Fleming discovered penicillin, opening the door to effective treatments for bacterial-caused venereal diseases.

In the 1920s and 1930s, Margaret Mead and Bronislaw Malinowski studied the sexual customs and development of Samoan, Trobriander, and other South Pacific cultures. No longer could Westerners claim their sexual ways and views were the only way and the most accurate view. Marxist Wilhelm Reich shocked Americans with his views of sexual orgasm and morality. In the 1940s, entomologist Alfred Kinsey turned his talents to studying American sexual mores. In the 1960s, William Masters and Virginia Johnson gave us detailed insights into the physiology of human sexual responses and created the first behavioral therapies for sexual dysfunctions.

In this brief history of sexology lies the origin and the rationale for this *Descriptive Dictionary and Atlas of Sexology*. The history of sexology encompasses philosophers, religious thinkers, Marxists, biologists, anatomists, artists, politicians, economists, explorers, social workers, entomologists, historians, psychiatrists, psychologists, anthropologists, sociologists, and poets. The explosion of sexological research and knowledge in recent years has thus created a serious problem of language and its precise usage.

Two examples will illustrate the need for and usefulness of this dictionary.

First, consider an entomologist studying the mating behavior and sexual responses of fruit flies who talks about "the rare male advantage." He will ignore a presentation by an expert on the mating behavior of rats who talks about the "Coolidge effect" and a psychologist writing about monogamous instincts or drives conflicting with the experience of "variety being the spice of life." All three are talking about much the same reality. Yet they do not communicate because each is using a different language rooted in their own respective disciplines.

Our second example led to the conception of this project. It surfaced when I began working on the second edition of my college textbook *Becoming a Sexual Person.* I found the definitions of sociological and psychological terms in textbooks written by social scientists very helpful; however, their definitions of biological and anatomical sexual terms often left much to be desired in terms of precision, accuracy, and clarity, for example, syphilis was defined simply as "a sexually transmitted disease," leaving out of the definition its bacterial origins, distinction from other STDs, its stages of development, and treatment. On the other hand, textbooks written by biologists had excellent definitions of anatomical and physiological terms but often fell short of clarity and accuracy in defining terms common in the social sciences.

Obviously our modern knowledge of sexuality comes from many different disciplines in many different languages. This dictionary provides a common basis for communication by bringing together terms and definitions from all the disciplines.

In preparing this dictionary, we consulted the following resources:

Alternative Approaches to the Study of Sexual Behavior. Donn Byrne and Kathryn Kelley, eds. Hillside, NJ: Lawrence Erlbaum Associates, 1986.

The Concise Science Dictionary. New York: Oxford University Press, 1984.

Cyclopedic Lexicon of Sex. J. E. Schmidt. New York: Brussel & Brussel, 1967.

Dictionary of Medical Slang and Related Esoteric Expressions. J. E. Schmidt. Springfield, IL: Charles C. Thomas, 1959.

Dictionary of Psychology. 2d ed. J. P. Chaplin. New York: Dell/Laurel, 1985.

Encyclopedia and Dictionary of Medicine, Nursing, and Allied Health. Benjamin F. Miller and Claire Brackman Keane. Philadelphia: W. B. Saunders, 1978.

Encyclopedia of Sex Education. Hugo G. Beigel. New York: William Penn Publishing Corp., 1952.

The Encyclopedia of Sexual Behavior. Rev. ed. Albert Ellis and Albert Abarbanel, eds. New York: Jason Aronson, 1973.

Encyclopaedia Sexualis. Victor Robinson, ed. New York: Dingwall-Rock, Ltd., 1936.

A Feminist Dictionary. Cheris Kramarae and Paula A. Treichler. London: Pandora Press, 1985.

Journey into Sexuality: An Exploratory Voyage. Ira L. Reiss. Englewood Cliffs, NJ: Prentice-Hall, 1986.

The Language of Sex from A to Z. Robert M. Goldenson and Kenneth N. Anderson. New York: World Almanac, 1986.

The Language of Sexuality. Alan Richter. Jefferson, NC: McFarland & Company, 1987.

Mosby's Medical and Nursing Dictionary. Laurence Urdang, ed. St. Louis: C. V. Mosby Company, 1983.

The Penguin Dictionary of Sociology. New ed. Nicholas Abercrombie, Stephen Hill, and Bryan S. Turner. London: Penguin Books, 1988.

The Sex Atlas: A New Illustrated Guide. Erwin J. Haeberle. New York: Seabury/Continuum, 1978.

Our entries were also cross-checked against the glossaries and indexes in all available human sexuality college textbooks.

No dictionary of sexology today would be complete if it did not draw on the extensive list of new concepts and terms created by John Money, professor emeritus of medical psychology in the Department of Psychiatry and Behavioral Sciences and Professor of Pediatrics at the Johns Hopkins Hospital and School of Medicine. Besides formulating and defining such pivotal concepts as gender role and gender identity, John Money's prolific research and interest in linguistics has considerably enriched the language of sexology. Terms and definitions adapted from his extensive glossaries are found scattered through our *Descriptive Dictionary.* Our sources for Dr. Money's terms include: *Gay, Straight, and In-Between: The Sexology of Erotic Orientation* (1988), *Lovemaps: Clinical Concept of Sexual/Erotic Health and Pathology, Paraphilia, and Gender Transposition in Childhood, Adolescence and Maturity* (1986), *Venuses Penuses: Sexology, Sexosophy, and Exigency Theory* (1986), *The Destroying Angel: Sex, Fitness, and Food in the Legacy of Degeneracy Theory, Graham Crackers, Kellogg's Corn Flakes, and American Health History* (1985), *Love and Love Sickness: The Science of Sex, Gender Difference, and Pairbonding* (1980), *Man and Woman, Boy and Girl: The Differentiation and Dimorphism of Gender Identity from Conception to Maturity* (1972), and *Sex Research: New Developments* (1965).

Acknowledgments

We acknowledge the help provided by Peter Anderson, University of New Orleans; Linda L. Hendrixson, Fairleigh Dickinson University; Sharon King; Raymond Lawrence; Leigh Minturn, University of Colorado (Boulder); and Anne Bolin, Elon College (North Carolina). The editor-in-chief also wishes to acknowledge the invaluable assistance of Carrie Hudson and Ivan Stormgart in tracking down many of the books we needed to find terms and research their definitions. Dr. Perper wishes to thank The Harry Frank Guggenheim Foundation for two full-support grants defraying the costs of his research.

Introduction

Timothy Perper

Words are as much a part of sexuality as they are of any other aspect of human life. In fact, although one set of words—the "four letter words" or obscenities—have been banned in polite speech and much writing for many years and remain banned in the broadcast media, they are known to essentially all adolescent and adult Americans. Other vocabularies of sexuality also exist. They have arisen not from whatever impetus produces sexual maledicta but from other needs and social and historical processes.

One source is a desire to talk "politely" or "decently" about sexuality and its consequences, not in leering prurience or adolescent embarrassment but because we mate and reproduce sexually. Thus, the language of sexuality contains terms and phrases referring to love, to men and women in love, and to the procreative and antiprocreative consequences of sexuality. In this domain, we find words like *pregnancy*, *abortion*, *contraceptive*, *courtship*, and *wooing*.[1] With these words, we no longer have the bite of sexual slang. Instead we have entered a linguistically calmer domain, where men and women do not *fuck* but *make love* or *have intercourse*. A woman is not *knocked up* or *in a special way* but *pregnant*, *expecting*, or (even!) *enceinte*. A *condom* is no longer a *rubber* but a *prophylactic*. Once we enter the polite or courteous domain of sexual language, we find a virtually complete set of linguistic doubles for the socially impolite terms.

Still commonly and, indeed, traditionally always, the polite language was the language of women and the home, while the impolite language was that of the "street" and men. However, as changes have occurred in women's status and role, barriers between the parlor and the gutter have faded, and both forms of sexual language have become more equally frequent in the speech of men and women. Even so, the division remains, for it represents a perceived sense that sexuality comes in two forms: one pure, associated with love and procreation, and the other impure, associated with lust and corruption (Perper 1985). The same division underlies the extraordinarily elusive distinction between the words *pornography* and *erotica*. If we—or judicial and legislative authorities—use terms like *lewd, prurient,* or *salacious* about a book or film, we know immediately to what they are referring, though we cannot exactly put our finger on the difference.

Still another vocabulary of sexuality exists if one wishes to continue a division of sexual vocabularies according to the architectural places in which they occur or are supposed to occur. There are the languages of sexual intimacy between two lovers—the language of the bedroom, which rarely, if ever, comes to the attention of more than two people. These languages are essentially private and include personal terms for sexual activities and body parts. Often they are the language of recaptured childlike playfulness or sometimes of idiosyncratic invention, such as the personal or human names given to the sexual organs, such as *Mortimer* for the penis or *Peaches 'n' Cream* for the vulva. This is a language Martha Cornog (1986) calls "genital pet names." In addition, entire families may have their own terms for sexual body parts and bathroom activities, such as the often-parodied *number one* and *number two*. With rare exceptions, these personal or couple/family–specific languages have not been studied by those who should study them.

But when we leave the home and neighborhood—parlor, bedroom, or street—we encounter new environments, and, with them, we hear new vocabularies for sexual events and processes. In the faintly disinfectant air of a hospital, medical school, or laboratory, entirely new terms appear: *primary retarded ejaculation* or *impotence* for *not getting it up*; *menstruation* for *having one's period* or *being visited by Aunt Flo(w) from Redfield* (Ernster 1975); *penis* for *pecker* or *gnarled tree trunk* (Cornog 1986). But in the domain of medicine and biology, far less familiar terms also appear, referring to anatomical structures and physiological processes unknown or unfamiliar to most laypeople: *salpinx, fornix,* and *ventromedial hypothalamus*.

Another domain of sexual language also exists, although its importance is fading, at least for the urban cognoscenti, illuminati, and other citified trend-watchers. This is the language of the barnyard; even the word itself can evoke a slightly dystonic sense of "animalistic" sexuality. Yet animal sexuality was—and still is—infinitely important as a source of metaphor or euphemism. For a farmer or stock-breeder, it is an absolute necessity that animals reproduce, and no prudery can be attached to how they do so. Now we encounter terms like *copulation, mounting, heat, intromission, receptivity, sire,* and *dam*. To an urban adolescent, the word *teat* may evoke giggles and leering. To a boy or girl on a farm, it is simply a word for the anatomy of a cow's udder. These terms also have their dialect equivalents among farmers; the British veterinarian James Herriott (1973:72–73) gives *calf bed out* as the Yorkshire version of *everted cow uterus*.

But if there are boudoirs, parlors, medical schools, and farms, there are also brothels and clubs catering to (human) sexual needs called *sick* or *freaky* in one linguistic domain, *abnormal* or *perverted* in another, and *paraphiliac* or *variant* in still another. To some in the *leather scene*, *rough trade* needs no explanation. To others, it is as obscure as any other jargon or argot used in any self-identified subculture. Occasionally, through a watered-down spirit of *épater les bourgeois*, some of these phrases enter polite speech or trendy-chic versions of polite speech. Thus, one need not be *in the life* to know what a *trick* or *John* is; certain aspects of the prostitute's life have received sufficient media attention for many hearers to understand what is meant by these terms. Nonetheless, these terms are often limited in usage and occurrence to special domains and places; for example, few speakers of English would know what *Rice-A-Roni* refers to in its own sexual domain. It is, in that usage, a term used by necrophiliacs for a corpse that has reached a certain stage of decomposition (Ashley 1986–1987:180).

And, with that, we reach at least one crux of the language of sexuality: above all, it refers to parts of life that many individuals consider disgusting and horrible, aberrant and weird, filthy and unpleasant. But even if someone finds necrophilia nauseating, other parts of sexuality will be found equally nauseating by others. Yet—and this is a crux also—the limits of what is treated as filthy either linguistically or socially are not invariant or uniform across people in the modern United States. Not merely do languages change with milieu, they also change with historical trends toward great sexual explicitness and freedom. If everyone agreed on what is and is not pornography, no long court process would be needed to define it. It is only when standards of politeness, explicitness, and acceptability vary that we encounter troubles in defining sexual words and phrases. It is an often-quoted aphorism that erotica is what turns *me* on and pornography is what turns *you* on. A difficult and troubling thought is hidden here: definitions of sexual terms and phrases do not have a rock-hard basis in lexicographic truth but receive meaning only in the flux and change of usage among many people of varied background and sexual moralities.

Accordingly, it is difficult indeed to compile a dictionary of sexuality. For some, who adhere to what is called the "prescriptivist" school of dictionary writing and dictionary reading, a word has one or only a few meanings, as if a firm black line had been drawn around its limits. For such people, using a term outside those limits is *wrong*—inaccurate, sloppy, and careless. You get an F if you use *lie* instead of *lay* in what the teacher said was the wrong context. However, for others—and this group includes nearly all speakers and writers of English—words mean more or less what they are intended to mean, even if the exact spelling is not quite right or the exact term is a little off-kilter. Lexicographers who follow this standard—the descriptivists, to whom we number ourselves loyal—try valiantly to capture not an alleged real or right meaning of a word but its sense in the domain in which it is actually used.

But here problems arise. In some domains of usage, such as biomedical terminology and jargon, terms are defined very narrowly and have specific, sharply limited meanings, which stay put. Outside of anatomy and physiology, however, sexual language does not have the precision of the language of science.

Instead meanings are fluid and may be ardently debated. Here we include seemingly lucid terms like *homosexual*, *heterosexual*, *bisexual*, and *transsexual*. To you, perhaps, these terms mean this, that, or something else, all quite specific and well understood by you. You might argue that the thises, thatses, and something elses are the only way to define such terms. But in real life, matters are messier. Another person comes along and says that for him or her, these terms refer to slightly different concepts, actions, events, and processes. The circle you draw around your meanings is not the same as the circle drawn by someone else.

Still, when one listens to people talk about sexuality, as this dictionary's editor-in-chief, the editors, and collaborators have done for many years, one discovers that these circles or domains of meaning all overlap and come to center, if not upon a medically precise definition, then upon a restricted set of meanings or senses. In this dictionary, we have attempted to locate that set of meanings and senses for the reader rather than just supply a prescriptivist definition of what a term "really should mean." And, when doing so, we found ourself needing to include background information designed to illuminate briefly the nature and properties of the term being defined.

Here we have followed authoritative sources but only if they exist—and in many domains of sexual language, they do not. No single source, for example, provides an authoritative or true definition of a word like *homosexual*. For such terms—and they include most terms in sexual language, except for biological and medical terms—we have made every effort to locate the major senses of the words we have included. Thus, our definitions represent a domain or region of meaning in which more usage seems to circulate—for example, the term *orgasm*. If someone said that a person washing his hands was "having an orgasm," most speakers of English, native or otherwise, would agree that that "isn't what orgasm means," unless, of course, the person washing his hands was doing something else, for example, "washing" his penis. But putting masturbation aside and also the (likely) possibility that the phrase "to wash one's hands" means masturbation in a specific individual's personal sexual vocabulary, nonetheless the term *orgasm* has a range of meanings that, in observable usage, does not include washing one's hands. Put in this manner, the thought seems obvious. But what of someone who says that he or she has had an orgasm while having sexual intercourse? What, precisely, does the word *orgasm* mean now? Clearly—and empirically, it is clear—the experience and process of orgasm to one person is not what it is to another. Yet both people use the same word for their different experiences.

The only way to make sense of this linguistic process is to assume that a commonality of meaning exists between two people. Despite differences in emotional intensity, physical experience, and sexual intimacy, *orgasm* is widely used to refer to a peculiarly intense reaction to continued sexual stimulation, even though the details of how it is achieved and experienced differ among people. From such considerations emerges the common core of meaning, the domain of meaning mentioned previously.

Unfortunately, laypeople—and those who have not had to struggle with the recalcitrance of words as vehicles for expressing thoughts—believe that this manner of reaching a definition is sheerly and purely a matter of the lexicographer's personal idiosyncrasies. But it is not, and it has not been. To be sure, the accumulated years of professional sexological, pedagogical, and literary backgrounds of the editors have entered our choices of definitions, but our professionality itself has required that we delve extensively and thoroughly into a large number of published sources for our definitions. (A partial list is included in the Preface.) Background material was not put together as a crazy quilt of opinionated misinformation. Instead the extensive literature was examined, digested, and abstracted for presentation here. As with every other such effort, some highly valuable works appeared too late for us to include in this dictionary, for example, the dictionary of the language of sadomasochism compiled by Murray and Murrell (1989).

Several times we have been asked for a list of references and authorities to legitimate our background statements. No practical solution to this problem exists. A full bibliography, including page citations, would run as long as this dictionary itself. There is a real need for such a bibliography. Frayser and Whitby (1987) provide a start, and other sources also exist, but we cannot include all of them here. We regret this. Instead a few key references have been given to lead readers to the literature.

Another problem concerning length exists: what determined what terms should be included? If we defined every word and phrase even remotely connected to sexuality, we would encompass nearly the entire English language, plus an addendum for Latin, Greek, and other languages. Such a lexicographical work would be valuable, but its price—to say nothing of its sheer bulk in cubic feet—would prohibit its publication. So decisions about what to include had to be made.

One decision came rather easily: to exclude slang and jargon. Partly, this choice was made because the raw research material documenting the range and meanings of such terms does not exist. (An individual's own slang vocabulary is but a small sample of all slang.) Moreover, efforts in this direction have been begun by Reinhold Aman, the tireless editor of *Maledicta: The International Journal of Verbal Aggression*. For ten years, Aman and his authors have put together the beginnings of a genuine lexicography of sexual slang, particularly maledictions based on sexuality. For example, we have used his definition of *smegma* and want to point out that his article on the meaning of this term refers to ten different "definitions" contained in thirteen standard dictionaries of English and five contained in medical dictionaries.

In the great tradition of lexicography, which ranged from Samuel Johnson to Murray of the *Oxford English Dictionary*, developing dictionary entries required collecting, collating, and analyzing all extant definitions, followed by synthesis or resynthesis of "The Definition." Many years—indeed, whole professional lifetimes—can be and have been spent on such efforts. Fortunately (or not, depending on one's view), little of that was necessary or even possible for this dictionary. Although we examined existing dictionaries for their definitions, all too often their entries were too brief, too inexact, or too moralizing to be of much help.

Then, too, the editors at Greenwood Press insisted that we prune a manuscript that was three times the original estimated length. Exigencies of production costs and pricing have not, we hope, gutted the major thrust of our effort.

We have also omitted pronunciations of words and phrases. For most part, the omission should cause little trouble; only medical terms occasionally are drastically mispronounced by laypeople. (For example, the biomedical term *meatus* has three syllables, with the accent on the second, and is not a cognate to the word *meat*, a slang expression for the penis.) The major reason for this omission is that the editors are not phonologists and are not equipped to deal with the full range of variant pronunciations and, especially, of dialectical variations in how common sexual words are pronounced. Moreover, the raw research material for including pronunciations is often unavailable; dialectologists rarely ask for regional pronunciations of sexual slang.

Finally, each editor and collaborator examined every entry in the dictionary a number of times. Other experts also provided commentary so that the final entries are the result of collaboration and extensive refinement. Nonetheless, we cannot blame our collaborators and consultants for whatever errors may exist; for those we must take responsibility. Yet we hope that this dictionary will provide interested readers with a clear sense of meaning for its entries, and that, if the reader disagrees with us, he or she will share these views with the editors. Future revisions of this work, we hope, will some day make this dictionary a thoroughly comprehensive and authoritative dictionary of the language of sexuality.

NOTE

1. A linguistic domain is not a group of words that "mean almost the same thing." For that, one would speak simply of a group of synonyms or near synonyms. Nor is it a group of words psychologically associated, in someone's mind, as having an emotional or intellectual unity. Thus, the layperson might say that he or she would "not use words like *courtship* and *abortion* in the same sentence, so I don't understand why you say they're in the same domain. They mean such different things!"

As used here, *domain* refers to quite another concept: a type of discourse or speech performed in a certain social milieu, and more or less specific to that milieu. Mel Brooks's sex lecture in the film *High Anxiety* is amusing not because it is delivered in baby-talk (he says *wee-wee* for *penis*, for example) but because it is delivered at a scientific and scholarly meeting where baby words are out of their domain. It is a fact of language that people use different vocabularies, intonations, and sometimes syntax in different social conditions. So, while Brooks's lecture is satiric, it also illustrates how specific social situations presume and evoke the use of a type or kind of language deemed suitable to the situation.

Thus, despite the differences in meaning and emotional loading, words like *courtship* and *abortion* do belong to the same linguistic domain. Each, for example, could be used in a sermon delivered by a preacher or could be uttered on a television talk show. Few people would be embarrassed by hearing either word in a serious discussion of a man and woman's relationship. The domain in question can be called formal, polite, or courteous and stands in contrast to other domains discussed here. Some words occur in more than one domain; others have no exact synonyms outside their domain of use.

REFERENCES

Aman, R. (1983). Offensive words in dictionaries. I. *Smegma*. *Maledicta* 7:109–120.

Ashley, L. (1986–1987). Sexual slang: Prostitutes, pedophiles, flagellators, transvestites and necrophiles. *Maledicta* 9:143–198.

Cornog, M. (1986). Naming sexual parts: Preliminary patterns and implications. *Journal of Sex Research* 22(3):393–398.

Ernster, V. L. (1975). American menstrual expressions. *Sex Roles*. 1:1–13.

Frayser, S. G., and T. J. Whitby (1987). *Studies in Human Sexuality: A Selected Guide*. Littleton, CO: Libraries Unlimited.

Herriot, J. (1973). *All Creatures Great and Small*. New York: Bantam.

Murray, T. E., and T. R. Murrell (1989). *The Language of Sadomasochism: A Glossary and Linguistic Analysis*. Westport, CT: Greenwood.

Perper, T. (1985). *Sex Signals: The Biology of Love*. Philadelphia: ISI Press.

The Complete
Dictionary
of Sexology

A

A The first letter in the sacred alphabets of ancient Phoenicia and Greece; signifying beginning and birth (*qv*).

AASECT *See* American Association of Sex Educators, Counselors and Therapists.

abactio partus (L.) "Expelled offspring," an old European term for an illegal abortion (*qv*).

abandonment The voluntary separation of one spouse from the other without the latter's consent, without justification, and with no intention of reunion.

abdominal abortion A pregnancy (*qv*) that ends in the spontaneous or induced death of an embryo (*qv*) or fetus (*qv*) in the abdominal cavity. The abdominal abortion may follow a brief tubal pregnancy (*qv*) and tubal abortion (*qv*) when the embryo becomes too large to be retained in the distal portion of the tube and is expelled into the abdominal cavity. More rarely, it may follow an abdominal pregnancy (*qv*). After death of the fetus, the abortus (*qv*) may be reabsorbed, or it may become calcified if retained over a long period of time. Otherwise surgical removal is required. In very rare cases, an abdominal pregnancy (*qv*) may not end in an abdominal abortion but go to full term with Caesarean delivery (*qv*).

abdominal delivery *See* Caesarean section.

abdominal pregnancy A very rare type of ectopic pregnancy (*qv*) in which the *conceptus* (*qv*) implants in the abdominal wall or in the outer intestinal wall. The embryo (*qv*) grows in the peritoneal cavity, usually but not always surrounded by an amnion (*qv*). The abdominal or visceral peritoneum where implantation (*qv*) occurs is highly vascularized and can thus support development of the placenta (*qv*), which develops from both the embryonic trophoblast (*qv*) and from the induced vascular maternal tissue. Less than 100 such pregnancies have gone to term (*qv*) and live birth through a Caesarean section (*qv*).

An abdominal pregnancy is extremely dangerous because of the deep placental involvement. Caesarean section is often complicated by massive severe hemorrhaging and the impossibility of removing all the placenta, which causes postoperative complications. Abdominal pregnancies account for 2 percent of all ectopic pregnancies and approximately 0.01 percent of all pregnancies. The condition results in perinatal death of the fetus (*qv*) in 90 percent of cases and maternal death in about 6 percent of cases.

abdominal testes Undescended testes (*qv*). *See* cryptorchidism.

abduction In law, the taking of a woman or a minor by fraud, persuasion, or force for the purpose of marriage, concubinage (*qv*), or prostitution (*qv*). *See also* Mann Act.

Abelard, Pierre (1079–1142) A medieval French philosopher and theologian renowned as author, with Heloise, of the most famous love letters of all time. After falling in love with his seventeen-year-old student, the brilliant Heloise, Abelard eloped with her, married, and had a son. Pursued by ruffians hired by Heloise's uncle, he was caught and castrated (*qv*). Abelard then retired to the monastery of St. Denis while Heloise became a nun. Later, as abbot of St. Gildas-en-Rhuys, he established Heloise as head of the sisterhood in the Paraclete. The two lovers were buried together in the Paraclete. Resources: R. J. Lawrence, *The Poisoning of Eros*. (New York: Augustine Moore Press, 1989), pp. 151–158; I. Singer, *The Nature of Love*, vol. 2: *Courtly and Romantic* (Chicago: University of Chicago, 1984).

aberrant sex (aberration) *See* deviance, natural sin, unnatural sin.

ablation Surgical removal, by amputation or excision, of a part of the body.

abnormal Having the attribute or characteristic of not being normal (*qv*), average, typical or usual; in sexual usage, abnormal usually implies deviance (*qv*).

abominable crime A sexual crime or act considered contrary to nature; sodomy (*qv*) or anal intercourse (*qv*). In nineteenth-century England, the abominable crime was the equivalent of buggery (*qv*). In American civil law, abominable crime refers to anal intercourse and/or bestiality (*qv*) in a context where such specific terms are, by convention, "unmentionable among Christians."

abort To miscarry (*qv*) or deliver a fetus (*qv*) before it is viable outside the uterus (*qv*). *See also* abortion.

aborticide Destruction of the fetus (*qv*) in the uterus (*qv*), or an abortifacient (*qv*).

abortifacient Any agent or procedure deliberately used to induce an abortion (*qv*).

abortion Termination of a pregnancy (*qv*) by any means before the fetus (*qv*) is sufficiently developed to survive outside the uterus (*qv*). In the United States, abortion is induced, it is almost always performed before the twenty-sixth week of gestation (*qv*). Abortions are classified as (1) spontaneous, (2) therapeutic when done for the purpose of safeguarding the health of the mother, or (3) elective if induced at the request of the pregnant woman. Surgical techniques for an abortion include: (1) cervical dilation and evacuation (*qv*) of the uterine contents (D&E), (2) dilation and curettage (*qv*) (D&C) or scraping of the uterine cavity with removal of the uterine contents, (3) vacuum aspiration (*qv*) (D&A), vacuum curettage (*qv*), or vacuum suction, and (4) in the case of third-trimester abortions, laparotomy (*qv*) with hysterectomy (*qv*) or hysterotomy (*qv*). Abortion may be medically induced (1) by intravenous injection of oxytocin (*qv*) early in pregnancy, (2) by intra-amniotic infusion or injection of a saline/urea solution into the amniotic sac (*qv*), (3) by administration of prostaglandins (*qv*) into the uterus, or (4) by some combination of these three. The term miscarriage is often used for a spontaneous abortion. *See also* abortion law; abortus; infanticide; personhood; preemptive abortion; Roe v. Wade; social birth; viability.

abortion, preemptive Use of an abortifacient (*qv*) chemical to prevent implantation (*qv*) of an embryonic mass in the event fertilization (*qv*) has occurred following unprotected intercourse (*qv*). Three methods are currently used: the morning-after pill, diethylstilbesterol (*qv*) taken by a woman for three to seven days, prostaglandins (*qv*) in vaginal suppositories, and RU 486 (*qv*). Menstrual extraction (*qv*) gained some popularity in the 1970s but is no longer recommended or used.

abortionist Although the term refers to anyone who deliberately induces an abortion (*qv*), it usually refers to someone who operates outside the law in performing abortions rather than to a physician whose practice includes performing legal abortion.

abortion law Any law regulating the practice of abortion (*qv*). In the United States, the reference is most frequently to the 1973 U.S. Supreme Court decision on Roe v. Wade (*qv*), which legalized abortion. Much of American law on abortion has been derived from English common law. Under this law and in colonial American law, abortion prior to the fifth month was not considered a crime. Before the advent of the Industrial Revolution, having a large number of children was an economic advantage to a couple but of no interest to the state, so laws regulating abortion were nonexistent. With the Industrial Revolution in the early 1800s, government and business began encouraging large families since child labor in the mills and mines and on the canals was an important economic consideration. In the nineteenth century, economic interests were joined by a humanitarian movement seeking to protect women from the crude and dangerous methods used in performing abortions. In 1803, English law declared abortion a crime except when the woman's life or health was in danger. The first American antiabortion laws were passed in 1821. By the late 1800s, abortion was a criminal act throughout the United States. In the 1960s, New York and California enacted less restrictive abortion laws. The British legalized abortion in 1968, followed five years later by the decision on *Roe v. Wade*. *See* Appendix D.

abortion on demand A concept promoted by pro-choice (*qv*) health care advocates who maintain that a pregnant (*qv*) woman has a right to terminate her pregnancy when and if she chooses. Some advocates make this an absolute right that applies at any time during a pregnancy; others would limit this right. *See also Roe v. Wade; Webster v. Reproductive Health Services.*

abortus (L.) The nonviable fetal product of an abortion (*qv*). In medical usage, this Latin term is combined with limiting adjectives, as in *abortus artificialis* for an induced abortion, *abortus completus* for a complete abortion or miscarriage (*qv*), *abortus imminens* for an impending miscarriage or abortion, *abortus incipiens* for a miscarriage or abortion that is already in progress and thus inevitable, *abortus incompletus* for an incomplete miscarriage or abortion in which some fetal tissue remains in the uterus (*qv*), *abortus septicus* for an incomplete abortion or miscarriage that has become infected, and *abortus spontaneous* for a spontaneous miscarriage.

abruptio placenta (L.) Separation of a normally implanted placenta (*qv*) after 20 weeks of gestation (*qv*) or during labor (*qv*) prior to delivery (*qv*). It occurs in approximately one in 200 pregnancies and is a significant cause of fetal and maternal mortality. Complete separation of the placenta brings immediate death to the fetus (*qv*) and requires immediate Caesarean section (*qv*) with removal of all hemorrhaged blood. Partial separation may not interfere with fetal respiration and may be compatible with live birth if properly managed. *See also* preeclampsia.

absolute inversion In psychoanalytic theory, an exclusive homosexual (*qv*) orientation in which the person shows no erotosexual (*qv*) interest in persons of the other sex and may even have an aversion for them.

absolutist ethic A system of values and beliefs in which what is right or wrong is unchanging and absolute, based either in divine revelation or in the laws of nature. *See also* hedonism; natural law theory; relativistic ethics; situation ethics.

abstinence, sexual The voluntary decision not to engage in sexual/genital relations of any kind. Abstinence may be lifelong as part of a religious commitment to celibacy (*qv*) as practiced by Buddhist monks and Roman Catholic priests, monks, and women religious. Periodic abstinence from sexual intercourse (*qv*) is used as a natural contraceptive method in the Billings' contraceptive (cervical mucus) method (*qv*), basal body temperature (*qv*), and rhythm (*qv*) or calendar methods of contraception. Abstinence is also required as a religious practice by Muslims during the daylight hours of Ramadan, the month of fasting. The practices of Tantric yoga (*qv*) recommend short periods of sexual abstinence to concentrate one's sexual energy (*qv*) and prepare for more intense responses when sexual intercourse is resumed. Eastern traditions of sexual abstinence are more positive in their image of sexual relations and lack the ascetic (*qv*) tradition and negative dualism (*qv*) common in the Christian traditions. A definition of abstinence may include not engaging in masturbation. *See also* chastity; Platonic love; virginity.

abstinence rule In psychoanalytic practice, the recommendation that the patient refrain from all self-indulgences, such as smoking and sexual activity (*qv*), that might reduce the energies available for commitment to the therapy.

abuse The misuse, wrong use, or excessive use of anything; injurious, harmful, or offensive treatment. *See also* child abuse; child sexual abuse; incest; pedophilia.

abuse-dwarfism Growth and mental retardation consequent to child abuse (*qv*), somatosensory deprivation (*qv*), and neglect.

acceptive stage The second or middle phase of a sexuoerotic (*qv*) relationship in which the genital organs are mutually involved in bodily contact, typically coitus (*qv*) or intercourse (*qv*). The acceptive stage is preceded by the proceptive phase (*qv*) and followed by the conceptive phase (*qv*) with the possibility of conception (*qv*) and gestation (*qv*). The acceptive stage is also known as receptivity (*qv*).

acceptor In a developmental-descriptive profile, an individual who has learned to cope with unresolved personality conflicts by accepting them instead of denying them. In the case of an individual with an unresolved inadequate personality, he or she may cope by accepting the perceived inadequacy, using seduction (*qv*) to regain control over one's life, which may then lead to antisocial behavior as a confidence artist or embezzler. In the case of an individual with an unresolved inadequate personality combined with an unresolved early sexual trauma (*qv*), he or she may cope by accepting the perceived inadequacy, using seduction to regain control over one's life, which may then lead to antisocial behavior as a seductive pedophile (*qv*), a seduction-motivated exhibitionist (*qv*), a passive homosexual (*qv*), voyeur (*qv*), sexually motivated arsonist (*qv*), or obscene phone caller (*qv*) with seduction fantasies (*qv*). The acceptor personality type satisfies his or her need for acceptance by others by pleasing and seducing the victim. The acceptor personality "gives up" because he or she is convinced that it is impossible ever to be on a par with one's peers. *See also* active sexual trauma; denier; inadequate personality; passive sexual traumas.

accessory chromosome An X or Y chromosome (*qv*) beyond the normal XX or XY complement, or a trisomic (*qv*) autosome (*qv*).

accessory gland An alternate, rarely used term for the prostate (*qv*) gland.

accessory urethral canal A congenital birth defect (*qv*) resulting in a second urethral canal, usually only a short pouch rather than an actual duct. The occurrence of two complete urethras (*qv*) extending from the bladder through the penis (*qv*) is extremely rare. When this condition is limited to a pouch, the partial accessory urethral canal is a common site of sexually transmitted infections.

accidental homosexuality An inaccurate and misleading term for a bisexual (*qv*) or heterosexual (*qv*) male who engages in homoerotic (*qv*) activity because he is in prison, the armed services, or otherwise deprived of available female partners. Accidental homosexuality is also referred to as functional or situational homosexuality. *See also* homosexuality, facultative.

accommodation In sociology and experimental psychology, the process whereby individuals adapt to situations of conflict without resolving the basis of the conflict or changing the system of inequality it involves; the process whereby an individual modifies his or her activity to fit the requirements of the external social world. *See* acculturation.

accouchement (Fr.) An archaic term for the period of confinement or "lying in" just prior to childbirth (*qv*), or for childbirth; common in Victorian society when it was thought improper for an obviously pregnant (*qv*) woman to appear in public.

accoucheur (Fr.) Archaic term for an obstetrician (*qv*).

accoucheuse (Fr.) Archaic term for a midwife (*qv*).

acculturation The process of contacts and interactions between different cultures or between individuals in different cultures, and the outcome of such contacts. *See also* accommodation.

achnutshik In Greenland, a transvestite (*qv*) male, raised in the female gender role (*qv*), who, between the ages of 10 and 15 years, becomes a quasi-legal "wife" for an older man. *See also* berdache; hijra.

acid phosphatase An enzyme with a pH optimum of 5.4 associated with the prostate (*qv*) where it is found in high concentrations. Acid phosphatase is associated with the androgenic hormones (*qv*) and considered by some to be a chemical characteristic of males. It is normally present in male urine, although some researchers claim it is also present in the fluid expelled in the phenomenon known as female ejaculation (*qv*). In the case of the female, acid phosphatase may be produced in the Skene's or paraurethral glands (*qv*), which are homologous (*qv*) to the male prostate (*qv*).

Ackerman breast types A four-category system of classifying breast (*qv*) tumors. In Ackerman Type I, the cancer cells have not penetrated a membrane barrier and can be removed with a simple lumpectomy (*qv*). In Types II and III, the most commonly detected forms, the duct and alveoli (*qv*) are involved. In Type IV, the malignancy is invasive, having spread through the bloodstream to invade the lymph nodes and other tissues.

acme (Gr.) A summit, said in reference to orgasm (*qv*).

acne syphilitica (L.) An acne condition characterized by pustules, or pimples with sharp caps, and associated with secondary syphilis (*qv*). *See also* acne vulgaris.

acne vulgaris (L.) Common acne; an inflammatory, papulo-pustular skin eruption (pimples) occurring usually on the face, neck, shoulders, and upper back. The cause is unknown, but the condition involves bacterial breakdown of sebum into fatty substances irritating to surrounding subcutaneous tissue. Acne is associated with the hormonal changes of puberty (*qv*) and adolescence (*qv*). Cysts and nodules may develop, with scarring common. Treatment includes topical and oral antibiotics, topical vitamin A derivatives, benzyl benzoate, and dermabrasion.

acquaintance rape Rape (*qv*) by an assailant known the the victim. *See also* date rape.

acquired immune deficiency syndrome (AIDS) An infection with the human immunodeficiency virus HIV-I (*qv*) or HIV-II (*qv*), which damages the body's immune system, leaving it incapable of fighting off infections and cancers. AIDS is the most serious of currently known sexually transmitted diseases (*qv*). There is no current cure or vaccine and only a few ameliorating drugs aimed at controlling or curing the secondary infections. Secondary infections, tumors, emaciation, and/or nervous system damage, not the virus, are responsible for death. Approximately 60 percent of AIDS death are caused by *Pneumocystis carinii pneumonia* (*qv*), a lung infection. Among the opportunistic cancers, the most common is *Kaposi's sarcoma* (*qv*), a cancer of the blood vessel walls. Other important infections associated with AIDS are tuberculosis, cryptococcosis, Candidiasis (*qv*), Toxoplasmosis, Herpes zoster, and Cryptosporidosis. The fatality rate for AIDS victims is extremely high, with an estimated 80 percent dying within three or four years of diagnosis.

The documented modes of transmission are through exchange of certain infected body fluids—blood, semen (*qv*), urine, and feces. This may occur (1) through the sharing of contaminated needles during intravenous drug use, (2) when the virus passes from infected semen into the rectal lining, which often tears during anal intercourse (*qv*), (3) through vaginal intercourse (*qv*), from male to female, or from female to male, especially during menstruation (*qv*), (4) possibly during fellatio (*qv*), (5) through transfusions with contaminated blood or blood products, and (6) for the fetus-infant by exposure to the virus in the womb (*qv*), during childbirth (*qv*), or directly after birth through breastfeeding (*qv*).

Infected individuals are usually classified in three types. Sero-positive individuals show no signs of immune system damage but have antibodies (*qv*) to the human immunodeficiency virus, indicating they have been exposed to a person with this virus and are most likely still infected with it. Sero-positive persons can infect other persons. Persons with AIDS-related complex (ARC) (*qv*) are sero-positive and exhibit some damage to the immune system. In persons with AIDS, the most critical stage, damage to the immune system results in any or all of the following: opportunistic infections, certain cancers, emaciation, and dementia. Another model suggests that all infected persons progress through 12 stages at varying individual rates.

AIDS testing detects antibodies for the HIV-I virus that usually appear between several weeks and several months after infection. Recent evidence suggests that some infected persons may not develop antibodies for a year or more after infection. The ELISA test (*qv*) detects antibodies for the HIV-I virus with a very high accuracy rate, although false positive (*qv*) results may occur because of the presence of very similar non-HIV-I antibodies. The Western Blot test (*qv*) is more expensive but very specific and therefore more accurate.

The incubation period before symptoms appear can be from six months to several years. Symptoms include fever; night sweats; swollen glands in the neck, armpits, or groin; unexplained weight loss; yeast infections; diarrhea; persistent unexplained dry cough; white spots or unusual blemishes on the tongue or mouth; pink or purple blotches or bumps on or under the skin, inside the mouth, nose, eyelids, or rectum; fatigue; and loss of appetite but without the opportunistic secondary infections. High-risk groups include sexually promiscuous (*qv*) gay (*qv*) and bisexual (*qv*) men, past or present intravenous drug users, heterosexuals with many sexual partners, and children born to mothers with AIDS.

AIDS appears to have originated in Africa and is a worldwide health problem. It was first recognized in the United States in 1981. As of 1990, there were an estimated 1-1/2 million people infected in the United States and 10 million worldwide. The causative virus has been given several names since its identification: HIV-I or human immunodeficiency virus, HTLV-III or human T-lymphotrophic virus type III, LAV or lymphadenopathy associated virus, and ARV. *See also* AIDS-related complex.

acrai (Arabic) Nymphomania (*qv*) and satyriasis (*qv*).

acrosome A membrane-covered organelle located at the front of the spermatozoon (*qv*); contains proteolytic enzymes, essential in the fertilization (*qv*) process, which allow the sperm (*qv*) to penetrate the layer of follicular cells and membranes surrounding the ovum (*qv*).

acrotomophilia A paraphilia (*qv*) in which sexuoerotic (*qv*) arousal and orgasmic facilitation are responsive to and dependent on a partner who is an amputee or on the fantasy of such a partner. When the erotic response is limited to the stump(s) of the amputee, the proper term is acrotophilia (*qv*). In the reciprocal paraphilic condition, apotemnophilia (*qv*), sexuoerotic stimulation is dependent on self-amputation. In John Money's taxonomy, one of the eligibilic paraphilias. *See* Appendix A.

ACTH *See* adrenocorticotropic hormone.

active sexual trauma The psychologically premature active involvement of a child in sexual activity (*qv*). The involvement and activity may be immediately traumatic or initially pleasurable and rewarding, only to be perceived later in life as taboo and therefore traumatic as a result of negative reactions from adults or peers. Either pattern may occur in cases of incest (*qv*) and pedophilia (*qv*). *See* passive sexual trauma.

Acton, William (1813–1875) A British physician and author of the influential book *The Functions and Disorders of the Reproductive Organs in Youth, in Adult Age, and in Advanced Life*. Considered an authority at the time on venereal disease (*qv*), prostitution (*qv*), chastity (*qv*), and, most important, masturbation (*qv*), Acton was highly respected by John Kellogg (*qv*) and thus influential in the American campaign against "the evils of self-pollution," or masturbation. Two quotations are typical of his thoughts about the sexual innocence of women and children:

Married men, medical men, or married women themselves, would, if appealed to, tell a different tale, and vindicate female nature from the vile aspersions cast on it by the abandoned conduct and ungoverned lust of a few of its worst examples. There are many females who never feel any excitement whatever. Others, again, immediately after each period, do become, to a limited degree, capable of experiencing it; but this capacity is only temporary, and will cease entirely until the next menstrual period. The best mothers, wives, and managers of households know little or nothing of sexual indulgences. . . . She submits to her husband, but only to please him.

Previous to the attainment of puberty, the normal condition of a healthy child is one of entire freedom from sexual impressions. . . . During a well-regulated childhood, and in the case of ordinary temperaments, there is no temptation to infringe this primary law of nature. . . . Thus it happens that with most healthy and well brought up children no sensual idea or feeling has ever entered their heads, even in the way of speculation.

These and other beliefs of Acton have since been shown to be both inaccurate and medically unsound, although they remain deeply embedded and influential in our culture.

actual effectiveness (failure) rate The effectiveness or failure rate for a contraceptive method (*qv*), which includes both failure of the method and failure due to improper use. *See also* theoretical effectiveness or failure rate.

actual intercourse rate A term indicating an attempt to compensate for the alleged tendency of women to overestimate and of men to underestimate the number of times per week or per month the couple has sexual intercourse (*qv*).

actus brevis (L.) Medical term for premature ejaculation (*qv*).

acyclovir An antiviral medication that enters cells infected with the herpes (*qv*) and other viruses and interferes with their ability to reproduce the virus. Acyclovir is used to treat the symptoms of Herpes I (*qv*), Herpes II (genital herpes) (*qv*), and other viral infections. In the case of genital herpes, its main effect appears to be a speeding up of the healing process and possibly shortening of the infectious period. To be effective, it must be used at the first sign of an outbreak. Acyclovir's trade name is Zovirax.

acyesis A rarely used term for the absence of pregnancy (*qv*) or the condition of female sterility (*qv*).

Adam/Eve Plan (principle) *See* Adam Plan; Eve Plan.

adamite An obsolete term for a nudist (*qv*). This modern usage is derived from a Christian sect in Germany and Holland, the Adamites, who practiced ritual nudity and extramarital sexual intercourse (*qv*) at their secret meetings in the belief that as God's chosen they had already been reborn into a state of heavenly innocence where all the elect were obliged to love one another.

Adam Plan An interpretation based on a variety of animal research data indicating that in order for a fetus (*qv*) to differentiate as a male, genetic factors and hormonal additions are needed to divert the fetus from the basic Eve Plan (*qv*) whereby female differentiation proceeds independent of any hormone influence prior to birth. Differentiation of a fetus as a male involves two concurrent processes. First is masculinization (*qv*) which is regulated by testosterone (*qv*) and its derivative, dyhydrotestosterone (*qv*). These hormones trigger the male differentiation of the internal and external male sexual and reproductive structures. The second, parallel process of anatomical defeminization, regulated by Mullerian inhibiting substance or MIS (*qv*), prevents the Mullerian duct (*qv*) system from development. The effects of masculinization (*qv*) and defeminization (*qv*) on the neural templates (*qv*) for gender identity/role (*qv*), sexual orientation (*qv*), and such sexually dimorphic (*qv*) tendencies as cyclic/acyclic hypothalamic hormone secretion, earlier/latter puberty (*qv*), touch and visual arousability, proceptivity (*qv*), and masturbation (*qv*) drive have yet to be ascertained. Because hormone balances fluctuate during pregnancy (*qv*) and have varied effects depending on critical periods (*qv*), differentiation as a male may be total or partial.

Adam's apple In males, the prominent projection of the thyroid cartilage of the larynx at the front of the neck. Because of its obvious association with maleness, male-to-female transsexuals (*qv*) commonly seek plastic surgery to have it reduced in size.

addict, sexual An individual whose preoccupation with sexual matters or compulsive sexual behavior interferes with everyday living. The concept of sexual addiction (*qv*) is a controversial one. Advocates of the concept believe that a large percentage of sexual addicts were sexually abused as children. Since the partner of a sexual addict often comes from a similar background, both partners usually need therapy. An addict needs to be told of the impact of normal sexual activity because he or she is often disassociated during the compulsive activity and is unaware of what a normal relationship involves in terms of intimacy. *See also* Sexaholics Anonymous.

addiction, sexual A compulsive dependence on frequent repetition of highly ritualized sexual activity (*qv*). The addiction is not to sexual activity but to a particular sexuoerotic (*qv*) stimulus that has been incorporated into a ritual activity and endowed with a psychoneurological basis. The activity itself may or may not qualify as being paraphilic (*qv*).

The use of the term *addiction*, which implies an analogy with alcoholism and its treatment, has been defended by Patrick Carnes. Carnes suggests the sexual addict progresses through an ever-accelerating cycle involving (1) a trancelike preoccupation with sex that creates a compulsive search for sexual stimulation, (2) creation of special rituals that intensify sexual arousal and excitement, (3) a compulsion to have sex no matter the cost or risk, and (4) a feeling of utter hopelessness and an inability to control one's compulsions. Those who object to this use of the term point out that treatment of the sexual addict (*qv*) does not require the person to give up sexual experience, whereas treatment of alcohol addiction involves abuse of a substance which must given up totally. The concept of sexual addiction is also subject to the vagaries of subjective and cultural judgements. Resources: P. Carnes, Sex can be an addiction, *SIECUS Report* (1986) 14(6); M. T. Levine & R. R. Troiden, The myth of sexual compulsivity, *Journal of Sex Research* 25(3) (1988):347–363.

Addison's disease A chronic condition in which the production of the adreno-cortical hormones (*qv*)—cortisol (*qv*), aldosterone (*qv*), and androgen (*qv*)—is variably deficient. In mild forms, clinical manifestations include fatigue and hyperpigmentation. In less severe forms, marked dehydration occurs. In the severe form, mild infections lead to shock and death. Although both sexes are affected, women tend to be more affected by sex hormone deficiency, decreased libido (*qv*), and ovarian failure. Long-term treatment includes replacement therapy with adrenocortical hormones.

adelphogamy A marriage custom in which two or more brothers share one or more wives. *See also* levirate law, polygyny.

adenosis An abnormal development or enlargement of glandular tissue, particularly the presence of nodules less than half an inch in diameter on the outer surface of the female breast (*qv*), usually occurring in nonparous (*qv*) women after age 40.

adipso-genital dystrophy *See* Frohlich's syndrome.

Adler, Alfred (1870–1937) An Austrian psychiatrist and founder of individual psychology, Adler's major contributions to personality therapy and psychotherapy have been overshadowed by the influence of Sigmund Freud (*qv*) until recently. Adler broke with Freud over his interpretations of inferiority feelings and compensatory striving for power as basic factors in the development of personality. Adler's concept of masculine protest (*qv*) is particularly relevant to sex education (*qv*).

adnexa uteri (L.) Medical term for the fallopian tubes (*qv*) and ovaries (*qv*).

adnexitis (L.) Infection and inflammation of the fallopian tubes (*qv*) and ovaries (*qv*).

adnexopexy The surgical repositioning of the fallopian tubes (*qv*) and ovaries (*qv*) in the abdominal cavity to restore or improve fertility (*qv*).

adolescence The psychosocial developmental period between the onset of puberty (*qv*) and early adulthood during which the young person refines his or her sex role (*qv*), self-concept, and relationships with persons of one's own and the other sex. The period of adolescence, which may extend from puberty (*qv*) to the mid- or late twenties, is distinct from the briefer period of physical and sexual maturation known as puberty. Sociologists point out that the notion of a separate and specialized age group called *adolescence* is the product of late-nineteenth-century social changes in Europe and North America. Some historians claim that the concept of adolescence can be traced back to at least the sixteenth century in France. The vernacular equivalent is *teens* or *teenage*.

adolescent growth spurt The period of rapid bone growth usually occurring in the early or middle teen years as a response to the rising levels of the growth hormone somatotropin (*qv*) and sex hormones associated with puberty (*qv*).

adolescent gynecomastia The growth in a boy of glandular tissue and enlargement of the mammae or breasts (*qv*) in response to the hormones of puberty (*qv*). Typically the enlargement is minimal and self-correcting, though in rare cases it may be significant and require corrective surgery or mastectomy (*qv*). The etiology of gynecomastia is obscure, being attributed either to an atypical utilization of low levels of estrogen (*qv*) normally produced by the cells of Leydig (*qv*) in the testes (*qv*) of the male or to an atypical lack of response to the masculinizing (*qv*) and antiestrogenic effects of testosterone (*qv*).

adolescent homosexuality Sexual contacts occurring with persons of the same gender during adolescence (*qv*), usually as part of the self-exploration common in the psychosocial upheaval of adolescence rather than as a sign of a true homosexual (*qv*) orientation. *See also* homoerotic; sissy boy syndrome.

adolescentilism, paraphilic A paraphilic (*qv*) response in which an adult impersonates an adolescent (*qv*) and responds to being treated as an adolescent by the partner. In John Money's taxonomy, one of the stigmatic eligibilic (*qv*) paraphilias. *See also* infantilism; juvenilism; gerontophilia; ephebophilia.

adolescent sterility A supposed period of relative female infertility (*qv*) believed to occur in the year or two following puberty (*qv*) during which the reproductive system, although mature, has not reached its balanced full reproductive capacity. Validity of this supposed period of infertility, based on circumstantial evidence from nonindustrial cultures that encourage sexual activity (*qv*) as soon as puberty is reached but have a low incidence of teenage pregnancy, has been challenged by the growing incidence of early teenage pregnancies, especially in the United States where many sexually active teenagers do not use contraceptives (*qv*).

adoption The social and legal process in which custody and responsibility for a child, usually born to a single mother, is assumed by a couple or single person other than the child's biological parents. Infertility (*qv*) of the adoptive parents is often the reason behind the adoption, which is usually handled through specialized government-regulated agencies. Third-party or prenatal adoptions may be arranged by physicians and/or lawyers for the offspring of specially contracted surrogate mothers (*qv*).

adosculation A rarely used term for fertilization (*qv*) by external contact only.

adrenal cortex The outer three layers of the adrenal gland (*qv*) as contrasted with the innermost part, the medulla. The adrenal cortex produces the gluco-corticoids, mineralcorticoids, and sex hormone precursors that are converted by the liver to testosterone (qv) and estrogens (qv).

adrenal-cortical hyperfunction *See* adrenogenital syndrome.

adrenal gland A pair of small endocrine glands (*qv*) located on top of the kidneys in the dorsal (back) side of the abdominal cavity. The three outer layers of the adrenal cortex and the inner medullary region are actually two distinct glandular systems, secreting their hormone (*qv*) products directly into the blood for transport to cells throughout the body. Controlled by pituitary (*qv*) adreno-corticotropic hormone (*qv*), the cortical layer produces three classes of steroid hormones: (1) the glucocorticoids (cortisol or hydrocortisone, cortisone, and corticosterone) (*qv*), (2) the mineralocorticoids (aldosterone, desoxycorticoste-rone, and corticosterone, and less potent androgens) (*qv*), and (3) small amounts of progesterone (*qv*) and estrogen (*qv*). The glucocorticoids help control metab-olism of protein, fat, and carbohydrates. The mineralocorticoids influence sodium and potassium concentrations in body fluids to maintain electrolyte balance. Under hypothalamic control, the medulla produces the vasoconstrictors, epi-nephrine (*qv*), and norepinephrine (*qv*), which regulate cardiac activity, gas-trointestinal mobility, metabolic rate, and arterial pressure.

adrenalin A common name for epinephrine (*qv*).

adrenal rest A small mass of adrenal tissue separated from the adrenal glands (*qv*) proper that develops elsewhere in the abdominal cavity. This additional, ectopic tissue may cause a surplus of adrenal cortical hormones and occasionally be the cause of precocious puberty (*qv*) or premature testicular enlargement.

adrenal virilization The development of masculine traits, both physical and possibly mental, as a result of abnormal production of androgenic (*qv*) hormones by the adrenal glands (*qv*).

adrenarche An early sign of puberty (*qv*) marked by appearance of pubic hair (*qv*) and sometimes menstruation (*qv*). When this occurs before the normal age for the onset of puberty, it may be caused by an adrenal malfunction or tumor.

adrenocortical hyperfunction *See* adrenogenital syndrome.

adrenocortical tumor A tumor of the adrenal cortex (*qv*), which results in some degree of premature puberty (*qv*) in males, although the testes (*qv*) remain infantile. In affected females, the genitalia (*qv*) may be ambiguous. *See also* congenital virilizing adrenogenital hyperplasia.

adrenocorticotropic hormone (ACTH) A peptide hormone (*qv*) produced by the anterior pituitary (*qv*) that stimulates the growth of the adrenal gland (*qv*) and the secretion of corticosteroids (*qv*) by the adrenal cortices (*qv*). *See also* congenital virilizing adrenogenital hyperplasia.

adrenogenitalism A condition characterized by oversecretion of androgens (*qv*) by the adrenal glands (*qv*), resulting in somatic masculinization (*qv*). Adreno-genitalism may be caused by a virilizing (*qv*) adrenocortical (*qv*) tumor, con-genital adrenal hyperplasia (*qv*), or an inborn enzyme deficiency. Girls born with this condition may be pseudohermaphroditic (*qv*). Males may show premature puberty (*qv*) but with small, immature testes (*qv*). Virilizing (*qv*) tumors are more common in women, usually occurring between ages 30 and 40, or after menopause (*qv*). *See also* adrenogenital syndrome; congenital virilizing adre-nogenital hyperplasia.

adrenogenital syndrome A hereditary disorder involving an enzyme deficiency in the adrenal gland (qv). Affected females are frequently masculinized (*qv*) in their external genitalia (*qv*), while affected males appear normal. *See also* con-genital virilizing adrenogenital hyperplasia.

adult A mature individual, a grownup; a person who is legally of age (i.e., no longer a minor), and therefore fully responsible for his or her actions before the law; a euphemistic adjective for sexually explicit or pornographic (*qv*) in such phrases as *adult bookstore*, *adult movie*, *adult entertainment*. *See also* adulthood.

adultery In legal, religious and moral terminology, sexual intercourse (*qv*) en-gaged in by a married person with a partner other than the spouse. In modern usage, adultery is sexual activity (*qv*) unacceptable to the spouse, whether it is known or unknown to that person. This usage distinguishes between adultery as an unacceptable extramarital relationship or "cheating" behavior and consensual extramarital relations that are acknowledged and accepted by both married part-ners. *See also* affair; open marriage; closed marriage; comarital; satellite rela-tionship; intimate friendship; hot sexual values; cool sexual values.

adulthood The period of maturity following adolescence (*qv*). The passage to adult stage varies in different cultures. In European countries and the United States, legal recognition as an adult varies between 18 and 21, with the age of consent for sexual activity (*qv*) often coming earlier.

adventitious *See* adventive.

adventive Anything that happens in one's life history that is unique and does not fit in with a universal system. *Antonym*: imperative.

affair A colloquial term for the sexual relationship of a married person with a partner other than his or her spouse. The affair may be consensual, with foreknowledge and acceptance of the spouse, or extramarital (*qv*), secretive, and viewed as infidelity (*qv*) or "cheating." *See* adultery; open marriage; closed marriage; comarital; satellite relationship; intimate friendship; hot sexual values; cool sexual values.

affiliation In medical law, the procedure of establishing paternity of a child.

affinial A relationship based on marriage (*qv*) rather than on the real or attributed ties of descent. The mother-in-law relationship is an affinial relationship, in contrast with the mother-child relationship based on descent.

affinity A relationship arising from a marriage (*qv*) between one of the married persons and a blood relative of the other. In some legal jurisdictions, affinity can be an impediment to marriage. *See also* consanguinity.

affirmative action A policy adopted by the federal government on the basis of Executive Order (EO) 11246 (as amended by EO 11375) issued by President Lyndon Johnson in 1964 requiring that all companies, universities, and other institutions that do business with or receive funding from the federal government shall not only refrain from racial, sexual, and religious discrimination in hiring, promotion, and admissions but also shall "take affirmative action to ensure that applicants are employed, and that employees are treated during their employment, without regard to their race, color, religion, sex, or national origin."

AFP *See* alpha fetoprotein.

A-frame orgasm The uterine-centered orgasm (*qv*) in women that is believed to result from stimulation (*qv*) of the Grafenberg spot (*qv*) in the vaginal wall (*qv*). Erotic response is transmitted by the pelvic nerve to the spinal reflex center with the myotonic discharge associated with orgasm occurring in the deeper muscles of the pelvis (*qv*), causing the uterus (*qv*) to contract and descend and the orgasmic platform (*qv*) to distend. *See also* tenting orgasm; uterine orgasm; blended orgasm.

afterbirth The blood, fluid, placenta (*qv*), fetal membranes, and portion of the umbilical cord (*qv*) that are expelled from the uterus (*qv*) usually within an hour after delivery (*qv*).

afterglow A colloquial term for the feelings of physical relaxation, emotional togetherness, and warmth that often follow orgasm (*qv*) as part of the resolution phase (*qv*). Although the more obvious elements in the afterglow may be the result of the orgasmic release of building sexual tension, the sense of fulfillment from intimacy (*qv*) and interpersonal communion is essential in this feeling.

afterpains Contractions of the uterine muscles common during the first days after delivery (*qv*) as the greatly distended uterus (*qv*) returns to its pregestational state. Afterpains tend to be stronger in nursing mothers, possibly due to high levels of oxytocin (*qv*) in the blood associated with breastfeeding (*qv*) and in multiparous (*qv*) women. They spontaneously cease within a few days.

afterplay The affectionate, sensual, and erotic interaction that follows sexual intercourse (*qv*) or orgasm (*qv*). J. Halpern and M. Sherman (*Afterplay: A Key to Intimacy* [New York: Stein and Day, 1979]) note that the term appeared in some earlier books on human sexuality and was apparently coined to counter the heavy emphasis on performance and coitus (*qv*) and to stress the importance of noncoital pleasuring (*qv*) both before and after intercourse (*qv*). In the same context, the term *loveplay* is gaining popularity as a replacement for the goal-oriented character of foreplay (*qv*).

agametic Asexual (*qv*), without recognizable sex organs or gametes (*qv*).

agamic Reproducing asexually, without the union of gametes (*qv*).

aganic descent *See* patrilineal.

agape (Gr.) An altruistic, spiritual, or religiously motivated form of love. In the Christian tradition, agape is extolled over the negative sensuality of lusty Eros (*qv*). *See also* lust.

agapemone A term for group marriage (*qv*) and spouse exchange as practiced in the mid-nineteenth century by an English communal group. *See also* Oneida Community; Church of the Latter Day Saints.

agastopia A rarely used term for admiration of any particular part of the body.

age avoidance A culturally conditioned constraint on self-disclosure to persons in a different age cohort than one's own age group. This taboo affects erotosexual (*qv*) behavior and communications. *See also* erotophobia; intimacy avoidance.

âge critique (Fr.) The climacteric period or menopause (*qv*).

agenesis Partial or complete failure of an organ or structure to form or develop normally. *See also* atrophy; dysgenesis.

agenitalism A complex of symptoms due to the lack of secretion of sex hormones (*qv*) caused by the absence or malfunction of the ovaries (*qv*) or testes (*qv*).

agennesic A rarely used term for impotence (*qv*) or sterility (*qv*).

agenocratia A rarely used term for opposition to contraception (*qv*).

agenosomia A congenital (*qv*) malformation characterized by the absence or defective formation of the genitals (*qv*) and the herniated protrusion of the abdominal viscera through an incomplete abdominal wall.

agents of socialization Family members, peers, and associates from whom one learns sexual and other values. *See also* script.

age of consent The legal age at which a minor (*qv*) is considered capable of consenting to sexual intercourse (*qv*); the age below which marriage (*qv*) is illegal without parental approval. Each state or legal jurisdiction determines its own age of consent for sexual intercourse and for marriage. In the 1970s, the age of consent for intercourse ranged from 7 years in Delaware to 21 years in several other states. If a male has intercourse with an underage female, her consent is irrelevant since a minor cannot legally consent to sexual intercourse. A male in this situation may be charged with statutory rape (*qv*), child molestation (*qv*), or another felony depending on the individual state statute.

age-specific marital fertility rate (ASMFR) The number of live births per 1,000 married women of a specific age in a given year. *See also* birthrate.

agglutination test A pregnancy test based on the presence of human chorionic gonadotropin (*qv*) in the woman's urine. *See also* immunological pregnancy test; Elisa Test; beta subunit HCG radioimmunoassay; home pregnancy test.

AGI *See* Alan Guttmacher Institute.

agonadal The absence of the gonads (*qv*) in either a male or female, either as a congenital (*qv*) malformation or as the result of surgery or an accident.

agonic behavior (society) A behavioral and interactive social pattern observed among primates in which social cohesion is achieved by attention drawn to a spatially central, focal individual by controlled aggression and threat from the focal individual. *See also* hedonic behavior.

agonistic In the behavioral sciences, being combative or in opposition to something; in pharmacology, an agonistic drug competes with another drug or with a naturally occurring substance at receptor sites. *See also* agonic behavior; synergistic action.

AI *See* artificial insemination.

AID Artificial insemination (*qv*) with a donor's semen (*qv*) instead of the husband's semen. *See also* AIH.

aidoiomania An abnormally strong desire for sexual intercourse (*qv*). *See also* addiction, sexual; nymphomania; satyriasis.

aidoitis A rarely used term for inflammation of the vulva (*qv*).

AIDS *See* acquired immune deficiency syndrome.

AIDS-related complex (ARC) An early stage in acquired immune deficiency syndrome (AIDS) (*qv*), in which a person tests seropositive for the HIV-I virus (*qv*) and exhibits damage to the immune system with a disturbed ratio of T4 helper cells (*qv*) to T8 suppressor cells. A person with ARC does not show dementia, emaciation, or certain opportunistic infections, lymphomas, or sarcomas listed by the Center for Disease Control as characteristic of AIDS. There are roughly five persons with ARC for every one person with the full AIDS condition. Many persons with ARC will convert to AIDS, but an undetermined number may not for reasons as yet unknown.

AIDS-related virus (ARV) An obsolete name proposed for the human immunodeficiency virus (*qv*) which causes acquired immune deficiency syndrome (*qv*).

AIH Artificial insemination (*qv*) with the husband's semen (*qv*) from several ejaculates (*qv*) concentrated and frozen until a sperm count (*qv*) sufficient for fertilization (*qv*) is achieved. *See also* artificial insemination donor.

aischrolatreia A rarely used term for the love of filth, dirt, or obscenities. *See also* coprophilia; mysophilia; narratophilia; scatophilia; autonephiophilia.

Alan Guttmacher Institute (AGI) A family-planning research and information association; affiliated with Planned Parenthood/World Population. Address: 360 Park Avenue South, New York, NY 10010.

Albright's disease A disorder characterized by fibrous dysplasia of the bones, isolated brown patches on the skin, endocrine dysfunction, and premature puberty (*qv*). In females, Albright's disease commonly results in early development of pubic hair (*qv*), breasts, and menstruation (*qv*); premature puberty is less common in males.

alcahueta (Sp.) A female matchmaker (*qv*), or procuress; the masculine form, *alcahuete*, refers to a male pimp (*qv*).

alcoholic jealousy A form of jealousy common in alcoholic persons whose anger and fear of partner loss are directed at a suspected rival and accompanied by suspicion of the partner's infidelity (*qv*).

alcoholic paranoia A paranoid state of mind in which an alcoholic person develops a pathological jealousy based on the irrational suspicion that the partner or spouse has been unfaithful despite all evidence to the contrary. *See also* alcoholic jealousy.

aldosterone A steroid (*qv*) hormone produced by the adrenal cortex (*qv*) that regulates the sodium and potassium balance in the blood.

aleydigism An endocrine abnormality in which the testicular interstitial cells, the cells of Leydig (*qv*), do not produce normal amounts of androgens (*qv*).

algolagnia A psychiatric term for taking pleasure in pain and cruelty; sadism (*qv*) is *active algolagnia*; masochism (*qv*) is referred to as *passive algolagnia*.

algomenorrhea Medical term for painful menstruation (*qv*). *See also* premenstrual syndrome.

algopareunia *See* dyspareunia.

algophilia *See* masochism.

alibido An absence of sexual desire or libido (*qv*). *See also* desire phase dysfunction.

alienation In sociological and psychological usage, the feeling of being estranged from one's self and from others. The term originally had philosophical and religious meanings until 1844, when Karl Marx gave it a sociological context that saw human estrangement in terms of objectification and denial of a person's essential human nature. In existentialist philosophy, alienation refers to the separation of the individual from the real self because of preoccupation with abstractions and the necessity of conforming to the wishes and dictates of others and society. In the 1950s and 1960s, American social scientists emphasized the subjective or psychological aspect of alienation. Alienation is still used in medicolegal writings as a general term for mental disorders.

alimentary orgasm A psychoanalytic concept referring to the tension relief and gratification thought to be experienced by infants during breastfeeding (*qv*). According to Sandor Rado, an alimentary orgasm is a prototype of the sexual orgasm (*qv*) in the adult. An adult's desire to recapture this infant experience is thought by some to lead to substance abuse.

alimony Payments by a former husband ordered by the court to provide financial support for a former wife. *See also* palimony.

allantois In fetal development, a tubular extension of the yolk sac (*qv*) endoderm that extends from the posterior intestine with allantoic (*qv*) blood vessels into the body stalk of the embryo (*qv*). In the human embryo, externally, the allantoic vessels become the umbilical vessels (*qv*) and part of the placenta (*qv*). Internally, it forms the bladder. *See also* amnion; chorion.

allele One of two or more alternate or mutant forms of a gene (*qv*) occupying the same locus on homologous (*qv*) chromosomes (*qv*). Following Gregor Mendel's second principle, alleles segregate during meiosis (*qv*), and the offspring normally receives one allele for each gene from each parent. The alleles for any particular gene may both be dominant (*qv*), both recessive (*qv*), one dominant and one recessive, or both codominant.

alloeroticism A psychoanalytic term for that phase of psychosexual development (*qv*) in which an individual is capable of directing his or her libido (*qv*) and love away from self and toward another person. *See also* autoeroticism.

alloiophilic An outdated term for a heterosexual (*qv*) person.

alloplasty A psychoanalytic term for the ability or capacity to direct one's libido (*qv*) and sexual interest away from oneself and immediate satisfactions and diverting this energy to relations with others or outside activities.

allosex avoidance A socially dictated or culturally conditioned restraint that limits self-disclosure to members of the other sex but not to members of one's own sex. Nudity in gym showers and locker rooms and gender-based limits on the use of street language, sexual slang, and sexual jokes are examples of allosex avoidance. *See also* age avoidance; intimacy avoidance.

alpha fetoprotein (AFP) A protein normally synthesized by the fetal yolk sac (*qv*), liver, and gastrointestinal tract. An elevated level of AFP in the amniotic fluid (*qv*) is an early indication of fetal neural defects, particularly spina bifida (open spinal cord) and anencephaly (lack of cerebral development). Elevated serum levels of AFP may also be associated with ataxiatelangiectasia, hepatitis, and other diseases.

alpha-interferon A biologically active, antiviral substance produced by the body but now mass-produced by genetic engineering and being tested in the treatment of acquired immune deficiency syndrome (*qv*).

altrigenderism A tendency of a young child to be attracted to children of the opposite sex and to engage in social, nonsexual play with them.

altruism A selfless regard for and interest in the welfare of others. In psychoanalytic theory, the libido (*qv*) is initially directed toward oneself, with the infant being purely egotistic and narcissistic. As the infant grows up, it learns to direct its libido toward the interests of the parents and others and replace its egotistic hedonism (*qv*) with pleasure derived from altruistic behavior. In sociobiology (*qv*), behavior that reduces the altruist's own life-expectancy or reproductive potential while increasing the reproductive potential of close genetic kin.

alveolus (pl. alveoli) Small saclike structures; milk-secreting cells in the breast (*qv*); also refers to the air sacs in the lungs.

amastia Absence of the breasts (*qv*) in a woman. *Amastia* may be a congenital defect (qv), a primary endocrine disorder resulting in faulty development, a secondary endocrine disorder arising during the prepubertal (*qv*) and pubertal (*qv*) period resulting in the absence of one or more secondary sex characteristics (*qv*) or the result of mastectomy (*qv*).

amative intercourse Sexual intercourse (*qv*) in which vaginal intercourse (*qv*) does not culminate in male ejaculation (*qv*). This form of intercourse was used as a contraceptive method by members of the Oneida Community (*qv*) (1831–1881), a utopian community in upstate New York. Within the community amative intercourse expressed friendship and nonexclusive love. Only those members selected by the community elders were allowed to engage in procreative sexual intercourse. *See also* maithuna; coitus reservatus.

amazon(s) In classic Greek mythology, a warrior tribe of women who lived independently of men, and who mated briefly with men from neighboring tribes and killed their male offspring. Their queen, Hippolyta, was captured by Theseus and wedded to him in Shakespeare's *Midsummer Night's Dream*. In later colloquial English, an Amazon was a strong woman who bent under no man's rule, and the term was therefore sometimes used contemptuously for suffragettes. Also colloquially, an amazon can be a dominatrix (*qv*). In modern feminist (*qv*) writing, the amazon is the ideal, collective Great Woman, who symbolizes in herself all women's strengths, autonomy, independence, and sisterhood.

ambierastia An outdated, rarely used term for bisexuality (*qv*).

ambiguous genitalia A congenital birth defect (*qv*) of the genitalia (*qv*) in which development from the embryonic undifferentiated state into a clear and unambiguous male or female sexual anatomy is either incomplete or mixed at birth so that gender (*qv*) cannot be assigned with certainty based solely on visual examination of the genitals. Embryologically, the external sexual anatomy cannot be ambisexual (*qv*) but must be male, female, intersexual (*qv*), or hermaphroditic (*qv*).

ambisexual Having characteristics of both sexes; characterized by absence of dominance of traits from one or the other gender. *Ambisexual* also can refer to men or women who have no preference or bias about the gender (*qv*) of their sexual partners. *See also* bisexualism.

ambisexuality Having characteristics shared by both sexes (e.g., nipples, pubic hair). A birth defect (*qv*) of the genitalia (*qv*), which are sexually ambiguous, intersexed (*qv*), or hermaphroditic (*qv*). Mating (*qv*) behavior that is shared by both sexes; *see also* bisexualism; hermaphroditism.

ambitypic A term applied to the development of sexual dimorphism (*qv*) in the genitalia (*qv*), brain, or behavioral patterns in which both male and female primordia or anlagen (*qv*) coexist initially followed by continued development of one gender-specific system and degeneration of the other system. In the early embryo (*qv*) paired male Wolffian (mesonephric) ducts (*qv*) coexist with paired female Mullerian ducts (*qv*). In the male fetus (*qv*), MIS (*qv*) triggers degeneration of the Mullerian ducts, while testosterone (*qv*) triggers development of the Wolffian ducts (*qv*) into the vasa deferentia (*qv*) and associated structures. In the female fetus, the Wolffian ducts degenerate, and the Mullerian ducts fuse and develop into the vagina (*qv*), uterus (*qv*), and fallopian tubes (*qv*).

amelia A congenital (*qv*) birth defect (*qv*) marked by the absence of one or more limbs.

amelostasis An amputation fetish (*qv*); having an erotic (*qv*) inclination toward the stump of an amputated limb missing in the partner either because of a congenital defect or amputation. *See also* acrotomophilia; apotemnophilia.

amenorrhea Absence or suppression of the menstrual cycle (*qv*) and menstrual periods (*qv*). A person with *primary amenorrhea* has never had a normal menstrual cycle and menses (*qv*). A person with *secondary amenorrhea* experiences sporadic or irregular cycles. Amenorrhea is normal prior to puberty (*qv*), during pregnancy (*qv*), and after menopause (*qv*). Otherwise it is caused by a dysfunction of the hypothalamus (*qv*), pituitary gland (*qv*), ovary (*qv*) or uterus (*qv*); by the congenital absence of the uterus; by medication as sometimes occurs in the adjustment period when a woman stops using an oral contraceptive (*qv*); or by surgical removal of either the ovaries or uterus. *See also* dysmenorrhea.

American Association of Sex Educators, Counselors and Therapists (AASECT) A national professional association for sex educators, counselors, and therapists founded in 1967. AASECT certifies sex educators, counselors, and therapists, and publishes the *Journal of Sex Education and Therapy*. Address: 435 N. Michigan Ave., Suite 1717, Chicago IL 60611.

amixia A lack of interbreeding or mixing of the races. *See also* miscegenation.

amniocentesis Transabdominal puncture of the amniotic sac (*qv*) in order to remove amniotic fluid (*qv*) containing fetal somatic cells for diagnostic purposes; usually performed between the sixteenth and twentieth weeks of pregnancy (*qv*). Karyotypes (*qv*) of fetal chromosome (*qv*) number and structure are helpful in identifying Klinefelter (*qv*), Turner (*qv*), Down, and other syndromes associated with chromosome anomalies. Enzyme assay and biochemical analysis of the amniotic fluid allow identification of phenylketonuria, Mediterranean and Cooley's thalassemias, and spinal cord anomalies. DNA probes (*qv*) are being developed to ascertain the presence of genetic defects in fetal chromosomes obtained by amniocentesis such as cystic fibrosis and Huntington disease. Amniocentesis can be used to ascertain the viability (*qv*) of a fetus (*qv*) but not before the thirty-fourth week of gestation (*qv*). *See also* chorionic villi sampling; perculation umbilical blood sampling.

amniography A diagnostic technique for placenta praevia (*qv*) in which radiopaque dye is injected into the amniotic sac (*qv*) so the site of the placenta (*qv*) can be seen on an X-ray film. A preferred technique is ultrasonography (*qv*).

amnion One of the four extraembryonic fetal membranes, immediately surrounding the embryo (*qv*) and fetus (*qv*) during its development in the uterus (*qv*). The other extraembryonic membranes are the chorion (*qv*), yolk sac (*qv*), and allantois (*qv*). The amnion is continuous with and covers the fetal side of the placenta (*qv*) proper or decidua basalis (*qv*). Initially it creates the amniotic sac. In later pregnancy, as the fetus enlarges, the amnion is pressed against and fuses with the chorion, eliminating the extraembryonic coelom. In late pregnancy, the amnion and chorion or decidua capsularis (*qv*) and the uterine wall or decidua parietalis (*qv*) are contiguous but not fused as the fetus fills the uterine cavity. The amnion is shed as part of the afterbirth (*qv*) following delivery.

amniotic fluid The fluid within the amnion (*qv*) or amniotic sac (*qv*) in which the developing fetus (*qv*) is suspended. The amniotic fluid allows the fetus to move freely, provides insulation against thermal changes and physical shock, prevents fetal adhesion to the amnion, provides a temporary storage place for fetal excretions, and permits symmetrical external body growth. It is ingested by the fetus to help prime functioning of various gastrointestinal and excretory organs. A medium of active chemical exchange, the amniotic fluid is secreted and reabsorbed by cells in the lining of the sac at a rate of 50 milliliters per hour. At term, it usually totals about 1,000 milliliters. *See also* oligohydramnios.

During labor (*qv*) it effects the uniform transmission of the force of uterine contractions to the cervix (*qv*) for dilation (*qv*). Since this fluid contains sloughed-off fetal skin cells, it is used in genetic and chromosomal screening following amniocentesis (*qv*).

amniotic sac The thin-walled, fluid-filled bag surrounding the fetus (*qv*) with a capacity at term of 4 to 5 liters. Rupture of the amniotic sac, known as the breaking of the waters, is a sign of impending labor (*qv*). *See also* amnion; amniotic fluid.

amniotomy Induction of labor (*qv*) by puncturing the amniotic sac (*qv*).

amoral Lacking in any sense of morality. The first of four stages in Jean Piaget's (*qv*) model of moral development, extending from birth to roughly the age of 2, during which time the infant lacks any moral awareness and is totally self-centered; *see also* egocentric stage; heteronomous stage; autonomous stage; preconventional morality; conventional morality; postconventional morality.

amor insanus (L.) Outdated term for erotomania (*qv*).

amorph An inactive gene (*qv*) or mutant allele (*qv*) with little or no effect on the expression of a trait (e.g., the O blood type allele).

amour (Fr.) A love affair (*qv*). *See also* adultery; extramarital sex.

amourette (Fr.) A diminutive expression for a short-term affair (*qv*).

amour socratique (Fr.) An obsolete euphemism for homosexual (*qv*) or homoerotic (*qv*) love. The term refers to Socrates and the ancient Greek custom of older men having younger male lovers (*qv*). The homosexual liaisons between men and boys were, in large part, directed toward initiating boys into the power of the male fraternity. That relationship was supposed to terminate when the boy reached manhood, at which time he became even more attractive because of his intellectual abilities. Both Socrates and Plato viewed all physical sexuality, including that between men, as ontologically and qualitatively inferior to abstinence (*qv*) because it involved the body rather than the soul. *See also* dualism; Platonism.

ampallang Wooden or metal balls implanted in the penile shaft (*qv*) or glans (*qv*) to increase clitoral stimulation. Use of the ampallang is common in many cultures, particularly in Indonesia. *See also* Ben-Wa balls.

amphetamine A central nervous system (*qv*) stimulant that increases blood pressure and acts as a weak respiratory stimulant. *Slang*: speed.

amphierotic (amphieroticism) A person whose bisexual (*qv*) orientation is predominantly but not exclusively homosexual (*qv*)—4 or 5 on the Kinsey Six Scale (*qv*). Also, a psychiatric disorder so named by Sandor Ferenczi, a Hungarian psychoanalyst.

amphigenetic Produced by the union of gametes (*qv*) from both sexes; a bisexual (*qv*) or truly hermaphrodite (*qv*) with both ovaries (*qv*) and testes (*qv*).

amphigenous inversion The condition of being sexually attracted to and active with persons of both sexes. *See also* bisexuality.

amphigony Sexual reproduction (*qv*) in which ovum (*qv*) and sperm (*qv*) are joined in fertilization (*qv*).

amphimixis In biology, the union of ovum (*qv*) and sperm (*qv*) in sexual reproduction (*qv*) so that both maternal and paternal genetic material are combined and expressed in the resulting offspring. In psychoanalysis, the union and integration of oral, anal, and genital libidinal impulses in the development of sexuality (*qv*).

amphiphilia *See* bisexuality.

amphoteric Having the properties or characteristics of both sides of what is usually considered dichotomous, for example, being androgynous (*qv*) and expressing both male or masculine and female or feminine traits and/or behaviors.

amplexus The copulatory position adopted by internal fertilizing animals, for example, amphibia, that lack an intromittant penis and internal vagina, and in which the male mounts and clasps the female so that the openings of his and her cloacas (*qv*) are adjacent. Sperm are then released and move across the cloacal junction into the female's reproductive tract, where fertilization occurs.

ampligen An experimental immunity-stimulating drug with possible antiviral effects being tested in the treatment of acquired immune deficiency syndrome (*qv*).

ampulla A funnel-shaped opening, for example, the ampulla of the fallopian tube (*qv*).

ampulla ductus deferentis (L.) In the human male, Henle's ampulla (*qv*), the dilated portion of the ductus deferens (*qv*) just before it enters the ejaculatory duct (*qv*).

ampullary tubal pregnancy An ectopic tubal pregnancy (*qv*) in which implantation (*qv*) occurs in the ampulla (*qv*) of one of the fallopian tubes (*qv*).

amputation fetish *See* acrotomophilia; apotemnophilia.

amulet A magical charm worn to ward off evil, attract a lover (*qv*), or enhance one's sexual prowess. A common Roman amulet was shaped like the male genitalia (*qv*).

amygdala A structure in the paleocortex, or limbic system (*qv*) of the brain, situated close to the temporal lobe of the neocortex (*qv*).

amyl nitrite A muscle-relaxant and vasodilator drug commonly prescribed to relieve the pain of angina pectoris. Amyl nitrite is usually inhaled. It is also used by some who claim that it prolongs or intensifies the experience of orgasm (*qv*).

anabolic Constructive metabolic processes that build up tissue, especially muscle. *See also* catabolic.

anabolic steroid Any one of several compounds derived from testosterone (*qv*) and used to promote masculinizing (*qv*) effects, especially in muscle and bone growth; estrogens (*qv*) are mildly anabolic.

anacampserote A rarely used term for a potion or charm whose use is claimed to bring back a lost love or lover (*qv*).

anaclisis A condition in which a person, consciously or unconsciously, chooses a love object because that person resembles the father, mother, or another person who was an important source of love and comfort in infancy; a condition of emotional dependence on other people, normal in children but pathological in adults.

anaclitic choice *See* anaclisis.

anaclitic depression A syndrome occurring in infants following sudden separation from the primary caregiver. Symptoms include apprehension, withdrawal, incessant crying, refusal to eat, sleep disturbances, and eventually severe impairment of physical, social, and intellectual adjustment. Recovery is complete and quick if the caregiving figure becomes available within one to three months. If unresolved, it can have severe effects on adult psychological functioning. *See also* hospitalism; maternal deprivation syndrome; somatosensory affectional deprivation.

anaclitic identification The tendency of children to identify with parents who are nurturing and warm.

anacreontic A rarely used term for erotic (*qv*) verse.

anadidymis Conjoined twins (*qv*) united in the upper body trunk but separated below the waist.

Anadrynes A secret aristocratic lesbian (*qv*) society of eighteenth-century France, the Anadrynes society was founded by Madame de Fleury and had branches in major European cities and London.

anaesthesia sexualis (L.) A term, coined by Krafft-Ebing (*qv*), for lack of sexual desire (*qv*) or response in a female; frigidity (*qv*).

anagapesis A rarely used term for a loss of interest in ex-lovers.

anakatadidymis (Gr.) Conjoined twins (*qv*) united in the middle of the body trunk but separated at both the upper and lower parts of the body.

anal Referring to the anus (*qv*).

anal aggressive character In psychoanalytic theory (*qv*), an obstinate and defiant personality that first expresses itself during the anal stage (*qv*) of psychosexual development (*qv*) when the individual repeatedly asserts him- or herself by refusing to defecate.

anal birth In psychoanalytic theory (*qv*), dreams and fantasies (*qv*) in which anal eroticism (*qv*) is symbolically expressed in wishes to be reborn through the anus (*qv*).

anal-castration anxiety In psychoanalytic theory (*qv*), fears of castration (*qv*) expressed in toilet phobias, for instance, the fear of being flushed down the sewer or that a devil or monster will emerge from the toilet bowel and enter one's body through the anus (*qv*).

anal character (personality) In psychoanalytic theory (*qv*), a personality pattern originating in fixations in the anal stage (*qv*) of psychosexual development (*qv*) with the erotic (*qv*) pleasure of resisting defecation leading to obstinacy, stinginess, and orderliness and the erotic pleasure of releasing the feces leading to generosity, conceit, and ambition.

anal coitus *See* anal intercourse.

anal eroticism In psychoanalytic theory (*qv*), a libidinal fixation, arrested development, or regression to the anal stage (*qv*) in which defecation and elimination are primary sources of pleasure. This type of arrested personality development may lead to an exclusive focusing of eroticism (*qv*) on elimination, anal masturbation (*qv*), and anal intercourse (*qv*). In the anal-retentive stage, anal eroticism is said to be characterized by miserliness, stubbornness, and over-scrupulousness. The anal-expulsive stage is characterized by generosity, conceit and ambition. *See also* anal character; oral eroticism.

anal fantasies Daydreams and mental images of anal intercourse (*qv*), anal rape (*qv*), and/or anal birth (*qv*).

anal fetishism A paraphilic (*qv*) condition in which sexual arousal and orgasm (*qv*) is responsive to and dependent on a passive focus on one's own anus (*qv*) or an active focus on another person's anus. *See also* autonepiophilia; coprophilia; klismaphilia; mysophilia; urophilia; undinism.

anal fixation In psychoanalytic theory (*qv*), the persistence of pleasure needs and character traits rooted in the anal stage (*qv*) of psychosexual development (*qv*); believed to lead to anal eroticism (*qv*) and a desire for anal intercourse (*qv*).

analingus Oral stimulation of the anal (*qv*) region.

anal intercourse (anal sex) Insertion of the penis (*qv*) into the rectum (*qv*). Although illegal in some jurisdictions of the United States as sodomy (*qv*) or buggery (*qv*), and although often socially and colloquially condemned as an "act against nature," anal intercourse is nonetheless a widely practiced form of sexual activity among heterosexual (*qv*) and homosexual (*qv*) couples. It can involve the insertion of the penis (*qv*) into the anus and rectum of the partner or the use of a dildo (*qv*). In brachioproctic intercourse, the lubricated hand is inserted, fingers outstretched and held together, into the partner's anus; then the hand is made into a fist (colloquially, "fist fucking" or "fisting).

Both women and men report enjoying and desiring anal intercourse, and it is not restricted to homosexual men. However, if the receptive partner is not relaxed and comfortable, or if external lubrication is not used, anal intercourse with penis dildo can cause pain or trauma and tearing to the anal and rectal tissue.

Since the emergence of acquired immune deficiency syndrome (AIDS) (*qv*) as a public health menace, anal intercourse has widely become considered a dangerous practice that can transmit the causative agent of AIDS (*see* HIV-I). Moreover, anal intercourse followed by vaginal intercourse can transmit fecal microorganisms to the woman's reproductive tract, which may cause serious genitourinary infections. Thus, sexological health authorities strongly urge the use of a condom whenever the penis is inserted into the rectum, and with a dildo (*qv*) when the dildo is also used in the vagina.

Anal rape (*qv*) can be used to dominate, humiliate, or punish another person. In such cases, both physical and psychological damage is inevitable, particularly if the victim is frightened and tense, as would be common. Psychoanalysts have argued that fear of anal rape is widespread among heterosexual men, and that homophobia (*qv*) and behavioral submission (nonsexual masochism [*qv*]) may result from such fears.

Condom-protected, mutually agreeable, and lubricated anal intercourse is said by the recipients to involve a pleasurable fullness of the rectum that is completely distinct from the feelings of rectal distention associated with the need for a bowel movement. Aficionados of anal intercourse sometimes employ enemas to remove fecal material from the rectum and thereby present a cleaner environment for intercourse. Resource: J. Morin, *Anal Pleasure and Health*, 2d ed. (San Francisco: Down There Press, 1986). *See also* fisting (*Addendum*).

analipsation An obsolete term for anal (*qv*) self-masturbation.

analist A person whose erotic (*qv*) fantasies (*qv*) and activities are focused on the anus (*qv*) and anal intercourse (*qv*).

anal itch A burning, irritated soreness in the anal (*qv*) region, often accompanied and aggravated by diarrhea. Pruritis, the medical term for *anal itch*, may result from a fungal infection (jock itch), pinworms, moniliasis (*qv*), and the use of tetracycline antibiotics. It may also be the consequence of physical abrasions associated with anal intercourse (*qv*).

anality A psychological condition in which one's libido (*qv*) is expressed in erotic (*qv*) fantasies (*qv*) and activities are focused on the anus (*qv*) and anal intercourse (*qv*).

anal masturbation Sexual arousal and orgasm (*qv*) achieved through self-stimulation of the anal region, using fingers, a vibrator (*qv*), dildo (*qv*), or other means of stimulation; both males and females may engage in this form of masturbation (*qv*).

analogous organs Organs in the male and female with similar functions but different embryonic origins. The eye of an animal and the photoreceptors of a plant allow the organism to react to light, but these structures have totally different evolutionary and embryonic origins. In contrast, homologous organs (*qv*) have the same embryonic origins but different functions or structures in the adult; for example, the male testes (*qv*) and female ovaries (*qv*) are homologous since both arise from the same primordial, undifferentiated gonads (*qv*).

anal personality *See* anal character.

anal phase *See* anal stage.

anal-rape fantasy The not-uncommon fantasy (*qv*) or fear of being forced into anal intercourse (*qv*).

anal response A part of the normal sexual response of orgasm (*qv*) in which a few reflexive contractions of the anal sphincter and associated muscles occur at 0.8 second in conjunction with orgasmic contractions in the prostate (*qv*) and the penile urethra (*qv*) or the vagina (*qv*) and orgasmic platform (*qv*).

anal sadism In psychoanalytic theory (*qv*), a sadistic (*qv*) form of anal eroticism (*qv*) manifested in aggressiveness and selfishness resulting from punishment received during toilet training. In the anal sadistic stage, the infant focuses on anal eroticism (*qv*) and sadistic impulses directed toward a parent. In a form of anal sadism, some rapists resort to defecating or urinating on their victims in order to degrade and humiliate them.

anal sex *See* anal intercourse; sodomy; buggery.

anal stage In Sigmund Freud's (*qv*) theory of psychosexual development (*qv*), the stage occurring between ages 1 and 3 years when a child's sexual energies (*qv*) are focused on the anus (*qv*) and the sensations associated with the eliminative functions. Adult behavior patterns associated with fixation in this stage include either extreme neatness, orderliness, cleanliness, perfectionism, and punctuality or their opposite extremes. *See* oral stage; genital stage; latency.

anal stimulation A form of loveplay (*qv*) and eroticism (*qv*) in which the anus (*qv*) is stimulated either lingually in anilingus (*qv*) or rimming, digitally, or mechanically with a vibrator (*qv*), dildo (*qv*), or other means. This may be self-stimulation or engaged in with a partner.

anal triad In psychoanalytic theory (*qv*), a combination of personality traits involving obstinacy, stinginess, and an obsession with orderliness observed in the anal personality or character (*qv*).

anandria The absence of male characteristics.

Ananga Ranga *The Theater of God*, a beautifully illustrated fifteenth-century Indian sex manual detailing the sexual organs and erogenous areas (*qv*) of men and women, the cycles of erotic passion as they relate to lunar cycles, and an encyclopedic review of lovemaking positions.

anaphrodisiac A substance that decreases libido (*qv*) or sexual functioning. Two such drugs are currently used in treatment of sex offenders (*qv*): Cyproterone acetate (*qv*) and Depo-Provera (*qv*). Most medically used drugs are anaphrodisiacs if the dose is high enough. Lack of sexual desire and decreased erectile (*qv*) intensity and ejaculations (*qv*) are common complaints from men using central nervous system (*qv*) depressants, especially barbiturates. With drugs that affect the autonomic sympathetic (*qv*) nerves, males may experience retarded ejaculation, and women will not be able to achieve orgasm (*qv*). With drugs that overstimulate the sympathetic (*qv*) system, premature ejaculation (*qv*) and vaginal spasms may result. Since the parasympathetic (*qv*) nerves control vasocongestion (*qv*) in the sexual organs, a drug that inhibits this system will also inhibit erection (*qv*) and vaginal lubrication (*qv*). Diuretics lower the level of arousal in women. Nondiuretic drugs used for hypertension may decrease libido and cause erection problems.

anaspadia A congenital (*qv*) deformity in which the urethra (*qv*) opens along the top of the penile shaft (*qv*); more commonly known as epispadia. *See also* hypospadia.

"Anatomy is destiny" Sigmund Freud's (*qv*) commonly repeated statement declaring that women are defined by their reproductive capacity and that their role and place in society is reduced to their biological function.

Andrade syndrome An inborn metabolic error caused by an autosomal dominant (*qv*) gene (*qv*). Progressive degeneration of the autonomic nervous system (*qv*) due to amyloid deposits, which results in disorders of the sensory nerves, paralysis, and impotence (*qv*) in males and premature menopause (*qv*) in females.

androgen A general term for male sex hormones (*qv*) secreted mainly by the testes (*qv*) but also by the adrenal cortex (*qv*) and the ovaries (*qv*). There are several forms of androgens, each slightly different in the composition, structure, strength, and nature of its biochemical activity. The main androgens are testosterone (*qv*), aldosterone (*qv*), and androsterone (*qv*).

androgenic flush An area of reddish pigmentation around the neck caused by an excess production of 17–ketosteroids (*qv*).

androgen-induced hermaphroditism A congenital (*qv*) syndrome resulting in masculinized (*qv*) development of the genitalia (*qv*) of a 46,XX gonadally female fetus (*qv*) induced by an excess of exogenous masculinizing (*qv*) hormone (*qv*) transmitted from the mother across the placental barrier (*qv*). In the current classification, this condition is a pseudohermaphroditism (*qv*). This condition can be experimentally induced in animals by testosterone (*qv*) injection into the pregnant female. In humans, the condition results from an androgen-producing tumor.

androgen-insensitivity syndrome A congenital (*qv*) condition in which a single gene (*qv*) mutation in a 46,XY gonadally male individual renders all the somatic (*qv*) cells incapable of responding to the masculinizing (*qv*) messages of the androgens (*qv*) produced in normal amounts by the fetal testes (*qv*), thereby producing an anatomical female. Since the somatic cells of the affected genetic male cannot respond to the androgens, testosterone (*qv*) does not cause the Wolffian ducts (*qv*) to develop into the internal male system. However, the Mullerian inhibiting hormone (*qv*) prevents female development of the Mullerian ducts (*qv*). The external genitalia (*qv*) differentiate as female, except for a short, blind vagina (*qv*) that is usually not deep enough to allow for coitus (*qv*) unless dilated or surgically lengthened during adolescence. At birth, such individuals appear to be anatomically normal females and are so assigned and raised by their parents. Such individuals have no menstrual cycle (*qv*) and are infertile (*qv*). Breast development is normal for a female, but lactation (*qv*) does not occur. The condition is also known as testicular feminization or testicular feminizing syndrome.

androgenital syndrome A 46,XX chromosomal gonadal (*qv*) female whose adrenal glands (*qv*) produce an excess of masculinizing (*qv*) hormones. *See also* congenital virilizing adrenal hyperplasia.

androgyne An individual who shows a mixture or merging of traditionally masculine and feminine characteristics, psychologically and/or behaviorally. Formerly the term was used as a synonym for *male pseudohermaphrodite* (*qv*), while gynandroid was a synonym for the *female pseudohermaphrodite*. *See also* pseudohermaphrodite; hermaphrodite.

androgyneity In anthropology, the cultural assumption that the individual has a bipolar potentiality in sex until he or she is turned into a definite gender by a tribal ritual. *See also* circumcision.

androgynophilia The erotosexual (*qv*) bonding of a man or woman simultaneously or sequentially with a member of both sexes; this bonding includes limerence (*qv*) (falling in love). *See also* bisexuality.

androgynous Having the characteristics of both sexes. A theory that holds that social roles, behaviors, personality, and appearances are reflections of individuality and are not determined by biological factors. *See also* androgyny.

androgyny In the broadest sense, the combination of both male/masculine (andro) and female/feminine (gyne) physical, personality, and/or behavioral characteristics in one individual. In the psychology of C. G. Jung (*qv*), androgyny is an archetype inherent in the human psyche, an archaic or primordial type, a universal and collective image that has existed in the human psyche from remotest times and has been represented in myths and symbols explaining the origin of the two separate sexes from a primordial being. In contemporary use, androgyny refers to the ability of males and females to express the personality traits and stereotyped behaviors attributed separately to both genders. *See* androgyne; androgyneity. Resources: C. G. Heilbrun, Androgyny and the psychology of sex differences, in H. Eisenstein and A. Jardine, eds., *The Future of Difference* (Boston: G. K. Hall, 1980); J. Singer, *Androgyny* (New York: Anchor/Doubleday, 1976).

andrology A subspeciality of urology (*qv*) that studies male fertility (*qv*).

andromania An obsolete term for nymphomania (*qv*).

andromimesis (andromimetic) A condition in which a female impersonates a male and relates sexuoerotically (*qv*) only with women. In andromimesis, a girl or woman mimics male bodily appearance, wears masculine dress, and displays stereotypic masculine behavior. An andromimetic woman may request surgical removal of her breasts (*qv*) and in some cases use hormones (*qv*) to achieve further masculinization (*qv*). Generally genital surgery and gender reassignment (*qv*) are not sought in this condition. *See also* gynecomimesis.

andromimetophilia A paraphilic (*qv*) condition in which sexual attraction (*qv*) is predominantly or exclusively toward an andromimetic (*qv*) female or a preoperative female-to-male transsexual (*qv*). In John Money's classification, andromimetophilia is an eligibilic paraphilia (*qv*).

androphilia Literally, "love of a male"; erotosexual (*qv*) pairing and limerence (*qv*) of a woman with a man (female androphilia) or of a man with a man (male androphilia). *See also* androphobia; heterosexuality; homosexuality.

androphobia An intense, neurotic fear of men. *See also* androphilia; homophobia; heterophobia.

androsperm A male-determining sperm (*qv*), containing 22 autosomes (*qv*) and a Y chromosome (*qv*). Androsperm are shorter lived, lighter, and faster swimming than gynosperm (*qv*), with a rounder head and greater sensitivity to the acidic vaginal environment. *See also* gynosperm.

androstenedione A natural, weak androgen (*qv*) produced by the adrenal cortices (*qv*) and, in lesser amount, the gonads (*qv*). Androstenedione is a direct precursor of testosterone (*qv*), a potent androgen. It can be measured in the blood of both sexes.

androsterone Originally believed to be the principal male sex hormone (*qv*), this relatively weak androgenic (*qv*) hormone has little influence on male sexual characteristics but does affect normal development and functioning of the prostate (*qv*). Since the discovery of testosterone (*qv*), it has been of little medical or biological interest.

anerotic The condition of not being erotic (*qv*) or responding to erotic stimuli; lacking in eroticism.

aneroticism An obsolete term for lack of sexual interest or response. *See also* desire phase dysfunction.

anesthesia, penile or vulval Lessening of erotosexual (*qv*) sensations in the penis (*qv*), or vagina (*qv*) and vulva (*qv*) and its replacement with some degree of numbness.

anestrous Lacking in the estrous cycle; an animal that is not in estrous (*qv*) or sexual heat.

aneuploid(y) A chromosome (*qv*) complement that is not an exact multiple of the haploid (*qv*) number. In humans, a cell that does not have some multiple of 23 chromosomes.

anhedonia A lack of enjoyment and pleasure in doing or experiencing something; doing something out of simply obligation or duty. *Antonym*: hedonia.

anililagnia A rarely used term for a sexual interest in older women. *See also* desire phase dysfunction.

anilingus Oral stimulation of the anal (*qv*) region. *See also* sodomy; buggery.

anima (L.) In Carl Jung's (*qv*) early analytical psychology formulation, a person's true, inner, unconscious personality or being as distinguished from the overt personality or persona. In his later thought, anima is an archetype representing the female component of the male personality. *See also* animus.

animal copulatory behavior A speciality within the broad field of sexology (*qv*), given a scientific basis by Frank Beach, Robert Goy, and William Young, among others. The field has immense importance in breeding programs for endangered and domesticated species. The breeding of horses, cattle, swine, and poultry requires detailed knowledge of their sexual behavior, as does the more avocational breeding of dogs, fish, and fancy birds. *See also* estrus; heat; lordosis; mounting; proceptivity; rut.

animalist An obsolete term for a person who engages in bestiality (*qv*); also a hedonist (*qv*).

animal sexuality Sexual behavior of nonhuman animals. The sexual and reproductive behavior of animals ranges from conjugation processes with multiple mating types in lower invertebrates, complex parthenogenetic (*qv*) mechanisms in higher invertebrates like insects, simple release of eggs (*qv*) and sperm (*qv*) into the water in some marine invertebrates, to vertebrate mechanisms that include internal fertilization (*qv*), sequential hermaphroditism (*qv*), gonochorism (*qv*), and the development of stable sexual phenotypes with sharp differences in sexual behavior between males and females.

   Symbolically, animal sexuality has been seen as beastlike in its innateness and instinctiveness. Although the image is grossly oversimplified, metaphors based on animal sexuality nonetheless abound and persist, especially for male sexuality.

animation In philosophy and religious beliefs, the moment in human development when the soul is joined with or infused into a body; also known as ensoulment (*qv*). Various belief systems locate the moment of animation at conception (*qv*), implantation (*qv*), quickening (*qv*), later in gestation (*qv*), birth, or some time after birth ranging up the age of reason when the child has the ability to understand the customs and mores of its society. *See also* immediate animation theory; mediate animation theory; personhood; social birth.

animus (L.) In Jungian psychology, the male component of the female personality stored in the collective unconscious; in psychiatry, a deep-seated, usually controlled antagonism capable of erupting with violence under stress.

ankh An Egyptian hieroglyph representing the vulva (*qv*) and womb (*qv*). A symbol of life and protection, the *ankh* is a cross with the upper vertical arm forming a loop rather than a single straight bar.

anlage (pl. anlagen) (Gr.) In embryology (*qv*), the initial structure or element that develops and differentiates into a more complex organ or structure.

annular hymen A ringlike or perforated hymen (*qv*) that allows passage of the menstrual (*qv*) discharge.

annulment A civil or ecclesiastical decree that a putative marriage (*qv*) never existed and was always in fact null and void. The various grounds for civil annulment, which prevail in different states, may include a previous undissolved marriage, impotence (*qv*), the refusal of either spouse to have sexual intercourse (*qv*), insanity, a forced marriage, and a blood kinship or consanguinity (*qv*) that makes the marriage illegal. Grounds for a religious annulment vary in the different churches but are similar to the civil grounds. *See also* abandonment; divorce; get.

anogenital intercourse An obsolete term for anal intercourse (*qv*).

anomaly A metabolic process, structure, or individual that differs significantly from the normal pattern. Havelock Ellis (*qv*) used *anomaly* as a neutral word to describe homosexuality (*qv*) as an irregular biological type. Examples of anomalies in the human chromosome complement include numerical anomalies such as Turner syndrome (45,XO) (*qv*) and Klinefelter syndrome (47,XXY) (*qv*) and structural anomalies with deletion, duplication, and translocation of chromosome (*qv*) segments. Examples of anatomical or developmental anomalies include hermaphroditism (*qv*) and pseudohermaphroditism (*qv*).

anorchia Congenital (*qv*) absence of one or both testes (*qv*). In anorchia, the fetal gonads (*qv*) either fail to develop or differentiate as testes (*qv*) and subsequently degenerate. Treatment includes testosterone (*qv*) replacement and prosthetic testicles surgically implanted in the scrotum (*qv*). *Compare*: hyporchia.

anorexia A medical condition marked by absence of appetite, deficient nutritional intake, and emaciation sometimes ending in death from self-starvation. Anorexia has a suspected association with sexual anxieties since the phenomenon is most common among adolescent girls who unconsciously may be expressing a desire to be thin, like a boy, and thereby avoid growing up to assume the role of a woman. Anorexia may alternate with bulimia (*qv*), eating binges followed by induced vomiting. Anorexia leads to amenorrhea (*qv*) when the percentage of body fat drops below the normal range of 18 to 25 percent to around 12 percent.

anorgasmia A hypophilic (*qv*) condition marked by the absence of or inability to experience sexual orgasm (*qv*). Anorgasmia may be primary or always present, secondary and occurring only with certain partners or in certain circumstances, or random. In men, anorgasmia is known as orgasmic incompetence (*qv*) or retarded or delayed ejaculation (*qv*). In females, it is often confused with frigidity (*qv*). The condition may result from a variety of organic and psychological causes.

anosmia In the strict sense, a total inability to smell anything; in a looser sense, anosmia may be hyposmia or a lack of acuity in the olfactory system with diminished ability to distinguish different odors. This condition may affect sexual desire (*qv*). *See also* pheromone.

anovaria Congenital (*qv*) absence of the ovaries (*qv*). *See also* Turner syndrome; Hunter syndrome.

anovular *See* anovulation; anovulatory menstrual cycle.

anovular stage The period between the first menstrual period (*qv*) and the first ovulation (*qv*). The start of ovulation may occur anywhere between one month and seven years after the onset of menstruation (*qv*).

anovulation (anovulatory) The failure of the ovaries (*qv*) to produce mature ova (*qv*) or to release them from mature follicles. Anovulation is a common organic cause of infertility (*qv*). It may be due to immaturity or senility of the ovary, to primary ovarian dysfunction, to ovarian dysgenesis (*qv*), to disturbances of the hypothalamus (*qv*), pituitary gland (*qv*), or ovary caused by stress or disease, or medications. It may be remedied by ovulation-inducing drugs such as Perganol (*qv*) or Chlomid (*qv*). *See also* follicle stimulating hormone; luteinizing hormone; releasing hormone.

anovulatory menstrual cycle A pattern of controlled menstruation (*qv*), with suppression of normal cycles in the ovaries (*qv*), ovulation (*qv*), and menses (*qv*). This condition, induced by use of the oral hormonal contraceptive pill (*qv*), results in infertility (*qv*).

antaphroditic A rarely used term for a venereal disease (*qv*) remedy.

antenatal An obsolete term for *prenatal* ("before birth").

antenuptial agreement (contract) *See* premarital contract.

antepartal In reference to a pregnant (*qv*) woman, the period of time between conception (*qv*) and the beginning of labor (*qv*).

anterior pituitary *See* pituitary.

anterior pituitary gonadotropin *See* follicle stimulating hormone; gonadotropin; luteinizing hormone; pituitary; releasing hormone.

anterior urethritis An infection and inflammation of the penile urethra (*qv*), between the base of the penis (*qv*) and the glans (*qv*).

anti-abortion movement A coalition of anti-abortion activists, including conservative Roman Catholics, religious fundamentalists, Evangelicals, Moral Majority Protestant groups, rightwing conservative politicians, and others opposed to the performance of abortion and its legal acceptability. Some anti-abortion activists have lobbied for a constitutional amendment that would declare the fetus (*qv*) a person with inalienable rights from the moment of conception (*qv*). Other aims of the anti-abortion movement include gaining legal protection for the fetus, restriction of the use of federal or state funds for abortions, restriction of federal funds for local or international programs providing abortion counselling or performing abortions, and closing clinics that perform abortions. *See also* pro-life movement; pro-choice movement; Appendix D.

antiandrogen A hormone (*qv*) or hormone analog or substitute that acts competitively to replace androgen (*qv*) within the nuclei of target cells. An antiandrogen inhibits the secretion of testosterone (*qv*) from the testis (*qv*) by inducing a negative feedback to the hypothalamus (*qv*) and/or pituitary (*qv*), thus reducing the release of gonadotropic-releasing hormones (*qv*) and follicle-stimulating hormone (*qv*). An antiandrogen is itself either biologically inert or has a very weak masculinizing function. *See also* cyproterone (acetate).

antiandrogenic agent A drug, such as cyproterone (acetate) (*qv*), administered to counter the overproduction of naturally occurring androgens (*qv*). An antiandrogenic agent may be used to control hirsutism (*qv*) and virilization (*qv*) in females and premature puberty (*qv*) in boys. It is used in a form of chemical castration (*qv*) to reduce or eliminate the sex drive (*qv*) of compulsive, repetitive sex offenders (*qv*) as an alternative to imprisonment. When used with males, antiandrogenic agents can block testicular development in young patients. In older men, such agents have a demasculinizing effect, producing erectile dysfunction (*qv*), sterility (*qv*), and gynecomastia (*qv*).

antibiotic A drug or chemical agent that kills microorganisms or inhibits their growth. Some antibiotics have a broad spectrum, being active against a variety of bacteria; others are very specific in their effect on a particular bacterial strain. Antibiotics are important therapeutic agents for syphilis (*qv*), gonorrhea (*qv*), non-gonococcal urethritis (*qv*), and hemophilus vaginalis (*qv*). Some antibiotics have a teratogenic (*qv*) effect on the fetus (*qv*).

antibody An immunoglobulin molecule formed by immunocompetent cells in response to an antigenic stimulus from a foreign substance or antigen (*qv*). Antibodies bind complementarily with their specific antigens to remove the foreign substance from the organism.

antigen A foreign molecule capable of eliciting the immunocompetent cells of an organism to produce an antibody (*qv*) specific to the stereochemical character of the antigen (*qv*).

antigonadotropin A chemical substance that counteracts or neutralizes one or more of the gonadotropic hormones (*qv*), follicle-stimulating hormone (*qv*), luteinizing hormone (*qv*), interstitial cell-stimulating hormone (*qv*), or human chorionic gonadotropin (*qv*). It is found in the blood serum, more often in individuals who have received repeated doses of gonadotropins as part of infertility (*qv*) treatment.

antipudic A rarely used term for a covering for the genitalia (*qv*).

antrum Any cavity, such as the antrum of the maturing Graafian follicle (*qv*).

anuloma A rarely used term for a man's mating with a woman judged socially inferior; the opposite of hypergamy (*qv*).

anuptaphobia A rarely used term for the fear of staying unmarried.

anus The termination of the alimentary tract or digestive system. Both involuntary and voluntary sphincters (*qv*) at the external opening of the rectum (*qv*) relax to allow defecation or penile insertion during anal intercourse (*qv*).

anxiety, sexual Strong, all-encompassing feelings of apprehension, danger, and powerlessness arising, often unconsciously, within the individual when confronted with sexual desires (*qv*) or impulses. Sexual anxieties result from conflicts in the person's psyche between sexual desires or impulses on one side and insecurities, taboos, and feelings of guilt or shame instilled by authority figures. In general, anxiety is marked by a variety of physical signs of tension, increased heart rate, rapid breathing, sweating, and trembling.

apandria Aversion for the male sex. *See also* androphobia.

apareunia The inability to engage in sexual intercourse (*qv*) or abstinence (*qv*) from sexual intercourse.

apathy, erotic A lack of interest in sexual relations (*qv*) and lack of sexual arousal (*qv*) at the possibility of such.

Apgar score The evaluation of a newborn's (*qv*) physical condition in terms of his or her ability to adjust to life outside the uterus (*qv*). Based on observations performed 1 minute and 5 minutes after birth, the Apgar score involves five factors: skin color, heart rate, respiratory effort, muscle tone, and reflex irritability. The evaluation was devised by Virginia Apgar (1909–1974), an American anesthesiologist.

aphanisis An obsolete term coined by Ernest Jones, a psychoanalyst, for the inability to enjoy sex, which he believed was the root of all neuroses.

aphilophrenia A rarely used term for the fear of being unloved.

aphoria A medical term for female infertility (*qv*). An accompanying adjective usually indicates the cause for the failure to reproduce, as *aphoria impercita*, an infertility resulting from sexual aversion (*qv*).

aphrodisiac A food, drug, or scent alleged to increase sexual interest or vigor. Folklore suggests enhancement of sexual desire is associated with mandrake (*qv*) root, ginseng, licorice, yohimbine (*qv*), oysters, fennel seed, and a variety of other substances, none of which has been shown to be effective biological agents. *See also* Welbrutin; yohimbine.

aphrodisiomania An obsolete term for erotomania (*qv*), nymphomania (*qv*) or satyriasis (*qv*).

Aphrodite In Greek mythology, the goddess of love, beauty, and sexuality, called Venus (*qv*) in Roman myth. She was the mother of Eros (*qv*) or Cupid, the god of love, and of Priapus, whose name refers to the penis (*qv*) and who is the god of procreation (*qv*) and phallic worship (*qv*). In classic Greek mythology, Aphrodite represented sensual sexuality as opposed to domestic fertility and motherhood, the domain of Demeter as well as other goddesses. In Plato's *Symposium*, a distinction is drawn between the "common" Aphrodite, who draws inferior men to women and boys, and a "heavenly" Aphrodite, who draws superior men to the beauty of the soul and mind rather than to the body. For Renaissance and later Western artists, Aphrodite became the ultimate symbol for female beauty and sexuality (*qv*) (e.g., Botticelli's *The Birth of Venus*, 1480–1485). From her name arises the word aphrodesiac (*qv*), referring to any substance imputed to enhance sexual prowess and pleasure. When conjoined with the god Hermes as Hermaphrodite, Aphrodite became a mythological and artistic symbol for the coexistence of male and female anatomical and psychological qualities in one individual. Resources: P. Friedrich, *The Meaning of Aphrodite* (Chicago: University of Chicago Press, 1978); E. C. Keuls, *The Reign of the Phallus: Sexual Politics in Ancient Athens* (New York: Harper and Row, 1985).

apistia A rarely used term for marital infidelity (*qv*).

apodysophilia A rarely used term for the desire to strip or appear naked in public.

apotemnophilia The paraphilic (*qv*) condition of being dependent on being an amputee or fantasizing being an amputee in order to obtain erotic arousal (*qv*) and facilitate orgasm (*qv*). Apotemnophilia may be accompanied by obsessional scheming to carry out a self-contrived amputation or to obtain this surgery. The reciprocal paraphilic condition in which the partner is the amputee is acrotomophilia (*qv*).

appendix testis A small, functionless vestige of the Mullerian (*qv*) or paramesonephric duct attached to the testis (*qv*) near the head of the epididymis (*qv*); also known as hydatid of Morgani.

appetitive behavior In motivation theory, a behavior that draws an animal or human closer to the thing it wants or needs. The appetitive search for food or a sexual partner may be followed by consummatory behavior (*qv*), eating, or coitus (*qv*). *See also* drive; instinct.

approach-avoidance conflict The coexistence of conflicting responses to a single stimulus, as when a man or woman wants to marry but fears the responsibilities or sexual aspects of being married.

APS *See* artificial placentation system.

Aquinas, Thomas (1225–1274) Dominican philosopher; Roman Catholic theologian, and, later, Roman Catholic saint, Aquinas is generally accepted as the towering figure in medieval theology because of his application of the philosophy of Aristotle to Christian thought in a way that has influenced all subsequent thinking in theology and philosophy. His master work, the *Summa Theologica*, contains many discussions of sexual matters and morality. His defense and extension of Aristotle's mediate animation theory (*qv*) allowed for abortion (*qv*) prior to quickening (*qv*) and is useful today in abortion discussions. His articulation of the natural law (*qv*) applied to sexual matters is still the basis of Roman Catholic positions that view masturbation (*qv*), contraception (*qv*), and anal (*qv*) and oral sex (*qv*) as unnatural acts (*qv*) and immoral. Because his training included studies with Albert the Great, a prominent biologist and theologian, Aquinas was able to use the scientific knowledge of his time as a basis for his philosophical and theological speculations. *See also* immediate animation; preformation; epigenesis; natural sin; unnatural sin.

Arabic erotology A classic tradition in Arab cultures that led to such love manuals as the sixteenth-century book *The Perfumed Garden of the Shaykh Nefzawi* (*qv*), translated into English in the late nineteenth century by Sir Richard Burton. Such love manuals are explicit and sensuous, although often deemed pornographic (*qv*) in Europe and America until recently.

ARC *See* AIDS-related complex.

archetype In Carl Jung's (*qv*) conception, the primeval content of the species unconsciousness with its inherited ideas and predispositions. *See also* phylism; template.

archistriatum (L.) In lower animals, the structure corresponding to the amygdala (*qv*) of mammals.

ardor urinae (L.) A dated medical term for a burning sensation accompanying urination.

areola (pl. areolae) A circular area of darker pigmented skin immediately surrounding the nipple (*qv*) of the breast (*qv*), containing oil-secreting glands whose secretions prevent drying and breaks in the skin during nursing (*qv*).

areolar gland One of the large sebaceous or oil-secreting glands in the areola (*qv*) encircling the breast (*qv*) nipple (*qv*) of women. Areolar glands protect the nipple during nursing (*qv*). They are surrounded by smooth muscle bundles that cause nipple erection when sexually stimulated.

areola umbilicus (L.) A pigmented area occasionally occurring around the navel in pregnant women.

Aretino, Pietro (1492–1557) A serious Italian writer, better known for his pornographic writings, *Figurae* [Postures], and *Ragionamenti* [Dialogs]. He is said to have blackmailed Michaelangelo for his homosexual (*qv*) activities.

Aristotle (384–322 B.C.E.) One of the greatest philosophers of history, this pupil of Plato and teacher of Alexander the Great was the son of a Greek physician. His interests included all philosophy, from logic and rhetoric through poetry to science and biology. His writing, based on personal observations, dissections, and attempts to find natural causes, include studies of the natural history and classification of animals, and the sexual reproduction (*qv*) and fetal development of cuttlefish, octopuses, chickens, insects, and mammals (*qv*). He discussed the causes and merits of homosexuality (*qv*) and suggested homosexuality may be a functional and acceptable adaptation to overpopulation. With Plato, he suggested the concept of a natural law (*qv*) in which the morality of use or abuse of anything was determined by the eternal and unchangeable laws of nature written in the essence of each creature. He supported the idea of epigenesis (*qv*), which influenced later philosophical theories of human development and abortion (*qv*). Through Thomas Aquinas (qv) in the Middle Ages, Aristotle has had a major influence on all subsequent Western thought, especially Christian philosophy and ethical thought.

arousal, sexual The physiological and psychological state of being sexuoerotically (*qv*) stimulated or excited. *See also* desire phase; excitement stage; plateau phase; orgasm; resolution phase; vasocongestion.

arpagee A rarely used term for a raped (*qv*) woman.

arranged marriage The negotiation of a marital contract or union of a male and female by the parents of the bride and groom or by family elders. In an arranged marriage, the consent or knowledge of the couple may be irrelevant, as is the concept of love existing at the beginning of the marriage. If the contract is agreed to while the couple are minors, the marriage is consummated after puberty (*qv*) or adult status is achieved. *See also* child marriage.

arrested testes Undescended testes. *See also* cryptorchidism.

arrha In the Germanic traditions of the early Middle Ages, a token remnant of the old brideprice (*qv*). *See also* bridegift; dowry; dower; endowment; Morgengabe.

arrhenoblastoma A rare, malignant tumor of the ovary (*qv*). This type of tumor may sometimes secrete an androgenic (*qv*) hormone, which has a masculinizing (*qv*) effect on the woman's body or, if she is pregnant (*qv*), on her female fetus (*qv*).

artificial embryonation The transfer of an embryo (*qv*) from one female to another after artificial insemination (*qv*). The embryo is flushed from the uterus (*qv*) before it implants in the first female. The menstrual cycle (*qv*) of the host woman is synchronized so that her uterine condition is optimal for implantation (*qv*).

artificial hymen Plastic surgery performed to recreate a hymen (*qv*). Popular in developed countries where virginity (*qv*) of the bride is highly valued, particularly in Japan, and in such developing nations as Morocco. The surgery is banned in Italy.

artificial impregnation *See* artificial insemination; artificial embryonation; self-insemination.

artificial insemination The introduction of semen (*qv*), fresh or frozen, into the vaginal canal (*qv*) or uterine cavity by any means other than sexual intercourse (*qv*). Artificial insemination is used to bypass the husband's sterility (*qv*) and produce a pregnancy or to impregnate a single or lesbian (*qv*) woman who does not want to have sexual intercourse. Human artificial insemination was first accomplished around 1800 in England but was not very successful until the mid-1930s because, prior to that time, insemination was done around the time of the menstrual period (*qv*), wrongly believed to be the most fertile period in the woman's cycle. *See also* artificial insemination donor; artificial insemination husband; self-insemination.

artificial insemination donor (AID) The introduction of fresh or frozen semen (*qv*) from a donor into the vaginal canal (*qv*) by any means other than sexual intercourse (*qv*). The identity of the donor is usually unknown to the woman being inseminated and her husband. AID is used when the husband is sterile (*qv*) or is a carrier for some serious hereditary defect, which, when combined with the mother's genome (*qv*), would place the resulting fetus (*qv*) at risk. To facilitate legitimization of the AID offspring, written consent of the husband and wife is usually required. In some states the husband may formally adopt his wife's AID offspring. *See also* self-insemination.

artificial insemination husband (AIH) The introduction of the husband's semen (*qv*), fresh or frozen, into the vaginal canal (*qv*) or uterine cavity by any means other than sexual intercourse (*qv*). In the case of oligospermia (*qv*) in the husband, several ejaculates (*qv*) may be frozen, stored, and combined for a single insemination.

artificial penis A dildo (*qv*) made of alabaster, plastic, marble, rubber or other material.

artificial placentation system (APS) A laboratory system capable of supporting a fetus (*qv*) outside the uterus (*qv*). An APS consists of a glass tank with artificial amniotic fluid (*qv*) and mechanical substitutes capable of replacing the respiratory, circulatory, excretory, and nutrient transfer systems of the placenta (*qv*); also known as an artificial womb.

artificial selection In animal husbandry and plant breeding, artificial selection refers to the selection of specific individuals as parents for the next generation. Selection is made on the basis of traits or characteristics possessed by the chosen animal or plant that are considered useful, valuable, or attractive (e.g., artificial selection for flower color or scent). The result of artificial selection is the enrichment of the next generation in the genes of the selected parents and the reduction of other genes. *See also* natural selection.

artificial womb *See* artificial placentation system.

ARV An obsolete name for the human immunodeficiency virus (HIV) (*qv*), which causes acquired immune deficiency syndrome (*qv*).

asceticism A value system and life-style that emphasizes self-discipline and self-denial of the body, sensual pleasures, and the senses in deference to the cultivation of purely spiritual values and goals. *See also* dualism; hedonism; Platonism; Stoicism (Stoics).

Ascheim-Zondek test (AZ test) An obsolete biological test for pregnancy (*qv*). Urine from a woman is injected into a female mouse where ovarian changes occur within 100 hours if the woman is pregnant. *See also* ELISA Test; beta subunit HCG radioimmunoassay; home pregnancy test.

asexual Lacking interest in sexual interaction, nonsexual; a form of reproduction (*qv*) without gametes (*qv*), by budding, fission, spore formation, parthenogenesis, or vegetative reproduction.

asexualization Castration (*qv*), sterilization (*qv*), or removal of the testes or ovaries (*qv*).

ASMFR *See* age-specific marital fertility rate.

aspermia Lack of semen (*qv*) or the inability to ejaculate (*qv*) semen.

asphyxiophilia *See* autoerotic (asphyxia) death; erotic self-strangulation.

aspro A professional male homosexual (*qv*) prostitute (*qv*).

ass An expression with several meanings: a contemptuous person, the buttocks (*qv*), the anus (*qv*), the vagina (*qv*), or sexual intercourse (*qv*) as in the expression ''get a piece of ass.''

assault In common speech, an attack or an onslaught; in law, the threat to attack or do bodily harm to an individual when there is immediate and present ability to do the threatened harm. In law, an actual attack is battery (*qv*), while threatening someone is assault. In sexology, assault typically refers to rape (*qv*) or the threat of rape. *See also* criminal assault.

assaultive marital rape *See* marital rape.

assertiveness training A flexible but loosely structured teaching method that seeks to help a client acquire assertive skills through role playing and practice. Four basic procedures are involved: (1) teaching the difference between assertion and aggression and between politeness and the lack of assertiveness, (2) helping to identify and accept both one's own personal rights and the rights of others, (3) reducing obstacles such as irrational thinking, excessive anxiety, guilt, insecurity, and lack of self-assuredness or self-image that prevent a person from being assertive, and (4) developing assertiveness skills through supervised practice sessions. Directed originally at helping middle-class women, assertiveness training has been criticized by some feminists (*qv*) as treating the symptoms of pervasive economic and social repression of women without acknowledging the underlying causes.

assignation A lovers' rendezvous, a tryst.

assigned sex (gender) The sex of a newborn, male or female, that is officially declared and recorded on the birth certificate. One's assigned sex is the basis for all future gender scripting (*qv*) by parents and others. A transsexual's (*qv*) assigned sex is officially and legally changed following surgery. *Synonym*: gender of assignment.

assisted breech An obstetrical procedure used for a baby being born feet or buttocks (*qv*) first. The delivery is natural and unassisted until the umbilicus (*qv*) appears, when obstetric extraction is begun.

assortative mating The pairing and mating of individuals on the basis of reciprocally matching features, behaviors, or other characteristics; the opposite of random mating. *See also* artificial selection; natural selection; sexual selection.

astringent treatment The use of alum or other chemicals to shrink the mucous membranes of the vaginal wall (*qv*). Occasionally used by young prostitutes (*qv*) to simulate virginity (*qv*). In some Eastern and South Pacific cultures, this treatment is believed to enhance the sexual attractiveness of young women.

astyphia Medical term for male impotence (*qv*). *See also* erectile dysfunction.

asymmetric hypomastia A congenital (*qv*) condition in females in which one breast (*qv*) is significantly smaller than the other.

asymptomatic Lacking in clinically significant or observed symptoms. *See also* pathognomonic.

atavism The presence in an individual of traits or characteristics more like those of an earlier ancestor than the immediate parent; a reversion to or reappearance of an early form. The term is not in current usage.

atocia A rarely used term for female infertility (*qv*).

atresia (L.) Congenital absence or closure of the opening of a tubular structure or organ.

atresia folliculi (L.) Degeneration of a corpus luteum (*qv*) into the scar tissue of a corpus albicans (*qv*) when the ovum (*qv*) is not fertilized (*qv*).

atresia vaginae (L.) A general term for closure of the vagina (*qv*), correctible by surgery. This condition may be due to an imperforate hymen (*qv*) or, more rarely, to fusion of the vaginal walls (*qv*).

atrophic vaginalis Degeneration and inflammation of the vaginal mucosa (*qv*) in postmenopausal (*qv*) women, resulting from a less than minimum estrogen (*qv*) level. Treatment is with combined estrogen and progesterone (*qv*) replacement.

atrophy (adj. atrophic, atrophied) Degeneration of an organ, tissue, or structure. A failure of cell nutrition manifested in decrease in size or healthiness of a tissue, organ, or system. *See also* agenesis; dystrophy.

attachment A psychological bonding (*qv*) that forms between an infant and the mother, father, and/or other caregiver. *See also* bonding.

attachment disorder A consequence of somatosensory-affectional deprivation (SAD) (*qv*) in which an infant (*qv*) fails to develop the ability to interact and relate with others because he or she was emotionally neglected and socially isolated at critical periods (*qv*) in early life. A pattern of apathy, lack of response, and failure to thrive is characteristic of children in institutions and children who are unloved or ignored at home.

attitude A relatively stable system of beliefs concerning some object and its value. Attitude surveys are common in sexological research. Psychologists tend to use the term *attitude* with a clearly defined meaning; social scientists are more flexible in its use. *See also* attitude scale.

attitude scale Sets of standardized statements with which research subjects are asked to agree or disagree. The development of an attitude scale assumes that an attitude (*qv*) toward a particular sexual behavior, for instance, might embrace aspects such as socioeconomic, religious, ethnic, and gender differences that allow respondents to be ranked along a continuum representing varying degree. The most commonly encountered attitude scales are the Guttman, Likert, and Thurston scales.

attraction The way in which a person is drawn to evaluate another person positively or negatively.

attribution The tendency to ascribe a cause to one's subjective experience. The process of attribution can also shape and contribute to the subjective experience.

atypical paraphilia A classification of the American Psychiatric Association that includes the more unusual and rarer paraphilias (*qv*). *See also* acrotomophilia; apotemnophilia; asphyxiophilia; autoassassinatophilia; coprophilia; erotophonophilia; klismaphilia; mysophilia; necrophilia; stigmatophilia.

Augustine of Hippo (Aurelius Augustinus) (354–430) A Christian theologian and a brilliant thinker and writer, Augustine was, next to St. Paul, the greatest influence on Christian thought, both Protestant and Catholic. In his youth, Augustine was a disciple of Manicheanism, a philosophy derived from dualistic Persian Zoroastrianism. His later Christian writings on the passions, sex, women, and marriage show this influence in the emphasis he places on the struggle between good and evil, light and darkness, matter and spirit. Augustine wrote dogmatically on the ''shame which attends all sexual intercourse'' even when engaged in by a married couple for the purpose of procreation (*qv*). According to Augustine, ''sexual intercourse is always performed with lust and therefore needs to be hidden.'' Having described the sexual organs of males and females as ''obscene parts,'' he argued that if Adam and Eve had not sinned in the Garden of Eden, they would have reproduced by the equivalent of a chaste, asexual (*qv*) handshake.

aulophobia A morbid, obsessive fear of any musical instrument resembling the penis (*qv*).

autoagonistophilia A paraphilic (*qv*) condition in which sexuoerotic (*qv*) arousal (*qv*) and orgasm (*qv*) is responsive to and dependent on being observed or being on stage or on camera while engaging in sexual activity (*qv*). In the reciprocal paraphilic conditions, mixoscopia (*qv*), scoptophilia (*qv*), and voyeurism (*qv*), sexual arousal and orgasm are dependent on watching another person engage in sexual activity.

autoassassinatophilia The paraphilic (*qv*) condition of being dependent on the staging of one's own masochistic (*qv*) death in order to achieve sexual arousal (*qv*) and orgasm (*qv*). The reciprocal paraphilia is lust murder (*qv*) or erotophonophilia (*qv*).

autocunnilingus Masturbation (*qv*) achieved by a woman through sucking or tonguing her vulval (*qv*) area.

autoerastia An obsolete term for autoeroticism (*qv*).

autoerotic (asphyxia) death A death that results inadvertently and accidentally from a paraphilic (*qv*) sexuoerotic (*qv*) ritual involving self-strangulation or self-applied electric current. Autoerotic death occurs more often with adolescent males than females, who often wear female underclothes while masturbating (*qv*). The partial asphyxiation heightens the intensity of masturbatory orgasm (*qv*). Various techniques are described in the writings of the Marquis de Sade (*qv*) and in pornographic (*qv*) literature and films. Between 500 and 1,000 deaths are estimated to be due to this paraphilic behavior each year in the United States. Most of these deaths are misinterpreted as suicides or homicides. *See also* autoassassinatophilia.

autoeroticism Erotosexual (*qv*) activity directed toward one's self and engaged in without a partner. The most common form of autoerotic activity is masturbation (*qv*), which may include stimulation of one's own genitals (*qv*), pelvic thrusting (*qv*), fondling (*qv*) of the testes (*qv*), nipples (*qv*), breasts (*qv*), and other erogenous areas (*qv*) of the body. *See also* alloeroticism; allosexual. A second meaning of the term occurs in psychoanalytic theory (*qv*) where the reference is to an early phase of psychosexual development (*qv*), occurring in the oral (*qv*) and anal stages (*qv*).

autofellatio Fellatio (*qv*) performed on one's self.

autofetishism A paraphilic (*qv*) form of narcissism (*qv*) in which one's own body becomes a sexual obsession and the stimulus for all erotosexual (*qv*) responses. *See also* automonosexualism.

autoflagellation An extreme form of stigmatophilia (*qv*) or automasochism (*qv*) in which a person whips and beats oneself in order to become sexually aroused (*qv*) and achieve sexual satisfaction (*qv*).

autohedonia An obsolete term for masturbation (*qv*).

autoinoculation The spread of an infection from one part of the body to another, as with fecal bacteria spreading from the rectum (*qv*) to the vagina (*qv*) or a sexually transmitted disease (*qv*) spreading from the penile/vaginal region to the oral cavity through oral sex (*qv*).

automasochism *See* apotemnophilia; asphyxiophilia; autoassassinatophilia; stigmatophilia.

automonosexualism A syndrome described by Magnus Hirschfeld (*qv*) in which a man is so self-centered and narcissistic he can achieve sexual satisfaction only by masturbation (*qv*) or autofellatio (*qv*).

automutilation *See* apotemnophilia.

automysophobia A morbid, neurotic fear of being dirty and smelling unclean. Because of the natural body odors and "messiness" of sexual relations (*qv*) and the close association of the sexual organs with the organs of defecation and urination, this fear may inhibit or prevent the affected person from engaging in sexual relations.

autonecrophilia A paraphilic (*qv*) condition in which one achieves sexual arousal (*qv*) and orgasm (*qv*) by imagining oneself as a corpse.

autonepiophilia A paraphilic (*qv*) condition in which sexuoerotic arousal (*qv*) and orgasm (*qv*) are responsive to and dependent on impersonating a baby in diapers and being treated as an infant by one's partner. Autonepiophilia may be adjunctive to masochistic (*qv*) discipline and humiliation. In the reciprocal paraphilic condition, nepiophilia (*qv*), an individual is dependent on playing the parent role with a partner who plays the infant role. *Synonym*: paraphilic infantilism.

autonomic nervous system That part of the nervous system normally outside voluntary control that regulates a variety of involuntary physiological reactions, especially those concerned with vital digestive, respiratory, cardiovascular, and glandular functions. This system is based in paired ganglionic chains and a variety of plexuses alongside the vertebral column. *See also* central nervous system; sympathetic nervous system; parasympathetic nervous system.

autonomous stage The last of three stages in Jean Piaget's (*qv*) model of moral development in which moral awareness and decision making are based on co-operation and internalized values rather than on the constraint of an outside authority. *See also* heteronomous stage; egocentric stage.

autopedophilia *See* autonepiophilia.

autophilia Love of one's self instead of a partner, characterized by masturbation (*qv*). *See also* autoeroticism; autosexual.

autoplasty A psychoanalytic term for using one's libidinal energies and drive to change the self as a means of adapting to reality. Psychoanalytic treatment is sometimes described as autoplastic adaptation.

autosadism A nonspecific, outdated term for a variety of paraphilias (*qv*) involving infliction of pain on one's self. *See also* apotemnophilia; asphyxiophilia; autoassassinatophilia; stigmatophilia.

autoscophilia A paraphilic (*qv*) condition in which sexual arousal (*qv*) and orgasm (*qv*) is facilitated by and dependent on looking at one's own body and sexual organs.

autosexual Sexual activity (*qv*) engaged in alone, usually masturbation (*qv*) with or without an accompanying erotic fantasy (*qv*) or ritual.

autosite The larger, more normally formed member of unequal or asymmetrical, conjoined twins (*qv*) upon whom the other, smaller twin is physiologically dependent.

autosomal inheritance An inherited trait produced by a gene (*qv*) or genes carried on one or more of the nonsex chromosomes (*qv*) or autosomes (*qv*). *See also* sex-limited trait; sex-influenced trait; X-linked trait.

autosome In the human, any one of the 22 paired homologous (*qv*) chromosomes (*qv*) other than the sex chromosomes, the X or Y.

autospermatoxin An agglutinating agent found in the blood serum of some males that immobilizes the sperm (*qv*) and results in sterility (*qv*).

autosuck vagina An artificial vagina (*qv*) that produces a vacuum and suction sensation when a penis (*qv*) is inserted into it.

autotomy Self-mutilation. *See also* apotemnophilia.

Availability Index *See* Marital Opportunity Ratio.

aversion therapy A form of behavioral (modification) therapy (*qv*) that utilizes negative conditioning to modify or eliminate a particular behavior or response. In a clinical setting, an unpleasant or painful experience is associated with the undesirable sexual stimulus, such as child pornography (*qv*), to develop in the patient an aversion for the stimulus.

avisodomy A form of bestiality (*qv*) involving sexual intercourse (*qv*) with a bird—usually a goose, duck, chicken, or turkey.

axillary hair Hair found under the axilla or arm at its junction with the shoulder following puberty (*qv*).

axillary intercourse Sexual intercourse (*qv*) engaged in by inserting the penis (*qv*) in the armpit where the upper arm joins the shoulder.

azidothymidine (AZT) The most commonly used drug in treating acquired immune deficiency syndrome (*qv*). Originally used in treating cancer, this drug is a synthetic nucleotide, which is incorporated into DNA (*qv*) when the RNA (*qv*) of the HIV I virus (*qv*) is transcribed into DNA. When azidothymidine replaces thymidine in the base sequence of the DNA, the next nucleotide cannot be attached. The resulting incomplete DNA chain prevents the formation of new viruses. However, since this synthetic nucleotide affects all rapidly dividing cells in the patient's body, the production of new red blood cells is especially affected, resulting in anemia.

azoospermia Complete absence of motile sperm (*qv*) from a semen sample (*qv*). Azoospermia may be caused by testicular dysfunction (*qv*), blockage of the tubules in the epididymis (*qv*), or vasectomy (*qv*). The result is sterility (*qv*), without impairment of the ability to have vaginal intercourse (*qv*). *See also* oligospermia.

AZT *See* azidothymidine.

B

baby An infant (*qv*) or young child from birth to about 2 years of age, especially one who is not able yet to walk or talk; lay term for infant.

baby boom The sharp rise in the American birthrate (*qv*) that followed World War II and extended through 1964. Advances in birth control (*qv*), concern over the population explosion, and socioeconomic factors led to a significant drop in the birthrate after the early 1960s. Children born during this era are referred to as *baby boomers*.

bacchanalia A relatively modern term for orgies (*qv*) in ancient Roman society, derived from the Greek and Roman god of wine and revelry, Bacchus. While popular images suggest that bacchanalia were characteristic of licentious life in ancient Rome, a more accurate reading indicates that the Greco-Roman tradition had a long history of careful and reflective, even fearful and inhibited attitudes, toward sexual pleasure. Contrary to popular image, Stoicism, the prevailing philosophy of Rome, stressed the need to control sexual drives and expression. In 185 B.C.E., the Roman government launched a brutal suppression of the cult of Bacchus and the bacchanalia. *See also* Dionysian.

bachelor An unmarried adult male.

bachelor mother An obsolete term for a single, never-married mother.

bacterial STDs Any sexually transmitted disease (*qv*) caused by a bacterium (*qv*). *See also* gonorrhea; syphilis; Hemophilus vaginalis; nongonococcal urethritis.

bacterium (pl. bacteria) Living organisms, characteristically microscopic in size, consisting of a single cell that differs from other single-celled organisms in lacking a cell nucleus and true chromosomes (*qv*) of the kind found in higher organisms, among other differences. As a group, bacteria are called prokaryotes to distinguish them from eukaryote organisms, whose cells have nuclei and true chromosomes. Based on cell shape, bacteria fall into three broad groups: spherical cocci (singular: coccus), rod-shaped bacilli (singular: bacillus), and the spiral, elongated spirochetes. Bacteria are also classified by their pathogenicity for humans, animals, and plants. Pathogenic bacteria are responsible for a wide variety of diseases, including syphilis (*qv*), caused by the spirochete *Treponema pallidum* (*qv*); and gonorrhea, caused by the coccus *Neisseria gonorrhoeae*. The study of bacteria is bacteriology, which, in modern usage, is now called microbiology. A sound knowledge of bacteriology or microbiology is essential for understanding the sexually transmitted diseases (STDS) (*qv*) and their prevention.

bad breast In the psychoanalytic (*qv*) model proposed by Melanie Klein, the theory that, during infancy, part of the mother's breast (*qv*) is experienced as a bad object reflecting the death instinct.

bad object In the psychoanalytic model proposed by Melanie Klein, the theory that the superego (*qv*) is focused on good and bad objects, with the bad objects representing something dirty and sexual (*qv*).

Baer, Karl Ernst von (1792–1876) An Estonian embryologist (*qv*) and biologist who taught in Russia and Germany, Baer is considered the founder of modern embryology. He discovered and described the mammalian (dog) ovum (*qv*) inside the Graafian follicle (*qv*) in 1827, individual zygotes (*qv*) in the uterine tube, and blastocysts (*qv*) in the uterus (*qv*). He investigated the embryology of the chicken and demonstrated the derivation of various vertebrate organs from primary germ layers (*qv*) by differentiation. He favored epigenesis (*qv*) and opposed preformation theory (*qv*).

bag of waters The membranous amniotic sac (*qv*) with its amniotic fluid (*qv*) surrounding the fetus (*qv*) in the uterus (*qv*) of a pregnant woman.

balanic Of or pertaining to the glans (*qv*) of the penis (*qv*) or clitoris (*qv*).

balanitis Inflammation of the penile or clitoral glans (*qv*), often with involvement of the foreskin (*qv*). Balanitis may be bacterial (*qv*), amebic (*qv*), diabetic, monilial (*qv*), or trichomonal (*qv*) in origin. It may also be caused by medication or drug side effects.

balanitis xerotica obliterans (L.) A chronic skin disease of the penis (*qv*) characterized by a white, hardened area on the glans (*qv*). The external urethral opening and damage to the glans may result. Treatment is with local antibacterial and anti-inflammatory agents.

balanoplasty Plastic surgery on the penile glans (*qv*).

balanoposthitis A generalized inflammation of the glans (*qv*) of the penis (*qv*) and foreskin (*qv*) characterized by soreness, irritation, and discharge and usually caused by a bacterial or fungal infection.

balanorrhagia An infection of the penile or clitoral glans (*qv*) with copious discharge of pus.

balanorrhea *See* balanorrhagia.

B and D Bondage and dominance or bondage and discipline (*qv*).

banns An announcement of an intended marriage (*qv*), generally made in church on three consecutive Sundays.

barbiturate One of several pharmacological agents used as an anticonvulsant, sedative, or elixir. They may have a masculinizing (*qv*) effect on the fetus (*qv*) when taken during pregnancy (*qv*). The street expression for barbiturates is ''downer.''

bar mitzvah (mizvah) (Hebrew) A Jewish ceremony celebrating the arrival of a 13-year-old Jewish boy at the age of responsibility and manhood. The term also applies to the youth undergoing the ceremony. The female counterpart is *bat mitzvah* (*qv*).

Barr body A condensed, partially inactive X chromosome (*qv*) appearing as a small, dense, dark-staining mass of the nuclear membrane of some somatic (*qv*) cells. Normal females have one active X and one partially inactivated X. The single X chromosome in somatic cells of males is active. In cells with two or more X chromosomes, the number of Barr bodies is always one fewer than the total number of X chromosomes. The presence of one Barr body and a Y chromosome indicates a 47,XXY Klinefelter syndrome (*qv*). Individuals with Turner syndrome (*qv*), 45,XO, have no Barr body. Inexpensive and rapid screening for Barr bodies is available. Also known as sex chromatin and X chromatin.

barren Childless. The term was commonly used in earlier times when women were believed to be the sole cause of sterility (*qv*).

barrenness *See* sterility.

barrier contraceptive A device designed to prevent conception (*qv*) by physically preventing the sperm (*qv*) from contacting the ovum (*qv*). Barrier contraceptives include the condom (*qv*), diaphragm (*qv*), vaginal sponge (*qv*), cervical cap (*qv*), and pessary (*qv*). They should be used in conjunction with a spermicidal (*qv*) foam or jelly to increase effectiveness.

bartholinitis An inflammation and swelling of the Bartholin's glands (*qv*) caused by *Trichomonas vaginalis* (*qv*) or other pathogens that obstruct the ducts of the glands. Surgical drainage and antibiotic treatment are usually required to restore normal function.

Bartholin's glands Two small, reddish-yellow glands on either side of the vaginal opening, which secrete a mucoid lubricating fluid at the opening; also known as greater vestibular or vulvovaginal glands.

Barton forceps *See* obstetric forceps.

basal body temperature (BBT) method of contraception A method of reducing the chance of pregnancy (*qv*) by limiting sexual intercourse (*qv*) to relatively safe, anovulatory (*qv*) times in the monthly female cycle. BBT uses daily checks of basal body temperature taken with an oral or rectal thermometer before rising after at least 5 hours sleep. A small dip in temperature followed by a sudden progesterone-mediated rise of between 0.5 and 1.0 degree F indicates ovulation (*qv*) has occurred. After several cycles are charted, abstinence (*qv*) is required for six days before the earliest day of ovulation in the previous six cycles and for the subsequent five days at the higher temperature. Actual failure rate among highly motivated married women is cited at 10 pregnancies among 100 women in a year. When combined with the Billings' contraceptive method (*qv*), advocates claim only a 2 percent failure rate. The BBT method may be referred to as the rhythm method of contraception (*qv*) or confused with the unreliable calendar method of birth control (*qv*).

basial A rarely used term for kissing (*qv*).

basilar squeeze technique *See* squeeze technique.

bas mitzvah (mizvah) *See* bat mitzvah (mizvah).

bastard (bastardry) A child born outside wedlock. In some civil jurisdictions, the status of the child is legitimized when the parents marry. While *bastard* originally referred to the status of the child's parents, both the term *bastard* and the term *illegitimate* (*qv*) are used in a pejorative and judgmental way against the child. *Bastard* is also a common insult signifying offensive or unpleasant behavior.

bastardy proceedings Legal procedure to establish paternity (*qv*) of a child born out of wedlock (*qv*).

bath (house), gay In large cities, a meeting place for male homosexuals (*qv*). These facilities may have originally served urban immigrant families at a time when tenements did not contain bath facilities. When apartments were built with modern bath and toilet facilities, public bath houses continued to serve the less advantaged citizens of large cities, gradually becoming meeting places for male homosexuals (*qv*).

bat mitzvah (mizvah) The ceremony in Jewish ritual celebrating the arrival of a 12- or 13-year-old Jewish girl at the age of responsibility. The male counterpart is bar mitzvah (*qv*).

battered woman (wife) syndrome (BWS) A pattern of repeated physical assaults and psychological abuse on a woman by a man with whom she lives. The violence usually follows a predictable pattern starting with a verbal argument, escalating to accusations, and verbal and physical abuse. Increasing male irritability and tension mark the initial phase, followed by acute violent activity, with the woman unable to defend herself or placate the male's anger and his claims of "teaching her a lesson." This culminates in apologies, remorse, and promises from the male not to repeat the abuse. Personal, cultural, and ethnic attitudes affect the incidence of BSW.

The personality profile of a battered woman typically includes being reserved, withdrawn, depressed, anxious, with low self-esteem, a poorly integrated self-image, a general inability to cope with life's stresses, and a tendency to accept blame of anything that goes wrong. The assaulter's profile is usually a close complement to the victim's personality. The same abusive pattern can occur with the male partner being the victim and the female the abuser.

battery A legal concept that describes any unconsented to, unjustified touching of another person. Sexual battery and assault are used in new legal definitions of various forms of rape (*qv*) and sexual assault (*qv*).

battledore placenta A placenta (*qv*) in which the umbilical cord (*qv*) is attached at the outer edge rather than in the middle so that the placenta resembles a battledore, or paddle.

bawdyhouse A brothel (*qv*) or house of prostitution (*qv*).

Bayle's disease A form of syphilis (*qv*) characterized by cerebral cortex atrophy and deterioration of the meninges that surround and protect the brain and spinal cord. Deterioration of the central nervous system (*qv*) results in an inability to concentrate, delusions, apathy, disorientation, and emotional instability—hence the other names for this condition: *dementia paralytic* and *general paralysis of the insane*.

BBT *See* basal body temperature method of contraception.

B/D Bondage and dominance or bondage and discipline (*qv*).

Beal v. Doe A 1977 decision of the U.S. Supreme Court ruling that the federal government is not required to fund elective abortions (*qv*).

beast fetishism Krafft-Ebing's (*qv*) term for the sexually stimulating effect of contact with animal skin or fur. *See also* hyphenophilia.

Bee-cell pessary *See* pessary.

beget To procreate (*qv*).

behavioral therapy The systematic application of learning principles and techniques to the treatment of undesirable or maladaptive behavioral patterns. Behavioral therapy is in contrast with psychotherapy in which thoughts, feelings, and unconscious conflicts are the focus of the therapeutic effort. In behavioral therapy, attempts are made to modify observable, maladjusted patterns by substituting a new response or set of responses to a given stimulus. Behavioral therapy focuses on reeducation by exercises that concentrate on the problem behavior rather than on its prior psychic or unconscious origins. Prime examples of behavioral therapies in sex therapy are the sensate focus exercises (*qv*) of Masters and Johnson, the stop-and-go technique (*qv*) and the squeeze exercise (*qv*). Behavioral therapies may include assertiveness training (*qv*), aversion therapy (*qv*), contingency management, flooding, modeling, operant conditioning (*qv*), and systemic desensitization (*qv*). Behavioral therapy is also known as behavioral modification. *See also* behaviorism; biofeedback.

behavior genetics That branch of genetics that studies if and how behavior patterns are inherited and how the genes influence behavior. Behavior genetics is among the most complex subfields of genetics because the path from gene (*qv*) to behavior is itself highly complex. Genes directly determine only the sequence of amino acids in proteins, but, because proteins are crucial to all aspects of cellular metabolism and physiology, genetic changes in protein structure can have effects on organ physiology. In turn, organ-level effects can alter overall body metabolism and physiology, with effects on behavior occurring in turn. This branching set of interactions is called *pleiotropy*. No direct path, therefore, exists from gene to behavior; instead, a web of interactions exists between levels. Furthermore, at all levels, environmental effects, such as the activities of other cells, organs, and organ systems, reciprocally interact with genetically caused alterations in protein structure to produce interactively and reciprocally multidetermined effects in which no one component is more important than another.

However, this view, which has strong support in the research database of behavior genetics, is often poorly understood by lay people, who wish to believe that somehow ''nature'' controls, determines, or predestines human behavior (*see* biology, biologism, biological reductionism). Likewise, critics of biologism and biological reductionism sometimes themselves fail to understand how genes in fact do act, and therefore conclude that the genes are irrelevant to human behavior. Neither viewpoint is correct because each is based on a lack of knowledge of the complex, but real, web of mutual interacting effects that exists between molecular, genetic, cellular, organ, personal, and social levels of human existence. In brief, the actuality is far more complex than simplistic arguments about nature and nurture would lead one to believe (*see* biosocial viewpoint).

behaviorism A school of psychology and a theoretical approach to the study of humans or other animals that emphasizes the observation, recording, and interpretation of activities as responses to stimuli, without reference to consciousness, mental states, emotions, or other subjective phenomena. Although the viewpoint of behaviorism is old, John B. Watson formalized this school of psychology in 1913. B. F. Skinner made behaviorism popular in the 1960s.

Behçet's syndrome An inflammatory disease characterized by ulcers and lesions on the genitalia (*qv*), mouth, eyes, and other body parts. Blindness, paralysis, thrombosis, and aneurysms are complications of this disease, whose etiology is suspected to be viral or autoimmune. It is rare in North America.

being love A concept of adult love (*qv*), proposed by Abraham Maslow (*qv*), that characterizes a love based on choice rather than on psychological need. Being love emphasizes a mutuality and concern for the other's welfare. It contrasts with deficiency love (*qv*), characterized by possessiveness, dependence, and a limited concern for the other.

bejel A nonvenereal form of syphilis (*qv*) prevalent among Middle East and North African children and caused by the spirochete *Treponema pallidum II*. It is spread by person-to-person contact and sharing contaminated eating implements. A primary lesion, usually on or near the mouth, is followed by pimplelike sores on the arms, legs, and body, with chronic ulcers of the nose and soft palate in the advanced stage. The severe and lethal consequences of genital syphilis rarely follow this nonvenereal infection. Treatment is with penicillin.

Bellotti v. Baird A 1979 U.S. Supreme Court decision overturning a Massachusetts law requiring parental consent for minors seeking abortions (*qv*). The eight-to-one decision implied that states may be able to require pregnant unmarried minors to obtain parental consent to an abortion as long as the state law provides an alternative, such as allowing the minor to seek a judge's approval instead.

BEM Sex Role Inventory (BSRI) A personality test of masculinity-femininity in which the subject rates statements of sex roles (*qv*) on the degree to which they represent Western societal values. The ranking is for a masculine, feminine, or androgynous (*qv*) personality. This scale was devised by developmental psychologist Sandra Lipsitz Bem in 1981.

benign orgasmic cephalgia A type of headache associated only with orgasm (*qv*). The headache is felt on both sides of the head starting with orgasm and lasting an hour or longer. It affects men more than women.

benign prostatic hyperplasia or hypertrophy (BPH) A nonmalignant condition common in older men characterized by multiple fibrous nodules pushing from the prostate (*qv*) gland into the urethral (*qv*) canal and blocking the passage of urine. BHP is associated with increased frequency of urination, especially at night, and with a diminished urinary flow. These early symptoms are followed by burning sensation during urination, chills, and fever. Kidney stones due to urine retention and blood in the urine may follow. Treatment is by transurethral (*qv*) resection in which the urethral canal is cleared by curettage (*qv*) through the urethra rather than by pelvic surgery, as was common in the past.

Benjamin, Harry (1885–1986) A physician, endocrinologist, and geriatric specialist, Benjamin was the first to recognize the phenomenon of transsexualism (*qv*), a term he coined to distinguish this condition from homosexuality (*qv*) and transvestitism (*qv*). He also pioneered sex change surgery (*qv*). Born in Berlin, Benjamin studied at universities in Berlin and Germany before coming to the United States in 1913. He was the author of *The Transsexual Phenomenon* (1966) and other books. In summarizing his work, he often repeated one sentence: "I ask myself, in mercy, or in common sense, if we cannot alter the conviction to fit the body, should we not, in certain circumstances, alter the body to fit the conviction?" As a geriatrics specialist, Benjamin advocated controversial injections of estrogen (*qv*) and testosterone (*qv*) to retard the aging process.

Ben-Wa balls Balls of stainless steel, gold, silver, or weighted plastic about an inch in diameter inserted into the vagina (*qv*), where they supposedly stimulate the woman as she moves; also known as *geisha balls*, *Burmese bells*, *Thai beads*, and *Rino Tama*.

berdache Among North American Indians, a berdache is a male who holds a special spiritual status as a shaman (*qv*), seer, and/or healer. An effeminate or androgynous (*qv*) male homosexual (*qv*), the berdache assumed a woman's role, including becoming a wife and mother. Following the devastating effects of persecution by Spanish and other colonists, the berdache tradition lost its prestige and went underground, emerging only recently with a cultural renaissance among native Americans. *See also* hijra. Resource: Walter L. Williams, *The Spirit and the Flesh: Sexual Diversity in American Indian Culture* (Boston: Beacon Press, 1986).

bestiality Physical contact between a human and animal that facilitates human sexual arousal or orgasm. Bestiality can involve oral or anal copulation, oral-genital stimulation, masturbation of the animal, or various body contacts. The practice is rare, but more common among men than women. Zoophilia, zooerasty, sodomy (*qv*) and buggery (*qv*) are terms used inconsistently for this behavior. *See also* mixoscopic zoophilia.

beta specific monoclonal enzyme-linked immunosorbent assay test (ELISA) A convenient, rapid, and sensitive qualitative test for pregnancy (*qv*) based on presence of human chorionic gonadotropin (HCG) (*qv*) detectable in female urine as early as seven-to-ten days following conception. HCG contains alpha and beta peptide chains, the beta subunit of HCG conferring both the biological and immunological specificity and distinguishing HCG from similar hormones, follicle-stimulating hormone (*qv*), luteinizing hormone (*qv*), and thyroid stimulating hormone (TSH). Two specially selected mouse monoclonal antibeta HCG immunoglobins are used to create two-site enzyme-linked immunosorbent assay molecules. These are coated on a test paddle. Results of the ELISA test can be available in 20 minutes.

In a positive test, while HCG beta subunits are captured by the monoclonal antibodies, the monoclonal antibody enzyme conjugate binds with the unbound portions of the ''captured'' HCG. After the test molecules coating the paddle are rinsed of all unbound specimen and reagent components, they are immersed in chromogen solution. If HCG is bound by the test molecules on the paddle, they turn blue, indicating a pregnancy.

In a negative test, the absence of HCG prevents ''capturing'' of the antibody-enzyme conjugate. When rinsed, all the conjugate is removed. When the test paddle is immersed in the chromogen, no enzyme is present to catalyze a reaction leaving the paddle colorless.

beta subunit HCG radioimmunoassay A sensitive and highly accurate test for pregnancy (*qv*) based on the presence of human chorionic gonadotropin (HCG) (*qv*) in the blood detected by a probe for the beta subunit of HCG. This test can be done as early as 9 days after fertilization. When performed very early in pregnancy, a positive finding should be confirmed by ultrasound scan since a noninvasive hydatidiform mole (*qv*) or highly malignant chorioepithelioma (*qv*) can continue producing HCG after embryo-death giving a false positive. *See also* beta-specific monoclonal enzyme-linked immunosorbent assay test (ELISA).

betrothal A civil or religious promise or contract to enter into marriage (*qv*) with a person; also known as an espousal or engagement. In some European societies, the espousal may carry the right to live together and have sexual intercourse (*qv*). In this context, the espousal may actually be more important than the civil marriage ceremony.

bhoga In Hindu philosophy, physical pleasure. Bhoga, or sexual pleasure, is viewed as one of two paths leading to nirvana, the Buddha, and final deliverance. Yoga (*qv*), spiritual exercise, is the alternate, and more demanding, path to liberation and the merging of the individual with the universal.

bias An attitude for or against something or someone; an attitude that influences an observer's judgment; technically a systematic error representing the difference between the true value of a characteristic and the average value obtained by repeated investigations. The idea of a bias assumes that there is a true or objective value. Bias and sampling error (*qv*) are said to be the cause for any discrepancy between the true value and the research value obtained from a single investigation.

biastophilia A sacrificial/expiatory type of paraphilia (*qv*) in which sexuoerotic (*qv*) arousal and orgasm (*qv*) are dependent on a surprise attack and violent assault on a nonconsenting, terrified, and struggling stranger. Biastophilia may be either heterosexual (*qv*) or homosexual (*qv*), although the former type is predominant whether the assaulter is male or female. The reciprocal or complementary philia, in which one is dependent on staging one's own brutal rape (*qv*) by a stranger, probably exists only in an attenuated form and rarely moves from fantasy (*qv*) into actuality. The term is derived from *biastes*, the Greek for forced sexual violation. *See also* raptophilia.

bicornate uterus An abnormal development of the uterus (*qv*) in which the Mullerian tubes (*qv*) do not fuse but remain separated, creating a double-horned or Y-shaped uterus.

bidet A toiletlike fixture, common in Europe, on which one sits to wash the genitalia (*qv*) and anal (*qv*) region before and after sexual intercourse (*qv*) and after defecation.

bigamy The state of entering into a putative marriage (*qv*) with one person while still legally married to a first spouse. Bigamy is a statutory offense in most societies where monogamy (*qv*) prevails. The penalty for violating an antibigamy law does not apply in cases where the first spouse has been missing for several years and is presumed or legally declared dead.

bilateral (bilineal) descent A lineage system in which descent is reckoned equally through both the father and mother. *See also* matrilineal; patrilineal.

Bilitis In ancient Greece, a courtesan (*qv*) to whom the poet Sappho wrote love letters. Pierre Louys published *Chanson de Bilitis* around 1900. In 1955, the Daughters of Bilitis (*qv*) was established as the first large-scale organization to provide support for lesbians (*qv*).

Billig exercises A series of exercises and posture training designed to reduce the symptoms of premenstrual syndrome (*qv*) and menstrual cramps (*qv*); developed during World War II in an effort to reduce absenteeism in the factories.

Billings' contraceptive method A natural contraceptive (*qv*) method that depends on ascertaining the time of ovulation (*qv*) by monitoring cyclic changes in the cervical mucus (*qv*) over several months and then not having intercourse (*qv*) during the estimated fertile (*qv*) periods between three or four days before ovulation (*qv*) and four or five days after ovulation. During ovulation, normally cloudy cervical mucus becomes clear and slippery and can be stretched between the fingers. The method was developed by Evelyn Billings and John Billings in Australia. *See also* Spinnbarkheit.

biofeedback An enhancement or therapeutic modality in which a person is provided with visual or auditory information about the autonomic physiological functions of his or her body. With an awareness of the involuntary function, the person may learn to control a response previously considered completely involuntary (e.g., blood pressure, muscle tension, brain wave activity, and the heart rate).

biogenetic law A sweeping and misleading generalization that each individual organism repeats in its early development the major stages of development its evolutionary ancestors passed through. The so-called biogenetic law is technically expressed as "ontogeny recapitulates phylogeny." Its originator, Ernst Haeckel (1834–1919), wrote "Ontogenesis is a brief and rapid recapitulation of phylogenesis." In the late 1800s, this theory was widely invoked as evidence for evolution. In its much more cautious and very restricted modern meaning, it is true that during development the embryo (*qv*) may show fragments of some of its ancestral developmental stages. However, some structures are eliminated or bypassed, some developmental phases are shortened or prolonged, and some appear out of chronology. The biogenetic law is also know as the theory of recapitulation.

biological clock A general term for the internal physiological mechanisms that regulate diurnal (*qv*), circadian, or other cycles in bodily functions, respiration, heartbeat, temperature regulation, hunger, sleep, elimination, sexual hormonal cycles, libido (*qv*) cycles, menstruation (*qv*), ovulation (*qv*), nocturnal penile tumescence (*qv*), and female nocturnal lubrication (*qv*).

biological parent (father, mother) Traditionally, the biological mother of an infant is the woman who was impregnated, bore the fetus, and gave birth to it, while the biological father was the man who impregnated her via vaginal intercourse. However, in the context of new reproductive technologies, especially embryo transplants (*qv*) and artificial insemination (*qv*), a distinction is made in parental roles among the genetic parent who donates the ovum (*qv*) or sperm (*qv*), the biological mother who gestates (*qv*) or biological father who impregnates (*qv*), and the social parent who raises the offspring. In this usage, the biological ''father'' could be a female gynecologist (*qv*) who performs the artificial insemination. The term biological parent is also used to refer to the genetic parent, or gamete (*qv*) donor.

biological rhythm Any physiological and psychological pattern that falls into a regular and predictable cycle (e.g., the menstrual [*qv*], sleep, and respiratory cycles). *See also* biological clock; diurnal rhythm.

biology, biologism, biological reductionism Biology is the science that studies life, living organisms, and characteristics associated with life. The range and variety of phenomena studied by biology, or open to potential biological study, is immense. However, in recent years, many social scientists and social critics, including many feminists (*qv*), have equated biology with a doctrine best called biologism, which asserts the primacy of biology over other aspects of human life, particularly human culture and the human capacity for learning, change, and social improvement. Biologism, often called biological reductionism, denies that cultural or learning processes can change allegedly ''innate'' or ''genetic'' characteristics of human beings, such as sexual behavior patterns and gender roles (*qv*) and relationships. Biologism has no warrant in the science of biology, and the two should not be confused. Nonetheless, racist and sexist uses of biologism have made the science of biology so suspect to many scholars that they often confuse biology with the biologism of particular political or social doctrines.

''Biology is destiny'' *See* ''Anatomy is destiny.''

biopsy Surgical removal of a small piece of living tissue for microscopic examination to facilitate a diagnosis, estimate a prognosis, or follow the course of a disease. The term may refer to the tissue as well as to the procedure.

biorhythm Any cyclic or rhythmic phenomenon or event observed in the life or an organism or species. *See also* biological rhythm.

biosocial viewpoint A theoretical position, also called biocultural viewpoint, that sees the relationship between biology and human behavior as a complex web of connections among all levels of human life, from the molecular, cellular, and organismic levels to the social (historical, cultural, and economic). Adherents of this view argue that it clarifies and replaces antiquated arguments about the supremacy of either nature or nurture because it sees neither as supreme or all-determining, and because it replaces the linear arrow of causation typical of older theories with a model of interactively and reciprocally determined influences among all levels.

Sexuality and reproduction provide one example of the differences among such viewpoints. Adherents to the nature side of the nature/nurture debate (*qv*) hold that male-female differences are mandated by, and inherent in, human nature and the properties of the universe. These differences are, in this view, difficult or impossible to change. Adherents to the nurture side of the debate tend to deny any role to nature, and argue that because gender relations are the products primarily or solely of specific social and economic arrangements between men and women, they can therefore be altered. The biosocial viewpoint argues that historically it has been a biological given that human reproduction occurs by heterosexual (*qv*) intercourse, and that differences in gender roles (*qv*) and in economic and social arrangements between men and women arose partly when the irreducible fact of sexual reproduction has interacted with highly variable political, economic, and social aspects of human life. To the proponents of the biosocial view, gender relationships and roles are rooted in a variety of aspects of overall life, in which the realities of biology are as important as the realities of economics. In this view, social change, often drastic and rapid, can occur when technology alters prior biological realities, as has happened when recent developments in contraceptives, sexually transmitted disease (STD) (*qv*) treatments, abortion (*qv*), and reproductive technologies were accompanied by social reform and activism producing shifts in gender roles and relationships. However, like many commonsense solutions to problems, the biosocial viewpoint has not been widely adopted in the politicized and polarized atmosphere of the nature/nurture debate.

biostatistics Numerical calculations and data on births, deaths, injuries, disease incidences, and other variables related to the general health and condition of human or subhuman populations. The science of analyzing data related to biological variables to ascertain validity or significance of the data. Also known as vital statistics.

biovular Medical term for release of two ova (*qv*) in the same cycle, or for dizygotic twins (*qv*).

biparental inheritance The inheritance of biological traits from both parents. *See also* amphigony.

biphasic oral contraceptive pill A low-dose combination contraceptive pill (*qv*) designed to reduce breakthrough bleeding and spotting associated with other low-dose pills. A typical biphasic pill provides a constant low daily dose of 35 micrograms of estrogen (*qv*) with half a milligram of progesterone (*qv*) in the first 10 days of the cycle and 1 milligram of progesterone in the second 10 days. The biphasic pill appears to have the same effectiveness rate as other combination pills (*qv*). *See also* triphasic contraceptive pill; progestin-only contraceptive pill.

birth The event of being born, either by passage of the fetus (*qv*) from the uterus (*qv*) through the vagina (*qv*) or surgically by Caesarean section (*qv*), to a life independent of the mother; the act of childbirth (*qv*) or delivery (*qv*). Human birth occurs approximately nine months after fertilization (*qv*), or 280 days after the first day of the last menstrual period (*qv*). Birth may be unassisted or assisted by a trained midwife (*qv*) or other attendant. *See also* delivery; labor; personhood; social birth; viability.

birth, multiple Two or more fetuses (*qv*) delivered at the same time by the same woman. If two infants are involved, they may be fraternal, dizygotic twins (*qv*) or identical, monozygotic twins (*qv*). Multiple births of three (triplets), four (quadruplets), five (quintuplets), or six (sextuplets) may include both fraternal and identical newborns. Multiple births are a decreasing but still significant risk when ovulation (*qv*) is induced in anovulatory (*qv*) women by exogenous (*qv*) hormones (*qv*).

birth adjustments The drastic and sudden adaptations a newborn must make at the end of its life in the uterus (*qv*). These adjustments include a shift in temperature from 98.6 degrees Fahrenheit to room temperature, the unmuffled sounds of everyday life instead of the near-soundproof womb, natural and artificial lights, respiration through breathing and the lungs, and taking food by mouth. According to Sigmund Freud (*qv*) and Otto Rank (*qv*), these adjustments are traumatic and anxiety producing. Modern rebirthing exercises are designed to help an adult get in touch with these anxieties and retroactively accept this transition as a basis for improved mental health and control of one's life. *See also* Leboyer method of childbirth.

birth bonus Financial or other incentives offered by a government to encourage couples to have children. Pronatalist policies, including a variety of birth bonuses, are used in France, West Germany, and other European countries where the birthrate (*qv*) is below replacement levels. Birth disincentives are used in the People's Republic of China and other countries to discourage couples from having more than one or two children.

birth canal The passage through which the fetus (*qv*) is delivered from the uterus (*qv*), through the cervix (*qv*) and vagina (*qv*) at the end of gestation (*qv*).

birth control Contraception (*qv*); a general term for a variety of natural, barrier, chemical, and surgical methods whose purpose is to prevent conception (*qv*) and/or implantation (*qv*) of the zygote (*qv*) in the uterus (*qv*). The term is commonly used despite its being less precise than *contraceptive*. *See also* birth control pill; cervical cap; condom; diaphragm; eugenics; intrauterine device; Sanger, Margaret; spermicide; vaginal suppository.

birth control clinic Any facility that provides contraceptive (*qv*) information, instruction and prescriptions. *See also* Planned Parenthood.

birth control pill A general term for any one of the several oral hormonal contraceptives (*qv*). Hormonal contraceptives are commonly known simply as "the pill." *See also* DES; RU 486; biphasic oral contraceptive pill; triphasic contraceptive pill; combination oral contraceptive pill; progestin-only contraceptive.

birth cry The reflexive wail of a newborn that accompanies the beginning of pulmonary respiration.

birthdate The date on which an infant was born. In normal gestations (*qv*), the birthdate occurs 280 days after the mother's last menstrual period (*qv*) started. In some cultures, one's age is counted from the date of conception (*qv*) rather than the date of birth (*qv*). In other cultures, the newborn's official presentation to and acceptance by the community or elders a few days after biological birth mark the official date of birth. *See also* social birth.

birth defect Any gross physical abnormality observed at birth (*qv*) or within the first year after birth. Approximately 3 percent of all live-born infants have a birth defect. An additional 3 percent are diagnosed as having a birth defect in their first year. A birth defect may also be known as a congenital defect (*qv*) or anomaly.

birthing center A freestanding medical facility specializing in childbirth (*qv*), associated or affiliated with a hospital, or operating independently.

birthing chair A specially designed chair that permits the mother to sit upright or recline at an angle during labor (*qv*) and delivery (*qv*), thereby improving the efficiency of parturition. The upright position appears to shorten the time in labor (*qv*), particularly the expulsive stage. Use of a birthing chair is not advised when anesthesia is needed. Modern birthing chairs are derived from birthing chairs common in America and Europe in the seventeenth and eighteenth centuries. These were three-legged stools with a high, sloping back and a circular seat with a central hole.

birthmark A congenital (*qv*) localized pigmentation of the skin present at birth (*qv*) or appearing shortly after birth. A birthmark may be flat or raised, a mole or a collection of fragile surface blood vessels, a hemangioma. Many birthmarks disappear naturally during childhood.

birth order The position of a child in the family in relation to other siblings (i.e., the first, second, third or later born). Some evidence exists that first-born offspring are at an advantage because there is no competition for parental care and attention as there is with later-born children. According to Alfred Adler (*qv*), birth order is an important influence on a child's emotional and personality development.

birth position The uterine (*qv*) position of the fetus (*qv*) just prior to birth (*qv*). Approximately 96 percent of deliveries (*qv*) begin with head-first presentation (*qv*) into the cervix (*qv*). Breech (*qv*) or buttocks (*qv*) presentations account for 4 percent of births. Breech presentation, which increases the risk of generalized joint laxity, may require manipulation by the obstetrician (*qv*).

birthrate The number of births during a given period, usually a year, to the total population in a specific area. The *crude birthrate* is given as the number of live births in one year per 1,000 persons of all ages in a population. The *refined birthrate* is the ratio of total births to the total female population during the period of one year. The *true birthrate*, or fertility rate, is the ratio of total births to the female population of child-bearing age (between the ages of 15 and 45).

birth ratio The proportion of male to female live births, usually considered to be between 105 and 114 males to 100 females in the United States. The heterogametic (*qv*) character of the human male dictates that equal numbers of X- and Y-bearing sperm (*qv*) be produced. However, at conception (*qv*), 150–160 males are conceived for every 110 females conceived. Male fetuses (*qv*) are more likely than female fetuses to miscarry, being more susceptible to respiratory infections, hepatitis, slow viral diseases, stillbirth (*qv*), and neonatal (*qv*) death. Poor maternal nutrition and lack of prenatal (*qv*) care in lower socioeconomic groups result in 8 to 9 percent more male miscarriages (*qv*) than in middle- or upper-class pregnancies (*qv*). After birth, higher rates of death from accidents, violence, and drugs for males further reduce the male-to-female ratio. *See also* conception ratio; implantation ratio.

birth trauma Any physical injury suffered by an infant during the birth process. According to Otto Rank (*qv*), birth trauma refers to the psychic shock and "primal anxiety" supposedly suffered in delivery (*qv*). *See also* birth adjustments; Lamaze method of childbirth; Leboyer method of childbirth.

birth weight The measured heaviness of a baby when it is born. In the United States, this is usually about 3,500 grams or 7.5 pounds, and 97 percent of newborns (*qv*) weigh between 2,500 and 4,500 grams, or 5.5 and 10 pounds. Low birth weight, a common consequence of poor prenatal (*qv*) care and nutrition, may place the newborn (*qv*) at a developmental disadvantage that has lifelong consequences.

bisexualism, bisexuality (adj. bisexual) The condition of being attracted to and enjoying sexual (*qv*) contacts with both males and females. Bisexual contacts may be either concurrent or sequential, heterosexual (*qv*) at one time and homosexual (*qv*) at another period of life. The proportion of same- and other-gender contacts experienced by a person may be 50:50, in which case the term *Kinsey 3* is applicable. In the Kinsey Six Scale (*qv*), individuals who are predominantly heterosexual but have had some or significant homosexual experiences are classified as being *Kinsey 1* or *2*, while homosexuals with significant or some heterosexual experiences-fantasies are described as being *Kinsey 4* or *5*. A *Kinsey 0* status indicates an exclusive heterosexual person; *Kinsey 6* indicates a person who is exclusively homosexual. Bisexualism, like homosexualism, is not a paraphilia (*qv*). The term is inappropriate when used to mean hermaphroditic (*qv*) or having gonads (*qv*) of both sexes. In the view of some, bisexuality is a way station between heterosexuality and complete homosexuality, but others consider it an acceptable life-style in its own right. *See also* monosexual; Sexual Orientation Grid.

bitterling test An obsolete pregnancy test (*qv*) in which a small, carplike bitterling fish is immersed in a quart of fresh water with 2 teaspoons of urine from the woman being tested. Pregnancy is indicated when a long oviduct protrudes from the fish's abdomen.

blastocoel The fluid-filled cavity of the blastocyst (*qv*).

blastocyst An early stage of mammalian embryonic development between early cleavage of the fertilized ovum (*qv*) and implantation (*qv*) at about 5 to 6 days. The blastocyst (blastula) consists of a spherical mass of embryonic cells with a hollow eccentric cavity, the blastocoel (*qv*). An inner cell mass develops into the embryo (*qv*) proper, while the outer layer of cells, the trophoblast (*qv*), develops into the extraembryonic chorion (*qv*) and amnion (*qv*).

blastomere One or more cells of a morula (*qv*), the solid mass of embryonic cells that develops from the zygote (*qv*) before it hollows out and forms a blastocyst (*qv*).

blastula *See* blastocyst.

blended orgasm A combination of the tenting orgasm (*qv*) resulting from clitoral stimulation and the A-frame or uterine orgasm (*qv*) resulting from stimulation of the vagina (*qv*) and Grafenberg spot (*qv*).

blenorrhagia A profuse gonorrheal (*qv*) discharge from the penis (*qv*) or vagina (*qv*).

blighted ovum A fertilized (*qv*) ovum (*qv*) or zygote (*qv*), that fails to develop normally and instead becomes a fluid-filled cyst (*qv*) attached to the uterine wall. The cyst may contain amorphous embryonic parts or only fluid. Blighted ova are common in first-trimester spontaneous abortions (*qv*). Suction curettage (*qv*) may be necessary if blighted ovum is retained.

blindfolding A common part of bondage (*qv*) games in which the vulnerability of the mock victim is highlighted and the element of surprise enhanced, thereby increasing the sexual enjoyment of both partners.

blissom An obsolete adjective for the state of sexual heat (*qv*); as a verb, it refers to copulation (*qv*) with a ewe.

Bloch, Iwan (1872–1922) A Berlin physician, Bloch's extensive research and writings on sexual matters make him one of the pioneers of modern sexology (*qv*). An expert on sexually transmitted diseases (*qv*), Bloch was active in the sexual reform movement. His major works are the three-volume *Handbuch der gesamten Sexualwissenschaft* (*Handbook of sexual science in its totality*), published between 1912 and 1925, and the 1907 *Das Sexualleben unserer Zeit* (*The sexual life of our times*).

blood group A variety of classifications of blood based on the presence of antigenic (*qv*) factors on the surface of the red blood cells and complementary antibodies (*qv*) in the plasma. The best-known blood groups, ABO and Rh positive/negative (*qv*), are the basis of transfusion incompatibilities. Rh is also the basis of maternal-fetal Rh incompatibility (*qv*) and erythroblastosis fetalis (*qv*). Most of the over 40 blood groups have little clinical or diagnostic use. Prior to the advent of human leukocytic antigens (*qv*), ABO, Rh, and MN blood groups were used to resolve cases of disputed paternity (*qv*). *See also* human leukocytic antigen.

blood test The analysis of blood components used to ascertain blood group (*qv*), human leukocytic antigens (*qv*), or the presence of sexually transmitted diseases (*qv*), drug usage, diabetes, anemias, and mononucleosis (*qv*). Specific blood tests may be required by law for applicants for marriage licenses and employment in certain professions.

bloody show A bloody discharge occurring during labor (*qv*) as a result of pressure from the fetus (*qv*) against the cervix (*qv*).

bloomers A women's garment with loose trousers gathered at the ankles and worn under a skirt. Designed in 1850 by Elizabeth Smith Miller and promoted by Amelia Bloomer, editor of the *Lily*, a women's temperance and suffrage paper, bloomers were popular until the mid-nineteenth century.

blue baby A newborn (*qv*) with cyanosis—a bluish tinge in the skin due to lack of oxygen caused by a congenital heart defect or by incomplete expansion of the lungs, or anemia due to erythroblastosis fetalis (*qv*).

blue discharge A dishonorable discharge from the U.S. Army during World War II based on charges of homosexual (*qv*) behavior.

blushing An involuntary reddening or flushing of the face resulting from embarrassment, modesty, self-consciousness, or confusion. Persistent and repeated blushing may be symptomatic of shame (*qv*) or guilt related to sexual reactions or behaviors. *See also* sex flush.

body cells The diploid (*qv*) somatic cells of an organism as distinct from the haploid (*qv*) germ cells, the ovum (*qv*) or sperm (*qv*).

body exploration Precoital or loveplay (*qv*) activity in which the partners explore, touch, stroke, and caress each other's body and the erogenous areas (*qv*). *See also* sensate focus exercises.

body-fat trigger A control mechanism regulating the presence or absence of menstruation (*qv*) in females. For menstruation to occur, between 18 and 25 percent of a woman's total body weight must be fat. In some female athletes, body fat may be as low as 12 percent, resulting in amenorrhea (*qv*). Estrogen (*qv*) production may be dependent on a normal amount of body fat.

body image An individual's personal and subjective self-image or mental picture of one's body, one's sexual attractiveness and competence. One's body image is constructed out of self-observations, the reactions of others, and one's own attitudes, emotions, memories, fantasies, and experiences. Since a positive body image is a critical factor in how one responds sexually, sex therapy (*qv*) often deals with improving the client's body image.

body language A colloquial term for body and facial movements and behavior that convey, or seem to convey, messages about a person's emotional or mental state. Called nonverbal communication or nonverbal behavior by experts, body language is a misleading term because the messages conveyed by most body movements, postures, and gestures do not have specific and exact meanings as do words or movements in true nonspoken language like the American Sign Language for the deaf. Instead, the meanings and intentions conveyed by so-called body language are highly context- and individual-specific, and change over time as new behavior patterns are learned. Sexual behavior, particularly courtship (*qv*) and rejection, utilizes nonverbal behavior extensively, with misunderstanding and miscommunication a common consequence. Resource: T. Perper, *Sex Signals: The Biology of Love* (Philadelphia: iSi Press, 1985).

body monitoring A psychological process in which a person becomes an outside observer of his or her own sexual performance, monitoring and grading his or her own sexual activities (*qv*) and performance. Body monitoring often results in sexual dysfunction (*qv*) because of the tendency to get caught up in a carousel of anxiety and performance pressures. *See also* carousel dynamics effects; spectatoring.

body narcissism An abnormal awareness of and concern about one's body, particularly one's sexual organs (*qv*). According to psychoanalytic theory (*qv*), this tendency originates in early childhood when a child begins to explore his or her body, is preoccupied with elimination and sexual responses, and experiences a fear of injury to the sexual organs.

body stalk In the second week of embryonic development, the mesenchymal (*qv*) mass that forms a bridge between the caudal end of the elongating embryonic disc and amniotic sac (*qv*) and the future placental (*qv*) region of the trophoblast (*qv*). Later the stalk shifts to a midventral position and merges with the yolk sac (*qv*) and allantois (*qv*) to form the umbilical cord (*qv*).

body-work therapist *See* sexual surrogate; surrogate therapy.

Bolger v. Youngs Drug Products Corp. A unanimous 1982 decision of the U.S. Supreme Court ruling as unconstitutional a federal law, the last vestige of the Comstock law (*qv*), that made it a crime to send through the U.S. mail unsolicited advertisements for contraceptives (*qv*).

bondage and discipline, bondage and dominance (B/D, B & D) A sexual relationship in which erotosexual (*qv*) arousal (*qv*) and orgasm (*qv*) are facilitated by or dependent on often highly stereotyped and individualistic scenarios in which one partner, the submissive, is bound, chained, or restrained and then disciplined, chastised, or punished, physically or mentally, by the other (dominant) partner. Such scenarios are characteristically heavily symbolic, and may rely on little or no physical pain or discomfort being administered to the submissive partner. Sexual arousal is nearly always mutual, and such scenarios can be negotiated beforehand by the partners to their mutual satisfaction. While alarming to the non-aficionado, such scenarios are claimed to be extraordinarily arousing sexually and are sometimes employed by prostitutes (*qv*) to arouse otherwise hard to arouse clients. Because of its mutually pre-planned nature, the B&D scenario must be distinguished from the often punitive and chastizing behavior of a partner directed to another person who is disliked. *See also* sadism; masochism; sadomasochism.

bondage harness A set of leather or cloth straps with ankle and wrist cuffs and/ or chest harness used as a restraint device in bondage and discipline (*qv*) or sadomasochist (*qv*) scenarios.

bonding The reciprocal emotional and psychosocial linking between parent and child produced primarily by the eye and physical contact. Bonding is the psychosocial process whereby closeness, personal commitment, a sense of security, and love develop between a parent or other adult and a newborn (*qv*), infant, or child. It is especially important immediately after birth (*qv*) when the newborn is alert and reactive—crying, sucking, clinging, grasping, and following with his or her eyes. These periods of responsiveness stimulate the parenting instinct in the mother and father. Bonding increases the survival of premature and high-risk infants. The concept is valued in new natural delivery (*qv*) modalities in which the woman consciously assists in the delivery and the father participates in the whole process. *See also* maternal deprivation syndrome; somatosensory affectional deprivation (SAD); Bradley method; Lamaze method of childbirth; LeBoyer method of childbirth.

Pair-bonding (*qv*) refers to the mate selection, the emotional bonding of love or limerence (*qv*), and the mating relationship of two adults.

bone marrow An ancient, alleged aphrodisiac (*qv*) celebrated by the poet classic Roman Horace, an epicurean.

bordel, bordello French-Italian term for a house of prostitution (*qv*). *Synonyms*: bawdy house, cat house, whorehouse.

bosom The female breasts (*qv*).

Boston marriage A colloquial term for a middle-class Victorian (*qv*) American lesbian (*qv*) relationship. Unlike the hidden world of Victorian working-class female couples in which one member passed as a man, Boston marriages were commonly visible and accepted. According to D'Emilio and Freedman, lesbian couples "lived together, owned property jointly, planned their travels together, shared holidays and family celebrations, and slept in the same bed. The temporary separations that might normally ensue in two busy lives elicited love letters of extraordinary emotional intensity, which provide a window into the passion shared by women lovers who have been euphemistically described as close friends and devoted companions." Resource: J. D'Emilio and E. B. Freedman, *Intimate Matters: A History of Sexuality in America* (New York: Harper & Row, 1988), pp. 191–192.

Boston Women's Health Book Collective (BWHBC) A nonprofit organization devoted to education about women and their health. The major publication of BWHBC, *Our Bodies Our Selves* (1979), is available in over 14 foreign language editions, with a second edition entitled *The New Our Bodies Our Selves* (1984). The BWHBC also publishes *Ourselves and Our Children* and the *International Women and Health Resource Guide*. Other projects include the Women's Health Information Center open to the public and extensive distribution of free educational materials to women's groups. Address: 465 Mt. Auburn Street, Watertown, MA 02172.

bottle feeding Feeding an infant or young child with a maternal milk substitute from a bottle with a rubber nipple. *See also* breast feeding; nursing.

boudoir (Fr.) An upper-class woman's private dressing or sitting room.

bouillabaisse A spicy French fish and seafood chowder made with wine and herbs and believed by some to be an aphrodisiac (*qv*) because legend suggests that Venus (*qv*) created the first bouillabaisse to arouse the sexual interest of Vulcan, her husband.

bowdlerized An expurgated edition of a work of art or literature. The term is derived from Dr. Thomas Bowdler, a self-appointed Victorian (*qv*) censor, who produced and published *The Family Shakespeare* with all of Shakespeare's sexual references and euphemisms deleted.

Bowers v. Hardwick A 1986 U.S. Supreme Court decision upholding an 1816 Georgia law prohibiting all people from engaging in oral (*qv*) or anal (*qv*) sex. In this bitterly debated five-to-four decision, the Court ruled that the Georgia law could be used to prosecute acts of sodomy (*qv*), "regardless of whether the parties who engaged in it are married or unmarried, or of the same or different sexes."

bowser *See* merkin.

boy marriage A real or temporary marriage between an adolescent (*qv*) male and an older male. *See also* pederasty. Among the East Bay Melanesians, adolescent males and females have segregated domiciles. In the male house, the teenage male is allowed simultaneous homosexual (*qv*) relations with a peer and an older male. Among the Australian Nambutji, every adolescent male becomes the homosexual ''boy-wife'' of the older male who performs his circumcision (*qv*). When the youth reaches adulthood, he may marry the daughter of his ''husband.''

BPH *See* benign prostatic hyperplasia.

brachioproctic eroticism Technical term for fisting (*qv Addendum*)

Bradley method A method of psychophysical preparation for childbirth (*qv*) developed by Robert Bradley, a physician. The Bradley method emphasizes education about the physiology of birth, exercise and nutrition during pregnancy (*qv*), and techniques for breathing and relaxation during labor (*qv*) and delivery (*qv*). The father is extensively involved in the classes and acts as a coach for the mother during labor. Also known as husband-coached childbirth. *See also* Lamaze method of childbirth; Read birth method; Leboyer method of childbirth.

brahmacharya In Hindu philosophy, the custom of premarital sexual abstinence (*qv*), followed by marriage (*qv*) and active sexual relations (*qv*) during the young and middle adult years, and sexual asceticism (*qv*) in the later years. The best-known recent advocate of brahmacharya was Mohandas (Mahatma) Gandhi; his position of spiritual and political leadership in modern-day India has made brahmacharya a living tradition. Resource: S. Kakar, *Intimate Relations: Exploring Indian Sexuality* (Chicago: University of Chicago Press, 1989).

braid cutting A rare sadistic (*qv*) fetish (*qv*) in which sexual arousal (*qv*) and orgasm (*qv*) is facilitated by or dependent on cutting the hair of a victim. In a psychoanalytic interpretation, this fetish is an unconscious attempt to cope with the anxiety of castration (*qv*) because of the knowledge that cut hair will grow back.

brain differentiation The complex and as yet poorly understood process of neurophysiological and anatomical differentiation, specialization, regionalization, and modularization of the brain. Originally conceived of in the oversimplified model of right and left lateralization of the cerebral (*qv*) hemispheres, with the right hemisphere supposed to be generally specialized in handling spatial relations and coordination, nonverbal skills, mathematics, and geometry while the left hemisphere specializes in language, analytical functions, and rote memory. The implications of brain differentiation are just beginning to be explored in terms of sexual differentiation (*qv*), gender roles (*qv*), lovemaps (*qv*), and sexual orientations (*qv*).

brank An iron cage or mask for the head with a bit or tongue clamp, used in medieval times as a punishment and remedy for gossipy, noisy, and quarrelsome women; sometimes used in modern bondage and dominance (*qv*) games.

Braxton-Hicks contractions Painless, short, irregular episodes of uterine muscle contractions (*qv*) sometimes mistaken for labor (*qv*) contractions. *See also* false labor; couvade.

breach of contract (promise) A general legal term for willful or negligent failure to fulfill the conditions of a legally binding contract or promise. In sexology, the term refers to violation or willful nonfulfillment of an espousal, prenuptial (*qv*), or nuptial (*qv*) agreement; for example, the fraudulent and willful failure to marry an individual (typically a woman) after promising to do so and after having had sexual intercourse with him or her. Depending on local, state, and federal contract law, breach of promise to marry may be grounds for a lawsuit that seeks compensation for the aggrieved party. Colloquially and in American folklore, a promise to marry a woman made solely as a seduction strategy can lead to payment of court-ordered damages and perhaps a socially enforced (''shotgun'') marriage. If the man is already married when he makes such a promise, the situation can lead to physical violence if the woman's angered relatives decide to take action.

breast amputation *See* mastectomy.

breast augmentation A cosmetic plastic surgery technique in which the size of the breast (*qv*) is increased by silicone or polyurethane gel implants.

breast binder A cosmetic prothesis used after modified or radical mastectomy (*qv*) and following reconstructive surgery.

breast cancer A malignant, neoplastic disease of the breast tissue; the most common occurring malignancy in American women. Its incidence increases exponentially from the third to fifth decade, with a second peak at age 65. Its incidence may be related to ovarian (*qv*) hormonal function in menstruating (*qv*) women and to adrenal function in postmenopausal (*qv*) women. A high fat diet may be a causative factor, although known risk factors include a family history of breast cancer, nulliparity (*qv*), exposure to ionizing radiation, early menarche (*qv*), late menopause (*qv*), obesity, diabetes, hypertension, chronic cystic disease (*qv*) of the breast, and possibly, postmenopausal estrogen replacement therapy (*qv*). Treatments may include controlled diet, vitamin and mineral therapy, and surgical lumpectomy (*qv*) or mastectomy (*qv*).

breast complex In psychoanalytic theory, the theory that after weaning (*qv*), the penis (*qv*) becomes a substitute for the mother's breast (*qv*) and nipple (*qv*). Some believe a possible consequence of breast envy may be a homosexual (*qv*) orientation in which the individual's own penis and the penis of his partner are a subconscious compensation for the loss of the mother's breast and nipple.

breast envy *See* breast complex.

breast examination A procedure in which the breasts (*qv*) and their accessory structures are observed and palpated (*qv*) by a trained health professional to ascertain the presence of changes or abnormalities that might indicate a malignant condition. Breast examination may be performed by a physician or nurse during a routine physical examination. Breast examinations can also be done by a woman herself on a regular, monthly basis as a health awareness and disease preventative procedure. *See also* breast self-examination.

breast-feeding Suckling, nursing (*qv*), or feeding an infant or young child with milk from the female breast (*qv*). Besides promoting bonding (*qv*) between mother and infant, breast-feeding reduces the risk of obesity and dental mal-occlusions. The infant's suckling naturally stimulates the mother's nipple (*qv*), enhancing the ejection of milk. This normal stimulation may result in an un-expected but natural reflexive erotic (*qv*) pleasure and even culminate in uterine contractions (*qv*) similar to those that accompany orgasm (*qv*). Breast-feeding also encourages postpartum (*qv*) uterine involution (*qv*) and slows the return of the menses (*qv*). This last effect tends to reduce the chance of conception (*qv*) until after the mother ceases nursing. *See also* breast milk; breast milk jaundice; lactation; bottle feeding.

breast lift A cosmetic plastic surgery in which sagging or pendulous breasts (*qv*) are raised by tightening the skin and other tissues above them.

breast milk Human milk produced by the female mammary glands (*qv*) under the stimulation of hypophyseal lactogenic (*qv*) hormone (*qv*). Breast milk, which is easily digested by most infants, confers some passive immunity on the infant. Bronchiolitis and gastroenteritis are rare in breast-fed infants. *See also* breast feeding; breast milk jaundice.

breast milk jaundice A yellow discoloration of the skin and mucosa due to high bilirubin in the blood of a breast-fed infant. In the first weeks of breast-feeding (*qv*), a metabolite in the mother's milk inhibits the infant's ability to bind the pigment bilirubin to a protein so it can be excreted.

breast phantom The feeling that a breast (*qv*) removed in a mastectomy (*qv*) is still intact and present. This phenomenon may be based on the persistence of an intact body image and a denial of the amputation.

breast prosthesis A padded, hemispheric, teardrop-shaped cosmetic replacement used by a woman following a masectomy (*qv*).

breast ptosis A medical term for a pendant or drooping female breast (*qv*); often occurs in middle-aged women who have breast-fed several children. It is the result of a partial atrophy of breast tissue and loss of elasticity in the breast skin. The condition may be corrected by cosmetic plastic surgery.

breast pump A device for withdrawing milk from the lactating female breast (*qv*).

breast reconstruction Surgical reconstruction of the female breast (*qv*), using a silicon or other prosthetic implant, to improve a woman's self-image following a mastectomy (*qv*).

breast reduction surgery Surgery to reduce the size of unacceptably large breasts (*qv*) by removing adipose (fat) tissue in the breast. This surgery may be performed for a male with gynecomastia (*qv*).

breasts A pair of glandular structures on the anterior aspect of the chest or upper body region and supported by the rib cage of the sexually mature woman. Each glandular component of the breast contains milk-producing grape-like clusters of secretory cells, alveoli (*qv*), and collecting ducts that terminate in a main duct. Fifteen to 20 such glandular clusters empty their products into the nipple. Fatty and fibrous tissue surround each mammary cluster. The nipple is surrounded by a darkly colored areola (*qv*) containing sebaceous (*qv*) and sweat glands, which lubricate the nipple during nursing (*qv*). Breast tissue changes naturally during the menstrual cycle (*qv*) and with the seasons of the year.

In anatomy, *breast* (singular) always refers to the upper anterior portion of the chest; however, in nonhuman mammals, the breasts, defined as milk-producing organs, can be located in a variety of positions ranging from the upper chest (as in primates) to the lower abdomen (as in cows). This variation in position occurs because embryonic development of the breasts depends on two parallel lines of tissue (the milk lines) that run from the axilla of the arms to the region of the groin. In cases where additional breasts are present in human males or females, they occur on the milk lines.

Socially, the human breasts are an important secondary sexual characteristic (*qv*) to which fashion, fad, history, culture, and individual preference have attributed varying degrees of importance for women's overall sexual attractiveness. At different times and in different groups, large and small breasts have been considered attractive or not; no uniform tradition of beauty exists to assert that only one breast size or shape is attractive to all. At some times and to some people, extremely thin fashion models or the slender "flapper" figures may be deemed the ultimate in beauty; at other times and to other people, voluptuousness and prominence of the breasts may be thought the centerpiece of sexual love-liness.

The breasts' natural size and shape vary considerably in women, and may change during post-adolescent life, particularly as a result of lactation and nursing. However, with the exception of surgical techniques for removing breast tissue or for implanting substances, like silicones, to increase breast size, breast dimensions are not otherwise readily alterable, for example, by diet or exercise. Nonetheless, exercise may change the tone and strength of the chest muscles underlying the breasts, and may therefore alter the woman's carriage and appearance.

The circumstances and frequency with which women cover their breasts vary with culture and climate; in societies where the breasts are usually uncovered, breast shape may not be a major aspect of sexual attractiveness nor play a large role in sexual activity. In societies such as the modern United States and the West generally, where the breasts are usually covered, breast exposure and nudity have become powerful symbols and elicitors of sexual interest in either men or other women. Brassieres can be designed as purely functional or as cosmetic enhancements to a woman's sexual attractiveness, as in uplift bras or erotic apparel such as the peekaboo bra, which exposes the nipples. In recent years, the manufacture, advertising, and selling of erotic brassieres and other items of apparel has become a growth industry, attesting to widespread erotic (*qv*) fascination with the breasts.

In some women, foreplay (*qv*) involving the breasts is extremely arousing sexually, while in others it is less so. Men, too, vary in the degree of sexual arousal produced by seeing or touching a woman's breasts, and vary themselves in responsiveness to stimulation of their own nipples. Colloquially, a man who is specifically aroused by breast shape (often large breasts) is a "tit man," a term that demonstrates implicitly the fact that other men are not as concerned by breast size and shape. A good deal about the role of the breasts in sexuality has been written by psychologists, particularly psychoanalysts, who seek the ultimate origin of the sexuality of the breasts in the infant's need for, and pleasure in, suckling. Various paraphilias (*qv*) concerning the breasts also exist; for example, the specific arousal (*qv*) of some men by lactating women's breasts.

See also bad breast; breast augmentation; breast binder; breast cancer; breast complex; breast-feeding; breast lift; breast phantom; breast ptosis; breast pump; breast reduction surgery; breast reconstruction; breast self-examination (BSE); broken breast; lumpectomy; mammary gland; mastectomy.

Resource: D. Ayala and I. J. Weinstock, *Breasts: Women Speak about Their Breasts and Their Lives* (New York: Summit Books, 1979); this work contains hundreds of photographs that show different breast sizes, and shapes, and that comment on the wide variability of breast shape in women.

breast self-examination (BSE) A simple, three-step visual and palpation (*qv*) examination of the female breasts (*qv*) recommended for all woman after puberty (*qv*) as a monthly routine. BSE should be done about a week after the monthly period when the breasts are usually not tender or swollen. After menopause (*qv*), the exam can be done on the first of every month.

Step 1: While showering or bathing, glide hands gently over the wet skin of the breasts with the fingers flat to check for any lump, hard knot, or thickening. Step 2: Before a mirror, inspect the breasts visually with arms resting at the sides, with the arms raised over the head, and then with the palms pressing down firmly on the hips to flex the chest muscles, looking for any swelling, dimpling of the skin, or change in the nipples. Step 3: While lying down, with a pillow or folded towel under the right shoulder and the right hand under the head, the flat left hand is used to palpate or gently press the right breast in a circular motion starting at the outer edge and moving the fingers as if around the face of a clock back to a 12 o'clock starting point. The circular movement is repeated three or four times in decreasing circles until the areola (*qv*) is included. The nipple (*qv*) should be squeezed gently to detect any clear or bloody discharge. This third step is repeated with the left breast using the right hand.

Any unusual finding should be checked promptly by a physician. The monthly BSE should be supplemented by a physician examination every three years between ages 20 and 40. After age 40, an annual physician examination is recommended with a baseline mammography (*qv*) between ages 35 and 40 followed by a mammogram every other year between ages 40 and 49 and every year after age 50.

breech birth/presentation A positioning of the fetus (*qv*) in the uterus (*qv*) just prior to birth (*qv*) so that the buttocks (*qv*) or legs instead of the head enter the cervical canal (*qv*) first. This occurs in approximately 3 percent of labors (*qv*).

breech extraction An obstetrical operation in which an infant being born feet or buttocks (*qv*) first is grasped and delivered by traction. In an assisted breech delivery, traction is not applied until the umbilical cord (*qv*) appears.

bridal night The first night a married couple spend together after the wedding. The increasing incidence of premarital sex (*qv*) and cohabitation (*qv*) have reduced the importance of the bridal night for many couples, although it still retains an importance for those who hold to premarital virginity (*qv*). *See also* defloration; jus primae nocte; droit du seigneur.

bridal sheet A marriage (*qv*) custom in which the bloodied sheet from the nuptial bed is publicly displayed or paraded by the groom's family or friends to announce that the bride was indeed a virgin (*qv*) whose intact hymen (*qv*) was ruptured by the groom when the marriage was consummated (*qv*).

bride capture A marriage (*qv*) in which the bride is captured or abducted from the house of the bride's father or from a neighboring or enemy tribe.

bridegift In contrast with the earlier Germanic tradition of a brideprice (*qv*) paid to the bride's family, the bridegift was money, land, or goods paid to the bride by the groom or the groom's family as part of the marriage (*qv*) arrangement. The bridegift, usually supplemented by the Morgengabe (*qv*) in Germanic traditions of the early Middle Ages, was usually defined in monetary terms, although it was increasingly made in land. Taken together, the bridegift and Morgengabe amounted to an endowment (*qv*) of bride and the new household. *See also* arrha; dower; dowry.

brideprice A marital custom wherein the groom or groom's family present money, gifts, or property to the bride's family. Historically, payment of a brideprice occurs in cultures where the bride is considered property to be purchased. As the position of women improves, the brideprice, or bridewealth, is often replaced by a new custom of a bridegift (*qv*) paid to the bride herself. *See also* arrha; dowry; dower; endowment; Morgengabe.

bridewealth *See* brideprice.

British Abortion Act of 1963 This abortion (*qv*) reform law legalized termination of a pregnancy (*qv*) when two physicians certify that continued pregnancy threatens the mother's life, or the mental or physical health of the mother or any of her children. The British Abortion Act also allows abortion if the fetus (*qv*) is at risk for a serious mental or physical handicap if carried to term. *See also* abortion law; *Roe v. Wade* decision.

broad ligament A wide, folded sheet of peritoneal tissue draped over the Fallopian tubes (*qv*), uterus (*qv*), and ovaries (*qv*), supporting these structures and binding them to the sidewalls of the pelvis (*qv*).

broken breast Medical term for an abscessed mammary gland (*qv*).

bromidrosiphobia A rarely used term for a fear of body smells.

brood cell In cytology and cytogenetics, the original parental cell used to start a clone (*qv*) of daughter cells.

brothel A house of prostitution (*qv*); also known as a bawdy house or cat house.

brother-sister marriage A socially accepted exception to the incest taboo (*qv*) prohibiting marriage (*qv*) of close blood relatives. This exception, usually restricted to royal or aristocratic lines, occurred in Pharonic Egypt, precolonial Hawaii, and among the Incas. Marriage of half-brothers and half-sisters, with a single common parent, was allowed among the ancient Persians and Greeks. In some cultures, such as Bali and the Amyara of South America, twin brothers and sisters are allowed to marry because they are believed to have been already intimate in the womb (*qv*). *See also* cousin marriage.

Brown-Sequard, Edward A nineteenth-century French physician who claimed virility (*qv*) could be restored by injection of an extract of dog testes (*qv*).

BSE *See* breast self-examination.

BSRI *See* BEM Sex Role Inventory.

buccal intercourse An obsolete expression for fellatio (*qv*) or cunnilingus (*qv*).

buccal onanism An obsolete expression for fellatio (*qv*).

buccal smear A simple cytological check of chromosomes (*qv*) in the epithelial cells scraped from the inside of the oral cavity. Examination of a buccal smear provides information on chromosome status, abnormal chromosome number and structure, and genetic gender by way of evidence of the X (*qv*) and Y (*qv*) chromosome.

Buck's fascia A sheath of connective tissue enclosing the three corpora of the penis (*qv*) in a single bundle. Buck's fascia extends from the penile glans (*qv*) to the base of the penis where it meets the perineal (*qv*) and other pubic muscles.

buggery The legal term for anal intercourse (*qv*) or sodomy (*qv*) in England. The term was derived from Bulgaria, the center for the medieval, heretical Catharist movement. Medieval Christians alleged that the real reason the Cathar women did not become pregnant (*qv*) was that the Cathars, who condemned sexual intercourse (*qv*), practiced anal intercourse. Resource: R. Aman, Offensive words in dictionaries, *Maledicta: The International Journal of Verbal Aggression* 9 (1986–1987):227–268.

bulb, penile The enlarged oval portion of the corpus spongiosum (*qv*) embedded in the perineal membrane. *See also* urethra.

bulbitis Inflammation of the urethra (*qv*) in the base of the penis.

bulbocavernosus muscle In females, the muscle encircling and supporting the vaginal entrance where it decreases the diameter of the vaginal orifice and aids in clitoral erection (*qv*). In males, it encircles the base of the penis (*qv*) where it helps in expelling the last drops of urine during urination, contributes to penile erection (*qv*) by compressing the deep dorsal vein of the penis during sexual stimulation, and aids in ejaculation (*qv*) of semen (*qv*).

bulbospongiosus muscle An alternate, infrequently used term for bulbocavernosus muscle (*qv*).

bulbourethral duct or gland Associated with the bulb or internal base of the penis or with the urethra in the female. *See also* Cowper's glands; paraurethral ducts; Skene's glands.

bulbus vestibuli (L.) Two oval masses of erectile (*qv*) tissue located one on either side of the vaginal opening and joined by a pars intermedia; homologous to the corpus spongiosum (*qv*) in the male.

bulimia A syndrome of increased appetite and excessive intake of food typically followed by self-induced vomiting. Bulimia may alternate with depression and anorexia nervosa (*qv*). Some believe it is associated with sexual repression (*qv*) or the avoidance of the consequences of sexual maturation, or indulged in as a compensation for sexual frustration (*qv*).

bundling A colonial American courtship (*qv*) custom adapted to the frontier necessities in which a young man and woman who were courting slept together at night to conserve heat and eliminate the need for the young man to ride back to his home after dark. Premarital sex (*qv*) was discouraged by enclosing the woman up to her armpits in a bundling bag or separating the couple with a board. While not publicly expected, premarital sex in such a situation was common and tolerated. *See also* Fensternl; "taking your night feet for a walk."

burdock A garden plant long popular as a love potion.

bust A euphemism for the bosom or breasts (*qv*) of a woman.

butterfly vibrator A flat, nonpenetrating vibrator held in place with straps designed specifically to fit over the mons (*qv*) and anterior vulva (*qv*) and provide stimulation to the clitoris (*qv*) and/or other erogenous areas (*qv*).

buttocks The nates, or large, fleshy protuberances at the lower posterior portion of the body trunk. The buttocks are comprised of fat and the gluteal muscles.

The buttocks, like the breasts, legs, face, and other anatomical regions, are an important component of sexual attractiveness, at least to some people at some times. Fashion and fad have dictated that sometimes thin, muscular buttocks are the pinnacle of attractiveness in both men and women while at other times fleshy and well-rounded buttocks have been socially considered more sexually attractive in women. No universal standard exists asserting that only one buttock shape or size is always sexually attractive, and individual men and women differ considerably in how attractive they find thin or fleshy buttocks either in themselves or in other people. In periods when athletic muscularity is considered sexually attractive in both men and women, individuals with large buttocks can suffer psychologically and socially, and often go to considerable extremes, including surgery, to alter what they perceive as an ugly part of their body. However, even at such times, there are people who find plump or round buttocks extremely attractive and dislike what they see as thin, bony buttocks. This difference is an example of how social fashion and fad fails to correspond to personal preference, and it can be argued that psychosexual (*qv*) maturity requires understanding that not everyone adheres to social fashions when making sexual choices or when experiencing sexual interest.

button A cervical cap (*qv*).

butyl nitrite A vasodilating drug alleged by some to prolong or intensify the experience of orgasm (*qv*); its use can lead to a cerebrovascular accident.

BWS *See* battered woman syndrome.

C

Caesarean hysterectomy Surgical removal of the uterus (*qv*) at the time a newborn (*qv*) is delivered (*qv*) by Caesarean section (*qv*) that results in intractable hemorrhage or other complications.

Caesarean section (C section) A surgical procedure in which a baby is delivered through an incision in the abdominal and uterine walls. A C section is performed when abnormal maternal or fetal conditions indicate vaginal delivery (*qv*) would be hazardous. Approximately 15 to 20 percent of births in the United States are by C section with a much lower frequency in other countries. A fear of medical malpractice suits is admitted by many to be the main reason for the continuing increase in C section deliveries. A previous C section delivery is no longer considered a barrier to a subsequent vaginal delivery. The Roman Emperor, Julius Caesar, was allegedly born in this way; hence the name.

CAH *See* congenital (virilizing) adrenal hyperplasia (CVAH).

caked breast An inflammatory condition of the breast (*qv*) associated with an increased blood flow prior to lactation (*qv*), characterized by fullness, hardness, and a flushed skin tone. Caked breast may also result from blockage of one or more of the milk ducts, resulting in engorgement.

calendar method of birth control A natural method of contraception (*qv*) based on limiting sexual intercourse (*qv*) to nonfertile times in the woman's cycle. The projected nonfertile time can be estimated by taking the average of the woman's menstrual cycles (*qv*) for 6 months, calculating the time of ovulation (*qv*) at 14 days before the beginning of the average cycle, and abstaining from intercourse for 3 to 4 days before and after the projected day of ovulation in each succeeding cycle. The safe period in subsequent cycles can be calculated as extending from the fourth day prior to the earliest ovulation recorded to the fourth day after the latest ovulation noted in a 6 month period. The calendar method of birth control, or rhythm, is widely regarded as unreliable. *See also* basal body temperature method of contraception; Billings' contraceptive method.

call boy A male homosexual (*qv*) prostitute (*qv*) who works by telephone appointment only, catering to more affluent clients, unlike the male prostitutes who work streets and bars.

call girl A female prostitute (*qv*) who works by telephone appointment only, catering to more affluent clients, business executives, and professional and business men, unlike prostitutes who work the streets, bars, and massage parlors (*qv*).

callomania Pathologic delusions of one's extraordinary beauty.

camp, camp culture A complex set of gay (*qv*) affectations in dress, personal manner, conversational style, language, and humor, all marked by exaggeration, insult, extravagance, and a satiric sense of the ludicrous and the artificiality of social convention, both gay and straight. In some large urban settings, camp is a life-style enjoyed for its fast-paced sophistication by both gay and nongay individuals.

Candida (L.) A genus of yeastlike fungi including the common pathogen *Candida albicans* (*qv*).

Candida albicans vaginalis (L.) A common, microscopic, yeastlike fungus normally present without symptoms in the mucous membranes of the mouth, intestines, and vagina (*qv*), and on the skin of healthy people; also known as *Monilia vaginalis*. *See also* candidiasis.

candidiasis An infection of the sexual-genital system, rectum (*qv*), or oral cavity caused by an excess growth of the naturally occurring *Candida albicans vaginalis* (*qv*). Infection may follow antibiotic therapy and direct sexual contact with an infected partner, including oral (*qv*) and anal sex (*qv*). Use of the oral contraceptive (*qv*), pregnancy (*qv*), and diabetes increase the infection risk. The oral infection is known as thrush. Candidiasis can cause balanitis (*qv*) in an uncircumcised male. It also occurs in patients with AIDS-related complex (*qv*) and acquired immune deficiency syndrome (*qv*).

Infected males are usually symptomless, while infected females have a thick, white, cream-cheese-like vaginal discharge, a yeastlike odor, irritation, and itching. Diagnosis is by microscopic examination of smears from suspected infection sites. Treatment is with vaginal or oral nystatin. Symptoms may be relieved by cool tub baths, Vaseline, and cool, wet presses. Recurrence of infections may be lessened by reducing sugar and carbohydrate intake and, some claim, by reestablishing proper bacterial flora by vaginal insertion of plain, unflavored yogurt.

Cannabis (L.) *See* marijuana.

cannibalistic phase In psychoanalytic theory, the second half of the oral stage (*qv*) in which the infant's (*qv*) aggression and anger is expressed by biting the mother's breast (*qv*) and nipple (*qv*), or the bottle nipple during feeding. If development is arrested at this stage, fantasies (*qv*) and impulses may later become focused on biting, chewing, and swallowing.

canon law The system of laws and decrees enacted by a Christian church to regulate all aspects of its institutional functioning, including standards for its members' behavior. *See also* civil law.

cantharides A white crystalline powder made from the dried bodies of *Cantharis vesicatoria*, a beetle native to France and Spain, and *Lytta vesicatoria*, a common Spanish fly. Although praised as an aphrodisiac (*qv*), in reality the extract causes inflammation and irritation of the urinary tract, capable of producing priapism (*qv*) and even death. Cantharides are popularly known as Spanish fly.

cap *See* cervical cap, pessary.

capacitation The physiological process whereby sperm (*qv*) are made capable of penetrating the cells surrounding the ovum (*qv*) and the ovum membrane. Capacitation involves physiological changes in the proteolytic enzymes in the sperm acrosome (*qv*) as it passes through the vaginal and uterine environments.

capote allemande (or anglaise) A condom (*qv*).

cardinal ligament A transverse sheet of subserous fascia extending across the floor of the pelvic cavity as a continuation of the broad ligament and associated with the vagina (*qv*), cervix (*qv*), and urinary bladder.

carezza *See* coitus reservatus; karezza.

Carile, Richard (1790–1843) An English social reformer and publisher of *Every Woman's Book; or What Is Love?* the first pamphlet on birth control (*qv*) in the English language.

caritas (L.) Spiritual and brotherly love. *See also* agape; love.

carnal abuse Legal term for forced sexual intimacies (*qv*).

carnal desire *See* eros; libido; lust.

carnal knowledge A legal term for sexual intercourse (*qv*).

carousel dynamics effect A model for the synergistic interaction of sexual performance fears and communications problems leading to a sexual dysfunction (*qv*). Either partner can ''get on the carousel or merry-go-round'' as a result of a single frustrating experience. When unresolved, this frustration leads to frustration in the other partner. When unresolved by communication, the cycle leads to hurt or anger in one partner, followed by getting even on both parts as the merry-go-round pattern is repeated and builds in intensity.

carpopedal spasm An involuntary, spastic contraction of the voluntary muscles of the hands and feet, sometimes associated with orgasm (*qv*). In the foot, the carpopedal spasm causes the big toe to extend straight, while the other toes bend back and the foot arches.

carrier A person or animal who harbors a pathogenic organism without showing its effects and spreads this organism to others; a heterozygous (*qv*) person with one normal dominant (*qv*) gene (*qv*) and one recessive (*qv*) mutant gene who is not affected by the abnormal gene but can pass that gene to offspring who will show the condition if they inherit the same defective gene from both parents.

caryncula Small, fleshy tags or remnants of the ruptured hymen (*qv*).

Casanova, Giovanni Giacomo (1725–1798) An Italian diplomat, historian, mathematician, chemist, composer, and playwright, remembered mainly for the 12–volume *Memoires* of his numerous amorous encounters with women. Although a compulsive seducer of women, Casanova approached his relations with women not simply as an exploitive conquest as the fictional Don Juan (*qv*) did but with an emotional and spiritual intimacy. Casanova was an intellectual associate of Boswell, Benjamin Franklin, Goethe, Frederick the Great, Voltaire and d'Alembert.

cassolette (Fr.) The natural odor of the vulva (*qv*), highly praised as an erotic (*qv*) stimulus in Eastern love manuals but frowned on by many Western women as a sign of a lack of cleanliness.

caste system A form of social stratification in which distinct hereditary social groups are hierarchically organized and separated from each other by rules of ritual (*qv*) purity.

castration Surgical removal of one or both testes (*qv*) or ovaries (*qv*); or of the testes and penis (*qv*). "Male castration has four degees: the clean-shaven (penis and testicles removed), stoned (testicles removed), tailless (penis removed), and crushed balls" (K. Schwartz, *The Male Member* [St. Martin's Press, 1985], p. 93). If castration is performed before puberty, side effects include decreases in libido (particularly in the male) and secondary sex characteristics (*qv*). Whether performed before or after puberty, castration produces sterility (*qv*) in both sexes and amenorrhea (*qv*) in the female.

Modern-day castration of the testes or ovaries is done to reduce the production of sex hormones (*qv*) that may stimulate malignant cell growth in female breast cancer (*qv*) and male prostatic cancer (*qv*). At other times and in other cultures, various types of male castration have been used as punishment for sex criminals, prisoners of war, victims of lynch mobs, and to produce eunuchs (*qv*) or *castrati* (*qv*). Spay is the term for female castration in animal husbandry. Removal of the clitoris (*qv*) is termed clitorectomy.

castration anxiety *See* castration complex.

castration cell Ring-shaped cells found in the anterior pituitary (*qv*) of men who have been castrated (*qv*).

castration complex In psychoanalytic theory (*qv*), the unconscious fear boys are said to experience that their penis (*qv*) will be cut off as punishment for masturbation (*qv*) or incestuous desires. The term also refers to the fantasy (*qv*) a girl may have that her mother has already cut off her penis as punishment for some incestuous desire or sexual offense.

castratus (pl. castrati) (L.) A male castrated (*qv*) in order to preserve his prepubertal soprano voice.

catamenia (catamenial discharge) Medical term for menstruation (*qv*) or menses (*qv*).

catamite An obsolete term for a malè homosexual (*qv*), or for a boy kept for the purposes of pederasty (*qv*).

catatonia A psychiatric syndrome in which a person appears immobile and unresponsive to sensory stimuli even though he or she is not unaware of them.

catharsis model of pornography research A hypothesis used in research on pornography (*qv*) that theorizes that pornography provides a necessary release of sexual tension in a repressive society. *See also* imitation model of pornography research.

caul A portion of the amniotic sac (*qv*) which may cover the face and head of the fetus (*qv*) during birth (*qv*). In folklore, a piece of caul was considered good luck, especially by sailors, who believed it could protect them from drowning.

cavernosum *See* corpus cavernosum.

CBR *See* crude birthrate.

cecum condom A condom (*qv*) made of the lining of animal intestines rolled over the erect penis (*qv*) before vulval contact and vaginal penetration. A space at the tip of the condom retains the ejaculate (*qv*).

celibacy A temporary or lifelong abstinence (*qv*) from sexual activity, especially sexual intercourse (*qv*). Celibacy is the official life-style for monks in the Eastern religions and among Catholic clergy and members of religious orders. *See also* asceticism; chastity; virginity.

cells of Leydig *See* Leydig, cells of.

cenotrope (coenotrope) An acquired behavior pattern shown by all members of a biological group in a common environment. The behavior is assumed to be the result of genetic factors and common experiences. *See also* phylism.

censorship, sexual The application of the law to prohibit publication, distribution, or possession of obscene (*qv*) or pornographic (*qv*) material, or sexually explicit material. Obscenity laws began after the invention of movable type and the printing press allowed rapid and inexpensive reproduction of books and pictorial material. An ongoing controversy exists over the relationship between censorship, obscenity (*qv*), and the First Amendment to the U.S. Constitution. *See also* Comstock law; Commission on Pornography and Obscenity: 1970, 1986; *Roth v. United States*.

central nervous system (CNS) That part of the body's nervous system, distinct from the peripheral nervous system, consisting of the brain and spinal cord. The CNS contains the cerebrum (*qv*) or cerebral hemispheres, the diencephalon with the hypothalamus (*qv*), the midbrain, hindbrain with the cerebellum (*qv*), and the spinal cord. The CNS processes information to and from the peripheral nerves, serving as the main network for coordination and consciousness, controlling sleep, sexual activity, muscular movement, hunger, thirst, cognition, memory, and the emotions. The spinal cord serves as a switching and relay terminal between the sensory and motor peripheral nerves and the brain. *See also* autonomic nervous system; parasympathetic nervous system; sympathetic nervous system.

central nervous system (CNS) depressant Any drug or medication that decreases the activity or functioning of the central nervous system (*qv*). The main types of CNS depressants—alcohol, barbiturates (*qv*), and hypnotics—can interfere with sexual functioning (*qv*).

central nervous system (CNS) stimulant Any drug or medication that quickens the activity of the central nervous system (*qv*). In contrast with a CNS depressant (*qv*), stimulants like caffeine and amphetamines are not known to affect sexual functioning (*qv*).

central placenta praevia A placenta (*qv*) abnormally located in the neck of the uterus (*qv*) where it lies in front of the fetus (*qv*) and blocks its passage through the cervix (*qv*) to the birth canal (*qv*). When diagnosed before labor (*qv*) begins, delivery (*qv*) is by Caesarean section (*qv*).

cephalic presentation In childbirth (*qv*), a delivery (*qv*) in which the fetal head passes through the cervix (*qv*) and vagina (*qv*) first.

cephalopelvic disproportion (CPD) An obstetric condition in which the fetal head is too large or the birth canal (*qv*) too small to permit normal delivery (*qv*). It may be managed by the use of forceps or by Caesarean section (*qv*).

cerebellum In the brain, a pair of hemispheric lobes beneath the posterior base of the cerebral hemispheres (*qv*) and above the brain stem. The cerebellum, known classically as the modulator and integrator of motor functions, has a major role in modulating all autonomic nervous system (*qv*) functions, all sensory efferents including tactile perceptions and alterations of pain thresholds, and emotional-social behaviors that range from the tranquil to the sexual to rage. J. W. Prescott has proposed that the cerebellum is a master integrating and regulating system of sensory, emotional-social, and motor functions of the body and that it provides the primary bridge between the neocortex (*qv*), or "conscious brain," and the limbic system (*qv*), or "unconscious brain." *See also* somatosensory affectional deprivation. Resource: J. W. Prescott, Affectional bonding for the prevention of violent behaviors: neurobiological, psychological and religious/spiritual determinants, in L. J. Hertzberg et al. (eds.), *Violent Behavior: Assessment and Intervention*, vol. 1 (New York: PMA Publishing Corp, 1989).

cerebral cortex In the brain, the neopallium, neocortex, or external gray layer of the cerebrum (*qv*) consisting of nerve cell bodies that govern and moderate conscious responses, muscular control, sensory input, the special senses, as well as processing, integrating, and interpreting sensory information and formulating motor responses. The cerebral cortex is divided into right and left hemispheres, with specialized areas clinically identified with specific functions. *See also* paleocortex; limbic system.

cerebrum The largest, uppermost, conscious section of the brain, divided by a central groove into right and left cerebral hemispheres, the cerebrum mediates sensory and motor functions and the less easily defined integration functions associated with various conscious mental activities, including cognition, memory, speech, writing, and emotional responses. The two hemispheres are connected by the corpus callosum. Each hemisphere is composed of an extensive outer cerebral cortex composed of gray matter, an underlying layer of white matter, and the central and medial structures of the limbic system (*qv*). The cerebral surface is convoluted and lobed, each lobe bearing the name of the skull bone under which it lies. The various electrical waves generated by neural functions may be recorded on an electroencephalogram to localize areas of brain dysfunction, identify altered states of consciousness, or establish brain death. *See also* neopallium; paleopallium.

ceremonial defloration *See* defloration.

cervical canal The passageway from the vagina (*qv*) to the uterine cavity or fundus (*qv*) through the cervix (*qv*). The cervical canal allows the passage of the monthly menstrual flow (*qv*), the semen (*qv*) into the uterus (*qv*) and fallopian tubes (*qv*), and the fetus (*qv*) during delivery (*qv*). The mucus secreted by endocervical glands changes in appearance and consistency during the monthly cycle. *See also* cervical mucus; spinnbarkheit.

cervical cancer A neoplastic, malignant growth in the uterine cervix (*qv*). Cervical cancer is easily detected by the Pap(anicolaou) test (*qv*) and curable if detected early. Factors associated with its etiology include coitus (*qv*) at an early age, multiple sexual partners, genital herpes (*qv*) and other viral venereal (*qv*) infections, multiparity, and poor obstetric and gynecological care.

cervical cap A small plastic or rubber thimble-like device worn on the cervix (*qv*) as a barrier contraceptive (*qv*). Like the diaphragm (*qv*), the cervical cap must be fitted to the size of the cervix and the user shown how to insert it properly. The cervical cap, which equals or exceeds the effectiveness of the diaphragm, is popular in Great Britain and Europe and has only recently become available in the United States.

cervical carcinoma *See* cervical cancer.

cervical erosion A chronic, degenerative inflammation of the mucosa of the cervix (*qv*) that may lead to sterility (*qv*) by blocking passage of the sperm (*qv*).

cervical evaluation A diagnostic study of the cyclic changes in the cervix (*qv*) and its mucus production. Abnormalities in the cervical mucus (*qv*) can be the cause of infertility (*qv*).

cervical fistula An abnormal passage from the uterine cervix (*qv*) to the vagina (*qv*) or bladder that may be caused by injury during childbirth (*qv*), surgical trauma, radiotherapy, or a malignant lesion.

cervical mucus A viscous, slippery secretion of the endocervical glands of the uterine cervix (*qv*) that changes in consistency and appearance during the monthly menstrual cycle (*qv*). For the first few days after menses (*qv*), little mucus is secreted. As ovulation (*qv*) approaches, increasing amounts of sticky, cloudy-white, or yellowish mucus are produced. Around the time of ovulation, the mucus volume increases, and it is clear, slippery, and elastic, somewhat like the uncooked white of a chicken egg. After ovulation the mucus becomes cloudy, thick, sticky, and gradually reduced in volume as menstruation approaches. *See also* Billings' contraceptive method; Spinnbarkheit; ferning.

cervical mucus method of contraception *See* Billings' contraceptive method; Spinnbarkheit.

cervical os The outer opening of the canal in the cervix (*qv*) connecting the uterine and vaginal cavities. Just before ovulation (*qv*), the outer os (*qv*) becomes soft and projects farther into the vagina (*qv*). In multipara (*qv*) women, the opening changes from a small circle to a wide slit. *See also* cervical mucus.

cervical pregnancy An ectopic pregnancy (*qv*) in which the conceptus (*qv*) implants in the cervical canal (*qv*). A cervical pregnancy is marked by abnormal bleeding and is life threatening. Management is by surgical removal of the conceptus.

cervical smear A small amount of secretions and superficial cells obtained from the external os of the uterine cervix (*qv*), the vaginal vault, and endocervical canal used for diagnosis of cervicitis (*qv*) or for a Pap(anicolaou) test (*qv*).

cervical sponge *See* vaginal sponge.

cervicitis An acute or chronic inflammation of the uterine cervix (*qv*). Acute cervicitis is a cervical infection marked by redness, edema, and bleeding. Other symptoms may include a copious, foul-smelling vaginal discharge, pelvic pain, and vulvar itching or burning. The usual causes are *Trichomonas vaginalis* (*qv*), *Candida albicans*, (*qv*), and *Haemophilus vaginalis* (*qv*). Such infections are often recurrent because of reexposure, undertreatment, or predisposing factors. Chronic cervicitis is a persistent inflammation characterized by thick, irritating, foul-smelling vaginal discharge, with a congested appearance of the cervix (*qv*) often with enlarged cysts (*qv*). Antibiotic treatment is seldom effective for chronic cervicitis.

cervix The neck of an organ, most commonly the external neck or lower part of the uterus (*qv*) leading into the vaginal canal (*qv*). The cervix provides an entrance passage for the sperm (*qv*) from the vagina (*qv*) into the uterine cavity and a passageway for menstrual flow (*qv*) and for the fetus (*qv*) during childbirth (*qv*). *See also* cervicitis, Pap(anicolaou) test.

Cesarean section (C section) *See* Caesarean section.

C-film *See* contraceptive film.

chador The traditional dress of Islamic women, consisting of a head-to-foot, flowing robe with a face veil or head hood. The chador was adapted from the Arabic desert garment, the burka.

Chadwick's sign A violet discoloration of the vaginal mucosa below the urethral opening, appearing after the fourth month of pregnancy (*qv*).

Chakra (Skt.) In Tantra (*qv*), a mystic circle or wheel; a psychic center or focal point, located primarily in the sexual organs (*qv*), spleen, navel, heart, throat, and head. Each Chakra acts as a transformer of energies, converting impulses from one frequency to another. Often referred to as the lotuses, the Chakras are believed to open and close depending on psychophysical conditions, which Tantric yoga (*qv*) postures and exercises seek to control. A gathering of Tantrics is also known as a Chakra.

chancre A small, painless, craterlike sore. If caused by the *Treponema pallidum* (*qv*) spirochete (*qv*), the hard chancre(s) (*qv*) heal without treatment, leaving no scar. Soft chancres (*qv*) are typical of chancroid (*qv*).

chancroid A highly contagious venereal (*qv*) ulcer caused by the bacterium *Hemophilus ducreyi*. A chancroid infection characteristically begins as a papule on the skin of the external genitalia (*qv*) that grows and ulcerates. It is common in the tropics and rare in the temperate climate of the United States and Europe. A skin test is more reliable than diagnosis by smear and culture. Treatment is with sulfa drugs. If left untreated, the infection spreads to form enlarged, inflamed lymph nodes in the groin. It may coexist with syphilis (*qv*) and lymphogranuloma venereum (*qv*), with which it may also be confused. *See also* chancre.

change of life A common, colloquial expression for menopause (*qv*), climacteric.

chastity (chaste) For unmarried persons and those who have chosen a celibate (*qv*) life-style, chastity requires abstinence (*qv*) from all sexual activity (*qv*). A married person is chaste if he or she has sexual relations (*qv*) only with the spouse. *See also* double moral standard; virginity.

chastity belt A variety of lockable devices for both males and females in use from medieval through Victorian (*qv*) times designed to prevent sexual (*qv*) indulgence. Male chastity belts were designed to prevent involuntary nocturnal seminal emissions (*qv*) and masturbation (*qv*). Female chastity belts were designed to secure the wife's sexual fidelity (*qv*) when the husband was absent.

chauvinism, male A set of attitudes, beliefs, habits, and customs asserting that men are superior to women in some or all aspects of life. The term chauvinism derives from Nicolas Chauvin, an intense patriot of France during the Napoleonic era, and has been applied wherever an individual or group asserts its own superiority over others. The phrase male chauvinist implies that the chauvinist holds derogatory and contemptuous opinions of women, and is therefore related to the concept of misogyny (*qv*). Sometimes, but not always, a male chauvinist holds that legal or social rules should forbid women certain rights, for example, education, job opportunities, pay, or advancement in job or career. Feminist (*qv*) theoreticians, although disagreeing over the causes of male chauvinism, all tend to agree that men in modern society are raised and nurtured in male chauvinist traditions. Loosely and colloquially, the phrase can be used to describe someone who insults women or who behaves in socially unacceptable ways toward them.

chelating agent A chemical substance that traps specific atoms or molecules and prevents them from forming their normal chemical combinations. Naturally occurring chelating agents protect sperm (*qv*) from traces of toxic metals in the vaginal fluids (*qv*) and semen (*qv*).

Chiari-Frommel syndrome A failure of lactation (*qv*) to stop following weaning (*qv*), usually resulting from a decrease in pituitary gonadotropins (*qv*) and an excess of prolactin (*qv*).

child A young person of either sex between the end of infancy (*qv*) and the start of adolescence (*qv*); a prepubescent (*qv*) boy or girl; a son or daughter. *See also* childhood.

child abuse The physical, emotional, and/or sexual maltreatment of a child. Child abuse often results in permanent physical injury, psychiatric injury, mental impairment, or death. Unless treated, child abuse can lead to a repetition of the abuse when the abused child becomes a parent. Child abuse is the result of multiple and complex factors involving a stressful environment, marital strife or other crisis, inadequate emotional and physical support within the family, and the lack of adequate stress-coping skills of the parents. Parents at high risk for child abuse usually have unsatisfied needs, difficulty in forming healthy interpersonal relations, unrealistic expectations of the child, and often a history of abuse or lack of nurturance when they were children. Predisposing factors in abused children include congenital or genetic abnormalities, difficult or uncomfortable pregnancy (*qv*) or delivery (*qv*), premature birth (*qv*), first or last birth order (*qv*), being under the age of 3 years, and being extremely irritable or crying often. *See also* child neglect; child sexual abuse.

childbearing period The reproductive period (*qv*) in a woman's life, between puberty (*qv*) and menopause (*qv*).

childbirth *See* birth; labor.

childbirth fear An intense, morbid fear of childbirth; maieusiophobia (*qv*).

childhood The period between infancy (*qv*) and the onset of puberty (*qv*). In the United States, according to Public Law 98–292, the Child Protection Act of 1984, childhood is the period of development prior to the eighteenth birthday. Sociologists, following the historical research of Philippe Ariès, have concluded that the child and childhood, as social categories, began to develop in the eighteenth century among the European nobility. The emergence of childhood as a distinct category was connected with the emergence of English public schools as a special institution for the cultivation of the elite and educational theories, particularly those of Jean-Jacques Rousseau in the 1700s. A growing awareness of the social rights of children led to the Factory Acts of the 1840s, which sought to protect children against exploitation at work.

childlessness *See* infertility; sterility.

child marriage Marriage (*qv*) between an adult (*qv*) and a child (*qv*) or infant (*qv*), usually an older male and younger female. Although most countries have enacted laws setting a minimum age for marriage, the practice of child marriage still exists in many remote areas. Although the betrothal (*qv*) or marriage may be formalized when the female spouse is still an infant or juvenile (*qv*), consummation (*qv*) of the marriage does not occur until she reaches puberty (*qv*).

child molestation *See* child abuse, child sexual abuse, pedophilia.

child neglect The failure of parents, guardians, or caregivers to provide the basic physical and/or emotional nurturance to the point where the deprivation interferes with normal growth and development or places the child's health and life in jeopardy. *See also* child abuse; somatosensory affectional deprivation.

child-penis wish In psychoanalytic theory (*qv*), the replacement of the Electra complex (*qv*) and penis envy (*qv*) of a girl with the wish to have a child by her father.

child pornography Pornography (*qv*) in which children are displayed in ways that can sexually arouse adults, typically men. Child pornographic depictions can range from indirect photographic or drawn representations of child-like characteristics, such as a child's hairless pubic area, to lengthy and detailed filmed and videotaped episodes of child-adult sexual intercourse and exploitation. In the United States, child pornography, also called "kiddy porn," is illegal to possess, buy, sell, exchange, manufacture, or produce. Despite recent federal government prosecution of the producers of child pornography, pedophiles (*qv*) have found a new, readily available source of sexual stimulation in the advertising media, which is increasingly using provocatively posed prepubescent or young girls in advertising. *See also* cybersex (*Addendum*).

child sexual abuse (or molestation) The sexual abuse (*qv*) of an infant (*qv*) or child (*qv*) by an adult (*qv*). Molestation may involve exhibitionism (*qv*), fondling or stroking the child's genitals (*qv*), and/or oral (*qv*), anal (*qv*), or vaginal (*qv*) sex. The extent of the problem is unknown, although recent publicity has led to an increase in reporting of the sexual abuse of minors. *See also* pedophilia.

chimera (Gr.) In developmental biology, the natural or experimentally induced combination of two or more individuals from the same or different species. This phenomenon is more commonly referred to now as a genetic or sexual mosaic (*qv*). Chimeras are produced experimentally by joining two embryos (*qv*), as in the case of a "gheep" in which early embryos of a sheep and goat are fused into a single animal that exhibits the distinct characteristics of sheep and goat in different body parts. A blood chimera can result from fusion of the placenta (*qv*) and a blood supply shared between dizygotic twins (*qv*).

Chlamydia (L.) Currently the most common sexually transmitted disease (*qv*) in America and a major cause of pelvic inflammatory disease (*qv*) in women, *Chlamydia* is caused by *Chlamydia trachomatis*. While the majority of females with *Chlamydial* infections show no symptoms, female symptoms may include vaginal discharge (*qv*), pelvic pain, abnormal bleeding, and painful urination. In males, *Chlamydia* is a major cause of nongonococcal urethritis (*qv*) and epididymitis (*qv*) in the United States. Symptoms in men include painful urination and discharge. The newborns (*qv*) of infected women are subject to eye infection, infant pneumonia, premature delivery, and low birth weight (*qv*). Infections are treated with tetracycline or erythromycin.

Chlamydia trachomatis (L.) One of several strains of intracellular parasitic microorganisms in the genus *Chlamydia*; currently classified as a bacterium. *See also* Chlamydia.

chloasma (gravidarum) (L.) Temporary brown-pigmented spots, usually on the face, which may be caused by use of oral contraceptives (*qv*) or by hormones (*qv*) associated with pregnancy (*qv*).

chocolate An alleged aphrodisiac (*qv*). Popular among the Aztecs, chocolate was introduced by the conquistadors to Europe. In reality, chocolate is rich in phenylethylamine (*qv*), a chemical that mimics the amphetamine-like psychological "high" that accompanies falling in love (*qv*). When a love affair collapses, one is left with a depression similar to amphetamine withdrawal, which sometimes leads to unconscious compensation in a chocolate binge.

chocolate cysts Small cysts of displaced endometrial tissue found in the ovaries (*qv*); similar displaced endometrial tissue from the uterine lining may be found elsewhere in the abdominal organs. *See also* endometriosis.

chordee A congenital anatomical deformity of the penis (*qv*) or clitoris (*qv*), characteristic of hermaphroditism (*qv*) and often associated with hypospadia (*qv*). In males, the penis may have a fixed ventral curvature caused by a fibrous band of tissue instead of the normal skin along the corpus spongiosum (*qv*). In females, the clitoris may be enlarged.

chorditis Inflammation of the spermatic cord (*qv*) and vas or ductus deferens (*qv*).

chorea gravidarum (L.) Involuntary, irregular muscle movements, especially in the eyes, associated with some first-trimester pregnancies (*qv*) or occurring as a side effect of oral contraceptives (*qv*). An affected woman may also experience clumsiness or difficulty in eating and dressing.

choriocarcinoma An epithelial malignancy that develops from the chorionic (*qv*) portion of the products of a conception (*qv*), usually from a hydatidiform mole (*qv*), or less frequently from an abortion (*qv*), teratoma (*qv*), or pregnancy (*qv*). The primary tumor is usually unobserved as it invades and destroys the uterine wall. Later, it metastasizes into the vaginal wall, vulva (*qv*), lymph nodes, lungs, liver and brain. Usually, the growth is first observed in the vagina (*qv*) near the cervix (*qv*) as purple wartlike tissue. It is more common in older than younger women, but may rarely occur also in the testes (*qv*) or pineal gland (*qv*).

chorioepithelioma *See* choriocarcinoma.

chorion The outermost and largest of the four extraembryonic membranes, the chorion is a major component in the placental formation. The chorionic surface is at first covered with fingerlike villi that remain in the area of the placenta (*qv*) while degenerating elsewhere and forming the smooth surface of the chorion laeve. The chorion is vascularized by allantoic blood vessels in the third week of gestation (*qv*). In later pregnancy (*qv*), the chorion laeve, and underlying amnion (*qv*) fuse with the uterine wall as the fetus (*qv*) grows and fills the uterine cavity. *See also* allantois; yolk sac.

chorionic gonadotropin A hormone (*qv*) produced by the placenta (*qv*) during pregnancy (*qv*), that affects ovarian (*qv*) function and helps support pregnancy by maintaining sex hormone secretion by the corpus luteum (*qv*) during the first trimester. The presence of chorionic gonadotropin in urine or blood is the basis for pregnancy tests. *See* follicle-stimulating hormone; luteinizing hormone; immunological urine test; beta-specific monoclonal enzyme-linked immunosorbent assay; beta subunit HCG radioimmunoassay test.

chorionic plate That portion of the fetal placenta (*qv*) that gives rise to the chorionic villi (*qv*) and attaches to the uterine wall to form the full fetal/maternal placenta (*qv*).

chorionic villi Fingerlike projections of the trophoblast (*qv*), originally covering the whole surface of the blastocyst (*qv*) at implantation (*qv*) but later restricted to the placenta (*qv*) where they form into villar trees to facilitate exchanges between fetal circulation and the maternal lake of blood inside the placenta.

chorionic villi biopsy or sampling (CVB or CVS) A prenatal (*qv*) screening technique that relies on analysis of fetal placental (*qv*) tissue to detect an abnormal chromosomal condition or metabolic defect. The tissue is obtained by biopsy (*qv*) done through the cervical canal (*qv*) between the sixth and tenth week of pregnancy (*qv*). The risk of miscarriage (*qv*) and fetal damage is higher with CVS than with amniocentesis (*qv*). *See also* perculation umbilical blood sampling.

chorionitis An inflammation of the chorion (*qv*) due to a bacterial or viral infection.

chrematisophilia (Gr.) A paraphilic (*qv*) condition in which sexuoerotic arousal (*qv*) and attainment of orgasm (*qv*) respond to and depend on being charged or forced to pay for sexual services. There is no known reciprocal paraphilia in which arousal and orgasm depend on enforcing a charge or robbing the partner.

chromatin The basic structural fiber of the chromosome (*qv*), composed of the nucleoprotein deoxyribonucleic acid (*qv*). Chromatin is visible during interphase as a diffuse, granular, and poorly staining net in the nucleus. Chromatin can be studied when it condenses into chromosomes during mitosis (*qv*) or meiosis (*qv*). *See also* sex chromatin.

chromatin negative A cell with a single X chromosome (*qv*) in its nucleus and therefore showing no sex chromatin (*qv*) or Barr body (*qv*). Absence of sex chromatin is diagnostic for a chromosomal male (46,XY) and for a Turner syndrome (*qv*) female (45,XO).

chromatin positive A cell showing sex chromatin (*qv*) in one or more Barr bodies (*qv*). The presence of one or more Barr bodies is diagnostic for a chromosomal female (46,XX), a sexual mosaic (*qv*) with 46,XX/46,XY or 46,XX/45,XO, and Klinefelter syndrome (*qv*) (47,XXY).

chromosomal gender *See* chromosomal sex.

chromosomal mosaic An individual with two distinct cell lines with different chromosomal content. Chromosomal mosaics are more commonly the result from post-fertilization mitotic nondisjunction (*qv*). The condition may also result from fertilization (*qv*) of an ovum (*qv*) by two sperms (*qv*) or from the fusion of two very early embryonic masses. In the former case, one cell may be lacking a chromosome (*qv*), while the other cell line is trisomic for the same chromosome. Typical mosaics include: two variations of Turner syndrome (*qv*), 46,XX/45,XO and 46,XY/45,X0; a mosaic trisomy 21 (Down syndrome); 46/47,21 + ; and others such as 46,XX/47,XXX and 47,XXX/48,XXXX. *See also* chimera.

chromosomal sex That aspect of one's biological sex determined at fertilization (*qv*) when the haploid (*qv*) number of chromosomes (*qv*) in the ovum (*qv*) and sperm (*qv*) are united to produce a single-cell diploid (*qv*) zygote (*qv*). In humans, the fertilized ovum or zygote normally contains 44 autosomes (*qv*) in 22 homologous (*qv*) pairs plus either two X chromosomes (*qv*) for a female or an X and a Y (*qv*) sex chromosome for a male. Deviations from this normal pattern result when the ovum or sperm contains more than one sex chromosome or autosome following nondisjunction (*qv*) during meiosis. Deviations include Turner (45,XO) syndrome (*qv*), Klinefelter (47,XXY) syndrome (*qv*), 47,XYY syndrome, 47,XXX, and various polysomies of either the X or Y or both X and Y chromosomes. The chromosomal sex of an individual may be at variance with his or her other sex variables (i.e., anatomical, hormonal, or psychological).

chromosome Microscopic, linear structures found in virtually all cells, composed of deoxyribonucleic acid (DNA) (*qv*) and various proteins, and responsible for the transmission of inherited characteristics. Functionally, DNA consists of a linear array of the inherited units called genes (*qv*), which are replicated when the chromosomes replicate at cell division, thereby accounting for the inheritance of characteristics controlled by the genes.

In mitosis (*qv*) and cell division, each chromosome replicates itself exactly so that the two cells formed after cell division are genetically identical to each other and to the original cell. In meiosis (*qv*) and germ cell formation, the chromosomes replicate and are then distributed to the sperm (*qv*) or ovum (*qv*) in such a way that each sperm or ovum receives only one-half of the total chromosome complement. When sperm and egg rejoin at fertilization (*qv*), the full chromosome complement is reestablished.

In humans, normally there are 22 pairs of homologous (*qv*) chromosomes, known as autosomes, plus 2 sex chromosomes, either 2 X chromosomes (in women), or one X chromosome and one Y chromosome (in men). Occasionally, due to abnormalities in meitosis or meiosis, additional or missing chromosomes are found in human cells (*see* Turner syndrome, Klinefelter syndrome, Down syndrome). *See also* chromosomal sex.

The term chromosome comes from *chromo* (color, Greek) and *soma* (body, Greek), and is so named because chromosomes take up dyes used for staining cells for microscopic examination. They were first identified in the late nineteenth century by Walter Fleming.

chronic hyperestrogenic syndrome A naturally occurring or induced over-production of estrogens (*qv*); a common cause of gynecomastia (*qv*).

Chueh-Chen (Ch.) Crescent-shaped pillows used by the Chinese to support the buttocks (*qv*) during lovemaking (*qv*).

Church of Latter Day Saints The religious denomination founded by Joseph Smith in 1830 in upstate New York and later based in Salt Lake City, Utah, commonly known as the Mormons. Following an 1843 revelation, Smith insti-tuted the practice of polygyny (*qv*). Polygyny ensured salvation for women and a high place in heaven, especially if they married a prominent member of the church. This practice was opposed by federal and state governments and led to the founding of the Republican party. An 1862 federal antipolygyny law was enforced after the Civil War. In 1890, with over 1,000 members in jail, the church officially disavowed polygyny, although some splinter groups still con-tinue the practice.

cicatrization Body beautification using deliberately produced scars; a common practice in the Sudan.

cilium (pl. cilia) (L.) A microscopic cytoplasmic thread projecting from the surface of an animal cell, capable of causing movement by rhythmic contraction or beating. Cilia lining the vas deferens (*qv*) propel the sperm (*qv*). Cilia also move the ovum (*qv*) through the fallopian tube (*qv*) from its fibriated os (*qv*) toward the uterus (*qv*).

circulus venosus of Haller (L.) The circle of veins beneath the areola (*qv*) of the nipple (*qv*).

circumcision Surgical removal of the foreskin (*qv*) of the penis (*qv*) in the male, or the clitoris (*qv*) and minor labia in the female.

Female circumcision: Surgical removal of the clitoris and/or minor labia. In nineteenth-century America, clitorectomy was used as a therapy for so-called oversexed women who expressed more interest in or enjoyment of sexual relations (*qv*) than their father, husband, physician, or religious adviser thought suitable. Such hyperesthesia (*qv*) was seen as a threat to male dominance and motherly purity.

Clitorectomy is a common ritual in many tribal cultures in Africa, Indonesia, and Malaysia. A 1980 survey found that 90 percent of Egyptian women had had some part of their clitoris or labia (*qv*) removed. Usually an older female performs this surgery in the home, without anesthesia, as part of a rite of passage (*qv*) for a girl entering puberty (*qv*). The mildest form involves removal of the clitoral hood (*qv*), or prepuce, although the whole clitoris and part of the minor labia may be removed. In Pharaonic circumcision (*qv*) or infibulation, the minor labia are removed and the two sides of the vulva are pinned or sewn together, leaving only a small hole for urine (*qv*) and the menstrual flow (*qv*). Infibulation ensures female virginity (*qv*) since the entrance to the vagina (*qv*) is not reopened until just before the wedding night by a midwife (*qv*), a female relative, or the husband himself when he consummates (*qv*) the marriage (*qv*). Efforts to eradicate this custom often lead to serious ethical dilemmas and cultural conflicts. Resources: T. Baasher, (1989). Psycho-social aspects of female circumcision, in T. Baasher, R. Bannerman, H. Rushwan, and I. Sharaf, eds, *Traditional Health Practices Affecting the Health of Women and Children*, World Health Organization Regional Office for the Eastern Mediterranean Region, EHO EMRO Technical Publication, 2(2) 1982): 162–180; M. Badawi, Epidemiology of female sexual castration in Cairo, Egypt, *The Truth Seeker* 1(3):31–43; F. P. Hosken, Female genital mutilation: Strategies for eradication, *The Truth Seeker* 1(3) (1989):22–30.

Male circumcision: Among prehistoric farmers, males ensured the fertility (*qv*) of their fields by offering their foreskins (*qv*) to the gods in the fields. Early Egyptians believed humans were created with both a masculine and a feminine soul. Since the male's feminine soul was thought to be located in the foreskin and the woman's masculine soul in her clitoris (*qv*), circumcision at puberty made the boy fully male and the girl fully female. African and Arabic cultures adopted circumcision from the Egyptians as a religious rite for both males and females. Male circumcision passed into the Jewish world with Abraham, who had his sons circumcised. Joshua required it for all Jewish males as a sign of the covenant between the Jews and God. Although popularly regarded as one of the essentials of a true believer, neither male nor female circumcision has any warrant in the Qu'ran. In the Islamic cultures, circumcision is usually performed after age 8 or 9 and before puberty. Resources: J. DeMeo, Desertification and the origins of armoring: The Saharasian connection, *Journal of Orogonymy* 21(2):185–213; B. Z. Goldberg, *The Sacred Fire: The Story of Sex in Religion* (New York: University Books, 1958); G. A. Larue, Religious traditions and circumcision, *The Truth Seeker* 1(3):4–8.

Circumcision became widespread in the United States in the 1800s when the Victorian culture believed it could prevent or cure asthma, epilepsy, venereal disease (*qv*), and cancer of the penis, and reduce the risk of masturbation (*qv*) by young males. After 1940, it became a routine postnatal surgery in the United States where, until recently, 80 percent of males were circumcised. In Canada less than 30 percent of males are circumcised, in Australia less than 25 percent, and in Great Britain, West Germany, and Scandinavia, about 1 percent undergo circumcision. In the 1980s, the popularity of circumcision was attacked by the American Pediatric Association, which later modified its opposition because of evidence that uncircumcised males have a higher risk of urinary tract infections and sexually transmitted diseases (*qv*). *See also* phimosis; subincision; superincision.

ciscisbeism (Ital.) A custom found among seventeenth- through nineteenth-century upper-class European families in which the wife took on a lover, theoretically with her husband's official knowledge and approval. The lover was her *ciscisbeo*, and had the privilege of being socially recognized as her official escort and companion. In the extended meaning of a sexual partner chosen by a married woman with social approval, ciscisbeism must be distinguished from adultery (*qv*), in which the liaison is unofficial, unrecognized, and often clandestine; and from polyandry (*qv*), in which a woman officially married one or more additional husbands and is recognized as their wife. In turn, the ciscisbeo himself must be distinguished from a gigolo (*qv*), a man who attaches himself financially and emotionally to a woman for the purpose of his gain. Presumably, because the terms ciscisbeism and *ciscisbeo* were associated linguistically with the customs and morals of the nobility and upper classes, both terms fell out of linguistic favor among middle-class speakers although the custom itself has remained alive.

cisvestism Magnus Hirschfeld's (*qv*) term for wearing apparel considered socially appropriate for one's own gender but that conveys specific sexual messages to members of heterosexual (*qv*) or homosexual (*qv*) groups or subcultures. In this definition, the key concept is that the clothes worn are appropriate to one's own gender, as socially defined in general or for specific situations, and not the opposite gender (as in cross-dressing [*qv*]). For example, homosexual men involved in sadomasochistic subcultures may wear symbolically hypermasculine attire, such as military uniforms, during a sadomasochistic scenario. A heterosexual example of male cisvestism is a man at a beach who wears flesh-tight bathing trunks to reveal or accentuate his genitals, thereby, he hopes, attracting women. In women, heterosexual cisvestism can include wearing scanty or revealing clothing in order to attract a specific man or type of man. A prostitute (*qv*) wearing high heels, black stockings, a miniskirt with a slit side, and a transparent blouse is yet another example. In lesbian culture, cisvestism has sometimes been considered problematic, either as deference to patriarchy or in the butch-femme dichotomy, where a lesbian (*qv*) woman might wear hyperfeminine clothing and accessories to convey sexual messages to other lesbians. Outside the sexual domain, the term cisvestism refers to wearing clothes or attire that convey illusory messages about one's status or job, for example, a civilian who wears a military uniform at a social gathering.

The prefix *cis-* is Latin, and means "on this side of." Its opposite is *trans-*, also Latin, meaning "on the other side of." The suffix *-vest-* refers to garments in general (as in the word *vestments*). Accordingly, by derivation, cisvestism means wearing the garb of one's own sex, while transvestism (*qv*) means wearing the garb of the other sex. To this derivation, sexology adds the concept of the purpose or reason for so dressing, to obtain the definition given above. Cisvestism is a potentially useful word, which, however, is not widely used in discussions of apparel, sex appeal, and sexuality (*qv*).

City of Akron v. Akron Center for Reproductive Health One of three cases joined in a single 1983 decision of the U.S. Supreme Court that struck down a variety of restrictions on abortion (*qv*). In this six-to-three decision, the Court said states and local communities may not require that all abortions for women more than three months pregnant be done in a hospital. Among other regulations declared unconstitutional was a requirement of a 24-hour waiting period between signing the consent form for an abortion and the medical procedure. The other two cases in this decision were *Planned Parenthood of Kansas City v. Ashcroft* and *Simopolous v. Virginia*.

civil codes of law The body of statutes, court rulings, case law, governmental decrees, and legal opinion enacted or held legally binding by secular authorities such as legislatures and courts, and that regulates a variety of noncriminal activities, such as property rights, contract rights, and marriage (*qv*) and divorce (*qv*), among others. In part, civil law exists to resolve and regulate conflicts that arise between individuals (or groups of individuals, as in a class action suit), a goal met by a case-by-case determination of the individuals' rights, duties, and obligations toward one another. In its broad sense, civil law is distinguished from criminal law, in which legislative bodies and courts determine that a specific action is illegal and establish punishments for the perpetrator of such actions. Sometimes civil law is defined narrowly to mean contract and property law, as distinct from family law, the laws of slander and libel, and so forth. Sexological examples of civil law broadly defined include legal statutes determining the grounds for divorce, property rights in marriage, and other issues, all distinct from the enactment, in the criminal codes, of laws against rape (*qv*), prostitution (*qv*), and similar crimes. In civil law, suit is brought by an aggrieved party against someone else, whereas in criminal law, court action is brought by the state against an individual. In both civil and criminal law, all parties to the action are subject ultimately to the United States Constitution and its protections, for example, the right to cross-examine witnesses and the right to refuse to testify against oneself.

clan A large descent group that claims a common ancestor. A clan exists independently of its members and can own land and exert political power. In contrast, a kindred (*qv*) has no existence as a separate body and exists only in relation to an individual. Clans may be patrilineal (*qv*) or matrilineal (*qv*). *See also* family.

clap thread A slender mucoid (*qv*) filament containing tissue and white blood cells extruded from the urethra (*qv*) of a person with chronic gonorrhea (*qv*).

cleavage Mitotic divisions of the fertilized ovum (*qv*) until it reaches a 16-cell blastula (*qv*) stage and begins differentiation into an inner cell mass and trophoblast (*qv*). Cleavage is also used to refer to the cleft between a woman's breasts, particularly in women with large busts.

Clerambault-Kandisky syndrome A sexuoerotic (*qv*) condition in which a person falls in love with an unattainable person along with the unshakable and false conviction that his or her own life is controlled by the reciprocated love of that person.

climacteric The physical and psychological phenomena that characterize reduction in sex-steroid hormones (*qv*) in about 5 percent of men over 60. Symptoms in men include weakness, fatigue, poor appetite, decreased sexual drive (*qv*), reduction or loss of erectile capacity, irritability, and impaired ability to concentrate. Climacteric may be associated with depression, melancholia, or involutional psychosis and a desperate attempt to prove one's sexual capacity. In the female, climacteric refers to the period of gradual decline in ovarian function leading to menopause (*qv*).

climax The sudden release of sexual arousal (*qv*) and tension in orgasm (*qv*), marked by involuntary muscle spasms throughout the body and in muscles of the pelvic cavity and acceleration of heart and respiratory rates.

clinical research method A technique involving observations of a clinical or therapeutic population that may describe and correlate symptoms in patients exhibiting a particular condition or the particular course of treatment as it affects subjects.

clitoral glans The exposed head of the clitoris (*qv*); homologous to the penile glans (*qv*).

clitoral hood The fold of skin covering the clitoris (*qv*), formed by the anterior junction of the labia minora (*qv*); sometimes referred to as the female foreskin (*qv*).

clitoral hypertrophy A hormone-induced enlargement of the clitoris (*qv*), associated with pseudohermaproditism (*qv*), an intersex condition (*qv*), or premature puberty (*qv*).

clitoral orgasm An orgasm (*qv*) produced by direct stimulation of the clitoris (*qv*) and involving tenting (*qv*) of the uterus (*qv*).

clitoral shaft The main structure of the clitoris (*qv*) composed of two small erectile cavernous bodies enclosed in a fibrous membrane and ending in a glans (*qv*).

clitorectomy *See* circumcision.

clitoridectomy *See* circumcision.

clitoriditis An inflammation of the clitoris (*qv*).

clitoridotomy Surgical removal of the clitoral foreskin. *See also* circumcision.

clitoris In the anatomy of the female, the erectile, hooded organ at the upper, external junction of the labia (*qv*), superior to the opening of the urethra (*qv*) and the vagina (*qv*). According to the Federation of Feminists Women's Health Centers (*A New View of a Woman's Body* [New York: Simon and Schuster, 1981, p. 33]), the clitoris is "a complex structure which includes the inner lips, hood, glans, shaft and legs, muscles, urethral sponge, bulbs, networks of nerves and blood vessels, the suspensory ligaments and pelvic diaphragm." Accordingly, the clitoris can be defined to contain an erectile shaft with a glans (*qv*), a clitoral hood formed by the junction of the labia minora (*qv*), and a pair of crurae, or legs, composed of erectile *corpora cavernosa* (*qv*).

Embryologically, the clitoris and penis (*qv*) develop from the same undifferentiated structure in the fetus, the genital tubercle (*qv*). In female embryogenesis, the tubercle develops to include sensory nerves, blood vessels, and the expandable tissue of the *corpora cavernosa*, but excludes the urinary ducts, which open to the exterior immediately below the clitoris. It is common in medical and anatomical textbooks and dictionaries to call the genital tubercle the "phallus" and to call the clitoris the homologue of the penis. Taken as purely technical terms, such descriptions are acceptable, but for most purposes such terms are phallocentric.

Sexologically, the function of the clitoris is erotosexual (*qv*) stimulation, enjoyment, and pleasure. In societies where the clitoris is excised or removed (*see* circumcision), the stated purpose often is to curb or control female sexuality and a woman's pleasure in sex. Psychologically, the same anti-clitoral purpose can be achieved non-surgically by prohibiting female masturbation (*qv*) or by making oral-genital contact illegal, as a form of sodomy (*qv*). Nonetheless, stimulation of the clitoris and associated areas of the vulva (*qv*) can produce intense emotional and sexual pleasure and can lead to orgasm (*qv*).

Textbooks and manuals of sexual pleasure often recommend that the clitoris be gently stimulated during foreplay (*qv*), but linguistically, it is not clear what the term "gentle" may mean. In this context, it has strong overtones of emotional, not physical, gentleness; assuredly, direct stimulation of the clitoris with a vibrator is gentle only as a description of intention and not of the physiological intensity of neural stimulation of anatomically underlying nerves. It is also clear, however, that advice offered to men to be gentle while stimulating the clitoris manually or orally is intended to redirect the man's sexual attentions solely from his own pleasure to achieving pleasure for both the woman and himself.

The clitoris can be stimulated (e.g., manually) with the tongue and lips (*see* oral-genital sex) or with a vibrator (*qv*). Women differ considerably in the sensitivity of the clitoris to each of these kinds of stimulation, and also differ greatly in how much clitoral stimulation will evoke orgasm. Penile-vaginal intercourse in the ventral-ventral, male-above, missionary position (*qv*) only rarely achieves direct clitoral stimulation, although it has been claimed that penile thrusting provides indirect stimulation through rhythmically extending the clitoral hood (*qv*).

In the old psychoanalytic literature it is widely stated that orgasm achieved through clitoral stimulation is immature, incomplete, or otherwise inadequate when compared to orgasm achieved through intravaginal stimulation with the penis, fingers, or a dildo (*qv*). However, experimental research by William Masters and Virginia Johnson showed that orgasm achieved through clitoral stimulation is physiologically indistinguishable from orgasm achieved in any other fashion. Psychologically, it is possible that multiple orgasmic women find large differences in different types of orgasm; nonetheless, in modern sexological thought, clitoral orgasm is not considered inadequate or immature in any way. Resource: T. P. Lowry and T. S. Lowry (eds.), *The Clitoris* (St. Louis: Warren H. Green, 1976).

clitorize An obsolete term for female masturbation (*qv*).

clitoromania An obsolete term for nymphomania (*qv*).

clitoromegaly An enlarged clitoris (*qv*), usually caused by an excess of male sex hormones (*qv*).

cloaca In those non-mammalian vertebrates that lack a penis and a specialized internal organ for receiving the penis, such as a vagina, the cloaca is a cavity into which the urinary, excretory, and reproductive ducts open. The cloaca thus serves as a common passageway for voiding urine and digestive wastes and for the transfer of sperm from the male to the female; *see* amplexus. The term is Latin and means "sewer" or "common sewer," as in the Cloaca Maxima in classic Rome, the city's great sewer into the river Tiber. Linguistically, the term cloaca either represents a now old-fashioned tendency to give unpleasant Latin names to structures associated with excretion and reproduction, or, perhaps, the namers wished to hide under opaque and obscure Latinisms what they thought were distasteful and unpleasantly nasty bodily functions. Either way, sexological terminology is littered with such nomenclatural relics, which are often phallocentric (*qv*) as well as pejorative.

cloaca theory In psychoanalytic theory (*qv*), the belief of some children (*qv*) and adults (*qv*) that babies can be born through the anal (*qv*) canal of either the father or mother.

clomiphene citrate A nonsteroidal fertility drug (*qv*). *See also* estrogen.

clone A group of genetically identical organisms derived asexually (*qv*) from a single organism.

clonic spasm Involuntary muscle contractions and relaxations in muscles around the prostate gland (*qv*) and in the urogenital organs that produce ejaculation (*qv*) in the male.

cloning The process of asexually reproducing genetically identical offspring from a single parent. *See also* clone.

closed marriage A marriage based on monogamy (*qv*) and sexual exclusivity; a marital relationship based on traditional values of clear, fixed sex stereotypes and roles, male dominance, togetherness, sexual exclusivity, and possessiveness. *See also* open marriage; hot sexual values; cool sexual values.

closed swinging A limited arrangement for extramarital sex (*qv*) or sex with other than one's usual partner in which several couples meet together, trade partners, pair off privately to have sexual relations (*qv*), and then return to their original partners. *See also* open swinging, swinging.

closeting An informal and widespread term for keeping one's sexual orientation (*qv*) a secret from friends, relatives, coworkers, or the public. ''Being or coming out of the closet'' means publically declaring one's sexual orientation. The term is often used in reference to homosexuality (*qv*).

clubbing An abnormal, clublike growth at the ovarian opening of the fallopian tube (*qv*) resulting from an involution of the fimbriae (*qv*) caused by chronic inflammation.

clunes *See* buttocks.

cluster analysis Statistical techniques used to analyze data containing several variables in order to identify internal structure and relationships. Cluster analysis may be used to identify distinct groups or clusters of responses in an attitude survey or to establish patterns of behavior in a survey of activities. *See also* content analysis; factor analysis.

cluster marriage *See* group marriage.

Clytemnestra complex An emotional-erotic triad in which a woman falls in love with a male relative of her husband and murders her spouse in order to be with that relative. The term is derived from the Greek myth in which Clytemnestra falls in love with her husband's cousin and kills her husband to be with the cousin.

CNS *See* central nervous system.

Coca-Cola douche An ineffective contraceptive method that relies on the mild acidity of the carbonated beverage in a douche (*qv*) following unprotected sexual intercourse (*qv*). The acidic fluid does not reach all the sperm (*qv*) and may force some into the cervical canal (*qv*), thus increasing the risk of conception (*qv*). The manufacturers of Coca-Cola have spent time and money to combat this misuse of their product.

cockscomb papilloma A benign, small, red lesion that may project from the uterine cervix (*qv*) during pregnancy (*qv*) and normally regresses after delivery (*qv*).

coding, research A research procedure designed to divide responses to a particular question or measure into clear categories. As an example, responses to a question about how often the research subject participates in a particular behavior may be coded into categories of: never, once a year, two-to-three times a year, monthly, weekly, or daily. Coding research is an essential part of quantitative research.

codpiece In male fashions from the Middle Ages through the sixteenth century, a bag or flap of fabric intended to accent the male genitalia (*qv*). "Cod" is an early term for the testes (*qv*); *codpiece* later became a euphemism for the penis.

cognitive aversion therapy A therapeutic modality that attempts to modify or eliminate undesirable behavior by linking the undesirable behavior with an unpleasant imagined event. *See also* aversion therapy.

cognitive dissonance L. Festinger's theory holding that when people find dissonance, or a lack of fit between attitudes or between their attitudes and behavior, unacceptable, they will try to reduce the tension by modifying their attitudes or adding new ones. Resource: L. Festinger, *A Theory of Cognitive Dissonance* (Evanston, IL: Row, 1957).

cognitive ideology A view of life emphasizing the place of intellectual activity and choice in human decision making.

cohabit (cohabitation) The act of living together as a sexually active heterosexual (*qv*) or homosexual (*qv*) couple in a primary relationship without civil or religious documentation of the relationship as a marriage (*qv*).

cohabitation contract An agreement intended by the signees as a legally and emotionally binding contract and entered into by two or more people who wish to live together as sexual partners with certain reciprocal and mutual rights, privileges, and obligations, but who do not wish to enter into a civil or religious marriage (*qv*). Such contracts may be written between an individual man and woman, between two homosexual (*qv*) men or women, or among several people who wish to form a group marriage (*qv*) arrangement. Subject matter covered by the contract may range from purely financial matters through complex documents listing many or all aspects of the relationship, sexual rights and privileges included.

The purposes of such contracts may also range widely. Sometimes they are purely emotional, symbolic, and psychological, and record the signees' devotion to each other and to an ideal of living together along with clearly specified duties and pleasures owed to one another. Often the intention is to create a relationship unhindered by what are perceived as the restrictive or exploitative elements of formal marriage. Other individuals may enter into cohabitation contracts in order to clarify for legal purposes their financial relationship, particularly if one, both, or all partners own valuable properties (e.g., a house) or have otherwise entangling legal relationships with relatives (e.g., through divorce settlements or inheritance law). Other contracts may blend these purposes.

As emotional and symbolic agreements, cohabitation contracts differ little from the informal verbal agreements made by all couples, including married couples, about matters of life together. However, cohabitation contracts can become extremely complex legally, particularly if the partners separate and conflict develops or if one partner dies and the provisions of the contract are contested by others who might inherit from the deceased partner. These complexities arise primarily when specifically sexual matters are described by the contract or if they may be inferred in court from evidence or testimony. A court might then rule that the contract is utterly without legal force and that its provisions are null and void in their entirety.

The legal reasoning behind such judgments is that anyone contemplating writing and signing a cohabitation contract should be well aware of the legal complexities that can evolve from an apparently simple document. In general, for any contract to be binding it must be lawful in the sense that it does not violate existing civil codes or criminal laws, and it must be enforceable in the sense that a court can order one of the contractees to perform contracted duties. However, if the cohabitation contract mentions sex, it may fail on either or both these criteria.

In jurisdictions in which it is illegal to sell sexual services or to offer them in trade or exchange for other services or goods, a cohabitation contract may be ruled nonbinding by a court if sexual activities between the partners can be inferred from the contract or from evidence offered in court. For example, if those laws make it illegal, as a form of prostitution (*qv*), to exchange sexual services for financial gain, a cohabitation contract explicitly or implicitly specifying that the woman will have intercourse with the man provided he pays her household and domestic bills in full or in part may be construed as describing a type of prostitution and be deemed nonbinding (as well as subjecting the woman to legal penalties for prostitution). The reason is that existing statutes already regulate sexual matters in the legal codes and case law of marriage, divorce (*qv*), prostitution, bigamy (*qv*), polygamy (*qv*), rape (*qv*), and the like, and no contract between individuals can set aside the provisions of the law for their convenience or advantage. The laws of the state bind individuals no matter what agreements they may make. If a cohabitation contract violates such laws, a court will rule it nonbinding even if the intention of the signees was not to break the law.

Furthermore, the Thirteenth Amendment to the U.S. Constitution, which forbids involuntary servitude, makes it impossible for a court to order a party to a cohabitation contract to fulfill his or her contracted sexual duties unwillingly. All laws about prostitution aside, doing so forces the unwilling individual into being the involuntary sexual servitor of another person, who, in the case of a man, is legally a rapist if he forces the woman to have intercourse with him in the mistaken belief that his cohabitation contract requires her to fulfill his sexual needs. A court, therefore, cannot order the woman to have sexual intercourse with the man because a court can neither create nor allow involuntary, contractual prostitution, nor tolerate or permit rape.

These issues sometimes arise in somewhat more specific form in so-called master-slave agreements made in the course of a sadomasochistic (S/M) relationship. In these relationships, one person agrees to become the powerless and obedient sexual slave of another person. However, regardless of the sexuerotic (*qv*) appeals of S/M, such a contract is not legally binding. Instead, it is an integral part of the entire sadomasochistic scenario between the individuals, and its purpose is enhancement of sexual pleasure and not its enforceability at law.

Individuals planning on writing and signing a cohabitation agreement, even if it seems innocent of all intent to break the law, are well advised to seek a lawyer's advice and assistance or to treat the contract as purely emotional, personal, and symbolic, thereby recognizing that it may have no force at all in law. *See also* prenuptial agreement (contract).

cohort A group of individuals who share a common characteristic (e.g., the same gender or age group).

coil A plastic contraceptive (*qv*) device inserted by a physician into the uterine cavity (*qv*) where it interferes with implanting of the 5-6-day-old embryo (*qv*) in the uterine wall or accelerates passage of the embryo through the tube before the uterine endometrium (*qv*) is prepared for implantation (*qv*). *See also* intra-uterine contraceptive device.

coital aninsertia The inability of a man to engage in penile-vaginal intercourse or of a woman to accept penile intromission or penetration (*qv*) of the vagina (*qv*). Such Latin medical terms usually refer only to penis-vagina intercourse, but the term can be extended to include any form of inability to engage in penile intro-mission, whether vaginal, oral, or anal. Coital aninsertia can be psychogenic in origin, arising from phobic anxiety or avoidance, or it can be physiological and anatomical if the vagina is not fully developed or if the penis will not remain erect. The term would not be used in cases where the person freely rejects inter-course. *See also* vaginal spasms.

coital death Death resulting from coronary or respiratory failure experienced during sexual intercourse (*qv*). Although coital death is very rare for males who have not previously experienced a heart attack, it is four times more likely to occur if the male is engaging in a stressful relationship, such as an extramarital affair (*qv*), in which a heavy dinner and drinking are followed by intense sexual activity (*qv*) with the emotional stress of guilt.

coital fear Also known as coitophobia. *See also* coital aninsertia.

coital movements A stereotypical pattern of bodily movements made during coitus (*qv*) or penile-vaginal intercourse, involving penile and pelvic thrusting (*qv*) by the man and pelvic thrusting and rotation by the woman. Initially, penile thrusting is shallow and relatively slow, but it tends to accelerate as the man nears ejaculation (*qv*). He then thrusts steadily and deeply, often with hip rotation, as the woman reciprocates the hip movement pattern. Although classic Latin had separate terms for the movements of the man and woman (*ceueo* and *criso*, respectively), as did Middle English (*swive* [*qv*] and *quim* [*qv*], respectively), modern English uses the same term for both. Broadly, the term can refer to all bodily movements made during coitus rather than those specifically associated with the man's pre-ejaculatory behavior.

coital wheel A coital position in which one partner bends backward in an arch.

coition An Anglicized form of coitus (*qv*). A distinction is sometimes made between the general process of coition and coitus as a specific act of intercourse (*qv*).

coitus A somewhat technical synonym for copulation (*qv*). In its most narrow medical-anatomical sense, coitus means the insertion of the erect penis (*qv*) into the vagina (*qv*), and is a synonym for sexual intercourse (*qv*) or intromission (*qv*). However, like many terms in sexuality, it has a series of extended meanings as well as referring to specific forms of intercourse.

The word derives from Latin *co-*, meaning "together," and *-ire*, a verb form meaning "to come" or "to go." It is one of two classic Latin terms used in neutral, educated, or standard discourse (*uenus*, meaning "desire," and *coire*, as defined above); like modern English, classic Latin had a full range of obscenities and euphemisms for coitus and related concepts, including the vulgar terms *stuprum* and *futeo*, the latter being a cognate with the obsolete slang *futter*. As in classic Latin, modern English also distinguishes between neutral or technical terms, such as coitus, copulation, intercourse, and the like, and vulgar or obscene terms and phrases such as do it, fuck, get it on, and so on.

Usages of *coitus* and *coition* given in the *Oxford English Dictionary* and dating from the 1500s and 1600s imply that the word once had two related meanings in English. One referred specifically to sexual union, and the other to conjunction in general. The latter meaning has vanished with time, and today *coitus* refers solely and explicitly, if neutrally, to sexual intercourse. *See also* copulation, intercourse, intromission, swive, and quim. Resource: J. N. Adams, *The Latin Sexual Vocabulary* (Baltimore: Johns Hopkins University Press, 1982).

coitus, axillary Intercourse (*qv*) with the penis (*qv*) inserted in the armpit of the partner.

coitus, femoral Intercourse (*qv*) with the penis (*qv*) inserted between the thighs of the partner. Also known as coitus ante portas and perineal coitus.

coitus, mammary Intercourse (*qv*) with the penis (*qv*) inserted between the woman's breasts (*qv*).

coitus, perineal Intercourse (*qv*) with the penis (*qv*) inserted between the upper thighs so that it rubs against the perineal (*qv*) region. *See also* coitus, femoral.

coitus ante portas (L.) *See* coitus, femoral.

coitus a tergo (L.) Sexual intercourse (*qv*) with the male making vaginal entry from behind the woman.

coitus in ano (L.) Technical term for anal intercourse (*qv*).

coitus incompletus (L.) An obsolete term for coitus interruptus (*qv*).

coitus in os (L.) Technical term for fellatio (*qv*).

coitus interruptus (L.) The withdrawal of the penis (*qv*) from the vagina (*qv*) prior to male ejaculation (*qv*). Coitus interruptus is an ineffective contraceptive practice. *See also* onanism.

coitus prolongatus (L.) The practice of various exercises and techniques designed to extend the duration of sexual intercourse (*qv*). *See also* coitus reservatus; karezza; Tantric sexual traditions; Taoist sexual traditions.

coitus reservatus (L.) Sexual intercourse (*qv*) in which erection (*qv*) and penile insertion (*qv*) are prolonged with minimal thrusting and without ejaculation (*qv*). Originating in the Orient and Tantric (*qv*) yoga (*qv*) tradition, extended intercourse allows an equality of male and female orgasm (*qv*) and time for spiritual meditation. Known as Maithuna or coitus prolongatus (*qv*), it was adopted by the nineteenth-century Oneida Community (*qv*) as a natural way of preventing unwanted pregnancies (*qv*) in a community that practiced group marriage (*qv*) and limited procreation (*qv*). *See also* Tantric sexual traditions; Tao; karezza.

coitus saxonicus (L.) A contraceptive (*qv*) method of sexual intercourse (*qv*) in which the male squeezes the urethra (*qv*) at the base of the penis (*qv*) just before orgasm (*qv*), thereby forcing the semen (*qv*) into the urinary bladder. Germanic Saxons, who invaded England in the fifth century, allegedly used this as a method of contraception (*qv*). *See also* retrograde ejaculation.

coitus sine ejaculatione (L.) A medical condition, not to be confused with coitus reservatus (*qv*) or with impotence (*qv*), in which ejaculation (*qv*) does not occur during sexual intercourse (*qv*). This condition may be natural, associated with aging, or the result of a pathological retrograde or retarded ejaculation (*qv*).

cold punch A transurethral (*qv*), surgical treatment for benign prostatic hyperplasia (*qv*). An instrument containing a small tubular knife, fiber optics, and suction tube is inserted into the male urethral meatus (*qv*) and into the prostatic region where the surgeon can guide the knife and suction tube to remove the overgrown tissue.

collaborative victim In victimology (*qv*) theory, a victim of sexual assault (*qv*) whom the evidence indicates did not resist the sexual activity (*qv*). *See also* incest; victim precipitation.

Collauti v. Franklin In this 1979 six-to-three decision, the U.S. Supreme Court ruled a Pennsylvania law unconstitutional and gave physicians broad discretion in ascertaining when a fetus (*qv*) is viable. While the states may seek to protect a viable fetus, determination of viability (*qv*) is left to the doctors.

colliculitis An inflammation of the seminal vesicles (*qv*) and the colliculus seminalis of the male. *See also* colliculus seminalis.

colliculus seminalis (L.) An anatomical term for a small elevation in the posterior wall of the prostatic urethra (*qv*) of a male. The colliculus seminalis is the site of the openings of the paired ejaculatory ducts (*qv*) and the vestigial cul-de-sac utriculus prostaticus (*qv*); also known as the verum montanum or urethral crest.

collusional marriage A relationship between married persons in which one partner instigates or engages in deficient, socially deviant, or illicit conduct, which the other partner covertly accepts, covers up, or endorses while ostensibly playing the role of martyr or victim.

colostomy The surgical creation of an artificial anus (*qv*) on the abdominal wall by cutting the colon (*qv*) and bringing it to a new opening in the abdominal surface. A colostomy is commonly performed in cases of cancer of the colon and benign obstructive tumors. Counseling is usually needed for colostomy patients to make necessary adaptations in their sexual relations (*qv*).

colostrum The thin, yellowish fluid secreted by the maternal mammary glands (*qv*) just before and after birth (*qv*); high in proteins and maternal antibodies important to the newborn's (*qv*) health.

colpo-, colp- Pertaining to the vagina (*qv*).

colpitis An inflammation of the vagina (*qv*); vaginitis (*qv*).

colpocystitis (L.) Inflammation of the vagina (*qv*) and urinary bladder.

colpopathy Any diseased or abnormal condition of the vagina (*qv*).

colpopoiesis (L.) Plastic surgery to create or reconstruct a vagina (*qv*); commonly used in the management of a hermaphroditic (*qv*) or male-to-female transsexual (*qv*) condition.

colporrhaphy Surgical suturing of the walls of the vagina (*qv*).

colposcope A plastic or metal vaginal (*qv*) speculum (*qv*) allowing visual examination of the vagina and cervix (*qv*).

colposcopy Visual examination of the vagina (*qv*) and cervix (*qv*).

colpotomy Any surgical incision into the vaginal (*qv*) tissues.

comarital Sexual relations (*qv*) of a married person with a third party that are accepted by the spouse, in contrast with adultery (*qv*) in which the spouse is not aware of and does not consent to the extramarital sexual activity. *See also* communitas; sexually open marriage; intimate friendship; satellite relationship.

combination oral contraceptive pill A hormonal contraceptive pill (*qv*) containing estrogen (*qv*) and progestin (*qv*) in a daily dosage that produces a physiological mimic of the normal female menstrual cycle (*qv*) but without ovulation (*qv*). The combination pill is the most popular of the hormonal contraceptives. Beginning on day 5 of the cycle, the pill provides more estrogen (*qv*) than is usual in the body at this time. This amount is enough to block the usual follicle-stimulating hormone (*qv*) message from the pituitary (*qv*) for a new ovum (*qv*) to develop. When the pill is continued for 21 days, no ovum is developed in that cycle. The small amount of progestin keeps the mucus plug in the cervix (*qv*) of the uterus (*qv*) thick and dry so sperm (*qv*) have a hard time getting through. It also keeps the uterine epithelium from developing properly so that implantation (*qv*) is unlikely in the event that ovulation is not suppressed. The sudden drop in estrogen and progestin after day 26, when the last pill is taken allows menstruation (*qv*) on day 29 and day 1 of the new cycle. The daily pill is resumed on day 5 of the next cycle. Although the theoretical failure rate is given at 0.5 percent, actual failure rate is about 2 percent because the response of individual females to the set hormone levels varies.

Commission on Obscenity and Pornography, Presidential, 1970 Appointed by President Richard Nixon, this commission spent two years with a budget of $2 million before concluding that neither hard-core nor soft-core pornography (*qv*) leads to antisocial behavior and that pornography provides a useful safety valve in an otherwise sexually repressive culture. The commission's recommendation that obscenity (*qv*) laws be abolished was rejected by three commissioners in a minority report, by the president as "morally corrupt," and by a 60-to-5 vote of the Senate. *See also* Commission on Obscenity and Pornography, Presidential, 1986.

Commission on Obscenity and Pornography, Presidential, 1986 (the "Meese Commission") A commission appointed by President Ronald Reagan, on the occasion of signing the Child Protection Act of 1984 (*qv*), to document the connection between pornography (*qv*) and child abuse (*qv*), incest (*qv*), and rape (*qv*); commonly referred to as the Meese Commission. Eleven commissioners chosen by U.S. Attorney General Edwin Meese were given one year and a budget of $500,000 to conclude its study. The commission recommended stricter penalties to regulate pornography traffic, enactment of laws to keep hard-core pornography off home cable television and home telephone service, and more vigorous prosecution of obscenity cases. It also encouraged private citizens to use protests and boycotts to discourage marketing of pornography. Among the contested findings of the commission was reliance on the concept of "the totality of evidence" to give credence to the testimony of fundamentalist ministers, police officers, antipornography activists, and putative victims of pornography and allow the conclusion that the causal connection between violent pornography and sexual assaults was proven. *See also* obscenity; Commission on Obscenity and Pornography, Presidential, 1970.

common-law marriage A marriage (*qv*) that is not solemnized by civil or religious ceremony but effected in the agreement of a man and woman to live together as husband and wife. Some states grant automatic legal recognition to common-law marriages if public cohabitation (*qv*) lasts a certain number of years. *See also* palimony.

communal living The cohabitation (*qv*) of several adults sharing economic resources, personal energies, and emotional support. This may or may not involve sexual openness and sharing. *See also* commune.

commune A life-style in which men and women bind themselves together in a community with a central residence or group of residences, and agree to share their resources, energies, and responsibilities. Some communes have a religious basis, others a secular or nationalist philosophy and goal. Most communes are communistic, holding all property and monies in common. Most are utopian. Some are anarchistic, but all communes seek to create a new and more perfect society. Some communes, like the Shakers (*qv*) and Rappites, were celibate (*qv*). Others, like the Society of Brothers (Bruderhof) and the Hutterites, are monogamous. Still others, like the Oneida Community (*qv*), practiced group marriage (*qv*).

Despite their small numbers, nineteenth-century American communes were influential in the formation of American sexual values, pioneering a positive view of female sexuality, self-health, knowledge of one's body, the intellectual equality of men and women, the social aspects of sex apart from reproduction (*qv*), the right of women to enjoy sex, and the right to easy divorce (*qv*).

communitas In the structural anthropology of Victor Turner, communitas is a significant interpersonal involvement that promotes change in a stable society while strengthening stable, normative structures; the supportive relationship of those persons in a society under liminality (*qv*). Social structures, according to Turner, provide the clear boundaries and status hierarchies without which no culture can be stable, function, and thrive. However, for human institutions to thrive, stable institutional structures must engage in an inner dialectic with experiences and relationships that promote change. In Turner's anthropology, the other side of the dialectic is antistructure. The antistructure is not a negative element. It is, in fact, a generative, positive pole, promoting change and creating communitas—any significant interpersonal involvement or relationship, a profound, paradoxical experience of interpersonal connectedness (love), that simultaneously violates the social structure and reinforces it.

Raymond Lawrence finds in Turner's theory of communitas and the dialectics of structure-antistructure a diagnostic tool in relation to the institution of marriage in the twentieth-century industrial West. The paucity of marital status reversal rituals or any clear dialectic between structure and antistructure in the marital images indicate a brittle, inflexible social structure headed for disaster. Turner's work suggests to Lawrence "that, when it comes to marriage, we take ourselves much too seriously in the modern West and are imperiled both by our exaggerated respect for [marital] structure and our loss of communitas values." Lawrence finds positive examples of antistructure, status reversal, and communitas in the literature of comarital relations (*qv*), sexually open marriages (*qv*), intimate friendships (*qv*), satellite relations (*qv*), swinging (*qv*), and gay (*qv*) and lesbian (*qv*) unions. Resources: V. Turner, *The Ritual Process: Structure and Anti-Structure* (Ithaca NY: Cornell University Press, 1969); R. J. Lawrence, *The Poisoning of Eros* (New York: Augustine Moore, Press, 1989), pp. 263–266.

community property Property acquired by a husband and wife during their marriage (*qv*).

companionate love A relationship between two persons based on friendship, caring, and commitment to the welfare of each other.

companionate marriage A trial marriage (*qv*) in which a couple cohabit (*qv*), use contraceptives (*qv*) to prevent any offspring being born during the trial period, and renounce any financial claim on each other in case they mutually agree to separate before entering into a formal, parental marriage. The concept was first proposed in 1927 by Judge Ben Lindsay of Denver and endorsed by Bertrand Russell and Havelock Ellis (*qv*).

competitive identification The subconscious modeling of one's personality and behavior on that of another person as a means of outdoing or bettering the other person.

complementation The psychological process whereby one learns responses and behaviors appropriate to one's assigned gender by adopting behavior, activities, and reactions that are the opposite of those observed in persons of the opposite gender. This concept is particularly applicable to the differentiation of a child's gender identity (*qv*) and gender role (*qv*). *Synonym*: reciprocation. *See also* identification.

complement fixation An immunological reaction in which an antigen (*qv*) combines with an antibody (*qv*) and its complement to inactivate or "fix" the complement. Complement fixation tests are commonly used to detect antibodies in infectious diseases, especially syphilis (*qv*) and viral illnesses.

complete abortion Termination of a pregnancy (*qv*) in which the full conceptus (*qv*) and afterbirth (*qv*) are expelled from the uterus (*qv*).

complete breech Fetal presentation (*qv*) in which the legs are folded on the thighs and the thighs on the abdomen so that these structures enter the cervical passage (*qv*) first during delivery (*qv*); the reverse of the normal vertex presentation (*qv*).

complete Oedipal complex The simultaneous occurrence of both the positive and negative Oedipal reactions (*qv*); a male child who identifies with his father and has an incestuous (*qv*) desire for his mother while at the same time identifying with his mother and expressing an incestuous desire for his father.

complete precocious puberty A male with interstitial cell (*qv*) tumors in both testes (*qv*) resulting in abnormally high levels of male sex hormones (*qv*) comparable at times with those normal for an adult male; the result is premature puberty (*qv*).

complex Literally, an "embrace"; a psychological term popularized by Sigmund Freud (*qv*) and Carl Jung (*qv*).

complex marriage A form of group marriage (*qv*) practiced by the Oneida Community (*qv*) in the mid-1800s. In the perfectionist interpretation of Methodism propounded by John Humphrey Noyes (*qv*), truly perfect Christians could hasten the Second Coming of Christ by anticipating the life hereafter in the Kingdom of God where all the saints will love one another. The sexual and emotional exclusivity of monogamy (*qv*), according to Noyes, promoted selfishness and was the greatest apostasy of Christianity. Since all the members of Oneida were married to each other, any person interested in a sexual relation (*qv*) with another member could approach an elder, who served as an intermediary. If the interest was mutual, the couple was allowed to engage in amative intercourse (*qv*). Procreative intercourse was limited to men and women selected by the elders as part of their stirpiculture (*qv*) experiment.

compulsion A persistent, irrational, and uncontrollable urge to engage in a particular behavior or act, regardless of the risk and the brevity of gratification following the act. *See also* paraphilia; addiction, sexual.

compulsory heterosexuality As used by Adrienne Rich in 1980, "the enforcement of heterosexuality (*qv*) for women as a means of assuring male right of physical, economical, and emotional access." One of the many means of enforcement of compulsory heterosexuality, according to Rich, is the pervasive attempt to make the lesbian (*qv*) culture as invisible as possible. Resource: A. Rich (1980), Compulsive heterosexuality and lesbian existence, *Signs* 5(4):647.

Comstock, Anthony (1844–1915) The most prominent Victorian (*qv*) censor of sexual material, widely known as "the nation's censor" for his antipornography and antiprostitution campaigns. As a soldier in the Civil War, Comstock waged a tireless war against swearing, drinking, and chewing tobacco among his fellow soldiers. After the war, his crusade shifted to erotic (*qv*) and pornographic (*qv*) material. In 1868, he used a new antiobscenity law sponsored by the Young Men's Christian Association (YMCA) to make his first arrests of two New York book dealers selling erotic material.

In 1873, as secretary of the Society for the Suppression of Vice and an inspector for the post office, he engineered passage of a broadly worded federal law allowing the confiscation of any painting, photograph, drawing, book, or other material considered obscene (*qv*). This law prohibited as illegal "every article or thing designed, adapted, or intended for preventing conception or producing abortion, or for any indecent or immoral use." Known as the Comstock prohibition, this law remained in effect until the U.S. Supreme Court declared unconstitutional a much-ignored ban on the sale of over-the-counter contraceptives (*qv*) to married women in 1963. The ban against public display and over-the-counter contraceptive sales to single women was overturned in 1972, and the entire law declared unconstitutional in 1977.

Comstock law (prohibition) *See* Comstock, Anthony.

conception The implantation (*qv*) or "nidation" of the blastocyst (*qv*) in the uterine endometrium (*qv*). The term refers in a looser sense to fertilization (*qv*), the union of the ovum (*qv*) and sperm (*qv*). *See also* impregnation; magnetic conception.

conceptional age The age of a fetus (*qv*) based on 38 weeks between conception (*qv*) and normal delivery (*qv*). Since the difference between fetal age (*qv*) measured from the last day of the last menstrual cycle (*qv*), or gestational age (*qv*) and from conception is 2 weeks, assigning fetal age based on conceptional age can be crucial in determining the legality of an abortion (*qv*) in a case of questionable viability (*qv*).

conception control *See* contraception.

conception ratio While the 46,XY chromosome (*qv*) complement of male somatic cells dictates a 1:1 proportion of sperm (*qv*) containing a Y chromosome (*qv*) to those carrying an X chromosome (*qv*), the sex ratio (*qv*) after conception (*qv*) is 160 males to 110 females. Many males fail to develop to term because of a higher incidence of chromosome damage and genetic defects (*qv*). Because male fetuses (*qv*) are more susceptible to miscarriage (*qv*), the birth ratio (*qv*) is between 105 and 114 males for every 100 female live births. *See also* implantation ratio; sex ratio; man shortage.

conceptive phase In a sexuoerotic (*qv*) relationship, the third and final phase, characterized by conception (*qv*), pregnancy (*qv*), and parenthood. *See also* acceptive stage; proceptive phase.

conceptus (L.) In the strict sense, the embryonic blastocyst (*qv*) when it implants in the uterine mucosa (*qv*). A less specific usage refers to the zygotic product of conception (*qv*), the embryo (*qv*), or even the fetus (*qv*).

concordance rate The statistical frequency with which both members of a pair of twins (*qv*) can be expected to exhibit an inherited trait when one twin shows it. A concordance rate of 1.0 means the trait always occurs in both identical twins when it occurs in one of the twins. A concordance rate less than 1.0 indicates a combination of hereditary and environmental factors involved in expression of the trait. A concordance rate less than 1.0 but above 0.5 indicates a predominance of the genetic but a growing environmental influence as the rate approaches 0.5. Rates below 0.5 indicate a predominance of environmental factors. Concordance rates for fraternal twins are lower than those for identical twins and often equal those of nontwins.

concubine A woman who shares a residence and has sexual relations with a man but lacks the full social status of a wife or equal partner. A concubine may be considered a secondary wife with a social and legal status inferior to that of the wife. Among wealthy Muslims, Turkish sultans, and the early Jews, concubinage was a legally accepted custom. King Solomon had 300 wives and 600 concubines as a sign of his political power and prestige. The term *concubine* is sometimes loosely applied to a mistress (*qv*).

concupiscence Lust; a strong, inordinate, excessive, or abnormal sexual desire. In Christian theology, concupiscence is the naturally occurring inducement or tendency to personal sin that every human experiences as a result of Adam's original sin. Whereas Augustine of Hippo (*qv*) and other early Christian writers identified concupiscence with the guilt of original sin, modern theologians regard concupiscence as a natural instinct, not in itself vicious but impeding the supernatural so long as it is not subject to the moral control of the individual. The term is often loosely equated, in popular religious thought, with the body, sex, and sin.

conditional love Eric Fromm's term for a type of love based on fulfillment of the lover's expectations.

condom A sheath, usually now made of latex or natural mucus membrane, that is rolled over the erect penis (*qv*) prior to intercourse (*qv*) to reduce the risk of pregnancy (*qv*) and sexually transmitted diseases (*qv*). Cecum condoms, made of the lining of animal intestines, are not an effective barrier to the HIV virus (*qv*) that causes acquired immune deficiency syndrome (*qv*). With a 15 percent actual failure rate, the contraceptive and prophylactic effectiveness of the condom is enhanced by using it with a spermicidal vaginal foam (*qv*).

Condoms were reportedly used by the Egyptians in 1350 B.C.E. The anatomist Fallopius described condoms made of linen in 1564. Vulcanized rubber condoms were first produced in the 1840s. Although the term condom is usually attributed to the legendary but mythical Dr. Condom, the term is more likely derived from the Latin *cunnus* for the female pudendum (*qv*), and *dum*, implying an inability to function. The term first appeared in print in *A Panegyric upon Cundum*, by the notorious rake John Wilmot, earl of Rochester, in 1665. *See also* safe sex (safer sex); vulcanization.

condonation A legal concept in which an illegal act (e.g., adultery [*qv*] or fornication [*qv*]) is not prosecuted or used as a grounds for a lawsuit because the aggrieved partner forgives the offending party. In keeping with condonation, a spouse who resumes sexual relations (*qv*) with an adulterous partner, in effect, condones and forgives the partner's behavior, thereby preventing use of this behavior in any subsequent lawsuit or divorce (*qv*) proceedings.

condyloma acuminatum (L.) A soft, wartlike growth common on the warm, moist skin and mucous membranes of the genital region caused by the extremely contagious human papillomavirus (HPV). Venereal warts (*qv*) spread from an infected person to the partner during oral (*qv*), vaginal (*qv*), or anal (*qv*) intercourse (*qv*). The first warts appear between 3 weeks and 3 months after exposure, but the infection can be transmitted before they appear. In women, the first warts are small, painless, nearly invisible, hard spots on the cervix (*qv*) or vaginal wall (*qv*). In males, the small, hard, and yellow-gray warts appear around the anus (*qv*) or on the tip and shaft of the penis (*qv*). Later they may become soft, pink or red, cauliflower-like, in single or multiple clusters. Venereal warts are more common in uncircumcised than in circumcised (*qv*) men. A Pap(anicolaou) test (*qv*) is usually needed to detect the virus. Treatment is with Podyphyllin, surgery, cryotherapy or freezing, electrodesiccation, or laser. Abstinence (*qv*) or use of a condom (*qv*) is essential until all the warts are removed. If not removed, the warts eventually block the vaginal and/or rectal openings. Vaginal or cervical warts can infect a newborn (*qv*) during delivery (*qv*). Vaginal warts carry an increased risk of cervical cancer (*qv*).

condyloma latum (L.) A flat, moist, wartlike growth in the perineal region or on the penile glans (*qv*), characteristic of secondary syphilis (*qv*).

confinement In social history, the custom of secluding women during the later stage of pregnancy (*qv*); in obstetrics, the stage of labor (*qv*) and childbirth (*qv*).

conflict-habituated relationship A relationship between two partners or spouses that appears filled with hostility but is actually a compatible and satisfying relation in which aggressive behavior is important in the couple's role playing (*qv*) and sex scenario.

congenital Associated or occurring with birth (*qv*) as distinct from hereditary, which denotes inheritance from parents. *See also* congenital birth defect.

congenital adrenal hyperplasia (CAH) *See* congenital virilizing adrenal hyperplasia.

congenital birth defect A gross physical defect present at birth (*qv*) or observed within the first year of infancy (*qv*). Such defects occur in about 6 percent of all live births.

congenital hypertrophy of the urethral verumontanum A proliferation of embryonic remnants of the Mullerian ducts (*qv*) that blocks the prostatic urethra (*qv*); thought to be caused by excess female hormones (*qv*) in the male fetus (*qv*). If not treated, kidney damage and death can result.

congenital syphilis Syphilis (*qv*) contracted by a fetus (*qv*) from an infected mother, resulting in bone disorders, general wasting during infancy (*qv*), blindness, deafness, stillbirth (*qv*), deformities or neonatal death (*qv*). Symptoms may not appear until early childhood. If treated before the fourth month of gestation (*qv*), the fetus is unlikely to be affected.

congenital virilizing adrenal hyperplasia (CVAH) A genetic defect (*qv*) resulting in ambiguous female genitalia (*qv*) at birth (*qv*) and possibly premature puberty (*qv*) in affected males. Affected females experience salt loss, dehydration, and severe virilization (*qv*). Affected males are usually not diagnosed until salt loss, dehydration, and/or premature puberty occur. CVAH results from varying degrees of cortisol (*qv*) and aldosterone (*qv*) deficiencies and adrenal androgen (*qv*) and pituitary adrenocorticotropin (*qv*) excesses. Adrenal malfunction begins before birth and continues unless treated. When left untreated, the severe form is lethal. Treatment can prevent premature death and postnatal virilization, although prenatally virilized female require plastic surgery. *Synonyms*: congenital adrenal hyperplasia; adrenogenital syndrome.

congested ovaries Unrelieved vasocongestion (*qv*) in the ovaries (*qv*) and vulva (*qv*) following prolonged sexual arousal (*qv*) or foreplay (*qv*) that does not culminate in orgasm (*qv*). Even without orgasm, the pain and pressure will dissipate in a few hours unless the stimulation is repeated. *See also* congested testes.

congested testes The result of unrelieved vasocongestion (*qv*) and seminal pressure in the testes (*qv*), epididymis (*qv*), and prostate (*qv*) following prolonged sexual arousal (*qv*) or foreplay (*qv*) that does not culminate in ejaculation (*qv*). The pain and pressure will dissipate in a few hours unless the stimulation is repeated. Persistent congestion can result in chronic prostatitis (*qv*) and permanent damage to the prostate gland (*qv*). *Slang*: "blue balls."

congress An obsolete term for sexual intercourse (*qv*).

coning Medical term for the reshaping of the female breast (*qv*) during mammoplasty (*qv*) or cosmetic breast surgery.

conizing of the cervix A biopsy (*qv*) performed to obtain cervical tissue for microscopic examination. Conizing gives more accurate and reliable results than a Pap(anicolaou) smear (*qv*), especially in cases of a cervical carcinoma (*qv*).

conjoined twins Monozygotic (*qv*) fetuses (*qv*) who fail to separate fully at the embryonic disc stage and are born partially joined. The union may be superficial or involve shared vital organs. Development of conjoined twins may be equal or unequal. Viability (*qv*) depends on the presence of normal development and the extent to which each twin has its own vital organs.

conjugal Associated with the legal status or relationship of marriage (*qv*); also applied to a man and woman living together. *See also* conjugal duties; conjugal rights; conjugal role.

conjugal duties The legal obligations accepted by a man and woman entering the marital state. The primary conjugal duty is that of participating in marital intercourse (*qv*) when the spouse requests it. Continued refusal may be grounds for divorce (*qv*) in some states. Other conjugal duties are financial support and sexual fidelity (*qv*), although these may be redefined by contract or informal consent. *See also* conjugal rights; conjugal role; sexually open marriage; consensual adultery.

conjugal infidelity *See* adultery.

conjugal paranoia An irrational jealousy and conviction that one's marital partner has been sexually unfaithful. *See also* alcoholic jealousy; alcoholic paranoia.

conjugal rights Conjugal rights are based on the voluntary acceptance of certain obligations or duties associated with the marital state that the spouse has both a legal and moral right to expect the partner to fulfill. *See also* conjugal duties; conjugal role.

conjugal role The tasks typically assumed by the husband and wife in the daily maintenance of a household. *Segregated conjugal roles* in which the husband and wife have quite different tasks are distinguished from *joint conjugal roles* in which domestic tasks are more or more less shared and interchangeable. The latter style is fostered by the trend toward dual career and egalitarian marriages.

conjugated estrogen A mixture of sodium salts of estrogen sulfates blended to approximate the composition of naturally occurring estrogens (*qv*); prescribed to relieve postmenopausal (*qv*) vasomotor symptoms (hot flashes), atrophic vaginalis (*qv*), female hypogonadism, osteoporosis, and primary ovarian failure.

conjugation A biological term for the reproductive union of single-celled organisms like bacteria (*qv*), algae, fungi, and protozoa. During conjugation, genetic material is exchanged between the cells or moves unilaterally from one cell to the other through specialized conjugation structures. The term is not used to describe the union of eggs and sperm (*qv*) produced by multicellular organisms. *See also* fertilization.

connecting stalk *See* body stalk.

connubial Associated with the legal status of marriage (*qv*) or being married. *See also* conjugal.

consanguineous marriage Marriage (*qv*) between two persons sharing the same common ancestor and forbidden by law or social custom. *See also* cumulative connubial association; cousin marriage; brother-sister marriage; incest.

consanguinity A measure of relationship or genetic kinship (*qv*) between two individuals who have one or more ancestors in common. The closest degree of consanguinity is that between parent and offspring, followed by brothers and sisters (siblings) with the same parents. Marriage (*qv*) or sexual relations (*qv*) between persons thus related are usually considered incestuous (*qv*). Various terms define the degree of consanguinity beyond those of siblings (e.g., half-siblings, first- and second-degree cousins, first or second cousin once removed). *See also* cousin marriage; brother-sister marriage; incest.

conscience The individual's system of moral values; in psychoanalytic theory (qv), the negative side of the superego (*qv*). The awareness of right and wrong that theologians formerly believed was innate or due to a natural law (*qv*) is now generally held to be learned. *See also* preconventional morality; conventional morality; postconventional morality; egocentric morality; heteronomous morality; autonomous morality.

consciousness-raising (CR) Small support groups designed to facilitate the sharing of experiences to gain strength and self-appreciation and to take control of one's life. First outlined by Kathie Sarachild at the First National Women's Liberation Conference in 1968, it is a major technique of analysis, structure of organization, method of practice, and theory of social change of the women's movement (*qv*).

consensual extramarital sex Sexual relations (*qv*) engaged in by a married person or persons with the consent and agreement of the spouse or spouses. *See also* open marriage; intimate friendship; satellite relationship.

consensual sex *See* consenting adult laws.

consent In law, the voluntary agreement or acceptance given by a mentally competent person who has achieved legal adulthood (*qv*) as defined by the local law. The age of consent for sexual intercourse (*qv*) in various states ranges from 7 years to 21 years of age. The age of consent for marriage (*qv*) also varies. Parents or a legal guardian can give consent for the marriage (*qv*) of a minor within the age limits set by law. *See also* child marriage; statutory rape.

consenting adult laws A specific law or code of criminal law that attaches criminal penalties for sexual (*qv*) behavior engaged in by two or more consenting adults as long as such behavior does not create a public nuisance. The trend toward consenting adult laws began in 1962 when the American Law Institute recommended the Model Penal Code (*qv*) and abolition of all criminal sanctions for sexual behavior engaged in by consenting adults in private. Forced sexual intercourse (*qv*), seduction (*qv*) of minors (*qv*), sexual assaults (*qv*), indecent exposure (*qv*), and prostitution (*qv*) would still be criminal offenses. In 1962, Illinois became the first state to adopt such a code of law.

constrictor vaginae (L.) The muscle surrounding the external opening of the vagina (*qv*) with extensions inserting on either side of the clitoris (*qv*). This muscle contributes to the transfer of penile thrusting (*qv*) stimulation to the clitoris and at the same time constricts the vaginal opening to stimulate the penis (*qv*).

constructionism In sexology, the viewpoint held by some social scientists and social critics that all or most aspects of gender (*qv*), including male-female differences, derive from society, culture, and learning rather than from biology, anatomy, or the physical nature of the universe. Constructionism is a version of the anthropological truism that all members of a culture see their lives through lenses provided by their own culture and its traditions. In more extreme forms, constructionism holds that categories such as ''nature,'' ''biology,'' ''sex,'' and even ''humankind'' are socially constructed and have no existence outside the culture of the people who define such words. In this view, constructionism comes close to the philosophical position of solipsism, where one argues that no realities exist outside one's personal perceptions. In its less extreme forms, constructionism has been a valuable counter to the excesses of biologism (*qv*).

consummate, to The first act of marital intercourse (*qv*) which is considered to complete, or consummate, the marital contract. Failure to consummate a marriage can be used as grounds for a civil or religious divorce (*qv*) or annulment (*qv*) depending on the applicable laws. Some couples may be content with an unconsummated marriage for a variety of reasons, in some cases because they prefer other sexual outlets to coitus (*qv*) or simply because they have little or no interest in expressing their love genitally.

consummatory behavior In motivation theory, acts that follow appetitive behavior and eliminate or reduce whatever need caused the behavior in the first place. In sexuality, appetitive behavior consists of flirtation behavior (*qv*) and courtship (*qv*), while consummatory behavior consists of mating (*qv*) and copulating (*qv*). Accordingly, in servomechanism fashion, intercourse extinguishes the drive state that originally led the organism to seek a mate. Many psychological theoreticians do not accept this phase description of behavior or the self-extinguishing concept implicit in this model.

contact comfort The physical and emotional warmth and nurturance an infant (*qv*) derives from touching the mother or other care provider; contact comfort is also an important aspect of normal sexual relations (*qv*). *See also* hospitalism; somatosensory affectional deprivation.

content analysis In quantitative social research, the analysis of the communications content of documentary or visual material, although the term is also applied to the content of interview data. Clear definition of content categories is essential to minimize bias resulting from the judgments of different investigators. *See also* cluster analysis; factor analysis.

continence Sexual abstinence (*qv*) or restraint. *See also* chastity.

continuum of sexual orientation *See* Kinsey Six Scale.

contraception (adj. contraceptive) The process of preventing conception (*qv*) by preventing ovulation (*qv*), fertilization (*qv*), or implantation (*qv*) of the fertilized ovum (*qv*) in the uterine wall. (The removal of an already implanted ovum is technically abortion [*qv*].) Contraceptive methods may be temporary, for example, the use of a condom (*qv*), diaphragm (*qv*), or contraceptive pill (*qv*), or permanent, for example, ligation of the fallopian tubes (*qv*) in the woman or cutting the *vasa deferentia* (*qv*) in a man. Contraceptive techniques differ in how they work: steroid contraceptives, like the birth control pill, prevent the release of the ovum from the ovary (*qv*) and are therefore anti-ovulatory; chemical contraceptives or spermicides act by killing the sperm (*qv*) and are applied intravaginally in cream, foam, or jelly form; barrier contraceptives, like condoms and the diaphragm, physically prevent the movement of sperm into the woman's reproductive tract; and natural or rhythm contraceptive techniques depend on sexual abstinence during periods of the woman's maximum fertility. Intrauterine devices (IUDs) (*qv*) are thought to work by preventing implantation of the fertilized ovum. Other techniques that function contraceptively include withdrawal of the penis before intravaginal ejaculation (*qv*) and the adoption of nonvaginal sexual behavior, such as fallatio (*qv*), in place of intravaginal ejaculation. Contraceptive techniques differ in their effectiveness and safety. Questions of the safety of the steroid birth control preparations cannot be answered generally but must be determined by each woman in consultation with a physician. Socially, contraception and contraceptive education has had a long and extremely controversial history, and only recently in the United States have contraceptive methods become available and acceptable for both men and women. Moreover, contraceptive use is still prohibited by conservative religions, such as Roman Catholicism and Orthodox Judaism. Even so, it can be argued that contraception is of worldwide biological, social, and psychologial importance to many hundreds of millions of women and men.

See also sexual abstinence; natural family planning (rhythm); barrier contraceptive; condom; contraceptive (oral) pills; vasectomy; tubal ligation; sterilization; vaginal suppository; contraceptive diaphragm; spermicide; contraceptive sponge; contraceptive foam; contraceptive jelly; pessary; cervical cap.

contraceptive diaphragm A barrier contraceptive device consisting of a thin rubber hemisphere bonded to a flexible ring. The contraceptive diaphragm is available in sizes of 0.5 centimeter increments between 5 1/2 and 10 centimeters. It is fitted to insert between the pubic symphysis (*qv*) and posterior fornix (*qv*) of the vagina (*qv*) and covers the cervix (*qv*). For increased effectiveness, it should be covered inside and out with a spermicide (*qv*). The actual effectiveness rate is 5 to 10 unwanted pregnancies per year in 100 women when used properly with a spermicide.

contraceptive effectiveness A statistical measurement of the success rate a particular contraceptive (*qv*) has in preventing pregnancy (*qv*). The theoretical effectiveness, based on ideal use, is higher than the actual effectiveness rate which compares the success of the contraceptive with its actual failure in preventing pregnancy in every day use. The actual failure rate includes failure of the method and failure due to improper use. A contraceptive method that results in less than 10 pregnancies a year for every 100 sexually active women in their reproductive years using the method is considered highly effective. On balance, most contraceptive methods are extremely effective and differ mostly in whether they are used properly and consistently. Resource: J. Trussell and K. Kost (1987). Contraceptive failure in the United States: A critical review of the literature. *Studies in Family Planning*, 12(5):246–249.

contraceptive film A thin, 2-inch square sheet of gel containing the spermicidal nonoxynol-9 (*qv*), that dissolves in the normal vaginal fluids and clings to the cervix (*qv*), where it blocks passage of the sperm (*qv*). Also known as vaginal contraceptive film.

contraceptive foam An aerosol contraceptive containing a spermicide (*qv*). The foam should be inserted with an applicator at the cervical end of the vaginal canal (*qv*) no more than 15 minutes prior to intercourse (*qv*) and left undisturbed for 6 hours after intercourse. Foam is best used in conjunction with a barrier contraceptive (*qv*) such as a condom (*qv*) or diaphragm (*qv*). *See also* vaginal foam.

contraceptive jelly A spermicidal (*qv*) gel designed to be used with a diaphragm (*qv*) to increase its effectiveness in preventing contraception (*qv*). When used alone, its effectiveness is poor. *See also* vaginal jelly.

contraceptive (oral) pills *See* biphasic oral contraceptive pill; triphasic contraceptive pill; combination oral contraceptive pill; progestin-only contraceptive.

contraceptive sponge A synthetic sponge containing a spermicide (*qv*), moistened and inserted manually into the vagina (*qv*) to cover the cervical opening (*qv*). The sponge can be inserted up to 24 hours prior to intercourse (*qv*) and should be left undisturbed for 6 hours after intercourse.

contraceptive suppository A meltable or effervescing oval containing a spermicide (*qv*) inserted deep in the vaginal canal (*qv*) within 2 hours of sexual intercourse (*qv*). It should be left undisturbed for 6 to 8 hours after intercourse.

contrasexual An obsolete term for a homosexual (*qv*) person. Carl Jung (*qv*) subsequently applied the term to that portion of the bisexual (*qv*) psyche that is repressed—in males, the anima (*qv*); in females, the animus (*qv*).

contrection Technical term for sexually arousing (*qv*) another person by handling the other's genitals (*qv*).

control group In social and biological science experiments, a group of people or subjects matched as closely as possible on relevant variables with an experimental group. Without parallel data from a control group, the investigator cannot tell whether an effect observed in the experimental group is due to the experimental variable (*qv*) being tested or to some other feature of the environment.

controlled variable A variable (*qv*) or independent factor subject to regulation by the experimenter.

conventional morality In Lawrence Kohlberg's scheme of moral development, that developmental stage characterized by a "good boy–nice girl" conformity to society's conventions and a general respect for society's laws. *See also* preconventional morality; postconventional morality; Piaget, Jean.

convergent validity A description of identical results from two or more research methods applied to the same research question. *See also* replicability; validity.

Coolidge effect A sexual (*qv*) and behavioral response pattern in which the introduction of a new sex partner to a male or female who has become sexually unresponsive restores that animal's interest in mating (*qv*) more quickly than the continued presence of the first partner. The Coolidge effect is expressed in the colloquialism, "Variety is the spice of life." The term is derived from a widely circulated anecdote regarding President Calvin Coolidge and his wife who visited a farm outside Washington in the 1920s. The First Lady, it is alleged, gently chided the president about the amorous enthusiasm and energies of one of the bulls (or in a second version, one of the roosters) and suggested it would be delightful if her husband were half as energetic. In reply, Mr. Coolidge called his wife's attention to the fact that her idolized bull (or rooster) seldom visited the same female twice. The Coolidge effect has been demonstrated by experiments with mice, rats, guinea pigs, dairy bulls, water buffaloes, sheep, swine, boars, and cats, and, in folklore, in human beings. It may play a role in the therapeutic effect of surrogate partners (*qv*) in sex therapy.

cool sexual values A system of sexual values and attitudes based on egalitarian relations, flexibility in roles and types of relationships, lack of sex stereotypes, and a diffused, open sensuality. *See also* hot sexual values; closed marriage; open marriage. Resource: A. K. and R. T. Francoeur, *Hot and Cool Sex: Cultures in Conflict* (New York: Harcourt Brace Jovanovich, 1974).

cooperative interaction An arrangement, usually negotiated by a therapist, in which both individuals in a relationship agree to assist each other actively in their joint effort to overcome a sexual dysfunction (*qv*).

coprography The irresistible urge to create graffiti involving words or drawings concerning excrement and sexual activities involving the anus (*qv*.) *See also* anal eroticism; coprophilia; mysophilia; narrotophilia. *See Addendum:* graffiti.

coprolagnia A paraphilic (*qv*) condition in which sexual arousal (*qv*) and achieving orgasm (*qv*) are facilitated by or dependent on thinking about, seeing, smelling, or handling feces. *See also* anal eroticism; coprophilia; mysophilia.

coprolalia An unconscious, irresistible urge to utter obscene (*qv*) words and phrases, particularly words about feces and defecation. Coprolalia may be a result of disturbances in the brain mechanisms as in Tourette's syndrome (*qv*) or a cultural phenomenon as in latah (*qv*).

coprology An obsolete term for obscenity (*qv*).

coprophagia A condition occasionally found in deteriorated schizophrenia in which the person eats feces. In psychoanalytic theory, it is interpreted as a regression to the anal stage (*qv*) of psychosexual development (*qv*). *See also* anal eroticism; coprophilia; mysophilia; narrotophilia; coprolagnia; coprography.

coprophemia *See* narratophilia.

coprophilia A paraphilic (*qv*) condition in which sexual arousal (*qv*) and the facilitation of orgasm (*qv*) responds to or is dependent on the smell or taste of feces or the sight and sound of a person defecating. This paraphilia may be expressed in constant jokes about defecation and feces, in hoarding feces or soiled clothing, in fecal fantasies, sexual arousal during defecation, and, in some schizophrenic patients, in smearing feces on the walls or furniture. Developmentally this response may have its origins in mammalian hygiene whereby infants are licked clean. In a paraphiliac, the condition has varied origins and may be related to masochism (*qv*) and self-deprecation. *See also* anal eroticism; mysophilia.

coprophobia A pathologic phobic reaction or fear of defecation and excrement, symbolically expressed as a fear of dirt, contamination, and disease; in psychoanalytic theory, a defense against anal eroticism (*qv*).

coprophrasia *See* coprolalia.

copula carnalis (L.) A legal term for sexual relations (*qv*) between husband and wife. *See also* carnal knowledge; fornication; adultery.

copula fornicatoris (L.) A legal term for sexual intercourse (*qv*) between a man and a prostitute (*qv*) or between two unmarried persons. *See also* carnal knowledge; adultery; fornication.

copulate, to (copulation) Sexual intercourse (*qv*) involving insertion of the penis (*qv*) in the vagina (*qv*). The word derives from Latin, meaning to "fasten" or "link together." The earliest reference to sexual copulation in the *Oxford English Dictionary* dates from 1483; today, the term is used primarily in animal behavior and zoology. *See also* coitus; intercourse, sexual; mount.

copulation fantasy An erotic (*qv*) fantasy (*qv*) that precedes and/or accompanies loveplay (*qv*) and/or sexual intercourse (*qv*); the fantasy may involve one's partner or a third party. *See also* masturbation fantasy.

copulatory behavior Behavioral patterns associated with the proceptive phase (*qv*), coital positions, and the acceptive phase (*qv*) of sexual relations. Such patterns vary greatly depending on the species of animal, or on the human culture involved.

copulin The pheromone (*qv*) from the vagina (*qv*) that attracts and stimulates the male to copulate (*qv*). The name was proposed by Richard Michael and coworkers who studied rhesus monkey matings in experimental conditions and in 1971 isolated and analyzed the substance as composed of odiferous short-chain aliphatic acids.

coquette (coquettry) A coquette is a woman who uses her sexual attractions and psychological wiles to attract men without intending to consummate (*qv*) any sexual relationship with them. Synonyms in colloquial English are flirt, tease, or cockteaser. Coquettry refers to the arts of flirtation and seduction when they fall short of actual intercourse. The term is of French origin but appeared in English in the early 1600s. The masculine form, *coquet*, is not used, although it accurately describes some men.

corditis *See* epididymitis.

core gender identity (CGI) The innermost experience of oneself as a male or female that develops in the first few years of childhood; also referred to as gender identity (*qv*). In one psychoanalytic theory, CGI refers to an infant's developing sense of self as a boy or girl in the second year of life, well in advance of the classic Oedipal phase (*qv*) to which the origin of gender differences is attributed in traditional psychoanalytic theory. In a third usage, CGI is the combination of physical characteristics, sex chromosomes (*qv*), fetal gonads (*qv*) and sex hormones (*qv*) that determine the development and function of the external genitalia (*qv*). CGI usually develops in concordance with one's external sexual anatomy. However, a transsexual (*qv*) experiences a transposition of or crosscoding for CGI with gender dysphoria (qv) a likely outcome. *See also* gender identity/role.

cornual pregnancy An ectopic pregnancy (*qv*) in which implantation (*qv*) occurs in the fallopian tube (*qv*) near the uterus (*qv*).

corona glandis, coronal ridge The sensitive, raised rim of the penile glans (*qv*).

corpus albicans (L.) Remnants of the corpus luteum (*qv*) when pregnancy (*qv*) does not follow ovulation (*qv*) or, after a pregnancy, when the corpus luteum regresses and is overgrown by scar tissue; literally, "white body."

corpus cavernosum (pl. corpora cavernosa) (L.) The paired, cylindrical, spongelike bodies of the penis (*qv*) or clitoris (*qv*) that transverse the length of the shaft, one on either side. The two corpora are enclosed in the dartos (*qv*) tunic and Buck's penile fascia (*qv*). At the root, they diverge into tapering crura (*qv*). At the distal end, they converge and are embedded in the glans (*qv*). Erection (*qv*) of the penis or clitoris occurs when the corpora become engorged with blood during sexual stimulation.

corpus fibrosum (L.) Fibrous tissue surrounding several Graafian follicles (*qv*) that start developing each month but fail to mature as only one follicle (*qv*) produces a mature ovum (*qv*).

corpus hemorrhagicum (L.) The brief period when the ruptured Graafian follicle (*qv*) fills with hemorrhaged blood before the secretory cells of the corpus luteum (*qv*) develop.

corpus luteum (L.) The spherical "yellowish body," the remains of the Graafian follicle (*qv*) following ovulation (*qv*) when the empty follicle fills with hemorrhaged blood and is overgrown by secretory cells. Granulosa-lutein cells lining the corpus luteum produce progesterone (*qv*), while the theca-lutein cells produce estrogen (*qv*) during the first trimester (*qv*) of pregnancy (*qv*) until placental hormone (*qv*) production takes over. In the event pregnancy does not follow ovulation, the corpus luteum ceases hormone production, regresses, and is overgrown by scar tissue. *See also* corpus albicans.

corpus mammae (L.) The functional tissue of the female breast (*qv*), composed of the secretory cells, collecting tubules, and mammary ducts.

corpus spongiosum (L.) A cylindrical body of spongy, erectile (*qv*) tissue surrounding the penile urethra (*qv*) and ending in the glans (*qv*); smaller than the paired corpora cavernosa (*qv*), which lie above it. Previously known as corpus cavernosum urethra.

corpus uteri (L.) The main body of the uterus (*qv*), above the cervix (*qv*); the fundal cavity where gestation (*qv*) occurs.

correlation (correlation coefficient) In statistics, a relationship between two variables in which if one variable changes, the other does as well. The strength of the relationship is measured by the correlation coefficient, a class of mathematically defined terms that range from +1 for complete correlation, through 0 for no relationship at all, to −1 for a complete but inverse relationship. When two variables are correlated, knowing about one correlated variable provides information about the other. In sexuality, correlational studies seek to understand how a given sexual variable such as frequency of intercourse might relate to other variables such as socioeconomic status, religion, or sex guilt (*qv*).

cortex (pl. cortices) The outer layer of an organ, for example, the adrenal cortex (*qv*) or ovarian cortex (*qv*).

cortical inductor substance An embryonic hormone (*qv*) responsible for the differentiation of the cortices (*qv*) of the primordial gonads (*qv*) into ovaries (*qv*); active after the sixth week of gestation (*qv*).

corticosteroid Any one of several natural hormones (*qv*) associated with the adrenal glands (*qv*) that influence or control key metabolic processes and functions of the cardiovascular and skeletal muscle systems, kidneys, and other organs.

cortisol In humans, the main glucocorticoid hormone (*qv*) produced by the adrenal cortices (*qv*); essential for the maintenance of life; available in synthetic form. Also known as hydrocortisone and 17-hydroxycorticosterone.

cortisone In current usage, a metabolite of cortisol (*qv*).

cotherapist A male and female team of sex therapists (*qv*) who work together in treating patients with sexual dysfunctions (*qv*). The use of a cotherapist was suggested by William Masters and Virginia Johnson to encourage rapport with and input from both partners. The cotherapists may work at different times and separately with the same- or opposite-gender patient, or together.

countertransference The conscious or subconscious emotional response of a therapist to a patient. *See also* transference.

courtesan Originally the term referred to a lady in a royal or noble court who was the mistress of one of the nobles, a sense retained today for mistresses of men highly placed in industry, government, or finance. More loosely, a courtesan is a well-paid, elegant prostitute (*qv*) with a high social status. *See also* paramour.

courtesan fantasy An erotic fantasy (*qv*) in which a woman imagines she is a prostitute (*qv*), concubine (*qv*), or courtesan (*qv*) or a male fantasying he is having intercourse (*qv*) with such a woman. Such fantasies may be used as an escape mechanism that allows a man or woman of strict morals to have and enjoy sexual relations (*qv*). *See also* madonna syndrome.

courtly love A revolutionary medieval view of love that viewed woman as far superior to man, almost unattainable and beyond the reach of passion, to be worshipped and honored by men. The roots of courtly love lie in the exaltation of earthly love among the Arab poets of Spain, especially the writings of Ibn Hazm (994–1064), Al Hallaj (857–922), and Ibn Arabi (1165–1240). Adopted by troubadours (*qv*) in southern France in the twelfth century, courtly love enlarged the concept of love beyond the biological urges of Eros (*qv*) and spiritual agape (*qv*) to introduce the idea of amor or love as a person-to-person relationship. At first, the object of a man's love or amor was the noble wife of a local lord, opening the door to adultery (*qv*) in our modern sense of an emotional relationship rather than a mere satisfying of lusty urges. When the troubadours and courtly love were associated in the ecclesiastical mind with the Manichean and Albigensian heresies, the troubadour tradition was persecuted in the so-called Albigensian Crusade of 1209.

After the Albigensian Crusade, the last troubadors adopted a platonic idealization of woman and male-female love. Rooted in the medieval world, the courtly love tradition died out. Courtly love was popularized by the image of Beatrice in Dante's *Divine Comedy* and in the poetry of Guinizelli, which extolled personal love as the "dolce stil nova" (*qv*) and adapted the new conception of love to the changing social conditions in Italy. The English writer C. S. Lewis is responsible for exaggerating the cultic aspects of courtly love and creating the myth of the total separation of courtly love from the marital state in the medieval period. Resources: I. Singer, *The Nature of Love: Courtly and Romantic* (Chicago: University of Chicago Press, 1984); H. A. Kelly, *Lore and Marriage in the Age of Chaucer* (Ithaca: Cornell University Press, 1975); G. Erasmi, Earthly love and divine love, in B. Gupta, ed., *Sexual Archetypes, East and West* (New York: Paragon House, 1987).

court-order state Term for a state that has responded to Reagan administration prohibitions on use of federal funds to provide abortion (*qv*) to indigent women by allocating state funds to pay for such abortions.

courtship Narrowly defined, the word courtship traditionally means endeavoring to win or gain the emotional and sexual affections and favors of another person, often with the goal of marriage (*qv*). More broadly, courtship refers to a complex combination of interpersonal feelings and behavior, often expressed symbolically, that communicate sexual and emotional interest, and that, if successful, precede and elicit sexual relations. In the broad sense, courtship includes all precoital interactions and communications.

In formal heterosexual (*qv*) traditions in the United States, courtship is synonymous with wooing, a socially defined and constrained set of behavior patterns enacted reciprocally by the man and woman and often involving extremely complex rules of dating (*qv*), touching, kissing (*qv*), and the like. In recent years, informal traditions of courtship have appeared for which no exact term exists (e.g., placing personals ads [*qv*] in newspapers or magazines). By default, these new patterns can be defined as modern courtship; *see* flirtation; proceptivity.

In non-human animals and human beings, courtship involves overtures and signals sent by each individual to the other. In no organism, and in no human society, are these interindividual signals sent only by the male. In addition, a courting female sends specific proceptive signals directed to a selected male who, in turn, sends signals to her in an ongoing, reciprocated fashion; *see* female choice. In modern and traditional heterosexual American courtship, these signals are often highly stereotyped and have considerable symbolic meaning attached to them (for example, he sends her flowers or she telephones him with a dinner invitation). Simultaneously, the two individuals are exchanging nonverbal signals (body language [*qv*]) that convey sexual interest or reluctance. Together, these symbolic exchanges plus bodily or nonverbal signals create a shared experience of mutual and accepting erotosexual (*qv*) interest, and they therefore represent courtship.

Psychologically, courtship is a period of intense emotion, including love (*qv*), limerence (*qv*), jealousy (*qv*), anticipation, exalted happiness, and anxiety. These internal experiences and feelings blend with the social events of courtship to create a unique period in the lives of most Americans.

However, in other cultures, social and personal events preceding either sexual intimacy or marriage may be quite unemotional, for example, if marriages are arranged or if sexual liaisons occur simply or casually. Likewise, within America, courtship customs and traditions vary considerably among ethnic groups and between geographic regions. However, despite these variations, courtship contains a core of sequentially developing and mutually communicated sexual and emotional interest.

In middle-class America, the great stress placed on courtship, and particularly on falling in love, makes it hard for many people to imagine that courtship elsewhere might be simple, direct, or relatively unemotional. American cultural stress on the profound emotional importance of courtship and choosing the right partner also makes it hard for many Americans to see similarities between parts of the middle-class American courtship system, such as interindividual signal exchange, and courtship patterns that occur elsewhere or among non-human species. Resources: B. L. Bailey, *From Front Porch to Back Seat: Courtship in Twentieth-Century America* (Baltimore: Johns Hopkins University Press, 1988); T. Perper, *Sex Signals: The Biology of Love* (Philadelphia: iSi Press, 1985).

cousin marriage Marriage (*qv*) in which the spouses are related by first-, second-, or third-degree cousin kinship. Judaism does not prohibit marriage of any cousins. Catholicism allows marriage of second cousins and, with a dispensation, first cousins. Most Protestant churches and the Islamic tradition allow first-cousin marriages. Two-thirds of the 762 cultures in the Human Relations Area File (*qv*) forbid marriage between any degree of cousin kinship. However, many societies require some sort of cousin marriage (e.g., cross- or parallel-cousin marriages). *See also* brother-sister marriage; consanguinity.

couvade (CS) (Fr.) The symptoms of pregnancy (*qv*) experienced by a man; from the French term for "to brood or hatch." Couvade has been documented in most Western societies, with the incidence in the United States ranging from 22 percent to 79 percent. Physical manifestations include the whole range of discomforts experienced by pregnant women, with the most common being nausea, vomiting, heartburn, constipation, backache, abdominal swelling, unintentional weight gain or loss, tachycardia, muscle tension, appetite changes, excessive fatigue, and general feeling of ill health. Psychological symptoms include headache, depression, difficulty in concentrating, restlessness, irritability, generalized anxiety, and insomnia. Originally regarded as a neurotic phenomenon, couvade syndrome is now associated with developmental crisis theory.

In some nontechnological cultures, a male ritualistically imitates the pregnancy and delivery (*qv*) of his wife in order to draw evil spirits away from her. The ritual may be so intense it triggers a psychosomatic response, with the husband actually experiencing the symptoms of pregnancy and labor. Resource: J. Clinton (1987) *Medical Aspects Human Sexuality*, 21(11):115,132.

covenant A religious commitment having its origins in the Jewish and Christian biblical covenants; a personal agreement between two persons in an ongoing relationship. In the Protestant tradition, marriage (*qv*) is often viewed as a covenant rather than as a sacrament or contract.

covert desensitization In psychotherapy (*qv*), linking an anxiety-producing stimulus with a fantasy (*qv*) of punishment. *See also* aversion therapy; behavior modification; operant conditioning.

covert homosexual A homosexual (*qv*) who conceals his or her sexual orientation (*qv*); a "closet homosexual" or "closet queen." *See also* closeting.

covert sensitization A type of aversion therapy (*qv*) in which a patient with a socially unacceptable sexual behavior is taught to use a negative or disagreeable fantasy (*qv*) as punishment for a fantasy he or she wants to get rid of but is still attached to; in psychotherapy (*qv*), the linking of a rewarding stimulus with a fantasy of punishment. *See also* covert desensitization.

coverture A feudal doctrine incorporated into English common law and Napoleonic law holding that after marriage a woman must turn over all her property and money to her husband, leaving the wife unable to engage in legally binding contracts. During the existence of the marriage or coverture, the wife's children are considered the legitimate offspring of the husband and legally belong to him. Such laws were gradually abolished in the United States and elsewhere starting in the nineteenth century.

Cowper's glands Two pea-sized glands at the base of the penis (*qv*), under the prostate (*qv*), which secrete a clear alkaline fluid into the urethra (*qv*) during sexual arousal (*qv*). This preejaculation leakage may contain some viable sperm (*qv*). *See also* Bartholin's glands.

Coyote Acronym for "Call Off Your Old Tired Ethics," a California prostitutes' (*qv*) labor union founded by Margot St. James.

CR *See* conditioned response; consciousness-raising.

crab louse A very small parasite generally limited to human hosts where it infests the coarse hair of the anogenital region, the armpits, chest, and eyebrows; *Phthirus* or *Pediculosis pubis*. Eggs are laid at the base of hair shafts. The lice burrow under the skin, causing tiny blue specks or small, crustlike lesions that itch intensely. Other signs of infestation are pinhead blood spots and feces specks on underwear. Treatment is with an over-the-counter cream, lotion, or prescription shampoo. Since adult lice die within 24 hours and their eggs take 6 days to hatch, all possibly infected clothing and bed linens must be washed in very hot water and kept in a sealed plastic bag for at least 7 days before using them again. Dry-cleaned or boiled clothes can be used immediately.

craniopharyngioma A congenital (*qv*) tumor of the pituitary (*qv*) that interferes with the hypothalamus (*qv*) and pituitary. In children, the tumor causes infantile genitals (*qv*). For men, the result is impotence (*qv*); for women, amenorrhea (*qv*).

creative singlehood A life-style based on the absence of an exclusive emotional, sexual, and financial dependence on any one person.

cremasteric reflex The reflexive retraction of the testis (*qv*) occurs when the outside temperature drops or when the skin on the front and inner surface of the thigh is stimulated. Retraction, due to the cremasteric muscle attached to the testes and crest of the pubis (*qv*), occurs only on the side stimulated.

cremaster muscle A scrotal (*qv*) muscle that elevates the testis (*qv*); an extension of the internal oblique abdominal muscle. *See also* cremasteric reflex.

cribriform hymen An intact hymen (*qv*) perforated with numerous small openings, which allow passage of the menstrual flow (*qv*).

crime against nature An ambiguous legal and philosophical term that can include oral sex, anal sex, bestiality; and/or homosexual acts of any kind. The basis of the expression is the belief that only heterosexual (*qv*), coital (*qv*), and noncontraceptive sexual activity (*qv*) are in accord with natural law (*qv*) or the divinely established nature and purpose of sex; all other sexual activities are an affront to nature. Various legal codes speak of an "abominable and detestable crime against nature," the "abominable crime of buggery," an "unnatural and lascivious act," a "deviate sexual conduct," an "infamous crime against nature," or simply "sexual misconduct" without describing or defining the specific sexual acts included under the vague legal terminology. *See also* natural sin; unnatural sin; sodomy; buggery. Resource: R. Aman, What is this crime that dare not speak its name? *Maledicta* 9 (1986–1987):247–268.

crime of passion Historically, in some Western societies, a husband could kill his wife and her lover, without fear of legal punishment, if he caught them in the act of adultery (*qv*).

criminal abortion Intentional termination of a pregnancy (*qv*) under any conditions prohibited by law. *See also* abortion.

criminal assault A euphemism for rape (*qv*).

criminal codes of law Secular laws designed to protect citizens from injury and harm by punishing violations with fines or imprisonment. Criminal laws are distinct from church law and from secular family and civil codes (*qv*) of law.

criminal conversation A quaint legalism for unlawful intercourse with a married woman.

critical period A period in fetal (*qv*) or postnatal (*qv*) development when the organism is responsive to a particular stimulus. The development of a specific organ, neural template (*qv*), or behavioral pattern is established when a specific stimulus occurs during the critical period. If the proper stimulus is not available during the critical period, the organ, neural template, or behavioral skill may not become established. Presence of a teratogen (*qv*) during the critical period may leave an organ or system deformed or undeveloped. The concept of a critical period is essential in understanding the interaction of biological and sociological factors in all development. *See also* nature/critical period/nurture; sensitive period.

crossbreeding In animal husbandry and plant breeding, hybridization or the mating (*qv*) of individuals from different strains or cultivars, or from different species. The term is not used for matings (*qv*) or marriages (*qv*) between individuals of different human races or sociocultural groups unless the speaker intends racist and supremacist meanings. Biologically, it is not possible for humans to crossbreed with any other animal species.

crosscoding In gender and psychosexual development (*qv*), a discordance or conflicting coding for any two aspects of sex or gender development—the genetic, gonadal, hormonal, anatomical, neural, or psychosocial. *See also* cross-gender behavior; transsexual; transvestite; transgenderist; gender dysphoria; gender transposition; sex variables; gender coding.

cross-complementation In terms of gender differentiation and gender-identity/role (*qv*), an agreement in gender between the self and the complementation figure or model. *See also* cross-identification; cross-coding.

cross-cousin The child of your father's sister or your mother's brother.

cross-cultural research Observational (*qv*) research that investigates and compares the behavior, customs, and values of people in different cultures; ethnographic research.

cross-dressing Dressing in the clothes of the other gender for purposes of entertainment, homosexual (*qv*) role playing (*qv*), or paraphilic (*qv*) need or to accommodate a gender dysphoria (*qv*): transvestism (*qv*). As a paraphilic compulsion, cross-dressing cannot be resisted and must be expressed in reality or fantasy to achieve sexual arousal (*qv*) and orgasm (*qv*). *See also* female impersonator; gynemimetic; transsexual; hijra; berdache; drag queen; sissy boy syndrome.

cross-fertilization Reproduction (*qv*) involving two different species or strains resulting in a hybrid (*qv*); allogamy.

cross-gender behavior Adopting and expressing the social role of the other sex; adopting the garb, fashions, hair styling, speech, and gesture patterns socially attributed to and accepted for the other gender. *See also* crosscoding; female impersonator; gynemimetic; transvestite; transsexual; hijra; berdache; drag queen; sissy boy syndrome; cisvestism.

cross-identification In terms of gender differentiation and gender-identity/role (*qv*), a disconcordance or dysphoria in the gender (qv) of the self and the complementation figure or model. *See also* crosscoding; cross-complementation; transsexual; transvestite; transgenderist; gender dysphoria.

cross-sectional research Research that draws comparisons between different groups over the same time period.

cross-sex parent The father of a girl or the mother of a boy.

croupade (Fr.) Sexual intercourse (*qv*) using a rear entry position in which the male is behind the woman. *See also* cuissade.

crowning In childbirth (*qv*), the appearance of the fetal head at the external opening of the vagina (*qv*) when the labia (*qv*) are stretched in a crown around the emerging forehead.

crude birthrate The number of births per 1,000 people in a population during one year. This statistic does not compensate for the variable percentage of fertile people per 1,000. *See also* birthrate.

cruising The overt and public search for a sexual partner. Often, the partner may be anonymous and cruising is undertaken for a purely sexual release. Among homosexual (*qv*) men, cruising often involves moving from one bar, club, bath house, or party to another during the search. Some sexologists feel that cruising is a sexual addiction (*qv*) involving a repeated and never-satisfied search for an idealized or lost sexual partner or experience. *See also* tea-room trade.

crus (pl. crura) (L.) The leg or trunk of a structure, for example, the internal base of the corpus cavernosa (*qv*) of the penis (*qv*) and clitoris (*qv*).

cryptomenorrhea Retention of the menstrual products within the uterus (*qv*) or vaginal canal (*qv*), resulting from an imperforate hymen (*qv*), rectocoel (*qv*), cystocoel (*qv*), or blocked cervical canal (*qv*). Symptoms include severe abdominal pain and reduced or absent menstrual flow (*qv*), peritonitis, and endometriosis (*qv*).

cryptorchidism A developmental anomaly in which one or both testes (*qv*) remain in the abdominal or pelvic region or in the inguinal canal instead of migrating perinatally into the scrotum (*qv*). If not corrected by hormones (*qv*) or surgery, usually before age 5, there is a high risk of eunuchoid (*qv*) features and sterility (*qv*) due to testicular atrophy (*qv*) and testicular cancer (*qv*). One in 50 American boys reaches puberty (*qv*) with one or both testes still undescended into the scrotum. For adult men, the incidence of cryptorchidism is about one in 500 males.

CS *See* couvade.

C section *See* Caesarean section.

C-20 block Medical term for an enzyme deficiency that affects the C-20 position of the cholesterol molecule, thereby preventing normal production of sex hormones (*qv*) from the cholesterol molecule. The autosomal (*qv*) mutation affects males more than females because male differentiation is dependent on androgenic hormones, while prenatal (*qv*) female development is hormone independent. Males with this condition develop external female genitalia (*qv*) despite having a chromosome (*qv*) complement of 46,XY. *See also* pseudohermaphrodite; hermaphrodite; DHT deficiency syndrome.

cuckold A derogatory Victorian (*qv*) term for a man whose wife has had an extramarital sexual affair.

cuissade (Fr.) A coital position in which the male is positioned astride the woman's thighs.

culdoscope A fiber optics instrument, often attached to a television monitor, that allows visual inspection of the internal organs of the pelvic and abdominal cavities; used in videolaseroscopy (*qv*) treatment for endometriosis (*qv*) and as a guide for tubal ligation (*qv*), as well as for diagnostic purposes.

culdoscopy Direct visual examination of the female viscera through a culdoscope (*qv*) or endoscope (*qv*) introduced into the pelvic cavity through the posterior vaginal fornix (*qv*); used for diagnostic or surgical purposes. *See also* videolaseroscopy.

cultural evolution The transformation over time of a social group from a putatively more primitive state of economic, social, or kinship organization to one that is putatively more advanced. Cultural evolution is distinct from the concept of history since it involves the idea of progress towards a ''higher'' form of social structure and organization. In biological anthropology, the term refers to the gradual evolution of the capacity for culture itself as human beings evolved from non-cultural hominid ancestors. It can also mean the set of changing patterns of behavior and social structure that result from the interaction of cultural or social processes with biological processes and factors such as disease and climate.

cultural lag A cultural lag exists when two or more social variables, which had been in agreement and functioned smoothly together, become dissociated and in tension because of their differential rates of change. The term is commonly used to refer to the tensions and lack of adaptation between relative stable sexual attitudes and values and technologies that can change rapidly. Resource: W. F.

Ogburn, *On Culture and Social Change* (Chicago: Chicago University Press, 1950).

cultural relativism In anthropology, the ideology and belief that a culture must be judged relative only to its own, internal standards of good and evil and not according to modern Western ideas of right and wrong. The doctrine asserts that no culture, no matter how seemingly primitive, can be called inferior or inadequate in comparison to any other, including our own. Critics of this view argue that some cultural traditions (e.g., suttee [*qv*], or clitorectomy [*qv*]) may be rooted deeply in the values of a society but are nonetheless wrong in some deeper, panhuman sense.

cultural sadism An ideology and value system that assumes that male aggression, violence, and sadism are to some degree normal, if not biologically determined.

cultural scripts Normative statements shared by a social group articulating the ways in which group members should relate, act, think, and feel.

culture In the social sciences and anthropology, a collective noun for the symbolic and learned, nonbiological aspects of a human society; colloquially, a particular historical and geographic tradition, with its institutions, ideologies, and intellectual attributes (e.g., Western culture). In the Anglo-French tradition, culture is synonymous with civilization, as opposed to barbarism. In Germany, culture, the repository of artistic, literary, and individual perfection, is contrasted with civilization regarded as the process of material and industrial development that threatens culture by creating an urban mass society. In anthropology, culture refers to the unifying social characteristics or features of a people, comprising both mental and material culture, as expressed in a people's institutions, customs, mores, traditions, beliefs, religions, ideologies, norms, myths, and folklore, together with behavior as related to material objects and processes, especially those involved with spoken and/or written language, tools, techniques, and economic practices.

Although anthropologists differ in precisely how they define culture, nonetheless, a common denominator of most definitions is that culture is shared among members of a given group. The result is that members of the group are more like each other than they are like anyone else outside the culture, and this common core of similarity in beliefs, traditions, customs, and so on, represents "culture." The term is therefore not synonymous with "society," in part because societies like that of the United States can be multicultural. (Other societies, like the Basques of Spain, are monocultural.) *See also* society; culture, sexual.

In biology, the word culture is used very differently. A culture of bacteria (*qv*) is a population of the bacterium grown in the laboratory, usually in artificial or semi-artificial nutrient media. The phrase "to take a culture" means to take a sample of tissue, body fluid, or exudate and to grow from it populations (cultures) of the microorganisms it contains for antibiotic and other testing for therapeutic purposes. Some bacteria, such as *Treponema pallidum* (*qv*), the causative agent of syphilis (*qv*), cannot easily be cultured in the laboratory.

culture, sexual Aspects of a culture that pertain specifically to the sexual beliefs, institutions, and behavior of a people. Male or female culture refers to those aspects of sexual culture that men or women share only with members of their own gender. These include different aspects of, or beliefs and behaviors about, sex and gender roles, reproductive and family duties and responsibilities, and a division of labor in economic and domestic spheres of activity.

Culture is also used as a euphemism for various sexual activities, for example, French culture referring to a preference for oral-genital sex (*qv*); Greek culture, anal intercourse (*qv*) and pederasty (*qv*); English culture, spanking or bondage and dominance (*qv*) as a sexual stimulus; and Roman culture, orgies (*qv*) and swinging (*qv*).

culture bound The tendency to think that the customs and behavioral patterns prevailing in one's own society are ''natural'' and ''normal.'' *See also* ethnocentrism; stereotypes.

culturistic Developmentally induced by the scripting (*qv*) of society or culture (*qv*); the opposite of nativistic (*qv*).

cummulative connubial association In upper-class continental Portuguese families and other cultures, a pattern of consanguine (*qv*) marriages that extends the family in intrafamilial ways and closes the system to the outside community.

cunna (L.) *See* cunnus.

cunnilingam *See* cunnilingus.

cunnilingus Erotic (*qv*) stimulation of the vulvar (*qv*) area with the lips, mouth, or tongue by a male or female partner. Cunnilingus, a form of oral sex (*qv*), may or may not be continued to orgasm. It is considered by sexologists to be a normal part of love play (*qv*) but some legal and religious codes may make it unlawful or sinful, treating it as an unnatural act (*qv*) or as nonprocreative.

Cunnilingus has not been conclusively shown to transmit acquired immune deficiency syndrome (AIDS) (*qv*); however, some writers recommend the use of dental dams as a prophylaxis in all forms of oral sex. The term is derived from the Latin *cunnus* (''vulva'') and *lingus* (''tongue''). *See also* fellatio; irrumatio; oral sex; soixante-neuf.

cunnophile A person who loves to perform cunnilingus (*qv*).

cunnus (pl. cunna) (L.) The vulva (*qv*) or female genitalia (*qv*); derived from the Latin for wedge, as in cuneiform writing. It is the root of the word *cunt*.

curettage Scraping tissue from the inside wall of an organ to remove a tumor, polyp, or product of conception (*qv*). *See also* dilation and curettage abortion.

curette A scoop-shaped instrument for scraping tissues, as used in a dilation and curettage abortion (*qv*).

Cushing syndrome A condition resulting from chronic over-secretion of cortisol (*qv*) by the adrenal cortices (*qv*) or by administration of large doses of gluco-corticoids. This condition is associated with pituitary (*qv*) malfunction, adrenal hyperplasia (*qv*), or an adrenal cortical neoplasm. ACTH (*qv*) from the pituitary normally stimulates cortisol (*qv*) production with surplus cortisol operating in a negative feedback loop to halt further ACTH production. Clinical symptoms are a marked decrease in linear growth, muscular atrophy, edema, decreased glucose tolerance, flabby obesity, and a moon-shaped face. Adult symptoms include hirsutism (*qv*) and menstrual (*qv*) irregularities in women and male impotence (*qv*). Treatment involves surgical removal or radiation of the primary lesion.

custom A social behavior that has been present and functional in a group usually for several generations.

cutting A behavioral pattern involving repetitive wrist slashing frequently associated with depression, dysmenorrhea (*qv*), and gender dysphoria (*qv*). Cutting is more common in women than among males. Some psychoanalysts interpret this behavior as an autosadistic distortion of masturbatory activity that is both a defense against and a gratification of sexual desire. *See also* autoassassinatophilia; apotemnophilia; erotophonophilia; stigmatophilia; autoerotic depression.

CVAH *See* congenital virilizing adrenal hyperplasia.

CVB *See* chorionic villi biopsy.

CVS *See* chorionic villi sampling.

cyclicity *See* menstrual cycle.

cyesis A medical term for pregnancy (*qv*).

cypridophobia An intense, paranoid fear of contracting a sexually transmitted disease (*qv*). The term is derived from Cypris, a Greek name for Venus (*qv*), who was supposed to have been born on the island of Cyprus.

cyproterone (acetate) A synthetic steroid hormone (*qv*) related to progesterone (*qv*); a potent antiandrogen used to reduce the libido (*qv*) of compulsive repetitive sex offenders (*qv*) and to control premature puberty (*qv*) in male children. Cyproterone is also used to counter the effects of excess male sex hormones in women who develop facial hair and other masculine features as the result of an adrenal disorder. *See also* Depo-Provera; medroxyprogesterone acetate.

cyst A body tissue cavity lined with inflamed or degenerating tissue. *See also* fibrocystic condition.

cystic breasts *See* fibrocytitis condition.

cystic carcinoma A malignant neoplasm characterized by cysts (*qv*) or cystlike spaces; common in breast (*qv*) and ovarian (*qv*) tumors.

cystitis A common inflammation of the bladder caused by an infection, injury, irritation, or presence of a foreign body such as a catheter, calculus (stone), or tumor. So-called ''honeymoon cystitis'' may occur when a woman begins to engage in frequent sexual intercourse (*qv*).

Symptoms include the urge to urinate every few minutes and a burning sensation even though very little urine (*qv*) is passed. Blood and pus appear in the urine. Cystitis is usually not a serious problem. In mild cases, symptoms may disappear in a day or two. Drinking fluids help flush the urinary tract of bacteria if the condition is caused by bacteria. Emptying the bladder before intercourse and use of a lubricating jelly for intercourse may also be helpful. If symptoms last more than 48 hours or recur frequently, an ordinary urinalysis should be done. Most urinary tract infections respond quickly to antibiotics. *See also* candidiasis.

cystocele Protrusion or herniation of the urinary bladder through the fascia (*qv*) of the anterior vaginal wall (*qv*).

cystoscopy Use of fiber optics to examine the urinary bladder.

cystostomy Surgical implantation of a urinary drainage tube directly into the bladder, usually as a temporary bypass following genital (*qv*) surgery.

cystourethrocele Prolapse (falling or slipping out of place) of the female urethra (*qv*) and bladder.

cytogenetics The science of genetics (*qv*) devoted to the cellular constituents concerned with heredity, the chromosomes (*qv*). Clinical cytogenetics is concerned with the relations between abnormalities in chromosome number and structure with particular pathologies.

D

Dalkon shield A plastic intrauterine contraceptive device (IUD) (*qv*) shaped like a small shield. Manufactured by Robbins Pharmaceutical and marketed between 1971 and 1974, this IUD was withdrawn when it was implicated as the cause of pelvic inflammatory disease (*qv*) and spontaneous abortions (*qv*).

dammed-up libido In psychoanalytic theory (*qv*), the frustration or inhibition of the pleasure or sexual drive (*qv*) by the lack of opportunity or suitable partners, the inability to respond normally to sexual stimuli or to achieve orgasm (*qv*), or by parental, religious, or societal pressures.

danazol A synthetic androgen (*qv*) used in treatment of endometriosis (*qv*). This drug suppresses the release of pituitary gonadotropins (*qv*) and thus also suppresses the menstrual cycle (*qv*) for several months. *Trade name*: Danocrine.

Danocrine *See* danazol.

Daoism *See* Taoism.

dartos muscles A layer of loosely organized, involuntary muscle fibers immediately beneath the skin of the scrotum (*qv*). Also known as *tunica dartos*. This muscle reacts to temperature and tactile stimulation to maintain the proper temperature for sperm (*qv*) production by drawing the scrotum closer to the body wall.

dasypygal Having hairy buttocks (*qv*).

date *See* dating.

date rape The use of psychological and/or physical coercion to pressure or force an unwilling partner into engaging in sexual intimacies and/or intercourse (*qv*) in a relationship where the couple know each other or are dating (*qv*). Date rape has no legal or statutory definition per se; accordingly, if a woman's accusation of date or acquaintance rape is brought to the attention of the authorities, the accusation will be treated as one of rape (*qv*) itself. In the literature, the terms date rape and acquaintance rape are used in a variety of ways by researchers and others concerned with sexual ethics and women's rights and issues.

Date rape may be termed acquaintance rape if it is perpetrated by a classmate, teacher, neighbor, coworker, or casual friend, in contrast to stranger rape, where the rapist and victim are not acquainted. The definition of date rape can be both broader and narrower than the definition of forcible rape involving strangers. It is narrower because it is situation-specific, occurring in the social context of dating and therefore in a special type of relationship. The definition is broader because the force is less often physical than emotional, persuasive, seductive, and manipulative. Thus, date rape is not defined solely as unwanted sexual intercourse with an acquaintance but may also incorporate aspects of forcible rape, including behavior and motives of anger, control, power, and degradation.

In date rape, individual motivations and the interpretations of these are extremely complex because of the conscious and unconscious desires of both parties at the time of the incident. The motivations of the perpetrator may range from a need to control, dominate, and degrade the victim, through sexual desire and arousal, to the need to conciliate and please the partner. After the assault, faulty memories, rationalizations, and, at times, mendacious reconstructions and reinterpretations affect the understanding of what happened and why it happened. After the assault, the victim may also be influenced by the definitions, ideologies and interpretations of peers and counselors.

Deeper motivations are often subconscious or unconscious, such as feeling anger, seeking power, or the sense of privilege—"I paid, I have a right to expect it." These deeper motivations of the perpetrator often differ from the admitted motivations (e.g., of being aroused and not being able to stop). The victim's interpretation at the time of the incident and afterward also vary widely. The victim may cooperate because he or she perceives the risk of physical harm, because of an internalized desire for dominance by the partner, or an inability to admit a partially formed desire for intercourse. The victim may also cooperate because the incident is not perceived as an assault at the time or out of a need to be accepted or liked.

The victim's postrape reinterpretation of her or his motivations and of the perpetrator's motives may lead the victim to accept full responsibility for the assault or to blame it all on the other person. A victim's terrified and upset response to a date rape may become a later recognition that the subjugation and assault was, in fact, pleasurable. This reinterpretation may lead to seeking similar reenactments with a consenting partner in a sadomasochistic-like scenario. Alternatively, the victim may use this as a growth experience, becoming aware that sexuality and intimacy require clear and frequent communication as well as self-awareness and assertiveness.

The perpetrator's interpretations and reinterpretations are also complex. The perpetrator may feel so guilt-ridden by accepting full blame for the incident that he or she experiences a complete aversion to any further sexual intimacy. Or the perpetrator may totally deny using any force or coercion and blame the incident on the victim.

The inability or failure to communicate one's actual desires and current limits on intimacy in the dating situation are an important factor in date rape. Alcohol and drug use are common factors in date rape. Awareness of these factors is an important element in date rape prevention.

In studies of college men and women, 20 to 25 percent of the males have admitted to sexual aggression in a dating situation, and half to four-fifths of the college women report being victims of such aggression. Increasing evidence suggests that date rape perpetrated by a female on a male partner is not uncommon.

The trauma of date rape can be as devastating as that of stranger rape, although some have come to believe that rapelike interactions are a normal part of dating and are not traumatic. Because of the range of reactions and the prevalence of date rape, especially on college campuses, it is important for educational and therapeutic programs to include discussions, prevention programs, and services for persons involved in such situations.

dating (n. date) Colloquially, a date is an appointment to meet someone at a specific time and place, but it can also refer to the individual whom one is meeting. Dating refers to the American custom of (originally heterosexual [*qv*]) courtship (*qv*) in which a male and female meet each other with various social, emotional, and sexual purposes in mind. Dating could (and can) be casual and nonsexual (''Platonic''), in which the two people have no long-term plans for a relationship with each other, or serious or ''heavy,'' in which an ongoing sexual and emotional relationship is already established. As a form of courtship, dating provides time for the two people (heterosexual or homosexual [*qv*]) to be with each other while they learn about each other and assess each other's potential for a long-term relationship or even marriage.

In the culture of heterosexual dating that evolved particularly on college campuses between World Wars I and II, and which persisted (and, in some places, continues to persist) after World War II, dating consisted of a series of stages graded according to the level of emotional and sexual intimacy. Casual dating became serious dating as the couple became sexually and emotionally involved and when they began tentatively to make public commitments toward one another by ''going steady.'' Thereafter, the young woman was ''pinned'': The young man gave her his fraternity pin or athletic letter, jacket, or sweater to wear as an emblem of his affection and the seriousness of his purpose toward her (a later generation of critics would say as an emblem of his social and sexual ownership of her). Next was the engagement, with a formal announcement, followed by the wedding. The sequence was (and is) highly ritualized, with subtle and complex tests made at each step concerning how to proceed next.

Following the Korean War, and, especially, following the sexual revolution of the 1960s, this complex dating scene broke down on many college campuses, though it is still retained on conservative campuses in the South. With the widespread availability of contraceptives (*see* contraception) and the emergence of sexually egalitarian ideologies, dating altered considerably and the strict progression of dating through a graded and carefully tested series of stages essentially disappeared on campuses. Furthermore, as increasing numbers of older people became divorced, their strategies for finding mates and partners did not simply recreate the earlier model of dating just described. These factors worked together to create the singles scene (*qv*) to replace the dating and marriage scene characteristic of the earlier part of this century in America. Moreover, the increased openness of homosexual courtship has resulted in some of the old patterns of dating being modified or discarded by various sexual minority (*qv*) groups.

In consequence, today the concept of dating has a somewhat old-fashioned flavor to it, and the word is not as widely used as it once was. For many people, *dating* evokes the days of acutely embarrassed adolescence together with a sense that old-fashioned dating is male chauvinist (*see* chauvinism, male) or, at least, does not treat the woman as an equal partner. However, no term has arisen to replace the word dating, with the possible exception of "getting together" or "seeing each other." The very blandness of these terms belies their emotional, sexual, and symbolic complexities, in which people still try to meet, assess each others' strengths and weaknesses, and form long-term relationships.

The term *dating* is an excellent example of how a word can attain highly specialized meanings and then fall out of use when the customs that underlie it fadeaway. Resource: B. L. Bailey, *From Front Porch to Back Seat: Courtship in Twentieth-Century America* (Baltimore: Johns Hopkins University Press, 1988).

dating service A business established to put single persons in contact with suitable partners for dating (*qv*), courtship (*qv*), and marriage (*qv*). Dating services may use computerized personal profiles or personal interviews and arranged introductions to match suitable couples. Others services provide videotaped interviews and leave to the individual the selection of persons who seem suitable and interesting as prospective partners. *See also* marriage broker; schadchen.

Daughters of Bilitis A lesbian (*qv*) organization founded by Del Martin and Phyllis Lyon in 1955 in San Francisco; named for the recipient of love letters from the Greek poet Sappho. *See also* Bilitis; Mattachine Society.

D&C Dilation and curettage (*qv*).

D&E Dilation and evacuation (*qv*).

de-analize In psychoanalytic theory (*qv*), the transference of sexual impulses from the anal (*qv*) region to other excretory or filth-related outlets, such as coprophilia (*qv*), finger painting, smearing mud, and telling of obscene (*qv*) jokes, or to the reverse, obsessive cleanliness.

debauch, to To seduce (*qv*) a person into sexual promiscuity (*qv*); to deflower (*qv*) a virgin (*qv*).

debauchery A derogatory term for intemperate and excessive indulgence in sexual and sensual pleasures, especially participation in sexual orgies (*qv*) or seduction (*qv*) of the young.

decidua (L.) The uterine endometrial tissues shed in the menses (*qv*) or afterbirth (*qv*). The decidua basalis is the uterine endometrium (*qv*), which becomes the maternal half of the placenta (*qv*). The decidua capsularis is the combined amnion (*qv*), chorion (*qv*), and uterine endometrium surrounding the developing embryo (*qv*) and fetus (*qv*) prior to its fusion with the decidua parietalis. The decidua parietalis is the inner lining of the uterine cavity outside the placental area, which fuses with the decidua capsularis (*qv*) in later pregnancy (*qv*). The combined decidua basalis and capsularis are sometimes referred to as the decidua vera.

de Clerambault's syndrome *See* Clerambault-Kandisky syndrome.

decriminalization The abolition or revocation of criminal penalties for an activity previously defined as illegal. Decriminalization of prostitution (*qv*), for instance, does not legally recognize or legitimize the behavior nor does it set up regulatory mechanisms under the law, but it illuminates legal penalties for prostitution. *See also* legalization; consenting adult laws.

deep fascia of the penis *See* Buck's fascia.

deep kiss An open-mouth kiss (*qv*) with tongue contact and caressing of the inside of the mouth; colloquially, a French or soul kiss.

deerotization In psychoanalytic theory (*qv*), the reduction, elimination, or sublimation of one's pleasure drive or libido (*qv*). Also known as delibidinalization and desexualization.

defeminization In embryology, a term referring to aspects of the development of a genetically male embryo into an anatomically male fetus (*qv*). In mammals, development of the masculine phenotype (*qv*) requires two conceptually and experimentally distinct processes, called defeminization and masculinization (*qv*). Defeminization refers to the reduction or elimination of embryonic structures that would otherwise develop into components of the female sexual and reproductive systems. Simultaneous with defeminization, masculinization causes the development of components of the male sexual and reproductive system. In the absence of defeminization, a genetic male would possess some internal structures of both male and female. Defeminization also refers to effects, some only hypothetical, that affect the developing brain and that, for instance, eliminate the capacity for cyclic release of luteinizing hormone releasing factor (*qv*). These processes are often described metaphorically by speaking of a basic Eve Plan (or principle) (*qv*) that in male embryos is surplanted by the Adam Plan (*qv*) or principle.

Anatomically the male fetus is defeminized through the action of Mullerian inhibiting substance (*qv*), which directs degeneration of the Mullerian ducts (*qv*). Elimination of the natural tendency of the hypothalamus (*qv*) to be programmed for a luteinizing hormone (*qv*) surge pattern and a cyclic production of gonadotropic releasing hormones (*qv*) and low proceptivity are two known outcomes of neural defeminization. The control for defeminization of the brain during prenatal life is not known. *See also* masculinization; feminization; and demasculinization.

defense mechanism A subconscious method of coping with unacceptable or negative emotions, knowledge, attitudes, or behavior. A defense mechanism is used to avoid recognizing personal motives or characteristics that might lead to anxiety, guilt, or lowered self-esteem.

deferent duct *See* ductus deferens.

deficiency love Abraham Maslow's term for a type of love between two people in which one partner depends on the other to fulfill his or her needs.

definition A statement or explanation of what a thing is. A *nominal definition* is an agreement to use a particular word or words to describe something or a phenomenon; for instance, at first French and American scientists named the virus causing acquired immune deficiency syndrome (*qv*), respectively, LAV and HTLV-III, before agreeing to a compromise name, HTLV-III/LAV, and finally the simpler HIV (human immunodeficiency virus) (*qv*). An *operational definition* asserts the specific measurements used in a measurement, as when Alfred Kinsey (*qv*) used the relative proportions of homosexual (*qv*) and heterosexual (*qv*) fantasies and sexual experiences to orgasm (*qv*) to define homosexual, bisexual (*qv*), and heterosexual orientations in the Kinsey Six Scale (*qv*). A *real definition* attempts to describe the essence or real nature of a phenomenon or thing in a way that has truth values.

defloration (V. to deflower) The rupture of a virgin's (*qv*) hymen (*qv*), or "flower," through sexual intercourse (*qv*) or by another means. Ritual or ceremonial defloration is an important pubertal (*qv*) or marital ritual in many cultures. In the Middle Ages, defloration of the bride was a prerogative reserved to the lord of the manor or prince. Canonically, this right was termed *jus primae noctis* (*qv*); in French, *droit du seigneur* (*qv*).

In cultures where virginity is sacred, it is the god, operating through a priest, who is believed to deflower the maidens. In Indonesian and South American cultures, finger defloration is performed on infant girls. In India, ceremonial defloration is usually done by squatting on a lingam (*qv*) or stone penis symbolizing Shiva, the god of sex and reproduction. In African and near East cultures where female circumcision (*qv*) is practiced, defloration may be done by an older female, a tribal leader, or female relatives of the groom to document the virginity of the bride.

degeneracy theory The dogma that all diseases are caused by the loss of semen (*qv*) or other vital fluids. In the Middle Ages, when medical knowledge about diseases was still backward, a belief in demon possession was used to explain all human afflictions, including epidemics and plagues. Epidemics were God's punishment for heresy and a failure to accept Christianity. The infamous *Malleus Maleficarum* (*qv*) detailed ways to find, torture, and dispose of witches. A study of witchcraft, which included sexual relations (*qv*) with demons, incubi (*qv*), and succubi (*qv*), revealed how one could be the victim of demons even without copulating (*qv*) with them. Demons collected semen from masturbation (*qv*) and nocturnal emissions (*qv*) and used it to create new bodies for themselves. In the demon-possession theory, sexuality, women, and illness were causally linked.

In the 1600s, this demon-possession theory was seriously challenged by new theories about the nature and transmission of diseases. However, the new medical knowledge could not yet satisfactorily explain disease as demon possession had. The gap was filled in the 1750s when Simon André Tissot (*qv*) revived and popularized the theory that loss of semen (vital body fluid) could explain all disease. Tissot claimed that all illnesses, diseases, and even death itself were due to the degeneracy caused by loss of semen: "The symptoms which supervene in females, are explained like those in men. The secretion which they lose, being less valuable and less matured than the semen of the male, its loss does not enfeeble so promptly, but when they indulge in it to excess, as their nervous system is naturally weaker and more disposed to spasms, the symptoms are more violent" (Source: J. Money, *Destroying Angel*, p. 52). Although the loss of semen in masturbation was seen as much more dangerous than loss of semen in intercourse, any loss of semen or vital fluids was dangerous. All diseases could be remedied by abstinence (*qv*) from sex, exercises, and proper nutrition. *See also* Graham, Sylvester; Kellogg, John.

Although fully debunked by the germ theory of disease, degeneracy theory still plays an influential role in modern thinking about sexuality. Resource:

J. Money, *The Destroying Angel: Sex, Fitness and Food in the Legacy of Degeneracy Theory, Graham Crackers, Kellogg's Corn Flakes and American Health History* (Buffalo: Prometheus Books, 1985).

degenerate A derogatory and colloquial term for a person who is believed to be involved in socially undesirable or illegal sexual activity; a person of depraved or low moral standards; often applied to rapists (*qv*) or sodomists (*qv*).

dehydroisoandrosterone A very low potency androgen (*qv*) produced almost entirely by the adrenal cortices (*qv*). Promoted as an aphrodisiac (*qv*), its sale for this purpose has been prohibited by the Food and Drug Administration.

delayed ejaculation *See* retarded ejaculation; inhibited male orgasm; orgasmic dysfunction.

delayed male puberty The failure of pituitary (*qv*) hormones (*qv*) to trigger the onset of puberty (*qv*) after age 16, the upper limit for the normal onset of puberty. Although growth and height may be normal, the genitalia (*qv*) remain juvenile.

delay of gratification In psychoanalytic theory (*qv*), the ability to reduce or sublimate one's instinctual drive for pleasure and tolerate the frustration and tension coming from unsatisfied libidinal needs, especially sexual needs.

DelCastillo syndrome Congenital (*qv*) absence of the germinal cells (*qv*) and epithelium in the testes (*qv*). In this condition, no viable sperm (*qv*) are produced, although Sertoli cells (*qv*) are present and functioning normally.

delibidinalization In psychoanalytic theory (*qv*), the elimination or sublimation of one's pleasure drive or libido (*qv*). Also known as deerotization (*qv*) and desexualization (*qv*).

Delilah syndrome A behavioral pattern in which a female is motivated by a desire to control and manipulate men and seeks multiple partners to exercise this desire.

delivery The birth (*qv*), or delivery, of a child; parturition (*qv*). *See also* labor.

delusional jealousy A paranoid form of jealousy (*qv*) in which one's partner is constantly watched for any possible sign of infidelity (*qv*). Innocent coincidences are interpreted in the worst light, and evidence of infidelity may be manufactured to support the paranoid suspicion of infidelity.

demasculinization The prenatal (*qv*) developmental process in which anatomical and/or neurological masculinization (*qv*) is inhibited or suppressed. Developmentally the female fetus (*qv*) is normally demasculinized through the absence of threshold levels of androgens (*qv*), which allows degeneration of the Wolffian or mesonephric ducts (*qv*). *See also* masculinization; feminization; defeminization.

dementia paralytica *See* paresis; syphilis.

demimonde (Fr.) The so-called half-world or twilight zone of the Parisian cafés and music halls between 1880 and 1900, in which women provided companionship and excitement for business men and men of society without the stigma of engaging in prostitution (*qv*); a woman of dubious reputation and sexual virtue.

demivierge (Fr.) A technical virgin (*qv*) who has not had penile-vaginal intercourse (*qv*), but who may have engaged in any other type of sexual activity (*qv*), including mutual masturbation (*qv*), oral sex (*qv*), and petting (*qv*) to orgasm (*qv*).

denidation The shedding or sloughing off of the superficial endometrial (*qv*) lining of the uterus (*qv*) during menstruation (*qv*).

denier In a developmental-descriptive context, an individual who has learned to cope with unresolved personality conflicts by denying them instead of accepting them. In the case of an unresolved inadequate personality (*qv*), the individual may cope by overcompensating and denying his or her perceived inadequacy, using anger and rage-motivated psychological fear and physical force to regain control over his or her life in antisocial behavior. In the case of an unresolved inadequate personality combined with an unresolved early sexual trauma (*qv*), the individual may cope by denial, using anger-motivated psychological terror and physical force to regain control in antisocial behaviors such as sadistic sexual murder, rape (*qv*), anger-motivated exhibitionism (*qv*), "passive" homosexuality (*qv*), voyeurism (*qv*), or obscene phone calls (*qv*) accompanied by rape fantasies (*qv*).

The denier personality satisfies his or her need for acceptance by others by degrading and forcing the victim to engage in unacceptable behaviors. *See also* acceptor; inadequate personality; active sexual trauma; passive sexual trauma.

Denman's spontaneous version or evolution The natural, unassisted turning of the full-term (*qv*) fetus (*qv*) from a transverse to a cephalic presentation (*qv*) so that the head is closest to the uterine cervix (*qv*).

dental dam A sheet of thin latex, about 4 inches square, used by dentists to isolate a tooth during a root canal or other operation. Use of a dental dam during cunnilingus (*qv*) is recommended by some epidemeologists and experts of acquired immune deficiency syndrome (*qv*) as a safer sex (*qv*) practice to reduce the risk of transmitting the HIV-I virus (*qv*).

deorality Transfer of the pleasure and satisfaction originally associated with the mouth to another part of the body or another activity; for example, the pleasure and satisfaction associated with breast feeding (*qv*) may be derived, later in life, from a spouse who represents a maternal figure.

deoxycorticosterone acetate A mineralocorticoid (*qv*) hormone (*qv*) used in treatment of congenital adrenal hyperplasia (*qv*).

deoxyribonucleic acid (DNA) A highly polymerized molecule found in most cells that is the carrier of genetic information in all organisms except a few viruses. In higher organisms, DNA is found primarily in the chromosomes (*qv*), where it constitutes the genetic material, in other words, the genes (*qv*). Structurally, DNA consists of two long molecular strands twisted around each other in a double helix, like a twisted ladder. The rungs of the ladder are composed of molecules called nucleotides, whose physical arrangement encodes the genetic information, as follows.

There are four types of nucleotide in DNA, known as adenosine (A), cytidine (C), guanidine (G), and thymidine (T). Normally, these pair up across the ladder as AT and CG. However, if one examines the sequence of A, C, G, and T molecules up and down the length of the DNA molecule, one finds that the order of these molecules determines, in extremely complex ways, the structure of other molecules in the cell. These sequences of the four nucleotides lengthwise along the DNA molecule are called the genes. Furthermore, DNA possesses the profoundly important capacity to replicate itself. When it does so, the newly synthesized DNA molecule contains an exact replica of the nucleotide sequence of the original DNA molecule, accounting for the capacity of genes to reproduce themselves.

During chromosome division and distribution in mitosis (*qv*) and meiosis (*qv*), the replicated DNA—and therefore the genes—are distributed to offspring cells in the organism, including the egg and sperm (*qv*). When, in turn, the egg is fertilized (*qv*) by the sperm, the newly fertilized zygote (*qv*) now contains the genes carried by the egg itself plus those of the sperm. This process, accomplished during sexual reproduction, accounts for the genetic composition of the new organism. Thus, if one looks at sexuality from the viewpoint of the DNA molecule, sexual behavior would appear to be only an extremely complex way of making sure that the self-replicating DNA can transmit itself from one generation to the next. Such a viewpoint is sometimes called reductionist because if one looks at the DNA molecule from the viewpoint of the sexually behaving organism, the transmission of the DNA seems to be a minor consequence of sexual love and intimacy. However, in a sense, each viewpoint has some truth, though both together make a more complete picture of the entirety of sexuality and its biological consequences. *See also* nature/nurture debate.

dependent variable In scientific research, a general term for any measured response or reaction of experimental subjects to experimental treatment(s) or intervention(s). Dependent variables are so named because they are hypothesized to depend on changes in specific factors or variables controlled by the experimenter: the so-called independent (or experimental) variables (*qv*) or the research procedure.

depersonalization disorder A feeling of alienation, strangeness, and unreality that leads to a dreamlike state pervading the consciousness. A person with a depersonalization disorder may feel like an observer of his or her own body, viewing otherwise important events with detachment and equanimity. *See also* spectatoring. This reaction is common in various forms of schizophrenia and in severe depression.

depilation (depilatory) The removal or extraction of hair from the body. Such removal may be temporary by waxing or chemical means, or permanent by electrolysis, which destroys the hair follicles.

Depo-Provera Trademark for medroxyprogesterone acetate (*qv*), a progestin-like (qv) and antiandrogenic (*qv*) hormone, Depo-Provera is used to help compulsive repetitive sex offenders (*qv*) gain self-control over their sexuoerotic (*qv*) behaviors and as an injectable contraceptive (*qv*) to suppress ovulation (*qv*) in Third World nations. Because its possible side effects include permanent infertility (*qv*), irregular bleeding, and possibly cancer, the Food and Drug Administration has not approved it for contraceptive use in the United States.

deprivational homosexuality Situational homosexual (*qv*) relations prompted by the unavailability of partners of the other sex. *See also* facultative homosexuality; homoerotic.

dermatitis medicamentosa (L.) A superficial skin infection of the scrotum (*qv*) induced by an allergic reaction to a medication.

dermatitis venenata (L.) A superficial scrotal (*qv*) skin infection caused by reaction to an irritant such as fabric dyes in underclothing.

dermatome In embryonic (*qv*) development, that portion of the mesodermal layer that develops into the dermal layers of the skin, as opposed to the sclerotome, which gives rise to the skeleton, and the myotome, which produces muscles. Dermatome may also refer to an area on the surface of the body innervated by nerve fibers from a single spinal root.

dermatomycosis (L.) A superficial infection of the skin, usually in the groin area or feet, caused by one of several fungi.

dermoid cyst A teratoma (*qv*) or tumor, usually benign, consisting of assorted partially differentiated embryonic tissues, usually skin, hair, sweat glands, and bits of cartilage, bone, and teeth. About 10 percent of all ovarian (*qv*) tumors are dermoid cysts. They may also occur in the thyroid and fallopian tube (*qv*). Some dermoid cysts may result from an unfertilized ovum (*qv*) that undergoes spontaneous parthenogenesis (*qv*).

DES *See* diethylstilbesterol.

De Sade, Marquis Donatien-Alphonse-François (1740–1814) A Provençal noble and aristocratic Parisian, de Sade's life revolved around sexual excitement and pleasure achieved by inflicting pain and torture on his victims. Starting at age 26, de Sade sought out prostitutes (*qv*), whom he whipped, knifed, and half-poisoned with overdoses of Spanish fly (*qv*). He progressed to abusing children of both sexes and to orgies (*qv*) focused on sexual sadism (*qv*). Between 1777 and 1790, he spent much of his time in the Bastille and in an asylum for the insane. His sadistic practices and fantasies are detailed in several books, the best known being *120 Days of Sodom*, *Justine*, and *Juliette*. Despite his brutality, he was widely admired by the romantics, surrealists, Baudelaire, Lamartine, Swinburne, Nietzsche, Cocteau, and others who made his idée fixe of the incorrigibly virtuous maiden being tortured a common theme in fiction.

descensus (L.) The descent of the testes (*qv*) into the scrotum (*qv*) around the time of birth (*qv*); the descent of the uterus (*qv*) from the false into the true pelvic cavity after the cessation of effective sexual stimulation.

descent group Any social group in which membership depends on common descent from a real or mythical ancestor. A lineage is a unilineal descent group in which membership rests either on patrilineal descent, through male ancestors only, or on matrineal descent, through female ancestors only. In *cognatic descent*, any combination of male or female linkage confers group membership. In *totemic descent*, membership is based on descent from a mythic ancestor, periodically affirmed and reinforced by common rituals. Resource: R. M. Keesing, *Kin Groups and Social Structure* (New York: Holt, Rinehart & Winston, 1975).

desensitization, systematic A technique used in behavioral therapy (*qv*) and sexuality education in which the person is exposed to a series of anxiety-producing stimuli of increasing intensity until the stimuli no longer elicit the initial response of fear or rejection. *See also* Sexual Attitudes Reassessment workshop.

desertion The act of abandonment (*qv*) whereby a spouse leaves his or her partner without justification or legal separation (*qv*).

desexualization Removing sexual significance from an object or activity; in psychoanalytic theory (*qv*), the reduction, elimination, or sublimation of one's pleasure drive or libido (*qv*). Also known as deerotization (*qv*) and delibidinalization (*qv*).

desidua *See* decidua.

desire phase The first of three general divisions of the sexual response cycle (*qv*) in which the desire for sexual activity (*qv*) increases, leading to the physiological changes of sexual arousal (*qv*) in the excitement phase (*qv*) and possible culmination in orgasm (*qv*). The desire phase was suggested by sex therapist Helen Singer Kaplan as a prelude to the four stages of the physiological sexual response cycle proposed by William Masters and Virginia Johnson Masters. Resource: H. S. Kaplan, *Disorders of Sexual Desire and Other Concepts and Techniques in Sex Therapy* (New York: Bruner/Mazel, 1979). *See also* desire phase dysfunction; excitement phase; plateau phase; orgasmic phase; resolution phase.

desire phase dysfunction Any conflict, abnormal function, or lack of normal function in the proceptive phase (*qv*) of erotosexual (*qv*) response that inhibits and affects the desire for sexual intimacy (*qv*) and activity (*qv*). Three general types of desire phase dysfunction are sexual aversion (*qv*), lack of sexual desire (*qv*), and sexual desire conflict (*qv*). In sexual aversion, an emotionally based anxiety is expressed in sweating and trembling whenever the person is faced with the possibility of sexual intimacy. A lack of sexual desire in one partner or conflicting levels in the amount of sexual intimacy desired can cause tensions within an intimate relationship. The origin of desire phase dysfunction may be either psychogenic or organic.

detumescence The loss of vasocongestion (*qv*) and the return of an erect penis (*qv*) or clitoris (*qv*) to the flaccid, unaroused state. While cessation of sexual stimuli or failure to reach orgasm (*qv*) results in rapid detumescence of the penis within a few minutes, clitoral detumescence may be somewhat slower.

deuterophallic phase A psychoanalytic (*qv*) distinction in the phallic phase (*qv*) of psychosexual development (*qv*) in which the child, usually between ages 3 and 7 years, first suspects that males and female have different genitals (*qv*).

deviance (n. deviate, adj. deviant) A behavior, idea, or attitude, that is not in conformity with what is considered normal, standard, or ideal according to some authority or consensus. In criminology, deviance is narrowly defined as an infraction of legal norms. A more common broader usage refers to any deviation from a social norm. Until recently, deviant was also a technical and common term for paraphilic (*qv*) behavior. In *Models of Madness, Models of Medicine*

(New York: Macmillan, 1974), M. Siegler and H. Osmond suggest five models of sexual deviance: (1) a religious model in which demonic possession or temptation leads to a sin that must be confessed, repented, and exorcised by a religious authority in order for the deviant to be saved; (2) a legal model in which the deviant's criminal behavior is punished and the criminal person rehabilitated by civil authorities if proved guilty; (3) a medical model in which an illness, due to some known or unknown natural cause, is treated by a physician to restore health to the sick person; (4) a psychoanalytic (*qv*) model in which arrested or impaired psychosexual development (*qv*) that has not been faced and resolved is symbolically acted out unconsciously in emotionally disturbed ways; and (5) a labeling model in which a group that cannot tolerate differences labels as criminal or sick those whose behavior differs from theirs, punishing the deviant, who has no rights. Resources: D. Downes and P. Rock, *Understanding Deviance* (Oxford: Oxford University Press, 1982); I. Taylor, P. Walton and J. Young, *The New Criminology: For a Social Theory of Deviance* (London: Routledge & Kegan Paul, 1973).

devitalized relationship A marriage (*qv*) or sexual relationship (*qv*) that has become increasingly passive. The transition from the intensity of limerence (*qv*) to a more down-to-earth, less sexual, and more routine commitment is a normal evolution in a relationship. However, some relations go beyond this natural transition as the partners drift away from each other. This dyadic shift may result from pregnancies (*qv*) and parental commitments, career involvements, or the loss of privacy in the home. The change may or may not be acceptable to the partners.

dexamethasone A synthetic, biologically very active adrenocortical hormone (*qv*), resembling cortisol (*qv*), used to suppress the pituitary's (*qv*) release of adrenocorticotrophic hormone and to control premature puberty (*qv*) in males.

DHEA *See* dehydroepiandrosterone.

DHT deficiency syndrome (dihydrotestosterone deficiency, 5-alpha-reductase deficiency) A form of pseudohermaphroditism (*qv*) resulting from a genetic mutation that creates a deficiency of the enzyme delta-4-steroid-5-alpha steroid reductase needed to convert testosterone (*qv*) into dihydrotestosterone (DHT), which will then trigger external male development. Chromosomally and gonadally, affected individuals are male. The affected newborn (*qv*) has ambiguous external sexual anatomy with a clitoral-like phallus (*qv*), a more or less fused scrotal-like labia (*qv*), and testes (*qv*) either in the inguinal canal of the pelvic girdle or in the labioscrotal folds (*qv*). Internal duct differentiation is normally male. The affected infant is usually assigned and raised as a female. However, the surge of pubertal testosterone in such individuals may be sufficient to trigger partial virilization (*qv*) with the clitoral-like phallus developing into a small penis and development of weak male secondary sex characteristics (*qv*). In the small rural village of Salinas in the Dominican Republic where most cases have been reported, the ''conversion'' of a daughter into a son is acceptable because of the strong patriarchal (*qv*) tradition, although the affected children are subject to some ridicule being referred to as *guevote* ("penis at 12") or *machihembra* ("first woman, then man"). When the condition occurs in more developed countries, the result is less likely to be accommodated by the family and the individual without severe psychological trauma. In cases where DHT-deficient children have been clinically and socially raised and conditioned as girls from birth onward with surgical feminization (*qv*), they become women with a heterosexual (*qv*) orientation as a woman, despite chromosomal and gonadal status as male. The extent of pubertal adjustment is hotly debated. Also known as girl-boy syndrome.

diabetic vulvitis An inflammation of the vulva (*qv*) common in women with diabetes. The high sugar content of diabetic urine promotes the excess growth of the yeast Candida (*qv*).

Diagnostic and Statistical Manual of Mental Disorders (DSM, DSM-III) A manual published by the American Psychiatric Association standardizing and describing mental and emotional disorders.

Diana complex A psychiatric term referring to any deep-seated, repressed desire of a woman to be a man. The usage is derived from the masculine role of the Roman goddess of hunting, Diana. *See also* transsexual.

diaphragm (vaginal) A dome-shaped latex cup with a flexible spring steel rim inserted into the vaginal canal (*qv*) to cover the cervix (*qv*) and serve as a contraceptive (*qv*) barrier against sperm (*qv*). Since diaphragms are available with diameters between 5 1/2 and 10 centimeters, fitting for the appropriate size is necessary. The optimal size may change following childbirth (*qv*), or significant weight loss or gain. The diaphragm is inserted up to 2 hours before intercourse (*qv*) and left undisturbed for 6 to 8 hours afterward. It should then be washed, dried, and dusted with cornstarch for storage. Effectiveness of the diaphragm is increased when it is used with a spermicidal (*qv*) jelly or cream.

dichorial twins Dizygotic twins (*qv*), each of which has its own chorionic sac (*qv*).

dichoric A species in which individuals are sexually dimorphic, males with testes or females with ovaries, or in which individuals are functional hermaphrodites (*qv*) with both ovaries and testes. *See also* monochoric.

Dickinson, Robert Latou (1861–1950) A gynecologist (*qv*) who pioneered the scientific study of human sexuality, marital sex, contraception (*qv*), and gynecology with his many books, over 200 research papers and reports on obstetrics (*qv*), diseases of women, and sex problems. In 1895, he coedited the *American Text Book on Obstetrics*. His major writings include *A Thousand Marriages* (1931), *Control of Conception* (1931–1938), *Atlas of Human Sex Anatomy* (1933), *The Single Woman, Her Sex Education* (1933), *Sex Variants* (1941), *Birth Atlas* (1941), *Techniques of Conception Control* (1941), and *Human Sterilization* (1950).

Dick-Read, Grantly (1890–1959) An English obstetrician (*qv*) famous for his books, lecturing, and promotion of natural childbirth (*qv*). His major books were *Natural Childbirth* (1933), *Childbirth Without Fear* (1944), *Birth of a Child* (1947), *Introduction to Motherhood* (1951), *No Time for Fear* (1955), and *Antenatal Illustrated* (1955). He is recognized for introducing prepared or natural childbirth to the United States.

didym- A combining form referring to the testes (*qv*).

didymus A combining form meaning a pair of similar structures (e.g., para- or epididymis, alongside or on top of the paired testes [*qv*]).

diecious (dioecious) Having male and female reproductive systems in two different individuals; as opposed to monecious or hermaphroditic (*qv*), in which both male and female reproductive systems occur in the same individual.

diestrus In animals with an estrous (*qv*) rather than menstrual (*qv*) cycle, a brief period of sexual quiescence in females before they come into estrus (*qv*), or sexual heat.

diethylstilbesterol (DES) A biologically active, synthetic female sex hormone (*qv*). Currently DES is used as an early abortifacient (*qv*) or "morning-after" pill. Between 1941 and 1971, 3 million to 6 million American women were given this drug to prevent spontaneous abortions (*qv*). DES is now known to increase the risk of vaginal and cervical cancer (*qv*), problem pregnancies (*qv*), and structural changes in the cervix (*qv*) and uterus (*qv*) in daughters born to mothers who used DES during pregnancy. Some studies suggest there may also be an increased incidence of breast (*qv*), uterine (*qv*), and ovarian (*qv*) cancer. One in 700 to 7,000 women experiences such side effects. For the sons of DES mothers, side effects include underdeveloped testes (*qv*), benign cysts (*qv*) on the epididymis (*qv*), undescended testes (*qv*), and abnormal semen (*qv*). Information on DES, which was prescribed under a variety of trade names, is available from: DES Action, Long Island Jewish Hospital, New Hyde Park, NY 11040.

differential socialization The dimorphic (*qv*) or gender-specific ways in which parents and other adults respond differently to boys and girls and reward and reinforce gender-specific behavior for the two sexes. *See also* scripting; sex stereotype; gender role; gender role scripting.

dihydrotestosterone (DHT) A powerful androgenic (*qv*) hormone (*qv*) converted from testosterone (*qv*) in peripheral target cells through the enzymatic action of 5-alpha-reductase. In embryonic development, DHT controls differentiation of external male genitalia (*qv*). *See also* testosterone; DHT deficiency syndrome.

dilation Enlarging a passageway or cavity, such as the enlargement of the cervical opening during childbirth (*qv*).

dilation and curettage (D&C) An abortion (*qv*) method involving dilation of the uterine cervix (*qv*) and scraping of the uterine endometrial wall (*qv*). D&C is also used for menstrual (*qv*) and uterine problems, to remove uterine tumors, and to remove placental fragments following delivery (*qv*) or an incomplete abortion (*qv*). Also known as vacuum curettage.

dilation and evacuation (D&E) A combination of vacuum curettage or modified endometrial aspiration (menstrual extraction) (*qv*) and cervical dilation (*qv*) with curettage (*qv*), used in second-trimester (*qv*) abortions (*qv*). Also known as vacuum aspiration.

dilators A series of graduated plastic or vinyl artificial penises (*qv*) used in behavioral modification exercises (*qv*) to overcome the psychological fears of vaginal (*qv*) penetration. *See also* vaginismus. Dilators are also used to enlarge the cervix (*qv*) and allow for a dilation and curettage procedure (*qv*).

dildo An artificial penis (*qv*), usually made of rubber or soft plastic, used in autoerotic masturbation (*qv*) by women or men and by lesbian (*qv*) or heterosexual (*qv*) women who wish to play the insertor role. The term may be derived from *diletto*, the Italian word for ''delight.''

dimorphism Characterized by having two forms or manifestations within the same species (e.g., distinct male and female forms, and masculine and feminine behaviors). *See also* diecious.

dinoprost An abortion (*qv*)-causing prostaglandin (*qv*).

dinoprostone A naturally occurring form of prostaglandin (*qv*) administered in a vaginal suppository (*qv*) to cause contraction of the smooth muscles of the uterus (*qv*).

dioecious *See* diecious.

Dionysian Orgiastic; pertaining to the emotional as opposed to the intellectual; in reference to Dionysos, the Greek god of wine, orgiastic (*qv*) religion, and fertility (*qv*). *See also* bacchanalia, sattvic foods.

diploidy (diploid) Having two complete sets of homologous chromosomes (*qv*), as in somatic (*qv*) cells. *See also* meiosis; mitosis; haploid; gamete.

dippoldism The spanking or whipping of children in order to achieve sexual arousal (*qv*) and facilitate orgasm (*qv*). The term is derived from a sadistic German schoolteacher, Dippold.

discharge The male ejaculate (*qv*); an unusual or abnormal secretion of the vagina (*qv*) or urethra (*qv*) symptomatic of a sexually transmitted disease (*qv*).

disinhibition The loss of rational control over one's sexual impulses, as occurs with the use of alcohol or psychogenic drugs. *See also* desensitization.

dispareunia *See* dyspareunia.

displaceability of libido In psychoanalytic theory (*qv*), the belief that impulses and aspects of the oral, anal, phallic, and genital stages (*qv*) of psychosexual development (*qv*) can substitute for each other in the sexual life of an adult, particularly during the foreplay (*qv*) that precedes sexual intercourse (*qv*).

display Courtship (*qv*) behaviors involving display of colorful plumage, body decorations, or other signs of masculinity (*qv*) or femininity (*qv*) to attract a partner while distracting or intimidating the approach of possible competing members of the same sex. *See also* proceptivity; flirtation.

dissociated virilization The unequal or out-of-sequence development of secondary male characteristics (*qv*), which may result from a hormonal disturbance.

distal urethra An alternate term for the Skene's glands (*qv*), associated with the female urethra (*qv*); homologous (*qv*) to the male prostate (*qv*).

distillate of love A archaic reference to the precoital (*qv*) secretions of the Cowper's glands (*qv*).

diurnal Any event that recurs daily or in a daily cycle. The incidence of erection (*qv*) men often experience when awakening in the morning may be due to a diurnal cycle of male sex hormone production, which rises from 4 A.M. to peak about 9:30 A.M., and then drops to a daily low about 12:30 A.M.

divorce A civil or religious dissolution of a lawfully contracted and valid marriage (*qv*) while both partners are still alive, thereby freeing each partner to remarry. Grounds for divorce may include adultery (*qv*), incompatibility, physical or mental cruelty, desertion (*qv*), nonsupport, and refusal or denial of sexual relations. *See also* annulment; no-fault divorce.

divorce counseling Mediation with a third party to negotiate a mutually acceptable, out-of-court agreement on a divorce (*qv*).

dizygotic twin Two infants (*qv*) conceived by simultaneous fertilization (*qv*) of two different ova (*qv*) in one woman so that, even though the twins share the same delivery (*qv*), they are as genetically unique as two siblings born at different times to the same mother. Such fraternal or nonidentical twins account for two-thirds of all twin births. Roughly one in 90 live births is a twin birth. The incidence of dizygotic twins is highest among blacks and lowest in Orientals. The highest incidence occurs with mothers between ages 35 and 39. Although fathers may transmit the disposition toward double ovulation to their daughters, the main hereditary effect is in the female.

DNA *See* deoxyribonucleic acid.

DOB *See* Daughters of Bilitis.

Doderlein's bacillus A species of *Lactobacillus* normally found in the human vagina (*qv*). This anerobic bacterium acts on glycogen molecules in the vaginal cells and secretions to produce lactic acid, which destroys or inhibits some potentially harmful bacteria entering the vaginal canal (*qv*).

Doe v. Bridgeton Hospital Association A 1977 decision by the U.S. Supreme Court ruling that private, nonsectarian hospitals must allow abortions (*qv*) to be performed.

Doe v. Bolton In this 1973 seven-to-two decision, issued the same day as the *Roe v. Wade* decision (*qv*), the U.S. Supreme Court struck down all restrictions on the facilities that can be used for an abortion (*qv*). This decision gave rise to the abortion clinic (*qv*).

Doe v. Commonwealth Attorney for Richmond A summary affirmation without opinion issued by the U.S. Supreme Court in 1976 supporting a lower court decision that Virginia's antisodomy law did not chill the exercises of the constitutional right of freedom of association.

Dogiel's corpuscles The sensory nerve endings in the skin of the genitalia (*qv*) and in the mucous membranes of the mouth and nose.

dolce stil nova (Ital.) Emerging in Bologna and then Florence in the second half of the thirteenth century, "the sweet new style" of romantic and mystical love asserted that earthly love for a human could open the way to the revelation of divine love. This new conception of love as a person-to-person amor (*qv*) went beyond the platonic idealism of courtly love (*qv*) advocated by the troubadors (*qv*). It emphasized the "gentle heart" as a material and formal condition for the existence of true love. Love became a trepid adoration of a perfect being in whom one finds happiness and comfort and from whose goodness and beauty radiates a higher spirituality. The term is derived from a line in Dante's *Purgatorio*.

domestic partners A legal term for two persons of the same gender who share a long-term, committed relationship, equivalent to a marriage (*qv*) except that they are of the same gender rather than being a man and woman. In 1989, the Court of Appeals of New York State granted limited legal recognition to some rights of domestic partners. On the municipal level in the United States, several cities have statutes recognizing the status and some rights of domestic partners. Sweden was the first nation to grant legal recognition to domestic partners, placing these same-gender unions on a par with heterosexual (*qv*) nonmarital cohabitation (*qv*). In 1989, Denmark became the first nation to grant full legal recognition of the rights and responsibilities of domestic partners, save for the right to adopt or retain child custody. *See also* gay unions.

dominant gene The gene controlling a trait that is expressed even when the gene is present in only one chromosome (*qv*) of a pair of homologous (*qv*) chromosomes. A gene is dominant when its alternate form, or allele (*qv*), is not expressed in the heterozygous (*qv*) condition. When two different alleles for the same trait are simultaneously expressed, the alleles are said to be codominant (*qv*). *See also* recessive gene; sex-influenced trait; sex-linked trait; sex-limited trait.

dominatrix A female partner who plays the dominating role in bondage and dominance (*qv*) or S/M (*qv*). A female prostitute (*qv*) may specialize in this role, serving the needs of male clients seeking a sexual relationship in which they can be submissive.

domineering father A father who tends to dominate the life of a family, making the wife and children totally subordinate to his desires and decisions. Psychologists suggest that a domineering father may be a cause of secondary erectile dysfunction (*qv*).

domineering mother A mother who tends to dominate the life of a family and her children in such a way that the husband-father and male offspring are emasculated (*qv*). Often suggested as a cause of male homosexuality (*qv*), although research does not support this conclusion. A domineering mother may be a cause for a secondary erectile dysfunction (*qv*).

Don Juan (colloq.) A seductive, sexually promiscuous (*qv*) male; a philanderer, rake, or libertine interested only in sexual contacts with no personal involvement. Don Juan was a legendary Spanish nobleman with insatiable sexual urges that led him to seduce (*qv*) countless women. His conquests and escapades are found as themes in many poems, plays, novels, and operas by Molière, Mozart, Lord Byron, Richard Strauss, George Bernard Shaw, and others.

Donovania granulomatis The rod-shaped bacterium associated with granuloma inguinale or venereum (*qv*).

Donovan's body The rod-shaped bacterium associated with granuloma inguinale or venereum (*qv*).

dopamine A neurotransmitter essential to brain function. Dopamine appears to serve as a short-term sexual activator. *See also* serotonin.

Dorian love An outdated term for male homosexuality (*qv*) and pederasty (*qv*); derived from the alleged practices of the Dorian tribe, which conquered the Peloponnesians of southern Greece in the twelfth century B.C.E.

dosage compensation The result of partial inactivation in Barr bodies (*qv*) of X chromosomes (*qv*) in the somatic cells so that males and females have only one active X chromosome, which produces roughly the same amount of gene (*qv*) products.

double-blind study A study or experiment in which neither the subjects nor the person collecting the data know whether a particular subject is in the experimental or control group (*qv*). *See also* single-blind study.

double entendre (Fr.) A word or expression that can be interpreted in a nonsexual way but also having an implied risqué sexual interpretation.

double-lumen implant A female breast (*qv*) implant with an inner compartment filled with a silastic gel and an outer sack whose size can be adjusted by injection of a saline solution.

double (moral) standard A dual set of moral standards and principles for males and females, usually with stricter standards applied to females, especially for premarital virginity (*qv*) and the amount of sexual behavior acceptable. *See also* masculine protest.

double vagina A congenital (*qv*) malformation in which the paired Mullerian ducts (*qv*) do not fuse to form a single vagina (*qv*) and uterus (*qv*) but remain separate and develop a complete system of two side-by-side vaginas and uteri, each with a single fallopian tube (*qv*). The parallel structures are seldom equal in development or size.

douche A hygienic or therapeutic procedure in which a mild medication or cleansing agent dissolved in warm water is introduced into the vagina (*qv*) under low pressure from a hanging bottle or squeeze container. When the vagina is distended, the flow is stopped to allow the fluid to flow out of the vagina. Douching is ineffective as a contraceptive (*qv*) method and may in fact enhance the movement of sperm (*qv*) into the cervix (*qv*). *See also* Coca-Cola douche; postcoital douche.

dowager's hump A colloquial term for the curvature of the upper spine and the accumulation of tissue in the neck and shoulder region caused by osteoporosis as the vertebral bones collapse more at the front of the spine. This condition, more common in older women than in men, can be controlled by sufficient calcium in the diet and hormone (*qv*) monitoring.

dower The wife's share of the husband's patrimony or inheritance; a portion of the groom's estate specified at the time of betrothal (*qv*) or marriage (*qv*) to provide for her support in case of his death. *See also* arrha; dowry; endowment; Morgengabe.

dowry Money or property given to the groom by the bride's family at the time of betrothal (*qv*) or marriage (*qv*), sometimes consisting of her share of her family inheritance. Increasingly the custom is being outlawed in developing nations, although it often continues illegally, as in India. Also known as the marriage portion. *See also* arrha; bridegift; brideprice; dower; endowment; Morgengabe.

Dreadnaught The trade name of the first rubber condom (*qv*) produced with a reservoir for the ejaculate (*qv*) at the tip; introduced in 1901.

dressing ring A metal ring, about an inch in diameter that is inserted surgically through the glans (*qv*) of the penis (*qv*) in order to increase sexual stimulation during vaginal intercourse (*qv*). During the Victorian era (*qv*), men used a dressing ring to secure the penis in the leg of their trousers; hence its other name, Prince Albert.

drive A behavior commonly exhibited by members of a species that appears to have a phylogenetic origin in the biological and neural evolution of the species. The term *instinct* (*qv*), commonly used in the past, is no longer popular in technical literature because of the difficulty of specifying the exact nature of the instinctive behavior. Because it is not as deterministic as the term *instinct*, the term *drive* allows for variations in the responses of individuals within a species.

droit du seigneur (Fr.) The "right of the lord," a historically questionable name for the custom in which a medieval Norman, Frank, or Viking lord of the manor had the right to deflower (*qv*) the bride of any serf. The more authentic term for this custom is *jus primae noctis* (*qv*) ("the right of the first night"). *See also* defloration. Resource: B. I. Murstein, *Love, Sex and Marriage through the Ages*. (New York: Springer, 1974), p. 137.

dromostanolone proprionate An androgen (*qv*) used in treating female breast cancer (*qv*).

dry days The day or two immediately following the cessation of the menstrual (*qv*) flow when the cervical mucus (*qv*) is at its lowest production and thickest texture.

dry orgasm A male orgasm (*qv*) that occurs without ejaculation (*qv*). A non-pathological experience for males before puberty (*qv*) as well as for older men, this phenomenon may also be due to incompetence of the inner prostatic sphincter, which allows for retrograde ejaculation (*qv*) of the semen (*qv*) into the urinary bladder. *See also* retarded ejaculation; inhibited male orgasm.

DSM-III The third edition of the *Diagnostic and Statistical Manual of Mental Disorders* (DSM) (*qv*) published by the American Psychiatric Association in 1980.

DTC *See* diethyldithiocarbamate.

dualism A worldview (*Weltanschauung*) in which there are two mutually exclusive and antagonistic forms of reality, principles, powers, or creators. In philosophy and religious thought, a dualistic (*qv*) perspective holds that the world is ultimately composed of or is explicable in terms of two basic entities: spirit or matter, body or soul, good or evil, and light or darkness. In a dualistic philosophy, sexual desires and behavior are relegated to the negative side. Dualistic philosophy can be traced from early Persian Zorastrian religious philosophy, through the Greek philosophy of Plato, to the Manicheans and Christian St. Augustine in the third century c.e., the Albigensians of southern France and Spain in the Early Middle Ages, to the Jansenists of France and Puritans. In Christianity, there has been a 2,000–year struggle with Stoic, Platonic dualist views of human nature and sexuality (*qv*), often suppressing the humanistic Jewish construct, which is not dualistic. Most of the antisexual attitudes blamed on Christianity and its Bible are in fact due to Greek Platonism and Roman Stoicism.

The Eastern religions also have a dualistic view of reality—matter and spirit, masculine and feminine—but the two poles of reality are seen as complementary and inseparable. Although they have a patriarchal bias, Eastern religions, especially Taoism (*qv*), lack the antisexual attitudes of Western dualisms and see the female as the sexual initiatrix. *See also* asceticism. Resource: R. J. Lawrence, *The Poisoning of Eros: Sexual Values in Conflict* (New York: Augustine Press, 1989).

dual orgasm A psychoanalytic theory (*qv*) that the clitoris (*qv*) is the prime site of sexual excitement (*qv*) and orgasm (*qv*) in young women but that as psychosexual maturity is achieved, the site of sexual pleasure and orgasm shifts to the vaginal (*qv*) region. In the original Freudian view, persistence of the clitoral orgasm in an older woman represents an immature and arrested form of psychosexual development (*qv*), a view widely rejected today. The work of William Masters and Virginia Johnson in the 1960s suggested that only a clitoral orgasm exists in women and that the vaginal orgasm is fiction. However, more recent studies suggest the possibility of several types of orgasm in women. *See also* tenting orgasm; blended orgasm; A-frame orgasm; Grafenberg spot.

dual-sex therapy The use of male and female cotherapists (*qv*) in the treatment of sexual inadequacy (*qv*) and dysfunction (*qv*). This approach was developed by William Masters and Virginia Johnson because they believe that a male counselor or therapist working alone cannot be expected to understand and appreciate fully the feelings and reactions of the female partner, while a female therapist will not be able to understand fully the male partner's perspective. Working at times as a team and then in one-on-one sessions, cotherapists are better able to gain a full perspective of the couple's problem and apply effective remedies.

DUB Dysfunctional or abnormal uterine (*qv*) bleeding.

ductless glands *See* endocrine glands.

ductus arteriosus (L.) A vascular channel in the fetus (*qv*) that joins the pulmonary artery directly to the descending aorta, thereby diverting most of the blood that would normally go into the pulmonary circulation to the somatic and placental circulation. At birth (*qv*), the ductus arteriosus closes, thereby maximizing the pulmonary circulation. *See also* foramen ovale; fetal circulation.

ductus deferens (L.) The ducts leading from the testes (*qv*) to the penile urethra (*qv*). *See also* vas deferens.

ductus efferens (L.) *See* vas efferens.

Dumas cap A type of cervical cap (*qv*) used as a contraceptive (*qv*).

Dutch cap A contraceptive rubber diaphragm (*qv*) with a semirigid ring.

dwarf, hypopituitary An individual of short stature, under 4 feet in an adult or at least four standard deviations below the mean for an age group, whose small stature is due to failure of the pituitary (*qv*) to produce sufficient growth hormone (*qv*). In a hypopituitary dwarf, other pituitary hormones may also be missing, in particular the gonadotropins (*qv*) follicle-stimulating hormone (*qv*) and luteinizing hormone (*qv*), so that sexual infantilism (*qv*) may persist into adult life. Supplying exogenous growth hormone may result in normal growth; treatment with appropriate steroid hormones will induce reasonable sexual maturity, although the male beard may not be induced.

dyad A pair or couple, as in dyadic marital therapy.

dydo Short metal rods with small balls screwed on both ends, inserted in holes made in the corona of the penile glans (*qv*), used to increase sexual stimulation (*qv*) for both the male and female during vaginal intercourse (*qv*).

dysfunctional An abnormal or impaired response or behavior (e.g., a sexual dysfunction). Sociologically the term also refers to that part of a social system that disrupts the functioning of another part of the system.

dysgenesis A defective or abnormal formation of an organ or structure, usually occurring during embryonic development.

dysgenitalism Any condition involving abnormal development of the genital (*qv*) organs and structures.

dysgerminoma A solid ovarian tumor (*qv*) associated with pregnancy (*qv*), adolescence (*qv*), and, in some cases, with premature puberty (*qv*).

dysmaturity The structural or functional failure of an organism to develop or mature.

dysmenorrhea Painful menstruation (*qv*) with symptoms usually including lower back and abdominal pain, headache, cramps, and a bloated feeling. The pains of dysmenorrhea are the result of factors intrinsic to the uterus (*qv*) and the menstrual process. *See also* premenstrual syndrome.

dyspareunia A technical term for a hypophilic (*qv*) sexual dysfunction (*qv*) characterized by difficult or painful intercourse (*qv*) or by an inability to enjoy sexual intercourse; recurrent or persistent genital pain in a male or female before, during, or after sexual intercourse. In women, causes of dyspareunia may be psychogenic, including a variety of fears, anxieties, and previous traumatic experiences, which lead to sexual inhibition (*qv*). Incomplete sexual arousal (*qv*), leading to a lack of vaginal lubrication (*qv*) followed by forced coitus (*qv*), can result in dyspareunia. A vaginal or pelvic infection and vaginal atrophy in post-menopausal (*qv*) women may also be a cause. In men, the cause is usually organic and involves Peyronie's disease (*qv*), a deformity of the penis (*qv*).

dyspermia, dyspermasia An early term for difficult or pain-producing orgasm (*qv*) during vaginal intercourse (*qv*). *See also* dyspareunia.

dysphoria A generalized feeling of ill-being, anxiety, discontent, or even physical discomfort, as in a gender dysphoria (*qv*).

dystrophy Partial atrophy (*qv*) or degeneration of a tissue or organ as a result of deficient cellular nutrition.

dysuria Painful or difficult urination, usually resulting from a bacterial infection or obstruction of the urethral passage.

E

---

early ejaculation *See* premature ejaculation; retarded ejaculation; ejaculatory dysfunction.

ear pulling In some interpretations, the habit of tugging at one's ear is seen as a substitute for masturbation (*qv*) or as a partial regression to the oral stage (*qv*) in which thumb sucking is a primary source of pleasure.

EBV *See* Epstein-Barr virus.

eccentric implantation The implantation of the blastocyst (*qv*) within a fold or recess of the uterine wall (*qv*), which then closes off from the uterine cavity.

eccyesis *See* ectopic pregnancy.

ecdysiasm (n. ecdysiast) A form of exhibitionism (*qv*) in which a person experiences a compulsion to undress in public as a means of arousing sexual excitement in others; a colloquialism for stripper.

echinococcus cyst An infection of the connective tissue of the fallopian tube (*qv*) or ovaries (*qv*) by parasitic tapeworm larvae *Taenia echinococcus*, which invades these tissues from the intestinal tract through the lymphatic or blood system. The condition occurs in Europe, Australia, and Latin America but is rare in North America.

eclampsia A condition occurring during the second half of pregnancy (*qv*) marked by high blood pressure, edema, excess protein in the urine (*qv*), and convulsions. Also known as toxemia of pregnancy. Sometimes eclampsia results in coma or death for the pregnant or puerperal (*qv*) woman. Early prenatal (*qv*) care, including frequent blood pressure measurement and urinalysis, provides early detection for preeclampsia and allows treatment to forestall further complications. Symptoms of eclampsia include dizziness, stomach pains, vomiting, visual disturbances, mental confusion, muscular twitching, and cyanosis (*qv*).

ecouteurism A paraphilic (*qv*) condition in which sexual arousal (*qv*) and orgasm (*qv*) are dependent on listening to accounts of sexual encounters or to the sounds made by a couple during sexual intercourse (*qv*). *See also* scoptophilia; narratophilia.

ecstasy In sexology, the peak of erotosexual (*qv*) pleasure and excitement and altered state of consciousness associated with orgasm (*qv*).

ectoderm The outermost of three embryonic tissue layers, defined by location and the tissues that arise from it, such as the skin and its derivatives—hair, nails, skin glands, and the nervous tissue, including the brain, spinal cord, and all nerves. *See also* mesoderm; entoderm.

ectopic pregnancy A pregnancy (*qv*) resulting from implantation (*qv*) of the blastocyst (*qv*) outside its normal nidation (*qv*) site in the uterine cavity (*qv*). The blastocyst may implant in the ovary (*qv*), in the walls of the abdomen and pelvic cavity, in the fallopian tube (*qv*), or in the lower uterine or cervical (*qv*) region where the placenta (*qv*) will prevent normal vaginal delivery (*qv*). Ectopic pregnancies are associated with nonfunctional tubal cilia, pelvic inflammatory disease (*qv*), or other conditions that leave pockets in the tubal walls. Tubal pregnancies usually rupture in the third month of gestation (*qv*) with serious, often lethal consequences, although abdominal pregnancies may go to term (*qv*) with delivery by Caesarean section (*qv*). Ecotopic pregnancies are three times more common in women from the lower socioeconomic level than among middle-class women.

ectopic testis A testis (*qv*) that develops or becomes lodged in a location other than either its original embryonic site in the abdomen or along the path taken by the testis in its perinatal migration into the scrotal sac (*qv*). *See also* cryptorchidism.

ectopotomy Surgical removal of the fetus (*qv*) or other product of conception through an incision in the abdominal wall. *See also* Caesarean section.

edema (adj. edematous) Swelling due to retention of excess fluid in the intercellular spaces of a tissue.

Edipus complex *See* Oedipus complex.

EEG *See* electroencephalogram.

effacement Shortening of the vaginal (*qv*) end of the cervix (*qv*) and flattening or thinning out of its walls as the fetus (*qv*) passes into the vaginal canal (*qv*) during delivery (*qv*).

effeminacy (adj. effeminate) Derogatory terms for the bearing and manner of a man who consciously or unconsciously imitates what he takes to be women's behavior, dress, and body movements. *See also* effeminate homosexual; sissy boy syndrome; female impersonator; transvestism.

effeminate homosexual A homosexual (*qv*) man whose mannerisms, voice inflections, body movements, and behavior imitate those of women, or which can be taken as imitating women's behavior. Such individuals are often stigmatized as unmanly and called sissies, fairies, pansies, or other derogatory terms by cynics and homophobes (*see* homophobia). However, these mannerisms may be expressions of camp (*qv*) rather than deliberate or unconscious imitations of women. *See also* female impersonator; sissy boy syndrome; transvestism.

effleurage The circular stroking with the fingertips in long, light, or firm strokes used in massaging the abdomen in the Lamaze method (*qv*) of childbirth (*qv*).

egg The female reproductive cell (*qv*) or gamete (*qv*). *See also* ovum.

egg lavage A nonsurgical technique whereby ova (*qv*) are flushed from the fallopian tube (*qv*) and then used for *in vitro* fertilization (*qv*) and embryo transplant (*qv*) to a surrogate mother (*qv*).

ego An individual's concept and awareness of self as distinct from others; in psychoanalytic theory (*qv*), the rational level of personality which tempers the primitive drives of the id (*qv*) and the demands of the superego (*qv*). In Sigmund Freud's (*qv*) model, the ego represents the superficial portion of the id and develops from it in response to stimulation from the infant's physical and social environment. The chief functions of the ego are reality testing, learning to distinguish between self and environment, and mediating between the id and superego.

ego-alien *See* ego dystonic.

egocentric stage The second of four stages in the model of moral development proposed by Jean Piaget (*qv*) in which the child, usually between ages 2 to 7, bends the rules and reacts instinctively to its environment. *See also* amoral; heteronomous stage; autonomous stage.

ego dystonic In psychiatry, the identification of an individual with a particular proclivity or behavioral tendency with which he or she is uncomfortable and which he or she tries to be rid of or to deny. For example, a male transsexual (*qv*) who wants to be rid of his male sexual anatomy and assume the sexual anatomy of a female experiences ego dystonia. *See also* ego syntonic.

ego ideal The positive side of the superego (*qv*).

ego identity The more or less consistent unity and persistence of one's self-identity or individuality, especially as it is experienced in self-awareness and behavior.

ego libido In psychoanalytic theory (*qv*), the concentration of the sex drive (*qv*) on the self. *See also* narcissism; autoeroticism.

Ego Psychology Erik Erikson's theory of personality development extends that outlined by Sigmund Freud (*qv*) and describes our lifelong psychosocial development in terms of a choice between two directions at eight stages. In Erikson's model, we negotiate each stage by making a fundamental choice in our orientation toward ourselves and others. In the first 18 months, Freud's oral stage (qv), the infant develops a basic sense of trust or mistrust of others. Between 18 months and 3 years, Freud's anal stage (*qv*), the child develops a greater sense of autonomy or a sense of self-doubt and shame (*qv*). Between ages 3 and 5, Freud's phallic stage (*qv*), the child continues exploration and initiative when rewarded or develops guilt when initiative is discouraged. During Freud's latency period (*qv*), ages 5 to 11, Erikson sees a choice between industry and self-accomplishment, or a growing sense of inferiority. In the genital stage (*qv*) of adolescence (*qv*), we move toward a firm self-identity or role confusion. In young adulthood (*qv*), we choose between intimacy (*qv*) with others or isolation and withdrawal. In adulthood, the choice is between creativity or stagnation, and in the mature years, between a sense of contentment and integrity, or despair. In each of these stages, we encounter crises that must be coped with either successfully or unsuccessfully.

ego syntonic In psychiatry, the term used to identify an individual who is comfortable with and accepting of a nonstandard proclivity or behavioral tendency. The term frequently refers to an individual who is comfortable with and accepting of his or her nonstandard gender-identity/role (*qv*), such as a male homosexual (*qv*) who is comfortable with and accepts his sexual status, orientation, and emotional needs. *Ego syntonic homosexuality* was dropped from the mental and emotional disorders listed in the 1980 third edition of the *Diagnostic and Statistical Manual of Mental Disorders* (*qv*). *See also* ego dystonic.

Eisenstadt v. Baird In this 1972 decision, the U.S. Supreme Court ruled a Massachusetts law prohibiting distribution and sale of contraceptives (*qv*) to unmarried people unconstitutional.

ejaculatio deficiens (L.) *See* ejaculatory incompetence.

ejaculation, ejaculate (v. to ejaculate) The expulsion of the seminal fluid (*qv*) through the penile urethra (*qv*), usually at the time of orgasm (*qv*). Ejaculation or propulsion follows the emission phase (*qv*), when seminal fluid pressure increases in the prostatic region (*qv*) and ejaculatory ducts (*qv*). Expulsion of 2 to 5 milliliters of semen, containing 100 million to 500 million spermatozoa (*qv*), occurs when the outer urethral valve reflexively opens while the inner valve remains closed to prevent retrograde ejaculation (*qv*). Propulsion is caused by two or three intense contractions of the penile urethra and the muscles around the base of the penis (*qv*) at intervals of 0.8 of a second, followed by a series of weaker, slower contractions. Despite a common misconception, orgasm and ejaculation are two distinct processes. *See also* ejaculatory incompetence; premature ejaculation; female ejaculation; retarded ejaculation; inhibited male orgasm; ejaculatory inevitability; nocturnal emission.

ejaculation center A cluster of nerve cells believed to control ejaculation (*qv*) and other genital (*qv*) activities and thought to be located in the sacral region of the spinal cord.

ejaculatio praecox (L.) *See* premature ejaculation.

ejaculator seminis (L.) The bulbocavernosus muscle (*qv*) encircling the shaft of the corpus spongiosum (*qv*), which helps produce an erection (*qv*) by compressing the erectile tissue of the penis (*qv*) and empties the penile urethra (*qv*) after the bladder has been voided.

ejaculatory duct Paired tubelike structures, about an inch long, through which sperm (*qv*) from the vasa deferentia (*qv*) and fluid from the seminal vesicles (*qv*) enter the prostatic urethra (*qv*).

ejaculatory incompetence The inability of a male to ejaculate (*qv*) within the vagina (*qv*); the inability to ejaculate during coitus (*qv*) or masturbation (*qv*). The condition may be classified as primary (*qv*) or secondary (*qv*). *See also* retarded ejaculation; inhibited male orgasm.

ejaculatory inevitability The feeling, occurring in the emission (*qv*) phase of ejaculation (*qv*), when a male becomes aware his arousal has passed the point where he can control ejaculation and where it is now a reflexive process involving the involuntary contractions of the vasa deferentia (*qv*), seminal vesicles (*qv*), and prostate (*qv*).

elective abortion Induced termination of pregnancy (*qv*) performed at the request of the mother and not for a medical reason; commonly but incorrectly referred to as a therapeutic abortion. *See also* abortion.

Electra complex In psychoanalytic theory (*qv*), the sexual attraction (*qv*) experienced by a girl to her father, usually accompanied by competition with and hostility to the girl's mother. In the Greek myth, Aegisthus helps his lover, Clytemnestra, murder her husband, Agamemnon, so they could marry. Electra, Clytemnestra's daughter, then induced her brother Orestes to kill their mother. In current psychoanalytic usage, the term has been replaced by *Oedipus complex* (*qv*), which is applied to the attachment of both sons and daughters to the opposite-gender parent.

electrolysis A method of hair removal in which an electric needle is inserted into the hair-growing follicle to kill it with an electrical pulse; a cosmetic treatment commonly used by women with unwanted facial or body hair, as well as by male-to-female transsexuals (*qv*).

Elisa Test A general acronym for any Enzyme-Linked IimmunoSorbent Assay test used to detect specific antibodies in the blood. The Elisa test for pregnancy (*qv*), is also known as the beta-specific monoclonal enzyme-linked immunosorbent assay test (*qv*).

A different Elisa test detects the presence of antibodies to the HIV-I virus (*qv*), which causes acquired immune deficiency syndrome (*qv*). False negative (*qv*) results occur when the test is performed before the body's immune system has had time to respond to the low-level antigenic effect of the HIV-I virus. Several months to a year or more may elapse after exposure and infection before the antibodies are at a level detectable by the Elisa test. Most HIV-infected persons, however, show a high level of antibodies by 12 weeks. False positive (*qv*) results also occur because of the presence of similar nonHIV-I antibodies. An initial sero-positive result with an Elisa test should be confirmed by a Western Blot Test (*qv*).

Eliza technique (test) A test used to detect antigens (*qv*) for the gonorrhea (*qv*) bacterium in cervical (*qv*), anal (*qv*), or urethral (*qv*) specimens. Although this test can give results within an hour or two, it is more complicated and much more expensive than the widely used gram-negative stain test. *See also* Transformation Test.

Ellis, Havelock (1859–1939) An English scholar, essayist, and physician, Ellis was an early champion of sex education (*qv*) for children, contraception (*qv*), changes in the divorce (*qv*) laws, the emancipation of women, experimental premarital (*qv*) sexual relations, and the elimination of criminal laws against consenting adult homosexual acts (*qv*). Ellis's classic work, a seven volume series, *Studies in the Psychology of Sex*, written between 1896 and 1928, was legally available in the United States only to members of the medical profession until 1935. A correspondent of Sigmund Freud (*qv*) who adopted some of his terms and ideas, Ellis was the first to recognize and discuss the importance of touch and other senses in lovemaking (*qv*), the nature of erotic (*qv*) dreams, the prevalence of masturbation (*qv*), and paraphilic (*qv*) behaviors.

elopement The act of secretly leaving home to marry without parental permission. From the birth of romantic love in medieval courtly love (*qv*) and the Renaissance on, elopement was seen as an affirmation of a young person's right to marry someone he or she loved rather than to have an marriage (*qv*) arranged by one's parents.

emasculate To castrate (*qv*). *See also* eunuch; castrati.

embarrassment dream In psychoanalytic theory (*qv*), a dream of undressing in public derived from a similar experience that provoked shame (*qv*) and embarrassment when the person was a child.

embryatrics Fetology, the scientific study and medical treatment of the fetus (*qv*) during gestation (*qv*).

embryectomy Surgical removal of an embryo (*qv*), particular in an ectopic pregnancy (*qv*). *See also* abortion.

embryo Any organism in its earliest stage of development when the major organ systems and the main external features are established. In humans, the embryonic stage extends from the second to the end of the eighth week of gestation (*qv*). In the third week after fertilization (*qv*), formation of the neural tube, thyroid, and heart begin. In the fourth week, the heart begins beating; primordia of the eyes, ears, and face form along with the arm and leg buds. In the fifth week, the nose and mouth take shape as the eyes, brain, and limbs continue developing. In the sixth week, the inner mouth and hands develop. In the seventh week, the face approaches a definite human appearance while the genital primordia begin developing. In the eighth week, the ovaries (*qv*) and testes (*qv*) can be distinguished, although the external genitalia (*qv*) have not differentiated into male or female form. Since all major organ systems are being established during these six weeks, the embryo is most vulnerable to teratogenic agents (*qv*), which can cause congenital birth defects (*qv*). *See also* zygote; blastula; fetus.

embryo adoption A reproductive technology in which a wife is naturally or artificially inseminated (*qv*) with the husband's or a donor's semen (*qv*) and the resultant zygote (*qv*) flushed from the uterus (*qv*) before it can implant (*qv*) to allow its transfer to a surrogate mother (*qv*) for a full-term pregnancy (*qv*). Embryo adoption is used when the genetic and social mother is unable to support a full-term pregnancy. In embryo adoption, the gestational mother is a partial surrogate mother because she serves only as a ''prenatal wetnurse.'' The gestational mother is not the genetic mother or donor of the ovum (*qv*). *See also* embryo transplant; surrogate mother; artificial embryonation; GIFT.

embryoctony Intentional destruction of a living embryo (*qv*) or fetus (*qv*) in the uterus (*qv*); feticide (*qv*). *See also* abortion.

embryogenesis The developmental processes, lasting about 8 weeks, during which a fertilized ovum (*qv*) is transformed into an embryo (*qv*) with all major organ systems. *See also* fetus.

embryo lavage A nonsurgical technique whereby fertilized ova (*qv*) or blastocysts (*qv*) are flushed from the uterine cavity (*qv*) for subsequent transfer to a surrogate mother (*qv*). *See also* embryo transplant.

embryology The study of the origin, growth, development, and functions of an organism from fertilization (*qv*) to birth (*qv*).

embryonate Impregnated; containing an embryo (*qv*); pertaining to or resembling an embryo.

embryonic competence The ability of an embryonic cell (*qv*) or tissue to respond to the stimulation of another embryonic tissue or artificial implant whose chemical influence organizes or induces continued normal growth and differentiation.

embryonic disc The thickened plate in the blastocyst (*qv*) from which the embryo (*qv*) develops in the second week of gestation (*qv*). Cells on the dorsal surface of the embryonic disc lining the floor of the amniotic sac (*qv*) migrate toward the midline and beneath the surface to form a mesodermal (*qv*) layer between the upper ectoderm and lower endoderm of the yolk sac (*qv*). The neural plate and, later, the neural tube form along the midline of the embryonic disc.

embryo replacement (ER) Removal of an ovum (*qv*) from a woman by laparoscopy (*qv*), followed by *in vitro* fertilization (*qv*), and return of the embryo to the same woman; used to bypass blocked fallopian tubes (*qv*). *See also* embryo transplant; GIFT.

embryotomy Dismemberment or mutilation of a fetus (*qv*) to facilitate its removal from the uterus (*qv*) when normal delivery (*qv*) is not possible. *See also* abortion.

embryo transplant (ET) A reproductive technology in which fertilization (*qv*) is accomplished outside the reproductive system (*qv*) of the woman producing the ovum (*qv*). When a woman has functional ovaries (*qv*) but blocked fallopian tubes (*qv*) that prevent her becoming pregnant (*qv*), her ovum may be surgically removed as ovulation (*qv*) occurs. The ovum is fertilized in an artificial culture medium, incubated for approximately two and a half days, and then introduced via the vaginal (*qv*) and cervical (*qv*) canals into her uterus (*qv*) where a normal gestation (*qv*) can follow. If the genetic mother who produces the ovum has had a hysterectomy (*qv*) or is otherwise unable to become pregnant, the embryo can be transplanted to a surrogate mother (*qv*). In the event the woman who produces the ovum has intact and functional fallopian tubes, the ovum may be flushed from the uterus, fertilized, incubated, and then transferred to the uterus of a surrogate mother, who carries the developing fetus (*qv*) full term. In another form of embryo transplant, a woman has coitus (*qv*) with her husband or is artificially inseminated (*qv*) with donor semen (*qv*). The resulting zygote (*qv*) is then flushed from her uterus and transferred to the uterus of a surrogate mother for full-term pregnancy. *See also* artificial insemination; embryo adoption; embryo replacement; in vitro fertilization; GIFT.

embryotroph The liquid nutritive material produced by the uterus (*qv*) from degenerative tissues and glandular secretions that nourishes the mammalian embryo (*qv*) until the placental (*qv*) circulation and support is established.

embryulcia Surgical removal of the embryo (*qv*) or fetus (*qv*) from the uterus (*qv*). *See also* abortion.

emission phase The buildup of seminal fluid (*qv*) pressure by myotonic contractions (*qv*) in the prostatic (*qv*) region and ejaculatory ducts (*qv*) prior to the expulsion of the seminal fluid (*qv*) out of the penile urethra (*qv*) during orgasm (*qv*). Emission is characterized by the psychological awareness of ejaculatory inevitability (*qv*). Closure of both the inner and outer urethral sphincters facilitates the buildup of pressure. *See also* ejaculation.

emmenology The medical specialty dealing with the physiology and abnormalities of menstruation (*qv*).

emotion A strong, generalized feeling or state of psychological excitement, as opposed to a rational ideation. A *primary emotion* is one that is considered to be basic and universal to all humans (e.g., anger, fear, happiness, surprise, disgust, sadness). A *secondary emotion* is derived from some combination of primary emotions (e.g., jealousy, which may arise from anger, fear of loss, and sadness).

emotional incest A form of incest (*qv*) in which a parent uses a son or daughter as a surrogate spouse emotionally and affectionally. Although sexual relations (*qv*) are not part of emotional incest, the disruption of normal parent-child relations and the violation of parental trust often results in a child who is overly attached to the parent and thus incapable of forming mature relationships with a peer of the opposite sex.

emotive ideology A life view or philosophy holding that the emotions should have priority in decision making.

empty nest syndrome A response common among parents who experience feelings of loss, emptiness, loneliness, mild depression, and sometimes actual grief when their children mature and move out of the parental home to begin life on their own. The reaction is more common with parents who build a major part of their life and activities around their children and do not prepare for the time when those children will leave.

encoding The transformation of informational messages into signals, as in the digital encoding of information in a computer memory, the transforming of sensory input and thought processes in the neural circuits of the brain and memory, and the prenatal encoding of neural templates (*qv*). *See also* genomic imprinting; imprinting; lovemaps.

encounter group A form of psychotherapy designed to encourage personal growth and improve interpersonal communications through intensive interactions in a small group. *See also* assertion training; consciousness raising; sensitivity training.

enculturation The process of adapting to a new culture (*qv*).

endocervical canal The tubelike passage between the mouth of the cervix (*qv*) and the uterine cavity (*qv*) containing numerous secretory, mucous-producing glands.

endocervical insemination Artificial insemination (*qv*) in which the semen (*qv*) is deposited inside the cervical canal (*qv*) instead of at the cervical end of the vagina (*qv*).

endocrine gland A ductless gland that discharges its hormone (*qv*) products directly into the bloodstream, such as the pituitary (*qv*), hypothalamus (*qv*), pineal gland (*qv*), thyroid, parathyroid glands, adrenal glands (*qv*), ovaries (*qv*), and testes (*qv*). Some endocrine glands have other functions besides producing hormones. Specializd tissue in other structures, such as the pancreatic Islands of Langerhans, the placenta (*qv*), and gastric and intestinal mucosa have some endocrine functions. *See also* exocrine gland.

endocrinology The scientific study of the endocrine glands (*qv*), their hormone (*qv*) products, and the physiological functions and effects of the hormones.

endoderm The inner of three primordial tissue layers in the very early embryo (*qv*), which gives rise to the linings of the gastrointestinal tract, lungs, and urinary bladder. Also spelled *entoderm*. *See also* mesoderm, ectoderm.

endogamy The social limitation of marriage (*qv*) to members of the same ethnic (*qv*), kinship (*qv*), cultural (*qv*), or religious group. Endogamy is more common in societies where elders or parents arrange marriages (*qv*) for their young. *See also* exogamy.

endometrial aspiration *See* menstrual extraction.

endometrial cancer A malignant neoplasm of the endometrium (*qv*), most often occurring in women in their fifties or sixties.

endometrial cycle The monthly cycle involving the endometrium (*qv*). *See also* menstrual cycle; menstruation.

endometrial hyperplasia An abnormal condition characterized by overgrowth of the endometrium (*qv*), the mucous lining of the uterus (*qv*), due to a sustained stimulation from estrogens (*qv*) and the absence of progesterone (*qv*). Normally the proliferation of the endometrium is stimulated by estrogens in the first part of the menstrual cycle (*qv*) prior to ovulation (*qv*). Following ovulation, endometrial proliferation continues, and estrogens are countered by progesterone until the endometrial lining is shed in the menses (*qv*). If the estrogenic stimulus continues for 3 to 6 months without progesterone control, the endometrium becomes abnormally thick and glandularized, and a cystic, premalignant, or malignant condition may follow.

endometriosis A painful condition caused by tissue of the uterine endometrium (*qv*) attaching to the inside of the fallopian tube (*qv*), the lining of the abdominal cavity, and the outer surface of the urinary bladder, ovary (*qv*), intestines, or uterus (*qv*). The ectopic tissue is subject to the hormonal control and menstrual (*qv*) response of the monthly female hormone cycle. Inflammation, secondary infection, and sterility (*qv*) are typical consequences. Etiology is uncertain, although evidence suggests the endometrial tissue is regurgitated from the uterine fundus (*qv*) through the fallopian tubes during menstruation spontaneously or as a side effect of the oral contraceptive pill (*qv*). Women who defer pregnancy (*qv*) are more likely to experience this condition. Black women are rarely affected. The most effective treatment is videolaseroscopy (*qv*). *See also* chocolate cysts.

endometritis An acute or chronic inflammation of the endometrium (*qv*). Acute inflammation is usually the result of a bacterial infection, usually gonococci or hemolytic streptococci. Chronic endometritis may result from an incomplete abortion (*qv*), irritation from an intrauterine contraceptive device (*qv*), fibroids (*qv*), or thinning and atrophy of the endometrium that accompany menopause (*qv*).

endometrium The innermost of the three layers of the uterine (*qv*) walls, composed of highly vascularized, spongy, specialized mucosal tissue, which also contains glands and lymphoid follicles. The endometrium consists of two main types of tissue: the outer portion, which is shed during menstruation (*qv*), and the inner basal portion, which proliferates during the menstrual cycle (*qv*). The outer portion is subdivided into compact and spongy zones, the latter facilitating implantation (*qv*) of the fertilized ovum (*qv*). The spongy endometrium is shed in the monthly menstrual flow when implantation does not follow ovulation (*qv*). *See also* endometrial cycle.

endorphin A general term for all the endogenous (*qv*) morphinelike substances produced by the pituitary gland (*qv*). Chemically similar in structure and action to morphine, endorphins are neuropeptides composed of many amino acids elaborated by the pituitary gland. As analgesic or pain-reducing neurotransmitters and neuromodulators in the peripheral and central nervous system (*qv*), endorphins are involved in orgasm (*qv*). *See also* enkephalin.

endowment Property or monetary payments made by the groom or the groom's family to the bride as part of a marriage (*qv*) agreement. The endowment included payments immediately available to the bride and also her dower (*qv*). *See also* arrha; brideprice; bridewealth; dowry; Morgengabe.

engagement In a social context, the period prior to marriage (*qv*) when a man and woman have agreed to marry and have formalized this commitment by an announcement and the exchange of gifts or rings. *See also* breach of contract; espousal; prenuptial contract.

In medical usage, engagement refers to the settling of the fetal (*qv*) head into position against the pelvic bones in preparation for birth (*qv*). Engagement usually occurs during the last three or four weeks of pregnancy (*qv*) in a woman having her first-born and during labor (*qv*) in subsequent pregnancies. Also known as dropping, lightening.

engagement ovaries The painful swelling of the internal female sexual organs (*qv*) due to vasocongestion (*qv*) from prolonged petting (*qv*) that does not culminate in the orgasmic release of sexual tension.

English culture A colloquial term for flagellation or spanking as a facilitator of sexual arousal. *See also* culture.

engorgement *See* vasocongestion.

enkephalin One of the endorphins (*qv*), a morphinelike neurotransmitter and neuromodulator found in the brain, pituitary (*qv*), and gastrointestinal tract. Two basic types of enkephalins are known: methionine enkephalin and leucine enkephalin. Each enkephalin is composed of five amino acids, four of them identical. Enkephalins are believed to inhibit neurotransmitters in the pathway for pain perception, thereby reducing the emotional and physical impact of pain. The pleasurable sensations and euphoria that accompany orgasm (*qv*) are due to a sudden increased release of beta enkephalins.

enosiophobia *See* sin phobia.

Enovid Trade name for the first successful oral hormonal contraceptive pill (*qv*), containing mestranol, an estrogen (*qv*), and norethynodrel, a progestin (*qv*), developed by Dr. Gregory Pincus and colleagues in 1956 and first marketed in the early 1960s.

ensoulment A religious or philosophical belief regarding the time at which a developing human organism is endowed with a human soul and thus regarded as a person with inalienable rights. Religious and cultural definitions of the time of ensoulment vary from conception (*qv*) to after the child reaches the age of reason and can understand the customs and mores of society. *See also* immediate animation theory; mediate animation theory.

Anthropological data suggest that most societies have some sort of belief about the existence of souls that leave the human body at death. Different societies have quite different beliefs about human souls, some holding that people have more than one soul, either a masculine and feminine soul or a good and an evil soul, while others believe a person has only one soul. *See also* infanticide; personhood; social birth.

entoderm *See* endoderm.

envy *See* penis envy; womb envy; vagina envy.

enzygotic twin *See* monozygotic twin.

eonism The term used by Havelock Ellis (*qv*) for male cross-dressing (*qv*), now known as transvestophilia (*qv*). The term is derived from Chevalier d'Eon (1728–1810), a French diplomat and transvestite at the court of Catherine the Great.

ephebiatrics The branch of medical science that deals with the medical concerns of adolescents (*qv*) and youths between puberty (*qv*) and adulthood (*qv*).

ephebophilia A paraphilic (*qv*) condition in which an adult's sexual arousal (*qv*) and orgasm (*qv*) depends on being involved, or fantasizing involvement, with a postpubertal (*qv*) or adolescent (*qv*) partner. Fantasies of past ephebophilic activity may be replayed during masturbation (*qv*) or copulation (*qv*) with an older partner. The reciprocal condition is paraphilic adolescentilism (*qv*), in which an older person impersonates an adolescent in order to achieve sexual arousal and orgasm. *See also* nepiophilia; pedophilia.

epicene An individual who exhibits the characteristics of the other sex, as an effeminate (*qv*) male or tomboy (*qv*) girl. The term may also mean androgynous (*qv*).

epidemiology The study of the incidence, distribution, and modes of transmission of diseases and illnesses in human populations.

epididymis A tube, 15 to 18 feet long, tightly coiled and folded against the back (posterior) side of the testes (*qv*), where sperm (*qv*) produced by the testes are stored and mature. During sexual stimulation (*qv*) and the emission phase (*qv*), the sperm move from the epididymis into the vas deferens (*qv*).

epididymitis Inflammation and pain due to an infection of the epididymis (*qv*), such as tuberculosis, syphilis (*qv*), a cyst (*qv*), spermatocoel (*qv*), or a tumor.

epigenesis A theory in evolutionary science and embryology (*qv*) that maintains that organ systems develop from undifferentiated cells and tissues in the zygote (*qv*), blastocyst (*qv*), and early embryo (*qv*) and not from some preformed pattern. The "preformed" hereditary instructions in the chromosomal DNA (*qv*) are translated by undifferentiated cells depending on their location and differing microenvironments within the embryo, but embryonic development is not the unfolding of some totally preformed, miniaturized pattern in the ovum (*qv*) or sperm (*qv*) as proposed by preformation theory (*qv*). *See also* homunculus.

epimenorrhagia A profuse, frequent menstrual flow (*qv*), often an early sign of menopause (*qv*).

epimenorrhea An abnormally frequent and brief menstrual flow (*qv*).

epinephrine A hormone secreted by the inner core of the adrenal gland (*qv*) that is involved in emotional excitement and responses thereto; also known as adrenalin.

epiphysis The end of a long bone separated from the bony shaft or diaphysis by cartilage in juvenile years but later fusing with the shaft. After epiphyseal fusion is completed toward the end of the teenaged years, no further growth in height is possible. Therapeutic steroid hormones (*qv*) used in the treatment of sexual anomalies may trigger premature epiphyseal closure. Adolescent (*qv*) males who produce excessive testosterone (*qv*) will simulate bone growth in length, followed by early fusion of the epiphysis and diaphysis, resulting in a cessation of growth. This accounts for some males being tall at age 12 compared with peers and later being much shorter in the same group.

episiotomy A surgical incision made from the posterior edge of the vaginal (*qv*) entrance, toward the anus (*qv*), to prevent tearing or injury of the perineal (*qv*) tissue during childbirth (*qv*). Episiotomy has been a standard procedure in American obstetrics although increasingly avoided in natural childbirth methods (*qv*) in which prior massaging and stretching of the perineal tissues during labor (*qv*) prevents tearing. It may be needed if a delivery (*qv*) proceeds too rapidly to allow normal stretching of the perineal tissues, if the fetus (*qv*) is too large, or if additional room is needed to allow use of forceps.

epispadias A congenital (qv) defect in which the urethral opening occurs on the upper surface of the penile glans (*qv*) or shaft, usually correctible with surgery. *See also* hypospadias.

epithelioma The type of cancer most often occurring first in the epithelial cells in the skin of the penis (*qv*) or elsewhere. As the cancerous cells invade the tissues underneath the skin, they enter the lymphatic system, forming bulges in the inguinal area and at the base of the penis.

epoophoron A functionless vestige of the Wolffian or mesonephric duct (*qv*) in females. The short, rudimentary duct, with several short tubules converging toward the ovary (*qv*), is usually situated in the mesosalpinx between the ovary and fallopian tube (*qv*).

Epstein-Barr virus The herpes (*qv*) virus that causes infectious mononucleosis (*qv*).

equal rights amendment (ERA) A statement that "equality of rights under the law shall not be denied or abridged by the United States or by any State on account of sex" proposed as the twenty-seventh amendment to the U.S. Constitution by the National Women's Party in 1923. The U.S. Senate passed the ERA in 1949, 1953, and 1959, but with a rider that exempted all sex-specific legislation, thereby rendering the amendment meaningless. The House refused to hold hearings until 1970 but then passed the original amendment in 1970 and 1971. The Senate passed it in 1972. Almost half the states approved the amendment immediately. The required three-fourths approval was not obtained, even with a three-year extension of the 1979 ratification deadline.

equity theory A social science theory of relationships, for example, marriage (*qv*), arguing that coupled individuals perceive themselves as satisfied and happy when there is a balance (equity) in each person's self-perceived benefits and costs. In plain English, equity theory claims that marital happiness depends on making fair bargains and fair trades openly and willingly, even if an outsider to the relationship might perceive inequalities or imbalances in the relationship. Equity theoreticians suggest that when negotiated balances break down, one member of the pair will feel exploited, tension and anger will develop, and the relationship will be at risk. *See also* exchange theory.

ER *See* embryo replacement.

ERA *See* equal rights amendment.

erectile *See* erection.

erectile dysfunction The inability of a male to have or maintain an erection (*qv*) sufficient for vaginal intercourse (*qv*) or, in a broader context, sufficient for masturbation (*qv*). Erectile dysfunction may be either primary (having always existed) or secondary (e.g., temporary, sporadic, or situational). This dysfunction, formerly known as impotence, may be due to psychological conflicts or organic causes. Among common psychological causes are an unresolved sexual trauma (*qv*), depression, sexual guilt (*qv*), anxieties, or a variety of fears, including the fear of failure, pregnancy (*qv*), or of contracting a sexually transmitted disease (*qv*). If the cause is psychological, the male usually can have an erection that allows masturbation but not intercourse. Possible organic causes include a low testosterone (*qv*) level, diabetes mellitus, multiple sclerosis, spinal cord injuries, pelvic surgery, drugs that affect the autonomic nervous system (*qv*), and some diuretic antihypertensive drugs. Deteriorating penile vascular circulation may be a factor in older men. Negative results on a test for nocturnal penile tumescence (*qv*) indicate an organic rather than psychological etiology. Erectile dysfunction may also be the result of interacting organic and psychological factors. Erectile dysfunction is also known as inhibited male sexual response (*qv*). The main behavioral treatment is sensate focus exercises (*qv*).

erectile tissue Spongy, cavernous tissue that becomes engorged with blood as a result of sexual stimulation and vasocongestion (*qv*), resulting in stiffening and erection (*qv*) of the clitoris (*qv*), minor labia (*qv*), penis (*qv*), and nipples (*qv*).

erection The stiffening and projection of the penis (*qv*) or clitoris (*qv*) as a result of sexual stimulation and vasocongestion (*qv*). Engorgement of the labia minor (*qv*) and nipples (*qv*) may also be included in this phenomenon.

erection center A nerve complex in the sacral or lumbar region of the spinal cord that controls erection (*qv*).

ergot alkaloid One of a large group of alkaloids derived from a common fungus that grows on rye and other grains in temperate climates, used as an abortifacient (*qv*), to induce completion of an incomplete or missed abortion (*qv*), and to assist in restoring normal uterine muscle tone following delivery.

Erikson's Ego Psychology *See* Ego Psychology.

erogenous area (zone) Those regions or parts of the body that, when stimulated by touch, create a subjective erotic arousal (*qv*). These include the primary erogenous areas of the clitoris (*qv*) and penis (*qv*), the labia (*qv*) and scrotum (*qv*), the mouth and lips, the perineal (*qv*) region and anus (*qv*). Secondary areas include the breasts (*qv*) and nipples (*qv*), the back of the neck, cheeks, ears, buttocks (*qv*), and inner thighs. Other areas of the skin may also serve as erogenous zones, depending on the individual.

Eros In Greek mythology, the young god of love, son of Aphrodite (*qv*) and lover of Psyche, and known also as Cupid. As a god, Eros personifies physical and sexual love (*qv*), particularly for members of the other sex. In later, especially modern, writing, Eros has come to represent the life force itself, as in Sigmund Freud's notion of Eros and *thanatos* (*qv*), the psychological forces of life and death, respectively. In psychoanalysis (*qv*), eros more specifically refers to the basic drive or instinct that expresses an individual's sexual and reproductive urges. Also, in lower-case spelling, *eros* can refer to a type of love in which the other person's sexual and physical attributes are considered primary; eros then contrasts with agape (*qv*), philia (*qv*), and storge (*qv*). *See also* courtly love; dolce stil nova; libido; love; sex.

erotic That which causes or is associated with sexual feelings or arousal (*qv*).

erotica Sexually explicit or descriptive material meeting some aesthetic standard and generally depicting socially approved sexual activities; usually also designed to stimulate sexual arousal. Erotica is usually distinguished from pornography (*qv*) although actual definitions may vary widely. In one common distinction, erotica is said to celebrate the equality of the persons involved in sharing the positive aura of sexual and physical pleasure while pornography depersonalizes sexual relations (*qv*); degrades men, women, and children; and often involves exploitation and violence in its depiction of sexual interactions. Depending on the social and legal context, erotica may or may not be considered pornographic and/or obscene (*qv*).

erotic apathy A condition or syndrome in which the ability to experience sexuoerotic (*qv*) arousal under normally conducive circumstances is absent or defective. A form of hypophilia (*qv*), erotic apathy may be due to one or more of a variety of organic and/or psychological causes. Erotic apathy may also refer to a lack of sexual desire (*qv*).

erotic bondage *See* bondage and dominance.

erotic code Those signs and actions that, given an appropriate context, convey sexual interest and arousal (*qv*), or enhance a sexual expression. Erotic codes vary widely depending on the culture. For instance, the penile extenders or codpieces (*qv*) that are part of some tribal cultures would be totally unacceptable in the erotic code of Victorian (*qv*) American society. The erotic code of dancing has changed radically as Western culture moved from the waltz and minuet to rock'n'roll, disco, and heavy metal music and dancing. The term erotic code was proposed by anthropologist William H. Davenport, Sex in cross-cultural perspective, in F. A. Beach, ed., *Human Sexuality in Four Perspectives* (Baltimore: Johns Hopkins University, 1977).

erotic delusion (paranoia) A mental disorder in which an individual becomes convinced that he or she is in love with and having a secret love affair (*qv*) with a wealthy or socially prominent person or celebrity.

erotic folklore Traditional tales, jokes, poetry, songs, and graffiti that have sexual themes or boast of or lampoon sexual behavior, particularly when considered deviant. Erotic folklore includes dirty jokes, bawdy songs ("rugby songs" in Great Britain), limericks, sexual insults, and graffiti. Examples of such erotic folklore have been found from the Orient, ancient Egypt, and classical Rome down to modern times. Resource: G. Legman, *Rationale of the Dirty Joke*, vol. 1 (New York: Grove Press, 1968), vol. 2 (New York: Breaking Point, 1975).

erotic hanging *See* asphyxiophilia; autoassassinatophilia; erotic self-strangulation.

erotic hunger strike Alfred Adler's (*qv*) term for the fear of and resistance to eating experienced by some adolescent (*qv*) girls who attempt to maintain their juvenile figure because, in Adler's view, they are afraid of assuming the normal role of a sexually mature woman. *See also* anorexia; bulimia.

erotic inertia A condition or syndrome in which one is unable to make a sexuoerotic (*qv*) initiative or maintain sexuoerotic activity under normally conducive circumstances. A form of hypophilia (*qv*), the condition may be either organic or psychogenic in origin. *See also* erotic apathy.

erotic instinct *See* libido; Eros.

eroticism (adj. erotic) The sexual impulse or desire; the personal sensual and psychological experience and expression of one's genitals (*qv*), bodily arousals (*qv*), and sexual functioning, either alone or with a partner, with an emphasis on ideation, imagery, and sensory stimuli. Eroticism refers particularly to the pleasurable sensory stimuli and responses associated with sexual arousal (*qv*) as distinguished from sexual behaviors involved in coitus (*qv*) and reproduction (*qv*). *See also* erotosexual; sexual; sexuoerotic.

eroticization *See* erotization.

erotic paranoia *See* erotic delusion.

erotic pyromania A condition in which sexual arousal (*qv*) and orgasm (*qv*) are dependent on the person's exercising control and manipulating others by staging a disaster by arson. *See also* symphorophilia.

erotic revulsion A hypophilic (*qv*) condition in which sexuoerotic (*qv*) activity is experienced as repulsive and disgusting. This response may be experienced in general or in relation to a particular partner. The response may be learned from social scripting (*qv*), religious teachings, or family attitudes or may be the result of some early traumatic experience that has not been faced and resolved.

erotic self-strangulation A rare paraphilic (*qv*) condition in which a person, usually an adolescent (*qv*) male, is dependent on partial asphyxiation, often achieved by hanging, or by restaging of this in fantasy (*qv*), in order to achieve erotic arousal (*qv*) and orgasm (*qv*). An estimated 50 adolescent and young American males annually die as an unintended result of an erotic self-strangulation that goes awry. In some cases this paraphilia appears to be associated with cross-dressing (*qv*), since some victims have been found cross-dressed. *See also* asphyxiophilia; autoassassinatophilia.

erotic/sexual *See* erotosexual.

Erotic Stimulus Pathway Model A model, proposed by David M. Reed, a psychologist at Jefferson Medical College, Philadelphia, that adds a four-stage psychological cycle of seduction (*qv*), sensations, surrender, and reflection to the four-stage physiological sexual response cycle (*qv*) proposed by William

Masters and Virginia Johnson. The psychological component of the desire stage is seduction, when we learn to seduce ourself into being sexually interested in another person at the same time trying to interest and attract that person. This seduction carries over into the excitement stage (*qv*) of the Masters and Johnson model.

Sensations overlay the excitement and plateau phases (*qv*). Our senses are nature's aphrodisiacs (*qv*), triggering conscious messages of sexual arousal (*qv*) and pleasure in the brain. The sight and voice of a beloved, the erotic (*qv*), pleasurable, healing touches, and the sights, tastes, smells, and sounds of sex play (*qv*), which are vital in the excitement-plateau stage, are processed in the conscious centers of our brain.

As the intensity of these psychological reactions builds to orgasm (*qv*), we enter the third phase of surrender. For orgasm to be a pleasurable experience, one needs to let go and give control over to the shared experience. If one has been taught to be overcontrolled or there are power struggles in the relationship, then the psychophysiological response of orgasm will be inhibited or otherwise affected.

During the resolution phase (*qv*), reflection plays an important psychological role. How a person feels immediately after the sexual experience builds a background for future sexual experiences with that person. If the immediate reflection is positive, warm, loving, and pleasurable, then the desire will likely reoccur. If the loveplay (*qv*) was not what one expected or left a negative feeling about the partner or situation, the person will be unlikely to repeat it.

erotic transference The redirection of erotic (*qv*) feelings from one person to another, usually from an individual in one's past to a person in one's current life. In psychoanalysis, the process of erotic or libidinal transference may occur when the patient transfers feelings of love for a parent to the analyst.

erotic type In psychoanalytic theory (*qv*), a personality preoccupied with loving and being loved. *See also* narcissistic type; obsessional type.

erotism *See* eroticism.

erotization In psychoanalytic theory (*qv*), the process whereby an individual gradually associates sexual pleasure and gratification with various parts of the body, such as the association of kissing (*qv*) and oral sex (*qv*) with the mouth, the enjoyment of nude art with the eyes, and erotic smells with the nose. In Freudian theory, this process is normophilic (*qv*) when the associations are integrated within a mature sexual personality. Sigmund Freud (*qv*) contended that this normal process may be diverted when a person becomes arrested or fixated in the oral (*qv*), anal (*qv*), or phallic stage (*qv*) or when a paraphilic (*qv*) orientation becomes obsessive and compulsive. In Freud's view, many seemingly asexual activities (e.g., scientific pursuits and the arts) are expressions of the libidinal drive (*qv*). *See also* esthetic pleasure.

erotogenesis In psychoanalytic theory (*qv*), the origins of sexual instincts and impulses in the oral (*qv*), anal (*qv*), and phallic (*qv*) regions of the body.

erotographomania A morbid and obsessive delight in writing love letters, usually anonymously, that express erotic and sexual interests in poetic and religious symbolisms. *See also* pornography, erotica.

erotography Written or graphic material dealing with erotic (*qv*) topics in a positive, nondegrading way. *See also* pornography; erotica.

erotolalia The use of sexually explicit talk as a means of expressing sexual interest or to enhance sexual arousal (*qv*) during loveplay (*qv*) and intercourse (*qv*). *See also* narratophilia.

erotomania A morbid exaggeration of or preoccupation with sexuoerotic (*qv*) images and activity. This condition, often stemming from doubts about one's sexual adequacy, may be limited to fantasy (*qv*) or lead to compulsive repetitive sexual activity. *See also* Casanova; Clerambault-Kandisky syndrome.

erotophilia Feeling comfortable with and positive about one's sexual nature and responses. *See also* erotophobia.

erotophobia Feelings of guilt and fear associated with one's sexual nature and responses. *See also* erotophilia.

erotophonophilia A paraphilia (*qv*) in which sexual arousal (*qv*) and orgasm (*qv*) are responsive to and dependent on stage-managing and carrying out the murder of an unsuspecting sexual partner. Also known as lust murder. The reciprocal paraphilia is autoassassinatophilia (*qv*). Despite the etymological validity of this term, combining the Greek, *eros* for "sexual love," *phonein*, "to murder," and *philia*, "love," the neologism is easily misinterpreted as referring to an obscene phone caller (*qv*).

erotosexual Combining both the erotic (*qv*) sensual response and sexual (*qv*) or reproductive behavior with more emphasis on the erotic and sensual than on the copulatory.

ERT *See* estrogen replacement therapy.

erythema (adj. **erythmatous**) Reddening of the skin due to vasocongestion (*qv*).

erythematous rash Redness of the skin resulting from superficial vasocongestion (*qv*). *See also* sex flush; sex skin.

erythroblastosis fetalis (L.) A type of hemolytic anemia occurring in newborns (*qv*) as a result of a maternal-fetal blood group (*qv*) incompatibility. The most common type of erythroblastosis fetalis involves the Rh blood factor (*qv*). The immune system of a mother who lacks the Rh blood factor will react to the Rh blood antigen (*qv*) in the circulation of an Rh-positive fetus (*qv*) if this antigen leaks across the placental barrier (*qv*). Subsequent leakage of the maternal anti-Rh antibody back cross the placental barrier will trigger destruction of the fetal red blood cells and their removal by the spleen, which undergoes hypertrophy under this stress. The fetal liver also experiences hypertrophy as it seeks to remedy the anemia by producing inefficient nucleated red blood cells. If the anemia is severe, it can result in fetal death. After birth, bilirubin pigments from the destroyed red blood cells may cause brain damage, cerebral palsy, deafness, mental retardation, or death. If the neonatal effect is severe, subsequent siblings run a higher risk of damage from this condition. Treatment is with RhO-GAM (*qv*). Once the immune system is sensitized to the Rh antigen and antibodies have been produced by the mother's immune system, all subsequent pregnancies run the risk of this condition. Also known as HDN (hemolytic disease neonatal) and Rh blood incompatibility.

erythrophobia An intense anxiety and morbid fear of the color red, expressed in a fear of blushing or displaying embarrassment. Erythrophobia may become associated sexually with erotophobia (*qv*) because of the fear of sex flush (*qv*) and reddening of the sexual organs (*qv*) during sexual arousal (*qv*).

erythroplasia of Queyrat Medical term for a premalignant, well-circumscribed, reddish, flat, and shiny patch on the glans (*qv*) or corona (*qv*) of the penis (*qv*); easily remedied by surgical removal of the patch.

ESO Extended sexual orgasm (*qv*). *See also* maithuna; coitus reservatus.

essential dysmenorrhea A form of menstrual (*qv*) dysfunction in which abdominal or menstrual pain occurs in the absence of any detectable pelvic abnormality. "Essential" means basic rather than necessary. Symptoms, including a dull, constant pain to sharp, spasmic cramps, often accompanied by nausea, headaches, diarrhea, and increased urination, may begin just before the menstrual flow (*qv*) and peak within a day before subsiding. More common in younger women, essential dysmenorrhea may result from abnormal uterine contractions or from obstruction in uterine circulation.

esthetic pleasure The sensual and mental pleasures associated with viewing, contemplating, and appreciating beauty in any form. Although the term is frequently used without any reference to sexual (*qv*) or erotic pleasure (*qv*), in the Freudian view, much, if not all, artistic appreciation and enjoyment results from libidinal pleasure drive (*qv*).

Estinyl Trade name for an estrogen (*qv*), ethinyl estradiol.

Estrace Trade name for an estrogen (*qv*), estradiol.

estradiol The most biologically potent, naturally occurring estrogen (*qv*), produced chiefly in the ovary (*qv*) by the Graafian follicle (*qv*). At puberty (*qv*),
estradiol regulates development of secondary female characteristics and the ducts
of the mammary glands (*qv*). It also controls proliferation of endometrial (*qv*)
tissues during the menstrual cycle (*qv*). Estradiol is used in oral hormonal contraceptive pills (*qv*), to inhibit lactation (*qv*), to prevent threatened abortion (*qv*),
to treat ovarian disease, and to palliate menopausal (*qv*) and postmenopausal
(*qv*) conditions such as osteoporosis and vagina atresia (*qv*). *See also* estrogen
replacement therapy. In males, estradiol has been used as an antiandrogen (*qv*)
in treating cancer of the prostate (*qv*).

estrin An estrogen (*qv*); an ovarian hormone (*qv*) whose exogenous injection
results in enlargement of genitalia (*qv*) and accompanying sexual response (*qv*).
Also known as folliculin.

estriol A relatively weak estrogen (*qv*), a metabolic product of estradiol (*qv*)
and estrone (*qv*) synthesized in the liver, placenta (*qv*), and uterus (*qv*) and found
in high concentrations in the urine (*qv*). Estriol is used in the treatment of
menopause (*qv*) and dysmenorrhea (*qv*).

estrogen A group of steroid sex hormones (*qv*) commonly referred to as female
sex hormones although they are produced naturally by both sexes. Estrogens,
including naturally produced estradiol (*qv*), estriol (*qv*), and estrone (*qv*), are
produced chiefly by the ovaries (*qv*), but also in small amounts by the adrenal
cortex (*qv*), the fetoplacental unit, and the interstitial cells of the testes (*qv*). In
mammalian females, the estrogens promote proliferation of the uterine endometrium (*qv*), producing a suitable environment for implantation (*qv*) and support
of the early embryo (*qv*) as well as enhancing breast growth. *See also* progesterone.

   In both males and females, estrogens are responsible for development of
secondary female sexual characteristics (*qv*) and inhibition of male secondary
traits. Some forms of estrogens are more biologically potent than others, the
more potent being used as antiandrogens (*qv*). A variety of synthetic estrogens,
including diethylstilbesterol (*qv*), are used therapeutically. These hormones induce sexual heat or estrus (*qv*) in lower animals, hence the name.

estrogenic Producing estrus (*qv*), or having biological properties or activities
similar to an estrogen (*qv*).

estrone An estrogen (*qv*) prescribed for menstrual irregularities (*qv*), prostatic cancer (*qv*), and menopausal (*qv*) vasomotor symptoms. Estrone is second only to estradiol (*qv*) in potency. Isolated from pregnancy (*qv*) urine (*qv*), the human placenta (*qv*), and palm kernel oil, estrone is also produced synthetically for use in contraceptive pills (*qv*).

estrus (adj. estrous) In subprimate vertebrates, the cyclic, restricted period of sexual receptivity (*qv*) that signals ovulation (*qv*). An estrous female is said to be in estrus when she is sexually receptive and fertile (*qv*). The estrous cycle is divided into preovulatory (*qv*), ovulatory (*qv*), and postovulatory (*qv*) phases with maximum proceptivity (*qv*) and receptivity around the time of ovulation. Estrus is controlled externally by environmental factors such as light and temperature, which affect the internal control mechanisms of the endocrine and reproductive systems. Persistent estrus can be experimentally produced in some newborn animals by injection of exogenous androgens (*qv*). Also known as rut, sexual heat, or heat. *See also* anestrous; menstrual cycle.

eternal suckling Sigmund Freud's (*qv*) term for a person who seeks and demands constant attention, nurturing, and protection.

ethnic group A group of people who share a common cultural or ethnic heritage. The concept of ethnicity is much debated by sociologists, who prefer to define groups in terms of a shared culture (*qv*) with a common language, customs, and institutions rather than in terms of common genetic constitution. A group may claim ethnic distinctiveness to set itself apart from others for a variety of reasons, or such distinctiveness may be imposed by some politically more powerful group seeking to maintain dominance.

Ethnographic Atlas The collection of computer-available information on some 1,200 cultures (*qv*) developed by George Peter Murdock as an extension of the Human Relations Area Files (*qv*). *See also* Standard Sample.

ethnography The direct observation, description, and interpretation of the culture, customs, and values of members of a social group. *See also* culture.

ethology The comparative study of animal behavior in its natural setting, as opposed to laboratory experimentation. Ethology often focuses on unlearned aspects of behavior, and therefore complements the concern behavioral scientists have for what is learned and socially created. *See also* sociobiology.

etiology The study of, or a theory regarding, the origin or cause of any condition; used in reference to the origin or cause of a disease or disorder.

eugenics The techniques of genetics (*qv*) and artificial selection (*qv*) as applied to the putative improvement of the genetic composition of human groups. Coined by Francis Galton in 1883, eugenics has often been associated with racist political and social programs. As a social movement, eugenics was influential in the United States between 1890 and 1920. The aim of the American Genetic Association, founded in 1913, was to maintain and improve human populations. The association's positive eugenics program provided financial incentives for parents who were thought to be in some way superior, while a negative eugenics program sought to prevent reproduction by parents who were allegedly inferior. In 1907, the state of Indiana introduced the idea of negative eugenics into its social policy by adopting a law that required sterilization (*qv*) of certain types of people. Today, these aims are discredited by most geneticists. *See also* euthenics; euphenics; social Darwinism; sociobiology.

Eulenspiegel Society An organization devoted to sadomasochistic (*qv*) liberation and education. Since its founding in 1971, this organization has broadened its activities to provide a social environment and activities for persons who enjoy bondage and dominance (*qv*), sadomasochism (*qv*), and other paraphilic (*qv*) activities. The term, derived from Tyll Eulenspiegel, a semifictitious prankster in fourteenth-century Germany, refers to the playful character of the gatherings and activities sponsored by the society. Address: Eulenspiegel Society, Box 2783, Grand Central Station, New York, NY 10163.

eunuch (adj. eunuchoid) A male whose testicles (*qv*) and sometimes the penis (*qv*) have been removed. When removal occurs before puberty (*qv*), the voice remains high-pitched, and the body does not develop male musculature. The prepubertal or juvenile male physique is referred to as the eunuchoid body type. Castration (*qv*) after puberty produces infertility (*qv*) but may not reduce sexual desire (*qv*) or erectile (*qv*) capacity because of testosterone (*qv*) produced by the adrenal glands (*qv*). The term is derived from the Greek for "guardian of the bed," referring to the use of eunuchs to guard the wives and concubines (*qv*) kept in a harem (*qv*). *See also* castratus.

eunuchoid Having the body build and physical characteristics of a prepubertal (*qv*) juvenile (*qv*). In a characteristic eunuchoid, the lower half of the body (from the feet to the pubic symphysis [*qv*]) is longer than the upper part (from the pubic symphysis to the head). The distance between the fingertips of the outstretched hands also exceeds the standing height. One type of Turner syndrome (*qv*) has a eunuchoid body and is over 5 feet tall. A sex hormone deficiency (*qv*) is the usual cause. The condition is more common in males than in females. *See also* eunuch; eunuchoidism; castrati.

eunuchoidism A deficiency in the function of testosterone (*qv*), or in its formation by the testes (*qv*), leading to sterility (*qv*), abnormal tallness, small testes, poorly developed secondary male sexual characteristics (*qv*), and reduced libido (*qv*) and potency (*qv*).

eupareunia Coitus during which an orgasm (*qv*) is achieved. *See also* dyspareunia.

euphemism A socially inoffensive term that is commonly used instead of a term that is socially unacceptable and embarrassing; for example, the use of the adjective adult (*qv*) as a substitute for sexual (*qv*) in adult bookstore, adult movies, or adult entertainment.

euphenics Any treatment or manipulation of a physiological or anatomical deficiency that allows an individual to lead a relatively normal life. *See also* eugenics; euthenics.

eurotophobia A morbid fear of the female sexual organs (*qv*).

euthenics Environmental manipulations designed to provide the best possible conditions for each individual's genotype (*qv*) to be expressed to the maximum. *See also* eugenics; euphenics.

Eve Plan (or principle) A biological principle metaphorically describing the tendency for sexual (*qv*) differentiation as a female to occur spontaneously in the absence of fetal (*qv*) testicular (*qv*) secretions of Mullerian inhibiting substance (MIS) (*qv*) and testosterone (*qv*), regardless of the individual's genetic and/or gonadal sex (*qv*). The addition of exogenous (*qv*) testosterone at the critical period (*qv*) in the sexual differentiation of a gonadal female brings into play the Adam plan (*qv*) and results in male differentiation. Because MIS blocks the anatomical development on the internal sexual anatomy of a female, it is said to be a defeminizing (*qv*) hormone (*qv*), while testosterone is a masculinizing (*qv*) hormone.

evirate A dated term for a eunuch (*qv*) or castrated (*qv*) male; also a male who believes he has turned into a woman.

exaltolide effect The ability of postpubertal (*qv*) females to perceive the musklike odor of the synthetic chemical exaltolide. The ability of women to detect musklike odors is at a maximum around the time of ovulation (*qv*), suggesting the evolution of an olfactory response that optimizes fertilization (*qv*) and fertility (*qv*). Neither men nor prepubertal females can detect this odor. *See also* pheromones.

exchange theory In anthropological theory, the conceptualization and explanation of social interaction, structure, and order in terms of exchanges, that is, what each party gains and gives in maintaining a particular relationship. Exchange theory emphasizes the shared values and trust of three or more individuals who relate with each other because they expect each person to fulfill his or her obligations to the group and not pursue purely self-centered interests. For some American sociologists, exchange theory assumes that individuals seek to maximize their own private gratification in their interactions with others and that decisions are made on the basis of a balancing of calculated or projected rewards and costs. Marriage (*qv*) and other relationships can be viewed in terms of exchange theory as an exchange of resources. *See also* equity theory.

excitement stage The first of the four stages in the physiological sexual response cycle model proposed by William Masters and Virginia Johnson. In the female, the excitement stage is characterized by vasocongestion (*qv*) and erection (*qv*) of the clitoris (*qv*), flattening and separating of the labia minora (*qv*), deepened color and two or three times increase in the size of the labia majora (*qv*), lengthening and distention of the inner two-thirds of the vagina (*qv*), nipple (*qv*) erection, breast (*qv*) enlargement, and the beginning of vaginal sweating (*qv*) within a short time after the beginning of sexual stimulation. In the male, the flaccid penis (*qv*) becomes erect, the skin and muscles of the scrotum (*qv*) thicken as the testes (*qv*) partially elevate, and Cowper's glands (*qv*) may secrete a small amount of acid-neutralizing lubricant into the urethra. *See also* Erotic Stimulus Pathway Model; plateau phase; orgasm phase; resolution phase; desire phase.

exhibitionism (exhibitionist) The paraphilic (*qv*) condition in which an individual, the exhibitionist, sexually responds to or depends on the embarrassment and shock a stranger, usually a female, expresses when unexpectedly confronted with the sight of male genitalia (*qv*). Fantasies of past exhibitionism may be replayed during masturbation (*qv*) or coitus (*qv*). The reciprocal paraphilia is voyeurism (*qv*) or scoptophilia (*qv*).

exogamy The social limitation of marriage (*qv*) to members outside one's own ethnic (*qv*), kinship (*qv*), cultural (*qv*), or religious group; marriage with a partner who is outside the individual's immediate group. *See also* endogamy.

exogenous Produced artificially outside the body and introduced into a body orally or by injection for diagnostic or therapeutic purposes. *See also* endogenous.

exoletus (pl. exoleti) (L.) In ancient Rome, a male prostitute (*qv*) with exaggerated masculine traits; the opposite of the effeminate male prostitutes known as *pueri* (little boys) or as *pathics*.

exorcism syndrome A sexual condition of repeatedly stigmatizing, assaulting, or punishing people who manifest symptoms or behavior that are at odds with one's own values. The person who seeks to exorcise the unacceptable behavior of others is often driven by the need to exorcise his or her own repressed desire to engage in the same forbidden behavior.

experimental marriage An informal or public agreement of a couple to live together before entering into a formal marriage (*qv*). In agricultural societies where the wife's ability to produce children to work the farm is important, an experimental marriage may be socially acceptable to test the woman's fertility (*qv*) prior to marriage. *See also* betrothal; espousal; trial marriage; window courting; fensternl.

extended family Conventionally an extended family consists of the biological parents, their children, the parents' parents, and perhaps other relatives living under one roof. In current usage, an extended family refers to the looser set of relationships whereby a nuclear family (*qv*) keeps in contact with its wider kin network and receives from them practical assistance in its daily life. In this usage, the typical family in modern industrial societies is not a true nuclear family but a modified extended family.

extended sexual orgasm *See* maithuna; coitus reservatus.

external cervical os The outer opening of the uterus (*qv*) located in the center of the cervix (*qv*) as it projects into the upper vaginal (*qv*) cavity.

external fertilization The union of sperm (*qv*) and ovum (*qv*) outside the bodies of the animals producing these gametes (*qv*); a reproductive pattern common in many invertebrates. *See also* amplexus; cloaca; internal fertilization.

external genitals The penis (*qv*) and scrotum (*qv*) in the male; in the female, the vulva (*qv*), or mons veneris (*qv*), major and minor labia (*qv*), clitoris (*qv*), and vaginal opening (*qv*).

external urethral sphincter One of two bundles of circular muscle fibers controlling the flow of urine (*qv*) and semen (*qv*) through the male urethra (*qv*), the external sphincter is located around the urethra just below the prostate (*qv*). During urination, both the internal and external sphincters open. During sexual arousal (*qv*) and the emission phase (*qv*) of male ejaculation (*qv*), both sphincters are closed. When the propulsion phase (*qv*) begins, the outer or external sphincter opens. In retrograde ejaculation (*qv*), the outer sphincter remains closed and the internal urethral sphincter (*qv*) opens so that semen is expelled into the bladder.

exteroreceptor Any sensory nerve ending, particularly those located in the skin, mucous membranes, or sense organs, that respond to stimuli originating from outside the body such as touch, sound, visual stimuli, heat-cold, pressure-pain, smell, and taste.

extragenital Originating outside or positioned outside the genital (*qv*) or sexual (*qv*) organs. *See also* sex flush; excitement phase; plateau phase; orgasm phase; erogenous area.

extramarital polygamy *See* man sharing.

extramarital sex Sexual intimacy and/or intercourse (*qv*) engaged in by a married person with someone other than his or her spouse. Extramarital sex may be consensual comarital relations (*qv*) as in a sexually open marriage (*qv*) or intimate network (*qv*), or it may be nonconsensual adultery, an affair (*qv*), or "cheating."

extrauterine pregnancy *See* ectopic pregnancy.

extravasate To seep out through a vessel into the tissue space. *See also* vaginal sweating.

F

F₁ In breeding experiments and genetics (*qv*), the parental generation is known as the P generation, their offspring as the F1 or first filial generation, and the grandchildren as the F2 or second filial generation.

F₂ *See* F₁.

factor analysis A statistical technique used to analyze survey data and identify common components in the data or factors that underlie a set of items. In an attitude scale (*qv*) derived from a survey of sexual attitudes, a single general factor, such as authoritarianism or religious adherence, may contribute to all items.

facultative Not obligatory; having the ability to adapt to more than one condition. For example, in facultative homosexuality (*qv*), a heterosexual person engages in homoerotic (*qv*) activity because heterosexual partners are not available. *See also* faute de mieux; obligate homosexuality; occasional inversion.

failure rate for contraceptives *See* contraceptive effectiveness.

fallectomy The surgical removal of a fallopian tube (*qv*). Also known as a salpingectomy (*qv*).

falling in love The personal experience and open expression of being intensely, and possibly suddenly, attracted, both sexually and emotionally, to another person. If reciprocated by the other person, it is the source of emotional ecstasy; if unreciprocated, it is the source of great anguish. *See also* courtship; dating; limerence; love.

fallopian tubes A pair of tubes, 3 to 4 inches long, reaching laterally from the cranial lateral corners of the uterus (*qv*) toward the two ovaries (*qv*) and embedded in the broad ligament supporting the uterus. The bell-shaped, fimbriated (*qv*) opening of each fallopian tube is positioned to facilitate entry of the ovum (*qv*) after ovulation (*qv*). Aided by rhythmic beating of ciliated cells lining the canal, the ovum passes into the fundal cavity (*qv*) of the uterus. Fertilization (*qv*) usually occurs in the tube. Following fertilization, the blastula (*qv*) passes into the uterine cavity, where it implants four or five days after fertilization. The fallopian tubes are the most common site for ectopic pregnancies (*qv*). These tubes, named after the Italian anatomist Gabriello Fallopius (1523–1562), develop from the Mullerian ducts (*qv*). Also known as oviducts, uterine tubes, and salpinx.

Fallopius, Gabriello (1523–1562) A sixteenth-century anatomist at the University of Padua who identified the oviducts or fallopian tubes (*qv*).

false erection The normal erect or projecting position of the nipples (*qv*) of the female or male breasts (*qv*), as distinct from the true nipple erection experienced by many men and women as a result of vasocongestion (*qv*) accompanying sexual arousal (*qv*).

false labor Irregular uterine contractions (*qv*) felt by a pregnant (*qv*) woman mainly in the lower abdomen and groin, in contrast with true labor (*qv*) contractions felt in the back and abdomen. Instead of increasing in frequency and regularity as true labor contractions do, false labor contractions usually occur only once or twice an hour before stopping for some time. *See also* Braxton Hicks contraction; couvade.

false negative A diagnostic test result that mistakenly indicates the absence of a condition or disease.

false ovary A congenital (*qv*) malformation in which a small mass of ovarian tissue is connected by fibrous tissue to the main ovarian structure.

false passage A medical term for any injury to the penile urethra (*qv*) or corpora cavernosa (*qv*) caused by the insertion of a foreign object into the urethra, which results in a dead-end diverticulum in the penile urethra. This may be an iatrogenic (*qv*) result of catherization or the result of insertion of a foreign object into the urethra to increase sexual arousal (*qv*) during masturbation (*qv*). A false passage often becomes a site of infection and an abscess.

false pelvis That part of the pelvis or lower body cavity above the iliopectineal line; below this line is the true pelvis or pelvic cavity.

false positive A diagnostic test result that mistakenly indicates the presence of a condition or disease. *See also* false negative.

false pregnancy A psychosomatic condition resulting in all the normal symptoms of pregnancy (*qv*) but without actual conception (*qv*) and pregnancy (*qv*) occurring. *See also* couvade.

false twins A misnomer for a pair of dizygotic twins (*qv*), the implication being that two infants born following a simultaneous gestation (*qv*) in one mother must be monozygotic twins (*qv*).

familial sexual hormonal disorder A congenital condition (*qv*) in which abnormally low levels of fetal sex hormones (*qv*) result in poor development of the genitalia (*qv*). Along with impaired sexual characteristics, affected individuals may suffer from dysmenorrhea (*qv*), mental retardation, deafness, and poor muscular coordination. This condition, also known as Koennicke's syndrome, is at least in part hereditary.

familiarism In sociology, the tendency of members within a family (*qv*) to maintain extremely close relations and a strong sense of family solidarity. This bonding may make it difficult for individuals to establish independent and mature relationships outside the family circle.

family In Western cultures, the smallest kinship (*qv*) whose core normally consists of two parents and their offspring. The word *family*, in the sense of a residential and biological unit, is relatively new. Before the eighteenth century, no European language had a term for the mother-father-child grouping. From Roman times through the Middle Ages and into the early modern period, the Latin cognate *familia* signified a house and all its inhabitants, including slaves, servants, and blood relatives. In modern usage, the word *family* has three meanings: (1) a lineage or line of descent; (2) a given person's living biological relations, including parents, siblings, grandparents, aunts, uncles, and cousins, whether or not they share the same domicile; and (3) one or two parents living together with their children and constituting a household.

Historians commonly speak of three types of families. In a *stem family*, three generations live together: parents, the eldest son and his family, and younger unmarried siblings. In a *joint family*, the parents share the same domicile with several married children and their families. In the *nuclear family*, parents and their children live together, but the children move out to establish their own families when they marry. *Single-parent families*, usually headed by a woman, may result from divorce (*qv*) of the original parents or from birth to an unwed mother. *See also* matrifocal. A *reconstituted* or *blended family* results from the divorce of two sets of parents and remarriage of former spouse from each of the original families, with children of one or both first marriages being integrated into the second marriage and family. Non-Western cultures have quite different definitions of family and kinships (*qv*). *See also* clan; extended family; kinship; matrilineal; nuclear family; patrilineal; patriarchal. Resource: F. Gies and J.

Gies, *Marriage and the Family in the Middle Ages* (New York: Harper & Row, 1987).

family codes of law Laws related to family issues such as marriage (*qv*), divorce (*qv*), adoption (*qv*), child support and custody, child neglect and abuse (*qv*), spouse abuse (*qv*), and the protection of minors. *See also* civil codes of law; criminal codes of law.

family institution The normative ways in which a small kinship (*qv*) group performs the key function of nurturant socialization of the newborn (*qv*).

family planning A colloquial term for contraception (*qv*).

fantasy (phantasy) The unrestrained, free play of the imagination; a series of mental images connected by a story line or dramatic plot; a daydream or dream occurring during the rapid eye movement phase of sleep. Sexual fantasies play a major role in psychogenic erotic arousal (*qv*) and orgasm (*qv*) resulting from masturbation (*qv*). They may also be an important psychogenic factor in erotic encounters with a partner. Enhancement of fantasy skills is often part of sexual enrichment exercises and therapies. A sexual fantasy may be a program of future expectations or hopes, a replay of past experiences, or a combination of both. It may be based on conscious or subconscious wishes and unfulfilled impulses. Erotosexual (*qv*) fantasies may be completely unrelated to a current sexual activity with a partner. This is the case with paraphilic (*qv*) fantasies in which the person reenacts in fantasy a previous experience in order to achieve sexual arousal and orgasm in a current relationship. In paraphilic reenactment fantasies, the fantasy eventually loses its erotic potential and the paraphilic behavior must be repeated to revitalize the fantasy. *See also* forced fantasy; guided fantasy.

FAS *See* fetal alcohol syndrome.

Fascinating Womanhood A best-selling book of the 1970s by Helen Andelin (New York: Bantam Books, 1965) that advocated a philosophy of male dominance and leadership and voluntary female submission (*qv*) in keeping with biblical injunctions about the proper roles for men and women. *See also* Total Woman.

father, fatherhood, fatherly Biologically, in sexually reproducing species, the father is the male parent (*qv*), the individual that contributes sperm (*qv*) for fertilization (*qv*) of the ovum (*qv*). This definition applies to all sexually reproducing species except those with isogametes (*see* isogamy) or that reproduce by conjugation (*qv*) or parthenogenesis (*qv*).

In many species, males interact with females only during periods of sexual activity and have little or no role in the care, feeding, protection, or nurturance of the offspring. In other species, such as the social canids (e.g., wolves) and primates (e.g., gorillas and marmosets), the male parent interacts extensively with the young in protective and recreational/playful ways.

When the term father is applied to human beings, its definition in English combines in one word the concept of biological fatherhood with a variety of culturally variable, socially instituted roles, duties, obligations, and benefits. The precise balance of meanings among these aspects of fathering depends on history, economics, and social and cultural traditions. On the other hand, classic Latin distinguished biological and social aspects of fatherhood under different words: *genitor* for the impregnator, and *pater* for the social father or for the male head of the family and household (*paterfamilias*). Accordingly, definitions of the word father are intimately linked to definitions of the family and to the existence of socially distinct gender roles (*qv*) for men and women, as well as to the biological processes of sexual reproduction.

In addition, the term father has a number of metaphorical or extended meanings that center on the idea that the father is the founder, originator, or creator of something, or is the chief or head of a group. In those parts of male society that are overtly hierarchical, a man who is the oldest, most powerful, most wealthy, or most revered may be called by the honorific title of father or patriarch (Greek, "father-ruler"), even if that individual has no biological relation to the people he rules or governs. Common English retains this sense of father in the phrase "George Washington was the father of his country," in which Washington's role in the American revolution and as first president is likened simultaneously both to his being the figurative progenitor of the nation as well as its first ruling or dominant male figure. This hierarchical sense of the word has led feminist writers to use the term patriarchal to characterize male society and, more generally, to characterize American society as a whole.

Legally, the term father has meanings that depend on family and marriage (*qv*) law, and on whether a nation allows legal divorce (*qv*). In countries that do not permit divorce, legal codes often define the father of the wife's children as her husband no matter who the actual biological father may be. In the United States, complex legal processes may be needed to determine the identity of a child's biological father (*see* paternity suit), although socially it is usual to assume that all the children of a married woman are her husband's offspring, even if the speaker might know to the contrary. Thus, both informal social rules (e.g., courtesy) and complex legally and institutionally defined codes interact to define a given man as the father of a given child.

Ethnographically, the customs of fathering and fatherhood are quite varied, and depend on differences in history, economics, and culture. Non-Western customs associated with fatherhood also have been subject to great change following colonialization and the imposition of Western legal codes.

Fatherly usually refers to emotional aspects of fathering rather than to biological, social, or legal concepts. Broadly, it means acting in supportive and loving yet firm ways toward children and possibly adults. Because such paternal behavior can be condescending and unpleasant, to say that individuals or institutions are "paternalistic" means that they are controlling, manipulative, and anti-egalitarian.

Fathering and its emotional and legal complexities have become a significant part of the men's liberation (*qv*) movement, especially aspects of the rights of fathers to visit or participate in the upbringing of their children after a divorce.

father figure A substitute or surrogate (*qv*) for a father (*qv*) or the father's role. A father figure is usually an authority figure, often a male relative or family friend, who performs the typical functions of a father and serves as a role model of the male parent who is absent or detached.

father fixation In psychoanalytic theory (*qv*), an irrational and inordinate attachment of a child to the father (*qv*). Fixation is said to prevent a son from establishing mature sexual relations (*qv*) or from falling in love (*qv*) with a woman, or a fixated daughter from falling in love with a man. *See also* Oedipal complex; Electra complex.

father imago Latin for father figure (*qv*).

father surrogate *See* father figure.

faute de mieux (Fr.) In psychiatric terminology, facultative homosexuality (*qv*) or homoerotic (*qv*) behavior resulting from the lack of an available heterosexual partner. Literally, the French phrase means "for want of something better."

fecundation Impregnation (*qv*) or fertilization (*qv*).

fecundity As used in demography, fecundity refers to the biological ability to produce offspring as distinct from actual reproduction (*qv*) or fertility (*qv*). In this usage, the fertility rate is always lower than the fecundity rate.

feedback An enrichment and therapeutic modality based on a control system (technically, a servomechanism) in which a signal generated from monitoring a generally unconscious process or activity is presented in a visual or aural signal. This allows the patient to respond to the changing signal with a conscious effort to alter the original autonomic process or activity (e.g., monitoring blood pressure by an audio or light signal and consciously trying to lower it). *See also* biofeedback; feedback, hormonal.

feedback, hormonal A physiological-biological control system, or servomechanism, in which the release into the body of a metabolic product serves as a regulator for the initiating mechanism so that neither too much nor too little of the end product is produced. In the human sexual system, (1) the hypothalamic gonadotropic releasing factors (*qv*) activate (2) gonadotropin (*qv*) production in the pituitary (*qv*), which (3) in turn activates estrogen (*qv*) and androgen (*qv*) production by the ovaries or testes (4). These sexual hormones (*qv*) then circulate in the blood to affect target organs throughout the body. At the same time, (5) circulating estrogens or androgens inhibit their excess production by inhibiting production of releasing factor and gonadotropins in a negative feedback.

Feline T-cell lymphotrophic virus-I (FeTLV-I) A T-cell retrovirus (*qv*) that infects the lymphocytes of cats, producing symptoms similar to human acquired immunodeficiency syndrome (AIDS) (*qv*). Because of the similarities between human and feline AIDS, the FeTLV-I virus may provide a useful research model.

fellatio Stimulation of the penis (*qv*) with the lips, mouth, or tongue by a male or female partner. Fellatio, a form of oral sex (*qv*), may or may not be continued to orgasm (*qv*) and ejaculation (*qv*), and the partner may or may not swallow the ejaculate. Fellatio is considered by sexologists to be a normal part of love play (*qv*), but some legal and religious codes may make it unlawful or sinful, treating it as an unnatural act (*qv*) or as nonprocreative.

Because fellatio is often performed without a condom (*qv*), it can be an avenue for the transmission of venereal diseases (*see* sexually transmitted disease) such as syphilis (*qv*), gonorrhea, herpes II (*qv*), and perhaps acquired immune deficiency syndrome (AIDS) (*qv*). Fears of AIDS transmission in particular have led to the use of condoms (*qv*) by some individuals, although it is not epidemiologically proven that AIDS is transmitted by oral sex.

There is a large literature on fellatio in modern sexological writing, particularly in sexual advice manuals, and it is a commonplace in visual and written pornography (*qv*) and erotica (*qv*). Classic and older written material is collected and analyzed in G. Legman's *Oragenitalism: Oral Techniques in Genital Excitation* (New York: Julian Press, 1969).

The term itself is borrowed without change from classic Latin, where *fello* originally meant "to suck the teat," a parallel also occurring in Sigmund Freud's idea that fellatio is a substitute for the infant's gratification in suckling the breast (*qv*). However, etymology and psychoanalytic speculation aside, in classic Latin and common modern English usage, fellatio refers specifically to sucking the penis. In Latin and in some modern sex manuals (*qv*), a distinction is drawn between fellatio and irrumatio (*qv*) according to who is the actively moving partner. In Latin, *irrumatio* meant "to thrust the penis vigorously in the partner's mouth," as opposed to fellatio, in which the partner actively moves his or her head and mouth around the penis. In modern English, this distinction has largely vanished and fellatio refers to both types of sexual activity. *See also* cunnilingus; soixante-neuf. Resource: J. N. Adams, *The Latin Sexual Vocabulary* (Baltimore: Johns Hopkins University Press, 1982).

female In biology, the individual who produces ova (*see* ovum) or who gestates (*qv*) and gives birth (*qv*) to the young. This definition is intended by biologists to be as general as possible, and its domain includes nearly all sexually reproducing organisms with the exception of a few microorganisms that produce interfertilizing gametes (*qv*) of equal size and mobility (*see* isogametes) or that reproduce by conjugation (*qv*).

In comparative zoology, females may have additional characteristics associated with internal fertilization and live birth: a canal for the transfer of sperm (*qv*) and for birth—the vagina (*qv*); a vascular, nutritive organ, the uterus (*qv*) or uteri, in which embryos (*qv*) develop; milk glands and teats for suckling; and, in the brain and endocrine system, specializations relating to the cyclic release of hormones (*qv*) involved with ovulation (*qv*) and uterine development.

The reproductive behavior of female mammals is quite varied. In some species, for example, rodents, the female displays an estrous cycle (*see* estrus), in which periods of sexual receptivity (*qv*) and fertility (*qv*) alternate with periods of nonreceptivity and infertility. Females in other species, for example, deer, display seasonal receptivity and fertility. In some primates and in humans, receptivity is not periodic, although in the underlying menstrual cycle (*qv*) there is periodic release of ova and shedding of the uterine lining. Characteristically, female mammals also display proceptive behavior (*qv*) in which the female actively seeks and solicits males. Following the birth of the young, mammalian females display ''maternal'' behavior, a loosely defined set of behavior patterns associated with suckling, retrieving the young if they stray from the nest, and social/sanitary activities such as licking the young. The social behavior of female mammals is likewise complex, involving at a minimum a period of obligate interaction with the newborn but often involving extensive, lifelong associations with other females, usually kin (a matriline).

Genetically, females and males are often, but not universally, distinguished by possessing different gene complexes or chromosomes that are functionally associated with sexual dimorphism (*qv*); *see* sex chromosomes. In mammals, including humans, the female normally has two X chromosomes whereas males normally have one X and one Y chromosome in addition to the autosomes. In other vertebrates, like birds, the arrangement can be reversed, with the male having two Z chromosomes and the female one Z and one W chromosome. In invertebrates, particularly insects, there is a wide variety of chromosomal and genetic differences between males and females.

When, however, the domain of definition of female is narrowed to refer only to human beings, the word becomes extremely complex because it is associated with far more attributes and connotations than biological characteristics and refers to socially defined aspects of women's social, sexual, intellectual, and cultural lives. Because the latter are distinguished in common speech and social life from the activities or characteristics of males, when we speak of someone as ''female'' we implicitly accept a division of human beings into two distinct sexes (*see* sex). Typically, the existence of this division is taken for granted by speakers and users of language, who often feel (consciously or unconsciously) that the distinctions between females and males are "natural" and are subject to social constructions of gender (*qv*). Linguistically, then, the word female blends within itself references to biological characteristics with references to social attributes of gender role (*qv*), to create a single word for what seems to be an indivisible whole—a female—rather than an integrated compound of conceptually distinct characteristics—a "person with female anatomy and with a woman's gender role." In brief, the word creates a unifying image or mask for a complex mixture of attributes.

The same is true for the word male, and it can therefore be argued that words such as female and male, feminine and masculine, and girl and boy all serve to simplify and dichotomize what otherwise would be an immense variety of differences among individuals with different biological heritages, sexual preferences (*qv*), and careers, and, in general, roles in society. In this specific sense, the term female is reductionist or, at best, a mere abbreviation for a much wider range of phenomena all lumped into a convenient, if inaccurate, term.

Like many words of very broad meaning and emotional importance, the word female carries with it a series of connotations, some positive and some negative. Its positive connotations revolve around the capacity to give birth and seemingly to create life, while its negative connotations center on ideas of passivity, inactivity, and emotional lability. In this phenomenon, it appears that the term has become the receptacle for stereotypes and prejudices, both positive and negative but always limited in their scope of understanding.

The word itself has a long and complex history, deriving from Middle English, Old French, and, originally, Latin. In spite of its spelling, the word female is not a derivation or modification of male but rather a diminutive of Latin *femina*, meaning "woman," as in *femella* and the like. However, from its earliest uses in English in the late 1300s, the term has meant approximately "women in general, seen in their reproductive and sexual contexts." It is therefore not surprising that in modern English the word is heavily burdened with an extraordinary range of social, biological, and psychological meanings, denotations, and connotations.

female choice An informal term referring to one aspect of sexual selection (*qv*) in which mate selection results from female solicitation (*qv*) of one or more males as a mate and rejection of other males. In Darwinian evolutionary theory, it is often argued that males are not as selective about their sexual or reproductive partners as are females. Female choice plays a large role in sociobiological (*qv*) theorizing, but the phenomenon of female choice exists in animals and humans independently of Darwinian and sociobiological thinking.

female circumcision *See* clitorectomy.

female ejaculation The controversial phenomenon of fluid expulsion from the female urethra (*qv*) reported by some women following stimulation of the Grafenberg spot (*qv*). In the seventeenth century, the Dutch embryologist Regnier de Graaf described some small glands and ducts surrounding the urethra in women. These glands, de Graaf reported, produced a clear fluid "which makes women more libidinous with its pungency and saltiness." In the 1930s, Theodore H. Van de Velde also spoke of female ejaculation:

It appears that the majority of laymen believe that something is forcibly squirted or expelled from the woman's body in orgasm, and should so happen normally, as in the man's case . . . I cannot venture to decide whether it should so happen, according to natural law. There is no doubt that it does happen to some women. But whether these are a majority or minority, I am unable to determine.

(Cited by J. L. Sevely and J. W. Bennett, 1978, Concerning female ejaculation and the female prostate. *Journal of Sex Research.* 14:1–20.)

Clinical studies and laboratory analyses suggest that the fluid expelled is a female parallel to the male prostatic fluid, secreted by the Skene's glands (*qv*), which are homologous to the male prostate (*qv*). The "ejaculate" may be produced in a trickle or sometimes in a "gushing stream." Researchers suggest that about 10 percent of women experience this phenomenon. Resource: A. Ladas, B. Whipple, and M. Perry, *The G Spot and Other Discoveries in Female Sexuality* (New York: Holt Rinehart & Winston, 1982). *See also* A frame orgasm; tenting orgasm; blended orgasm.

female impersonator A male who dresses in feminine clothing and adopts a feminine role as part of an entertainment or comedy act. The episodic adoption of feminine dress and role may or may not be associated with transvestism (*qv*) and/or homosexuality (*qv*). *See also* transsexual.

female liberation movement *See* women's liberation.

female orgasmic dysfunction *See* orgasmic dysfunction.

female sexual desire peak Any phase of the menstrual cycle (*qv*) when a significant portion of women experience an increased desire for sexual activity (*qv*). Research indicates three periods of heightened sexual desire: about 50 percent of women report a peak after the start of the menstrual flow (*qv*), 30 percent report a peak just before the menstrual flow begins, and the remaining 20 percent peak about the time of ovulation (*qv*).

female sperm The female-determining sperm (*qv*), containing 24 autosomes (*qv*) and an X chromosome (*qv*). *See also* androsperm; gynosperm.

female vindictiveness A concept used occasionally in legal proceedings to suggest that a woman's complaint of acquaintance, date, or marital rape (*qv*) is actually motivated by an attempt to punish a boyfriend or estranged husband.

feminine (n. femininity) Behavior, characteristics, appearance, and/or attire traditionally or culturally attributed to the woman; the quality or state of being womanly, expressing the physical, social, and sexual roles that a particular culture or society considers appropriate to the female gender and sex; *see* female.

According to Casey Miller and Kate Swift, feminine and masculine are "perhaps the most culturally biased words in the language. Rarely employed in a biological sense, they are used instead to describe what a group or society has decided female and male persons should (or should not) be." Resource: C. Miller and K. Swift, *The Handbook of Nonsexist Writing for Writers, Editors, and Speakers* (New York: Lippincott and Crowell, 1980). *See also* feminine identity.

High among the prescriptive meanings of feminine are the deprecatory senses of weak, womanish (*qv*), effeminate, passive, and dependent: terms listed by various dictionaries as secondary meanings of feminine. Here, usage contrasts feminine with masculine (*qv*), in its perceived strength, activity, and steadfastness. Although such usages may be stereotyped at best, and sexist and phallocentric at worst, they are nonetheless significant for understanding the range of meanings associated with sex and gender terms. Likewise, in some usages, *feminine* refers to delicate attractiveness mixed with charm and prettiness. Once again, there is an implicit linguistic contrast to masculine, now perceived as forthright, unmannered, rude, and socially maladept. As with the words female (*qv*) and male (*qv*), the word feminine does not exist alone but is used and defined in contrast and comparison with a cognate term, masculine. Whether or not the term feminine receives positive connotations depends on the speaker's intentions and beliefs, a fact that explains how one word can carry seemingly contradictory meanings.

However, in patriarchal or male chauvinist (*see* male chauvinism) thoughts, femininity has most often been valued negatively as irrational, illogical, emotional, noncompetitive, nonaggressive, sexually passive, and even frigid (*see* frigidity), as well as interested only in nurturing, child rearing, and homemaking. In the past century these stereotypes have been challenged by feminism (*qv*) and a growing emphasis on androgynous (*qv*) values.

In 1789, the feminist pioneer Mary Wollstonecraft (*qv*) defined femininity as "weak elegancy of mind, exquisite sensibility, and sweet docility of manner." According to Katherine MacKinnon, femininity "means attractiveness to men, which means sexual attractiveness, which means sexual availability on male terms." A counterpart to the machismo (*qv*) stereotype of masculinity (*qv*), in this view femininity depersonalizes women. Resource: C. Kramarae and P. A. Treichler, *A Feminist Dictionary* (London: Pandora Press, 1985).

feminine hygiene Measures taken by a woman to ensure absence of any odor from the sexual organs (*qv*), especially during menstruation (*qv*) and pregnancy (*qv*). These measures are more frequently advertised and promoted in the United States than in European countries. They include shaving the legs, arms, and underarms, and the use of vaginal douches (*qv*), vaginal sprays, and body powders. The term is also a euphemism for sanitary napkins (*qv*), contraceptives (*qv*), vaginal suppositories (*qv*), and vaginal jellies (*qv*). When feminine hygiene products are used to mask or disguise persistent malodors, significant pathological processes may go unnoticed. Natural health practitioners and other health professionals therefore often urge the use of soap and water for cleaning, rather than relying on commercial vaginal sprays.

feminine identification *See* sissy boy syndrome.

feminine identity A core gender identity (*qv*) or inner awareness that one is a female rather than a male. *See also* gender identity transposition; gender role transposition; sexual orientation transposition; sissy boy syndrome; transsexual.

feminine masochism A psychoanalytic term for a pattern of passivity and receptivity, which Sigmund Freud (*qv*) considered characteristic of the ''feminine nature.'' The term also refers to a male who seeks to satisfy a need to be punished by fantasizing he is suffering the pains of childbirth (*qv*) or being forced into prostitution (*qv*).

feminine mystique The title of Betty Friedan's 1963 best seller, *The Feminine Mystique*, which discusses the outcome of the then popular cultural identification of womanhood with the roles of wife and mother. The myth of the feminine mystique indoctrinated women with the belief that ''the highest value and only commitment for women is the fulfillment of their femininity . . . . The new mystique makes the housewife-mother, who never had a chance to be anything else, the model for all women.'' Friedan identified a ''nameless aching'' produced by the split between the cultural ideal of feminine (*qv*) fulfillment and the reality of isolation, frustration, and despair women found when they conformed to the myth. The popularity of Friedan's book led to founding of the National Organization for Women in 1966 and to a rebirth of the women's liberation movement (*qv*).

feminine traits Characteristics actually or supposedly associated with women and with femininity, including behavior, appearance, manners, attire, and personality. *See also* feminine.

femininity *See* feminine.

femininity complex A concept proposed by psychoanalyst Melanie Klein that maintains that boys respond to the fear of castration (*qv*) by wishing they had a vagina (*qv*) and breasts (*qv*), but at the same time dreading the feminine role so strongly they become sexually aggressive.

femininosexual An obsolete term for lesbian (*qv*).

feminism The political, social, cultural, economic, intellectual, and personal theory and movement for achieving equal rights for women, socially, politically, economically, and sexually; the "women's rights movement." In 1911, Teresa Billington-Greig defined feminism as

a movement seeking the reorganization of the world upon a basis of sex-equality in all human relationships; a movement which would reject every differentiation between individuals upon the ground of sex, would abolish all sex privileges and sex burdens, and would strive to set up the recognition of the common humanity of woman and man as the foundation of law and custom.

Throughout its history, feminism has been characterized by three different positions: (1) a conscious stand that opposes defamation and mistreatment of women by men, (2) a belief that males and females are culturally and not just biologically formed, and (3) an outlook that transcends the accepted value systems of the time by exposing and opposing cultural prejudices and narrowly defined gender roles (*qv*) in a desire for equal opportunities for both sexes.

From the middle of the nineteenth century and throughout the twentieth century in America, the feminist movement has supported a variety of reform, liberal, radical, and revolutionary goals. These have included voting rights for women; feminist activism in the labor movement and labor unions characterized by the slogan "Equal Pay for Equal Work"; reform and revision of family (*qv*) and marriage (*qv*) customs and laws, particularly in the areas of divorce (*qv*), child support, free access to contraception (*qv*), and abortion (*qv*); the Equal Rights Amendment (*qv*) effort; radical alteration of male–female sexual and emotional relationships, ranging from proposals for the abolition of marriage (*qv*) through the establishment of lesbian (*qv*) communes (*qv*); and socialist/Marxist efforts to establish socialism as a precursor to a fully egalitarian state. Feminism has also involved a major attempt to escape the patriarchal biases of traditional religions by articulating, primarily through art, a contemporary space-age, ecologically oriented theology of GAIA (the whole earth considered as a single living organism) based in but also transcending the ancient Earth Mother religious traditions (Resources: E. W. Gadon, *The Once and Future Goddess: A Symbol for Our Time* [New York: Harper and Row, 1989]; M. Gimbotas, *The Language of the Goddess* [New York: Harper and Row, 1989]).

Other issues associated with feminism have centered on linguistic reform and the elimination of sexist language, particularly masculine pronouns; the establishment with corporate and educational institutions of maternal leave and day-care centers; and the development of egalitarian ideologies and career possibilities.

Feminism can, also refer to a body of philosophical and theoretical writing that develops principles and strategies for achieving feminist goals. In this sense, feminism is closely associated with women scholars who have systematically been reexamining social life and history in order to eliminate and replace anti-female and misogynist biases, as well as to correct errors in fact and interpretation about women and history. Accordingly, the literature on feminism is immense. Resource: C. Kramarae and P. A. Treichler, *A Feminist Dictionary* (London: Pandora Press, 1985).

feminist A person, particularly a woman, who endorses and strives to achieve the purposes and aims of feminism (*qv*), either in her own life or in broader social, cultural, economic, or intellectual arenas; a woman who is an active member in support of feminist organizations or of the women's movement (*qv*). The right to define this term has itself become an issue within feminism, with many feminist writers and theoreticians objecting in principle when men try to define it. It is thus controversial within feminism whether or not a man can be, or can call himself, a feminist. Some writers in the male liberation movement speak of men who are "feminist-identified" to indicate that they support the goals of feminism without trying to preempt or co-opt those goals.

Broadly, historians of the women's movement have distinguished several strands of meaning within the concept of feminist. A "liberal" feminist advocates equal status and rights for women and men, equal pay for equal work, and equal employment opportunities within the existing social and economic system of modern America, and denies that feminist goals necessarily require radical or revolutionary restructuring of American or other patriarchal societies. By contrast, "radical" feminists argue that attaining such short-term goals are mere anodynes for an infinitely deeper structural and profound disequality between men and women that can be overcome only by seeking total or near-total change in American politics, economics, family and marital life, and sexual customs. Among these are some "lesbian feminists," who may speak of themselves as "woman-identified" and who may refuse social and sexual contact with men. "Socialist" or "Marxist" feminists specifically hold that equality for women cannot be achieved until the American capitalist system has been replaced with a socialist economy wherein the family (*qv*) and marriage as institutions will be subject to planned change in directions of equality and a justice not believed to exist at present. These theoretical differences are the source of much writing and concern to activists within feminism.

feminization To make or become feminine (*qv*); the anatomical and neurological differentiation of the fetus (*qv*) as a female. In human fetal development, feminization proceeds naturally in the absence of the threshold levels of Mullerian inhibiting substance (*qv*) and other as-yet-unidentified defeminizing (*qv*) hormones (*qv*). Feminization may occur simultaneously with either masculinization (*qv*) controlled by threshold levels of androgens (*qv*) or with demasculinization (*qv*) when androgens are not present in sufficient amounts at critical periods (*qv*). In a 46,XY genetic male with testicular feminization (*qv*), androgenic hormones are present in sufficient amounts at the proper times, but the target cells are incapable of responding to their masculinizing message so that the inherent feminizing process takes precedence. *See also* defeminization. In sociological usage, an occupation is said to be feminized when women enter it in significant numbers.

feminization of poverty The socioeconomic trend that increasingly puts women at an economic disadvantage and increases their proportion among the poor. In the United States, two out of three poor adults are women, and one out of five children is poor. Single women head half of all poor families, and over half the children in female-headed households are poor. No-fault divorce (*qv*), which was supposed to reduce the feminization of poverty for divorced women and mothers, has in effect had the near-opposite outcome.

feminizing neoplasm An ovarian tumor (*qv*) that increases the level of estrogens (*qv*) and may thereby cause a premature puberty (*qv*) in a young girl, or, in a sexually mature woman, irregular uterine bleeding, breast enlargement, and/or endometrial hyperplasia.

feminizing testes (testicular) syndrome *See* androgen insensitivity syndrome; testicular feminization syndrome.

femme fatale (Fr.) A reputedly irresistible, seductive woman; in the Hollywood mystique, a woman with a throaty, sexy voice who dresses in a mysteriously seductive way.

femme sole (Fr.) The legal term for a single, widowed, divorced, or separated married woman. Also spelled feme sole.

femoral testicle An ectopic (*qv*) testis (*qv*) that has migrated from the fetal abdomen to the medial side of the thigh opposite the scrotum (*qv*) instead of to the scrotum.

Fensternl (Germ.) A German custom of prenuptial courtship (*qv*) which functions in rural areas to ensure a young woman's fertility (*qv*) before she marries. In an agrarian culture, a young man seeking a bride would be concerned about the ability of a potential bride to produce offspring to help with farm work. Fensternl, "window courting," provided this assurance in a socially acceptable way. At about the age of 18, young women alert young men that they are courting by hanging a lighted lantern or other signal in their bedroom window. When young men stop by, assisted, if need be, by a ladder, the woman may invite the young men who interest her to spend the night and leave before the parents and rest of the family arise in the morning. When the young woman becomes pregnant (*qv*), she announces her choice of a husband, without concern for the identity of the actual father of the first child. The custom persists in rural areas and smaller German villages where it provides a simple way for young people to meet and court. In the modern context, pregnancy is no longer one of the goals of Fensternl. On Scandinavian farms, a similar custom is known as "taking your night feet for a walk." A similar colonial American custom that endured into the late eighteenth and early nineteenth centuries was known as bundling (*qv*).

ferning A crystalline, fernlike pattern shown by uterine cervical mucus (*qv*), sampled at the time of ovulation (*qv*), as it dries when spread on a glass microscope slide. Before and after ovulation, the cervical mucus dries in a granular pattern because of the influence of progesterone (*qv*). *See also* Spinnbarkheit.

fertile Capable of reproducing or bearing offspring; by extension, capable of generating anything new.

fertile days *See* fertile period.

fertile period In a woman's menstrual cycle (*qv*), the period 2 to 3 days before and 2 to 3 days after ovulation (*qv*) during which fertilization (*qv*) may occur—between the eleventh and seventeenth days of a typical 28 day cycle. The estimate of the fertile period is based on the fact that the ovum (*qv*) can be fertilized for at least 24 hours after ovulation and spermatozoa (*qv*) can fertilize for 48 to 72 hours after ejaculation (*qv*). *See also* basal body temperature; calendar method of birth control; Billings' contraceptive method; rhythm method of contraception.

fertility Biologically, the ability to reproduce; sociologically, the actual number of live births in a population in one year. In the biological-medical usage, a distinction may be made between *natural fertility* and *potential fertility*, the latter taking into account the use of various therapies and fertility drugs to overcome infertility problems. *See also* fertility cohort; fecundity; birthrate.

fertility awareness *See* Mittleschmerz.

fertility cohort The number of live births for a group or cohort (*qv*) of women during their fertile years.

fertility cycle The monthly reoccurrence of ovulation (*qv*) and fertility (*qv*) in women between menarche (*qv*) and menopause (*qv*). In women, the menstrual cycle (*qv*) integrates production of one or more ova (*qv*) with preparation of the uterus (*qv*) for implantation (*qv*) by cycling variations in the release of follicle-stimulating hormone releasing factor (*qv*) and luteinizing hormone releasing factor (*qv*) from the hypothalamus (*qv*), follicle-stimulating hormone (*qv*) and luteinizing hormone (*qv*) from the anterior pituitary (*qv*), and estrogens (*qv*) and progesterone (*qv*) from the ovaries (*qv*) and uterus to facilitate fertilization (*qv*) and implantation of the resultant zygote (*qv*). Despite individual variations in the length of the menstrual cycle, the beginning of each menstrual flow (*qv*) occurs 14 days after ovulation. The fertility potential is highest for the 4 or 5 days surrounding ovulation.

fertility drug Any of several synthetic hormone (*qv*) preparations administered to stimulate ovulation (*qv*) in an anovulatory (*qv*) woman, such as the nonsteroidal drug Clomid (*qv*) or clomiphrene citrate, or Perganol (*qv*), a human menopausal gonadotropin (*qv*). While the risk of multiple ovulation, and thus a multiple pregnancy, has been reduced with the smaller doses of fertility drugs currently used, the risk of multiple pregnancy is still higher than with a naturally ovulating woman. This increased risk brings an increased risk of miscarriage (*qv*).

fertility rate The number of pregnancies per year per 1,000 women of child-bearing age in a population. In a population where no contraceptive (*qv*) methods are used, the natural fertility rate is estimated at approximately 800 pregnancies per year per 1,000 women of childbearing age.

fertilization The union of ovum (*qv*) and sperm (*qv*); in the human this restores the normal diploid (*qv*) 46-chromosome (*qv*) complement to the zygote (*qv*). In most fish and amphibians, fertilization is external, occurring outside the female body. In higher animals, primates, and humans, fertilization is internal and usually occurs in the fallopian tube (*qv*). Once a single sperm has penetrated the outer membrane of the ovum, rapid changes prevent other sperm from entering the ovum. This penetration also triggers maturation of the ovum and release of the second polar body (*qv*), giving the ovum a haploid (*qv*) chromosome complement that combines with the haploid complement of the sperm. Fertilization is sometimes loosely referred to as conception (*qv*), a term more properly used for the implantation (*qv*) of the blastocyst (*qv*) in the uterine wall several days after fertilization.

fertilization membrane A barrier that develops around the ovum (*qv*) due to changes in the ovum membrane and the zona pellucida (*qv*) surrounding the ovum, which prevents other sperm (*qv*) from entering the ovum after it is fertilized (*qv*). When the first sperm makes contact with the ovum and penetrates the zona and ovum membrane, polarity in the zona is reversed to repel any other sperm attempting to enter the ovum. In sea urchins and frogs, the viscosity of the ovum membrane is also increased as cortical granules under the membrane break down and fuse with the ovum membrane and zona pellucida. This reinforcement may also occur in primate and human fertilization.

fetal abortion Termination of a pregnancy (*qv*) after the twentieth week of gestation (*qv*) but before the fetus (*qv*) is able to survive outside the uterus (*qv*). *See also* abortion.

fetal activity The movements of the fetus (*qv*) that the mother usually begins to feel in the seventeenth to twentieth weeks of pregnancy (*qv*) when the fetus measures about 11 inches head to toe and weighs over a pound. Commonly known as quickening (*qv*), fetal activity was believed in the Middle Ages to mark the beginning of human life. Thus, abortion (*qv*) prior to quickening was often morally acceptable. *See also* mediate animation theory.

fetal adrenal androgen A masculinizing (*qv*) hormone (*qv*) produced by the adrenal glands (*qv*). Excessive production of this androgen (*qv*) when the external genitalia (*qv*) are undergoing rapid differentiation, weeks 8 through 12, can result in masculinization of a female fetus (*qv*), leading in some cases to pseudohermaphrodism (*qv*).

fetal age The age of the conceptus (*qv*) computed from the time of fertilization. Also known as fertilization age. *See also* gestational age.

fetal alcohol syndrome (FAS) The variable teratogenic (*qv*) results of alcohol consumption during pregnancy (*qv*). The full teratogenic effects are observed in 33 to 43 percent of infants born to alcoholic women. Symptoms in the fetus (*qv*) include cardiac abnormalities, hyperactivity, poor attention span, fine-motor dysfunction, weak grasp, facial deformities, retarded physical growth, visual disorders, low birth weight (*qv*), and reduced mental capacity. Recent studies suggest that consumption of as little as 1 or 2 ounces of alcohol at critical periods (*qv*) in fetal development can result in fetal alcohol syndrome. Historically, the connection between maternal consumption of alcohol was known in early Greece and Rome where laws sometimes prohibited newlywed couples from drinking alcohol to avoid having mentally or physically handicapped offspring.

fetal asphyxia A condition in which fetal respiratory exchange is disturbed so that the oxygen level is abnormally low while the carbon dioxide level is elevated. An elevated carbon dioxide level results in acidosis, which can cause brain damage and even fetal death.

fetal blood vessels The blood vessels of the umbilical cord (*qv*), usually two arteries, that carry waste products from the embryo (*qv*) or fetus (*qv*) to the placenta (*qv*) and one vein that carries nutrients and oxygen from the placenta to the embryo or fetus.

fetal circulation The circulation of blood between the embryo (*qv*) or fetus (*qv*) and its placenta (*qv*) where nutrients and waste products are exchanged between the fetal and maternal blood. Until fetal circulation is established, the zygote (*qv*) and early embryo are provided with nutrients and eliminate metabolic waste products by diffusion. As the embryo grows, a more efficient circulatory system with placental exchange replaces diffusion. In the third week of pregnancy (*qv*), blood cells begin forming in the yolk sac (*qv*), allantoic wall (*qv*), and chorion (*qv*). Primitive blood vessels begin forming a few days later. By the end of the third week, the primitive heart is formed and pumping blood.

Blood enters the right atrium of the fetal heart via the superior and inferior vena cava. Most of the blood flows through the right atrium into the left atrium via a small hole, known as the foramen ovale (*qv*), in the interatrial septum. From the left atrium, the blood enters the left ventricle and then the fetal aorta. Any blood not passing through the foramen ovale enters the right ventricle and leaves the heart through the pulmonary trunk. Most of this blood is diverted from the pulmonary circulation by a shunt known as the ductus arteriosus between the pulmonary trunk and the aorta. This shunt prevents overloading the lungs with blood during their development. At birth, the foramen ovale and ductus arteriosus close, establishing the normal cardiac cycle of an adult.

Blood in the aorta is distributed throughout the fetal body, including the umbilical arteries, which bring some of the blood to the placenta for removal of wastes and for the uptake of oxygen and nutrients. This oxygenated blood returns to the fetus via the umbilical vein, which diverts most of the blood directly into the inferior vena cava via the ductus venosus, which runs through the liver. Some of the blood from the umbilical vein nourishes the fetal liver and then enters the inferior vena cava.

fetal distress A compromised condition of the fetus (*qv*), usually discovered during labor (*qv*) and characterized by a markedly abnormal rate or rhythm of cardiac activity. Among the various factors that may result in fetal distress are toxemia of pregnancy (*qv*), fetal alcohol syndrome (*qv*), a variety of infections transmitted across the placental barrier (*qv*), erythroblastosis fetalis (*qv*), maternal drug addiction, or a maternal abdominal injury. Caesarean section (*qv*) may be necessary if the baby cannot be stabilized. *See also* fetus at risk.

fetal erections Penile erections (*qv*) experienced by the fetus (*qv*) in the second and third trimesters (*qv*) of gestation (*qv*), observable by ultrasonography (*qv*).

fetal infection The transmission of an infectious disease from the mother to a fetus (*qv*) before or during labor (*qv*). Viral and bacterial pathogens can enter the fetus by transmission across the placental barrier (*qv*). They can also be transmitted by infected amniotic fluid (*qv*) swallowed by the fetus or by contact when passing through the birth canal (*qv*). The most common fetal infections acquired during birth are herpes genitalis (*qv*), *Chlamydia* (*qv*), *Candida albicans* (*qv*), hemolytic streptococcus (*qv*), and *condyloma* (*qv*). Infections acquired in utero are syphilis (*qv*), rubella (*qv*), and HIV-I virus (*qv*).

fetal-maternal exchange The transfer of substances from the mother to the fetus (*qv*) and from the fetal circulation to the maternal circulation across the placental barrier (*qv*). Placental transfer is based on five mechanisms: simple and facilitated diffusion, active transport, pinocytosis, and some minor leakage of cells between the maternal and fetal system. Transport mechanisms are responsible for the exchange of oxygen, carbon dioxide, water, fatty acids, water-soluble vitamins, glucose, unconjugated steroid hormones (testosterone [*qv*] and some synthetic progestins [*qv*]), electrolytes, antibodies, metabolic wastes, most drugs, and drug metabolites, including heroin, alcohol, and methadone. Viruses, some pathogenic bacteria, and some teratogenic (*qv*) substances regularly cross the placental barrier.

fetal-maternal incompatibility *See* Rh factor incompatibility; erythroblastosis fetalis; hemolytic disease neonatal.

fetal membranes Four extraembryonic membranous sacs essential to the support of fetal development: the chorion (*qv*), amnion (*qv*), yolk sac (*qv*), and allantois (*qv*). In mammals (*qv*) and humans, the yolk sac and allantois contribute to the gut and bladder. The main fetal membranes in the higher animals are the two sacs that enclose the fetus (*qv*): an inner amnion and an outer chorion. As the fetus grows in size, these two membranous sacs are forced together and fuse into a single enveloping sac with the placenta (*qv*) on one side. *See also* afterbirth; decidua.

fetal monitor Electronic equipment used during labor (*qv*) to check the progress of the fetus (*qv*) during the delivery (*qv*) process; monitoring of the fetal heartbeat and the duration, frequency, and intensity of maternal uterine contractions (*qv*) are a prime concern.

fetal period *See* fetus.

fetal response The reactions and responses of a fetus (*qv*) to environmental conditions such as the mother's smoking, use of alcohol, or emotional stress. *See also* fetus at risk.

fetal testicular androgen The hormone (*qv*) produced by the cells of Leydig in the fetal testes (*qv*) and responsible for masculinization (*qv*) of the external genitalia (*qv*). *See also* dihydrotestosterone.

fetation The process of fetal development in the uterus (*qv*). *Synonym*: pregnancy (*qv*).

feti- A combining form referring to fetal or the fetus (*qv*).

feticide *See* abortion; embryoctomy.

fetish (fetishism) The attribution of erotic (*qv*) or sexual (*qv*) significance to some nonsexual inanimate object or to a nongenital body part; an inanimate object venerated for its alleged magical powers. Fetishism involves a paraphilic (*qv*) condition in which the fetishist is dependent on a fetish object, substance, or part of the body in order to achieve sexual arousal (*qv*) and orgasm (*qv*). The erotic symbolism of a fetish results from associations usually developed unconsciously during the prepubertal (*qv*) or early adolescent (*qv*) period.

FeTLV-I *See* feline T-cell lymphotrophic virus-I.

feto- A combining form referring to fetal or the fetus (*qv*).

fetus The unborn offspring from the end of the embryonic (*qv*) period at 8 weeks through to birth (*qv*) at about 26 weeks. In the ninth and tenth week of pregnancy (*qv*), the external genitalia (*qv*) differentiate, and the face assumes a recognizably human profile. Since all basic organ systems and structures are established by the end of the embryonic period, fetal processes involve further differentiation and enlargement of these structures and organs.

fetus at risk A fetus (*qv*) whose normal development is threatened by parental or uterine factors. Maternal factors that place a fetus at risk include deficient prenatal care, use of alcohol (*See also* fetal alcohol syndrome), medication or controlled substances, stress, and exposure to herpes (*qv*), syphilis (*qv*), acquired immune deficiency syndrome (*qv*), or other sexually transmitted diseases (*qv*). Other factors that place a fetus at risk are maternal-fetal incompatibility associated with the Rh blood factor (*qv*), heritable familial tendencies to schizophrenia and bipolar manic depressive state, and parental dominant or recessive genes for inherited disorders such as hemophilia and cystic fibrosis. *See also* fetal distress.

fetus in fetu (L.) A fetal anomaly in which a small, imperfectly formed twin (*qv*), incapable of independent existence, is contained within the body of the normal twin.

fetus papyraceus (L.) A twin fetus (*qv*) that has died early in its development and been retained in the uterus (*qv*) in a desiccated state until its twin is delivered.

F factor A fertility (*qv*) factor that facilitates reproduction (*qv*) in some primitive organisms like bacteria or in genetic material that otherwise cannot reproduce.

fiancé A man engaged to be married. *See also* espousal; engagement.

fiancée A woman engaged to be married. *See also* espousal; engagement.

fibrocystic condition or disease The presence of a single or multiple cysts (*qv*) in the breasts (*qv*). Although cysts are in themselves benign and fairly common in women, they may be potentially malignant and therefore should be carefully monitored. A fibrocystic condition may be managed with a dietary and vitamin-mineral supplement or, if needed, by surgery. This condition appears to show a genetic (*qv*) familial tendency.

fibroid *See* fibroma.

fibroma A benign neoplastic tumor consisting largely of fibrous or fully developed connective tissue, usually occurring in the uterus (*qv*) or in the vulva (*qv*).

fibromyoma A smooth muscle and fibrous connective-tissue tumor associated with hypertrophy of the prostate (*qv*) in older men. When the tumor blocks the urethral canal (*qv*) so that urination becomes painful or difficult, surgical opening of the canal becomes necessary.

fibrous hymen An abnormally thick and tough hymen (*qv*); usually surgical incision is required to permit sexual intercourse (*qv*).

fictive image A mental image that is not perceived through the senses but constructed in the imagination by drawing on past perceptions and experiences retrieved from the memory and reconstituted in the mind. *See also* perceptive image.

fidelity, marital In the sexual sense, the limiting of sexual intimacy (*qv*) to a monogamous relationship. The traditional sense of marital fidelity is expressed in the marital vow a man and woman exchange "to foresake all others, and cleave to each other as two in one flesh." *See also* comarital relations; intimate network; intimate friendship; sexually open marriage; polyfidelity; infidelity; extramarital sex.

field study (research) A form of observation in which a researcher studies a sample or population in its natural surroundings and situation rather than in a laboratory or clinical setting. *See also* clinical method; observational study.

figurae veneris (L.) Positions for coitus (*qv*).

filial generation *See* F$_1$.

filter theory of mate selection A theory proposed to explain marital choice in which similar values (e.g., religious affiliation, socioeconomic class) are viewed as the basic factor utilized in selecting a partner for an intimate relationship, thereby filtering or screening out all others who have dissimilar values.

fimbria (pl. fimbriae) Fingerlike projections at the os (*qv*) of the fallopian tube (*qv*) whose rhythmic movements sweep the ovum (*qv*) into the fallopian tube for transport to the uterine cavity (*qv*).

finger defloration *See* defloration.

first stage orgasm The emission phase (*qv*) of male orgasm (*qv*).

fitness, reproductive The measurement of reproductive success and the capacity to transmit one's genes (*qv*) to the next generation.

5-alpha-reductase A naturally occurring enzyme necessary for the conversion of testosterone (*qv*) to dihydrotestosterone (*qv*). Male differentiation of fetal external genitalia (*qv*) is dependent on dihydrotestosterone, whereas internal differentiation responds to testosterone and Mullerian inhibiting substance (*qv*). *See also* DHT deficiency syndrome.

five-digit coding system A parity classification system used to record (1) the number of pregnancies (*qv*), (2) the number of deliveries (*qv*), (3) the number of premature deliveries (*qv*), (4) the number of abortions (*qv*), and (5) the number of living children. Thus, 3-2-0-1-2 indicates a woman who has had three pregnancies, two deliveries, one abortion, no premature deliveries, and two viable infants.

fixation An arrested psychosexual development (*qv*), the persistence in adult life of an early psychosexual stage or gratification, or a reversion under stress to an early stage of development; also a strong attachment to an idea, theory, or person.

flaccid Soft, relaxed, nonerect, weak; used particularly in reference to the penis (*qv*) and clitoris (*qv*) in their unaroused state. *See also* erection.

flagellant A person who undergoes whipping or scourging as an expiatory action, either as a religious penitent or as part of a sexual masochistic (*qv*) scenario.

flagellantism (flagellation) A religious doctrine of asceticism (*qv*) that emphasizes the infliction of pain by being whipped or whipping oneself as a means of mortifying the "flesh" and disciplining the body and its emotions to bring them into submission to higher spiritual goals. Originating in the medieval culture of the twelfth century, flagellation is still practiced in some Hispanic and Latin American cultures and the Philippines. The term is used today in the practice of sadomasochism (*qv*), where it is associated with sexual excitement (*qv*) and arousal.

flagellomania Sexual excitement (*qv*) aroused by whipping. *See also* flagellantism.

flagrante delicto, in (L.) *See* in flagrante delicto.

flat condyloma Large, flat lesions occurring near the anus (*qv*) or on the vulva (*qv*), often in clusters, and characteristic of secondary syphilis (*qv*); may occur also in children with congenital syphilis (*qv*).

flirtation behavior (flirtatiousness) Behavior patterns enacted by men or women that elicit sexual interest without necessarily preceding or promising sexual intimacy. Flirtation is highly culture-specific and varies from individual to individual, but characteristically involves body postures or "body language" (*qv*), looks, touches, and talking, often with extensive sexual/nonsexual dual meanings. If flirtation precedes sexual intimacy, it is more accurately called courtship (*qv*). Flirtatiousness can be part of an individual's general interpersonal repertoire or it can be restricted to certain social settings, for example, parties. The word flirt is usedly solely for women and vary rarely for men; it typically connotes a lack of seriousness of sexual and emotional purpose and has a strong derogatory tone. Resource: T. Perper, *Sex Signals: The Biology of Love* (Philadelphia: ISI Press, 1985).

flocculation A medical term for the association or clumping of minute, submicroscopic particles into larger masses that are visible with or without magnification. *See also* VDRL.

flogging *See* flagellantism.

floppy infant syndrome A general term for a variety of spinal muscular atrophies affecting newborns (*qv*) and infants (*qv*).

fluorescent antibody (FA) test A clinical test that uses an antibody (*qv*) labeled with a fluorescent dye that does not alter the antibody-antigen (*qv*) reaction and allows identification of a pathogen under a fluorescence dark-field microscope. An FA test is commonly used to detect the bacterium *Neisseria gonorrhoeae* in an individual who shows no symptoms of gonorrhea (*qv*). It is also the most commonly used serological screening test for syphilis (*qv*).

Fluorescent Treponemal Antibody Absorption Test (FTA-ABS) A clinical test to detect the presence of the *Treponema pallidum* (*qv*) bacterium that causes syphilis (*qv*). It uses an antibody (*qv*) labeled with a fluorescent dye that attaches to the bacterium, rendering it visible under ultraviolet light.

fluoxymestrone A drug used to increase testosterone (*qv*) production in a male experiencing erection (*qv*) problems due to an abnormally low testosterone level.

flush, sex *See* sex flush.

foeti-, foeto- A combining form referring to fetal (*qv*) or the fetus (*qv*).

foetus *See* fetus.

Foley catheter A catheter with an inflatable balloon tip, the balloon anchoring the catheter to prevent its accidental expulsion. This type of catheter is sometimes used to expand a blocked prostatic urethral (*qv*) canal.

follicle, cystic An ovarian or Graafian follicle (*qv*) that has enlarged into a fluid-filled cyst (*qv*).

follicle, Graafian or ovarian The composite structure that provides a locus for maturation of the ovum (*qv*) prior to its release in ovulation (*qv*). The follicle develops from the germinal and nutritive cells of the ovarian cortex. Originally the primitive ovum is surrounded by a single, then a double envelope of nurse or follicle cells. As the follicle and ovum mature, a fluid-filled cavity appears inside the follicle, and the growing ovum lodges in a hill-like structure projecting inward from the follicle surface into the follicle cavity. After release of the ovum, the ruptured follicle and its remaining nutritive cells are converted into a secretory corpus luteum (*qv*), which produces progesterone (*qv*) and estrogen (*qv*) to develop the uterine lining further. If pregnancy (*qv*) does not occur, the corpus luteum degenerates into the scar tissue of a corpus albicans (*qv*).

follicle-stimulating hormone (FSH) Produced by specialized cells of the anterior lobe of the pituitary gland (*qv*) in both males and females, this steroid hormone stimulates gametogenesis (*qv*). In the female, FSH stimulates formation of the ovarian follicle (*qv*) in the ovary and production of estrogens (*qv*). *See also* follitropin. FSH secretion peaks when the follicle ripens, approximately 14 days before the start of the next menstrual period (*qv*). At that time, luteinizing hormone (*qv*) takes over to trigger ovulation (*qv*) and begin the second or luteal phase of the ovarian cycle in which the ruptured follicle becomes a progesterone-secreting corpus luteum (*qv*). In males, FSH increases significantly at puberty (*qv*) and is believed to influence the growth of seminiferous tubules (*qv*) in the testes (*qv*). It then regulates all stages of spermatogenesis (*qv*). In both males and females, production of FSH by the pituitary is regulated by FSH releasing factor (*qv*) produced by the hypothalamus (*qv*). When used therapeutically, FSH is derived from the urine (*qv*) of postmenopausal (*qv*) women, hence the term menotropin.

follicular phase or stage The first of two phases in the ovarian cycle, during which an ovum (*qv*) matures within an ovarian or Graafian follicle (*qv*) until ovulation (*qv*) occurs. The ovarian follicular phase is paralleled by the uterine proliferative phase (*qv*). *See also* follicle stimulating hormone; luteal phase; uterine cycle.

folliculitis gonorrheica (L.) An inflammation of the Littre's glands (*qv*) and their associated recesses in the roof of the urethra (*qv*), due to a gonorrheal (*qv*) infection.

folliculogenesis Formation of Graafian or ovarian follicle (*qv*) in the ovary (*qv*).

follitropin Follicle-stimulating hormone (*qv*) isolated and purified from the urine (*qv*) of postmenopausal (*qv*) women, used in treatment of male infertility (*qv*) due to oligospermia (*qv*) and female infertility due to ovulatory dysfunction. When used with infertile women, follitropin, also known as menotropin, carries a multiple birth risk of about 30 percent. In males, the extract increases sperm count (*qv*) and motility.

fondling A general term for caresses and touches of the erogenous (*qv*) parts of the body and the genitalia (*qv*) that are often a part of foreplay (*qv*). *Fondling* is also used legally to refer to unwanted touching. *See also* sensate focus exercises.

food taboos Cultural prohibitions of certain foods because of their association with or resemblance to the genitalia (*qv*) (e.g., the prohibition of bananas and coconuts by Europeans missionaries when they converted natives of the South Pacific).

foot binding An ancient Chinese custom in which the feet of upper-class women were tightly bound from the age of 5 or 6 on to produce small, deformed feet that were considered both highly erotic (*qv*) and a leisure-class status symbol. This custom also served to keep the upper-class women home-bound and dependent because it made walking difficult, if not impossible. It was discontinued with the end of imperial rule in the early 1900s.

foot fetishism The paraphilic (*qv*) dependence on viewing, handling, or kissing the feet and toes as a means to sexual arousal (*qv*) and orgasm (*qv*). In non-Western cultures, feet are associated with sexual pleasure as part of a medical or religious tradition and without the paraphilic addiction. In the traditions of oriental acupuncture, specific areas of the feet have subtle connections with all the vital organs of the body. In the Hindu culture, the feet are revered as the "microcosms of the body," washed, anointed with fragrant oil, and decorated with flowers because they not only bear the weight of the whole body but are also important in sexual arousal and foreplay (*qv*). A foot fetish is distinct from a paraphilic dependence on shoes. Resources: W. A. Rossi, *The Sex Life of the Foot and Shoe* (New York: Dutton, 1976).

foramen ovale (L.) An opening in the wall of the fetal heart between the right and left atrium that closes after birth. *See also* fetal circulation.

Forbes-Albright syndrome An endocrine disease characterized by amenorrhea (*qv*) and lack of prolactin (*qv*) caused by an adenoma of the anterior pituitary (*qv*).

forced fantasy An emotionally charged fantasy (*qv*) deliberately stimulated by the analyst or therapist.

forceps delivery An obstetric operation in which instruments are used to deliver a baby. Used to quicken delivery of an infant experiencing toxemia (*qv*) or fetal distress (*qv*), or more often to shorten a normal delivery, forceps delivery requires anesthesia and an episiotomy (*qv*).

forceps rotation An obstetric procedure in which forceps are used to turn the baby's head when it stops normal rotation in the birth canal (*qv*).

Fordyce's disease The appearance of sebaceous, acnelike (*qv*) cysts (*qv*) on the penile (*qv*) shaft.

foreplay The traditional term for erotosexual (*qv*) activity during the proceptive phase (*qv*) in which caressing, stroking, kissing (*qv*), and other skin-body contact and stimulation promotes penile erection (*qv*), vaginal lubrication (*qv*), and the urgency of being ready for coitus (*qv*) and/or orgasm (*qv*). Feminists (*qv*) have criticized the term foreplay as a concept created by men in a heterosexual (*qv*) culture that sums up sexual relations in terms of penetration and conquest. Current usage suggests *loveplay* (*qv*) as a more appropriate term for this activity because it emphasizes the value of these erotic activities in their own right and avoids the performance (coital) pressure and goal-oriented message of the term *foreplay*.

forepleasure A psychoanalytic term for the pleasure associated with foreplay (*qv*).

foreskin The loose sheath of skin, or prepuce, covering the glans (*qv*) of the penis (*qv*) or clitoris (*qv*); in the male, it is continuous with the thin skin of the penile shaft (*qv*). Although hairless, the outer surface of the foreskin has a number of small papillae. The inner surface contains the preputial glands, also known as Tyson's glands (*qv*), which secrete an oily, odorous substance, which when mixed with dead skin cells becomes the smegma (*qv*). In American males, the foreskin is commonly removed in circumcision (*qv*), for supposed hygienic reasons, shortly after birth. Male circumcision is a religious ritual for Jews and Muslims. Female circumcision (*qv*), as practiced in African and Arabic cultures, commonly involves removal of the clitoris and labia minora (*qv*), not just the clitoral foreskin. In some cultures where circumcision is not practiced, the foreskin of males may be tied with a cord to protect the glans during athletic competition or in everyday circumstances. The cord is loosed or removed to allow urination and intercourse (*qv*).

formal values Values that express the idealized socially accepted concept of what is right and wrong in human behavior; society's clearly articulated values or a group's formal statement of its values. *See also* informal values.

forme fruste (L.) The phenotypic (*qv*) expression of a gene (*qv*), disease, or syndrome in a form so mild that it is not clinically significant or goes undiagnosed.

formicophilia A subvariety of zoophilia (*qv*) in which an individual is dependent for achieving sexuoerotic arousal (*qv*) and orgasm (*qv*) on the sensations produced by small creatures, ants, and other insects, snails and frogs, creeping, crawling or nibbling the genitals (*qv*), perianal region, and nipples (*qv*).

fornication Sexual intercourse (*qv*) between two unmarried persons. Fornication is a sinful or forbidden act in most religious value systems. It is also a crime in some civil jurisdictions that do not have consenting adult laws (*qv*) or still adhere to early English common law. The term *fornication* is derived from the Latin term *fornix* (*qv*) because Roman prostitutes (*qv*) plied their trade under the arches of viaducts. *See also* adultery.

fornix The arch-like vault or upper space of the vaginal canal (*qv*); also an archlike nerve fiber bundle in the midbrain.

45,XO *See* Turner syndrome.

45,XO/46,XX *See* Turner syndrome.

45,XO/46,XY *See* Turner syndrome.

45,XY/47,XXY *See* Klinefelter syndrome.

45,XO/47,XXX *See* Turner syndrome.

47,XXX *See* XXX syndrome.

47,XXY syndrome *See* Klinefelter syndrome.

47,XYY syndrome *See* XYY syndrome.

48,XXXX *See* XXXX syndrome.

fossa navicularis vulvae (L.) A shallow depression between the labial (*qv*) folds and the hymen (*qv*) at the vaginal entrance. Also known as the vestibular fossa.

fourchette A fold of mucous membrane usually found in virgins (*qv*) at the posterior junction of the labia minora (*qv*). Also known as the labial frenulum.

Fournier's gangrene The sudden onset of painful swelling resulting from tissue necrosis and subsequent putrefaction in the scrotum (*qv*) of a healthy male. This condition may be due to a streptococcal infection of the scrotal tissue, to a urinary tract infection, or to an interruption of normal circulation.

fractional dilation and curettage A diagnostic technique for endometrial cancer (*qv*) in which specimens are obtained by curettage (*qv*) from all regions of the uterine cavity (*qv*).

fractured penis A rupture of the corpora cavernosa (*qv*) and associated tissues in the penile shaft (*qv*) as a result of an external trauma inflicted while the penis (*qv*) is erect.

fragile X syndrome An abnormal, inherited secondary constriction near the end of the long arm of the X chromosome (*qv*). This constriction is the cause of the second most commonly diagnosed form of mental retardation. Affected individuals have an intelligence quotient in the range of 30 to 70 but generally show no other physical symptoms.

frank breech An intrauterine position of the fetus (*qv*) in which the buttocks (*qv*) are presented first in the maternal pelvic inlet.

fraternal twins Siblings (*qv*) resulting from the simultaneous ovulation (*qv*) and fertilization (*qv*) of two ova (*qv*), hence the designation dizygotic (*qv*), and resulting in the birth of two offspring in the same delivery (*qv*); the opposite of identical or monozygotic twins (*qv*).

free love A philosophical, often anarchistic movement in late nineteenth- and early twentieth-century American society that advocated the abolition of marriage (*qv*) and the right of each person to live without government regulation of inter-personal relations. More specifically, the advocates of free love claimed that love, not marriage (*qv*), should be the precondition for sexual relations (*qv*). Although the philosophical and political advocates of free love never numbered more than a few thousand, they deeply influenced American sexual attitudes down to the present with their emphasis on sexual freedom for women, the social aspects of sexuality (*qv*) as distinct from reproduction (*qv*), the intellectual equality of men and women, and self-health and knowledge of one's own body and its functioning. Central among the leaders of this movement was the feminist Victoria Woodhull. Other advocates included George Sand, George Bernard Shaw, Bertrand Russell, and H. G. Wells.

freemartin A male calf's twin sister that has been partially masculinized (*qv*) before birth by the male twin's testicular (*qv*) hormones (*qv*) communicated through fusion of the two placentas (*qv*). The female freemartin is sterile (*qv*) and partially hermaphroditic (*qv*) as a result of exposure to androgenic (*qv*) hormones at critical periods (*qv*) in its fetal development.

Frei test A confirming skin test for the *Lymphogranuloma venereum* (*qv*) virus. Development of a reddish thickened area at the site where a killed viral antigen (*qv*) is injected under the skin indicates presence of the Lymphogranuloma virus in the body.

frenulum Any fold of skin or mucous tissue. The small triangular fold of highly sensitive skin on the underside of the penis (*qv*) just behind the glans (*qv*), connecting the glans with the foreskin (*qv*). The frenulum of the clitoris (*qv*) results from the junction of the labia minora (*qv*) below the clitoral glans.

frenum The very sensitive area of the penile shaft (*qv*) immediately behind the raised edge of the corona of the glans penis (*qv*).

frequency The statistical measure of how often an individual or group gives or performs a particular activity or experiences a particular response during some unit of time. The concept was used by Alfred Kinsey (*qv*) in the context of the frequency of total sexual outlets (*qv*), meaning an individual's weekly average of all sexual activities—coital (*qv*), masturbatory (*qv*), sexual dreams (*qv*), petting (*qv*) or foreplay (*qv*), homosexual activities (*qv*), and animal contacts.

Freud, Sigmund (1856–1939) The Austrian psychiatrist and neurologist who created the theory and practice of psychoanalysis. Freud's major contributions included recognizing and researching the dominant role of the unconscious in both normal and neurotic behavior, the role of sexual drives (*qv*) or libido (*qv*) in psychosexual development (*qv*), and the importance of dreams. In the midst of Victorian (*qv*) repression, Freud recognized and stressed the existence of sexual drives in women and children. His contributions to sexology (*qv*) include theories on the interpretation of sexual dreams (*qv*), on the analysis of the unconscious and unresolved sexual conflicts developing during childhood and adolescence, a model for psychosexual development including the oral (*qv*), anal (*qv*), phallic (*qv*) and genital (*qv*) stages, theories of the Oedipal (*qv*) and Electra complexes (*qv*), and a theory for the interaction of the id (*qv*), ego (*qv*), and superego (*qv*).

Freudian fixation *See* fixation.

Freudianism A set of observations and hypotheses derived from the work and writings of Sigmund Freud (*qv*), including the importance of the unconscious, the construct of id (*qv*), ego (*qv*), and superego (*qv*), the oral (*qv*), anal (*qv*), phallic (*qv*), and genital (*qv*) stages of psychosexual development (*qv*), and the efficacy of helping patients resolve their problems by exploring their earliest experiences. *Synonym*: psychoanalysis (*qv*).

frictation A sexual practice engaged in by two male homosexuals (*qv*) who achieve sexual satisfaction by rubbing against each other in a face-to-face position. When engaged in by two lesbians (*qv*), the practice is known as tribadism (*qv*).

Friedman's test An obsolete pregnancy test (*qv*) using a rabbit and urine (*qv*) from the woman being tested. *See also* Achheim-Zondek test.

frigidity (adj. frigid) An outdated derogatory expression for female anorgasmia (*qv*), preorgasmia (*qv*), orgasmic dysfunction (*qv*), or desire phase dysfunction (*qv*); a general term for lack of sexual response in a woman.

Frohlich's syndrome A disorder occurring in adolescent (*qv*) boys, characterized by genital hypoplasia, female secondary sexual characteristics (*qv*), and female distribution of body fat. Other symptoms may include diabetes insipidus, visual impairment, and mental retardation. The condition may be caused by a malfunction of the hypothalamus (*qv*) or by a tumor in the anterior pituitary (*qv*). Treatment may include administration of testosterone (*qv*), a weight reduction program, removal or destruction of the tumor, and hormone replacement. Also known as adiposogenital dystrophy or syndrome.

frottage The paraphilic (*qv*) condition in which a person, a frotteur (*qv*), is dependent on rubbing against and feeling the body of a stranger, especially in a crowded public area, in order to obtain erotic arousal (*qv*) and achieve orgasm (*qv*); a paraphilia of the solicitational-allurative type.

frotteur A person for whom the most effective stimulus for erotosexual arousal (*qv*) is achieved by rubbing up against another person's body, especially a stranger in a crowded or public place. The act of rubbing is an end in itself and may be sufficient to produce an orgasm (*qv*).

frotteurism *See* frottage.

FSH *See* follicle-stimulating hormone.

FTA-ABS *See* Fluorescent Treponemal Antibody Absorption Test.

fuck A slang and colloquial term for sexual intercourse (*qv*), generally considered quite vulgar; although its public use is becoming more common. *Fuck* and words derived from it are often used as expletives and intensifiers in a nonsexual sense. Fuck is derived from a Germanic verb that originally meant to strike, move quickly, or penetrate. The term is akin to or perhaps borrowed from the Middle Dutch *fokken*, meaning to strike or to copulate with.

fugue state An altered state of consciousness in which what is happening now is unrelated to or dissociated from what has happened in the past. A condition resembling sleep walking in which a person, though awake, flees from familiar surroundings and dissociates or is unable to recall his or her previous history or experiences. When the fugue state ends, the events that occurred during it are largely unrecallable or dissociated as in a dual or multiple personality. Psychologically this syndrome appears to be caused by an inability to cope with a severe conflict or with a chronically stressful situation. It can also be induced by drugs.

functional Capable of operating or behaving in the way and degree expected of an average or healthy individual; a part of a social system that tends to support another part of that system (e.g., norms supporting autonomy and mobility for teenagers functionally support premarital (*qv*) sexual experiences); a condition that develops in response to the environment and is not obligate (*qv*).

functional homosexuality *See* facultative, faute de mieux.

functional impotence The failure or inability to achieve a penile erection (*qv*) sufficient to allow vaginal penetration (*qv*). *See also* erectile dysfunction.

functional vaginismus *See* vaginismus.

fundiform ligament One of the ligaments supporting the penis (*qv*), extending like a sling from the front of the abdomen to the pubic symphysis (*qv*) and around the tip and sides of the penis.

fundus The base or deepest part of an organ; the rounded upper portion of the uterus (*qv*), farthest from the cervical opening.

fungal infection Any infection that is caused by a fungus, mold, or yeast. *See also* candidiasis.

funicular encysted hydrocele A swelling of the scrotum (*qv*) caused by inflammation of the spermatic cord (*qv*), similar in appearance to the swelling associated with an inflammation of the tunica vaginalis of the testis (*qv*).

furor amatorius (L.) An insatiable sexual desire (*qv*). *See also* nymphomania, satyriasis.

G

---

galactopoiesis The maintenance of milk secretion by the human breast (*qv*), involving the interaction of prolactin (*qv*), somatotropin (growth hormone), adrenocortical hormones (*qv*), estrogens (*qv*), progesterone (*qv*), and oxytocin (*qv*).

galactorrhea Abnormal lactation (*qv*) occurring without any association with pregnancy (*qv*) or nursing (*qv*). This condition may occur following discontinuation of the oral contraceptive pill (*qv*) and tends to disappear as the woman's hormones (*qv*) return to natural cycling. *See also* Forbes-Albright syndrome.

game In the sociological theory of George Herbert Mead (*qv*), the second stage in the development of the self (*qv*), following the play stage (*qv*), in which the child at age 4 or 5 begins to learn for the first time to take a number of roles simultanously and thereby to achieve a unified concept of self. In order to be a part of the game, the child must consciously take the role of the entire group with which he or she wants to interact. As the child's awareness of self matures, role-taking (*qv*) and games become more complex. *See also* sexual games.

gamete A reproductive cell, the sperm (*qv*), or the egg or ovum (*qv*). The gamete results from meiosis (*qv*) and is haploid (*qv*) in chromosome (*qv*) number.

gamete intrafallopian transplant *See* GIFT.

gametocide Any agent that destroys gametes (*qv*) or germinal cells (*qv*). *See also* spermicide.

gametocyte An immature ovum (*qv*) or spermatozoan (*qv*); an oocyte (*qv*) or spermatocyte (*qv*).

gametogenesis Production of gametes (*qv*), ova (*qv*) or sperm (*qv*). *See also* oogenesis; spermatogenesis.

gamogenesis Sexual reproduction (*qv*) through the union of gametes (*qv*). *See also* fertilization.

gamomania A pathological preoccupation with a desire to marry.

gamone A hormonelike substance supposedly produced by the male and female gametes (*qv*) to attract the opposite-sex germ cells (*qv*) to facilitate fertilization (*qv*). An androgamone allegedly attracts the ovum (*qv*) and a gynogamone the sperm (*qv*).

gamophobia An intense, morbid fear of marriage (*qv*).

-gamy A combining suffix meaning a particular type of marriage (*qv*) specified by the prefix, for example, monogamy (*qv*), bigamy (*qv*), polygamy (*qv*).

gang bang Sexual activity (usually sexual intercourse [*qv*]) between one female and a series of males in rapid succession.

gang rape A sexual assault (*qv*) or rape (*qv*) of a single victim by two or more assailants. Also known as party or frat(ernity) rape.

gangrene of the scrotum A severe condition involving deterioration and necrosis of the scrotal tissue, usually due to interruption of circulation, injury, burns, or seepage of infected urine (*qv*) into the scrotum (*qv*).

gangrenous balanitis A rapidly destructive, erosive infection of the genitals (*qv*) that may start with a spirochete infection of the penile glans (*qv*). *See also* balanitis.

Gardnerella vaginalis (L.) *See* Hemophilus vaginalis.

gastrodidymus Conjoined (*qv*), equally developed twins (*qv*) joined in the abdominal region.

gastromenia A psychogenic conversion in which the bleeding of menstruation (*qv*) occurs in the stomach rather than in the uterus (*qv*).

gastrula (gastrulation) An early embryonic stage marked by the formation of the three primary tissue germ layers: entoderm (*qv*), mesoderm (*qv*), and ectoderm (*qv*); formation of a gastrula.

gates, psychosexual development *See* sex; sex variables; transference.

gay A common, nonperjorative expression for a homosexual (*qv*) or for a homosexual life-style; sometimes the term refers exclusively to male homosexuality. In the thirteenth and fourteenth centuries, the Provençal word *gai* was used in reference to courtly love (*qv*) and its literature as a designation for "the art of poesy" (*gai saber*), for a lover (*gaiol*), and for an openly homosexual person. Courtly love (*qv*) was popular in southern France, an area noted for gay sexuality. Both courtly love and its troubadours (*qv*), some of whose poetry was explicitly homosexual, were associated with southern French heretical Christian sects, especially the Cathars and Albigensians who were widely suspected of favoring homosexuality. In the early twentieth century, *gay* became a code or password in the English homosexual subculture. Its first public use in the United States, outside pornographic literature, appears to have been in the 1939 movie *Bringing Up Baby*, when Cary Grant, wearing a dress, proclaimed he had "gone gay." Currently *gay* is a political term preferred by many persons with a homosexual orientation. *Antonym*: straight (*qv*). *See also* Manicheanism (*Addendum*).

gay liberation The movement for legal recognition of the rights of homosexual (*qv*) men and lesbians (*qv*) in the United States is commonly traced to the 1969 Stonewall Inn riot (*qv*) in Greenwich Village, New York City. *See also* Daughters of Bilitis; Lamda Legal Defense and Education Fund; Mattachine Society.

Gaylord v. Tacoma School District A 1977 decision of the U.S. Supreme Court not to hear the appeal of a Washington State public school teacher who was dismissed after years of outstanding work because he acknowledged he was gay (*qv*) when asked by school officials. In refusing to hear the appeal, the Court let the lower court decision stand.

gay marriage *See* gay union.

gay pneumonia *See* Pneumocystis carinii.

gay-related immune deficiency *See* GRID; acquired immune deficiency syndrome.

gay union A public ceremony acknowledging the mutual commitment of two homosexual (*qv*) men or lesbian (*qv*) women to live together and share the responsibilities and commitments normally associated with the marital state (*qv*). Although gay marriages or gay unions are not recognized by civil law, some religious representatives will consent to witness such unions insofar as they can as representatives of a church. *See also* domestic partners.

geisha In the Japanese culture, a woman specially trained as a professional hostess, entertainer, and companion of men. Geishas are trained in conversation, playing musical instruments, singing, dancing, the traditional tea ceremony, and in serving meals. In some cases, their services include sexual relations (*qv*) with male customers, although geishas are not considered prostitutes (*qv*). In many respects, geishas hold a position of respect and honor in Japanese society similar to that of the hetaerae (*qv*) in ancient Greece.

gemellary Of or pertaining to twins (*qv*).

gemellipara A woman who has given birth to twins (*qv*).

gender One's personal, social, and/or legal status as a male (*qv*) or a female (*qv*) or as a person of mixed gender. In its simplest usage, gender is one's social role as a sexual person as opposed to the genital anatomy with which one is born or the social concomitants of being biologically male, female, or intersex (*qv*). Adjectives that describe gender are *masculine* (*qv*) and *feminine* (*qv*). Adjectives describing sex (*qv*) are *male* (*qv*) or *female* (*qv*). Gender is a cultural construct applied to the newborn (*qv*). In some cultures, gender is subject to later change, based on somatic and behavioral criteria that are wider than the criteria of one's genitalia (*qv*) and/or erotic responses. A major theoretical and political debate persists about the extent to which gender as a socially constructed phenomenon is related to or influenced by one's biological sex. *See also* Adam plan; core gender identity; Eve plan; gender coding; gender identity/role; masculinization; template.

   See also multiple listings under "gender ——," "sex ——," and "sexual ——." Because of varying preferences in ideology and constructs, what some refer to as "sex" or "sexual," others define as "gender." In this Dictionary, we have listed such phrases under their more common usage, relying on the reader to check possible alternate listings. Thus, while some speak of "gender orientation," the definition of this term is listed under the more common usage of "sexual orientation." Similarly, "gender identity" may be the equivalent of "sexual identity," and "sex" a synonym for "gender."

gender, sociology of *See* sociology of gender.

gender change The process of changing one's sex (*qv*), as in transsexual (*qv*) surgery. *See also* gender transposition; sex change operation.

gender coding The designation of any biological characteristic, psychological response, or behavior as belonging to the male, female, or both sexes. The combined genetic, hormonal, and social labeling or coding of a person's physical, mental, and/or behavioral traits as belonging either exclusively to the male, to the female, or shared in an androgynous (*qv*) way by both sexes. The criteria for coding are multivariate and sequentially derived from the interaction of biological and social variables. In sex-irreducible gender coding (*qv*), biological factors are the predominant, almost exclusive determinants; social determinants are predominant in sex-adventitious gender coding (*qv*). No gender coding is exclusively biological or exclusively social. *See also* sexual scripting; social scripting. Resource: J. Money, *Gay, Straight, and Inbetween: Sexology of Erotic Orientation* (New York: Oxford University Press, 1988).

gender coding, sex-adjunctive Behaviors ascribed to one or the other, or both, genders (*qv*) that are (1) based on the anatomical consequences of prenatal (*qv*) hormonal differences and (2) are then applied to division of labor between males and females. Conceptually sex-adjunctive gender coding develops from sex-derivative coding (*qv*) through social scripting (*qv*) of the division of labor between the sexes because of their different physiques and physical abilities. Despite variations and contradictions, gender-coded division of labor occurs in all cultures and is socially transmitted. The recent shift to an information-based economy and social structure and away from brute strength and physical abilities derived from hormone differences has radically altered gender coding for occupational roles, often resulting in a unisex gender coding for some occupations. *See also* gender coding. Resource: J. Money, *Love and Love Sickness* (Baltimore: Johns Hopkins University Press, 1980).

gender coding, sex-adventitious Sex-coded behaviors extending sex-adjunctive coding (*qv*) through social scripting (*qv*) to support the dimorphic and unequal distribution of power between the sexes. These behaviors include feminine ornamentation, clothing style, grooming, cosmetics, and etiquette that present women as dependent on men and display them as showpieces of male wealth and power. In various cultures, body mutilation, piercing, scarifying, tattooing, painting, and hair styles serve as gender coding for power. Two common examples are foot binding (*qv*) in imperial China and genital mutilation (*qv*), especially female circumcision (*qv*), in northern and eastern Africa. Sex-adventitious gender coding may extend to food taboos (*qv*) designed to preserve male power. *See also* gender coding.

gender coding, sex-derivative Male and female distinctions arising from the biological differences between male and female in reproduction (*qv*) and caused by estrogen (qv) or androgen (qv) hormone (*qv*) production. Sex-derivative gender coding includes dimorphic secondary sexual characteristics (*qv*) such as facial hair, breast (*qv*) growth, pubertal voice changes, bone structure, muscular development, and subcutaneous body fat deposition. Since gender dimorphism (*qv*) is not absolute, most sex-derived gender coded traits can, under certain circumstances, appear in both genders, such as facial hair in women especially after menopause (*qv*), idiopathic gynecomastia (*qv*) induced in males by drugs or hormonal disturbances, and changes induced as part of transsexual (*qv*) treatment. *See also* gender coding. Resource: J. Money, *Love and Love Sickness* (Baltimore: Johns Hopkins University Press, 1980).

gender coding, sex-irreducible Sex or gender differences that are immutable and irreducible because of biological determinants, for example, in mammals, males impregnate (*qv*) while females menstruate (*qv*), ovulate (*qv*), gestate (*qv*), and lactate (*qv*). Reproductive differences exist independently of one's sexual orientation (*qv*) and all other forms of gender coding (*qv*). The immutability of this form of gender coding is modified by the common use of infant formula milk, the future possibilities of hormone-induced male neonatal breast-feeding, and surgically aided male abdominal pregnancy (*qv*) followed by Caesarean section (*qv*). Resource: J. Money, *Love and Love Sickness* (Baltimore: Johns Hopkins University Press, 1980).

gender coding, sex-shared/threshold dimorphic Based on experimental animal and human clinical data, sex-shared/threshold dimorphic gender coding refers to characteristics that appear to be the long-term consequences of prenatal (*qv*) and neonatal (*qv*) coding of the brain. Gender differences produced by early hormonal coding are not absolute or irreducible but depend for their manifestation on different thresholds for responses in males and females. Such behaviors appear to be widely shared across species of higher animals, especially the primates and subhuman species. These behaviors can be experimentally altered by administration of exogenous hormones. In this category, John Money lists (1) kinesis (overall muscular energy expenditure), (2) roaming, (3) competitive rivalry, assertiveness and jockeying for position in a dominance hierarchy of one's peers, (4) aggression in repelling intruders and predators, (5) parental aggression in defense of young, (6) nestling progeny, (7) parentalism threshold, (8) positioning in sexual rehearsal play, and (9) visual sexuoerotic response threshold. *See also* gender coding. Resource: J. Money, *Love and Love Sickness* (Baltimore: Johns Hopkins University Press, 1980).

gender constancy The hypothesis that one's core gender identity (*qv*) or gender role/identity (*qv*) does not normally change once established in early childhood.

gender differences A general reference to differences in physique, ability, attitude, and/or behavior found in or attributed to males or females. *See also* gender coding; gender role.

gender dysphoria The subjectively experienced state of incongruity between one's genital anatomy and one's gender-identity/role (*qv*). Gender dysphoria is particularly obvious in transsexualism (*qv*) and transvestism (*qv*). *See also* gender transposition.

gender identification operation Synonym for a sex change operation (*qv*), or transsexual (*qv*) surgery.

gender identity The internalized sense of being male, female, or having an ambivalent sexual status; the self-awareness of knowing to which sex one belongs; the private experience of gender role (*qv*). In native American Indian cultures, gender identity may include the status of berdache (*qv*) and in some areas of India, the status of a hijra (*qv*). The term gender identity may be used to include the three concepts of core gender identity (*qv*), gender role (*qv*), and sexual orientation (*qv*). *See also* gender scripting; gender identity/role.

gender identity conflict (disorder) The term is also applied to a male whose macho (*qv*) needs prevent him from using a condom (*qv*) to prevent an unwanted pregnancy (*qv*) or to reduce the risk of acquired immune deficiency syndrome (*qv*), or to a female whose need to have a child conflicts with safe sex (*qv*) practices. *See also* gender dysphoria; gender transposition.

gender-identity disorder of childhood According to the American Psychiatric Association definition, a clinical disorder in which a child experiences gender dysphoria (*qv*), a strong discontent with and rejection of one's own sexual anatomy, and a persistent desire to become a member of the opposite sex. *See also* sissy boy syndrome; transsexual.

gender identity/role (G-I/R) A term devised by John Money to emphasize the inseparable nature of one's gender identity (*qv*) —the private experience of one's maleness or femaleness— and one's gender role (*qv*) or public manifestation of gender identity as a male, female, or ambivalent individual. The unity of G-I/R is expressed as two sides of a coin, thereby emphasizing the lifelong interaction of biological and cultural factors at critical periods (*qv*) in one's development. *See also* gender coding; nature/critical period/nurture. Resource: J. Money, *Love and Love Sickness* (Baltimore: Johns Hopkins University Press, 1980).

gender of assignment The public assignment of male or female sex and gender status to a newborn (*qv*), usually based on its external genital (*qv*) anatomy.

gender orientation A more general, less genitally-focused term for what has traditionally been labeled sexual orientation (*qv*). Gender orientation includes (1) a person's erotic or sexual orientation, i.e., homosexual (*qv*), bisexual (*qv*), or heterosexual (*qv*) orientation, (2) the gender orientation of their sexual fantasies, and (3) their affectional or romantic orientation. Taken together, one's core gender identity, gender role, and gender orientation constitute one's gender or psychosexual identity and status.

gender reassignment *See* sex change operation.

gender role The combination of everything an individual does and says to indicate to others or to self the extent to which one's gender identity (*qv*) is male, female, or ambivalent; the public expression of one's gender identity. Gender role may also refer to that culturally determined cluster of behavioral patterns and attitudes that members of one or the other gender are socially expected to fulfill. In another usage, gender role includes erotosexual (*qv*) arousal and response or sexual orientation (*qv*). However, since this broader usage of the term gender role leads to confusion, it is more accurate to speak of sexual orientation or sexual preference as a distinct part of one's gender role/identity (*qv*). *See also* gender coding; gender scripting; sexual script.

gender role dysphoria (nonconformity) A behavioral pattern in which an individual adopts the gender role (*qv*) of the opposite sex, either chronically as in a transgenderist (*qv*) or episodically as in a transvestite (*qv*). Gender role dysphoria can be distinguished from gender (identity) dysphoria and from transpositions in sexual orientation (*qv*), as occurs in persons with a homosexual (*qv*) or bisexual (*qv*) orientation. *See also* sissy boy syndrome.

gender role socialization The scripting (*qv*) or training of children by parents, caregivers, and others in behavior, attitudes, and expectations considered appropriate to the child's gender (*qv*) in that society or culture.

gender role stereotyping The designation by society of dimorphic, specific, and fixed roles for every individual depending on his or her gender (*qv*).

gender scripting *See* gender role; scripting.

gender status A person's psychosexual status as male, female or a member of a third gender such as hijra (*qv*) or berdache (*qv*), as this status is recognized by others or by society. Gender status is the other side of the coin to gender identity (*qv*), the individual's personal self-awareness of his or her gender. *See also* gender orientation.

gender stereotype Commonly accepted beliefs, not necessarily grounded in reality, about the characteristics of a person based on his or her gender (*qv*) and culturally determined gender role (*qv*).

gender transposition The exchange or crossing over from one set of gender-coded attributes, expectations, or stereotypes in one's gender-identity/role (*qv*) from male to female or from female to male. This transposition or exchange can be (1) total, partial or adventitious, (2) chronic or episodic, and (3) either significant or insignificant in its consequences and repercussions for the individual.

In terms of total gender transposition, the crossing over may be total chronic transposition as in transsexualism (*qv*) or total episodic as in transvestism (*qv*). Partial transpositions can be either partial chronic as in gynemimesis (*qv*) or andromimesis (*qv*) or partial episodic as in bisexualism (*qv*). In adventitious crossing over, the gender transposition may be chronic as in androgynous (*qv*) gender-coded education, work, legal status, and so forth, or adventitious episodic as in androgynous gender-coded play, body language, grooming, dress, and so forth. *Resource*: J. Money, *Gay, Straight, and Inbetween: Sexology of Erotic Orientation* (New York: Oxford University Press, 1988).

gene In biology, the gene is defined as the fundamental unit of biological inheritance, and genetics as the science that studies the transmission, inheritance, and function of genes. Genes were discovered in the mid-nineteenth century by Gregor Mendel, who established the basic rules for their inheritance; *see* allele, dominant gene, recessive gene, sex-influenced trait, sex-linked trait, sex-limited trait. Biochemically, the genes are regions in deoxyribonucleic acid (DNA) (*qv*), or, in some viruses, in ribonucleic acid (RNA) (*qv*). In organisms with true chromosomes (*qv*), the gene or genetically functional region of DNA is located at a specific place or "locus" on a chromosome and is inherited with the chromosome that carries the gene. Accordingly, the transmission of chromosomes during fertilization (*qv*) allows the transmission of the genes, and fertilization is therefore the physical mechanism by which inheritance occurs.

At the molecular level, genes function by encoding the structure of cellular proteins, and have no other direct effect. However, indirect effects build extensively from this primary genetic level because proteins are essential to every aspect of cellular or organismic life and activity. These indirect effects are called pleiotropic and can ultimately affect behavior; *see* multiplier effect; behavior genetics. Color blindness is one example, because at the genetic and molecular level the gene affects structures and functions of cells in the eye, which, in turn, affects vision as a whole, and can therefore affect such social matters as a person's ability to distinguish green and red traffic signals.

Colloquially, the term gene is often used loosely and carelessly to mean an innate or built-in biological characteristic of an organism, as in the expression, "Color blindness is genetic." To the biologist, the phrase means that a pleiotropic sequence from molecule to behavior has been rigorously established by detailed investigation of all levels from molecule to society. To the layperson, the expression means vaguely that somehow nature controls how we see colors. From this interpretation emerges a complex web of symbolic meanings about nature, nurture, and biological predestination that have no warrent in either the science of biology or genetics. *See also* nature/critical period/nurture; biology, biologism, biological reductionism.

gene flow The slow transfer or diffusion of genes (*qv*) between two or more populations as they interbreed.

gene pool The total of all genes (*qv*) in a population at a particular time.

general fertility rate (GFR) The number of live births (*qv*) per 1,000 women of childbearing age (15 to 49) in a given year.

generalized other In the sociological theory of George Herbert Mead (*qv*), the viewpoints, values, norms, and attitudes of a group or community. Mead's concept of the generalized other parallels Sigmund Freud's (*qv*) concept of the superego (*qv*), except that the superego develops unconsciously while the development of the generalized other is a conscious process.

general marital fertility rate (GMFR) The number of live births per 1,000 married women of a specific age in a given year.

general paresis An organic mental disorder and form of generalized paralysis caused by chronic syphilis (*qv*). Three types of general paresis are associated with late-stage syphilis, each characterized by a different psychosis: a despondent type characterized by depression; an expansive type characterized by euphoria and grandiose delusions; and a paranoid type with delusions of persecution. Also known as dementia paralytica and general paralysis of the insane.

generation The act or process of reproduction (*qv*); a group of contemporary individuals; the period of time between the birth of an individual and the birth of its offspring.

generation gap The disparity in values, attitudes, and expectations held by older and new generations (*qv*), which results in a general lack of understanding and communication, particularly between adolescents (*qv*) and their parents.

generative organs A somewhat old-fashioned term for the male and female genitalia (*qv*) or sex organs (*qv*).

genesial cycle The female's reproductive period, from menarche (*qv*) to menopause (*qv*).

genetic balance theory In biology, a genetic theory that seeks to explain how sex chromosomes (*qv*) and autosomes (*qv*) together determine sex (*qv*) at the molecular, cellular, and organ level during embryogenesis. The theory first was developed about 1916 in the work of geneticist Calvin Bridges. It has subsequently encompassed a large body of theoretical and experimental work.

In humans, genetic balance theory broadly suggests that during initial stages of gonadal development, the X chromosomes (*qv*) and Y chromosomes (*qv*) and their associated genes (*qv*) act in dynamic balance to produce developmental tendencies toward male or female differentiation, or in cases of chromosome imbalance, toward pathological syndromes such as Klinefelter syndrome (*qv*) and Turner syndrome (*qv*). Later development then proceeds as a further dynamic balance between already existing gonadal differentiation and the differential intensity of effects of androgenic (*qv*) and estrogenic (*qv*) hormones produced by the ovaries (*qv*) and testes (*qv*) to achieve a unique individual blend of masculinization (*qv*), demasculinization (*qv*), feminization (*qv*), and defeminization (*qv*).

In non-mammalian species, particularly insects, genetic balance theory suggests that the balance is between female-directing genes on the X chromosomes and male-directing genes on the autosomes and not the Y chromosome, which in insects often contains no genes at all. The result, however, is a similar complex web of gonadal and organ-level differentiation for final sexual phenotypes (*qv*). Resources: J. J. Bull, *Evaluation of Sex Determining Mechanisms* (Menlo Park, CA: Benjamin/Cummings, 1983); W. G. Eberhard, *Sexual Selection and Animal Genitalia* (Cambridge, MA: Harvard University Press, 1985).

genetic code To the biologist, the phrase genetic code refers solely to a list of 64, and only 64, equivalencies between sequences of nucleotides (*qv*) in deoxyribonucleic acid (DNA) (*qv*) and the sequence of amino acids in proteins; *see* gene. However, when lay speakers use the expression, they often intend a vague and imprecise concept that maintains that somehow the genes encode, determine, or predestine an individual's behavior, temperament, and gender-specific behavior, among other characteristics. Although genes sometimes have quite strong effects on behavior, these effects arise through extensive and characteristically extremely complex pathways between cellular metabolism and behavior. There is no direct connection between the genetic code, as biologists define the term, and behavior; *see* biology; biologism; biological reductionism; multiplier effect.

genetic defect Any metabolic or anatomical abnormality whose primary expression is due to a single gene (*qv*), multiple interacting genes, or a defect in either the number or structure of a chromosome (*qv*).

genetic drift The random change in the frequency of a particular gene (*qv*) occurring in a small population, sometimes after it has separated from a larger parent population.

genetic father The male whose sperm (*qv*) fertilizes an ovum (*qv*), either by natural insemination (*qv*) following coitus (*qv*) or by artificial insemination (*qv*). A distinction can be made between the genetic father or sperm provider and the biological father, physician, or layperson, who does the impregnation (*qv*) when this is achieved by artificial insemination. *See also* social parent; father; mother.

geneticism The belief that behavior is inborn. In the nature/nurture debate (*qv*), the doctrine of instincts and the Freudian stages (*qv*) of psychosexual development (*qv*) represents an extreme in biological reductionism. *See also* nature/critical period/nurture. *See also* biology; biologism.

genetic lethal A genetically determined trait one of whose consequences is that affected individuals die before reaching reproductive age or are incapable of reproducing.

genetic mother The woman whose ovum (*qv*) is used in test tube fertilization (*qv*), or whose uterus (*qv*) is flushed following artificial insemination (*qv*) to provide a zygote (*qv*) for embryo transplant (*qv*); distinguished from the gestational or biological mother (*qv*) who bears the child and the social mother (*qv*) who raises it.

genetic sex The sex (*qv*) of an individual based on the chromosome (*qv*) complement as determined at fertilization (*qv*), 46/XX being the typical genetic sex of a female and 46/XY typical of a male. Also known as chromosomal sex (*qv*).

genital character *See* genital stage.

genital corpuscles *See* Dogiel's corpuscles.

genital eroticism Sexual arousal (*qv*) produced by stimulation of the genitalia (*qv*).

genital femoral nerve One of two branches of the lumbar plexus, which innervates the cremaster muscle (*qv*), the skin of the scrotum (*qv*), and the labia majora (*qv*); the other branch, known simply as the femoral nerve, innervates the skin and muscles of the thigh.

genital herpes A sexually transmitted disease (*qv*) caused by the herpes genitalis or herpes simplex II virus. Genital herpes is transmitted directly in any intimate sexual contact with open sores or blisters. The clusters of small, painful blisters burst after a few days, leaving small, infective ulcers, which heal within two or three weeks. The infection is more common in women than in men. During dormant periods, the virus lives in nerves, being reactivated by stress, hormonal changes, sunbathing, food allergies, cold, and fatigue. There is no effective cure, although the painful symptoms of infective outbreak may be relieved by local or systemic analgesics, warm sitz baths, and sulfa cream to prevent secondary infections, and wet dressings. Acyclovir (Zorivax) speeds healing of blisters and possibly shortens the infective period by entering infected cells and halting their ability to reproduce the virus but only if used in the first days of an outbreak.

genitalia The internal and external sexual (*qv*) or reproductive (*qv*) organs and systems; usually the term refers only to the external male sex organs—penis (*qv*), testes (*qv*), and scrotum (*qv*)—or the external female organs—clitoris (*qv*), labia (*qv*), and vulva (*qv*).

genital intercourse Coitus (*qv*) in which the penis (*qv*) is inserted in the vagina (*qv*).

genitality The ability to concentrate one's sexual excitement (*qv*) and energies (*qv*) on the genitalia (*qv*). *See also* genital stage.

genital libido In psychoanalytic theory (*qv*), the focusing of sexual interests and stimulation on the genitals (*qv*), following a transition through the oral (*qv*), anal (*qv*), and phallic stages (*qv*) of psychosexual development (*qv*). *See also* genital stage.

genital love *See* genital libido; genital primacy; genital stage.

genital mutilation Any ritualistic or paraphilic (*qv*) motivated injury or damage done to the genitalia (*qv*). Male circumcision (*qv*) is probably the most common form of genital modification or mutilation, widely practiced for hygienic and religious reasons in both industrial and Third World cultures. Other ritualistic and religiously motivated mutilations are female circumcision (*qv*), the subincision (*qv*) and superincision (*qv*) of the penis (*qv*) practiced by some Australian and South Pacific natives, and the self-castrations practiced by Islamic Dervishes, the Skoptsy (*qv*) sect, and the hijra (*qv*) of India. Religious penance and extreme body-denying asceticism (*qv*) is often a motive in genital mutilation. In some societies, ampallangs (*qv*), rings, bells, and other jewelry are inserted in the labia (*qv*), penis, or scrotum (*qv*) as decoration. Self-mutilations may be paraphilic in their origins, as with apotemnophilia (*qv*) and stigmatophilia (*qv*).

genital organs *See* genitalia; genitals.

genital penetration phobia A hypophilic (*qv*) condition involving irrational panic and disabling fear that prevents a female or male from engaging in penile-vaginal intercourse (*qv*). In females, the fear may be of bleeding or other expected pain believed to be associated with penetration (*qv*) of the vagina by the penis, finger, or other object. This fear results in vaginal spasms that prevent penetration. In males, the fear may be related to the myth of vagina captiva (*qv*) or vagina dentata (*qv*).

genital phase *See* genital stage.

genital primacy According to the Freudian model of psychosexual development (*qv*), the subordination in the mature personality of all sexual components under the primacy of the genital zone (*qv*) and genital eroticism (*qv*). *See also* genital stage.

genital reflex In males, a reflex (*qv*) in which tactile or cerebral stimulation results in penile erection (*qv*) or ejaculation (*qv*). *See also* psychogenic; reflexogenic.

genital ridge *See* gonadal ridge.

genitals *See* genitalia.

genital stage In psychoanalytic theory (*qv*), the culminating stage of psychosexual development (*qv*), beginning at puberty (*qv*) as a result of biological and hormonal forces and characterized by a synthesis of the previous oral (*qv*), anal (*qv*), and phallic (*qv*) stages in an adult genital-coital sexuality (*qv*), a growing sense of personal independence and autonomy, and establishment of a stable and meaningful heterosexual (*qv*) relationship.

genital tubercle The small primordium, a fingerlike projection of tissue that normally develops into a penis (*qv*) or clitoris (*qv*) in the second and third months of fetal life.

genital tuberculosis A chronic granulomatous infection caused when the bacterium *Mycobacterium tuberculosis* invades the reproductive system. In men, the affected organs are the prostate (*qv*), testes (*qv*), and epididymis (*qv*). In women, the uterus (*qv*) and fallopian tubes (*qv*) are most commonly involved. About 2 percent of all upper genital tract infections in women involve genital tuberculosis.

genital warts A sexually transmitted viral disease resulting in painless, soft, pink or red, cauliflowerlike, single or multiple clusters of warts. Genital warts appear one to three months after infectious contact in moist regions of the body— the oral cavity and anal (*qv*), penile (*qv*), and vulval (*qv*) areas. These highly contagious growths can block vaginal (*qv*), urethral (*qv*), or anal openings. Also known as condylomata. Treatments include cryotherapy and the drug podophyllin.

genital zones *See* erogenous zones.

genitoerotic Any erotic (*qv*) feeling or activity associated with the genitalia (*qv*) in imagery and/or activity.

genitourinary (GN) system The genital and urinary systems of the body. *See also* urogenital system.

genome The complete set of genes (*qv*) in the chromosomes (*qv*) of somatic cells of an individual. *See also* genotype.

genomic imprinting (inactivation) A genetic mechanism that allows a gene (*qv*) contributed by a mother to her offspring to differ functionally from an identical gene contributed by the father. Mendelian and classical genetics assumes that when an offspring inherits two genes with exactly the same DNA (*qv*) sequence, one from the father and one from the mother, both genes will function exactly the same regardless of whether the gene came from the mother or the father and regardless of the sex of the offspring. In an elementary example, Mendelian and classical genetics claim that a gene for blue eyes is a gene for blue eyes, whether it is inherited from the father or mother. The revolutionary evidence of genomic imprinting, announced in 1989, says it matters very much whether the gene comes from the father or the mother. In the developing egg (*qv*) or sperm (*qv*), different genes may be turned off depending on the sex of the individual producing the gamete (*qv*). These genes remain turned off in the offspring. When that offspring begins producing its own eggs or sperm, these genes may be turned on depending on the sex of the offspring. Genetic imprinting is now considered one of the most fundamental molecular manifestations of maleness and femaleness. *See also* imprinting; encoding; template. Resource: R. Weiss, A genetic gender gap, *Science News* 135(1989):312–315.

genophobia An intense, morbid fear of sex (*qv*).

genotype The complete genetic constitution of an individual or group, the sum of an individual's genes (*qv*) and chromosomes (*qv*). The genotype is expressed only in interaction with the organism's environment, creating an observable product in the organism's phenotype (*qv*). May also refer to the specific alleles (*qv*) at a particular chromosome (*qv*) locus in an individual. *See also* phenotype.

gens An anthropological term used to characterize the division of an ethnic (*qv*) group whose line of descent is traced through the male. *See also* patrilineal.

gentle birthing *See* Leboyer method of childbirth.

genuine victim A quasi-legal term used to distinguish the victim of a rape (*qv*) by a stranger from the victim of date (*qv*), acquaintance (*qv*), or marital rape (*qv*). Since use of this term is based on a personal judgment of the victim's possible partial responsibility for the assault, it is not acceptable in court.

German measles *See* rubella.

germ cell *See* gamete.

germinal cell A primordial or immature gamete (*qv*) or the mature ovum (*qv*) or spermatozoan (*qv*).

germinal cell aplasia The absence of germinal epithelium from the seminiferous tubules (*qv*) resulting in total absence of spermatogenesis (*qv*). This condition does not affect the normal functioning of the Sertoli cells (*qv*) in the testes (*qv*).

germinal disc *See* embryonic disc.

germinal epithelium The epithelial covering of the gonadal ridge (*qv*) from which the gonads (*qv*) develop in the second month of gestation (*qv*); the epithelial covering of the ovary (*qv*), previously thought to be the origins of the oogonial cells.

germinal nucleus The pronucleus, the haploid (*qv*) nucleus of the ovum (*qv*) or spermatozoan (*qv*) after fertilization (*qv*) when it swells in preparation for pronuclear fusion and restoration of the diploid (*qv*) chromosome number to the zygote (*qv*).

germinal period (stage) The period between fertilization (*qv*) and the development of the embryonic disc (*qv*) in the first half of the third week of gestation (*qv*), when the neural plate and three primary germ layers (*qv*) develop. This period includes the zygote (*qv*) stage, morula (*qv*), and blastocyst (*qv*) with an inner cell mass (*qv*), trophoblast (*qv*), and fetal membranes (*qv*).

germinal ridge *See* gonadal ridge.

germinal spot The nucleolus (*qv*) of the mature ovum (*qv*), prior to fertilization (*qv*).

germinal stage *See* germinal period.

germinal vesicle The germinal nucleus (*qv*), or pronucleus, of a mature ovum (*qv*) prior to fertilization (*qv*). *See also* meiosis, oogenesis.

germination The period of gestation (*qv*) between fertilization (*qv*) and formation of the embryo (*qv*); in humans, roughly the first two weeks following fertilization.

germ layer theory A trilaminar model of early embryonic development that pictures the formation of three primordial cell layers—ectoderm (*qv*), mesoderm (*qv*), and endoderm (*qv*)—during the process of gastrulation (*qv*) in the embryonic disc (*qv*). All tissues, organs and structures are derived in some way from a single germ layer or a combination of germ layers. *See also* germinal period.

germ nucleus *See* germinal nucleus; pronucleus.

germ plasm theory The reproductive and hereditary material as distinct from the somatic cells (*qv*). This distinction was introduced by August Weismann (1834–1914), a German biologist who mistakenly believed that a certain type of protoplasm was transmitted substantially unchanged from generation to generation via the gametes (*qv*). After fertilization (*qv*), the germ cells divided rapidly into germ plasm and somatic cell lines.

gerontophilia (adj. gerontophilic) The psychological condition or dependence in which a young adult is responsive to and needs erotosexual (*qv*) activity with a much older partner in order to achieve sexual arousal (*qv*) and orgasm (*qv*).

gerontosexuality *See* gerontophilia.

gestagen A synthetic form of progesterone (*qv*). *Synonyms*: progestogen, progestin.

Gestalt psychology A school of psychology that maintains that a psychological phenomenon is perceived as a total configuration or pattern developing from the relationships among the constituent elements rather than as an aggregate of discrete elements, each with its own distinct characteristics. Because of the synergistic interactions of the components, the gestalt is more than a sum of all the parts. *See also* gestalt therapy.

Gestalt therapy A form of psychotherapy that stresses the unity of self-awareness, behavior, and experience and incorporates elements of psychoanalytic, behavior and humanistic-existential therapies. *See also* Gestalt psychology.

gestate To carry a developing fetus (*qv*) in the uterus (*qv*).

gestation The period of pregnancy (*qv*) in a viviparous animal, the time from conception (*qv*) until birth (*qv*); in women, roughly 266 days if calculated from conception or 280 days if the calculation is made from the end of the last menstrual period (*qv*).

gestational age The age of the fetus (*qv*) expressed in weeks and calculated from the first day of the mother's last menstrual period (*qv*). *See also* conceptional age.

gestational mother The woman who bears and gives birth to a child. Until the recent introduction of embryo transplants (*qv*) and test tube fertilization (*qv*), the gestational mother was also always the genetic mother (*qv*).

gestosis Any disorder or toxemia (*qv*) associated with pregnancy (*qv*). *See also* eclampsia; preeclampsia.

get (Hebrew) The decree of religious divorce (*qv*) in the Jewish tradition.

getting partner The partner in couple sex therapy who is the recipient in the sensate focus exercises (*qv*). Although the getting partner does not engage in touching, caressing, or exploring the partner's body while in the getting role, he or she is encouraged to give verbal feedback as to what is enjoyable or unpleasant. Verbal feedback and even manual directions can be provided for the giving partner (*qv*). Directing a more or less firm touch, longer or briefer, and encouraging the exploration of certain areas are also appropriate in the getting role. At different times in the sensate focus exercises, the couple reverse their roles of giving and receiving.

getting together model of courtship A nontraditional, unstructured, and flexible pattern of courtship (*qv*) that allows for a variety of marital and nonmarital relationships, egalitarian male-female relations, and a strong emphasis on openness and sensuality. First described by Roger Libby. *See also* primrose path model of courtship. Resource: R. Libby, Social scripts for sexual relationships, in S. Gordon and R. W. Libby, eds., *Sexuality Today and Tomorrow* (North Scituate, MA: Duxbury, 1976).

GFR *See* general fertility rate.

giant mammary myxoma A usually benign tumor of the breast (*qv*) consisting of connective tissue cells in a loose mucoid matrix, which sometimes develops in women entering menopause (*qv*). Such tumors, which may grow to weigh 6 or 7 pounds and exceed 10 inches in diameter, are removed by a simple mastectomy (*qv*).

gichigich A sexual custom engaged in by the Yap women of the Caroline Islands of the Western Pacific in which the woman sits astride the male while he slowly massages her major labia (*qv*) with his penis (*qv*) until she has multiple orgasms (*qv*). Because of the strenuous nature of this form of coitus (*qv*), it is usually only practiced by young couples before marriage (*qv*).

GIFT The acronym for *gamete in fallopian tube transfer*, a form of artificial in vivo fertilization (*qv*) in which an ovum (*qv*) and semen (*qv*) are deposited in the fallopian tube (*qv*) of a childless woman in hope of fertilization and normal pregnancy (*qv*).

gigantism An abnormal condition characterized by excessive size and stature, usually caused by oversecretion of the growth hormone. It occurs less frequently in hypogonadism (*qv*) and in certain genetic disorders such as Klinefelter syndrome (*qv*).

gigolo A man who provides social and/or sexual companionship to women for money or other compensation. To the extent that the relationship is sexual, a gigolo may be a male prostitute (*qv*). The term may be applied in a derogatory way to a ''womanizer'' who exploits his female companions for cash gifts and expensive presents. *See also* ciscisbeism.

ginseng A plant of the genus *Panax* much prized particularly in the Orient for its reputed but undocumented benefits as a medicine, tonic, and stimulant and for its aphrodisiac (*qv*) uses. Both psychological and physical benefits are attributed to ginseng.

G-I/R *See* gender identity/role.

girl A female child or adolescent (*qv*). Depending on changing customs, the term has been applied to a female servant or employee, a young unmarried woman, or a girlfriend of any age, although such usage is increasingly considered to be sexist (*qv*) and demeaning to women. In Middle English, *girl* referred to a young person of either sex, with the adjective *knave* used to refer to a male girl and *gaye* used to indicate a female girl. The term is also used as a demeaning epitaph for women by people who need to see women in narrow, nonthreatening, and dependent terms, much as *boy* is use as a demeaning term for male adults of color. The term *girl* referring to a female adult implies childishness, conformity, dependency, purity, delicacy, nonaggressiveness, noncompetitiveness, frivolity, and immaturity.

giving partner The partner in couple sex therapy who is active in touching and exploring the receiving or getting partner (*qv*) during the sensate focus exercises (*qv*). At different times in the exercises, the giving and receiving roles are reversed.

glandulae preputialis (L.) Secretory glands around the corona of the penile glans (*qv*) and under the foreskin (*qv*) that produce smegma (*qv*).

glans A general term for a small rounded mass, or glandlike body; a glans may or may not be erectile.

glans clitoris (or clitoridis) (L.) The smooth, erectile, darker colored, enlarged end of the clitoris (*qv*), continuous with the intermediate part of the vaginal vestibular bulbs and consisting of two corpora cavernosa (*qv*) enclosed in a dense, fibrous membrane connected to the pubis (*qv*) and ischium.

glans gonorrhea (L.) An irritation of the prepuce (*qv*) or foreskin (*qv*), often mistaken for a gonorrhea (*qv*) infection by the layperson, hence the name.

glans penis (L.) The smooth, rounded tip of the penis (*qv*), the enlarged end of the corpus spongiosum (*qv*). The urinary meatus (*qv*) is located at the center of the distal portion of the glans. The glans is covered by the thin, hairless foreskin (*qv*) in uncircumcised males.

gleet An abnormal gonorrheal (*qv*) discharge of urethral mucus; a slang expression for gonorrhea.

glucocorticoid A class of hormones (*qv*) that has its main effect on carbohydrate metabolism; the chief natural glucocorticoid is cortisol (*qv*), produced by the adrenal cortex (*qv*).

gluteal Referring to the buttocks (*qv*).

GMFR *See* general marital fertility rate.

Gn-RH *See* gonadotropic releasing factor.

godemiche An obsolete term for a dildo (*qv*).

gonad The primary reproductive organ, the ovary (*qv*) or testis (*qv*), which produces gametes (*qv*) and the gender-appropriate balance of sex hormones. Also applied to the undifferentiated embryonic reproductive gland that develops into an ovary or testis.

gonadal dysgenesis Defective or abnormal development of the ovary (*qv*) or testis (*qv*), particularly during the embryonic-fetal period; characteristic of Turner (*qv*) and Klinefelter (*qv*) syndromes. *See also* vanishing testes syndrome.

gonadal gender (or sex) An individual's sex status determined by the presence of ovaries (*qv*), testes (*qv*), or ovariotesticular gonads (*qv*). Gonadal sex may be in nonconformity with other variables that contribute to one's gender identity/role (*qv*), as in androgen insensitivity syndrome (*qv*), adrenogenital syndrome (*qv*), and transsexualism (*qv*).

gonadal ridge The earliest stage in the development of the fetal gonads (*qv*). The paired gonadal ridges arise from primordial germinal cells that migrate from the yolk sac (*qv*) to the surface of the paired mesonephric (*qv*) kidneys in the seventh week of fetal development. As the gonads develop, they separate from the mesonephros, which then degenerates as it is replaced by the definitive metanephric kidneys. The Wolffian or mesonephric ducts (*qv*) become the vasa deferentia (*qv*) in the male fetus (*qv*) and attach to the testes (*qv*). In the female, the Wolffian ducts degenerate. The paired Mullerian ducts (*qv*), which develop alongside the Wolffian ducts, become the posterior vagina (*qv*), uterus (*qv*), and fallopian tubes (*qv*) in the female but degenerate in the male fetus.

gonadectomy Surgical removal of one or both of the gonads (*qv*), either by ovariectomy (*qv*) or castration (*qv*).

gonadocentric That stage of psychosexual development (*qv*) beginning with puberty (*qv*) when the libido (*qv*) becomes fully focused on the genitalia (*qv*). *See also* genital stage.

gonadopause A reduction or cessation of sexual activity that sometimes accompanies aging.

gonadostat theory In analogy with a thermostat, the hypothetical mechanism whereby hormones (*qv*) secreted by the ovaries (*qv*) or testes (*qv*) regulate by a feedback mechanism (*qv*) the secretions of the hypothalamus (*qv*) and pituitary (*qv*). This process depends on both threshold levels of a particular hormone or metabolic product and on critical periods (*qv*) at which the gonadostat mechanism is sensitive to or capable of responding to the feedback stimulus.

gonadotropin Any hormone (*qv*) that stimulates or influences the functioning of the ovaries (*qv*) or testes (*qv*). Two types of gonadotropins are produced by the anterior pituitary gland (*qv*) in both males and females: the follicle-stimulating hormone (*qv*), which controls early spermatogenesis (*qv*) and oogenesis (*qv*), and luteinizing hormone (*qv*) or ICSH (*qv*) in males, which regulates testosterone (*qv*) production; sperm (*qv*) maturation, and ovulation (*qv*). In early pregnancy (*qv*), the placenta (*qv*) produces a third gonadotropin, human chorionic gonadotropin (*qv*), which maintains the corpus luteum (*qv*) of the ovary (*qv*).

gonadotropin-releasing factor or hormone (Gn-RF or Gn-RH) The hormone or factor produced by the hypothalamus (*qv*), which controls the production and release of luteinizing hormone (*qv*) and follicle stimulating hormone (*qv*) or interstitial cell stimulating hormone (*qv*) in different regions of the pituitary (*qv*). Originally, Gn-RH was thought to be two distinct hormones, luteinizing hormone-releasing factor (*qv*) and follicle-stimulating hormone-releasing factor (*qv*). The release of Gn-RH is controlled by a negative feedback (*qv*) mechanism involving FSH and LH.

gonapodium *See* gonopodium.

gon-, gono- A combining form referring to semen (*qv*) or seed.

-gonic A combining form referring to any agent, process, or product of sexual generation or reproduction (*qv*).

gonoblast A gamete (*qv*) or germ cell (*qv*).

gonochorism In biology, the occurrence in adults of some species, for example, certain fish, of a change of sexual phenotype (*qv*) from male to female or from female to male. Such changes occur within the lifetime of an individual, and both male and female phases are fertile and capable of enacting species-specific reproductive and copulatory behavior (*qv*).

gonococcal arthritis *See* gonorrheal arthritis.

gonococcal conjunctivitis *See* gonorrheal conjunctivitis.

gonococcus (pl. gonococci) (L.) A gram-negative intracellular bacterium of the species *Neisseria gonorrhoeae*, the cause of gonorrhea (*gv*).

gonocyte A gamete (*qv*) or germ cell (*qv*).

gonopodium In certain fish, anal fins modified with claspers, which assist the male in achieving intromission (*qv*) or copulation (*qv*).

gonorrhea A common sexually transmitted bacterial infection of the vagina (*qv*), penis (*qv*), rectum (*qv*), throat, or eyes caused by the bacterium *Neisseria gonorrhoeae* (*qv*). Symptoms in males include a greenish or yellow-green penile discharge, anal irritation, painful urination or defecation, and swollen glands and sore throat. Female symptoms include a vaginal discharge and itching. Symptoms appear 1 to 14 days after contact. Many females usually show no early symptoms, while 5 to 20 percent of males also show no symptoms. The gonococcal bacterium, transmitted by sexual contact, may involve the epipidymis (*qv*), prostate (*qv*), seminal vesicles (*qv*), and external genitalia (*qv*) of the male and the cervix (*qv*), uterus (*qv*), fallopian tubes (*qv*), and ovaries (*qv*) of the female. In both sexes, the rectum and throat may become infected by anal (*qv*) or oral sex (*qv*). In pregnant women, a gonorrheal infection may result in inflammation or premature rupture of the fetal membranes (*qv*), premature labor (*qv*), low birth weight (*qv*), respiratory problems, or even death of the newborn (*qv*). A gram stain test of cultures from swabs taken from suspected infected areas gives reliable, quick results. Treatment is with penicillin or other antibiotic. A recent strain, known as PPNG or more commonly Vietnam Rose, produces an enzyme that inactivates penicillin; in this case treatment is with spectinomycin unless the strain is also resistant to that antibiotic.

gonorrheal arthritis An acute or chronic gonococcal (*qv*) infection of the joints of the body. The infection may be limited to a single joint or involve many joints. Reduced and painful joint movement may be accompanied by fever. If left untreated, the infected joint may become frozen or immobilized.

gonorrheal bubo A swelling of the lymph glands in the inguinal (*qv*) region; an early sign of a gonococcal (*qv*) infection.

gonorrheal conjunctivitis A severe, destructive prurulent infection of the mucous membrane lining the inner surface of the eye of a newborn (*qv*) caused by the gonococcus *Neisseria gonorrhoeae* (*qv*). Inflammation and a copious puslike exudate are symptoms of this infection, which may lead to blindness if left untreated.

gonosome The X or Y sex chromosome (*qv*), as distinct from autosomes (*qv*).

Gonosticom Dri Dot test An inexpensive, easily used test for the antibodies (*qv*) of the gonorrhea (*qv*) bacterium in blood, not recommended by the Centers for Disease Control because of the risk of false positive (*qv*) and false negative (*qv*) results. Some physicians find the test is useful in detecting a gonorrheal cause for abdominal pelvic inflammatory disease (*qv*) or arthritis. *See also* Eliza test; Transformation Test.

-gony A combining suffix meaning "birth" or "origin."

Gordon-Overstreet syndrome A form of Turner syndrome (*qv*) with partial virilization (*qv*). Individuals with this form of Turner syndrome show the typical characteristics of Turner's with virilizing enlargement of the clitoris (*qv*) and hirsutism (*qv*).

gossypol An extract of cotton seed that has been tested for use as a male contraceptive (*qv*) because of its suppression of spermatogenesis (*qv*); of limited use because of the prolonged sterility (*qv*) that results after the drug use is stopped.

gothic (romance) novel A popular form of fiction primarily written for and read by women, with an often formulaic story line typically beginning when a vulnerable, innocent young woman is kidnapped, taken away forcibly, and given in marriage (*qv*) to an older, aloof, and seemingly cruel but irresistibly attractive man who takes her to a remote castle or estate where she learns that he truly loves her. *See also* romance novels, Harlequin romance.

Graaf, Regnier de (1641–1673) In 1672, this Dutch physician and anatomist observed vesicular follicles on the surface of the rabbit ovaries (*qv*). He mistook these ovarian follicles for the ovum (*qv*), which is actually much smaller, being contained within the ovarian follicle, now known also as the Graafian follicle (*qv*). De Graaf also provided the first modern descriptions of the human male and female sexual anatomy.

Graafian follicle The capsulelike structure in the ovary (*qv*) that nurtures the development of the ovum (*qv*). Development of the Graafian follicle, 10 to 12 millimeters in diameter when mature, is stimulated during the follicular phase (*qv*) by follicle stimulating hormone (*qv*). The follicle is surrounded by a single and, later, a double layer of protective and nutritive nurse cells. These cells secrete fluid into the growing follicular cavity, eventually causing the follicle to rupture and release the ovum into the abdominal cavity near the opening of the fallopian tube. After ovulation (*qv*), the ruptured follicle is invaded by secretory cells, becoming the corpus luteum (*qv*), which produces progesterone (*qv*) and estrogens (*qv*) to maintain early pregnancy (*qv*) and prevent further ovulation in the event of fertilization and uterine implantation. *See also* Graaf, Regnier de.

Grafenberg, Ernst A German obstetrician and gynecologist, Grafenberg and his collaborator Robert Latou Dickinson (*qv*) described a "zone of erogenous feeling . . . located along the suburethral surface of the anterior vaginal wall." This modern rediscovery of a finding originally reported by Regnier de Graaf (*qv*) is the basis for renaming this region the Grafenberg spot (*qv*). Resource: E. Grafenberg, The role of urethra in female orgasm, *International Journal of Sexology* 3(1950):145–148.

Grafenberg spot A very sensitive tissue located in the anterior wall of the vagina (*qv*), just under the urinary bladder, an inch or two beyond the vaginal orifice, and usually halfway between the back of the pubic bone and the front of the cervix (*qv*). Stimulation of this area produces an initial feeling that one must urinate, sometimes followed by intense sexual arousal, which may result in an A-frame (*qv*) or uterine orgasm (*qv*). The Grafenberg spot, or G spot, may be associated with female ejaculation (*qv*).

Graham, Sylvester (1794–1851) An influential minister of the 1800s noted for his advocacy of temperance, vegetarianism, exercise, and sexual abstinence (*qv*) as a remedy for an epidemic of cholera in the early 1830s and to counter the sexual degeneracy of Americans. In his many lectures and in a magnum opus, *Lectures on the Science of Human Life*, Graham warned about the consequences of "excessive venereal indulgence," advising men they were not strong enough to engage in sexual intercourse (*qv*) until about age 30. Even then he urged they engage in marital intercourse for procreative purposes only about once every three years. Graham also denounced masturbation (*qv*), warning of the dire consequences of any loss of "vital fluids" or semen (*qv*). Graham recommended bread and crackers made from whole wheat or Graham flour as a replacement for red meat and spicy, hot foods that irritate the digestive system and in turn stimulate the sexual organs. Resource: J. Money, *The Destroying Angel* (Buffalo, NY: Prometheus Press, 1985).

granuloma inguinale (L.) A sexually transmitted disease (*qv*) characterized by ulcers of the skin and subcutaneous tissues of the groin and genitalia (*qv*) and caused by infection with *Calymmatobacterium granulomatis*, a small gram-negative rod-shaped bacterium. Diagnosis is made by microscopic examination of cells taken from the lesions. Streptomycin is standard treatment. Syphilis (*qv*) is a common concurrent infection.

granulosa cells The cells lining the Graafian follicle (*qv*) that proliferate after ovulation (*qv*) to form the corpus luteum (*qv*). The granulosa cells are stimulated by the follicle-stimulating hormone (*qv*) to produce the liquid that fills the antrum or cavity of the developing follicle.

granulosa cell tumor An ovarian tumor (*qv*) in which the neoplastic cells resemble the granulosa cells (*qv*) surrounding the Graafian follicle (*qv*). In postmenopausal (*qv*) women, such tumors can cause irregular menstrual bleeding. In girls, the excess estrogens (*qv*) can produce premature puberty (*qv*).

granulosa-theca-cell tumor An ovarian tumor (*qv*) involving the granulosa (*qv*) and theca (*qv*) cells surrounding the Graafian follicle (*qv*). Production of excess estrogens (*qv*) may cause premature puberty (*qv*) in a female child.

gravid Pregnant (*qv*); carrying a fertilized ovum (*qv*) or a fetus (*qv*).

-gravida A combining form referring to a pregnant (*qv*) woman (e.g., *nonigravida* meaning "never pregnant," *primigravida*, *unigravida*, and *gravida I* referring to a first pregnancy, *gravida II* to a second pregnancy, and *gravidocardiac* indicating a maternal heart problem associated with pregnancy).

Great Imitator Syphilis (*qv*) is commonly referred to as the Great Imitator because many of its symptoms, if considered separately, would indicate several different nonsyphilitic infections. More recently, chlamydia (*qv*) has been accorded this title because its symptoms are often misinterpreted as indicating a gonorrheal (*qv*) infection.

green discharge A dishonorable discharge for homosexual (*qv*) behavior used by the U.S. Navy during World War II.

GRID Literally, "gay-related immune deficiency," an acronym used before 1982 for what is now known as acquired immune deficiency syndrome (*qv*).

Griselda complex A psychiatric term for one type of unresolved Oedipal complex (*qv*) in which a father is reluctant to allow his daughter to marry.

Griswold v. Connecticut In this 1965 decision, the U.S. Supreme Court overturned laws prohibiting doctors from prescribing contraceptives (*qv*) and others from selling them. *See also* Comstock Law.

gross indecency A nineteenth-century British legal term for anal intercourse (*qv*). *See also* buggery; sodomy.

group In sociology, a group is a collective of individuals who interact and form social relationships. A primary group, according to sociologist C. H. Cooley, is small and defined by face-to-face interactions and solidarity to their own norms of conduct. Examples include the family (*qv*), groups of friends, and many work groups. Secondary groups are larger and do not involve direct contact of all members with each other. Resource: C. H. Cooley, *Social Organization* (New York: Scribner's, 1909).

group B streptococcal infection A bacterial streptococcal infection with possible serious complications, particularly for pregnant (*qv*) women. This pathogen can be sexually transmitted. Fetal complications of this infection result in about 5,000 fetal deaths a year in the United States from abortion (*qv*), perinatal death, premature birth, and a variety of neonatal diseases.

group marriage A life-style in which three or more people live together as spouses; often similar to traditional monogamous (*qv*) marriages (*qv*) except that in a group marriage all adults work out mutually agreeable arrangements for sharing of income-producing employment, household tasks, and child rearing. *See also* Oneida Community.

group sex Sexual activity shared by three or more people at the same time in the presence of each other. Group sex may be strictly heterosexual (*qv*), homosexual (*qv*), or include a mix of heterosexual and lesbian (*qv*) activities. Rarely does group sex include homosexual relations between the participating males. *See also* swinging.

group superego That portion of the superego (*qv*) derived from one's peers as opposed to that portion inculcated by one's parents.

group therapy The use of psychotherapeutic techniques within a small group of patients or clients who, under the direction of a psychotherapist, sex counselor, or therapist, provide support for each other and insights into shared or similar problems. Group therapy is useful in sex therapy, in sexual enrichment, in working with rape (*qv*), incest (*qv*), and abuse (*qv*) victims, in rehabilitation of sex offenders (*qv*), and in work with sexual addicts (*qv*).

G spot *See* Grafenberg spot.

guevedoces (guevote) (Sp.) A Spanish phrase, literally "penis at twelve," used to describe individuals who appear to change from females to males at puberty (*qv*). *See also* DHT deficiency syndrome. Synonym: *Machihembra*, "first woman, then man."

guiche A metal ring about 1 inch in diameter inserted in the perineal region (*qv*), between the anus (*qv*) and vulva (*qv*). Gentle tension or pulls on the ring during sexual intercourse (*qv*) are said to increase sexual pleasure.

guilt The sense or belief that one has violated some social or religious norm (*qv*), done a wrong, or committed an offense or sin. In some cultures, guilt, experienced in the internal sanctions of conscience, religion, and punishment imposed after the fact, is the primary social control over an individual's behavior. *See also* shame.

guilt, sexual A generalized expectancy for self-monitored punishment for violating or anticipating the violation of internalized standards of socially acceptable behavior regarding sexually related thoughts and behaviors. Resource: D. Mosher, The meaning and measurement of guilt, in C. E. Izard, ed., *Emotions in Personality and Psychopathology* (New York: Plenum Press, 1979).

gumma A granuloma characteristic of tertiary syphilis (*qv*). *See also* intracranial gumma.

Guttmacher Institute *See* Alan Guttmacher Institute.

gymno- A combining form meaning "pertaining to nakedness" (e.g., *gymnophobia* meaning a morbid fear of the naked body).

gynandroblastoma A rare, usually benign, ovarian tumor (*qv*) that produces both androgens (*qv*) and estrogens (*qv*), characteristically marked by hirsutism (*qv*) and abnormal uterine (*qv*) bleeding.

gynandroid A synonym for a female pseudohermaphrodite (*qv*). *See also* androgyne.

gynandromorph An individual possessing both male and female characteristics, usually as the result of a genetic mosaic condition. *See also* sexual mosaic. Gynandromorph birds and insects are not uncommon. Among higher animals and humans, it is a very rare condition. *See also* hermaphrodite; he/she; pseudohermaphrodite.

gynandromorphy Having some of the body characteristics of an average man and some of an average woman but without being at either extreme; etymologically, "woman-man-shape."

gynandrous (gynandry) An alternate term for androgyny (*qv*); a man or woman who has some of the physical characteristics usually attributed to the other sex. *See also* pseudohermaphrodite.

gyneco-, gyn-, gyne-, -gyne, gyno- Combining forms meaning pertaining or referring to the female sex or to a woman.

gynecoid Having the physical appearance of a female.

gynecologic examination A medical examination of the female reproductive and sexual system; also called a pelvic exam. A complete gynecological examination has four parts: inspection of the external genitalia (*qv*) or vulva (*qv*); viewing the vagina (*qv*) and cervix (*qv*) with the aid of a speculum to separate the vaginal walls and allow the taking of samples for Pap smear (*qv*) analysis; palpation of the lower abdomen with one hand and two fingers of the other hand inside the vagina to feel the size and shape of the uterus (*qv*) (called a bimanual exam); and a rectal exam with the rectum penetrated and palpated by one finger. It is recommended that all women have a gynecological examination at puberty (*qv*) and yearly thereafter.

gynecologist A physician who specializes in the diagnosis and treatment of the female sexual organs (*qv*) and reproductive system. *See also* gynecology.

gynecology That branch of medical science specializing in the diagnosis and surgical and nonsurgical treatment of the female sexual organs (*qv*) and reproductive system, usually practiced in conjunction with obstetrics (*qv*).

Gyn/Ecology A feminist term coined by Mary Daly in 1978 to indicate "a way of wrenching back some word power. The fact that most gynecologists are males is in itself a colossal comment on 'our' society . . . *Gyn/Ecology* is by and about women amazing all the male-authored world tapestries *of our own kind*. That is, it is about dis-covering, de-veloping the complex web of living/loving relationships *of our own kind*." Resource: M. Daly, *Gyn/Ecology: The Metaphysics of Radical Feminism* (Boston: Beacon Press, 1978).

gynecomastia (gynecomasty) Unilateral or bilateral female breast (*qv*) development occurring in a male. Gynecomastia may result from a genetic (*qv*) anomaly such as Klinefelter syndrome (*qv*), from a hormone-secreting tumor in the testes (*qv*), pituitary (*qv*), lung, or breast, from the failure of the liver to inactivate circulating estrogens (*qv*) as in alcoholic cirrhosis, from exogenous hormone treatment, or from the use of nonmedical drugs, particularly marijuana whose active ingredient THC can trigger gynecomastia. When gynecomastia is induced in a male-to-female transsexual (*qv*) prior to surgical removal of the male genitalia (*qv*), the individual is known as a he/she (*qv*). *See also* andromimetic; gynecomimetic.

gynecomastia-aspermatogenesis syndrome A form of Klinefelter syndrome (*qv*), 47,XXY, characterized by female breast (*qv*) development, gynecomastia (*qv*), and absence of spermatogenesis (*qv*).

gynecomimetic (n. gynecomimesis) A boy or man manifesting the features or characteristics of a female in bodily appearance, dress, and behavior. A gynecomimetic may be a drag queen (*qv*) or a male homosexual (*qv*) who lives the role of a woman while retaining his male genitalia (*qv*). Some gynecomimetics may take hormones (*qv*) to stimulate female breast (*qv*) development. Also referred to as a he/she (*qv*). *Compare*: andromimetic.

gynemimetophilia A paraphilia (*qv*) of the stigmatic-eligibilic type in a person who is aroused by and dependent on a partner who is a transvestite (*qv*), a gynecomimetic (*qv*), or a preoperative male-to-female transsexual (*qv*).

gynephilia *See* gynophilia.

gynephobia *See* gynophobia.

gynetresia A congenital anomaly characterized by total absence of the vagina (*qv*) or a very shallow vagina. The condition can be remedied by plastic surgery performed after puberty (*qv*) when full body size is achieved and the artificially constructed vagina can be regularly dilated.

-gynic A combining form meaning "relating to the human female."

gyno- *See* gyneco-.

gynogamone A hormonelike substance believed to be produced by the ovum (*qv*) to attract sperm (*qv*). *See also* gamone; androgamone.

gynomonoecism A developmental anomaly in which an individual who appears to be female produces spermatozoa (*qv*).

gynophilia (adj. gynophilic) Literally, "love of a woman"; a male or female who falls in love with a woman. *See also* homosexuality; heterosexuality; lesbian.

gynophobia An anxiety disorder characterized by a morbid fear of women, usually originating in an unresolved frightening childhood experience with women; treated with psychotherapy, behavioral therapy (*qv*), and gradual desensitization (*qv*). As used by feminists like Adrienne Rich, *gynophobia* or *gynephobia* is "the age-old, cross-cultural male fear and hatred of women, which women too inhale like poisonous fumes from the air we breathe daily." Resource: A. Rich, *On Lies, Secrets, and Silence: Selected Prose 1966–1978* (New York: W. W. Norton, 1979), p. 289.

gynosperm One of the dimorphic forms of sperm (*qv*), containing 22 autosomes (*qv*) and one female-determining X chromosome (*qv*). The gynosperm is longer lived, slower swimming, and heavier than the androsperm (*qv*) and has an oval-shaped head. Gynosperm are differentially inhibited by the alkaline cervical and uterine environments, characteristics that may be utilized to alter the sex ratio (*qv*) at conception (*qv*).

-gynous A combining form meaning "pertaining to female characteristics."

H

habitual abortion The spontaneous termination of three successive pregnancies (*qv*) before the twentieth week of gestation (*qv*). Habitual abortion may be due to a chronic infection, maternal hormonal dysfunction, or uterine abnormalities.

half-sibling One of two or more children who share one parent in common; half-brother, half-sister.

Hall, G. Stanley (1884–1924) An American psychologist and specialist in human development and sexual behavior. His two volume *Adolescence: Its Psychology and Its Relations to Physiology, Anthropology, Sociology, Sex, Crime, Religion and Education* (1905, reprinted in 1981) is still a standard reference.

hamartophobia *See* sin phobia.

Hamm, Stephen An early embryologist (*qv*), one of the first to observe human spermatozoa (*qv*) in 1677, although he did not understand their role in fertilization (*qv*).

haploid A cell or animal, usually a gamete (*qv*) produced by meiosis (*qv*), with only one set of nonhomologous chromosomes (*qv*) instead of the usual diploid (*qv*) chromosome complement found in somatic cells. In humans, the diploid number is 44 autosomes (*qv*) plus XX or XY chromosomes. The haploid chromosome number in the human ovum (*qv*) is 22 autosomes plus one X chromosome; the sperm has 22 autosomes plus either one X or a Y chromosome.

haptephobia A morbid fear of being touched, in some cases due to a repressed fear of the possibility of sexual activity (*qv*).

haptic Having to do with touch or the sense of touch.

hard chancre The primary lesion in syphilitic (*qv*) infections. The chancre appears first as a silvery pimple on the glans (*qv*) of the penis (*qv*), under the foreskin (*qv*), on the penile shaft (*qv*), scrotum (*qv*), mucous tissues of the mouth area, the vaginal wall (*qv*), vulva (*qv*), anus (*qv*), or rectum (*qv*). The pimple erodes into an ulcerated crater with a raised rim, filled with *Treponema pallidum* (*qv*). The chancre is painless and will regress as the bacteria spread and the infection enters the second stage of syphilis (*qv*).

harem A secluded part of a Muslim's house where all the women of the household live. Because of the Islamic recognition of the power of female sexuality and the consequent belief that men must be protected by female isolation or purdah (*qv*), Moslem households often have a special quarters for the wife, mother, female relatives of the householders, concubines (*qv*), and female servants, if any. The customs of harem and purdah result in a sex-segregated society that allows men to maintain power while isolating women. Variations of the harem occur in Near East, Siamese, Peruvian, and Hindu societies.

In certain non-human mammals, especially social mammals (e.g., deer), females frequently form lifelong, closely bonded groups. In the mating season, these groups attract otherwise solitary males. The term harem has been used for these female groups since characteristically only one adult male is associated with the group of females. In this usage, the term is quite misleading, since the female group predates the male's attachment to it and will continue its existence after he has left. This usage is an example of how a word for a specific human cultural arrangement is projected onto a biological phenomenon which is then erroneously seen as a natural basis for human culture. Mammalogists prefer the term "one-male group" for such multi-female groups at those times when they are associated with a male. *See also* biology; biologism; biological reductionism.

harlequin fetus A newborn infant (*qv*) whose skin is composed of thick, horny scales divided by deep red fissures.

Harlequin romance A best-selling series of romance novels (*qv*). The classic early Harlequin novels dealt with a young, vulnerable heroine in a dead-end job who meets an arrogant, moody, sometimes violent male who is at least 10 years older than she, besides being rich and powerful. The hero's moods alternate between gentle romance and brutal hitting. In the end, the heroine learns that her hero truly loves her and only appeared brutal, insensitive, and aloof because he feared she was a gold-digging adventuress. More recent Harlequin novels have independent heroines in well-paying careers and sensitive heros who believe in the equality of the sexes. The "cold bitch other woman" has been dropped and, in some cases, even the mandatory "happy ever after" ending. *See also* gothic (romance) novel.

Harris v. McRae A 1980 decision of the U.S. Supreme Court upholding the Hyde Amendment (*qv*) and declaring that the federal government and individual states are under no constitutional obligation to pay for abortions (*qv*) of women on welfare even when medically necessary.

Hartigan v. Zbaraz A 1987 four-to-four split vote of the U.S. Supreme Court that invalidated an Illinois law that could have restricted access to abortion (*qv*) for some teenagers.

harvesting of ova *See* ovum lavage.

HCG *See* human chorionic gonadotropin.

HCG radioreceptor assay A laboratory test for pregnancy (*qv*) based on detection of human chorionic gonadotropin (*qv*) in the urine (*qv*) of a test patient. *See also* beta subunit HCG radioimmunoassay.

HCS *See* human chorionic somatomammotropin.

HDN Hemolytic disease neonatal. *See also* erythroblastosis fetalis.

head flattening A custom of body adornment in which a child's forehead and skull are flattened and reshaped to slope backward to a point, thereby increasing his or her beauty and sexual attractiveness (*qv*). From early childhood on, the forehead and back of the skull are bound between two boards, reshaping the orientation of the cranial bones while the cartilagenous sutures are still flexible. This custom was practiced by native Americans in the Northwest and in parts of France as late as the early twentieth century.

heat A period of sexual receptivity (*qv*) in some mammals. *See also* estrus; rut.

hedonic behavior (society) A behavioral and interactive social pattern observed among primates in which social cohesion is achieved by attention drawn to a spatially central, focal individual and by reassuring, bonding touches, and strokes. *See also* agonic.

hedonism The philosophical belief that pleasure is the principal good and should be the aim of all action. Hedonism is commonly traced to the Greek philosopher Epicurus (341–270 B.C.E.) who held that the human goal should be a life of pleasure (hedone), regulated by morality, temperance, serenity, and cultural development. The Epicurean philosophy did not endorse gross indulgence in sensual pleasures but rather the difficult mastery of the lower senses by the higher ones and the cultivation of the higher arts. Like Stoicism and the Aristotelian "Golden Mean," Epicureanism or hedonism emphasized self-denial, not self-indulgence, in an austere and existentialist ethics.

Hedonism was popularized in the eighteenth and nineteenth centuries by British utilitarian philosophers. Jeremy Bentham argued that "right" and "wrong" have been distorted by Christian and other erroneous views of human nature, his view being that humans naturally seek pleasure and avoid pain while Christian philosophies believe that suffering is a passport to eternal bliss and that sensual pleasures are actually immoral. John Stuart Mill added to the pursuit of pleasure a concern for producing the greatest amount of good in human actions. Both Epicureanism and utilitarianism have been repeatedly and falsely pictured as philosophies advocating swinish self-indulgence of sensual appetites in the pursuit of materialistic pleasure. In Western cultures, the popular and uncritical association of hedonism and pleasure with immoral self-indulgence is at the opposite pole of the true hedonistic philosophy.

hedonophobia A morbid fear of experiencing sensual pleasure, especially from sexual arousal (*qv*). *See also* hedonism.

Hegar's sign A softening of the isthmus of the uterine cervix (*qv*) early in pregnancy (*qv*); a probable indication of pregnancy.

helper lymphocyte (or T cell) *See* lymphocyte.

he-man An especially masculine male. *See also* machismo.

hematocolpos (hematometra, hematosalpinx) (L.) An abnormal condition in which menstrual products (*qv*) are retained because of an imperforate hymen (*qv*). Hematocolpos involves the vagina (*qv*) only, hematometra the vagina (*qv*) and uterus (*qv*), and hematosalpinx the vagina, uterus and fallopian tubes (*qv*).

hematrophic metabolism The physiological functions of the placenta (*qv*), or trophoblast, and its blood transport system, which are essential to early embryonic nutrition, hormone synthesis, and placental transfer. Early in pregnancy (*qv*), the placenta synthesizes glycogen, cholesterol, and fatty acids, human chorionic gonadotropin (*qv*), somatomammotropin (*qv*), and progesterone (*qv*).

hemiacephalus (L.) A fetus (*qv*) lacking a brain and most of the cranium. *See also* hemicephalus.

hemicastration A now-rare form of castration (*qv*) in which only one of the two testes (*qv*) is removed; practiced in the belief that it prevents the birth of twins (*qv*), which were considered unlucky.

hemicephalus (L.) A congenital (*qv*) anomaly characterized by absence of the cerebrum. *See also* hemiacephalus.

hemihypertrophy *See* unilateral sexual precocity.

hemikaryon (L.) A haploid (*qv*) cell, such as the ovum (*qv*) or sperm (*qv*).

hemipagus (L.) Conjoined twins (*qv*) united at the thorax.

hemizygote (hemizygous) An individual, organism, or cell that has only one of a pair of alleles (*qv*) for a specific trait. Hemizygous genes (*qv*) are expressed regardless of whether they are recessive or dominant. Classic examples of hemizygotes are the genes on the long arm of the X chromosome (*qv*) of a male since the Y chromosome (*qv*) carries no matching alleles for these genes.

hemocytometer An instrument used to count blood cells or spermatozoa (*qv*) in ascertaining male fertility (*qv*).

hemolytic disease neonatal *See* erythroblastosis fetalis.

Hemophilus vaginalis (L.) A gram-negative bacterium associated with and a possible cause of human vaginitis (*qv*), transmitted by intimate sexual contact with an infected person. A vaginal infection of *Hemophilus vaginalis* is characterized by a profuse creamy white or gray vaginal discharge (*qv*) with a foul odor, although infected women may have no symptoms and men serve as asymptomatic carriers. Infected males are treated with oral antibiotics and females with antibiotic and sulfa vaginal suppositories (*qv*). *Hemophilus vaginalis* has no known complications, and dangers to the fetus (*qv*) of an infected woman are unknown.

hemospermia vera (L.) A benign condition in which blood and seminal fluid (*qv*) are found mixed together in the seminal vesicles (*qv*).

hepatitis A A form of liver infection caused by the hepatitis A virus and characterized by slow onset of symptoms and signs. Hepatitis A is transmitted by direct contact or through contaminated food or water. The infection occurs most often in young adults and is usually followed by complete recovery. *See also* hepatitis B.

hepatitis B A form of liver infection caused by the hepatitis B virus and characterized by rapid onset of acute symptoms and signs. Hepatitis B is transmitted by sexual contact (*qv*), by contaminated blood transfusions, and the use of contaminated needles or instruments. The infection may be severe and result in prolonged illness, destruction of liver cells, cirrhosis, or death. Also known as serum hepatitis. *See also* hepatitis A.

hereditary Pertaining to a condition, characteristic, or disease transmitted from parent to offspring through the genes (*qv*). *See also* heritable; multifactorial.

heritable (n. heritability) In genetics and biology, heritable and heritability are technical terms referring to the degree to which a trait responds to artificial selection (*qv*) or, in a population, the numerical ratio of genetic variance to overall phenotypic (*qv*) variance. Unfortunately, each term reminds the reader of the rules of English word formation, in which both terms would mean "capable of being inherited because the trait is controlled by genetic factors." However, geneticists do not imply this in their usage of these terms. To express the extent to which a given trait is controlled by genetic factors, geneticists would speak of the "coefficient of genetic determination" or use a similar statistically defined concept. Because these terms have such drastically different meanings to the geneticist and the layperson, it is best to avoid them except in clearly defined technical discourse.

herm A sculptured stone column so named because it was often capped by the head of Hermes, the messenger of the Greek gods, with an erect penis (*qv*) at the base of the column. Since the herm marked shrines where the Greeks paid homage to the divinities of reproduction (*qv*) and growth, the pillar usually had a prominent phallus (*qv*) carved on its surface. Herms were paraded during the Dionysian (*qv*) cultic processions in ancient Greece, not as a sign of sexual eroticism (*qv*) but in veneration of the male generative principle and as a symbol of male power. Resource: R. J. Lawrence, *The Poisoning of Eros* (New York: Augustine Moore Press, 1989), pp. 12–13.

hermaphrodism *See* hermaphrodite.

hermaphrodite An individual having the genital (*qv*) characteristics of both sexes. In humans, this birth defect has four general types: (1) a male hermaphrodite or pseudohermaphrodite (*qv*) with testes (*qv*) and female sex organs (*qv*), (2) a female hermaphrodite or pseudohermaphrodite with ovaries (*qv*) and male sex organs, (3) a true hermaphrodite with the gonadal tissue of both sexes in ovotestes (*qv*), and (4) the agonadal (*qv*) hermaphrodite with gonadal dysgenesis (*qv*) or undifferentiated gonads for whom the discordance is between his or her chromosomal sex (*qv*) and the external sexual anatomy and gender identity (*qv*).

Some invertebrates are simultaneous hermaphrodites, with functional reproductive systems of both sexes. Other organisms, including some fish, are sequential hermaphrodites, changing their sex, usually from female to male, when stimulated by an appropriate change in their environment. Etymologically, the term is derived from the names for the Greek god and goddess of love, Hermes and Aphrodite, respectively, or more directly from the name of the son of those deities, Hermaphroditus. *See also* intersexuality.

hermaphroditism *See* hermaphrodite.

hermaphroditism, cryptorchid hypospadia A hermaphroditic (*qv*) condition in which the testes (*qv*) are undescended and the penis (*qv*) has an open urinary sinus or trough instead of an enclosed urethral tube, which gives ambiguous or intersexual external genitalia (*qv*).

herpes Any one of five related viruses, including the *herpes simplex* viruses 1 and 2 (*qv*), responsible for cold sores and genital herpes, the *varicellazoster* or *zoster* virus (*qv*), which causes chicken pox in children and "shingles" in adults, the Epstein-Barr virus (*qv*) responsible for infectious mononucleosis (*qv*) and the cytomegalovirus (*qv*).

Herpes genitalis (L.) An infection caused by type 2 *herpes simplex* virus (HSV2), which is usually limited to the genital and rectal areas, although it can also occur in the oral cavity and throat. Herpes genitalis is one of the most common sexually transmitted diseases (*qv*), infecting over 30 million Americans. The virus can be transmitted by sexual contact with an infected person if contact is made with infectious lesions during kissing (*qv*), oral sex (*qv*), and vaginal (*qv*) or anal sex (*qv*). A fetus (*qv*) can also contract the disease if vaginally delivered (*qv*) when the mother has an outbreak of infectious lesions.

The first sign of an infection is a burning, tingling, or itching sensation in the site of infection within a week or two of contact with an infected person. These sensations also may signal a new outbreak in a previously infected person. The initial sensations are followed several hours later by the appearance of small, red, transient, irritating, and sometimes painful fluid-filled blisters on the genital skin and associated mucous membranes. Other effects may be a mild fever, malaise, urinary dysfunction, and/or enlargement of the lymph nodes in the inguinal (*qv*) region or neck. Within a week after onset of the symptoms, thin yellow crusts form on the vesicles (*qv*) as natural healing begins. In males, the glans (*qv*) and foreskin (*qv*) are more likely to be infected; in females, infections occur on the surface of the cervix (*qv*), vagina (*qv*), or perineum (*qv*). Blisters may also appear on the skin near the genitalia (*qv*). Recent evidence indicates that an infected person may still be infectious even though no symptoms are present. Infectious outbreaks subsequent to the initial outbreak generally have milder symptoms. Infectious outbreaks, occurring four to five times a year, may be activated by hormone changes, sunbathing, food allergies, cold, or fatigue. Experts believe about two-thirds of infected people have no symptoms.

Laboratory tests detect presence of the HSV2 virus. Treatment of uncomplicated HSV2 infection is mainly by cleaning the lesions with mild soap and water followed by a drying medication; loose, nonbinding, cotton underwear is recommended. Acyclovir (*qv*) speeds healing of lesions and possibly reduces the infective period by entering infected cells and halting their ability to reproduce the virus if used in the first few days of an outbreak. Antibiotics and sulfa drugs may be prescribed for secondary bacterial or fungal infections. The dangers to the fetus of an infected woman include miscarriage (*qv*), stillbirth (*qv*), and brain damage in the newborn (*qv*).

herpes gestationis (L.) A *Herpes simplex* (*qv*) infection causing a rash of small blisters and severe itching on the skin and mucous membranes of some women during the latter half of pregnancy (*qv*). The symptoms disappear several weeks after delivery (*qv*) but often reappear with subsequent pregnancies. The infection is associated with an increased risk of miscarriage (*qv*).

herpes labialis (L.) *See Herpes simplex I; Herpes simplex II.*

herpes progenitalis (L.) A *Herpes simplex* (*qv*) infection of the penis (*qv*) or vulva (*qv*).

Herpes simplex encephalitis (L.) A *Herpes simplex I* (*qv*) infection that has spread along the nerve tracts from the nasal passages to the frontal and temporal lobes of the brain. Initial symptoms include headache, runny nose, fever, nausea, and vomiting, followed by a loss of appetite, insomnia, sensitivity to light, dizziness, and disorientation. If left untreated with antiviral medications, the infection progresses to seizures, personality changes, hallucinations, tremors, loss of muscle coordination, paralysis, coma, and death.

Herpes simplex I (HSV-1) The virus responsible for cold sores in the mouth and nasal passages. Also known as oral herpes or Herpes labialis. The incubation period is usually 1 to 2 weeks, although symptoms may appear within 2 days of exposure. The small, fluid-filled pimples or blisters ulcerate within a few days and disappear without leaving a scar. This virus may be transmitted by kissing (*qv*), or through orogenital contact (*qv*).

Herpes simplex II (HSV-2) The virus responsible for *Herpes genitalis* (*qv*). *HSV-2* is very similar to *HSV-I* (*qv*) but can usually be distinguished from it in laboratory tests.

Herpes zoster An infection caused by the varicellazoster virus and resulting in a painful skin eruption known as shingles and chicken pox.

Herpes zoster virus (HVZ) The herpes virus responsible for chicken pox.

herstory A feminist (*qv*) term created to emphasize the androcentric bias of history, the story of men written by men; herstory is the past as seen through the eyes of women, the human story as told by women about women (and possibly men).

he/she A colloquial expression for a male-to-female transsexual (*qv*) who has begun hormonal therapy for female breast (*qv*) development but has not had surgery for removal of the testes (*qv*) and penis (*qv*). A he/she may be a temporary status prior to complete sex reassignment (*qv*) or a long-term life-style.

heterae (Gr.) An educated, sophisticated class of prostitutes (*qv*) in ancient Greece who provided intellectual as well as sexual stimulation for their patrons. *See also* geisha.

hetero- As a prefix, hetero- means "other" or "different"; however, in sexology, as a prefix hetero- carries with it the tacit meaning of "other or different sex." *See also* homo-.

heteroeroticism (heteroerotism) A general and psychoanalytic term for the focusing of libido (*qv*) on persons or objects outside the self. *See also* autoeroticism.

heterogamy (adj. heterogametic, heterogamous) Producing two kinds of gametes (*qv*), as the heterogametic human male produces two types of sperm (*qv*)—one type carrying the X chromosome (*qv*) and the other a Y chromosome (*qv*)—while the female is homogametic (*qv*). In birds and some other species, the female is the heterogametic sex.

heterogenesis The alternation of sexual (*qv*) and asexual (*qv*) reproduction (*qv*) in different generations, the asexual stage usually involving parthenogenic (*qv*) or hermaphroditic (*qv*) reproduction.

heterogenous strain A strain or line of animals that is not inbred for genetic homogeneity but where individuals mate (*qv*) or are bred to promote genetic diversity.

heterologous artificial insemination *See* artificial insemination by donor.

heterologous twins *See* dizygotic twins.

heteronomous stage A pattern of moral decision making in which constraints by an outside authority provide the basis for judgments and behavior; the middle stage in the moral development model proposed by Jean Piaget (*qv*), preceded by the egocentric stage (*qv*) and followed by the autonomous stage (*qv*). *See also* conventional morality.

heterophilia An orientation in which limerence (*qv*) or love (*qv*), lust (*qv*), and sexual bonding are directed to those of the other sex. *Synonyms*: heteroerotic, heterosexual. *See also* homoerotic; homosexual.

heterophobia A fear of heterosexuals (*qv*) whose limerence (*qv*) or love (*qv*), lust (*qv*), and sexual bonding are directed to persons of the opposite sex. *See also* homophobia.

heteroploid An individual, organism, or cell that has a variation in the normal somatic chromosome (*qv*) number—either a single chromosome or an entire set of chromosome added or missing. Common examples of heteroploid individuals are individuals with Klinefelter syndrome (47,XXY) (*qv*), Turner syndrome (45,XO) (*qv*), and Down syndrome (47,21 +).

heterosexism Heterosexism is a value system that claims heterosexuality (*qv*) is the norm for all social and sexual relationships and imposes this model on all individuals through homophobia (*qv*). Heterosexism continues the institutionalization of heterosexuality in all aspects of society, including legal and social discrimination against homosexuals (*qv*) and the denial of homosexual rights as a political concern.

The term heterosexism was developed by British homosexual activists to indicate the sexual orientation biases in advertisements that show men paired with women but not men paired with men or women paired with women. In 1985, the Greater London Council was presented with guidelines that encourage advertisements with same-sex pairing as well as heterosexual couples.

heterosexual (n. heterosexuality) In the strict sense, a heterosexual person is characterized by the ability to fall in love, have limerence (*qv*) with, and pair-bond in a sexuoerotic (*qv*) way only with a person of the other morphologic sex. *See also* homosexual; bisexual; heterosexism; heterosexualism. Alfred Kinsey (*qv*) cautioned that

It would encourage clearer thinking on these matters if persons were not characterized as heterosexual or homosexual, but as individuals who have had certain amounts of heterosexual experience and certain amounts of homosexual experience. Instead of using these terms as substantives which stand for persons, or even as adjectives to describe persons, they may be better used to describe the nature of overt sexual relations, or of stimuli to which an individual erotically responds.

A. Kinsey, W. Pomeroy, and C. Martin, *Sexual Behavior in the Human Male* (Philadelphia: W. B. Saunders, 1948), p. 617.

heterosexual anxiety (panic) The fears associated with the potential for intimate relationships with members of the opposite sex. Such anxieties are a common part of the insecurities of adolescence (*qv*) and usually lessen as one gains experience in socializing with the opposite sex in various settings. The fears may be complicated or exaggerated by sex-negative (*qv*) conditioning and repressive religious views of sexuality (*qv*), by concern over one's sexual attractiveness, and fear of being inadequate sexually.

Heterosexual-Homosexual Behavior Rating *See* Kinsey Six Scale.

heterosexualism Contact with a person of the other gender, either as a genital act (*qv*) or as a long-term gender orientation (*qv*). The term, proposed by John Money, is used much as right-handedness to indicate a condition that conforms to a statistical or ideological norm (*qv*) and is not in itself pathological, although it is subject to other pathology. Heterosexualism refers to a person's ability to fall in love (*qv*) with and pair-bond (*qv*) with a sexuoerotic (*qv*) partner of the other sex. Resource: J. Money, *Lovemaps* (New York: Irvington Publishers, 1986), p. 286.

heterosexual precocity A form of premature puberty (*qv*) in which the secondary sexual characteristics (*qv*) of the opposite sex develop instead of those of one's own sex.

heterosociality The tendency to socialize and to establish strong friendships with members of the opposite sex without necessarily expressing a sexual interest in them.

heterospecific mating A crossbreeding (*qv*) between different species or types (e.g., mating a tiger with a lion to produce a liger or tigron).

heterotypic hormones Hormones (*qv*) typical of one sex that are given for therapeutic or experimental purposes to the other sex.

heterozygosis The formation of a zygote (*qv*) by the union of two gametes (*qv*) with dissimilar genes (*qv*). *See also* hybrid.

heterozygous (heterozygote) Having two different alleles (*qv*) of a gene (*qv*) at the same locus (*qv*) on homologous chromosomes (*qv*). In a heterozygous individual, one of the alleles may be dominant and the other recessive and unexpressed, or the two alleles may be codominant (*qv*). In a trait controlled by a single gene, a homozygous (*qv*) individual will exhibit the characteristic of the two identical alleles, except in the rare case of being inhibited by another gene.

hexenmilch *See* witch's milk.

hexoestrol A synthetic estrogen (*qv*) used in the radioactively labeled form as a tracer or indicator in investigative studies of estrogen uptake by various cells and tissues of the body.

hierarchy of needs *See* motivational hierarchy.

hieroduli (Gr.) Male prostitutes (*qv*), often transvestite (*qv*) priests, associated with temple worship in Greece and other ancient Near Eastern cultures.

high sex ratio A society in which males outnumber females, particularly in the 20-30 year-old age group. Orthodox Jews have a high sex ratio because regulations limiting marital intercourse (*qv*) to the few days around the time of ovulation (*qv*) increase the odds of fertilization (*qv*) by androsperm (*qv*). In Russia between 1860 and 1880, census figures indicate that Jewish men outnumbered Jewish women by 146 to 100. In actuality, the ratio was likely higher because the birth of males was underreported to avoid the czar's taxes and conscription for his army. Since Orthodox Jews oppose marriage (*qv*) with outsiders, the shortage of suitable brides is a problem. In limiting couples to only one child, China's current population control program is producing a high sex ratio. Since a male child is much preferred, a first-born girl is often discretely abandoned or suffocated. The couple can then try again for a boy. Differential migration of females from rural areas to domestic service in large cities often leaves rural areas with a high sex ratio. *See also* low sex ratio; Marital Opportunity Ratio; marriage squeeze. Resource: M. Guttentag and P. Secord, *Too Many Women? The Sex Ratio Question* (Beverly Hills: Sage, 1983).

hijra In India, the term for a full-time female impersonator (*qv*), a gynemimetic (*qv*). In some cases, the hijra is a eunuch (*qv*) with partial surgical sex reassignment (*qv*). The hijra are a traditional Hindu social organization, part cult and part caste, that worships the goddess Bacuchara Mata. They play the sexuoerotic (*qv*) role of a woman in relations with men.

hilar cells Ovarian cells responsible for the production of androgenic hormones (*qv*). Estrogenic (*qv*) hormones and progesterone (*qv*) produced primarily by the granulosa cells (*qv*) and theca cells surrounding the Graafian follicles (*qv*) offset the androgens from the hilar cells to give females a predominance of feminizing hormones.

Hindu genital classification A traditional Hindu classification of the lingam (*qv*), or penis (*qv*), and yoni (*qv*), or vagina (*qv*), based on size and compatibility. In the classic *Kama Sutra* (*qv*) and *Ananga Ranga* (*qv*), fully erect lingams are classified as "hare" for those up to 5 inches long, "bull" between 5 and 7 inches, and "horse" larger than 7 inches. The "deer" yoni is up to 5 inches deep, the "mare" yoni between 5 and 7 inches deep, and the "elephant" over 7 inches deep. A variety of compensating coital positions are recommended for couples with nonmatching genitalia (*qv*). *See also* Rite of the Five Essentials.

Hindu coital positions The complete range of positions humans can assume in engaging in sexual intercourse (*qv*) as described and illustrated in the classic Hindu love manuals (*qv*), the *Kama Sutra* (*qv*) and the *Ananga Ranga* (*qv*). Each position is described in detail and illustrated in these manuals. Each position bears a poetic name or a reference to an animal or something in nature, such as the "fluttering, soaring butterfly position" for the female-above position, "playing the flute" for fellatio (*qv*), "conjunction of sun and moon," and "position of the monkey."

Hindu love ritual *See* Rite of the Five Essentials.

Hirschfeld, Magnus (1868–1935) A German physician who pioneered sexuality research, particularly on the psychological and social problems of homosexuals (*qv*) and advocated repeal of antihomosexual laws. In 1897, Hirschfeld founded the Wissenschaftlich-Humanitares Komitee to promote the scientific study of sexuality (*qv*). As editor of the journal *Yearbook for Sexual Intermediate Stages*, Hirschfeld published articles by such experts as Sigmund Freud (*qv*), Iwan Bloch (*qv*), and Havelock Ellis (*qv*). By the turn of the century, the committee had grown into the Institute for Sex Science with laboratories, a research library, and massive collections of sexual materials. His major writings, *Sexual Pathology* (New York: Julian Press, 1932) and *Sex Anomalies and Perversions* (London: F. Aldor, 1944), drew a distinction between transvestism (*qv*) and homosexuality. Among his many contributions to sexology (*qv*) was a survey on sexual behavior obtained from interviews from 10,000 persons using a 130-item questionnaire. In 1921, Hirschfeld founded the International Congress for Sexual Reform, which developed into the World League for Sexual Reform with support from Bertrand Russell, Judge Ben Lindsey, Freud, and others. The institute was destroyed by the Nazis in 1933, launching a persecution that sent homosexuals and other "deviants" to the concentration camps. Hirschfeld died in exile in France, but his work bore fruit in the late 1960s when German homosexuals were finally accorded full sexual and civil rights.

hirsuitoid papilloma of the penis Small, white, raised lesions occurring around the corona of the glans (*qv*) of the penis (*qv*), and occasionally accompanied by hair growth on the lesions.

hirsutism Hairiness, especially excessive body hairiness, in a masculine distribution due to heredity, a hormonal dysfunction, or medication.

histocompatibility The quality of a cellular or tissue graft that allows its acceptance and functioning when transplanted to another organism. When the histocompatible genes (*qv*) of the donor and host do not match, the host's immune system is activated, and the grafted tissue or organ is rejected. In the case of the H-Y antigen (*qv*), histocompatibility means that the histocompatibility antigen associated with the Y chromosome (*qv*) is expressed only in male cells, and thus male cells may be recognized as foreign by the female immune system if transplanted to a female.

historical bisexuality A person who has had some sexual experience with or attraction to both sexes at some time in the past.

histrionic personality disorder A psychological disorder characterized by dramatic, reactive, self-centered, and intensely exaggerated behavior with irrational angry outbursts, tantrums, manipulating threats, and continuous demands for reassurance because of feelings of helplessness and dependence. *See also* hysterical character disorder.

Hite Report on Female Sexuality (1976), Hite Report on Male Sexuality (1981) The first book details the responses of 3,000 women who responded to 100,000 questionnaires distributed by Shere Hite to readers of women's magazines and members of women's groups, churches, and women's centers. Respondents ranged in age from 14 to 78 and came from many life-styles, although only 35 percent were currently married. The second book summarizes the views of 7,200 men, ages 13 to 97, who responded to Hite's questionnaires, which were distributed mainly through women's groups and organizations and magazine readerships.

Both studies rely heavily on self-reported behavior and attitudes quoted extensively in brief anecdotal form. Hite's viewpoint is strongly feminist (*qv*). In both books, the majority of pages are devoted to the informative, candid, and sometimes anguished comments of the respondents.

HIV-I The causative agent for acquired immune deficiency syndrome (*qv*). *See also* human immunodeficiency virus-I.

HIV-II *See* human immunodeficiency virus-II.

HLA *See* human leukocytic antigen.

H. L. v. Matheson In this 1981, six-to-three decision, the U.S. Supreme Court upheld a Utah law requiring doctors to try to inform the parents of immature minors seeking an abortion (*qv*) before performing the requested procedure.

Hodgson v. Minnesota A Minnesota law that requires unmarried persons under 18 and still living with a parent to provide written notice to both parents, if possible, before obtaining an abortion (*qv*). The law also imposes a 48-hour waiting period and criminal penalties for doctors who perform abortions in violation of the law. This law was accepted for a hearing before the U.S. Supreme Court following its 1989 ruling on *Webster v. Reproductive Health Services (qv).*

holandric inheritance (trait) *See* Y-linked trait.

hologynic inheritance (trait) The acquisition or expression of traits or inherited conditions exclusively through the maternal line, transmitted by genes (*qv*) located on attached X chromosomes (*qv*). This type of inheritance does not occur in humans. However, the term is sometimes applied to inherited traits associated with the maternal line, as the tendency for multiple ovulation (*qv*) and dizygotic twin (*qv*) births.

home pregnancy test A variety of over-the-counter test kits for pregnancy (*qv*), based on detection of human chorionic gonadotropin (*qv*) in the urine (*qv*) that can be used without training.

homicidophilia *See* lust murder; erotophonophilia.

hominid That taxonomic family within the primate order of which humans are the only contemporary representatives.

homo- As a prefix, homo- means "the same." Strictly speaking, then, a term like homophobia (*qv*) should mean "fear of sameness," but it does not. Instead, in sexology, homo- carries with it the tacit meaning of "same sex," just as hetero- carries with it the tacit meaning of "other sex." This specialization of meaning may offend purists but it is a fact of usage, both in technical and lay speech and writing. As a result, homophobia means a "fear of homosexuality or homosexuals (*qv*)," and not a "fear of sameness." *See also* hetero-.

homochronous inheritance The phenotypic (*qv*) expression or clinical onset of a genetic trait occurring in an offspring at the same age it appeared in the parent or in its monozygotic twin (*qv*).

homoerotic Sexual activity (*qv*) engaged in by two persons of the same sex, motivated by the need for sexual release, power, or control, rather than by pair-bonding (*qv*) or limerence (*qv*); often used as a synonym for homosexual (*qv*). As distinct from homosexual activity, homoerotic activity may be a temporary, functional adaptation to an environment in which heterosexual (*qv*) relations are not possible, such as prison or unisex summer camp, or while on isolated service in the armed forces. *See also* facultative homosexuality; homosexuality; bisexual; heterosexual.

homoerotophobia *See* homophobia.

homogamy Inbreeding (*qv*) among the members of a geographic or cultural isolate that may increase the risk and incidence of phenotypic expression of all recessive traits.

homogenic An obsolete term for homosexual (*qv*).

homogenitality An obsessive interest in the genitalia (*qv*) of one's own sex; homosexual (*qv*) relations.

homologous (homolog) In developmental terms, structures or organs with the same embryonic origins although their function may differ as, for instance, the penis (*qv*) and clitoris (*qv*), or the female labia (*qv*) and the male scrotum (*qv*); two chromosomes (*qv*) similar in size and structure and carrying the same genes (*qv*) at corresponding loci.

homologous artificial insemination *See* artificial insemination husband.

homophile *See* homosexual.

homophilia The condition or orientation in which love (*qv*), lust (*qv*), limerence (*qv*), and sexual bonding are directed to persons of the same sex. *See also* homoerotic; homosexual; homophobia; heteroerotic; heterosexual; heterophilia; heterophobia.

homophobia An intense dislike and fear of homosexual (*qv*) persons, often expressed as an obsessive hostility for those whose love (*qv*), lust (*qv*), and sexual bonding are directed to persons of the same sex. The fear of feelings of love and sexual attraction for members of one's own sex can lead to hatred of those feelings in others. *See also* heterophobia; homoerotic; homophilia; hetero-erotic; heterosexual; heterophilia; heterophobia.

homoseductive mother The theory that an overly protective mother who is also overly close to her son and the dominant figure in the family causes homosexuality (*qv*) in the son. In the 1960s, Irving Bieber, a psychiatrist, originated the idea of the homoseductive mother, suggesting that a male teenager turns to homosexual relations out of fear of heterosexual (*qv*) relations. This fear results from the mother's seductiveness and her jealous possessiveness, which places her son in the position of the father-lover, triggering Oedipal anxieties (*qv*). Bieber later traced the origins of homosexuality to a detached or openly hostile father. Hating and fearing such a father, the son also yearns for his father's love and seeks this in homosexual relations. Resource: I. Bieber et al., *Homosexuality* (New York: Vintage Books, 1962).

homosexual (homosexuality) Few terms in sexuality are as difficult to define as these two words. Very broadly, each refers to the occurrence or existence of sexual attraction, interest, and genitally intimate activity between an individual and other members of the same gender. Beyond that broad definition, the difficulties begin.

One problem is that *homosexual* can be an adjective or a noun. As an adjective in the sentence, ''Mutual penile masturbation by two men is a homosexual act,'' the word homosexual indicates the basic concept of sexual activity between people of the same sex. However, it leaves unclear what acts are and are not to be called homosexual. If a man kisses another man when greeting him in a gay (*qv*) bar, is that a ''homosexual kiss''? The usage here varies immensely, and many would answer depending on whether the men self-identified themselves as gay (*qv*).

Use of the word homosexual as a noun refers to a person who engages in a certain act or experiences a certain emotional state of sexual attraction (*qv*) or limerence (*qv*) with a person of the same gender (*qv*). Few concepts are as difficult to define, or to defend once defined, as the assertion that someone is a homosexual. If, at age 15, a woman engaged in erotic caresses with another woman, is she a homosexual? A question such as this poses three crucial problems in defining homosexuality and, by extension, heterosexuality as well. (1) Labelling someone a homosexual in his or her entirety because of a possibly small portion of their overall life and existence is using a part to define the whole. (2) Homosexuality is an arbitrary term that is not subject to defensible definition: How many homosexual acts make a person a homosexual? (3) It also represents a dangerous philosophical essentialism to speak of a person as being a homosexual or a heterosexual (*qv*) because in so doing we impute to that person's essential nature a certain quality or characteristic when it is still questionable what human nature really is.

Partly in response to these equivocations, ambiguities, and ambivalences, many writers and speakers prefer to use ''gay'' and ''lesbian'' (*qv*) instead of ''homosexual.'' These terms, of course, refer today to life-styles and to self-declared community/sexual/political commitments, matters far transcending genital (*qv*) activities or definitions based on genital activities. However, they do not solve all the definitional problems because each term merely replaces one word, homosexual, with another, gay or lesbian, without resolving the part-for-whole or frequency-of-activity problems just mentioned.

An additional complexity arises because terms like homosexual, gay, and lesbian can be used either by speaker A to describe speaker B (attributive labelling) or by speaker A to refer to him- or herself (self-identifying labelling). One can reasonably argue that if speaker A calls herself a lesbian, she accepts whatever part-for-whole, frequency, and essential connotations she feels the word carries, or, at the very least, is willing to debate with another person. However, when person B calls speaker A a lesbian, it is entirely unclear whether person A will accept being so labelled by someone else, particularly when many speakers intend insulting or thoughtlessly careless meanings in using words like homosexual, gay, and lesbian. Accordingly, an individual can self-identify using one of these terms and still stoutly reject being so labelled by another person.

Before the mid-nineteenth century, the term homosexual did not exist. It was coined in 1869 by a Hungarian physician, Karoly Maria Benkert, writing under the pseudonym Kertbeny. Kertbeny's intention was to create a value-neutral expression to replace value-laden words like pederasty (*qv*), sodomy (*qv*), buggery (*qv*), catamite, and ganymede. Similar intentions underlay the use of ''urning'' by Ulrichs in 1862 and ''inversion,'' which was popularized by Havelock Ellis in the early twentieth century although used earlier. These labels had the advantage of openly disavowing the pejorative meanings of terms like sodomite, but they did not eliminate the other problems mentioned above.

In today's usage, the terms homosexual and homosexuality retain a somewhat formal quality, and are perhaps more encountered in technical writing and formal discourse than in casual speech. In technical discourse, the part-for-whole labeling problem is avoided by the attempt to use *homosexual* only as an adjective and not as a noun. Thus, the phrase ''homosexual act'' is legitimate, but not the phrase, ''She is a homosexual.'' The frequency-of-activity problem is theoretically soluble in technical discussions by using the Kinsey Six (0–6) scale (*qv*) or the more qualified sexual orientation grid (*qv*) devised by Fred Klein. The Kinsey scale is based on the proportion of same- and other-gender sexual activities and fantasies. Klein's orientation grid uses seven factors, including activities and fantasies, with each of the seven factors being rated on the Kinsey 0–6 proportional scale. Klein's grid also uses a 3-point temporal spectrum of ''five years ago,'' ''today,'' and ''ideal,'' so that 21 ratings are generated, totaled, and divided by 21 to obtain a basic 0–6 rating for the individual in question. While avoiding the seductive simplicity of the Kinsey rating and appearing to make the definitions of homosexual, heterosexual, and bisexual (*see* bisexualism) more quantified, qualified, and scientific, Klein's grid actually renders the terms less distinct. Moreover, many sexologists now distinguish between sexual and erotic orientation (the common meaning of homosexual, bisexual, and heterosexual), sexual fantasy orientation, and affectional orientation, and include these three elements in the umbrella term gender orientation (*qv*).

When all is said and done, however, these efforts are stopgaps, and the concepts of homosexual, heterosexual, homosexuality, and heterosexuality remain among the most difficult words in sexology to define with clarity, sensitivity, and rationality. *See also* homosexualism; heterosexualism.

homosexual anxiety (panic) Sudden, acute anxiety precipitated by fear of a sexual approach or assault (*qv*) by a person of the same sex; fear of being considered a homosexual (*qv*) by peers or associates; an unconscious fear that one is in fact homosexually oriented; fear of not being able to function in a homosexual relation; or the depression and anxiety associated with a long-term homosexual partner. *See also* heterosexual anxiety.

homosexualism Contact with a person of the same gender (*qv*), either as a genital act or as a long-term gender orientation (*qv*). The terms, proposed by John Money, is used much as left-handedness is to indicate a condition that, although it does not conform to a statistical or ideological norm (*qv*), is not in itself pathological or exempt from other pathology. Homosexualism refers to a person's ability to fall in love (*qv*) with and pair-bond (*qv*) with a sexuoerotic (*qv*) partner of the same sex. Resource: J. Money, *Lovemaps* (New York: Irvington Publishers, 1986), p. 286. *See also* homosexual; bisexual; gender-identity/role; heterosexualism, heterosexual.

homosexuality, facultative A technical term for sexual orientation (*qv*) and sexual activity (*qv*) with persons of the same sex that does not exclude sexual relations with the opposite sex; the opposite of obligate or exclusive homosexuality (*qv*). In effect, such persons may be considered bisexual (*qv*), although the same-sex activity may be engaged in only for sexual release, power, or control and without the occurrence of limerent bonding or pairing, as in prisons. *See also* bisexuality; homoerotic.

homosexuality, obligative (obligate) A condition in which a person can only bond or pair with limerence (*qv*) with a person of the same sex. Exclusive or obligative homosexuality leaves no option for bisexual (*qv*) or heterosexual (*qv*) bondings. *See also* homosexual.

homosexual marriage In most usages, an informal but emotionally binding commitment between two gay (*qv*) men or two lesbian (*qv*) women in which they publicly avow their mutual love, respect, commitment, and desire to become a couple with a life together. Such marriages currently have no legal status in the United States, although the Netherlands has granted full legal status to homosexual marriages and some local jurisdictions in the United States have accorded some recognition to "domestic partners." Also known as a gay union.

homosexual rape Sexual assault (*qv*) or sexual activity (*qv*) forced on a person of the same sex as the perpetrator. *See also* facultative homosexuality.

homosexology Sexological science as applied to homosexuality (*qv*) and its relationship to heterosexuality (*qv*) and bisexuality (*qv*).

homosociality Narrowly used, the term refers to the tendency of certain persons to socialize primarily with persons of their own gender (*qv*). Homosocial groups can involve two or many people. They can involve occasional, sporadic groupings or constitute a major portion of an individual's life. Homosocial groups often form first in childhood and adolescence, with a tendency to homosociality persisting in most, though not all, adults. In some cultures, men and women live most of their lives in gender-segregated groups, interacting only during ritual occasions or sexual encounters. In other societies, homosociality is rare, with boys and girls, men and women, interacting continuously throughout most of their lives.

homozygous (homozygote) Having identical alleles (*qv*) of a gene (*qv*) at the same locus (*qv*) on the homologous chromosomes (*qv*). In a trait controlled by a single gene, a homozygous individual will exhibit the characteristic of the identical alleles.

homunculus (L.) In embryology (*qv*), the preformation theory (*qv*) held that a "miniature human," a homunculus, was preformed in either the ovum (*qv*) or sperm (*qv*). The theory of preformation (*qv*) proposed by philosophers like Leibnitz (1646–1716) and Charles Bonnet (1720–1793) and by embryologists like Malpighi (1628–1694) and Spallanzani (1729–1799) as a remedy against the "insolent presumption" of early evolutionary theory. In this theory, evolutionary change was explained by the existence of preformed homunculi in every sperm or ovum. Advocates of an ovist version of the preformation theory claimed they could see a well-developed, though minute human being, the homunculus, curled up into the Graafian follicle (*qv*), which was mistaken for the ovum. Other advocates of preformation, Leuvenhoek, Hamm, and Hartsoeker, claimed the homunculus was contained in the newly discovered sperm. The preformation theory was experimentally refuted by Caspar Wolff (*qv*) in 1759.

honeymoon cystitis *See* cystitis.

hormonal cyclicity Regular, recurrent changes in the blood levels of one or more hormones, for example, the synchronized, cyclic monthly release of pituitary gonadotropins (*qv*) and ovarian estrogen (*qv*) and progesterone (*qv*) in the menstrual cycle (*qv*).

hormonal gender (sex) Sexual status as indicated by a balance of male and female sex hormones (*qv*) in which estrogens (*qv*) and progesterone (*qv*) predominate in a female and androgens (*qv*) in a male. Hormonal sex is responsible for differentiation of the sexual anatomy and neurological encoding of sex-differentiated potentials or tendencies before birth and for control of pubertal development of the body as male or female. An individual's hormonal sex may differ from other sex variables, particularly with one's genetic sex (*qv*).

hormonal therapy The therapeutic administration of exogenous (*qv*) hormones (*qv*) and/or the surgical removal of the endocrine (*qv*) to supplement, reduce, or otherwise alter the balance of hormones (*qv*) to facilitate treatment of a hormone-related condition.

hormone A chemical substance produced and secreted into the blood by an endocrine (*qv*) gland or by specialized glandular cells in the viscera, brain, and neuroendocrine systems. Hormones are vital in regulating most physiological functions of the body. They circulate through the bloodstream to reach and affect specific target organs (*qv*). The production of individual hormones may be regulated by other hormones, by neurotransmitters, or by negative feedback loops (*qv*) in which an excess of target organ product signals a decreased need for the stimulating hormone. *See also* testosterone; androgens; estrogens; follicle-stimulating hormone; luteinizing hormone; lactogenic hormone; progesterone; human chorionic gonadotropin; gonadotropin; pheromone.

Hormonin Trade name for a fixed combination oral contraceptive containing estriol (*qv*), estrone (*qv*), and estradiol (*qv*).

hospitalism The adverse reaction of infants to prolonged hospitalization so that they fail to thrive and do not develop normally. *See also* somatosensory affectional deprivation.

hot flash (flush) A transient, recurrent sensation of warmth experienced by some women during or after menopause (*qv*). Although they result from autonomic vasomotor disturbances associated with changes in the hormonal activities of the ovaries (*qv*), pituitary (*qv*), and hypothalamus (*qv*), the etiology of hot flashes is unknown. Most menopausal women do not experience hot flashes. For those who do, their frequency, intensity, and duration vary widely. Symptoms may be relieved by administration of exogenous estrogen (*qv*).

hot sex values A sexual value system based on patriarchy (*qv*), a genital definition of sex, sexual exclusivity, clear sex roles (*qv*) and stereotypes, exclusive monogamy (*qv*) as the only acceptable adult life-style, a double moral standard (*qv*), emphasis on female premarital virginity (*qv*), sexual performance, and partners or spouses viewed as property. *See also* cool sexual values; closed marriage; open marriage.

Hottentot bustle *See* steatopygia.

HPL *See* human placental lactogen.

HPV The viral cause of genital warts (*qv*). *See also* papillomavirus.

HRAF *See* Human Relations Area Files.

HSI *See* herpes simplex I.

HSII *See* herpes simplex II; herpes genitalis.

HSV1 *See* herpes simplex I.

HSV2 *See* herpes simplex II; herpes genitalis.

Ht-H rating The heterosexual-homosexual ratio or rating. *See also* Kinsey Six Scale.

HTLV-I *See* human T-lymphotrophic virus type I.

HTLV-II *See* human T-lymphotrophic virus type II.

HTLV-III *See* human T-lymphotrophic virus type III.

HTLV-IV *See* human T-lymphotrophic virus type IV.

HTLV-III/LAV A name for the human immunodeficiency virus (*qv*) proposed as a political compromise between French and American researchers and used prior to 1987. *See also* acquired immune deficiency syndrome.

Humanae vitae (L.) "On human life," a 1968 official document or encyclical issued by Pope Paul VI supporting the traditional anticontraceptive position of the Roman Catholic church.

human chorionic gonadotropin (HCG) A hormone (*qv*), produced by the chorionic villi (*qv*) and then by the placenta (*qv*) during pregnancy (*qv*), whose main function with placental progesterone (*qv*) is to maintain the corpus luteum (*qv*) and its secretions of estrogens (*qv*) and progesterones (*qv*). With properties similar to those of luteinizing hormone (*qv*), HCG stimulates formation of interstitial cells (*qv*) and secretion of testosterone (*qv*) in the testes (*qv*) of male fetuses (*qv*). It is found in substantial amounts in the urine (*qv*) of pregnant women, hence its use in pregnancy testing (*qv*). It may also be produced by a choriocarcinoma (*qv*) and a hydatid mole (*qv*), resulting in a false positive (*qv*) on a pregnancy test. It is also produced in a male with testicular cancer.

human chorionic somatomammotropin (HCS) A hormone (*qv*) secreted by the placenta (*qv*) that prepares the mammary glands (*qv*) for milk production. Also known as HPL (human placental lactogen).

human immunodeficiency virus (HIV-I) The current universally accepted name for the virus responsible for the complex of opportunistic infections associated with suppression of the immune system and resulting in the clinical condition known as AIDS, or acquired immune deficiency syndrome (*qv*). HIV-I is a fragile retrovirus containing a short strand of ribonucleic acid (*qv*) enclosed in a glycoprotein envelope. The viral coat lacks sufficient antigenic (*qv*) character to trigger the immune system to protect against it. The virus is transmitted by anal (*qv*) and vaginal intercourse (*qv*) with an infected partner, by intravenous drug use with contaminated needles or syringes, through transfused infected blood or blood products, and from an infected mother to her baby in the womb (*qv*) or during breast-feeding (*qv*). HIV-I preferentially infects T4 or helper lymphocytes (*qv*), some neuroglial cells in the central nervous system (*qv*), macrophages, endothelial cells, some intestinal cells, and the B lymphocytes (*qv*). With a depressed immune system, a person infected with HIV-I is open to a wide range of opportunistic bacterial, protozoan, fungal and viral infections, emaciation, dementia, and development of certain cancers that characterize the disease AIDS. HIV-I was previously known as: AIDS-associated retrovirus (ARV), lymphadenopathy associated virus (LAV), human T-lymphotrophic virus-III (HTLV-III), and HTLV-III/LAV.

human immunodeficiency virus (HIV-II) A fragile retrovirus (*qv*) containing a short strand of ribonucleic acid (*qv*) enclosed in a glycoprotein envelope, HIV-II may be a more virulent form of HTLV-IV (*qv*). HIV-II was isolated by Montagnier of the Pasteur Institute from West African patients with the symptoms of acquired immune deficiency syndrome (*qv*) who nevertheless lacked signs of HIV-I (*qv*) infection.

human leukocytic antigen (HLA) One of five pairs of genetic (*qv*) markers located on chromosome 6, which code for specific cell membrane antigens (*qv*), known as HLA-A, HLA-B, HLA-C, HLA-D, and HLA-DR. Each of the five general types is broken down into more specific subtypes based on modifications of the protein coded for by the gene (*qv*) in question. Each individual inherits a set of five closely linked HLA genes from the father and a second set from the mother. This gives every individual, except monozygotic twins (*qv*), a genetic fingerprint that is unique. HLAs are used to assess tissue compatibility for grafts and transplants, to ascertain an individual's predispositions for certain diseases, and in determining parentage.

human menopausal gonadotropin (HMG) A synthetic preparation of follicle-stimulating hormone (*qv*) and luteinizing hormone (*qv*), used to stimulate ovulation (*qv*) in anovulatory (*qv*) women.

human papillomavirus (HPV) The virus causing genital warts (*qv*). *See also* papillomavirus.

human placental lactogen (HPL) *See* human chorionic somatomammotropin.

Human Relations Area Files (HRAF) The first cross-cultural reference files that brought together in a single data base all available knowledge about a specific behavior, value, or custom in whatever cultures had been studied. HRAF was started in the late 1930s by George Peter Murdock. These files were later expanded into the Ethnographic Atlas and then into the Standard Cross-cultural Sample.

human T-cell leukemia virus (HTLV) An alternate name for the human T-lymphotrophic virus, types I, II, III, and IV (*qv*).

human T-lymphotrophic virus-I (HTLV-I) The human T-lymphotrophic virus type I is the first virus shown to cause cancer in humans, a rare and fatal form of lymphocytic leukemia, and less often a neurological disorder resembling multiple sclerosis. HTLV-I was first isolated in 1978 by Robert C. Gallo at the National Cancer Institute. It is found among black, Hispanic, and white Americans in rural southeastern United States and among intravenous drug users, in the southern islands of Japan, among some Japanese in Hawaii, and in Jewish communities in Ethiopia and is widely spread in the Caribbean. It is spread by blood, body fluids and sexual contact. Although not as virulent as the acquired immune deficiency syndrome (*qv*) virus, HIV-I or HTLV-III, HTLV-I does attack the T lymphocytes (*qv*) in the immune system. However, HTLV-I stimulates uncontrolled multiplication of lymphocytes, producing lymphomas, whereas the HTLV-III virus depletes the T4 lymphocytes. HTLV-I may lie dormant for up to 40 years, and only 1 percent of those infected with it are thought to develop a recognizable disease. Some Japanese virologists believe it was introduced to their country some 12,000 years ago during conquests by Central Asians.

human T-lymphotrophic virus-II (HTLV-II) Similar to human T-lymphotrophic virus-I (*qv*) but genetically distinguishable from it, HTLV-II is a retrovirus (*qv*) that infects lymphocytes (*qv*), leading to uncontrolled multiplication, lymphocytic leukemia, and lymphomas.

human T-lymphotrophic virus-III (HTLV-III) The name proposed by Robert Gallo of the National Cancer Institute in the United States for the human immunodeficiency virus, currently known as the human immunodeficiency virus-I (*qv*), which causes acquired immune deficiency syndrome (*qv*).

human T-lymphotrophic virus-IV (HTLV-IV) A seemingly less virulent, perhaps nonpathogenic retrovirus similar in structure to HIV-I (HTLV-III) (*qv*), which causes acquired immune deficiency syndrome (AIDS) (*qv*). It is believed that HTLV-IV has a slightly different surface coat from that of HTLV-III and therefore has a different immunogenic reaction. HTLV-IV was isolated by Max Essex of the Harvard School of Public Health from AIDS-asymptomatic prostitutes (*qv*) in Senegal in West Africa. The relationship of HTLV-III, HTLV-IV, HIV-II (*qv*), STLV-III (*qv*), and FeLV-I (*qv*) is not clear.

hunger and love The central expression of the Life Urge, which, according to psychiatrist Wilhelm Stekel, suggests that persons of power and position have an advantage in securing for themselves the best food and most attractive sex partners.

Hunterian chancre The classic hard chancre (*qv*), characteristic of primary syphilis (*qv*), identified and described by John Hunter in the 1700s.

husband Legally, a man who is married to a woman. The word is old English and derives from *hus*, cognate with modern *house*, as in "householder," and *bonda*, meaning "property owner" or "freeholder." Etymologically, a husband is therefore a man who owns a house as a freeholder. This early usage changed broadly as modern English evolved, and today two classes of meanings can be broadly distinguished. One is *husbandman*, meaning an agriculturist or farmer, affiliated with the verb *to husband*, meaning "to save, gather, or protect" (e.g., resources or food). The other meaning, of husband as a married man, arises from the custom that landowners and householders were, or should be, married men, as Jane Austen noted in the opening sentence of *Pride and Prejudice* (1815): "It is a truth universally acknowledged, that a single man in possession of a good fortune must be in want of a wife." Accordingly, the word husband is deeply and directly connected to the social history of English-speaking cultures of specific forms of land tenure and freeholding, as well as to marriage (*qv*) and family customs.

The modern term househusband, meaning a man who cares for the house while his wife works, is derived from *housewife* by simple substitution of *husband* for *wife*. Nonetheless, the word househusband linguistically contains a duplication of the first syllable (house/hus-); etymologically both syllables mean the same thing. However, such is the nature of the English language and the inventiveness of its speakers. *See* wife and woman for an even more complex example of social history and linguistic duplications. *See also* adultery; concubine; conjugal duties; mistress.

Hutchinson-Gilford syndrome A hormonal disorder characterized by a combination of infantilism and premature aging. The genitalia (*qv*) of an affected person develop normally until puberty (*qv*) but go no further. The pubic hair (*qv*) fails to develop. Baldness and a potbellied condition are common. The skin becomes elastic and atrophied with prominent veins.

hyaluronidase A proteolytic enzyme secreted by sperm (*qv*) that facilitates fertilization (*qv*) by allowing the sperm to penetrate the protective layer of nurse or follicle cells surrounding the ovum (*qv*).

H-Y antigen An antigenic (*qv*) product of the H-Y gene (*qv*) thought to be located on the Y chromosome (*qv*). This histocompatibility factor is believed to adhere to the surface of all male mammalian cells, making them immunologically incompatible with female cells when transplanted or grafted artificially. In the course of normal embryonic development, it programs the cells of the undifferentiated gonads (*qv*) to develop into testes (*qv*). If the H-Y antigen is absent, the undifferentiated gonads become ovaries (*qv*).

hybrid (hybridization) An offspring produced by genetically different parents with two different forms of a trait or from different strains or species; the result or process of crossbreeding (*qv*) between genetically different parents. Colloquially, anything that has qualities or aspects of several, usually distinct, things or processes; for example, in electronics, a hybrid integrated circuit contains both analog and digital circuitry. The colloquial use illustrates how a sexual/ reproductive term can become a metaphor.

hybristophilia A paraphilic (*qv*) condition in which sexual arousal (*qv*) and orgasm (*qv*) depend on and respond to being with a partner known to have committed a crime, particularly murder, rape (*qv*), or armed robbery. The partner may have served a prison sentence or may be provoked and instigated to commit a crime by the hybristophiliac.

hydatidiform mole *See* hydatid mole.

hydatid mole An abnormal embryonic growth resulting from proliferation of the epithelial covering of the chorionic villi (*qv*) and formation of grapelike cysts in villi that have no blood supply. Hydatid moles are more common in women under 20 years of age and over age 40. Oriental women are also more susceptible. Since the hydatid mole is composed of placental tissue, it produces human chorionic gonadotropin (*qv*), which can result in a false positive (*qv*) pregnancy test (*qv*) result.

hydatid of Morgani *See* appendix testis.

Hyde amendment A 1977 legislative amendment designed to restrict the use of federal funds for abortion (*qv*) to cases in which the mother's life would be in jeopardy if her pregnancy (*qv*) is continued to term. This amendment was first attached to the 1977 annual appropriation bill for the Departments of Labor and Health and Human Services by Congressman Henry J. Hyde (R-Illinois). The legislation is still referred to as the Hyde amendment though it has been sponsored by other congressmen since 1978. The term is also commonly used in a loose sense to refer to any legislation restricting the use of federal or state funds to abortions in which the mother's life is threatened. The Hyde amendment was ruled constitutional by the U.S. Supreme Court in the 1980 case of *Harris v. McRae* (*qv*).

hydramnios An excess of amniotic fluid (*qv*) occurring during a pregnancy (*qv*), often associated with toxemia of pregnancy (*qv*), multiple gestation (*qv*), and diabetes mellitus.

hydradenoma A benign tumor of the sweat glands in the labia majora (*qv*) or surrounding tissues that may perforate the surface and become a small, bleeding ulcer.

hydrocele A painless swelling of the scrotum (*qv*) caused by fluid accumulation in the outermost covering of the testes (*qv*), the tunica vaginalis testes. A hydrocele may be the result of a congenital abnormality, an injury, or an infection. *See also* spermatocele.

hydrophallus (L.) A swollen condition of the penis (*qv*) caused by the accumulation of lymph or other fluids in the corpora cavernosa (*qv*).

hydrops fetalis (L.) A massive, usually fatal edema (*qv*) in the fetus (*qv*) or newborn (*qv*) usually associated with the Rh factor (*qv*) and severe erythroblastosis fetalis (*qv*).

hydrops folliculi (L.) A fluid-swollen ovarian follicle (*qv*) cyst (*qv*) that may be several inches in diameter. *See also* pyosalpinx.

hydrosalpinx A fluid-swollen fallopian tube (*qv*) that, if it ruptures, may cause peritonitis.

hydroxycorticosteroid *See* 17–hydroxycorticosteroid.

H-Y gene *See* H-Y antigen.

hymen A thin membrane partially covering the entrance to the human vagina (*qv*). Types include: an *annular hymen*, with a single large opening; a *septate hymen*, with two semicircular side-by-side openings; a *cribriform hymen*, with multiple small openings; and an *imperforate hymen*, with no opening. *See also* hematocolpos; hematometra; hematosalpinx. Although absent from birth in many women, the presence of an intact hymen has often been considered the hallmark of female virginity (*qv*). Since the hymen can be broken in the normal course of physical activities, such as athletics or exercise, this equation of an intact hymen with virginity has caused many young women much anguish and anxiety. Breaking the hymen of a virgin during vaginal intercourse has historically sometimes been considered a right reserved to a powerful civil or religious leader; *see* defloration; droit du seigneur. Hymen reconstruction with plastic surgery is popular in Japan, India, and Islamic cultures, where the value of female virginity coexists with a shift to modern liberated sexual life-styles for women. *See also* hymenolatry.

hymenolatry A cultural or individual attitude emphasizing the presence of an intact hymen (*qv*) as evidence of female virginity (*qv*) and following a well-defined sexual double standard (*qv*) requiring virginity of the bride.

hymenoplasty Plastic surgery to reconstruct the hymen (*qv*).

hyperadrenocorticism *See* adrenogenital syndrome; Cushing syndrome.

hyperemesis Episodes of severe vomiting occurring during pregnancy (*qv*). Mild forms of this condition are usually psychogenic and found in women who react to stress with intestinal disorders. More severe forms are usually of undetermined etiology. The condition usually requires hospitalization and, in some cases, a therapeutic abortion (*qv*). If left untreated, hemorrhage and miscarriage (*qv*) are likely. *See also* nausea gravidarum.

hyperesthesia A Victorian (*qv*) term for a supposed condition in women of enjoying or wanting sex more than the propriety of the era deemed suitable and proper in a woman of the genteel classes. Clitorectomy (*qv*) was sometimes recommended as a remedy; *see also* nymphomania.

hypergamy In sociology, a term referring to a tendency among some people to select partners or spouses who are perceived to have a higher economic, social, educational, or professional status and rank than themselves; also known as "marrying up." In traditional American marriages (*qv*), women have tended to hypergamy more than men, who therefore are hypogamous (*see* hypogamy). Female hypergamy appears to have two broad origins: One is the desire for a husband who offers wealth, career, or status that the woman herself lacks (or believes she lacks); the other is a male desire for a wife who does not challenge the man's self-perception of his own intelligence, power, or status. She marries a rich man; he marries a woman who is not a threat to him. As a potential strategy for mate choice, hypergamy is possible only to women of the middle class for only they have traditionally been able to meet and court men wealthier than themselves. Very wealthy women cannot marry up because few men exceed them in status. Poor or working-class women have not traditionally had the chance to marry men in socioeconomic classes higher than their own—the rich son seldom marries the chambermaid, although he may have sex with her. With the widespread emergence of relatively class-blind higher educational systems in the United States, hypergamy appears to be dwindling, at least in women, as an ideology of "marriage between equals" gains acceptance among educated Americans. *See also* isogamy.

hypergenitalism A state characterized by excessive development of the sexual organs (*qv*).

hypergenital body type A body type characterized by premature and exaggerated appearance of primary (*qv*) and secondary sexual characteristics (*qv*). In females, this condition is marked by early menarche (*qv*) and an elevated fecundity (*qv*).

hypergonadotropic hypogonadism A failure of the ovaries (*qv*) to respond to gonadotropic hormones (*qv*) resulting in an elevated level of circulating gonadotropins (*qv*) and below-normal levels of estrogens (*qv*). The condition is more common in menopausal (*qv*) women, although it can occur in younger women as the result of an ovarian inflammation or tumor.

hypermania A psychopatholological state characterized by excitability, heightened sexual interest, hyperactivity, irritability, quick anger, and optimism.

hypermenorrhea *See* menorrhagia.

hypermobile testes A condition in which the testes (*qv*) migrate back and forth between the scrotal sac (*qv*) and the lower pelvic cavity through an open inguinal hernia (*qv*) that did not close off after the initial perinatal descent of the testes. Migration is temperature dependent, with the testes migrating to the scrotum when it is warmer than usual, as in a hot bath. The condition can be remedied by surgically closing the passage. This condition is not the same as testicular retraction, which is a normal occurrence.

hypernephroma A nodular yellow tumor on the mucous membrane of the vaginal wall (*qv*), following migration of metastatic (cancer) cells from a primary tumor in the kidneys.

hyperorgasmia The phenomenon of experiencing more orgasms (*qv*) in a given time period than established by a given social or cultural standard.

hyperphilia A syndrome with varied etiology and diagnoses in which sexuoerotic (*qv*) activity or functioning in either the proceptive (*qv*) or acceptive phase (*qv*) is significantly above a social or cultural standard or beyond the level preferred by the individual.

hyperplasia An increase in the number of cells in an organ, and thus usually in the overall size of the organ or structure. *See also* hypertrophy.

hyperprolactinemia An excess of prolactin (*qv*) in the blood resulting from a pituitary (*qv*) gland dysfunction. In men, an excess of prolactin may be associated with certain psychotropic medications and result in decreased libido (*qv*) or erectile dysfunction (*qv*). In women, an excess of prolactin may be associated with abnormal breast (*qv*) development and function and with secondary amenorrhea (*qv*).

hypersexual (n. hypersexuality) Having an unusually high libido (*qv*) according to a social, cultural, or psychiatric standard; this is not a precise term. *See also* satyriasis; nymphomania; hyposexuality.

hyperspadias A congenital birth defect (*qv*) in males in which the urinary opening lies on the upper surface of the penile shaft (*qv*), somewhere between the glans (*qv*) and the base of the penis (*qv*).

hypertrophy Excessive cell growth or enlargement of an organ or structure. *See* also hyperplasia.

hyphenophilia A paraphilic (*qv*) condition in which sexual arousal (*qv*) and orgasm (*qv*) are associated with and dependent on touching, rubbing, or the feel of skin, hair, leather, fur, and fabric, especially if they are worn in proximity to erogenous (*qv*) parts of the body.

hypoactive sexual desire Lack of sexual desire (*qv*) or the loss of interest in sexual activity (*qv*), judged by comparison with a social, cultural, or psychiatric standard. *See also* desire phase dysfunction.

hypogamy In sociology, the tendency among certain people to choose partners or spouses who are perceived to be of lower social, economic, educational, or professional status than themselves; also known as "marrying down." In traditional American marriages, men have tended to hypogamy more than have women because it has been widely believed that a man makes an acceptable marriage even if his bride is less wealthy, less educated, or less socially acceptable than he or his family; *see* hypergamy. However, for very wealthy men and men of old, established, or traditional families, hypogamous marriage (*qv*) may be impossible because family and social pressure may compel them to marry a social peer. Such men may form a long-term liaison with a beloved "other woman" of the "wrong class" while remaining married for purposes of social appearance and form. This option of an affair with a hypogamous partner is also open to wealthy or high-status women; however, such matters are often well-kept secrets although they may be tacitly acknowledged and regulated by social customs; *see* ciscisbeism. Hypogamy is not strictly an option of the American working classes, although female hypergamy may be a possibility, especially if the young woman is educated.

In recent years, as relatively class-blind higher educational systems have developed, and as an ideology of "marriage between equals" has emerged, hypogamy is less obviously a matter of social rank or wealth than it is of age, education, and career. Thus, a hypogamously marrying man may have a wife who is college-educated but who is much younger, does not seek a career, or does not otherwise advance in the outside world as fast as her husband. Such marriages, in which, for example, the wife puts the husband through graduate school and remains a housewife, have been the source of immense tension and anger for many American women. This experience has produced some of the strongest feminist (*qv*) critiques of American sexual and gender relationships, of which Betty Friedan's *The Feminine Mystique* remains the *locus classicus* of this anger and the analyses it has produced.

hypogenital type *See* eunuchoid.

hypogonadism A failure in the development or a reduced functioning of the ovaries (*qv*) or testes (*qv*).

hypoleydigism Reduced secretion of testosterone (*qv*) from the interstitial cells (*qv*) or cells of Leydig (*qv*) in the testes (*qv*), resulting in reduced libido (*qv*) and male secondary sexual characteristics (*qv*).

hypomastia Underdevelopment of the female mammary glands (*qv*) or breasts (*qv*), usually resulting from low levels of estrogenic (*qv*) hormones.

hypomenorrhea An abnormally brief or reduced menstrual flow (*qv*). *See also* amenorrhea; dysmenorrhea.

hypophallus A micropenis (*qv*)

hypophilia An impaired, deficient, or less than normal incidence of sexual or genital responsiveness judged according to a social, cultural, or psychiatric standard. *See also* sexual dysfunction.

hypophysectomy Surgical removal of the pituitary gland (*qv*).

hypophysis The anterior pituitary gland (*qv*).

hypopituitarism A generalized endocrine (*qv*) deficiency produced by partial or total failure of the pituitary gland (*qv*) to secrete its proper hormones (*qv*), including the gonadotropins (*qv*). In males, this condition may be marked by small genitalia (*qv*), reduced libido (*qv*), low blood pressure, and small stature with gynandromorphic (*qv*) features. In females, the condition may be indicated by infertility (*qv*), lack of libido, small breasts, and hirsutism (*qv*). Following pituitary surgery, endocrine failure is usually complete, while unexplained failure may be either partial or complete. Partial failure may involve mainly the pituitary gonadotropins (*qv*), which are needed to stimulate sperm (*qv*) and ovum (*qv*) production along with other hormonal functions of the testes (*qv*) and ovaries (*qv*).

hypoplasia Abnormal smallness of a structure, such as a micropenis (*qv*), which is too small to function in coitus (*qv*). Hypoplasia may result from failure in embryonic growth and differentiation or from subsequent lack of response to growth-promoting factors. *See also* hyperplasia.

hyporchia A degeneration of the testes (*qv*) following their fetal differentiation; testosterone (*qv*) replacement may be necessary at puberty (*qv*) in severe cases. *See also* anorchia.

hyposexuality A partial or complete lack of sexual desire (*qv*), interest, and activity according to a social, cultural, or psychiatric standard. Hyposexuality can be caused by low levels of androgenic (*qv*) hormones, negative conditioning, or sexual anxiety or phobias. *See also* desire phase dysfunction; hypophilia.

hypospadias A congenital birth defect (*qv*) in males in which the urinary opening is on the underside of the penile shaft (*qv*), somewhere between the glans (*qv*) and the perineum (*qv*). Hypospadias near the glans are known as primary or mild hypospadias; openings located closer to the perineal region are severe, penoscrotal, or tertiary hypospadias. Artificial hypospadias may occur as a sequel to accidental injury during circumcision (*qv*) or insertion of foreign objects in the urethra (*qv*) during masturbation (*qv*). A hypospadiac penis may be normal or small in size. In the latter case, when combined with penoscrotal hypospadias, the effect may be a female pseudohermaphrodite (*qv*).

hypothalamic amenorrhea Interruption of the normal menstrual cycle (*qv*) due to interference with the normal production of the gonadotropic releasing factors (*qv*) by the hypothalamus (*qv*). This condition may result from anxiety, from a drop in the body fat level from a normal 18 to 25 percent to around 12 percent in athletic or anorexic women (*qv*), or other organic conditions.

hypothalamus A portion of the diencephalon of the brain, which activates, controls, and integrates the peripheral autonomic nervous system (*qv*), endocrine (*qv*) processes, and many somatic functions such as body temperature, sleep, appetite, and sexual and mating behaviors. The hypothalamus produces gonadotropic releasing factors (*qv*), FSH-RF and LH-R, which trigger follicle-stimulating hormone (*qv*) and luteinizing hormone (*qv*) production by the pituitary (*qv*). Structurally it forms the floor and part of the lateral wall of the third brain ventricle and cerebral hemispheres. Developmentally, the inherently female or bipotential neural templates of the hypothalamus must be defeminized and/or masculinized to produce male physiological patterns. *See also* Adam plan; Eve plan.

hypoxyphilia *See* asphyxiophilia.

hysterectomy Surgical removal of the uterus (*qv*). Hysterectomy is performed to remove fibroid tumors of the uterus, to treat chronic pelvic inflammatory disease (*qv*), severe recurrent endometrial hyperplasia (*qv*), uterine hemorrhage, and precancerous and cancerous conditions of the uterus. The two main types are *total hysterectomy*, with removal of uterus and cervix (*qv*), and *radical* *hysterectomy* in which the ovaries (*qv*), oviducts (*qv*), lymph nodes, lymph channels, uterus, and cervix are removed.

hysteria A neurotic disorder characterized by histrionic (*qv*) behavior and the conversion of unconscious conflicts into physical symptoms. Sexual consequences may include penile or vulvar anesthesia (*qv*). Sigmund Freud (*qv*) interpreted hysteria as a guilt or defense mechanism against masturbation (*qv*). Also known as a conversion disorder. *See also* testeria.

hysterical character disorder In psychoanalytic theory (*qv*), the consequence of an unresolved Electra complex (*qv*) in a woman, leading to a seductive, manipulative, exhibitionistic, and domineering woman who enjoys humiliating and psychologically ''castrating'' men. *See also* histrionic personality disorder; narcissism.

hysterical pregnancy A false pregnancy (*qv*). *See also* pseudocyesis.

hysterorrhea Any discharge from the uterus (*qv*), including the menses (*qv*).

hysterorrhexis Any rupture in the uterus (*qv*).

hysterosalpingo-oophorectomy Surgical removal of the uterus (*qv*), one or both fallopian tubes (*qv*), and one or both ovaries (*qv*).

hysteroscope (hysteroscopy) A tubular instrument with a built-in light and lenses that permits hysteroscopy, direct visual examination of the inner lining of the uterus (*qv*) and cervix (*qv*).

hysterotomy Surgical incision of the uterus (*qv*) to remove a second trimester (*qv*) fetus (*qv*) whose abortion (*qv*) by saline injection (*qv*) was incomplete; loosely, any incision in the uterus.

hystersalpingography The introduction of a dye opaque to X-rays into the uterus (*qv*) and fallopian tubes (*qv*) so that structural defects, adhesions, and blockages can be detected by x-ray examination.

HZV *See* herpes zoster virus.

I

I In the sociological theory of G. H. Mead (*qv*), the spontaneous, impulsive, and innovative dispositions of the individual that have not yet come under the control of society. In Mead's theory, the I is the counterpart phase of the Me (*qv*) in the development of the self (*qv*). Every action of an individual begins with an I and ends with a Me as the individual's initial impulsive behavior comes under the control of society and is evaluated by its internal representation, the Me phase.

IAG *See* idiopathic adolescent gynecomastia.

iatrogenic A condition that generally arises as an unintended and unexpected side effect of a diagnosis or therapeutic treatment; for example, iatrogenic traumas may occur during diagnosis and treatment of adolescent (*qv*) sexual anomalies (*qv*), incest (*qv*) and child molestation (*qv*). An iatrogenic condition or symptom may also be undesirable or desirable.

ICSH *See* interstitial cell stimulating hormone, luteinizing hormone.

icthyosis-hypogonadism An X-linked (*qv*) condition marked by scaly skin and small genitalia (*qv*), and in some cases by mental retardation and loss of the sense of smell.

id (L.) In psychoanalytic theory (*qv*), that part of the psyche, functioning in the unconscious, which is the source of instinctive energy, impulses, and drives, including the libido (*qv*). Rooted in and governed by the pleasure principle (*qv*), the id expresses itself in animalistic, chaotic impulses that demand self-preservation and gratification. The id is in contact only with the body and not with the outside world. Thus, it centers its demands on the body. This brings it into constant conflict with the ego (*qv*), which is governed by the reality principle (*qv*). *See also* id-ego; superego.

ideal lover template A hypothesized, neurophysiological gestalt (*qv*) of an ideal man or woman, a "specific proto-image of a woman who, once seen, and I stress *seen*, will trigger off an immense network of thoughts and emotions that center on love, sex, intimacy—and marriage." Resource: Timothy Perper, *Sex Signals: The Biology of Love* (Philadelphia: ISI Press, 1985), pp. 15–17.

id-ego In psychoanalytic theory (*qv*), the organization of the psyche into the original primitive mind of the infant, the id (*qv*), ruled by the pleasure principle (*qv*), and the ego (*qv*), or reality-oriented aspect of the mind, which develops out of the id.

identical twins Two offspring developing from the same zygote (*qv*). A single sperm (*qv*) fertilizes an ovum (*qv*), which subsequently separates into two embryos (*qv*) to produce two infants with identical hereditary traits. *See also* monozygotic twins.

identification The process of copying and imitating someone's behavior, attitudes, and reactions so as to become like that person; a child's attempt to become like the same-sex parent in order to gain the affection of the opposite-sex parent. Identification may be a normal function of personality development and learning, contributing to the acquisition of new interests and ideas, or an unconscious defense mechanism, competitive in motivation and either positive or negative in outcome. Also applied to the differentiation of one's gender identity/role (*qv*). *See also* complementation.

identity The condition or fact of being aware of oneself as a unique person or self; one's awareness of one's self and what sets one apart from others. Also, two things that are the same in all essential characteristics. *See also* gender identity; gender identity/role.

identity crisis A period of personality disorientation involving an individual's sense of self and role in society. An identity crisis is most common during adolescence (*qv*) and the so-called midlife crisis when a person is more likely to question and become confused about personal worth, abilities, values, goals, choices, and one's place in the world. Erosion of family life, social fluidity, mobility, shifting career expectations, and changing roles, values, and expectations in sexual relationships may contribute to the onset of an identity crisis. The concept was developed by Erik Erikson.

ideogogic (ideogogy) In sex therapy (*qv*), a treatment that involves discussing the abstract and social meanings that one's behavior has for other people who are affected by it. *See also* somesthetic.

idiogamy (idiogamist) A person who is unable to respond fully in a sexual way with anyone other than his or her spouse or someone closely resembling the spouse.

idiographic (idiography) Specific and unique to one's own self and personal autobiography.

idiopathic Any primary disease, condition, or syndrome with no currently known or postulated origin or cause.

idiopathic adolescent gynecomastia The unexplained occurrence of female breast (*qv*) development in an adolescent (*qv*) male. *See also* adolescent gynecomastia.

ileostomy Surgical formation of an opening of the ileum, the distal part of the small intestine, onto the surface of the abdomen so that fecal matter can bypass the normal rectal (*qv*) and anal (*qv*) passage and be collected in an external ileostomy bag. *See also* colostomy.

ilioinguinal nerve A branch of the first lumbar spinal nerve that supplies both sensory and motor fibers to the skin and muscles of the genitalia (*qv*) and nearby inner thigh region.

illegitimate child A child born to an unmarried woman or to a married woman whose husband is not the child's biological father. Colloquially, an illegitimate child may be referred to as a "bastard," "love child," or "natural child." Because of the dramatic increase in the number of children born to single mothers in United States, these derogatory terms are often avoided, and the child is accepted and described in terms of its mother's unmarried or single status. In many cultures, no distinction is made between legitimate and illegitimate. Thus, the English creole of the Virgin Islands speak of a *bush child* born to a woman and her casual acquaintance, an *inside child* born within marriage, an *outside child* whose father is married to a woman other than the child's mother, a *spree child* born to a known woman and unknown father, and a *yard child* fathered by a man other than the mother's husband.

illicit relations A general term referring to (1) sexual acts between partners who are not legally accepted as sexual partners, such as incest (*qv*), adultery (*qv*), pedophilia (*qv*), or fornication (*qv*); or (2) to sexual acts prohibited by either civil or religious law, such as sodomy (*qv*) and oral sex (*qv*). *See also* natural act; unnatural act; natural law.

imagery A vivid representation or mental picture based on actual persons, things, and experiences, on a perceptive image (*qv*), on a fictive (*qv*) image constructed in the mind, or on a combination of both perceptive and fictive imagery in the imagination; a dream or fantasy (*qv*).

imago (L.) In embryology (*qv*), the initial structure or element that develops and differentiates into a more complex organ or structure. *See also* anlage. In analytic psychology, an unconscious, usually idealized mental image of a significant individual in the person's early formative years.

imitation model of pornography research A research hypothesis theorizing that people learn patterns of exploitation and violence from the role models provided by pornography (*qv*). *See also* catharsis model of pornography research.

immediate animation theory A medieval philosophical theory holding that the human soul or animating principle is infused into prime matter at the moment of conception (*qv*) and that therefore the conceptus (*qv*) is fully human from then on. *See also* mediate animation theory. Animation theories were central in the debates over preformation (*qv*) and epigenesis (*qv*) in the 1600s and 1700s. *See also* ensoulment; personhood.

immisio penis (L.) A legal term for penile (*qv*) penetration (*qv*) of the vagina (*qv*) or anus (*qv*). Depending on the legal jurisdiction, the term may indicate simple contact between the penile glans (*qv*) and vulva (*qv*) or anus or actual penetration of the penile glans beyond the vaginal introitus or anal sphincter.

immune system A cellular and biochemical system in the body that protects it against pathogenic organisms. In humans, the immune system incorporates, in part, the humoral immune response of B-lymphocytes to produce antibodies (*qv*) that counter specific antigens (*qv*) and the cell-mediated response that uses T cells (*qv*) to mobilize tissue macrophages in the presence of a specific foreign body. The production of interferons (*qv*) represents a nonspecific response of the immune system.

immunological pregnancy test The basic and most common test to ascertain if a gestation (*qv*) has begun, based on the presence of human chorionic gonadotropin (HCG) (*qv*) in the urine (*qv*) of the female in question. Test urine is exposed to HCG antibodies (*qv*) and then to polymer spheres coated with HCG. If the woman is pregnant, the HCG in her urine will bind with the antibodies, thus neutralizing them. No agglutination occurs when the coated spheres are added. If the woman is not pregnant, the HCG antibodies remain free because the urine contains no HCG. However, the free HCG antibodies will bind with the HCG-coated spheres when these are added to the urine. This secondary clumping indicates the woman is not pregnant. The test is 85 to 98 percent accurate after 6 to 8 weeks of gestation. *See also* beta specific monoclonal enzyme linked immunosorbent assay (Elisa); beta subunit HCG radioimmunoassay test; home pregnancy test.

immunosuppression An abnormal condition of the immune system (*qv*) characterized by a marked inhibition of the body's ability to respond to antigenic (*qv*) stimuli. Immunosuppression may be congenital or disease induced, as with acquired immune deficiency syndrome (*qv*). It may also be induced deliberately to prevent rejection of a transplanted organ by the immune system of the recipient or incidentally as a side effect of chemotherapy. Immunosuppression may affect the B-lymphocytes (*qv*) of the humoral immune response and/or the T-lymphocytes (*qv*) of the cell-mediated immune system.

imperative A behavior or developmental pattern that is predetermined or obligatory for all members of a species. *See also* adventive.

imperforate anus Any of several different congenital (*qv*) malformations in which the newborn lacks an anal (*qv*) opening for the rectum (*qv*). This condition can be corrected by surgery.

imperforate hymen A congenital (*qv*) condition in which the hymen (*qv*) is unusually thick and contains no opening to allow the menstrual flow (*qv*) to exit. Minor surgery can correct this condition. *See also* hematocolpos.

implantation The process of attachment in which the blastocyst (*qv*), or early embryo (*qv*), embeds itself in the endometrium (*qv*) of the uterine wall (*qv*). In humans, this occurs about the sixth day after fertilization. *See also* nidation.

implantation ratio The proportion of XY (*qv*) male to XX (*qv*) female zygotes (*qv*) that embed in the uterine wall (*qv*). Normally the ratio is about 120 male concepti (*qv*) to 100 female. *See also* birth ratio; conception ratio; sex ratio.

impotence An outdated but still common term for the inability of the male to have and maintain an erection (*qv*) sufficient for completion of penile-vaginal intercourse (*qv*). This condition, now called erectile dysfunction (*qv*), may be primary (*qv*) or secondary (*qv*) in its occurrence and either organic (*qv*) or psychogenic (*qv*) in its etiology. *See also* inhibited male sexual arousal.

impregnate, to (impregnation) To inseminate (*qv*) and make pregnant (*qv*); the process of producing a pregnancy by introduction of the semen (*qv*) during penile-vaginal intercourse (*qv*) or artificial insemination (*qv*). *See also* intromission.

imprinting In ethology, imprinting refers to certain kinds of stage-specific interactions between animals, often an adult and its offspring, that have permanent effects of the offspring's behavior. This definition can cause much confusion because its important ethological distinctions are not readily apparent, and because imprinting is not a synonym for general learning or parental influence.

The most widely known example of imprinting illustrates some of these distinctions. In many birds, for example, geese, the newly hatched gosling will follow the first moving object it sees, normally its mother. In Konrad Lorenz's well-known study of this phenomenon, he was able to show that following behavior is elicited not specifically by the mother goose but by any object that moves (including Lorenz himself). Once the gosling has seen this object, it will follow it only, and will ignore all other moving objects. Ethologists say that the goslings are "imprinted on" the moving object.

In this type of imprinting, the offspring's behavior is not *itself* imprinted but rather arises from internal neurological and physiological sources within the chick. Instead, the *object* to which the behavior pattern is attached is imprinted. In a computer programming analogy, the behavior pattern is already programmed into the memory, but the identity of the object that elicits the behavior is input from outside. It is as if the organism were programmed in two steps: (1) Before hatching, neural pathways are input for the posthatching response of following object X when it moves; and (2) the identity of object X will be input after hatching, thereby triggering the behavioral response.

Empirically, ethologists have found that such imprinting can occur only during limited periods of early development. Thus, if gosling chicks are raised in incubators without any moving object to follow, they will, when later exposed, never imprint on any moving object, and accordingly will never follow any moving object. The time window during which imprinting is possible is called the critical period (*qv*). Its exact duration varies between individuals and is not rigidly set, but after this period passes, imprinting becomes impossible.

The question of whether or not human infants imprint is controversial, partly because the concept of imprinting is not simple. Thus, a newborn will watch people as they move, but this phenomenon is not imprinting because it is elicited by nearly any moving object, not just one, and because it does not display a critical period. A mother might say that her baby is "imprinted" on her because it smiles at her more than at other people, but this is not ethologically accurate. Babies smile at many adults, and they soon learn situation-specific habits in which they smile more at some people than at others.

Areas in which imprinting seems theoretically possible in human development include aspects of native language acquisition and acquisition of one's basic gender identity (*qv*). Thus, small children can learn a language thoroughly and completely even though they have never been formally taught grammar, vocabulary, or pronunciation. In most people, this ability dwindles with time, so that adults may have considerable trouble learning a new language. Although other processes are involved in language acquisition, the phenomenon of childhood language learning appears reminiscent, in part, of imprinting.

Likewise, some sexologists have proposed that the development of one's internal sense of gender identity, and, in particular, of the characteristics of people to whom one will later be sexually attracted, also resemble imprinting in some ways. First, it appears that the development of one's gender identity occurs during a time window in early childhood. Second, it appears that certain childhood experiences can permanently alter later sexual development in marked and specific ways; *see* Somatosensory Affectional Deprivation syndrome. More significantly for the parallel between imprinting and gender acquisition, it has been suggested that the specific characteristics of the people whom one will find attractive in adulthood are input or programmed in some sense during childhood. One speculation is that young children have a broad template or model of what will later be attractive and that this template is completed by a process akin to imprinting. Thus, many little boys may be neurologically and physiologically prepared to input the visual details of women's faces, bodies, hair, and voice to complete their internal images, models, or templates of what is sexually attractive. Similarly, little girls may be neurologically and physiologically prepared to input details of men's bodies and voices, and in particular, of how men's bodies feel to the touch, to complete their internal images, models, or templates of what is sexually attractive in men. These internal images, whether imprinted or not, do not fully describe or explain gender (*qv*) differentiation, but their development plays a role in gender acquisition and seems similar in some ways to ethological imprinting.

It has been further argued that details of an individual's sexuoerotic (*qv*) script are likewise imprinted or programmed during critical periods in childhood. In this view, the child develops a "lovemap" (*qv*) which is a mental visual/tactile/emotional representation of a sequence of events that will be considered as genuinely and deeply arousing in adulthood. The central component of this view is that the lovemap is highly personalized and idiosyncratic because it arises from imprinting-like events that are unique to each individual. Evidence of this viewpoint comes from cases where such lovemaps are "vandalized" or "distorted," that is, where the child is prevented from developing a complete or pain-free representation of what is arousing. In these cases, the lovemap becomes paraphilic (*see* paraphilia) as opposed to normophilic. Paraphilic or vandalized lovemaps are extremely resistant to change by psychotherapy or other treatment modalities, suggesting that they are deeply embedded in the child's development.

Imprinting thus defined is distinct from genomic imprinting (*qv*). *See also* ideal lover template; encoding; scripting theory; template. Resources: Eibl Eibesfeldt, *Love and Hate: The Natural History of Behavior Patterns* (New York: Holt, Rinehart and Winston, 1972); John Money, *Lovemaps* (New York: Irvington Publishers, 1986); T. Perper, *Sex Signals: The Biology of Love* (Philadelphia: ISI Press, 1985).

impuberty The lack of primary and secondary sexual characteristics (*qv*) in a postpubertal (*qv*) male or female; the persistence of juvenile characteristics beyond the time when sexual maturation would be expected to produce adult development. *See also* delayed male puberty; neoteny; Turner syndrome.

impulse rape A spontaneous, unplanned sexual assault (*qv*) or rape (*qv*), committed because the opportunity arises in the execution of some crime, usually burglary, or in an argument. Also known as situational or opportunistic rape.

inadequate character A dependent, socially incompetent individual whose social functioning is built on dependency relationships.

inadequate personality A psychological condition in which an individual perceives himself or herself as always being inadequate and in no way equal to peers. An inadequate personality is marked by a lack of physical stamina, emotional immaturity, social instability, poor judgment, reduced motivation, ineptness, especially in interpersonal relations, and inability to adapt effectively to new or stressful situations. If the inadequate personality remains unresolved, the individual may compensate in one of two ways: by denial, overcompensation, and seeking to control others by physical or psychological force or by accepting one's perceived inferiority and relying on seduction to gain acceptance by others. *See also* acceptor; denier. The term may also be used to refer to an individual who lacks good judgment and motivation or to a social failure.

inappetence A lack of sexual desire (*qv*) or libido (*qv*). *See also* desire phase dysfunction.

inborn Innate (*qv*); acquired or occurring during prenatal (*qv*) life.

inbred strain (inbreeding) In biology, an inbred strain of plants or animals is a population that has been deliberately bred to increase the likelihood of genetic homozygosity (*see* homozygous); characteristically, inbreeding protocols involve mating close genetic relatives. The purpose is to increase the frequency of or "fix" desired genes in the population that produce advantageous traits such as commercial productivity or yield, leaner meat, a tastier product, or outstanding show quality.

In human genetics, inbreeding refers to marriages (*qv*) and matings (*qv*) occurring in a small population, and not to matings between close kin (*see* incest). One genetic consequence is the appearance of recessive alleles (*qv*) in homozygous form. These alleles may then have deleterious consequences, or they may simply be idiosyncratic to the population. The phenomenon occurs most readily in isolated populations.

Colloquially, inbreeding is believed to produce extensive genetic anomalies and defects among the offspring, a consequence that does not always follow. As a result, to call someone "inbred" is to accuse him or her of an ancestry of near incest that has produced physical monstrosities and mental retardation. The best-known historical examples, the Jukes and the Kallikaks, appear to have been invented by journalists to help spread eugenic (*qv*) propaganda. Nonetheless, the terms inbreeding and inbred, and the names of these mythic families, remain as part of the repertoire of sexual and social insult in the United States. *See also* hybrid; crossbreeding.

incentive motivation Motivation inspired by an external stimulus rather than by an internal need, desire, or drive (*qv*). Specific sexual desires (*qv*) are largely motivated by incentives, whereas the basic libido (*qv*) appears to be a more generalized drive.

incest Sexual contact between two persons of close kinship (*qv*) for whom such intimacy is forbidden by custom, law, and/or religious tradition. The degree of kinship within which sexual intimacy (*qv*) is prohibited may be based on genealogical, clan (*qv*), tribal, or totemic descent or on kinship by marriage (*qv*) or adoption (*qv*). Overt incest may involve sexual intercourse (*qv*), oral (*qv*) or anal sex (*qv*), sexual fondling (*qv*), mutual masturbation (*qv*), or other sexual intimacies. Covert sexual abuse, or emotional incest (*qv*), occurs when a child is used emotionally as a substitute for an adult partner or spouse.

Sibling incest appears not to have predictable traumatic results. In incest involving individuals of widely differing ages and power roles, however (e.g., parent-child incest), the psychological trauma is similar to that observed in rape-trauma syndrome (*qv*). An important additional trauma in incest involves the breaking of trust betwen the child and the adult authority figure, which, unless dealt with in therapy, can render the victim unable to fully trust again. *See also* incest fantasy; mother-son incest; rape counseling.

incest barrier In psychoanalysis (*qv*), a defense mechanism against naturally occurring incestuous impulses and fantasies (*qv*) that develop during the latency period (*qv*) before puberty (*qv*). The psychological barrier develops as the child recognizes and internalizes the social taboos (*qv*) and proscriptions against incestuous relations. The prohibitions of the incest barrier free the individual and his or her libido (*qv*) from family attachments and open up the possibility of developing an intimate, satisfying relationship with someone outside the family circle. *See also* incest taboo.

incest fantasy The tendency of children between ages 3 and 7 to dream or fantasize a sexual relationship with the other-sex parent. *See also* Oedipal complex; Electra complex. Adults occasionally have sexual dreams with an incest theme, without consciously desiring to enact this behavior. *See also* rape fantasy.

incest taboo A prohibition of sexual intimacy (*qv*) between persons of close blood or social kinship (*qv*). *See also* incest.

incestuous ties Erich Fromm's term for a pattern of close, nonsexual, but dependent relationships within a family that interferes with a healthy maturing and separation of the offspring and their involvement with persons outside the family circle.

inclusional cyst A cyst (*qv*) in the vagina (*qv*), perineal region (*qv*), or fouchette (*qv*) of a woman.

incompetent cervix In obstetrics (*qv*), the dilation (*qv*) of the cervical os (*qv*) of the uterus (*qv*) before term (*qv*) and labor (*qv*). This condition may result in a miscarriage (*qv*) or premature delivery (*qv*).

incomplete abortion Termination of a pregnancy (*qv*) in which not all the products of conception (*qv*) are expelled or extracted. An incomplete abortion may require curettage (*qv*) and surgical evacuation (*qv*) and/or treatment with oxytocin (*qv*) and blood transfusion to prevent hemorrhagic anemia and infection.

incontinence A lack of voluntary control over the functions of urination, defecation, or one's sexual impulses.

incubus (pl. incubi) (L.) In European folklore, a demon or evil spirit that assumes the form of a male and is believed to lie on top of sleeping people, mainly women, in order to have sexual intercourse (*qv*) with them. *See also* succubus.

indecency Conduct, generally sexual in character, that is commonly considered socially unacceptable or illegal.

indecent exposure A legal term for the public display of a part of the body that is prohibited by law, usually the genitalia (*qv*), buttocks (*qv*), or breasts (*qv*) in a woman, and the male genitalia (*qv*).

independent variable A factor in an experimental design or environment that the experimenter or observer can manipulate or vary in order to ascertain the effects on other variables under study. *See also* dependent variable.

index case In genetic research, the individual who is first identified in a family as showing the trait being studied.

indolamine One of a subgroup of biogenic amines, which functions as a neurotransmitter (*qv*) in the brain. *See also* serotonin; dopamine.

induced abortion The intentional termination of a pregnancy (*qv*) before the fetus (*qv*) is viable (*qv*) outside the uterus (*qv*), as opposed to spontaneous abortion (*qv*) or miscarriage (*qv*). *See also* abortion.

induced labor An obstetrical procedure in which labor (*qv*) is artificially initiated by means of amniotomy (*qv*) or administration of oxytocin (*qv*).

induction In embryology (*qv*), the process of stimulating and directing morphogenetic differentiation in a developing embryo (*qv*) through the action of chemical substances transmitted from one part of the embryo to another.

inductive method In the sciences and social research, a process whereby the truth of a proposition is made more probable by the accumulation of confirming evidence. A conclusion derived from the inductive method can never be ultimately validated because there is always the possibility of refuting the previously gathered evidence. *See also* deductive method.

inductor theory A theory of sexual development (*qv*) suggesting that male sexual organs (*qv*) are an adaptation of the more basic and primordial female sexual organs and that male sexual development is induced by the presence of male hormones (*qv*) at critical periods (*qv*) in fetal development. The inductor theory was proposed by Mary Jane Sherfey, *The Nature and Evolution of Female Sexuality* (New York: Random House, 1966). *See also* Adam principle; Eve principle.

inertia Apathy or lack of sexual responsiveness and/or arousal (*qv*) in the proceptive (*qv*) phase extending into the acceptive (*qv*) phase; a complete lack of sexual desire (*qv*) or libido (*qv*). *Antonym*: ultraertia.

infancy The beginning of early childhood; the period between birth and years 2 or 3, during which the infant learns to talk and walk.

infanticide The intentional killing of a newborn (*qv*) or infant. In modern Western societies, infanticide is legally defined as murder, although in history, infanticide and infant abandonment have both been used as a drastic means for limiting family size. The distinction between infanticide and abortion (*qv*) is that abortion occurs before birth, at a time when legal status and social and cultural customs do not necessarily assign full personhood (*qv*) to the fetus (*qv*). In some cultures—in China, for instance—the distinction between abortion and infanticide is complicated by recognition of a hiatus between the biological birth and recognition of the newborn's personhood in a social birth (*qv*) ritual. During the hiatus between biological and social birth, killing the newborn may be viewed as an extra-uterine abortion because personhood is not attributed to the infant, just as it is not to the fetus.

Cross-culturally, infanticide is not uncommon, although its frequency is sometimes exaggerated in travellers' tales and missionaries' reports. When it does occur, it is usually a response to acutely limited resources, for example, famine or chronic crop failure, or to other forms of acute social stress, such as war. Infanticide may be culturally permissible if the infant is deformed or otherwise abnormal. When an illegitimate infant is killed the act may be called infanticide, but if the killer is not the infant's mother, it is more properly a form of murder representing a punishment of the mother. Infanticide of female infants is commonly reported as more frequent than that of males, leading some to suggest that infanticide is a form of population growth control. *See also* viability.

infantile fallopian tube A thin, weak, underdeveloped fallopian tube (*qv*). Also known as a hypoplastic tube.

infantile seduction A psychoanalytic term for the sexual flirtation (*qv*) and seductive behavior (*qv*) of a child with an unresolved Oedipal (*qv*) or Electra complex (*qv*).

infantile sexuality The capacity of infants for sexual desire and experience. *See also* oral stage; anal stage; genital stage; sexual rehearsal play.

infantilism A condition in which various anatomical, physiological, and/or psychological characteristics of childhood persist in the adult; regression of an older person to a level of behavior more appropriate to a child.

infantilism, paraphilic A paraphilic (*qv*) condition in which sexual arousal (*qv*) and orgasm (*qv*) are dependent on being able to impersonate an infant (*qv*) and being treated as such by one's partner. *See also* autonepiophilia; adolescentilism; gerontalism; juvenilism; nepiophilia.

infant mortality The statistical rate of infant (*qv*) death during the first year after birth, expressed as the number of such deaths per 1,000 live births in a specific area or institution. About 70 percent of infant mortality is neonatal mortality (*qv*).

infatuation A foolish, irrational, generally short term, and intensely passionate involvement with another person; a love affair that is not approved or accepted by the couple's families or social or religious group.

infected abortion A spontaneous or induced termination of a pregnancy (*qv*) in which the products of conception (*qv*) have become infected.

infectious mononucleosis *See* mononucleosis.

infertile period The period in the menstrual cycle (*qv*) when a woman is unlikely to conceive (*qv*); often, but sometimes erroneously, thought to be all the days of the monthly cycle excluding the two to three days before and after ovulation (*qv*).

infertility The inability to conceive and carry a fetus (*qv*) to term (*qv*) and delivery (*qv*). Infertility is usually defined as the inability to conceive within one year's time with regular sexual intercourse (*qv*). About one-third of all infertility cases are due to the male, a third to the female partner, and the remaining third to male and female combined factors.

infibulation *See* Pharonic circumcision; female circumcision.

infidelity Sexual intercourse by a married person with someone other than the spouse, unfaithfulness to the marital promise that the spouses will "forsake all others and cleave to each other as two in one flesh." *See also* adultery; communitas; consensual adultery; open marriage; intimate network; intimate friendship; polyfidelity.

in flagrante delicto (L.) A legal term for "being caught in the act of committing a crime"; commonly applied to a married person observed in the act of adultery (*qv*). *See also* crime of passion.

inflatable breast implant An empty plastic sac inserted through a small incision in the female breast (*qv*) and filled by injecting a saline solution into the sac through a valve.

inflatable pessary *See* pessary.

informal value A moral judgment or value expressed in what a person actually does; a personal informal value may conflict with the formal value (*qv*) endorsed by the family or ethnic group, society, or church to which that individual belongs.

infundibulum The fimbriated, funnel-shaped, open end of the fallopian tube (*qv*), proximate to the ovary (*qv*).

infusion cavernosography The injection of a radioactive substance into the penis (*qv*) to monitor the blood supply and flow; used in diagnosing erectile dysfunctions (*qv*).

ingler An obsolete term for the passive partner in anal intercourse (*qv*).

ingravidation Medical term for impregnation (*qv*) followed by fertilization (*qv*) and nidation (*qv*).

inguinal Associated with the groin, the region or crease between the abdomen and thigh.

inguinal adenopathy A tender swelling of the lymph nodes in the groin area.

inguinal canal In the male, the oblique passage in the lower anterior abdominal wall through which the testes (*qv*) descend into the scrotum (*qv*) shortly before birth; in the adult, it is about 5 centimeters long. The spermatic cord (*qv*) with vas deferens (*qv*), nerve, and blood vessels also pass through it. In the female, the round ligament passes through it.

inguinal hernia The protrusion of the intestine into the inguinal canal (*qv*). It can occur when the temporary extension of the abdominal cavity that allows the descent of the testes (*qv*) into the scrotum (*qv*) does not close off after testicular descent.

inhibited orgasm The inability to reach orgasm (*qv*) during vaginal intercourse (*qv*) due to psychogenic, organic, or a combination of psychogenic and organic factors. *See also* orgasmic dysfunction; sexual dysfunction.

inhibited sexual arousal (ISA) In the male, failure to obtain or maintain an erection (*qv*) capable of allowing penile-vaginal intercourse (*qv*) and ejaculation (*qv*); in females, the inability to achieve vaginal lubrication (*qv*) sufficient to allow sexual intercourse (*qv*) without pain or physical discomfort. *See also* inhibited sexual excitement.

inhibited sexual desire (ISD) A persistent or temporary lack of sexual desire (*qv*) or libido (*qv*). In the terminology of the American Psychiatric Association, inhibited sexual desire is both persistent and pervasive and due primarily or exclusively to psychological causes. *See also* desire phase dysfunction.

inhibited sexual excitement (ISE) In the terminology of the American Psychiatric Association, a psychologic disorder characterized by persistent lack of sexual arousal (*qv*) despite adequate sexual stimulation. *See also* inhibited sexual arousal.

inhibition The often unconscious control and restraint of natural impulses and behavior arising from emotional insecurity, fear of consequences, or moral imperatives. *See also* incontinent, chastity.

initiation rite In anthropology, a ritual or ceremonial that marks the transition in an individual's life from one status or role to another; also called a rite of passage (*qv*). Quite frequently, initiation rites center on biologically marked transitions such as the onset of puberty (*qv*), the first menses (*qv*), marriage (*qv*), or the elevation to the rank, status, and role of a socially defined adult. Often an initiation rite involves the removal of the person from society and his or her sequestering in ritual solitude, followed by a ceremony that allows the person to reenter society in the new status or role. The intermediate stage of solitude, sequestration, or ritual training and discipline is called the liminal period (*qv*), from *limen*, meaning "threshold" in Latin. In anthropologist Victor Turner's often quoted phrase, during the liminal period the individual belongs to neither the prior nor the future status or group, but is "betwixt and between." Examples include male circumcision (*qv*) in the West, other forms of genital surgery or mutilation (e.g., subincision [*qv*] in non-Western societies), sequestration of boys during puberty and of girls at the onset of menstruation, ceremonies marking the elevation of a young man to full adult masculinity (often warriorhood), and, in the West, the engagement-wedding-honeymoon period. Initiation rites are heavily imbued with symbolic meaning and are often led by religious or spiritual figures in the society. *See also* bar mitzvah; bas mitzvah; ritual multiple intercourse; ceremonial defloration. Resource: V. Turner, *The Forest of Symbols: Aspects of Ndembu Tribe* (Ithaca, NY: Cornell University Press, 1967).

innate A no longer widely used term meaning inborn, indwelling, inherited, or congenital (*qv*); an innate trait or characteristic is one that is deemed to belong to the individual from conception (*qv*) or birth (*qv*). Innate behavior patterns are sometimes also referred to as instinctive or, simply, instincts.

With the development of modern genetics (*qv*), particularly behavioral genetics, these terms have fallen into disuse because it has become clear that behavior patterns as such are never present from conception or birth and are always developmental consequences of gene-environment interactions. However, laypeople, as well as critics of biologism (*see* biology; biologism; biological reductionism), often believe that the concept of innateness is a necessary part of the biologist's worldview. The factual database that has made the concept of innateness outdated has arisen primarily from genetic analyses of development and behavior. A variety of social critics have argued theoretically, often with great passion, that the concept of behavioral innateness is useless and serves only repressive social ends and political purposes. On twin grounds, then, the idea that behavior is innate no longer has empirical or theoretical support, and the term is best avoided. Nonetheless, lay speakers often use the term loosely to mean that a characteristic was not taught to a child but seemed always to be present. *See also* imprinting; nature/critical period/nurture; nature/nurture debate.

inner cell mass A cluster of cells inside the blastocyst (*qv*) of placental (*qv*) mammals from which the embryo (*qv*) proper develops. *See also* trophoblast.

inner labia *See* labia minora.

insemination In biology, the act of introducing sperm (*qv*) into the reproductive tract of the female (*qv*) so that fertilization (*qv*) of the ovum (*qv*) can occur. Often the word is taken to mean that the sperm is ejaculated into the vagina (*qv*), but in artificial insemination fertilization may be achieved external to the female's reproductive tract, or the sperm may be inserted using artificial or mechanical means. Metaphorically, the word has the extended meaning of initiating a process or event. *See also* artificial insemination donor (AID); artificial insemination husband (AIH); coitus; copulation; *in vitro* fertilization; impregnate.

insertee In male homosexual (*qv*) relations, the partner who accepts another's penis (*qv*) into his mouth or anus (*qv*).

inserter (insertor) In male homosexual (*qv*) relations, the partner who puts his penis (*qv*) into his partner's mouth or anus (*qv*).

inspectionalism A psychiatric term for voyeurism (*qv*).

instinct A no longer widely used term denoting a behavior pattern, or the motivation for performing a behavior pattern, that is considered built into the biology, genes (*qv*), or "nature" of the individual. In this sense, instinctive is approximately synonymous to innate (*qv*) or inborn. In a second, related meaning, an instinct is an unlearned or unpracticed behavior pattern, response, attitude, or reaction. In psychoanalytic theory (*see* psychoanalysis), an instinct is a biological excitation that leads to mental activity or to behavior.

These usages place "instinct" in the nature/nurture debate (*qv*), and represent an old language in which it is argued that certain aspects of human individual and social life are the products of an inborn, indwelling, and universal "human nature" that causes all people at all times to behave in similar ways. Modern formulations of this type often attribute to the genes (*qv*) the ability to transmit these allegedly inborn characteristics. Thus, in nineteenth- and twentieth-century sexology (*qv*), it was often claimed that sexual behavior and arousal (*qv*) were "instinctive," meaning that they were a basic part of human nature and an ineradicable component of human biology. Characteristically, such arguments such as the Oedipal theory (*see* Oedipus complex), were projections by the theorist from his culture and worldview onto what he perceived was the universal canvas of Nature (most instinct theorists are men, justifying the pronoun "his"). In more recent formulations, for example, those of certain sociobiologists (*see* sociobiology), the word instinctive is less frequently used than synonyms like inborn or genetic, although the meaning is the same.

During the middle and late twentieth century, as both genetics and sexology developed, it became clear that sexuality is an immensely complex web of biological, psychological, social, cultural, historical, and economic processes mutually and reciprocally interacting. Thus, as long as biotechnology offered no alternatives to fertilization (*qv*) and birth (*qv*), it was possible for the layperson to believe that biology created an "instinct" toward sexual reproduction. However, with the emergence of contraception (*qv*) and abortion (*qv*), it has become obvious to most people that no indwelling "instinct" mandates reproduction. This drastic shift in mindset and worldview has been powerfully reinforced by social and cultural changes that have in many cultures stressed the plasticity and reformability of personal and social behavior, in opposition to the perception of permanence that is at the root of the concept of sexual instinct.

Critics of instinct theorizing have flourished particularly in the social and psychological sciences, which historically had its origins in heavily instinct-ridden thinking, for example, that of Sigmund Freud (*qv*). The modern trend in such fields is to eschew all forms of instinct theorizing and to look with great suspicion at all theories that seem to recall its themes and tenets. Feminist (*qv*) writers especially have rejected instinct theorizing, and have subjected it to detailed and powerful critiques.

Nonetheless, because there is no generally acceptable term for behavior patterns that appear early in infancy and childhood, or that occur universally or nearly universally among the peoples of humankind, words like instinct, inborn, and innate have retained their power and continue to occur in casual or lay speech and writing about sexuality. However, their association with antiquated theorizing about human nature makes their use questionable at best, and utterly confusing at worst. *See also* behavior genetics; biology, biologism; biosocial viewpoint; drive; maternal instinct.

intercalary cells Long, slender cells in the fallopian tube (*qv*) lining which are believed to secrete nutrients that maintain the ovum (*qv*) and sperm (*qv*) prior to fertilization (*qv*) and the zygote (*qv*) during its passage to the uterine lumen.

intercourse, axillary *See* axillary coitus.

intercourse, femoral *See* interfemoral intercourse.

intercourse, interruptus *See* coitus interruptus.

intercourse, mammary *See* coitus, mammary.

intercourse, oral *See* fellatio; cunnilingus.

intercourse, prolongatus *See* karezza, maithuna.

intercourse, reservatus *See* coitus reservatus; coitus sine ejaculatio; karezza; maithuna.

intercourse, Saxon *See* coitus saxonicus.

intercourse, sexual A technical synonym for coitus (*qv*) or copulation (*qv*); the act of inserting the erect penis (*qv*) in the vagina (*qv*) or anus (*qv*). The term is also used in conjunction with qualifying or descriptive adjectives (e.g., anal, interfemoral, or oral intercourse). More broadly, placing the emphasis on sexual communications and interactions, sexual intercourse includes the entire proceptive (*qv*) and acceptive (*qv*) interaction from loveplay (*qv*) through intromission (*qv*), orgasm (*qv*), and afterplay (*qv*).

interfemoral intercourse Sexual intercourse (*qv*) engaged in by moving the penis (*qv*) between the thighs.

interferon A class of small, soluble proteins released by cells when they are invaded by viruses. The interferon induces uninfected cells to form antiviral protein to inhibit multiplication of the virus. Production of interferons is not restricted to viral infections but may also be triggered by certain nonviral agents.

intermarriage Marriage between two individuals belonging to different racial, ethnic, or religious groups. *See also* miscegenation; xenophobia.

intermediate sex An obsolete term for homosexual (*qv*).

intermenstrual fever A small but detectable rise in basal body temperature that occurs at the time of ovulation (*qv*). *See also* basal body temperature (BBT) method of contraception; mittleschmerz.

internal cervical os The inner opening of the cervical canal (*qv*) that leads from the uterine lumen (*qv*) into the canal; the external os (*qv*) projects into the vaginal canal (*qv*).

internal fertilization The union of ovum (*qv*) and sperm (*qv*) within the body of the female, as distinct from external fertilization (*qv*), which is common among fish and amphibians. Internal fertilization is characteristic of mammals (*qv*).

internalization The process of socialization or enculturation by which an individual learns and accepts as binding the values and norms of conduct appropriate to his or her family, social group, or society. *See also* scripting.

internal morphologic sex The accessory organs of the sexual-reproductive anatomy located within the body cavity but not including the ovaries (*qv*) and testes (*qv*). In females, these include the fallopian tubes (*qv*), uterus (*qv*), and vagina (*qv*) which develop from the Mullerian ducts (*qv*); in males, the epididymis (*qv*), vasa deferentia (*qv*), prostate (*qv*), seminal vesicles (*qv*), and Cowper's glands (*qv*) derived from the Wolffian (*qv*) or mesonephric ducts (*qv*).

internal oval migration The passage of an ovum (*qv*) from the fallopian tube (*qv*) on one side of the body through the uterine cavity (*qv*) into the fallopian tube on the other side.

internal urethral sphincter One of two bundles of circular muscle fibers controlling the flow of urine (*qv*) and semen (*qv*) through the male urethra (*qv*), is located between the upper surface of the prostate (*qv*) and the base of the urinary bladder. During urination, both the internal and external sphincters open. During sexual arousal (*qv*) and the emission phase (*qv*) of male ejaculation (*qv*), both sphincters are closed. When the propulsion phase (*qv*) begins, the outer or external urethral sphincter (*qv*) opens. In retrograde ejaculation (*qv*), the outer sphincter remains closed, and the internal sphincter opens, releasing semen into the bladder.

International Professional Surrogates Association (IPSA) An international association and accrediting agency for sexual surrogates (*qv*) or body work therapists; address: IPSA, P.O. Box 74156, Los Angeles, CA 90004.

interoceptor Any sensory receptor located in the viscera that responds to and transmits sensory information from viscera to the central nervous system (*qv*).

intersex A nonspecific term for an individual who has anatomical characteristics of both sexes or whose external genitalia (*qv*) are ambiguous or inappropriate for a normal male or female. *See also* hermaphrodite; intersexuality.

intersexuality An alternate term for hermaphroditism (*qv*).

interstitial cells *See* Leydig cells; interstitial cell-stimulating hormone (ICSH).

interstitial cell-stimulating hormone (ICSH) In the male, this hormone is produced by the anterior pituitary (*qv*) and stimulates the cells of Leydig (*qv*) in the testes (*qv*) to produce testosterone (*qv*). A negative feedback system (*qv*) regulates the production of testosterone. ICSH is identical to luteinizing hormone (*qv*) in the female.

interstitial implantation The complete embedding of the blastocyst (*qv*) within the uterine endometrium (*qv*). *See also* interstitial pregnancy.

interstitial pregnancy An ectopic pregnancy (*qv*) occurring in any body tissue outside the uterus (*qv*). *See also* interstitial implantation.

intertrigo A fungal-related inflammation of the skin of the genitalia (*qv*). Reddish-brown discolorations of the skin appear where the skin of the penis (*qv*) and scrotum (*qv*) or labial (*qv*) tissue rub against the thighs.

interview A research technique in which subjects are personally asked survey questions; a diagnostic technique in which a subject is asked specific questions about the nature, onset, history, and symptoms of a problem behavior. *See also* sexual history; sexual problem history.

intimacy *See* intimate.

intimacy avoidance A socially dictated constraint or reduction in what one discloses about oneself to specific individuals or groups; a prohibition on discussion of specific topics. Intimacy avoidance may negatively affect interpersonal communications and sexual behavior. *See also* age avoidance; allosex avoidance.

intimacy principle The principle that because a gestalt (*qv*) is an integrated whole that is greater than its individual parts, all parts in the gestalt are so interrelated that no one part can be changed without changing the whole.

intimate An intimate is a person with whom one has a deep and close friendship, and from whom one keeps no secrets. Intimates may relate as equals, but intimate friends can also be of different social status. Intimacy is the state of being intimate friends with another person, and can involve intellectual, physical or sexual, emotional, and spiritual affinities and sharing. Often "intimacy" is used as a euphemism for sexual relations, which may or may not be intimate in the sense defined above. The sexual sense of "intimate" which specializes the broader meaning just given probably arises from the belief that sexuality conjoins people deeply and profoundly. *See also* sex; sexuality.

intimate friendship A friendship in which sexual intimacy (*qv*) and expression are acceptable to the two friends as well as to other persons with whom they have an ongoing intimate relationship or to whom they may be married. *See also* communitas; intimate network; satellite relationships; sexually open marriage.

intimate network A social network including married and single persons who participate in multilateral relationships that include primary (*qv*) and secondary or satellite relationships (*qv*), with sexual intimacy (*qv*) acceptable where couples find it appropriate; an informal but somewhat structured intentional family (*qv*) or kinship (*qv*) linked by voluntary commitments and intimacies but without the incest (*qv*) taboos usually associated with families. Resource: James Ramey, *Intimate Friendships* (Englewood Cliffs, NJ: Prentice-Hall, 1976).

intra-amniotic infusion (injection) Injection of prostaglandin (*qv*) or a salt solution into the amniotic fluid (*qv*) to cause an abortion (*qv*) by triggering circulatory failure in a second-trimester (*qv*) fetus (*qv*). Also known as saline injection.

intracanicular fibroma A benign growth of the glandular and fibrous tissues of the female breast (*qv*).

intracanicular papilloma A benign wartlike growth in the breast (*qv*).

intracranial gumma A soft, degenerating tumor of the brain associated with tertiary syphilis (*qv*), resulting in loss of recent memory, delirium, and emotional instability. *See also* general paresis.

intracrural intercourse *See* interfemoral intercourse.

intraductal carcinoma A malignancy of the milk ducts in the female breast (*qv*).

intramural fallopian tube That portion of the fallopian tube (*qv*) which is embedded in the wall of the uterine (*qv*) horn.

intrapartal The period between labor (*qv*) and birth (*qv*).

intrapreputial movement Rhythmic movements of the clitoris (*qv*) back and forth under the clitoral or preputial hood during the plateau phase (*qv*) of sexual arousal (*qv*), caused by tension between the labia minora (*qv*) and clitoral hood during coitus (*qv*).

intrauterine (contraceptive) device (IUD, IUCD) A contraceptive (*qv*) device made of plastic inserted into the uterine cavity (*qv*) and left there. The IUD appears to speed up transport of the ovum (*qv*) through the fallopian tube (*qv*) and to prevent implantation (*qv*) of the fertilized ovum. The IUD is inserted just before or just after the menstrual period (*qv*) when the cervix (*qv*) is slightly open and menstruation ensures that a pregnancy (*qv*) does not exist. A fine monofilament tail extends through the cervix into the upper vagina (*qv*), where its presence confirms retention of the IUD. Failure rate is two to four unplanned pregnancies in 100 women using the device for a year. The most serious complication is infection. Other complications include cervicitis (*qv*), uterine perforation, salpingitis (*qv*) causing sterility, ectopic pregnancy (*qv*), miscarriage (*qv*), endometritis (*qv*), bleeding, pain, cramping, undetected expulsion, and embedding of the IUD in the uterine wall.

Major manufacture and availability in the United States was severely restricted by lawsuits in 1986. The IUD is recommended for use only with women who have had at least one full term pregnancy and are not yet ready to have an irreversible tubal ligation (*qv*).

introcision A surgical procedure to enlarge the vaginal (*qv*) opening for childbirth (*qv*). *See also* episiotomy.

introitus (L.) The entrance or orifice to a cavity or tubular structure, for example. the vulval (*qv*) entrance of the vagina (*qv*).

introitus vaginalis (L.) The external opening to the vagina (*qv*), surrounded by the vulva (*qv*).

intromission Insertion of the penis (*qv*) into the vagina (*qv*) or anus (*qv*) during copulation (*qv*), coitus (*qv*), or intercourse (*qv*).

in utero (L.) Literally, "within the uterus (*qv*)."

inversion A term used by early sexologists (*qv*), particularly Sigmund Freud (*qv*) and Havelock Ellis (*qv*), classifying homosexuals (*qv*) as having an absolute or total inversion, an amphigenous or bisexual (*qv*) inversion, or an occasional or facultative inversion.

invert An obsolete term for a male or female homosexual (*qv*), still used for nonhuman animals that show sexual patterns of the other sex.

inverted nipples A congenital (*qv*) condition in which the nipples (*qv*) of the breast (*qv*) do not protrude from the areola (*qv*) but rather project inward. Inverted nipples seldom interfere with nursing (*qv*). In older women, this condition may be an indication of breast cancer (*qv*).

inverted Oedipus complex In psychoanalytic theory (*qv*), a reversal of parental roles during the Oedipal stage (*qv*) so that the same-sex parent becomes the object of the child's libidinal attachment.

in vitro fertilization A procedure in which an ovum (*qv*) is removed surgically or by lavage (*qv*) from the ovary (*qv*) or fallopian tube (*qv*), fertilized in a culture medium with sperm (*qv*), artificially cultured for 2 days, and then transferred to the uterus (*qv*) of the original woman to bypass her blocked fallopian tubes. It may also be transferred to a surrogate mother (*qv*) if the ovum donor does not wish to or cannot carry a gestation (*qv*) full term (*qv*). *See also* in vivo fertilization.

in vivo fertilization Natural fertilization (*qv*) of an ovum (*qv*) by sperm (*qv*) within the reproductive tract of a female, following coitus (*qv*) or artificial insemination (*qv*). *See also* in vitro fertilization.

involution A regressive change or deterioration in either psychological or physical functions associated with aging; the return of an enlarged organ, such as involution of a puerperal (*qv*) uterus (*qv*) to its normal size.

involutional Pertaining to or associated with menopause (*qv*) or climacteric (*qv*).

involutional depression (melancholia) An emotional disturbance occasionally associated with menopause (*qv*) or climacteric (*qv*), characterized by gradual onset of depression, a negative outlook on life, insomnia, lack of appetite, irritability, and restlessness.

involutional gynecomastia Breast (*qv*) enlargement in an older male. *See also* gynecomastia.

involutional psychotic reaction An emotional disturbance occasionally associated with menopause (*qv*) or climacteric (*qv*), characterized by severe agitation, feelings of worthlessness and depression, persistent insomnia, and, in some cases, hypochondria and paranoid delusions of persecution.

IPSA *See* International Professional Surrogates Association.

ipsation Self-induced sexual excitement (*qv*). *See also* autoeroticism, masturbation.

irrumated Forced to perform fellatio (*qv*).

irrumation (n) (L.) A term for the act of fellatio (*qv*) when the movements of the penis (*qv*) mimic the coital (*qv*) penile thrusting (*qv*) and the mouth is used as a passive receptacle.

irrumator A male who takes the active, insertor (*qv*) role in fellatio (*qv*) with another male.

ischomenia The arrest or suppression of the menstrual flow (*qv*).

ISD *See* inhibited sexual desire.

isogamy Fertilization (*qv*) involving two gametes (*qv*) that are identical in size; the opposite of heterogamy (*qv*), in which ovum (*qv*) and sperm (*qv*) are unequal in size. A second usage of this term applies to the tendency to choose a partner or spouse who is on the same economic, educational, career, and/or social status levels, as distinct from hypergamy (*qv*), or "marrying up," and hypogamy (*qv*), or choosing a spouse from a lower economic, education, and/or social level.

isoimmune hemolytic disease of the newborn *See* erythroblastosis fetalis; Rh factor.

isosexual Pertaining to or of the same sex; an obsolete term for homosexual (*qv*).

isosexual precocity Premature puberty (*qv*) in which the secondary sexual characteristics (*qv*) are appropriate to the child's adult gender.

isthmus The narrow, central portion of the fallopian tube (*qv*) or the narrowing cavity of the uterus (*qv*) just above the cervical canal (*qv*).

ithyphallic (Gr.) Pertaining to or causing an erection (*qv*) of the penis (*qv*).

IUCD *See* intrauterine device.

IUD *See* intrauterine device.

ius primae noctis (L.) More properly, jus primae noctis (*qv*) "the right of the first night." *See also* defloration; droit du seigneur.

J

Jacquemier's sign An almost purplish hue in the vaginal mucosa (*qv*) just behind the urethra (*qv*), sometimes associated with pregnancy (*qv*). This change usually appears in the second month of gestation (*qv*).

janiceps Conjoined or Siamese twins (*qv*) with fused heads and faces that look in opposite directions.

Jarisch-Herxheimer reaction A sudden, transitory inflammatory reaction that may accompany the use of antibiotics or other chemical treatments in the treatment of syphilis (*qv*). Symptoms include a fever and exacerbation of chancres (*qv*), which last about 24 hours before disappearing without treatment. An insufficient dose of the therapeutic agent may be the cause.

jealousy, sexual On a cultural or group level, sexual jealousy is an emotional response developed to set boundaries and limit sexual access to those relationships that a group defines as important. On an individual and interpersonal level, sexual jealousy is an emotional response to a perceived threat from an outsider to an important relationship in which one is involved. On the personal level, cross-cultural research (*qv*) indicates that jealousy in males usually involves the primary emotion of anger since men are almost invariably in the position of power, while jealousy in women is associated with the primary emotions of fear of loss and sadness or depression. The normalcy of jealousy was questioned by influential psychologists and popular writers on sex and marriage during the 1960s and 1970s who suggested that jealousy is evidence of personal insecurity and lack of faith in the partner and in the primacy of the relationship. In attempting to resolve the "problem of jealousy," individuals and couples need to consider the important role of sexual jealousy in setting boundaries. In adapting to the radically altered social systems in which modern male-female relations develop, couples may utilize a variety of strategies involving diverting, segregating, and integrating the taboo (*qv*) relationship. *See also* sexually open marriage; extramarital sex; crime of passion; alcoholic jealousy; paranoid jealousy. Resources: I. L. Reiss, *Journey into Sexuality* (Englewood Cliffs, NJ: Prentice-Hall, 1986); G. Clanton & L. G. Smith, *Jealousy* (Englewood Cliffs, NJ: Prentice-Hall, 1977); N. Friday, *Jealousy* (New York: Morrow, 1985).

Jennifer fever Barbara Gordon's term for compulsion that drives many males to marry a much younger woman in order to cope with the midlife crisis they experience in aging and finding their sexual vigor slacking. Resource: B. Gordon, *Jennifer Fever: Older Men, Younger Women* (New York: Harper & Row, 1988).

Jobst breast support An elastic brassiere used during the early healing process following a mammoplasty (*qv*).

Jocasta complex The morbid attachment of a mother for her own son.

jock itch A fungal infection of the superficial skin in the groin region caused by *Tinea cruris* (*qv*) and easily cured with nonprescription medication.

Jorgensen, Christine (1927–1989) The name adopted by George Jorgensen following male-to-female transsexual surgery (*qv*) in December 1952. A photographer from Long Island, New York, George Jorgensen was 26 years old when he became a celebrity following transsexual surgery (*qv*) in the Danish clinic of Dr. Christian Hamburger. The resulting publicity helped society recognize and accept the problems of gender transpositions (qv).

Jung, Carl (1875–1962) A Swiss psychoanalyst and founder of analytical psychology, Jung studied in Basel and Paris. In 1906, he became a member of Sigmund Freud's (qv) circle. Seven years later, he broke with Freud over the nature of the unconscious and libido (qv). Jung was particularly interested in the study of primitive peoples—their myths, religions, folkways, and mores. *See also* anima; animus.

jus primae noctis (L.) *See* droit du seigneur.

juvenile A young person, a youth.

juvenile paresis A form of partial paralysis associated with congenital syphilis (*qv*). Neurological symptoms first occur between ages 10 and 15 after an asymptomatic childhood. These symptoms include visual difficulties and loss of muscular coordination, memory, and judgment. A maternal syphilitic infection in the first four months of pregnancy (qv) does not pose a threat to the fetus (qv) if it is treated promptly. Passage of the *Treponema* bacterium across the placental membrane is blocked by Langhans' membrane, which degenerates in the fifth month. Maternal syphilitic infections in the second half of gestation (qv) can pass to the fetus.

juvenilism, paraphilic A paraphilic (*qv*) condition in which achieving sexual arousal (qv) and orgasm (qv) is dependent on the actual or fantasized impersonation of a juvenile (*qv*) and being treated as such by one's partner. In the interpretative schema of paraphilias proposed by John Money, paraphilic juvenilism is one of the stigmatic-eligibilic paraphilias. *See also* adolescentilism; ephebophilia; infantilism; gerontalism; nepiophilia; pedophilia; Appendix A.

K

Kahn test A serological, blood-precipitation test for syphilis (*qv*). A white precipitate appears when an alcohol extract of normal heart muscle is added to a syphilitic blood serum; a modification of the Sachs-Georgi Reaction test.

Kallman syndrome A rare condition characterized by insufficient release of gonadotropic (*qv*) hormones from the pituitary (*qv*) to stimulate maturation of the testes (*qv*) or ovaries (*qv*), resulting in infertility (*qv*). Treatment is with exogenous gonadotropin releasing hormone (*qv*).

Kama (Kamadeva) (Skt.) The Hindu god of love, similar to the Roman god Cupid. The son of Vishnu and Lakshmi, the god Kama is believed to be present during all acts of love. His wife, Rati, is the embodiment of sensual love. Kama also represents "the pursuit of love of pleasure, both sensual and aesthetic," one of the four goals of life in the Hindu tradition. Two manuals, the *Kama-Shastra* and the *Kama Sutra* (*qv*), were allegedly written by the gods and sages as comprehensive guides for the disciplined enjoyment of sexual pleasures.

Kama Sutra One of the best known of ancient sex manuals (*qv*) of India, written in the second century B.C.E. *Kama Sutra* discusses the spiritual aspects of sexuality (*qv*), with details on a great variety of positions and techniques for increasing the sensual enjoyment of sexual intercourse (*qv*). The *Kama Sutra*, written by Vatsyayana, was first translated into English and published secretly by Sir Richard Burton in 1883.

Kantner and Zelnik Surveys Two landmark surveys of "The Sexual Experience of Young Unmarried Women in the United States" conducted in 1971 and 1976 by John F. Kantner and Melvin Zelnik. A probability sampling method was used in both of these studies of 15– to 19–year-old unmarried women, allowing for comparisons between black and white populations. In the years between the two studies, the incidence of premarital sexual intercourse (*qv*) rose from 27 to 35 percent, the average age of first intercourse dropped from 16.5 to 16.2 years, the number of girls with two or more sexual partners rose from 25 to 31 percent, and the use of the contraceptive pill (*qv*) and intrauterine contraceptive device doubled. Kantner and Zelnik are also noted for other surveys of teenage sexual behaviors, all published in *Family Planning Perspectives*. Resources: J. F. Kantner & M. Zelnik, Sexual experience in young unmarried women in the United States, *Family Planning Perspectives* 4(4) (1972):9–18; M. Zelnik & J. F. Kantner, Probabilities of intercourse and conception among U.S. Teenage women, 1971–1976, *Family Planning Perspectives* 11(3) (1979):177–183; M. Zelnik & J. F. Kantner, Contraceptive patterns and premarital pregnancy among women aged 15–19 in 1976, *Family Planning Perspectives* 10(3) (1978):135–142; M. Zelnik & J. F. Kantner, Sexual and contraceptive experience of young unmarried women in the United States, 1976 and 1971, *Family Planning Perspectives* 9(2) (1977):55–71; M. Zelnik & J. F. Kantner, Sexual activity, contraceptive use and pregnancy among metropolitan-area teenagers: 1971–1979, *Family Planning Perspectives* 12(5) (1980):230–237.

Kaposi's sarcoma An opportunistic cancer commonly associated with acquired immune deficiency syndrome (*qv*) in male homosexuals (*qv*), but otherwise a rare malignancy of the blood capillaries and connective tissue. Kaposi's sarcoma is a multifocal neoplasm that begins as soft brownish or purple papules on the feet. In HIV-infected males, the lesions often appear first on the upper torso. These papules slowly spread in the skin and into the lymph nodes and viscera. Under normal conditions, this sarcoma occurs most often in Jewish, black, and elderly males of Mediterranean descent. It occasionally occurs in association with diabetes and malignant lymphoma.

karezza A technique for prolonging sexual intercourse (*qv*) without ejaculation (*qv*), practiced both as a means of contraception (*qv*) and as a way of concentrating and retaining sexual energies (*qv*) released by intercourse. This custom originated in ancient Persia and was introduced into India, from whence it spread throughout the Orient. Hindu men are taught how to use breathing control, meditation, postures, and finger pressure to prevent ejaculation (*qv*) while repeatedly bringing themselves to that point just before ejaculatory inevitability (*qv*). This custom spread throughout the Orient and entered the United States in the early 1900s. This custom is different from the Taoist and Tantric approach to prolonged vaginal intercourse which also stresses the conservation of male semen but complements this with transforming and circulating the sexual energy upward in the body and in exchanges with a partner, thereby extending the enjoyment of many orgasms without ejaculation. *See also* coitus reservatus; maithuna; Oneida community.

karyogamy The fusion of the sperm (*qv*) and egg (*qv*) pronuclei (*qv*), which concludes the process of fertilization (*qv*).

karyotype The structural characteristics of the chromosome (*qv*) complement of an individual or species, including information about the number, form, and size of chromosomes within the nucleus. A karyotype is obtained from a photomicrograph taken during the metaphase stage of mitosis (*qv*) or at synapsis in meiosis (*qv*). The karyotype is a pictorial or diagrammatic representation of the chromosome complement in which a greatly enlarged photomicrograph of a metaphase chromosome smear (*qv*) from a single somatic (*qv*) cell is cut up and the chromosome images arranged on a white background in homologous pairs in descending order of size and according to the position of the centromere (*qv*).

katasexual *See* necrophilia.

Kegel exercises *See* pubococcygeal muscle exercises.

Kellogg, John Harvey (1852–1943) Appointed medical superintendent at the Western Health Reform Institute run by the Seventh Day Adventists in 1876, Kellogg invented granola and corn flakes as organic, nutritious alternatives to Sylvester Graham's (*qv*) graham bread in the fight against moral degeneracy and sexual passion. Resource: J. Money, *The Destroying Angel* (Buffalo: Prometheus Press, 1985), pp. 17–27.

Kempf's disease An acute psychological condition, described by the American psychiatrist Edward Kempf, marked by an intense, recurring fear and anxiety of being sexually assaulted by a homosexual (*qv*) or being identified as a homosexual.

ketone Any compound with a carbonyl group (CO) and hydrocarbon groups attached to the carbonyl carbon at the seventeenth carbon atom. *See also* 17-ketosteroid; 21-hydroxylase deficiency.

ketosteroid *See* 17-ketosteroid.

Kielland rotation An obstetric operation in which Kielland forceps are used to turn the fetal head to correct an arrest in the active stage of labor (*qv*). Because of risk to mother and child, a Caesarean section (*qv*) is often preferred.

killer T lymphocyte *See* lymphocyte.

kimilue A culture-dependent syndrome characterized by extreme apathy, loss of interest in life, and vivid sexual dreams (*qv*) found among the Diegueno Indians of lower California.

kindred The network of an individual's relatives. Unlike a clan (*qv*), in which the common ancestor is remote, a kindred includes only the living blood relatives of an individual. A kindred is said to be ego centered since its composition differs for each member of the kindred, except siblings. The kindreds of a given community form a series of overlapping circles. Kindreds are defined as bilateral or cognatic if they include relatives on both the father's and the mother's side or as patrilateral (*qv*) or matrilateral (*qv*) if only one side of the family is included. *See also* lineage, family.

Kinsey, Alfred Charles (1894–1956) An entomologist at Indiana University who gained fame in the 1940s and 1950s as a premier researcher in the field of human sexuality (*qv*). His two major studies of human sexual behavior in the United States, popularly referred to as the Kinsey Reports (*qv*), are landmarks in scientific sexology (*qv*). When asked to develop and teach a course on marriage (*qv*), Kinsey, a careful scientist, was surprised to find little data on human sexual behavior. Even more disturbing was his discovery that what was known was mostly based on poorly designed studies and questionable surveys. Applying skills honed in collecting and cataloging over 4 million insect specimens, Kinsey developed an intensive interview with 300 to 521 questions. Encouraged by the university administration and by a grant from the National Research Council, Kinsey recruited and trained Clyde E. Martin, Wardell B. Pomeroy, and Paul Gebhard to administer his questionnaire. He also established the Institute for Sex Research, known now as the Kinsey Institute for Research in Sex, Gender, and Reproduction. Resource: W. B. Pomeroy, *Dr. Kinsey and the Institute for Sex Research* (New York: Harper & Row, 1972).

Kinsey Institute for Research in Sex, Gender, and Reproduction The premier center for scientific research into all aspects of human sexuality (*qv*), founded by Alfred Kinsey (*qv*) as a not-for-profit corporation affiliated with Indiana University. Originally known as the Institute for Sex Research, the institute published the results of Kinsey's early research, *Sexual Behavior of the American Male* (1948) and *Sexual Behavior of the American Female* (1953). After Kinsey's death in 1956, the institute was headed by his associate, Paul H. Gebhard. Major studies published in the Gebhard years were *Pregnancy, Birth and Abortion* (1958), *Sex Offenders: An Analysis of Types* (1965), *Homosexualities: A Study of the Diversity among Men and Women* (1978), and *Sexual Preference: Its Development in Men and Women* (1981). Reorganized in 1981, the institute appointed its third director in 1982, June Machover Reinisch. Along with a major publication, *Masculinity/Femininity: Basic Perspectives* (1987), the institute staff produces numerous monographs, journal articles, and book chapters every year. Two current staff projects focus on prenatal development and reproductive cycles. The institute's library and collections are the world's most impressive on the subject of sexuality. Resource: W. B. Pomeroy, *Dr. Kinsey and the Institute for Sex Research* (New York: Harper & Row, 1972).

Kinsey Reports Two landmark surveys, conducted by Alfred Kinsey (*qv*) and coworkers, *Sexual Behavior in the Human Male* (1948) and *Sexual Behavior in the Human Female* (1953). The Kinsey Reports were based on data gathered between 1938 and 1949 from nonprobability, random interviews with 5,300 males and 5,940 females. No data on blacks were included in either report, and unskilled laborers, devout Jews, Catholics, minorities, rural dwellers, the less educated, and midwesterners and westerners were underrepresented. Each interview characteristically lasted about 2 hours, covering social and economic data, a marital history of each marriage, sex education (*qv*), physical and physiological data, nocturnal sex dreams (*qv*), masturbation (*qv*), heterosexual (*qv*) and homosexual (*qv*) activities histories, and sexual contacts with animals. Despite their limitations, these surveys provided the first scientific information about the sexual behaviors of American men and women. Resources: A. C. Kinsey, W. B. Pomeroy, & C. E. Martin, *Sexual Behavior in the Human Male* (Philadelphia: Saunders, 1948); A. C. Kinsey et al., *Sexual Behavior in the Human Female* (Philadelphia: Saunders, 1953).

Kinsey Six Scale A discontinuous scale of 0 to 6, rating the proportion of heterosexual (*qv*) and homosexual experiences (*qv*) and fantasy, with 0 being the rating for an exclusively heterosexual person, 3 the rating for a true bisexual (*qv*) (equally attracted to both men and women), and 6 the rating for an exclusively homosexually oriented person. This scale was developed by Alfred Kinsey (*qv*) and his coworkers to illustrate the results of their surveys of sexual behavior (*qv*) in the American male and female. Based on sexual experiences and fantasies (*qv*), roughly 50 percent of the American men interviewed were exclusively heterosexual, or Kinsey 0, 46 percent were in the bisexual range of Kinsey 1–5, and 4 percent in the exclusive homosexual category of Kinsey 6. *See also* Sexual Orientation Grid.

kinship A social relationship defined by real or supposed blood ties and marriage. Kinships exist in all societies and in most cases play a significant role in socialization of individuals and in maintaining group solidarity. In nonindustrial societies, kinships may be so extensive and significant that they account for the whole social system. In other societies, other relationships may reduce the importance of kinships. In some societies, fictive kin ties are based on religious bonds such as those of godparent-godchild.

kinship model family group A family unit composed of the biological parents and their offspring. A kinship model family group, which is similar to a nuclear family (*qv*) but more closely tied to an extended family (*qv*), has clearly delineated sex roles (*qv*), is resistant to change, and is dominated by the maternal grandmother who raises the children and makes most of the decisions.

kiss A touch or caress with the lips; a form of greeting in many societies, an expression of friendship, affection, reverence, sexual desire, or love. In cultures where kissing is not customary, it is often replaced by nose rubbing (*qv*).

Klein Sexual Orientation Grid *See* Sexual Orientation Grid.

kleptolagnia Sexual excitement (*qv*) or gratification produced by stealing. *See also* kleptophilia.

kleptomania (kleptophilia) A psychological condition in which compulsive stealing or fantasizing (*qv*) about stealing is sometimes associated with sexual arousal (*qv*) and/or facilitating or achieving orgasm (*qv*).

Klinefelter syndrome Klinefelter syndrome, the most common numerical sex chromosome (*qv*) anomaly in males, involves at least one extra X chromosome (*qv*), usually 47,XXY; the condition is characterized by hypogonadism (*qv*) and sterility (*qv*). Roughly 80 percent of Klinefelter cases have a karyotype (*qv*) of 47,XXY. Much rarer is 48,XXXY. Mosaics, with different genotypes (*qv*) in two cell lines, occur with two or more X chromosomes and one or two Y chromosomes (*qv*) (i.e., 46,XY/47,XXY). The overall incidence of this condition is 1 in 400 to 1 in 1,000 births. Although the condition is diagnosed in childhood because of very small testes (*qv*), diagnosis is more common in adolescence (*qv*) since clinical symptoms appear mostly at puberty (*qv*) and vary widely from normal to severe. Dysgenesis (*qv*) of the testes (*qv*) and sterility (*qv*) with no sperm (*qv*) production result when elastic connective tissue replaces the germinal cells (*qv*). The small testes are distorted by hyalinization and fibrosis. An affected male is still capable of erection (*qv*) and coitus (*qv*), although secondary erectile dysfunction (*qv*) may result from response to lowered libido (*qv*) and gynecomastia (*qv*). Other symptoms include a eunuchoid (*qv*) body with poor male secondary sex characteristics (*qv*), which give a feminine appearance. The gynecoid impression is accented in half of the Klinefelter cases by female breast (*qv*) development or gynecomastia (*qv*). Penile size is usually normal, although pubic hair (*qv*) may be sparse and female in pattern. The axillary (*qv*) and facial hair is also usually sparse. Klinefelter males are tall and slim, with long legs. The span of the outstretched arms exceeds the individual's height. Some experts report that most Klinefelter individuals are retarded, some severely, while others report a majority have a normal intellectual development. Social adjustment may be poor, in part in response to tall, eunuchoid body and gynecomastia. Personality and character trait disturbances, emotional and behavioral troubles, alcoholism, minor criminality, and outright psychosis are common, but their frequencies are not documented. This condition is also known as testicular dysgenesis. *See also* 45/XO, Turner syndrome.

klismaphilia (adj. klismaphilic) A paraphilic (*qv*) condition in which a person is dependent on being given an enema or on restaging this experience in a fantasy in order to obtain erotic arousal (*qv*) and facilitate or achieve orgasm (*qv*).

Kluge's sign A bluish coloration of the vulva (*qv*) and vaginal (*qv*) walls usually occurring during the second month of pregnancy (*qv*). Also known as Chadwick's sign. *See also* Jacquemier's sign.

Kluver-Bucy syndrome A pattern of changed behavior experimentally induced in animals by surgical removal of the amygdala (*qv*), characterized by a change from aggressiveness to docility in undomesticated monkeys, indiscriminate food choice, and bizarre changes in the regulation of sexual behavior with a loss of sexual inhibitions (*qv*). This condition was first demonstrated in the late 1930s by H. Kluver and P. C. Bucy.

Knaus method of family planning An outmoded and unreliable method of natural family planning based on abstinence (*qv*) from sexual intercourse (*qv*) for a week midway between a woman's menstrual periods (*qv*). Also known as the calendar method. *See also* Billings' contraceptive method; cervical mucus method of contraception.

knee-chest position A technique designed to remedy cryptorchidism (*qv*) or undescended testes (*qv*). The patient is seated with knees flexed on a straight-backed chair, with his feet on the seat of the chair close to the buttocks (*qv*) and the knees tight against the chest. By increasing pressure on the abdomen and inguinal canals (*qv*), this position may force the descent of the testes into the scrotum (*qv*) without resorting to surgery.

"knowing" ("knowledge") In Hebrew and the biblical tradition, *yahdah*, or "knowing," is not a euphemism for sexual intercourse (*qv*) but rather an expression suggesting that the intimacy (*qv*) of sexual intercourse involves the deepest, most complete, and intimate knowledge of the other person available to humans. The term has been adopted in legal terminology in the phrase *carnal knowledge*.

Koennicke's syndrome *See* familial hormonal disorder.

koro A culturally induced psychological disorder in which an affected male develops a morbid, obsessive fear his penis (*qv*) is shrinking and being reabsorbed and the female believes her breasts (*qv*) and labia (*qv*) are shrinking and being sucked inside her body. Occurring primarily in southern China, Malasia, and Borneo, this obsession may be associated with guilt associated with masturbation (*qv*) or promiscuity (*qv*). The affected person often calls on family members and friends to help prevent the reabsorption of the genitalia (*qv*).

Krafft-Ebing, Baron Richard von (1840–1902) A neurologist specializing in forensic psychiatry who pioneered in the detailed and comprehensive clinical study of deviant sexual behaviors. His major work, *Psychopathia Sexualis* (1886), was published despite the prevailing antisexual Victorian (*qv*) attitudes. Krafft-Ebing described and named both sadism (*qv*) and masochism (*qv*). His clinical investigations also documented that the general paralysis and other consequences of syphilis (*qv*) are due to an organism that attacks the central nervous system (*qv*). By modern standards, his work is moralizing and anti-pleasure oriented.

kraurosis penis A degenerating condition of the glans (*qv*) of the penis (*qv*) and foreskin (*qv*) associated with stenosis (*qv*) of the urethra (*qv*).

kraurosis vulvae (L.) A skin disease of older women characterized by dryness, itching, and atrophy of the external genitalia (*qv*) and a predisposition to carcinoma of the mucous membranes and vulva (*qv*).

kundalini (Skt.) In the traditions of yoga (*qv*), the kundalini represents Shakti (*qv*), the feminine aspect of the creative force, the serpent power or mystical fire in the subtle body. Yoga teachers stress a physiology in which a great vein runs from the serpent power at the lowest part of the spine to the lotus (*qv*), or the highest and most powerful psychic center. Normally latent at the lowest psychic center at the base of the spine, the kundalini endows a person with self-awareness and normal consciousness. When aroused, the kundalini can be channeled to rise through the seven chakras (*qv*) of the central channel of the Subtle Body until it merges with the eternal Shiva (*qv*) to confer freedom and immortality. By arousing the serpent power and channeling it upward, yogi hope to gain spiritual energy, cosmic consciousness, and salvation. *See also* reverse kundalini; Tantra; lotus; Tao.

L

labeling theory In the sociology of deviance (*qv*), labeling theory explains deviance as a product not of individual psychology or biological tendencies but of social control by which the group in control labels certain behaviors as deviant. Two propositions support the labeling theory. The first contends that deviant behavior is not simply deviant by its own nature or a violation of a universal social norm but is declared such because a society successfully labels or defines it as deviant. The second proposition claims that labeling a behavior as deviant causes the person who engages in that behavior to accept a self-image or self-definition of himself or herself as permanently locked in the deviant role as an outsider.

labia (s. labium) (L.) The fleshy, liplike edges of an organ or tissue. *See also* labia majora; labia minora.

labia majora (L.) Two long, liplike pads of skin, one on either side of the vaginal opening (*qv*) outside the labia minora (*qv*) and extending from the anterior labial commissure to the posterior labial commissure or fourchette. Each labium contains areolar tissue, fat, a thin layer of nonstriated muscle, and may be covered with pubic hair (*qv*). The labia majora are homologous to the male scrotum (*qv*).

labia minora (L.) Two delicate, erectile folds of skin between the labia majora (*qv*), which extend from the clitoris (*qv*) posterior on both sides of the urethral and vaginal orifices.

labioscrotal Having the shape and appearance of female labia (*qv*) that are partially fused to resemble a scrotum (*qv*) instead of being completely separated; a divided scrotum that resembles labia.

labioscrotal folds The innermost of two paired embryonic ridges on either side of the developing external genitalia (*qv*) that appear between 6 and 8 weeks of development. In the female, the folds remain separate, developing into the minor labia (*qv*). In the male, the folds fuse to form the underside of the penis (*qv*). *See also* labioscrotal swellings (*qv*).

labioscrotal fusion A consequence of abnormal androgenic (*qv*) hormone (*qv*) production in a female fetus (*qv*) before the twelfth week of gestation (*qv*) that results in fused labia resembling a scrotum (*qv*).

labiocrotal swellings The outer of two paired embryonic ridges enclosing the urogenital sinus, the labioscrotal folds (*qv*), and the developing external genitalia (*qv*) between the sixth and eighth weeks of development. In the female, the folds remain separate and develop into the labia majora (*qv*). In the male, they fuse to form the scrotum (*qv*).

labor The period and the processes during parturition (*qv*) from the beginning of cervical dilation (*qv*) through childbirth (*qv*) to the delivery of the placenta (*qv*) or afterbirth (*qv*).

lack of sexual desire *See* desire phase dysfunction; inhibited sexual desire; sexual apathy.

lactation The synthesis and secretion of milk from the female breasts (*qv*) or mammae (*qv*), usually beginning within a few days after birth (*qv*); the period of suckling or nursing (*qv*) the young until weaning (*qv*).

lactational amenorrhea The tendency for lactation (*qv*) and breast-feeding (*qv*) to suppress the monthly menstrual cycle (*qv*) and ovulation (*qv*), thereby reducing the woman's fertility (*qv*). This is not effective as a form of birth control (*qv*).

lactogenic Stimulating the production of milk from the mammary glands (*qv*).

lactogenic hormone The pituitary hormone (*qv*) that stimulates the production of milk from the mammary glands (*qv*). Also known as prolactin (*qv*).

Ladin's sign The softening of the uterine (*qv*) tissues at the junction with the cervix (*qv*) during the fifth or sixth week of gestation (*qv*).

Lamaze method of childbirth The most popular form of natural childbirth (*qv*), involving instruction on all aspects of childbirth, practice of relaxation, breathing, and muscle control exercises, and coaching during labor (*qv*) and delivery (*qv*). Frederick Lamaze, a French obstetrician (*qv*), developed this method in the 1950s after observing childbirth in Russia. This method involves a psychophysical preparation for childbirth based on the work of Pavlov and Nicolaiev with hypnosis and stimulus-response, hence its other name, psychoprophylaxis childbirth. *See also* Bradley method; Leboyer method of childbirth; Read birth method.

Lambda Legal Defense & Education Fund, Inc. A groupd founded in 1973 that pursues litigation to counter discrimination against gay men (*qv*) and lesbians (*qv*), as well as sponsoring education projects to raise public awareness of gay legal rights. Address: 666 Broadway, 12th floor, New York, NY 10012. *See also* National Gay Rights Advocates.

Laminaria (L.) A brown marine alga used as an abortifacient (*qv*). When inserted into the cervical canal (*qv*), the dried seaweed absorbs moisture, expands, and forces the uterine cervix (*qv*) to open, triggering expulsion of the fetus (*qv*).

lanugo Soft, downy hair that appears all over the developing fetus (*qv*) during the fifth or sixth month of pregnancy (*qv*), normally disappearing before birth (*qv*). Also known as vellus hair.

laparoscope A type of endoscope (*qv*), consisting of an illuminated tube with a fiber optic system, inserted through an incision in the abdominal wall, flank, or loin to allow examination of the surfaces of intestinal organs, ovaries (*qv*), and fallopian tubes (*qv*), or to allow sterilization (*qv*) of the oviducts (*qv*).

laparoscopy Examination of the abdominal organs using a laparoscope (*qv*) under a general or local anesthesia. To facilitate examination of the internal organs, carbon dioxide gas is injected into the abdominal cavity, thereby lifting the abdominal wall and allowing the internal organs to be spread for exploration. Laparoscopy is useful in the diagnosis of female infertility (*qv*), pelvic inflammatory diseases (*qv*), endometriosis (*qv*), ectopic pregnancies (*qv*), unexplained abdominal pain, and various cancers of the abdominal organs, and for female sterilization via tubal ligation or cauterization. *See also* laser laparoscopy; open laparoscopy.

laparotomy Any surgical incision into the peritoneal cavity to allow visual examination of the abdominal and pelvic organs.

lascivious Having the character of arousing sexual desire (*qv*). *See also* lewd; obscene; erotic.

lascivious cohabitation A old-fashioned legal term referring to an unmarried couple sharing the same domicile as sexual partners.

laser laparoscopy A medical procedure in which a physician uses a laparoscope (*qv*) to guide a laser in burning away uterine endometrial tissue that has become displaced into the abdominal cavity and organs. *See also* endometriosis.

latah (lattah) A disorder in which passive, submissive women unexplainably develop an extreme fear and hallucinations with a sexual content, mimic the behavior of others, and compulsively utter profanities and obscenities (*qv*). This reaction, triggered by a sudden fright, has been reported in Malaya, Thailand, the Philippines, Siberia, and the Congo but does not occur elsewhere. *See also* Tourrette syndrome.

late androgenic stimulation An abnormally high level and activity of androgens (*qv*) in a female fetus (*qv*) after the twelfth week of gestation (*qv*). The normal critical period (*qv*) for androgenic influences on the development of the genitalia (*qv*) is the eighth through twelfth weeks of gestation. After the twelfth week, formation of the vagina (*qv*), clitoris (*qv*), and labia (*qv*) is complete. However, abnormally high levels of fetal androgens (*qv*) after the critical period can cause hyperplasia (*qv*) of the clitoris (*qv*).

latency (period) In psychoanalytic theory (*qv*), a stage in psychosexual development (*qv*) alleged to last from about 6 years of age until puberty (*qv*) during which there is little interest in sexual activity (*qv*) and what little interest there is is sublimated into nonsexual behaviors and interests. Manifestations of the latency period are culturally influenced and vary greatly, being totally absent in those cultures that are positive toward sexual rehearsal play (*qv*) among prepubertal (*qv*) children. Most psychologists believe the evidence disproves the existence of a latency period.

latent homosexual A psychoanalytic term used to describe a person who may fantasize about homosexual (*qv*) relations but does not engage in such behavior. The concept of latency is used by some psychologists to explain the emergence of homosexual behavior after considerable heterosexual (*qv*) activity. A person with a latent homosexual orientation may indulge defensively in vocal homophobia (*qv*) and strong criticism of homosexuals out of anxiety over his unacknowledged same-gender orientation. More recent theory has replaced the idea of latency with a more dynamic and flexible image of sexual orientation (*qv*).

latent stage of syphilis The third phase in the developmental course of syphilis (*qv*) when skin rashes, flulike symptoms, mouth sores, and patchy balding disappear even without treatment. During this stage, the now-noncontagious bacteria attack the internal organs in one-third of untreated cases. *See also* tertiary syphilis.

Laurence-Moon-Biedle syndrome An inherited syndrome characterized by some combination of eye disorders, obesity, underdeveloped genitalia (*qv*), poor secondary sexual characteristics (*qv*), anomalies of the hands and feet, and mental retardation. Although few individuals exhibit all these symptoms, affected members within a single family may show the full range. Eye problems and sexual hypoplasia (*qv*) are the most common symptoms. Sexual effects in males include gynecomastia (*qv*), erectile dysfunction (*qv*), azoospermia (*qv*), and absence of cells of Leydig (*qv*) in the testes (*qv*). Underdeveloped breasts (*qv*), amenorrhea (*qv*), and an increased risk of miscarriage (*qv*) are common in females.

LAV *See* lymphadenopathy-associated virus; human immune deficiency virus.

lavage The process of washing out an organ for therapeutic purposes. In reproductive or infertility (*qv*) medicine, uterine lavage is used in nonsurgical collection of ova (*qv*) for *in vitro* fertilization (*qv*). *See also* embryo lavage; ovum lavage.

lawful abortion Any abortion (*qv*) that conforms to the guidelines of the 1973 *Roe v. Wade* (*qv*) decision of the U.S. Supreme Court and local state laws. According to the decision, any woman may have an abortion performed by a licensed physician for any reason in the first trimester (*qv*). Because of the increased medical risks of second-trimester abortions, states are free to restrict the circumstances of such abortions but cannot outlaw them. Abortion may still be lawful in the third trimester, even though the fetus is viable (*qv*), to save the mother's life or in cases of rape (*qv*) or incest (*qv*).

LBW *See* low birth weight.

leather fetish A paraphilic (*qv*) preoccupation with and interest in clothing made of leather, particularly jackets, pants, boots, shoes, and caps, often decorated with metal. The symbolism is one of a hypermasculinity. Leather fetishes are more common among individuals with a sadomasochistic (*qv*) or bondage and dominance (*qv*) interest.

Leboyer method of childbirth An approach to childbirth (*qv*) devised by Charles Leboyer, a French obstetrician (*qv*), that stresses (1) a gentle, controlled delivery (*qv*) in a quiet, dimly lit warm room, (2) avoidance of pulling the newborn's head, (3) avoidance of overstimulating the newborn's sensory intake, and (4) encouragement of maternal/paternal/infant bonding. *See also* Bradley method; Lamaze method of childbirth; Read birth method.

lechery (lecher) A hedonistic overindulgence in sexual pleasure and activity; *lecher* is a colloquial term for a man who expresses a frequent and socially inappropriate or undesirable sexual interest in others; lasciviousness, lewdness.

Leeuwenhoek, Anton van (1632–1723) Owner of a drapery shop and lifetime janitor at the Delft City Hall whose hobby led him to improve the primitive microscopes of the time. Using lenses he ground himself, he was able to study and describe accurately for the first time a variety of animal and plant tissues.

His work produced the first description and illustration of spermatozoa (*qv*) and a contribution to the refutation of the theory of spontaneous generation.

legal codes The division of legal responsibilities to cover specific areas of human behavior. Criminal, civil, and family codes are central to the system of jurisdiction in the United States and most Western countries.

legal jurisdictions The division of legal responsibilities to specific authorities or jurisdictions within a society. In the United States, the *federal jurisdiction* includes all American citizens, the *military jurisdiction* includes only military personnel, and *state* and *local jurisdictions* include all persons within the appropriate territory.

lek A mating ground or territory staked out by a male who then waits for prospective females to arrive and select a mate. *See also* lekking.

lekking Courtship (*qv*) behavior in which male antelopes assemble on a mating ground, or lek (*qv*), at the beginning of the mating (*qv*) season and wait for the females to arrive. Although the females bypass some males, the males left out do not resort to fighting their successful rivals. Lekking is also common among some birds. *See also* proceptive phase; flirtation pattern.

Leriche syndrome A blood-clotting obstruction of the terminal aorta. This results in oxygen deprivation of the lower extremities with consequent fatigue in the hips, thighs, and calves when exercising and, for males, in the loss of erectile (*qv*) capacity.

lesbian "A woman whose primary erotic, psychological, emotional and social interest is in a member of her own sex, even though that interest may not be overtly expressed" (Del Martin and Phyllis Lyon, cofounders of the Daughters of Bilitis [*qv*]). Like other definitions developed by lesbian and feminist (*qv*) thinkers, the Martin and Lyon definition transcends clinically oriented descriptions of a lesbian as a "female homosexual" (*qv*), in which sexuality is in the fore above other matters and in which a woman is labelled in a part-for-whole manner (*see* discussion under homosexuality). Currently, many lesbian and feminist writers and speakers would insist that a lesbian is involved not merely with one woman, as the Martin and Lyon definition seems to suggest, but with all women, and has identified fully with all women. Some writers speak of a "woman-identified" lesbian—defining the woman by what she is, whereas other writers stress the rejection of social, emotional, and sexual contact with men as crucial for defining "lesbian"—defining her by what she is not. Feminist theologian Mary Daly uses both criteria to contend that only women-identified women who have rejected false loyalties to men are lesbians; all other women are female homosexuals or heterosexuals (*qv*).

The term itself comes from the Aegean island of Lesbos where Sappho, a great poet of ancient Greece, lived (ca. 600 B.C.E.). Her love poetry to women has been interpreted as indicating her commitment to a panhistoric, universal "lesbian" life-style that is believed by some lesbian writers to unify all women; hence, the occasional use of "Sapphist" as a synonym for lesbian.

Nonetheless, because the terms lesbian and Sapphist both refer specifically to portions of Western history, they can be considered ethnocentric. However, no general and non-ethnocentric term has arisen in common English usage to replace lesbian, and few speakers will try to use non-English terms to describe non-Western women whose primary affiliations are with women and not with men. *See also* feminism; lesbianism; women; wimmin; womon; womyn. Resource: C. Kramarae and P. A. Treichler, *A Feminist Dictionary* (London: Pandora, 1985).

lesbianism The status or fact of being a lesbian (*qv*); a commitment to lesbian political, social, and feminist (*qv*) goals. For many modern lesbian feminists, lesbianism is a political and cultural movement and position that rejects sexual, social, and definitional submission to male-centered needs, systems, and frameworks in order for women to become independent of phallocentric culture (*qv*) and patriarchal power (*see* patriarchy). Rita Mae Brown, author of *Ruby Fruit Jungle*, maintains that lesbianism means that one forgets the male power system and gives women primacy in one's life—emotionally, personally, and politically. In this and other feminist definitions, matters of sexual preference are not placed in the fore, as they are in clinical definitions which describe a condition or set of behavior patterns entailing woman-woman sexual activity. A wide variety of definitions, commentary, and descriptions of lesbianism have been developed by feminists and lesbians as part of recent activism and efforts to reject phallocentric power. No single definition has gained wide acceptance, nor should it given the broad usage- and meaning-based criteria adopted; *see* J. Johnson, *Lesbian Nation: The Feminist Solution* (New York: Simon and Schuster, 1973); C. Kramarae and P. A. Treichler, *A Feminist Dictionary* (London: Pandora, 1985). Indeed, feminist lexicographers might argue that the ideal of a single "true" definition is itself a phallocentric notion, incompatible with the diversity and variation of women's involvement with other women. Even so, the central core of meaning of lesbianism today appears to be that of autonomy, independence, and self-definition of women's sexual and social lives, combined with a social and philosophical focus on the community of women. *See also* lesbian separatism.

lesbian separatism A central philosophical and pragmatic component of certain, though not all, radical/lesbian feminist (*qv*) viewpoints, "lesbian separatism" seeks to repudiate and reject male or patriarchal culture (*see* patriarchy) in order to uncover and realize a fully autonomous, women-centered culture, history, and society. This term is not defined merely in negatives, as a rejection of the sexist (*see* sexism) and sexual society of men, for then institutions feminists consider as prototypically patriarchal, such as the convent or the nunnery, would qualify. Instead, the emphasis of lesbian separatism is to create a community of women independent of phallocentric (*see* phallocentrism) and patriarchal needs, systems, and institutional frameworks.

lesbophobia The fear of lesbians (*qv*), as homophobia (*qv*) is a fear of gay (*qv*) men.

lesophobia A fear of strong women.

lethal factor A naturally produced chemical within the vaginal (*qv*) environment of some women that immobilizes sperm (*qv*). The term has other meanings in genetics and chemistry.

leukoplakia Thick, slightly raised, white patches found on the oral mucosa; the term is no longer applied to similar premalignant patches found on the skin, especially the penis (*qv*) or vulva (*qv*).

leukorrhea A whitish viscous vaginal discharge (*qv*) frequently caused by a fungal infection, by oversecretion of the cervix (*qv*) during pregnancy (*qv*), or by hormone (*qv*) changes in the uterus (*qv*) or cervix early in gestation (*qv*). *See also* candida albicans.

Leuwenhoek, Anton van *See* Leeuwenhoek, Anton van.

levirate law A custom of the early Jewish people requiring that the younger brother of a man who married and died without offspring marry the widow and conceive a son by the widow so that he can then inherit the deceased older brother's name and property. The term *levirate* is derived from the injunctions of Moses (Deut. 25:5–10). A broader type of levirate custom is common in Polynesia and most of the rest of the nonindustrial world where a younger brother is allowed to have extramarital sexual intercourse (*qv*) with the wife of an older brother. *See also* Onanism.

Leviticus The third book of the Pentateuch in the Jewish sacred texts, traditionally ascribed to the authorship of Moses, Leviticus records the detailed laws, prescriptions, and ritual and social taboos (*qv*) received by Moses from Yahweh. Leviticus is the probable source of many menstrual (*qv*) and sexual taboos common in Western civilization.

lewd (lewdness) A generally derogatory term for arousing sexual desire; concerning sexuality presented in an offensive way; a legal term that may include prostitution (*qv*), fornication (*qv*), exhibitionism (*qv*), and other sexual activities. *See also* obscene; lust; chaste; debauchery; lascivious.

Leydig cells The cells located outside the seminiferous tubules (*qv*) but within the testes (*qv*) proper that secrete testosterone (*qv*) and some estrogenic (*qv*) hormones. The cells of Leydig are named for Franz von Leydig, the German histologist who first described them. Also known as interstitial cells. *See also* interstitial cell-stimulating hormone (ICSH).

Leydig cell tumor A usually benign hyperplasia (*qv*) of the testicular interstitial cells or Leydig cells (*qv*) that can cause premature puberty (*qv*) or, after puberty, gynecomastia (*qv*).

LH *See* luteinizing hormone.

LHRH *See* luteinizing hormone-releasing hormone; gonadotropin-releasing hormone.

liaison An illicit premarital (*qv*) or extramarital (*qv*) relationship, lacking in civil or religious recognition.

libertine An obsolete term for a hedonistic (*qv*) person who indulges in illicit and promiscuous (*qv*) sexual relations (*qv*). *See also* Casanova; Don Juan.

libidinal development A synonym for psychosexual development (*qv*). In psychoanalytic theory (*qv*), the growth of the libido (*qv*) and the differentiation of the self through the oral (*qv*), anal (*qv*), phallic (*qv*), latent (*qv*), and genital stages (*qv*).

libidinalization *See* erotization.

libidinal types Sigmund Freud's (*qv*) tripartite classification of personalities based on the prevailing focus of libidinal (*qv*) or sexual energy. In the narcissistic (*qv*) personality, the libido (*qv*) is centered in the ego (*qv*), and the principal interest is in self-love and personal gratification. In the obsessional personality, the libido is invested primarily in the superego (*qv*) and the moral imperatives of the conscience. In the erotic personality, the libido remains concentrated in the id (*qv*), and the individual focuses on loving interpersonal relations.

libido The subjectively experienced and self-reported sexual drive (*qv*) or urge; the primary, possibly instinctual, seeking of erotosexual (*qv*) gratification activated by testosterone. Although libido is considered by psychoanalysts to be innate, the behaviors that allow for gratification of this need are learned. On average the erotosexual impulse peaks in the late teens for males and in the thirties for most women. Generally, libido may taper off with the later years, but it may remain alive and strong as long as life lasts. Lack of sexual desire (*qv*), a hypophilic (*qv*) condition, may be psychological in origin or organic as the result of a low testosterone level or a medication that blocks the action of testosterone in activating libido. In psychoanalytic theory (*qv*), libido is the positive life force or psychic energy of Eros (*qv*) as contrasted with the aggressive, self-destructive death force of Thanatos. In Jungian theory, libido is a general life force that expresses itself in all types of activities. *See also* dammed-up libido; genital libido; oral libido; summa libido.

In the higher primates and humans where a menstrual cycle (*qv*) occurs, a woman's libido may exhibit some monthly fluctuation, but such effects are highly variable. Nevertheless, the hormones (*qv*) of the menstrual cycle make the human female receptive to intercourse (*qv*) any time, whereas female estrous (*qv*) mammals are sexually receptive only at the time of estrus (*qv*) and ovulation.

libido analog A libidinal substitute; an object that represents the life force of libido (*qv*); in personal sexual behavior, a fetish (*qv*). An example of a public libido analog is the use of the lingam (*qv*) and yoni (*qv*) in Hindu rituals.

licentiousness Unrestrained, promiscuous (*qv*) sexual activity (*qv*). *See also* hedonism; lewdness; lust.

lichenification A condition of thickened, leathery skin around the genitals resulting from inflammation due to excessive scratching, rubbing, or irritation.

lichen planus A nonmalignant, chronic skin disease of unknown cause, characterized by small, flaky, very itchy plaques. The condition may appear anywhere on the penis (*qv*) or scrotum (*qv*), where the lesions last a month or two before disappearing and reappearing elsewhere, on the wrists and mouth. After several more months, the plaques disappear, even without treatment. On mucous membranes, the lesions are gray and lacy. On other tissues, they are purplish. Steroid creams can relieve the itching.

life force A mystical or metaphysical concept in which life is seen as having characteristics and features not fully inherent in molecules and matter of which living organisms are composed; also called vital force. Metaphorically, life force can refer to the enthusiasm and vigor of individuals or societies that appear to have zest and creativity. Also metaphorically, the life force can be seen as the urge, thought immanent in all life, toward creating and realizing more life. Accordingly, for modern thinkers like Wilhelm Reich (*qv*), the life force is the essentially sexual source of energy that pervades the universe and, as the orgone (*see* orgone energy), is the ultimate source of all vitality, health, and sensual-sexual completeness. For others, for example, George Bernard Shaw, the life force is essentially a feminine principle in the universe that can seize a man and elevate him toward panhistoric consciousness of his role as a catalyst in the realization of new life. *See also* libido.

life instinct In psychoanalytic theory (*qv*), the equivalent of eros (*qv*), the tendency to preserve and reproduce the self. *See also* instinct; thanatos.

life-only standard A legal term describing laws that prohibit the use of public funds for any abortions (*qv*) except those where the pregnancy (*qv*) directly threatens the life of the mother. *See also* abortion on demand; British Abortion Act of 1963; Roe v. Wade.

Likert scale A type of attitude scale (*qv*) on which a subject is asked to indicate his or her degree of agreement or disagreement with specific statements of attitudes. A three-point scale contains "Agree," "Uncertain," "Disagree"; a five-point scale ranges from "Agree strongly," "Agree," "Uncertain," "Disagree," to "Disagree strongly."

limbic system A portion of the brain that governs emotions such as fear, rage, pleasure, anger, and sexual arousal. Structurally, it consists of portions of the cerebrum (*qv*), thalamus (*qv*), hypothalamus (*qv*), amygdala (*qv*), hippocampus (*qv*), preoptic area, and paraolfactory area. Although all stimuli reach the limbic system, sensations of smell have the most pronounced effect on memory, particularly when associated with sexual activity (*qv*), punishment, or pleasure. The system also influences such diverse activities as defensive behavior, libido, motor activities, ovulation (*qv*), and regulation of the autonomic nervous system (*qv*). *See also* paleocortex.

limerence (adj. limerent) This easily misspelled word was coined by Dorothy Tennov to refer to the unique and often extremely unpleasant combination of love, attraction, lust, anxiety, depression, and elation that sometimes accompanies sexuoerotic (*qv*) interest in another person; in older English, a synonym is love sickness (*qv*). Limerence is not sexual frustration, but instead is an all-encompassing emotional state in which one is completely preoccupied by the other person's every act and statement and oblivious to most other concerns. The preoccupation seems obsessive to the limerent individual, and is felt as being beyond conscious control.

In the United States and Western culture generally, limerence is often considered a normal and inevitable consequence of sexual attraction (*qv*), but it is not. Instead, limerence arises as a combination of sexuoerotic attraction plus unclear or paradoxical communication in which the desired partner sends messages that *might* mean that interest *might* be reciprocated. It is the uncertainty of the response, not the sexuoerotic attraction itself, that generates limerence. Limerence only rarely cures itself, although a folk saying implies that time is the best doctor. It can, and perhaps often should, be treated psychotherapeutically, because a limerent individual may be crippled emotionally by a pattern of repeated anxiety, preoccupation bordering on obsession, and depression alternating with elation. It can also be treated if a professionally trained third party can bring the two individuals together in order to clarify the nature of their miscommunication. It then sometimes turns out that the individual who has stimulated the limerence is well aware of it and enjoys the seeming power that it gives him or her over the other person. Alternatively, the limerent individual may decide to withdraw from the entire situation—the colloquial expression being "to cut bait." This is often advisable if limerence is prolonged past several months and communication remains cloudy and unclear.

Historically and culturally, limerence is akin to the romantic notion of an all-powerful emotional "elective affinity," such as gripped Werther in Johann Wolfgang Goethe's *The Sorrows of Young Werther* or as was described in W. Somerset Maugham's novel *Of Human Bondage*. Many folksongs, especially the blues, deal with limerence, as does a great deal of modern rock music of the "she done left me" variety. Shakespeare nearly never described limerence past the point of transient anxiety in the earliest stages of love, implying that limerence is a culturally and historically influenced phenomenon. Romeo and Juliet are not limerent but rather are "in love," since each knows with complete certainty that the feelings of love and sexual desire are mutual and reciprocated. Their tragedy is therefore not internal but external, in the prohibition of their marriage. By contrast, in Margaret Mitchell's *Gone with the Wind*, Scarlett O'Hara is limerent over Ashley Wilkes.

Limerence, however, is not by any means a recent phenomenon. Hippocrates, the ancient Greek physician and "father of medicine," described limerence, pointing out that it is usually an affliction of the young, both male and female. He observed the pallor, lack of appetite, and depression associated with limerence, and commented that the physician can distinguish it from similar afflictions by taking the victim's pulse while simultaneously mentioning the loved one's name.

Full-blown limerence almost never develops if the two individuals are mutually attracted to each other, but only when the interest is one-sided and communication is opaque. For this experience, common English speaks of "unrequited love," a condition known to its victims as peculiarly unpleasant. The physiological sequellae of limerence suggest that it has, in part, a physiological basis, a proposition that obtains some support from the fact that limerence is described in ancient Egyptian love poetry and is therefore not solely nor purely the result of a recent emergence of romantic ideals of love or their existence in romantically minded individuals of Hippocrates' Greece.

Curiously, some individuals rarely or never experience limerence, regardless of occasional one-sided romances. Such people move on to another romance quickly when their interest is not reciprocated. However, other individuals appear limerence-prone and cannot imagine any other way of being in love. In addition, some men and women are able to inspire rapid and intense limerence in other people while others only rarely inspire it.

Resources: M. V. Fox, *The Song of Songs and the Ancient Egyptian Love Songs* (Madison: University of Wisconsin Press, 1985); John Money, *Love and*

Love Sickness (Baltimore: Johns Hopkins University Press, 1980); T. Perper, *Sex Signals: The Biology of Love* (Philadelphia: ISI Press, 1985); D. Tennov, *Love and Limerence: The Experience of Being in Love* (New York: Stein and Day, 1979).

liminal (liminality) According to anthropologist Victor Turner, a liminal period is a socially defined time when an individual is in transition from one socially defined status to another. The term is derived from the Latin *limen* for "threshold." Thus, a boy who is being trained for his initiation rites (*qv*) into manhood is no longer a boy and not yet a man. He is "betwixt and between": liminal, or in a liminal state. Cross-culturally, liminal periods and states typically culminate in rites and rituals that celebrate the transition from the prior state to the new state and officially mark its social occurrence.

An important example from modern America is the courtship-wedding-honeymoon period, in which the couple has left the single state but have not yet established their household as a couple. The feasting, dancing, and celebration of the wedding are typical of ceremonials that mark liminal states and transitions. Also characteristic of the closure of the liminal transition of the wedding is the custom of the husband carrying the bride across the threshold of their new home. Rites of reversal also exist in which the usual rules of social behavior are reversed, as in the Carnival and Mardi Gras. *See also* communitas. Resources: T. Perper, *Sex Signals: The Biology of Love* (Philadelphia: ISI Press, 1985); V. Turner, *The Ritual Process: Structure and Anti-Structure* (Ithaca, NY: Cornell University Press, 1969), pp. 94–130.

lineage A descent group in which ancestry can actually be traced through specific, known persons to a common ancestor. In a large clan (*qv*), a common ancestry is claimed, but usually the common ancestor is so remote clan members cannot trace their descent back to the clan's founder through intermediate ancestors over hundreds of years. *See also* descent group; kindred.

linea nigra (L.) A dark, pigmented line in the abdominal skin extending from the umbilicus (*qv*) to the mons veneris (*qv*) that appears in some women following pregnancy (*qv*).

lingam A stylized sculpture symbolic of the Hindu god Lord Shiva and the penis (*qv*), often used in Hindu phallic worship. Miniature lingams are worn as sexual amulets to promote male potency. Lingam is the Sanskrit word for penis. *See also* yoni.

lingam ring An early sexual aid, popular in the Hindu and Chinese cultures; an ivory, jade, or metal ring that fits around the base of the erect penis (*qv*) during intercourse (*qv*) in such a way that it provides clitoral stimulation.

linkage, social The ways in which one part of a society is connected with another part, such as the interconnection between the differential social power of males and females in society and the masculine and feminine roles and customs endorsed by that society.

lipoid hyperplasia An endocrine (*qv*) disorder involving lack of the enzymes that convert cholesterol (*qv*) into androgens (*qv*) and estrogens (*qv*), resulting in excess fatty tissue.

lipoma, vulvar A nonmalignant, fatty tumor that develops usually on one side of the vulva (*qv*), under the labia (*qv*).

Lippes loop A nonchemical intrauterine device (*qv*), available in several sizes, developed by Jack Lippes, but withdrawn from sale in the United States in 1987.

lips, inner, outer, or vulvar *See* labia minora; labia majora; vulva.

lips of the vulva *See* labia minora; labia majora.

lithopedion Medical term for a calcified fetus (*qv*), usually found outside the uterus (*qv*).

lithotomy position A patient posture sometimes used in some types of gynecological (*qv*) and prostate (*qv*) examinations, in which the patient lies on the back with the hips and knees flexed and the knees separated.

Littre's glands (Fr.) Several small mucous glands opening into the urethra (*qv*) of both males and females.

live birth The delivery (*qv*) of an infant that exhibits any sign of life, irrespective of gestational age (*qv*) and regardless of whether it survives the neonatal period (*qv*).

living together Cohabitation (*qv*), usually with the implication that the couple living together are sexually intimate (*qv*). *See also* trial marriage; lascivious cohabitation; comarital relations; satellite relations; sexually open marriage.

LMP Abbreviation for "last menstrual period" (*qv*), commonly used in medical records.

lochia A discharge from the uterus (*qv*) and vagina (*qv*), that occurs naturally during the first few weeks after childbirth (*qv*). For the first three or four days, the discharge, known as a *lochia cruenta*, is made up of blood, endometrial decidua (*qv*), and fetal lanugo (*qv*). As the blood content diminishes and the placenta (*qv*) exudes serous material and lymph, the darker and thinner discharge is known as a *lochia serosa*. By the third week after delivery, the discharge has become mucoid and gray-white in color and is known as a *lochia alba*. The lochia ceases about six weeks after delivery.

locomotor ataxia *See* tabes dorsalis.

longitudinal research (study) Research that compares the same population or subjects, called a panel, at different periods in their life span or development.

lordosis In certain quadrupedal mammals, for example, rodents, when a male mounts a female in estrus (*qv*), the female arches her back sharply downward, thus lifting her haunches and exposing the genitalia (*qv*) for intromission; the back arch is lordosis. Medically, lordosis can also refer in humans to an exaggerated lumbar curve in the spinal column in both men and women; it is not a sexual behavior pattern. *See also* acceptive stage, proceptivity.

loss of consortium A legal term for compensation damages paid for the loss of conjugal (*qv*) relations. A claim for loss of consortium may be in response to the impairment or loss of the ability to engage in sexual relations (*qv*) resulting from medical treatment or as the consequence of a wrongful injury incurred in an accident or deliberate assault. Loss of consortium may also be claimed from a third party whose activities or relationship with the spouse resulted in the alienation of affections leading to conjugal separation (*qv*) or divorce (*qv*).

lotus In the traditions of yoga (*qv*), the lotus represents the highest and most powerful psychic center; *lotus flower* is a Tantric (*qv*) term for the female sexual organs (*qv*) or vulva (*qv*). Yoga teachers stress a physiology in which a great vein runs from the lowest part of the spine, where serpent power, the kundalini (*qv*), rests, to the lotus, or the highest and most powerful psychic center. By arousing the serpent power, the yogi hopes to gain spiritual energy and salvation when the kundalini is united with the highest lotus.

love (v. to love) The personal experience and manifest expression of being attached, committed, and bonded to another person, group of persons (e.g., one's kin), or an ideal. The *Oxford English Dictionary* gives four pages of definitions of the word, the first of which is "that disposition or state of feeling with regard to a person which (arising from recognition of attractive qualities, from instincts of natural relationship, or from sympathy) manifests itself in solicitude for the welfare of the object and usually also in delight in his presence and desire for his approval; warm affection, attachment."

Today, scholars would not say that the love for one's family is an instinct based on natural relationships, nor would we use the pronouns "he" and "she" in this definition. Nonetheless, the *Oxford English Dictionary*'s definition contains the essential elements for defining the word love: strong feeling; an attachment arising from the qualities of the person, persons, or ideal to whom one is attached; and a desire to affiliate oneself with the loved one. From this sense, which implies that the essence of love is to connect or relate to someone or something external to oneself, there arise the many meanings of the word found in phrases like "love of country," "love of God," "mother love," and "male-female love," among many others.

In its sense of tender and passionate desire for someone else, love refers at least implicitly to sexuality (*qv*), and this sense seems never to have been lost in the many changes of meaning of the word. Philosophers and historians argue that the modern Western sense of love as an all-encompassing emotion pertaining specifically to a bonded couple is of recent historical origin, and certainly chivalric or courtly love (*qv*) did not include modern ideals of a consumated love between man and woman or husband and wife. Today, however, the word love does evoke a sense of deep bonding, consumated ideally by sexual and loving union. At the same time, Western culture is ambivalent and radically uncomfortable about the union of love above and below the belt, in other words; of spiritual love and lusty love; *see* lust.

The word love derives from Old English *lufu*, which has the general sense of "holding dear or desirable." Etymologically, this meaning is perhaps at the root of all other meanings of the word.

The Feminist Dictionary cites several aspects not usually found in typical dictionaries: "a deep personal experience no longer considered the viable foundation for a woman's existence"; "to be cared for, thought of and valued, not abstractly, as men often value women, but in the accumulation of daily minutiae that make life dense and intricate and worthy." Radical feminist Andrea Dworkin defines romantic love as the "mythic celebration of female negation . . . . For the women, the capacity to love is exactly synonymous with the capacity to sustain abuse and the appetite for it . . . . For the woman, love is always self-sacrifice, the sacrifice of identity, will and bodily integrity, in order to fulfill and redeem the masculinity of her lover." Resource: C. Kramarae & P. A. Treichler, *A Feminist Dictionay* (London: Pandora Press, 1985).

The exact specifications needed for a feeling of commitment and bonding to qualify as love vary in different cultures. In contemporary Western cultures, love involves three aspects—commitment, passion, and intimacy—in varying proportions. Various forms of love have been described, endorsed, and feared over the centuries. These distinctions have included: sacred and profane love, platonic (*qv*) or affectional love as in a friendship, eros (*qv*) or erotic desire/sexual love, familial love, filial love, parental love, marital love, romantic love (*qv*), person-to-person amor (*qv*), courtly love (*qv*), and spiritual love or agape (*qv*). The term is also used as a synonym for *like*.

According to Shakespeare, "Love is not love which alters when it alteration finds." For Rilke, "Love consists in this: that two solitudes protect and touch and greet each other."

See also eroticism; free love; hunger and love; limerence; love affair; lovemap; love child; love needs; love object; love play; lover; love sickness; pregenital love; productive love; romance; transference love.

Resources: B. Ehrenreich, E. Hess, and G. Jacobs, *Re-Making Love: The Feminization of Sex* (Garden City, NY: Doubleday Anchor, 1986); M. M. Hunt, *The Natural History of Love* (New York: Minerva Press, 1967); B. I. Murstein, *Love, Sex, and Marriage through the Ages* (New York: Springer, 1974); T. Perper, *Sex Signals: The Biology of Love* (Philadelphia: iSi Press, 1985); I. Singer, *The Nature of Love*, vols. 1–3 (Chicago: University of Chicago Press, 1984, 1984, 1987); D. Tennov, *Love and Limerence: The Experience of Being in Love* (New York: Stein and Day, 1979).

love affair A short- or long-term romantic relationship that usually involves sexual activity (*qv*), although in some love affairs emotional intimacy may be the primary motivation and sexual intimacies avoided. *See also* affair; extramarital relations; satellite relations; intimate friendship; polyfidelity.

love at first sight A strong and immediate reaction to another person in a totally engrossing attraction or infatuation. *See also* limerence; ideal lover template; lovemap.

loveblot A person or image who resembles the person or image in someone's lovemap (*qv*) sufficiently to become the recipient in a limerent (*qv*) love affair. The term *loveblot* is used in reference to a Rorschach inkblot. While most people fall in love with a partner who matches their lovemap fairly closely, others project their idealized and highly idiosyncratic lovemap onto a person who does not match that lovemap. In this case, the lover falls in love with the loveblot rather than with the person, much as a person projects meaning onto a Rorschach inkblot. Resource: J. Money, *Lovemaps* (New York: Irvington, 1986).

love child A dated colloquial term for an illegitimate (*qv*) or natural child (*qv*); also refers to adolescents and young adults of the 1960s whose credo was "make love, not war."

lovemaking A euphemism for sexual intercourse (*qv*); any activity between individuals that involves sexual pleasure and/or satisfaction. In nineteenth-century American and Victorian England, lovemaking referred to courtship (*qv*) customs.

lovemap A personalized, developmental template or representation in the mind and brain depicting an idealized lover (*qv*) and the idealized program of sexuoerotic activity (*qv*). A lovemap may be projected and enjoyed in fantasy or actually engaged in with that lover. A lovemap is said to be normophilic (*qv*) if it falls within the range of what the community or authorities say is statistically normal (*qv*). The uniquely personalized character of each lovemap is the result of some prenatal phylogenetic programming overlaid by each individual's post-natal idiosyncratic combination of sexual and erotic scripting (*qv*). Thus, what one person finds a strong sexual attraction is not for another person. The gender aspect of the neurological template appears to be laid down before birth as a prenatal part of gender identity/role (*qv*) and one's sexual orientation (*qv*), al-though it is elaborated on by a variety of social factors after birth. *See also* paraphilia; vandalized lovemap; loveblot. Resource: J. Money, *Lovemaps* (New York: Irvington, 1986).

lovemap displacement The process whereby a normal lovemap (*qv*) is changed into a paraphilic (*qv*) lovemap when an element that is intrinsic in courtship (*qv*) and loveplay (*qv*) becomes dislocated from its normal place, repositioned and exaggerated. The element of voyeurism (*qv*) or exhibitionism (*qv*) that plays a normal, healthy role in courtship and loveplay can be exaggerated to the point where it, rather than intercourse (*qv*) and orgasm (*qv*), becomes the focus of sexual arousal and satisfaction. *See also* lovemap inclusion. Resource: J. Money, *Lovemaps* (New York: Irvington, 1986).

lovemap inclusion The process whereby a normal lovemap (*qv*) is changed into a paraphilic (*qv*) lovemap when some element extraneous to courtship (*qv*) and loveplay (*qv*) becomes incorporated into a developing lovemap. Enemas, spank-ing, and fetishes (*qv*) are typical extraneous elements that are incorporated into paraphilic lovemaps that create a dependence on the element for sexual arousal and satisfaction. Resource: J. Money, *Lovemaps* (New York: Irvington, 1986).

love needs A general term applied by Abraham Maslow (*qv*) in his hierarchy of needs theory to those needs for emotional support, affection, respect, accep-tance, affiliation, and belonging that come into play after the basic survival and physiological needs and security-safety needs are met. *See also* needs hierarchy.

love object In psychoanalytic (*qv*) terminology, the person toward whom one directs and in whom one invests libido (*qv*) or sexual energy (*qv*); the person who is the object of one's affection, romantic interests and sexual desire. *See also* limerence; lovemap.

loveplay An inclusive term covering all sexuoerotic (*qv*) activities from the least intimate first stages of flirtation (*qv*) to the full sexual intimacies and varieties of mutual autoeroticism (*qv*), oral (*qv*), anal (*qv*), and coital (*qv*) activities; any mutually shared activity that leads, more or less, to sexual pleasure and grati-fication. Loveplay is a recent alternate term for the more traditional term *foreplay* (*qv*), kissing (*qv*) of all types, and touches and caresses of the erogenous (*qv*) parts of the body and genitalia (*qv*). Some prefer the term *loveplay* because it does not imply the performance pressure of an overriding goal of intercourse (*qv*) and orgasm (*qv*) for all erotosexual activities. *See also* proceptive phase; outercourse.

love powder *See* aphrodisiac.

lover A man or woman who is romantically and sexually involved with another person who is not his or her spouse; also applied to the same-gender partner of a homosexual (*qv*) male or lesbian (*qv*). *See also* limerence.

love sickness The personal and painfully traumatic emotions experienced when the partner with whom one has fallen in love or is limerent (*qv*) responds unsatisfactorily or with indifference.

low birth weight (LBW) A newborn infant (*qv*) that weighs less than 2,500 grams (5 pounds, 8 ounces). Contributing factors may include premature birth (*qv*), a lack of proper maternal nutrition during pregnancy (*qv*), and use of alcohol or drugs by the pregnant woman. *See also* fetal alcohol syndrome.

low sex ratio A society in which females outnumber males, particularly in the 20- to 30-year-old age group. When females outnumber males, the society tends to grant more equality of the genders (*qv*), allow for more sexual freedom, and accept life-style options for women that are not limited to marriage (*qv*) and child rearing. *See also* high sex ratio; Marital Opportunity Ratio; marriage squeeze. Resource: M. Guttentag & P. Secord, *Too Many Women? The Sex Ratio Question* (Beverly Hills: Sage, 1983).

LRF *See* luteinizing hormone releasing factor.

LRH Luteining releasing hormone. *See also* luteinizing hormone releasing factor; gonadotropin-releasing hormone.

LTH *See* luteotropic hormone.

lubricant The naturally produced slippery fluid that passes from blood vessels in the vaginal (*qv*) walls between the vaginal wall cells and into the vaginal cavity during sexual arousal (*qv*). In males, the secretions produced by Cowper's glands (*qv*) during sexual arousal and prior to ejaculation (*qv*). A water-soluble commercial cream or jelly may be use as a substitute for the natural vaginal lubricant is used to facilitate intercourse (*qv*) when natural vaginal sweating (*qv*) is not sufficient. *See also* transudate.

lues (L.) The Latin term for a plague or discharge, a common medical synonym for syphilis (*qv*).

luetin A extract of a killed culture of *Treponema pallidum* (*qv*), the causative agent for syphilis (*qv*), used in the Noguchi reaction (*qv*) skin test for syphilis.

lumpectomy A surgical procedure in which a noninvasive malignant growth in the breast (*qv*) and surrounding tissue are removed, leaving the rest of the breast intact. Recent studies comparing the long-term outcome of lumpectomy and radiotherapy with other more invasive forms of mastectomy (*qv*) show no real advantage for the more radical surgeries when dealing with stage 1 malignancies. Often lumpectomies are combined with chemotherapy, particularly when malignant cells are found in regional lymph nodes.

lupae (L.) An obsolete Latin term for prostitutes (*qv*), derived from their custom in ancient Rome of attracting customers with wolf calls.

lust A strong sexual desire (*qv*), especially when it is considered excessive, illicit, or improper; by extension, any strongly felt need or desire. Standard dictionary definitions often described lust as unrestrained, uncontrolled or uncontrollable, sinful, and degraded or degrading. However, each of these terms fails to characterize lust because none of them points to the standard(s) by which sexual feelings can be evaluated as too strong, too excessive, or too great. However, in its pejorative usage, lust implicitly refers to belief and value systems in which sexuality (*qv*) should and must be restrained lest it otherwise destroy a person's sanity or a society's integrity. Accordingly, the word records a fear of sex as personally and socially dangerous. In a second set of related meanings, lust refers to sexual activities that offend against decency. Here, too, usage points to socially accepted standards and rules against which one can offend. However, when such standards are changing, or when a variety of standards exist, as they do in a culturally pluralistic society, the word lust has no single or even particularly clear group of meanings outside the sense of sexuality gone too far in seizing control where the speaker believes it ought not to do so.

To counter the traditional distinction between spiritual love and decadent lust, and to rescue the word from its anti-sexual milieu of love above and lust below the belt, some use the word to mean a healthy and desirable intensity of feeling for another person or ideal, as in "a lust for truth." These efforts are designed to affirm what is seen as a human right to enthusiasm, dynamism, eagerness, and passion in personal and sexual relationships. *Lusty* means virgorous and enthusiastic, and lacks much of the pejorative sense of *lust*. *See also* agape; chastity; concupiscence; lewd; love. Resource: C. Kramarae and P. A. Treichler, *A Feminist Dictionary* (London: Pandora Press, 1985).

lust dynamism Harry Stack Sullivan's term for an active, powerful sex drive (*qv*). Resource: H. S. Sullivan, *Interpersonal Theory of Psychiatry* (New York: Norton, 1953).

lust murder Homocidophilia (*qv*), a rare paraphilic (*qv*) condition in which a person is dependent on sadistic (*qv*) homicide of the partner, or on restaging this in fantasy, in order to achieve sexual arousal (*qv*) and orgasm (*qv*). Coitus (*qv*) with the victim is usually not part of the lust murder; rather orgasm is the outcome of the mutilation and murder of the victim. The converse condition is the staging of one's own murder, or autoassassinatophilia (*qv*). *See also* snuff film.

luteal Of or pertaining to the corpus luteum (*qv*)—its functions or effects.

luteal phase The second half of the menstrual cycle (*qv*), following ovulation (*qv*) and lasting 14 days, during which the corpus luteum (*qv*) is stimulated by luteinizing hormone (*qv*) to produce progesterone (*qv*) and small amounts of estrogen (*qv*). Progesterone causes the uterine endometrium (*qv*) to move from the proliferative to the secretory state and become a rich, dense wall suitable for implantation (*qv*) of the fertilized ovum (*qv*). If implantation (*qv*) does not occur, progesterone secretion slowly declines until menstruation (*qv*) begins 14 days after ovulation. *See also* follicular phase; menses.

luteinizing hormone (LH) A gonadotropic (*qv*) glycoprotein hormone secreted by the anterior lobe of the pituitary (*qv*). In females, LH works with follicle-stimulating hormone (*qv*) to stimulate secretion of estrogens (*qv*) in the maturing follicle (*qv*). High estrogen concentrations then stimulate a surge of LH, which triggers ovulation (*qv*), after which LH stimulates conversion of the follicle to a corpus luteum (*qv*), which secretes estrogens and progesterone (*qv*). High levels of progesterone inhibit the production of LH in a negative feedback (*qv*). If the ovum (*qv*) is not fertilized, the level of LH declines in the second week after ovulation until the end of the menstrual flow (*qv*), when its secretion again increases.

In males, where LH is known as interstitial cell-stimulating hormone (*qv*), LH stimulates testosterone (*qv*) production in the interstitial cells (*qv*) of the testes (*qv*). Testosterone then works with follicle-stimulating hormone to induce maturation of the seminiferous tubules (*qv*) and sperm (*qv*) production. *See also* luteinizing hormone releasing factor.

luteinizing hormone-releasing hormone (factor) (LH-RH, LH-RF) *See* gonadotropin-releasing hormone.

luteoma A granulosa cell tumor in the ovarian follicle that cytologically appears as miniature corpora lútea (*qv*). Such tumors may be benign or malignant. They may lead to endometrial hyperplasia with excessive secretion of estrogens (*qv*) by the tumor cells. If not surgically removed, these tumors can grow to weigh 50 pounds.

luteotropic hormone (LTH) Another name for the lactogenic hormone (*qv*) or prolactin (*qv*) produced by the anterior lobe of the pituitary (*qv*) and responsible for milk production at the end of a pregnancy (*qv*).

lying-in The time before, during, and after childbirth (*qv*); the condition of being in confinement or childbirth.

lymphadenopathy Chronically swollen lymph nodes. Specific or generalized swelling of lymph nodes is a symptom of many diseases, including several sexually transmitted diseases (*qv*), such as acquired immune deficiency syndrome (*qv*) and lymphogranuloma venereum (*qv*).

lymphadenopathy associated virus (LAV) The name given by Luc Montagnier of the Pasteur Institute in France to the human immune deficiency virus, or HIV-I (*qv*), which causes acquired immune deficiency syndrome (*qv*).

lymphocyte One of two kinds of small leukocytes or white blood cells with nongranular cytoplasm that develop in the bone marrow. Normally lymphocytes comprise 25 percent of the total white blood cell count. However, their number increase greatly when the body is challenged by an infection, especially if this is a major or chronic infection. The two forms of lymphocytes are B cells and T cells.

When B lymphocytes are exposed to an antigen (*qv*) matching their specific surface antibody, they are activated and multiply to produce both plasma B cells and memory B cells. The plasma cells secrete large amounts of the antibody specific to the antigen. The memory B cells are not immediately active but remain in the body. If the body is reexposed to the same antigen, the memory B cells convert into antibody-secreting plasma cells.

The T lymphocytes become competent after they pass through the thymus gland early in life. When exposed to an antigen, they divide rapidly, producing a large number of new T lymphocytes sensitized to that antigen, as well as memory T cells. Secretions of these killer T cells, also called lymphokines, are essential to the cell-mediated immune response. One type of T lymphocyte, the helper T or T4 cells, activates the B cells and other T cells, thus turning on the immune response system. Meanwhile, suppressor T or T8 cells suppress the immune system to prevent an overreaction that could possibly injure the host's own tissue. T lymphocytes also appear to play an important role in controlling the proliferation of certain cancers.

The HIV-I virus (*qv*), which causes acquired immune deficiency syndrome (*qv*), attacks the helper T lymphocytes, thereby reducing the immune defenses of the body and leaving it open to opportunistic infections like pneumocystis carinii pneumonia (*qv*) and cancers like Kaposi's syndrome.

lymphogranuloma venereum (LGV) An infection caused by *Chlamydia trachomatis* (*qv*), an intracellular parasitic microorganism currently classified as a bacterium. Until recently *Lymphogranuloma venereum* was considered a tropical and subtropical disease; however, its incidence in temperate zones of the United States has been increasing. The disease is characterized by initial transient ulcerative genital lesions, followed by marked swelling of the lymph nodes of the groin, headache, fever, nausea, and malaise. Rectal wall ulcerations are less common. Transmission is by intimate sexual contact. A serologic test can identify LGV antibodies (*qv*) in the blood. Treatment is with tetracycline or erythromycin.

Lyon hypothesis *See* dosage compensation; Barr body.

M

McDonald's sign The suddenly easy flexion of the upper portion of the uterus (*qv*) in the seventh or eighth week of gestation (*qv*) and detectable by a physician as a sign of pregnancy (*qv*).

machismo (adj. macho) (Sp.) The concept and cultural imperatives associated with masculinity (*qv*) in Latin American cultures; the Latin American word for the mystique of manliness. Machismo stresses male physical aggressiveness, high risk taking, breaking the rules, casual and uninvolved sexual relations (*qv*) with women, and elective active penile insertion in other men. Though useful to describe an extreme male chauvinism, the term as used by non-Latinos to some extent represents a stereotype with deep-rooted value judgments and cultural assumptions. The term is said to be derived from *macho* in the classical Aztecan language, meaning "image," "reflection of myself." *See also* marianismo; testeria.

Mackenrodt's ligaments The lateral ligaments connecting the cervical (*qv*) neck of the uterus (*qv*) with the sides of the pelvis.

Mackintosh Society A British organization for rubber fetishists (*qv*). In 1823, the Scottish chemist Charles Mackintosh produced the first practical waterproof cloth by cementing together two layers of fabric with a solution of naphtha and rubber. Raincoats made from this material were called mackintoshes.

macrogenitosomia (L.) A congenital condition resulting from excess fetal androgens (*qv*); characterized by enlarged external genitalia (*qv*) in boys and by pseudohermaphroditism (*qv*) in girls. *See also* macrogenitosomia praecox.

macrogenitosomia praecox (L.) Pellizzi's syndrome, a precocious sexual development (*qv*) due to a tumor of the pineal gland.

macromastia An unusually large breast (*qv*) development, either unilateral or bilateral, resulting from hypertrophy of the mammary or milk glands (*qv*) and a simultaneous abnormal increase in the fatty and fibrous connective tissue of the breast.

maculopapular Having the characteristic of being spotted and raised or elevated. *See also* sex flush.

madam Although madam, a contraction of the French for "my lady," became a form of address for one's beloved in the fourteenth or fifteenth centuries, the term has also been applied since the Renaissance to a prostitute (*qv*) or a woman who runs a brothel (*qv*).

Madonna complex or syndrome A sexually inhibiting factor in which a man separates lust (*qv*) and love (*qv*) and attributes sinful lust to whores (*qv*) and pure, innocent love to madonnalike women, especially wives and mothers. This attribution allows a man to have intercourse (*qv*) and enjoy sex in illicit relations, but not with a wife or the mother of his children. *See also* prostitute-versus-madonna syndrome.

maeitics A medical term for obstetrics (*qv*).

Magna mater (L.) In Jungian theory, the symbol or archetype of the universal primordial mother that exists in the collective unconscious of humanity.

magnetic conception A seventeenth-century theory proposing that fertilization (*qv*) and conception (*qv*) were the result of penile thrusting (*qv*) allegedly that magnetized the female reproductive tract and the spark of life in the male semen (*qv*).

Maher v. Roe In this 1977 decision, the U.S. Supreme Court ruled that states are not required to fund elective abortions (*qv*).

Mahu In Polynesian societies, a male, usually one in each village, who is a transvestite (*qv*) and appears to prefer same-sex relations. This custom provides a casual sexual outlet for the otherwise heterosexual (*qv*) males of the village.

maidenhead A colloquial term for the hymen (*qv*).

maidenhood The state of being a virgin (*qv*); virginity (*qv*).

maieusiophobia An intense and morbid fear of childbirth (*qv*). Grantly Dick-Read (*qv*) and other advocates of natural childbirth (*qv*) believe that this fear is the cause of difficult labor (*qv*).

maithuna, maithuna sadhana (Skt.) A Hindu, Buddhist, Tantric (*qv*), and Taoist (*qv*) term for sexual intercourse (*qv*). In these traditions, maithuna may refer also to any form of ritual sexual intercourse in which the sexual union is prolonged and transformed into a ceremonial act through which the couple figuratively become a divine pair. The ceremonial union of Shiva, the male principle, with Shatki, the female principle, imitated by a couple to raise the kundalini (*qv*) through physical union. Maithuna also refers to sculptures depicting mithuna (loving couples) in sexual embrace. *See also* Kama Sutra; Tantric love ritual; Rite of the Five Essentials.

male (maleness) Of or pertaining to the individual or sex (*qv*) that impregnates (qv) or fecundates (*qv*); of or pertaining to a man (*qv*) or to men in contrast to that which pertains to women (*qv*). These definitions, which paraphrase those given in the *Oxford English Dictionary*, illustrate both a linguistic/lexicographic and a sexological point: one cannot define "male" as that which pertains to the "male sex" without begging the question. Accordingly, the problem is in isolating and identifying the core characteristics that, in actual usage, seem to underlie the concept. Thus, it is difficult to gainsay the characteristic chosen by the editors of the *Oxford English Dictionary*, although many social critics would argue that a definition of "male" solely in terms of biological reproductive function misses much of the point because it focuses on one behavior that is a minor episode in the life of any male, and not experienced by all males. Yet it is difficult to locate another sufficiently universal characteristic of maleness that would serve in place of the biological/procreative characterization. This conundrum can be resolved by recognizing that the word "male" has different domains of usage, of which perhaps the broadest is in biology. Thus, reproductively, "male" refers to characteristics of that class or group of organisms that transfer genetic (*qv*) material to the egg (*qv*) or the female (*qv*), defined as that class or group of organisms that produces eggs and possesses the internal organs for the nurturance of the fertilized egg in animals with internal fertilization (*qv*). We may now unambiguously ascertain which of several Rotifers, for example, are male and which are female without reference to any social, personal, economic, or cultural facts or phenomena. Furthermore, this sense of male can be used to characterize, in part, what it means to be a human male.

However, in human history and society, the domain of usage of "male" is broader and includes characteristics associated with gender (*qv*) as well as sex and reproduction. In these broader domains, "male" refers to characteristics and features of a socially defined group of human beings called "men" in English, and contrasted in common usage with that group called "women" (*qv*). This dichotomy of *all* human beings, mature or not, into two and only two genders is a fundamental feature of the English language. Thus, in the English language, a homosexual (*qv*) individual is not considered as belonging to a third sex, although German and some non-Western languages would permit that characterization. Instead, English speakers and writers say "homosexual man" or "homosexual woman," thus preserving the dichotomy of human beings into men and women as more fundamental than their sexual behavior. The fact that one can say "*hetero*sexual man" or "*hetero*sexual woman" without being redundant implies that the truly basic linguistic distinction is between "men" and "women," independent of how or with whom they may choose to express sexual interest.

Nor is it possible to define "male" and "maleness" solely in terms of social or economic power. A so-called definition of "male" as "pertaining to that group of people who have political and economic power" can serve as a secondary commentary on a fact of male/female relationships in much of modern history, but, at root, it would force one to conclude that Queen Victoria was a "male." Accordingly, one is again forced to seek the basic groundwork for defining "male" and "female" in linguistic usage that perceives a fundamental dichotomy of all people into two groups according to their real or potential reproductive roles. One can argue that this linguistic dichotomy is not at all neutral with respect to how we think and act, a version of the Sapir-Whorf hypothesis (*qv*), and hopelessly out-of-date in terms of reproductive technologies. Still, it remains a fact of English that "male" and its correlative "female" are two of the basic terms in the worldview built into the English language. Etymologically, "male" derives from the Old French *masle*, which in turn derives from the Latin *mascula*, meaning of or pertaining to the sex that impregnates. Later borrowings from classic Latin included words like "masculine," which now exists in modern English as a doublet for "male." Currently, "masculine" tends to refer more to gender and "male" to biological or reproductive characteristics, but there is considerable overlap between the two.

male accessory organs Structures in the male reproductive system that serve as adjuncts to the penis (*qv*), testes (*qv*), vasa deferentia (*qv*), ejaculatory ducts (*qv*), and the urethra (*qv*). These include the prostate gland (*qv*), paired seminal vesicles (*qv*), and bulbourethral glands (*qv*).

male anomalies Congenital birth defects (*qv*) involving the male genitalia (*qv*) and reproductive system. Structural defects include unilateral or bilateral cryptorchidism (*qv*), micropenis (*qv*), hypospadia (*qv*), hyperspadia (*qv*), and the absence of a functional prostate (*qv*), one or both of the vas deferens (*qv*) or seminal vesicles (*qv*).

male-breast carcinoma A malignant condition of the rudimentary male breast (*qv*) occurring mostly in men in their fifties and similar to female breast cancer (*qv*).

male chauvinism A philosophical, political, and social viewpoint holding that men are inherently superior to women in all or some ways, that is, intellectually, emotionally, and/or psychologically; and that men should therefore possess political, social, cultural, sexual, and economic powers over women. Often, male chauvinist philosophy argues that this perceived male (*qv*) superiority over women (*qv*) is innate to, or inherent in, a biology or nature that has endowed men with traits superior to those of women. In practice, male chauvinism in the United States has had as its goals the retention and enhancement of traditional divisions of labor (e.g., that a woman's place is in the home), as well as maintaining unequal opportunities between men and women for owning property, obtaining an education, having political rights such as voting, or having a job or career opportunities. Colloquially, the term can also refer to a man who expresses offensive and derogatory opinions about women in general or who attributes negative qualities in a particular woman to the fact of her sex. The phrase, together with ''male chauvinist pig,'' became current in American English during the 1960s, although the term ''chauvinism'' (*qv*) predates that period, especially in Left politics as a synonym for white supermacist or racist. *See also* feminine mystique; ''Total Woman''; ''Fascinating Womanhood.''

male climacteric The medical term for the so-called male change of life (*qv*) or male menopause (*qv*), supposedly homologous in its psychological effects to female menopause (*qv*).

male-determining sperm *See* androsperm.

male estrogen Estrogens (*qv*) and estrogen metabolites produced by the cells of Leydig (*qv*) in the testes (*qv*) and found in the urine of males. The function of male estrogens is unknown, although some suggest it may act as a balance to potential overproduction of testosterone (*qv*) and other androgens (*qv*).

male gender identity The internal conviction one has of being a male (*qv*), of belonging to the male gender (*qv*). The internalized conviction one has of being a male is distinct from, although related to, one's gender role (*qv*). It is also distinct from although related to one gender or sexual orientation (*qv*). *See also* gender identity; gender identity/role; cross-coding; transsexual.

male hermaphroditism A generic term applied to several different syndromes involving congenital (*qv*) ambiguity of the sex organs (*qv*) in which male characteristics dominate, usually occurring in a 46,XY genetic-gonadal male. The ambiguity results from the failure of full hormonal masculinization (*qv*) due to either the type or quantity of androgenic (*qv*) hormones (*qv*) available at critical periods (*qv*) or to the insensitivity of tissues to specific androgenic hormones during the process of fetal masculinization (*qv*). *Synonym*: male pseudohermaphroditism.

male liberation *See* men's liberation.

male menopause A colloquial but inaccurate term for the physiological and psychological changes experienced by some men between ages 50 and 65 when androgen (*qv*) production may slow. Varying symptoms include flushes or hot flashes (*qv*), indecision, fatigue, and depression. An exaggerated belief in male menopause may lead to fears of a waning sexual capacity and a need to reaffirm sexual potency by having sexual affairs (*qv*) with younger women or the desire to divorce (*qv*) and marry a younger woman. *See also* Jennifer syndrome.

male motherhood In American folklore and in some non-Western societies, the belief that men can be impregnated and bear children. The fact that this phenomenon has never been documented does not alter the conviction of some people that it does in fact occur. In biology, male motherhood refers to the fact that in a few species, for example, seahorses, the fertilized eggs are transferred to internal structures in the male's body, from which the young later hatch and are cared for by the male. *See also* male pregnancy.

maleness *See* male; masculine.

male organ A colloquial and medical term for the penis (*qv*).

male pregnancy The belief among some peoples that a male can become pregnant (*qv*) under certain circumstances, as when a young male has anal intercourse (*qv*) with a much older male or if a man allows the female-above position for intercourse. Modern reproductive technology, particularly *in vitro* fertilization (*qv*) and embryo transplant (*qv*) techniques, may someday permit a male to become pregnant if the blastocyst (*qv*) were surgically implanted in the abdominal wall and supported for 6 weeks with exogenous hormones (*qv*) until the placenta's pregnancy-supporting endocrine functions can take over. Delivery would be by Caesarean section (*qv*), as in a naturally occurring female abdominal pregnancy (*qv*). Despite misconceptions to the contrary, a sex change operation (*qv*) does not allow a male-to-female transsexual (*qv*) to conceive or bear a child. *See also* male motherhood.

male prostitution The exchange of sexual services by a male for money or other compensation. The male prostitute's partner may be a homosexual (*qv*) male, or a heterosexual (*qv*) woman. In some cultures, male prostitutes are transvestites (*qv*) and gynemimetics (*qv*). *See also* prostitution.

male pseudohermaphroditism *See* male hermaphroditism.

male reproductive system assessment An evaluative procedure combining a health-oriented sexual history (*qv*) and thorough physical examination, including semen (*qv*) analysis and sperm count (*qv*), to assess the condition of the patient's genitalia (*qv*), reproductive history, and genitourinary infections and disorders.

male sexual dysfunction *See* painful intercourse; erectile dysfunction; inhibited orgasm; premature ejaculation; retarded orgasm.

male sexual functioning The three components of male sexual behavior essential to natural reproduction (*qv*): production of motile sperm (*qv*) capable of fertilization (*qv*), penile erection (*qv*) sufficient to allow for vaginal penetration, and ejaculation (*qv*). *See also* male reproductive system assessment.

male sperm *See* androsperm.

Malinowski, Bronislaw (1884–1942) A major force in the empiricist tradition of British anthropology who concentrated on intensive, detailed empirical study of small societies, emphasized direct participation with native informants, and adhered to functionalist theory, treating cultural institutions as direct expressions of human needs. Malinowski's fieldwork was done in the Trobriand Islands, New Guinea, after World War I. His academic life was spent at the London School of Economics. His major works were *Argonauts of the Western Pacific* (1922), *Sex and Repression in Savage Society* (1927), *Coral Gardens and Their Magic* (1935), and *A Scientific Theory of Culture* (1944).

Malpighi, Marcello (1628–1694) In 1675, Malpighi, an Italian biologist, microscopist, and physician, found embryos (*qv*) in what he thought were unfertilized chicken eggs. He concluded that the chicken egg must already contain the preformed, miniature chick and that the role of the sperm (*qv*) was merely to trigger development of this preformed miniature being. Malpighi's role as papal physician was crucial in the subsequent debate between the advocates of the new preformation theory (*qv*) and advocates of the mediate animation theory (*qv*), which philosophers had argued made termination of a human pregnancy (*qv*) prior to quickening (*qv*), or fourth month, morally acceptable.

malpositioned testes A condition characterized by the failure of one or both of the testicles (*qv*) to migrate into their usual position in the scrotum (*qv*) before or shortly after birth (*qv*). Because of the privacy associated with sexuality (*qv*) in American society, one in 50 boys reaches puberty (*qv*) with one or both testes (*qv*) still undescended into the scrotum. For adult men, the incidence of cryptorchidism (*qv*) is about one in 500 males.

Malthus, Thomas Robert (1766–1834) A British writer, clergyman, and political economist best known for his *Essay on Population* (1789), which argued that, unless checked, the human population increases in a geometrical ratio while food production supporting this population increases only in an arithmetic ratio. Malthus argued that the living conditions of the working class could not be improved unless the population increased but that simultaneously an increased population would reduce the living standard because of a food shortage. Growth in the human populations, Malthus argued, was controlled by family, disease, war, late marriage, and sexual abstinence (*qv*). Unless the reproduction rate (*qv*) of humans is voluntarily controlled by sexual restraint, especially in the working class, poverty, war, and widespread starvation will provide a natural control for overpopulation. *See also* malthusianism.

malthusianism A theory proposed by Thomas Robert Malthus (*qv*) maintaining that the mid-nineteenth-century world was overpopulated and on the verge of mass famine. Malthusianism was widely challenged by the late nineteenth century when major advances in agriculture and industrial output, at least in the Western world, appeared to reduce the immediate threat. More recently, worldwide efforts to control population growth and the natural reduction in birthrates as Third World nations become industrialized have added new insights into the basic fallacy behind malthusianism. The awareness of the threat of global overpopulation, new contraceptive (*qv*) methods suitable for Third World nations, and the need for new food and energy sources have highlighted the much more complex nature of the issues Malthus was the first to address.

mamilla (L.) The teat or nipple (*qv*) of the breast (*qv*); any nipplelike structure.

mamilliplasty Theleplasty; plastic surgery reconstruction of the nipple (*qv*).

mamillitis *See* mammitis.

mamma (pl. mammae) (L.) *See* breast; mammary gland.

mammal (mammalia) Any member of the class Mammalia, a group of warm-blooded four-limbed vertebrates with body hair and mammary glands (*qv*). The class Mammalia contains three subclasses: the primitive egg-laying monotremes (duck-billed platypus); the marsupials, which give birth to premature young, which are nursed (*qv*) in pouches (opossums, kangaroos); and the eutherians or placental mammals which carry their young in the uterus (*qv*) where they are nourished through the placenta (*qv*) until birth (*qv*).

mammalingus Sexual stimulation of the female by sucking of her breasts (*qv*).

mammarized society A culture that places great emphasis on the female breast (*qv*) for its appeal as an erotic (*qv*) and sexual stimulation, as well as a sign of true femininity (*qv*) and fertility (*qv*).

mammary abscess A swollen, inflamed, and pus-filled abscess of the breast (*qv*), usually occurring during nursing (*qv*) or weaning (*qv*).

mammary amputation *See* mastectomy.

mammary gland Milk-producing structures or glands in the breast (*qv*) of mammals (*qv*). The term *mammary gland* may refer to the whole female breast or to an individual milk-producing cluster within it. In the latter usage, each mammary gland contains grapelike clusters of milk-producing cells, alveoli, and collecting ducts, which terminate in a main duct and reservoir. Fifteen to 20 such clusters of mammary glands empty into the nipple (*qv*). Fatty and fibrous tissue surround each cluster. Estrogens (*qv*) and progesterone (*qv*) interact to regulate growth of the female breast. Milk production depends on pituitary lactogenic hormone (*qv*); expression of milk during breast-feeding (*qv*) depends on oxytocin (*qv*). Breast tissue naturally changes during the estrus (*qv*) or menstrual cycle (*qv*) and with the yearly seasons. The mammary glands of males and prepubescent females are rudimentary. *See also* areola.

mammary neuralgia *See* mastalgia.

mammary ridges Two parallel lines of thickened epidermis that develop about the sixth week of gestation (*qv*) and extend from the armpits to the groin region, marking the first stage in development of the mammary glands (*qv*). In the human, these ridges quickly regress except in the chest region, where they form a single pair of mammary buds. These buds gradually penetrate the underlying mesenchyme (*qv*) to form the lactiferous ducts of the breasts (*qv*) in the eighth month. If regression is not normal, a condition of polythelia (*qv*) or polymastia (*qv*) may result. Total regression of the mammary ridges, resulting in amastia (*qv*), is rare.

mammectomy *See* mastectomy.

mammilla Teat; the nipple of the female breast (*qv*).

mammitis An inflammation of the breast (*qv*) or mammary glands (*qv*).

mammogram A diagnostic radiography or X-ray of the soft tissues of the breast. *See also* xenography.

mammography A diagnostic X-ray of the breast (*qv*), with or without the injection of an opaque substance into the ducts, used to screen for abnormal growths. The mammogram cannot distinguish a malignant from a benign growth.

mammometer A device used to measure the volume of the female breast (*qv*) to detect any significant deviation in the size of the two breasts or as part of breast reconstruction following mastectomy (*qv*).

mammoplasty Augmentive, reductive, reshaping, or reconstructive plastic surgery of the breast (*qv*).

mammose Having unusually large breasts (*qv*).

mammothermography A diagnostic procedure using thermography (*qv*) to detect abnormal growths in the breast (*qv*).

mammotrophic *See* mammotropic.

mammotrophic hormone Prolactin (*qv*).

mammotropic Having a stimulating effect on the breast (*qv*).

mammotropin *See* prolactin.

man (men, manhood) One or more adult male (*qv*) human beings; a generic term for any individual or group of individuals, especially when used as a suffix, as in the word policeman; in the singular, the species *Homo sapiens* (synonym mankind; now usually humankind or humanity). Manhood is the state of being a man.

Setting aside specialized uses—for example, the nautical use of *man* to mean "ship" in compounds like man-of-war for a naval battleship or Gloucesterman for a commercial fishing schooner (named after the town of Gloucester)—the sexological and gender (*qv*) uses of the words man and men fall into two broad categories of meaning, one narrower than the other. In each category, the word man stands in linguistic opposition to a series of correlative terms that help define the word's domains of meaning.

The narrower sense of *man* and *men* refers to people of the male sex (*qv*) or masculine (*qv*) gender, and stands in contrast to *woman* (*qv*) and *women*. However, in this use, *man* also stands in contrast to *boy* or *lad*, so that *man* in the narrower sense means a sexually and socially mature human male. Accordingly, the word is subject to legal, cultural, and historical definitions that have differed considerably from place to place and from time to time. In jurisdictions of the United States, the calendar age of 18 or 21 years alone determines whether a male human is an adult (i.e., a man), and subject to adult civil and criminal codes of law, or still considered a child. The same holds for the age of majority for women, since this definition of adulthood is gender-blind. Socially, however, strong distinctions are made between boys and men that are not so strongly made between girls and women. Indeed, feminist (*qv*) critics of sexism (*qv*) in language have argued that the word girl has only chauvinistic (*see* chauvinism, male) uses and meanings, because a young female can be the object of sexual attentions no matter what her age. However, boyhood—culturally considered to be a time of schooling, playfulness, and mischief—is sharply distinguished from manhood. In many non-Western cultures, ceremonials or rites of passage (*qv*) mark the liminal (*qv*) transition from boyhood to manhood; *see* bar mitzvah. In still other cultures, male societies may contain more than the two age-graded ranks of boy and man. In these cultures, a long time period may intervene between sexual and social maturity at the end of boyhood and the achievement of full social, legal, and/or symbolic status of manhood. For example, in certain hunter and warrior cultures, a boy becomes a warrior or hunter before he is allowed to be married, an event that seems nearly universally to be deemed a privilege of manhood itself. (Childhood betrothals and marriages done for dynastic purposes are an exception.) By contrast, a young female (e.g., 11 years old) may be deemed in some cultures to be fully marriageable as a woman. Within this diversity of definition of man and manhood, the generalization appears to hold that socially, manhood is a status or rank, and is not solely or even primarily a matter of personal maturity or precocity, psychological growth, intelligence, health, strength, or sexual capability. In such societies, a man is an older male, socially fully mature, who is married and who has passed through a series of transitions from boyhood to manhood.

With the growth of gay (*qv*) male culture in the United States, it might seem that this definition would have changed, in part because gay manhood is not associated with marriage (*qv*) to a woman and the privilege of becoming a socially recognized father (*qv*) of children. However, this change has not occurred. Even if details of how one becomes sexually mature differ between gay and nongay men, ''being gay'' means achieving the status of being a (gay) male member of a community of other like men, and is therefore not synonymous with merely ''being homosexual (*qv*).'' Thus, coming out means coming out as a gay *man*, where the italics mean that the individual normatively recognizes his social and emotional responsibilities to others, and that others recognize his full membership and social rights and privileges within the self-defined community of gay men. Even if a gay man responds that not all gay males meet such standards of adulthood, the comment is less a refutation of the definition of manhood than a reiteration of an assumption that inheres in the definition itself, that not all human beings with penises (*qv*) are men—that is, truly men in the social and symbolic sense.

However, this self-defined social collectivity of men, whether gay or not, differs from other human social collectivities by virtue of a unique relationship to members of the socially defined collectivity of women. Potentially, any adult male may marry or impregnate (*qv*) a human female, but this biological capacity does not provide the crucial definitional basis of what *man* means. Instead, being a member of the collectivity called men, gay or not, requires that the man recognize his relationship to women as a group and individually, so that male-female relationships are regulated by social principles rather than being the province of the boy's whimsicality or mischieviousness, or the outlaw's criminality. Accordingly, the word man, meaning an adult male human being, requires the additional qualifications that manhood is a socially defined and socially achieved status, often defined by age or age-related responsibilities or roles, and that represents social and symbolic membership in a collectivity of like individuals, all of whom interact with women in potentially reproductive, but socially regulated and defined, ways.

An important component of this definition is its dependence on socially determined principles rather than on the individual's male psychology or gender preference. Thus, although a 16-year-old male may call himself a man and demand to be treated as an adult, adults are more likely to treat him as a boy and will only occasionally, and in a condescending way, accord him adult treatment. Moreover, a gay man, who considers himself as sexually uninterested in women and therefore as not having a potentially reproductive relationship with them, will still be treated by society at large and by women in particular as a potentially able sexual partner for women. Therefore, even if his socially ascribed manhood is defined symbolically, the fact that he is called a man arises directly from the sexual fact that men are defined in the United States as socially and sexually mature males erotically and reproductively related to women.

The male human beings who are left over from this definition are not seen as men but as boys, or are excluded in part or whole from the community of other men, often as outlaws or outcasts. To be sure, individuals in the latter category are legally treated as masculine when sequestered in sex-segregated prisons, or when they are members of a (possibly illegal) community inside or outside prison. Nonetheless, other male individuals—for example, the lone rapist, the sociopathic killer, and the pedophile (*see* pedophilia)—are widely considered in police and prison sociology as being utterly outside the pale and lacking in the status of being men, masculine though they may be. These people are defined as loners, mavericks, kooks, or crazies, terms that place them on the other side of a fuzzy boundary apart from socially defined men. Again, we return to the point that the status of being a man is defined by social rules that include a potentially reproductive relationship with women, and not by self-labelling or choice.

The social realities that have led to this definition have been widely criticized by writers in the men's liberation movement (*qv*) for their rigid structuring of roles and statuses, especially their rigid distinction between manhood and womanhood. These critics see such rigidity as psychologically destructive and socially pernicious. However, no single nor consensual alternative has been suggested in such writings, although commonalities in attempts at redefinition include role model (*qv*) flexibility; willingness to transcend traditional gender role (*qv*) distinctions and behavior; openness to accepting others—for example, those of different ages—as intrinsically one's own equals, friends, or compatriots; and accepting or seeking relationships with women that transcend reproductive modalities and the restrictions on male-female relationships found in older traditions of manhood and fatherhood. Often these critics espouse radical or alternative political and economic ideas, if only because most critics of traditional definitions of manhood see them lodged in specific economic or political systems, arising, for example, from the nature of post-industrial capitalism. However, other critics have based their ideas on religious or aesthetic principles; for example, the belief that the godhead is essentially both male and female.

Feminist (qv) writers have also strongly criticized the social realities underlying the definition of manhood. However, unlike male critics, feminist writers often begin their analyses with aspects of male-female relationships; for example, the idea that it is a near-mandatory privilege of manhood to be a father. This feature of the definition has led to the widespread use of the term patriarchy (qv) for the values implicit in the traditional definition of manhood. Men sometimes find this emphasis on the patriarchy bewildering. For them the greater realities of being a man exist in the entire web of social rules and customs that limit and define a man's actions and feelings rather than residing primarily in his relationship to women. However, when the seeming right of being a father can potentially be enforced without the woman's consent (e.g., in rape [qv]), feminist criticisms of patriarchal values and definitions are important aids in efforts to redefine manhood.

However, the reader should understand that these criticisms, for both men and women, are attempts at social reform, and are revisionary efforts to substitute one definition for another. They are not necessarily efforts to understand how current spoken and written usage defines the words man, men, and manhood. Even if some critics wish it otherwise, these words have all been socially, historically, and culturally defined in relation to the sorts of age-graded rules, identities, and statuses discussed above.

Much has been written about these topics, ranging from the extraordinary misogyny of Otto Weininger, a nineteenth-century German philosopher, to works of modern male liberationist writers such as Warren Farrell and Herb Goldberg. A brilliant novelistic treatment of this definition is Lois McMaster Bujold's science fiction parable, *Ethan of Athos*. Ethan, the hero, comes from a planet called Athos, which is inhabited only by men, and whose culture and social order is hierarchically structured around the fact that they reproduce by artificial insemination (qv) of imported and cultured ovarian tissue. Ethan's off-world experiences with women, and one woman in particular, Elli Ouin, provide Bujold with an opportunity to characterize male society and culture as it presently exists.

Resources: Eugene August, *Men's Studies: A Selected and Annotated Bibliography* (Littleton, CO: Libraries Unlimited, 1985); Donald Bell, *Being a Man: The Paradox of Masculinity* (Lexington, MA: Lewis Publishing Company, 1982);

Lois McMaster Bujold, *Ethan of Athos* (New York: Baen Books, 1986); Warren Farrell, *Why Men Are the Way They Are: The Male-Female Dynamic* (New York: McGraw-Hill, 1986); Warren Farrell, *The Liberated Man: Beyond Masculinity: Freeing Men and Their Relationships with Women* (New York: Random House, 1974); Herb Goldberg, *The New Male: From Self-Destruction to Self-Care* (New York: Morrow, 1979); Michael Korda, *Male Chauvism: How It Works* (New York: Random House, 1973); R. E. L. Masters and Eduard Lea, *The Anti-Sex: The Belief in the Natural Inferiority of Women: Studies in Male Frustration and Sexual Conflict* [*An Anthology of Male Misogyny*] (New York: Julian Press, 1964).

The second usage of the word man, as a synonym for person or humanity in general, has led to major changes in American speech and writing over the past several decades. Of Germanic origin the root word man means "person," "individual," or "human being," as found in the word mankind, meaning all humans—males, females, and children—collectively. *Man* has often been used as a suffix; thus, a policeman is an officer of the law and not necessarily a male. More recent usage has systematically substituted gender-neutral terms for such expressions: for example, police officer for policeman, fire fighter for fireman, and mail carrier for mailman. Most modern handbooks of usage and style say these substitutions are now necessary, not optional, in both formal and informal writing and speech.

In part, these changes have arisen from feminist criticisms of sexist language, but they have also appeared in bureaucratic contexts (e.g., on federal income tax returns), where feminist concerns are unlikely to have any effect. Instead, another linguistic process appears to underlie the shift away from terms with gender-specific suffixes. This process illustrates a crucial fact of how the English language speaks of sexuality (*qv*) and gender.

As women have entered historically male professions, terms like fireman have become ambiguous. The use of *man* as a suffix meaning "person" and its equally historical meaning of a person specifically of the masculine sex results in a contradiction. Less abstractly stated, the suffix *man* is a marker with two, presently contradictory, meanings. Languages, or the users of languages, do not tolerate such contradictions. Accordingly, one usage or the other has to give way. In modern American English, the use of *man* as a generic for "person" has given way to *man* as a specific for "male person."

Latent in this dry observation is a crucial fact. When given a choice about interpreting a word or suffix such as -*man*, speakers of English put the gender meaning first; that is, linguistically, one's membership in a specific gender has greater salience than one's membership in any other category. Linguistically, in English, one is a man or a woman before one is a human being. If it were the other way around, then expressions like fireman could be used without discomfort to women. Accordingly, one can conclude that in English a division of people into males and females is *the* fundamental distinction of the language. Aphoristically, to speak English is to see people as sexual and gendered before all else.

A good example occurs when the individual's sexual preference (*qv*) is for persons of his or her own gender. One then speaks of a "homosexual man" or a "lesbian woman," where the adjective represents a sort of subcategorization of the broader, more basic terms man and woman. A male individual who prefers individuals of his own gender as sex partners is not therefore called a "woman," nor referred to as a third sex or gender. Instead, he remains a man before all else. In other languages, alternative expressions are possible, for example, "the third sex," an English translation of a German expression meaning a male homosexual. However, "the third sex" never obtained currency in English; instead, the basic rule of English comes into play, and all human beings are typecast as either one sex or gender or the other.

Terms like auntie and queen, current in gay camp (*qv*) speech, might seem to contradict this conclusion, but they do not. Both terms are used with overtones of sarcasm and even dislike (e.g., "He's an old queen" or "He's a real auntie"), and they are not the primary terms for describing gay individuals. Nor do lesbian writers use *man* or *fellow* for those individuals who adopt anti- or non-feminine dress, manners, and speech. While the earlier dichotomous terminology of *butch* in contrast to *femme* is less acceptable today, many lesbian writers will use the term *dyke*, rescued, as it is said, "from the patriarchy," as a term with specific meaning about a person's style and manner. Once again, the fundamental dichotomy has been retained because of deep, seemingly ineradicable roots in the concept of sexually and socially mature gendered human beings. Accordingly, the words man and woman represent two of the deepest categories in the English language, the perceived division between which flavors and shapes virtually all speech and writing about human beings and their sexuality. *See also* phallocentrism; Sapir-Whorf hypothesis.

The word man itself is Old English, and derives from a Germanic root meaning "human being" or person. In other Germanic languages, the dual meanings of "human being" and "adult male" are expressed in different words; for example, German *Mensch* and *Menschen* for "human being" and "people" and *Mann* for an adult male human being. Old English has distinct words meaning man and woman in the sexual senses: *wer-* for man and *wif-* for woman (*see* wife); *wer-* survives today in the English word werewolf, a man who turns into a wolf at the full of the moon as depicted in mythology and horror movies.

Mandragoris An alternative name for Aphrodite (*qv*), derived from the Greek for "mandrake," the legendary universal aphrodisiac (*qv*).

mandrake *Mandragora officinarum*, a herb native to northern Africa and southern Europe and widely used from ancient times as an aphrodisiac (*qv*), hallucinogen, narcotic, and analgesic.

manly Characterized by qualities attributed to men, in the sense of adult male human beings. Usually these qualities are related to bravery, valor, strength, and heroism, and the emotional qualities associated with them. Originally, the term referred to soldiers and warriors, with an honorable connotation. It is rarely applied to women, and is not considered sexist (*see* sexism). *See also* man; mannish.

Mann Act *See* White Slave Act.

mannish When said of a woman or women's dress, speech, manner, and, possibly, sexual preference (*qv*), having qualities not usually associated with femininity (*qv*). In nineteenth- and early twentieth-century English, a "mannish woman" was a euphemism for a lesbian (*qv*), especially one who fit the stereotypes of a butch or dyke lesbian. Today, lesbian writers reject the adjective as male chauvinist (*see* chauvinism, male) and phallocentric (*see* phallocentrism). As a result, the word is now seen as strongly pejorative.

Mann test A technique for ascertaining the condition of the female cervix (*qv*) by inserting a balloon treated with radiopaque dye that can be visualized on an X-ray film.

man-sharing A colloquial and sociological term for a kind of informal polygyny (*qv*), in which a married man with a wife (*qv*) and children develops a second-household family (*qv*) typically with an unmarried woman who has children. Man-sharing has been described among urban American blacks, possibly as a response to economic pressures and a shortage of marriageable males; also known as extramarital polygamy.

man shortage *See* marriage squeeze; Marital Opportunity Ratio; sex ratio; high sex ratio.

mantra In Hindu and Buddhist philosophies, a sound, series of sounds, or phonetic verse repeated aloud or mentally to focus the mind during meditation, relax the body, and release the primal forces. In the Tantric love rite (*qv*) and Hindu philosophy, repetition of one's mantra during lovemaking (*qv*) is believed to awaken sexual energy and prepare the couple for the highest form of transcendent sexual union.

manustupration An obsolete term for masturbation (*qv*).

mar'a The Arabic term for woman. In classical Islam, women are regarded as intellectually inferior to men and hold a subordinate legal status. In urban Islam, female seclusion, or purdah (*qv*), limits women's contacts with males outside their family circle. Secular trends and Islamic modernism, beginning with Qasim Amin (1865–1908), have improved the position of women somewhat.

maraichinage A form of intense, prolonged deep kissing (*qv*) in which the lovers use their tongues to caress and explore the partner's mouth. Believed to have originated among the Maraichins of Brittany, France, this practice has been used as a form of contraception (*qv*), at times being engaged in to the exclusion of penile-vaginal intercourse (*qv*).

Margulies spiral IUD An intrauterine contraceptive device (*qv*) shaped like a coil with a beaded tail. Introduced in 1959, this IUD has not been popular because it causes discomfort during coitus (*qv*).

marianismo The view, especially in Latin America, that women have a special and deep spiritual affinity and connection to the Virgin Mary that makes them morally superior to most men in their purity and virtue. *See also* machismo.

marijuana The hemp plant *Cannabis* whose flowering tops provide a commonly used psychoactive drug, tetrahydrocannabinol (THC) (*qv*). Of the several cannabinoids extracted from *Cannabis*, the isomers of THC appear to be the most psychoactive components. Characteristic psychological responses associated with ingesting or smoking marijuana are alterations of mood, memory, motor coordination, cognitive ability, and self-perception. The effects depend on the dosage, type of administration, and past usage and experience of the user. The senses of touch, taste, and smell may be enhanced. Pharmacological effects of smoking marijuana are evident within minutes, with peak plasma concentrations of THC occurring within 10 to 30 minutes. The effects seldom last more than 2 or 3 hours. Studies reported by the National Institutes of Health indicate the cannabinoids inhibit secretion of the luteinizing hormone (*qv*), follicle-stimulating hormone (*qv*), and prolactin (*qv*). They also cause changes in ovulation (*qv*), reduced testosterone (*qv*) levels causing gynecomastia (*qv*) in males and shorter menstrual cycles (*qv*) in females. Studies of the effects on fetal (*qv*) development are inconclusive. However, the National Institutes of Health suggest that marijuana does interfere with normal fetal growth and may affect the visual or other neurologic responses of the fetus.

marital adjustment Adaptation to the responsibilities and demands of being married (*qv*), including adjustment to the idiosyncrasies and differing views, interests, sexual needs, and preferences of the spouse (*qv*). Adjustment is also essential in the process of couple decision making, childbearing (*qv*) and child rearing, domestic tasks, financial and social responsibilities, and other practical problems.

marital aids A colloquial term for sexual devices and erotic (*qv*) materials such as vibrators (*qv*), dildoes (*qv*), exotic lingerie, and equipment for bondage and dominance (*qv*) or sadomasochism (*qv*).

marital conflict Severe and periodic or mild and persistent tensions and disagreements between husband and wife, usually triggered by divergent positions on sexual relations (*qv*), child rearing, money or the power balance in the relationship, and life-style. *See also* marital discord.

marital discord A persistent and severe form of marital conflict (*qv*), often leading to separation (*qv*) and divorce (*qv*).

marital duty *See* conjugal duty.

Marital Opportunity Ratio (MOR) The ratio of men in a society available for and seeking marriage (*qv*) to the number of socially suitable women, eliminating homosexuals (*qv*) and committed single persons. In the early 1980s, the Availability Index or Marital Opportunity Ratio for white women in 38 metropolitan areas was favorable only to women 20 to 24 years old. For every 100 white women ages 20 to 24 in San Diego, there were 179 available males. Houston had 149 males, Baltimore 133, Chicago 129, with Pittsburgh, Buffalo, and Miami tied with 117 males for every 100 women aged 20 to 24. Once a woman passes her twenty-fifth birthday, the MOR drops precipitously. Most urban areas have roughly three single women in their late forties or early fifties competing for every one suitable male. The opportunities become fewer as white women age.

Among American urban blacks, the overall sex ratio (*qv*) is between 63 and 80 men to 100 women. Poor nutrition and a lack of prenatal care in lower economic groups result in 8 to 9 percent more male fetuses (*qv*) dying than in middle- or upper-class pregnancies (*qv*). Single mothers are also more likely to miscarry (*qv*) a male than a female fetus. With a higher proportion of single mothers in the black population, this adds to the overall shortage of black males. Increasing the shortage is a penal system that sends a disproportionate number of young black males to prison. Proportionally more blacks than whites serve overseas in the armed forces. Violence and drugs add to the shortage of young black males. Black women in college outnumber black males 8 to 5, adding to the marriage squeeze (*qv*). *See also* high sex ratio. Resources: M. Guttentag & P. F. Secord, *Too Many Women? The Sex Ratio Question* (Beverly Hills: Sage, 1983); C. F. Westoff & N. Goldman. Figuring the odds in the marriage market, *Money Magazine* 13(1984):34–35.

marital rape The act of forcing the spouse, usually the wife, to engage in sexual relations (*qv*) against her will. Since the marriage contract traditionally assumed the husband had a right to sexual relations and the wife the conjugal duty (*qv*) to acquiesce, courts and others commonly assumed that the husband's sexual relations with his wife could never be considered rape (*qv*), even if she was uninterested or unwilling. The wife could not licitly refuse her husband's request or demand for sexual relations. The reverse situation—a wife raping her husband—was even more inconceivable.

In 1980, the California marital rape bill altered the existing rape code to include sexual intercourse (*qv*) with one's spouse if accomplished under force, violence, or threat of great and immediate bodily harm. Since 1980, over half of the states have passed laws making it a felony for a husband to force his wife to engage in sexual relations against her will. Some of these statutes are gender neutral, leaving open the possibility that the actor or perpetrator can be either the husband or wife. *See also* acquaintance rape; date rape.

marital relations Sexual intimacy and intercourse (*qv*) engaged in by two persons who are married to each other, in distinction to premarital sexual relations (*qv*), extramarital relations (*qv*), comarital relations (*qv*), and adultery (*qv*). In this usage, the term *relations* originated as a British legal euphemism for coitus (*qv*).

marital status A colloquial term used on forms and questionnaires to indicate whether the respondent or applicant is single, cohabiting, married, separated, divorced, or divorced and remarried. Population statistics usually give data on the marital status distribution, the number or ratio of individuals in each of the categories.

marital therapy Psychological counseling and psychotherapy for married couples. Marital therapy may include sex(ual) therapy, but it is broader because it focuses on the dynamics of the relationship between husband and wife, especially their grievances, conflicts, emotional aspects, and communication skills. Marital therapy is also known as marriage therapy.

Marquis de Sade *See* de Sade, Marquis.

marriage The social and legally recognized ceremony and state in which a man and woman are considered husband and wife and their offspring accepted as legitimate; any social structure designed to regulate sexual relations (*qv*), parenting, and various duties, including economic support, owed by each partner or spouse to the other; the term also refers to the more or less permanent union of two or more persons, the state of being married. In every society and culture, mate selection leading to marriage operates rather like a market in which the rules of selection determine the forms of exchange between the couple and their households. In a closed market, the parents arrange the marriage of their children to consolidate property and form family alliances. In such arranged marriages, initial affection and love (*qv*) are unimportant. In open markets, affection, love, and the personal decision of the partners are the basis of mate selection. Various courtship (*qv*) rites may precede the formal marriage, unless the choice of spouse is arranged by the parents or elders.

Traditionally marriage was justified by Christians for reproduction (*qv*) and to avoid fornication (*qv*), with partnership and passionate love in the background. Modern Christians have virtually reversed this order, although official Roman

Catholicism and some fundamentalists remain uncomfortable with sexual pleasure and distrustful of sexual passion. Roman Catholicism, Eastern Orthodox Christians, and some Anglicans view marriage as a sacrament. Divorce (*qv*) is officially forbidden by Catholicism and Anglicanism, although decrees of nullity or annulments (*qv*) can be obtained. Many Protestant churches and Eastern Orthodox Christians recognize legal divorces while holding to the ideal of lifelong marriage. In Judaism, marriage is a positive duty. Religious divorce, get (*qv*), is permitted. In Islam, marriage is a civil contract, and polygamy (*qv*), though discouraged, is still allowed. Similarly, while unilateral divorce by the husband remains valid, modern laws have mitigated the disadvantage for the wife.

See also arranged marriage; banns; boy marriage; brother-sister marriage; child marriage; cluster mrriage; group marriage; common-law marriage; companionate marriage; consummate; cousin marriage; endogamy; exogamy; experimental or trial marriage; fensternl; gay union; homosexual marriage; intermarriage; Levirate marriage; cross-cousin marriage; marriage of convenience; monogamy; multiple marriage; plural marriage; polyandry; polygamy; polygyny; renewable marriage; sexually open marriage; symbiotic marriage; taking your night feet for a walk.

marriage, cross-cousin In a matrilateral cross-cousin marriage, a male child marries his mother's brother's daughter; a female child marries her mother's brother's son. In a patrilateral cross-cousin marriage, a male child marries his father's sister's daughter; a female child marries her father's sister's son. *See also* cousin marriage.

marriage broker A go-between who arranges marriages (*qv*); in Jewish communities, a *schadchen*. *See also* matchmaker.

marriage certificate The religious or civil document confirming that a couple have entered into the marital state. Depending on the laws or customs in a particular society, the marriage certificate is witnessed by a civil or religious official and one or more other individuals.

marriage contract The general legal agreement a man and woman make implicitly when their marriage (*qv*) is recognized by a civil or religious authority. The details of the contract in terms of responsibilities for mutual financial support, financial assets, conjugal duty (*qv*), child rearing, and child support are usually specified by state because of its compelling concern for the good of society. This marriage contract is different from a prenuptial agreement or contract (*qv*), which may be negotiated by the parents in an arranged marriage (*qv*) or by a couple entering a second marriage into which they bring financial obligations and assets.

marriage encounter A type of marriage-enrichment group (*qv*) with a strong religious character, popular in charismatic and fundamentalist movements.

marriage-enrichment group A support and mutual therapy group in which married couples meet regularly with a trained group leader to discuss all aspects of the marriage relationship and the problems, tensions, conflicts, and responsibilities they personally encounter. *See also* marriage encounter.

marriage fear *See* gamophobia.

marriage license A civil legal document certifying that no obstacles to a marriage (*qv*) are known. Some states require a waiting period after a license is issued before the marriage can take place. More than half the states require a blood test for syphilis (*qv*) and gonorrhea (*qv*). Some states are considering legislation to require a test for the HIV (*qv*) virus. Such tests may be made either by a private physician or by a health department laboratory.

marriage of convenience A marriage (*qv*) based on familial, monetary, or social advantages rather than on mutual affection or love (*qv*). Aliens seeking citizenship in the United States sometimes resort to a marriage of convenience because marriage to an American citizen carries with it naturalized citizenship. *See also* arranged marriage.

marriage portion *See* dowry.

marriage squeeze The shortage of men available for marriage (*qv*) in proportion to the number of single women seeking a spouse. One example of the marriage squeeze occurs because the shifting birthrates (*qv*) during the baby boom (*qv*) created a shortage of mates available today for women born between the 1940s and late 1960s. If the 1,417,000 girls born in 1947 all looked for a mate among the 1,217,000 boys born in 1946, 200,000 would not find partners. However, for males in the 1990s who were born as the baby boom waned, the marriage squeeze is reversed, with more females available in the traditional pool for the males seeking younger wives. Another major factor in the marriage squeeze is the fact that women tend to "marry up," while men traditionally seek younger wives who also complement and do not challenge their status. In recent years, more women than men are attending and graduating from college, adding to the marriage squeeze. *See also* Marital Opportunity Ratio; sex ratio. Resource: M. Guttentag & P. F. Secord, *Too Many Women? The Sex Ratio Question* (Beverly Hills: Sage, 1983).

masculine (n. masculinity) Having the characteristic of or attributed to the male gender (*qv*). In the sexist (*see* sexism) biases of Western cultures, masculine traits ideally include self-reliance, self-confidence, strength, purposefulness, rationality, vigor, power, controlling one's environment, commitment to career, and autonomy. These traits may also be applied in metaphor to inanimate objects and plants. When masculine traits are attributed to women, it is usually in a demeaning way, the more so when the gender role (*qv*) differences are sharply drawn and stereotyped. The behaviors and attitudes considered appropriate to a male are often stereotyped and determined in unique combinations by a particular society. *See also* sex adjunctive characteristics; sex (or gender) adventitious characteristics; sex derivative characteristics; sex irreducible characteristics; testeria.

masculine-feminine continuum A model of masculinity (*qv*) and femininity (*qv*) in which masculine and feminine characteristics are pictured at opposite ends of the spectrum as black-and-white opposites with graduated shades of gray in between the extremes.

masculine-feminine dichotomy A model of masculinity (*qv*) and femininity (*qv*) in which masculine and feminine are viewed as mutually exclusive opposites with no overlap.

masculine habitus The composite of physical features associated with a typical postpubertal male, including facial and body hair, deeper voice, mature genitalia (*qv*), distinct musculature, bone structure, and fat distribution. *See also* sex derivative characteristics; secondary sexual characteristics.

masculine identity *See* male gender identity.

masculine protest In the psychological construct proposed by Alfred Adler (*qv*), both men and women can adopt exaggerated behavior attributed by the culture to males as a form of masculine protest. In women, according to Adler, masculine protest means a rejection of the traditional feminine (*qv*) role of submission and dependence coupled with an endorsement and adoption of traditional masculine aggressive behavior. In men, Adler claimed that masculine protest is an excessive drive to overcompensate for an insecure masculine self-image. The extreme of either pattern of masculine protest is said to be neurotic and maladoptive. Both women and men can express masculine protest in the sense of the healthy desire to be strong, to dominate, and to be superior. According to Adler, a misdirected desire for superiority is the driving force behind the neurosis of masculine protest. *See also* machismo.

masculine traits *See* masculine.

masculinity *See* masculine.

masculinity-femininity scales, tests Psychological tests designed to measure the ratio or degree of masculinity (*qv*), femininity (*qv*), and androgyny (*qv*). The most widely used test available is Sandra Bem's Sex-Role Inventory (*qv*), although the Minnesota Multiphasic Personality Inventory (*qv*), the Guilford-Zimmerman Survey, and the Gough Femininity Scale are also used.

masculinization The developmental process of differentiating and/or assimilating masculine (*qv*) features and characteristics. The process of masculinization involves a constant interaction of biological and sociological factors at critical periods (*qv*), both before and after birth (*qv*). In the third and fourth months of pregnancy (*qv*), anatomical masculinization centers on differentiation of the internal and external genitalia (*qv*)—the penis (*qv*), testicles (*qv*), scrotum (*qv*), and male accessory organs (*qv*). Internally the primordial gonads (*qv*) develop into testes (*qv*), the Mullerian ducts (*qv*) degenerate, and the Wolffian ducts (*qv*) differentiate into the vasa deferentia (*qv*) with accessory structures. Externally the genital tubercle (*qv*) develops into a penis and the genital swellings and folds (*qv*) into the scrotum. This is followed by masculinization of the hypothalamus (*qv*) for acyclic production of gonadotropic-releasing factors (*qv*) and possibly other traits associated with males. Masculinization of the brain and neural pathways is not supported by strong evidence at present and remains highly controversial. From birth on, socialization and gender scripting (*qv*) interact with the developing biological substrate and neural templates to produce a male. *See also* premature puberty; virilization.

masculinizing (virilizing) neoplasms Pituitary (*qv*) or adrenal gland (*qv*) tumors or nonendocrine tumors that produce an excess of androgens (*qv*), causing development of male secondary sex characteristics (*qv*) in a female, including hirsutism (*qv*), an enlargement of the clitoris (*qv*), deepening of the voice, and masculine muscular development.

masculinizing surgery Plastic surgery that alters the genitalia (*qv*), giving a female-to-male transsexual (*qv*) the external sexual organs of an anatomical male; also used in the clinical treatment of some intersex (*qv*) and hermaphroditic (*qv*) children with ambiguous genitalia. *See also* transsexual surgery; sex change operation.

masculinovoblastoma A tumor of the ovary (*qv*), possibly derived from adrenal cortical tissue, which has a masculinizing (*qv*) or virilizing (*qv*) effect on a female. *See also* adrenal rest.

mask A disguise or covering for the face with openings for the eyes, nostrils, and mouth. In cultures that Margaret Mead (*qv*) terms sexually repressive guilt cultures, masks are often incorporated into annual ritual celebrations when people can indulge in normally forbidden sexual activities. Typical examples occur at the Carnival in Rio de Janeiro and the Mardi Gras in New Orleans. In Brazilian culture, a common expression typifies the safety valve function of the mask in such celebrations: ''Behind the mask, there is no guilt.'' Other anthropologists have proposed different interpretations. Masks are also sometimes used in sadomasochistic (*qv*) scenarios and in other sexual games.

masked homosexuality According to the psychoanalyst Wilhelm Stekel, masked homosexuality is expressed by men who engage in pedophilic (*qv*) relations with boys and in sex with much older women. *See also* gerontophilia. In other contexts, masked homosexuality refers to an exclusive preference among heterosexual (*qv*) individuals for sexual acts usually engaged in by homosexual (*qv*) persons, such as a male's exclusive preference for heterosexual anal intercourse (*qv*).

mask of pregnancy *See* chloasma.

Maslow, Abraham H. (1908–1970) An American psychologist, Maslow is known for his advocacy of humanistic psychology, his studies of self-actualizers, and his motivational hierarchy (*qv*), a theory of human motivation and peak experiences (*qv*). Maslow rejected the dominant American schools of behaviorism (*qv*) and psychoanalysis (*qv*) as too narrow. He urged a more humanistic "third force," which he conceived of as being concerned with higher human motives and the need for self-realization, knowing, understanding, and aesthetic needs. His major writings include *Principles of Abnormal Psychology* (1941), *Motivation and Personality* (1954), *Toward a Psychology of Being* (1962), and *Religion, Values and Peak Experiences* (1964). *See also* self-actualization.

Maslow's hierarchy of needs *See* motivational hierarchy.

masochism (adj. masochistic) The paraphilic (*qv*) condition of responding to or being dependent on receiving punishment, bondage, discipline, humiliation, and/or servitude in order to become sexually aroused (*qv*) and reach orgasm (*qv*). A person may play the masochist role to please a sadist (*qv*) partner or for commercial gain. The reciprocal paraphilia is sadism. Masochism is named for Leopold von Sacher-Masoch (1836–1895) (*qv*), an Austrian author who wrote about this sexual practice in *Venus in Furs*. *See also* bondage and dominance; feminine masochism; mental masochism; moral masochism; sadomasochism.

masochist *See* masochism.

masochistic fantasies Fantasies that create or relive sexual encounters in which one imagines himself or herself being humiliated, degraded, choked, whipped, and otherwise abused and mistreated for purposes of sexual arousal (*qv*). Many people may occasionally enjoy a masochistic fantasy without wanting to engage in masochistic practices. Masochistic and rape fantasies (*qv*) are common for men and women raised in a sexually repressive, moralistic tradition because they allow one to fantasize being forced to engage in and enjoy otherwise forbidden pleasures. Masochistic fantasies play an important role in sadomasochistic scenes (*qv*).

masochistic sabotage An openly destructive behavior designed to satisfy the unconscious need to bring punishment on one's self.

massage Stroking, rubbing, kneading, and/or tapping of the soft tissues of the body for sensual pleasure, to improve circulation and muscle tone, and/or to relax the recipient. Massage exercises may be included in sensate focus exercises (*qv*).

massage parlor A colloquial term for an establishment that advertises body massage and perhaps a sauna but is in reality a business providing sexual services, ranging from masturbation (*qv*) by a masseuse to oral sex (*qv*) and intercourse (*qv*). Massage parlors may also cater to various paraphilias (*qv*) such as enemas, urophilia (*qv*), bondage (*qv*), and sadomasochist (*qv*) sex. *See also* prostitution.

mastalgia Pain in the breast (*qv*) caused by congestion or "caking"; may be associated with lactation (*qv*), an infection, fibrocystic disease (*qv*), especially prior to or during menstruation (*qv*), or with advanced cancer. *See also* caked breast.

mastectomy Surgical removal of the glandular tissue of the breasts (*qv*), often as a treatment for cancer. In a *simple mastectomy*, only breast tissue is removed. In a *radical mastectomy*, some muscles of the chest are removed with the breast tissue and all the lymph nodes in the axilla. In a *modified radical mastectomy*, the large chest muscles that move the arm are preserved. The term is commonly applied to surgery performed on females with a malignancy of the mammary glands (*qv*). It also refers to treatment of a male with a malignancy or gynecomastia (*qv*). Since mastectomy commonly has a negative impact of the woman's body self-image, postsurgery follow-up with participation in a mastectomy support group is an important part of the surgery and recovery procedure. *Synonym*: mammectomy. *See also* lumpectomy.

master gland A nontechnical term for the pituitary gland (*qv*).

mastitis An acute or chronic inflammatory condition of the mammary gland (*qv*) or breast (*qv*), usually caused by a streptococcal or staphylococcal infection.

masto-, mast- A combining form meaning "of or pertaining to the breast (*qv*)."

mastodynia *See* mastalgia.

masturbation Self-stimulation of the genitalia (*qv*) by touch or pressure, usually with the hands or vibrator (*qv*), and with orgasm (*qv*) as a common but not inevitable or necessary outcome. In masturbating, many women may combine vaginal and breast stimulation with clitoral stimulation. Women, and to a lesser extent men, use a vibrator in masturbating. *Mutual masturbation* may be engaged in by a couple as an alternative to sexual intercourse (*qv*). Various studies from the time of Alfred Kinsey (*qv*) on have documented the high incidence of masturbation, with about 95 percent of American men and 85 percent of American women reporting they masturbate at least occasionally. Ultrasonic scanning of male fetuses (*qv*) has revealed that they not only have penile erections (*qv*) in the womb but that they also engaged in penile stroking. In some cultures, it is considered an admission of sexual inadequacy for a male to acknowledge he masturbates because he is not man enough to find a woman. In some religious systems, masturbation is considered a crime or sin against nature since it allows enjoyment of sexual pleasure in a nonreproductive, noncoital expression. The etymological derivation is "hand" (Latin: *manus*) plus "rape" or "ravishment" (Latin: *stuprare*). Many slang expressions for masturbation play on this derivation; for example, "visit the widow with five children" or, "have a date with Mary Five-Fingers." *See also* degeneracy theory; Tissot; Sylvester Graham.

masturbation fantasy An erotosexual fantasy (*qv*) that precedes or accompanies masturbation (*qv*). Like the imagery of a sleeping dream that arises in the subconscious, the imagery and ideation (*qv*) of the conscious fantasy have a high degree of autonomy and individual specificity to stimulate arousal (*qv*) and orgasm (*qv*). *See also* coital fantasy.

matchmaker An intermediary other than the parents who arranges a marriage (*qv*) for a young couple. In many Jewish and Hispanic traditions, the role of the matchmaker, or marriage broker, is an honored and well-paid role. It was much more common in eighteenth- and nineteenth-century Europe in the upper and upper-middle class. It continues today among the Orthodox and Hasidic Jews and other communities. Today's dating counselors, and video or computer dating services serve some of the traditional functions of the matchmaker in bringing eligible single men and women together by matching their interests and values. *See also* marriage broker.

mate One's partner or spouse. *See also* domestic partner; mating. (*Addendum*).

mate exchange A situation or relationship in which two married couples change partners for purposes of sexual intercourse (*qv*); mate exchange or swinging (*qv*) usually does not include emotional involvement with the other spouse. *See also* consensual adultery; open marriage; comarital relation.

maternal age The age at which a female can become pregnant (*qv*) and bear a child. According to the *Guinness Book of World Records*, the youngest documented maternal age is for a Peruvian—some say Chilean—girl with premature puberty (*qv*), who gave birth at age 5 via Caesarean section (*qv*). The oldest documented human birth was to a 57-year-old American woman.

maternal androgen Masculinizing (*qv*) androgens (*qv*) produced by the mother's adrenal glands (*qv*) or by a virilizing (*qv*) tumor of the ovary (*qv*) or adrenal gland. The androgens pass through the placental barrier (*qv*) to affect the fetus (*qv*). The effect of early exposure of a female fetus to maternal androgens can be fetal virilization (*qv*), resulting in an enlarged clitoris (*qv*), and some masculine body features. Maternal androgen may also be exogenous, coming from hormonal medications taken by the mother during pregnancy. *See also* diethylstilbesterol.

maternal-child attachment *See* bonding; maternal-infant bonding.

maternal-child separation syndrome *See* separation anxiety.

maternal deprivation syndrome A postnatal (*qv*) condition characterized by developmental retardation occurring in an infant or child as a result of being deprived of maternal physical or emotional nurturance. Symptoms typically include retarded physical growth with weight below the third percentile for the child's age and size, pronounced withdrawal, silence, apathy, and irritability. Posture and body movement patterns are unnaturally stiff and rigid, with slow responses to the approach or touch of others. Causes may include unfavorable socioeconomic conditions that prevent the mother or other primary care provider from giving normal nurturance and contact with the child, parental indifference, emotional instability or insecurity of the mother, failure of the mother to bond with the child, and rejection of the child because of his or her appearance, gender, or behavior. Emotionally deprived children often remain below age norms in intellectual development, fail to develop socially, and as adults are unable to form trusting, meaningful relationships. The nature and extent of the condition vary considerably, depending on the child's age when the deprivation occurs, the degree of deprivation, the child's constitution, and whether substitute care or intervention can be provided. If deprivation occurs early and is prolonged, the damage is difficult to reverse. *See also* anaclitic depression; somatosensory affectional deprivation.

maternal drive In psychology, a basic urge or impulse to nurture, feed, and protect one's offspring; in anthropology, a species-specific trigger-releasing mechanism for nurturing, feeding, and protective behavior exhibited by the mother toward her offspring. The term *instinct* (*qv*), commonly used in the past for what is now termed a drive, is no longer popular in technical literature because of the difficulty of specifying the exact nature of the instinctive behavior.

The term *drive* is not as deterministic as is *instinct*. It also allows for variations in the responses of individuals within a species who exhibit the particular drive and for evidence that many components of maternal behavior are learned. *See also* maternal instinct.

maternal impression The discredited theory that pregnant (*qv*) women can influence the fetus (*qv*) indirectly by engaging in certain kinds of behavior, such as listening to classical music or reading extensively. Birthmarks (*qv*) were previously attributed to a frightening maternal impression.

maternal-infant bonding A complex process of psychological/emotional attachment on the part of the mother with her newborn infant. According to M. Klaus & J. Kennell's *Maternal-Infant Bonding* (St. Louis: C. V. Mosby, 1976): "This original mother-infant bond is the wellspring for all the infant's subsequent attachments and is the formative relationship in the course of which the child develops a sense of himself. Throughout his lifetime, the strength and character of this attachment will influence the quality of all future bonds to other individuals." There is a certain sexism (*qv*) and heterosexual (*qv*) bias evident in this standard definition, which assumes that only a woman, the mother, can effect this kind of bonding, and at the same time it appears to be talking only about the bonding of male children with their mothers.

maternal instinct In many animals, an assumed innate drive of the female to feed, protect, and nurture her offspring. The term *instinct* (*qv*) has been questioned because animal and human studies have shown that female animals raised in isolation and not allowed to observe older females mothering do not learn these skills and are not as successful nurturing, feeding, and protecting their offspring. These experiments clearly refute the concept of maternal instinct. It has been suggested that prolactin (*qv*) and early maternal-infant bonding play important roles in what is currently termed the maternal drive (*qv*) rather than maternal instinct.

maternalism A theory that nurturing and mothering is an instinct (*qv*) possessed only by the female of the species. *See also* maternal instinct.

maternal mortality The death rate for women during childbirth (*qv*). Both the age and socioeconomic level of women are major factors in maternal mortality. The death rate is highest among mothers 10 to 14 and over 40 years of age. The next highest rates occur among women ages 15 to 18 and 35 to 39. Poor women are also at a higher risk than the general population because of the lack of prenatal care and poor nutrition. *See also* infant mortality.

maternal nondisjunction *Nondisjunction* (*qv*) or unequal distribution of a homologous (*qv*) pair of chromosomes (*qv*) during oogenesis (*qv*). When *maternal nondisjunction* involves the X chromosome (*qv*), two types of ova (*qv*) can result:

one ovum with two X chromosomes and the other with no X chromosome. Fertilization (*qv*) of the XX ovum will result either in a female with 47,XXX or in a male with 47,XXY or Klinefelter syndrome (*qv*). Fertilization *qv*) of the ovum with no sex chromosome results in a lethal 45,YO or a sexually immature female with 45,XO (Turner syndrome [*qv*]).

maternal virilization syndrome The congenital (*qv*) condition of a female fetus (*qv*) virilized (*qv*) by prenatal exposure to maternal androgens (*qv*); the appearance of secondary gender characteristics (*qv*) as a result of exposure of the fetus to maternal androgens.

maternity blues *See* postpartum blues.

maternity cycle A medical term for the period including conception (*qv*), the 9 months of gestation (*qv*), labor (*qv*), delivery (*qv*), and the first 6 weeks after birth (*qv*).

mating Coitus (*qv*), copulation (*qv*), or intercourse (*qv*); the potentially reproductive physical union of male and female partners or male and female organs in the case of hermaphroditic (*qv*) animals. A secondary definition includes bonding (*qv*) and marriage (*qv*). Mating is essentially the process of proceptivity (*qv*) and receptivity (*qv*) leading to conceptivity (*qv*); the process of mate selection and copulating (*qv*) in order to reproduce.

mating dance A colloquial expression for flirtation (*qv*), or the ritualized signs, behaviors, and expressions couples develop to signal sexual interest or the lack thereof.

matriarchy A term used in nineteenth-century anthropology and by modern faminisats (*qv*) to designate a society in which mothers and women are recognized as the major source of power and the head of the family, tribe, or collectivity, with offspring inheriting the mother's name, property, and status. In contemporary use, matriarchy refers to a form of family in which the mother is the head, and descent is reckoned through her. Matriarchy is distinguished from a matrilineal (*qv*) society in which descent and lineage are traced through the female even though the female may not have much authority or power in the culture. *See also* patriarchy; patrilineal.

In 1884, Friedrich Engels argued that a "primitive matriarchy" characterized prehistoric nomadic human societies before the development of agriculture, urban life, private property, and the male-dominated state. No modern culture is a matriarchy; however, myths of such cultures, such as the Amazons, are common. The concept of matriarchy is widely used to support the feminist (*qv*) perspective on the differences between gender (*qv*) and biologically determined sex roles (*qv*). Resources: Frederick Engels, *The Origin of the Family, Private Property and the State* (New York: International Publishers, 1942); Karl Jaspers, *The Origin and Goal of History* (New Haven: Yale University Press, 1953).

matrifocal family A family unit comprised of a mother and her children with the children's father either temporarily or permanently absent; also known as a single-parent family since most single-parent families are headed by a woman.

matrilineal Designating descent, kinship (*qv*), or derivation of lineage through the mother instead of through the father or other male relatives; descent is traced only through one of the four grandparents, the mother of one's mother's. Although in matrilineal cultures the father is usually recognized as playing some role in conception (*qv*), he is not a member of his child's maternal kinship group and hence not of particular social importance. Matrilineal societies permit women much greater latitude in extradomestic activities and power than do bilineal (*qv*) or patrilineal (*qv*) cultures.

matrilocal A residence system, usually occurring in matrilineal (*qv*) cultures, in which the bride brings her husband to live with her in or near her maternal home. Also known as uxorilocal. *See also* patrilocal.

matrimonial agency *See* matchmaker; marriage broker; dating service.

matrimonial duty *See* conjugal duty.

matrimony (adj. matrimonial) The state of marriage (*qv*) or wedlock; also the marriage ceremony.

matrix A dated term for the uterus (*qv*).

matron An older, mature married woman whose behavior distinguishes her from younger women; a woman of some authority or power.

Mattachine Society The first major homophile (*qv*) organization in the United States, founded in Los Angeles in 1951. The Mattachine Society has chapters in every major city, working to promote equal treatment of homosexuals (*qv*) and to deter abuse and prejudice toward homosexuals. The society publishes the *Homosexual Citizen* and the *Mattachine Newsletter*. The name is derived from a group of outspoken medieval court jesters. *See also* Daughters of Bilitis.

mau ar (Portug.) An evil aura allegedly transmitted by a menstruating (*qv*) woman and capable of preventing dough from rising, causing wounds to become infected, and turning wine sour.

Mayer-Rokitansky-Kuster (MRK) syndrome A 46,XX female with ovaries (*qv*), vaginal atresia (*qv*), possibly defective fallopian tubes (*qv*), and a rudimentary cordlike uterus (*qv*) leading to amenorrhea (*qv*). Individuals with MRK syndrome and those with 46,XY androgen-insensitivity syndrome (*qv*) both have vaginal atresia and amenorrhea, the difference being that persons with MRK have 46,XX, ovaries and female hormones (*qv*) while those with AIS have 46,XY, testes (*qv*), and male hormones. When 18 MRK and AIS subjects were compared, all were exclusively heterosexual as women in imagery, ideation, and practice, suggesting that chromosome status, gonadal status, and hormonal cyclicity are not essential in developing feminine sexual orientation. *See also* androgen-insensitivity syndrome.

Mayoral test The Mayoral and Jiminez test for paternity (*qv*); now replaced by more sophisticated HLA blood tests and deoxyribonucleic acid probes (*qv*).

Me In the sociological theory of George Herbert Mead (*qv*), that aspect of the self (*qv*) that is the internal agent of conformity and social control. *See also* ego; I; role taking.

Mead, George Herbert (1863–1931) A sociologist who developed a positive, mutually supportive model of the relationship between the individual and society, emphasizing that it is by living and interacting with others that we develop our full human potential. According to Mead, the self emerges through the process of interaction with significant others (*qv*) and the generalized other (*qv*) or social group to which one belongs. Gestures and conversation are vital to the symbolic interaction in which the individual can imaginatively assume a variety of social roles and internalize the responses these roles would generate in the generalized other. Mead's theory contrasts with that of Sigmund Freud (*qv*), who implied that people would be happier as individuals without the discontents imposed by society and civilization. *See also* I; game; Me; play; role-taking. Resource: G. H. Mead, *Mind, Self and Society* (Chicago: Chicago University Press, 1934).

Mead, Margaret (1901–1978) A pioneering student of Franz Boas who helped establish, with her colleague Ruth Benedict, the modern science of cultural anthropology. Mead gained renown for her research on personality, childhood and adolescent development, and sexual behavior (*qv*), mainly in South Pacific and Oceanic cultures. Her early work, which emphasized the importance of nurture (*qv*) over nature (*qv*), provided significant support for feminism (*qv*). Among her many works are several classic studies of sexuality (*qv*): *Coming of Age in Samoa* (1928), *An Inquiry into the Question of Cultural Stability in Polynesia* (1928), *Growing Up in New Guinea* (1930), *Sex and Temperament in Three Primitive Cultures* (1935), *Male and Female* (1949), *Childhood in Contemporary Cultures* (1955), *New Lives for Old* (1956), and *American Women* (1966). Immense numbers of readers were introduced to anthropology through her work.

After her death, the objectivity and accuracy of Mead's reports of sexual behaviors in Samoa were challenged by Derek Freedman, who claimed that Mead did not speak Samoan, that her informants were not reliable, and that her data did not support her theories. Supporters of Mead's work maintain she did not deny or neglect the influence of heredity and that her subsequent research more than adequately replicated her early Samoan work. Resource: D. Freedman, *Margaret Mead and Samoa: The Making and Unmaking of an Anthropological Myth* (Cambridge, MA: Harvard University Press, 1983).

meatometer An instrument for measuring the opening of the urethra (*qv*) in the glans (*qv*) of the penis (*qv*) or in the vulva (*qv*). The term is derived from *meatus* (*qv*), the Latin word for an opening, and is pronounced me-a-*tom*-e-ter.

meatorrhaphy Suturing of the cut end of the urethra (*qv*) to the glans (*qv*) of the penis (*qv*) following surgery to enlarge the urethral meatus (*qv*); pronounced me-a-*tor*-ra-phy.

meatoscopy Visual examination of any opening, especially the urethral opening, usually performed with the aid of a speculum (*qv*); pronounced me-a-*tos*-co-py.

meatotome The surgical instrument used in a meatotomy (*qv*); pronounced me-a-*tot*-o-me.

meatotomy A surgical incision to enlarge the urethral meatus (*qv*); pronounced me-a-*to*-to-my.

meatus (L.) A relatively small opening or passageway to a body organ (e.g., the urinary meatus); pronounced me-*a*-tus.

median bar hypertrophy A type of overgrowth of the prostate (*qv*) in which a mass of rapidly proliferating fibromuscular tissue extends laterally across the urethral opening of the bladder, obstructing the flow of urine (*qv*).

median lobe hypertrophy A lobe of prostatic (*qv*) tissue that develops as an overgrowth upward into the urinary bladder, obstructing the urethral inlet and blocking the flow of urine (*qv*).

mediastinum testis (L.) The thickened region of the tunica albuginea (*qv*) behind the testis (*qv*) from which arise the septa, which subdivide the testis into conical lobes.

mediate animation theory A theory of human development proposed by Aristotle and adopted by later Christian thinkers in which the fetus (*qv*) is said to be sequentially animated by three different life principles or souls. According to the mediate animation theory, a vegetative life principle controls development from fertilization (*qv*) through the early embryonic (*qv*) stage. An animal life takes over as the fetus develops animal functions. Finally, in the third month, when a human form is achieved, a human life principle, or soul, takes over. Since the human form and soul was not believed to be present until 40 days after conception (*qv*) for a male fetus and 80 days for a female fetus, this theory allowed termination of pregnancy prior to quickening (*qv*) from around 300 C.E. to 1600 C.E. in Christian Europe. *See also* ensoulment; epigenesis; immediate animation theory; preformation theory.

medicalization The tendency to attach medical labels to behaviors regarded as socially or morally unacceptable, as when homosexuality (*qv*) or paraphilias (*qv*) are described as diseases and treated medically.

medical model The basic paradigm of medicine since the development of the germ theory of disease in the nineteenth century, the medical model has three assumptions: (1) all diseases and dysfunctions can be traced to a specific causative agent or factor; (2) the patient is treated as a passive target of therapeutic intervention rather than as a person in a complex social environment; and (3) restoring health or equilibrium requires the use of medical technology and advanced scientific procedures. The use of the medical model in sex research and therapy has been criticized because its search for a single simple cause and therapy precludes the use of nonmedical procedures. When used in sex research and therapy, this model also depersonalizes the patient by treating him or her as a dysfunctional organism that can be fixed, instead of taking into consideration the psychological and social factors in sexual orientation (*qv*), paraphilias (*qv*), and dysfunctions (*qv*).

medroxyprogesterone acetate A synthetic progestin (*qv*) with many physiological properties of progesterone (*qv*), although structurally it is an androgen (*qv*). Medroxyprogesterone acetate is used in hormonal contraceptive pills (*qv*) to suppress ovulation (*qv*). As a male contraceptive, it prevents spermatogenesis (*qv*). It is also used as a reversible antiandrogen (*qv*) to suppress androgen release and eliminate libido (*qv*) in male sex offenders. Medroxyprogesterone acetate is the generic chemical name for Depo-Provera (*qv*) or Provera (*qv*).

medulla The inner core of any organ or gland. *See also* cortex.

medullary cancer of the prostate The softer of two types of cancer of the prostate (*qv*), more difficult to palpate and detect than the scirrhus (*qv*) type, which is hard, fibrous, and particularly invasive.

medullary inductor substance A hormonal influence responsible for triggering differentiation of the medullary region of the primitive gonad (*qv*) into testicular tissue with cells of Leydig (*qv*), nurse cells, seminiferous tubules (*qv*), and

Sertoli cells (*qv*). The medullary inductor substance should not be confused with the Mullerian inhibiting substance (*qv*).

Meese Commission *See* Commission on Obscenity and Pornography, Presidential, 1986.

meiosis The two-stage process of cell division involved in the production of gametes (*qv*). During the resting or interphase stage, before meiosis begins, the chromosomes (*qv*) of the primordial germ cell replicate. In the prophase I of Meiosis I, the homologous (*qv*) pairs of duplicated chromosomes synapse, or pair up. The extranuclear centrioles replicate and move to the nuclear poles to form a spindle necessary for chromosome migration. In metaphase I of Meiosis I, the paired chromosomes arrange themselves on an equatorial plate, bisecting the nucleus at a right angle to the spindle fibers. During anaphase I of Meiosis I, spindle fibers pull the homologous chromosomes apart. During telophase I of Meiosis I, one duplicated chromosome from each homologous pair migrates to one pole of the spindle while the matching duplicated chromosome migrates to the opposing pole.

During prophase II of Meiosis II, a new spindle is formed at each of the two poles of the original spindle. During metaphase II of Meiosis II, the duplicated chromosomes arrange themselves on new equatorial plates. During anaphase II of Meiosis II, the duplicated strands of each chromosome are pulled apart and begin migrating to opposite poles. During telophase II of Meiosis II, each of the four resulting nuclei develops into cells. In oogenesis (*qv*), the products of meiosis are three polar bodies that disintegrate and die and a single ovum (*qv*). In spermatogenesis (*qv*), the result is four functional sperm (*qv*), from a single spermatogonial cell.

The sperm or ovum produced by meiosis contain half the normal number of chromosomes in somatic cells (*qv*), being haploid (*qv*) instead of diploid (*qv*). The human ovum and sperm contain 22 autosomes plus one sex chromosome, an X in the ovum and either an X or a Y in the sperm. After union of a sperm and ovum, the zygote (*qv*) contains the diploid number.

melatonin This hormone (*qv*), secreted into the blood by the pineal gland (*qv*) in the brain, appears to inhibit endocrine (*qv*) functions, including the gonadotropins (*qv*) and ovulation (*qv*). In humans, light impulses from the eyes are split by the optic nerve, with stimuli going both to the visual cortex and to the hypothalamus (*qv*). A hypothalamic releasing factor then stimulates the pineal gland and regulates its production of melatonin. The secretion of melatonin has a marked diurnal (*qv*) rhythm, being tenfold higher at night than in daylight. In subpolar countries, melatonin production is lowest and the number of conceptions (*qv*) peak in June and July when daylight lasts 20 hours. A marked decrease in melatonin results in premature puberty (*qv*).

membranous urethra That portion of the male urethra (*qv*) extending from just below the prostate (*qv*) to the bulb at the base of the penis (*qv*); it connects the prostatic and penile portions of the urethra.

membrum virile (L.) The male sex organ; penis (*qv*).

Meme The brand name for a polyurethane material used in breast enlargement surgery for women; a unit of cultural transmission.

menacme That portion of a woman's life between menarche (*qv*) and menopause (*qv*).

ménage à trois (Fr.) A household, or a sexual encounter or relationship, involving three adults. The more common form of ménage à trois is a heterosexual (*qv*) couple with a second woman. The two women are usually bisexual (*qv*), with the husband relating to both women sexually and engaging in voyeurism (*qv*) when the two women interact sexually. In ciscisbeism (*qv*), an upper-class, usually married, woman arranges to have a male companion or attendant for social and sexual services. Resource: A. Karlen, *Threesomes: Studies in Sex, Power, and Intimacy* (New York: Beech Tree Books, William Morrow, 1988).

menarche The onset of menstrual cycles (*qv*) in a pubertal (*qv*) female. Menstruation (*qv*) usually begins between the ages of 9 and 17 years, with an American average of 12.5 years and a British average of 13.0 years. Climate has little, if any, effect on the time of menarche. However, the average age for menarche appears to rise by one month for every additional 1,000 feet females are above sea level. Correlation studies (*qv*) of monozygotic (*qv*) and dizygotic (*qv*) twins indicate a strong genetic (*qv*) influence. Strenuous exercise can delay the onset of menstruation when the body fat drops below 20 percent. The variety of food and proper nutrition has been implicated in promoting earlier menarche, although the theory that the age of menarche has decreased significantly for European and American women since the 1500s has been questioned by V. Bullough (*Science* [1981]213:365–366). *See also* pubarche.

menigeal neurosyphilis A severe form of syphilitic infection of the meninges occurring several years after the initial infection. Symptoms may include headaches, stiff neck, insomnia, lethargy, neurasthenia, and convulsions or epilepticlike seizures.

meningovascular syphilis An inflammation of the meninges and vascular tissue covering the brain, spinal cord, and nerve roots caused by a syphilitic infection. Symptoms may include visual disturbances, headaches, stiffness in the neck, dizziness, and mental confusion.

meno- A combining form referring to menses (*qv*) or menstruation (*qv*).

menopausal depression Feelings of depression and dejection accompanying menopause (*qv*) in women who have a previously existing tendency to depression, dissatisfaction with life, and feelings of inadequacy. A severe psychotic type is characterized by delusions of sin and guilt and/or an obsession with death. This condition is a form of involutional depression or melancholia (*qv*).

menopausal myopathy A muscle disorder affecting some women during or after menopause (*qv*), characterized by inflammation and/or atrophy of some muscle tissues.

menopause The natural and gradual cessation of menstruation (*qv*) in a human female, usually between ages 45 and 60. Menopause may also occur earlier as a result of illness or surgical removal of the uterus (*qv*) or both ovaries (*qv*). In natural menopause, the production of pituitary gonadotropins (*qv*) and ovarian estrogen (*qv*) decreases, ovulation (*qv*) stops, and menstruation becomes less frequent and eventually stops. Hot flashes (*qv*) are the only nearly universal symptom of menopause. The cessation of menstrual cycles and fertility (*qv*) does not mean a cessation of sex drive or libido (*qv*). Menopause is also used to refer to the broader phenomenon of climacteric (*qv*) or change of life.

menorrhagia Abnormally heavy or prolonged menstrual (*qv*) bleeding. Menorrhagia may occur in association with a benign growth in the uterus (*qv*) such as polyps and fibroids, with lesions, with malignancies, with an excess of estrogens (*qv*), with leukemia, and with aplastic anemia. If the condition is chronic, it may result in anemia. If the condition occurs after menopause (*qv*), a benign or malignant growth in the uterus may be the cause.

menorrhea The normal menstrual flow (*qv*) or menses (*qv*).

menoschesis Amenorrhea (*qv*); the suppression of menstruation (*qv*) caused by a psychological condition.

menostasis An abnormal condition in which the products of menstruation (*qv*) cannot escape the uterus (*qv*) or vagina (*qv*) because of a blockage; inaccurately used to refer to amenorrhea (*qv*) or menopause (*qv*).

menotropins A hormone (*qv*) preparation containing gonadotropins (*qv*) extracted from the urine (*qv*) of postmenopausal (*qv*) women and used to induce ovulation (*qv*) in anovulatory (*qv*) women and spermatogenesis (*qv*) in men.

menoxenia Any irregularity in the menstrual cycle (*qv*).

menses In women between menarche (*qv*) and menopause (*qv*), the monthly flow or uterine discharge (*qv*) consisting of uterine lining cells, blood, and vaginal and cervical mucus (*qv*). The menstrual flow (*qv*) begins 14 days after ovulation (*qv*) when fertilization (*qv*), implantation (*qv*), and pregnancy (*qv*) do not follow. Menses usually lasts 3 to 7 days, with the discharge amounting to between 6 and 8 ounces of fluid. Roughly a half-ounce of blood is lost each day of the menstrual flow, with the remainder of the discharge composed of cellular debris, mucus, and other substances. *See also* menstrual cycle; menstrual phase.

men's liberation A term, coined as an analogy with women's liberation (*qv*), for a movement on behalf of men to achieve sexual and family (*qv*) reform, and to eliminate or reduce preceived inequities, prejudices, and discriminations against men. Members of the men's liberation movement have focussed on issues like child visitation rights for divorced fathers; elimination of judicial prejudices against automatically assigning the children of a divorce (*qv*) to the woman; equalization of alimony (*qv*) payments; establishment of support payments by the divorced woman to the divorced man if appropriate; elimination of sexist (*see* sexism) stereotypes of men, particularly those that see men in general as sexual brutes, rapists, or exploiters; and elimination of customs that de facto penalize the man in a marriage (*qv*) such as the expectation that he should or must support his wife. In the area of sexual rights, men's liberation issues include the woman taking equal contraceptive (*see* contraception) responsibility with the man, the woman paying for her share of a social event (as on a date [*qv*]), and women in general abdicating what is seen by men's liberationists as their sole right to determine if a sexual encounter proceeds to intercourse. An example of the last issue is redefining date rape (*qv*) so that it is not immediately presumed that the man is guilty.

Despite the identification of inequities of these sorts, the men's liberation movement has achieved little of the fame or success gained by the women's liberation movement. Men's liberationists are often perceived by women as chauvinists (*see* chauvinism) and perhaps even dangerous, for example, when male liberationists talk of assigning some or equal complicity to the woman in a date rape situation. The men's liberation slogan, "I am an equal-responsibilities feminist (*qv*)," means that the male speaker supports the goals of the women's movement but simultaneously wants women to take equal responsibilities for sex, child support, and the like. This slogan has not made friends among feminists, who perceive only old-fashioned patriarchy (*qv*) under the seeming support for feminism. In consequence, there has been little or no cooperation between feminists and men's liberation groups to achieve changes in law, custom, or habit. Moreover, a wide variety of loosely defined viewpoints and positions can be subsumed under the term "men's liberation," not all of which are necessarily compatible theoretically or politically. Important books in the field include Warren Farrell's 1974 *The Liberated Man* (New York: Random House) and his 1986 *Why Men Are the Way They Are* (New York: McGraw-Hill), which contains political-economic analyses of male-female relationships; and Herb Goldberg's 1979 *The New Male* (New York: Morrow), which is more psychological in emphasis than Farrell's two books.

menstrual age *See* menstrual weeks.

menstrual aids Various sanitary pads (*qv*) and tampons (*qv*) made of disposable material that absorbs the menstrual flow (*qv*). *See also* menstrual sponge; toxic shock syndrome.

menstrual calendar A record kept by a woman documenting the beginning and end of her menstrual flows (*qv*). When used to predict the time of ovulation (*qv*) and fertility (*qv*) and estimate nonfertile periods, the menstrual calendar used alone has a very low reliability record. *See also* calendar method of birth control; rhythm method of birth control. The calendar is, however, useful to a physician in detecting irregularities in a woman's cycles that may require medical attention.

menstrual cramps Spasms in the pelvic muscles resulting from uterine contractions associated with shedding of the uterine lining in the menstrual flow (*qv*) and the subsequent release of prostaglandins (*qv*). The cramps, centered in the lower back and varying from woman to woman, can be relieved by over-the-counter medications, by noncoital or coital orgasm (*qv*), and by asperin or a prescription medication that blocks either the synthesis or action of specific prostaglandins.

menstrual curse *See* menstrual taboo.

menstrual cycle In women after puberty (*qv*) and before menopause (*qv*), the monthly cycle during which the inner lining of the uterus (*qv*) proliferates in preparation for implantation (*qv*) and is sloughed off in the menses (*qv*) when implantation does not occur. The menstrual cycle is regulated by the hormones (*qv*) of the hypothalamus (*qv*), pituitary (*qv*), ovary (*qv*), and uterus. In common usage, the cycle runs from the start of one menstrual period through to the start of the next menstrual flow. Following a menstrual flow of 3 to 7 days, the developing ovarian follicle stimulates proliferation and vascularization in the lining of the uterus. Following ovulation (*qv*), the empty Graafian or ovarian follicle develops into a hormone-producing corpus luteum (*qv*) that secretes both progesterone (*qv*) and estrogens (*qv*). These hormones stimulate accelerated proliferation, secretion, vascular congestion, and edema in the inner lining of the uterus.

If fertilization (*qv*) and pregnancy (*qv*) do not follow ovulation, the corpus luteum degenerates, and the uterine mucosa is sloughed off in the menses (*qv*), or menstrual flow. However, if ovulation is followed by fertilization and pregnancy, hormonal feedback from the uterine mucosa and conceptus (*qv*) maintains the corpus luteum and its hormone production until the placenta (*qv*) can assume maintenance of the pregnancy.

The average cycle is 29.5 days but can vary widely. Five out of six women have cycles that vary more than seven days in length. *See also* amenorrhea; ovarian cycle; proliferative phase; secretory phase; uterine cycle.

menstrual disorders Psychological, emotional, and/or physical effects associated with menstruation (*qv*), including irritability, inhibitions, emotional changes, menstrual cramps (*qv*), menstrual migraines (*qv*), and guilt feelings and internal conflicts arising from negative messages about sex and menstruation (*qv*) received from parents or religious authorities. *See also* premenstrual syndrome.

menstrual extraction A preemptive form of abortion (*qv*) typically used within two or three weeks after fertilization (*qv*). In menstrual extraction, a small vacuum tube, inserted through the vaginal (*qv*) and cervical canals (*qv*), is used to remove the uterine endometrium and very young embryo (*qv*) by suction. *See also* vacuum aspiration; vacuum curettage.

menstrual flow *See* menses.

menstrual hut In some non-Western nations and among some American Indian tribes, a shelter at the edge of a village where menstruating (*qv*) women can be isolated.

menstrual migraines Migraine headaches that occur during the premenstrual days or just after the menses (*qv*) begins.

menstrual period *See* menses.

menstrual phase The final, or first, of four phases in the menstrual cycle (*qv*) during which mucosa of the uterine endometrium (*qv*) is shed, leaving the spiral arteries of the basal layer bleeding until they repair; the menses (*qv*).

menstrual regulation A euphemism for a very early abortion (*qv*). *See also* menstrual extraction.

menstrual sponge A small natural or synthetic sponge inserted into the vagina (*qv*) to absorb the menstrual flow; not commonly used by women in industrial nations because of the availability of inexpensive sanitary pads (*qv*) and tampons (*qv*). *See also* toxic shock syndrome.

menstrual synchrony The biological phenomenon whereby the menstrual cycles (*qv*) of women living in physical proximity for a few months become synchronized within a few days of each other. Resource: M. McClintock, Menstrual synchrony and suppression, *Nature* (London) 229 (1971):244–245.

menstrual taboo Customs, rituals, and taboos associated with menstruation (*qv*) that make the menstruating woman, her menses (*qv*), and relationships with her subject to complex social regulation. Many, though not all, non-Western societies establish complementary duties and rituals for women and for men concerning menstruation. Often, menstruating women sequester themselves in their house or in specially constructed "menstrual huts" during the time of active menstrual flow, effectively making menstruation a liminal (*qv*) event or period. At such times, the woman does not involve herself in the production of food or in other duties. As a result, the term menstrual hut, which is often used in anthropological literature, is a misnomer, since it evokes images of confinement and even imprisonment. In actuality, these aspects of menstrual ritual are part of female, not male, culture, and in part create a socially legitimate time away from often arduous family (*qv*) and marital duties. It can be argued that for non-Western women who are susceptible to premenstrual tension, the menstrual hut represents a safe and calm environment.

Also common worldwide are prohibitions or restrictions on sexual intercourse (*qv*) during the time of the menstrual flow. Men and women attach very different values to these sexual taboos (*qv*). For women, who may be subject to considerable unwanted sexual advances, the taboo can offer a temporary, recurring respite from their husbands. For men, however, menstruating women are typically surrounded by a complex mythology of uncleanliness and danger. For example, it is not uncommon for men to believe that menstruating women can ruin a planned hunt or spoil a weapon. Such beliefs encourage them to avoid such women. It is not at all clear how frequently women believe such myths, but they do serve a social function of establishing rules for how men and women relate.

In English- and European-derived American culture, there are a number of such beliefs about the alleged powers and dangers of menstruating women, particularly in older, farm-based traditions; for example, the belief that contact with a menstruating woman can make milk or wine go sour. Even today, some men believe that sexual intercourse with a menstruating woman can be medically or physically dangerous to the penis (*qv*) and to overall health and strength. While one may be tempted to dismiss such beliefs as mere superstition, they represent an acknowledgment of a woman's fertility (*qv*) and a woman's broader sacred powers of procreation (*qv*), in the sense that an amenorrheic (*see* amenorrhea) woman is not fertile and prepubescent girls and postmenopausal women do not bear children.

Accordingly, many religions hold that male contact with menstruating women is dangerous. In ancient Rome, Pliny recorded what appear to be folklore beliefs that menstrual blood can turn new wine sour, make fruit fall off trees, turn crops barren, rust iron, and corrode bronze. Although Tantric traditions encourage intercourse during menstruation, traditional religions and cultures of Japan, China, Persia, Hindu India, and Africa, as well as native American cultures, have forbidden it. This taboo is also found in early Hebrew scriptures, from whence it passed into Christianity. "And if any man lie with her at all, and her flowers be upon him, he shall be unclean seven days, and all the bed whereon he lieth shall be unclean" (Leviticus 15:24, 20:18)—"flowers" is the euphemism the translators of the King James version used for menstrual blood. After the destruction of the temple in Jerusalem in 70 C.E., when ritual purity ceased to play a major role in Jewish life, the only surviving prohibition on a menstruating woman was that she not have sexual intercourse (*qv*) with her husband until she took a ritual bath, the mikveh (*qv*), a week after menstruation had ceased.

In all these traditions, it is not body exudates in general that inspire the taboos or rituals; for example, no customs exist prohibiting contact with individuals who have recently urinated. Instead, the focus is on a specific aspect of woman's physiology that conveniently can be used to symbolize a far wider range of matters related to fertility, sexuality (*qv*), and procreation. Moreover, the various spiritual and physical ills associated with menstruation are, in fact, not associated with menstruation at all but rather with making contact with a person who is in a taboo or sacred state. In none of these taboos is a woman's menstruation believed to be harmful to her or to other women with whom she may have contact. The taboo is directed toward men making social or sexual contact with her. The putative ills and disasters that follow upon illicitly contacting a menstruating woman are punishments visited on the contactor for violating a religious and social custom or taboo, which, in societies with menstrual taboo, is associated with the sacredness of fertility, reproduction, and procreation. Menstrual taboos commonly symbolize deep and sacred conceptualizations that, however, are not always obvious initially.

menstrual weeks A system for calculating the length of a pregnancy (*qv*) using the last menstrual period (LMP) as a starting point, even though ovulation (*qv*), fertilization (*qv*), and conception (*qv*) take place about 2.5 weeks after LMP.

menstruation (v. to menstruate) The physiological process whereby the monthly menses (*qv*) is expelled from the uterus (*qv*). Also known as catamenial discharge; menstrual phase or cycle; period. In many cultures, women's (and men's) colloquial expressions for menstruation include colorful euphemisms and slang terms, for example, "Aunt Flo(w)," and "ride the cotton pony."

mental masochism A form of masochism (*qv*) in which the individual seeks to be punished mentally and emotionally rather than physically.

meretrix (L.) An obsolete term for a prostitute (*qv*).

merkin In the sixteenth to eighteenth centuries, a term for the female pubic hair (*qv*) or female genitalia (*qv*); its current use is for a small wig used to change the color of the pubic hair. The merkin as a genital wig appears to have developed prior to 1796 when the loss of body hair was a common occurrence in the widespread smallpox and scarlet fever epidemics. After Jenner's discovery of a smallpox vaccine, merkins remained popular with prostitutes (*qv*) because their use allowed them to satisfy the preference of customers for a bare or haired mons, as well as for particular colors of pubic hair.

mesoderm In embryology (*qv*), the middle of the three primary germ layers of the developing embryo (*qv*), from which develop the bone, connective tissue, muscle, blood, vascular, and lymphatic tissues. *See also* endoderm; ectoderm.

mesonephric duct Paired ducts in the abdominal cavity of embryos (*qv*) of both genders in the first trimester (*qv*) that serve a temporary excretory function and then are incorporated into the reproductive system. In the third through eighth week, the mesonephric or Wolffian ducts (*qv*) drain the mesonephros (*qv*) or mesonephric kidneys. As the mesonephros degenerate and their function is taken over by the metanephric or definitive kidneys, the Wolffian ducts attach to the testes (*qv*) in the male fetus (*qv*), developing into the internal vasa deferentia (*qv*) and associated structures: the epididymis (*qv*), Cowper's glands (*qv*), seminal vesicles (*qv*), and prostate (*qv*). This male differentiation is controlled by fetal testosterone (*qv*). In females, in the absence of sufficient testosterone, the Wolffian ducts degenerate, leaving only functionless vestiges. The mesonephric ducts are named for Kaspar F. Wolff (*qv*). *See also* Mullerian ducts.

mesonephros A transitory pair of kidneys in the mammalian fetus (*qv*), the mesonephros develops in the late fourth week and degenerates towards the end of the eighth week after fertilization (*qv*). The mesonephros develops as the short-lived non-functional pronephros degenerates. Each of the two long ovoid mesonephric kidneys consists of about 40 elongated tubules attached to a common mesonephric duct (*qv*). These differentiate first in the cranial region and later in the caudal region. In the male fetus, the mesonephric duct and parts of the tubules persist as the vasa deferentia (*qv*) and associated structures. An alternate name for the mesonephric duct is Wolffian duct (*qv*), derived from its discoverer, Kaspar F. Wolff (*qv*). In the female fetus, the mesonephric ducts and their tubules disappear. The definitive kidneys, or metanephros (*qv*), begin developing in the eighth week of pregnancy and serve the excretory needs from that time on.

mesosalpinx The cephalic, free border of the broad ligament containing the fallopian tubes (*qv*).

mesovarium A short fold in the broad ligament that suspends the ovary (*qv*) on either side.

Messalina syndrome A seldom-used term for nymphomania (*qv*), the term referring to the alleged promiscuous sexual appetite of Valeria Messalina, the wife of the Roman Emperor Claudius.

metagenesis The regular alternation of sexual with asexual reproduction within the same species, as in the jellyfish or coelenterates.

methallenstril An estrogen (*qv*) used in treatment of menstrual cycle (*qv*) irregularities.

methyltestosterone A synthetic androgen (*qv*) used in the treatment of testosterone (*qv*) deficiency, osteoporosis, and female breast cancer (*qv*).

metralgia Tenderness or pain in the uterus (*qv*).

metria- A combining form referring to the uterus (*qv*).

metritis Inflammation of the uterine walls; also known as uteritis.

metro-, metra- A combining form referring to the uterus (*qv*).

metrodynia Tenderness or pain in the uterus (*qv*).

metrorrhagia Uterine bleeding other than that caused by menstruation (*qv*); may be caused by uterine lesions or the result of a urogenital malignancy, especially cervical cancer (*qv*).

microgenitalia A condition characterized by abnormally small external genitalia (*qv*). *See also* micropenis.

microIF *See* microimmunufluoresence test.

microimmunufluoresence test An immunological (*qv*) test using fluorescent labeled antigens (*qv*) to identify specific antibodies in the diagnosis of certain sexually transmitted diseases (*qv*).

microorchidism A congenital birth defect (*qv*) in which the testes (*qv*) are abnormally small.

micropenis A congenital birth defect (*qv*) in which the penis (*qv*) is exceptionally small. The maximum stretched length for a flaccid micropenis is no greater that 2.5 standard deviation units (SDU) below the average mean length for the affected individual's age group. For example, since the average stretched length of adult penises is 6.6 inches, with a standard deviation of 0.77 inch, a stretched adult micropenis would be less than 4.68 inches. The diameter of a micropenis is correspondingly reduced, with the corpora cavernosa (*qv*) being hypoplastic. A micropenis may contain a normal or hypospadiac (*qv*) urethra. *See also* ambiguous genitalia. Also known as microphallus or penile agenesis.

microphallus *See* micropenis; ambiguous genitalia.

micturation Urination or excretion of the urine (*qv*).

middle germ layer *See* mesoderm.

midline episiotomy *See* episiotomy.

midpain *See* Mittelschmerz.

midwife A person trained as a birth attendant and assistant; in developed nations, midwives are usually licensed as nurses or nurse practitioners.

Mien-Ling (Ch.) A Chinese variation of a common Oriental sexual aid, Mien-Ling has one hollow silver sphere containing a drop of mercury and a second sphere with a metal tongue that vibrates. Mien-Ling are inserted in the vagina (*qv*), where they are said to produce pleasurable sensations when the woman moves. In Japan, Mien-Ling balls are known as Ri-no-tama, and elsewhere, as Ben-Wa balls (*qv*) or Burmese balls.

MIF The Mullerian inhibiting factor. *See also* Mullerian inhibiting hormone.

Mifepristone *See* RU 486.

Mignon delusion A child's false belief that he or she is living with foster parents rather than real parents who are rich and famous. This delusion, often associated with schizophrenia, is interpreted by some psychoanalysts as a defense mechanism against unresolved aggression occurring during the Oedipal (*qv*) period.

migratory (gonorrheal) polyarthritis A progressive arthritis with variable signs of inflammation, joint pain, and a mild fever developing a few days to a few weeks after the onset of gonorrheal (*qv*) urethritis (*qv*). Unless prolonged, the arthritic inflammation lasts one to five days. In chronic cases, the pain in the joints originally affected diminishes as new joints become involved. Chronic cases are treated with antibiotics.

MIH Abbreviation for Mullerian inhibiting hormone (*qv*).

mikveh In Judaism, the ritual purification bath in spring or rain water required of a woman a week after her menses (*qv*) and after childbirth (*qv*) before she resumes her normal domestic duties and sexual relations (*qv*) with her husband. The mikveh, also spelled mikvah, is the only remaining biblical injunction for menstruating women. The rabbis of the Talmud explained the laws of family purity, which include the prohibition of intercourse (*qv*) during menstruation and before the mikveh, not in terms of religious ritual purity but as necessary to prevent the husband from taking sexual relations with his wife for granted. The laws of family purity and the mikveh are strictly adhered to today by Orthodox Jews but not by Conservative or Reform Jews. *See also* menstrual taboo.

milk An opaque white or bluish-white liquid produced by the mammary glands (*qv*) of mammals to suckle and nourish their newborn (*qv*). The main components of milk, besides water, are carbohydrate, usually lactose, protein, mainly casein with some lactalbumin and lactoglobulin, suspended fat, calcium and phosphorus, and various vitamins. Mother's natural milk is generally considered more beneficial and healthful than synthetic formulas.

milk duct The excretory duct that connects the lobe of a mammary gland (*qv*) with the opening in the nipple (*qv*) of the female breast (*qv*). *See also* lactation.

milk incest An incest (*qv*) taboo (*qv*) prohibiting sexual relations (*qv*) or marriage (*qv*) between a man and his wet nurse (*qv*) or between a man and a woman who have been nursed by the same woman. This form of incest taboo has been reported among Eastern Orthodox Christians, Italian Roman Catholics, and Muslims as well as in west Africa, Egypt, and the Middle East.

milk line *See* mammary ridges.

Miller v. United States A 1973 decision of the U.S. Supreme Court that attempted to tighten the restrictions on obscene (*qv*) material by requiring that defenders of an alleged obscene work prove that it has "serious literary, artistic, or scientific merit." Although the intent was to close the door on some material that became legal under the 1957 *Roth v. United States* (*qv*) decision, the Miller decision left prosecutors and the courts with the quandaries of the *Roth* decision unchanged. The courts still faced the near-impossible task of determining what has "literary, artistic, or scientific merit," who represents the "average community member," and what the "community" is.

mind-body problem A debate and issue in philosophy and psychology, dating back to the earliest philosophies of Greece, Persia, India, and China, regarding the exact relationship between body and mind. The central issues are the nature of body and mind, whether they are separate substances, and the nature, if any, of their interaction. The view that body and mind are two separate, independent substances with no interaction is represented by Plato's dualistic (*qv*) philosophy. Monistic (*qv*) views accept the existence of either body or spirit while rejecting the reality of the other pole. Interactive philosophies and psychologies accept the reality and interaction of mind and body, or body and soul or spirit. *See also* biosocial viewpoint.

minipill A contraceptive pill (*qv*), taken daily, containing small doses of progesterone (*qv*) and no estrogens (*qv*).

Minnesota Multiphasic Personality Inventory (MMPI) A test designed to measure nine aspects of personality, including masculine-feminine interests. *See also* BEM Sex Role Inventory.

minor (minority) In law, a person below the legal age of majority and adult status; in industrial nations, a minor is usually under age 18 or 21. The specific age of minority varies from state to state and country to country. Unemancipated minors cannot consent to their own medical treatment, except in the case of abortion (*qv*) and access to contraceptive information and services.

minx Colloquial term for a woman, characteristically young, who is considered sexually available and very much inclined to enjoy sex.

MIS Abbreviation for Mullerian inhibiting substance, now known as Mullerian inhibiting hormone (*qv*).

misattribution The erroneous subjective interpretation of something another person does or says, as when a nonsexual response is misinterpreted as a sexual overture, or when a male misinterprets a woman's statement that she is not interested in sexual intimacy as meaning she really is interested but is saying no because women are expected to say no.

misbegotten A derogatory term for a child born out of wedlock; a curse often used in a sexual or scatological context.

miscarriage A spontaneous, natural abortion (*qv*), usually before the twenty-eighth week of gestation. About 10 to 15 percent of all pregnancies (*qv*) end in miscarriages. In early pregnancy, a miscarriage is usually due to chromosomal abnormality and grossly abnormal fetal development.

miscegenation A racist legal term for sexual relations (*qv*) or marriage (*qv*) between persons of two different races. In the United States, miscegenation usually refers to sexual relations or marriage between whites and blacks, although such laws have also prohibited sexual relations and marriage between Caucasians and Orientals. All state laws against interracial marriages were declared unconstitutional by the U.S. Supreme Court in 1967.

mislabeling *See* misattribution.

misogamy A pathological aversion to marriage rooted in a fear of sexual intimacy, in an unwillingness or inability to assume the responsibilities of the married state, or, in psychoanalytic theory (*qv*), in an unresolved Oedipal complex (*qv*).

misogyny (n. misogynist) A pathological and extreme aversion to or hatred of women. Both men and women can be misogynists. In men, the attitude may arise from feelings of being intimidated or threatened by women, by homosexual (*qv*) tendencies, or gender dysphoria (*qv*). In women, the attitude may stem from a daughter's awareness that her parents really wanted a boy or from a disdain for effeminate behavior and things associated with being a woman. In psychoanalytic theory (*qv*), misogyny may be the result of an unresolved Oedipal complex (*qv*).

misopedia A morbid hatred of and aversion to children. Some psychiatrists regard this condition as a response to the subconscious belief that children are the product of incest (*qv*).

missed abortion A condition in which a dead embryo (*qv*) or fetus (*qv*) is not expelled from the uterus (*qv*) for two or more months. As the necrotic fetus degenerates, uterine infection may occur.

missionary position The position for sexual intercourse (*qv*) in which the male reclines above the female partner, who lies on her back facing him. Common opinion attributes the term to Christian missionaries in the South Pacific or Africa who advocated this coital position even though the natives preferred a variety of other positions. This advocacy of the missionary position was allegedly due to an interpretation of the story of Genesis in which man is created first and given primacy over woman in all things. Hence the supposed immorality of woman being in any position superior to or above a man. However, Artemidorus, a second century B.C.E. Greek philosopher, advocated this face-to-face, man-on-top position as the only proper one for Greeks because it affirmed the domination of men over women. Artemidorus also denounced oral eroticism as "an awful act." Although the position is assumed to be universally popular, *A Feminist Dictionary* observes dryly that the missionary position is unknown and unmissed in many cultures. Resource: R. J. Lawrence, *The Poisoning of Eroticism* (New York: Augustine Moore Press, 1989), p. 12.

mistress In its narrowest and most male-centered sense, a woman who provides sexual favors (*qv*) and companionship for a man for a more or less extended period of time without being married to him; a generic term for an adult woman. In fourteenth-century France, mistress originally denoted a woman who rules or is in command. The term, however, was quickly deprived of its sense of power and given a sexual connotation. Traditionally the mistress was the paramour (*qv*) of a married man who provided for her support and a place to live. In contemporary developed nations, the mistress is often financially self-supporting as a single career woman. In the S/M (*qv*) culture, mistress refers to a dominant woman. *See also* intimate friendship; comarital relations; sexually open marriage.

mithuna In the Hindu and Buddhist worlds, a loving couple, or sculpture depicting a loving couple. *See also* maithuna.

mitosis Chromosome (*qv*) replication followed by division of the chromosomes and cell to form two identical daughter cells with the same chromosome complement as the original parental cell. *See also* meiosis.

Mittelschmerz (Ger.) A sharp, brief abdominal pain or cramps occurring in many women at the time of ovulation (*qv*); German for "middle pain."

mixed chancre A genital (*qv*) lesion caused by a combined infection of *Haemophilus ducreyi* (*qv*) and *Treponema pallidum* (*qv*). *See also* hard chancre; soft chancre; syphilis.

mixed gonadal dysgenesis *See* ovotestis; true hermaphrodite.

mixoscopia A paraphilic (*qv*) condition in which sexual arousal (*qv*) and orgasm (*qv*) are dependent on watching a loved one engage in sexual relations (*qv*) with another person. *See also* voyeurism.

mixoscopia bestialis A paraphilic (*qv*) condition in which sexual arousal (*qv*) and orgasm (*qv*) are dependent on watching a loved one engage in sexual relations (*qv*) with an animal.

MMPI *See* Minnesota Multiphasic Personality Inventory.

mobility of libido A psychoanalytic term for the shifting of sexual energy (*qv*) from one object to another (e.g., from one person to another or from one part of the body to another). *See also* fetish, partialism.

modeling theory A theory of pornography's (*qv*) effects based on the assumption that a person who observes sexual acts is likely to engage in such acts. Also known as imitation theory (*qv*). *See also* catharsis theory; null theory.

Model Penal Code A guide for revision of American penal codes recommended in 1962 by the American Law Institute. The Model Penal Code advocated abolition of all criminal sanctions for any sexual behavior engaged in by consenting adults in private. In this proposal, forced or imposed sexual intercourse (*qv*), seduction (*qv*) of minors and the mentally impaired, sexual assaults (*qv*) of all types, indecent exposure (*qv*), and prostitution (*qv*) would still be criminal offenses. In 1962, Illinois was the first state to adopt such a code of law, now known as consenting adult laws (*qv*).

modesty The sense of privacy; behaving according to the public standard of what is proper or decorous; decent, pure, and not displaying one's body. The requirements and standards of modesty vary greatly from one culture (*qv*) to another and within a single culture from one period to another. Thus, while a bikini swimsuit might be modest in the United States of the 1960s or 1980s, a Victorian woman who showed a naked ankle was considered immodest. In Islamic cultures, modesty requires women to wear the chador (*qv*) in public, while bare-breasted women in Africa or the islands of the South Pacific are in keeping with the standards of modesty in those cultures. In some cultures, it is considered inappropriate and immodest for a woman to make direct eye contact with a male.

Modicon Trade name for an oral contraceptive (*qv*) containing ethinyl estradiol, an estrogen (*qv*), and norethinodrone, a progestin (*qv*).

modified radical mastectomy *See* mastectomy.

mohel The Hebrew word for the individual who performs the religious rite of circumcision (*qv*) on a male 8 days after his birth.

moist warts *Condylomata acuminata* (*qv*), or venereal warts (*qv*) caused by the human papilloma virus (*qv*).

molar pregnancy A pregnancy (*qv*) in which a benign hydatid mole (*qv*) develops from the trophoblastic (*qv*) tissue of the early embryo (*qv*). In a molar pregnancy, all the signs of pregnancy are exaggerated. Because of the risk of cancer developing in the placental tissues, the growth must be surgically removed.

molestation Sexual advances (*qv*) and assault against a child or mentally retarded person who cannot give legal consent. Sexual molestation usually involves persuasion but may also involve physical force. Molestation may involve fondling (*qv*) of the genitalia (*qv*), oral-genital contact, and intercourse (*qv*). *See also* sexual harassment.

Moll, Albert (1862–?) A contemporary of Sigmund Freud (*qv*), the German physician Moll was the first to engage in a scientific study of the sexual development of children and adolescents. The American translation of his *Das Sexualleben des Kindes* (1909) bore the title *The Sexual Life of the Child* (1912). Unlike Freud, who created a new theory of infantile and childhood sexuality (*qv*), Moll worked within the confines of the doctrines of his day, deferring to the degeneracy theory (*qv*) and antimasturbatory biases of the day. His work also focused more on sexological pathology and criminology than on the normal. An important feature of Moll's work was his clinical studies of children, sometimes with long-term outcome data. His work prepared the way for development of a sexology (*qv*) of childhood that does not focus on psychosexual abnormalities and pathologies.

momism A colloquial term for a pattern of excessive concern, care, and attention showered on a child by an overly protective mother or, in some cases, father. Momism may be an unconscious compensation for an unspoken rejection of the child or a substitute for sexual satisfaction in marriage. Momism can be a form of emotional incest. *See also* mother-son incest. The term, coined by the American novelist Philip Wylie, is often used contemptuously for women's behavior in general.

monecious A species in which male and female reproductive structures occur in the same individual. In plants, both male and female structures may occur in the same flowering structure or separately in different flower structures. A species is also said to be monecious if it has only one sex, parthenogenetic (*qv*) females, as do brine shrimp and many other vertebrates. The term is also sometimes applied to species in which the male and female cannot be distinguished by external appearance. *See also* diecious; hermaphrodite.

moniliasis *See* candidiasis.

Monilia vaginitis (L.) *See* Candida albicans.

monism (adj. monistic) In philosophy, a doctrine that there is only one ultimate substance or principle in the universe. For philosophical idealists, this principle may be mind. For materialists, it may be matter. For others, the single ultimate substance may be a combination of matter-spirit. From a theological perspective, monism involves a denial of any distinction between God and the world and the belief that spirit, matter, and all life constitute a single reality. *See also* dualism.

monitrice A labor (*qv*) coach, usually a registered nurse or midwife (*qv*) who has special training in the Lamaze method of childbirth (*qv*).

monochoric A species in which all members have ovaries, the ovum is diploid (*qv*) and only females are produced. *See also* dichoric.

monochorial twins Fetal (*qv*) twins (*qv*) who share a single chorion (*qv*). *See also* monozygotic twin.

monogamy (adj. monogamous) Marriage (*qv*) or cohabitation (*see* cohabit) with only one person at a time; the practice of having only one mate. Applied to a heterosexual (*qv*), gay (*qv*), or lesbian (*qv*) couple, the term usually implies sexual exclusivity. Monogamy can exist in a single lifelong adult relationship, or in a series of two or more monogamous relationships. The traditional Western definition of monogamy has centered on two values, "forsaking all others" or sexual exclusivity, and "until death do us part." However, in recent years some people have modified these values in various ways. Some monogamous couples stress emotional exclusivity in a way that allows or accepts extramarital sexual (*qv*) relations that are not emotional and based on sexual release rather than love (*qv*). Others allow emotional and sexual relationships to coexist alongside but subordinate to the primary marital relationship. More common is a modification of the lifelong value with a series of monogamous relationships but only one mate at a time in a sexually exclusive relationship. *See also* adultery; bigamy; comarital relationship; polyfidelity; polygamy; polygyny; polyandry; satellite relationship; serial monogamy; sexually open marriage.

monomorphism A species having only one sexual form instead of the dimorphic (*qv*) male and female sexual forms, for example, the parthenogenetic (*qv*) females of the whip-tail lizards. *See also* monecious.

mononucleosis, infectious An acute herpes-type viral infection caused by the Epstein-Barr virus (EBV); symptoms include fever, malaise, sore throat, swollen lymph glands, atypical lymphocytes, enlargement of the spleen and liver, and abnormal liver function. Transmission is by respiratory infection, but the disease is not highly contagious. When infected, children have mild, often unnoticed symptoms. The older the person, the more severe the symptoms are likely to be. Infection usually confers permanent immunity. Treatment is mainly for the reduction of symptoms.

monopediomania A psychological dependency on and sexual attraction to a one-legged partner; a paraphilic (*qv*) variation of acrotomophilia (*qv*) in which sexual arousal (*qv*) and satisfaction are dependent on the partner's, usually a female, being an amputee.

monoploid *See* haploid.

monorchidism (monorchism) Having only one testicle (*qv*) descended into the scrotum (*qv*).

monosexual (n. monosexuality) Having all the characteristics of either the female or male gender (*qv*) or associating only with persons of the same gender. In one usage, monosexual means having the characteristics and traits of one gender only, without any transposition (*qv*) or cross-coding (*qv*) for the anatomy, hormones (*qv*), gender identity (*qv*), gender role (*qv*), or sexual orientation (*qv*) of the other gender. *See also* gender identity/role. In a second usage, monosexual refers to an individual who is either exclusively heteroerotic (*qv*) or exclusively homoerotic (*qv*) in sexual activities or in long-term gender orientation. In the later usage, monosexual is the opposite of bisexual (*qv*). Monosexual can also refer to a species with only parthenogenetic (*qv*) females and no males.

monosomy A cell or individual lacking a single chromosome in the normal diploid (*qv*) complement. Monosomy of the X chromosome (*qv*), 45,XO, is known as Turner syndrome (*qv*). Most monosomies involving one of the 22 pairs of somatic chromosomes are lethal to the developing embryo (*qv*) unless the missing chromosome is one of the smaller autosomes (*qv*). Somatic monosomies that survive to birth have severe deformations.

monospermy The fertilization (*qv*) of a single ovum (*qv*) by a single sperm (*qv*), as opposed to polyspermy (*qv*). Monospermy is normal for some species, including humans. Polyspermy—more than one sperm fertilizing an ovum—occurs in bees.

monotrophy A phenomenon in which a mother is able to bond with only one infant at a time. If the mother of twins (*qv*) leaves the hospital with one twin but leaves the other behind for a few days, Klaus and Kennell suggest she may not bond with the second child because of doubts that the child is in fact hers. Monotrophy is used to explain why many mothers of twins dress the twins alike as a way of facilitating bonding with both simultaneously. Resource: M. Klaus and J. Kennell, *Maternal-Infant Bonding* (St. Louis: C. V. Mosby, 1976).

monovulatory Routinely releasing one ovum (*qv*) during each ovarian cycle (*qv*), as opposed to diovulatory, a tendency in some families and individuals to produce two ova instead of one in each cycle. A tendency to diovulation increases the incidence of dizygotic twins (*qv*).

monozygotic Twins (*qv*) resulting from the fertilization (*qv*) of a single ovum (*qv*), which subsequently divides into two embryos (*qv*) that become genetically identical offspring; the opposite of dizygotic (*qv*) or fraternal twins, which result from the simultaneous ovulation (*qv*) of two ova, which are fertilized and develop into genetically different twins. One in 90 live births currently is a twin birth, with two-thirds of these twins being dizygotic and one-third monozygotic.

mons (pubis) *See* mons veneris.

monster A dated and pejorative medical term for a grossly deformed and usually nonviable fetus (*qv*).

monster myths Folklore that offers simplistic, nonscientific explanations of the origin and cause of severe birth defects (*qv*). Among the more common monster myths are those that associate deformed offspring with sexual intercourse (*qv*) during menstruation (*qv*).

mons veneris (L.) In human females, a soft, fatty, triangular-shaped mass of tissue covering the pubic bone, above and anterior to the vulva (*qv*). Literally, "mountain of Venus." The mons veneris is covered with pubic hair (*qv*) after puberty (*qv*). Also known as mons pubis; the mons.

Montgomery's tubercle One of several types of sebaceous glands in the areolae (*qv*) of the breasts (*qv*). They enlarge during pregnancy (*qv*) and secrete a lubricant that protects the breast from infection and trauma during nursing (*qv*). *See also* Morgagni's tubercle.

monthly period *See* menses.

mooning A recurring fad among adolescents (*qv*) in which youths expose their bare buttocks (*qv*) from the windows of a moving automobile. *See also* streaking.

Moral Majority A coalition of American fundamentalist, evangelical, and charismatic Protestants dedicated to a literal interpretation of the Bible and strongly opposed to sex education (*qv*) in the schools, any deviation from traditional sex roles (*qv*), premarital sex (*qv*), sexual permissiveness (*qv*), uncensored literature and art, abortion (*qv*), and other "secular" or "humanist" trends. The key figure in the political efforts of the movement in the 1980s was the Reverend Jerry Falwell.

moral masochism A psychoanalytic (*qv*) term for an unconscious need to be punished by an authority figure representing the father. Sigmund Freud (*qv*) theorized that this need arises from a desire for passive intercourse (*qv*) with the father, which the child blocks and transforms into a desire to be punished by him.

mores Patterns of cultural and moral action that contribute to the continuity of a group because they represent traditional and prescriptive standards that regulate individual behavior. *See also* deviance.

Morgagni's tubercle One of several small, soft nodules occurring on the surface of the areola (*qv*) of the breast (*qv*) in association with large sebaceous glands just under the surface that secrete a bacteriostatic, lubricating substance during pregnancy (*qv*) and lactation (*qv*). *See also* Montgomery's tubercle.

Morgengabe (Ger.) In the early Middle Ages, the money paid by the groom to the bride the day after the marriage in recognition of the bride's surrender of her virginity (*qv*) and the groom's acquisition of sexual rights to her; literally, the "morning gift." A Germanic marriage custom, the Morgengabe originated in the sixth and seventh centuries as the economic direction of Germanic marriages shifted significantly. *See also* arrha; bridegift; brideprice; dower; dowry; endowment.

Mormons *See* Church of the Latter Day Saints.

morning-after pill Colloquial term for a large dose of contraceptive estrogen (*qv*) or an estrogenlike compound, usually diethylstilbesterol (*qv*), given orally to a woman within 24 to 72 hours after sexual intercourse (*qv*) to prevent pregnancy (*qv*); used in emergency situations such as rape (*qv*) or incest (*qv*).

morning drop A grayish-white mucoid fluid that seeps from the external opening of the male urethra (*qv*) at the tip of the penis (*qv*), usually upon rising in the morning; may be a symptom of gonorrhea (*qv*).

morning erection An erection (*qv*) commonly experienced by men as they awaken.

morning sickness A colloquial term for the medical condition known as nausea gravidarium (*qv*), sometimes experienced by pregnant (*qv*) women.

morphodite A colloquial expression for a hermaphrodite (*qv*); also a colloquial term for a lesbian (*qv*). The origin of the word is obscure.

morphogenesis (adj. morphogenetic) The development and differentiation of the structures, organs, and form of an organism during its embryonic (*qv*) development.

morphologic sex The male, female, or intersex status of an individual as determined by the structure of internal and external sexual anatomy. An individual's morphologic or anatomical sex may or may not be in accord with the chromosomal or genetic gender (*qv*), gonadal gender (*qv*), hormonal gender (*qv*), or gender role/identity (*qv*), and gender orientation (*qv*).

morphophilia A paraphilic (*qv*) condition in which erotosexual (*qv*) arousal and facilitation of orgasm (*qv*) are responsive to and dependent on a partner whose body characteristics are selectively particularized, prominent, or different from one's own bodily characteristics; in John Money's typology, a stigmatic/eligibilic paraphilia. *See also* Appendix A.

mort douce (Fr.) A French phrase, literally "sweet death," with several meanings: (1) death occurring during sexual intercourse (*qv*), (2) the warmth and calm that follow orgasm (*qv*), and (3) euthanasia or mercy killing.

morula (L.) A round, solid mass of embryonic cells that develops in a few days after fertilization (*qv*); derived from the Latin for "mulberry." In mammalian development, the morula stage is followed by the blastocyst (*qv*) stage when the solid ball develops a cavity and differentiates into an inner cell mass (*qv*), which becomes the embryo proper, and the outer trophoblast (*qv*), which becomes the chorion (*qv*).

mosaicism, chromosomal An individual with two or more distinct types of body cell, each with slightly different chromosomal content. Chromosomal mosaicism is usually the result of mitotic (*qv*) nondisjunction (*qv*), which occurs immediately after fertilization (*qv*) in the zygote (*qv*) or later in the blastocyst (*qv*). In the case of nondisjunction in the zygote (*qv*), one cell line may lack a chromosome while the other cell line is trisomic for the same chromosome. If nondisjunction occurs later in embryonic development, the result will be a majority of the body cells with a normal chromosome complement and two other cell lines—one monosomic (*qv*) and the other trisomic (*qv*). Monosomic cell lines are usually not viable, although monosomy of the X chromosome (*qv*), Turner syndrome (*qv*), and monosomies involving a small autosome (*qv*) may be viable. Chromosomal mosaicism also results from the fertilization of an ovum (*qv*) by two sperm or from the fusion of two very young embryonic masses. Typical mosaics include: variations of Turner syndrome (e.g., 46,XX/45,XO and 46,XY/45,X0), a mosaic trisomy 21 or Down syndrome, (e.g., 46/47,21 +), and mosaic such as 46,XX/47,XXX and 47,XXX/48,XXXX.

mosaicism, sexual An individual whose body tissues contain cells with two distinct chromosome (*qv*) complements—an individual with two types of body cells, one with a male chromosome complement of 46,XY and the other female complement of 46,XX, or some other combination of multiple normal and/or abnormal male and female karyotypes (*qv*).

Mosher Forced-Choice Guilt Inventory Having defined guilt as "a generalized expectancy for self-monitored punishment for violating or anticipating the violation of internalized standards of socially acceptable behavior," Donald Mosher operationalized this definition in a *Forced-Choice Guilt Inventory*, which elicits self-reports of an individual's level of guilt. Three areas are delineated in this scale: sex guilt, hostility guilt, and morality-conscience guilt. The sex guilt area, of interest in sexological research, deals with guilt about sexually related thoughts and behaviors. Guilt in this area has been correlated with other influences (e.g., religious affiliation, sex-negative parental attitudes, and the lack of sexual experience).

mother The female parent; one who gives birth (*qv*), originates, nurtures, has responsibility for, and authority over a child. Because *mother* is associated with birth and the primary nurturing parent, the term is combined with other terms as a modifier in a variety of metaphors, as in mother earth, mother nature, mother country, mother superior, mother tongue, mother wit, and mother copy or tape.

Because of the recent advent of reproductive technologies separating functions traditionally performed by a single female parent, a distinction can be drawn between the genetic or gametic mother (*qv*), who provides the ovum (*qv*), the biological or gestational (*qv*) mother, who carries the fetus (*qv*) from conception (*qv*) to term, and the social and/or adoptive mother (*qv*), who nurtures and raises the newborn. *See also* homoseductive mother; phallic mother; surrogate mother.

mother archetype In Jungian theory, the primeval concept of mother that resides in the human unconscious and is evident in the importance of the mother figure in mythologies around the world.

mother attachment *See* mother fixation.

mother complex A strong emotional attachment to one's mother, usually with sexual overtones.

mother figure *See* mother surrogate.

mother fixation In psychoanalytic theory (*qv*), an irrational and inordinate attachment of a child to the mother that is alleged to prevent the fixated son from establishing mature sexual relations (*qv*) or from falling in love (*qv*) with a woman, or the fixated daughter from falling in love with a man. *See also* Oedipal complex; Electra complex. The abnormally persistent, close, and often paralyzing attachment of mother fixation is characteristic of this form of arrested development. This definition reflects a common sexist (*qv*) bias current when the concept was originally proposed.

mothering The provision by a mother (*qv*), mother surrogate (*qv*), or the father of the nurturance, physical care, and emotional support essential for a child to develop a sense of self-identity, security, and self-worth. *See also* somatosensory affectional deprivation syndrome. Terms like *mothering* are based on assumed sexist (*qv*) distinctions between socially stereotyped male and female sex roles (*qv*). Attempts to overcome such bias by including the other gender are seldom effective because the user of the term automatically assumes the gender distinction implied by the terms *mothering* and *fathering*.

mothering one A term for a male or female who provides the basic care, love, and protection required by an infant or child; the term was coined by psychologist Harry Stack Sullivan.

mother instinct An alternative term for maternal instinct (*qv*).

mother-son incest Sexual relations (*qv*) between a mother and her son. This form of incest is much rarer than father-daughter incest. Its occurrence is usually associated with an absent father, marital conflict, alcoholism, or mental disturbances. In one form of mother-son incest, termed emotional incest, sexual relations do not occur, even though the mother places the son in the emotional role usually associated with her male partner and uses the son as a surrogate partner emotionally and affectionally. Whether or not the mother-son incest involves sexual intimacies, the effects are similar, resulting in a son who is overly attached to the mother and incapable of forming mature relationships with other females.

mother surrogate A term used to designate a person who fulfills the social role of the natural mother.

motile (motility) Exhibiting the ability to move under its own power, as a motile spermatozoan (*qv*), which is capable of swimming with the aid of its undulating tail.

motivational hierarchy In Maslow's (*qv*) humanistic psychology, a hierarchical or pyramidal categorizing of basic human needs and motives with first priority given to the physiologic or biologic (air, food, water, shelter, clothing), followed by the feeling and knowledge of being secure, a sense of belonging to a group or family and being loved, satisfaction of the need to be respected and held in esteem, and finally the need to be self-actualizing (*qv*). Resource: Abraham Maslow, *Motivation and Personality* (New York: Harper & Row, 1970).

motoro A term for a premarital courtship (*qv*) practice, common among the Mangaians of the South Pacific, in which young men crawl into the huts of single girls at night and leave before dawn. Motoro, or nightcrawling (*qv*), is done without permission of the young woman's parents and, in some cases, the young woman's permission. *See also* bundling; fensternl.

mount, to A specific type of sexual interaction in quadrupedal animals in which the male straddles the female atop her back and thrusts with his pelvis. Animal behavioral specialists distinguish mounts with and without penile intromission (*qv*). In response, the female may arch her back in lordosis (*qv*), or may attempt to fight off the male. The term is only rarely used to describe human sexual behavior. *See also* coitus; copulate; present.

mount of Venus *See* mons veneris.

mouth-genital contact *See* oral-genital sex.

MPC Mucopurolent cervicitis (*qv*). *See also* nongonococcal urethritis.

mucoid *See* mucus.

mucopurolent cervicitis *See* nongonococcal urethritis.

mucosa A mucous membrane; a thin, delicate tissue with a moist surface; the innermost layer of any cavity or tubelike structure within the body—the lining of the mouth, trachea, intestinal tract, urethra (*qv*), uterus (*qv*), or vagina (*qv*). *See also* mucus.

mucous plug The mucus (*qv*) secreted by cells in the cervix (*qv*) under the influence of the female hormone cycle. During ovulation (*qv*), the possibilities of fertilization (*qv*) are enhanced by changes in the cervical mucus, which becomes watery and provides stringy fibers that guide the sperm (*qv*) through the cervix into the uterine cavity (*qv*). At other times, the mucus forms a barrier plug that protects against the penetration of sperm and microorganisms that might cause infection of the abdominal organs. *See also* cervical mucus; Billings' contraceptive method; ferning; spinnbarkheit.

mucus (n.), mucous (adj.) A viscous, slippery secretion of certain membranes and glands lining the mouth, digestive tube, respiratory passages, and the urogenital tract; contains mucopolysaccharide mucin, white blood cells, water, inorganic salts, and cellular debris.

mucus method of contraception *See* Billings' contraceptive method; cervical mucus.

mujerados (Sp.) Male transvestites (*qv*) or homosexuals (*qv*) who assume the female gender role (*qv*) and serve as shamans (*qv*) among the American Indians in the New Mexico area. *See also* berdache; hijra.

mulatto A racist term for an individual with one black and one nonblack parent. *See also* octoroon; quadroon.

Muller, Johannes Peter (1801–1848) A German physiologist, discoverer of the Mullerian ducts (*qv*), and founder of modern experimental physiology.

Mullerian ducts Paired tubular structures in the pelvic/abdominal cavity of the fetus (*qv*) that in females develop into the inner two-thirds of the vagina (*qv*), the uterus (*qv*), and fallopian tubes (*qv*). In females with low levels of Mullerian inhibiting hormone (MIH) (*qv*), the posterior region of the tubes fuse to form the upper vagina and uterus, while the anterior region remains separate and develops into the fallopian tubes. In the male fetus, a high level of MIH reduces the Mullerian tubes to functionless vestiges. The ducts were named for their discoverer, Johannes P. Muller (*qv*), a German physiologist. *See also* Wolffian ducts; mesonephric duct.

Mullerian inhibiting hormone (MIH) A hormone that prevents the growth and differentiation of the primordial paired Mullerian ducts (*qv*) that otherwise form into the upper vagina (*qv*), uterus (*qv*), and fallopian tubes (*qv*). In the male fetus, MIH is produced by the testes (*qv*) in amounts that defeminize (*qv*) the internal sexual anatomy by reducing the Mullerian ducts to functionless vestiges. Prior to a standardizing of the terminology, MIH was also known as Mullerian inhibiting substance (MIS), and Mullerian inhibiting factor (MIF).

Muller's tubercle A small extension of the fused Mullerian ducts (*qv*) into the urogenital sinus in the ninth week of gestation (*qv*) of a female fetus (*qv*); the terminal end of the uterovaginal canal with the posterior side of the urogenital sinus, which thickens and elongates before hollowing out to form the vagina (*qv*) and uterus (*qv*).

multifactorial inheritance A trait that is the result of the interaction of several genes (*qv*) and environmental factors. The degree of genetic control over a multifactorial trait can be expressed in terms of concordance (*qv*), based on studies of the trait in monozygotic (*qv*) and dizygotic (*qv*) twins.

multimodal therapy A therapeutic approach that combines two or more modalities, such as behavioral therapy (*qv*), transactional analysis (*qv*), modern psychoanalysis (*qv*), or a variety of psychological approaches.

multiorgasmic *See* multiple orgasm.

multipara (adj. multiparous) A woman who has given birth to two or more viable offspring. *See also* nullipara.

multiparous labia The labia majora (*qv*) and minora (*qv*) of women who have given birth (*qv*). During the resting state, the minor labia of parous women are different from those of a nulliparous (*qv*) woman, usually being more pendulous. The labia of multiparous women may have varicose veins. During sexual arousal (*qv*), the minor labia of a multipara have a deeper, more intense wine red color, while the nulliparous minor labia are pink or bright red. During arousal, the multiparous major labia become engorged, doubling or tripling in size, while the nulliparous major labia flatten, thin out and are more widely separated. *See also* sex skin.

multiphilia A paraphilic (*qv*) compulsive condition involving recurrent short-term limerence (*qv*) or falling in love (*qv*) and pair-bonding (*qv*) with new partners. The presence of limerent pair-bonding, despite its brevity, distinguishes this condition from nymphomania (*qv*) and satyriasis (*qv*) in which limerence is allegedly absent. A form of ultraertia (*qv*).

multiple marriage A nonspecific term for polygamy (*qv*), polygyny (*qv*), polyandry (*qv*), plural marriage (*qv*), serial polygamy (*qv*), divorce (*qv*) and remarriage (*qv*), or group marriage (*qv*).

multiple mothering The care and nurturance of children by several women who provide the social role associated with mothering, as in a kibbutz, the Oneida Community (*qv*), or an adoption center (orphanage).

multiple orgasm Having more than one orgasm (*qv*) in a brief space of time, without a refractory period (*qv*). In the female, Shere Hite reports a distinction between sequential multiple orgasms, a series of orgasms with short resolution phases (*qv*) between the orgasms, and a rarer form of multiple orgasm, with no breaks between the orgasms while stimulation is continued (*The Hite Report* [*qv*]). Multiple orgasm in males, especially in the younger years, was reported by Alfred Kinsey (*qv*) (1947). William Hartman and Marilyn Fithian maintain that the ability of a male to have multiple orgasms is a learned ability, associated with the practice of orgasm without ejaculation (*qv*). Multiorgasmic males may experience the emission phase (*qv*) of ejaculation during their multiple orgasms but refrain from the propulsion phase (*qv*), which is under voluntary somatic muscle control and triggers a refractory period. *See also* maithuna; karezza. Resource: W. Hartman and M. Fithian, *Any Man Can* (New York: St. Martin Press, 1984); A. Kinsey et al., *Sexual Behavior in the Human Male* (Philadelphia: Saunders, 1948).

multiple personality A colloquial term for schizophrenia in which a person experiences self as two or more different personalities, each dissociated from the other, with variable degrees of overlap and shared memory or mutual amnesia. A multiple personality may be a factor in paraphilic (*qv*) sex crimes, commonly committed in a fugue state (*qv*).

multiplier effect The interaction between the organism and the environment in which initial differences between males and females in predispositions to behave in certain ways are magnified with time as each individual interacts with his or her human environment in different ways. In theory, such interactions can enhance differences (positive multiplier effect) or reduce them (negative multiplier effect).

Each interaction alters the individual organism slightly, so that it perceives and responds to the environment increasingly differently. In the theory, stereotypical gender role behavior (*qv*) finally emerges from these dynamic interactions among biological, psychological and social factors. *See also* sex variables.

mummified fetus A fetus (*qv*) that died in the uterus (*qv*) and has been desiccated. *See also* fetus papyraceus.

musgami (Ch.) An Oriental contraceptive (*qv*)—a kind of cervical cap (*qv*) made of oiled silk paper.

mut'a An early Muslim tradition that allows a man to contract with a woman for a ''temporary marriage,'' a marriage of pleasure, in return for a certain payment. The duration of the mut'a might be a single night, several weeks, or longer. In fundamentalist Iran, the mut'a has been revived in response to the growing number of widowed and single women for whom husbands are not available because of the Iraqi-Iranian war of the late 1980s.

mutagen Any chemical or physical agent that induces a genetic mutation or an increase in the rate of mutation (*qv*) of a gene (*qv*). *See also* teratogen.

mutagenesis The induction or causing of a change in the genetic code or deoxyribonucleic acid (*qv*).

mutation An inheritable change in the sequence of the deoxyribonucleic acid (*qv*) bases coding for a gene (*qv*) and its expression.

mutilation An accidental or deliberate injury, maiming, or damage done to an organ or part of the body. Self-mutilation may be part of a paraphilic (*qv*) orientation, as in apotemnophilia (*qv*) and stigmatophilia (*qv*). Mutilation may also be part of a ritual or cosmetic tradition within a culture. *See also* acrotomophilia; circumcision; female circumcision; sadism; stigmatophilia.

mutual absorption In Tantric yoga (*qv*) and Taoist traditions, the belief that during sexual intercourse (*qv*) the man and woman should each absorb the other's vital energies—the man's absorbing the woman's female essence to counteract his loss of semen (*qv*), or male essence, and the woman's absorbing the man's ejaculate (*qv*) with its male essence to balance her loss of female essence. *See also* ying, yang.

mutual masturbation Sexual activity (*qv*) in which the partners handle each other's genitalia (*qv*) and bring each other to orgasm (*qv*) through manual masturbation (*qv*), cunnilingus (*qv*), or fellatio (*qv*).

mutual orgasm A sexual interaction in which both partners achieve orgasm (*qv*) simultaneously. With the growing interest in and emphasis on female orgasm starting in the 1960s, mutual orgasm became for many couples a performance expectation and a source of anxiety when it was not achieved. Mutual orgasm may provide more enjoyment for a couple, but it can also create a destructive performance pressure.

Mycostatin Trade name for an antifungal drug, often used to treat candidiasis (*qv*).

myelacephalus A abnormal fetal condition—usually a separate monozygotic twin (*qv*) with barely recognizable parts and form.

myoma A benign muscle tissue tumor whose growth is often accelerated by increased estrogens (*qv*) associated with pregnancy (*qv*) and estrogen therapies. Uterine fibromyomas occur in more than one-quarter of all women over the age of 35. Myomas tend to regress after menopause (*qv*).

myomectomy The surgical removal of a myoma (*qv*). In the case of uterine fibromyomas, removal is commonly done by dilation and curettage (*qv*).

myometrium The middle of three layers of the uterine wall; a muscular layer with muscle cells arranged horizontally, vertically, and diagonally around the uterus (*qv*). The myometrium is lined on the inside by the endometrium (*qv*) and on the outside by a thin membranous covering called epimetrium.

myotonia The buildup of muscle tone or tension, especially during sexual arousal (*qv*). *See also* vasocongestion. Myotonia resulting from sexual arousal during the excitement (*qv*) and plateau (*qv*) stages is released during orgasm (*qv*) with the involuntary, rhythmic contractions of the muscles and organs in the genital (*qv*) system and, to a lesser extent, all over the body.

mysophilia (adj. mysophilic) A paraphilic (*qv*) condition in which a male is dependent on contact with or fantasy (*qv*) about something soiled or considered filthy in order to be sexually aroused and achieve orgasm (*qv*).

myxoma, mammary A tumor of the breast (*qv*) in premenopausal women, usually benign and treated by surgical removal.

MZ Abbreviation for monozygotic twin (*qv*).

N

N The number of items in a set.

n, 2n, 3n, 4n Symbols for the haploid (*qv*), diploid (*qv*), triploid (*qv*), and tetraploid (*qv*) number of chromosomes in a cell, individual, or strain.

Nabothian cyst A small, pearly white, firm cyst formed in a Nabothian gland (*qv*) of the uterine cervix (*qv*) and commonly found in women of reproductive age, especially those who have borne children.

Nabothian glands Many small, mucus-secreting glands in the uterine cervix (*qv*).

nadle A third gender in the Navaho culture, in addition to the more traditional male and female genders (*qv*). Two paths can lead to the status of nadle. One can be born with ambiguous genitalia (*qv*) that makes assignment to the male or female gender difficult, or a person who is dissatisfied with being in either the male or female gender role may decide to adopt the role of nadle. The nadle gender combines the rights and duties of both male and female genders except that the person is forbidden to hunt or participate in war parties. A nadle may marry, dress in any way he or she wishes, and perform a wide variety of tasks.

Nagele's rule A method of calculating the estimated time of delivery (*qv*) based on the mean length of gestation (*qv*). To calculate the expected day of delivery, 3 months are subtracted from the first day of the last normal menstrual period (*qv*) and 7 days added to that date.

nakedness fear (phobia) *See* gymnophobia.

nameless crime An obsolete term for sodomy (*qv*). In many criminal codes, the terms *sodomy*, *anal*, and *oral sex* are considered unmentionable, hence the general term *nameless crime* used for any taboo (*qv*) sexual activity whose mere mention is socially unacceptable. *See also* crime against nature.

nandrolone decanoate An androgen (*qv*) used in the treatment of testosterone (*qv*) deficiency and female breast cancer (*qv*).

nandrolone phenopropionate An anabolic androgen (*qv*) used in treatment of metastatic breast cancers (*qv*).

narcism, narcissism (adj. narcistic, narcissistic) The condition of being dominated by self-love or being self-centered based on an idealized self-image. In psychoanalysis (*qv*), an early stage of development characterized by an extreme concern for the self and lack of concern for others. Also in psychoanalysis, a condition in which the sexual self-interest normally associated with the phallic stage (*qv*) occurs as the infantile ego (*qv*) acquires a libido (*qv*). In an adult, narcissism may be an abnormal fixation or a regression. It is a trait common to immature and neurotic personalities. The term is derived from the Greek myth of Narcissus, a youth who fell in love with his own image reflected in a pond.

narcissistic object choice A psychoanalytic (*qv*) term for the tendency to choose a sexual or marital partner who is similar to oneself as an expression of self-love.

narcissistic neurosis In an adult, narcissistic neurosis represents a developmental fixation (*qv*) or regression (*qv*) to a very early, pregenital phase of development that prevents the individual's developing a mature attachment to another person. *See also* oral stage; anal stage; genital stage.

narcissistic object choice The investment of the libido (*qv*) in the self or in a person very similar to one's self.

narcissistic personality A personality characterized by behavior and attitudes that indicate an abnormal self-centeredness and self-love. A narcissistic personality tends to be extremely unrealistic about personal attributes and goals and what one is entitled to and can expect from the other person in a relationship. At the same time, a narcissistic personality devalues and deprecates other persons. *See also* narcissism.

narcissistic personality disorder A condition characterized by an exaggerated sense of one's own importance, qualities, and uniqueness, an abnormal need for attention and admiration, a preoccupation with grandiose fantasies, and problems in interpersonal relations involving exploitation of others and a lack of empathy. *See also* narcissism; narcissistic personality.

narratophilia (adj. narratophilic) The paraphilic (*qv*) condition of being responsive to or dependent on using or hearing dirty or obscene words or on reading or listening to erotic narratives in the presence of one's partner in order to achieve sexual arousal (*qv*) and orgasm (*qv*).

natal Referring to birth (*qv*), or to the buttocks (*qv*) or nates (*qv*).

natality *See* birthrate.

natal sex The gender (*qv*) of a newborn (*qv*).

nates The buttocks (*qv*).

natimortality The proportion of stillbirths (*qv*) to the general birthrate (*qv*).

National AIDS Hotline A Public Health Service resource and information service for inquiries regarding acquired immune deficiency syndrome (*qv*) operating 7 days a week and 24 hours a day. Telephone: 1–800–342–7514.

National AIDS Network A national organization promoting cooperation between groups working with persons with acquired immune deficiency syndrome (*qv*). Address: 729 Eighth Street S.E., Suite 300, Washington, D.C. 20003.

National Association of People with AIDS A national support group providing information and services for persons with acquired immune deficiency syndrome (*qv*). Address: P.O. Box 65472, Washington, D.C. 20003.

National Coalition of Gay Sexually Transmitted Disease Services A national organization coordinating gay (*qv*) and lesbian (*qv*) groups that deal with sexually transmitted diseases (*qv*). Address: P.O. Box 239, Milwaukee, WI 53201.

National Gay and Lesbian Task Force Hotline A national telephone hotline providing information on acquired immune deficiency syndrome (*qv*): 1–800–221–7044.

National Gay Rights Advocates A public interest law firm that handles litigation in the area of civil rights and discrimination issues concerning acquired immune deficiency syndrome (*qv*). Address: 540 Castro Street, San Francisco, CA 94114.

National Sexually Transmitted Diseases Hotline Run by the American Social Health Association, this telephone hotline provides information on all sexually transmitted diseases (*qv*). Telephone: 1–800–227–8922.

native lovemap As used by John Money, in an analogy with native language, the lovemap (*qv*) one assimilates as his or her own personal, inalienable possession, regardless of its degree of conformity or difference to the lovemaps of others. Resource: J. Money, *Lovemaps* (New York: Irvington, 1986).

nativism A theory that gender variations, especially homoerotic orientation, are inborn and due to genetic (*qv*) or biological factors rather than to social influences and learning.

nativistic A point of view that emphasizes the role of heredity as opposed to environment. *See also* nature/nurture debate; nature/critical period/nurture. Native or natural to an organism or species; the converse of acquired or culturally induced. *See also* scripting; conditioning.

natural act (sex, sin) A sexual act that, although considered sinful and immoral by adherents of the natural law theory (*qv*), nevertheless does not interfere with the procreative goal of sexual relations; for example, rape (*qv*), incest (*qv*), adultery (*qv*), and fornication (*qv*). Unnatural sexual sins include oral (*qv*) and anal sex (*qv*), masturbation (*qv*), and contraceptive coitus (*qv*). *See also* natural law.

natural child An obsolete term for a child born out of wedlock; also used to distinguish a child born in wedlock from an adopted child.

natural childbirth A method of labor (*qv*) and parturition (*qv*) using little or no medical intervention. Natural childbirth is based on the belief that the pain experienced in giving birth is almost entirely the result of fear and tension and that this pain can be reduced to a minimum by understanding the processes of birth, by learning to coordinate breathing with relaxation, and by doing exercises that develop the abdominal and uterine muscles used in the final stage of labor. This method of delivery was described by Grantly Dick-Read (*qv*), a British physician, in his 1942 book *Childbirth Without Fear*, written after his observations of childbirth in Russia. *See also* Lamaze method of childbirth; Leboyer method of childbirth.

natural family planning (NFP) Any form of spacing and controlling the number of pregnancies (*qv*) by timing intercourse (*qv*) in terms of the ovulatory cycle instead of using barrier contraceptives (*qv*), exogenous hormones (*qv*), or surgical interventions. *See also* Billings contraceptive method; cervical mucous method of contraception; rhythm method of contraception.

natural fertility The reproductive capacity and performance of an individual or a group unaffected by the use of any contraceptive (*qv*) or induced abortion (*qv*).

natural homosexual period A misleading term occasionally applied to the period of same-gender socialization that precedes the onset of puberty (*qv*) when boys tend to avoid the company of girls and socialize with others of their own gender and girls socialize with girls and develop emotional crushes for older women, particularly teachers and counselors. This period ends with the awakening of heteroerotic (*qv*) interests during adolescence (*qv*).

natural law theory In theological and philosophical thought, the divine law and purpose of all natural phenomena as revealed in nature; the belief that the justice and validity of laws and social institutions depend on their conformity to certain universal laws of nature. Natural law includes the sum of the rights and duties that of themselves follow directly from the nature of man. The immutability of this law is an important theme in Catholic ethics. Applied to sexual morality, the belief that sexual activity and sexual relations (*qv*) are natural and morally good only when they occur within the heterosexual marital union and are open to reproduction (*qv*). In this philosophical context, anal sex (*qv*), contraceptive intercourse (*qv*), masturbation (*qv*), and homosexual (*qv*) relations are immoral because they allow enjoyment of sexual pleasure without acceptance of the "natural" goal of sexual relations—procreation. Oral sex may be accepted provided it culminates in vaginal intercourse. In terms of natural moral law and sexuality, the divinely determined nature, function, and purpose of human sexuality are revealed in the Genesis story of Adam and Eve. The basic assumptions of natural law theory have been challenged by the secularization of Western culture and intellectual relativism.

natural selection According to Darwinian evolutionary theory, variations in reproductive success of different individuals within a species or population promote the survival of those individuals producing the most offspring and their inherited traits and, at the same time, cause a gradual decrease of less successful individuals and their inherited traits. Natural selection is the basic mechanism behind the evolution of new species. It is based on the fitness of the individual genotypes (*qv*) and their adaptability to the environment. *See also* sexual selection.

nature/critical period/nurture This new paradigm of development states that biological factors or nature and cultural determinants or nurture combine and interact at critical periods (*qv*) in development, both before and after birth (*qv*), to leave a permanent residual or imprint on behavior. The old reductionist theories of biological and cultural determinism have been disproved by research showing that prenatal (*qv*) and neonatal (*qv*) antecedents or templates may facilitate certain behaviors and sexual orientation (*qv*) provided the postnatal determinants in upbringing and socialization facilitate elaboration and fixing of these tendencies. *See also* nature/nurture debate. Resources: J. Money, Homosexual genesis, outcome studies, and a nature/nurture paradigm shift. In P. Pancheri et al., eds.,

Endorphins, Neuroregulators and Behavior in Human Reproduction (Amsterdam: Excerpta Medica, 1984); J. Money, *Gay, Straight, and In-Between: The Sexology of Erotic Orientation* (New York: Oxford University Press, 1988).

nature/nurture debate The long-standing debate over the relationship, relative influence, and interaction of biological and social factors in the development of the individual. There are two extreme positions in the nature/nurture debate: biological and cultural determinism. Biological determinism is a form of reductionist theory arguing that the characteristics of individuals can be explained exclusively in terms of biological factors and genetic inheritance. The biological reductionism of Sigmund Freud's (*qv*) classic phrase that "anatomy is destiny" reflects the patriarchal biases of Victorian (*qv*) society. On the other side, cultural determinism argues that individual differences and group character can be explained entirely by socialization and scripting (*qv*). While sociologists and psychologists reject all forms of biological reductionism, T. Parsons has suggested a more fruitful theoretical relationship between biological and social systems that draws on the parallel between symbols, information and cybernetics in social systems and the communication of "information" through deoxyribonucleic acid (*qv*) and hormones (*qv*) in biological systems. Recent studies of neurological differences between male and female brains and of neural templates for behavioral tendencies and gender identity suggest that both extremes in the nature/nurture debate lack validity, and that a more accurate picture is presented by the phrase nature/critical period/nurture (*qv*). The reduction of prenatal factors to biology and postnatal factors to social influences only is counterproductive since the postnatal learning and socialization enter the brain as messages from the senses and are processed by the physiological activities of the brain as learning and memory. Also, psychosexual development (*qv*) involves multiple biological and social factors interacting over time, from fertilization (*qv*) on through birth (*qv*) and continuing through adolescence (*qv*). Resources: J. Money, *Gay, Straight, and In-Between: The Sexology of Erotic Orientation* (New York: Oxford University Press, 1988); T. Parsons, *Social Systems and the Evolution of Action Theory* (New York: Free Press, 1977). *See also* biology, biologism, biological reductionism.

naturism A health movement originating in Germany around 1900 that emphasizes the health aspects of nudism. Naturism and naturist clubs, also known as sun clubs and open-air clubs, promote a family atmosphere and encourage sunbathing, sports, and family activities in the nude without any sexual connotation.

nausea and vomiting of pregnancy *See* nausea gravidarum.

nausea gravidarum (L.) A common condition of recurrent, brief periods of nausea and vomiting associated with the first trimester (*qv*) of pregnancy (*qv*), usually between the sixth and twelfth to fourteenth weeks of gestation (*qv*). More commonly known as ''morning sickness,'' though some women experience the symptoms in the afternoon or evening. The symptoms may also occur when a woman is not pregnant. The etiology is poorly understood with various factors involved: the hormonal changes of early pregnancy, infections, emotional disturbances, allergies, and altered reactions to foods and odors. The mild condition of morning sickness should not be confused with two other conditions, persistent nausea and vomiting of pregnancy and hyperemesis gravidarum, both of which involve *prolonged* vomiting and may require hospitalization.

navel The umbilicus, a depression near the center of the abdomen marking the site where the umbilical cord (*qv*) from the placenta (*qv*) entered the fetus (*qv*). When the umbilical cord is tied off after birth, the remnant dries up and is sloughed off in a few days, leaving a small, circular depression. In some, the navel is flush or projects.

navel cord *See* umbilicus.

naviculans (L.) The clitoris (*qv*).

NBAS *See* Neonatal Behavior Assessment Scale.

neck stretching A cosmetic custom in the Padaung culture of Burma in which rings are gradually added to a woman's neck to increase her sexual attractiveness by doubling the normal length of her neck.

necromania A pathologic desire for sexual relations (*qv*) with a corpse, usually accompanied by a morbid interest in anything associated with dead bodies, such as autopsies, funerals, morgues, and cemeteries. This condition is almost exclusively found among males. *See also* necrophilia.

necrophilia (adj. necrophilic) A severe but rare paraphilic (*qv*) condition of being responsive to or dependent on sexual activity (*qv*) with a dead body in order to achieve erotic arousal (*qv*) and facilitate or achieve orgasm (*qv*). This condition almost always occurs in psychotic males who have no interest in relating sexually with live persons. In necrophilia, the obsession is with death; in lust murder (*qv*) or erotophonophila (*qv*), the obsession is with killing as a source of sexual arousal and orgasm. The two conditions may also coexist. *See also* necromania.

necrophiliac A person with necrophilia (*qv*).

necrosis Localized tissue death resulting from disease or injury.

necrospermia A condition in which the spermatozoa (*qv*) in seminal fluid (*qv*) are immobile or dead.

need The physiological and/or psychological lack of something required for proper functioning; more generally, any lack or deficiency experienced by an individual as harmful to his or her welfare; an animal drive or physiological motive. Satisfaction of basic biological or physiological needs for food, sleep, and shelter is essential to survival. The satisfaction of psychological needs is more flexible and culturally conditioned. Thus, a need for sexual satisfaction may be satisfied in a heteroerotic (*qv*) or homoerotic (*qv*) relationship, in marriage (*qv*) or celibacy (*qv*), in a socially acceptable outlet, or in paraphilic (*qv*) behavior. *See also* motivational hierarchy.

negative Electra complex *See* negative Oedipus complex.

negative feedback loop *See* feedback, hormonal.

negative nuclear sex (gender) A cell nucleus whose chromosome (*qv*) complement contains a single X chromosome (*qv*) and no Barr body (*qv*). A 46,XY male shows a normal negative nuclear sex, as do most 45,XO females with Turner syndrome (*qv*). Also known as chromatin negative (*qv*). *See also* chromatin positive.

negative Oedipus complex A psychoanalytic (*qv*) term for a son who experiences an erotic attraction for his father rather than for his mother as in the standard Oedipus complex (*qv*); a daughter who is sexually attracted to her mother rather than to her father as in the Electra complex (*qv*). Also known as an inverted Oedipus or Electra complex.

negative relationship In research, an inverse relationship between two variables (*qv*) (e.g., as one variable increases the other decreases).

negative sexual conditioning A social and cultural indoctrination, both verbal and nonverbal, during the formative years that creates in a child a complex of negative attitudes and values related to human sexuality and sexual behavior. The sex-negative attitudes absorbed during the formative years are a common cause of psychogenic sexual dysfunctions (*qv*).

Neisseria gonorrhoeae (L.) The gram-negative, nonmotile bacterium that causes gonorrhea (*qv*).

neobehaviorism A school of psychology that applies the general principles of behaviorism (*qv*) in a broader and more flexible way, stressing experimental research and laboratory analyses of overt behavior as well as less quantifiable behaviors such as fantasies, stress, love, empathy, trust, and personality.

neocortex That part of the pallium, the outermost surface of the cerebral hemispheres, showing stratification and organization of the most highly evolved and conscious type. In terms of evolution, the neocortex evolved much more recently than the paleocortex (*qv*) or the limbic system (*qv*), which it encapsulates. Also known as isocortex; neopallium.

neo-Freudian Characterizing a psychoanalyst or psychoanalytic theory that follows Sigmund Freud's (*qv*) major doctrines but adds theoretical formulations and concepts that depart significantly from his original premises. The term is commonly applied to the systems of Harry Stack Sullivan, Karen Horney, Clara Thompson, Alfred Adler (*qv*), Carl Jung (*qv*), Erich Fromm, and others.

neo-Malthusianism A movement advocating the limitation of population growth by means of voluntary birth control rather than legal restraints on the right of individuals to reproduce. *See also* Malthus.

neonatal Pertaining to the first 4 weeks following birth (*qv*).

Neonatal Behavior Assessment Scale (NBAS) A scale for assessing and evaluating an infant's neurological condition and behavior in terms of alertness, motor maturity, irritability, consolability, and interaction with people.

neonatal death Death of a live-born infant during the first 28 days after birth (*qv*).

neonatal developmental profile An evaluation of the developmental status of a newborn (*qv*) based on a gestational age (*qv*) inventory, a neurologic examination, and the Neonatal Behavior Assessment Scale (NBAS) (*qv*).

neonatal mortality The statistical rate of infant deaths during the first 28 days after live birth (*qv*); expressed as the number of such deaths per 1,000 live births in a specified population or institution in a given period of time.

neonate The newborn infant (*qv*) up to 28 days after birth.

neopalium *See* neocortex.

neoplasm A new and abnormal growth of cells, a tumor, which may be benign or malignant.

neoteny The persistence of embryonic or juvenile stages of development in the sexually mature adult form. Neoteny has probably been very important in evolution of many groups, including humans, who have resemblances to young stages of apes.

nepiophilia A paraphilic (*qv*) condition, similar to pedophilia (*qv*), except that the sexual partner is an infant; sexual arousal (*qv*) and achievement of orgasm (*qv*) are responsive to and dependent on having or fantasizing sexual activity (*qv*) with an infant sexual partner. The reciprocal paraphilia is infantilism (*qv*) in which a person impersonates an infant in order to be aroused and achieve orgasm. *See also* ephebophilia; gerontophilia; pedophilia.

nervi erigens (L.) The nerves in the sacral region of the spinal cord responsible for an erection (*qv*) of the penis (*qv*).

neuroendocrine Pertaining to the nervous and endocrine (*qv*) systems, particularly their interaction; also structures that function as both an endocrine gland and as nervous tissue, such as the neurons in the hypothalamus (*qv*) that produce the hormone (*qv*) oxytocin (*qv*) and release this hormone into the vascular bed of the pituitary gland (*qv*).

neurogenic A condition caused by a problem or dysfunction in the nervous system.

neurohormone A hormone (*qv*) that stimulates the neural mechanism. *See also* neurotransmitter.

neuromodulator A neurochemical substance that influences or modulates the action of a neurotransmitter (*qv*) or neurohormone (*qv*).

neuron A nerve cell consisting of a central body and branches, an axon and one or more dendrites, and characterized by the capacity to be stimulated by other nerves and by conductivity or the ability to conduct neural impulses.

neuronal spiking Large neuronal electrical (voltage) discharges from nerves or brain tissue, characterized by a very sharp peak of the waveform typically two to five times the magnitude of background neuronal activity, which is in the range of 20 to 100 microvolts. Neuronal spiking can be detected in deep brain structures by way of implanted electrodes, as well as in the scalp-recorded electroencephalogram. Neuronal spiking has been linked diagnostically with somatosensory affectional deprivation (*qv*).

neuropeptide Those biochemical substances, related to peptide hormones (*qv*) that are active in the brain and nervous system. *See also* neurotransmitters; peptide hormone; endorphin.

neurosyphilis A syphilitic (*qv*) infection that has spread into the central nervous system (*qv*). The bacterium *Treponema pallidum* (*qv*) infects the central nervous system, the meninges, and cerebrovascular system in about 10 percent of all untreated cases of syphilis. Clinical signs that can be detected before physical signs of neurological involvement include significant increases in white blood cells and proteins in the cerebrospinal fluid. The cerebrospinal fluid also gives a positive reaction to a syphilis blood test. Physical symptoms include a gradual weakening and wasting of muscles in the upper extremities, followed by pain in the lower limbs and a loss of feeling that makes walking difficult, culminating in general paresis (*qv*) or paralysis. Other major symptoms include visual disturbances, tremors of the mouth and tongue, loss of tendon reflexes and muscle coordination, loss of bladder and rectal sphincter control, and impotence (*qv*). Destruction of the posterior columns of the spinal cord leads to a loss of conscious position sense. *See also* tabes dorsalis.

neurotransmitter One of a variety of biochemical substances produced and released by the brain or nerve cells and responsible for conductivity between nerve cells. A neurotransmitter may be released at the synapse or the point of contact between the tip of a terminal branch of the nerve fiber belonging to one nerve cell and the cell body or a dendrite of another nerve cell. Neurotransmitters induce activity in susceptible cells of the brain and nervous system. Some neurotransmitters are classified as neurohormones. *See also* peptide hormone; endorphin.

neurula An early embryonic stage during the formation of the neural tube; the third stage of embryonic development, following the morula (*qv*) and blastocyst (*qv*) stages.

neurulation The development of the neural plate and neural tube in the early embryo (*qv*). *See also* neurula.

newborn A recently born infant, a neonate (*qv*).

new impotence A colloquial and semitechnical term for an alleged increase in impotence (*qv*) among young men in the 1960s and 1970s, attributed to growing feelings of insecurity as a result of the feminist movement (*qv*) and women's liberation (*qv*).

NGU *See* nongonoccocal urethritis.

nidation The implantation (*qv*) of the developing blastocyst (*qv*) in the endometrial (*qv*) wall of the uterus (*qv*) at the beginning of pregnancy (*qv*).

night courting A courtship (*qv*) practice in which a young man and woman share the same bed, purportedly without having sexual intercourse (*qv*). In colonial America and through to the early 1800s, night courting was known as bundling (*qv*). The custom was prevalent in the colder European, English, Scotch,

Scandinavian, and American rural areas where homes, lacking central heat, were heated by wood fireplaces. *See also* fensternl; night crawling.

night crawling A courtship (*qv*) and sexual practice in which a young man crawls into bed with a young woman during the night without disturbing or waking the young woman's family. Genital fondling (*qv*), various sexual activities, and intercourse (*qv*) may be part of night crawling depending on the culture (*qv*). This custom is common in Polynesian, Philippine, and various cultures of the Americas. *See also* bundling; night courting; fensternl.

nipple bud The embryonic primordium of the mammary gland (*qv*) and nipple (*qv*). The mammary glands and their nipples are derived from a pair of primitive mammary ridges (*qv*), epidermal thickenings that become visible in the seventh week of gestation (*qv*). The ridges rapidly regress everywhere except in the chest region, where the mammary buds form and eventually develop into mammary glands.

nipple graft The cosmetic relocation of the nipple (*qv*) of the female breast (*qv*) or mammary gland (*qv*) following surgical correction of ptosis (*qv*) or drooping breasts or hypertrophic, overly large breasts.

nipples The rounded, pigmented, erectile tips of the mammary gland (*qv*) or breast (*qv*) in both male and female mammals (*qv*). In the female mammal, the nipples increase in size during pregnancy (*qv*) and nursing (*qv*). They are the channels through which milk is secreted when a woman is breast-feeding (*qv*) or nursing. The nipples are subject to vasocongestion (*qv*) and erection (*qv*) during sexual arousal (*qv*) or when stimulated by touch or friction. Females as well as males vary greatly in the pleasure they experience from nipple stimulation. The nipples may be everted, flat, or, more rarely, inverted. *See also* areola; polythelia; polymastia.

nipple shield A soft latex device used to allow the nipples (*qv*) of a lactating (*qv*) woman to heal from cracking.

nit The egg of a parasitic louse, usually found attached to human hair or clothing fibers. *See also* pediculosis.

nocturnal emission A wet dream (*qv*); subconscious and involuntary sexual arousal (*qv*) and ejaculation (*qv*) during sleep occurring in roughly 80 percent of adolescent males and, rarely, adult males. Nocturnal emissions are associated with erotosexual (*qv*) dreams occurring during the rapid eye movement phase of sleep. *See also* spermatorrhea. Nocturnal emissions decrease in frequency for males who masturbate (*qv*) or have other sexual outlets. Unexpected and unexplained nocturnal emissions can be a source of concern and anxiety to an adolescent male, as unexpected and unexplained onset of menstruation (*qv*) can be to an adolescent female.

nocturnal orgasm An orgasm (*qv*) reached as a result of a sexuoerotic (*qv*) nocturnal dream. According to the Kinsey (*qv*) survey of American males, close to 100 percent of men in his sample had experienced erotic dreams, with close to 85 percent of these culminating in orgasm, with the peak incidence occurring in the late teens and early twenties. For females in the Kinsey sample, about 70 percent reported having sexual dreams, but only 50 percent reported orgasm accompanying these dreams, which reach their peak when women are in their forties.

nocturnal penile tumescence (NPT) The spontaneous and natural erection (*qv*) of the penis (*qv*) during sleep. Healthy men typically experience three episodes of NPT a night for a total duration of 2 to 3 hours. NPT is associated with the rapid eye movement phase of sleep. Male NPT, which occurs from birth (*qv*) through advanced old age, can be measured by harnessing the penis in an expandable ring attached to a sensory recorder for changes in pressure. In cases of male erectile dysfunction (*qv*), absence or abnormality in the pattern of NPT is indicative of an organic rather than psychological etiology. Less is known about the female counterpart of NPT because of the difficulty in measuring vasocongestion (*qv*) in the female genitalia (*qv*). *See also* plethysmograph.

nocturnal pollution *See* nocturnal emission.

no-fault divorce A type of divorce (*qv*) stating that a marriage (*qv*) may be dissolved without the need to demonstrate in court that one of the spouses is guilty of any particular misconduct and therefore subject to a punitive financial settlement. The first no-fault divorce statute was enacted in 1980 by California. Elimination of punitive financial settlements usually results in equal division of financial assets accumulated by the couple, with provisions made for any pre-nuptial agreement (*qv*) or contract the couple may have agreed to. While the theory of no-fault divorce was endorsed by feminists (*qv*) and others concerned about the disadvantages of the previous divorce procedures created for women, the reality is that no-fault divorce has placed women in even worse financial situations. Equal division of marital property usually requires sale of the couple's house, forcing the wife to move at a time when she does not have the financial assets to purchase another home. Under no-fault divorce settlements, mothers commonly retain custody of any children, receive less in child support and alimony, and are required to pay for expensive child-care services while they work.

Noguchi reaction A skin test for syphilis (*qv*) that uses injection of an extract of several strains of killed *Treponema pallidum* (*qv*). Appearance of a red pimple at the site of injection indicates a syphilis infection.

noma An acute necrotizing ulceration of the mucous membranes of the mouth and genitalia (*qv*), probably caused by a spirochete bacterium. Noma affects primarily youngsters with poor nutrition and hygiene. The ulcers spread rapidly, causing a painless destruction of soft tissues and bone, which leaves disfiguring scars when the lesions heal.

nonage A person who is below the legal age for some activity, usually for consenting to sexual intercourse (*qv*) or marriage (*qv*), drinking, driving, or voting; a minor (*qv*).

nonbacterial prostatitis A chronic inflammation of the prostate gland (*qv*) caused by something other than a bacterial infection. Nonbacterial prostatitis may be an autoimmune disease with the person's own immune system activated to attack the prostate tissues. No cure is known; however, avoiding all alcohol and aggravating medications plus increasing the amount of water normally drunk can reduce the symptoms.

nonconsummation Never having had penile-vaginal intercourse (*qv*) within a marriage (*qv*) or cohabitation (*qv*). The lack of sexual intercourse may be due to ignorance about what intercourse actually involves, to an exclusive preference for other sexual behaviors and outlets, to a fear of hurting or being hurt, to vaginismus (*qv*), or to persistent male erectile dysfunction (*qv*) or premature ejaculation (*qv*). Nonconsummation may be grounds for divorce (*qv*) or annulment (*qv*). *See also* consummate.

nondemand pleasuring A behavioral exercise in which a person caresses the partner's body, gradually increasing the degree of intimacy but without expecting sexual arousal (*qv*) from the partner. *See also* sensate focus exercises.

nondisjunction In genetics, the failure of two homologous (*qv*) chromosomes (*qv*) to separate, one to each of the two daughter cells during anaphase (*qv*) of the first division of meiosis (*qv*); the failure of two chromatids (*qv*) to separate equally between the two daughter cells in anaphase of the second meiotic division (*qv*); or the failure of a chromosome pair to separate equally between the two daughter cells at anaphase in the mitotic (*qv*) division of a somatic cell. As a result of nondisjunction, one cell is missing a chromosome, and the other has two of the same chromosome. Fertilization (*qv*) of a sperm (*qv*) or egg following meiotic nondisjunction results in monosomic conditions such as Turner syndrome (*qv*) (45,XO), or trisomic conditions, Down syndrome (trisomy 21, 47,21 +) and Klinefelter syndrome (*qv*) (47,XXY). Postfertilization somatic nondisjunction results in a chromosome mosaic (*qv*) condition.

nonfilarial elephantiasis A swelling of the legs, scrotum (*qv*), labia (*qv*), breasts (*qv*), or other body parts caused by an obstruction of the lymphatic (*qv*) circulation by a streptococcal (*qv*) or other nonfilarial infection.

nongonococcal urethritis (NGU) A sexually transmitted infection of the urethra (*qv*) not caused by the *Neisseria gonorrhoeae* (*qv*) bacterium. Until recently, NGU was mostly ignored. In the late 1980s, 2 million new cases occurred annually among American men. *Chlamydia trachomatis* (*qv*) is the leading cause of NGU, an infection of the urethra. Other microorganisms causing NGU are *Mycoplasma hominis*, *Candida albicans* (*qv*), *Trichomonas vaginalis* (*qv*), *Ureaplasma urealyticum* (*qv*), and the *Herpes simplex* (*qv*) virus. In addition to being transmitted by sexual contact with an infected partner, the infection can be spread to the eyes by contaminated fingers. A rectal infection can result from anal intercourse (*qv*). Infection can also be transmitted by nonsexual contact.

Symptoms appear within 1 to 3 weeks, usually a slight white, yellow, or clear discharge from the vagina (*qv*) or penis (*qv*), and, for males, a mild to moderate pain when urinating. Although 9 of 10 men infected with Chlamydia have some symptoms, many men ignore the mild discomfort of painful urination and a watery discharge. Females often experience no symptoms even though they are infected and can transmit the infection to a partner. NGU is frequently misdiagnosed as gonorrhea (*qv*) by a physician unaware of the difference between NGU and gonorrhea. An NGU infection can also coexist with a gonorrheal or other infection. Antibiotics are the treatments of choice. Sexual partners should be treated whether or not they are symptomatic. Follow-up tests are recommended since the infection can recur within 2 to 6 weeks after treatment, possibly due to reinfection or to the life cycle phase of the bacteria at time of treatment. Physical or emotional stress can trigger a recurrence of NGU.

If undiagnosed and untreated in women, NGU can lead to severe pelvic infection, infertility (*qv*), and a tendency to miscarriage (*qv*). Each year, 500,000 men in the United States get epididimitis, an inflammation of the testes (*qv*), as a result of NGU. Infants born to infected women should be routinely treated for disease because of the risks of pneumonia, conjunctivitis of the eye, miscarriage, low birth weight (*qv*), infant death, and infections of the middle ear, rectum, intestines, and sexual organs. Also known as nonspecific urethritis (NSU). In women, the infection is more properly known as mucopurulent cervicitis.

nonmarital sex A general term for any sexual activity (*qv*) between 2 persons who are not married to each other. *See also* adultery; extramarital sex; fornication; intimate networks; masturbation.

nonoxynol-9 A member of the nonoxynol chemical group effective as a spermicide (*qv*). Because Nonoxynol-9 has been proved effective in in vitro tests in killing the HIV-I virus (*qv*), its use is recommended with condoms (*qv*) as part of safe sex (*qv*) practices (*qv*) to reduce the risk of acquired immune deficiency syndrome (*qv*).

nonparous (n. nonpara) The condition of not having given birth (*qv*) to a viable baby. *See also* nulliparous.

nonreactive phase *See* refractory period.

nonsadistic sexual assaulter The least dangerous of three psychological types of sexual assaulters, characterized by shyness, passivity, and a tendency to avoid social exchanges, usually with little heterosexual (*qv*) experience. This type of assaulter uses only as much force or threats as necessary to persuade the victim to submit. *See also* sadistic psychotic sexual assaulter; sadistic nonpsychotic sexual assaulter.

nonsexual fetish A fetish (*qv*) involving a nonsexual part of the body or an inanimate object.

nonspecific urethritis (NSU) *See* nongonoccocal urethritis.

noradrenaline, norepinephrine A hormone (*qv*) secreted by neurons that acts as a transmitter at peripheral sympathetic nerve (*qv*) endings and possibly other synapses (*qv*) in the central nervous system (*qv*).

norethindrone A progestin (*qv*) used in treating endometriosis (*qv*) and abnormal uterine bleeding.

norgestrel A progestin (*qv*) used in some oral contraceptives (*qv*).

norm A standard of behavior shared by members of a group against which all other behavior is measured. *See also* normal; sexual values. A social norm often, but not always, refers to the actual behavior of the majority of a group. While behavior that deviates from a norm is punished by sanctions when disclosed, the basic effectiveness of a social norm depends on the extent to which a group can socialize its members to internalize the norm.

normal Conforming with or constituting an accepted standard, model, or pattern for a particular group, population, or species; that which does not deviate significantly from the norm (*qv*); the median or average of a large group; in statistics, a distribution of data that follows a bell-shaped or Gaussian curve; in medicine, consistent with a healthful state. *See also* deviance; norm; normal deviance.

normal deviance A socially or legally deviant (*qv*) sexual behavior that is nevertheless commonly practiced; the phrase contains an inherent contradiction because of the opposing meanings of normal and deviance. In various American legal jurisdictions and social value systems, masturbation (*qv*), oral sex (*qv*), anal sex (*qv*), and extramarital sex (*qv*) are viewed as deviant behavior though they are commonly practiced and seldom prosecuted. Normal deviance, however, is frequently prosecuted when engaged in by a person in a socially unacceptable life-style. Thus, a heterosexual (*qv*) couple may engage with impunity in oral or anal sex, while a homosexual (*qv*) couple may be arrested for this normal deviance. *See also* formal values; informal values.

normative Establishing a norm (*qv*), value, or standard of behavior; also, typical of the average response or of the majority of individuals in a population. *See also* deviance.

normophilia A condition of conforming erotosexually with the norms dictated by custom, religious, or civil authorities; the opposite of paraphilia (*qv*) or deviant (*qv*).

Norplant A commercial name for an implantable, time-released hormonal contraceptive (*qv*) that provides pregnancy protection for up to five years. Microcapsules, hollow silastic tubes about the diameter of a round toothpick, are surgically implanted under the skin, where they release continuous low-level doses of levonorgestrel, a progestin (*qv*). This hormone (*qv*) inhibits ovulation (*qv*) and causes a thickening of the cervical mucus (*qv*), which prevents sperm (*qv*) penetration. The contraceptive effect can be reversed by removal of the implant. The implant is not recommended for women who are breast-feeding (*qv*), or who have liver disease, breast cancer (*qv*), or undiagnosed uterine bleeding.

nose rubbing A form of greeting or sexual expression used in some cultures instead of kissing (*qv*).

nosocomial Belonging to or associated with a hospital, clinic, or other health care facility. *See also* nosocomial abuse.

nosocomial abuse A form of psychologically traumatizing abuse inadvertently and unintentionally imposed on a patient in the course of diagnosis and treatment, as when a child with ambiguous genitalia (*qv*) is traumatized by being used as a demonstration case and exposed to physical examination by a group of interns or other health professionals.

nosology The science or classification of diseases.

notifiable Pertaining to certain medical conditions, diseases, and events that by law must be reported to a governmental agency. Individual localities, states, and the federal government vary on which conditions, diseases, and events must be reported.

Noyes, John Humphrey (1811–1886) A ministerial graduate of Yale Divinity School, Noyes founded and directed one of the best-known and most influential sexual communes of nineteenth-century America, the Oneida Community (*qv*).

A follower of Charles Finney's perfectionist faith, Noyes believed that Christians could lead a perfect life on earth and anticipate the community of love promised by Jesus in the afterlife. By the 1840s, Noyes, his wife, Harriet, and a few friends had a small community in Putney, Vermont. In 1848, the community moved to Oneida, New York, where at its peak it had about 350 members, with branches in Newark, New Jersey, and Brooklyn, New York. The Oneida Community practiced a form of group marriage (*qv*) and considered sexually exclusive monogamy (*qv*) the most dangerous and selfish of heresies. *See also* maithuna; stirpiculture.

NSU Nonspecific urethritis. *See also* nongonoccocal urethritis.

nubile An adolescent (*qv*) or young adult female of marriageable age.

nubilis A legal term for someone who is legally old enough to marry.

nuchal cord An umbilical cord (*qv*) that encircles the neck of the fetus (*qv*). An umbilical cord twisted around the neck during gestation (*qv*) or delivery (*qv*) occurs in about a quarter of all deliveries. It is usually remedied by slipping the cord over the fetal head in a normal presentation (*qv*) or by clamping and cutting it to prevent fetal distress (*qv*).

Nuck canal In females, a peritoneal pouch in the inguinal (*qv*) region of the pelvic cavity.

Nuck canal cyst A cyst (*qv*) in the Nuck canal (*qv*), which may begin with an inflammation of the labia majora (*qv*).

nuclear family A two-generational family model consisting of parents and their biological or adopted children. The nuclear family is believed by some social scientists to be the standard of Western family life following World War II, when it replaced the early extended, multigenerational family model (*qv*). In reality, less than a third of all families in Europe and North America fit the nuclear family model. Other models include married and cohabiting couples with no children, cohabiting couples with children, a growing number of single-parent families, couples whose children have left home, blended or reconstituted families where the husband and/or wife are in their second marriage and children from the first and second marriages are combined in one household, and single persons living alone or with other persons sharing economic responsibilities but not sexual intimacies in a household.

One theoretical position assumes that the nuclear family has become more common because its flexibility and mobility are well adapted to the needs of industrialization. However, recent research shows that the extended family did not dominate Western society before the industrial revolution, that isolated conjugal households are not the dominant form in industrial societies, and that industrialization was actually accompanied by considerable use of extended kin contacts and support.

nucleotide The basic unit in both deoxyribonucleic acid (DNA) (*qv*) and ribonucleic acid (RNA) (*qv*) genetic material composed of a 5–carbon sugar attached to a phosphate group and a nitrogen base. In DNA, the nitrogen base is adenine, cytosine, guanine, or thymine. In RNA, thymine is replaced by uracil.

nude-group therapy A form of group therapy (*qv*) in which the therapy is believed to be enhanced by the practice of nudity (*qv*). Nude-group therapy is based on the belief that because clothing provides a safe refuge behind which people can hide their true emotions and feelings, the vulnerability of being nude in public allows one more easily to break through some of the most deeply rooted taboos of society, thereby facilitating emotional disclosures and therapy.

nudism The social practice or cult of nudity for hygienic reasons. *See also* naturism.

nudist A person who believes in or practices nudism (*qv*).

nudity The state or quality of being nude, undressed, or naked. In Western civilization and cooler climates, nudity in public is not a socially acceptable practice and is often associated with sexual overtures and stimulation. Nudity has been traditionally accepted in the visual arts and more recently in the performing arts, movies, and television. The degree of partial nudity varies widely with different time periods in Western cultures, ranging from the total body clothing of the Victorians to miniskirts and bikini bathing suits. In other cultures, especially in tropical climates, the genitalia (*qv*) are usually covered although body covering may be very scant. *See also* naturism.

null hypothesis (H$_o$) In research, a hypothesis that predicts no significant difference or relationship exists among the variables or observed sample estimates that could not have occurred by chance or random variation alone.

null theory The hypothesis that exposure to pornography (*qv*) neither stimulates nor depresses sexual behavior. *See also* catharsis model of pornography research; imitation model of pornography research; modeling theory.

nulliparous (n. nullipara, nulliparae) The condition of not having given birth to a viable baby; nonparous. The distinction between parous and nulliparous is apparent in several anatomical variations. For instance, in nulliparous women the major labia (*qv*) are thinner, flatter, and more widely separated that in parous women. When a nulliparous woman is sexually aroused, the major labia appear almost to disappear unless sexual stimulation is prolonged, in which case they become swollen.

Nupercainal A local anesthetic used to desensitize the glans (*qv*) of the penis (*qv*) and thereby delay ejaculation (*qv*) in a male suffering from premature ejaculation (*qv*).

nuptial Pertaining to marriage (*qv*) or a wedding ceremony.

nurse cells *See* Sertoli cells.

nursing (to nurse) *See* breast-feeding; lactation.

nurture Giving emotional response, protection, comfort, and/or support.

nymph In Greek and Roman mythology, one of the minor nature goddesses personified as a beautiful maiden living in the river, mountain, or forest; an attractive, apparently sexually free young woman; a developmental stage in certain arthropods (e.g., ticks).

nymphae (L.) The labia minora (*qv*) of the female genitalia (*qv*).

nymphectomy A form of female circumcision (*qv*) involving excision of the labia minora (*qv*).

nymphitis An inflammation of the labia minora (*qv*).

nympho- A combining form meaning "of or pertaining to labia minora" (*qv*).

nympholepsy A sexual ecstasy (*qv*) or frenzy.

nymphomania (nymphomaniac) A pejorative psychiatric term for a very sexually active woman; also used to refer to a woman who is sexually active with several partners but reports no sexual pleasure from the activity itself. The term is not applied to a woman who has a great deal of sex with her husband but with little or no sexual pleasure. Falling in love (*qv*) or limerence (*qv*) is not part of this behavior, nor is payment from male partners sought and wanted. *See also* sexual addiction. The male counterpart is satyriasis (*qv*) or Don Juanism (*qv*).

O

OB Abbreviation for obstetrics *(qv)* or an obstetrician *(qv)*; commonly used in the combination OB/GYN (obstetrics and gynecology).

object cathexis (object finding, object libido, object love) Psychoanalytic *(qv)* terms for the investment of libidinal energy in persons, relations, and activities outside oneself; the opposite of ego libido *(qv)*.

object fetish An inanimate object to which is attributed sexually arousing qualities. *See also* fetish.

object loss In psychoanalytic theory *(qv)*, the threatened or actual loss of love because of the rejection, illness, or death of a loved one.

object relation In psychoanalytic theory *(qv)*, a relationship with persons, activities, or things from which gratification is obtained for one's sexual drive *(qv)*, libido *(qv)*, or one's self-destructive, aggressive, thanatos drive *(qv)*.

obscene phone caller *See* telephone scatophilia.

obscenity (adj. obscene) As a social or moral concept, anything that is offensive to modesty or decency. The current legal definition of obscenity in the United States is based on the 1957 U.S. Supreme Court decision in *Roth v. United States (qv)*. All definitions and applications of the term obscenity, both social and legal, vary historically. In the social and moral context, obscenity refers to the lewd, disgusting, filthy, or repulsive. It is often equated with pornography *(qv)*, defined as any form of communication deemed offensive by a society or a subculture within a specific period of time. *See also* Commission on Obscenity and Pornography, 1970 and 1986.

Obscenity and Pornography, White House Commission on *See* Commission on Obscenity and Pornography, 1970 and 1986.

obsessive-compulsive reaction A psychological condition in which a person is driven to repetitive behavior in response to persistent and obsessive thoughts. Fetishes (*qv*) and sexual addiction (*qv*) are considered by some to represent obsessive-compulsive behavior.

obstetric canal The vaginal canal (*qv*) from the uterine cervix (*qv*) to the vulva (*qv*), through which the infant is born.

obstetric forceps Forceps, similar to a large pair of pliers with two handles, shanks, and blades, used to assist in the delivery of the fetal head. They vary in weight, length, shape, and mechanism of action.

obstetrician A physician who specializes in obstetrics (*qv*).

obstetrics The branch of medicine concerned with pregnancy (*qv*) and childbirth (*qv*), including the normal and pathologic functioning of the female reproductive tract and the care of the mother and fetus-infant from conception (*qv*) through the immediate postpartum (*qv*) period.

O.C. *See* oral contraceptive.

occasional inversion Sigmund Freud's (*qv*) term for situational (*qv*) or facultative homosexual (*qv*) behavior in which sexual activities with persons of the same gender are prompted by the prolonged lack of sexual partners of the opposite sex rather than by a true homosexual orientation.

Oceanic kiss A kiss (*qv*) in which the face is placed on the cheek of the other person in order to smell his or her skin; a traditional greeting in Polynesia. The term is derived from Oceania, which includes the Pacific islands of Melanesia, Micronesia, and Polynesia.

Oceanic position A coital position, prevalent in the islands of the Pacific, in which the woman is prone on her back while the man kneels or squats between her spread legs and embraces her while engaging in intercourse (*qv*). The term is derived from Oceania, which includes the Pacific islands of Melanesia, Micronesia, and Polynesia.

octoroon A racist term for a person with one black great-grandparent and seven nonblack great-grandparents. *See also* mulatto; quadroon.

odalisque A female slave or concubine (*qv*) in an Oriental harem (*qv*), particularly a chambermaid in the entourage of a Near Eastern sultan. Social custom frequently gave to the ruler's mother or to some state official the right to choose suitable concubines for him. In cultures where local rulers were allowed multiple wives and concubines, sultans theoretically had the right to have sexual relations (*qv*) with any odalisque within his jurisdiction.

oe- In words like estrus and estrogen, the usual British spelling replaces the initial "e" with "oe" (oestrus and oestrogen).

Oedipal *See* Oedipus.

Oedipal stage (Oedipal phase) A psychoanalytic (*qv*) term for the phallic phase (*qv*) in psychosexual development (*qv*), occurring usually between ages 3 and 7, when the Oedipal complex (*qv*) allegedly expresses itself.

Oedipus (Oedipal) complex (Oedipus situation) In psychoanalytic theory (*qv*), the sexual attraction (*qv*) of a child for his or her other-gender parent accompanied by a mixture of rivalry and fear toward the same-gender parent. In boys, the fear focuses on the threat of castration (*qv*) by the father as punishment for the son's sexual desires for the mother. In girls, the fear is one of having already been castrated for incestuous desires. Originally Sigmund Freud (*qv*) distinguished between an Oedipal complex in boys and an Electra complex (*qv*) in girls. More recently, the term Oedipal complex has been used for both genders. This complex allegedly manifests itself during the phallic phase (*qv*) of psychosexual development (*qv*). It is resolved when the child overcomes castration fears, represses incestuous desires, and identifies with the same-gender parent. The name is based on the Greek myth and play about King Oedipus who killed his father and unknowingly married his mother. *See also* Electra complex.

oestrum, oestrus *See* estrus.

Ogino-Knaus rule An obsolete method of family planning based on the estimation that ovulation (*qv*) and conception (*qv*) are most likely halfway between any two menstrual periods and unlikely just before and after menstruation (*qv*). *See also* rhythm method of contraception; cervical mucous method of contraception; Billings' contraceptive method; basal body temperature method of contraception.

Ohio v. Akron Center for Reproductive Health An Ohio state law requiring any doctor asked to perform an abortion (*qv*) on an unmarried person under 18 to contact one of her parents or an adult sibling, stepparent or grandparent, at least 24 hours before the procedure. In its 1989 ruling in *Webster v. Reproductive Health Services* (*qv*), the U.S. Supreme Court agreed to hear an appeal of this law.

olfactophilia A paraphilic (*qv*) orientation in which sexuoerotic arousal (*qv*) and achievement of orgasm (*qv*) require particular body odors, especially the sexual areas. *See also* osmolagnia; pheromones; renifleur.

oligohydramnios An abnormally low level of amniotic fluid (*qv*) in the third trimester (*qv*) of a pregnancy (*qv*)—about 400 milliliters compared with the normal level of about 1,000 milliliters reached by 37 weeks. In most cases, the oligohydramnios condition is believed to result from a diminished placental blood flow.

oligomenorrhea An abnormally light or infrequent menstruation (*qv*). *See also* amenorrhea; dysmenorrhea.

oligospermia A sperm count (*qv*) below the level usually considered necessary for male fertility (*qv*). A normal sperm count is 100 million sperm per milliliters of semen with about 3 milliliters of semen in an ejaculate (*qv*). Levels below 20 million are considered in the range of oligospermia. The complete absence of viable, motile sperm is termed azoospermia. It is sometimes possible to combine several ejaculates from a male with oligospermia, centrifuge them to concentrate the sperm, and use the concentrate in artificial insemination (*qv*) to allow impregnation (*qv*).

olisbos A dildo (*qv*) or artificial phallus (*qv*) commonly made from leather and used by lesbians (*qv*) in ancient Greece.

Ombredaane's surgery A surgical procedure for the repair of hypospadia (*qv*) in a newborn infant. The new urethra (*qv*) is constructed from skin taken from the scrotum (*qv*) and under the surface of the penis (*qv*). This skin is later replaced by transplanting the foreskin (*qv*) or prepuce (*qv*) to the underside of the penis.

OMI *See* oocyte maturation inhibitor; prophase arrest.

onanism As commonly used, onanism refers to masturbation (*qv*) or to withdrawal of the penis (*qv*) from the vagina (*qv*) before ejaculation (*qv*). This usage is based on a misinterpretation of the biblical story of Onan (Gen. 38). Onan was required by Levirate law (*qv*) to marry the childless widow of his deceased brother Er in order to provide a son to continue Er's lineage and inherit his property. Onan practiced withdrawal (*qv*) and "spilled his seed on the ground." God punished him for his defiance of the law and his selfishness. Theologians and physicians in the eighteenth century reinterpreted the story of Onan as a condemnation not only of withdrawal or coitus interruptus (*qv*) but also of masturbation.

oncogene A gene (*qv*) capable of converting a normal cell into a malignant cell.

Oneida Community A nineteenth-century American utopian community of perfectionist Methodists, famous for their inventions, craft work, denunciation of monogamy (*qv*), the practice of group marriage (*qv*), and eugenic selection of parents. Founded in the 1830s in Putney, Vermont, the Oneida Community had about 350 members at its peak in the 1870s, with communities in Oneida and Brooklyn, New York, and Newark, New Jersey. *See also* Noyes, John Humphrey; stirpiculture; maithuna. Resource: C. Robertson Noyes, *Oneida Community: An Autobiography, 1851–1876* (Syracuse: Syracuse University Press, 1970).

oneirogmus A nocturnal emission (*qv*), ejaculation (*qv*) during a sexual dream (*qv*).

ontogeny (ontogenesis, ontogenetic, ontogenic) In biology, the developmental history of a single individual or organism from conception to maturity, in contrast with phylogeny (*qv*), or the developmental history of a species or phylum.

oo- A combining form meaning "of or pertaining to an ovum (*qv*) or egg"; pronounced "oh-oh."

ooblast The primordial germ cell (*qv*) from which the mature ovum (*qv*) develops. *See also* oogonium.

oocenter *See* ovocenter.

oocyte An immature ovum (*qv*) before it is capable of being fertilized (*qv*). In mammals (*qv*), a diploid (*qv*) parent cell or oogonium (*qv*) derived from a germinal cell in the ovary (*qv*) develops into a primary oocyte as the ovarian follicle (*qv*) matures. The first meiotic (*qv*) division, started during fetal development, is completed with formation of a secondary oocyte and a first polar body at ovulation (*qv*). The latter disintegrates while fertilization causes the secondary oocyte to complete the second phase of meiosis, forming a haploid (*qv*) ovum and a second polar body and immediately a diploid zygote (*qv*).

oocyte maturation inhibitor (OMI) A substance that stops meiosis (*qv*) and produces the phenomenon of prophase arrest (*qv*); secreted by the follicle or nurse cells (*qv*) surrounding the primary oocytes (*qv*) in the mammalian fetal ovaries (*qv*).

oocytin An acrosomal (*qv*) enzyme in the mammalian spermatozoan (*qv*), released in the process of fertilization (*qv*), which changes the surface membrane of the ovum (*qv*) to prevent additional sperm (*qv*) from entering the ovum.

oogamy Sexual reproduction (*qv*) by fertilization (*qv*) of a large, nonmotile female gamete (*qv*) by a smaller, motile male gamete. *See also* heterogamy; isogamy.

oogenesis The process of gametogenesis (*qv*) or ovum (*qv*) production in a female, involving the transformation through the 2 stages or divisions of meiosis (*qv*) of a diploid (*qv*) germinal cell to produce a haploid (*qv*) ovum and nonfunctional polar bodies. All mammalian ova begin developing in the fetus (*qv*) and then go dormant until puberty (*qv*) when individual ova resume development on a cyclic basis. *See also* follicular stage; luteal stage; oocyte; ovarian cycle; ovulation; menstrual cycle; prophase arrest.

oogonium The stage in mammalian oogenesis (*qv*) between a primordial germ cell and the primary oocyte (*qv*). The primordial germ cells multiply rapidly during gestation (*qv*) and near the time of birth (*qv*) begin the first meiotic (*qv*) division when further development of the oocyte is arrested. Individual primary oocytes resume their meiotic division after puberty (*qv*). *See also* prophase arrest.

ookinesis The replication and division of chromosomes (*qv*) occurring in the nucleus of an oocyte (*qv*) or egg cell during its maturation and the restoration of the diploid (*qv*) chromosome complement during fertilization (*qv*). *See also* meiosis; gametogenesis; oogenesis; spermatogenesis.

oolema The membrane confining the ovum. *See also* zona pellucida.

oophor- (oophoro-) A combining form meaning "of or pertaining to the ovary" (*qv*).

oophorectomy The surgical removal of an ovary (*qv*), performed to remove an ovarian cyst (*qv*) or tumor as a source of estrogen (*qv*). The excess estrogen can stimulate certain types of cancer in women or aggravate endometriosis (*qv*). If both ovaries are removed, sterility (*qv*) results, and menopause (*qv*) is induced. The operation, which often accompanies a hysterectomy (*qv*), is also known as an ovariectomy.

oophoritis An inflammation of one or both ovaries (*qv*), usually occurring with salpingitis (*qv*).

oophorosalpingectomy Surgical removal of one or both ovaries (*qv*) and the corresponding fallopian tube(s) (*qv*), performed to remove a cyst (*qv*), abscess, or tumor or to treat endometriosis (*qv*). If both ovaries are removed, sterility (*qv*) results, and menopause (*qv*) is induced. The operation often accompanies a hysterectomy (*qv*).

oophorotomy *See* oophorectomy.

ooplasm The cell material or cytoplasm of the ovum (*qv*), including the yolk (*qv*) in lower animals.

oosperm An obsolete term for the zygote (*qv*), or fertilized ovum (*qv*).

ootheco- *See* oophor-.

ootid The mature ovum (*qv*) after the spermatozoan (*qv*) has penetrated the ovum's surface membrane and the second meiotic (*qv*) division is completed but before fusion of the male and female pronuclei. *See also* polar body; meiosis; oogenesis.

open laparoscopy A technique for direct visual examination of the abdominal and pelvic organs through a small incision in the umbilical (*qv*) region. The fiber optics of the laparoscope (*qv*) allow for visualization of the internal organs on a television monitor screen. Closed and vaginal laparoscopy are more commonly used today. In closed laparoscopy, a laparoscope is introduced through a small abdominal incision; in vaginal laparoscopy, the incision is made in the anterior vaginal wall near the cervix (*qv*). *See also* laser laparoscopy.

open lewdness A legal term for lascivious and public cohabitation (*qv*).

open marriage A marriage (*qv*) that is adaptable to change and allows flexibility in roles, personal identity, and private space for personal growth and incorporates other relationships as growth-oriented companionships, with an emphasis on honest, open love and open trust. In its current usage, the term usually implies that the spouses have agreed to allow for comarital (*qv*) or extramarital sexual relationships. *See also* communitas; sexually open marriage; closed marriage; satellite relationship; intimate network. Resource: N. O'Neill & G. O'Neill, *Open Marriage* (New York: Evans, 1972).

open swinging A form of consensual sexual relations (*qv*) outside one's marriage or usual sexual partnership in which two or more couples exchange partners and engage in sexual relations (*qv*) in the same room. *See also* closed swinging, swinging, orgy, group sex.

operant Any act or response defined in terms of its effects on the environment. The specific stimulus or stimuli need not be known to identify an operant behavior or response. *See also* operant conditioning.

operant conditioning The process of changing the frequency of a behavior (the operant) by following its occurrence with reinforcement or punishment. Operant conditioning is often used in sex therapy (*qv*) and in the treatment of paraphilias (*qv*). The term was applied to the development of sexual behaviors by A. Bandura & R. H. Walters. Resources: A. Bandura, *Principles of Behavior Modification* (New York: Holt, Rinehart & Winston, 1969); A. Bandura & R. H. Walters, *Social Learning and Personality Development* (New York: Holt, 1963); R. J. McGuire et al., Sexual deviation as conditioned behavior, *Behavioral Research & Therapy* 2 (1965):185–190.

operational definition Defining a concept in terms of its measurements; a functional and provisional, as opposed to definitive and absolute, definition or description of a concept or term.

operculum A lid or covering such as the mucous plug blocking the cervical os (*qv*) of the gravid (*qv*) uterus (*qv*), or the gill covering in fish.

ophthalmia neonatorum (L.) A gonorrheal (*qv*), streptococcal, syphilitic (*qv*), or other infection of the eyes of a newborn (*qv*), resulting in a discharge of pus usually within the first month after birth (*qv*). Routine prophylaxis, a topical administration of a silver nitrate solution or antibiotic ointment in the eyes of every newborn, has practically eliminated this condition.

opiate A narcotic derived from the opium poppy that induces relaxation, euphoria, and sleep. *See also* opioid.

opioid A naturally occurring peptide found in the brain and elsewhere in the body whose effect resembles that of opium or a morphinelike synthetic opiate (*qv*).

opponent-process theory A psychological theory suggesting that the powerful aversion or attraction to a particular activity or experience undergoes reversal under appropriate circumstances, as when pain is reversed into pleasure for the masochist (*qv*), tragedy into triumph, terror into euphoria, or the proscribed into the prescribed. The term was proposed by Richard Solomon as an augmentation to the traditional stimulus-response learning theory. Resource: R. L. Solomon, The opponent-process theory of acquired motivation, *American Psychologist* 35(1980):691–712. It has been applied to paraphilic addiction by J. Money, *Lovemaps* (New York: Irvington, 1986). *See also* stimulus-response learning theory.

opportunistic sex Sexual intimacy and intercourse (*qv*) that occurs spontaneously and without anticipation so that the participants may not take precautions against sexually transmitted diseases (*qv*) and pregnancy (*qv*).

opportunistic rape *See* impulse rape.

oral-aggressive *See* anal-sadistic phase.

oral-anal sex Sexual activity (*qv*) in which the mouth and tongue are used to stimulate the anus (*qv*). *See also* anilingus; anal sex.

oral-biting period An alternate term for the oral-sadistic phase (*qv*).

oral character In psychoanalysis (*qv*), a complex of personality traits rooted in the oral stage (*qv*) of psychosexual development (*qv*). In this theory, it is proposed that a child who is able to satisfy his or her libido (*qv*) needs with adequate suckling satisfaction and nurturance from the mother during the oral stage will develop into a socially cooperative, generous person with an optimistic outlook on life. Failure to meet this basic need results in an aggressive, overcompetitive, and critical individual.

oral coitus An uncommon, alternate term for fellatio (*qv*) or cunnilingus (*qv*).

oral contraceptive A hormonal pill taken daily to suppress ovulation (*qv*). Oral contraceptives, commonly referred to as the birth control pill or more simply the pill, were introduced in the early 1960s. The physiological mechanism of the hormonal contraceptive pill works through the natural negative feedback system (*qv*) of the female hypothalamic-pituitary-ovarian-uterine cycle. A steady supply of estrogen (*qv*) and progesterone (*qv*) from the oral contraceptive causes a reduction in the secretion of the gonadotropic-releasing hormones (*qv*) from the hypothalamus (*qv*), inhibiting production of the pituitary hormones, follicle-stimulating hormone (FSH) (*qv*) and luteinizing hormone (LH) (*qv*). Lack of FSH and LH prevents ovulation (*qv*). *See also* combination oral contraceptive pill; sequential oral contraceptive pill; minipill.
   Anthropologist Ashley Montagu ranks the social impact of the pill, which allows sexual relations (*qv*) without the risk of pregnancy, "with the discovery of fire, the creation of and employment of tools, the development of hunting, the invention of agriculture, the development of urbanism, scientific medicine, and the release and control of nuclear power." Resource: A. Montagu, *Sex, Man and Society* (New York: Putnam, 1969).

oral dam *See* dental dam.

oral dependency A psychoanalytic (*qv*) term for the tendency to be dependent on and seek out other people who can provide the security, care, protection, and emotional nurturance claimed to be important during the oral stage (*qv*) of infancy.

oral eroticism A psychoanalytic (*qv*) term for the satisfaction of libido (*qv*) in any pleasurable activity involving the mouth, lips, and tongue, especially sucking, eating, smoking, kissing (*qv*), biting, suckling at the breast (*qv*), thumb sucking, fellatio (*qv*), and cunnilingus (*qv*). *See also* oral fixation.

oral fixation A psychoanalytic (*qv*) term for a fixation on or regression to the satisfaction of libido (*qv*) in pleasurable activities involving the mouth, lips, and tongue. In an oral fixation, behaviors associated with the oral stage (*qv*) in the psychosexual development (*qv*) of an infant are engaged in despite their allegedly regressive character. This includes thumb sucking, nail biting, baby talk, passivity, insecurity, oversensitivity, and a psychological dependence on others for care, nurturance, and protection.

oralgenitalism A variant for oral sex (*qv*). *See also* cunnilingus; fellatio; irrumation; soixante-neuf.

oral-genital sex A variant for oral sex (*qv*). *See also* cunnilingus; fellatio; irrumation; soixante-neuf.

oral herpes *See* herpes simplex I.

oral impregnation A not-uncommon myth that a woman can become pregnant from ordinary or deep kissing (*qv*) or fellatio (*qv*).

orality A general psychoanalytic (*qv*) term for any activity, behavior, or sexual gratification associated with the mouth, lips, and teeth, including kissing (*qv*), sucking, biting, licking, fellatio (*qv*), cunnilingus (*qv*), anilingus (*qv*), breast-feeding (*qv*), eating, and smoking. *See also* oral stage; oral eroticism; oral sadism; oral fixation; oral character; oral dependency.

oral libido A psychoanalytic (*qv*) term for the association of the sexual energy (*qv*) or libido (*qv*) with sensual and erotic gratifications associated with the mouth.

oral phase *See* oral stage.

oral progesterone test An obsolete test for pregnancy (*qv*) previously used when a woman had missed a menstrual period (*qv*). Following an oral dose of progesterone (*qv*), the woman being tested will menstruate within a few days if she is not pregnant. If she is pregnant, the exogenous progesterone produces no response.

oral sadism A psychoanalytic (*qv*) term for an occasional or regular regression to the second phase of the oral stage (*qv*), experienced by an adult who uses the mouth, lips, and teeth as means of sadistic sexual pleasure and to express aggression and hostility. *See also* oral sadistic phase.

oral sadistic phase In psychoanalytic theory (*qv*), the second phase of the oral stage (*qv*) of psychosexual development (*qv*) during which the infant derives pleasure from chewing on objects and expresses anger through biting. In theory, as the infant moves through the oral stage, sucking is replaced by biting and chewing. In articulating its emerging individuality, the infant between roughly the eighth and eighteenth months derives sexual pleasure from chewing anything it can get into its mouth and at the same time expresses its need for independence and anger at its continued dependence by biting the mother's breast (*qv*) or nipple (*qv*). *See also* oral sadism.

oral sex A general term for any use of the tongue, lips, or mouth to stimulate sexually a partner's erogenous zones (*qv*) and genitals (*qv*) by licking, sucking, biting, and/or kissing (*qv*). *See also* cunnilingus; fellatio; irrumation; soixante-neuf. Resource: G. Legman, *Oragenitalism* (New York: Julian Press, 1969).

oral stage In psychoanalytic theory (*qv*), the eighteen months of an infant's life prior to toilet training when sexual energies (*qv*) or libido (*qv*) are focused on oral stimulation, especially sucking, nursing, eating, and crying. *See also* anal stage; phallic stage.

orchi- (orchio-, orchido-) A combining form meaning "of or pertaining to the testes" (*qv*).

orchidectomy The surgical removal of one or both testes (*qv*). If both are removed, the result is sterilization (*qv*) and removal of the main source of androgens (*qv*). *See also* cryptorchidism.

orchidopexy One of several surgical methods for relocating an undescended testis (*qv*) into the scrotal sac (*qv*). *See also* orchipexy.

orchiectomy *See* orchidectomy.

orchipexy Surgical relocation of an undescended testis (*qv*) into the scrotal sac (*qv*) with the relocated testis anchored to the sac so that it cannot return to the abdominal cavity. *See also* cryptorchidism.

orchis (Gr.) The Greek term for testicle (*qv*); also the botanical name for a group of plants commonly known as orchids. The sexual reference is based on the resemblance of the lady slipper's flower, an orchid, to the scrotum (*qv*) with its two testicles. This is also the basis for the attribution of aphrodisiac (*qv*) qualities to the orchid.

orchitis An inflammation of the testis (*qv*), a condition most commonly associated with mumps but also occurring as a consequence of epididymitis (*qv*) and with gonorrhea (*qv*), syphilis (*qv*), and genital tuberculosis (*qv*).

organic In medicine, *organic* refers to the body, to something derived from an animal or plant source, or to a complex chemical that contains the element carbon. Simple organic compounds like carbon monoxide and carbon dioxide are referred to as inorganic even though they contain the element carbon.

An organic sexual dysfunction (*qv*) may have its origins in a hormone imbalance, in a vascular or circulatory inadequacy, in an anatomical defect, or some other cause directly related to the body and its functioning. Organic sexual dysfunctions (*qv*) are distinct from psychogenic (*qv*) sexual dysfunctions, which have their origins in the psychological processes of the brain. Most sexual dysfunctions are now thought to have a combined organic and psychogenic etiology rather than being a simple case of one specific organic or psychological cause.

organic impotence The inability of a male to achieve and maintain an erection (*qv*) sufficient for vaginal intercourse (*qv*) due to vascular insufficiencies or to defects in the erection reflex or central nervous system (*qv*) controls over erection. Organic causes include a degenerative disease, trauma, or the side effect of some medication, surgery, or radiotherapy. *See also* psychogenic.

organ libido Erotic response associated with a specific bodily organ.

organ of Giraldes *See* paradidymis.

organogenesis In embryology (*qv*), the period of prenatal development from the second to the eighth week of gestation (*qv*) during which all the main organ systems and structures of the the body are established. Because of the rapid development of major organ systems during this six-week period, the embryo (*qv*) is most susceptible to the teratogenic (*qv*) agents.

organogenic In psychologic and psychiatric theory, the principle that some mental conditions or syndromes attributed to the mind are in reality due to a somatic or organic (*qv*) cause in the brain, involving neurotransmitters (*qv*) and/ or functioning of the neural cells in the brain.

orgasm (adj. orgasmic) The intense, reflexive, physiological release of sexual tension (*qv*) following sexual stimulation and the buildup of sexual arousal in intercourse (*qv*), oral sex (*qv*), anal sex (*qv*), or masturbation (*qv*); the third and shortest of the four phases of the sexual response cycle as described by W. Masters and V. Johnson. The pleasurable sensations and euphoria that accompany orgasm are due to a sudden increased release of beta enkephalins (*qv*), fragments of endorphins (*qv*), which normally reduce pain. The somatic aspects of orgasm involve a reflexive release of myotonic (*qv*) tension built up by sexual stimulation and excitement throughout the body. This reflexive release involves the total body and typically lasts less than a minute.

Orgasmic responses experienced by both men and women include reduction in voluntary muscle control and involuntary muscle spasms throughout the body. It may include the carpopedal spasm in the foot with the big toe held straight while the other toes bend back and the foot arches. The external rectal sphincter contracts at 0.8 second intervals. Involuntary rapid pelvic thrusting (*qv*) may occur immediately prior to orgasm particularly in the male. In the female, orgasm includes uterine contractions and 3 to 15 rhythmic contractions of the orgasmic platform (*qv*) with an initial intense 3 to 6 contractions at 0.8 second intervals followed by less intense and slower contractions. In males, orgasm may or may not be accompanied by the emission (*qv*) and propulsion (*qv*) phases of ejaculation (*qv*). The classic and most widely accepted classification of climactic or orgasm is threefold: clitoral and vaginal in females, and penile orgasm in males. *See also* ejaculation; excitement stage; plateau stage; resolution phase; orgasmic platform; A-frame orgasm; tenting; blended orgasm; orgasmic dysfunction; inhibited orgasm.

orgasm disclosure ratio The number of persons who have seen one experience an orgasm (*qv*) in a given period of time divided by the total number of people with whom one is interacting sexually in that same time period.

orgasmic dysfunction The inability of a male or female to reach orgasm (*qv*) following normal sexual stimulation, either alone or with a partner. Orgasmic dysfunction may occur with only intercourse (*qv*) or masturbation (*qv*), or with both. It may have a variety of psychological and/or organic etiologies. It may be primary, having always existed, or secondary and situational, occurring sporadically or only with a particular partner or situation. Orgasmic dysfunction in women is also known as anorgasmia or preorgasmia. The term *inhibited orgasm* (*qv*) is also used for orgasmic dysfunction in both males and females. The terms *impotence* and *frigidity* are no longer used in the technical literature because of their accusatory and denigrating tone.

orgasmic impotence (inadequacy) An alternate term for inhibited female orgasm (*qv*), preorgasmia (*qv*), or orgasmic dysfunction (*qv*) when this is psychogenic rather than organic in etiology.

orgasmic peak The moment of orgasm (*qv*) or sexual climax (*qv*).

orgasmic phase *See* orgasm; sexual response cycle.

orgasmic platform The thickening of the walls and tightening and elevation of the outer third of the vagina (*qv*) due to vasocongestion (*qv*) of the vestibular bulbs (*qv*) during sexual arousal. The orgasmic platform facilitates gripping of the penis (*qv*) during intercourse (*qv*), increasing the pleasure for both partners.

orgasmic reconditioning A therapeutic approach used to condition a person away from an unsuitable or inappropriate fantasy by instructing the person to begin masturbating (*qv*) with the unsuitable fantasy and shift to a more acceptable and appropriate fantasy just before orgasm (*qv*). *See also* operant conditioning.

orgasmic stage The third phase of the four-phase sexual response cycle proposed by William Masters and Virginia Johnson during which the rising tension of vasocongestion (*qv*) and sexual arousal (*qv*) is released in a myotonic (*qv*) burst, orgasm (*qv*). In the sexually mature male, orgasm is usually but not necessarily accompanied by ejaculation (*qv*). In the female, orgasm may be accompanied by female ejaculation (*qv*). Multiple orgasms (*qv*) in a brief space of time without a refractory period are a possibility for both females and males. *See also* excitement stage; plateau phase; resolution phase; orgasmic platform; A-frame orgasm; tenting; blended orgasm; orgasmic dysfunction; inhibited orgasm.

orgastic impotence The inability of a male to reach orgasm (*qv*) despite a normal erection (*qv*) and ejaculation (*qv*). *See also* inhibited male orgasm; orgasmic dysfunction.

orgastic potency The capacity of a male or female to achieve orgasm (*qv*) after appropriate sexual stimulation.

orgone accumulator *See* orgone box.

orgone box A wood and metal enclosure resembling a telephone booth, developed by Wilhelm Reich (*qv*), who claimed that it captures and concentrates orgone energy (*qv*), transferring it to the patient inside who can then direct this energy to the genitalia (*qv*), thereby restoring sexual potency, or to an ailing organ, thereby restoring it to a healthy condition.

orgone energy According to psychologist Wilhelm Reich (*qv*), a primal force permeating the entire universe. This reservoir of cosmic energy can be tapped by body massage, the orgone box (*qv*), and other means to cure a wide range of human diseases and to increase orgastic potency (*qv*). *See also* orgone therapy.

orgone therapy Wilhelm Reich's (*qv*) controversial therapy based on the belief that full orgastic potency (*qv*) is the key to psychological health. According to Reich, full orgastic potency can be enhanced by releasing cosmic orgone energy (*qv*) with body therapy, massage, and the use of an orgone box (*qv*), which concentrates orgone energy. Orgasm, Reich held, regulates the emotional energy of the body and relieves sexual tensions that otherwise would be transformed into neuroses.

orgy A common, usually humorous or derogatory, term for simultaneous sexual activity involving more than two persons. *See also* swinging; group sex. In ancient Greece and Rome, the term was applied to an uninhibited group revelry with drinking, singing, dancing, and unrestrained sexual activities (*qv*) associated with ceremonies in honor of Dionysius (*qv*) or Bacchus (*qv*).

original sin The sin of disobedience committed by the original or first human, Adam, in the Garden of Eden. In Catholic theology, the state in which all human beings are born, insofar as this condition is caused by the disobedience of Adam, the first human, their ancestor and head. This original sin placed every individual human being in a situation of inward alienation from God. Original sin should not be confused with a real, that is, personal and voluntary, sin. According to Augustine of Hippo and other early Christian theologians, coitus (*qv*) in particular was tainted with the guilt consequences of original sin and thereby transformed into a "shameful lust," which could be morally accepted only when engaged in by a married couple for purposes of procreation (*qv*). Even in this situation, sensual enjoyment of the marital union could be venially sinful. This interpretation of original sin, strongly influenced by Augustine's early association with the dualistic (*qv*) Manichean philosophy, has been rejected by later theologians. *See also* concupiscence.

orogenital contact *See* fellatio; cunnilingus; oral sex.

orolabial stimulation A technical term for cunnilingus (*qv*).

orthogenital Pertaining to sexual patterns considered normal; usually limited to heterosexual (*qv*) and coital (*qv*) behaviors.

os (L.) An opening or mouth of an organ of the body, as the cervical os (*qv*); also the Latin term for "bone."

oscheo- A combining form referring to the scrotum (*qv*).

osmolagnia (L.) Sexual arousal (*qv*) caused by certain odors, a response believed by some to be a facilitating factor in the enjoyment of or preference for fellatio (*qv*) and/or cunnilingus (*qv*). *See also* olfactophilia; renifleur.

os penis (L.) A bone located in the fibrous tissue between the corpora cavernosa of many mammals, in bats, rats, and some primates, but not in humans. Also known as the baculum.

os priapi (L.) *See* os penis.

Ota IUD The first plastic intrauterine device (*qv*), introduced in 1959 by the Japanese physician T. Ota.

Othello syndrome A form of paranoid jealousy in which a spouse, usually the wife, is suspected of sexual infidelity (*qv*), triggering jealous rage and violence in the husband. The term is derived from the Shakespearean play *Othello* and its retelling in nineteenth-century operas by Rossini and Verdi. When Othello, a noble Moor, is made madly jealous by the villainous Iago, he kills his faithful and loving wife, Desdemona.

outbreeding The mating (*qv*) and breeding of genetically unrelated individuals, as opposed to inbreeding (*qv*).

outercourse Any form of sexual pleasuring (*qv*) or expression of sexual intimacy other than penile-vaginal intercourse (*qv*). The term outercourse was coined in the late 1980s to contrast with intercourse, to counter the phallocentrism (*qv*) of the American culture, and to give credibility to the many noncoital forms of sexual pleasuring that are underutilized because of our cultural equation of "sex" and "sexual pleasure" with penile-vaginal intercourse. *See also* penile-vaginal fixation.

outer labia An alternate term for the labia majora (*qv*). *See also* labia minora.

outing A term referring to an effort of the AIDS Coalition to Unleash Power (ACT-UP) to force the government to fund more research and support for the fight against AIDS by threatening to reveal the gender orientation of closeted homosexual politicians. In 1989, the term was adopted by Dignity, a gay Catholic organization, seeking to counter the expulsion of their chapters and members from church property by revealing the gender orientation of antigay closeted homosexual priests and bishops.

ova The plural of ovum (*qv*).

ovari- (ovario-) A combining form meaning "of or pertaining to the ovary" (*qv*).

ovarian Of or pertaining to the ovary (*qv*).

ovarian agenesis A congenital failure to develop functional ovaries (*qv*). Turner 45,XO syndrome (*qv*) is also known as ovarian agenesis or dysgenesis syndrome because the primary effect of this monosomy of the X chromosome (*qv*) is nonfunctional "streak ovaries."

ovarian cancer A malignant, neoplastic condition usually affecting both ovaries; most common in women ages 40 to 60 but occasionally occurring in adolescents (*qv*). Risk factors include a history of infertility (*qv*), nulliparity (*qv*) or only one or two pregnancies, repeated spontaneous abortion (*qv*), delayed childbearing (*qv*), and a family history of ovarian cancer. This condition is usually not diagnosed until it is well advanced. Some tumors, such as granulosa cell tumor (*qv*), may produce sex hormones (*qv*).

ovarian calculus An abnormal combination of proteins and inorganic minerals, usually calcium phosphate, forming in the corpus luteum (*qv*) after ovulation (*qv*).

ovarian carcinoma *See* ovarian cancer.

ovarian cycle That aspect of the female monthly cycle centered in the ovaries (*qv*), their production of a Graafian follicle with a mature ovum (*qv*), ovulation (*qv*), and a corpus luteum (*qv*). Following menstruation (*qv*), the ovaries enter a follicular phase (*qv*) of variable duration in which blood levels of hypophyseal follicle-stimulating hormone (FSH) (*qv*) rise and then taper off while luteinizing hormone (LH) (*qv*) rises and then levels off, causing one or more ovarian follicles (*qv*) to develop. When the ovum is mature, ovulation is triggered by a peak and drop in FSH, LH and ovarian estrogen (*qv*). A 14–day ovarian luteal phase (*qv*) follows. In this phase, the ruptured and collapsed follicle changes into a corpus luteum, which produces some estrogens and progesterone (*qv*), the latter temporarily suppressing LH production by the pituitary (*qv*). If implantation (*qv*) occurs 6 or 7 days after ovulation, the developing placenta (*qv*) of the embryo (*qv*) produces human chorionic gonadotropin (HCG) (*qv*) and progesterone, which promote continued growth of the corpus luteum through early pregnancy (*qv*). If implantation does not occur, there is no HCG, and the corpus luteum degenerates into a corpus albicans (*qv*), bringing a drop in estrogens and progesterone which triggers menstruation (*qv*). *See also* menstrual cycle.

ovarian cyst A cystic (*qv*) growth occurring in the ovary (*qv*). An ovarian cyst may occur in a mature Graafian follicle (*qv*) that does not move close enough to the ovarian surface to allow rupture and release its ovum. In this case, the ovarian cyst will be small, fluid filled, and usually nonmalignant, although the pressure may cause lower abdominal pain and menstrual irregularities. Ovarian cysts usually regress spontaneously. Uterine endometrial (*qv*) tissue may be deposited on the ovary forming an endometrial cyst filled with old blood and cellular debris. *See also* dermoid cyst.

ovarian fossa A small recess in the lateral wall on either side of the pelvic cavity in which the ovary (*qv*) is located.

ovarian ligament A round, tubelike structure of connective tissue enclosed within the broad ligament that helps suspend the ovary (*qv*) in its proper position.

ovarian pregnancy An ectopic pregnancy (*qv*) in which the embryo (*qv*) implants (*qv*) in the ovary (*qv*) instead of in the uterus (*qv*). It invariably ends either in an early miscarriage (*qv*) with reabsorption of the embryonic mass or in an ovarian tumor, which may require surgical removal.

ovarian varicocele A varicose swelling of the ovarian veins in the broad ligament supporting the uterus (*qv*). *See also* varicocele.

ovariectomy *See* ovariotomy.

ovaries *See* ovary.

ovariotomy The surgical removal of an ovary (*qv*), or a portion thereof. Access to the ovary may be obtained through an abdominal or vaginal incision. An ovariotomy performed to remove an ovarian cyst is termed an oophorectomy or oophorotomy.

ovary (pl. ovaries) The paired female gonads (*qv*) that produce ova (*qv*), estrogens (*qv*), and progesterone (*qv*), located in the lower abdominal cavity on either side of the uterus (*qv*). The paired ovaries produce one or more ova on a monthly cycle between puberty (*qv*) and menopause (*qv*). Ovaries also produce estrogenic hormones (*qv*) and progesterone, essential to the menstrual cycle and in gestation (*qv*). The ovaries are located on either side of the lower abdominal cavity and are attached to the uterus and fallopian tubes (*qv*) by ligaments. The human ovary is approximately the shape and size of an almond. The ovaries are homologous (*qv*) to the male testes (*qv*).

overnight sensation An obsolete term for nocturnal emission (*qv*).

oversexed *See* nymphomania; satyriasis; sexual addiction.

overt homosexuality A homoerotic (*qv*) orientation that is recognized and expressed in the individual in obvious same-gender activity or admitted intent, as distinguished from an unconscious or latent homosexual orientation (*qv*) in which acceptance and expression of this orientation are held in check.

ovi- A combining form meaning ''of or pertaining to the ovum (*qv*) or egg.''

oviduct *See* fallopian tube.

oviferous Having the capability of producing ova (*qv*).

oviparous Reproduction (*qv*) in which the female lays eggs containing the developing embryo (*qv*). In oviparous eggs the embryo has developed very little at the time the egg is laid; birds and most reptiles are oviparous. *See also* ovoviparous; viviparous.

ovo- A combining form meaning of or pertaining to the ovum (*qv*) or egg.

ovogenesis *See* oogenesis.

ovogonium *See* oogonium.

ovotestis A gonad (*qv*) that develops abnormally, appearing to contain both ovarian and testicular tissues; very rare. *See also* hermaphrodite.

ovoviparous Reproduction (*qv*) achieved by laying eggs in which internal fertilization (*qv*) and incubation of the fertilized egg produce an embryo (*qv*) that is already well developed and close to hatching when the egg is laid (e.g., some fish and viper reptiles).

ovulation (v. to ovulate) The monthly expulsion of an ovum (*qv*) from the surface of an ovary (*qv*) following spontaneous rupture of a mature ovarian or Graafian follicle (*qv*). Ovulation is regulated by the hormones (*qv*) of the ovarian cycle (*qv*) and may be accompanied by a brief, sharp lower abdominal pain on the side of the ovulating ovary. *See also* Mittelschmerz. In humans, if the ovum is not fertilized (*qv*) and implanted (*qv*) in the uterine lining, ovulation is followed 14 days later by the start of menstruation (*qv*).

ovulation method of contraception *See* Billings' contraceptive method; cervical mucus method of contraception; rhythm method of contraception.

ovulum (L.) A small ovum (*qv*).

ovum (pl. ova) (L.) The female gamete (*qv*) or mature reproductive cell, capable when fertilized by a sperm (*qv*) of developing into a new individual. The human ovum contains a haploid (*qv*) number of chromosomes—22 autosomes (*qv*) and one X chromosome (*qv*). Also commonly referred to as an egg.

ovum harvesting (ovum lavage) *See* egg lavage; transvaginal ovum recovery.

oxytocic agent Pertaining to a number of drugs which stimulate contraction of the smooth muscle of the uterus (*qv*). Oxytocic agents include the hormone oxytocin (*qv*), certain prostaglandins (*qv*), and the ergot (*qv*) alkaloids. These agents are used to augment labor contractions (*qv*), control postpartum hemorrhage, correct a postpartum lack of muscle tone, and restore uterine muscle tone following a Caesarean section (*qv*).

oxytocin A hormone (*qv*) secreted by the posterior pituitary that stimulates uterine contractions during delivery (*qv*) and stimulation of lactation (*qv*). When the infant sucks on the nipple (*qv*) in nursing (*qv*), the stimulus triggers release of oxytocin from the posterior pituitary. The oxytocin causes contraction of the alveoli in the mammary glands (*qv*), forcing milk into the ducts that lead to the nipple.

oxytocin challenge test A stress test for assessing intrauterine functioning of the fetus (*qv*) and placenta (*qv*) and ascertaining the capacity of the fetus to tolerate continuation of the pregnancy or the anticipated stress of labor (*qv*) and delivery (*qv*). Following intravenous administration of an oxytotic agent to the mother, the fetal heart is monitored during a series of uterine contractions. If it appears the fetal heart is not capable of taking the stress of continued pregnancy or labor and delivery, the fetus may be delivered by Caesarean section (*qv*).

P

P₁ In genetics, the symbol for the parental generation. *See also* F_1, F_2.

paederastia *See* pederasty.

-pagus A combining form meaning "conjoined twin" (*qv*).

painful intercourse Sexual intercourse (*qv*) accompanied by physical pain resulting from the lack of vaginal lubrication (*qv*), a vaginal infection, an allergic reaction, or psychological cause in women or from a sexual deformity in men. In women, painful intercourse may result from a number of psychological precedents, including hostility, anger, or resentment directly or indirectly aimed at the partner, fears connected with intercourse and penetration, the sequelae of an unresolved early sexual trauma (*qv*) or assault (*qv*), negative religious messages, or inadequate loveplay (*qv*) and stimulation. It can also arise from organic causes like vaginal infection, pelvic trauma or lacerations, endometriosis (*qv*), allergic reactions to spermicides (*qv*) or douches (*qv*), spinal cord injury, or discomfort in certain coital positions. In females, the condition is also known as dyspareunia (*qv*). When psychogenic in origin, the physiological pathway in both males and females involves inhibition of the parasympathetic (*qv*) cholinergic (*qv*) nerves and vasocongestion (*qv*), which reduces arousal and lubrication. When the condition occurs in a man, it is usually organic in etiology. The condition may be chronic and primary (*qv*) or sporadic and secondary (*qv*).

pair bonding Development of a strong and long-lasting closeness and emotional attachment or bonding (*qv*) between two lovers or between parent and child.

Palace of Yin A Taoist (*qv*) term for the sexual center of women, deep in the womb (*qv*); this center is believed to produce profuse secretions when stimulated.

paleocortex (paleopallium) The limbic system (*qv*); that part of the cerebral cortex (pallium) containing three major neural circuit systems: (1) the septal circuits, which are particularly important in sociability, procreation, and preservation of the species; (2) the neighboring amygdala circuits, which meet the needs for feeding, fighting, self-protection, and sexuality (*qv*); and (3) the anterior thalamic nuclei, which connect the hypothalamus (*qv*) with the cingulate gyrus and with the medial dorsal nucleus of the thalamus (*qv*), which in turn projects into neocortical regions involved in anticipatory planning. The paleocortex, the second of three phyletic systems comprising the human brain, develops in association with the olfactory system. On the most primitive level of central neurological control and in terms of phylogenetic development, the olfactory or reptilian brain facilitates sexual behaviors characteristic of reptiles. The addition of paleocortex overlaying the olfactory brain allows sexual behavior increasing in complexity to that of a mammal (*qv*) somewhat more lowly than the rabbit. The addition of the outermost neopallium (*qv*) allows the more complex sexual behavior characteristic of primates and its maximal expression in humans.

Evidence suggests that a gate or funnel for eroticism and mating behavior is situated in proximity to the hypothalamus, not far from the optic chaisma where rich communications exist with the septum in the paleocortex. The model of a triune organization in the brain, the olfactory, paleocortex and neocortex, was first proposed by Paul D. MacLean, *A Triune Concept of the Brain and Behavior* (Toronto: Toronto University Press, 1973).

palimony A colloquial term for financial compensation and support awarded by the court or mutual agreement to a woman after a nonmarital cohabitation (*qv*) dissolves. Palimony may be based on a long-standing concept of an implied, verbal, or written contract and commitment to support in nonmarital relations. The term originated in 1977 as the result of suit brought in California State Supreme Court by Michelle Triolla when her six-year relationship with actor Lee Marvin broke up. In some jurisdictions, the concept has been applied to same-gender couples. The term is derived from a contraction of *pal* and *alimony*.

pallium (L.) *See* cerebral cortex; neocortex; paleocortex.

palmate folds Small columns of tissue on the walls of the cervical canal (*qv*) in the uterus (*qv*), containing glands that produce the cervical mucus (*qv*) and dovetail so as to help close the cervical canal except around the time of ovulation (*qv*).

palpation Examining by touch and gentle pressure the surface of an organ for unusual or abnormal conditions, as in palpating the breasts (*qv*), prostate (*qv*), or testicles (*qv*).

pampiniform plexus Three veins that drain blood from the testicles (*qv*). Blockage or compression of any one of these veins results in a varicocele (*qv*).

pander To act as an intermediary in satisfying someone else's sexual needs or desire by, for instance, supplying a prostitute (*qv*) for a client, or designing or selling publications or products that cater to certain sexual preferences; frequently used pejoratively; to procure, to pimp.

panerotic potential A theory suggesting humans are born with a potential to react erotically to almost any person or thing within their experience and that this potential is gradually narrowed down by scripting (*qv*) and conditioning to certain socially acceptable objects. Resource: William Stayton, A theory of sexual orientation, *Topics in Clinical Nursing* 1(4)(1980):1–7.

pangenesis Charles Darwin's now-rejected explanation of the inheritance of traits based on the theory that each specialized cell in the parent's body sends some kind of informational particle to the gonads (*qv*) where all the hereditary information, pangenes, are incorporated in the ovum (*qv*) or sperm (*qv*) and transmitted to the offspring. The theory of pangenesis provided Darwin with a mechanism for inherited traits on which natural selection (*qv*) acted in the evolution of species. At the same time Darwin was proposing his pangenesis theory, Gregor Mendel devised an explanation of inheritance, later associated with chromosomes (*qv*) and genes (*qv*) that, is now universally accepted. Mendel's explanation was ignored until the early 1900s. *See also* Mendelian laws of inheritance.

panhypopituitarism A form of abnormally low endocrine (*qv*) activity in the anterior pituitary (*qv*), usually caused by a tumor and resulting in a regression of secondary sexual characteristics (*qv*) and the genitalia (*qv*) as the secretion of follicle-stimulating hormone (*qv*) and luteinizing hormone (*qv*) decreases. This condition also includes decreased secretion of one or more other hormones— growth hormone, adrenocorticotropic hormone, thyroid-stimulating hormone, and/or prolactin.

panhysterectomy Complete surgical removal of the uterus (*qv*), cervix (*qv*), fallopian tubes (*qv*), and ovaries (*qv*). *See also* hysterectomy.

panmixis In genetics, population-wide mating that is at random with respect to genotype (*qv*). Also known as random breeding, panmixis occurs only if the likelihood of mating between two individuals is independent of differences or similarities in their genotypes. The opposite, assortative mating, means that individuals of like genotypes tend to mate more often than chance alone would dictate (positive assortative mating) or less often (negative assortative mating).

pansexualism A doctrine in psychology and philosophy that asserts that all phenomena, both natural and cultural, are underlaid by sexual (*qv*) urges or at least by sexual energies. Critics of psychoanalysis (*qv*) have often charged that Sigmund Freud's (*qv*) view of human behavior was a form of pansexualism, because in their view he reduced all human activity to an interplay between sexual urges and repression. This view is inaccurate, however, since Freud counterposed *Thanatos* (*qv*), a "death instinct," to his concept of Eros (*qv*), a "life instinct" that is basically libidinous. Later psychological philosophers, like Wilhelm Reich (*qv*), have held ideas closer to pansexualism; *see* orgone box, orgone energy, orgone therapy.

pantagamy An alternate term for group marriage (*qv*). *See also* Oneida community; amative intercourse.

Papa In Polynesian creation myths, Papa, the earth mother, joined with Rangi, the sky father, and gave birth to the gods. Their son Tane made his wife, the first human, out of earth from Papa's body.

Papanicolaou (Pap) smear or test A simple cytological smear used most often to test for a cancerous or precancerous condition of the cervix (*qv*); also used to detect ovarian (*qv*), vulvar (*qv*), endometrial (*qv*), fallopian tube (*qv*), and vaginal (*qv*) cancers in cytological smears taken from these organs. In the standard Pap test, scrapings of cells are taken from the posterior outer wall or fornix of the cervix, the endocervix, and the cervix itself. Cell samples are obtained by a wood or plastic spatula and cotton swab during speculum-assisted vaginal dilation without anesthesia. Findings are usually reported in terms of five classes: Class I, only normal cells observed; Class II, atypical cells consistent with inflammation; Class III, mild dysplasia; Class IV, severe dysplasia and suspicious cells; and Class V, carcinoma cells observed. The test was developed by Dr. George N. Papanicolaou (1883–1962), who discovered that malignant uterine tumors slough off cancerous cells into the surrounding vaginal fluid and that these cells can be detected by cervical smears.

paper-doll fetus *See* fetus papyraeus.

Papez theory The theory that the hypothalamus (*qv*), the anterior thalamic nuclei, the gyrus cinguli, the hippocampus, and their connections constitute a harmonious system that may elaborate the functions of central emotion control as well as participate in the expression of emotions; proposed in 1937 by J. W. Papez.

papilla A small nipple-shaped projection; the nipple (*qv*) of the breast (*qv*).

papillary Composed of papilla (*qv*), small pimple- or nipple-shaped elevations, as in goose pimples.

papilloma A benign tumor that projects from an epithelial surface; in the urethra (*qv*), it can interfere with urination and ejaculation (*qv*).

pappus (L.) The medical term for the downy facial hair that appears early in puberty (*qv*) as a precursor of adult facial hair; colloquially referred to as "peach fuzz."

Pap smear *See* Papanicolaou smear.

Pap test *See* Papanicolaou smear.

papyraeus fetus *See* fetus papyraeus.

parabiotic twins Two organisms that more or less share the same bodily systems. Siamese twins (*qv*) are natural parabiotic twins; artificial parabiotic twins can be created by surgery for experimental purposes.

paracervical block A form of regional anesthesia injected into the nerve plexus of the uterine cervix (*qv*) during labor (*qv*).

paracyesis An ectopic pregnancy (*qv*).

paradidymis A functionless vestige of the Wolffian duct (*qv*) attached to the epididymis (*qv*) in the male fetus (*qv*); the other Wolffian duct vestige is the appendix epididymis. A similar vestigial structure, the paroophoron (*qv*), is found in the female.

paradoxical incontinence Frequent urination and leakage caused by pressure of the abdominal organs on the bladder and associated with benign prostatic hyperplasia (*qv*).

paradoxical refractory period The unexplained occurrence in older men of a refractory period (*qv*) of several hours duration during which an erection (*qv*) is not possible if the cycle of sexual excitement and plateau is interrupted and orgasm (*qv*) and ejaculation (*qv*) do not occur. Normally males experience a refractory period only after ejaculation (*qv*).

paragenital Pertaining to contraceptive (*qv*) coitus (*qv*).

parametrium The layer of connective tissue on the floor of the pelvis (*qv*), extending from the cervical portion of the uterus (*qv*) laterally between the layers of the broad ligament.

paramour The male or female partner in a love affair (*qv*); a lover or mistress (*qv*).

para I A woman who has had one live birth; primipara (*qv*).

paranoid (n. paranoia) An individual with a psychological condition, paranoia, characterized by thinking that is delusional and at times hallucinatory.

paraphile *See* paraphiliac.

paraphilia (adj. **paraphilic**) An erotosexual and psychological condition characterized by recurrent responsiveness to and obsessive dependence on an unusual or socially unacceptable stimulus, either perceptually or in fantasy in order to experience sexual arousal (*qv*) and achieve orgasm (*qv*). Paraphilias may arise as a result of vandalizing (*qv*) of a normophilic (*qv*) lovemap (*qv*) during childhood and/or preadolescent years, hence their resistance to reprogramming by behavioral modification, aversion therapy, or other treatments. Males are believed to be much more likely to have paraphilias than are females, probably because their psychosexual development (*qv*) is much more subject to distorting or traumatizing experiences at critical periods (*qv*) in their development than is female psychosexual development. *See also* Eve plan, Adam plan. A paraphilic experience may be replayed in fantasy during masturbation (*qv*) or intercourse (*qv*) with a partner to facilitate arousal and orgasm in a situation that would not be possible without the fantasy replay. The term paraphilia is a legal synonym for a perversion or deviant behavior. In colloquial usage, paraphilic is a synonym for kinky or bizarre sexual practices. See Appendix A.

paraphiliac A person with a paraphilia (*qv*), one whose sexual gratification (*qv*) is dependent on an unusual or socially unacceptable sexual fantasy or experience; a neutral term for sexual alternatives that formerly were termed deviant or perverted; a paraphile.

paraphimosis, tubular A complication of an inflammation of the fallopian tube (*qv*), resulting in partial or full closure of the distal tube just behind the fimbriated os (*qv*) near the ovary (*qv*). *See also* salpingitis. In the male, constriction of the foreskin (*qv*) is known as phimosis (*qv*).

paraplegia (adj. **paraplegic**) A condition characterized by paralysis in both legs. Paraplegia may or may not involve the back and abdominal muscles. The male incidence of paraplegia is double that of females, and highest between ages 16 and 35. Half of the approximately 11,000 spinal cord injuries each year in the United States involve paraplegia. *See also* quadriplegia. Paraplegia, whether the result of a congenital condition or trauma, requires adjustments in sexual functioning (*qv*).

parasexuality An abnormal, "perverted," or antisocial sexual behavior. *See also* paraphilia; perversion; sexual deviance.

parasitic fetus The smaller, usually malformed member of conjoined (*qv*), un-equal, or asymmetrical twins (*qv*) that is attached to and dependent on the more normal fetus (*qv*) for growth and development. *See also* twin transfusion syndrome.

parasympathetic system The craniosacral subdivision of the autonomic nervous system (*qv*) whose actions, mediated by acetylcholine, are primarily concerned with elimination, conservation, and restoration of the body's resources and with moderating the adrenergic actions of the sympathetic nervous system. The nerves of the parasympathetic nervous system decrease heart rate, constrict the bronchioles in the lungs, stimulate secretion of digestive juices, and increase motility in the digestive tract. They innervate blood vessels of the pelvic organs in both sexes, causing vasodilation (*qv*), and are thus responsible for erection (*qv*) of the penis (*qv*) and clitoris (*qv*) and tumescence (*qv*) of the labia minora (*qv*).

paraurethral duct One of two ducts that drain the bulbourethral glands (*qv*) into the vestibule of the vagina (*qv*). Also known as the Skene's duct (*qv*).

paravaginitis An infection and inflammation of the tissues around but not in the vaginal walls (*qv*); an infection of the external female genitalia (*qv*).

parenchyma (L.) The functional tissue of an organ, as distinct from the structural tissue or stroma.

parenchyma testis (L.) The functional portion of the testis (*qv*)—the seminiferous tubules (*qv*) and cells of Leydig (*qv*).

parenchymatous neurosyphilis The tertiary stage of syphilis (*qv*) in which the motor functions coordinated by the central nervous system (*qv*) are disrupted some 10 to 30 years after the initial infection; characterized by tabes dorsalis (*qv*) and partial paralysis.

parent A mother (*qv*) or father (*qv*); a person responsible for providing physical, social, and emotional support for a child; the male who impregnates (*qv*) or the female who conceives, gestates (*qv*), and delivers (*qv*) a child. Adoptive parents represent another legal and social use of the term parent. In view of today's reproductive technologies—artificial insemination (*qv*), frozen ova (*qv*), and embryo transplants (*qv*)—a distinction can be made among a genetic or biological parent (*qv*), a gestational mother (*qv*), and the social or adoptive parent.

parental suit A legal action to establish paternity (*qv*).

parent figure A parent (*qv*), substitute parent, or guardian who provides physical, social, and emotional support for the natural development of a child.

parental perplexity The incapacity of parents to understand and communicate effectively with their children and to provide needed guidance and support because of their own confusion, frustration, and inability to decide what is best for or needed by their children. *See also* generation gap.

parental rejection A pattern of consistent rejection and disapproval by a parent of a child that can undermine the child's self-confidence and prevent development of a strong self-image to the point where the child finds it difficult, if not impossible, to experience mature feelings of love and sexual bonding with a peer in an intimate adult relationship.

Parents Anonymous A self-help group for parents who have abused their children or feel that they may become abusive.

paresis A partial or general paralysis. *See also* parenchymatous neurosyphilis; syphilis; tabes dorsalis.

pareunia An alternate technical term for sexual intercourse (*qv*); literally, ''lying beside.''

parity The condition of having or not having given birth (*qv*) to a live child or children (e.g., nulliparity, uniparity). *See also* parous.

paroophoritis An inflammation of the paroophoron (*qv*) or the tissue surrounding the ovary (*qv*).

paroophoron A small, vestigial remnant of the mesonephric or Wolffian ducts (*qv*) and tubules embedded in the broad ligament between the ovary (*qv*) and the uterus (*qv*). *See also* epoophoron.

parous (-parous) Denotes a woman who has borne children; a combining form referring to the number of offspring produced in a single delivery (e.g., uniparous, diparous) or to the method of birth, as in viviparous or oviparous.

Parousia (Gr.) A biblical term for the saving presence of Christ, to be manifested in the Second Coming of the Redeemer at the end of the world. The common belief of Christians in the first century that the Parousia and the end of the world were imminent fostered a belief that celibacy (*qv*) was a more appropriate lifestyle than marriage (*qv*) and childbearing (*qv*).

parous introitus (L.) A vaginal (*qv*) opening fully stretched by delivery (*qv*).

parthenogenesis The development of an ovum (*qv*) into an organism without fertilization (*qv*) by a sperm (*qv*); virgin birth (*qv*). Some animal species regularly mix parthenogenetic or asexual reproduction with sexual reproduction (*qv*). In such species, both male and female individuals occur. Other species are monochoric; that is, all members of the species have the same gonadal type, in which case the ovum is diploid (*qv*) and only females are produced and these are genetically identical with the parent. Pathenogenesis has been clinically induced in a variety of species by producing a sublethal damage to the surface of the ovum by chemical or physical means. Parthenogenesis does not occur in humans.

parthenophobia A morbid fear of girls, especially virgins (*qv*).

partialism (partial love) The condition of a person who is able to be sexually responsive to and receive sexual gratification with another person only when that partner has some specific and required body attribute (e.g., a particular type of hair, breasts, leg, foot, or amputated limb). *See also* acrotomophilia; andromimetophilia; fetishism; gynemimetophilia; morphophilia; stigmatophilia.

participant observation Research conducted by an individual who is simultaneously engaging in the behavior of the group whose behavior is being studied. Some participant observers reveal their purpose to their subjects before beginning to collect data; others do not. *See also* observational research.

particular friendship A euphemism for an exclusive and emotional association or friendship of two persons of the same sex that is assumed to be sexual or potentially sexual. Prior to a new openness to sexual issues and discussion of homosexuality (*qv*), officials in Catholic seminaries and convents frequently preached about the dangers of particular friendships without ever explaining the basic concern about homosexual or lesbian (*qv*) behavior.

partner swapping An exchange of sexual partners by married or unmarried couples. *See also* swinging.

part object *See* fetishism; partialism.

partouse (Fr.) A French term for group sex (*qv*) or an orgy (*qv*).

partunate period The several-hour period immediately following birth (*qv*) when the newborn (*qv*) must adapt to life outside the uterus (*qv*) by breathing on its own, taking nourishment, and adjusting to a world filled with noise, light, and temperature changes.

parturition *See* childbirth.

Parvati (Skt.) In Hindu philosophy, Parvati is the daughter of the Himalaya Mountains, the gentle consort of Shiva (*qv*), the embodiment of sensuality (*qv*), and the personification of transcendental abundance and the delight of Tantric (*qv*) unions. *See also* Shakti.

passion An extreme, compelling emotion, drive, or excitement. *See also* eros; libido.

passive algolagnia *See* masochism.

passive-congenital relationship A relationship characterized by shared attitudes toward sexual relationships and other aspects of everyday life. *See also* conflict-habituated relationship.

passive immunity A form of acquired immunity resulting from the administration of antibodies (*qv*) to a recipient. The antibodies are made by injecting a specific foreign antigen (*qv*) into an animal and then isolating the antibodies it produces. Another form of passive immunity involves maternal antibodies, which cross the placental barrier (*qv*) to the fetus (*qv*) or are ingested with the colostrum (*qv*).

passive role A behavioral pattern characterized by submission and responding to another person's sexual initiatives; the insertee (*qv*) role in anal intercourse (*qv*); the behavioral pattern adopted by the submissive masochist (*qv*) in a bondage and dominant or sadomasochistic (*qv*) relationship.

passive scoptophilia A form of paraphilic (*qv*) exhibitionism (*qv*) in which a person is sexually aroused (*qv*) and achieves sexual gratification (*qv*) by having other persons view his or her sexual organs (*qv*).

passive sexual trauma A psychological trauma that develops as a result of a person observing some sexual behavior and associating it with something else physically or emotionally painful that occurs about the same time. Passive sexual trauma may become a factor in the etiology of sexual assault (*qv*) or rape (*qv*) later in life.

passivism *See* passive role.

paternal engrossment *See* bonding.

paternal nondisjunction Nondisjunction (*qv*) of a homologous (*qv*) pair of chromosomes (*qv*) during spermatogenesis (*qv*). Paternal nondisjunction may affect an autosomal (*qv*) pair or the sex chromosomes (*qv*). When paternal nondisjunction involves the sex chromosomes in the first meiotic (*qv*) division, the sperm (*qv*) produced contain either 22 autosomes and no sex chromosome, or 22 autosomes and both the X (*qv*) and Y (*qv*) chromosomes. Sperm with the former combination fertilizing a normal ovum will produce an individual with Turner syndrome, or 45,XO (*qv*). Sperm with the second complement fertilizing a normal ovum will produce an individual with Klinefelter syndrome, or 47,XXY (*qv*). When paternal nondisjunction occurs in the second meiotic division, three kinds of sperm are produced: one type with 22 autosomes and no sex chromosomes, a second type with 22 autosomes and XX, and a third type with 22 autosomes and YY. When fertilizing a normal ovum (*qv*), the first type of sperm results in a female with Turner syndrome or 45,XO, the second results in a female with 47,XXX (*qv*), and the third a male with 47,XYY syndrome (*qv*).

paternity The state or condition of being a father (*qv*).

paternity blues The transient feelings of mild depression experienced by a new father when he is unprepared for the changes in his life-style and marital relationship accompanying the birth of a child, especially a firstborn.

paternity suit In law, a civil suit brought against a man by a woman who charges that he fathered her child out of wedlock (*qv*) and therefore owes her and the child support or other reparation. An important part of a paternity suit is the evidence offered to substantiate the claim. Biologically, no amount of evidence is ever sufficient to prove paternity medically and without any question, whereas conclusive evidence may be provided that the man is not the father. Since tests of paternity depend on showing that the child's genes (*qv*) match those of the putative father, a single mismatch suffices to disprove paternity. However, it is theoretically possible that the woman has had lovers with very similar genes. In this case, a match of a dozen or more genes between the child and putative father can easily occur by chance, given that each individual has between 50,000 and 100,000 genes, many of which are said by geneticists to be ''public'' genes and thus widely prevalent in a population. Gathering, presenting, and interpreting legal genetic evidence of paternity is extremely difficult. Newer genetic techniques using antigen (*qv*) matches and deoxyribonucleic acid (DNA) (*qv*) comparisons offer some advantages, but their legal validity and interpretation remain for the courts to decide.

paternity test A clinical test designed to establish biological paternity (*qv*), based on matches and discrepancies between the HLA antigen (*qv*), ABO, Rh positive/negative, and other blood groups of the child, the alleged father, and the mother. *See also* paternity suit.

pathicism A form of homosexual (*qv*) behavior in which the partner who adopts the stereotypic feminine or passive role (*qv*) also adopts the behaviors and attire of the female in a chronic or episodic gender role transposition (*qv*). *See also* transgenderist; transvestite.

pathological arsonist A person who is sexually aroused by setting fires and dependent on this to achieve orgasm (*qv*). Setting fires gives the pathological arsonist control over his world that he does not otherwise have. *See also* pyromania.

pathological pornographer A person who is sexually attracted to children but photographs children in the nude and in sexual poses as a way of establishing contact and communication with a child because he finds a direct sexual approach uncomfortable. The camera serves as a safe insulator, protecting the adult from the young victim while allowing him or her to satisfy a pedophilic (*qv*) dependence on the child for sexual arousal (*qv*) and satisfaction.

pathologic deviance Sexual behavior contrary to social mores (*qv*) or illegal.

patriarchal family A family in which the father or eldest male is recognized as the head of the family or tribe. *See also* patriarchy.

patriarchy (adj. patriarchal) A form of social organization in which the father or eldest male is the supreme authority in the family, tribe, or clan (*qv*), with descent, kinship (*qv*), and inheritance traced through the male line; a society, community, or country based on this social organization. While patriarchy is often explained in terms of male strength and the need of the reproductive female for protection, most sociologists argue that patriarchy is the outcome of a variety of social factors, including compulsory heterosexuality (*qv*), male violence, the way men are organized in the workplace, and gender role (*qv*) socialization. Feminist (*qv*) usage of the term *patriarchy* emphasizes the male control of females and the lack of effective power for women in such a society. *See also* matriarchy. Resource: C. Kramarae and P. A. Treichler, eds., *A Feminist Dictionary* (London: Pandora Press, 1985), pp. 322–324.

patrilineal A system of tracing one's ancestry in which descent is traced only through the father. Patrilineal societies are often highly male dominated and may also require strict segregation of women from public life. *See also* bilateral descent; descent group; matrilineal; patriarchy; purdah.

patrilocal A residence system in which after marriage (*qv*) the husband brings his bride to live with or near his parents. Also known as virilocal.

patriophobia A morbid fear of inheriting a genetic defect (*qv*) or disease.

pausimenia An obsolete term for menopause (*qv*).

Pauthrier's giant lichenification Thick, hard, scalelike plaques of the genital (*qv*) skin caused by a variety of infections.

PC muscles *See* pubococcygeal muscles.

PC muscle exercises *See* pubococcygeal muscle exercises.

peak day That day in the monthly cycle when, according to one of the natural family planning methods, ovulation (*qv*) occurs and the woman is most susceptible to becoming pregnant (*qv*) if she has intercourse. *See also* Billings' contraceptive method; cervical mucus test; ferning; Spinnbarkheit; Mittelschmerz.

peak experience A term created by Abraham Maslow (*qv*) to describe moments of great awe, understanding, and rapture during which an individual loses self-consciousness and becomes one with the world. Peak experiences may be creative periods, contemplative experiences of compassionate and nonactive awareness, or an experience of oneness with another person and the cosmos during sexual relations (*qv*).

peak mucus sign *See* peak day; Billings' contraceptive method; cervical mucus test; ferning; Spinnbarkheit; Mittelschmerz.

peccatophobia *See* sin phobia.

pederast An older male who has anal intercourse (*qv*) with a prepubertal (*qv*) or early pubertal (*qv*) boy.

pederasty Sexual relations between a man and a boy. Common but incorrect usage of the term includes the limitation of anal intercourse (*qv*) performed by an older male on a prepubertal (*qv*) or early pubertal (*qv*) boy. The term is also incorrectly used to refer simply to anal intercourse without regard to the ages of the participant males. The term is not applicable to sexual relations (*qv*) between an older woman and a boy. *See also* pedophilia.

pederosis An obsolete term for pedophilia (*qv*).

pediatrics That branch of medicine concerned with the development and care of children.

pedication An obsolete term for pederasty (*qv*) or bestiality (*qv*).

pediculosis An infestation with the blood-sucking louse *Pediculus pubis*, also known as *Phthirius pubis*. Pediculosis usually occur in the pubic (*qv*) area but may also occur in other areas with hair—the eyelids and eyelashes, scalp, and skin. Pubic lice are often transmitted during sexual intercourse (*qv*), but may also be transmitted through infected bedding or clothing. Pediculosis is colloquially known as crabs.

pedigree A line of descent, lineage (*qv*), or ancestry. Genetic pedigrees are useful in tracing the inheritance of specific traits or diseases and estimating risks for the offspring of prospective parents.

pedomania An obsolete term for pedophilia (*qv*).

pedophilia The psychological, paraphilic (*qv*) condition in which an adult is responsive to or dependent on erotosexual (*qv*) activity with a prepubertal (*qv*) or early pubertal (*qv*) boy or girl, or fantasy of such, in order to achieve sexual arousal (*qv*) and orgasm (*qv*). The condition appears to be more common among men. The sexual activity may involve voyeurism (*qv*) and exhibitionism (*qv*), mutual fondling of the genitalia (*qv*), mutual masturbation (*qv*), and/or vaginal (*qv*), oral (*qv*), or anal (*qv*) intercourse. Pedophiliacs are much more commonly males who act heterosexual with adults, yet seek children they can seduce and control, often without regard for their gender. Fantasies that replay previous pedophiliac activity may fuel subsequent masturbation or copulation (*qv*) with an older partner. Commonly known as child molestation. *See also* pederasty; nepiophilia; ephebophilia; gerontophilia.

pedophiliac A person who is erotosexually (*qv*) attracted to prepubertal (*qv*) or early pubertal (*qv*) boys or girls. *See also* pedophilia.

pedophthoria In ancient Greece, the seduction of a boy by an older male. *See also* pederasty; pedophilia.

pedotribes In ancient Greece, an older male who has as a lover an adolescent boy. The older male served as a tutor and educator for his young lover and introduced him to the sexual arts. Similar socially structured relationships occur in other cultures, such as the East Bay Melanesians.

peeping Tom A colloquial term for a voyeur (*qv*). The term is derived from eleventh-century English folklore of a male citizen who peeped as Lady Godiva rode naked through her husband's town to protest his unjust taxation of the citizens.

peep show An adult book store or shop that rents or sells pornography (*qv*) and has facilities for showing such films or videos to individual customers in private or semiprivate cubicles.

peer group Any collective in which the members share some common characteristics such as age, sex, or ethnicity. Adolescent peer groups share a high degree of social cohesiveness, a hierarchical organization, and a behavioral code that rejects or contrasts with adult values and experience.

peer pressure Expectations and psychological pressure exerted by one's peers that play a major motivational role in much of teenage sexual activity (*qv*). In several studies of teenage sexual activity, peer pressure is listed as the main reason teens do not delay having sexual intercourse (*qv*).

Peggy Lee syndrome The feelings of disappointment often reported by teenage girls in their first sexual intercourse (*qv*) when it is not as thrilling as expected. The term was derived by sexologist David Weis from Peggy Lee's popular song "Is That All There Is?"

pelvic abscess A cavity-like, open sore containing pus and surrounded by inflamed tissue, resulting in lower abdominal pain and fever, and associated with pelvic inflammatory disease (*qv*), acute appendicitis, or diverticulitis of the colon.

pelvic cellulitis A secondary bacterial infection of the parametrium (*qv*) occurring after childbirth (*qv*) or an abortion (*qv*) as a result of a primary injury and infection in the external genitalia (*qv*), vagina (*qv*), or cervix (*qv*).

pelvic examination *See* gynecologic examination.

pelvic-floor exercises An uncommon term for pubococcygeal muscle exercises (*qv*).

pelvic inflammatory disease (PID) Any inflammatory condition of the female pelvic organs (*qv*), especially one due to bacterial or other sexually transmitted infection. PID may be characterized by fever, a foul-smelling vaginal discharge (*qv*), lower abdominal pain, abnormal uterine bleeding, painful coitus (*qv*), and tenderness or pain in the uterus (*qv*), ovaries (*qv*), or fallopian tubes (*qv*) during bimanual pelvic examination. PID can be detected by bacteriologic examination of cervical mucus (*qv*) samples and sonograms (*qv*). PID is a common cause of female sterility (*qv*) resulting from tubal blockage. Simultaneous antibiotic treatment for a partner is recommended to prevent reinfection. *See also* endometriosis; salpingitis.

pelvic minilaparotomy A surgical operation in which the lower abdominal cavity of a female is entered by way of a small incision to allow tubal sterilization (*qv*) or for diagnosis and treatment of eccyesis (*qv*), ovarian cyst, endometriosis (*qv*), or infertility (*qv*).

pelvic muscles A general term for two sets of muscles: the true pelvic muscles (the levator ani and coccygeus) and the pelvic wall muscles (the obturator internus and piriformis). *See also* pubococcygeal muscle exercises.

pelvic nerve The nerve involved in orgasm (*qv*); stimulated in males by deep pressure within the penis (*qv*); in females stimulation is possibly associated with Grafenberg spot (*qv*) stimulation.

pelvic thrusting The in-and-out thrusting by the male of the penis (*qv*) in the vagina (*qv*) and the reciprocal thrusting by the female of her pelvis (*qv*), as part of coitus (*qv*), and often culminating in ejaculation (*qv*) and orgasm (*qv*).

pelvis The lower portion of the body trunk composed of the coccyx, sacrum, and two innominate (hip) bones, surrounding and protecting the bladder and the internal sexual and reproductive organs.

pendulant breasts Breasts (*qv*), usually medium or large, that hang low on the chest. Normal in all women although more common as age increases.

pendulous urethra An alternate term for the penile urethra (*qv*).

penectomy Surgical removal of the penis, usually performed as part of the treatment for cancer of the penis. *See also* castration.

penetrance In genetics, a variable factor that modifies the regularity with which an inherited trait is manifested in an individual.

penetration The introduction of the penis (*qv*) into the vaginal canal (*qv*), or rectum (*qv*). The question of vaginal or anal penetration is sometimes critical in determining legally whether rape (*qv*) or child molestation (*qv*) has been committed. In some jurisdictions, penetration is said to have occurred if the glans (*qv*) of the penis makes contact with the vulva (*qv*), anus (*qv*), or mouth. In other jurisdictions, the penile glans must have actually been introduced into the vaginal introitus or rectum. Also known as intromission (*qv*).

penetration phobia An aversion or hypophilic (*qv*) condition involving irrational panic and disabling fear that prevents penetration of the vagina (*qv*), mouth, or anus (*qv*) by the penis (*qv*). A penetration phobia is usually psychogenic (*qv*) in etiology. The term is also applied to the fear of having the penis enveloped in something, particularly the vagina or mouth. *Synonym*: aninsertia. *See also* vaginal spasms; sexual aversion; vagina dentata.

penial Referring to the penis (*qv*).

penile Referring to the penis (*qv*).

penile bone A cartilaginous structure or bone found in some mammalian species but not in the human male; located above the corpus spongiosum (*qv*) and between the corpora cavernosa (*qv*) of the penis (*qv*). *See also* baculum; os penis.

penile cancer A rare malignancy of the penis (*qv*) occurring more frequently in uncircumcised men and associated with genital herpes (*qv*) and poor personal hygiene.

penile clamp A clamp designed to fit over the penis (*qv*) as an aid in controlling urinary incontinence (*qv*).

penile implant Any of several types of rigid silicone rods, flexible silicone-covered rods, or self-contained inflatable devices surgically inserted into the shaft of the penis (*qv*) to allow a male with organic (*qv*) erectile failure (*qv*) to have an erection (*qv*) and thus achieve vaginal penetration (*qv*). *See also* penile prosthesis.

penile meatus The opening of the penile urethra (*qv*) in the glans (*qv*) of the penis (*qv*). *See also* epispadia; hypospadia.

penile piercing The practice of inserting a ring or stud in one or more holes made in the foreskin (*qv*) or glans (*qv*) in order to increase stimulation and pleasure during intercourse (*qv*).

penile plethysmograph *See* plethysmograph.

penile prosthesis Any device used to assist a male with an organic erectile dysfunction (*qv*) to achieve and maintain an erection (*qv*) that allows vaginal penetration (*qv*). The simplest form is a plastic sheath slipped over the flaccid penis and sealed at the base to allow a suction device to create a vacuum that promotes an erection (*qv*). Rigid or flexible silicone rod implants, some with self-contained pump and hydraulic system, can be surgically embedded in the corpora cavernosa (*qv*) of the penis to allow vaginal penetration. *See also* penile splint.

A self-contained three-part inflatable system is the most sophisticated type of penile prosthesis. A small pump, implanted in the scrotal sac (*qv*), is used to pump fluid from a reservoir under the abdominal skin to a pair of collapsed cylinders embedded in the cavernous bodies of the penile shaft, resulting in an erection. Return to the flaccid state is achieved by pressing a release valve attached to the pump in the scrotum. A simplified form of this implanted inflatable system consists of the paired inflatable penile cylinders, with the pump and release valve embedded in the penile glans (*qv*). Penile prostheses are used in men unable to achieve an erection due to an organic condition such as spinal cord injury, multiple sclerosis, prolonged kidney dialysis, chronic diabetes, abdominal surgery, or prostatectomy (*qv*).

penile splint A soft rubber sheath reinforced with plastic ribs that covers much of the penile shaft (*qv*) but not the glans (*qv*), used to enhance an erection (*qv*) and allow for vaginal penetration (*qv*) for men with erectile problems.

penile urethra The most distal portion of the male urethra (*qv*), contained in the shaft of the penis (*qv*). *See also* membranous urethra; prostatic urethra.

penilingus (L.) An alternate term for fellatio (*qv*).

penis The male urinary and copulatory organ of mammals and some reptiles, composed of an internal root and an external shaft with a glans (*qv*) penis and the foreskin (*qv*) or prepuce at the distal end. In mammals, the body or shaft of the penis contains two parallel, erectile, cylindrical bodies—the corpora cavernosa (*qv*), and beneath them, surrounding the urethra, the erectile corpus spongiosum (*qv*). The corpus spongiosum expands at its distal end to form the mushroom-shaped glans penis. All three corpora are highly vascularized and erectile during sexual stimulation. The flaccid human penis averages between 3 and 4 inches in length and 1 inch in diameter. *See also* micropenis. The average erect dimensions are 5 to 7 inches in length and 1.5 inches in diameter. There is considerable variability in length and diameter for flaccid and erect penises. The homologous female structure is the clitoris (*qv*).

penis captivus (L.) A condition in which the erect penis (*qv*) cannot be withdrawn from the vagina (*qv*) until it returns to its flaccid condition. Although this condition is widely rumored to occur in humans, it has not been clinically documented. The condition does occur in many animals, where a vascular knot in the penis prevents its withdrawal before the flaccid state is reached. The myth of its occurrence in humans is probably rooted in the fear of castration (*qv*).

penis enhancer Any device designed to increase the size of the penis (*qv*) or alter its texture or structure, purportedly to enhance the stimulation provided during vaginal intercourse (*qv*). Among the more popular types of penis enhancers are textured, ribbed, nubbed condoms (*qv*); penile sheaths that extend penile length and width; penile rings that stimulate the clitoris (*qv*) during intercourse; and French ticklers, condoms with rubber projections alleged to stimulate the inner portion of the vagina (*qv*).

penis envy In psychoanalytic theory (*qv*), an alleged unconscious sense of sexual inadequacy (*qv*) and inferiority in a female because she lacks a penis (*qv*) and as a result envies the male. According to Sigmund Freud (*qv*), the girl becomes aware of her lack of a penis during the phallic stage (*qv*), between ages 3 and 7. It is suggested that the girl blames her mother for this castration (*qv*) and transforms her envy into a desire to become pregnant and have a child. Critics, like Margaret Mead (*qv*) and Karen Horney, have pointed out that Freud ignored motherhood except as a substitute for possession of a penis though the reverse envy might be closer to the truth. *See also* phallocentric culture; phallocentrism; uterine envy.

penis extender *See* penis sheath.

penis fear Phallophobia, a morbid fear of the penis (*qv*), especially when it is erect.

penis feminis (L.) The clitoris (*qv*).

penis holding A ritual of greeting or oath taking in some cultures. In Genesis 24:1–5,9, the servant of Abraham swears an oath by putting his hand under Abraham's thigh. Whether this meant he held Abraham's penis (*qv*) or testicles (*qv*) is not clear, although both variations have been reported in tribal cultures. The etymological derivation of "to testify" and "testicles" may originate in this custom.

penis muliebris (L.) The clitoris (*qv*).

penis ring A sex aid placed around the shaft of the penis (*qv*) (at its base) that restricts blood flow out of the penis and helps maintain an erection.

penis sheath A device that covers the penis (*qv*) for purposes of modesty, for protection, or to enhance its aesthetic and sexual appeal. Penis sheaths, phallocrypts, codpieces (*qv*), and penis extenders may be made of gourds, curled bark, cloth, or metal. They are often decorated or in the case of penis extenders, which can be 2 or 3 feet long and tipped with feathers, hair, or flowers. Penis sheaths are popular among native cultures in New Guinea and South America.

penis symbol *See* lingam; phallus; penis sheath.

penis/vagina fixation An obsession that reduces all sexual interaction to penile penetration (*qv*) of the vagina (*qv*); a misconception about the efficacy of penis/vagina intercourse (*qv*) in producing orgasm (*qv*) for women. *See also* clitoral orgasm; outercourse; vaginal orgasm.

penis wrapper *See* penis sheath.

penitis An inflammation of the penis (*qv*).

penoclitoris A medical term for the sexually ambiguous phallus (*qv*) of a newborn. *See also* intersex; pseudohermaphrodite.

penoscrotal raphe The scarlike line formed along the under-surface of the penile shaft (*qv*) and scrotum (*qv*) by fusion of the labioscrotal swellings (*qv*), which enclose the male penile urethra (*qv*) during the first trimester (*qv*) of gestation (*qv*).

pentamindine isethionate A drug originally used in treatment of protozoan infections, which is also used in treating pneumocystis carinii (*qv*) associated with acquired immune deficiency syndrome (*qv*).

peodeiktophilia The paraphilic (*qv*) condition of exhibitionism (*qv*), a solicitational-allurative type of paraphilia in which sexuoerotic arousal (*qv*) and attainment of orgasm (*qv*) depend on evoking surprise, dismay, shock, or panic from a stranger by exhibiting the flaccid or erect penis (*qv*). No term exists for the paraphilic act of a female's exposing her genitalia (*qv*). The reciprocal paraphilic condition in which sexual arousal and orgasm are facilitated by staring at the penis is included in the broader concept of voyeurism (*qv*).

percephalus A fetus (*qv*) or individual with a malformed head.

perculation umbilical blood sampling (PUBS) A method of fetal diagnosis, monitoring, and therapy in which fetal blood is withdrawn from the vein of the umbilical cord (*qv*) and subjected to chromosomal, genetic, and enzymatic/hormone analysis. Blood is withdrawn through a hypodermic syringe guided to the umbilical vein by an ultrasound scan (*qv*). This test can be performed as early as 17 weeks of gestation (*qv*). Blood analysis may reveal anemia, liver, or heart dysfunctions, and enzyme or hormone deficiencies, as well as the presence of the HIV virus (*qv*). When appropriate, therapeutic drugs may be introduced into the umbilical vein to control or remedy a deficiency or infection. *See also* amniocentesis; chorionic villi sampling.

perforate hymen A hymen (*qv*) with one or more openings to allow passage of vaginal secretions (*qv*) and the menstrual flow (*qv*), in contrast with an imperforate (*qv*) hymen. *See also* annular hymen; cribriform hymen.

performance anxiety The fear that one will not be able to perform adequately in a sexual relationship—by failing to achieve an erection (*qv*) or have an orgasm (*qv*), by not being able to be aroused and lubricated, or by not being able to satisfy the partner. Performance anxiety is experienced by most men and women at one time or another but most commonly in a new relationship and in the adolescent (*qv*) years. Such anxiety is often a psychogenic cause in desire phase dysfunction (*qv*), particularly sexual aversion (*qv*), and of erectile and excitement phase dysfunction (*qv*).

Perfumed Garden A sixteenth-century Arabic pillow book (*qv*) describing all aspects of the art of lovemaking (*qv*) with beautiful miniature illustrations.

perinatal Around the time of birth (*qv*) or associated with childbirth (*qv*).

perinatal mortality The statistical rate of fetal and infant death, including still-births (*qv*), occurring between 28 weeks of gestation (*qv*) and the end of the fourth week after birth, usually expressed as the number of deaths per 1,000 live births in a particular area or population.

perinatologist A medical specialist concerned with the health, diagnosis, and treatment of disorders in the mother and her child during pregnancy (*qv*), child-birth (*qv*), and the first month following birth (*qv*).

perineal Associated with or related to the perineum (*qv*).

perineal body The muscle and connective tissue between the vagina (*qv*), anus (*qv*), and lower rectum (*qv*) in the female and between the scrotum (*qv*), anus, and lower rectum in the male.

perineal coitus *See* femoral coitus.

perineal testicle A partially descended testicle (*qv*) lodged in the perineal (*qv*) tissues, under the bulb at the base of the penis. *See also* cryptorchidism.

perineum (adj. **perineal**) The hairless region bordered on the sides by the thighs and between the scrotal base or vulva (*qv*) and the anus (*qv*); an erogenous (*qv*) zone innervated by the perineal branch of the pudendal nerve (*qv*).

period A colloquial term for that phase in the female monthly cycle during which the functional layer of the uterine mucosa (*qv*) is shed; the time of the menstrual flow (*qv*); short for menstrual period. *Synonyms*: menses; menstrual period.

period, critical A time slot in fetal development or postnatal life during which the organism is competent and can respond to a particular stimulus. The tran-quilizer thalidomide is an excellent example of this phenomenon. It inhibits upper and lower limb development if administered during the critical period when the genes (*qv*) controlling limb development are functioning. At other times in a pregnancy, it has no teratogenic (*qv*) effect on the limbs. The language centers of the brain also have a critical period during which it is easy to learn a native language. If this critical period is passed and a native language not learned, it may be impossible for an individual to use language to communicate. *See also* nature/critical period/nurture.

periodic leukorrhea A whitish, mucous vaginal discharge (*qv*) occurring just before or during menstruation (*qv*).

peripheral androgen blocker A steroid (*qv*) drug used to block the virilizing (*qv*) effects of endogenous androgens (*qv*) in females and prevent or reduce the unwanted effects of hirsutism (*qv*).

peristalsis Rhythmic waves of muscle contraction passing along a tubular organ. In females, peristaltic movements and ciliary activity move the egg from the os (*qv*) of the tube to the uterine cavity (*qv*). In the male, rhythmic peristaltic contractions of the urethra (*qv*) are vital in ejaculation (*qv*).

peritonitis An inflammation of the peritoneal tissues lining the abdominal cavity, resulting at times from bacterial infections entering through the vagina (*qv*), uterus (*qv*), and fallopian tubes (*qv*), from rupture of an ovarian cyst, from an ectopic pregnancy (*qv*) in the fallopian tube, or from a ruptured pyrosalpinx (*qv*). *See also* pelvic inflammatory disease.

permissiveness with affection An attitude and value system that maintains that sexual relations (*qv*) between unmarried couples are justified and morally permissible if the man and woman are in love or engaged. This standard of behavior emerged in the 1960s and 1970s in the United States, replacing or modifying the double moral standard (*qv*) and the prohibition against all premarital sexual relations (*qv*) that had prevailed earlier.

pernicious vomiting of pregnancy *See* hyperemesis (gravidarum).

persistent puberism The arrested development or underdevelopment of the secondary sex characteristics (*qv*) due to lower-than-normal production of estrogens (*qv*) or androgens (*qv*) during adolescence (*qv*). If the condition persists beyond adolescence, the result may be the appearance of an eternal child or youth. This physical condition has a psychological counterpart, known as Peter Panism (*qv*).

personal ad A colloquial expression for an advertisement run in the "Personals" or "Hearts Only" want ad sections of newspapers and magazines by a man or woman seeking a suitable person with whom to develop a friendship, sexual relationship, or, possibly, a long-term relationship or marriage (*qv*). The individual who runs a personal ad identifies his or her background, usually giving age, race, perhaps with ethnic and/or religious group, and a further description designed to attract a partner desirable to the person placing the advertisement.

personality The quality or fact of being a person; an individual's habitual patterns and qualities of behavior as expressed by physical and mental activities and attitudes. A sampling of psychological definitions of personality indicates the range of current views: the individual's style of life or characteristic manner of responding to life's problems including goals in life (Adler [*qv*]); "the dynamic organization within the individual of those psychophysical systems that determine his characteristic behavior and thought'' (Allport); ''that which permits a prediction of what a person will do in a given situation'' (R. B. Cattrell); the integration of id (*qv*), ego (*qv*) and superego (*qv*) (Freud [*qv*]); the integration of the ego, the personal, and the collective unconscious, the complexes, archetypes (*qv*), persona, and the anima (*qv*) (Jung [*qv*]); ''the continuity of functional forms and forces manifested through sequences of organized regnant processes and overt behaviors from birth to death'' (H. A. Murray). Resource: J. P. Chaplin, *Dictionary of Psychology*, 2nd rev. ed. (New York: Laurel/Dell, 1985)

personhood Those biological, legal, social, and/or religious characteristics that designate a human infant as an acceptable member of its social group, included under the protection of its laws, and worthy of the effort and expense necessary to support and educate it until it becomes an adult. Since there are no scientifically verifiable criteria for personhood, this phenomenon is subject to a wide variety of philosophical and religious opinions. The concept of when personhood, or ensoulment (*qv*), is accomplished ranges from the moment of conception (*qv*) in Roman Catholic and other conservative religious views, to quickening (*qv*), viability (*qv*), biological birth, and circumcision (*qv*) or other social birth rituals that occur after biological birth. The criteria for attributing personhood to an individual are equally important at the end of human life in the case of comatose persons on life support systems.

The specific characteristics used to designate a human infant as an acceptable member of its social group vary considerably, depending on whether one adopts a biological, legal, social, or religious perspective. Infant personhood has traditionally been conferred by a birth ceremony, held after the newborn is judged to be healthy. However, ethnographic data suggest that the biological criterion is less important than social and religious criteria. Biological health is a often a necessary but not sufficient condition for conferring personhood on an infant. Both biological and social acceptability are usually required for the designation of an individual's personhood. In Chinese culture, for instance, biological, social, and religious factors are factors in the granting of personhood to an infant at its social birth (*qv*) three days after its biological birth.

The Fourteenth Amendment to the U.S. Constitution confers citizenship, and by implication personhood, on anyone born in the United States. The U.S. Supreme Court decision in *Roe v. Wade* (*qv*) cites biological viability (*qv*) at 24 to 28 weeks of gestation (*qv*) as an implicit indication of legal personhood. *See also* immediate animation theory; mediate animation theory.

perversion Used in a legal, religious or moral, and cultural context for any sexual behavior that differs from what is considered normal in a society at a given time in history. The term is used as a synonym for the equally judgmental term *sexual deviance* (*qv*). In psychiatric usage, perversion refers to extreme forms of paraphilia (*qv*), such as sadomasochism (*qv*), zoophilia (*qv*), necrophilia (*qv*), pedophilia (*qv*), urophilia (*qv*), coprophilia (*qv*), and lust murder (*qv*). In the religious context, perversion implies not only immoral but also an unnatural (*qv*) sexual act or behavior. A nonjudgmental near-synonym is *paraphilia*.

pessary A device, available in several forms, inserted in the vagina (*qv*) to treat a prolapsed uterus (*qv*) or uterine retroversion or to serve as a contraceptive vaginal diaphragm (*qv*) or cervical cap (*qv*). May also refer to a contraceptive spermicidal (*qv*) vaginal suppository (*qv*).

Peter Pan syndrome (Peter Panism) A compulsion to remain young forever, expressed by ignoring one's own birthdays, dying one's hair, using cosmetics that claim to rejuvenate the skin and prevent wrinkles, and seeking out cosmetic surgery. The term is derived from Peter Pan, the ever-young hero of Sir James M. Barrie's 1904 play, *The Boy Who Never Grew Up*.

Petri papyrus An ancient Egyptian papyrus, dated at between 1900 and 1800 B.C., that contains the first known medical description of a contraceptive (*qv*)— a vaginal suppository (*qv*) composed of loose fibers, crocodile dung, and honey.

petting Sexually intimate activity involving kisses (*qv*), caresses, and fondling (*qv*) the erogenous (*qv*) areas and genitalia (*qv*) but stopping short of vaginal penetration (*qv*) and intercourse (*qv*). *Petting* is not usually used to include oral-genital (*qv*) activities, although it may include mutual masturbation (*qv*) to orgasm. In many cultures, petting is a common prelude to vaginal intercourse. *See also* loveplay. A distinction may be made between light petting, or necking, above the waist, and heavy petting, below the waist and involving the genitals. *See also* technical virgin.

Peyronie's disease Fibrous growths in the connective tissue surrounding and dividing the corpora cavernosa (*qv*) of the penis (*qv*) that cause painful erections (*qv*) and/or distortion of the penile shaft (*qv*). If the fibrous growth invades the erectile bodies, erection may no longer be possible. The condition has no known cause and no known cure, although surgery and/or palliative measures may help. *See also* phallanastrophe.

PG An abbreviation for prostaglandin (*qv*).

Phaedra complex The sexual, incestuous love of a mother for her son, or the nonpathological attraction of a stepparent for a stepchild. The term is based on the Greek myth of Phaedra, the wife of Theseus, who fell in love with her stepson, Hyppolyte. When Hyppolyte refused her advances, she accused him of violating her and hung herself.

phallanastrophe An abnormal condition in which the penis (*qv*) is permanently bent upward. *See also* Peyronie's disease.

phallic aggression The aggressive, intimidating display of the male genitalia (*qv*), usually in the erect condition. A variety of male animals engage in phallic aggression during rut (*qv*) when males compete for the available females. Exhibitionists (*qv*) and rapists (*qv*) may engage in phallic display as a way of intimidating or seeking to impress their victims.

phallic identity The tendency of males to seek their identity in their penis (*qv*), with an emphasis on the belief that "bigger is better." *See also* penis envy; penis/vagina fixation; phallocentric culture.

phallicism *See* phallic worship; lingam.

phallic love In the psychoanalytic model, a term for the pride and affection displayed by boys for their penis (*qv*) and girls for their clitoris (*qv*) and for the interest in the pleasure derived from masturbation (*qv*). This awareness and focus of love emerges in the phallic stage (*qv*) of psychosexual development (*qv*), which Sigmund Freud (*qv*) claimed occurs between ages 3 and 7 years.

phallic mother A psychoanalytic theory (*qv*) that erectile dysfunctions (*qv*), homosexuality (*qv*), and hatred of women can be traced to a boy's feelings of dismay and disgust when he discovers that his mother does not have a penis (*qv*).

phallic-narcissistic character In psychoanalytic theory (*qv*), a male whose unresolved Oedipal complex (*qv*) drives him to a narcissistic and exhibitionistic Don Juan (*qv*) behavior as a defense mechanism against a castration anxiety (*qv*).

phallic oath An oath taken with the hand on the penis (*qv*) or testicles (*qv*). *See also* penis holding.

phallic phase (stage) In psychoanalytic theory (*qv*), the third of five stages in psychosexual development (*qv*); the period from about age 3 to 5 or 6 when the boy becomes aware of the pleasure-giving possibilities of his penis (*qv*) and girls become aware of its symbolic equivalent. It is during the phallic phase that a boy experiences sexual fantasies (*qv*) about his mother and a rivalry with his father, leading to the Oedipal complex (*qv*). In a parallel development, the girl is said to experience sexual fantasies about her father and a rivalry with her mother, leading to'the Electra complex (*qv*). The phallic stage is, according to Sigmund Freud (*qv*), followed by a latency period (*qv*) and finally, with puberty (*qv*), the beginning of the adult genital phase (*qv*). *See also* oral phase; anal phase.

phallic pride A psychoanalytic term for a boy's pride in his penis (*qv*) and the sense of superiority that it gives him as an aid to overcoming his anxiety at the possibility of being castrated (*qv*).

phallic primacy *See* phallic phase.

phallic sadism A psychoanalytic term for the sexual fantasies (*qv*) that supposedly accompany the phallic stage (*qv*); such fantasies picture sexual intercourse (*qv*) as a violent, aggressive act and the penis *(qv)* as a weapon of aggression and dominance. *See also* phallic aggression.

phallic symbol Any pointed or upright object that symbolizes the erect penis (*qv*). *See also* lingam.

phallic worship Religious ceremonies and rituals that pay reverence to the penis *(qv)*, In both ancient and modern Hindu and Buddhist traditions, the sacred phallus or lingam *(qv)*, made of stone or wood, is the principal icon of the god Shiva. The cults of Dionysius and Priapus in ancient Greece involved phallic worship as a symbol of male superiority, as do some modern Shinto rites. *See also* herm.

phallitis An inflammation of the penis (*qv*).

phallocampsis An abnormal curvature of the erect penis (*qv*) due to an inflammation on one side, which prevents a symmetrical erection. *See also* chordee; Peyronie's disease.

phallocentric culture A society in which male fertility (*qv*) and power are honored and worshipped in symbols of the phallus or penis (*qv*). *See also* lingam; phallic worship; Priapus.

phallocentrism An explanation of sexual development in which the penis (*qv*) is central and symbolically powerful. Psychoanalyst Karen Horney has challenged the phallocentrism of psychoanalytic theory (*qv*), suggesting that male envy of women's reproductive capacity is more powerful and more dynamic than penis envy (*qv*).

phallocrypsis The retraction of the penis (*qv*) to the point where it is hardly visible.

phallocrypt *See* penis sheath.

phallodynia Medical term for a pain experienced in the penis (*qv*).

phalloid Shaped like a phallus or penis (*qv*).

phallophobia *See* penis fear.

phalloplasty Plastic surgery designed to construct or reconstruct a penis (*qv*) to remedy the consequences of a birth defect (*qv*), accidental amputation of the penis, or as part of a female-to-male sex-change procedure (*qv*).

phallos, phallus (L.) The penis (*qv*) or male copulatory organ; the genital tubercle (*qv*) in the two-month-old, sexually undifferentiated embryo (*qv*). May also refer to an enlarged clitoris (*qv*) or to a penislike structure in a female hermaphrodite (*qv*).

phallus girl The fantasy of some male transvestites (*qv*) involving the imagery of being a girl but with a hidden penis (*qv*).

phanermania A compulsive behavior pattern involving the need to stroke or touch repeatedly one part of one's own body; often interpreted as expressing a subconscious sexual need.

phantom-lover syndrome A form of erotomania (*qv*) in which a delusionary, schizophrenic man or woman is convinced that an unknown person is irresistibly in love with him or her.

Pharaonic circumcision A more extreme form of female circumcision (*qv*) in which the minor or major labia (*qv*) are pinned, sewn, or otherwise fused together, leaving only a small hole for urine (*qv*) and the menstrual flow (*qv*). The medial surfaces of the minor labia may be abraded and the girl's legs tied together long enough to allow the labia to heal together (infibulation). In other variations, the minor labia are removed, and the two sides of vulva (*qv*) or major labia are sewn or pinned together. Pharaonic circumcision is used to ensure female virginity (*qv*) since the entrance to the vagina (*qv*) is not reopened until just before the wedding night by a midwife (*qv*) or female relative, or by the husband himself when he consummates the marriage on the wedding night.

Pharaonic mutilation *See* Pharaonic circumcision.

phenotype The physical characteristics, behavior, metabolic, or biochemical products resulting from the interaction of the genotype (*qv*) and environment; simplistically, the physical expression or manifestation of a single gene (*qv*).

pheromone An odorous secretion that acts as a chemical and sexual messenger between individuals. Unlike a hormone (*qv*), which acts as a chemical messenger transported by the bloodstream, mammals (qv) use pheromones to repel foes or competing males, mark boundaries, and assist offspring-parent recognition and attraction and as sex attractants.

philanderer A colloquial term for a man who is promiscuous or sexually drawn to and involved with many different women. *See also* Don Juan; Casanova.

philia (Gr.) Nonsexual love between friends; a friendship in which concern about the well-being of the partner is primary. Philia is also used as a combining form indicating a tendency or preference for something with descriptive prefixes to indicate the object of the tendency, such as homophilia (*qv*), pedophilia (*qv*), urophilia (*qv*). *Antonym*: phobia (*qv*). *See also* agape; eros; storge.

phimosiotomy A surgical procedure to relieve a constricted foreskin (*qv*). *See also* phimosis.

phimosis The narrowing of an opening; tightness of the prepuce (*qv*) or foreskin (*qv*) of the penis (*qv*), which prevents its retraction over the glans (*qv*). The inability to retract the foreskin can lead to accumulation of smegma (*qv*) with inflammation of the glans, or to painful erections (*qv*) or urination.

phimosis of the fallopian tube An involution of the fimbriae of the fallopian tube (*qv*), due to inflammation that closes the tube.

phimosis vaginalis A congenital narrowness or closure of the vaginal opening (*qv*) or cervix (*qv*).

phobia (adj. phobic) An anxiety disorder characterized by an obsessive, irrational, intense, and morbid dread or fear of something, as in homophobia (*qv*). *Antonym*: philia (*qv*).

phocomelia A developmental birth defect (*qv*) of a limb; development of a hand or foot attached directly to the body trunk by a single small, deformed bone and lacking an elbow or knee. A newer term, *meromelia*, indicates any absence of a limb component; a more colloquial term, *seal flipper*, is sometimes used. This condition can be experimentally inducible by the tranquilizer thalidomide (*qv*) and other drugs.

photoplethysmograph An instrument consisting of a transparent plastic cylinder containing a photoelectric cell and light source designed to measure volume and vascular changes in the vagina (*qv*) in response to sexual stimulation.

Phthirus pubis (L.) An alternate scientific term for *Pediculosis pubis*, a type of blood-sucking louse.

phylism (adj. phyletic) An element or unit of response or behavior in an organism that belongs to an individual through its phylogenetic (*qv*) heritage as a member of a particular species, as opposed to idiosyncratic traits and behaviors unique to an individual. Phyletic behavior and traits are the product of both prenatal genetic (*qv*) and postnatal determinants. Phylisms include everyday natural or spontaneous behaviors such as walking, breathing, crying, biting, grasping, swallowing, eating, drinking, laughing, touching, itching. Other phylisms include masturbation (*qv*), fellatio (*qv*), cunnilingus (*qv*), erection (*qv*), ejaculation (*qv*), orgasm (*qv*). The term was coined in 1983 by John Money. *Synonym*: phylon. In the genesis of a paraphilia (*qv*), a phylism that is not ordinarily programmed into a sexuoerotic function (*qv*) becomes separated from its regular context and enlisted in the service of eroticism and sexual response.

phylogenetic Characteristic of the phylogeny (*qv*) or evolutionary history of a species or race, in contrast to an ontogeny (*qv*), the developmental history of an individual. *See also* recapitulation theory.

phylon *See* phylism.

Piaget, Jean (1896–1980) A Swiss developmental psychologist and director of the Jacques Rousseau Institute in Geneva for 50 years, Piaget is world famous for his studies of cognitive and moral development. *See also* egocentric morality; heteronomous morality; autonomous morality.

piblokto A native term for an acute hysterical state affecting Eskimo women who suddenly burst into tears and, screaming, tear off their clothes, and run naked in the snow making animallike sounds. This hysterical episode, followed by amnesia and unconsciousness, is thought to be a social script triggered by the harsh environment and the frustration and sexual abuse (*qv*) associated with the woman's role in Eskimo society.

picket-fence injury A medical expression for any injury that penetrates the vaginal wall (*qv*), usually resulting from insertion of a foreign object into the vagina during masturbation (*qv*).

pictophilia (adj. pictophilic) The psychological or paraphilic (*qv*) condition of being responsive to or dependent on viewing erotic pictures, films, or videotapes alone or in the presence of a partner in order to become sexually aroused (*qv*) and facilitate or achieve orgasm (*qv*). The term is also applied to the reciprocal paraphilia in which a person is dependent on showing visual erotica to the partner in order to be aroused and reach orgasm. In J. Money's paradigm, a type of solicitational-allurative paraphilia. See Appendix A.

PID *See* pelvic inflammatory disease.

PIH Prolactin-inhibiting hormone. *See also* prolactin.

pili The microscopic, hairlike cilia such as occur on the surface of the gonococcal bacterium that enable the bacteria to attach to the epithelial cells lining the urogenital tract.

pill, the A prescription contraceptive oral medication containing estrogen (*qv*) and/or progesterone (*qv*) taken daily during a 28-day period to suppress ovulation (*qv*) and create a pseudomenstrual flow and, sometimes, to regularize otherwise irregularly occurring menses (*qv*). Development of the pill is credited to Gregory Pincus and John Rock in the 1950s. However, it is often forgotten that they were encouraged and funded by the 88-year-old Margaret Sanger (*qv*) who raised $150,000 to help Pincus find a "simple, cheap, safe contraceptive to be used in poverty-stricken slums and jungles and among the most ignorant people." The pill was first marketed in the early 1960s. *See also* oral contraceptive; biphasic contraceptive pill; triphasic contraceptive pill; combination contraceptive pill; progestin-only contraceptive pill; diethylstilbestrol.

pillow books Classic, often beautifully illustrated manuals containing advice on all aspects of lovemaking (*qv*) and sexuality (*qv*). Among the most famous pillow books are Ovid's *Art of Love*, an early Roman text; the fourth-century Hindu *Kama Sutra* (*qv*); the fifteenth-century *Theater of God* or *Ananga Ranga* from India; the Italian Pietro Arentino's Renaissance sonnets; and the sixteenth-century Arabic classic, *The Perfumed Garden* (*qv*). The Chinese and Japanese cultures have produce a variety of ornate and erotic pillow books and scrolls.

pimp Colloquial expression for a female prostitute's (*qv*) business manager and "protector."

pineal body or gland A small, cone-shaped organ, located in the midline of the midbrain in the region of the thalamus (*qv*) and attached to the posterior wall of the third ventricle of the cerebrum (*qv*), possibly related to reproductive functions. In certain amphibians and reptiles, the gland is thought to function as a light receptor. The pineal gland appears to secrete the hormone melatonin (*qv*), which may inhibit production of luteinizing hormone (*qv*) and affect fertility. The pineal gland, also known as the epiphysis cerebri, may function in triggering the onset of puberty (*qv*).

pinealoma A tumor of the pineal gland (*qv*) that can cause delayed or premature puberty (*qv*).

ping-pong infection A phenomenon of epidemiology in which a sexually transmitted infection is transmitted back and forth between two partners because only the partner showing symptoms is treated and the other partner, who may be asymptomatic but infectious, is not treated and therefore remains capable of reinfecting the treated partner. With any sexually transmitted disease (*qv*), it is highly recommended that all sexual partners be tested and treated if necessary.

pituitary An endocrine gland (*qv*) known as the master gland because the hormones (*qv*) it produces affect many vital functions of the body, including growth, sexual activity (*qv*), and reproduction (*qv*). The pituitary is situated in the midline behind the eyes and directly under the hypothalamus (*qv*), surrounded by a depression in the sphenoid bone in the base of the skull. The main hormones produced by the anterior pituitary include adrenocorticotropic hormone (*qv*), the growth hormone somatotropin (*qv*), prolactin (*qv*), and the two gonadotropic hormones—follicle-stimulating hormone (*qv*) and luteinizing hormone (*qv*). The posterior pituitary stores two hormones, oxytocin (*qv*), released during lactation (*qv*) and labor (*qv*), and vasopressin, an antidiuretic. Also known as the hypophysis.

pituitary-gonadal axis A hypothetical construct used to explain the two-way, reciprocal regulation involving hormonal production by the pituitary gland (*qv*) and the ovaries (*qv*) or testes (*qv*).

pituitary gonadotropin Hormones secreted by the pituitary (*qv*) gland that affect the ovaries (*qv*) or testes (*qv*). *See also* follicle-stimulating hormone; luteinizing hormone; interstitial cell-stimulating hormone.

Pityriasis rosea (L.) A skin disease that first appears as almost unnoticeable ring-shaped rashes (macules or papules) anywhere on the body, followed by itching scales, which soon disappear without treatment. Two to three weeks later, large areas of itching scales may appear on the penis (*qv*) and elsewhere. *Pityriasis rosea* is not a venereal disease (*qv*); its cause is unknown.

placenta The highly vascular fetal/maternal-derived organ formed early in pregnancy on the inner wall of the uterus (*qv*) through which the fetus receives oxygen and nutrients and eliminates waste products. Forming early in the second week of pregnancy (*qv*), the placenta is at first involved with synthesis of glycogen, cholesterol, and fatty acids important in nutrition of the embryo. The placenta is a major source of hormones, especially estrogen (*qv*), progesterone (*qv*), human chorionic gonadotropin (*qv*), and human chorionic somatomammotropin (*qv*) or human placental lactogen (*qv*). The exchange of substances across the placental barrier (*qv*) involves simple diffusion of oxygen and carbon dioxide, facilitated diffusion, and active transport of nutrients, hormones, electrolytes, antibodies, and wastes. The fetal/maternal exchange is facilitated by villar bushes containing umbilical capillaries surrounded by maternal blood within the compartments of the placenta. The placenta is ejected from the uterus through the vagina (*qv*) after childbirth as the afterbirth (*qv*). *See also* artificial placentation system; placentophagia; placenta praevia; placental insufficiency; placental barrier.

placental barrier The triple-membrane, semipermeable layer separating the fetal blood circulation in the placental villi from the maternal lake of blood in the placenta (*qv*), which prevents blood cells and large molecules from crossing from mother to fetus (*qv*) or from fetus to mother but allows for nutrient and metabolic waste exchange. In the hemochorial type of placenta found in humans, the placental barrier is composed of the endothelial lining of the fetal capillaries, some connective tissue, and the syncytiotrophoblast of the placental villi. The placental barrier is not completely effective in preventing damage to the fetus from infectious organisms or maternal foreign proteins. *See also* erythroblastosis fetalis.

placental hormone One of the hormones (*qv*) synthesized and secreted by the placenta (*qv*). *See also* human placental lactogen; human chorionic gonadotropin; estrogen; progesterone.

placental immunity A passive form of immunity experienced by the fetus (*qv*) as a result of maternal gamma immunoglobulins that cross the placental barrier (*qv*) and give the fetus immunity to many of the same diseases to which the mother has immunity.

placental infection A fetal infection caused by viruses such as the *Herpes genitalis* (*qv*), cytomegalovirus (*qv*), coxsackie, measles, polio, and Rubella (*qv*), the *Toxoplasma gondii* (*qv*) intracellular protozoan parasite, or the syphilis (*qv*) bacterium passing through the placental barrier (*qv*) from the mother to infect the fetus (*qv*).

placental insufficiency An abnormal condition of pregnancy (*qv*), manifested by slowing in the rate of fetal and uterine growth and resulting from a structurally abnormal placenta (*qv*), an infected placenta, or poor placental circulation.

placenta praevia (or previa) A complicating condition in a pregnancy (*qv*) caused by development of the placenta (*qv*) in such a way that it partially or completely blocks the cervical passage by covering the internal os (*qv*) of the cervical canal (*qv*). A placenta praevia may separate from the uterine wall (*qv*) during delivery (*qv*) or at any time during gestation (*qv*). If any hemorrhaging of the placenta occurs, a Caesarean section (*qv*) is usually performed immediately to save the life of both the mother and the fetus, even if the fetus is not term (*qv*).

placentitis Any infection or inflammation of the placenta (*qv*).

placentophagia Eating the placenta (*qv*) and afterbirth (*qv*). Placentophagia occurs in some mammals, for example, rodents, where ingestion of placental hormones (*qv*) facilitates or initiates lactation. It has been reported in some nonindustrial cultures. Some health faddists also recommend placentophagia for its alleged health benefits to the mother.

planned parenthood A philosophical conviction that every child should be a wanted child and that sexually active adults should have available to them and utilize effective contraceptives (*qv*) to avoid unwanted pregnancies (*qv*). *See also* Planned Parenthood/World Population.

Planned Parenthood Association of Kansas City v. Ashcroft In this 1983 six-to-three decision, the U.S. Supreme Court ruled on three cases, the other two being *City of Akron v. Akron Center for Reproductive Health* (*qv*) and *Simopolous v. Virginia*. The decision overturned a law requiring that second-trimester (*qv*) abortions (*qv*) be performed in hospitals, declared constitutional a parental consent requirement if it includes provisions for a judicial bypass, and ruled on other restrictions on abortion.

Planned Parenthood of Central Missouri v. Danforth In this 1976 decision, the U.S. Supreme Court overturned laws that required spousal or parental consent for abortions (*qv*).

Planned Parenthood/World Population Commonly known simply as Planned Parenthood, this family-planning and health services organization has local clinic affiliates in most U.S. cities. It also operates throughout the world as the International Planned Parenthood Federation, offering information and guidance on contraception (*qv*), unwanted pregnancies (*qv*), gynecological health services, and abortion (*qv*). Founded by Margaret Sanger (*qv*), the organization was first known as the American Birth Control League. The name Planned Parenthood was adopted in 1942. Planned Parenthood is the premier family-planning service organization in the world.

plateau phase The second of the four stages in the sexual response cycle described by W. Masters and V. Johnson, occurring after arousal (*qv*) and before orgasm (*qv*). In the male, the plateau phase is characterized by secretions of the Cowper's glands (*qv*), full enlargement and deepening color of penile glans (*qv*), full stable erection (*qv*), full elevation of testes (*qv*) against the body wall, a marked increase in testicular size up to 50 percent, a twofold increase in urethral bulb size, collection of seminal fluid (*qv*) in the prostatic urethra (*qv*), and at the end, a feeling of ejaculatory inevitability (*qv*). In females, plateau phase is characterized by formation of the orgasmic platform (*qv*) in the outer third of vagina (*qv*), full distention and tenting (*qv*) of the inner two-thirds of the vagina, full elevation of the uterus (*qv*), a color change in the labia minor (*see also* sex skin), secretions of the Bartholin's glands (*qv*), and shortening and withdrawal of the clitoris (*qv*) under the labial hood near the end of plateau. The duration of the plateau phase varies widely. Some sexologists see plateau phase as a continuation of the excitement phase (*qv*) rather that as a distinct phase. *See also* desire phase; orgasm; resolution phase.

platonic love Love of another person that is not sexually or genitally expressed; often referred to as spiritual love. *See also* agape; philia; Platonism; storge.

Platonism The philosophy and anthropology of Plato (427–347 B.C.E.), a leading thinker of ancient Greece and one of the most influential of Western thinkers. The Platonic anthropology is essentially a dualism (*qv*) of an exiled soul implanted in a tomb, the body. According to Plato, the soul is the spark of divinity and the body its prison and defilement. The worldly activities of the soul—thinking, reflecting, and philosophizing—create an affinity between the soul and mind. The body, with its senses and sexuality (*qv*), has to be overcome for the "fallen soul" to return to "the divine sphere of light." The antisexual dualism of Platonism was perfected by the Greek Plotinus and the Gnostics, before becoming the dominant theme of a Christian spiritualistic dualistic anthropology in the thought of Augustine (*qv*). *See also* Aphrodite; Dionynius; platonic love. Resources: P. Ricoeur, *The Symbolism of Evil* (Boston: Beacon Press, 1967); R. J. Lawrence, *The Poisoning of Eros* (New York: Augustine Moore, 1989), pp. 5–16.

play In the sociological theory of George Herbert Mead (*qv*), the first stage of self-development in which the child begins role taking (*qv*) while interacting with significant others (*qv*). During this stage, the child has not yet developed a full sense of self. Because the child has no awareness of a general set of social values and norms, that is, no generalized self (*qv*), he or she can easily move from one role to another depending on the situation encountered (e.g., a boy may pass from role playing mother, sister, or father, depending on the situation at the time). The play stage lasts until the age of 4 or 5, when the child moves into the game stage (*qv*).

Playboy Survey A survey sponsored by *Playboy* magazine and conducted by Morton Hunt in 1972 that tried to duplicate the Kinsey studies (*qv*) published in 1948 and 1953. The survey involved 982 males and 1,044 females, recruited in 24 U.S. cities. Each subject provided data on 1,000 to 2,000 items in a questionnaire. Follow-up interviews were conducted with 200 participants. Resource: M. Hunt, *Sexual Behavior in the 1970's* (Chicago: Playboy Press, 1974; New York: Dell Paperback, 1975); R. T. Francoeur. *Becoming a Sexual Person* (New York: Macmillan, 1982), pp. 346–355.

pleasure principle This central idea in psychoanalytic theory (*qv*) proposes that all human behavior is driven by an initial built-in striving for immediate sensual gratification, the need to maximize sensual pleasure and minimize pain. The pleasure principle is the basis of the id (*qv*). The ego (*qv*) and superego (*qv*) are also derived indirectly from the pleasure principle when the id comes into contact with society and reality. In every-day human experience, the pleasure principle is moderated by the limitations of society and the need to yield the reality principle (*qv*). The other basic drive in the Freudian model is that of thanatos (*qv*).

pleasuring Current usage of the term refers to loveplay (*qv*), petting (*qv*), necking (*qv*), kissing (*qv*), and other forms of nongenital sensual and erotic stimuli. In earlier English usage, pleasuring was a euphemism for sexual intercourse (*qv*).

plethysmograph An instrument for measuring and recording changes in the sizes and/or volumes of organs by measuring changes in their blood volume. A *penile plethysmograph* can be used to analyze a male's erectile ability, to detect nocturnal penile tumescence (*qv*) to distinguish organic from psychogenic (*qv*) erectile dysfunction (*qv*), and in the aversion behavioral (*qv*) treatment of paraphilias. *See also* photoplethysmograph.

plicamycin Generic name for an anticancer drug used in treating testicular cancer (*qv*).

PLISSIT model A model for the use of different levels of sex therapy, PLISSIT stands for four levels of therapy, starting with *p*ermission giving and often *l*imited *i*nformation, moving to *s*pecific *s*uggestions, and finally, in problems that are not resolved by the efforts of the first three levels, culminating in *i*ntense *t*herapy. On the simplest level of sexual therapy, the dysfunctional (*qv*) person is given permission to be sexual (*qv*) and to discuss any sexual issue of concern. As an authority figure, the therapist may also give permission for the patient to explore different sexual behaviors he or she may be curious about or interested in experiencing. The therapeutic effects of permission giving are usually reinforced and enhanced by providing limited information related to the patient's specific problem. If the problem is not resolved with application of permission giving and limited information, the therapist may make specific suggestions such as the use of sensate focus (*qv*), stop-and-go (*qv*), and squeeze (*qv*) behavioral exercises or suggest making changes in the lovemaking environment or behavior designed to address the specific sexual problem. Therapeutic efforts utilizing the first three levels of this approach to sex therapy may resolve up to 90 percent of common sexual problems. Intensive therapy with a skilled professional sex therapist (*qv*) is needed to resolve more complex dysfunctions. The PLISSIT therapy model was devised by Jack Annon and Ron Pion. Resource: Jack Annon, *Behavioral Treatment of Sexual Problems*, vol. 1 (Honolulu: Enabling Systems, 1974).

plural marriage A polygynous (*qv*) or polyandrous (*qv*) marriage (*qv*) in which a person has more than one spouse. *See also* group marriage; polygamy; intimate network; polyfidelity.

PMS *See* premenstrual syndrome.

PMT Premenstrual tension. *See also* premenstrual syndrome.

Pneumocystic carinii pneumonia (PCP) (L.) An opportunistic form of pneumonia occurring when the immune system is suppressed and characterized by fever, cough, labored breathing, and cyanosis. Pneumocystic carinii pneumonia is a major complication in many cases of acquired immune deficiency syndrome (*qv*). When combined with the suppression of the immune system that accompanies an infection with HIV-I (*qv*), Pneumocystic carinii pneumonia is invariably lethal.

pneumogynecography An X-ray film made of the ovaries (*qv*) and uterus (*qv*) after the peritoneal cavity has been distended by injection of carbon dioxide gas.

podophyllotoxin An extract of the root of the may apple or mandrake (*qv*) used as a topical treatment for venereal warts (*qv*).

Poelker v. Doe In this 1977 decision, the U.S. Supreme Court upheld the right of the city of St. Louis, Missouri, to refuse elective abortions (*qv*) in public hospitals but let stand a New Jersey Supreme Court ruling in *Doe v. Brideton Hospital Association* that private, nonsectarian hospitals must allow abortions to be performed.

point of no return Colloquial term for ejaculatory inevitability (*qv*).

polar body One of two or three small, nonfunctional cells in mammals (*qv*) produced by the unequal distribution of cytoplasm during the two meiotic (*qv*) divisions of oogenesis (*qv*). The polar bodies receive very little cytoplasm and consist mainly of chromosomes (*qv*). Normally they are not fertilized (*qv*) and quickly degenerate.

pollution A threatening, pejorative, obsolete term for the loss of seminal fluid (*qv*) through a nocturnal emission (*qv*) or masturbation (*qv*).

polyandry In anthropology, a broad term referring to customs in which one woman is simultaneously married to more than one man. Polyandry must be distinguished from other forms of multiple female sexual partnerships (e.g., an extramarital affair, ciscisbeism [*qv*], or serial monogamy [*qv*]), because in polyandry each man is a legal and social husband (*qv*) to the woman. Polyandry is known to occur in Tibet, Africa, the Philippines, and elsewhere. Often, as in Tibetan fraternal polyandry, the men are brothers and share the same wife. In other cases, the men belong to different kinship (*qv*) groups and are not related to each other. Reliable ethnographic data on polyandry has only recently been collected; in older field reports it was either ignored, unknown to the investigator, or considered as generalized promiscuity (*qv*) on the woman's part. Polyandrous marriages are not promiscuous but rather are an essential and structured feature of social and family (*qv*) life in areas where they occur.

polycyesis A multiple pregnancy, leading to birth of more than one infant.

polycystic ovaries An abnormal condition of the ovaries (*qv*) in which development of cysts (*qv*) is triggered by increased levels of testosterone (*qv*), estrogen (*qv*), and luteinizing hormone (*qv*) and decreased amounts of follicle-stimulating hormone (*qv*). The condition results in amenorrhea (*qv*), hirsutism (*qv*), and infertility (*qv*).

polyestradiol phosphate An estrogen (*qv*) compound used in treating prostate cancer (*qv*). Its possible side effects include impotence (*qv*), loss of libido (*qv*), and gynecomastia (*qv*).

polyestrous Having two or more reproductive cycles (*qv*) in a mating season or year.

polyfidelity (adj. polyfidelous) In analogy to the fidelity (*qv*) and commitment shared by marital or domestic partners, polyfidelity refers to the commitment shared by more than two persons in an ongoing intimate network (*qv*). The term was coined by Even Eve, cofounder in the early 1970s of Kerista Village, an egalitarian, nonmonogamous utopian community in San Francisco. As originally defined, a polyfidelitous family is "a group of best friends, highly compatible, who live together as a family unit, with sexual intimacy occurring equally between all members of the opposite sex, no sexual involvement outside the group, an intention of lifetime involvement, and the intention to raise children together with multiple parenting." The basic assumption is that one can have many primary relationships simultaneously. Resource: A. Pines and E. Aronson, Polyfidelity: An alternative lifestyle without jealousy? *Alternate Lifestyles* 4(3)(1981):373–392. Subsequent to this usage, *polyfidelity* has been applied with a more flexible meaning to the primary and secondary, comarital (*qv*), or satellite (*qv*) relationships in intimate networks and sexually open marriages (*qv*) with their varying negotiated degrees of emotional and sexual fidelity.

polygamy The practice or condition of having more than one spouse at the same time. Commonly misused when polygyny (*qv*) or polyandry (*qv*) would be a more specific term.

polygyny The practice or condition whereby a man has more than one wife or erotosexual (*qv*) partner at the same time; the opposite of polyandry (*qv*). Various forms of polygyny were or are practiced by the Church of the Latter Day Saints (*qv*), the Oneida Community (*qv*), Muslims for whom the Qu'ran allows four wives per male, and many nontechnological or preliterate cultures. In the Jewish tradition, Genesis 2:24 may seem to imply monogamy (*qv*), but this is hardly explicit, and the Jewish tradition is consistent in its acceptance of polygyny. Both the Mishna and the Talmud testify clearly to the practice of polygyny. The first Hebrew authority to call for a ban on polygyny was Rabbi Gershom ben Judah of Worms in 1040 C.E. Gershom realized that the Jewish practice of polygyny would not set well with the religio-political crusade of Pope Gregory the Great against the marriage (*qv*) of clerics. Gershon's ban affected German and French Jews and was not extended to Sephardic Jews until the mid-twentieth century when the chief rabbinate of the state of Israel made the ban universal. Resource: R. J. Lawrence, *The Poisoning of Eros* (New York: Augustine Moore, 1989), pp. 16–23.

polyiterophilia A form of hyperphilia (*qv*) in which a person's erotosexual response requires repeating the same sexual activity (*qv*)—manual, oral, anal (*qv*), vaginal (*qv*), or penile (*qv*)—many times over in order to achieve orgasm (*qv*) and satisfaction.

polymastia A condition characterized by more than the normal number of mammary glands (*qv*) due to incomplete regression of the embryonic mammary ridges (*qv*). *See also* amastia; polythelia.

polymorphous perverse Sigmund Freud's (*qv*) term for the capacity of humans to respond to many different types of pleasure or erotosexual stimuli, involving all senses of the body, in an early "pansexual" stage. This capacity is socially channeled and restricted as the child moves through the oral (*qv*), anal (*qv*), phallic (*qv*), latency (*qv*), and genital stages (*qv*) of psychosexual development (*qv*). As a manifestation of the pleasure principle (*qv*) or libido (*qv*), polymorphic perversity may be expressed in socially acceptable sexual behavior or in paraphilic (*qv*) or deviant (*qv*) behaviors. *See also* panerotic potential.

polyorchidism A condition characterized by having more than two testicles (*qv*).

polyps Small, benign tumors, often found in the uterus (*qv*) or cervix (*qv*).

polyspermy Fertilization (*qv*) of an ovum (*qv*) by more than one sperm (*qv*), resulting in the triploid or tetraploid organism.

polythelia The condition of having more than the usual number of nipples (*qv*). Like polymastia (*qv*), polythelia is due to incomplete developmental regression of the embryonic mammary ridges (*qv*), the difference being that polymastia represents supernumerary complete breasts with milk glands, ducts, and nipples while polythelia has only supernumerary nipples. *See also* amastia.

pompadour fantasy A sexual fantasy (*qv*) in which a woman imagines she is the mistress (*qv*) of an important, famous, and powerful person. The concept is named for Madame de Pompadour, a mistress of King Louis XV of France. *See also* courtesan fantasy.

pop the question An old-fashioned colloquialism for a man asking a woman to marry him; one of many allusive phrases and terms that exist in the English language for sexual and sexually related matters.

population at risk A group of people who share a characteristic that causes each member to be vulnerable to a particular event, as intravenous drug users, male homosexuals (*qv*), and men who engage in anal sex (*qv*) constitute populations at risk for acquired immune deficiency syndrome (*qv*) or prostitutes (*qv*) are a population at risk for syphilis (*qv*) and gonorrhea (*qv*).

pornographomania A paraphilic (*qv*) compulsion and need to write sexually obscene material, graffiti, and letters. *See also* narratophilia; pictophilia; telephone scatophilia.

pornography Speech, writings, pictures, images, or films depicting erotic behavior with the intent of sexually arousing (*qv*) the reader or viewer. Any definition of pornography is subject to social and legal debate, and the term may be applied to materials considered sexually arousing, whether so intended or not. Originally *pornography* meant writings about prostitutes (*qv*). Pornography may be considered socially unacceptable or forbidden. It may also be tolerated, as it is in current American society, or embraced as in the classic love manuals (*qv*) or pillow books (*qv*).

The legal prohibition of pornography is based on the technical definition of obscenity (*qv*). Some modern specialists make a distinction between pornography and erotica (*qv*). *See also* erotography. Another common distinction is made between *soft-core pornography*, characterized by frontal nudity and some sexual activity (*qv*), and *hard-core pornography*, characterized by close-ups of the genitalia (*qv*), explicit and close-up views of oral (*qv*), vaginal (*qv*) and anal intercourse (*qv*), as well as sadomasochism (*qv*) and other paraphilic (*qv*) behavior. *See also* Commission on Obscenity and Pornography, Presidential, 1970; Commission on Obscenity and Pornography, Presidential, 1986.

pornolagnia A paraphilic (*qv*) attraction to prostitutes. *See also* madonna complex.

positive feedback system The enhancement of one stimulus by another, as when a sexual stimulus is reinforced by a positive response. *See also* feedback.

positive nuclear sex *See* chromatin positive.

positive pregnancy signs *See* pregnancy signs.

positive transference A psychoanalytic term for a patient's transference of positive feelings of love, attachment, and idealization from the patient's parents to the therapist.

POSSLQ An acronym used by the U.S. Census Bureau to indicate "persons of the opposite sex sharing living quarters." *See also* domestic partners; cohabit (cohabitation).

postambivalent phase A psychoanalytic term for the final, or genital, stage (*qv*) of psychosexual development (*qv*) characterized by a positive integration of genital orgasm (*qv*) and a "love object." The prior oral (*qv*), anal (*qv*), phallic (*qv*), and latency stages (*qv*) are described as ambivalent because of the mixture of positive libidinal satisfactions with the negative means of their achievement by swallowing, biting, or consuming.

postcoital douche Insertion of chemical solutions into the vagina (*qv*) following sexual intercourse (*qv*) for hygienic or contraceptive (*qv*) reasons. Such douching is usually unnecessary for hygienic purposes. It is ineffective as a contraceptive method and may even increase the risk of conception by forcing sperm (*qv*) into the cervical canal (*qv*).

postcoital semen test A clinical test for male fertility (*qv*) based on examination of a semen (*qv*) sample collected from the vagina (*qv*) after sexual intercourse (*qv*). Sperm count, sperm morphology, and sperm motility are important criteria.

postcoitum triste (L.) A feeling of loss and depression following a satisfying sexual encounter, a normal feeling of letdown following orgasm (*qv*). *See also* Peggy Lee syndrome.

postconventional morality The third of three levels of moral development in the schema proposed by Lawrence Kohlberg in which decision making is based on an internalized morality and conscience. *See also* preconventional morality; conventional morality; Piaget, Jean.

postillionage (Fr.) The insertion and manipulation of a finger or small vibrator in the partner's anus (*qv*) for erotic stimulation (*qv*) during loveplay (*qv*), or in one's own anus during masturbation (*qv*). The practice is more commonly engaged in by men than by women.

postmastectomy exercises Exercises essential to prevent shortening of muscles and contraction of joints following a mastectomy (*qv*).

postmature infant An infant born after the end of the forty-second week of gestation (*qv*), usually showing the signs of placental insufficiency (*qv*).

postmenopausal That period of a woman's life following cessation of the monthly menstrual cycle (*qv*). *See also* menopause.

postmenopausal muscular dystrophy A progressive weakening of the hip and shoulder muscles without muscular atrophy following menopause (*qv*).

postorgasmic phase *See* resolution stage; refractory period.

postovulatory phase The ovarian luteal state (*qv*) and uterine secretory phase (*qv*) following ovulation (*qv*) in a woman's monthly menstrual cycle (*qv*).

postpartum The time immediately following childbirth (*qv*) or delivery (*qv*).

postpartum blues (or depression) A mild to moderate depression occurring in some women following childbirth (*qv*). This condition usually develops between 3 days and 6 weeks postpartum (*qv*). The etiology is not understood, although wide hormonal fluctuations, social, and psychological influences have been suggested. Some form of postpartum depression appears to affect about half of all women who give birth. Milder cases, colloquially referred to as the baby blues, are both common and normal. A severe form of postpartum depression is termed *postpartum psychosis* (*qv*).

postpartum eclamptic syndrome A poorly understood complication, with no known etiology, usually occurring within 48 hours of the onset of labor (*qv*), characterized by high blood pressure, severe headache, mental confusion, visual disturbances, vomiting, muscle twitching, and convulsions.

postpartum psychosis A recently identified, severe emotional disturbance experienced by some women following childbirth (*qv*), characterized by severe depression, withdrawal from reality, schizophrenic reactions, delusions, hallucinations, and, in some cases, homicidal attacks by the mother on her newborn (*qv*) and herself. Estimates of severe postpartum depression, recently termed *postpartum psychosis*, vary from one in 2,000 or 3,000 births to one in 100 births. Large fluctuations or disturbances in maternal hormones (*qv*), coupled with circumstances in the delivery (*qv*) that isolate the mother from her newborn (*qv*), lack of knowledge about mothering, lack of family support, and an extreme sense of isolation and helplessness are thought to be contributing factors.

postpartum taboo Any prohibition against engaging in sexual intercourse (*qv*) after childbirth (*qv*). The prohibition may be limited to the time of breast-feeding (*qv*), or to any specified time period of a few days, a week, or longer. In non-Western societies, the taboo (*qv*) may last a year or more.

post-pill amenorrhea The failure of normal menstrual cycles (*qv*) to resume within three months following discontinuance of use of an oral contraceptive (*qv*). This uncommon condition is poorly understood and is rarely permanent.

postpubertal panyhypopituitarism A deficiency in the production of pituitary hormones (*qv*) after the onset of puberty (*qv*), characterized by weakness, lethargy, failure to lactate (*qv*), amenorrhea (*qv*), loss of libido (*qv*), and other symptoms. It is treated with hormone replacement.

postpubescence The one- to two-year period following puberty (*qv*) during which skeletal growth slows after an initial spurt and the physiological processes of reproduction (*qv*) are established.

post-term infant A dated medical term. *See also* postmature infant.

potency In traditional colloquial and medical usage, the ability of a male to accomplish sexual intercourse (*qv*), including vaginal penetration and ejaculation (*qv*); in embryology (*qv*), the range of developmental possibilities of which an embryonic cell or part is capable.

potentia coeundi, potestas coeundi (L.) The ability to engage in penile-vaginal intercourse (*qv*). *See also* erection; vaginal lubrication.

potential fertility The statistical chance of pregnancy (*qv*) for a woman or group of women in a normal married situation using no contraceptive (*qv*) method.

Prader-Willi syndrome A syndrome associated with below-normal levels of pituitary gonadotropic hormones (*qv*) and characterized by compulsive overeating, cryptorchidism (*qv*), hypogonadism (*qv*), psychological disturbances, mental retardation, short stature, and extreme obesity. The condition usually results from a monosomy of a chromosome (*qv*) in group D or a partial deletion of chromosome 15.

preadolescence The period of psychosexual development (*qv*) preceding the onset of puberty (*qv*), characterized by a growth spurt and maturation of the ovaries (*qv*) and testes (*qv*). *See also* prepubescence; prepuberty; epiphysis.

precocious birth *See* premature birth.

precocious breast development Development of the female breast (*qv*) prior to 8 years of age. Precocious breast development is usually due to abnormal functioning or a tumor in the pituitary (*qv*), ovaries (*qv*), or adrenal cortex (*qv*). *See also* witch's milk; pubarche; premature puberty; thelarche.

precocious menstruation The abnormal onset of the menstrual cycle, or menarche (*qv*), before age 10, usually associated with a tumor or abnormal functioning of the anterior pituitary (*qv*), ovaries (*qv*), or adrenal cortex (*qv*). *See also* secular decline hypothesis.

precocious puberty *See* premature puberty; precocious breast development; precocious menstruation; pubarche.

precoital fluid The alkaline fluid secreted by Cowper's glands (*qv*) during sexual arousal (*qv*) in the male. Two or three drops of this thin fluid are usually produced toward the end of the plateau stage (*qv*), although it can appear during the excitement stage (*qv*). The fluid helps neutralize the acidic condition of the membranous and penile urethra (*qv*) and acts as a lubricant to allow for deep penile penetration (*qv*) just prior to ejaculation (*qv*). Sperm (*qv*) are found in this fluid, indicating the possibility that it could result in conception (*qv*).

preconventional morality The first of three levels of moral development in the schema proposed by Lawrence Kohlberg in which decision making is based on a total respect for authority and meeting one's own needs. *See also* postconventional morality; conventional morality; Piaget, Jean.

predatory rape *See* situation rape.

prednisone The generic name for one of the synthetic glucocorticoid hormones (*qv*) used therapeutically as a substitute for cortisol (*qv*), which is normally produced by the adrenal cortex (*qv*).

preeclampsia An abnormal condition of pregnancy (*qv*) characterized by onset of acute hypertension, protein in the urine (*qv*), and edema after the twenty-fourth week of gestation (*qv*). The cause is unknown, although it occurs in 5 to 7 percent of pregnancies (*qv*), most often in a first pregnancy and in young mothers. Complications include premature separation of placenta (*qv*), hemolysis, cerebral hemorrhage, eye damage, fetal malnutrition, pulmonary edema, and low birth weight (*qv*). Treatment includes rest and antihypertensive medication.

preemptive abortion The use of prostaglandins (*qv*), diethylstilbestrol (*qv*), or menstrual extraction (*qv*) to induce the menstrual flow (*qv*) or removal of the uterine endometrium (*qv*) when a pregnancy (*qv*) is suspected but not known for certain to exist.

preformation theory A philosophical theory of human development proposed by sixteenth-century microscopists and embryologists (*qv*), that maintained that the human form is fully contained in the egg or sperm (*qv*). Although early faulty observations were quickly refuted by observations with improved microscopes, the concept of a preformed embryo (*qv*), or homunculus (*qv*), in the ovum (*qv*) or sperm was used by theologians and moralists, especially in the Catholic tradition, to argue that because the human form is preformed and present in the gamete (*qv*), the human soul is also present from the moment of conception (*qv*). Thus, abortion (*qv*) is immoral at any time of gestation (*qv*). *See also* epigenesis.

pregenital love A psychoanalytic term for the first expressions of caring and attachment for another person, usually expressed by an infant during the oral stage (*qv*) when breast-feeding from the mother.

pregenital phase In psychoanalytic terminology, the oral (*qv*) and anal stages (*qv*) of psychosexual development (*qv*) when the libido (*qv*) and sexual satisfaction (*qv*) are focused on the oral or anal processes, before the genital phase (*qv*).

pregnancy The gestational (*qv*) process during which a new individual develops in a woman's uterus (*qv*), from conception (*qv*) through the embryonic (*qv*) and fetal (*qv*) periods to birth (*qv*). Pregnancy in humans lasts approximately 266 days or 38 weeks from fertilization to birth. Clinically pregnancy is said to last 280 days or 40 weeks, counting from the first day of the last menstrual period (*qv*). Following fertilization (*qv*) of the ovum (*qv*) in the outer third of the fallopian tube (*qv*), the zygote (*qv*) undergoes rapid cell division, forming a hollow cell mass or blastula by the time it reaches the uterine cavity (*qv*). Following implantation (*qv*) of the blastocyst (*qv*) in the uterine mucosa (*qv*), a placenta (*qv*) develops to provide a means of maternal-fetal exchange during the pregnancy. Pregnancy ends with labor (*qv*) and delivery (*qv*).

pregnancy fantasies Misconceptions, myths, or imaginary illusions about pregnancy (*qv*). *See also* pseudocyesis; couvade.

pregnancy rate In statistics, the ratio of pregnancies (*qv*) per 100 woman-years. The pregnancy rate is calculated as the product of the number of pregnancies in the women observed multiplied by 1,200 (months) divided by the product of the number of women observed multiplied by the number of months of observation. Thus, if 100 women used a particular contraceptive method for one year and five of them became pregnant, the pregnancy rate would be 5 per 100 woman-years (5 x 1200/100 x 12).

pregnancy signs Indications that suggest or clearly indicate that a woman is pregnant (*qv*). Presumptive signs include a missed menstrual period (*qv*), a tingling sensation in the nipples (*qv*), sensitive breasts (*qv*), fatigue, and/or morning sickness (*qv*). Presumptive signs may be caused by conditions other than pregnancy. Probable pregnancy signs can be detected by a physician after 6 weeks of gestation (*qv*), including an enlarged, soft cervix (*qv*), enlargement of the abdomen, and distention of the uterus (*qv*). Positive pregnancy signs, detectable after 3 months, include fetal heartbeat, fetal movement, indications of a fetal skeleton as seen on an ultrasonogram or X-ray film, and abdominal palpation of the fetus (*qv*). *See also* immunological (urine) pregnancy test; beta-specific monoclonal enzyme-linked immunosorbent assay test (ELISA test); beta subunit HCG radiommunoassay test; home pregnancy test.

pregnanediol A biologically inert urinary metabolite of progesterone (*qv*).

pregnanediol-urine pregnancy test *See* immunological (urine) pregnancy test.

pregnanetriol A urinary metabolite of 17–hydroxyprogesterone, the precursor of all biologically active steroid hormones (*qv*), including cortisol (*qv*) and the sex hormones (*qv*). Detection of an excess of this hormone in the urine (*qv*) indicates an overly active adrenal gland cortex (*qv*), the basis of adrenogenital syndrome (*qv*).

pregnenolone An intermediate hormone derived from cholesterol (*qv*) and precursor for progesterone (*qv*) and some androgenic (*qv*) hormones.

premarital agreement or contract *See* prenuptial agreement.

premarital counseling A series of discussion and guidance sessions in which a couple or several couples work with a trained marital counselor or member of the clergy to prepare for all aspects of married life.

premarital intercourse Sexual intercourse (*qv*) or coitus (*qv*) engaged in by two people who are not yet married; also known as fornication (*qv*) and premarital sex; generally refers to coitus (*qv*) between young, never married people.

premarital relations *See* premarital intercourse.

premarital sex *See* premarital intercourse.

premature Not fully developed or mature; occurring before the usual time; an infant born before 37 weeks of gestation (*qv*).

premature birth *See* premature infant.

premature delivery *See* premature infant.

premature ejaculation A sexual dysfunction (*qv*) or a hypophilic condition in which an individual is unable to sustain the preorgasmic period of sexuoerotic arousal so that ejaculation (*qv*) occurs too soon relative to the individual's own expectation or that of the partner. Premature ejaculation may occur during the acceptive phase (*qv*) or at intromission (*qv*). The condition has varied causes, more often psychogenic than organic. The Kinsey male survey (*qv*) indicates that a majority of American men ejaculate within 2 minutes of vaginal penetration (*qv*). Behavioral therapies commonly used in treatment of this condition are the stop-and-go (*qv*) and the squeeze technique (*qv*).

premature emission *See* premature ejaculation.

premature infant In the traditional sense, any neonate (*qv*) born prior to 37 weeks of gestation (*qv*); in practical usage, since gestational age (*qv*) is often difficult to determine, the term usually describes a newborn infant weighing less than 5 1/2 pounds, regardless of gestational age. A wide variety of predisposing factors may be associated with a premature infant, although the etiology is in most instances unknown. Prematurity is most common among women in low socioeconomic conditions where lack of prenatal care and poor nutrition may precipitate the condition. Complications experienced by a premature infant are associated with the immaturity of various organ systems, especially the respiratory, cardiac, and nervous systems.

premature labor Labor (*qv*) that begins earlier than normal, either before the fetus (*qv*) has reached a weight of 4 1/2 to 5 pounds (2,000 to 2,500 grams) or before 37 weeks of gestation (*qv*). The causes are poorly understood. *See also* premature infant.

premature menstruation *See* menarche; precocious menstruation.

premature pubarche *See* pubarche; premature puberty.

premature puberty Puberty (*qv*) that begins and is completed before the age of 9 in girls and before the age of 11 in boys. Premature puberty may be an error of timing only or associated with a brain lesion that alters the biological clock of puberty in the hypothalamus (*qv*) and pituitary (*qv*). *Synonym*: precocious puberty. *See also* pubertal delay; precocious menstruation.

premature thelarche *See* thelarche; precocious breast development.

prematurity *See* premature ejaculation; premature infant; premature labor; premature puberty.

premenopausal The time preceding the menopause (*qv*).

premenstrual congestion The physiological retention of water by a woman during the luteal phase (*qv*) of her monthly cycle, often resulting in a temporary, cyclic weight gain and loss.

premenstrual sex drive A peaking in sexual interest and receptivity experienced by some women just prior to menstruation (*qv*). Other women experience a peak in sexual interest and receptivity around the time of ovulation (*qv*).

premenstrual syndrome (PMS) A combination of mild to severe physical and psychological symptoms, including fatigue, a bloated feeling, depression, irritability, and lowered self-esteem experienced by some women a few days before menstruation (*qv*) and during the first day or two of menstruation. Various physical, psychological, and social conditioning causes have been suggested as causes, with no clear answer. It has been documented that women from strict backgrounds are more likely to experience this condition.

premenstrual tension (PMT) *See* premenstrual syndrome.

prenatal Occurring or existing in the 9 months between conception (*qv*) and birth (*qv*); referring to changes in or the care of the pregnant woman, as well as the growth and development of the fetus (*qv*) during the embryonic (*qv*) and fetal (*qv*) periods.

prenatal development The process of embryogenesis and organogenesis occurring between conception (*qv*) and birth (*qv*); the development, differentiation, growth, and maturation of the whole organism known successively as the embryo (*qv*) and fetus (*qv*) and its various tissues and organ systems. *See also* critical period; sex variables.

prenatal developmental anomaly *See* congenital birth defect.

prenatal diagnosis Any of several methods used to ascertain the presence or possibility of a genetic disorder (*qv*) or abnormal condition during fetal development. *See also* amniocentesis; chorionic villi sampling; fetoscopy; perculation umbilical blood sampling; thermography; ultrasonography.

prenatal masculinization The masculinizing (*qv*) effect of testosterone (*qv*) and other androgenic (*qv*) sex hormones on the fetal sexual anatomy and behavioral pathways in the brain before birth (*qv*). In the normal development of the male fetus (*qv*), the androgenizing hormones are endogenous (*qv*), being produced by the fetus itself. Anatomical masculinization (*qv*) of the male fetus consists primarily of differentiation of the internal vasa deferentia (*qv*), prostate (*qv*), seminal vesicles (*qv*), and Cowper's glands (*qv*) from the Wolffian ducts (*qv*) and the external penis (*qv*) and scrotum (*qv*) from the genital tubercle, swellings, and folds.

Concomitant with masculinization in the male fetus, defeminization (*qv*) is induced by Mullerian inhibiting hormone (*qv*), which blocks the development of the Mullerian ducts (*qv*). Variable degrees of masculinization and defeminization can coexist in behavior and/or anatomy.

Since the female fetus does not normally produce large amounts of androgenic hormones, it does not experience prenatal masculinization except in the rare case where it is exposed to endogenous androgens produced by an overactive adrenal cortex (*qv*). Exogenous androgens, diethylstilbestrol (*qv*), and some progestins (*qv*) can cause prenatal masculinization in female fetuses. Some researchers claim that high levels of androgens during critical periods (*qv*) in development may lead to a higher incidence of tomboy (*qv*) behavior and bisexual (*qv*) or lesbian (*qv*) orientation. Defeminization (*qv*) is not the opposite of masculinization but refers to a distinct function and process. *See also* feminization; demasculinization; Eve plan; Adam plan.

prenatal sexual development The genetic, anatomical, hormonal, and neural differentiation in a sexually dimorphic way (*qv*), following either the Eve plan (*qv*) for female development or the Adam plan (*qv*) for male development. *See also* psychosexual differentiation; sex variables; cross-coding.

prenatal syphilis Syphilis (*qv*) contracted by the fetus during gestation (*qv*). Prenatal syphilis is a common cause of stillbirths (*qv*). Neonatal blindness can be avoided by an antiseptic eye wash administered shortly after birth (*qv*). Harm to the fetus from maternal syphilis can be avoided in the vast majority of cases if treatment is begun before the fifth month of gestation (*qv*).

prenubile Prior to puberty (*qv*); incapable of marriage (*qv*) because of sexual immaturity. *See also* prepubescence.

prenuptial agreement (contract) A verbal or written agreement entered into by a man and woman prior to their marriage (*qv*). Prenuptial agreements specifying dowry (*qv*) and brideprice (*qv*) are often negotiated by parents when they arrange a marriage for their children. In Western societies, the increase in divorce (*qv*) and remarriage has resulted in a new awareness of the economic consequences of divorce and a desire to anticipate and avoid such problems in a second or third marriage. Prenuptial agreements are also popular in dual-career marriages where the bride and groom wish to protect their financial estates and perhaps financial obligations from a previous marriage. The legal weight of such agreements is still contested, especially when signing of the agreement is accompanied by subtle or overt psychological pressure with an impending marriage. Prenuptial agreements are increasingly overturned on challenge when they have not been updated by postnuptial revisions.

preoedipal period In psychoanalytic theory (*qv*), the oral (*qv*) and anal stages (*qv*) of psychosexual development (*qv*) when children focus their love on the mother. In the preoedipal period, the father has not yet emerged as a love object or rival in the child's subconscious. *See also* Oedipal complex; Electra complex.

preorgasmic Not yet having experienced orgasm (*qv*). In males, the term refers to the period of ejaculatory inevitability (*qv*) just prior to orgasm. The term is also used to refer to the brief period just before orgasm in both males and females when the heart rate, breathing rate, and blood pressure peak and the maximum penile erection, testicular elevation, and vaginal distention occur. A preorgasmic woman is someone who has not yet had orgasms, a condition formerly referred to by the pejorative term *frigid* or *frigidity*.

preorgasmic emission Two or three drops of mucoid fluid that seep from the urinary meatus (*qv*) of the male during the plateau stage (*qv*). This small emission, which comes from the Cowper's glands (*qv*), appears to neutralize the acidic environment of the membranous and penile urethra (*qv*). It normally contains active sperm (*qv*), which may be sufficient to cause conception (*qv*). *See also* precoital fluid.

preovulatory The period of the woman's monthly menstrual cycle (*qv*) preceding the release of the ovum (*qv*) from the ovary (*qv*). In the ovary, this would be the follicular phase (*qv*). In the uterus (*qv*), the preovulatory period is the pro-liferative stage (*qv*).

prepared childbirth *See* natural childbirth; Bradley method; Lamaze method of childbirth; Read birth method.

prephallic masturbatory equivalent In the psychoanalytic model, those auto-erotic (*qv*) activities that occur before the genitalia (*qv*) become the focus of sexuality (*qv*) and involve use of the mouth, thumb or finger sucking, defecation, urination, and general touching as sources of sensual and/or erotic pleasure. *See also* oral stage; anal stage.

prepubertal *See* prepubescence.

prepubertal growth spurt *See* pubescent growth spurt.

prepubertal panhypopituitarism A syndrome in children in which the anterior pituitary (*qv*) fails to produce adequate amounts of one or several hormones— follicle-stimulating hormone (*qv*), luteinizing hormone (*qv*), adrenocorticotropic hormone (*qv*), thyroid-stimulating hormone (*qv*), or prolactin (*qv*). Depending on which hormones are affected, the symptoms range from metabolic dysfunc-tions and stunted growth to sexual immaturity (*qv*) and delayed puberty (*qv*). Prognosis is good when hormone replacement is employed.

prepuberty *See* prepubescence.

prepubescence (adj. prepubescent) The approximately two-year period preceding puberty (*qv*) characterized by accelerated growth and the initial appearance of secondary sex characteristics (*qv*), foreshadowing sexual and reproductive maturity.

prepuce (adj. prepucial, preputial) The hairless foreskin (*qv*) or loose, retractable skin covering the penile glans (*qv*) in the male and the sheath of skin covering the top of the clitoris (*qv*) in the female. The prepuce may be surgically removed in circumcision (*qv*) either after birth or as part of the pubertal right of passage (*qv*). *See also* subincision; superincision; female circumcision.

preputial gland *See* Tyson's glands.

preputium (L.) The prepuce (*qv*) or foreskin (*qv*) of the penis (*qv*) or the hood of the clitoris (*qv*).

present, to In animal mating (*qv*), the position assumed by the female to allow the male to mount (*qv*) and engage in penile thrusting (*qv*). Generally a female presents by crouching with her buttocks (*qv*) elevated. In human sexual intercourse (*qv*), either sex may present to the other and be mounted. *See also* coitus; copulate; intercourse; acceptivity; proceptivity; conceptivity.

presentation In labor (*qv*), the manner in which the newborn's body appears at the cervical opening (*qv*) of the uterus (*qv*); in 96 percent of all presentations, the head is presented first. *See also* breech birth.

presumptive pregnancy signs *See* pregnancy signs.

presymphysial lymph node Located in front of the pubis symphysis (*qv*), this lymph node drains the lymphatics of the penis (*qv*) and connects with the inguinal (*qv*) lymph nodes. Because of its proximity to the genitalia (*qv*), the presymphysial lymph node is easily involved when microorganisms infect the penis.

preterm infant *See* premature infant.

preterm labor *See* premature labor.

prevalence model of contraception A statistical model for estimating the number of pregnancies (*qv*) prevented by different contraceptive methods (*qv*) based on survey data.

previa (L.) *See* placenta praevia.

previllous embryo An embryo (*qv*) of a placental mammal prior to the time when villi form on the chorionic (*qv*) surface. Villi are highly vascular, thin-walled, fingerlike projections that facilitate the exchange of metabolic nutrients and wastes between the fetus (*qv*) and the uterus (*qv*). Primary villi begin to develop in the area of the future placenta (*qv*) at the end of the second and beginning of the third week. They quickly spread to cover the entire chorionic surface before regressing in the seventh week everywhere except in the area of the placenta (*qv*).

Priapea (L.) A collection of 80 short poems widely regarded as the most erotically explicit poems surviving in Latin from antiquity. The first 27 are concerned with Priapus (*qv*) as a god, the second 27 with Priapus as a statue, and the remaining 26 poems with a degenerate and depraved Priapus who has become a cynical fornicator (*qv*), pederast (*qv*), and irrumator (*qv*). Variously attributed to Virgil, Ovid, and other Roman writers of lesser status, the collection is probably the result of several different writers.

priapism A rare, pathological condition involving prolonged and painful erection (*qv*) of the penis (*qv*), usually without sexual desire. The origin and causes of priapism are usually unknown, although a lesion within the penis or in the central nervous system (*qv*) may be a factor. The condition almost always results in destruction of the spongy tissues of the penis and eventually in chronic impotence (*qv*) due to persistent congestion. The term, derived from Priapus (*qv*), the name of a Greek and Roman god, is also used as a synonym for satyriasis (*qv*).

priapitis An obsolete term for inflammation of the penis (*qv*).

Priapus (L.) In Greek and Roman mythology, the male god of reproduction (*qv*), often depicted with an erect penis (*qv*). *See also* Priapea; priapism.

primacy zone Sigmund Freud's (*qv*) term for the erogenous (*qv*) area of the body dominant at any particular time in the oral (*qv*), anal (*qv*), phallic (*qv*), and genital stages (*qv*) in the Freudian model of psychosexual development (*qv*).

primal anxiety In the psychoanalytic model (*qv*), the first experience of separation that comes when the infant leaves the safety and comfort of the maternal uterus (*qv*) and is suddenly confronted with a variety of anxiety-producing stimuli.

primal fantasies In the psychoanalytic model (*qv*), the fragmented and scattered imaginations of a child about the various aspects of adult sexuality (*qv*), including sexual intercourse (*qv*), conception (*qv*), pregnancy (*qv*), and birth (*qv*), formed in the subconscious and expressed in dreams.

primal horde (stage) theory In psychoanalytic theory (*qv*), the idea that the original human family was ruled by a dominant male to whom the females and younger males were subordinate.

primal scene Generally the term refers to a child's real or imagined observation of parents' engaging in sexual intercourse (*qv*). A negative parental response to being discovered in the act of intercourse (e.g., slamming the door and screaming at the child) may result in a trauma that will adversely affect the child's sexual responses as an adult. Even if the child's observation is not known to the parents, the child's perception of assumed violence and pain may lead to fear of intercourse, inhibited sexual desire (*qv*), or other dysfunctions. Some have suggested that repetition of this childhood experience might establish an inclination to voyeurism (*qv*).

primary In terms of a sexual dysfunction (*qv*), a condition that has always existed, as distinct from a dysfunction that develops after a period of normal function; a response or condition that occurs only in a particular situation or with a particular partner.

primary amenorrhea *See* amenorrhea.

primary deviance A sociological term for behavior that deviates from a norm (*qv*) but that is not used as a basis for self-definition, as would sexual orientation (*qv*), cross-dressing (*qv*), or transsexualism (*qv*).

primary drive A drive or impulse originating in the basic needs of the body: hunger, thirst, sex, and elimination (urination and defecation). *See also* primary need.

primary erectile dysfunction *See* erectile dysfunction.

primary follicle A very early Graafian or ovarian follicle (*qv*) surrounded by a single or double layer of nurse or follicle cells; located near the surface of the ovary (*qv*).

primary homosexuality A homosexual (*qv*) orientation experienced or sensed more or less vaguely in childhood even though it may be resisted and not acted on until much later in life; in contrast to a homosexual orientation that is perceived and acted on only when the person is in his or her middle or later years.

primary hypogonadism Testicular failure caused by a basic defect in the testes (*qv*) rather than by an infection or disease, resulting in a deficiency in the production of sperm (*qv*) and testosterone (*qv*).

primary impotence *See* erectile dysfunction.

primary impulse *See* primary drive; primary need.

primary masochism According to Sigmund Freud (*qv*), a psychological linkage that results in a "lust for pain"; a psychological dependence on being the recipient of physical and/or psychological abuse in order to achieve sexual arousal (*qv*) and orgasm (*qv*).

primary narcissism A psychoanalytic (*qv*) term for the earliest manifestation of self-love in which the alleged pleasure principle (*qv*) or libido (*qv*) is satisfied in the sensations and needs of the infant's own body. This narcissistic (*qv*) orientation is believed to remain dominant until the infant begins to reorient him- or herself in relationships with other persons and the environment.

primary need In Abraham Maslow's hierarchy of needs (*qv*), that combination of basic survival needs including the physiological needs for food, air, water, shelter, and clothing.

primary oocyte The female germ cell (*qv*) as it enters the first meiotic (*qv*) division in the process of producing an ovum (*qv*). This stage follows the oogonial (*qv*) stage and precedes the secondary oocyte (*qv*) stage, which marks the beginning of the second meiotic division.

primary orgasmic dysfunction A condition in a man or woman who has never been able to reach orgasm (*qv*) by manual, oral, or coital stimulation. *See also* inhibited orgasm.

primary sex characteristics The genitalia (*qv*) that distinguish the male and female sex or gender; the nonconvertible male-female differences, specifically the male's ability to impregnate (*qv*) and the female's ability to ovulate (*qv*), menstruate (*qv*), gestate (*qv*), and lactate (*qv*). *See also* gender coding; sex-irreducible characteristics; sex characteristics; secondary sex characteristics.

primary sexual dysfunction Any sexual dysfunction (*qv*) that has always been experienced by an individual; for example, in the case of a primary orgasmic dysfunction, a woman who has never experienced an orgasm (*qv*), or primary inhibited sexual arousal in a male who has never had an erection (*qv*). *See also* secondary sexual dysfunction; situational sexual dysfunction.

primary spermatocyte The male germ cell (*qv*) as it enters the first meiotic division (*qv*) in the process of producing a sperm (*qv*). This stage follows the spermatogonial (*qv*) stage and precedes the secondary spermatocyte (*qv*) stage, which marks the beginning of the second meiotic division. *See also* spermatozoon.

primary testicular failure The failure of the testicles (*qv*) to respond adequately to the gonadotropic (*qv*) stimulation of the pituitary's follicle-stimulating (*qv*) and interstitial cell-stimulating hormones (*qv*) because of testicular atrophy (*qv*) or some other abnormality. The result is a lack of or deficiency of testosterone (*qv*) and sperm production. Also known as primary hypogonadism (*qv*).

primigravida (L.) A woman pregnant (*qv*) for the first time; also known as gravida I.

primipara (adj. primiparous) (L.) A woman bearing or having delivered only one child.

primogeniture An ancient familial tradition, evident among the early Hebrews and documented in the biblical tradition, in which one son, usually the eldest, was designated as the sole successor and heir of the father. In the history of the family in Western cultures, the Roman and Germanic traditions replaced primogeniture with an inheritance pattern in which all brothers, and in some cases all siblings, shared in the inheritance. In the eleventh-century Frankish culture, primogeniture reemerged among the nobility and gradually filtered down to the lower social classes. Resource: F. Gies and J. Gies, *Marriage and the Family in the Middle Ages* (New York: Harper & Row, 1987).

primordial germ cell Large spherical diploid (*qv*) cells in the ovaries (*qv*) or testes (*qv*) that multiply by mitosis (*qv*) and are precursors of the oogonial (*qv*) and spermatogonial (*qv*) cells that undergo meiosis (*qv*). In humans, the primordial germ cells first develop in the yolk sac (*qv*) and allantois (*qv*) about the twentieth day after fertilization (*qv*). After migrating to the gonadal ridges where the ovaries (*qv*) or testes (*qv*) develop, these cells may either continue undergoing cell division, eventually giving rise to the gametes (*qv*), or they may reorganize gonadal tissue, which then develop into the gametes while the primordial germ cells themselves disappear.

primordium The earliest recognizable embryonic (*qv*) or undifferentiated stage of a tissue, structure, or organ; an anlage (*qv*).

primrose path model of courtship A courtship (*qv*) model devised by sex educator Roger Libby to describe and explain a traditional pattern of courtship in the United States involving structured heterosexual (*qv*) activities, with early exclusive pair bonding and monogamous (*qv*), role-rigid marriage.

private parts A common euphemism for the genitalia (*qv*).

PRL Prolactin-releasing hormone. *See also* prolactin.

Pro-abortion movement *See* pro-choice movement.

probability sample A sample that matches the characteristics of a larger population by matching the proportion of subgroups in the sample to those in the general population. *See also* random sample.

probable signs of pregnancy *See* pregnancy signs.

"Problem that has no name" Sexism (*qv*), the problem that has no name, makes women into cultural, social, and economic nonpersons, robbing them of their names and histories. The phase was defined by Simone de Beauvoir in 1953 and popularized in the United States by Betty Friedan in 1963. *See also* feminism.

proceptivity In animal behavior and biology, behavior patterns performed by a female to solicit the male sexually, to arouse him, or to elicit his attempts to copulate (*qv*) with her. In mammals and other sexually reproducing vertebrates proceptive behavior patterns are highly varied, but often involve sudden physical movements by the female, which serve to focus the male's attention on her. In some species, such as rodents and some birds, the female will quickly dash away from the male and then stop, eliciting from him a strong following reaction and often an attempt to mount (*qv*).

In human sexuality, proceptivity can be defined as any behavior pattern a woman employs to express interest in a man, to arouse him sexually, or to maintain her sociosexual interaction with him. Such patterns are culture-specific but often seem to involve extensive nonverbal communication; for example, body language (*qv*), including looks, touches, shifts in posture toward to the man, and various voice tones, is used to express warmth or interest. These patterns are part of courtship (*qv*) and are often colloquially described as flirtation (*qv*). Proceptive repertoires among women are extensive, and similarities have been described, for example, between the proceptive behavior of modern college students and women in ancient Rome as described by Ovid at the beginning of the Common Era.

An important difference between the definition of proceptivity for animals and humans is that the consummatory (*qv*) behavior of animal proceptivity is intromission (*qv*) and ejaculation (*qv*), whereas in human beings it is much more complex. Because human proceptive behavior is part of courtship, it is part of a sequence that may lead to marriage (*qv*) as much as to mating (*qv*), and, indeed, may lead to marriage before sexual intercourse (*qv*). Immense communicatory confusion may exist if the man believes that the woman's behavior connotes interest in sexual intercourse while she believes it connotes interest in an emotional relationship prior to any sort of sexual involvement. The problem exists because a second woman may enact similar behavior—for example, she too may smile, move closer, and take the man's hand—with the intention of signalling specifically sexual interest. Two fundamentally different proceptive messages are intended by the two women, although each uses similar, if not identical, behavior to express their proceptive interest. No simple solution to this problem seems to exist, because if the man misreads the first woman's intentions as sexual when they are not, he risks embarrassing or sexually assaulting her, while in the second case his misinterpretation and seeming lack of interest may offend the woman. These problems appear to be virtually epidemic among young Americans, and are one of many causes for date rape (*qv*) as well as women's sexual dissatisfaction with men who seem either overly interested or unresponsive. The obvious solution—explicit and clear discussion of one's interests and plans—is extremely difficult because open discussions of sexual motivations are even more difficult to achieve for many individuals than an understanding of each other's nonverbal signals.

Strictly, proceptivity refers only to female behavior, although some sex researchers have employed it for behavior enacted by men. This later usage, however, has the problem of diminishing specifically female patterns in proceptivity, and of retreating to the views that only men express sexual interest overtly and that women are sexually passive, coy, reluctant, or hesitant. Women may be this way with some men but may be highly proceptive with others, and, despite the difficulties some men have in decoding women's proceptive behavior, women can indeed be clearly and explicitly interested in starting, escalating, and maintaining a sexual relationship with men. Resources: F. A. Beach, Sexual attractivity, proceptivity and receptivity in female mammals, *Hormones and Behavior* 7(1976):105–138; T. Perper, *Sex Signals: The Biology of Love* (Philadelphia: ISI Press, 1985); T. Perper and D. Weis, Proceptive and rejective strategies of U.S. and Canadian college women, *Journal of Sex Research* 23(1987):455–480.

process, vaginal A medical term for the herniated outpocketings of the abdominal cavity floor that develop in the seventh month of gestation (*qv*) to allow descent of the testicles (*qv*) into the scrotal sac (*qv*). Once the testicles enter the vaginal processes, the entrance to the outpocketings closes, and the pockets enclosing the testes (*qv*) are known as the tunica vaginalis.

pro-choice movement A broad term synonymous with organizations and individuals who favor freedom of reproductive choice for women, most importantly including the freedom to choose an abortion (*qv*) without state or legal interference or restriction. The term is preferred by advocates of this position because it stresses the woman's freedom and responsibility, and links these with other areas of American life in which individuals can make free choices among different life options. The term pro-abortion is often openly opposed by members of the movement because it is thought too narrow to encompass all the reproductive and marital possibilities open to women, at least in theory. Thus, a pro-choice advocate is likely to favor free access to contraception (*qv*) and to information on contraception rather than to focus solely or narrowly on abortion rights and issues. Nonetheless, in recent years the abortion issue has played a central role in the pro-choice movement, particularly as individuals and organizations seen as anti-woman and anti-freedom by pro-choice individuals have become increasingly more vocal and focused in their objections to abortion. *See also* pro-life movement; Right to Life.

procreation (v. to procreate) Biologically and medically, the process and/or acts of conceiving, gestating, or delivering offspring. In this narrow sense, procreation is synonymous with reproduction (*qv*). However, the term procreation has strong formal overtones, arising from religious and theological speech and writing, of humans cooperating with God, who creates new humans. The word nicely illustrates how the English language surrounds sexuality (*qv*) with words that differ in their nuances of meaning and usage. Approximate formal synonyms for "to procreate" would be "to beget" or "to engender"; however, the verb would not be used as a colloquial or casual equivalent for sexual intercourse (*qv*), which is essential to procreation. Etymologically, the word derives from classic Latin *procreare*, meaning to "beget," "bring forth," or "cause," from *pro-*, meaning "to favor" or "move forward," and *creare*, meaning "to create." Like the term reproduce, but unlike terms such as beget, father, and bring forth, procreate does not specify the gender of the individual who is doing the procreating. Thus, in origin as well as in meaning, *procreation* and *to procreate* both have a formal quality absent in seemingly synonymous terms.

procreation fantasy A daydream or fantasy (*qv*) associated with reproduction (*qv*). A woman may become so convinced she has engaged in sexual intercourse (*qv*) that a psychosomatic condition known as pseudocyesis (*qv*) may result.

procreative sex Sexual relations (*qv*) or coitus (*qv*) engaged in solely for the purpose of reproduction (*qv*). In some traditions, this is the only form of morally acceptable sexual relations. *See also* recreational sex.

proctophobia A pathological and obsessive fear of anything associated with the rectum (*qv*) and anus (*qv*), such as defecation, enemas, rectal examinations, and anal intercourse (*qv*).

procuring (v. to procure) Colloquial expression meaning to obtain customers for a prostitute (*qv*). *See also* pander; pimp.

prodromal labor The early period of parturition or labor (*qv*) before the cervical canal (*qv*) dilates.

productive love Erich Fromm's term for a healthy, constructive form of love and relationship that emphasizes mutual commitment, respect, responsibility, and interdependence without diminishing individuality.

progamic sex determination A mechanism whereby the sex of the offspring is determined not genetically by fertilization (*qv*), but by the size of the egg, with a large egg producing a female and a smaller egg producing a male offspring.

progenitor A parent or ancestor.

progeny Offspring or the descendants of a known or common ancestor.

progestagen, progestogen Any natural or synthetic form of progesterone (*qv*) that acts to prepare the uterus (*qv*) for reception of a fertilized ovum. Also known as gestagen; progestin.

progestational Of or related to a drug whose effects are similar to those of progesterone (*qv*). Natural and synthetic preparations of progesterone and of its derivative, medroxyprogesterone acetate (*qv*), are prescribed in the treatment of amenorrhea (*qv*) and abnormal uterine bleeding. Other progestational drugs, such as norethindrone (*qv*) and norgestrel (*qv*), are used in some oral contraceptives (*qv*). Progestational compounds may be used to treat threatened or habitual miscarriage (*qv*). However, since progestational compounds may contain progestins (*qv*), which may have a virilizing (*qv*) effect on the fetus (*qv*), caution is recommended in their use in women who plan to become pregnant (*qv*).

progesterone One of the two major female sex hormones (*qv*) progesterone is produced by the ovarian corpus luteum (*qv*) following ovulation (*qv*), by the adrenal gland cortex (*qv*), and by the placenta (*qv*) during pregnancy (*qv*). It is responsible for preparing the uterus (*qv*) for implantation of the fertilized ovum (*qv*) and for maintaining a pregnancy. Progesterone also stimulates growth of the mammary glands (*qv*). As progesterone levels increase in the blood, there is a negative feedback inhibition of luteinizing hormone (*qv*) production by the pituitary (*qv*). Progesterone is produced in small amounts by the male. In the metabolic pathway of steroid hormones (*qv*), progesterone is converted to androgen (*qv*) and then estrogen (*qv*).

progesterone block A genetic defect (*qv*) resulting in the lack of the enzyme needed to convert pregnenolone (*qv*) into progesterone (*qv*). The blockage of the metabolic synthesis leading to progesterone also restricts androgenic (*qv*) production. The result is usually male pseudohermaphroditic (*qv*) development.

progesterone test The use of progesterone (*qv*) injections or pills to ascertain possible causes of amenorrhea (*qv*). Following a 5– to 10–day regime of progesterone, menstruation (*qv*) will occur if the woman's estrogen (*qv*) levels are normal. This result indicates that a case of amenorrhea is due to progesterone deficiency.

progestin Synthetic progesterones (*qv*) used to maintain a pregnancy (*qv*). Originally the name given to what is now called progesterone. *Synonyms*: gestagen; progestogen. *See also* progestin-induced hermaphroditism.

progestin-induced hermaphroditism A hermaphroditic (*qv*) birth syndrome in which the sexual organs of a genetic (46,XX) and gonadal (*qv*) female fetus (*qv*) are masculinized (*qv*) by synthetic hormones (*qv*) such as exogenous (*qv*) progesterone (*qv*) and 19–noresterone. These synthetic hormones, previously used to prevent a threatened miscarriage (*qv*), are no longer used because of their ineffectiveness and because in some cases the synthetic hormone crossed the placental barrier (*qv*) and caused a masculinizing (*qv*) effect in the fetus.

progestin-only contraceptive Any of a growing number of hormonal contraceptives (*qv*) containing only progestin (*qv*). Two progestin-only contraceptives were available in the United States as of 1989, the progestin-only minipills (*qv*) and the Progestasert intrauterine device (*qv*). Progestin-releasing implants and long-acting injectable progestins are widely used in other countries. Alternative vehicles for delivering contraceptive progestin include biodegradable implants, injectable microspheres, and microcapsules, as well as progestin-releasing vaginal rings.

projected jealousy The tendency of a person who has been sexually unfaithful to accuse the spouse or lover of the same infidelity (*qv*).

prolactin The hormone (*qv*) that stimulates milk production, produced and secreted by the posterior pituitary gland (*qv*); also known as luteotropic hormone (LTH). Secretion of prolactin is regulated by hypothalamic prolactin-inhibiting and prolactin-releasing factors (PIF and PRF). Prolactin acts with estrogen (*qv*), progesterone (*qv*), thyroxine, insulin, growth hormone, glucocorticoids, and human placental lactogen (*qv*) to stimulate growth and development of the female breast (*qv*) and mammary glands (*qv*). After birth, it initiates and maintains milk production. The infant's suckling at the breast stimulates the central nervous system (*qv*) to mediate prolactin production. The hormone does not normally occur in males.

prolan Currently used as a synonym for placental human chorionic gonadotropin (*qv*). In the *Encyclopedia of Sex Education* (New York: Wm. Penn Publishing Corp., 1952), Hugo Biegel gives the now-common name of follicle-stimulating hormone (*qv*) as a synonym for prolan A, luteinizing hormone (*qv*) as a synonym for prolan B, and human chorionic gonadotropin for the prolan of pregnancy.

prolapse The falling, sinking, or sliding of an organ out of its normal position, as in a prolapsed uterus (*qv*).

prolapsed cord An abnormal condition in a pregnancy (*qv*) in which the umbilical cord (*qv*) is compressed until the blood supply to the fetus (*qv*) is cut off.

pro-life movement The self-identifying title chosen by a coalition of political right and conservative, fundamentalist, and evangelical religious groups opposed to any legalization of abortion. Studies by James Prescott have revealed inconsistencies in the values pro-life advocates hold—opposing abortion (*qv*), contraception (*qv*), sex education (*qv*), day care centers (*qv*), lunch programs for school children, but commonly supporting traditional sex roles (*qv*), the death penalty, and nuclear armament. Hence, some critics argue a more accurate title is the anti-abortion or anti-choice movement. Resource: J. W. Prescott, Abortion and the right to life. *The Humanist* (1978, July/August, & November/December). *See also* pro-choice movement.

proliferative phase The phase of the woman's monthly menstrual cycle (*qv*), following the cessation of the menstrual flow (*qv*), during which the uterine lining (*qv*) becomes dense and richly vascular in preparation for the secretory phase of the cycle, which starts with ovulation (*qv*). The proliferative phase varies in duration, with an average of 2 weeks. Stimulated by follicle-stimulating hormone (*qv*) from the pituitary (*qv*), the ovary (*qv*) produces increasing amounts of estrogen (*qv*), which causes the proliferation of the uterine mucosa (*qv*).

promiscuity (adj. promiscuous) A pejorative term for a pattern of behavior in which a person is casual and indiscriminate in sexual relations (*qv*) with multiple partners. Alfred Kinsey's informal definition of a promiscuous person was ''a person who has more sex than you think they should.'' In traditional thinking, *promiscuity* is applied to any sexual behavior outside the marital union. Traditionally women have been much more often victimized than men by accusations of promiscuity because of a prevailing double moral standard (*qv*), which holds women to much stricter standards than men.

promise of marriage *See* engagement; breach of contract.

pronucleus The enlarged nucleus of the ovum (*qv*) or the spermatozoon (*qv*) after fertilization (*qv*) but prior to fusion of the duplicated chromosomes (*qv*) to form a two-celled zygote (*qv*).

prophase The first of four stages of nuclear division in mitosis (*qv*) and in the two divisions of meiosis (*qv*). During prophase, the chromosome (*qv*) material progressively shortens and thickens to form individually recognizable chromosomes, each composed of two chromatids held together by a centromere. The nuclear membrane and nucleolus disappear, spindles form from the separated centrioles, and the chromosomes begin to migrate to the equatorial or metaphase plate.

prophase arrest A phenomenon in oogenesis (*qv*) in which oogonial cells begin meiosis (*qv*) before birth (*qv*) but stop at the first prophase (*qv*) stage and remain dormant until maturation of individual ova (*qv*) resumes after puberty (*qv*). All the primordial oogonial cells begin their two-stage meiotic division before birth. However, follicular or nurse cells surrounding the primary oocytes secrete an oocyte maturation inhibitor (*qv*), which quickly stops all chromosome activity at the prophase stage of the first meiotic division. Only years later, after puberty, does the process of cell division resume as individual primary oocytes mature in the monthly menstrual cycle (*qv*). This halt in cell division leaves the chromosomes in a delicate, unstable situation for many years between birth and menopause (*qv*) and vulnerable to chromosomal nondisjunction (*qv*).

prophylactic *See* prophylaxis.

prophylaxis (adj. prophylactic) Literally, "prevention of disease"; used in reference to reducing the risk of a sexually transmitted disease (*qv*); any drug, device, or treatment used to prevent infection or disease; prophylactic, or simply "pro," is a common colloquial term for a condom (*qv*) or "rubber."

proposal An offer of marriage (*qv*).

proposition (v. to proposition) A colloquial term for a verbal invitation to engage in sexual activity, usually sexual intercourse (*qv*).

proprioception (adj. proprioceptive) Sensory inputs arising from joints, tendons, and the inner ear giving information about changes in body position.

propulsion phase Expulsion or ejaculation (*qv*) of the seminal fluid (*qv*) from the penile urethra (*qv*) when the external or outer prostatic sphincter opens following the buildup of pressure in the prostate (*qv*). *See also* emission phase; ejaculation.

prostaglandin A class of potent, hormonelike, unsaturated fatty acids that act in exceedingly low concentrations on local target organs, exhibiting a large array of effects, including use as an abortifacient (*qv*) in termination of pregnancy (*qv*). Prostaglandins, secreted by a wide variety of tissues, effect changes in vasomotor tone, platelet aggregation, endocrine (*qv*) and exocrine (*qv*) functions, and the activity of the autonomic nervous system (*qv*). Because prostaglandins are rapidly metabolized, they can be injected locally to achieve a desired local effect. The name was devised by early investigators who found them in semen (*qv*) and attributed their production to the prostate (*qv*) gland. Later research revealed that the main source is the seminal vesicles (*qv*).

prostate A golfball-sized muscular and glandular structure in the urogenital system of males. Its secretion liquefies congealed semen (*qv*) received from the paired ejaculatory ducts (*qv*). The alkaline character of these secretions is essential for sperm motility (*qv*) and neutralizing the acidic environment of the male and female reproductive tracts. Prostatic secretions, which constitute more than 30 percent of the seminal fluid, consist of acid and alkaline phosphatases, citric acid, and various proteolytic enzymes.

The prostate surrounds the neck of the bladder (*qv*) and urethra (*qv*) and is ventral to the rectum (*qv*), below the caudal part of the pubic symphysis (*qv*) and above the seminal vesicles (*qv*). The prostate can be palpated through the rectum to detect a normal or enlarged condition. Skene's glands (*qv*) in the female are homologous (*qv*) to the male prostate. *See also* prostatitis; benign prostatic hypertrophy.

prostatectomy A partial excision of the prostate (*qv*) to enlarge the prostatic urethra (*qv*) when it is closed by benign prostatic hyperplasia (*qv*); in the case of a malignant growth, the surgical removal of the whole prostate gland (*qv*).

prostate enlargement *See* benign prostatic hyperplasia.

prostate massage A digital massage of an enlarged prostate gland (*qv*) to relieve a case of prostatitis (*qv*) or to obtain a seminal fluid (*qv*) sample for analysis. Using a lubricated, gloved finger inserted into the rectum (*qv*), a physician or other health professional massages each lobe of the prostate through the rectal wall from the outside to the center line, pressing the seminal fluid into the prostatic urethra.

prostatic acid phosphatase A chemical compound characteristically secreted by the prostate (*qv*) and apparently found also in female ejaculate. *See also* female ejaculation; Grafenberg spot.

prostatic cancer A cancer of the prostate gland (*qv*). Prostatic cancer, which often shows no symptoms until the malignancy is well established, affects between a quarter and a third of all men who live to age 80. Statistics from the American Cancer Society indicate that prostatic cancer claims the lives of approximately 22,000 American males each year. Cancer of the prostate gland claims the lives of more men past age 50 than any other form of cancer. This mortality rate could be greatly reduced by a simple annual prostatic examination. Therapy for prostatic cancer includes surgery, radiation, and a range of chemotherapies, including estrogen (*qv*), which acts as an antiandrogen (*qv*) to counter the action of testosterone (*qv*), a contributing factor in this form of cancer.

prostatic fluid An alkaline secretion of the prostate gland (*qv*) that constitutes 30 percent of the seminal fluid (*qv*) and consists of characteristic acid and alkaline phosphatases, citric acid, and various proteolytic enzymes.

prostatic pouch In the male, the utriculus prostaticus or prostatic utricle (*qv*), a vestigial remnant of the Mullerian ducts (*qv*), a cul-de-sac pouch in the floor of the prostatic urethra (*qv*).

prostatic urethra That portion of the male urethra (*qv*) contained within the prostate gland (*qv*) into which the bladder and ejaculatory ducts empty their contents for final transport through the membranous and penile portions of the urethra.

prostatic utricle A cul-de-sac in the prostatic urethra (*qv*) of males, derived from atrophied or vestigial Mullerian ducts (*qv*); homologous (*qv*) with the female uterus (*qv*) and thus also known as the uterus masculinis.

prostatitis An acute or chronic infection or inflammation of the prostate (*qv*), treatable with antibiotics, sitz baths, bed rest, and fluids. *See also* benign prostatic hypertrophy.

prosthetic penis *See* penile prosthesis.

prosthetic testis A soft, silicone substitute testis (*qv*) surgically implanted for cosmetic or psychological effect into an empty scrotum (*qv*).

prostitute A male or female who exchanges sexual favors (*qv*) for money.

prostitute-versus-madonna syndrome A stereotype of women common in American culture from the Victorian (*qv*) era through the 1950s in which women were believed to fall into two classes: whores or madonnas. Madonnas were stereotyped as blond, blue-eyed, fair-skinned "nice girls," "princesses," the "snow maiden" of Nathaniel Hawthorne's novels, and the "girl next door" whose purity and innocence made her a perfect candidate to become a wife and mother. On the other side were the "dark maidens," with long, black hair and flashing dark eyes, the "townies" sought out by college males, the "ladies of the night," who were available for man's enjoyment but totally unacceptable as wives and mothers. *See also* madonna complex.

prostitution The commercial exchange of sexual favors (*qv*) in return for money. While both males and females may engage in prostitution, the term usually applies to females serving male clients, unless otherwise qualified; *see* male prostitution. Prostitution, "the world's oldest profession," is found in almost every known culture. In ancient Greece, the fees of common prostitutes were set by the state, whether they plied their trade on their own or in a brothel (*qv*). A higher class of prostitutes, the *hetaira*, were educated and sophisticated women, often being the mistresses (*qv*) of some of the most influential leaders of classical Greece. Some *hetaira* served in temples as sacred prostitutes (*qv*). The Romans created an administrative system to organize prostitution, establishing brothels along all major thoroughfares at regular intervals convenient to traveling males. In the Roman era, prostitution lost its religious associations, becoming a simple commerce. At the height of the Middle Ages, Thomas Aquinas (*qv*) acknowledged that prostitutes serve a useful function, protecting the chastity and virtue of decent women much as sewers protect citizens of a city from pollution. Public baths, reintroduced from the East by the Crusaders, often served also as brothels.

In the seventeenth and eighteenth centuries, the Age of Reason and the Enlightenment, prostitution was common and accepted unless it was ill mannered. Some prostitutes, such as Madames du Barry and Pompadour, exercised considerable political power. Prostitution was very much a part of Victorian (*qv*) society, promoted by widespread poverty and the vulnerability of poor immigrant women who had limited opportunities for employment. On the western frontier, prostitution was often open and publicly known, especially after the gold rush started, with such flamboyant practitioners as Calamity Jane and "Cattle Kate" Watson. In the Storyville and French quarter of New Orleans, prostitution flourished until World War I.

In the last half of the twentieth century, prostitution in the United States has involved both male and female runaway teenagers, some forced into servicing pedophiles (*qv*); streetwalkers and masseuses; male hustlers servicing older males who are often covert homosexuals (*qv*) in heterosexual marriages; and high-priced call girls (*qv*). In many European countries and some counties of the state of Nevada, prostitution is either legalized or decriminalized (*qv*). *See also* pimp; procurer; reglamentation; Wolffenden Report. Resource: V. Bullough & B. Bullough, *Women and Prostitution: A Social History* (Buffalo: Prometheus Press, 1987).

Provera The trade name for medroxyprogesterone acetate (*qv*), a progestin (*qv*); also known as Depo-Provera (*qv*).

prudishness (n. prude) Exhibiting an excessive modesty and sense of propriety, especially in sexual matters, to the point of presenting oneself as being morally superior to others and shocked by their improper behavior. Prudishness may be a mask for hypocrisy and an obsessive interest in sexual matters.

prurient Medically, an intense itching condition, a characteristic and symptom of some sexually transmitted diseases (*qv*).

prurient interest Psychologically, an intense longing or desire for something considered immoral, lusty, lascivious, or lewd, or in the words of the U.S. Court of Appeals for the Ninth Circuit, "a shameful and morbid interest in nudity, sex, or excretion." An appeal to prurient interests is one of the three legal characteristics of obscenity (*qv*) specified by the 1957 decision of the U.S. Supreme Court in *Roth v. United States* (*qv*).

pruritis (adj. pruritic) An itching condition. *See also* prurient.

pseudocopulation Simulation of sexual intercourse (*qv*) by two persons who rub their genitalia (*qv*) together without vaginal or other penetration (*qv*) and thereby achieve sexual gratification (*qv*). *See also* femoral intercourse; tribadism.

pseudocyesis A false pregnancy (*qv*) marked by some of the hormonal changes of genuine pregnancy and possible enlargement of the abdomen even though no fetus (*qv*) is present. This condition, also known as pseudopregnancy, is more likely to occur in immature women with severe conflicting emotions about pregnancy and childbearing. *See also* couvade.

pseudoexhibitionism A male who occasionally, especially when under stress, exhibits his genitalia (*qv*) in public as a substitute for sexual intercourse (*qv*), which he prefers and would engage in if he had the opportunity. A true exhibitionist (*qv*) has a paraphilic (*qv*) dependence of displaying his genitalia in public in order to achieve sexual arousal (*qv*) and satisfaction (*qv*) and is often so timid in dealing with women that he cannot enter into a mature, intimate relationship.

pseudofamily A social unit of adults and children that does not fit the traditional definition of a biologic two-parents-with-children social unit, such as an adoptive or foster family, a single parent family, an Israeli kibbutz, a group marriage (*qv*), a commune (*qv*).

pseudohermaphrodite A condition in which both gonads (*qv*) are ovaries (*qv*) with discordant male external genitalia (*qv*) and sexual identity (*qv*), or both gonads are testes (*qv*) with discordant female external genitalia and sexual identity. In a true hermaphrodite (*qv*), the gonads are a combination of ovarian and testicular tissue. In current usage, the prefix *pseudo* has been dropped and a distinction made among four types of hermaphrodite: (1) a true hermaphrodite with ovariotestes, (2) a male hermaphrodite with testes and female genitalia, (3) a female hermaphrodite with ovaries and male external genitalia, and (4) a rarer form of agonadal hermaphroditism in which the discordance is between chromosomal sex and anatomical sex and gender identity.

pseudohomosexuality A sexual relationship (*qv*) or behavior involving 2 persons of the same gender in which the homosexual involvement is not based on a primary or true homosexual orientation (*qv*) but rather is motivated primarily by nonsexual needs of dependence or power, as occurs in prisons. Also known as homoerotic (*qv*).

pseudomucinous cystadenoma A nonmalignant, mucus-producing ovarian tumor; perhaps the most common type of ovarian tumor.

pseudoprecocious puberty Premature development of secondary sexual characteristics (*qv*) without concurrent early maturation of the gonads (*qv*); induced by an endocrine (*qv*) gland tumor.

pseudopregnancy A physiological mimicking of the suppression of ovulation (*qv*) that follows the hormone changes in a natural pregnancy (*qv*), induced by hormones in the contraceptive pill (*qv*). *See also* couvade; pseudocyesis.

pseudosexual precocity Premature thelarche (*qv*), lactation (*qv*), and menstruation (*qv*) in a juvenile female without the appearance of pubic hair (*qv*) and the growth spurt associated with puberty (*qv*). Caused by reduced thyroid activity and often by a tumor of the pituitary gland (*qv*).

pseudovoyeur A person who occasionally enjoys viewing a striptease (*qv*) show, pornographic (*qv*) movie, or magazine as a substitute for engaging in sexual intimacy when the opportunity for such is not available. A true voyeur (*qv*) has a paraphilic (*qv*) dependence on watching others to achieve sexual arousal and satisfaction and is incapable of participating in coitus (*qv*) without reenacting in fantasy (*qv*) voyeuristic activities.

psoriasis, genital A chronic, heritable skin disorder characterized by red patches covered by thick, dry, silvery, adherent scales that affect the genitalia (*qv*) and perineal region, although the condition more commonly manifests itself in the scalp, ears, knees, elbows, chest and abdomen. The condition may be acute or chronic and recurrent.

psychic impotence A general term referring to the psychological inability of a male to engage in vaginal intercourse (*qv*) and achieve orgasm (*qv*) in a satisfactory way, despite the desire to do so and despite having no organic impediment. Psychic impotence may be manifested in a psychogenic (*qv*) erectile dysfunction (*qv*), premature ejaculation (*qv*), retarded ejaculation (*qv*), or inhibited male orgasm (*qv*). A variety of psychological factors may underlie this condition, including the madonna complex (*qv*), a revulsion at the perceived messiness or dirtiness of sex, an unresolved attachment to the mother, or a deep-seated fear of castration (*qv*).

psychic masturbation Sexual gratification (*qv*) achieved through erotic fantasies without manipulation of the genitalia (*qv*) or other erogenous areas (*qv*) of the body.

psychic vaginismus *See* vaginal spasms; vaginismus.

psychoanalysis, psychoanalytic theory A psychological system and therapeutic program, originated by Sigmund Freud (*qv*) and developed by his followers, that probes into an individual's past conscious and unconscious experiences and memories to find the roots of present psychological problems, neuroses, and psychoses. *See also* oral stage; anal stage; phallic phase; latency; genital stage; ego; id; superego; pleasure principle; thanatos.

psychoendocrine *See* psychohormonal.

psychogender An alternate term for psychological and emotion gender identity (*qv*), as distinct from sexual anatomy.

psychogenic Originating in the mind. In psychology and psychiatry, the theory that the origins of some symptoms or syndromes can be explained and treated entirely in terms of mental or psychic processes, without reference to the organ systems of the body.

psychogenic arousal Sexual excitement (*qv*) or arousal resulting from consciously perceived stimuli—visual, aural, olfactory, and tactile. *See also* reflexogenic arousal; psychological conversion.

psychogenic aspermia An emotional or psychological barrier that prevents a male from ejaculating (*qv*). *See also* ejaculatory incompetence.

psychohormonal Related to the interactive relationship between mental states and hormones (*qv*). *Synonym*: psychoendocrine.

psycholagny Sexual excitement (*qv*) limited to fantasies (*qv*) and the imagination.

psychological conversion The phenomenon in which extremely strong emotional or psychological processes can cause the appearance of physical trauma.

psychopath A person who commits antisocial acts without any sense of guilt and without any internal controls that would stop such acts.

Psychopathia Sexualis (L.) The title of Richard von Krafft-Ebing's (*qv*) 1886 pioneering text classifying and describing varieties in human sexual behavior; Krafft-Ebing's term for psychosexual disorders (*qv*).

psychopathia transsexualis (L.) An early medical term for transsexualism (*qv*).

psychophysical preparation for childbirth One of several programs that prepares women by teaching them what happens during childbirth (*qv*). These programs involve exercise and relaxation techniques that promote control and comfort during labor (*qv*) and delivery (*qv*). *See also* Bradley method; Lamaze method of childbirth; LeBoyer method of chidlbirth; Read birth method.

psychoprophylactic preparation for childbirth A system of prenatal education using the Lamaze method of natural childbirth (*qv*).

psychosexual ''Pertaining to the mental and emotional aspects of sex life and sex behavior'' (Hugo Biegel, *Encyclopedia of Sex Education* [New York: Wm. Penn Publishing Corp., 1952]). The current usage is more generalized: ''pertaining to sexuality in its broadest sense, including both mental and somatic aspects'' (J. P. Chaplin, *Dictionary of Psychology* [New York: Dell Laurel, 1985]).

psychosexual development (differentiation) The developmental processes whereby an individual's psychosexual or gender identity/role (*qv*) gradually emerges and becomes established. In psychoanalysis (*qv*), the emergence of the personality through a series of infant-to-adulthood stages in which the focus and dominant mode of achieving libidinal (*qv*) pleasure shift from the oral (*qv*), to the anal (*qv*), phallic (*qv*), latency (*qv*), and finally genital (*qv*) stage. In broader terms, psychosexual development refers to the anatomical, hormonal, and neural differentiation during pregnancy (*qv*) and to all biobehavioral factors involved in continued sexual differentiation after birth. *See also* sex; sex variables; transference.

psychosexual development gates *See* sex variables.

psychosexual disorder or dysfunction A sexual maladjustment or disorder caused by an emotional or psychological problem rather than by an organic cause. *See also* gender dysphoria; sexual problem; sexual dysfunction; ego dystonic; paraphilia.

psychosexual identity *See* gender identity.

psychosexual incongruity An incompatibility or disagreement between part or all of the gender role (*qv*) and gender identity (*qv*) and one or more of the physical variables of sex. *See also* gender coding; gender transposition; gender dysphoria; transsexual.

psychosexual neutrality The theory that the infant is born a tabula rasa (*qv*), or "blank slate," with no prenatal (*qv*) tendencies or templates for gender identity (*qv*) encoded in the brain before birth and with actual gender identity emerging solely from postnatal scripting (*qv*) and learning.

psychosexual trauma *See* sexual trauma.

psychosurgery A surgical procedure designed to alter the psychological functioning and/or behavior of an individual.

pubarche The onset of puberty (*qv*); the first appearance of pubic hair (*qv*).

puber A child who has arrived at the age of puberty (*qv*).

puberism A delay in the normal development of secondary sexual characteristics (*qv*); a synonym for puberty (*qv*).

pubertal delay The failure of puberty (*qv*) to occur at the normal age for its completion—13 for girls and 15 for boys. Pubertal delay may originate in a endocrine (*qv*) timing error or in association with a hormonal deficiency in the hypothalamus (*qv*), pituitary (*qv*), or gonads (*qv*).

pubertal growth spurt *See* pubescent growth.

pubertal rites Any social ritual or initiation ceremony, sexual or not in content, that accompanies puberty (*qv*) and marks the transition of a young male or female to adult status. *See also* bar mitzvah; bat mitzvah; circumcision; female circumcision; ritual defloration; superincision; subincision.

pubertas praecox (L.) *See* premature puberty.

puberty The transitional biological stage between childhood (*qv*) and adulthood (*qv*) when a surge in sex hormones (*qv*) triggers development of secondary sexual characteristics (*qv*) and the achievement of reproductive capacity. The prepubescent processes of puberty begin with the appearance of pubic hair (*qv*), starting on average between 8 and 14 years for females and between 10 and 15 years for males, followed quickly by a growth spurt. During puberty proper in males, the testes (*qv*), scrotal sac (*qv*), and penis (*qv*) mature, and spermatogenesis (*qv*) and nocturnal emissions (*qv*) begin. In females, the ovaries (*qv*) start functioning, bringing menarche (*qv*) and breast (*qv*) development. Puberty is marked by an increasingly intense romantic and erotic interest. It also marks the beginning of the liminal period (*qv*), involving both the transition from childhood to adult status and from the single to the married state. *See also* adolescence; epiphysis; premature puberty; pubertal delay.

puberty rite *See* liminal; pubertal rites.

pubes The hairy region covering the parts around the genitalia (*qv*), especially the pubic bone; in the female, the mons veneris (*qv*). *See also* pubic hair.

pubescence The period of puberty (*qv*) or the developmental processes associated with it.

pubescent growth spurt The response of the body to a surge in somatotropin or growth hormone from the pituitary (*qv*) that triggers a rapid growth of bone and muscle. The average age of onset for girls is 11 years, with growth peaking at age 12. For males, the average age of onset is between 13 and 14 years.

pubic growth curve The period of sexual maturation starting with the onset of puberty (*qv*) and lasting an average of about six years until full secondary sexual characteristics (*qv*) are developed.

pubic hair The hair on the lower abdomen, mons veneris (*qv*), and genital region that appears at puberty

pubic lice *See* pediculosis.

pubic rite Any rite of passage (*qv*) or pubertal ceremony in which the genitalia (*qv*) are altered or mutilated. *See also* subincision; superincision; circumcision; female circumcision.

pubic wig *See* merkin.

pubis (L.) The anterior portion of the pelvic girdle or pelvis (*qv*).

public indecency *See* lewdness; exhibitionism.

pubococcygeal (PC) muscle Muscles in the pelvic (*qv*) region running from the pubic bone in the front, around both sides of the sexual organs, to the obturator canal. The right and left sides are separated medially by an interval called the genital hiatus which allows passage of the urethra (*qv*), vagina (*qv*) and rectum (*qv*). *See also* pubococcygeal muscle exercises

pubococcygeal (PC) muscle exercises A regimen of isometric exercises in which a woman executes a series of voluntary contractions of the muscles in her pelvic diaphragm and perineal region in an effort to increase the muscle contractability of the vaginal introitus (*qv*) or improve urine (*qv*) retention. PC muscle exercises are also used by males to increase and enhance sexual response and pleasure. The exercises were devised by Dr. Arnold H. Kegel, a gynecologist (*qv*), as a nonsurgical treatment for urinary incontinence following childbirth (*qv*), hence their other name—*Kegel exercises*. These exercises are useful as part of a natural childbirth (*qv*) preparation program.

puboscrotal testicle A testicle (*qv*) that has left the abdominal cavity but has not reached its normal postnatal position in the scrotum (*qv*), lodging instead in the floor of the pelvic cavity at the level of the base of the penis. *See also* cryptorchidism.

PUBS *See* perculation umbilical blood sampling.

pud Abbreviation for pudendum (*qv*).

pudendal nerve A nerve in the pelvic region, a branch of the pudendal plexus arising from the second, third, and fourth sacral nerves, which is involved in orgasm (*qv*). Branches of the pudendal nerve include the inferior rectal nerve, the perineal nerve, and the dorsal nerve of the penis (*qv*) or clitoris (*qv*). The pudendal nerve is stimulated by light pressure on the skin of the penis and by friction and touch of the clitoris.

pudendal plexus A network of motor and sensory nerves formed by branches of the second, third, and fourth sacral nerves, supplying the bladder, prostate (*qv*), seminal vesicles (*qv*), uterus (*qv*), external genitalia (*qv*), and some intestinal structures.

pudendum (adj. pudendal, pl. pudenda) (L.) The external sexual organs or genitalia (*qv*), usually applied to the female vulva (*qv*); literally, "shameful area." Commonly abbreviated pud; however, pud is also a colloquial term for penis.

pudendum muliebre (L.) The vulva (*qv*).

puer- A combining form referring to a child.

puer aeternus (L.) Carl Jung's (*qv*) term for the universal archetype of eternal youth. *See also* Peter Pan syndrome.

puerile Of or pertaining to children, or childhood; often synonymous with immature.

puerpera (L.) A woman from the beginning of labor (*qv*) until the pelvic organs have returned to their normal nongestational position. *See also* puerperium.

puerperal Of or pertaining to the period immediately after childbirth (*qv*), or to a woman who has just given birth.

puerperal disorder *See* postpartum depression; postpartum psychosis.

puerperal fever An often fatal syndrome associated with systemic bacterial infection and septicemia following childbirth (*qv*), usually resulting from unsterile obstetric techniques and therefore rare in current medical practice. Before childbirth in hospitals became common in the early 1800s, puerperal fever was rare. With the shift to hospital deliveries, it became epidemic, killing as many as 20 percent or more of mothers and their infants. Although the germ theory of disease was not yet formulated, Ignaz Semmelweis, a Viennese physician, became convinced that physicians were transmitting the infection because they did not wash their hands after performing autopsies and before examining patients and because they did not disinfect their instruments before using them with a new patient. Medical colleagues ignored or discredited the work of Semmelweis for half a century. While discovery and acceptance of sterilization and antiseptics greatly reduced the incidence of puerperal fever, it was not until the 1940s that the advent of penicillin and antibiotics practically eliminated the problem. The causative organism is most often one of the hemolytic streptococci bacteria.

puerperal mania A rare but acute mood disorder in women that sometimes follows childbirth (*qv*), characterized by a severe manic reaction. *See also* postpartum depression; postpartum blues.

puerperal metritis *See* puerperal fever.

puerperium The 6-week period following childbirth (*qv*) during which the anatomical and physiological changes brought about by pregnancy (*qv*) resolve.

pulsatile Pulsating, functioning rhythmically, or occurring in cycles.

punch biopsy Several small samples of cervical (*qv*) tissue excised with a knifelike, cone-shaped punch and used for various diagnostic procedures.

puppy love A colloquial term for a short-lived, intense, and highly romanticized infatuation commonly occurring in the preadolescent (*qv*) or adolescent years (*qv*). *See also* limerence.

purchase marriage A form of marriage (*qv*) in which a price is paid for the bride by the husband or his family. *See also* bridegift; brideprice; Morgengabe.

purdah The Islamic custom or institution of female exclusion that requires Muslim women to cover their entire bodies with a chador (*qv*) to prevent their being seen by any male except close relatives. Purdah preserves and protects the woman as the property of a male and keeps the perceived powerful and socially disruptive force of female sexuality (*qv*) within bounds so she does not bring shame upon male relatives and family.

puritan complex An acceptance of and compulsive adherence to a rigid moral code for sexual behavior and relationships coupled with an obsessive fear of violating the slightest aspect of this code. *See also* Puritans.

Puritans Whereas *Puritan* refers to a religious sect, *puritan* refers to someone who is a sexual moralist and against sex and sexual pleasure.

An English group of Protestants in the sixteenth and seventeenth centuries, also known as separatists, who wanted a reform of the Church of England and elimination of Roman Catholic rituals more thorough than that promoted by Queen Elizabeth, the Puritans placed a strong emphasis on the family (*qv*) and were intolerant of any sexual activity (*qv*) outside marriage (*qv*). Although they had nothing against sex as such, the Puritans followed the Old Testament morality and severely punished extramarital sex (*qv*), as well as any form of homosexuality (*qv*) or sex with animals. Their condemnation of premarital sex (*qv*) was less rigorous since the ancient Hebrews were not clear in their condemnation of this behavior. The Puritans endorsed strict codes for dress and public behavior in a life-style that appeared drab, joyless, and oppressive. When Oliver Cromwell and the Puritans came to power in England, they intensified their persecution of sexual deviance. In 1650, Parliament passed the Puritan Act with strong penalties for incest (*qv*), adultery (*qv*) and fornication (*qv*). Although they soon lost power in England, the Puritans established a totalitarian religious state in several New England colonies where they passed legislation calling for the death penalty for adultery, homosexual acts, and bestiality (*qv*). Occasional outbursts of antisexual hysteria led to witch-hunts with sexual overtones. This rigid culture was increasingly diluted by new waves of immigration from cultures more accepting of sexuality.

purity *See* chastity.

purulent Producing or containing pus.

pus tube *See* pyosalpinx.

pygmalianism A psychosexual disorder (*qv*) in which an individual creates erotic fantasies (*qv*) about an object he or she has created.

pygo- A combining form referring to the buttocks (*qv*).

pygoamorphus Asymmetrical, conjoined twins (*qv*) in which the parasitic member is an undifferentiated mass attached to the sacral region of the other fetus (*qv*).

pygomania A sexual obsession with the female buttocks (*qv*).

pygomelus A malformed fetus (*qv*) with one or more extra lower limbs attached to the buttocks (*qv*).

pygopagus Conjoined twins consisting of two fully or nearly fully formed fetuses united back to back in the sacral region.

pyosalpinx An inflamed, pus-filled, sausage-shaped fallopian tube (*qv*). Rupture of the tube can cause peritonitis (*qv*).

pyrimidionones A family of drugs that stimulate production of interferon (*qv*), a natural antiviral agent produced by the body; used experimentally in treatment of genital herpes (*qv*).

pyrolagnia Sexual arousal (*qv*) and satisfaction (*qv*) in response to setting or watching fires. *See also* pyromania.

pyromania, erotic A psychological compulsion to set fires that an individual associates with and depends on to achieve sexual arousal (*qv*) and orgasm (*qv*). Most arsonists are motivated by financial gain or vengeance. Those who use arson for erotic purposes are usually passive, shy persons with a weak self-image who find an outlet for their need to control something in their lives by setting a fire that requires the attention and efforts of firefighters.

Q

quadriplegia (quadriplegic) An abnormal condition characterized by paralysis of the arms, the legs, and the trunk of the body below the level of an associated spinal cord injury that severely restricts the individual's movements and sensations, thereby requiring major adjustments in his or her sexual relations (*qv*). Because of the altered sensations, body image, and self-image experienced by quadriplegics, sexual functioning (*qv*) is often compromised. Counseling can help a quadriplegic make an improved adjustment to the limitations imposed by paralysis. Trauma resulting from automobile and sporting accidents are the main cause of quadriplegia, which affects about 150,000 Americans, the majority of them males between the ages of 20 and 40. Spinal cord injuries, with damage between the fifth and seventh vertebrae, are the most common cause of injury-induced paralysis. *See also* paraplegic.

quadroon A racist term for an individual with one black grandparent and three nonblack grandparents.

quadruplet Any one of four offspring produced at one birth (*qv*).

quantitative inheritance *See* multifactorial inheritance.

queer A pejorative and insulting term for a male homosexual (*qv*).

questionnaire A set of questions given to research subjects and designed to provide specific information relevant to the study. The questions may be open-ended, with the respondents free to answer as they wish, or close-ended, with the respondents choosing from predetermined yes-no or multiple-choice answers.

quickening The first fetal movements perceived by the pregnant woman (*qv*), usually occurring in the sixteenth to twentieth week of gestation (*qv*). Until the modern renewal of the debate between advocates of mediate and immediate animation theories (*qv*), first proposed by philosophers and embryologists (*qv*) in the 1600s, quickening was considered to mark the infusion of the human soul. Thus, for those who accepted mediate animation, termination of the pregnancy before quickening might be allowed because the human soul was not yet present, only an animal life principle.

quim (to quim) According to Eric Partridge, a vernacular term for the female pudendum (*qv*) from the seventeenth to the twentieth centuries in such usages as *quimming* (or copulating), *quim-stick* for penis (*qv*), and *quim-sticking* meaning intercourse (*qv*). Revival of this term as a noun and verb was suggested in 1982 by John Money as an active female counterpart for the many technical and colloquial terms which present intercourse as a male-active behavior. As a verb, *to quim* would mean to take the penis (*qv*) into the vagina (*qv*) and perform on it grasping, sliding, and rotating movements of varying intensity, rhythm, and speed. As a noun, *quim* would refer to the practice of *quimming*. The term would be a female-in live complement to the gender-indifferent noun *copulation* and verb *to copulate* (*qv*), and the male-active noun *swive* and verb *to swive* (*qv*). Resource: J. Money, To quim and to swive: Linguistic and coital parity, male and female, *Journal of Sex Research* 18(2)(1982):173–176.

quintuplet Any one of five offspring produced at one birth (*qv*).

R

---

rabbit pregnancy test An obsolete test for pregnancy (*qv*) in which urine (*qv*) from the possibly pregnant woman is injected in a female rabbit whose ovaries (*qv*) react to the presence of human chorionic gonadotropin (*qv*) by showing signs of ovulation (*qv*) within a day or two. *See also* beta specific monoclonal enzyme-linked immunosorbent assay test (ELISA); beta subunit HCG radioimmunoassay test; home pregnancy test; immunological urine test.

race The human race; a group or population of persons related by common descent, blood, or heredity; in ethnology, a population characterized by a more or less distinctive combination of traits that are transmitted by descent. As an anthropological concept, *race* is vague and controversial, with many anthropologists now speaking only of three primary divisions, the Caucasian (loosely called white), the Negroid (loosely called black), and the Mongoloid (loosely called yellow) races. The term can also refer to a local geographic or ethnic group or to the whole human race. Because there are so many variations in physical traits, because there has been so much intermingling and migration of subpopulations of different racial backgrounds over the centuries, and because the term has so many unscientific connotations, the concept of racial differences is almost meaningless. In scientific usage, it is commonly replaced by ethnic group (*qv*).

Almost all racial or ethnic minority groups have been depicted by the majority group in derogatory and inferior terms: as being more sexually promiscuous (*qv*), having an offensive body odor, and being emotionally and morally less disciplined. These stereotypes are then used as the basis for discrimination.

Racine syndrome A swelling of the salivary glands occurring in some women beginning about five days before menstruation (*qv*) and returning to normal as the menstrual flow begins. Similar swelling may occur in the breasts (*qv*).

racism The institutionalized discrimination, prejudice, and oppression of people of one race or ethnic group by those of another, usually majority group; the social and political belief that uses race as a basis for economic, political and social segregation and exploitation. *See also* sexism.

radical mastectomy The surgical removal of an entire breast with the associated pectoral muscles, axillary lymph nodes, and all fat, fascia, and adjacent tissues performed in the treatment of breast cancer (*qv*). Alternates to radical mastectomy include modified radical mastectomy and simple mastectomy. *See also* lumpectomy; mastectomy.

rajasic foods Food that, according to the traditions of yoga, induce sexual passion and produce semen that is thick and sticky, characteristics associated with the yoni (*qv*). These foods include red meat, chicken, fish, root vegetables, spices, and salt.

random sample A number of cases or individuals chosen from a larger population in a way that ensures that any one selection has as much chance of being picked as any other, and that the sample will be a valid representation of the entire population. *See also* stratified sample; probability sample.

Rank, Otto (1884–1939) An Austrian psychoanalyst who departed from orthodox Freudian thought and is best known for claiming that neuroses are due to a birth trauma (*qv*). Rank also advocated short-term rather than long-term therapy. The separation anxiety and dependence that follow from the birth trauma can be overcome by the patient's developing a sense of independence within constructive relationships.

rape In English common law, forced sexual intercourse (*qv*) with a nonconsenting female other than one's own wife. This definition did not recognize marital rape (*qv*), rape of a male, or rape accomplished by nonphysical coercion. Hence, a more inclusive definition is currently used: vaginal (*qv*), oral (*qv*), or anal (*qv*) sexual intercourse or other sexual intimacies or contact forced on one person by another using physical force, the threat of physical force, coercion, or a weapon. A 1985 Federal Bureau of Investigation definition uses the phrase *forcible rape*, which it defines as ''the carnal knowledge of a female forcibly and against her will. Assaults or attempts to commit rape by force or threat of force are also included; however, statutory rape (without force) and other sex offenses are excluded.'' This definition implies that there may be consensual rape. It also implies that only women can be raped. The meaning of *forcibly* and *force* are left unexplained. Other experts avoid the term *rape* and speak of *sexual assault* or *sexual coercion*.

Careful and precise use of the term is essential since the specific legal definition of rape varies according to the statutes in question. Legal definitions of rape differ considerably from the casual, colloquial, and feminist (*qv*) uses of the term.

In legal usage, the specific meaning of rape is defined by statutory law in terms that may include actual vaginal penetration (*qv*) by the penis (*qv*) or some other degree of proximity of the genitalia (*qv*). Legal definitions of rape may limit this term to vaginal intercourse (*qv*), or include other sexual activities (*qv*). The relationship between the two parties may also be a factor in the legal definition, as it is with statutory rape (*qv*), incest (*qv*), acquaintance (*qv*) rape, date rape (*qv*), and marital rape. The legal use of the term is currently supplemented and detailed in legal definitions of the general category of sexual assault (*qv*), for example the New Jersey Penal Code speaks of four categories: (1) sexual assault, (2) aggravated sexual assault, (3) criminal sexual assault, and (4) aggravated criminal sexual assault.

While some laws limit the term *rape* to a male sexually assaulting a female, other legal definitions are gender neutral and allow for rape to include homosexual (*qv*), lesbian, and female rape of a male.

The most difficult aspect of defining rape is the issue of consent. To what extent can rape be alleged if the alleged victim is impaired by the use of alcohol or drugs—a major factor in date rape? To what extent can the term rape be applied to a mentally retarded adult? Some would regard rape of a mentally retarded adult as a type of statutory rape and date or acquaintance rape when the victim is impaired by the use of drugs or alcohol as a type of sexual assault lacking the full forced aspect of rape. In feminist literature, there is considerable debate over extensions of the term rape to sexual harassment (*qv*) and unwanted flirtation (*qv*). Equally difficult to define is the concept of psychological coercion: when does seduction (*qv*) become persuasion and then coercion? When does acceptance become hesitation then reluctance and then rejection? When does a "maybe" mean "yes" or "no"? These questions remain deeply perturbing to all concerned with sexual assault.

Psychologically, some forms of rape involve a paraphilic (*qv*), psychological addiction, and compulsive repetitive behavior. *See also* rapism. The paraphilic rapist (*qv*) uses unexpected physical violence and psychological terror and threats to achieve control over the victim. Because of the addictive nature of rapism and the need to repeat the violence to achieve sexual arousal (*qv*) and possibly orgasm (*qv*), the rapist may replay an actual rape in fantasy (*qv*) while masturbating (*qv*) or copulating (*qv*) in a nonrape situation. This usage is more or less distinct from date or acquaintance rape, which may be more sexually than control motivated. *See also* biastophilia; rape counseling; rape fantasy; rape prevention program; rape-trauma syndrome; raptophilia; spouse rape; victim precipitation.

rape counseling The provision of advice, interpretations, support, guidance, and therapy for the victim of a sexual assault (*qv*). Rape counseling is a recent development, evolving as the law enforcement, medical, and counseling professions have responded to feminist (*qv*) pressure. It has also been a response to a growing social awareness of the extent of sexual assault in marital (*qv*), acquaintance (*qv*), and stranger rape, and a newly developed sensitivity to the indepth support of the needs of the victim of a sexual assault needs to cope with and recover from the sequelae of rape. Ideally rape counseling begins as soon as the victim reports the assault to a friend, family member, teacher, or medical or law enforcement official. The one on one counseling immediately following the assault may remain one on one, or the victim may move into an ongoing support group. Rape counseling involves a combination of emotional support, assistance in dealing with the relationship adjustments that result, provision of support and guidance in handling the psychological sequelae (particularly the sense of personal violation and loss of control), a liaison between the victim and medical, legal, and law enforcement authorities, and guidance in coping with the criminal investigation and trial if this is pursued. Rape counseling may also involve counseling the victim's partner and/or family.

rape crisis center (program) A center or program providing advice, counseling, and support for the victims of rape (*qv*) on an individual or group basis.

rape fantasy A sexually arousing fantasy (*qv*) of being raped (*qv*) or forced to engage in sexual practices or of forcing a person to engage in sexual activity (*qv*). Both men and women may enjoy occasional rape fantasies without actually desiring to rape or be raped. Men and women raised in a sexually repressive, moralistic tradition may use a rape fantasy because it allows them to fantasize being forced to engage in and enjoy otherwise forbidden sexual practices. The vast majority of persons who occasionally indulge in a rape fantasy do not want to be raped. However, some people misinterpret the use of rape fantasies as an indication that women enjoy being forced to have sex. The myth that being forced to have sex is a source of ecstasy for a struggling yet willing female victim is commonly accepted by males. Persons may occasionally enjoy a masochistic fantasy without actually being a masochist (*qv*) or wanting to engage in masochistic practices.

rape prevention program A type of educational program designed to provide women and men with factual information about the different types of rape (*qv*) and sexual harassment (*qv*), the psychological uses of sexual assault (*qv*) and harassment (*qv*), personality profiles of the kinds of individuals who engage in such behavior, the situations, circumstances, and behaviors that place one at a high risk for sexual assault, coping techniques useful in the event of a sexual assault, and community resources. Standard recommendations for rape prevention include use of automatic timers for house lights, lighted residential and work entrances, safety locks on all windows and doors, looking inside the car front and back before entering it, insisting on good identification before letting any stranger in the house, not listing first names on a mailbox or in a telephone directory, walking only in lighted areas and being alert at all times about one's surroundings, and avoiding deserted or enclosed areas.

Recommendations for dealing with a rape situation vary greatly depending on the group making the recommendations. These usually include: escaping if one can, running toward the nearest residence and yelling "Fire"; if one cannot escape and is trapped, then not directly challenging the assaulter's control but resisting by talking and immediately stating forcefully one's refusal to go along with the assault; avoiding direct physical resistance when the assailant displays or threatens use of a weapon; and physically attacking the assailant only if one has thought this out and practiced different attacks beforehand or if one feels threatened with grievous bodily harm or death. *See also* acquaintance rape; date rape; marital rape; stranger rape.

rape-trauma syndrome A reaction pattern composed of strong emotions and feelings of shame (*qv*), humiliation, rage, personal violation, fear, confusion, the sense of having lost power or control over one's life, and possibly the feeling that one somehow caused or unknowingly invited the attack. *See also* victim precipitation. As part of rape trauma, the victim may experience a long-term fear of being alone, feelings of being followed, sexual phobias (*qv*), a compulsion to wash the body in an attempt to wash off the degradation and shame, sexual aversion (*qv*), and a sense of personal responsibility and guilt for not taking adequate precautions or for not having resisted the assault more. The acute phase of rape trauma may be characterized by anger, guilt, or embarrassment, fear of physical violence and death, humiliation, a desire for revenge, and multiple physical complaints (including gastrointestinal distress), genitourinary discomfort, tension, and a disturbance of the normal patterns of sleep, activity, and rest. The long-term phase of rape-trauma is characterized by nightmares, phobias, a need for support from significant others, friends, and family, and changes in the victim's usual patterns of daily life, including a change of residence and sometimes a sexual dysfunction (*qv*).

A compound reaction includes all the symptoms of rape trauma with a reliance on alcohol or drugs, and the recurrence of symptoms of prerape conditions, particularly psychiatric illness. A silent reaction sometimes occurs instead of the rape trauma or compound reaction. In this response, the victim's usual sexual relationships change abruptly. The victim refuses to discuss the rape and even denies it happened. Sudden, strong phobias are also part of the silent reaction.

raphe The line of fusion between two tissues, as the penoscrotal or scrotolabial raphe, which marks the fusion of the labioscrotal folds.

rapism The psychological condition in which a person is dependent on the terrified resistance of a nonconsenting stranger in order to obtain erotic arousal (*qv*) and achieve orgasm (*qv*).

rapist In common usage, any person, male or female, who physically or psychologically forces another person to engage in sexual activities (*qv*). Legally, the term is restricted to persons actually convicted of rape or sexual assault. In a restricted psychological usage common since the late 1970s, a rapist is psychologically motivated by the need to degrade and humiliate a nonconsenting victim in order to obtain erotic arousal (*qv*) and achieve orgasm (*qv*). *See also* rapism; acquaintance rape; date rape; spouse rape; victim precipitation; sadistic nonpsychotic rapist; sadistic psychotic rapist.

raptophilia *See* rapism.

Rati (Skt.) In Hindu thought, the wife of Kama, the god of love. Rati is the embodiment of eroticism (*qv*) and portrays the initiatory role of woman in sexual relations. The term can also refer to loveplay and sexual desire.

rational emotive therapy A form of psychotherapy (*qv*) that emphasizes a reorganization of one's cognitive and emotional functions, a redefinition of one's problems, and a change in one's attitudes in order to develop more effective and suitable patterns of behavior. Developed by psychologist Albert Ellis, this therapy can be used with individuals or with groups.

ravish To rape (*qv*).

Read birth method *See* natural childbirth; Dick-Read, Grantly.

reality ego In psychoanalytic theory (*qv*), the pleasurable objects of the external world that have been incorporated into the ego (*qv*).

reality principle An awareness of the demands of the environment and the need to adjust one's behavior to meet those needs by postponing immediate gratification in favor of achieving long-term goals. In psychoanalytic theory, the reality principle represents ego (*qv*) and runs counter to the pleasure principle (*qv*) which drives the id (*qv*) in its demands for immediate gratification of instinctual impulses. The reality principle allows an individual to deal rationally and effectively with the exigencies of everyday life.

rebellion A psychologic force or unconscious motivation that leads some adolescents (*qv*) to engage in sexual relations (*qv*) as an expression of independence from parents and authority figures.

rebirth fantasy The mental imagination of being born again. A rebirth fantasy may be part of a dream in which the individual emerges from water. Interpretations of rebirth fantasies vary from an unconscious wish to return to the peaceful existence of prenatal life in the womb, an attempt to deny death and mortality, an expression of belief in reincarnation, or an incestuous (*qv*) desire for the mother.

receptiveness A broad term for an individual's general willingness to interact with another in a potentially sexual manner. Receptiveness includes a variety of proceptive (*qv*) behaviors and interaction that may end with receptivity (*qv*) or rejective behavior. In terms of receptiveness in human couples, the flirtation (*qv*) sequence is delineated by several escalation points at each of which one partner indicates a desire to escalate the intimacy and the other responds either by accepting the escalation or rejecting it. *See also* acceptivity; courtship; lordosis.

receptivity In biology and animal behavior, a technical term that refers to species-specific female behavior patterns that facilitate penile intromission (*qv*) when the male mounts (*qv*) the female. In quadrupedal mammals, such behavior patterns often include lordosis (*qv*), a sharp arching of the back that exposes the female's genitalia (*qv*) to the male as he mounts, as well as movements of the pelvis that facilitate intromission and ejaculation (*qv*). The term is much narrower in meaning than receptiveness, and is not commonly used to describe human sexual behavior. If it were so used, it would be restricted to activities performed during sexual intercourse itself, for example, the woman lifting her buttocks (*qv*) as the man starts intercourse, thereby exposing her vagina (*qv*) to penetration by his penis (*qv*). Other behavior patterns that occur during human sexual intercourse (*qv*)—for example, the sharp head turn shown by some men and women during orgasm (*qv*)—do not facilitate intromission, and therefore cannot be defined as aspects of receptivity. Furthermore, sexologists distinguish receptivity from proceptivity (*qv*) and attractivity, which broadly refer to female behavior patterns that solicit specific males and act as an attractant to males in general. However, in common English such distinctions are only rarely made, in part because most casual observers of sexual behavior are rarely sufficiently objective to make them.

receptor A sensory neuron terminal that responds to a specific stimulus, such as heat, pressure, odor, or taste.

recessive gene A gene (*qv*) whose phenotypic (*qv*) expression or character trait appears only when two recessive alleles (*qv*) are simultaneously present in an individual's genotype (*qv*). *See also* dominant gene.

reciprocation Mutual giving and receiving; a psychological term for the mutual adaptative process that occurs when one person adapts his or her behavior to conform or respond to the behavior or orientation of the other; the principle or law that responses are the product of the stimulus's duration and intensity; in Jean Piaget's (*qv*) theory of cognitive and moral development, the child's belief that punishment should be logically related to an offense. *See also* complementation.

recreational sex A colloquial term for extramarital sexual relation (*qv*); sexual activity (*qv*) engaged in primarily for the pleasure it gives rather than as a means of procreation (*qv*). The extent of emotional involvement and intimacy may be deliberately limited. *See also* procreative sex; relational sex.

recruitment of ova *See* ova harvesting; ovum lavage.

rectocele A hernia, prolapse (*qv*), or protrusion of part of the rectum wall into the posterior floor of the vagina (*qv*) after the muscles of the vagina and pelvic floor have been weakened by a congenital defect (*qv*), childbearing (*qv*), aging, or surgery.

rectum The last segment of the large intestine, about 12 centimeters long, continuous with the descending sigmoid colon and terminating at the anus (*qv*).

red degeneration A hemorrhagic-necrotic fibroid tumor in the uterus (*qv*), incompatible with pregnancy (*qv*) if the woman is pregnant.

red light district A colloquial term for an area noted for its houses of prostitution (*qv*) and the availability of prostitutes on the street. The significance of the term *red light* has been variously traced to the red kerosene lantern Bavarian girls hung in their windows when engaging in fensternl (*qv*) or window courting or train men hung in front of houses of prostitution during stop-overs on the western frontier so the engineer could round up the crew when the train was ready to leave.

reduction division *See* meiosis.

reductionism. *See* biology; biologism; biological reductionism.

redundant prepuce An unusually large prepuce (*qv*) or foreskin (*qv*).

reeducation The restoration of a function or meaning that has been lost or left undeveloped in previous experience. *See also* behavioral therapy; desensitization; resensitization; sensate focus; systematic desensitization.

reference group The people or group against whom one judges one's self in terms of behavior, characteristics, and/or standards.

referred testicular pain The perception of a tactile stimulus or pain as occurring in the lower abdomen when it actually originates in the scrotum (*qv*) or testes (*qv*).

refined birthrate In demographic statistics, the ratio of total births to the total female population during the period of one year. *See also* birthrate; true birthrate; crude birthrate.

reflex arc A neural mechanism in which an impulse is carried to the spinal cord or brain stem via a sensory neuron and automatically returned via a motor neuron to a muscle or gland causing a motor or physiological response. This circuit does not require input from the higher conscious levels of the brain.

reflexogenic arousal Sexual arousal (*qv*) resulting from tactile stimulation that activates a reflex arc (*qv*) leading to relaxation of blood vessels of the cavernous tissues of the genitalia (*qv*), thereby producing tumescence (*qv*). *See also* psychogenic arousal.

refractory period A temporary period of psychophysiologic erectile incompetence (*qv*) immediately following ejaculation (*qv*) during which a male cannot be sexually aroused. The duration of the refractory period may be minimal in the teen years and longer in the later years. *See also* resolution stage.

regional fibrosis The overgrowth of a portion of an organ by fibrous tissues, as when fever associated with an infection or other noxious agent causes fibrous tissue to take over a seminiferous tubule (*qv*), thereby inhibiting germinal cell development and sperm (*qv*) production. The extent of reduction in the number of sperm produced depends on the number of seminiferous tubules affected by the fibrous growth. Similar overgrowths by fibrous tissue may occur in the breast (*qv*), ovary (*qv*), or uterus (*qv*).

reglamentation A Latin American custom of regulating prostitution (*qv*) by creating state supervised, licensed, or run brothels (*qv*).

regression A psychological defense mechanism by which one returns to an earlier behavioral pattern and the satisfactions of an earlier stage of development. *See also* oral stage; anal stage; phallic phase; genital stage; repression; sublimation.

Reich, Wilhelm (1897–1957) A controversial Austrian-American psychoanalyst who argued that Sigmund Freud (*qv*) and traditional psychoanalytic theory (*qv*) unduly neglected the social and economic conditions that contributed to psychological problems and concluded that the single measure of psychologic well-being is orgastic potency (*qv*). Originally a physicist, Reich studied medicine and joined Freud's psychoanalytic association in Vienna after World War I. He soon broke with Freud after refusing to accept the theory of a death instinct and Freud refused to psychoanalyze him. Reich moved to Berlin in 1930 and became an active Marxist, attempting to combine psychoanalytic and Marxist theories. He also worked with the German Association for Proletarian Sexual Politics to change civil laws regulating sexual behavior. Later he developed a theory of orgone energy (*qv*), the single psychic and physical force at work in the universe and in individuals.

Moving to the United States in 1939, he developed the orgone box (*qv*). In 1954, when the U.S. Food and Drug Administration declared the orgone box a fraud and banned practically all of his writings, Reich refused the injunction, was imprisoned, and died while under psychiatric care in prison. Today his work, with the exception of the orgone theory, has regained some general recognition. His therapeutic techniques, combining verbal communications with massage (*qv*), are used by many therapists. Recognized today as one of the most important writers on sexual issues, his major works include: *The Function of the Orgasm* (1927), *The Imposition of Sexual Morality* (1932), *Character Analysis* (1933), *The Mass Psychology of Fascism* (1933), and *The Sexual Revolution* (1936).

rejuvenant Any medication, aphrodisiac (*qv*), or substance alleged to restore a youthful vigor, particularly sexual vigor.

relational sex Sexual activity (*qv*) occurring within the context of emotional involvement and intimacy in a relationship. Relational sex usually involves some sense of mutual commitment and responsibility, either as part of a friendship, a premarital engagement (*qv*), or within a marriage (*qv*). *See also* satellite relationship; intimate friendship; sexually open marriage; recreational sex.

relational therapy A form of therapy in which the focus is on the relationship between two persons and the emphasis is on improving their intimacy (*qv*) and communication skills. *See also* marriage counseling.

relativistic ethics A system of values in which right and wrong are held to vary according to circumstances. *See also* absolutist ethic; natural law; situation ethics.

relaxation therapy A form of therapy in which the patient is taught how to relax and reduce psychological tensions, especially the pressure to perform sexually in a certain way. *See also* biofeedback; sensate focus exercise.

relaxin An ovarian (*qv*) hormone (*qv*) that relaxes the pelvic ligaments during gestation (*qv*); may also stimulate breast (*qv*) growth and prevent premature labor (*qv*).

releasing factor (RF) or hormone (RH) Any one of several peptides (*qv*), produced by cells in the hypothalamus (*qv*). One type, secreted directly into the anterior pituitary (*qv*) via a portal vein, stimulates the pituitary to secrete a specific tropic hormone (qv). The releasing hormone regulating production of luteinizing hormone (LH) (*qv*) and follicle-stimulating hormone (FSH) (*qv*) is known as gonadotropin-releasing hormone (Gn-RH) (*qv*). Other releasing hormones regulate production of the growth hormone and adrenocorticotropic hormone (ACTH) (qv). Regulation is by negative feedback (*qv*) by a hormone at the end of the sequence.

reliability The extent to which a measure or stimulus produces the same response when repeated under the same conditions. *See also* convergent validity; replicability; validity.

remarriage Marriage (qv) after the death of a spouse or after a divorce (qv). Some churches, especially the Roman Catholic and Anglican or Episcopal, prohibit divorce and remarriage, although annulments (*qv*) may make remarriage acceptable. Alimony (*qv*) may cease when a divorced woman remarries.

renewable marriage An alternative to a traditional marriage (qv), in which the commitment is not "until death do us part" but rather for a specific agreed-upon duration at the expiration of which the couple is free to terminate or continue the relationship. Several state legislators have considered legislation to recognize renewable marriage contracts.

renifleur (Fr.) In psychiatry, a person who is erotically stirred or gratified by smells. *See also* olfactophilia.

reorganization phase The period of readjustment and rehabilitation following a sexual assault (qv) during which the victim attempts to return to her or his normal preassault psychological state and life-style. The reorganization phase involves dealing with overcoming the feeling of having been personally violated and losing personal control of one's life, dealing with any feelings of guilt or of being responsible for or having invited the assault, and coping with the fears, anxieties, and phobias that often follow an assault. *See also* rape counseling.

representative sample *See* random sample.

repression A defense mechanism used to avoid dealing consciously with an impulse or memory because of the anxiety or guilt it provokes; an unconscious process whereby unpleasant memories and motives are driven from the consciousness, allowing the preservation of the ego-ideal (*qv*). *See also* regression; sublimation. Individuals commonly repress traumatic sexual experiences such as sexual abuse (qv), incest (qv), or rape (qv) to avoid the anxiety such memories trigger and preserve their self-image. When a specific sexual desire (qv) or impulse violates a taboo (*qv*) or is considered immoral or sinful, repression may lead to avoidance of the forbidden behavior. Repression may not lead to avoiding a particular behavior if the individual can repress the unacceptable motive for it and rationalize another, acceptable motive for acting.

reproduction The process by which animals and plants produce offspring; procreation. Asexual reproduction (*qv*), without gametes (qv), may involve budding, fission, or production of gemmae, spores, or vegetative offshoots. *See also* parthenogenesis. Sexual reproduction involves the union of gametes and fertilization (*qv*) either inside or outside the female's body or, more rarely, as in the seahorse, in the body of the male.

reproductive behavior Behavior usually or necessarily associated with reproduction (qv) or any of its facets; any activity that leads to mating (*qv*) and propagation of the species. Depending on the species, the term can include precoital courtship (*qv*), proceptivity (*qv*), receptivity (*qv*), conceptivity (*qv*), lactation (*qv*), and postnatal protection and training of the offspring by one or both parents until the offspring are self-sufficient and able to survive on their own. *See also* Somatosensory Affectational Deprivation (SAD) syndrome; flirtation behavior; maternal instinct.

reproductive freedom A brief phrase introduced by feminists (*qv*) in the 1970s to express a basic human right of women including the right to safe contraception (*qv*) and abortion (*qv*), health care during pregnancy (*qv*) and birth (*qv*), freedom from forced sterilization (*qv*), and, more recently, involuntary Cesarean section (*qv*). The concept emerged in the late nineteenth century among feminists and advocates of free love (*qv*), who claimed that women should have control over their reproductive potential. In the early 1900s, Margaret Sanger's (*qv*) efforts to popularize family planning and contraceptives (e.g., the slogan, "Every child a wanted child") marked a major step toward implementing this right.

reproductive period That time in a life span when an individual is fertile (qv) and capable of reproduction (qv). In human females, the refractory period extends from the onset of menses (*qv*) and ovulation (*qv*) during puberty (*qv*) to menopause (*qv*) or climacteric (*qv*). Human males can reproduce from puberty to death.

resolution phase The last of four phases in W. Masters and V. Johnson's model of the sexual response cycle (*qv*) in which, following orgasm (*qv*), the sexual system returns to its unaroused state. In the male after orgasm (*qv*), penile erection (*qv*) and testicular congestion quickly decrease to about half the aroused condition, with full return to the unaroused condition taking several minutes. In the female, the clitoris (*qv*), labia (*qv*), and vagina (*qv*) begin returning to their unaroused condition immediately after orgasm, with full unaroused state achieved in less than half an hour. Elevated respiratory and heart rates return to unaroused state as sex flush (*qv*) disappears. Perspiration may accompany loss of vasocongestion (*qv*). In the male, resolution may entail a refractory period (*qv*). *See also* excitement stage; plateau phase; orgasmic stage.

respiratory eroticism A psychoanalytic term for sexual pleasure (*qv*) achieved through smoking or some other respiratory activity. *See also* asphixophilia.

response The behavior or outcome that results from a stimulus; any muscular or glandular process elicited by a stimulus; an answer given to a test question or survey questionnaire. The term *response* is widely used in psychology, usually with a qualifier, as in response attitude, response hierarchy, response equivalence, or response threshold. Responses involving subtle physiological and neurological changes can often be measured and quantified with special electronic instruments.

RET *See* rational emotive therapy.

retained Mullerian syndrome A developmental anomaly in which the Mullerian ducts (*qv*) in a genetic male do not degenerate and instead continue to develop into female structures—fallopian tubes (*qv*), vagina (*qv*), and uterus (*qv*). In some cases, the uterine tissue may respond to endocrine stimulation, resulting in menstruation (*qv*) through the penile urethra (*qv*). *See also* defeminization; Mullerian inhibiting substance.

retarded ejaculation The inability of a male to reach an orgasm (*qv*) and ejaculate (*qv*) during vaginal intercourse (*qv*) and/or during masturbation (*qv*). Also known as inhibited male orgasm (*qv*).

retention cyst A cyst (*qv*) resulting from the abnormal retention of secreted substances, as a milk cyst in the breast (*qv*), a seminiferous cyst in the seminiferous tubule (*qv*) of the testis (*qv*), or a bulbourethral gland (*qv*) cyst.

rete testis (L.) A network of tubules situated between the converging seminiferous tubules (*qv*) in the testis (*qv*) and the head of the epididymis (*qv*). Roughly 800 to 1,000 seminiferous tubules empty their spermatozoa (*qv*) into the rete testis which empties into a dozen or so efferent ducts that enter the vas deferens (*qv*) in the convoluted epididymis (*qv*).

reticular activating system A functional rather than morphologic system in the brain essential for wakefulness, and attention, and concentration; composed of nerve fibers in the thalamus (*qv*), hypothalamus (*qv*), brain stem, and cerebral cortex (*qv*).

retifism A paraphilic (*qv*), erotic obsession with women's shoes. The term is derived from Rétif de la Bretonne, an eighteenth-century French novelist and educator famous for his paraphilic obsession with women's shoes. Shoe fetishists achieve sexual gratification (*qv*) and release by observing, wearing, licking, smelling, kissing, or masturbating with women's shoes.

retractile testis A testicle (*qv*) that is not properly suspended in the scrotum (*qv*) because of a spastic cremaster muscle (*qv*). A retractile testis is a common cause of cryptorchidism (*qv*) in adolescents (*qv*). This condition can often be remedied by gentle heat and manipulation by a physician.

retraction reaction The retraction of the clitoral body (*qv*) from its normal pudendal (*qv*) overhang position during plateau phase (*qv*).

retroglandular sulcus A constriction in the shaft of the penis (*qv*) between the base and glans (*qv*) of the penis.

retrograde ejaculation A form of male ejaculation (*qv*) in which a weakened internal urethral sphincter (*qv*) relaxes, allowing seminal fluid to flow into the urinary bladder during the buildup of pressure in the prostate (*qv*) and seminal vesicles (*qv*) in the emission phase (*qv*) of male orgasm (*qv*). Normally, the internal and external sphincters are closed during the emission phase. The external sphincter (*qv*) opens during the propulsion (*qv*) phase to allow ejaculation (*qv*). This condition is common in males with diabetes, multiple sclerosis, and after some prostatic surgery and in many paraplegics (*qv*). It can also be induced by squeezing the penis just before the propulsion phase of ejaculation, in which case it is sometimes used as an exotic form of male pleasure. *See also* coitus saxonicus.

retropubic A surgical approach used in the treatment of prostatic hypertrophy in which an incision is made through the lower abdominal wall, behind the pubic bone, so that the prostate (*qv*) can be approached directly rather than indirectly with a suprapubic incision that allows access to the prostate through the urinary bladder.

Retrovir A trade name for azidothymidine (*qv*), the best-known and most promising drug for treating symptoms of acquired immune deficiency syndrome (AIDS) (*qv*). Also known as AZT.

retrovirus A member of a family of viruses composed of ribonucleic acid (RNA) (*qv*) instead of deoxyribonucleic acid (DNA) (*qv*) as other viruses are. The best-known example is the human immunodeficiency virus (HIV-I and HIV-II [*qv*]) which causes acquired immune deficiency syndrome (*qv*). Retroviruses also contain reverse transcriptase enzyme, which allows the RNA to copy its information into DNA coding which can then be incorporated in the DNA complement of a host cell. Most retroviruses contain cancer-causing oncogenes (*qv*), although the HIV viruses are also included in this category.

reverse Kundalini A Tantric (*qv*) term for an unnatural, perverted sexual practice, such as anal sex (*qv*), which reverses the natural upward flow of sexual energy (*qv*).

reward-cost theory In psychology, the theory that each relationship has some distinct benefits and costs and that one must give up certain expectations, values, and goals in a relationship to gain other, more important values. Business management theory commonly refers to cost-benefit analysis in its decision-making processes.

RF releasing factor *See* releasing hormone.

RH A releasing hormone (*qv*) or releasing factor, a peptide produced by the cells of the hypothalamus (*qv*) which activates specific hormone production in the nearby pituitary (*qv*).

Rh blood group incompatibility *See* erythroblastosis fetalis.

Rh factor An antigenic (*qv*) protein found on the surface of red blood cells in 85 percent of American Caucasians and in similarly high percentages in other racial and ethnic groups. In reality, since there are two or three pairs of closely linked alleles, the description here, though common, is an oversimplification of a variety of possible immune reactions involving the Rh factor. Persons who are Rh negative have two recessive genes (*qv*) and do not produce the Rh protein. Persons who are Rh positive have one or two dominant alleles (*qv*) and produce the antigenic (*qv*) RH protein. The term is derived from its discovery in the blood of the Rhesus monkey. *See also* erythroblastosis fetalis.

rhinosporidosis A fungal infection characterized by fleshy red polyps on the mucous membranes of the nose, conjunctiva, pharynx, soft palate, and the vagina (*qv*) resulting from swimming or bathing in water contaminated with the microorganism *Rhinosporidium seeberi*.

Rh negative *See* Rh factor.

RhO-GAM The trade name for a synthetic antibody substance that binds with fetal Rh antigens (*qv*) before they can activate the immune system of an Rh-negative woman who is pregnant (*qv*) with an Rh-positive fetus. RhO-GAM should be administered to an Rh-negative woman within 72 hours of any abortion (*qv*), miscarriage (*qv*), or delivery (*qv*) to prevent possible sensitization of her immune system by fetal Rh antigens and subsequent formation of Rh antibodies in her body. *See also* erythroblastosis fetalis.

Rh positive *See* Rh factor.

rhythm method of contraception A method of birth control (*qv*) that involves abstinence (*qv*) from sexual intercourse (*qv*) during a woman's "fertile period," estimated by keeping accurate records of each menses (*qv*) and length of time between menses for at least six months. Using the longest and shortest cycles, the fertile days can be estimated by subtracting 18 from the shortest period to obtain the first fertile or unsafe day of the cycle and 11 from the longest cycle to obtain the last fertile day. The actual failure rate of this method is 21 pregnancies among 100 women using this method for a year. This method is seldom recommended by fertility specialists unless it is combined with cervical mucus (Billings' contraceptive method) (*qv*) or the basal temperature method of contraception (*qv*).

RIA *See* radioimmunoassay.

ribonucleic acid (RNA) A complex, single-stranded nucleic acid chain copied from a deoxyribonucleic acid (DNA) (*qv*) template and containing ribose sugar, phosphate molecules, and the bases adenine, cytosine, guanine, and uracil. The sequence of bases in messenger RNA carries the genetic code (*qv*) transcribed from the nuclear DNA to specialized sites within the cell known as ribosomes, where the information is translated into proteins. Single-stranded ribosomal RNA provides a base for the messenger RNA and protein synthesis. Molecules of transfer RNA bring specific amino acid molecules to the ribosomes, where they are incorporated into a protein chain by a polymerase enzyme that reads the coding of the messenger RNA.

right of the first night *See* droit du seigneur.

Right to Life A general term for any group whose ideology and philosophy is opposed to abortion (*qv*) under any circumstances. Since the 1973 *Roe v. Wade* (*qv*) decision by the U.S. Supreme Court recognizing a woman's constitutional right to privacy and legalizing abortion, the various Right to Life groups have focused on efforts to have the Supreme Court reverse *Roe*, to pass a constitutional amendment recognizing the fetus (*qv*) as a person with inalienable rights protected by the Constitution, and at least weaken the effects of legalized abortion by restricting the use of federal and state funds to pay for abortion counseling and for abortions for women who cannot afford to pay for an abortion. Members of the Right to Life movement believe that human life and personhood (*qv*) begins at conception (*qv*).

In the late 1980s and early 1990s, the Right to Life (*qv*) movement focussed its efforts on getting justices appointed to the United States Supreme Court who were anti-abortion and would vote to repeal *Roe v. Wade* (*qv*). A second focus has been efforts to get individual states (e.g., Louisiana, Pennsylvania, Ohio, Wisconsin, and the territory of Guam) to enact laws that on appeal would force the United States Supreme Court to consider reversing *Roe v. Wade*. *See also* anti-abortion movement; pro-life movement; pro-abortion or pro-choice movement.

ring *See* wedding ring.

rite of passage (Fr. **rites de passage**) Any public, formally recognized ritual (*qv*) performed to mark a person's change of social status or a transition at a critical point in the life cycle. Rites of passage are most commonly required in nonindustrial societies at the onset of puberty (*qv*) or at marriage (*qv*). *See also* bar mitzvah; circumcision; liminality.

Rite of the Five Essentials In the Tantric (*qv*) tradition, a secret sexual ritual in which five ingredients—cereal grains, fish, wine, meat, and sexual intercourse—are combined in a kind of holy communion.

ritual In anthropology, any formal actions that follow a set pattern that symbolically represents a shared meaning; in sociology, any regular pattern of interaction.

ritual abstinence Temporary abstinence from sexual intercourse (*qv*) during certain holy days. In Islam, true believers are required to abstain from sexual intercourse and passionate kissing (*qv*), as well as from food, during the daylight hours of the holy month of Ramadan. In early Christianity, sexual abstinence was recommended during the 40 days of Lent, the season of penance before Easter.

ritual bath A ceremonial bathing, showering, or washing of the body or the genitalia (*qv*) required by social or religious tradition after intercourse (*qv*) or menstruation (*qv*). An orthodox Jewish woman bathes in a mikveh (*qv*) when her menstrual flow ends. Arab and Muslim males bathe their whole body after intercourse and before going out in public. Similar customs of ritual purification are found in Hindu and Oriental cultures.

ritual defloration *See* ceremonial defloration; defloration.

ritual multiple intercourse Any public, formally recognized ritual (*qv*) or ceremony in which a woman has sexual intercourse (*qv*) with multiple partners to mark a change of social status, to celebrate a birth in the family, or to promote social cohesion and strengthen family or tribal alliances. Ritual multiple intercourse, known as *otiv-bombari*, is celebrated among the Marind Anim people of New Guinea to mark weddings, births, and other occasions. Depending on the society and its beliefs about the power of semen (*qv*), ritual multiple intercourse may serve a variety of nonsexual functions in addition to compensating for sterility (*qv*) of any husbands in the community. The Marind Anim, for instance, use semen to enrich their ritual foods and to mix in certain cosmetics. This custom may also serve an important social function in strengthening the bonding among the men. *See also* semen myths.

ritual mutilation Any ritual (*qv*) scarring or cutting of the genitalia (*qv*) or other body parts performed to mark a person's change of social status or a transition at a critical point in the life cycle. *See also* clitorectomy; circumcision; ceremonial defloration; defloration; scarification.

ritual rape Forced sexual intercourse (*qv*) required as part of an initiation ceremony by some teenage gangs in Western societies or associated with bride capture in some tribal cultures such as the Gusii of Africa.

ritual sexual intercourse Any sexual intercourse (*qv*) that is structured and required by social or religious traditions within a culture. Many nonindustrial cultures have incorporated ritual sexual intercourse into their social structure and behavior. Such rituals may serve a variety of social functions, as the ritual multiple intercourse (*qv*) of the Marind Anim does. In some cultures, ritual intercourse with an older woman is part of a rite of passage (*qv*) to manhood for a newly circumcised (*qv*) pubertal male. It may also be a healing ritual, as when a newly widowed woman is required to have intercourse with a stranger to cleanse herself of her husband's spirit or when a husband is required to have intercourse with his wife a certain number of days after delivery.

ritual wife exchange Beliefs and superstitions regarding the defloration (*qv*) of virgin (*qv*) brides have led some cultures to develop rituals (*qv*) believed to protect the bride and groom from sickness or evil spirits. Among Australian aborigines, a bride's hymen is ritually breached using a special instrument so she can have sexual intercourse (*qv*) with other men to protect her and her husband from sickness. *See also* ceremonial defloration; ritual defloration; ritual multiple intercourse.

Roe v. Wade In this landmark 1973 seven-to-two decision, the U.S. Supreme Court recognized women's constitutional right to privacy in decisions regarding abortion (*qv*) and legalized abortion nationwide. The Court ruled that prior to fetal viability (*qv*) outside the uterus (*qv*), the woman's right to privacy should have priority. In the first trimester (*qv*), this means that the woman and her physician have the sole decision regarding abortion. In the second trimester, a state may intervene only to protect the woman's health. In the third trimester, the state may regulate abortion to protect fetal life. *See also* Doe v. Bolton.

Rokitansky syndrome *See* Mayer-Rokitansky-Kuester syndrome.

role A set of culturally determined rights, duties, and obligatory behaviors that accompany one's position in a society, group, or institution; the function, characteristics, and behavior expected of an individual because of his or her gender (*qv*); the function of any variable in a cause-and-effect relationship; the ways in which an individual interprets the constructs and expectations of others with whom he or she associates. *See also* gender role; role taking; sex role stereotype; scripting.

role confusion An individual's persistent psychological discomfort and confusion regarding his or her gender role (*qv*) as a male or female. *See also* gender dysphoria.

role model A person used as a source of standards and as a pattern for learning about one's role in society.

role playing (role taking) In the sociological theory of George Herbert Mead (*qv*), the mental process whereby an individual determines the standpoint and intention of others based on their actions. If individual A sees individual B running at him with clenched fists raised, A imagines that B intends to harm him and decides whether to stay and fight, cower in fear, or take flight. A is able to evaluate the possibilities for his action by taking the role (role taking) of B. Infants imitate the behavior of others without any understanding of the meanings of its actions. Role taking begins on a very basic level when the child begins interpreting the behaviors and intentions of significant others (*qv*). *See also* gender role; play; game; scripting.

romance (n. romantic) In the broadest and original meaning, a narrative depicting marvelous, heroic achievement; colorful adventures; and chivalrous devotion, as in the Arthurian romances. In more common usage, the quality or characteristic of person-to-person intimacy, love (*qv*), excitement, passion, and being "starry-eyed"; having a wondrous, visionary, idealized, fairy-tale-like quality. In Western cultures, romantic love is characteristic of the proceptive phase (*qv*) of a relationship, especially in the initial stage of an intimate relation. In the early courtly love (*qv*) tradition, romantic love stopped short of the acceptive stage (*qv*) and was not consummated in sexual intercourse (*qv*) or marriage (*qv*). In later courtly love traditions from the sixteenth century on, consummation of romantic love was increasingly accepted in northern Europe, where romantic love was incorporated in marriage, and in southern Europe where it became part of the extramarital affair (*qv*). In the late nineteenth century, the romantic concept of a "one and only true love who would completely satisfy all one's needs for a lifetime" emerged in American culture from unknown roots. *See also* agape; amour; eros; limerence; love; philia; storge.

Resources: I. Singer, *The Nature of Love*, vol. 1–3 (Chicago: University of Chicago Press, 1984, 1984, 1987); B. I. Murstein, *Love, Sex, and Marriage Through the Ages* (New York: Springer, 1974); M. M. Hunt, *The Natural History of Love* (New York: Minerva Press, 1967); D. Tennov, *Love and Limerence: The Experience of Being in Love* (New York: Stein & Day, 1979); B. Ehrenreich et al., *Re-Making Love: The Feminization of Sex* (Garden City, NY: Doubleday Anchor, 1986).

romance novels A form of popular fiction for women readers; romance novels, including gothic novels (*qv*) and the Harlequin romances (*qv*), make up more than half the book sales in the United States. The novels vary from little to considerable sexual explicitness. The reactions of feminists (*qv*) to the romance novels vary from tolerance to vehement condemnation as female pornography (*qv*) that endorses, supports, and eroticizes male domination.

Roth v. United States A 1957 landmark decision of the U.S. Supreme Court that seriously undercut the 80-year-old Comstock law (*qv*) by establishing three new requirements for a work to be considered legally obscene (*qv*): a dominant theme that appeals to prurient (*qv*) or obsessive and depraving sexual interests. Under the Comstock law, a single page or even a single sentence could be picked out and used to declare the whole work legally obscene. The material must be offensive to the average community member and not merely to the most susceptible member, as had been previously allowed. Finally, the material must lack any redeeming social value.

In *Roth*, the Court had to state for the first time why obscenity (*qv*) was not protected by the First Amendment of free speech. The Court did this by declaring that obscenity has "no redeeming social value." Lawyers quickly twisted this criterion around, arguing that the works of Henry Miller and D. H. Lawrence, long-banned under the Comstock law, were "not utterly without social value" and were therefore protected by the First Amendment. *See also* Miller v. United States.

round vesicle An alternate term for the ovarian follicle (*qv*).

rubella A viral infection, also known as German measles; a childhood disease of little consequence to adults or children but with serious developmental consequences for a fetus (*qv*) if the mother is exposed in the first trimester (*qv*).

rubella embryopathy Any congenital (*qv*) anomaly in an infant caused by an exposure to the rubella (*qv*) virus early in gestation (*qv*).

Rubin test A procedure for checking for blockages in the fallopian tubes (*qv*). The uterus (*qv*) and tubes are filled with carbon dioxide to test whether the gas can pass through the tubes into the abdomen. The passage of gas through an open tube can be detected by X-ray imaging and by a characteristic sound it makes when entering the abdomen.

rudimentary testis A congenital (*qv*) anomaly in which one or both testes (*qv*) fails to develop and differentiate into a functional organ producing sperm (*qv*) and hormones (*qv*). Also referred to as testicular agenesis or dysgenesis.

RU 486 A drug sponsored by the World Health Organization and manufactured by a French pharmaceutical company, RU 486 is an effective and safe postcoital contraceptive (*qv*), menses (*qv*) inducer, or abortifacient (*qv*). RU 486 mimics the structure of the female hormone progesterone (*qv*). This allows RU 486 to bind to uterine receptor sites where progesterone usually binds. Since progesterone cannot bind at the RU 486–blocked sites, it cannot maintain a pregnancy (*qv*) and turn off menstruation as it usually does. This action results in a heavy menses with expulsion of any zygote (*qv*). This action has led the inventor of RU 486, Dr. Etienne Baulieu, to describe the drug as a contragestive—a contraction of ''contra-gestation'' as contraceptive is a contraction of ''contra-conceptive.'' Also known as mifepristone or mifegyne.

In the early weeks of pregnancy, it is 90 to 95 percent effective and 80 percent effective by the seventh week. When prostaglandins (*qv*), which induce uterine contractions (*qv*), are used with RU 486, the rate of successful nonsurgical abortions (*qv*) jumps to 95 percent in the first 12 weeks. Tests of RU 486 in France and California show that the only side effects of RU 486 are a temporary nausea and heavy bleeding. If approved by the Food and Drug Administration and marketed in the United States, RU 486 could replace 80 to 90 percent of the 1.5 million first-trimester surgical abortions performed every year in the country. RU 486 looks promising as a treatment for endometriosis (*qv*), and may be used to prevent almost a third of the Caesarean sections (*qv*). Despite strong advocacy by feminist (*qv*) groups, no American pharmaceutical company has yet expressed an interest in investing $125 million to get this drug approved by the FDA. This basic cost is not what worries possible investors. Because RU 486 is viewed as a ''do-it-at-home abortion drug,'' any company that applies for a license to market RU 486 would face an immediate nationwide boycott of all its products.

rugal (n. ruga, pl. rugae) Wrinkled, ridgelike, corrugated tissue, especially large folds in the mucous membrane of an organ such as the vagina (*qv*) and stomach. Rugae allow for expansion of an organ without tearing.

rule of abstinence *See* abstinence rule.

ruptured hymen A hymen (*qv*) that has been breached or torn. Rupture of the hymen may be the consequence of vaginal intercourse (*qv*), a gynecological (*qv*) examination, use of a vaginal tampon (*qv*), digital exploration, or sports activity. *See also* virginity; defloration.

rut The periodic sexual excitement (*qv*) and mating (*qv*) activity of many male animals including deer, sheep, goats, and camels. Also known as heat. *See also* estrus.

S

saccharomycosis A genital (*qv*) infection caused by a yeast-fungus of the genera *Candida* (*qv*) or *Cryptococcus*.

Sacher-Masoch, Leopold von (1836–1895) An Austrian lawyer and writer whose paraphilic (*qv*) need for pain and humiliation to obtain sexual pleasure prompted Krafft-Ebing (*qv*) to coin the term masochism (*qv*). Sacher-Masoch's fetish (*qv*) for pain, humiliation, and fur may have come from childhood experiences watching his aunt and her lover (*qv*) enact bondage and whipping scenarios in a fur closet. He described these events and his reenactment of them in a celebrated novel, *Venus in Furs*. He died shortly after being committed to a mental institution. *See also* Marquis de Sade.

sacred prostitution In some early religions, priests and priestesses (*qv*) devoted to fertility (*qv*) gods and goddesses engaged in sexual relations (*qv*) with worshipers in the temple. This custom, also known as temple prostitution, has been traced back to the fifth century B.C.E. in the ancient Near East, India, and Greece. It was vehemently condemned by the early Hebrew prophets.

sacred triangle The triangular mons veneris (*qv*) or mons pubis (*qv*).

sacrouterine Related to the sacrum or sacral region of the spine and to the uterus (*qv*); associated with or in the pelvic region of the body.

SAD *See* somatosensory affectional deprivation.

sadism A psychological dependence on inflicting humiliation, punishment, torture, restraint, and pain on one's partner in order to achieve sexual arousal (*qv*) and facilitate orgasm (*qv*). While sadism is generally used to refer to any cruel behavior, including sexual violence and rape (*qv*), the specific sexological use and meaning of the term depends on the consent or nonconsent of the recipient. In the context of a sadomasochistic scene (*qv*) or scenario, the masochistic partner is willing and in control of the interaction, by, for example, setting the limits and stopping it if it exceeds them. In the case of nonconsensual, unreciprocated sadism, the sadist is driven by a paraphilic (*see* paraphilia), often pathological, need, and the victim does not consent. *See also* autoassassinatophilia; homocidophilia; lust murder; sadomasochism.

sadistic nonpsychotic rapist A sexual assaulter or rapist (*qv*) who must control and dominate women using physical force in order to be sexually aroused (*qv*) and achieve orgasm (*qv*). This type of rapist is usually motivated by generalized anger against women. *See also* sadistic psychotic rapist.

sadistic psychotic rapist A psychotic sexual assaulter or rapist (*qv*) motivated by hatred and anger and sexually aroused (*qv*) by inflicting pain on his victim. This type of rapist often mutilates his victim and may murder her. *See also* lust murder; homocidophilia; sex-aggression-fusion rapist; snuff pornography.

sadomasochism (S and M, S&M, S/M, SM) A consensual activity involving polarized role playing (*qv*), intense sensations and feelings, actions, and fantasies (*qv*) that focus on the forbidden playing out or fantasizing dominant and submissive roles as part of a sexual scenario. In psychological terms, a complementary paraphilic (*qv*) condition in which one person is sexually aroused (*qv*) by inflicting pain on a partner who is aroused by and depends on painful stimuli in order to achieve orgasm (*qv*). *See also* bondage and dominance; sadism, masochism. Sadomasochism may involve elaborate scenes and scenarios, often scripted in advance by the partners, and equipment, called toys or paraphernalia. The humiliation often includes imposing obedience and servitude on the masochist (the "M" or "bottom") by the sadist (the "S" or "top"). Sadism is usually chronic in its expression and occurs predominantly in men. The reciprocal paraphilic condition is masochism. A nonsadistic person, especially a woman, may play the sadist role to oblige a masochistic (*qv*) partner either freely or for financial profit.

This paraphilia (*qv*) is named after the French author Marquis de Sade (1740–1814) (*qv*) whose novels extolled this kind of sexual role playing. Resources: R. R. Linden et al., eds., *Against Sadomasochism: A Radical Feminist Analysis* (East Palo Alto, CA: Frog in the Well, 1982); C. Moser & E. E. Levitt, An exploratory-descriptive study of a sadomasochistically oriented sample, *Journal of Sex Research* 23(3) (1987) 322–337; T. E. Murray & T. R. Murrell, *The Language of Sadomasochism: A Glossary and Linguistic Analysis* (Westport, CT: Greenwood Press, 1989); Members of SAMOIS, eds., *Coming to Power: Writings and Graphics on Lesbian S/M*, 2d ed. (Boston: Alyson Publications, 1982).

See also anal sadism; lust murder; phallic sadism; rape; rapist; sadistic non-psychotic rapist; sadistic psychotic rapist; sadomasochistic sacrifice.

sadomasochistic sacrifice A paraphilic (*qv*) ritual in which sexuoerotic arousal (*qv*) and orgasm (*qv*) depend on participation in a reciprocal interaction of a sadistic (*qv*) authority figure with a masochistic (*qv*) victim, with or without mutual consent of the victim. *See also* lust murder; homicidophilia; snuff film; erotophonophilia.

sadomasochistic scene A consensually created sadomasochistic (*qv*) interaction involving two or more partners in which sadist (*qv*) and masochist (*qv*) roles (*qv*) are mutually agreed to and enacted.

safe period A colloquial term for those days in a woman's menstrual cycle (*qv*) when she is not likely to conceive following unprotected intercourse. *See also* natural family planning.

safe sex (safer sex) A general term referring to sexual practices (*qv*) that reduce the risk of contracting the HIV (*qv*) virus in homosexual (*qv*) and heterosexual (*qv*) relationships, especially with a partner whose past sexual history places him or her at risk for having been exposed to the acquired immune deficiency syndrome (*qv*) virus. The primary safer sex practice is use of a condom (*qv*) impregnated with nonoxynol-9 (*qv*) with a spermicidal foam also containing nonoxynol-9. Condom use is recommended to prevent exposure to seminal or vaginal fluids. Safer sex practices also include avoiding anal (*qv*) and oral sex (*qv*) with any partner in high-risk groups such as intravenous drug users. Some authorities recommend outercourse (*qv*), mutual masturbation (*qv*), use of a dental (oral) dam (*qv*) when engaging in oral sex, fantasy (*qv*) exchanges, and noncoital sexual outlets such as sexual talk, bondage and dominance (*qv*), sadomasochism (*qv*) and exhibitionist-voyeurist (*qv*) scenarios. The original term *safe sex* practices has been modified to *safer sex* because although such practices significantly reduce the risk of infection, the only absolutely safe sex practice is abstinence (*qv*).

Saint-Hilaire, Etienne Geoffrey In 1818, Saint-Hilaire, a French naturalist, carried out the first significant studies of congenital birth defects (*qv*) and laid the foundation for the science of teratology (*qv*) by experimenting with animals to induce congenital birth defects.

saline injection *See* intra-amniotic infusion.

saliromania A general term for a paraphilic (*qv*) compulsion in which sexual gratification (*qv*) and orgasm (*qv*) are dependent on filth, ugliness, or deformity, saliromania includes mysophilia (*qv*), olfactophilia (*qv*), urophilia (*qv*), coprophilia (*qv*), autonepiophilia (*qv*), and narratophilia (*qv*). Psychoanalysts trace saliromania and its variations to an unsatisfied urge to play with feces during the anal stage (*qv*) of early childhood.

salpingectomy Surgical removal of one or both fallopian tubes (*qv*); performed to remove a cyst (*qv*) or tumor or to excise an abscess. Removal of both tubes results in sterilization (*qv*).

salpingitis An infection of the fallopian tubes (*qv*), accompanied by unilateral or bilateral abdominal pain, nausea, occasional dysmenorrhea (*qv*), and fever. *See also* pelvic inflammatory disease.

salpingitis isthica nodosa (L.) The development of nodules and an abnormal thickening of the fallopian tube (*qv*) wall close to the uterus (*qv*).

salpingo-oophorectomy Surgical removal of one or both sets of fallopian tubes (*qv*) and ovaries (*qv*).

salpingostomy Formation of an artificial opening in a fallopian tube (*qv*), performed to restore functioning to a tube blocked by infection or inflammation.

salpingotomy An incision in a fallopian tube (*qv*).

saltpeter Potassium nitrate, a diuretic with an unsupported reputation of being an anaphrodisiac (*qv*) or sexual depressant. Although saltpeter has been used since Sumerian times 4,000 years ago, it can have harmful side effects as a carcinogen precursor, as a cause of anemia, and as a lethal poison.

same-gender sex play The tendency of prepubescent (*qv*) children to engage in sexually exploratory activities with members of their own sex or gender. *See also* homoerotic. Also, the tendency for prepubescent children to enact the gender roles (*qv*) of adults of their own gender in sex rehearsal play (*qv*) with children of the other gender.

S and M, S&M *See* sadomasochism.

Sanger, Margaret (1883–1966) A sexual educator and reformer, and a community and obstetrical nurse in New York City, Sanger believed that every pregnancy (*qv*) should be wanted. Motivated by the conviction that much of the high infant and maternal mortality rates in the crowded slums of New York City at the turn of the century resulted from self-induced abortions (*qv*), Sanger campaigned for open access to contraceptives (*qv*). The self-appointed censor of the era, Anthony Comstock (*qv*), along with the police and religious leaders, opposed her every move to provide the poor with then-illegal contraceptive information and devices. Sanger argued that birth control, a term she introduced, was every woman's right. Her opponents argued that disseminating information about birth control would increase immoral behavior among single and married persons and would, by doing away with an unwanted pregnancy, eliminate ''the proper divine punishment for illicit sex.'' Spurred by her close friend Havelock Ellis (*qv*) and his reports of family planning in the Netherlands, Sanger published *The Woman Rebel*, later renamed the *Birth Control Review*. Her first birth control clinic opened in New York City in October 1916. In 1921, she founded the American Birth Control League and in 1927 organized the first World Population Conference in Geneva. In 1936, she succeeded in having the Comstock law (*qv*) modified to allow physicians to prescribe contraceptives. *See also* Planned Parenthood/World Population.

sanitary napkin (pad) A disposable pad of cellulose or other material designed to absorb the menstrual flow (*qv*) when held by adhesive backing to the underclothes or by an elastic belt between the legs in the vulval area. *See also* tampon.

Sapir-Whorf hypothesis In linguistics, a hypothesis based on work by linguists Edward Sapir and Benjamin Lee Whorf, which states that the worldview of a culture is constrained by and reflected in a given language. In this view, English-speaking people, for instance, have a worldview that differs systematically, if subtly, from the worldview of individuals who speak Chinese. The Sapir-Whorf hypothesis does not assert that English and Chinese cultures are different: That is a fact of anthropology and is not under debate. Instead, the hypothesis suggests that one reason these cultures differ is that the two languages differ, thereby creating subtly different ways of understanding, explaining, and interpreting the social and natural world.

It is very difficult to prove or disprove the Sapir-Whorf hypothesis. On the one hand, it seems nearly self-evidently true, but on the other hand, it is extremely difficult to find specific examples in which the hypothesis is substantiated. For example, it has been argued that different cultures have very different ideas of time because the language of one culture may contain an elaborate grammatical apparatus for making past, present, and future tenses of verbs, whereas the language of another culture may not have this apparatus. However, it still turns out that individuals of both cultures are perfectly able to tell time, both the hour of the day and the season. Nonetheless, linguists retain a belief that these differences do, in fact, affect people's concepts of time and its passage.

For sexuality (*qv*), the importance of the Sapir-Whorf hypothesis is that in many cultures, modern America included, men and women speak subtly or not-so-subtly different dialects of the same language. In modern American English, for example, it is commonly believed that men speak a language that is more crude, gross, coarse, and unrefined than the language women use. If this is so, a simple application of the Sapir-Whorf hypothesis would suggest that men's view of their world is also more crude, gross, coarse, and less refined than women's view. Many individuals would quickly agree with this stereotype, although men's liberationists (*qv*) would not.

In this example, the assumption that individuals—men, for example—speak only one language or dialect of a language poses a problem. For the Sapir-Whorf hypothesis to apply, men would always have to speak more crudely than women, and women would always have to speak in more refined ways than men. However, that is patently not the case. Accordingly, the usual applications of the Sapir-Whorf hypothesis to language, particularly sexual languages, do not take into consideration the range of variation of a speaker's language, and instead assume that he or she has one and only one language. As a result, no global conclusion about worldviews of men and women can be reached on the basis of their different use of words and expressions under some, but not all, circumstances. Even so, many writers about sexuality and gender (*qv*) hold to explicit or implicit versions of the Sapir-Whorf hypothesis, and claim, for example, that if the language of men were refined by the elimination of sexist (*see* sexism) terms and expressions, then men themselves would not think or behave in sexist ways, or at least not so frequently.

Although this conclusion seems intuitively self-evident, it is, in fact, not clear that language by itself has such power to shape behavior and thought. It may instead be the case that language reflects sexist or exploitative customs and institutions, and changes in language would merely disguise objectionable customs or make them sound more acceptable. There is, and can be, considerable debate about these issues, with language-oriented writers tending to believe one version of the Sapir-Whorf hypothesis or another, and activists and politically oriented individuals tending to deny any overarching significance to the hypothesis.

Sapphic love *See* lesbianism.

sapphism Lesbianism (*qv*). The term is derived from the early Greek woman poet Sappho (600 B.C.), who lived on the Aegean island of Lesbos and wrote lyrical accounts of women's sexual encounters with women. *See also* Bilitis; Daughters of Bilitis.

sapphist A lesbian (*qv*). *See also* sapphism.

SAR (Workshop) *See* Sexual Attitude Reassessment Workshop.

sarcoma botyroides A tumor derived from primitive striated muscle fibers and characterized by painful, swollen, grapelike growths in the upper vagina (*qv*), uterine cervix (*qv*), or neck of the urinary bladder; most frequent in young females.

sarcoma, prostatic A rare form of prostatic cancer (*qv*) occurring at any age but most common in infants and young boys. *See also* median bar hypertrophy; median lobe hypertrophy; medullary cancer of the prostate; scirrhous carcinoma.

Sarcoptes scabiei (L.) A mite that causes an intense itching by burrowing under the skin to lay its eggs and by its toxic products; transmitted by close physical or sexual contact. *See also* scabies.

satellite relationship Secondary, nonprimary relationships occurring in open marriages (*qv*), sexually open marriages (*qv*) and intimate networks (*qv*). Satellite relationships may or may not involve sexual intimacy (*qv*), but their participants view the relationship in the context of the primary relationship(s) of everyone involved. The dynamics of satellite relationships strive to make them synergistic rather than competitive with primary relationships. *See also* comarital relationship; communitas. Resource: A.K. Francoeur & R.T. Francoeur, *Hot and Cool Sex: Cultures in Conflict* (New York: Harcourt Brace Jovanovich, 1974).

sathon An ancient Greek term for the boy lover (*qv*) of an older male.

satii *See* suttee.

sattvic foods In the traditions of yoga (*qv*), foods that stimulate creativity and eroticism (*qv*): dairy products, honey, grains, nuts, and most fruits and vegetables growing above ground. These foods are believed to produce a sweet, nonirritating semen (*qv*).

satyr An old term for a male driven to compulsive sexual activity (*qv*) that gives only fleeting satisfaction. In Greek mythology, a satyr was a woodland deity who served as an attendant to the demigod Bacchus or Dionysius. The satyr was fond of merriment and lechery (*qv*), and usually depicted as a chimera with the hind end of a goat and the front end of a horned man.

satyriasis An old, largely pejorative term for an excessive and uncontrollable sexual desire in the male. *See also* satyr. Satyriasis may be organic or psychological in origin. Also known as Don Juanism (*see* Don Juan), or sexual addiction. The female counterpart is nymphomania (*qv*). Both terms leave unspecified what is meant by "excessive." *See also* addiction, sexual; promiscuity.

satyromania *See* satyriasis.

SBE Self-breast examination. *See also* breast self-examination.

scabicide Any drug or agent that kills or controls the mite responsible for scabies (*qv*).

scabies A contagious skin condition caused by the mite *Sarcoptes scabiei* and characterized by intense itching and excoriation from scratching. Treatment is with a sulfur ointment, benzyl benzoate, or another scabicide applied topically.

scaled behavior The sequence of increasingly more intimate sexual acts that most people in a particular culture (*qv*) follow when engaging in sexual relations (*qv*).

scatography Graffiti or other writing about excrement, filth, or obscenity (*qv*) designed to express or arouse sexual interest. *See also* erotic folklore.

scatology (adj. scatological) In the broad sense, the study of verbal and graphic material legally defined as obscene (*qv*) or filthy. Although the term literally means "study of excretory activity and products," it is commonly used in a sexual context. *See also* anal eroticism; telephone scatophilia.

scatophilia *See* coprophilia.

scatophobia *See* coprophobia.

schadchen (Heb.) A matchmaker (*qv*) or marriage broker (*qv*) in Jewish communities.

scirrhous carcinoma (scirrhus) A fibrous, especially invasive tumor of prostatic (*qv*) or mammary (*qv*) cancer easily diagnosed by its hardness when palpated. *See also* medullary cancer of the prostate.

sclerosing lymphangitis of the penis Inflammation, enlargement, and hardening of the lymphatic vessels of the penile shaft (*qv*).

scold's bridle In the Middle Ages, a mask or gag used to quiet quarrelsome, shrewish women. In modern times, this device has been modified for use in bondage and dominance (*qv*) games. *See also* brank; sadomasochism.

scopo- *See* scoptolagnia; scoptophilia; scoptophobia.

scoptolagnia Sexual excitement (*qv*) produced by looking at naked persons or their genitalia (*qv*).

scoptophilia A paraphilic (*qv*) dependence on viewing sexual acts and/or the sexual organs (*qv*) as a means of achieving sexual excitement (*qv*) and orgasm (*qv*). The reciprocal paraphilia is autagonistophilia (*qv*). Related paraphilia are voyeurism (*qv*) and exhibitionism (*qv*). Sigmund Freud (*qv*) distinguished between an active form of scoptophilia, where the pleasure is in looking, and a passive form, where the pleasure is in being looked at. *Synonyms*: mixoscopia; scopophilia; scoptolagnia.

scoptophobia A morbid fear of being looked at; an extreme form of shyness, most common in adolescence (*qv*) as an expression of sexual self-consciousness.

script In developmental and sociological terms, the personally internalized sets of behavior, attitudes, values, and expectations accepted as appropriate by an individual. As a metaphor, a script refers to "a repertoire of acts and statuses that are recognized by a social group, together with the rules, expectations, and sanctions governing these acts and statuses" (J. Laws and P. Schwartz, *Sexual Scripts: The Social Construction of Female Sexuality* [Hinsdale, IL: Dryden Press, 1977]). The script concept was developed by Eric Berne in his transactional analysis (1970) and by John Gagnon and William Simon (1973). The contention is that much of human behavior, and sexual behavior in particular, is scripted as a play is in a theater. Scripts are the mental plans we use to organize our behavior along socially appropriate lines. They are often gender specific and strongly influenced by the culture of the individual.

A sexual script has five key variables, which, on either the cultural or personal level, specify with whom one has sex, what one does sexually, when sex is appropriate, the proper setting for sex, and why one has sex. *See also* scripting theory; gender role; gender role socialization; socialization. Resources: J. H. Gagnon and W. Simon, *Sexual Conduct: The Social Origins of Human Sexuality* (Chicago: Aldine, 1973); J. H. Gagnon, *Human Sexualities* (Glenview, IL: Scott, Foresman, 1977); E. Berne, *Sex in Human Loving* (New York: Simon & Schuster, 1970).

scripting theory A theory that a long-lasting psychological linking develops between early sexual experiences and a particular circumstance, stimulus, or person. Scripting theory also refers to the discrete and sporadic social conditioning a person is subjected to by his or her family, parents, society, culture, religion, and peer influences. Scripting theory denies the existence of a biologically based sexual drive and claims that sexual learning and social contingencies almost completely account for what we do sexually. Also, scripting theory rejects any sharp distinction between what is sexual and what is nonsexual. *See also* script; gender role; gender role socialization; libido; nature/nurture debate; sex negative; sex positive; socialization.

scrotal angioma A tumor of the scrotum (*qv*) characterized by enlarged blood vessels and wartlike growths.

scrotal erysipelas An inflammation of the scrotal tissues, usually caused by a streptococcal infection following an injury, a chancroid infection, or a lymphatic disorder.

scrotal hypospadia A congenital birth defect (*qv*) in which the urethral opening develops in the scrotum (*qv*). *See also* hypospadia.

scrotal pouch The embryonic extension of the pelvic cavity, known as the vaginal process, which develops in the seventh month of gestation (*qv*) to facilitate the descent of the testicles (*qv*) into the scrotum (*qv*); it becomes the inner lining of the scrotum.

scrotal sac *See* scrotum.

scrotal xanthomata Chicken poxlike lesions on the skin of the scrotum (*qv*), genitalia (*qv*), and the perineal (*qv*) region due to excessive fat in the blood.

scrotitis An inflammation of the scrotum (*qv*), scrotitis may result from an infection, such as gonorrhea (*qv*), syphilis (*qv*), mumps, scarlet fever, typhoid fever, tuberculosis, or influenza or from a physical condition such as an intestinal-scrotal hernia, an undescended testicle (*qv*), hydrocele (*qv*), or twisting of the spermatic cord (*qv*).

scrotoplasty Plastic surgery to repair or refashion the scrotum (*qv*).

scrotoplexy Surgical removal of a portion of the scrotum (*qv*) to correct a defect.

scrotum The dark-colored, loose- and thin-skinned pouch containing the testes (*qv*), epididymis (*qv*), and parts of the spermatic cords (*qv*) in the male. The scrotum develops from fusion of the paired embryonic swellings. A thin-walled septum divides the scrotal cavity into a right and left side. The left portion usually hangs lower than the right, corresponding to the longer length of the left spermatic cord and its angle of entry into neighboring blood vessels. The scrotal skin is highly vascular and has thinly scattered kinky hairs and sebaceous (*qv*) follicles. The thin, subcutaneous layer of the dartos muscle (*qv*) controls the looseness or tightness of the muscular sac against the body wall, thus maintaining an optimal testicular temperature. The scrotum is homologous to the labia majora (*qv*) in the female.

seasonal sex *See* estrus.

sebaceous Fatty, oily, or greasy, usually referring to the oil-secreting glands of the skin or their secretions.

sebaceous cyst A cyst (*qv*) involving a sebaceous gland (*qv*) similar to an acne pimple. Sebaceous cysts occur in the labia minor (*qv*), anus (*qv*), penile glans (*qv*), and wherever else sebaceous glands are found.

sebaceous gland One of many small saclike organs in the dermis that usually empty their secretions into the hair follicles. Abundant in the scalp, labia minora (*qv*), and coronal region of the penile glans (*qv*), they are the source of a variety of fatty or oily secretions. *See also* smegma.

sebum The normal secretions of sebaceous glands (*qv*), composed of keratin, fat, and cellular debris.

secondary A descriptive term used to indicate that a condition has not existed from birth (*qv*) or puberty (*qv*), or a condition whose cause is due to another dysfunction. *See also* primary.

secondary areola A second, darker pigmented ring appearing during pregnancy (*qv*) around the areola (*qv*) and the breast nipple (*qv*).

secondary erogenous zones Areas of the body that have become erotically sensitized through learning and experience, in contrast with the primary erogenous zones of the genitalia (*qv*).

secondary gender characteristics *See* secondary sex characteristics.

secondary hypogonadism Underdevelopment of the testes (*qv*) due to a deficiency of pituitary gonadotropins (*qv*) that decreases testosterone (*qv*) production rather than being caused by a hormonal dysfunction within the testes themselves. Secondary hypogonadism accounts for about three-quarters of all cases of hypogonadism (*qv*).

secondary nonorgasmia A dysfunction (*qv*) in which the person is orgasmic (*qv*) during masturbation (*qv*) or with one partner but not with another partner. *See also* inhibited orgasm.

secondary oocyte In oogenesis (qv), the haploid (qv) product of the first meiotic (*qv*) division of the diploid (qv) primary oocyte. Since cytokinesis is unequal in oogenesis, one large secondary oocyte and a much smaller polar body (*qv*) are produced. This first polar body may undergo a second abortive division. The larger secondary oocyte divides a second time, again unequally, to produce an ovum (*qv*) and a second polar body, which degenerates.

secondary sex(ual) characteristics Physical characteristics that develop as part of puberty (*qv*) and distinguish the two sexes: in the female, breasts (*qv*) and characteristic fat deposits; in the male, beard, deepened voice and larynx development, and gender-characteristic muscle structures and skeleton. Secondary sexual characteristics are contrasted with primary and tertiary sexual characteristics (*qv*). *See also* gender coding.

secondary sexual dysfunction Any sexual dysfunction (*qv*) that follows a period of satisfactory sexual functioning. A secondary sexual dysfunction is complete or absolute when it is encountered in all situations and times and with any partner. It is incomplete when it occurs only in certain situations, with a certain partner, or at certain times. This condition should not be confused with temporary sexual satiation following intense sexual activity (*qv*). *See also* refractory period.

secondary spermatocyte In the male, the two haploid (*qv*) products of the first meiotic (*qv*) division; each divides into two spermatids (*qv*), which mature into spermatozoa (*qv*).

secondary wife In polygynous (*qv*) societies, any wife or concubine (*qv*) other than the first or primary wife. The concept refers to a temporal series of wives and not to the husband's emotional preference. Secondary wives usually have limited rights and authority and are often subject to the primary wife's authority.

second stage orgasm In the male, the propulsion phase (*qv*) of ejaculation (*qv*), in contrast with the primary stage or the emission phase (*qv*).

second testicular hormone A general term currently applied to those estrogens (*qv*) that can be isolated from the urine (*qv*) of males. It is assumed that these trace estrogens are produced, along with the higher levels of testosterone (*qv*), by the cells of Leydig (*qv*) in the testes (*qv*), since these estrogens are not found in men with nonfunctioning cells of Leydig.

Secret Dalliance A Taoist (*qv*) term for the lovemaking (*qv*) of a single man with more than one woman; viewed as a way of gaining magical power.

secret vice A Victorian expression for masturbation (*qv*). Also known as solitary vice or self-pollution.

secular decline hypothesis The unfounded theory that the onset of menstruation (*qv*) has been occurring at an increasingly earlier age over the past several centuries; its existence has been challenged by V.L. Bullough, Age of menarche: A misunderstanding, *Science*, 213 (1981) 365–366. *See also* menarche.

secular law A law enacted and enforced by the civil judiciary system, as opposed to church or canon law (*qv*); varies considerably depending on the society and jurisdiction. *See also* civil codes of law. In the U.S. system of jurisprudence, secular law includes criminal, civil, and family legal codes, framed by federal, state, local and military authorities. Each jurisdiction enacts codes of laws pertaining to sexual behavior within its jurisdiction.

secundine A technical term for the afterbirth (*qv*).

seduce, to (v.), seduction (n.) To persuade, induce, tempt, or otherwise entice someone to engage in a behavior in which they normally would not indulge, the connotation being an enticement to do something sexual (*qv*) and forbidden or against one's conscience and values. Depending on the state jurisdiction, sexual seduction accompanied by a promise to marry a woman may be a criminal act, with or without breach of promise (*qv*).

seductive behavior In psychoanalytic theory (*qv*), parental treatment of a child may be seductive and a subconscious expression of incestuous (*qv*) desire, even though the seduction may not be overt and may not result in actual incestuous acts.

segmentation Another term for cleavage (*qv*) of the zygote (*qv*) and morulla (*qv*) cells; mitotic (*qv*) cell division without any increase in cell size and without any differentiation of the cells.

selection *See* artificial selection; ideal lover template; lovemap; natural selection; sexual selection; stimulus/response/value model.

selective breeding *See* artificial selection.

selective gonadotropic failure A condition caused by a reduction in the levels of gonadotropic (*qv*) hormones, follicle-stimulating hormone (*qv*), and luteinizing hormone (*qv*) produced by the anterior pituitary (*qv*), which results in under-development of the male genitalia (*qv*) and prostate (*qv*) and a eunuchoid (*qv*) body.

self The individual as a conscious being; the ego (*qv*) or I (*qv*); the personality (*qv*); in the sociological theory of George Herbert Mead (*qv*), the self is the individual's capacity for self-awareness and self-evaluation. In contrast to Sigmund Freud (*qv*) who emphasized unconscious processes in the child's personality, Mead emphasizes the self. According to Mead, development of the self depends on the distinctly human ability for taking the role of the other or, more simply, role taking (*qv*), whereby an individual determines the intentions of others by their actions.

self-abuse An obsolete, moralistic term for masturbation (*qv*). *See also* secret vice; self-pollution; solitary vice.

self-actualization In humanistic psychology, the highest stage of motivation and personality development in which a person is self-motivated and self-actualized instead of being driven by outside needs; a central concept in Abraham Maslow's (*qv*) developmental motivational model of human needs. At the most elementary level of human existence, behavior is driven by basic survival and psychological needs. When these basic needs are met, security and safety needs come to the fore. On a third level, an individual focuses on meeting the needs for love and a sense of social belonging. The next step to self-actualization involves meeting the need for the respect and esteem of others. Only when all these lower-level needs are met can a person become self-actualizing. *See also* motivational hierarchy.

self-castration *See* self-emasculinization.

self-control A colloquial term for the practice of the virtues of temperance and chastity (*qv*); the ability to restrain and control sexual impulses, to moderate sexual responses, or to delay orgasm (*qv*) in order to match the partner's sexual pacing.

self-emasculinization A form of self-mutilation (*qv*), where a male castrates himself by amputating his penis (*qv*), testicles (*qv*), and scrotum (*qv*). Occasionally, a male transsexual (*qv*) who is unable to obtain sex reassignment (*qv*) surgery may emasculate himself as an act of desperation. Historically, self-emasculinization has been performed by adherents of some religious sects with a very strong ascetic (*qv*) tradition, such as the Skoptsy sect (*qv*) in eighteenth-century Russia and some early Christian ascetics. A notable example, Origen, a third-century writer and theologian, made himself a eunuch (*qv*) for the sake of the kingdom of God (Matthew 19:12). *See also* apotemnophilia; asphyxiophilia; autagonistophilia;, self-flagellation; stigmatophilia.

self-flagellation A religious ritual involving whipping one's self as expiation and penance for one's sins, especially those of a sexual nature. *See also* flagellantism.

self-induced abortion The termination of a pregnancy (*qv*) achieved through a woman's own efforts, either using a chemical abortifacient (*qv*) or a mechanical device. Self-induced abortions are extremely dangerous and may result in death.

self-insemination The introduction of donor semen (*qv*) into the vagina (*qv*) using a needleless syringe at the time of ovulation (*qv*) to produce a pregnancy (*qv*). Artificial insemination (*qv*) performed on one's self is advocated by the Feminist Self-Insemination Group for lesbians (*qv*) who want a biological child.

self-isolation A phobic (*qv*) withdrawal from and aversion to social interactions.

self-love (self-loving) An affirmative term for masturbation (*qv*). Also a pejorative term for narcissism (*qv*).

self-mutilation Any injury or disfigurement inflicted on one's own body either in expiation for one's real or supposed misconduct and sins or as an extreme of masochism (*qv*). *See also* apotemnophilia; asphyxiophilia; autagonistophilia; self-emasculinization; self-flagellation; stigmatophilia.

self-pleasuring A contemporary, positive term for masturbation (*qv*). *See also* self-pollution; secret vice.

self-pollution A moralistic, condemnatory term for masturbation (*qv*) common in religious writings of the seventeenth century through the early 1900s. *See also* self-pleasuring; secret vice; solitary vice.

self-stimulation A nonjudgmental term for masturbation (*qv*). *See also* self-pleasuring; self-pollution.

semen The thick, whitish (sometimes yellowish or grayish) secretions of the prostate (*qv*), seminal vesicles (*qv*), and Cowper's glands (*qv*) mixed with sperm (*qv*). Semen is usually ejaculated from the penis (*qv*) during orgasm (*qv*) or in a nocturnal emission (*qv*). A major component in semen is the sugar fructose which provides an energy resource for sperm motility (*qv*). Initially the semen is rather viscous, even congealed; after exposure to vaginal secretions, it liquefies to facilitate sperm motility. The average ejaculate (*qv*) contains about 3 milliliters of semen. Semen also contains about 8 calories per gram, mainly in proteins and fats, plus trace elements. Semen may contain and transmit the HIV-I (*qv*) virus, the bacterium that causes gonorrhea (*qv*), and the yeast *Candida albicans* (*qv*). Also known as seminal fluid. Colloquial usage inaccurately equates sperm with semen.

semen analysis The laboratory examination of a sample of semen (*qv*) to ascertain the number and percentage of normal, viable, and motile sperm. In normal semen, about 20 percent of the sperm are structurally deformed and/or nonmotile. A sperm count (*qv*) above 20 million sperm per milliliter is commonly considered essential to normal fertility. Some studies suggest that the sperm count in American males has been dropping over the past century due to increasing exposure to toxic substances which accumulate in the testes (*qv*) and interfere with or halt spermatogenesis. A 1929 study reported a median sperm count of 90 million per milliliter compared with medians of 65 million in 1974 and 60 million in 1979. Resource: R. C. Dougherty, Sperm counts decreasing in American men, *Sexual Medicine Today* 3(11) (1979) 14–15.

semen myths A variety of beliefs regarding semen (*qv*) occur in cultures around the world, most viewing semen as a vital fluid. Many semen myths embody the degeneracy theory (*qv*)—the belief that all diseases are caused by the loss of semen or vital fluids. Males in many cultures believe they are born with only so much semen (*qv*) and that if it is wasted in masturbation (*qv*) or sexual intercourse (*qv*), there may come a time when none is left. Others believe that loss of semen drains vital fluids from the brain, causing loss of memory and, in the extreme, death.

Traditional Chinese philosophy holds that semen loss diminishes the yang (*qv*), or male element, thereby reducing a man's strength and perhaps shortening his life. Hinduism teaches that since semen is the basis of a man's strength and long life, periodic abstinence (*qv*) and avoidance of masturbation and nocturnal emissions (*qv*) are important to health. Other semen myths include the belief that boys have no semen but can acquire enough semen for their adult lives by having oral sex (*qv*) with older men and the belief that multiple inseminations (*qv*) of an already pregnant woman are needed to insure fetal health and growth. Resources: G. H. Herdt, ed., *Ritualized Homosexuality in Melanesia* (Berkeley, CA: University of California Press, 1984); G. H. Herdt, ed., *Rituals of Manhood: Male Initiation in Papua New Guinea* (Berkeley, CA: University of California Press, 1982); J. Money, *The Destroying Angel* (Buffalo, NY: Prometheus Press, 1985); T. Gregor, *Anxious Pleasures: The Sexual Lives of an Amazonian People* (Chicago: University of Chicago Press, 1985). *See also* Graham, Sylvester; Kellogg; karezza; Tantric sexual traditions; Tao; ritual multiple intercourse.

semen reflux *See* retrograde ejaculation.

semen retention *See* coitus prolongatus; coitus reservatus; degeneracy theory; karezza; Tantric sexual traditions.

semenuria The presence of semen (*qv*) in the urine (*qv*), resulting from retrograde ejaculation (*qv*), prostate (*qv*) surgery, or a defect in the internal and external urethral sphincters (*qv*).

semidelivery A form of partial Caesarean section (*qv*) or intrauterine surgery involving the temporary removal of the fetus (*qv*) from the uterus (*qv*) to allow surgery or manipulation of the fetus before it is returned to the uterus to continue its gestation (*qv*) to term (*qv*). During its time outside the uterus, the fetus continues to receive oxygen and nutrients by way of the intact placenta (*qv*) and umbilical cord (*qv*).

seminal cyst A cyst caused by retention of sperm (*qv*) in the seminiferous tubules (*qv*) of the testicle (*qv*) or in the epididymis (*qv*).

seminal discharge The emission (*qv*) and expulsion or ejaculation (*qv*) of semen (*qv*) during sexual intercourse (*qv*), fellatio (*qv*), masturbation (*qv*), or nocturnal emission (*qv*).

seminal duct Any tubular passage for semen (*qv*)—the vas (ductus) deferens (*qv*), ejaculatory duct (*qv*), or penile urethra (*qv*).

seminal emission *See* ejaculation.

seminal fluid *See* semen.

seminalplasmin A component of seminal fluid (*qv*) containing a powerful natural antibiotic that may protect women and men from various sexually related infections. The existence of this substance is not reason to believe that it provides adequate protection against transmission of sexually transmitted diseases (*qv*). *See also* safe sex.

seminal pool The cavity that forms at the cervical (*qv*) end of the vaginal canal (*qv*) during the plateau (*qv*) and orgasmic stages (*qv*) to serve as a receptacle for the ejaculated semen (*qv*) and facilitate its access to the cervical canal.

seminal vesicles Located just posterior to the prostate (*qv*) in the male reproductive system, the seminal vesicles are a pair of glandular sacs that secrete part of the nutrient semen (*qv*) in which sperm (*qv*) are transported. The coiled tubes of the seminal vesicles are packed into two sacs, each about 3 inches long and located immediately dorsal to the prostate (*qv*) as outpocketings of the vasa deferentia (*qv*). The seminal vesicles were originally so named because they were falsely thought to store the semen.

seminal vesiculitis Inflammation of a seminal vesicle (*qv*).

semination The depositing of semen (*qv*) in the vagina (*qv*) or uterus (*qv*) during coitus (*qv*) or by means of artificial insemination (*qv*). *See also* impregnation.

seminiferous tubules Long, thin, coiled tubes within the testes (*qv*) that produce sperm (*qv*). Each testicle contains about 800 seminiferous tubules, each about 25 to 30 inches long. On the inside surface of the tubes, germinal cells (*qv*) undergo a two-stage meiotic (*qv*) division and maturation to produce spermatozoa. *See also* cells of Leydig; spermatogenesis.

seminoma The most common type of testicular tumor associated with cryptorchidism (*qv*), with cells resembling the germinal cells (*qv*) normally found in the seminiferous tubules (*qv*).

Seneca Falls The town in upstate New York where women gathered in July 1848 to discuss their social, civil, legal, and religious rights and declare their intention to work for equality of the sexes. The Declaration of Sentiments, passed at the convention, began with a line borrowed from the Declaration of Independence, ''We hold these truths to be self-evident: that all men and women are created equal.''

senile ovaries A medical term for the ovaries (*qv*) of a postmenopausal (*qv*) woman, containing mostly connective tissue, old corpora albicantia (*qv*), and a few Graafian follicles (*qv*).

sensate focus exercises Noncoital, nondemand, graduated pleasuring exercises developed by William Masters and Virginia Johnson for use in behavioral therapy (*qv*) of various sexual dysfunctions (*qv*). The exercises stress playful, non-goal-oriented touching, caressing exploration of the partner's body and sensual responses with continual verbal feedback. Later stages may incorporate verbal and manual guidance of the exploring partner's hand. The exercises are usually spaced over several weeks, with the therapist providing directions during counseling and the couple practicing each stage of the exercises in private. In special cases, the therapist may be present.

The object of these exercises is for the couple to become comfortable with each other, without the male's needing to have an erection (*qv*) or the female's needing to become aroused. By eliminating performance anxieties (*qv*), these exercises are useful in overcoming sexual aversion (*qv*) and anxiety, and erectile, arousal, and orgasmic dysfunctions in both males and females, particularly when combined with other therapeutic modalities in a multimodal therapy. Sensate focus exercises are also useful with nondysfunctional couples for sexual enrichment (*qv*). Resource: W. Masters & V. Johnson, *Human Sexual Inadequacy* (Boston: Little Brown, 1970).

sensitive period A period in development when learning a new behavior occurs most readily. *See also* critical period.

sensitivity-training group A group whose purpose is to offer members a supportive atmosphere in which to raise one's consciousness, discuss, experiment with, and alter behavioral patterns and interpersonal relations. Also known as encounter group or T-group.

sensitization In psychology, an acquired reaction to a naturally occurring or artificial stimulus. *See also* desensitization; resensitization; systematic desensitization.

sensual (n. sensuality) Pertaining to the effects of any of the senses; pertaining to, or consisting in, the gratification of the senses, or the indulgence of bodily appetites and desires; fleshly; devoted to the pleasures of the senses and appetite; voluptuous; sometimes lewd (*qv*). *See also* sensuous.

sensuous Of or pertaining to the senses or sensible objects; addressing the senses; characterized by sense impressions or imagery addressing the senses as in a ''sensuous description''; highly susceptible to influence through the senses; that which appeals to the senses in a pleasurable way. *See also* erotic; sensual;

sexuoerotic. The standard dictionary definitions of *sexual* (*qv*) and *sensuous* make a fine distinction between the two concepts, which appears to be eroding in modern American usage. All sexual responses are sensual, but *sensual* is a broader, more inclusive and less genitally oriented term than *sexual*. *Sensuous* refers to erotic pleasures that are sensual.

separate ova Two or more ova (*qv*) released in the same ovulation (*qv*). If several ova are fertilized (*qv*), the result is nonidentical, dizygotic twins (*qv*), nonidentical triplets (*qv*), or quadruplets (*qv*).

separation An agreement of a married couple to live apart without, at least for the time, divorcing (*qv*); a legal separation involves an agreement on division of properties, child custody, and domicile and is usually preliminary to a divorce.

separation anxiety The fear and apprehension caused by removal from familiar surroundings and significant persons, occurring commonly in infants (*qv*) separated from their mother or mothering figure.

sepsis An infection resulting from contamination by pathogenic (*qv*) bacteria or viruses in the blood. *See also* puerperal fever; septicemia.

septate hymen A hymen (*qv*) consisting of a single medial fold of tissue across the vaginal opening and two openings, one on either side. *See also* annular hymen; cribiform hymen; imperforate hymen.

septic abortion Spontaneous or induced termination of pregnancy (*qv*) where the mother's life is threatened by infection. Treatment involves immediate and intensive care, massive antibiotic therapy, uterine evacuation, and often an emergency hysterectomy (*qv*). Prior to the legalization of abortion (*qv*), septic abortions were a common consequence of self-induced abortions (*qv*) and abortions performed in unhygienic conditions.

septicemia A systemic infection in which pathogenic bacteria or viruses are spread through the body by the circulating blood.

septum Any dividing structure; a region of the limbic system (*qv*) associated with sexual behavior (*qv*), erection (*qv*), and orgasm (*qv*).

sequential bisexual A person who shifts between exclusive heterosexual (*qv*) and exclusive homosexual (*qv*) behavior at different times in life. Resource: F. Klein, *The Bisexual Option* (New York: Arbor House, 1978). In the view of some, bisexuality (*qv*) exists only as a transition stage; for others, it is a flexible gender orientation (*qv*) between heterosexuality and full homosexuality.

sequential oral contraceptive pill A hormonal oral contraceptive (*qv*) in which the pills taken on the first 15 days of the menstrual cycle (*qv*) contain only estrogen (*qv*), while the pills for the next 5 days contain both estrogen and progesterone (*qv*). This pattern of exogenous (*qv*) hormones mimics the natural ovarian hormone cycle. *See also* combination oral contraceptive pill; minipill; progestin-only contraceptive pill.

serial monogamy A life-style involving marriage (*qv*), divorce (*qv*), and re-marriage (*qv*) in which a male or female has only one spouse at a time, but two or more spouses in a lifetime. Also known as consecutive or serial polygamy, and serial marriage.

serial polygamy *See* serial monogamy.

serological test A test of the blood for presence of a particular pathogenic (*qv*) bacterium, virus, or antibody (*qv*). *See also* Elisa test; Eliza Technique; Western Blot test; Wassermann test.

seropositive The result of a test for presence of the HIV-I virus (*qv*), which causes acquired immune deficiency syndrome (*qv*). A seropositive response occurs when the serum being tested contains antibodies (*qv*) to the HIV-I virus that interact with the test material. *See also* Elisa test; Western Blot test.

serosa The outer covering of any organ within the abdominal, pelvic, and thoracic cavities; the membranous covering of the uterus (*qv*), derived embryologically from the peritoneum (*qv*).

serotonin A chemical substance, an indolamine, that serves as a neurotransmitter (*qv*) in the brain; believed to act as an inhibitor in sexual pathways. *See also* dopamine.

serous cyst A large cyst (*qv*) in the ovary (*qv*), filled with a serous, gray-to-amber fluid.

Sertoli cell A nurse or nutritive cell within the seminiferous tubule (*qv*) that develops cytoplasmic bridges to 100 or more developing spermatozoa (*qv*) and directs their synchronous maturation from the germinal cell stage to mature sperm.

Sertoli-cells-only syndrome An abnormal condition of the testis (*qv*) that contain Sertoli cells (*qv*) but no germinal epithelium or spermatogonia (*qv*).

sessile nodule In neutrophils or white blood cells with two or more X chromosomes (*qv*), the partial extrusion of all but one of the X chromosomes from the surface of the nucleus into the cytoplasm. If the extruded sex chromatin (*qv*) is completely contained in the extruded body, it is known as a drumstick appendage. Sessile nodules and drumstick appendages in the neutrophils are parallels of the Barr bodies (*qv*) in other somatic cells.

17–hydroxycorticosteroid A metabolite of cortisol (*qv*) that can be measured in the urine (*qv*).

17–hydroxylase An adrenal cortical (*qv*) enzyme essential in the synthesis of most steroids (*qv*), especially cortisol (*qv*).

17–ketosteroid Chemically a steroid (*qv*) containing a ketone group or a carbonyl group with hydrocarbon groups, at the seventeenth carbon atom of the steroid molecule. 17–ketosteroids produced by the adrenal cortex (*qv*) in both males and females are important in sexual development (*qv*) and functioning. At puberty (*qv*), they stimulate growth of the penis (*qv*), clitoris (*qv*), and pubic hair (*qv*). They also contribute to the problem of acne (*qv*) during adolescence. Ketosteroids stimulate amino acids incorporation into proteins, thus building muscle mass as well as the sexual organs (*qv*). *See also* 21–hydroxylase deficiency. 17–ketosteroids are androgen (*qv*) metabolites normally found in the urine. Excess ketosteroids in the urine (*qv*) indicate the presence of certain tumors or metabolic defects.

sex One's personal and reproductive status as a male, a female, or an individual of uncertain reproductive status; one's sex as male, female, or of ambiguous or uncertain anatomical status as determined by external genitalia (*qv*); a classification into male or female based on several physical and psychological criteria (*see also* sex variables); a colloquial expression for the act of sexual intercourse or genital interaction; in Victorian English, "the sex" was commonly used to mean "women generally."

Sex is derived from the Latin verb *secare*, meaning "to cut" or "to divide." The noun *sex* was introduced into the English language in a translation of the Latin Bible in 1382. Inspired by the religious reformer John Wycliffe, this translation said that God commanded Noah to select two specimens of every animal for his ark: "the maal sex and femaal" (Gen. 6:19).

A 1651 usage (cited in the *Oxford English Dictionary* under "sexual") uses *sex* to mean both "male" and "female," as well as to refer to reproductive capacities themselves: "these simples [small animals] are . . . of both sexes which truly would not come to passe if those simples had already a sex or sexuall powers within them." This dual sense of the word *sex* has remained alive in English. The sentence "mammals have two sexes" illustrates the first meaning, whereas "they reproduce by means of sex" illustrates the second meaning. The first sense directs attention to a basic, presumptively natural dichotomy of living things into two reproductive types, male and female, differentiated according to their perceived reproductive roles. In the second sense, the word *sex* is more closely synonymous with "sexual powers" or "sexual capacities," sexuality being considered a property or characteristic of living things as exemplified in their masculinity and femininity. Modern usage, especially scientific and scholarly, tends to employ the term *sexuality* for this second meaning.

The word sex has a broader meaning that generalizes from purely reproductive functions to include all characteristics of men and women that categorically distinguish them socially, emotionally, or personally. To say "She belongs to the female sex" imputes not merely a reproductive distinction, but also points to socially general and widespread differences believed to distinguish that person from someone who "belongs to the male sex." This sense of the word sex is close to the Latin *secare*, because it "cuts" the human race into two groups whose differences are recorded in words like masculine, feminine, and gender (*qv*). Simultaneously, the word sex in this sense evokes activities that can conjoin men and women; consequently, like the word cleave, which can mean "to break" and "to adhere," *sex* refers to characteristics that distinguish and separate men and women and to activities that bring them together. In actual usage, sex is one of the more complex words in English.

Perhaps the strongest influence on the Western concept of sex as sexuality has been the dualism (*qv*) of body-soul that came out of Platonism (*qv*) and Stoicism (*qv*) into Christian thought through Augustine of Hippo (*qv*). According to Plato, the gods were threatened by the original androgynous (*qv*) humans and solved their problem by splitting each original human into two sexual persons, two males, two females, or a male and a female, each of whom would then search for his or her other half. This view of human sexual nature was coupled with a body-soul dualism and with an ancient concept of sexuality as defilement. One of the great puzzles in human history, according to Paul Ricoeur, is the persistent association of sexuality (sex) with defilement, which he defines as a "quasi-material something that infects as a sort of filth, that harms by invisible properties . . . [and] works in the manner of a force in our psychic and corporeal existence." For Ricoeur, this "indissoluble complicity between sexuality and defilement" is preethical and reaches back to the roots of primitive human consciousness. Resource: P. Ricoeur, *The Symbolism of Evil* (Boston: Beacon Press, 1967), pp. 25–30.

According to historian Erwin Haeberle, until well into the eighteenth century, sex simply meant something like gender, sort, set, class, type, race, or breed. The word was commonly used to refer to a denomination, a school of thought, a faction, or a caste. Until the nineteenth century, the word was also used to refer to women as a class. By the eighteenth century, sexual was used to refer to the process of reproduction. The many current meanings of *sex*, *sexual*, and *sexuality* emerged gradually over many years. Resource: E. Haeberle, *The Sex Atlas* (New York: Seabury, 1978).

Accordingly there are many subtle gradations of meaning even in the simple-sounding concept of a sexual dichotomy of male and female sexes. In one direction, these meanings grade continuously toward concepts of gender (*qv*), social and cultural learning, and sexual scripting (*qv*), whereas in the other direction, the meanings reach toward modern biology and to complex, multistage theories of biopsychosexual development. *See also* sex variables. As a consequence, sex has no single, pure, or clear meaning; it refers to a range of complex phenomena.

See also multiple listings under *sex*, *sexual*, and *gender*. Because of varying preferences in ideology and constructs, what some refer to as *sex* or *sexual*, others define as *gender*. Thus, while some speak of *gender orientation*, the definition of this term is listed under the more common usage of *sexual orientation*. Similarly, *gender identity* may be the equivalent of *sexual identity*, and *sex* a synonym for *gender*. In this dictionary, we have listed such phrases under their more common usage.

sex act A colloquial term for copulation (*qv*), sexual intercourse (*qv*), or coitus (*qv*).

sex addict *See* addiction, sexual.

sex-adjunctive characteristics *See* gender coding, sex-adjunctive.

sex- (or gender-) adventitious characteristics *See* gender coding, sex-adventitious.

sex-aggression-fusion rapist A technical term for a rapist (*qv*) or sexual assaulter who associates inflicting pain and violence with sexual pleasure. In one developmental model, an extreme deprivation of nurturance—somatosensory affectional deprivation (*qv*)—alters neural connections in the pleasure and violence-pain centers of the hypothalamus (*qv*), leading to associations between pain and sexual behavior. The infliction of pain and violence on another person then becomes essential to the rapist's sexual arousal (*qv*) and satisfaction (*qv*). This type of rape is relatively rare, although it is widely publicized when it does occur. *See also* sadistic non-psychotic rapist; sadistic psychotic rapist; lust murder; homocidophilia.

Sexaholics Anonymous A network of self-help groups patterned on the 12–step program, like that of Alcoholics Anonymous, but for people with a particular sexual compulsion or addiction. *See also* addiction, sexual.

sex aid Any artificial device used to enhance or extend sexual excitement or pleasure. Sex aids include dildos (*qv*), penile extenders and sheaths with various surfaces designed to stimulate the vaginal wall and clitoris, vibrators (*qv*), vaginal balls (Ben-Wa balls) (*qv*), plastic vaginas, inflatable dolls, clitoral stimulators ("French ticklers" or love rings), drugs such as amyl nitrite (*qv*), marijuana (*qv*), cocaine and crack, and a wide variety of potions, creams, and pills alleged to have aphrodisiac (*qv*) effects.

sex (or gender) anomaly A major deviation from the normal (*qv*) in sexual anatomy or physiology; often used to describe nonbehavioral characteristics. *See also* perversion.

sex apparatus An obsolete term for the internal and external sexual organs (*qv*), including the genitalia (*qv*) the endocrine glands (*qv*), ovaries (*qv*), testes (*qv*), adrenal glands (*qv*), hypothalamus (*qv*), and pituitary (*qv*).

sex (sexual or gender) appeal Having the capacity to arouse sexual interest and desire. In colloquial American English, *sex appeal* has been called "it." However, sex appeal is very much a matter of culture (*qv*) and personal taste. What is considered sexually attractive in a man or woman in one culture may be viewed quite negatively in another culture or era. For instance, the ample, voluptuous women Rubens painted in the 1600s, the Victorian woman of the late 1800s, the turn-of-the-century Gibson girl, the tall women of the Ziegfeld Follies, the vamps of the 1920s, and the flat-chested Twiggy type of the 1970s are all examples of the varieties of sex appeal.

In non-Western cultures, the variety of what is considered sexually appealing has an even wider range. In southern Africa, women with an excessive accumulation of fat in the buttocks (*qv*) are highly prized. *See also* steatopygia. Sex appeal may focus on blackened or filed teeth, tattooing, elongation of the neck, devices that exaggerate the lips or nose, pendulous breasts, and flattened or pointed heads. The sex appeal of hair varies with personal as well as cultural taste. In modern Egypt, 90 percent or more of women remove all body hair except on the head. In the United States, women who do not shave their legs and under their arms may be considered sexually unappealing, although European women commonly do not shave body hair. The sex appeal of male beards and baldness and of long or short hair in women is often a matter of personal taste more than of cultural patterns. Resources: D. Morris, *Body Watching* (New York: Crown, 1985); D. Morris, *Manwatching: A Field Guide to Human Behavior* (New York: Abrams, 1977).

sex-appropriate (or gender-appropriate) behavior Specific behavioral patterns culturally associated with and considered appropriate to men and women. *See also* sex roles; sexually dimorphic behavior.

sex as defilement *See* asceticism; celibacy; degeneracy theory; dualism; Platonism; sex; Stoicism.

sex (or gender) assignment The attribution of an individual to the male or female sex or gender (*qv*), or to an ambiguous, intersex (*qv*), pseudohermaphrodite (*qv*), of hermaphrodite (*qv*) status. One's sex of assignment is usually determined at birth (*qv*) and based on external, visible sexual anatomy. In cases of ambiguous genitalia (*qv*), decisions for management take into consideration hormone balance and karyotype (*qv*), along with the prognosis for a sex change operation (*qv*) and the probable long-term outcome of sex reassignment (*qv*). In transsexuals (*qv*), the sex of assignment is consistent with the criteria of sexual anatomy, chromosomes (*qv*), and hormone balance but contradicts the individual's self-perceived sexual identity (*qv*). Following sex change surgery, the assigned sex of a transsexual is changed to match the new sexual anatomy and the old gender identity. *See also* sex reassignment.

sex bias *See* sex discrimination; sexism.

sex-blind Characteristic of laws or regulations that prohibit discrimination according to sex (*qv*) or gender (*qv*).

sex center of the brain A nontechnical term for the limbic system (*qv*), hypothalamus (*qv*), and pituitary gland (*qv*), which together regulate aspects of sexual development and behavior.

sex (or gender) change operation (surgery) Surgery performed to change the external sexual anatomy to that of the other sex or gender; also called sex or gender reassignment surgery (SRS or GRS), and the "Christine Jorgensen operation." Transsexuals (*qv*), who believe that their gender or sexual identity (*qv*) does not conform to their external anatomical sex, may seek a sex change operation to reduce or eliminate their gender dysphoria (*qv*). Advocates of such surgery often argue that because gender identity is established before birth or during very early infancy, it is therefore resistant to all forms of psychotherapy and counseling. Thus, they claim, the only viable solution is surgery, which will bring the external genitalia (*qv*) into conformity with the internal psychic experience of gender and facilitate the transsexual's social life as a member of the other sex. Other experts argue that transsexuals will respond to psychotherapy and that sex change surgery should be used only in rare cases.

According to the standards proposed by the Harry Benjamin (*qv*) International Gender Dysphoria Association, candidates for surgery should be carefully screened and required to live for a year or more in the gender role he or she wishes to assume prior to any surgery. During this time, hormone treatments may be undertaken to develop secondary sexual characteristics (*qv*) of the desired sex, particularly breast enlargement and decreased facial hair in male-to-female transsexuals, and facial hair and musculature in female-to-male transsexuals.

In the male-to-female sex change surgery, the testes (*qv*) and the erectile (*qv*) and urethral tissue of the penis (*qv*) are removed. The skin of the penis is used to create a vagina (*qv*) and clitoris (*qv*) while the scrotum (*qv*) and perhaps some transplanted tissue are used to create the major and minor labia (*qv*).

In a female-to-male sex change, skin from the labia (*qv*), abdomen and/or thighs is used to construct a nonfunctional penis and scrotum. Plastic prosthetic testicles are implanted in the scrotum, and a penile prosthesis (*qv*) may be implanted to make intercourse (*qv*) possible.

Male-to-female transsexuals outnumber female-to-male transsexuals by at least a four-to-one ratio. One authoritative estimate places the incidence of male-to-female transsexuals at 1 in 25,000 to 1 in 100,000 and for female-to-male transsexuals, between 1 in 100,000 and 1 in 400,000. Approximately 10,000 Americans have had sex change operations since 1965. Resources: B. W. Steiner, ed., *Gender Dysphoria: Development, Research, Management* (New York: Plenum Press, 1985); L. M. Lothstein, *Female-to-Male Transsexualism: Historical, Clinical and Theoretical Issues* (Boston: Routledge & Kegan Paul, 1983); R. F. Docter, *Transvestites and Transsexuals: Toward a Theory of Cross-Gender Behavior* (New York: Plenum, 1988).

sex (gender or sexual) character (or characteristics) Any structural, behavioral, or functional trait typically found more often in one sex (*qv*) than in the other. Also those visible bodily features associated with the sexual status and reproductive role of a male or female. Sexual characteristics are commonly classified as primary (*qv*), secondary (*qv*), and tertiary (*qv*). *See also* sex; gender coding, sex-adjunctive; gender coding, sex-adventitious; gender coding, sex-derivative; gender coding, sex-irreducible.

sex chromatin In genetics, the partially inactivated X chromosome (*qv*) found as a dark-staining Barr body (*qv*) on the nuclear membrane of a somatic (*qv*) cell. In normal female body cells, one X chromosome remains active and functional, and the second X chromosome is partially inactivated while remaining intact in the nuclei of the body's cells to form the sex chromatin. In cells with abnormal chromosome complements, such as 47,XXY and multiple X, the number of sex chromatin bodies is always one fewer than the number of X chromosomes in the cell. The presence or absence of sex chromatin in somatic cells obtained by buccal smear (*qv*), amniocentesis (*qv*), or chorionic villi sampling (*qv*) is used in ascertaining chromosomal sex status. Individuals with Turner syndrome (45,X0) (*qv*) and 46,XY males lack a Barr body; 47,XXY individuals with Klinefelter's syndrome (*qv*) have one Barr body. Also known as Barr body (*qv*) or X chromatin. *See also* Lyon hypothesis; sex chromosome.

sex chromosome In genetics, sex chromosomes are distinguished from autosomes (*qv*) because the former are different in the two sexes and contain genes related to sexual differentiation. Many, though not all organisms, possess specialized chromosomes that are associated with being either male or female. These specialized chromosomes segregate during meiosis (*qv*) so that each sex receives a different complement of sex chromosomes. In the animal kingdom, several different types of sex chromosomes exist. In mammals and humans, the two sex chromosomes are called X and Y. In mammals, the sex-related X and Y chromosomes are distinct from autosomes (*qv*), although the former do not contain all sex-determining genes.

The normal diploid (*qv*) chromosome (*qv*) complement of a human female is two X chromosomes and 44 autosomes (*qv*) arranged in two homologous (*qv*) or paired sets of 23 chromosomes. The normal diploid chromosome complement of a human male is 44 autosomes plus an X and a Y chromosome arranged in two homologous or paired sets of 23 chromosomes. At least one X chromosome is needed for embryonic development to proceed.

The X and Y chromosomes carry sex-determining genes or regions that influence prenatal differentiation of internal and external sexual anatomy. Two X chromosomes are needed in females for ovarian (*qv*) development. A Y chromosome is needed for male anatomical development. An individual with a Y chromosome will develop male primary sexual characteristics (*qv*), even in the presence of several X chromosomes. *See also* sex chromatin; Barr body; sex chromosome anomalies; Turner syndrome; Klinefelter syndrome; HY-antigen; testicular determining factor gene.

sex chromosome anomalies A variety of syndromes have their origin in variations in the number and type of sex chromosomes. The more common syndromes are listed here with their genetic designation. Descriptions are given elsewhere as indicated: 45,XO syndrome: *see* Turner syndrome; 45,XO/46,XY syndrome: *see* Turner syndrome; 45,XO/47,XXX: *see* Turner syndrome; 46,XY/47,XXY: *see* 47,XXY, Klinefelter syndrome; 47,XXX syndrome: *see* 47,XXX syndrome, and XXX or X trisomy; 47,XXY syndrome: *see* 47,XXY, Klinefelter syndrome; 47,XYY syndrome: *see* XYY syndrome; 48,XXXX: *see* XXXX; 48,XXXY: *see* Klinefelter syndrome; 49,XXXXX: *see* XXXXX.

sex chromosome mosaic An individual with two or more groups of cells with different complements or combinations of the X (*qv*) and Y (*qv*) chromosomes. Individuals with sex chromosome mosaicism may have a variety of mosaic patterns depending on when the nondisjunction (*qv*) occurred in the individual's development, which cells are affected, and which of the abnormal cells are viable or lethal. Sex chromosome mosaics often have sexual abnormalities, but because of the sex hormones, the overall phenotype may be concordant.

sex-controlled *See* sex-influenced trait.

sex cord In the early embryonic development of the fetal gonads (*qv*) on the surface of the mesonephros (*qv*), fingerlike epithelial sex cords grow into the underlying mesoderm (*qv*), where they participate in the differentiation of the ovary (*qv*) and testis (*qv*). In embryos with an XX (*qv*) sex chromosome complement, the outer cortical layer develops into the ovary (*qv*) while the sex cords degenerate. In embryos with an XY (*qv*) sex chromosome complement, the sex cords differentiate into the seminiferous tubules (*qv*) while the cortex degenerates.

sex counselor (counseling) A trained professional who provides an opportunity for a client to discuss sexual concerns and obtain information and advice about sexual behavior and relationships. A sex counselor may deal with a general sexual problem (*qv*) such as inhibitions, fears, anxieties, and negative views of sexual intimacy, or with specific problems, such as erectile dysfunction (*qv*) or inhibited orgasm (*qv*). Persons with deeply rooted sexual dysfunctions may require the assistance of a sex therapist (*qv*) or psychologist. The American Association for Sex Educators, Counselors and Therapists (*qv*) provides training and certification for sex counselors and therapists. *See also* PLISSIT.

sex-derivative characteristics Male-female differentiated traits derived from or based on ovarian (*qv*) or testicular (*qv*) hormone differences, such as the male beard and the female breast (*qv*). *See also* gender coding, sex-derivative.

sex desire *See* libido.

sex (or gender) determination In biology, the process whereby an individual's genetic sex or gender (*qv*) is determined at fertilization (*qv*) by the union of a homogametic (*qv*) gamete (*qv*) with a heterogametic (*qv*) gamete. In human sex determination, the heterogametic male produces two kinds of sperm (*qv*), androsperms (*qv*) and gynosperms (*qv*). The homogametic female normally produces only one kind of egg with a single X (*qv*) chromosome and 22 autosomes (*qv*). The result of a normal sperm with an X or Y (*qv*) chromosome fertilizing a normal egg with an X chromosome yields a genetic female with 46,XX (*qv*) or a genetic male with 46,XY (*qv*). *See also* sex variables.

In some animals, genotypic sex determination prevails, with the sex of the offspring decisively determined by chromosomal mechanisms. In animals which are hermaphroditic (*qv*) or which change sex during their life span, sex appears to be influenced by environmental factors (e.g., temperature, the amount of yolk in the egg, and presence or absence of ethologically dominant (alpha) individuals. For the later stages of sex determination, *see* sex (or gender) differentiation; sex variables. Resource: C. R. Austin & R. G. Edwards, eds., *Mechanisms of Sex Differentiation in Animals and Man* (New York: Academic Press, 1981).

Reproductive technologists and animal breeders have been experimenting with ways of separating androsperm from gynosperm in order to bias the ratio in sex determination. *See also* sex selection.

sex differences Those characteristics that distinguish the sexes or genders. *See also* berdache; hijra; male; female; intersex; sex-irreducible characteristics.

sex (or gender) differentiation The gradual appearance over time of characteristics associated with male and female sexual anatomy, physiology, gender behavior, and social role. Biologically sex differentiation involves embryonic (*qv*) and fetal (*qv*) developmental processes which translate the chromosomal-genetic code, established at fertilization (*qv*) into the sexual anatomy of the male (*qv*), female (*qv*), or, more rarely, an intersex (*qv*), hermaphrodite (*qv*), or pseudohermaphrodite (*qv*). Psychologically sex (or gender) differentiation refers to the intrapsychic and interpersonal processes that create and strengthen the internal perception of one's self as male or female. In particular, psychoanalytic theory (*qv*) has built elaborate constructs of sexual differentiation. Sociologically sex differentiation pertains to how an individual adopts culture- and society-specific sexual norms, attitudes, behavior patterns, and beliefs, as well as pertaining to how societies themselves produce different roles (*qv*) for men and women. The literature on sex differentiation in each field is huge.

Synoptic theories of sex differentiation attempt to relate biological, psychological, and social processes into a single coherent description of how a newly fertilized human ovum (*qv*) finally becomes a sexually mature individual living and reproducing in a particular social milieu. *See also* sex variables.

sex discrimination Any prejudicial treatment of an individual or group based on gender. According to feminist theory, patriarchal biases in most societies make women the victims of sex discrimination, with fewer opportunities in the job market, less compensation for equal work, less opportunity for promotion or job tenure, less access to certain recreational facilities and clubs, and fewer educational opportunities. *See also* sexism; Title IX; Title X.

sex distribution *See* sex ratio.

sex doll A plastic or rubber life-sized, inflatable doll with somewhat exaggerated sexual anatomy, used as a substitute for a sexual partner. *See also* dildo, Sybian.

sex drive *See* libido.

sex during menstruation *See* sexual intercourse during menstruation.

sex during pregnancy *See* sexual intercourse during pregnancy.

sex education Cognitive and affective instruction in the biological, psychological, cultural, social, moral, and ethical aspects of human sexuality (*qv*) and human reproduction (*qv*). Formal sex education may be conducted by teachers in a school setting or by church organizations. Informal sex education is provided by parents, older siblings, or peers. Also referred to as *family life education*. *See also* Sex Information and Education Council of the United States.

sex experimentation Sexual activities engaged in by prepubescent (*qv*) children that seem to foreshadow adult sexual behavior and test the limits of parental and social acceptance. In adults, sexual activities seen as expanding an existing repertoire of pleasurable or arousing behavior. Developmental psychologists and sexologists (*qv*) have stressed that childhood sex experimentation or sex play is essential for developing normal adult sexual behavior. *See also* sex play; sexual rehearsal play.

After marriage (*qv*), sex experimentation is recommended by many sex therapists and counselors to enrich a satisfying sex life, as a way to remove inhibitions against acts that seem frightening or anxiety producing, and to revitalize a sexual relationship that has become routine. Sex experimentation can also lead to discovery of new and satisfying sexual outlets to those faced with paralysis, a stroke, an injury, arthritis, a heart attack, or muscular dystrophy, which radically alters one's self-image and makes previously satisfying outlets no longer possible.

sex fiend *See* erotophonophilia; sex maniac; lust murderer.

sex flush A temporary reddish rash or color change in the skin that sometimes develops in both men and women as a result of vasocongestion (*qv*) during the plateau stage (*qv*) of sexual arousal (*qv*). Sex flush usually begins on the abdomen and breasts (*qv*) before spreading to the neck, face, hands and soles of the feet as arousal increases.

sex glands *See* gonads; ovaries; testes.

sex history *See* sexual history.

sex hormones Steroid or protein biochemicals produced by endocrine glands (*qv*) and secreted directly into the blood that regulate or affect sexual-gender differentiation and both sexual and reproductive functions. A variety of steroid sex hormones are derived from cholesterol (*qv*), including the main categories of androgens (*qv*), estrogens (*qv*), and progestational hormones (*qv*). The primary synthesis of these sex steroids (*qv*) occurs in the ovaries (*qv*), testes (*qv*), and adrenal cortices (*qv*). Protein sex hormones include lactogenic hormone (*qv*) or prolactin, and the gonadotropins (*qv*)—follicle stimulating hormone (*qv*) and luteinizing hormone (*qv*)—which are produced by the anterior pituitary. Human chorionic gonadotropin (*qv*) is produced by the placenta (*qv*).

sex hospitality A social custom in which a wife has sexual relations (*qv*) with an unrelated traveling male. This custom is most commonly observed in Siberia, the Aleutian Islands, Alaska and among the Eskimos of northern Canada, although it also occurs in the South Pacific and Africa. The traditional interpretation of this custom has been that the claims of hospitality allow, even mandate, that the host welcome a traveling male and offer him sexual access to his wife, or in some cultures a daughter, for the night.

A recent anthropological perspective offers a quite different interpretation of this custom among Eskimos. The harsh climate and nomadic life of the Eskimos make cooperation and kinship (*qv*) ties essential for survival. In Eskimo society men and women are equal. Both men and women can initiate courtship (*qv*), request marriage (*qv*), and pass on property to designated children. But no Eskimo exists as an individual. Eskimos are defined by their relationships and kinship ties. Thus, a stranger who enters an iglo or village is, by definition, not a real person because he has no kin ties with the residents. Because he has no known kin or spirit, he is a threat to the residents' survival and must be killed. The only way he can be saved is if a member of the group invites him into the kinship group by marriage.

Marriage, for the Eskimos, is not an elaborate ritual as it is in other cultures. It requires only a simple act of sexual intercourse (*qv*). However, for the Eskimo, marriage is much more than the union of a man and woman; it is an admission to a kin network that reaches back to ancestors and beyond the grave into the future.

It was a liaison so permanent that no European could—or would—understand. Once made, it could not be broken, even by divorce or death. The husband of the hour, no matter how brief [the sexual encounter], was the husband for all time. If his wife left, and his children were motherless, the transitory wife must care for them, even if her own children had less to eat, or even if her husband of many years must work harder to provide for them. [The same obligation was taken on by the stranger in terms of supporting his transitory wife and her children should her husband die.] The spiritual tie was permanent, a bond that could be frivolous in times of plenty, or life-threatening in times of starvation, but lasting forever. The Europeans, who recorded stories of wife-lending, and often told their stories as if they had participated in the rites reluctantly, never recorded that they understood their obligations in this kinship tie.

Resource: C. Moyers Gove, Wife lending: Sexual pathways to transcendence in Eskimo culture, in G. Feuerstein, ed., *Enlightened Spirituality: Essays on Body-Positive Spirituality* (Freedom CA: Crossing Press, 1989), p. 269.

sex hygiene The science of maintaining health and preventing disease in the area of sexual activity (*qv*). *See also* safe sex.

sex-influenced trait A gene (*qv*) on an autosomal (*qv*) chromosome (*qv*) whose expression differs in males and females; an allele (*qv*) that, because of hormonal differences in males and females, behaves as dominant (*qv*) in one gender and as recessive (*qv*) in the other gender. Patterned baldness and gout are two common sex-influenced traits.

Sex Information Education Council of Canada (SIECCAN) A nonprofit education and advocacy organization whose goals are to promote, encourage and assist in public and professional education about sexuality (*qv*); to collect, disseminate and assess resource material and information relating to human sexual behavior (*qv*); and to organize and present professional education workshops and seminars on various aspects of sex education (*qv*), counseling, therapy, and research. SIECCAN publishes a journal and newsletter. Addresses: SIECCAN, 150 Laird Drive, Toronto M4G-3V7, Quebec, Canada; or SIECCAN, 326 Gainsborough Rd., Toronto M4L 3C6, Ontario, Canada. *See also* Sex Information and Education Council of the United States.

Sex Information and Education Council of the United States (SIECUS) A nonprofit education and advocacy organization founded in 1964 by Mary Calderone, a physician, and others to provide information on all phases of human sexuality (*qv*) to educators and students on all levels. SIECUS publishes a bimonthly, *SIECUS Report,* with state-of-the-art articles, reviews of books, and reports on audiovisual materials and educational aids. The SIECUS library, is an important resource for research in human sexuality. Address: 130 West 52nd Street, Suite 2500, New York, NY 10036. Resource: 25 years of SIECUS' commitment to sexual health and education, *SIECUS Report* 17(4) (March-April 1989). *See also* Sex Information and Education Council of Canada.

sexing-stealing-lying syndrome A condition in which forbidden or illicit sexual activity (*qv*) coexists with compulsive stealing or shoplifting and/or with glib deceptive stories or pseudologia fantastica.

sex-irreducible characteristics Primary male-female differences, specifically the male's ability to impregnate (*qv*) and the female's ability to ovulate (*qv*), menstruate (*qv*), gestate (*qv*), and lactate (*qv*). *See also* gender coding, sex-irreducible.

sexism (adj. sexist) Any pattern of prejudice or discrimination based on the assumed superiority of men or women who thus claim endowments, rights, status, and prerogatives greater than those allowed the other, allegedly inferior gender; also attitudes, behavior patterns, beliefs, and ideologies alleging the superiority of one sex over the other. *See also* sex discrimination; sex-stereotyped behavior; sex roles; Title IX; Title X.

sex-limited trait A trait controlled by an autosomal (*qv*) gene (*qv*) transmitted by both parents but expressed only in one gender (*qv*). Differential sex hormone (*qv*) balances in males and females regulate or limit the expression of such genes, such as female breast (*qv*) development and male facial hair. *See also* sex-influenced trait; sex-derivative characteristic; sex-linked trait.

sex-linked trait An inherited trait produced by a single gene carried on the X (*qv*) or Y (*qv*) chromosome. Sex-linked genes on the X chromosome are said to be X linked (*qv*). The few traits produced by genes on the Y chromosome are termed holandric (*qv*) because they appear only in males (andros) and never in females, who lack the Y chromosome (*qv*).

sex maniac A colloquial term, not used by professionals, for a person (usually male) who is preoccupied with sexual exploits and sexual pleasure. The term is variously applied to exhibitionists (*qv*), voyeurs (*qv*), fetishists (*qv*), Don Juans (*qv*), ''jocks,'' nymphomaniacs (*qv*), and sex addicts (*qv*), as well as those who engage in antisocial, violent sexual assault (*qv*) such as rape (*qv*) and lust murder (*qv*).

sex manual Handbooks and guides designed to impart information about human sexual behavior, sexual intercourse (*qv*), and reproduction (*qv*). Sex manuals have been popular in many cultures, regardless of whether these qualify as sexually permissive or sexually restrictive cultures. The earliest extant sex manuals are the *Art of Love* by the Roman Ovid (43 B.C.-c.17 A.D.), the fourth-century Hindu *Kama Sutra* (*qv*), the Renaissance sonnets of Pietro Aretino (*qv*), the fifteenth-century Indian *Ananga Ranga* (*qv*), the sixteenth-century Arabic *Perfumed Garden* (*qv*), and the more recent classic bridal rolls of the Japanese and pillow books of imperial China. In the Victorian era, the very popular *The Wife's Handbook* (1866) by Dr. Alcott was followed by Marie Stopes's *Married Love* (1918), importation of the latter being banned by American Customs officials. The first of the modern sex manuals to draw on the new findings of the emerging field of sexology was *Ideal Marriage* (1926) by the Dutch physician T. H. van de Velde (*qv*), followed by Hannah Stone and Abraham Stone's *The Marriage Manual* (1952). The epitome of American sex manuals is Alex Comfort's famous *Joy of Sex* (1972) and *More Joy* (1974).

sex mosaic *See* sex chromosome mosaic.

sex-negative A term describing a society's values, cultural attitudes, or religious traditions or a personal value system that takes a restrictive, repressive approach to sexual behaviors, often condemning any indulgence in sexual pleasure outside heterosexual (*qv*) marital (*qv*) and procreative (*qv*) intercourse. Sex-negative implies the belief that the sexual drive (*qv*) is a dangerous and potentially destructive force that must be suppressed, sublimated, or otherwise controlled in order to protect society. *See also* degeneracy theory; dualism; sex-positive; Stoicism; Puritanism; Victorianism.

sex object An animal or inanimate object that is the focus of sexual interest and attraction; a person who is depersonalized or objectified as the focus of sexual interest, attraction, and gratification. With the growth of the feminist (*qv*) movement and consciousness, the concept of a woman, or a man, being treated as a sex object has become a sensitive issue, leading often to resentment and angry rejection of the objectification.

sex offender An individual who engages in sexual acts that violate a criminal law. The seriousness of their criminality varies from voyeurism (*qv*) and exhibitionism (*qv*) to rape (*qv*) and lust murder (*qv*). In a developmental descriptive model, some sex offenders, termed deniers (*qv*), use sex as a violent means of overcompensating or denying their social and sexual inadequacy (*qv*) and to vent their frustration and anger resulting from an unresolved early sexual trauma (*qv*) by controlling and degrading their victims. Other sex offenders, termed acceptors (*qv*), use seduction (*qv*) as a way of compensating for their feelings of inadequacy and an unresolved early sexual trauma. The majority of convicted sex offenders are in their late teens or early twenties, with 50 to 60 percent unmarried.

sexologist A professional trained in the scientific study of human sexuality. *See also* sexology.

sexology As defined by the American College of Sexology, the interdisciplinary science of sex including its anatomical, physiological, psychological, medical, sociological, anthropological, historical, legal, religious, literary, and artistic aspects. John Money distinguishes sexology from sexosophy (*qv*), defining the former as the body of knowledge that comprises the science of sex, or more precisely, the science of the differentiation and dimorphism (*qv*) of sex (*qv*) and of the erotic-sexual pairbonding (*qv*) of partners. Sexology can be subdivided into genetic, morphologic, hormonal, neurohormonal, neuroanatomical, neurochemical, pharmacologic, behavioral, sociocultural, conceptive-contraceptive, gestational-parturitional, and parental sexology, with life span subdivisions of embryonic, fetal, infantile, child, pubertal, adolescent, adult, and geriatric sexology. Resource: J. Money, *Venuses Penuses* (Buffalo: Prometheus Books, 1986).

sexophobia A dread or fear of the sexual organs (*qv*) and anything that pertains to them.

sex (sexual) organs The genitalia (*qv*) or reproductive organs that make possible the union of ovum (*qv*) and sperm (*qv*). In the female, the external female sex organs are the vulva (*qv*), major and minor labia (*qv*), clitoris (*qv*), and vagina (*qv*). The internal female sex organs are the two ovaries (*qv*), the uterus (*qv*), and the paired fallopian tubes (*qv*). The external male sex organs are the penis (*qv*) and the scrotum (*qv*) containing two testes (*qv*). The internal male sex organs are the paired vasa deferentia (*qv*), seminal vesicles (*qv*), ejaculatory ducts (*qv*), spermatic cords (*qv*), prostate gland (*qv*), Cowper's glands (*qv*), and urethra (*qv*).

sexosophy That body of beliefs comprising the philosophy, principles, and convictions people have about their own personally experienced sexuality (*qv*) and that of other people, singly and collectively. Sexosophy includes personal and shared values, as well as culturally transmitted value systems. Its subdivisions are historical, regional, ethnic, religious, and developmental or life span. While sexology (*qv*) deals with scientific evidence, sexosophy deals with beliefs and dogmas. Resource: J. Money, *Venuses Penuses* (Buffalo: Prometheus Books, 1986).

sex play The sexual rehearsal play (*qv*) of children, such as playing "doctor-nurse and patient" or "mommy and daddy." Masturbatory activities (*qv*), colloquially described as "playing with oneself." Any erotic activity or loveplay (*qv*) that does not culminate in sexual intercourse (*qv*). The loveplay that precedes sexual intercourse. *See also* outercourse.

sex-positive An attitude and value judgment that sees sexual pleasure, sexual intimacy, and sexual relations in a positive light, as a very natural part of human life. The core of sex-positive attitudes is an acceptance of pleasure and the seeking of pleasure as a constructive rather than destructive force in the life of the individual and for society in general. *See also* dualism; Platonism; sex-negative; degeneracy theory; sexual conditioning; scripting.

sex prediction The ascertainment of the male or female status of a fetus (*qv*) before birth (*qv*). Sex prediction can be made by amniocentesis (*qv*) and chorionic villi sampling (*qv*) based on the fetal chromosome complement. Visual examination of the fetal genitalia (*qv*) is also possible using an ultrasound scan. Sex prediction is commonly confused in the popular mind with sex selection (*qv*).

sex ratio The ratio of males to females in a particular population at a particular time or for a particular age cohort. Natural selection tends to keep the numbers of males and females balanced for maximum reproduction. Since the human male is heterogametic (*qv*), males probably produce about equal numbers of androsperm (*qv*) and gynosperm (*qv*). However, at conception (*qv*), the sex ratio appears to be three males to two females. Since roughly one in three male fetuses miscarries, males only slightly outnumber females at birth—roughly about 106 males to 100 females.

By age 20, after traffic accidents, street violence, war, and substance abuse take their toll, the ratio is roughly equal. (Before the advent of antibiotics and automobiles, contagious diseases and war were factors in maintaining the balance.) Social factors, particularly war and migration, also alter the sex ratio. In ancient Sparta, sickly newborn males were killed because they would not grow up to be strong soldiers. Females were protected because they could produce more soldiers. In nearby Athens, female infanticide was common because women were of little value in that city-state.

In societies with a high sex ratio (i.e., a male surplus), the male-dominated political structure supports social norms and attitudes favoring marital stability, monogamy (*qv*), female virginity (*qv*), and sexual fidelity (*qv*) for women. Strong barriers prevent women from exploring alternative life-styles other than marriage (*qv*), from divorcing (*qv*) once they are married, and from challenging male dominance in any way. In societies with a low sex ratio, sexual permissiveness is more acceptable for both men and women. Multiple or successive relationships with different partners are acceptable, and sexual intimacy (*qv*) is not limited to the marital bed. Women may be less valued and protected, but they are also freer to explore independent lives and to seek intimacy in different life-styles. *See also* man shortage. Resources: M. Guttentag & P. Secord, *Too Many Women? The Sex Ratio Question* (Beverly Hills, CA: Sage, 1983); W. Novak, *The Great American Man Shortage And What You Can Do About It* (New York: Bantam Books, 1983).

sex reannouncement *See* sex reassignment.

sex (or gender) reassignment The legal, social, and/or surgical/hormonal reassignment or redesignation of an individual's sex-gender. Sex reassignment follows transsexual surgery (*qv*). *See also* sex change operation. *Sex reannouncement* is the proper term when an ambiguous genital (*qv*), intersex (*qv*), hermaphroditic (*qv*), or pseudohermaphroditic (*qv*) condition is resolved in a newborn or child.

sex reassignment operation (surgery) *See* sex change operation.

sex rehearsal play *See* sexual rehearsal play.

sex reversal *See* sex change operation; transsexualism.

sex ritual Any rite or ceremony prescribed by a society or religious tradition that celebrates or regulates sexual activities (*qv*). *See also* circumcision; communitas; female circumcision; Hindu coital positions; karezza; mikveh; superincision; subincision; Tantric love ritual; Tantric sexual traditions; Tao; Rite of the Five Essentials.

sex (or gender) role Patterns of behavior and thought that are culturally stereotyped as typical of or especially suited to one or the other gender. Some sex roles, such as child care and nurturance, are related to reproduction (*qv*); others are independent of the reproductive function (e.g., breadwinner and competitive body-contact sports for males). The concept of sex (gender) role is basic to many social scientific and psychological theories of gender development, personal erotosexual behaviors, and the maintenance of sex stereotypes (*qv*) in societies. *See also* androgyny; gender-identity/role; gender role; sexually dimorphic behavior.

sex role identification *See* sexual identity; gender role.

sex role inventory A psychological test in which the subject rates himself or herself on a variety of items related to sex roles (*qv*) to arrive at ratings of masculinity (*qv*), femininity (*qv*), androgyny (*qv*), or undifferentiated personality. *See also* BEM Sex Role Inventory.

sex role orientation *See* sexual identity; gender role; gender-identity/role.

sex role preference *See* gender role; gender identity.

sex role stereotypes *See* gender role; gender role sterotypes; sex role; sex-stereotyped behavior.

sex selection *See* sex determination; sex prediction.

sex-shared, threshold-dimorphic sex characteristics *See* gender coding, sex-shared threshold-dimorphic.

sex skin The preorgasmic deepening color of the minor labia (*qv*) in the human female during the plateau stage (*qv*).

sex-stereotyped behavior Patterns of behavior and thought that are culturally established as expectations especially suited to one or the other gender (*qv*). Some sex-stereotyped behaviors are related to reproduction (*qv*); others are independent of reproductive function. The latter behaviors are culturally dependent and may change rapidly in periods of social disruption or transition. A good example occurred in the 1960s, when a newly militant feminism (*qv*) challenged many stereotyped behaviors, such as the belief that women are more emotional or unpredictable than men, less interested in sports, and more nurturing than men. *See also* androgyny; gender-identity/role; gender role; sexually dimorphic behavior; sex roles; testeria.

sex steroids *See* steroids; sex hormones.

sex surrogate *See* sexual surrogate.

sex therapist A professionally trained person skilled in helping people resolve their sexual problems (*qv*) and overcome their sexual dysfunctions (*qv*) with a variety of therapeutic modalities including behavioral therapy (*qv*), psychotherapy (*qv*), biofeedback (*qv*), hypnosis, transactional analysis (*qv*), and psychoanalysis (*qv*). Many sex therapists and sex counselors (*qv*) are certified by the American Association of Sex Educators, Counselors, and Therapists (*qv*).

sex typing A typology of the behaviors, attitudes, emotions, and reactions that a society or culture (*qv*) considers appropriate and typical for the normal male or the normal female. *See also* sex roles; gender roles; sex role stereotypes.

sexual Of or pertaining to sex. As an adjective, sexual refers to the experience and expression of one's status and/or identity as a male (*qv*), female (*qv*), or other, particularly in terms of the genitalia (*qv*) or sex organs (*qv*), and reproduction (*qv*); any activity related to the stimulation, response, and functions of the sex organs. *See also* sex.

  See also multiple listings under *sex*, *sexual*, and *gender*. Because of varying preferences in ideology and constructs, what some refer to as *sex* or *sexual*, others define as *gender*. Thus, while some speak of *gender orientation*, the definition of this term is listed under the more common usage of *sexual orientation*. Similarly, *gender identity* may be the equivalent of *sexual identity*, and *sex* a synonym for *gender*. In this dictionary, we have listed such phrases under their more common usage.

sexual aberration Any sexual behavior that deviates from what a society considers normal (*qv*) or typical, usually with the connotation that the aberrant behavior is criminal or at least antisocial. *See also* deviance; paraphilia.

sexual abnormality *See* sexual aberration; deviance.

sexual abstinence *See* abstinence, sexual; celibacy; virginity.

sexual abuse The psychological exploitation of or infliction of unwanted sexual contact on a person or animal for the purpose of one's own sexual excitement (*qv*) and gratification (*qv*). Physical sexual abuse involves hands-on touching in a sexual way. The range of abusive behaviors may include sexualized hugging or kissing (*qv*), touching or fondling erogenous areas (*qv*) or the genitalia (*qv*), oral (*qv*) and anal sex (*qv*), masturbation (*qv*) of the victim or forcing the victim to masturbate the perpetrator, and sexual intercourse (*qv*). Overt sexual abuse involves voyeurism (*qv*) and exhibition (*qv*), inside or outside the victim's home. Parents and other adults engage in overt sexual abuse when they are sexually stimulated as a result of intruding on the privacy of children. Covert sexual abuse may be verbal, involving inappropriate sexual talk with children or strangers, or a boundary violation, in which the privacy of a child or unwilling adult is violated. Emotional sexual abuse results from inappropriate, sexual (*qv*) and cross-generational bonding in which a sexually dysfunctional (*qv*) adult uses a child to meet his or her emotional needs. Resource: J. Bradshaw, *Bradshaw On: The Family: A Revolutionary Way of Self-Discovery* (Deerfield Beach, FL: Health Communications, 1988). *See also* child abuse; child neglect; child sexual molestation; incest; rape; lust murder; erotophonophilia; sadomasochism; sadism; molestation.

sexual activity Any individual or mutually shared activity involving stimulation of the sexual organs (*qv*) for the purpose of enjoying the erotosexual (*qv*) pleasure that comes from such stimulation; *See also* masturbation; kissing; necking; petting; outercourse; oral sex; anal sex; vaginal intercourse.

sexual addict (addiction) *See* addiction, sexual.

sexual advances Any deliberate attempt to arouse sexual interest (*qv*) and desire in another person; flirting (*qv*) behavior ranging from nonverbal, indirect approaches (e.g., winking, smiling, and prolonged direct eye contact), to physical contact in squeezing the hand, caressing the face, and on to direct verbal invitations to sexual intimacy. *See also* flirtation; proceptivity; seduction.

sexual affinity An immediate, strong, and mutually shared sexual attraction experienced by two persons of the same or opposite genders. *See also* eros; ideal lover template; libido; limerence; love; pheromone.

sexual-aim rapist A rapist (*qv*) who is interested in satisfying his own sexual pleasure needs and not in degrading or forcing the victim any more than is necessary to have sexual intercourse (*qv*) with the unwilling victim. Such rapists often apologize after they have achieved orgasm (*qv*), and may have fantasies (*qv*) of their victim's falling in love with them because of their sexual skills; *See also* date rape; acquaintance rape.

sexual analism *See* anal intercourse.

sexual anesthesia A psychological condition in which the individual does not experience any subjective pleasure from stimulation of the genitalia (*qv*) and reflexogenic (*qv*) sexual arousal (*qv*). *See also* inhibited sexual arousal; inhibited sexual desire; inhibited sexual excitement; dyspareunia.

sexual apathy A lack of motivation or interest in sexual interaction and coitus (*qv*), despite the availability of a suitable partner. Little is known about the origins of sexual apathy, although a variety of possible causes has been suggested, ranging from genetic inborn factors to a suppressed and unresolved previous sexual trauma (*qv*) or painful experience, a monotonous and unimaginative view of sexual relations by one or both partners, decreasing cellular receptors for testosterone (*qv*), pressure from or preoccupation with family or business, depression, or chronic fatigue. *See also* sexual aversion.

sexual appetite *See* libido; sexual desire.

sexual asceticism *See* abstinence; celibacy; dualism; sex; Stoicism; Platonism; Puritanism; Victorianism.

sexual assault The use of physical force and/or psychological coercion to force a nonconsenting victim to engage in or observe sexual activity. *See also* date rape; exhibitionism; frottage; incest; marital rape; obscene phone caller; rape; sexual abuse; sexual harassment.

Sexual Attitude Reassessment (SAR) Workshop An intensive multimedia workshop designed to break down inhibitions about sexual matters, facilitate communication of sexual issues, and convey basic information about sexual matters. SAR workshops, lasting from one or two days to a week, include a sequence of film sessions, lectures, and group exercises in which the whole group participates with facilitators. Each large-group session is followed by a discussion period in small groups of 10 to 15 participants facilitated by a skilled group leader. Because of the anxiety-producing nature of sexual topics in our culture, sexually explicit educational and pornographic (*qv*) films are used to desensitize the participants by sensory overload. Systematic desensitization (*qv*) is aided by showing the films in a dimly lighted room that allows participants to watch the films while also observing and learning from the reactions of other participants in a relaxing, permission-giving environment.

Resensitization (*qv*) is accomplished in small-group discussions with skilled facilitators who draw out the participants' feelings and emotional reactions to the films, lectures, and exercises as a springboard for discussion of sexual topics that are commonly accompanied by anxiety and inhibitions. Also known as SAR, SAR Workshop, or Sexual Attitude Restructuring.

sexual attraction *See* sex appeal.

sexual aversion A severe phobic (*qv*) reaction in which a sexual situation or even the possibility of sexual involvement triggers an anxious avoidance in an individual, often with strong reactions of disgust, anger, sweating, and fear. *See also* sexual desire; sexual desire conflict; lack of sexual desire.

sexual avoidance *See* sexual aversion.

sexual awakening The psychological changes associated with puberty (*qv*) when romantic (*qv*) and erotic (*qv*) feelings accompany the maturation of the child's sexual anatomy and functioning. The use of this term is based on the assumption that the child experiences a period of total sexual latency (*qv*) in the years before puberty.

sexual conditioning The verbal and nonverbal messages parents and other authority figures give to children, thereby molding or conditioning their attitudes and values about sexual intimacy and behaviors. Also refers to gender roles (*qv*), gender role socialization (*qv*), and scripting (*qv*). Sexual conditioning is often used by authority figures to provide sex-negative (*qv*) messages based on the belief that the sexual drive is a dangerous and potentially destructive force which must be suppressed, sublimated, or otherwise controlled in order to protect society. *See also* dualism; degeneracy theory; socialization; Stoicism.

sexual defilement *See* asceticism; celibacy; dualism; degeneracy theory; Platonism; sex; Stoicism.

sexual desire A strong, even urgent desire or internally perceived need for sexual intimacy and coitus (*qv*). *See also* desire phase dysfunction; lack of sexual desire; libido; sexual aversion; sexual desire conflict; inhibited sexual desire.

sexual desire conflict A tension or discordance between two or more persons in a relationship about their desire for sexual intimacy and relations. A classic case of sexual desire conflict was expressed by the characters played by Woody Allen and Diane Keaton in the movie *Annie Hall*. When the therapist asked how often the couple had sex, Annie replied, ''All the time, at least three times a week,'' while Alfie replied, ''Hardly ever, barely three times a week.'' *See also* inhibited sexual desire; sexual aversion.

sexual disease *See* sexually transmitted disease; sexually related disease.

sexual disorder A sexual dysfunction (*qv*), sexual problem (*qv*), paraphilia (*qv*), sexually related disease (*qv*), sexually transmitted disease (*qv*), infertility (*qv*), abnormal development of the sexual organs, or a benign or malignant growth in one of the sexual organs (*qv*).

sexual display The endless variety of ways men and women have developed to enhance and exhibit their sexual features and attract a partner. For women, sexual display often relies on cosmetics, perfumes, accenting jewelry, hair fashions, ways of walking and gesturing, and above all clothing (e.g., plunging necklines, tight clothing, slit skirts, miniskirts, bikini bathing suits). For men, sexual display may rely on tight trousers, shirts, and bathing suits that emphasize the genitalia (*qv*). At various times in European and American history, codpieces (*qv*) have been popular with men as a form of sexual display. The macho (*qv*) category of sexual display includes men who engage in body building, display of their muscular building, leather fashions, and motorcycle riding. In preindustrial cultures, sexual display often involved tattooing, scarification, body piercing jewelry, depilation (*qv*), and genital-exaggerating displays such as the penis sheath (*qv*). *See also* Coolidge effect; courtship; flirtation; proceptivity; sex appeal.

sexual dissatisfaction A term used by William Masters and Virginia Johnson for a homosexual (*qv*) person who is unhappy with his or her sexual orientation (*qv*) and seeks therapy to become a heterosexual (*qv*).

sexual double standard Moral or social standards that set different expectations for men and women. *See also* double moral standard.

sexual dream A nocturnal dream (*qv*) about sexual activities (*qv*), erotic situations, symbols, or relationships which are remembered after the dreamer awakens but do not result in a nocturnal emission (*qv*) or, in the case of a female, in orgasm (*qv*). An alternate term for nocturnal emission (*qv*) in males. Although nocturnal emissions occur during rapid eye movement sleep, the normal period when one dreams, many men are not aware of the erotic dreams that accompany their nocturnal emissions. In Alfred Kinsey's (*qv*) data, only about 4 percent of American women reported having had orgasmic sexual dreams, and most of these were reported by sexually experienced women.

Sexual dreams often bring to the surface suppressed or forbidden activities or relationships, especially episodes of incestous (*qv*), homosexual (*qv*), or masochistic (*qv*) activity. The emergence of such taboo (*qv*) subjects in sexual dreams may be useful in analyzing an individual's sexual desires but of themselves do not mean that one actually wants to experience the taboo sexual behaviors while awake.

sexual drive Libido (*qv*); the personal and subjective desire or feeling of readiness for an erotosexual (*qv*) experience. Because sexual drive is subjective, it is not by itself a scientific term. In psychology, drive theories were at one time popular. Today however, sexologists avoid the concept of sexual drive.

sexual dwarf An adult dwarf whose genitalia (*qv*) are normally developed.

sexual dysfunction The inability to react emotionally and/or physically to sexual stimulation in a way expected of the average healthy person or according to one's own standards. Sexual dysfunctions may affect various stages in the sexual response cycle (*qv*)—desire, excitement, and orgasm (*qv*). They have a wide range of psychological, physiological, or combined origins and may be either primary (*qv*) or secondary (*qv*). Most men and women at one time or another experience some sort of sexual dysfunction. In one analogy common among sex therapists, sexual dysfunctions are said to be about as common as the common cold. Currently there is a trend to speak of sexual difficulties instead of sexual dysfunctions because of the negative or pejorative connotation of the latter term. *See also* desire phase dysfunction; sexual aversion; desire conflicts; lack of sexual desire; painful intercourse; vaginal spasms; inhibited orgasm; erectile dysfunction; premature ejaculation.

sexual ecstasy *See* orgasm; climax.

sexual energy *See* eros; libido; pleasure principle.

sexual ethics *See* sexual values; hot sex values; cool sex values; formal values; informal values; Piaget, Jean.

sexual excitement Any noticeable increase of sexual desire that results in or from a physiological response in the genitalia (*qv*). Sexual excitement can be triggered subconsciously during sleep and result in a nocturnal emission (*qv*) or female orgasm (*qv*). It also occurs consciously with fantasies (*qv*), masturbation (*qv*), sexual daydreams, and erotic thoughts. *See also* desire phase; excitement stage.

sexual exploitation The depersonalized use or taking advantage of another person for one's own sexual gratification (*qv*) or financial profit. Incest (*qv*), sexual molestation (*qv*) of children, and pimping (*qv*) are typical examples of sexual exploitation.

sexual failure *See* sexual dysfunction.

sexual fantasies *See* fantasy.

sexual favors Consensual sexual intimacies undertaken with the implied or overt expectation that the giver or recipient of such sexual favors will be rewarded.

sexual frustration The thwarting or blocking of sexual desire (*qv*) and gratification (*qv*) with a resulting sense of disappointment, tension, and possibly anger. Sexual frustration can arise from circumstances beyond one's control, such as a shortage of suitable partners (*see also* sex ratio), lack of opportunities for meeting suitable partners, or an occupation or situation that limits a heterosexually oriented person to meet with persons of the same gender, as in prison, on shipboard, or at military outposts. It can also result from sex-negative (*qv*) warnings, strict social or parental regulations of courtship (*qv*), restrictive moral precepts, and from a lack of self-identity and confidence that keeps one from approaching potential partners.

sexual fulfillment The sense of personal accomplishment, success, and sexual gratification (*qv*) following a rewarding sexual encounter.

sexual functioning *See* sexual response cycle; sexual dysfunction.

sexual games A broad term for activities that go beyond penile-vaginal intercourse, particularly if they involve homosexual (*qv*) relations, bondage and discipline (*qv*), dressing up (*see* cisvestism; transvestism), sadomasochism (*qv*), or group sex (*qv*). The word games implies that the activities are playful and not intended as serious denials of social norms or laws. However, when used pejoratively, *sexual games* can refer to psychological efforts to control another person's emotions and behavior by withholding sex. This meaning of the term is close to Eric Berne's meaning in his book *Games People Play*, in which a *game* is a very serious interaction that often involves unpleasant outcomes for one, both, or all players.

sexual gratification A general term often implying orgasm (*qv*) without specifying how the gratification is achieved.

sexual guilt Shame (*qv*) and guilt (*qv*) associated with behavior that violates one's personal values and standards of proper sexual behavior or the norms held by the religious or social group to which one belongs.

sexual harassment Any unwelcome or unsolicited sexual overture, request for sexual favors (*qv*), or other verbal or physical conduct of a sexual nature whose acceptance or rejection is explicitly or implicitly used as a condition for employment, recognition, promotion, or grades. Sexual harassment can also be charged when the conduct has the purpose or effect of unreasonably interfering with an individual's work or academic performance, when the conduct creates an intimidating, hostile, or offensive work or academic environment, or when one is treated unfairly because another person used sexual favors to gain an advantage. *See also* date rape; rape; sexual assault.

sexual history An interview technique developed by Alfred Kinsey (*qv*) in the 1940s to gather a complete profile of a person's sexual behavior and experiences. Kinsey's sexual history interview usually lasted about 2 hours and, depending on responses to key lead questions, contained between 300 and 521 questions. Kinsey's approach relied on the interviewer memorizing all questions and recording the answers on a single page. Information on nine general categories of sexual behavior was recorded, including social and economic data, a history of each marriage (*qv*), sex education (*qv*), physical and physiological data, nocturnal sexual dreams (*qv*), masturbation (*qv*), heterosexual (*qv*) activities history, homosexual (*qv*) activities history, and sexual contact with animals. In each of these categories, the interviewer could pursue the history in depth.

sexual humor A funny, amusing, ironical, or ludicrous account, joke, pun, or story with a sexual (*qv*) theme. Sexual humor, in contrast with nonsexual humor, is often prompted by an urge or need to defy social conventions or release repressed sexual desires (*qv*) in an indirect, safe way. *See also* erotic folklore. Resource: G. Legman, *Rationale of the Dirty Joke*, vol. 1 (New York: Grove Press, 1968); vol. 2 (New York: Breaking Point, 1975).

sexual hygiene Steps taken to ensure that the sexual organs (*qv*) and reproductive (*qv*) system remain healthy and functioning. Traditionally, the term *sex* or *sexual hygiene* has been applied only to women. However, with a growing awareness of health issues, men in their teens and twenties are now advised to include a monthly self-examination of the penis (*qv*) and testes (*qv*). Penile-testicular cancer (*qv*) is the most common solid tumor in younger males. Annual prostate (*qv*) and rectal (*qv*) examinations are recommended for men over 50. Although breast cancer (*qv*) is rare in men, some men's health organizations recommend a monthly breast self-examination (*qv*).

For women, sexual hygiene involves regular attention to maintaining cleanliness during menstruation (*qv*), avoiding conditions that favor toxic shock syndrome (*qv*), a monthly breast self-examination (*qv*), an annual or semiannual gynecological examination (*qv*) with Pap tests (*qv*) and mammograms (*qv*) as medically recommended. Also recommended are regular washing of the genitalia (*qv*) with water and a mild, non-perfumed soap to remove smegma (*qv*) in the male and to cleanse normal vaginal (*qv*) and vulvar (*qv*) secretions in the female.

For sexually active persons, practical knowledge of contraceptive methods (*qv*) and use of an effective contraceptive when pregnancy (*qv*) is not desired are important. Also important are a practical knowledge of the symptoms and treatment of sexually related diseases (*qv*), taking precautions to reduce the risk of contracting sexually transmitted diseases (*qv*), and the use of safer sex (*qv*) guidelines with a prompt medical check-up for any unusual discharge, lump, sore, or bleeding in the urogenital (*qv*) organs. *See also* social hygiene; social purity movement.

sexual (or gender) identity A person's internalized conviction of his or her own gender (*qv*) status as a male (*qv*) or female (*qv*). Sexual identity is used by various authorities as a synonym for gender identity (*qv*), sex or gender role (*qv*), sex or gender role preference (*qv*), sex or gender role identification (*qv*), or sexual or gender orientation (*qv*)—heterosexual (*qv*), homosexual (*qv*), or bisexual (*qv*). In the classification suggested by Richard Green, sexual identity is synonymous with gender identity and contains three components: (1) core-morphologic identity or anatomic sexual identity, (2) gender-role behavior or sex-typed masculine and feminine behavior, and (3) sexual or gender orientation, sexual partner preference or sexual object choice. *See also* gender-role/identity. Resource: R. Green, *The "Sissy Boy Syndrome" and the Development of Homosexuality* (New Haven: Yale University Press, 1987).

sexual inadequacy Any degree of sexual response insufficient to meet the demand of the moment; this may be primary or constant inadequacy or a transitory, occasional deficiency in response and performance. *See also* sexual dysfunction.

sexual incompatibility The inability or unwillingness of two persons to reach agreement and compromise by adjusting their sexual desires, needs, and agendas. When such differences cannot be accommodated, the relationship is no longer rewarding, or viable. Sexual incompatibility commonly results from conflicting differences in sexual desire (*qv*), from emotional inhibitions, prejudices, and sex-negative (*qv*) attitudes, from conflicting expectations about the frequency of sexual activity (*qv*), and from conflicting interests in particular sexual activities such as oral (*qv*) or anal sex (*qv*), fetishistic (*qv*) behavior, bondage and dominance (*qv*), or cross-dressing (*qv*).

sexual infantilism The dysfunctional (*qv*) avoidance of sexual expressions associated with adult sexual intimacy (*qv*), particularly intercourse (*qv*), and a preference for sensual or erotic activities more characteristic of children, such as kissing (*qv*) and hugging. Some experts consider fetishes (*qv*) and voyeurism (*qv*) as expressions of sexual infantilism. *See also* autonepiophilia; adolescentilism; ephebophilia; infantilism, paraphilic; juvenilism; nepiophilia; pederasty; and pedophilia.

sexual inhibition A subconscious, involuntary suppression of sexual desires (*qv*) and needs. Sexual inhibitions may be due to sex-negative (*qv*) messages from parents and authority figures that associate guilt and shame with sexual behavior, fear of failure, lack of experience, or childhood abuse (*qv*) or trauma (*qv*).

sexual instincts The allegedly innate, unlearned drives and behavioral patterns for proceptivity (*qv*), acceptivity (*qv*) or receptivity (*qv*), conceptivity (*qv*), and parenting, that ensure reproduction (*qv*) sufficient to allow survival of a species. In psychoanalytic theory (*qv*), sexual instincts refers to all expressions of eros (*qv*) and the pleasure principle (*qv*) in the anal (*qv*), oral (*qv*), phallic (*qv*), and genital stages (*qv*). According to Sigmund Freud (*qv*), eros or the sexual instincts are often sublimated, leading to creativity in the arts, business, and scientific pursuits. There is considerable disagreement over the use and meaning of the term *instinct* (*qv*), and the terms is no longer used in an explanatory way in modern sexology. *See also* drive; sexual drive.

sexual insults Derogatory language directed at an individual or group and attributing socially disapproved sexual or personal attributes or habits such as filthy or inappropriately large-sized genitals, incestuous (*see* incest) or promiscuous (*see* promiscuity) behavior, illegitimate parentage, or preference for unusual sexual partners (same gender [*qv*], animals, children, or even inanimate objects). The insults may be applied directly to the person or to the person's ancestors, particularly the mother (*qv*). Cultures and languages differ in the thematic locus of the preferred insult forms, with some emphasizing sexual forms; others, scatological forms; and still others, the profane use of religious terms. The most common sexual insults in English are *motherfucker* and *cocksucker*. Resource: *Maledicta: The International Journal of Verbal Aggression*.

sexual intercourse *See* coitus; intercourse; loveplay; outercourse.

sexual intercourse during menstruation Although some cultures have strong menstrual taboos (*qv*), William Masters and Virginia Johnson found that only about 10 percent of American women find sexual intercourse (*qv*) during menstruation (*qv*) distasteful or objectionable. Both aesthetic and religious reasons are cited for avoiding menstrual intercourse. Masters and Johnson also found that masturbation may relieve cramps associated with menstruation. Resource: J. Delaney, M. J. Lupton and E. Toth, *The Curse: A Cultural History of Menstruation* (New York: New American Library Mentor, 1976).

sexual intercourse during pregnancy Modern medical opinion encourages pregnant (*qv*) women to continue their usual sexual relations (*qv*) until a week or so before expected delivery (*qv*) unless complications in the pregnancy or a tendency to miscarriage (*qv*) are encountered. As the pregnancy approaches term (*qv*), the couple may find it advisable to use coital positions (*qv*) that do not press on the abdomen or otherwise cause pain for the woman. Oral sex (*qv*) and other noncoital activities seldom pose any danger for the pregnant woman. *See also* outercourse.

sexuality The personal experience and expression of one's status as a male (*qv*) or female (*qv*). While the sexuality is often defined in terms of courtship (*qv*), pairbonding (*qv*), the function of the genitalia (*qv*) and reproduction, sexuality involves all aspects of one's personality and behavior that reflect and are affected by one's being male or female. *See more complete definitions under* sex; sexual.

sexualization In psychoanalytic theory (*qv*), the association of various parts of the body and their activities with sexual energy (*qv*) and sexuoerotic responses; the sublimation (*qv*) of sexual energy in nonsexual activities such as business and the creative arts. Sexualization as a social phenomenon refers to the appearance of sexual themes and material in nonerotic contexts such as advertising.

sexual liberation A social trend or shift away from repressive or restrictive sexual mores towards more sex-positive (*qv*) social standards that accept sexuality (*qv*) and sexual pleasure. The basic idea of sexual liberation is to treat a wide range of consensual sexual expressions as positive rather than destructive to the individual and society. The term also refers to the breakdown of phallocentrism (*qv*), patriarchalism (*qv*), and heterosexism (*qv*).

The shift from repressive Victorian (*qv*) standards to the more tolerant and permissive attitudes of the 1920s marked an earlier period of sexual liberation in this century. In the 1960s and 1970s, a second era of sexual liberation occurred with the advent of oral contraceptives (*qv*), women's liberation (*qv*), and gay liberation (*qv*). Researchers such as Albert Moll (*qv*), Sigmund Freud (*qv*), Havelock Ellis (*qv*), Magnus Hirschfeld (*qv*), Krafft-Ebing (*qv*), Margaret Sanger (*qv*), Marie Stopes (*qv*), Robert Latou Dickinson (*qv*), Alfred Kinsey (*qv*), and, in the 1960s, the team of William Masters and Virginia Johnson, have played major roles in setting the stage for recent sexual liberation, as did increasingly sexualized publications of the *Playboy/Penthouse* type. *See also* sexual revolution; free love.

sexual life-style The pattern of sexual expression and relationships a person develops as he or she matures and adjusts to his or her sexual or gender orientation (*qv*) and the need for emotional support, intimacy, and sexual gratification (*qv*). Sexual life-styles vary greatly in their profiles and in what types of behavior and relationships are judged acceptable. Fundamentalist religious groups tend to prohibit any sexual indulgence outside marriage (*qv*) and endorse only heterosexual (*qv*) relationships. In more permissive traditions, sexual life-styles may include acceptance of masturbation (*qv*), oral sex (*qv*), anal sex (*qv*), contraception (*qv*), abortion (*qv*), tolerance or even endorsement of premarital sex (*qv*), flexibility in the sexual and/or emotional exclusivity (*qv*) of marriage, homosexual (*qv*) and lesbian (*qv*) relationships, and an acceptance of divorce (*qv*) and remarriage (*qv*). *See also* domestic partner; gay liberation.

sexual love *See* courtly love; eros; platonic love.

sexually dimorphic behavior Behavior that is different in males and females; behaviors that distinguish one sex (*qv*) or gender (*qv*) from the other. *See also* gender roles; sex roles; sex role stereotypes.

sexually closed marriage A marriage (*qv*) in which both spouses freely accept sexual exclusivity and the obligation to limit their sexual relations to each other. *See also* monogamy; sexual monogamy; sexually open marriage; open marriage; closed marriage.

sexually open marriage (SOM) A marriage (*qv*) in which both spouses freely and openly accept the possibility of sexual relationships with individuals other than their spouse. *See also* communitas; intimate network; satellite relationship; open marriage; closed marriage.

sexually related disease (SRD) Any disease of the sexual organs that may be transmitted or develop from causes other than sexual relations (*qv*). Certain diseases of the sexual and reproductive systems, such as yeast infections, qualify as SRDs because they can result from nonsexual causes like diabetes, or hormonal disturbances that disrupt the natural balance of microorganisms in the vagina. *See also* sexually transmitted disease.

sexually transmitted disease (STD) A disease transmitted by genital intimacy with a partner; previously known as venereal disease (*qv*) or VD. Historically, STDs have been among the best known and most frightening of contagious diseases. Often, such diseases were given colloquial names, such as "the great pox" for syphilis (*qv*), in contrast to "small pox," a childhood disease. Other STDs include gonorrhea (*qv*), notable perhaps because it is easy to misspell and for its drastic effects on both the male and female urogenital systems, and a disease which has become infamous, acquired immune deficiency syndrome (*qv*). Often these diseases affect the sexual organs first but then spread to nongenital regions; for example, tertiary syphilis spreads to the spinal cord and brain. In women, undetected and untreated STDs can cause sterility.

Considerable effort has been expended by medical microbiologists, epidemiologists, physicians, and other health care professionals to treat and reduce the spread of STDs, especially to young people. Educational programs are particularly important because in recent years concern over the STDs has lessened with the dramatic effects of antibiotics. The appearance of viral STDs such as herpes (*qv*) and AIDS has reawakened the once rampant fears of disease transmitted sexually. *See also* sexually related disease; candida; chancroid; condyloma; granuloma; hemophilus; lymphogranuloma; non-gonococcal urethritis; pubic lice; scabies; and trichomonas.

sexual masochism A paraphilic condition or variant form of sexual behavior in which an individual is dependent on experiencing pain and humiliation intentionally inflicted by another person in order to achieve sexual arousal (*qv*) and orgasm (*qv*). *See also* masochism; sadism; sadomasochism.

sexual melancholia An obsolete term for a state of depression in a man resulting from the belief that he is becoming impotent (*qv*). Also known as bipolar disorder.

sexual minority A term referring to individuals or groups whose sexual orientation (*qv*), sexual preferences (*qv*), or sexual behaviors are considered different from stereotypes of what is thought to be normative heterosexual (*qv*) activity, namely, "vanilla sex" (*qv*). The term may refer to self-identified groups, such as gay (*qv*) or lesbian (*qv*) activist organizations, which speak of themselves as minorities in order to stress the civil rights aspects of their quest for full respect in a society they perceive as hostile to them.

sexual monogamy A sexually exclusive marriage (*qv*) of one man and one woman with no sexual relations (*qv*) permitted outside the marital union.

sexual mosaic An individual whose body tissues contain cells with two distinct complements of sex chromosomes (*qv*)— that is, with two cell lines, one male (46,XY) (*qv*) and the other female (46,XX) (*qv*)—or some other combination of multiple normal and/or abnormal male and female chromosome contents. *See also* sex chromosome mosaic.

sexual myths Misconceptions, folklore, fallacies, and superstitions about sexual behavior. J. McCary's *Sexual Myths and Fallacies* (New York: Van Nostrand Reinhold, 1971) is the most complete listing of sexual myths. Typical examples of such myths include: wet dreams (*qv*) are a sign of mental instability; menstruating (*qv*) women should not engage in sports; blacks have a greater sex drive (*qv*) than whites; alcohol is a sex stimulant; sterilization (*qv*) reduces a man's sex drive; sexual intercourse (*qv*) during pregnancy (*qv*) is dangerous; early menstruation means an early menopause (*qv*); a woman who swallows semen (*qv*) can become pregnant; you can't become pregnant having sex while standing up; douching with cola soda is a good contraceptive (*qv*); homosexuals (*qv*) are a menace to society; frequent masturbation (*qv*) leads to insanity.

sexual negativism Magnus Herschfeld's (*qv*) term for sexual apathy (*qv*) or a lack of sexual desire (*qv*), due possibly to a hormone imbalance.

sexual neuroses Emotionally disturbed, neurotic symptoms and behavior related to sexuality (*qv*). Sexual phobias (*qv*), fears, anxieties, compulsive behaviors, extreme preoccupations, morbid fears, and excessive feelings of shame (*qv*) and guilt can arise from deeply embedded emotional conflicts and tensions that have not been confronted and resolved.

sexual norms Standards endorsed by a society, group, or individual as determining what is acceptable and unacceptable in sexual behavior (*qv*) and relationships. *See also* sexual values; norms.

sexual oralism *See* oral sex.

sexual orientation A pattern of sexual attraction and limerence (*qv*) based on the gender (*qv*) of one's partners; heterosexual (*qv*) orientation leading to partners of the other gender, homosexual (*qv*) orientation to partners of the same gender, and bisexual (*qv*) orientation to partners of both genders. *See also* gender orientation. One view is that sexual orientation is established as a neurobiological tendency before birth and that this tendency is then elaborated on and confirmed or modified by postnatal social and sexual experiences, especially in the prepubertal (*qv*) years. Other views point to purely genetic determinants, or to childhood scripting and social learning. There is currently considerable debate over these views.

sexual orientation disturbance An obsolete psychiatric term for a condition in which a person with a homosexual (*qv*) or bisexual (*qv*) orientation is emotionally disturbed by this orientation. The current term is ego-dystonic (*qv*) homosexuality.

sexual orientation grid A two-dimensional scale or grid designed by Fred Klein to describe sexual orientation (*qv*) in terms of seven factors and three time frames. The seven factors are sexual attraction (*qv*), sexual behavior (*qv*), fantasies (*qv*), emotional preference, social preference, life-style, and self-identification. These are arranged on the vertical axis of the grid, while the horizontal axis is broken into the time frames of 5 years ago, the current year, and ideal or future goal. An individual can rate himself or herself in each of the 21 boxes, using the 0–6 rating criteria of the Kinsey Six Scale (*qv*). The total sum of the 21 ratings is then divided by the number of ratings to give an overall sexual orientation rating from 0 to 6. The divisor will be less than 21 if one or more boxes is not given a rating. Resource: F. Klein & T. J. Wolf, eds., *Bisexualities: Theory and Research* (New York: Haworth Press, 1985).

sexual outlet A term coined by Alfred Kinsey (*qv*) to refer to various sources of orgasm (*qv*).

sexual pathology In its scientific meaning, sexual aberrations and disorders. Sexual aberrations can be psychological—such as sadism (*qv*), masochism (*qv*), sexual dysfunctions (*qv*), and paraphilias (*qv*)—or congenital (*qv*) and developmental disorders such as Turner syndrome (*qv*), Klinefelter syndrome (*qv*), hermaphroditism (*qv*), pseudohermaphroditism (*qv*), intersexes (*qv*), adrenogenital syndrome (*qv*), and androgen insensitivity syndrome (*qv*). In the early 1900s, much of the research by pioneers such as Sigmund Freud (*qv*), Richard von Krafft-Ebing (*qv*), and Albert Moll (*qv*) focused on sexual pathology rather than on the normal expressions of sexuality (*qv*). *See also* sexual anomaly.

sexual permissiveness The belief or view that sexual activity (*qv*) between consenting adults should be as free as possible from government regulations and laws and other forms of social interference. A belief in sexual permissiveness is rooted in the conviction that sexual expression and pleasure are natural and good rather than the expression of some demonic, destructive urge that needs to be controlled and regulated for the good of society. Those who advocate sexual permissiveness seldom advocate or would tolerate elimination of social controls on pedophilia (*qv*), incest (*qv*), rape (*qv*), lust murder (*qv*), or the extreme of sadomasochist (*qv*) practices in which real physical or psychological damage is done. The term *permissiveness* has a culturally pejorative overtone in American society. *See also* degeneracy theory; promiscuity.

sexual perversion Any sexual behavior, orientation, preference, or life-style at odds with the norms (*qv*) and values of a society. *See also* deviance; paraphilia.

sexual phobia An intense, morbid fear about sexual behavior (*qv*), sexual relations (*qv*), or objects associated with sex. Sexual phobias are often the origin of different sexual dysfunctions (*qv*). *See also* Appendices A and B.

sexual precocity Premature sexual maturation; the premature development of the secondary sexual characteristics (*qv*) that usually accompany puberty (*qv*) and the teen years. Sexual precocity can be triggered by gonadal (*qv*) or adrenal (*qv*) tumors, or brain lesions that alter the production of gonadotropins (*qv*) by the hypothalamus (*qv*) and anterior pituitary (*qv*). The term is also applied to sex rehearsal play (*qv*) engaged in by prepubertal (*qv*) youths, or even adolescents (*qv*). *See also* adrenogenitalism; premature puberty.

sexual preference The sexual attraction (*qv*) for a particular type of person, erotic stimulus, object, or situation. When used as a synonym for sexual or gender orientation (*qv*), *sexual preference* is misleading since it implies that such orientation is no more than a casual preference that can be lightly taken on or discarded rather than an intrinsic part of one's sexual being.

sexual preoccupation An intense, often obsessive, and even morbid interest in or concern about sex (*qv*) and sexual (*qv*) matters. It is commonly suggested that, both for individuals and for cultures (*qv*) as a whole, sexual preoccupation is more typical of sexually restrictive cultures where sex and sexual matters carry a negative connotation. In more permissive cultures, sexual matters are taken more in a positive, natural, and therefore less attention-getting context. *See also* prudery; Stoicism; Victorianism.

sexual primordial reaction A tendency to immediately appraise a person sexually upon meeting him or her.

sexual problem A condition in which a person is not sexually dysfunctional (*qv*) but feels uneasy, uncomfortable, or guilty about his or her sexual behavior or has a communication problem with his or her mate; always psychological in origin.

sexual problem history A brief interview and screening technique consisting of five questions designed to obtain essential information about a person's specific sexual dysfunction (*qv*) as a basis for treatment. The brief sexual problem history focuses on (1) the nature of the presenting problem, (2) its origins, (3) its course or history, (4) previously attempted treatment, and (5) the goals of the person seeking treatment.

sexual proceptivity *See* proceptivity.

sexual psychopath Generally a person whose sexual behavior is so compulsive, repetitive, and often so bizarre that the person is considered a threat to society. This term is not a psychiatric diagnosis and its definition varies depending on the legal jurisdiction and on the speaker's viewpoint.

sexual reassignment *See* sex change operation; sex reassignment; transsexual.

sexual receptivity *See* acceptivity; conceptivity; proceptivity; receptivity.

sexual reflex In males, a reflexive, automatic response to tactile or mental stimulation resulting in penile erection (*qv*). In females, the sexual reflex results in vasocongestion (*qv*) and vaginal lubrication (*qv*). Also refers to the reflexive response of orgasm; *see* reflexogenic arousal.

sexual regression A phenomenon occurring in the second and third months of embryonic life when the bisexual (*qv*) potential of the internal sexual anatomy differentiates into the male or female path, with the regression of the Wolffian ducts (*qv*) in the female fetus (*qv*) and regression of the Mullerian ducts (*qv*) in the male fetus. *See also* Adam Plan; Eve Plan.

sexual rehabilitation The restoration of an individual to normal sexual functioning as a result of therapy for a sexual dysfunction (*qv*), counseling for a sexual trauma (*qv*) such as rape (*qv*) or incest (*qv*), or supportive advice and counseling for a person with a physical disability.

sexual rehearsal play Activities, motions, and positions, including presenting (*qv*), coital positioning, and pelvic thrusting (*qv*), spontaneously occurring as part of the play of human and nonhuman infants and juveniles. Sexual rehearsal play is a essential component of and prerequisite to a healthy sexuoerotic (*qv*) maturity in primates. *See also* sex rehearsal play; sex experimentation. With regard to the sexual rehearsal play of children, some believe that repression of this developmental experience can traumatize the normal lovemap (*qv*) and lead to sexual dysfunction (*qv*) or paraphilic (*qv*) behavior later in life.

sexual rejuvenation The restoration of youthful sexual vigor to an older person. A wide variety of aphrodisiacs (*qv*), animal testicle (*qv*) transplants, hormone (*qv*) injections, and drugs have been promoted as producing sexual rejuvenation, all without substantiated evidence. The most famous of these was Eugen Steinach's (*qv*) so called monkey gland treatment. *See also* Voronoff, Serge; Welbrutin; Exsativa.

sexual relations A general term for a sexually intimate relationship between two or more persons. *See also* adultery; carnal knowledge; coitus; oral sex; anal sex; fornication; heterosexual; bisexual; homosexual; premarital; extramarital; marital; comarital; intimate friendship.

sexual repression The restriction of certain sexual activities by means of social standards and values that view sexual energies as powerful and dangerous and therefore as requiring suppression either by taboos (*qv*) whose violation shames (*qv*) oneself and one's kin or by laws that emphasize guilt (*qv*) and punishment for any violation. In the psychoanalytic model (*qv*), sexual repression is a defense mechanism in which unacceptable sexual thoughts, desires, and impulses are pushed from the conscious mind because of the anxieties, shame, or guilt they produce. *See also* degeneracy theory; dualism; Platonism; Puritans; Stoicism; Victorianism.

sexual response cycle The cycle or stages of physiological and psychological changes males and females experience during sexual stimulation (*qv*) and gratification (*qv*), moving from a state of dormant sexual interest to sexual desire (*qv*), sexual arousal (*qv*), the release of sexual tension in orgasm (*qv*), and a return to the resting state where sexual interests are more or less quiescent. In 1942, Wilhelm Reich (*qv*) first proposed the division of the human sexual response cycle into four phases: (1) mechanical tension, (2) bioelectric charge, (3) bioelectric discharge, and (4) mechanical relaxation.

In the 1960s, William Masters and Virginia Johnson studied the reactions of muscles, blood pressure, pulse, respiration, sweating, and other physiological measures that occur during this cycle. They then gave Reich's four stages new names, which are now standard: the excitement (*qv*), plateau (*qv*), orgasm, and resolution (*qv*). Zilbergeld and Ellison have criticized this model for ignoring two important subjective factors: sexual desire and arousal. They suggested a five-phase model: (1) interest or desire; (2) arousal; (3) physiological readiness (erection and vaginal lubrication [*qv*]); (4) orgasm; and (5) satisfaction. Helen Singer Kaplan emphasized the role of sexual desire in a three-phase cycle of sexual desire, sexual arousal (excitement and plateau), and orgasm. Kaplan ignored the resolution stage because it is of no consequence in sexual therapy. David Reed, a psychologist at Jefferson Medical College in Philadelphia, has suggested an integration of these various insights to complete the psychological side and stress the connection between the physiological and psychological dimensions of our sexual responses. Resources: W. R. Stayton, A theology of sexual pleasure, *American Baptist Review* (8:2) (1989):94–108; W. Reich, *The Function of the Orgasm* (New York: Noonday, 1942). *See also* Erotic Stimulus Pathway model; Appendix E.

sexual response time The time from the onset of sexual contactor stimulation until orgasm (*qv*). This time varies greatly among individuals of both sexes, within the life span of an individual, and in different sexual encounters.

sexual revolution A relatively rapid and widespread shift in sexual attitudes, behavior, and values toward more permissive (*qv*), liberal standards, or to more restrictive and conservative standards. Two sexual revolutions are commonly identified in twentieth-century American culture. The first, following the demise of Victorian (*qv*) standards, was promoted by the social realignment, economic prosperity, and liberal politics after World War I, in the "roarin' twenties" and "flapper era." Factors in this revolution were new sexual values, more liberal norms for women, increasing education for women, a growing economic independence of women, increased effectiveness of contraceptives (*qv*), and the exposure of young Americans to more liberal European attitudes.

A second sexual revolution is commonly identified in the 1960s and 1970s. It started with long-range social changes brought on by World War II, especially exposure of young Americans to more permissive sexual values in the Orient and South Pacific. Among the major factors contributing to the sexual revolution of the 1960s and 1970s were the accelerating economic and political liberation of women, the advent of the contraceptive pill (*qv*) in the 1960s, individualism and alterations in family (*qv*) structure, growing tensions in dual-career families leading to increased divorce (*qv*), increased social mobility, a reduction in the size of the family and the number of children married couples wanted, an increase in sexual opportunities for men and women alike, the emergence of teenagers as a subculture with an identity of their own as consumers and leisure to explore their budding sexual energies and interests, the advent of rock music, the permission-giving publicity of alternate life-styles by television talk shows, the resurgence of feminism (*qv*) and the women's movement (*qv*), the advent of gay liberation (*qv*), and the civil rights movement.

In some respects, the effects of this latest sexual revolution have been greater for women than for men, with women adopting the sexual freedoms and values traditionally enjoyed by males, while male behaviors and, to some extent, attitudes have remained relatively stable. *See also* free love; sexual liberation.

sexual rights In America's post-liberation era, the individual's right to sexual self-expression, choice of sexual partner and orientation (*qv*), and choice of marriage (*qv*) or other life-style (*qv*). As used in anthropology and cross-cultural studies, sexual rights usually refer to the right of sexual access of a male to women other than his wife, such as the right to have sexual intercourse with a brother's wife. *See also* conjugal rights; jus primae noctis; levirate.

sexual sadism *See* masochism; sadism; sadomasochism.

sexual script A cultural script (*qv*) whose goal is to enhance, reduce or permit sexual arousal (*qv*) under acceptable conditions; an individual's unique set of attitudes, expectations, and values regarding sexual behavior, emotions, and relationships. A sexual script is the result of an individual's unique response to the scripting for attitudes, values, and expectations rooted in his or her ethnic, racial, and religious culture, as well as the ongoing scripting (*qv*) received from family, peers, and society. In fundamentalist cultures, sexual scripts tend to be relatively stable and intolerant of deviations. In less conservative cultures or subcultures, sexual scripts tend to be more inclusive, permissive, and flexible. *See also* gender role; stereotypes; socialization.

sexual selection In Darwinian evolutionary theory, sexual selection refers to preferential mate choice, usually made by the female, of only certain partners from a larger group of potential mates. In the theory, characteristics can evolve that have reduced survival value, but are retained in the species because they enhance the possessor's reproductive (*qv*) potential. Examples are the greatly enlarged antlers of the now extinct Irish elk and the peacock's tail.

In recent years, sexual selection theory has been dominated by the concept of parental investment and the possibility that males and females have different reproductive strategies that can bring them into conflict. It is not clear how important sexual selection has been in human evolution, nor if it is operating today.

sexual senescence *See* menopause; climacteric.

sexual standards *See* sexual norms; formal values; informal values.

sexual surrogate A member of a therapy team who teaches social and sexual skills by serving as a partner for the patient and assisting him or her in carrying out the clinician's suggestions for somatosensory (*qv*) exercises. Also known as body-work therapists or sex surrogates. The professional standards and ethics of sexual surrogates are regulated by the International Professional Surrogates Association (*qv*). *See also* surrogate therapy.

sexual synergism Sigmund Freud's (*qv*) term for the combined effect of different, sometimes contradictory, pleasant and unpleasant stimuli, such as love and hate, pleasure and pain, interest and fear, coming together to produce sexual arousal (*qv*) and excitement (*qv*).

sexual taboo Any relationship, behavior, word, or symbol related to sexuality (*qv*) prohibited by general public consensus or by religious proscription in a particular society. Incest (*qv*) is often cited as the most universal taboo (*qv*), but the meaning of incest and other forbidden relationships varies in different cultures, so that a culture that does not view first-cousin or sibling marriage as incest may have a strong taboo against other marriages within the kinship (*qv*) or clan (*qv*).

Menstrual taboos (*qv*) are perhaps the next most common sexual taboo. In Orthodox Judaism and other religions, any physical contact between a man and a menstruating woman is believed to make the man ritually or religiously unclean. *See also* mikveh. Sexual relations may also be taboo when a woman is pregnant (*qv*) or nursing (*qv*), before sports contests, planting, harvesting, the hunt, or war. Some cultures have sexual taboos regulating where sexual intercourse (*qv*) may or may not take place.

sexual trauma An emotionally and/or physically painful and disturbing sexual experience such as date (*qv*), acquaintance (*qv*), or marital rape (*qv*), incest (*qv*), or child sexual molestation (*qv*). Some draw a distinction between an *active sexual trauma* (*qv*) in which the individual was personally involved and a *passive sexual trauma* (*qv*) in which the individual was an observer. The long-term outcome of a sexual trauma depends on how able the victim is to acknowledge and deal emotionally with the negative experience so that it can be put to rest.

If the sexual trauma is not resolved, it may be repressed into the subconscious, where it can lead to a variety of psychological disturbances including hypophilic sexual dysfunctions (*qv*), such as a lack of sexual desire (*qv*), sexual aversion (*qv*), inhibited sexual arousal (*qv*), vaginal spasms (*qv*), or inhibited orgasm (*qv*). *See also* rape-trauma syndrome. An unresolved early childhood sexual trauma may also be a factor in a variety of criminal expressions, particularly rape (*qv*), incest, and pedophilia (*qv*).

sexual underactivity A condition in which an individual's sexual desire (*qv*) and/or activity (*qv*) falls in the lower portion of the frequency distribution curve for a population. *See also* hypophilia.

sexual values The norms or standards endorsed by a society or by an individual. A sexual value is termed *formal* (*qv*) when it expresses the public, official position of a religious or civil group. An *informal value* (*qv*) is one that is held by and expressed in the actual behavior of an individual or group of people. In relatively stable societies, formal and informal values tend to match each other. In transitional societies, the pressure for changes in formal values increases as more and more people adopt different informal and culturally alien values. *See also* communitas; hot sex values; cool sex values; sexual revolution.

sexual vandalism The compulsive need to deface or destroy the sexual features portrayed in statues, paintings, and other artistic expressions.

sexual variance A nonjudgmental term for sexual behaviors (*qv*), activities, preferences (*qv*), or orientations (*qv*) that do not conform to the conventions and norms (*qv*) of a society. Every society has its established norms for sexual behaviors. In more restrictive cultures, the range of what is considered acceptable in sexual behavior may be quite narrow, as it was in the Victorian (*qv*) age. In such cultures, sexual variances are commonly referred to as deviant, perverted, abnormal, and unnatural behaviors. In liberal or permissive societies sexual variances may not even be noticed.

sexuoerotic The unified experience of the sexual (*qv*) and the erotic (*qv*) with more emphasis on the sexual or genital than on erotic imagery.

sex variables In a descriptive model of developmental gates first proposed by John Money, each individual passes through a series of "gates" or "either/or forks" in psychosexual development starting with conception (*qv*) and reaching sexual maturation at puberty (*qv*).

Perhaps it will help if we elaborate the road map metaphor [of psychosexual development] a bit by picturing gates at the either-or forks in sexual differentiation. In species like [the fish] *Labroides dimidiatus*, all the gates stay open so that it's possible for an individual to pass back and forth, able to function fully as either a male or a female throughout its adult life . . . In the mammalian kingdom, some of the gates lock earlier, others stay open longer, and as you move up the scale to the primates, the sexual behavior gates gain some independence of the anatomical gates. . . .

As you approached each gated sex-differentiation point, you could have gone in either direction, but as you passed through, the gate locked, fixing the prior period of development as male or female. Your gonads, for example, could have become either testicles or ovaries, but once they became testicles, they lost the option of becoming ovaries, or if they became ovaries they could never again become testicles. In behavior, however, at first you drove all over the highway, but as you proceeded you tended to stick more and more to the lanes marked out and socially prescribed for your sex. The lines and barriers dividing male from female for each kind of sex-linked [gender role] behavior vary according to your culture and experience, and the kind of individual you have become makes a difference in the way you feel about crossing them, but you never lose these options entirely. A sufficiently strong stimulus—physical, hormonal, neural, or social— can push you over practically any behavior line or barrier. Your own experience and alterations in the gender stereotypes of your culture can obscure established lines and lower barriers so that crossing becomes easier or harder.

The gates originally proposed were: (1) chromosomal sex (*qv*), (2) gonadal sex (*qv*), (3) hormonal sex (*qv*), (4) internal sexual anatomy (*qv*), (5) external sexual anatomy, (6) assigned sex (*qv*) and rearing, and (7) gender role (*qv*) and identity (*qv*). Resource: J. Money & P. Tucker, *Sexual Signatures: On Being a Man or a Woman* (Boston: Little, Brown, 1975).

Recent research has prompted an expansion of this model by R. T. Francoeur, T. Perper and N. A. Scherzer to 12 "gates"—with 6 prenatal (*qv*) variables: (1) chromosomal sex, (2) gonadal sex, (3) hormonal sex, (4) internal morphologic sex, (5) external morphologic sex, and (6) neurological encoding, and 6 postnatal (*qv*) variables: (7) assigned sex, (8) gender scripting (*qv*), (9) gender role, (10) gender identity, (11) sexual or gender orientation, and (12) puberty. Resource: R. T. Francoeur, *Becoming a Sexual Person*, 2nd ed. (New York: Macmillan, 1991).

Shakers A radical Quaker sect flourishing from around 1800 into the early 1900s, the Shakers practiced celibacy (*qv*), common possession of property, separation from the rest of the world, segregation of the sexes, and carefully regulated interactions between male and female members of the community. The sect's name was drawn from their communal dances in which the men and women, on opposite sides of the hall, engaged in a trance-inducing ritual of orgiastic shaking. By 1988, celibacy and the inability to attract new members had reduced the Shakers to 7 women in their 80s and 90s.

Shakti (Skt.) In Hindu thought, the personification of the active, creative energy of femininity (*qv*). Shatki is the power of Tantra (*qv*); known in her benign aspect as Parvati and in her awesome aspect as Kali. *See also* kundalini; Shiva.

shaman A person of supernormal powers; a practitioner of the sacred; a healer, seer, or conductor of souls who achieves contact with the spirits in an ecstatic state in certain American Indian and Northeast Asian religions. Shamans frequently abstain from sexual intercourse (*qv*), particularly when they are in training. They also enforce the various sexual taboos (*qv*) prevailing in a particular culture. In many cultures, shamans are transvestites (*qv*) and/or homosexual (*qv*), since such individuals are thought to participate in both male and female spiritual realms. *See also* berdache. Resource: W. L. Williams, *The Spirit and the Flesh: Sexual Diversity in American Indian Culture* (Boston: Beacon Press, 1986).

shamanism The religion of certain peoples of northeast Asia and of native North Americans who believe that the workings of good and evil spirits can be influenced only by the shaman (*qv*).

shame The feeling of being embarrassed and humiliated by the exposure of one's involvement in forbidden activities or by one's lack of skills, faults, or other shortcomings. Shame is often associated with sexual matters. Sex-negative (*qv*) messages from parents or religious authorities regarding one's genitalia (*qv*) and natural functions such as menstruation (*qv*) and nocturnal emissions (*qv*) often result in feelings of shame and embarrassment. Self-consciousness about one's sexual anatomy and the supposed shortcomings of one's physical attractiveness may interfere with normal sexual functioning.

In many cultures, familial or kin sanctions designed to prevent actions that would shame the family are the primary control force, especially in preventing forbidden sexual relations (*qv*) and activity. In other cultures, guilt (*qv*), the internal sanctions of conscience, and punishment imposed after the fact are the primary social control over individuals' behavior.

shame-aversion therapy A form of behavioral-modification therapy (*qv*) in which the patient reenacts an undesirable, usually sexual (*qv*), activity in the presence of others in order to associate a sense of shame (*qv*) with that behavior and condition the person to avoid it in the future.

sheath Colloquial term for condom (*qv*).

Shiva (Skt.) The transcendent aspect of the Hindu triad of forces governing all phenomena; the Yogic ideal, "Lord over Death," the Eternal, Immortal Spirit. *See also* Shakti; kundalini.

Shiva Lingam (Skt.) The lingam (*qv*), or phallus, of Shiva (*qv*); the ever-erect sexual organ (*qv*) often idealized in a sculpture or stone.

shoe fetish A paraphilic (*qv*) dependence on handling or viewing a woman's shoe, particularly a high-heel shoe. *See also* retifism.

short hairs A colloquial term for the pubic hairs (*qv*). The most common usage is in the phrase "to have someone by the short hairs," meaning to have another person in one's control.

shot, the A colloquial term, analogous to "the pill," for an injection of Depo-Provera (*qv*) to prevent conception (*qv*) for a two-to-three-month period.

shotgun wedding A colloquial term for a marriage (*qv*) necessitated by pregnancy (*qv*).

show The slight bleeding from the vagina (*qv*) at the start of labor (*qv*).

Siamese twins Monozygotic (*qv*) twin fetuses (*qv*) physically joined to each other. Siamese twins result from incomplete separation of a single zygote (*qv*) into identical twins (*qv*). The extent of the union may range from superficial to deeply shared organ connections. Most Siamese twins can be successfully separated with modern surgical techniques, provided that each has its own complement of vital organs. The term refers to Chang and Eng (1811–1874), Chinese conjoined twins born in Siam who were turned into international celebrities by P. T. Barnum.

sib, sibling A brother or sister; two individuals related by blood by having the same parents.

sibling rivalry Competition between siblings (*qv*) for the attention, affection, and/or approval of a parent or for recognition by others.

sibship The state of being related by blood; a group of people descended from the same ancestor.

side girl A colloquial term for a married man's girlfriend or mistress (*qv*), popular in the English-speaking Caribbean and among blacks in the southern states.

SIECCAN *See* Sex Information and Education Council of Canada.

SIECUS *See* Sex Information and Education Council of the United States.

significant other (SO) In the sociological theory of George Herbert Mead (*qv*), any person with whom an individual interacts frequently and emotionally. The prototypical significant other is a parent, but significant others may also be other close relatives, or an intimate friend, lover, or spouse. Significant others play a large part in determining the individual's self or consciousness through role-taking (*qv*) The term is also commonly used for one's habitual sociosexual partner, whether spouse or not. *See also* generalized other.

significant symbols In the sociological theory of George Herbert Mead (*qv*), a set of symbols shared by members of a community. According to him, the basis for human action, cooperation, and order is an elaborate set of significant symbols, especially a common language, which permits members to share a common definition and interpretation of situations and to anticipate the behavior of one another. Significant symbols are arbitrary and vary from one culture to another.

silent rape reaction One of several possible responses to a sexual assault (*qv*) or rape (*qv*), this response involves a complete denial by the victim, to self and others, that she or he was sexually assaulted, though the assault may be clearly revealed by a dramatic change in the victim's sexual behavior and attitudes and by unexplained psychosomatic complaints, anxieties, fears, and depression. *See also* rape-trauma syndrome.

silver nitrate A topical antimicrobial agent used to prevent gonococcal (*qv*) eye infections in newborns (*qv*).

Simian T-cell lymphotrophic virus-I (STLV-I) A T-cell retrovirus (*qv*) that infects the lymphocytes of certain strains of monkeys, producing symptoms similar to human acquired immunodeficiency syndrome (*qv*). Because of the similarities between human and simian AIDS, the STLV-I virus may provide a useful model for the study of human AIDS.

Simmond syndrome A chronic, progressive hormonal disorder resulting from decreased endocrine (*qv*) activity in the anterior pituitary (*qv*) and characterized by decreased sexual activity (*qv*) and atrophy (*qv*) of the genitalia (*qv*). Among the symptoms are loss of pubic (*qv*) and axillary hair (*qv*), loss of facial hair in men, hypoglycemia, weight loss, emaciation, and premature aging.

Simopolous v. Virginia *See* City of Akron v. Akron Center for Reproductive Health; Kansas City v. Ashcroft.

simple mastectomy Surgical removal of a whole breast (*qv*), but leaving the skin, underlying muscles and adjacent lymph nodes intact, performed to remove small malignant mammary neoplasms. *See also* modified radical mastectomy; radical mastectomy; lumpectomy.

Sims-Huhne test An examination of the cervical mucus (*qv*) when a woman is ovulating (*qv*), usually performed within 2 to 3 hours after coitus (*qv*) to provide information about the viscosity of the cervical mucus as a possible cause of infertility (*qv*).

Sim's position A position assumed by a male to facilitate a prostate examination (*qv*). The patient rests on his left side with the right knee and thigh flexed upward toward the chest.

simulsex A colloquial term for bisexuality (*qv*).

simultaneous fertilization *See* superfecundation; superfetation.

simultaneous orgasm *See* mutual orgasm.

Singer v. U.S. Civil Service Commission A 1977 action by the U.S. Supreme Court on gay rights (*qv*) in employment that left no national precedent on this issue. Singer, a clerk-typist for the federal Equal Employment Opportunity Commission, was dismissed because of his gay rights activism. When he appealed to the Supreme Court, the Court remanded the case to the U.S. Civil Service Commission for review under its recently liberalized guidelines on sexual orientation (*qv*). Singer was reinstated with back pay because the Civil Service Commission guidelines, adopted after the case was filed in federal court, stated that termination cannot be solely on such basis. Although the case was resolved administratively in Singer's favor by remanding the case to the Civil Service, no national legal precedent was set.

single-blind study A research study or experiment in which either the subject or the person collecting the data does not know whether the subject is in the experimental or control group. *See also* double-blind study.

singles bar A bar whose clientele consists largely of single men and women seeking entertainment, companionship, and a possible partner. Different singles bars cater to particular customer populations, attracting men and women of different age cohorts and social classes. The same bar may serve two or three different singles populations at different times in the day, or on different days of the week.

singles groups Entrepreneurial, community, or other organized groups of unmarried people that provide social opportunities for their members to meet and perhaps form partnerships. Some singles groups have a religious affiliation or association, while others are special interest groups such as Parents Without Partners.

singles scene A general term applying to the activities of unmarried people in a city or region, focusing on their efforts to meet partners for social or sexual purposes. In some communities, the singles scene is identified with the singles bar (*qv*) while elsewhere it may involve personals advertisements. The singles scene is complex because a given community of singles can consist of never-married, divorced (*qv*), and widowed (*qv*) individuals, all of whom have very different social and sexual interests and needs.

single (moral) standard The application of a single set of behavior norms and values to both males and females within a particular culture. *See also* double moral standard.

sin phobia An intense, sometimes pathological fear of committing, or having committed an unpardonable sexual sin. This kind of phobia often results from the sexual anxieties (*qv*) and guilt (*qv*) instilled by parents or religious authorities as a means of controlling sexual impulses and behavior, particularly masturbation (*qv*) and premarital sex (*qv*). In its pathologic extreme, this phobia may interfere with normal social functioning. Also known technically as enosiophobia, hamartophobia, and peccatophobia.

sissy An offensive colloquial term for an effeminate male; a boy whose developmental differentiation of gender-identity/role (*qv*) is, in variable degree, in conflict with his genital anatomy. *See also* sissy boy syndrome.

sissy boy syndrome A behavioral-developmental condition in which a boy adopts what are viewed as "feminine" behavior patterns. A "sissy boy" prefers to be a girl as much as possible, dressing in girl's or women's clothes, preferring dolls to trucks, playing with girls, avoiding rough-and-tumble play and sports, and playing mommy in "mommy-daddy games." Longitudinal studies of the sissy boy syndrome suggest that this childhood condition may be related to an adult homosexual (*qv*) orientation. Resource: R. Green, *The "Sissy Boy Syndrome" and the Development of Homosexuality* (New Haven: Yale University Press, 1987).

sister A female sibling (*qv*); a colloquial term common in the male homosexual (*qv*) community for a fellow male homosexual; a bonding term and relationship between lesbians (*qv*) or feminists (*qv*). *See also* sisterhood.

sisterhood The solidarity of women; the bonding between lesbians or feminists, variously defined as: "an authentic bonding of women on a wide scale for our own liberation" (Mary Daly, *Beyond God the Father* [Boston: Beacon Press, 1973]); "female solidarity expressed in a discovery of shared oppression" (Dorothy E. Smith, *Feminism and Marxism* [Vancouver: New Star Books, 1977]); "for black women, the spiritual bonding that unites all black women brought from Africa to the Caribbean and the United States as slaves to be bred, traded, and bought" (Sylvia Witts Vitale, Growing up Negro, soon to be black, *Heresies* (1982) (Issue 15), 6(1):20–26). *Sisterhood is Powerful*, a ground-breaking book in the second wave of radical feminism, was edited by Robin Morgan (New York: Vintage, 1970). Resource: C. Kramarae & P. A. Treichler, *A Feminist Dictionary* (London: Pandora Press, 1985).

situational homosexuality Sexual activity (*qv*) engaged in by persons of the same sex because their present environment (e.g., a boarding school, summer camp, aboard ship, or in prison) does not allow for sexual contact with persons of the other sex. This kind of sexual activity, often referred to as homoerotic (*qv*), is usually only a temporary experience, with heterosexual (*qv*) relations resumed as soon as possible. *Synonyms*: accidental homosexuality (*qv*); faute de mieux (*qv*); occasional inversion (*qv*).

situational orgasmic dysfunction A type of secondary sexual dysfunction (*qv*) in which a man or woman who has in the past experienced orgasm (*qv*) as a result of masturbation (*qv*), oral sex (*qv*), or vaginal intercourse (*qv*), now finds himself or herself unable to reach orgasm in a particular situation or with a particular partner.

situational rape or sexual assault An unplanned and unexpected sexual assault (*qv*) or forced sexual activity (*qv*) that occurs incidentally in association with a burglary or argument or when the assaulter is discovered in some criminal activity. *See also* impulse rape; rape.

situation ethics As defined by its originator, medical ethicist Joseph Fletcher, and applied to sexual ethics, situation ethics is "the ethical system in which sexual behavior is morally acceptable in any form—heterosexual, homosexual, bisexual, autosexual, or polysexual, with the determination of whether any sexual act is right or wrong based on what it is intended to accomplish—its foreseeable consequences; sex is a means to an end beyond the sexual act itself; no sexual act is intrinsically right or wrong; no sexual act in and of itself should be either blamed or praised, apart from whatever human values motivated and guided it." Resources: J. Fletcher, *Situation Ethics: The New Morality* (Philadelphia: Westminster, 1966); J. Fletcher & T. Wassmer, *Hello Loves: An Invitation to Situation Ethics* (Washington: Corpus Books, 1970).

sixty-nine (69) A colloquial expression for mutual oral sex (*qv*), cunnilingus (*qv*), and/or fellatio (*qv*), engaged in by a man and woman, two men, or two women.

Skene's glands The largest of the glands opening into the female urethra (*qv*) just inside the urethral meatus (*qv*). The Skene's glands are homologous (*qv*) to the male prostate (*qv*) and are thus sometimes referred to as the female prostate. They produce an isozyme of the enzyme acid phosphatase, which was originally thought to occur only in male seminal fluid (*qv*). They are thought by some to be associated with female ejaculation (*qv*). The Skene's glands, also known as the paraurethral glands, may become inflamed as a result of infection.

skin brassiere A medical expression for the skin tissues that normally support the female breast (*qv*) in a forward projecting position.

skin decoration In many cultures, sexual attractiveness is enhanced by the facial and/or body decoration, including cosmetic coloring and painting or, less frequently, patterned and colored scars or tattoos.

skin eroticism Sexual excitement (*qv*) derived from physical stimulation of the skin or by the sight of a partially or fully undressed person. Because skin-to-skin contact in breastfeeding (*qv*) and maternal touches are an important and vital source of sensual pleasuring in infancy, it is natural that sexual stimulation resulting from caresses, rubbing, licking, and kissing (*qv*) the skin is especially pleasurable and a major component in loveplay (*qv*).

Cultural interpretations of nudity and the erotic message of bare skin vary widely among cultures (*qv*). In some cultures, bare female breasts (*qv*) may be considered erotically neutral, while an uncovered head of hair may be viewed as extremely erotic. In other cultures, particularly Western cultures, the reverse is true. *See also* nudism; nudity.

Skoptsy This eighteenth- and nineteenth-century ascetic sect, which broke with the Russian Orthodox church, practiced both male and female castration (*qv*). In keeping with their interpretation of the Gospel of Matthew (19:12), male members first excised their scrotum (*qv*) and testes (*qv*), and then removed the penis (*qv*) itself. Some women in the sect followed suit by having their breasts (*qv*) and even their ovaries (*qv*) excised. Also spelled Skoptsi.

sleeping together A colloquial term for a couple who are having sexual intercourse (*qv*), or cohabiting (*qv*) without being married. However, the fact that a couple is living together does not necessarily mean they are sexually active with one another. *See also* domestic partners.

sleep with, to A colloquial euphemism meaning "to have sexual intercourse (*qv*) with someone."

sloughing An abnormal condition in which immature germinal cells are released into the lumen of the seminiferous tubules (*qv*), which become clogged, producing infertility (*qv*) due to the lack of mature sperm (*qv*) in sufficient number to permit fertilization (*qv*).

slut A derogatory term for a promiscuous woman, namely, a woman with multiple sexual partners; a prostitute (*qv*). The term also implies an offensive boldness of manner and personal slovenliness. The term may be used for both men and women, sometimes humorously or sarcastically, for example, for someone who has "sold out" to a profession or occupation and is practicing it solely, and perhaps dishonestly and against his or her own values and ideals, for financial gain.

S/M (SM, S and M) Abbreviations for sadomasochism (*qv*) or submission-mastery.

small-penis anxiety (complex) An emotional concern and anxiety, common especially among adolescent (*qv*) males, that one's penis (*qv*) is significantly smaller than those of others. Erotic literature, pornography (*qv*), and folklore that associate a large penis with masculinity (*qv*) undoubtedly contribute to this anxiety. It has also been suggested that a man who looks down at his own penis inevitably perceives another man's penis as longer and thicker because of the different angle or perspective of viewing.

smear In cytology, cells that have been spread on a glass slide, fixed, and then stained in preparation for microscopic examination. Buccal smears using epithelial cells from the oral cavity are the most common preparation for ascertaining presence of Barr bodies (*qv*) and chromosomal sex (*qv*). *Smears* are also used for detecting some STDs; *See also* Pap smear.

smegma A whitish, cheesy, foul-smelling secretion of sebaceous (*qv*) glands that accumulates under the foreskin (*qv*) around the corona of the penile glans (*qv*) and around the labia minora (*qv*) near the clitoral glans (*qv*), containing dead epithelial cells, pheromones (*qv*), and possibly bacteria. Fresh, recently secreted smegma is colorless and odorless; when it becomes noticeable, its color is whitish, its consistency cheesy, and it smells foul. Resource: R. Aman, Offensive words in Dictionaries: I Smegma. *Maledicta (The International Journal of Verbal Aggression)* 7 (1983):109–120.

snake A reptile; an animal character common in creation myths as a symbol of knowledge, seduction (*qv*), fertility (*qv*), and the penis (*qv*). The similarities of the snake symbolism in the sixth century B.C.E. Sumerian Epic of Gilgamesh and the story of creation in the Hebrew story of creation are typical of these symbolisms.

snake phobia An intense, morbid fear of snakes (*qv*). Snakes are common features in dreams, fantasies (*qv*), folklore, myths, religious rituals, and works of art. When a snake is viewed as a symbol of the penis (*qv*), a snake phobia may be interpreted as a subconscious fear of sexual intercourse (*qv*).

snuff film (pornography) A sexually explicit, pornographic (*qv*) film in which sexual arousal (*qv*) is linked with and dependent on the torture and murder of a victim whose agony is recorded in every detail. True snuff films involve the actual torture and murder of a victim. More common are simulated snuff video and audio cassettes. Snuff pornography is a sexual stimulus for homicidophiliacs (*qv*). *See also* erotophonophila; lust murder.

social birth A public ritual (*qv*) in which an infant (*qv*) is formally presented to and accepted by the elder or elders of a family or community. At times in Chinese culture, a newborn who died or was killed before social birth was not mourned. In Orthodox Jewish tradition, a male infant who dies before circumcision (*qv*) eight days after its biological birth (*qv*) is not given a name or a formal burial. Circumcision is a necessary sign of the covenant between Yahweh and his chosen people and of incorporation into the people of God. In the autocratic family of ancient Rome, the head of the household, the paterfamilias, was a petty absolute monarch who had to accept formally any new recruit into the household, whether a newborn infant, bride, or a new servant or slave. The newborn was placed at his feet. If he picked up the child, he or she was admitted into the family and given a name. Otherwise the child was exposed or abandoned with the chance that it might be picked up by another family. This custom continued well into the Middle Ages in Western Europe. *See also* personhood; viability.

SO *See* significant other.

social disease A nonspecific colloquial euphemism for a sexually transmitted disease (*qv*).

Social Exchange Theory Social Exchange Theory has gained popularity in recent years for explaining the formation and development of intimate relationships (*qv*). According to exchange theorists, all relationships involve an exchange of rewards and costs. Each partner experiences some events and aspects in the relationship as rewarding or enjoyable and others as unpleasant costs. Since no relationship generates only rewards, each partner sustains some costs in any relationship. When the rewards exceed the costs, the relationship generates "profit." Such relationships tend to be satisfying and to grow more intimate. When the costs are greater than the rewards, the relationship operates at a loss.

These exchange principles operate at various stages of a relationship and influence who we find attractive, who we are willing to date a second time, who we see steadily, and if we marry. Moreover, the exchange of rewards and costs can shift over time. A relationship that was once highly rewarding can become costly, even to the point of a break-up. *See also* Stimulus-Value-Role model. Resource: F. I. Nye, Choice, exchange, and the family, in W. R. Burr, R. Hill, F.I. Nye, & I. L. Reiss, eds., *Contemporary Theories About the Family. Volume II: General Theories/Theoretical Orientations* (New York: Free Press, 1979).

social hygiene A term, common in the early 1900s, for education aimed at reducing and preventing the spread of what were then called social diseases— sexually transmitted diseases (*qv*). The social hygiene movement dealt also with social or community conditions, such as prostitution (*qv*), which spread sexually transmitted diseases. *See also* degeneracy theory. Today, the terms *social health* and the more inclusive *community health* have replaced *social hygiene*. *See also* sexual hygiene; social purity movement.

socialization Socialization is a broad term referring to how people learn the social norms, customs, roles, and beliefs appropriate to their society and gender. Socialization theorists see socialization beginning with the infant's first contact with its mother, and proceeding through childhood (*qv*), adolescence (*qv*), and into adulthood (*qv*). In different forms, socialization hypotheses are basic to all the social sciences. Socialization can also refer to how one learns particular manners and sexual customs. *See also* scripting; conditioning; role-taking.

social parent The adult who accepts and fulfills the role of a father or mother; the adoptive parent. *See also* genetic parent; biological parent; surrogate parent.

social purity movement A social movement in the United States in the late 1800s and early 1900s that successfully fought efforts to legalize and regulate prostitution (*qv*), worked to raise the age of consent for sexual intercourse (*qv*), and rejected middle-class reticence about discussing sex while at the same time seeking to return control of sexuality (*qv*) to the private sphere of the family. *See also* social hygiene; sexual hygiene. Resource: J. D'Emilio & E. B. Freedman, *Intimate Matters: A History of Sexuality in America* (New York: Harper & Row, 1988).

social vice A Victorian (*qv*) expression for promiscuous (*qv*) sexual activities (*qv*), chiefly with prostitutes (*qv*). *See also* social hygiene; social purity movement.

Society for the Scientific Study of Sex Founded in 1957, this international interdisciplinary society is dedicated to the advancement of scientific knowledge about human sexuality (*qv*), to quality research, and the clinical, educational, and social applications of research related to all aspects of sexuality, as well as the dissemination of accurate scientific information on sexual topics to interested researchers, practitioners, and public policymakers as well as to the public media. Commonly referred to as SSSS, Quad-S, or 4S, the Society publishes the quarterly *Journal of Sex Research*. Address: SSSS, P.O. Box 208, Mount Vernon, Iowa 52314. Telephone: 319–895–8407.

Society for the Second Self *See* Tri-Ess.

Society for Sex Therapy and Research (SSTAR) A professional multidisciplinary organization formed to enhance communication between clinicians and clinical investigators interested in the treatment of human sexual disorders. STARR sponsors a national meeting and a clinical seminar each year. Address: Robert Taylor Seagraves, University Hospital of Cleveland, 2074 Abington Rd., Cleveland, Ohio 44106.

sociobiology Sociobiology is a theoretical framework based on Darwinian evolutionary theory and population genetics that seeks to explain the social behavior of animals and humans by referring to evolved genetic constraints on behavior. Such causes for behavior, described as ultimate, contrast with proximate causes, such as events occurring within the lifetime of the individual. Sociobiologists have focused on aggressive and sexual behavior (*qv*), since these have direct effects on the individual's reproductive (*qv*) potential.

Sociobiological theorists have maintained that differences between males and females in the number of sexual partners over the lifetime result from the male's effort to maximize his fitness by having as many offspring as possible whereas, in this theory, females maximize their fitness by selecting fewer partners. *See also* sexual selection. Many social scientists and feminists (*qv*) have criticized sociobiology for what they perceive are its androcentric (*qv*) and biological determinist arguments.

Sociobiology was first proposed by E. O. Wilson in *Sociobiology: The New Synthesis* (Cambridge: Harvard University Press, 1975). Resources: D. Symons, *The Evolution of Human Sexuality* (New York: Oxford University Press, 1977); D. P. Barash, *Sociobiology and Behavior* (New York: Elsevier, 1977).

sociology of family The study of how sexual reproduction (*qv*) is structured and how the offspring are integrated in the kinship system (*qv*). The sociology of the family focuses on two issues: the relationship between industrialization and types of family structure, and the inequality and exploitation of wives, as masked by the intimacy and emotional attachments in the modern family. *See also* extended family; nuclear family.

sociology of gender The study of how physical differences between men and women are mediated by culture and social structure. Social and cultural conditioning affect four areas: (1) the specific personality traits attributed to women and their socialization (*qv*) into the feminine gender identity (*qv*); (2) the seclusion of women from public activities and the workplace by relegating them to the home; (3) the allocation of women to inferior and typically degrading productive areas; and (4) the stereotyping of women as weak and emotionally dependent on men.

sociopath A person who totally lacks any sense of social responsibility, conscience, or guilt. A sociopath has very little real emotional capacity, but may act very emotionally when blaming others, including victims. Some psychologists believe that sociopathy involves defense mechanisms that prevent a psychotic breakdown triggered by too much guilt and pressure.

sodoma imperfecta (L.) A medieval term for unnatural (*qv*) sexual activity, particularly anal intercourse (*qv*) between men. Because of the assumed unnatural character of this behavior, its punishment was reserved to the ecclesiastical court rather than being handled by the civil courts as were the natural (*qv*) crimes of adultery (*qv*) and rape (*qv*).

sodomite One who practices sodomy (*qv*); a colloquial and sometimes legal or religious term for a male homosexual (*qv*).

sodomy Generally any unnatural (*qv*) or noncoital sexual act. Depending on the legal jurisdiction and definition, sodomy may involve oral sex (*qv*), anal sex (*qv*), and both oral and anal sex, as well as sex with animals. The term is derived from the biblical story of Sodom and Gomorrah. In chapters 18 and 19 of Genesis, God punishes the inhabitants of these two cities because Lot refused to let the townsfolk abuse his two male angelic visitors and instead offered his virgin (*qv*) daughters. Originally sodomy meant only ''male homosexual anal (and oral) copulation.'' Over the centuries other ''unnatural vices'' or ''crimes against nature'' have been included in the term *sodomy*, resulting in a polysemous and now imprecise and useless word. Resource: R. Aman, Offensive words in dictionaries, *Maledicta: The International Journal of Verbal Aggression* 9 (1986–1987):227–268.

soft chancre A small, reddish pus-filled pimple which ruptures and develops a depressed center exuding pus; caused by a bacterial infection of *Haemophilus ducreyi* (*qv*). Unlike the hard chancre (*qv*) associated with syphilis (*qv*), soft chancres are quite painful and tend to occur in clusters.

soft media A colloquial term for sexual aids (*qv*) or fetish-like (*qv*) objects that are considered sexually arousing (e.g., lacy lingerie and fur).

soixante-neuf (Fr.) French for sixty-nine (*qv*).

solicitation In legal parlance, the crime of asking another person to participate in or commit a crime; commonly used to refer to the acts of a prostitute (*qv*) soliciting customers. In animal behavior, the term solicitation is used neutrally or broadly to refer to all forms of proceptive behavior by the female; *see* proceptivity.

SOM *See* sexually open marriage.

soma, somatic The body as distinct from the psyche or mind; body cells as distinct from germ or reproductive cells.

somatomammotropin, human chorionic (HCS) Produced late in pregnancy (*qv*) by the placenta (*qv*), this protein hormone (*qv*) is responsible for milk production in the mammary glands (*qv*). It is also known as human placental lactogen (HPL). An identical hormone, known as prolactin (*qv*) or lactogenic hormone, is produced by the anterior pituitary (*qv*). This pituitary hormone acts with estrogens (*qv*), progesterone (*qv*), thyroxin, insulin, growth hormones, and human placental lactogen to stimulate development and growth of the mammary glands. HCS is also identical with luteotropin, which stimulates formation of the corpus luteum (*qv*) in the ovary (*qv*).

somatosensory Pertaining to somatic or body sensations.

Somatosensory Affectional Deprivation (SAD) syndrome Neuronal changes in the brain resulting from the lack of body pleasure experienced when the body is not touched, caressed, and gently rocked or moved. SAD and the neuronal changes resulting from it have been correlated with an increased tendency to violent adult behavior and a difficulty or inability to relate with others in ways which involve body pleasuring. The primary source of somatosensory affectional stimulation (SAS) is provided by the mother to her newborn/infant with gentle touching, breastfeeding (*qv*), and carrying the baby on her body throughout the day. This SAS stimulates the vestibular-cerebellar system of the brain. In addition to touch and movement input, the emotional sense of smell provides a third component in the formation of the emotional brain. The developing brain requires these forms of sensory stimulation from the senses for the normal development and functioning of the emotional brain, or limbic-cerebellar-frontal/temporal lobe complex.

   Initially the primary focus of research on SAD was on postnatal environmentally induced somatosensory affectional deprivation occurring when the caregiver does not pick up, hold, cuddle, or caress the infant/child sufficiently, where there is no breastfeeding, or where breastfeeding is foreshortened. SAD, however, can also result when the sensory receptors and neural afferent tracts of the somatosensory affectional system are damaged during prenatal and/or postnatal development by alcohol, drugs, stress, illness or disease, anoxia, neurotoxins, or malnutrition. When the neurobiological system is damaged, the ability of the newborn or infant to assimilate and benefit from SAS can be seriously limited. Evidence suggests that the neuronal changes induced by SAD can be detected in neuronal spiking patterns (*qv*).

somatotropin The growth hormone (*qv*) produced by the pituitary (*qv*).

somesthetic In sex therapy (*qv*), a treatment that involves various pressures and touch, massage (*qv*), sensual body grooming, and sensations of hot, cold, wet, and dry. The sensate focus exercises (*qv*) are a good example of this modality.

somnophilia A paraphilic (*qv*) condition in which a person depends on intruding on and fondling a stranger who is asleep or on fantasizing about such an experience in order to be erotically aroused (*qv*) and reach orgasm (*qv*).

Soranos of Ephesus (98–138 A.D.) A Greek physician, Soranos appears to be the first Westerner to describe contraceptive (*qv*) methods and abortifacients (*qv*) in some detail.

Sorensen Report A 1973 study of the sexual behavior and attitudes of American teenagers conducted by Robert C. Sorensen and based on a probability sample of 411 13- to 19-year-old American adolescents (*qv*) who responded to an anonymous questionnaire and agreed to be interviewed. While the study included married and unmarried, and both sexually active (*qv*) and celibate (*qv*) teens, 75 percent of the males and 60 to 70 percent of the females, ages 13 to 15 reported masturbating. Fifty-nine percent of the males and 45 percent of the females reported having had sexual intercourse (*qv*). The study was published as *Adolescent Sexuality in Contemporary America* (New York: World, 1973).

sororal polygyny *See* sororate.

sororate A marriage (*qv*) custom requiring that when a sister dies, her surviving sister will marry the widower (*qv*). *See also* levirate. May also refer to the simultaneous marriage of a man with two or more sisters, a preferred form of polygyny (*qv*), sometimes referred to as sororal polygyny.

Spallanzani, Lazzaro (1729–1799) An Italian embryologist (*qv*) who disproved a commonly accepted theory of Aristotle (*qv*) that in egg-laying animals, the female is solely responsible for reproduction (*qv*) while in the high animals and humans the male semen (*qv*) is solely responsible for reproduction with the female merely providing a convenient incubator for the male "seed." After studying sperm (*qv*) cells fertilizing ova (*qv*), he experimented with artificial insemination (*qv*) of frogs in 1776 and dogs in 1780, gaining recognition as the father of artificial insemination.

Spanish collar A colloquial term for a foreskin (*qv*) that is so tight it irritates the penis (*qv*), causing frequent erection (*qv*) and painful swelling. This condition, easily corrected by circumcision (*qv*), should not be confused with phimosis (*qv*), Peyronie's disease (*qv*), or priapism (*qv*).

Spanish fly *See* cantharides.

spay To remove the ovaries (*qv*) of a female animal; used primarily in veterinary medicine.

spectatoring A psychological process whereby a person acts as an observer, monitor, or judge of his or her own sexual performance and/or that of the partner. Spectatoring is a common outcome and cause of sexual dysfunction (*qv*). It results from the individual's being overly conscious of performance and from the expectation that one should or must always perform perfectly. Spectatoring often leads to anxiety and to a failure to perform satisfactorily because "working at sex" inhibits one's spontaneous responses and reactions. Also known as body monitoring.

spectrophilia A morbid attraction to or obsession with spirits; the illusion of having sexual relations (*qv*) with spirits. This disorder was much more common in the religious atmosphere of the Middle Ages and during the time of the Inquisition when it was widely believed that humans could engage in sexual intercourse (*qv*) with demons. *See also* incubus; succubus.

speculum A blunt double-bladed, plastic or metal medical device used to dilate and separate the vaginal (*qv*) walls to allow examination of the vagina and cervix (*qv*). Some feminist (*qv*) self-health groups commonly encourage women to become familiar with their own internal sexual anatomy and do pelvic self-exams alone or in groups using a speculum. *See also* gynecologic examination.

sperm *See* spermatozoon; spermatid.

sperm agglutination In the male, a partial blockage of the ductus deferens (*qv*) or an infection of the testes (*qv*) that prevents exit of the sperm (*qv*). The blocked sperm trigger an immune response (*qv*) in which newly produced antibodies against sperm agglutinate or clump and immobilize the sperm so they have no motility (*qv*) when ejaculated (*qv*).

sperm analysis *See* semen analysis; sperm count.

sperm aster In cytology, a radiating structure of microtubules that forms around the sperm (*qv*) head or male pronucleus (*qv*) inside a fertilized ovum (*qv*) during the first mitotic (*qv*) cleavage (*qv*) of the zygote (*qv*).

spermatemphraxis An obstruction of the normal passage of the sperm (*qv*) or semen (*qv*) through the vas deferens (*qv*) and prostatic, membranous, and penile urethra (*qv*).

spermatic canal The inguinal canal (*qv*), or fetal extension of the pelvic cavity, through which the testicle (*qv*) descends into the scrotal sac (*qv*).

spermatic-cell arrest A cytogenetic blockage that stops the meiotic (*qv*) process, preventing the formation of secondary spermatocytes (*qv*) and resulting in azoospermia (*qv*).

spermatic cord A compound structure containing arteries, veins, lymphatics, nerves, and the vas deferens (*qv*) or spermatic duct and extending from the deep inguinal ring in the abdomen to the testis (*qv*) and supporting the latter. The left spermatic cord is usually longer than the right cord, allowing the left testis to hang lower than the right testis in the scrotal sac (*qv*).

spermatic duct *See* ductus deferens.

spermatic fistula An abnormal passage communicating with a testis (*qv*) or a seminal duct.

spermatid A male reproductive cell resulting from division of a secondary spermatocyte (*qv*) and structurally modified into a spermatozoon (*qv*) in the last phase of spermatogenesis (*qv*).

spermatocele A cystic swelling in the epididymis (*qv*) or rete testis (*qv*) containing sperm (*qv*); usually painless and does not require therapy.

spermatocelectomy Surgical removal of a spermatocele (*qv*).

spermatocide *See* spermicide.

spermatocyte In the seminiferous tubule of the testicle, the immature male reproductive cell produced by division of a spermatogonial cell (*qv*). Each primary spermatocyte subsequently divides into two haploid (*qv*) secondary spermatocytes, which modify their form and structure to become mature spermatozoa (*qv*) during spermiogenesis (*qv*).

spermatocytogenesis *See* spermatogenesis.

spermatogenesis The process of sperm (*qv*) production in the seminiferous tubules (*qv*) of the testes (*qv*); the male counterpart to oogenesis (*qv*). *See also* meiosis. In the final stage of spermatogenesis, known as spermiogenesis, round secondary spermatocytes lose their cytoplasm and modify their form to the tadpole shape of mature sperm.

spermatogenic cells The reproductive cells in the testes (*qv*), that divide by meiosis (*qv*) to produce spermatozoa (*qv*) in the seminiferous tubules (*qv*). The Sertoli cells (*qv*), a second type of cells in the seminiferous tubules of the testes, regulate and promote this spermatogenesis (*qv*).

spermatogonium (pl. spermatogonia) The germinal cell of the male that undergoes repeated mitotic (*qv*) divisions in the seminiferous tubules (*qv*) and eventually gives rise through two stages of meiotic (*qv*) division to spermatocytes and eventually spermatozoa (*qv*). *See also* spermatogenesis.

spermatolysin A vaginal secretion found in some women which lyses or destroys sperm (*qv*).

spermatophobia A morbid fear of semen (*qv*).

spermatorrhea A Victorian (*qv*) and obsolete medical term for an involuntary ejaculation (*qv*), wet dream (*qv*), or nocturnal emission (*qv*); a copious emission of semen (*qv*) without orgasm (*qv*), as in a nocturnal emission (*qv*). In a male who has had a vasectomy (*qv*), ejaculation of semen with no sperm may be termed a false spermatorrhea.

spermatorrhea dormientum (L.) *See* nocturnal emission.

spermatozoon (pl. spermatozoa) The mature male gamete (*qv*), reproductive cell, or sperm (*qv*). Roughly 55 to 75 microns in length, a spermatozoon has three regions: (1) an oval or round head containing dexoyribonucleic acid (*qv*) and capped by an acrosome (*qv*) body containing enzymes that aid fertilization (*qv*) of the ovum (*qv*), (2) a midpiece with spiral mitochondria that metabolize energy sources in the seminal fluid to produce rhythmic contraction of the microtubules in the (3) tail that allows the sperm to swim through the female reproductive tract. Spermatozoa are produced in the seminiferous tubules (*qv*) of the testes (*qv*). The meiotic divisions and maturation of a single sperm take 64 days, plus or minus 5 days. A spermatozoon contains the haploid (*qv*) number of chromosomes—22 autosomes (*qv*) and either an X (*qv*) or a Y (*qv*) chromosome. *See also* androsperm; gynosperm.

Prior to ejaculation (*qv*), the sperm are stored in the epididymis (*qv*). The average male ejaculate (*qv*) contains about 300 million sperm in about 3 milliliter of semen (*qv*). *See also* sperm count. A human spermatozoon moves at the rate of about 1.5 millimeters per minute, or about an inch in 15 minutes. While a sperm has a normal life expectancy of about 2 days in the vaginal environment, it may retain its ability to fertilize (*qv*) an ovum for only 12 to 24 hours. In cryogenic storage in liquid nitrogen, a sperm may live for 15 to 20 years with little effect on its capacity to fertilize when thawed. A spermatozoon that successfully travels through the vaginal, uterine, and tubal passages may then join with the ovum in fertilization to form a diploid zygote (*qv*) with 44 autosomes and two sex chromosomes, XX (*qv*) or XY (*qv*).

spermaturia *See* semenuria.

sperm bank A research or commercial facility for the cryonic storage of semen (*qv*) for future use in artificial insemination (*qv*). Human sperm banks are used by men who are planning to have a vasectomy (*qv*) or are engaged in occupations that endanger fertility (*qv*). Sperm banks are also commonly used to store sperm of endangered animal species or of prize animals whose semen is sold to animal breeders seeking to improve the genetic qualities of their stock.

sperm count An estimated count of the number of motile sperm (*qv*) in a sample of semen (*qv*). A sperm count above 20 million sperm per milliliter is commonly considered essential to normal fertility (*qv*). Some studies suggest that the sperm count in American males has been dropping in the past century because of increasing exposure to toxic substances, which accumulate in the testes (*qv*) where they interfere with spermatogenesis (*qv*). A 1929 study reported a median sperm count of 90 million per milliliter compared with a 65 million median in 1974 and a 60 million median in 1979. *See also* semen analysis. Resource: R. C. Dougherty, Sperm counts decreasing in American men, *Sexual Medicine Today*. 3(11) (1979):14–15.

spermia A combining form meaning ''pertaining to sperm'' (*qv*).

spermicide A chemical substance capable of immobilizing or killing sperm (*qv*); used in contraceptive vaginal foams (*qv*), suppositories (*qv*), and jelly (*qv*). *See also* nonoxynol-9.

spermin A prostatic secretion that gives seminal fluid its specific odor (*qv*). Resource: Hugo Biegel, *Encyclopedia of Sex Education* (New York: Wm. Penn, 1952).

spermiogenesis *See* spermatogenesis.

sphincter A ringlike structure of voluntary or involuntary muscle surrounding a natural body opening and allowing for its opening and closing, as in the bladder and anus. *See also* external urethral sphincter; internal urethral sphincter.

sphincter cunni (L.) The bulbocavernosa (*qv*) or bulbospongiosus (*qv*) muscle that in the female surrounds the opening of the vagina (*qv*) and in the male surrounds the base of the penis (*qv*). *See also* pubococcygeal muscle exercises.

spiking activity Distinctly abnormal spike patterns observed in electroencephalographic tracings that may be indicative of convulsive seizures, epilepsy, or developmental somatosensory affectional deprivation (*qv*) leading to violent and antisocial behavior. *See also* neuronal spiking.

Spinnbarkheit (Germ.) The stretchability of cervical mucus (*qv*), an easily discerned indication of ovulation (*qv*). Under the influence of increased estrogen (*qv*) associated with ovulation, the cervical mucus is altered so that it can be stretched several inches between the thumb and index finger. It is believed that this change facilitates the passage of sperm (*qv*) through the cervical canal (*qv*) by providing filaments the sperm can follow at the precise time when the woman is most fertile and most likely to conceive (*qv*). *See also* ferning; Billings' contraceptive method.

spinster An obsolete and now insulting term for a woman who has remained unmarried beyond the time when she would be normally expected to have married. In the Victorian (*qv*) era and through the early decades of the twentieth century, the implication was that there was "something wrong" with a woman, a spinster, whom no man wanted to marry. In the mores of the times, a spinster was expected to be celibate (*qv*). These judgments and expectations no longer hold for single women after their adolescent years, since many women now choose not to marry and yet are sexually active, some even choosing to become single mothers.

Spirochaeta pallida (L.) An alternate term for *Treponema pallidum* (*qv*), the organism causing syphilis (*qv*).

spirochete A spiral or cork-screw-shaped bacterium such as the one that causes syphilis (*qv*).

sponge, vaginal/cervical *See* vaginal sponge.

spongy body *See* corpus spongiosum.

spontaneous abortion A naturally occurring termination of a pregnancy (*qv*) prior to the twentieth week of gestation (*qv*) as a result of a fetal or uterine-maternal abnormality. More than 10 percent of all pregnancies end in spontaneous abortion. An ovum with a chromosomal (*qv*) or congenital (*qv*) defect that is incompatible with life is a common cause. Other possible causes are hormonal imbalances, trauma, malnutrition, and uterine (*qv*) or placental insufficiency (*qv*). Spontaneous abortion is more common in women below the age of 20 years than in other age cohorts.

spontaneous delivery A vaginal (*qv*) delivery (*qv*) without the assistance of forceps.

spousal rape *See* marital rape.

squeeze technique An exercise used in treating premature ejaculation (*qv*) developed by William Masters and Virginia Johnson. The partner sits between the man's legs and stimulates his penis (*qv*), gradually bringing about an erection (*qv*). When the man feels himself reaching the point of orgasmic inevitability (*qv*), he signals his partner to stop stimulation and to squeeze the glans (*qv*) between the partner's fingers with the thumb on the frenulum (*qv*). This momentary tolerable pain reduces the orgasmic impulse. After alternating stimulation and squeezing several times in different sessions, the male learns to experience intense penile stimulation without reaching an orgasm too early for his partner. Sometimes referred to as the pinch technique. It is seldom used today, having been replaced by the stop-and-go exercise (*qv*).

SRD *See* sexually related disease.

SRS Abbreviation for sex reversal or reassignment surgery. *See also* sex change operation; transsexual.

SSSS Acronym for the Society for the Scientific Study of Sex (*qv*).

SSTAR Acronym for the Society for Sex Therapy and Research (*qv*).

stag film A colloquial term for 10– to 15–minute, sexually explicit films, popular before the advent of video cassette soft- and hard-core pornography (*qv*), and usually shown at male-only gatherings (e.g., male clubs and premarital bachelor parties).

Standard Cross-cultural Sample A reference/research sample of 186 societies chosen by George Peter Murdock in 1969 as the best-described sample of non-industrialized cultures. *See also* Human Relations Area Files; Ethnographic Atlas.

status orgasmus (L.) A medical term for a rapid series of orgasms (*qv*) experienced by a woman as a single fluctuating or sustained orgasm, lasting 20 to 60 minutes.

statutory rape A legal concept of sexual intercourse (*qv*) between an adult and a legal minor; consent or its absence on the minor's part is irrelevant to the crime. In some legal jurisdictions, such as in the New Jersey Penal Code, sexual intercourse between a consenting minor female and an older male is classified as sexual assault (*qv*). If force is used, the crime is aggravated sexual assault. The degree of the crime can be affected by the difference in the ages of the perpetrator and the victim, the perpetrator's position of authority, and the relationship of the perpetrator and victim. *See also* rape; incest.

STD *See* sexually transmitted disease.

steatopygia An extreme accumulation of fat in the female buttocks (*qv*). Among the Hottentots and Bushmen of southern Africa, this trait is considered a mark of feminine beauty and sexual attractiveness (*qv*).

Steinach, Eugen (1861–1944) An Austrian physician who pioneered sex-change surgery (*qv*) for transsexuals (*qv*) in the 1920s and the use of animal testicular implants (the so-called "monkey gland" treatment) for sexual rejuvenation. *See also* Benjamin, Harry.

Stein-Leventhal syndrome A condition in females associated with abnormal ovarian function and marked by ovulatory failure, secondary amenorrhea (*qv*), and body hairiness. In this condition, the ovaries are usually polycystic (*qv*) with a thickened capsule, possibly resulting from overproduction of androgen (*qv*). Symptoms may be relieved by removal of part of the enlarged ovaries.

stereotype Rigid, exaggerated, and prejudicial conventional beliefs and expectations based on oversimplified evidence or uncritical judgments. Because stereotypes provide a sense of social solidarity, they are often resistant to change or correction even when strong evidence to the contrary is available. *See also* conjugal roles; gender; gender coding; gender stereotyping; racism; sexism; heterosexism; sex roles; sexual scripts.

sterile (n. sterility) Incapable of reproducing (*qv*), due to genetic, physiological, or anatomical causes. *See also* infertility; oligospermia; azoospermia; ovarian agenesis; testicular agenesis.

sterilization A surgical procedure that makes an individual incapable of reproducing (*qv*). The more common procedures are vasectomy (*qv*) in the male and tubal ligation (*qv*) in the female. *See also* castration; eunuch; ovariectomy; eugenics; salpingectomy; spay.

steroid A general term for the organic chemical compounds that share a common complex structure of three six-carbon rings and a fourth ring with five carbons. Although the steroids share a common basic structure, chemically minor changes in the steroid molecule can radically alter the physiological activity of two otherwise very similar steroids. Steroids are vital in body chemistry and include the male and female sex hormones—androgens (*qv*), estrogens (*qv*), and progesterone (*qv*))— the adrenal cortical hormones (cortisone), bile acids, and vitamins of the D group. The body synthesizes all steroids from cholesterol; the site of their synthesis depends on the particular steroid. *See also* peptide hormone.

stigma A distinguishing mark burned or cut into the flesh; some trait that detracts from the character or reputation of a person—a mark of disgrace or reproach such as a socially unacceptable sexual orientation (*qv*) or paraphilic (*qv*) condition; the pimplelike spot on the surface of the ovary (*qv*) that marks the site of a follicle (*qv*) approaching maturity and preparing for ovulation (*qv*). *See also* stigmatophilia.

stigmatophilia A paraphilic (*qv*) condition in which a person is responsive to and dependent on one's partner or one's self being tattooed, scarified, or pierced for the wearing of gold jewelry especially in the genital region, in order to achieve sexual arousal (*qv*) and orgasm (*qv*).

stilbesterol An alternate term for diethylstilbesterol (DES) (*qv*).

stillbirth The birth (*qv*) of a near-term (*qv*) but dead infant, caused by fetal distress (*qv*), abnormally long labor (*qv*), fetal immaturity, syphilis (*qv*), or erythroblastosis fetalis (*qv*).

stimulus-value-role theory (SVR) A theory explaining marital partner choice in terms of initial physical, mental, or emotional stimulus-attraction, followed by selection based on compatible values and negotiation of compatible roles. Resource: B. Murstein, Stimulus-value-role: A theory of marital choice, *Journal of Marriage and Family* 32 (1970):465–481.

stirpiculture A eugenics (*qv*) program developed and practiced by the members of the Oneida Community (*qv*) in the mid-1800s in which the elders of the community selected men and women to engage in procreative (*qv*) sexual intercourse (*qv*) and produce children because their traits were especially desirable. In the complex marriage (*qv*) pattern of Oneida, all men and women were free to engage in amative intercourse (*qv*) if they so desired. However, the community carefully limited reproduction (*qv*). John Humphrey Noyes (*qv*), Oneida's founder, argued that the community should put as much care and design into human reproduction as they devoted to breeding their farm animals. Although all members of the community were expected to take their turn in the children's house, certain males and females were chosen by the community to be full-time foster parents because of their special skills in this area.

STLV-I *See* Simian T-cell lymphotrophic virus-I.

Stockholm syndrome The emotional bonding (*qv*) and psychological dependence that sometimes develops between rapist and victim, a molester and the person molested, a captor and the captive, or a terrorist and the hostage. The term is derived from the clinical case of a female hostage in a Stockholm, Sweden, bank robbery who became so emotionally attached to one of the robbers that she broke her engagement to her fiancee and remained faithful to her captor during his term in prison.

Stoicism (Stoics) Originating with the philosophy of Zeno about 308 B.C.E., this early Greek philosophy taught that man should accept his fate and live calmly, free from passion, grief, and joy because everything that happened to humans was the result of divine decree. Stoicism was a preeminent philosophy in the Greco-Roman world. The Stoics were particularly suspicious of sex because the ecstasy of coitus seemed to subvert the rule of reason. Seneca, a contemporary of Jesus, tutor of emperors, and preeminent Stoic of his day, characterized sexual desire (*qv*) as "friendship gone mad." Musonius Rufus, the Stoic most admired by early Christians, wrote that "men who are not wantons or immoral are bound to consider sexual intercourse justified only when it occurs in marriage and is indulged in for the purpose of begetting children, since that is lawful, but unjust and unlawful when it is mere pleasure-seeking, even in marriage.'' This philosophical view of sex has been a major influence in Christian thought. Resource: R. J. Lawrence, *The Poisoning of Eros* (New York: Augustine Moore Press, 1989), pp. 9–16.

stone infant A fetus (*qv*) that dies in the uterus (*qv*), but which, instead of being miscarried (*qv*) or reabsorbed, is preserved as a mass surrounded by bonelike calcium salts. The calcium salts apparently protect the mother from the toxic effects of the dead fetus, which can remain undetected in the uterus for many years. *See also* fetus papyraceus.

Stonewall Inn riot (1969) Stonewall Inn was a gay bar (*qv*) in Greenwich Village, New York City, where police regularly harassed the homosexual (*qv*) patrons until one evening in June 1969 when the patrons fought back. The riot is commonly cited as the birth of the gay liberation (*qv*) movement. Each year, the Stonewall Inn riot is commemorated with gay liberation parades.

stop-and-go (stop-and-start) technique A therapeutic behavioral exercise, developed by James H. Semans to teach male control of orgasm (*qv*) and premature ejaculation (*qv*). The partner sits in a comfortable position, stimulating the male's penis (*qv*) manually or orally until he is just about to ejaculate (*qv*). At this point, stimulation is halted and resumed only when the man is again in control of his responses. Stimulation and rest are repeated several times in each session until the man is able to control his orgasmic response. This technique can be used during coitus (*qv*) with the female in the above-sitting position where she is able to control vaginal thrusting (*qv*). Males can use it during masturbation (*qv*) or if they assume the male-above position during intercourse (*qv*). *See also* squeeze technique; premature orgasm.

Stopes, Marie Carmichael (1880–1958) A scientist who opened the first British birth control clinic in 1921. Stopes's book *Married Love*, first imported to the United States in 1918, ran into trouble with U.S. Customs, allegedly because of her charts of the periodicity in women's sexual desire (*qv*). In 1931, Judge Woolsey ruled that her book was not legally obscene (*qv*). Both *Married Love* and her other book, *Wise Parenthood,* were widely read and influential in promoting the sexual knowledge and liberation of women. She also advocated use of the diaphragm (*qv*) and Stopes cervical cap (*qv*) for contraception (*qv*).

storge (Gr.) An early Greek term for the affectionate, generalized form of love one has for parents, children, and pets. Storge is clearly distinguished from eros (*qv*) or erotic, passionate love, from agape (*qv*) or spiritual, unselfish love, and from philia (*qv*), the nonsexual love shared by friends.

straddle trauma An injury to the glans (*qv*), urethra (*qv*), corpora cavernosa (*qv*), and/or corpus spongiosum (*qv*) of the penis (*qv*) and/or to the testicles (*qv*) caused by a man falling with one leg on either side of a hard object.

straight A colloquial term for a person with a heterosexual (*qv*) orientation. *See also* gay; bisexual.

strain A genetically inbred (*qv*) population within a species.

stranger rape A sexual assault (*qv*) or rape (*qv*) by a person unknown to the victim. *See also* acquaintance rape; date rape; impulse rape; marital rape.

strangulation, penile An interruption of the blood circulation in the penis (*qv*), artificially induced by inserting the penis through a tight metal ring after which swelling prevents removal of the ring. Penile strangulation occurs mainly in adolescent (*qv*) males engaged in sexual experimentation. The constricting ring must be quickly removed to prevent gangrene from developing because of the restricted blood flow. *Compare*: phimosis.

stratification, social A ranking of individuals according to their status and roles within a social system. Each rank, with its significant differences in power and prestige, shares a common subculture. The term *social class* describes a hierarchy in which one's rank depends on achievement. The term *caste* refers to a ranking based on birth in which a newborn (*qv*) is assigned to the caste of the parents.

stratified (quota) sample A subset of individuals whose demographic characteristics match those of the large population of which the subset is a part. *See also* random sample.

streaking A recurring fad among adolescents (*qv*), most recently among college students in the early 1970s, in which males and females race nude (*qv*) through a public place as a social protest. Also known as mooning when the buttocks (*qv*) are exposed from the window of a moving automobile.

streak ovaries A type of ovarian agenesis (*qv*) in which the ovaries (*qv*) do not develop but remain fibrous, nonfunctional cords. Streak ovaries are characteristic of individuals with Turner syndrome (*qv*) who have only one X chromosome (*qv*). Two X chromosomes are essential for normal ovarian development.

stretch marks A colloquial term for the linear scars of collagen that often result from rapidly developing tension in the skin and subsequent tears in the underlying dermis; often occur on the female abdomen after pregnancy (*qv*).

striae albicantes or atrophica (L.) *See* stretch marks.

stricture An abnormal narrowing or stenosis of a tube or passage. Strictures in the prostatic or penile urethra (*qv*) and in the vas deferens (*qv*) can seriously affect fertility (*qv*) in the male. In females, strictures involving the fallopian tubes (*qv*) are a common cause of infertility (*qv*). Strictures of the cervical canal (*qv*) can interfere with fertility by blocking passage of the sperm (*qv*) and can complicate a vaginal (*qv*) delivery (*qv*).

striptease A colloquial term for the eroticized, gradual undressing on stage by a female, or sometimes male, dancer. The prolonged undressing builds up the erotic tension for the audience as they urge the striptease artist on to the state of complete nudity. The role of the dancer is to play with the audience and slowly, teasingly indulge its voyeuristic (*qv*) needs.

structural-functionalism A sociological theory, much elaborated by various schools of thought, that views society as an interrelated set of structures functioning together to maintain a stable society. *See also* communitas.

Sturm und Drang (Germ.) An early view of adolescence (*qv*) as a period of "storm and stress." This view has been discredited and replaced by a view of adolescence as a series of less traumatic and more gradual changes. By extension, *Sturm und Drang* refers to any highly emotional, stress-filled reaction.

subcutaneous implant Surgical insertion of an object or substance, such as a contraceptive hormone pellet, under the skin.

subcutaneous mastectomy A surgical procedure in which breast (*qv*) tissue is removed, leaving the skin, areola (*qv*), and nipple (*qv*) intact. This surgery, which also leaves the adjacent lymph nodes and muscles intact, may be performed on a woman who is at high risk for developing breast cancer (*qv*). Prosthetic implants are used to restore the normal breast curve.

subfecundity A fertility (*qv*) level below that considered normal for a female, usually applied to a woman who has one child and then, despite not using a contraceptive (*qv*), cannot become pregnant (*qv*) again.

subincision A form of genital mutilation (*qv*) in which an incision is made along the underside of the penis (*qv*), opening up the urethra (*qv*) before it ends in the penile glans (*qv*); often performed as part of a tribal rite of passage (qv) as among the Australian aborigines. *See also* circumcision; superincision.

sublimation A psychological defense mechanism by which unacceptable or personally inappropriate sexual needs or desires (*qv*) are consciously or subconsciously channeled into socially or personally acceptable nonsexual activities;

the deflection of libidinal energy from a normal sexual outlet to a satisfying, socially accepted, and nonsexual activity. *See also* celibacy; substitution.

submission The act of yielding to another's wishes or desires. When it refers to sexual activities (*qv*) and stereotypes (*qv*) in traditional patriarchal (*qv*) cultures, the woman is expected to be sexually submissive and wait for the male to make overtures and take the lead in sexual interactions. The endorsement of the missionary position (*qv*) in Western culture was based on the belief that man was created first and woman created from Adam's rib so that woman should always be submissive to the male and never assume a position superior to him, either physically or mentally.

In bondage (*qv*) and discipline and in sadomasochism (*qv*), submission of one partner to the other is a prime source of erotic pleasure for both partners.

substitute sex partner *See* sexual surrogate.

substitution The replacement of an unacceptable activity with a socially or morally acceptable activity. It is commonly suggested, half seriously, half in jest, that the American frontier was conquered by young men who were constantly warned about the devastating consequences of masturbation (*qv*) and advised to chop down a few trees when tempted to masturbate. If they did succumb to the temptation, they were advised to chop down a dozen or more trees as penance. *See also* sublimation.

Subtle Body In Yoga (*qv*), a term for the normally invisible body of biovibrations present within and around the physical body as an aura; composed of plasma energies and ever-changing and interacting vortices, the Subtle Body is also known as the Brahmanda, or aura of Brahma.

subtotal hysterectomy Surgical removal of the uterus (*qv*) at or above the level of the cervix (*qv*). Also known as supracervical hysterectomy. *See also* hysterectomy.

succubus (L.) In the mythology and folklore of the Middle Ages, an evil spirit or demon who assumes a female form and is supposed to lie under sleeping men in order to have intercourse with them. *See also* incubus; spectrophilia.

sucking impulse The natural impulse or response of a newborn (*qv*) to purse the lips around a nipple (*qv*) and create suction when provided with the opportunity to nurse (*qv*). According to Freudian theory, this earliest source of autoerotic (*qv*) pleasure continues to exert its attraction throughout life when it can be expressed in a child's sucking his or her thumb, in deep kissing (*qv*) with sucking on the partner's tongue, or in the many oral sexual caresses in which sucking is a major source of erotic (*qv*) pleasure.

suckling An infant who is still nursing (*qv*).

suction abortion Termination of a pregnancy (*qv*) by removal of the fetus (*qv*) and other uterine (*qv*) contents by suction. *See also* vacuum curettage; dilation and evacuation; suction curettage.

suction curettage A method of abortion (*qv*) in which the products of conception (*qv*) are scraped from the wall of the uterus (*qv*) and removed by aspiration. Also used to obtain a specimen of endometrium (*qv*) for cytological examination.

suffragette Coined by the *London Daily Mail* around 1900 to belittle militant women fighting for the vote in Great Britain, the term suffragette was converted into a proud label by militant feminists (*qv*). Christabel Pankhurst edited a newspaper entitled, *Suffragette*, after 1913.

suicidal sex *See* autoerotic asphyxia.

suigenderism The prepubertal (*qv*) tendency of boys to associate and play with other boys and avoid girls and the parallel tendency in girls.

summa libido (L.) *See* acme.

superego In psychoanalytic theory (*qv*), that part of the psyche or aspect of personality that develops as the moral standards and sanctions of the parents and society are incorporated into the personality. The negative side of the superego, the conscience, results from parental prescriptions about behavior. It is the source of feelings of guilt (*qv*) when cultural prescriptions are not followed. The positive side of the superego, the ego ideal, also results as parental prescriptions are internalized and the child begins to feel a sense of internal pride in doing what he should do.

superego anxiety In psychoanalytic terms, an anxiety and sense of paralyzing guilt resulting from behavior that violates parental and social principles and taboos (*qv*). *See also* superego.

superfecundation The fertilization (*qv*) of two or more ova (*qv*), released in the same menstrual cycle (*qv*), by sperm (*qv*) from the same or different males during separate acts of sexual intercourse (*qv*). *See also* superfetation.

superfetation The fertilization (*qv*) of a second ovum (*qv*) after the onset of pregnancy (*qv*), resulting in the presence of two fetuses (*qv*) of different gestational ages (*qv*). Only a few cases have been documented. Also known as superimpregnation.

superimpregnation *See* superfetation.

superincision A ritual (*qv*) form of genital mutilation (*qv*) for adolescent (*qv*) boys in certain Polynesian and other societies. Superincision is usually performed as a pubertal (*qv*) rite of passage (*qv*) marking the passage of a youth from childhood to manhood. With the foreskin (*qv*) pulled over a wood or iron anvil to protect the glans (*qv*), an incision is made running the whole length of the upper surface of the penis (*qv*). No anesthesia is used, and poultices protect against infection until the incision is healed.

superior-kneeling position A coital position in which the female kneels astride the prone male to maximize her control over insertion and reduce the need for male pelvic thrusting (*qv*). This position is recommended for males with erectile dysfunction (*qv*) because it shifts the weight and control to the woman and reduces the demands for physical exertion on the male.

supernumerary breast *See* polymastia.

supernumerary chromosome An alternate term for a trisomy (*qv*) condition in which an organism has two complete set of homologous chromosomes (*qv*), being diploid (*qv*), plus an additional third autosome (*qv*) in one set of homologous autosomes or additional sex chromosome beyond the normal XX (*qv*) or XY (*qv*). Trisomy of the sex chromosomes has some effect on the development in 47,XXX (*qv*), 47,XXY (*qv*), or 47,XYY (*qv*). The effects of a trisomy of an autosome are much more serious (trisomy of chromosome 21, or Down syndrome).

supernumerary oviduct A developmental defect in which one of the Mullerian ducts (*qv*) divides and develops into two parallel fallopian tubes (*qv*) on one side. The additional tube may or may not be functional in transporting ova (*qv*) from the ovary (*qv*) to the uterine cavity (*qv*).

superovulation The maturation and release of multiple ova (*qv*), induced by administration of a fertility drug (*qv*) such as Clomid (*qv*) or Perganol (*qv*).

supportive therapy A form of psychotherapy that concentrates on providing emotional support and reassurance for a person with a problem.

suppository An easily melted, medicated, globular, egg- or pencil-shaped mass inserted in the vagina (*qv*), urethra (*qv*), or rectum (*qv*). Spermicide-containing vaginal suppositories are used for contraceptive purposes. Vaginal, rectal, and urethral suppositories with antibiotics or other medications may be used in treating sexually transmitted diseases (*qv*).

suprainfection A secondary, iatrogenic (*qv*) infection resulting from a primary treatment, as when antibiotic treatment for a bacterial sexually transmitted disease (*qv*) alters the vaginal environment and allows a secondary *Candida* (*qv*) infection.

suprapubic Literally, "above the pubic bone"; an incision in the lower abdominal region to gain access to a tumor or remedy a problem in the organs of the pelvic cavity.

suprarenal glands *See* adrenal glands.

surface papilloma A wartlike, usually benign but rapidly growing tumor on the ovarian (*qv*) surface.

surrogate A person who acts in the place of another person. An aunt, uncle, grandparent, cousin, or unrelated person may serve as a surrogate parent. A surrogate mother (*qv*) may serve as a "prenatal (*qv*) wet nurse (*qv*)" for a woman unable to become pregnant or to carry a child. Sexual surrogates (*qv*) are also sometimes used in sex therapy (*qv*).

surrogate, sex *See* sexual surrogate.

surrogate mother A woman who volunteers to gestate a child for a woman who cannot bear her own child. A partial surrogate mother is artificially inseminated (*qv*) with the semen (*qv*) of the childless husband. She then serves as a "prenatal wet nurse," carrying the child to delivery (*qv*) before giving him or her to the childless couple for adoption (*qv*). In embryo adoption (*qv*), the wife is naturally or artificially inseminated with the sperm (*qv*) of her husband or a donor. The resultant embryo (*qv*) is then flushed from the uterus (*qv*) for transfer to the full surrogate, who carries the child to term and then gives it up for adoption. Depending on the individual case, the surrogate mother may or may not be compensated for her time and labor over and above payment of all her medical and other expenses. *See also* artificial embryonation.

surrogate partner *See* sexual surrogate; surrogate therapy.

surrogate therapy The use of a professionally trained substitute partner who works to relieve anxieties, teaches intimacy skills, and provides guidance through various levels of loveplay (*qv*) and intercourse (*qv*) for a dysfunctional (*qv*) person with whom other more conventional psychotherapeutic and behavioral therapies have not been effective. Sexual surrogates (*qv*) or body-work therapists are especially effective with young, physically impaired persons who may benefit from experimenting with a skilled and able-bodied surrogate partner. The use of sexual surrogates (*qv*) was originated by William Masters and Virginia Johnson and discontinued by them in the 1960s. The use of surrogate therapy has been severely affected by the concern over acquired immune deficiency syndrome (*qv*).

survey A research technique in which subjects in a random (*qv*) or stratified sample (*qv*) are asked questions about the type and frequency of their particular behaviors, attitudes, values, beliefs, expectations, and so forth in order to provide insights into the behavior and values of the general population.

suspensory ligament A triangular fibrous sheath extending between the umbilical region, the base of the penis (*qv*), and the pubic symphysis.

sustentacular cells *See* Sertoli cells.

suttee A Hindu practice in which a widow (*qv*)—whether a child bride of an arranged marriage (*qv*) to an old man or an older widow—is expected (and forced, if necessary) to immolate herself with her husband's corpse on his funeral pyre. The custom is not universal in Hinduism, and was outlawed by British colonial authorities in 1829 although it continued well into this century. In modern India, suttee is defined as murder, and it is a hanging offense even to encourage someone to engage in suttee.

SVR *See* stimulus-value-role theory.

sweating reaction An involuntary perspiring reaction occurring during the immediate postorgasmic portion of the resolution phase (*qv*) of the sexual response cycle (*qv*) in both men and women. *See also* transudation.

sweating, vaginal *See* transudation; vaginal dryness; vaginal lubrication.

swing club An establishment, generally run for profit, that caters to heterosexual (*qv*) partner exchange or swinging (*qv*). Such facilities usually have a large open area for meeting and mixing plus a series of rooms with beds or padded floors to permit open or closed swinging. The clubs provide food and beverages, and often have such amenities as swimming pools and jacuzzis. The most famous such club in recent years was Plato's Retreat in New York City.

swinging (n.), to swing (v.) The exchange of partners for social-sexual recreation; a colloquial synonym for mate or wife swapping. In closed swinging, the participating couples exchange partners and each new couple has sexual relations (*qv*) in privacy. In open swinging, all participants engage in sexual relations in the same room. *See also* group sex, orgy.

swive, to (v.) Between the fourteenth and eighteenth centuries, the common English colloquial term meaning to copulate (*qv*) or to have sexual intercourse (*qv*). By the seventeenth century, *to swive* had become a vulgar term, unacceptable for public usage. Subsequently the term occasionally reappeared in some dialects and in verse and humor. In 1982, John Money proposed reviving the term as a legitimate, active male term complementing a revival in the female active term *quim* (*qv*) and the gender-indifferent term *copulation*. *To swive* means to put the penis (*qv*) into the vagina (*qv*) and perform sliding and rotating movements of varying intensity, rhythm, and speed. As a noun, *swive* refers to the practice of swiving. Resource: J. Money, To quim and to swive: Linguistic and coital parity, male and female, *Journal of Sex Research* 18(2) (1982):173–176.

Swyer syndrome A form of male pseudohermaphroditism (*qv*) in which a genetic male with 46,XY (*qv*) karyotype, develops the internal and external sexual anatomy of a female. At birth, such individuals are identified as female, assigned a female gender status (*qv*), and raised as females. Although they possess internal female organs, they do not menstruate (*qv*) or develop female secondary sexual characteristics (*qv*) at puberty (*qv*). *See also* androgen-insensitive syndrome.

sybarite Someone devoted to sensual pleasure.

symbiotic marriage A marriage (*qv*) characterized by a mutual, often neurotic dependence of the spouses on each other, often to the degree that neither partner can function without the other. *See also* synergic marriage.

symbol Any gesture, sign, concept, or artifact that stands for, signifies, or expresses something else. Symbols have received extensive study by social scientists and psychologists; a specialized discipline, semiotics or semiology, is devoted to the study of symbols in all their complex forms and meanings.

The study of symbols by cultural anthropologists and sociologists often yields important insights into sexual attitudes, behavior, gender roles (*qv*), and sexism (*qv*). In psychology, the study of sexual dream symbolism was pioneered by Sigmund Freud (*qv*) and later by others, such as Carl Jung. In psychoanalytic (*qv*) schools of thought, symbols represent ways in which unconscious sexual desires (*qv*) may reach through superego (*qv*) repression into the person's consciousness. In the arts, symbols are esthetically personalized and consciously chosen ways of expressing feelings and states that otherwise elude conscious knowledge.

symbolic masturbation A theory that interprets a variety of repetitive acts, such as pulling one's ear lobes, rubbing one's nose, or twisting a strand of hair, as substitutes for masturbation (*qv*).

sympathetic nervous system That division of the autonomic nervous system (*qv*) primarily concerned with regulation of bodily activities that expend energy. An increase in sympathetic activity causes an increase in heart rate, blood pressure, respiratory rate, blood flow to voluntary muscles, and so forth. The emission phase (*qv*) of ejaculation (*qv*) is under sympathetic control. *See also* parasympathetic nervous system.

sympatric species Two distinct biological species (*qv*) capable of breeding together.

symphorophilia A paraphilic (*qv*) condition in which a person is responsive to and dependent on stage-managing the possibility of a disaster, such as a traffic accident, fire, or flood, and then watching it happen in order to achieve sexual arousal (*qv*) and orgasm (*qv*). This term is also applied to the reciprocal paraphilic condition in which a person arranges to be at risk as the potential victim of an arranged disaster in order to achieve sexual arousal and orgasm.

symphysis pubis The cartilaginous junction of the pubic and ischial bones at the mid-ventral point of the pelvic girdle that provides a base of attachment for the root of the penis (*qv*) or clitoris (*qv*).

symptothermal method of family planning A natural method of family planning, in which monitoring the cervical mucus (*qv*) and basal body temperature (*qv*) is used to ascertain those times when sexual intercourse (*qv*) is not likely to result in conception (*qv*). The joint use of the Billings' contraceptive method (*qv*) and basal body temperature is more effective than either method alone. By permitting a more accurate determination of the fertile period (*qv*), it requires a shorter period of abstinence. *See also* Spinnbarkheit.

syndrome A group of clinical signs and symptoms which occur together and characterize a disease or disorder.

synergic marriage A marriage based on an equal partnership rather than an unequal status in which the individuality and identity of the husband and wife are both valued and promoted by mutual efforts. *See also* open marriage; closed marriage; symbiotic marriage.

synergistic action In pharmacology, the combined effect of two or more drugs that is greater than the sum of the effects of the drugs taken separately.

synorchidism Complete or partial fusion of the testicles (*qv*).

synoscheros A congenital birth defect (*qv*) in which the penis (*qv*) is incorporated into the scrotum (*qv*).

syphilis An infection caused by the spirochete *Treponema pallidum* (*qv*) and usually transmitted by sexual contact. The course of syphilis runs through three stages. In the primary stage, painless chancres (*qv*) appear at the point where the spirochetes entered in the body. These disappear in 1 to 5 weeks. Symptoms in the secondary stage include a rash, flulike symptoms, mouth sores, and patchy balding. These disappear naturally after several months, even without treatment. About one-third of the untreated cases then enter a tertiary stage in which the bacteria attack internal organs, the spinal cord, and brain, leading to loss of muscle control, blindness, deafness, paralysis, insanity, and eventually death.

Treatment is with penicillin or other antibiotics. Blood tests every 3 months for a year are important to ensure that the spirochete has in fact been eliminated. In sexual folklore, syphilis was thought to originate from bestiality (*qv*). The term *syphilis* is derived from the Greek name of a shepherd hero, Syphilis ("lover of swine"), in a play by the sixteenth-century writer Girolamo Fracastero. *See also* syphilization; prenatal syphilis; tabes dorsalis; VDRL.

syphilitic adenopathy A secondary infection of the lymphatic tissues of the body, especially in the groin and neck regions, associated with syphilis (*qv*).

syphilitic arteriosclerosis The loss of elasticity in arterial walls resulting from syphilis (*qv*).

syphilitic chancre *See* hard chancre.

syphilitic conjunctivitis An infection, chancres (*qv*), and/or soft tumors or gummas (*qv*) occurring in the inner lining of the eyelids, the conjunctiva, as a result of syphilis (*qv*).

syphilitic vitiligo The loss of pigmentation, especially in the neck region, during second-stage syphilis (*qv*).

syphilization The theory that repeated exposure to syphilis (*qv*) over several generations can lead to development of relative immunity to syphilis (*qv*). Clinical efforts to induce relative immunity to syphilis by inoculation with attenuated *Treponema pallidum* (*qv*) have not succeeded.

syphiloma A tumor, such as a gumma (*qv*), resulting from a syphilitic (*qv*) infection.

systematic desensitization A behavioral therapy in which deep relaxation is used to reduce anxiety associated with certain situations; a therapeutic technique in which a person is gradually exposed to increasing amounts of anxiety-producing stimuli. As originally developed by Joseph Wolpe, systematic desensitization provides a patient with a structure in which to experience a hierarchy of anxiety-producing situations under conditions of physical relaxation with the goal of reducing the anxiety responses. Systematic desensitization is used in conjunction with resensitization (*qv*) in a Sexual Attitudes Reassessment (SAR) workshop (*qv*) to facilitate communications about sexual matters. Systematic desensitization is achieved in a SAR by careful sensory saturation and overload using a sequence of lectures and sexually explicit films shown with dim lighting, which allows participants to observe the films while also observing and learning from the reactions of other participants in a relaxing, permission-giving environment. Resensitization (*qv*) is accomplished in small-group discussions with skilled facilitators who draw out the participants' feelings and emotional reactions to the films and lectures as a springboard for discussion of sexual topics that otherwise would be accompanied by anxiety.

T

TA *See* transactional analysis.

tabes dorsalis (L.) A degeneration (demyelination) of the posterior columns of the spinal cord, a consequence of advanced syphilis (*qv*), characterized by progressive loss of peripheral reflexes, severe locomotor disturbances, and sometimes accompanied by impotence (*qv*) and incontinence. People with tabes dorsalis become uncertain in their walk and cannot properly distinguish directions and distances. Studies indicate that about 10 percent of those with late syphilis and 40 percent of those with clinical neurosyphilis suffer from *tabes dorsalis*.

taboo, tabu, tapu Among nonindustrialized peoples, a prohibition attached to certain individuals, things, relationships, or acts that are sacred or potent and therefore prohibited, unmentionable, and/or untouchable. Can also refer to a highly developed system of social or religious prohibition that results from tradition or convention. Breaking a taboo generates fear, shame (*qv*), and guilt in those who violate it, thus enabling authorities to wield power over those who accept the taboo. The term taboo, which came into English after Captain Cook's travels in Polynesia, originally referred to anything prohibited by social or religious custom.

E. Durkheim claims that observation of a taboo serves as a symbol (*qv*) of group membership and binds a social group together with shared rituals and values. In totemist (*qv*) systems, C. Lévi-Strauss views taboo as a symbolic message expressing the interchange among nature, culture (*qv*), and society. *See also* menstrual taboo; sexual taboo; tahara. Resources: E. Durkheim, *The Elementary Forms of Religious Life* (London: Allen & Unwin, 1954); E. Durkheim, *On Institutional Analysis* (Chicago: University of Chicago Press, 1978); C. Lévi-Strauss, *Structural Anthropology* (London: Penguin Press, 1968).

tabu *See* taboo.

tabula rasa (L.) A seventeenth-century concept popularized by John Locke in an effort to emphasize that the infant's mind is totally blank, without ideational content, until it is exposed to experiences and socialization. Literally, "a blank tablet." *See also* nature/nurture debate; nature/critical period/nurture.

TACE Trade name for chlorotrianisene, an estrogen (*qv*).

tachycardia A rapid pulse.

tactile Of or pertaining to the sense of touch; whatever can be perceived by touch. Individuals differ in their sensitivity to touch and their interpretations of touch depending on early experiences in nurturance (*qv*) or the lack of it. *See also* somatosensory affectional deprivation syndrome. In sexology (*qv*), tactile stimulation refers to sexual arousal (*qv*) and excitement resulting from any activity that triggers sensations in the skin's touch receptors. The initial touch between two persons marks a critical escalation point in the flirtation (*qv*) process and proceptivity (*qv*). In addition, a large portion of the courtship (*qv*) and loveplay (*qv*) leading to sexual intimacy involves tactile stimulation, from holding hands and kissing to touching, licking, sucking and biting any part of the body, but especially the erogenous (*qv*) areas. Sensitivity varies as sexual arousal increases or decreases.

tahara In the Islamic tradition, ritual purity, a state required before one may participate in worship. Tahara is achieved when sexual intercourse (*qv*) or menstruation (*qv*) is followed by a major purification rite of washing. *See also* menstrual taboo.

"take back the night" A profound symbolic slogan and challenge, first used in Great Britain in 1977 and in the United States in 1980 as a rallying cry by feminists (*qv*) seeking controls over pornography (*qv*).

"taking your night feet for a walk" English translation of the Scandinavian phrase for a premarital courtship (*qv*) tradition, similar to the Bavarian custom of fensternl (*qv*) or window courting. In the Scandinavian tradition, single eligible women move into a loft over the barn for the summer and leave the ladder down at night as an invitation to young men seeking a bride. The young men who visit the women are said to "take their night feet for a walk." Like fensternl, this custom is not an invitation to open promiscuity (*qv*). Similar courtship traditions are found in many other agrarian and tribal societies. *See also* bundling; night crawling.

tampon A cylindrical-shaped pack of cotton or synthetic absorbent material inserted into the vaginal canal (*qv*) to absorb the menstrual secretions during the period of menstrual flow (*qv*). The use of tampons to absorb the menstrual flow and treat a variety of health problems is mentioned in the literature of ancient Egypt. The term, from the French *tapon* for a piece of cloth to stop a hole, appears to have entered English as a medical term around the time of the Civil War. Tampons were produced commercially in the United States in the 1930s, although their advantages and disadvantages were emotionally debated until the 1960s. *See also* toxic shock syndrome; virginity.

Tantra An Eastern spiritual philosophy or system that takes into account both "inner" and "outer" realities; originally a Hindu sacred text, usually dealing with sexual yoga (*qv*) and magical practices related to the cult of Shakti (*qv*). In the Buddhist tradition, tantra refers to a series of ritual texts delivered to humans by the Buddha. The Buddhist tantra were transmitted to initiates in relative secrecy until the fourth or fifth century, after which they were widely taught throughout India by the tantric saints, known as the "84 perfect ones." Tantric teachings later spread to Nepal, Tibet, China, Japan, Thailand, and Indonesia. The term may also refer to a specific text outlining specific tantric practices.

In contrast to the asceticism of Buddhist monks are the "left-handed" followers of Tantric Buddhism. Left-handed Tantra urges the cultivation of sensual pleasure in order to become Buddhas. Sexual imagery of the lingam (phallus) (*qv*) and the female yoni (*qv*) are common in the sensual mysticism of Vajrayana where male and female deities are portrayed in sexual embraces. *See also* Yab-Yum. Buddhist art, like Hindu art, often expresses the divine union of Buddha in sexual imagery.

The actual meaning and subtleties of the Tantric love ritual are difficult for Westerners to comprehend because of their Western dualistic (*qv*) views of sex, human nature, and the divine, and because of the arcane Tantric terminology with its pantheon of gods and goddesses. Tantric love rituals, and other Eastern rituals, are not merely ways to achieve heightened sexual pleasure; they are primarily ways of seeking a consciousness of and identification with the divine through one's own embodiment and interaction with another. For Tantra, the greatest energy in the universe is sexual (*qv*) and ritual intercourse (*qv*) and orgasm (*qv*) viewed as a transcendent and cosmic experience.

The Tantric love ritual (*qv*) begins with an enhancement of the environment, with flowers, incense, music, and candlelight. This is followed by the couple bathing and then oiling and massaging (*qv*) each other. After a period of meditation designed to hasten the ascent of kundalini (*qv*) and alternate-nostril breathing, the couple chant a Mantra and envisage themselves as an embodiment of Shiva and Shakti, the supreme couple. With the woman on his right, the man kisses and caresses her whole body, from feet to head and back to the toes. The woman then slowly arouses the male with caresses and kisses all over his body.

Finally, after the woman moves to the left of the male, the couple move through a series of coital positions until each of them experiences the "transcendental power of love." The male refrains from orgasm (*qv*) in order to retain the vital life energies of his semen (*qv*). *See also* semen myths; maithuna.

Early Tantric and Taoist teachings place special emphasis on breath control and meditation as a way of "redirecting" the vital energies of semen to the brain. Tantric yoga (*qv*) is the yoga of this form of transcendental sex, the blending of body control, ritual, and exercise that brings together in a complementary way male and female sexual energies (*qv*) of the two persons and of the male-female divinity.

Although early Buddhism, which began in Nepal in the sixth century B.C., spread into India, China, Korea, and Japan and separated into a variety of what in Christianity would be termed separate churches or sects, its early traditions were exclusively monkish and other-worldly with a strong ascetic flavor. Masturbation (*qv*) and any sexual contact were frowned on because sex would distract the monk from meditation and liberation for nirvana. Over the centuries, the ecstatic, and at times orgiastic, cults inspired by Tantric visions of cosmic sexuality were attacked by the more ascetic Hindu and Buddhist traditions, as well as by the British colonial government.

See also extended sexual orgasm; karezza; Ritual of the Five Essentials; Tantric love ritual; Tantric sexual traditions; Tao. Resource: N. Douglas & P. Slinger, *Sexual Secrets: The Alchemy of Ecstasy* (New York: Destiny Books, 1979).

Tantric love ritual A ritual (*qv*) form of sexual intimacy in both the Hindu and Buddhist Tantric yoga sexual tradition (*qv*) that creates a gradual progression of physical activities and spiritual concentration culminating in the concentration of sexual energy (*qv*) in the highest part of the body through an orgasm (*qv*) that involves the whole person. *See also* Tantra.

Tantric sexual traditions Tantric traditions, found in both Hinduism and Buddhism, involving worship of divinities whose main concern is with sexual (*qv*) and cosmic energy. *See also* Tantra.

Tao (Tao Chia, Tao Chiao) An ancient Chinese philosophy and religion that views nature and spirit as interdependent and mutually sustaining. Tao is "the way," the cosmic truth conceived of as the path trodden by the wise and the rhythmic source of all life seen in the living cycle of the seasons in harmony with which all life should be lived. Taoism is based on the teachings of Lao-Tse (c. 604–531 B.C.) who advocated simplicity and selflessness. The two main philosophical words of Tao are the *Tao Te Ching* by Lao-tse and the *Book of Chang Tzu*.

Taoist sexual traditions are applications of this ancient Chinese philosophy to sexual relations (*qv*) in a way that nature and spirit interact and sustain one another. Taoist sexual traditions are very similar to those of Tantric yoga (*qv*), only the Taoists do not personify the subtle energies with a pantheon of divine beings. Some Taoist masters recommend that a male release his semen two or three times out of ten intercourses (*qv*), in order to "direct" and "transform" the vital life energies of the semen to the brain. Similarly, women are taught to use proper breathing exercises and meditation as ways of circulating and transforming their egg energies. *See also* coitus prolongatus; coitus reservatus; karezza. Resources: M. Chia & M. Winn, *Taoist Secrets of Love: Cultivating Male Sexual Energy* (Santa Fe: Aurora Press, 1984); M. Chia & M. Chia, *Healing Love Through the Tao: Cultivating Female Sexual Energy* (Huntington, NY: Healing Tao Books, 1986).

taphophilia A paraphilic (*qv*) attraction to cemeteries, associated with necrophilia (*qv*) and necromania (*qv*).

tapu *See* taboo.

target cell, organ A specific cell or organ influenced or affected by a hormone (*qv*); for example, the target organs for the gonadotropic (*qv*) hormones are the ovaries (*qv*) and testes (*qv*). When a circulating hormone reaches its target organ, it is incorporated by a specific receptor site or molecule and becomes metabolically active. Its action also depends on the presence or absence of other hormones and on prior hormonal action, as in the menstrual cycle (*qv*).

tart An obsolete colloquial term for a prostitute (*qv*).

T-cell *See* lymphocyte.

T-cell-helper depletion Since the HIV-I (*qv*) virus destroys the T-cell-helper lymphocytes (*qv*), depletion of these cells in the body's immune system provides an indication of the progress of acquired immune deficiency syndrome (*qv*).

T-cell lymphotrophic virus I (HTLV-I) *See* human T-lymphotrophic virus type I.

T-cell lymphotropic virus II (HTLV-II) *See* human T-lymphotrophic virus type II.

T-cell lymphotropic virus III (HTLV-III) *See* human T-lymphotrophic virus type III; human immunodeficiency virus-I (HIV-I).

T-cell lymphotrophic virus IV (HTLV-IV) *See* human T-lymphotrophic virus type IV.

TDF gene *See* testicular-determining factor gene.

tearoom trade A British colloquial term for homosexual (*qv*) interactions in public places, such as public restrooms and truck stops. Resource: L. Humphreys, *Tearoom Trade: Impersonal Sex in Public Places* (Chicago: Aldine, 1970).

teasing To annoy or harass by persistent, irritating actions or remarks, or by poking fun. In flirtation, courtship (*qv*), and intimate relationships, teasing often has more of a playful character about it than is implied by the usual dictionary definition. Nevertheless, the colloquial *cock teaser* for a female who flirts with a male while rejecting any sexual response from him is clearly negative and more in line with the standard definition. *See also* date rape; sexual harassment.

teat The nipple (*qv*) of the female breast (*qv*); the milk-releasing nipple of a cow's udder.

technical virgin A woman who has not had vaginal intercourse (*qv*), although she has engaged in other intimate sexual activities such as oral (*qv*) or anal sex (*qv*), mutual masturbation (*qv*), or petting (*qv*).

teenage sex A general term referring to sexual relations (*qv*) or the incidence of sexual intercourse (*qv*) engaged in by persons less than 20 years old; the term may include consequences of teenage sex like teenage pregnancy (*qv*) and abortion (*qv*).

Reported Incidence. In 1976 and 1981, the Alan Guttmacher Institute (*qv*) documented that roughly half of the 11 million American teenagers were sexually active. Nearly one-third of all Swedish teenagers were reported to have had sexual intercourse by age 16, and 80 percent by age 18. In Canada, on the other hand, only 20 percent were sexually active at ages 16 to 17. While French and English teenagers were less likely than American teenagers to have experienced sexual intercourse by age 18, by age 19 French teenagers were second only to those in Sweden. The median age for first sexual intercourse, however, was very similar for girls in Great Britain, France, the Netherlands, and the United States, somewhere between 17 and 18. Statistical studies have yet to document the effect of concern over AIDS on the incidence of teenage sexual experience. Resources: Alan Guttmacher Institute, *11 Million Teenagers: What Can Be Done About the Epidemic of Adolescent Pregnancies in the United States* (1976); *Teenage Pregnancy: The Problem That Hasn't Gone Away* (1981).

Incidence of Pregnancy. Between 1975 and 1985, over a million American teenagers were newly pregnant each year. One of every five American mothers in the mid-1970s was a teenager, with a quarter of a million mothers between ages 15 and 17 and 13,000 under the age of 15 each year. While teenagers accounted for only 18 percent of the sexually active American women at risk for pregnancy, they accounted for 46 percent of the out-of-wedlock pregnancies, and 31 percent of all abortions. Among 32 developed countries, only Iceland, Greece, Hungary, and Rumania have a higher per capita rate of teenage pregnancy than the United States. Many much poorer and less developed nations (e.g., Tunisia and the Philippines) have far fewer pregnant teenagers per capita than the United States. Even when the statistics are limited to pregnancies among white teenagers, only East Germany, Iceland, Yugoslavia, Greece, Czechoslovakia, Hungary, Poland, and Rumania exceed the American rate. The rates of teenage pregnancies in western European countries are one-fifth to one-half the U.S. rate. Japan's rate is one-twentieth the American rate. Guttmacher Institute statistics for the late 1970s give the following rates for teenage pregancies among girls 15 to 19 years of age: 96 per 1,000 in the United States, 45 per 1,000 in England and Wales, 44 per 1,000 in Canada, 35 per 1,000 in Sweden, and 14 per 1,000 in the Netherlands.

These statistics on teenage sexual activity and pregnancy require careful interpretation because over half of those listed under these terms are 18 or 19 year olds who may be married.

Contraceptive Use. In recent years, the number of teenagers using effective contraceptives (*qv*) has increased significantly. In 1979, 7 in 10 teenagers said they had used some contraceptive the last time they had sex compared with only half the sexually active teenagers in 1971. On the other hand, nearly two-thirds of the teenage women said they either never used any contraceptive or used it only erratically. In this unprotected group, 41 percent said they were not worried because they had sex only at an "infertile time of their cycle." Even the teenagers who did use contraceptives waited about 9 months after they first started having sex before using a contraceptive. More than half the pregnancies reported to teenagers in the late 1970s occurred within 6 months of the first sexual intercourse and one-fifth within the first month. In 1986, Dawson found nearly one-third of all sexually active American teenagers had at least one premarital pregnancy. That means half a million teenage abortions and half a million American adolescents who give birth every year. Resources: D. Dawson, The effects of sex education on adolescent behavior, *Family Planning Perspectives* 18(4) (1986):162–170; J. Dryfoos, What the United States can learn about prevention of teenage pregnancy from other developed countries, *SIECUS Report* 14(2) (1985):1–7.

Abortion. In 1986, 30 percent of all sexually active American teenagers had had at least one premarital abortion. In the mid-1980s, half a million teenagers had abortions, and half a million gave birth every year. In the mid-1980s, about half the states had laws requiring some form of parental notification for minors seeking abortions, though lower courts had ruled that most of such laws were unenforceable. Resource: K. Luker, *Abortion and the Politics of Motherhood* (Berkeley: University of California Press, 1984).

Major Social Issues. Teenage sex has become a public health and political issue with many problems. The ideal of sex education (*qv*) is to provide sufficient information about intimacy, relationships, contraception, and sexually transmitted diseases (*qv*) so that teenagers will learn to make informed decisions. Other ideals stress the moral virtue of sexual abstinence. In these programs, the social concern is primarily to deny or restrict teenage sexual activity rather than to reduce its negative consequences. The European ideal accepts the reality of teenage sex and focuses on reducing the number of teenage pregnancies, abortions, and the risk of STDs. *See also* Appendix D.

telegony An erroneous belief that traits of a previous mate are likely to be inherited when the female has the offspring by subsequent mating (*qv*) with different males. Despite the fact that no scientific evidence supports telegony in mammals, it still has many adherents among animal breeders who believe the offspring of a prize female animal with a prize sire are jeopardized if that female has previously mated with a mongrel.

teleology The study of final causes; the fact or quality of being directed to a definite end or of possessing an ultimate purpose; a philosophical or religious belief that natural phenomena and everything in this world are determined by an overall design or purpose in nature. According to natural law (*qv*) theory, sexual pleasure and sexual organs (*qv*) are designed for reproduction within heterosexual (*qv*) marriage. Therefore all homosexual (*qv*) relations and behaviors and any nonmarital or contraceptive heterosexual behavior are considered immoral.

telephone scatalogia, telephone scatophilia, telephonicophilia A form of exhibitionism (*qv*) in which sexual arousal (*qv*) is achieved by talking about sexual (*qv*) or obscene matters (*qv*) over the telephone to an unknown listener. For the obscene phone caller, sexual arousal and orgasm (*qv*) depend on luring, threatening, or forcing a known or unknown person to listen to sexually explicit telephone conversations.

temperature eroticism The erotic and pleasurable sensation of contrasts in body temperature during intimate physical contact; the feeling of warmth or of being hot, which results from vasocongestion (*qv*) or increased blood flow in the skin. *See also* somatosensory affectional deprivation; nurturance; touch.

temperature method of contraception A technique of contraception (*qv*) that seeks to ascertain the time of ovulation (*qv*) by checking the basal body temperature (*qv*) and avoiding intercourse (*qv*) during the fertile period (*qv*). This contraceptive method involves daily measurements of slight changes in the basal body temperature, with avoidance of intercourse from the last day of the menstrual flow (*qv*) until 3 days after the small dip and sudden rise in the basal body temperature that marks ovulation (*qv*). The failure rate for this method is relatively high unless it is combined with the Billings' or cervical mucous method (*qv*).

template In psychosexual development (*qv*), a neurological pattern, encoded in the brain, that regulates or establishes tendencies that affect behavioral responses or thinking. *See also* ideal lover template. In genetics, the deocyribonucleic acid (*qv*) strand that acts as a coding pattern for the synthesis of messenger ribonucleic acid (*qv*) in the nucleus. Neural encoding presumably begins prenatally and continues during infancy and perhaps into preadolescence. Resources: T. Perper, *Sex Signals: The Biology of Love* (Philadelphia: ISI Press, 1985); J. Money, *Lovemaps* (New York: Irvington, 1986). *See also* imprinting.

temple prostitution *See* sacred prostitution.

tempt, to (n. temptation) To endeavor to persuade, incite, or induce someone into evil or sin. *See also* concupiscence. Colloquially, the term has come to have a positive meaning of being drawn to something pleasurable or nice, perhaps with a delicious tinge of guilt for seeking the forbidden.

tenderness The quality of being sensitive, caring, gentle, considerate, loving, and affectionate; the sensitivity to touch of an organ or structure, for example, the nipples (*qv*), clitoris (*qv*), testicles (*qv*), and penile glans (*qv*). Actions, such as cuddling, hugging, and kissing, that express these qualities are often simply described as tenderness.

tenting (tenting effect) Elevation of the uterus (*qv*) from the pelvic cavity into the abdominal cavity during sexual arousal (*qv*), resulting in expansion of the inner vaginal cavity (*qv*) and formation of a seminal pool (*qv*) where semen (*qv*) gathers after coital ejaculation (*qv*). Some believe that clitoral stimulation is associated with the tenting effect.

tenting orgasm A orgasm (*qv*) triggered by stimulation of the clitoris (*qv*), with nerve impulses traveling along the pudendal nerve (*qv*) to the sacral region of the spinal cord and returning to trigger formation of the orgasmic platform (*qv*) and produce a myotonic (*qv*) discharge in the various pelvic muscles including the pubococcygeal muscles (*qv*). This orgasm is contrasted with the A-frame orgasm (*qv*).

teratism Any congenital or developmental abnormality produced by inherited or environmental factors or by their combination; a severely malformed fetus (*qv*).

terato- A prefix meaning ''of or related to a monster or abnormal development.'' *See also* teratoma.

teratocarcinoma A tumor, usually in the testicle (*qv*) or ovary (*qv*), that contains embryonic or trophoblastic tissues. *See also* teratoma.

teratogen (teratogenesis) Any substance, agent, or process that interferes with normal prenatal development, causing malformations in one or more developing structures. Chemical substances and drugs such as thalidomide (*qv*) and alcohol, and agents such as radiation, bacteria, and viruses, are common teratogens. However, abnormalities in chromosome (*qv*) number, genetic (*qv*) mutations, and alterations of normal differentiation of an organ, structure, or whole organism can also be termed teratogenic. *See also* congenital birth defect.

teratologic effect An obvious physical deformity or abnormal development caused by maternal-fetal exposure to a teratogenic (*qv*) agent and apparent at birth (*qv*) or diagnosed in the first year after birth. *See also* congenital birth defect.

teratoma A tumor composed of different kinds of tissue, none of which normally occur together or in the same site. *See also* teratocarcinoma. Teratomas and teratocarcinomas are closely related, some fully benign, others highly malignant, and a third mixed type. The most common site for a teratoma is in the ovaries (*qv*) or testes (*qv*). Approximately one-third of all testicular cancers (*qv*) are teratocarcinomas. A teratomatous rest is a malignant, invasive tumor composed of ectopic (*qv*) embryonic tissue that produces human chorionic gonadotropins (*qv*). When a teratomatous rest occurs in a young male, the hormone-induced result is often premature puberty (*qv*). However, since this tumor is highly invasive and malignant, it usually results in death before the sexual precocity becomes evident. *See also* hydatid mole.

Teratomas derived from germ cells can develop into partly formed embryonic tissues and organs, an extreme case being the formation of mouse embryos without fertilization (*qv*) and within the testes of male mice of certain strains. Resource: C. R. Austin & R. G. Edwards, eds., *Mechanisms of Sex Differentiation in Animals and Man* (New York: Academic Press, 1981), pp. 301–328.

teratomatous rest *See* teratomas; hydatid mole.

teratophobia A morbid fear of monsters (*qv*), or more specifically, the fear of giving birth (*qv*) to a grossly deformed infant (*qv*).

term The end of a normal gestational (*qv*) period; any pregnancy (*qv*) that results in a newborn (*qv*) delivered (*qv*) after the end of the thirty-seventh and before the beginning of the forty-third week of gestation, regardless of birth weight. An infant born before the start of the thirty-eighth week of gestation is referred to as a premature or preterm delivery; a fetus delivered after the forty-second week is referred to as a postterm fetus, infant, or delivery.

territorial marking The marking by an animal of its home territory with an odorous substance or pheromone (*qv*) secreted by specialized glands or excreted in the urine (*qv*).

tertiary sex characteristics Sex differences that are in large part acquired or learned; the adoption of masculine and feminine sex roles (*qv*) based on sexual role stereotypes (*qv*) within a culture. These characteristics are distinct from primary and secondary sex characteristics (*qv*), which are part of the biological maturation process. *See also* gender coding: sex adventitious, sex adjunctive, sex irreducible, sex derivative.

testeria A feminist (*qv*) term for the crippling, often dangerously pathological, condition found in males who cannot express their emotions and must always remain rational, detached, calm, and efficient. *Testeria* is a wordplay on the etymology of "hysteria" (*qv*), which folklore attributed to a "wandering womb." *See also* masculinity; macho. Resource: C. Kramarae & P. A. Treichler, *A Feminist Dictionary* (London: Pandora Press, 1985), p. 445.

testes Plural of testis (*qv*).

testes determining factor (TDF) gene A small genetic region of the Y chromosome (*qv*) which was thought to induce testicular differentiation of the embryonic hipotential gonad. The TDF gene is distinct from the H-Y antigen gene, which had previously been thought to be on the Y chromosome and essential for directing testicular development. The function of this genetic region in determining testicular, and hence masculine, development was challenged in 1989 by Palmer and colleagues.

testis det factor (TDF) gene In 1990, three articles in *Nature* resolved the problem raised by Palmer and reported independent confirmations of the TDF gene in humans and a variety of mammals. Resources: J. Gubbay et al. A gene mapping to the sex-determining region of the mouse Y chromosome is a member of a novel family of embryonically expressed genes, *Nature* (Britain) 346(1990, July 19): 245–250; D. C. Page et al., The sex-determining region of the human Y chromosome encodes a marker protein, *Cell* 51(1987): 1091–1104; M. S. Palmer et al. Genetic evidence that ZFY is not the testis-determining factor, *Nature* (Britain) 342(1989, December 21/28): 937–939; A. H. Sinclair et al. A gene from the human sex-determining region encodes a protein with homology to a conserved DNA-binding motif, *Nature* (Britain) 346(1990, July 19): 240–244.

testicle (testicular) The testis (*qv*) and associated epididymis (*qv*); an alternative term for the testis (*qv*).

testicular agenesis A congenital (*qv*) absence or nondevelopment of normal testicular tissue, resulting in failure of the internal and external sexual organs to differentiate as male and/or in the lack of secondary male sexual characteristics (*qv*) at birth (*qv*).

testicular atrophy A degeneration and loss of function in the testes (*qv*), resulting from an interruption or degeneration of the testicular blood supply, syphilis (*qv*), filariasis, or the mumps.

testicular biopsy Surgical removal of a small sample of the testis (*qv*) to provide material for histological examination in cases of infertility (*qv*).

testicular cancer A malignant neoplasm (*qv*) of the testis (*qv*) occurring most commonly in men between the ages of 20 and 35. Trauma is not considered a causative factor, although diagnosis frequently follows a trauma. Tumors are more common in the right than the left testis. An undescended testis (*qv*) is often affected.

testicular cord *See* spermatic cord.

testicular elevation The involuntary contraction of the dartos muscles (*qv*) that lifts the testes (*qv*) within the scrotal sac (*qv*) and brings them closer to the pelvic floor. Testicular elevation occurs during sexual excitement (*qv*), when it is a precursor to and perhaps an essential component in male orgasm (*qv*). It also occurs when the testicles are exposed to cold.

testicular failure Any dysfunction of the testes (*qv*), either of the sperm-producing seminiferous tubules (*qv*) or of the androgen-producing cells of Leydig (*qv*), that results in infertility (*qv*) and/or failure to develop secondary sexual characteristics (*qv*).

testicular feminization syndrome The result of an X-linked (*qv*) recessive (*qv*) gene (*qv*) characterized by the inability of somatic cells (*qv*) in a chromosomal male (46,XY) (*qv*) to produce receptors for testosterone (*qv*) and its derivatives. The affected individual thus does not respond to the masculinizing (*qv*) effects of circulating androgens (*qv*). Although the affected individual has a male chromosome complement, a male balance of hormones, and testes, the anatomical phenotype (*qv*) is that of a sterile, amenorrheic (*qv*) female with normal external female anatomy and secondary female sex traits produced by testicular and adrenal-produced estrogens (*qv*). Also known as androgen insensitivity syndrome.

testicular tumor A benign or malignant growth in the testicle (*qv*), usually affecting only one testis. Testicular tumors frequently result in precocious production of pubertal (*qv*) hormones and thus in a premature sexual maturation. *See also* teratoma.

testis (pl. testes) The paired male reproductive glands, which produce sperm (*qv*) and androgenic hormones (*qv*). The testes are laterally compressed, oval spheroids, about 4 centimeters long and 2.5 centimeters wide. Each testis consists of several hundred conical lobules containing the tiny seminiferous tubules (qv), each about 75 millimeters long, in which the spermatozoa (qv) develop. The testes also produce a preponderance of testosterone (qv) with some estrogenic (qv) hormones from the interstitial cells of Leydig (qv). They are rich in nerve supply and sensitive to touch and pressure.

Originally the testes are situated in the fetal abdominal cavity behind the peritoneum. Toward the end of pregnancy (qv), they migrate downward though the inguinal canal (qv), creating a temporary herniation of the pelvic cavity, which is closed off after the testes become situated in the scrotal (qv) sac. The medical term for an arrested, undescended, or abdominal testicle is cryptorchidism (qv). Sterility (qv) results if both testes fail to descend.

Differences in the origins of the two internal spermatic arteries from the aorta account for the tendency of the left testis to hang below the right testis in the scrotum. The convoluted epididymis (qv), where sperm are stored prior to ejaculation (qv), rests on the upper posterior border of the testis. Each epididymis is a coiled tube, about 20 feet long, connected to the vas deferens (qv). *See also* appendix testis; congested testes; ectopic testis; femoral testicle; hypermobile testes; malpositioned testes; mediastinum testis; parenchyma testis; perineal testicle; puboscrotal testicle; retractile testis; rudimentary testis.

testis cords The primordia that appear in the genital ridges, or developing undifferentiated gonads (qv), in the sixth week of gestation. These quickly develop into the seminiferous tubules (qv) of the testes (qv). Also known as primitive sexual cords.

testolactone An estrogen (qv) inhibiting form of testosterone (qv) used therapeutically with infertile (qv) men suffering from low sperm count (qv) caused by high levels of estrogens (qv).

testosterone The most biologically active hormone (qv) in the androgenic (qv) family of steroids. Testosterone, mainly produced in the male by the testicular cells of Leydig (qv), stimulates masculine differentiation of internal fetal sexual anatomy, male secondary sexual characteristics (qv) following puberty (qv), and libido (qv) in both sexes. It also diverts the fetal brain from the Eve plan (qv) into the Adam plan (qv).

Testosterone or its metabolites can be measured in both blood plasma and urine. Artificially synthesized structural variants include testosterone proprionate and testosterone sulfate. Dihydrotestosterone (qv), a naturally occurring variant, directs differentiation of the external anatomy in male fetuses (qv). In females, testosterone is produced by the ovaries (qv) and adrenal glands (qv) from an estrogenic precursor.

testosterone cyclopentylproprionate *See* testosterone cyprionate.

testosterone cyprionate An injectable, long-acting form of testosterone (*qv*) sometimes used to treat men having low levels of testosterone and organic erectile dysfunction (*qv*).

testosterone enanthate, phenylproprionate, and proprionate Injectable, long-lasting forms of testosterone (*qv*).

test tube baby A colloquial term for a fetus (*qv*) or infant (*qv*) conceived in vitro or outside the uterus (*qv*), or by artificial insemination (*qv*). The ovum (*qv*) needed for in vitro fertilization (*qv*) is obtained by ovum lavage (*qv*) or surgically removed with the aid of an endoscope (*qv*). Following in vitro fertilization, the resultant embryo (*qv*) is transplanted back into the uterus of the woman who produced the ovum or into the uterus of a surrogate mother (*qv*), where it is carried to term (*qv*).

test tube conception *See* test tube baby; in vitro fertilization.

tetanic contraction A continuous or sustained muscular contraction. *See also* vaginismus.

tetrahydrocannabinol (THC) The psychoactive component in the hemp plant *Cannabis sativa*, marijuana, and hashish. THC is a rapidly metabolized beta-adrenergic antagonist that increases the pulse rate, produces a feeling of euphoria and has varying other psychological effects, including sexual enhancement for some. In large doses, THC can cause gynecomastia (*qv*) in males.

T-group *See* encounter group; sensitivity-training group.

Thai beads *See* Ben-Wa balls.

thalamus The major center of the brain involved in the transmission of sensory impulses to the cerebral cortex (*qv*). The thalamus translates crude sensations of pain, temperature, and touch. It participates in associating sensory impulses with pleasant and unpleasant feelings, in the arousal mechanisms of the body, and in the mechanisms of complex reflex movements. *See also* hypothalamus.

thalidomide A sedative-hypnotic used in Europe and Great Britain between 1953 and the early 1960s until it was withdrawn from the market because of its serious teratogenic (*qv*) effects, particularly on fetal limb development. While widely used in Europe, thalidomide was not legally available in the United States.

thanatos (Gr.) In psychoanalytic theory (*qv*), human life is dominated by two opposing basic instincts: thanatos, the death instinct that motivates the organism to return to its original inorganic state, and eros (*qv*), the life-preserving or life-enhancing instinct. *See also* libido.

theca externa (L.) A thick, dense, protective layer of connective tissue in the ovary (*qv*), which encloses the developing ovum (*qv*) with its follicle cells. *See also* theca interna.

theca interna (L.) The layer of cells immediately surrounding the ovarian follicle (*qv*), rich in capillary supply and lymph vessels. After ovulation (*qv*), the theca interna supports the formation of the corpus luteum (*qv*). *See also* theca externa.

thecoma An ovarian tumor that produces female sex hormones (*qv*); generally found in postmenopausal (*qv*) women, it causes irregular uterine bleeding, breast (*qv*) enlargement, and increased libido (*qv*). Only rarely is it malignant.

theelin An obsolete medical term from the 1940s for a female hormone (*qv*) produced by the ovaries (*qv*) and placenta (*qv*), and believed to be responsible for the development of the uterus (*qv*), vagina (*qv*), and breasts (*qv*) as well as influencing female libido (*qv*). Identified as estrone (*qv*), a metabolic derivative of the active hormone estradiol (*qv*), theelin is now a trade name for estrone (*qv*).

thel- A prefix meaning "of or pertaining to the nipple (*qv*)," as in *thelangia*, *thelarchy*, *theleplasty*, *thelitis*.

thelalgia Any pain experienced in the nipple (*qv*) of the breast (*qv*).

thelarche The beginning of female breast (*qv*) development, which normally occurs prior to the start of puberty (*qv*) during the beginning of the rapid body growth phase between ages 9 and 13. Premature thelarche is precocious breast development in a female without other evidence of sexual maturation. *See also* menarche.

thelasis A medical term for suckling (*qv*), nursing (*qv*), or breast-feeding (*qv*).

thelerethism The erection of the nipple (*qv*) due to stimulation of involuntary muscle fibers, contraction in the areola (*qv*) and nipple triggered by touch, sexual arousal, temperature, or simple friction with clothing.

-thelia A combining form meaning "of the nipples (*qv*)" or "being female."

thelitis an inflammation of the nipple (*qv*) of the breast (*qv*).

thelyblast An outdated term for the nucleus of a fertilized ovum (*qv*).

thelygenic The reproductive pattern of producing only female offspring.

thelygonia An ovum (*qv*) or sperm (*qv*) containing an X chromosome (*qv*). Since the mammalian female is homogametic (*qv*), human ova are all thelygoniae; in the heterogametic (*qv*) male, only half the sperm are thelygoniae since the other half contain a Y chromosome (*qv*).

thelymania An obsolete term for satyriasis (*qv*).

thelyplasm The X chromosome (*qv*) in a male or female gamete (*qv*). *See also* thelygonia.

theoretical effective or failure rate The effectiveness or failure of a contraceptive method (*qv*), measured by the number of unwanted pregnancies (*qv*) expected to occur under hypothetical conditions where the user consistently and accurately follows the manufacturer's directions. *See also* actual effectiveness (failure) rate.

therapeutic abortion Termination of a pregnancy (*qv*) deemed necessary by a physician to preserve the mother's life or her physical or mental health. Informally used for any legal abortion (*qv*).

therapeutic coitus A concept in Taoist (*qv*) and Tantric (*qv*) belief in which specific coital positions, rhythms, and rituals (*qv*) are said to have healing and health-enhancing effects by rectifying physiological and energy imbalances.

thermography A computerized diagnostic technique for measuring the heat given off by different organs or organ regions to assess the health or disease status of the organ; may be used in detecting certain vascular tumors of the breast (*qv*).

Thornburgh v. American College of Obstetricians and Gynecologists In this 1986 five-to-four decision, the U.S. Supreme Court struck down a Pennsylvania abortion (*qv*) regulation somewhat similar to those invalidated in 1983 in *Kansas City v. Ashcroft, City of Akron v. Akron Center for Reproductive Health* (*qv*), and *Simopolus v. Virginia* (*qv*). The Court said that states may not require doctors to inform women seeking abortions about potential risks and about the availability of prenatal care (*qv*) and childbirth care (*qv*).

threesome A simultaneous sexual interaction of three persons. Typically a man, or less commonly a woman, will initiate the addition of a third individual to his or her dyadic (*qv*) sexual activities. Depending on the gender of the three participants, a threesome may involve male or female homoerotic behavior. Males interested in threesomes often fantasize the main female partner in the role of a whore (*qv*). Some threesomes are transitory; others may last for years. *See also* ménage à trois; troilism. Resource: A. Karlen, *Threesomes: Studies in Sex, Power, and Intimacy* (New York: Beechtree Books, 1988).

thrush Candidiasis (*qv*) of the oral mucous membranes, characterized by white patches or plaques and caused by *Candida albicans*. Thrush may develop following use of a broad-spectrum antibiotic that suppresses the normal competing bacterial flora of the mouth, thereby allowing *Candida* to gain ascendancy.

thyme An herb considered by ancient Greeks and Romans to be an aphrodisiac (*qv*) because its flowers attract bees, which make honey, an ingredient in many aphrodisiacs.

Tijuana bible Eight-page, wallet-sized, cartoon-style, sexually explicit booklets popular in the 1930s and 1940s illustrating a variety of sexual activities, often with characters from the newspaper comics. The inexpensive Tijuana bibles provided young men with information about sexual behaviors in an era when little formal or public sex education (*qv*) was available. Also known as "eight pagers."

tinea cruris (L.) A superficial skin infection of the groin, caused by one of several fungal organisms; more common in the tropics and among males. Also colloquially known as jock itch (*qv*).

Tissot, Simon André (1728–1797) A Swiss physician who gave prominence and popularity to the degeneracy theory (*qv*), which held that the loss of "vital fluid" through masturbation (*qv*) or onanism (*qv*) caused insanity and other diseases. Tissot's *Treatise on the Disease Produced by Onanism*, first published in Latin and French, appeared in an English edition in 1776 and in an American edition in 1832. His writings strongly influenced American sexual thinking and morality during the Victorian (*qv*) era. *See also* Graham, Sylvester; Kellogg, John; semen myths; onanism. Resource: J. Money, *The Destroying Angel* (Buffalo: Prometheus Books, 1985).

titillatione mammarum (L.) A term once used by prostitutes (*qv*) who specialized in mammary coitus (*qv*).

Title IX A federal government statute mandating equal educational opportunity regardless of sex, including equal athletic opportunities for both males and females in schools.

Title X A U.S. Public Health Services act that provides public funding for contraceptive (*qv*), sterilization (*qv*), and abortion (*qv*) services. *See also* Title XIX; Appendix D.

Title XIX A U.S. Social Security Act that established Medicaid to provide public funding for state-operated programs of medical assistance to people with low incomes. Under broad federal guidelines, the individual states determine benefits, eligibility, rates of payment, and methods of administration. In the late 1980s, anti-abortion (*qv*) advocates were often able to have state laws enacted that totally prohibit the use of Medicaid and Title X (*qv*) funds for contraceptives (*qv*), sterilization (*qv*), and abortions (*qv*). Previously more than 30 percent of all public funding for these services came from these sources.

T-mycoplasma *See Ureaplasma urealyticum.*

tobacco stains A complication of endometriosis (*qv*) in which brown-colored cysts, caused by endometrial (*qv*) tissue, become ectopically implanted in the peritoneal membranes of the pelvic and abdominal cavities.

tobacco wife An eighteenth- and nineteenth-century colloquial expression for a woman brought from Europe, sight unseen, by an American colonist who paid her passage in tobacco. Also known as a trade wife when a frontiersman paid the passage of a woman to the western frontier.

toco- A combining form referring to birth (*qv*).

tocoergometry A measurement of the expulsive force of the uterine (*qv*) muscles in childbirth (*qv*).

tocomania A mental disturbance that sometimes follows childbirth (*qv*). *See also* postpartum depression.

tocophobia A morbid fear of childbirth (*qv*).

tomboy A colloquial expression applied to a prepubescent (*qv*) or adolescent (*qv*) girl whose behavior and/or interests are labeled as boyish in, for example, their focus on sports, physical activity, and choice of friends. The differentiation of gender identity-role (*qv*) for a tomboy, defined in terms of sex role stereotypes (*qv*), is judged more or less discordant with her gender. *See also* sissy boy syndrome.

topless A colloquial term referring to female dancers, waitresses, and other women in service or entertainment roles who appear in public naked to the waist. Also refers to nightclubs, restaurants, and other places of entertainment that feature bare-breasted women.

TOR *See* transvaginal ovum recovery.

TORCH An acronym for the five main organisms that can cause congenital birth defects (*qv*): Toxoplasma (*qv*), Other (syphilis) (*qv*), Rubella (*qv*), Cytomegalovirus (*qv*), and Herpes simplex (*qv*).

torsion of the testis An abnormal axial rotation of the spermatic cord (*qv*) that stops the blood supply to the testicle (*qv*), epididymis (*qv*), and related structures. Partial loss of circulation may result in testicular atrophy (*qv*), and complete loss of circulation for 6 hours may result in testicular gangrene. Prompt surgical correction is required in most cases.

TOSOS An acronym for The Other Side of Silence, a homosexual (*qv*) support group founded by the playwright Doric Wilson.

total hysterectomy The surgical removal of the entire uterus (*qv*) with the cervix (*qv*). Surgical removal is usually accomplished through an abdominal rather than vaginal (*qv*) approach. In a subtotal or partial hysterectomy, the cervical portion of the uterus is left in place.

Total Woman The title of a best-selling book of the 1970s by Marabel Morgan that draws heavily on the ethic of the old South and conservative biblical interpretations to defend and extol the traditional submissive role of woman-mother. Total Woman workshops were popular nationwide among antifeminist traditional women in the 1970s. Feminist Catherine MacKinnon argues that "*Total Woman* makes blasphemous sexuality into a home art, redomesticating what prostitutes have marketed as forbidden." *See also* Fascinating Womanhood; hot sexual values. Resources: M. Morgan, *The Total Woman* (New York: Pocket Books, 1973); C. A. MacKinnon, Feminism, Marxism, Method, and the State: An agenda for theory, *Signs* 7(3)(1982):96.

totem (totemism) A plant, animal, or natural object that is a symbol (*qv*) of and considered to be related by reproductive kinship (*qv*) to a given family (*qv*), tribe (*qv*), or clan (*qv*) and taken as its emblem. The totem is revered as the ancestor, tutelary spirit, and protector of the family, tribe, or clan. A totem plant or animal is taboo (*qv*) and considered sacred, although it may be eaten on ritual occasions. Among some primitive peoples, members of the groups with the same totem are forbidden to marry or have sexual relations (*qv*), a belief Sigmund Freud (*qv*) interpreted in his 1913 work, *Totem and Taboo*, as a primitive prohibition against incest (*qv*). Later anthropologists, notably structuralists, have interpreted totemism as part of a symbolic system involving kinship, reciprocal duties, and relationships between humans and nature.

touch Physical contact with one's own or another person's body or some object using the finger, hand, or some other part of one's body. Touch, the primal form of direct communication and nurturance, can express affection and provide stimulation to the erogenous (*qv*) areas of the body during loveplay (*qv*), or it can be painful and violent. Touch is a major component in the somatosensory affectional stimulation essential to normal physical and psychosexual (*qv*) development. *See also* somatosensory affectional deprivation (SAD) syndrome; frottage; toucherism.

touch deprivation *See* somatosensory affectional deprivation (SAD) syndrome.

toucheurism A paraphilic (*qv*) condition in which sexual arousal (*qv*) and orgasm (*qv*) respond to and depend on surreptitiously touching a stranger on an erotic (*qv*) body part, particularly the breast (*qv*), buttocks (*qv*), or genital (*qv*) area. *See also* frotteur.

Tourette syndrome A disorder, with childhood onset, characterized by episodes of involuntary muscle spasms in various body parts, vocal tics (barks, yelps, and grunts), and an uncontrollable urge to utter obscenities. *See also* coprolalia.

toxemia of pregnancy An infrequent complication of pregnancy (*qv*) characterized by high blood pressure, swelling, protein in the urine (*qv*), and possible convulsions. *See also* preeclampsia; eclampsia.

toxic shock syndrome (TSS) A condition in which vaginal (*qv*) inserts, particularly superabsorbent tampons (*qv*), allow the growth of life-threatening bacteria; first reported in 1980. The symptoms of TSS, caused by toxins from the bacterium *Staphylococcus aureus*, include fever, sore throat, nausea, vomiting, diarrhea, red skin flush, dizziness, and high blood pressure. Because the toxic reaction progresses rapidly, a physician should be consulted immediately when symptoms are first suspected. Treatment consists of supportive methods since there is no way to neutralize the toxin. TSS occurs more often during menstruation (*qv*) and in women between ages 15 and 24. Since TSS has occurred during use of a diaphragm (*qv*) and cervical cap (*qv*), these devices should not be left in place more than 24 and 48 hours respectively. Incidence is 10–15 per 100,000 women of menstrual age. When TSS occurs in nonmenstruating women and in men, it is due to an infection.

toxin A poisonous secretion or waste product produced by a virus, bacteria, plant, or animal.

Toxoplasma gondii (L.) An intracellular parasitic protozoan found in cats and other animal hosts. When this parasite infects a human adult, it causes toxoplasmosis, characterized by a rash, fever, malaise, central nervous system (*qv*) disorders, myocarditis, and pneumonitis. When the infection occurs in a fetus, it affects the liver and brain, causing congenital (*qv*) cerebral calcification, convulsions, blindness, microcephaly, or hydrocephaly, and mental retardation.

TPAL A classification system indicating (1) the total number of pregnancies (*qv*) a woman has had, (2) the number of premature infants (*qv*), (3) the number of abortions (*qv*), and (4) the number of living children.

trade wife *See* tobacco wife.

transactional analysis (TA) A form of psychotherapy based on a theory that three different, coherent, organized egos coexist throughout life in every personality, representing the parent, the adult, and the child. According to Eric Berne, who developed TA, each interaction between two persons is a transaction in which one of the three egos of both persons is expressed in meeting the person's need for recognition, or "strokes." The goal of transactional analysis is to help a person develop an adult ego decision-making power instead of inappropriately expressing the child or parent ego. Resources: E. Berne, *Sex in Human Loving* (New York: Pocket Books, 1971).

transcervical uterine aspiration The removal, by suction, of fluid, conception (*qv*) products, or abnormal endometrial (*qv*) tissue from the uterine cavity. *See also* vacuum curettage; vacuum aspiration; dilation and curettage.

transexual, transexualism *See* transsexual; transsexualism.

transexual surgery *See* sex change operation; transsexual.

transference In psychology and psychiatry, an unconscious defense mechanism where feelings originally directed to important people in one's early life are transferred to others in one's current life, like a therapist. In *positive transference* or transference love, feelings of love (*qv*) are directed towards the therapist. Such feelings are often sexualized. In *negative transference*, the redirected feelings are those of anger and fear. *See also* countertransference.

transformation test A test that detects a gonorrheal (*qv*) infection by isolating deoxyribonucleic acid (*qv*) from the gonorrhea bacterium in a cervical (*qv*) specimen. Cheaper and simpler than the standard culture test for gonorrhea, this test is still in the developmental stages. Research suggests that it may be adaptable as a self-administered test, using a tampon (*qv*) to collect the specimen. Also known as the C Test. *See also* Eliza Technique; Gonosticom Dri Dot test.

transgenderist A person, usually a male, who enacts the social role of the other gender; a transsexual (*qv*) who does not have sex change surgery (*qv*). A transgenderist is also defined as a person who is cross-coded for his or her gender role behavior (*qv*), or as a gynecomimetic (*qv*) or andromimetic (*qv*) individual who does not seek or want transsexual surgery. For some experts, transgenderism is synonymous with the chronic partial transposition of gender identity-role (*qv*). Transgenderism differs from transvestitism (*qv*) in that the former reflects a stable, continuous life-style, whereas the latter involves episodic cross-dressing (*qv*). *See also* female impersonator; gender transposition; transposition; transvestite.

transitional bisexuality In F. Klein's interpretation, a condition in which a person shifts from heterosexual (*qv*) to homosexual (*qv*) orientation through a temporary transitional period of bisexual (*qv*) activity. *See also* sequential bisexual. Resource: F. Klein, *The Bisexual Option* (New York: Arbor House, 1978).

transposition A shift from one side or path to another side or path, such as occurs in crosscoding for gender identity (*qv*) in the transsexual (*qv*), for gender role (*qv*) in the transvestite (*qv*), or for gender orientation (*qv*) in the homosexual (*qv*) or bisexual (*qv*).

transposition, gender-identity/role The interchange or crosscoding (*qv*) for gender identity (*qv*) and gender role (*qv*). The crosscoding may affect masculine and feminine expectations, behavioral stereotypes, or physical appearances. Various types of transposition have been described. *Total chronic transposition* is known as transsexualism *(qv)*. *Partial chronic transposition* involves gynecomimesis (*qv*) or andromimesis (*qv*), with the accepting love partner expressing male androphilia (*qv*) or female gynophilia (*qv*). *Total episodic transposition* results in transvestism (*qv*), and *partial episodic transposition* is characteristic of bisexuality.

Chronic and episodic transpositions are found in androgenous gender-coded education, androgenous legal status, androgeny (*qv*) of gender-coded play, body language (*qv*), grooming, and ornamentation. *See also* crossdressing; gender transposition; gender dysphoria. Resource: J. Money, *Love and Love Sickness* (Baltimore: Johns Hopkins University Press, 1980).

transsexual A person manifesting the symptoms of transsexualism (*qv*); a person, more often male than female, whose gender identity (*qv*) conflicts with his or her external sexual anatomy and who seeks a sex reassignment operation (*qv*); an individual gender-crosscoded (*qv*) for his or her core-morphologic identity (*qv*) and gender-role behavior (*qv*). A distinction is made by experts and transsexual advocates between preoperative and postoperative transsexuals depending on whether they have had sex change surgery.

transsexualism The condition of experiencing a persistent and profound sense of discomfort and inappropriateness about his or her anatomical sex and feeling compelled to have that anatomy surgically altered in order to live biologically and socially as a member of the other sex. Behaviorally transsexualism is the act of living and passing socially as a member of the opposite gender, with or without hormonal, surgical, or legal sex reassignment (*qv*). The need to identify as a member of the other sex may be so strong in male-to-female transsexuals that they may attempt self-castration (*qv*) or genital self-mutilation (*qv*). Preoperative and postoperative transsexuals often seek counseling and peer support in national and local gender dysphoria (*qv*) groups.

The cause or causes of transsexualism are unknown. However, psychologists have long theorized that profound abnormalities of infant and child development may cause this form of gender dysphoria (*qv*). Others, frequently including advocates of transsexual rights, argue that transsexualism is produced by prenatal (*qv*) biological factors resulting in a fixed condition resistant to psychological treatment. Such advocates argue that a sex change operation (*qv*) is the only solution for the transsexual.

In transsexuals, sexual orientation (*qv*) may or may not be transposed so that the postoperative transsexual may be oriented to partners of one or the other sex or to both sexes. *See also* hijra; xanith; berdache; gender transposition; transvestite; transgenderist; transposition gender identity-role. Resources: H. Benjamin, *The Transsexual Phenomenon* (New York: Ace Books, 1966); A. Bolin, *In Search of Eve: Transsexual Rites of Passage* (South Hadley, MA: Bergin & Garvey, 1988); R. F. Docter, *Transvestites and Transsexuals: Toward a Theory of Cross-Gender Behavior* (New York: Plenum, 1988).

transudate (transudation) The passage of a fluid through a membrane or squeezed through the spaces between the cells of a tissue; passage of a clear fluid or plasma from engorged blood vessels between the cells of the vaginal wall and into the vaginal canal (*qv*) where the fluid provides lubrication (*qv*) for intercourse (*qv*). *See also* vaginal sweating.

transurethral Any surgical process accomplished by entry through the urethra (*qv*), as in a transurethral prostatic operation. *See also* TURP; endoscope.

transvaginal ovum recovery (TOR) A surgical procedure for recovery of ova (*qv*) by introducing a laparoscope (*qv*) and suction instrument into the abdominal cavity through a small incision in the vaginal wall close to the cervix (*qv*) to gain access to the ovaries (*qv*) and harvest ova for in vitro fertilization (*qv*).

transverse presentation In childbirth (*qv*), the sideways positioning of the fetus (*qv*) in the uterus (*qv*) so that at birth a shoulder or arm is seen first in the vaginal opening; resolved by a Caesarean section (*qv*) if the fetus cannot be turned. *See also* breech birth; version, fetal.

transvestism (transvestite) A dependence on crossdressing (*qv*); behaviorally the act of dressing in the clothes of the opposite sex; psychologically the condition of feeling compelled to cross-dress, often in relation to sexual arousal (*qv*) and attainment of orgasm (*qv*) and/or to receive the attention afforded those of the female gender role (*qv*). Transvestism is usually a lifelong behavior pattern which rarely leads to transsexualism (*qv*) and is not necessarily linked to homosexuality (*qv*). Most transvestites are heterosexual (*qv*), and many are married. "Drag queens," another type of transvestite, are homosexual men who adopt elaborate feminine personas, garb, and mannerisms as part of camp culture (*qv*). Female impersonators (*qv*) are professional entertainers who may or may not be homosexual. In the strict sense, transvestism excludes drag queens and female impersonators and has been described as an episodic, total transposition (*qv*) of gender identity/role (*qv*). The reciprocal paraphilic condition is gynemimetophilia (*qv*). *See also* transposition of gender-identity/role; Tri Ess. Resource: R. F. Docter, *Transvestites and Transsexuals: Toward a Theory of Cross-Gender Behavior* (New York: Plenum, 1988).

transvestophilia *See* transvestism.

traumatic avulsion The separation or tearing away of any part of the body, as when the scrotum (*qv*) and/or penis (*qv*) are torn away by an abrasion. If the testicles (*qv*) are left exposed as the result of such an accident, they can be reimplanted under the skin of the thigh, or a new scrotum may be constructed from grafted tissue.

traumatic epididymitis A form of epididymitis (*qv*), an inflammation of the epididymis (*qv*) brought on by strenuous exercise in a young man. The condition may be caused by a reverse flow of urine (*qv*) up the urethra (*qv*) toward the bladder or by irritation of the prostatic urethra (*qv*) during physical exertion rather than by a direct injury to the epididymal tubes.

Treponema pallidum (L.) The microorganism that causes syphilis (*qv*); an actively motile, slender spirochete bacterium.

trial marriage A term for nonmarital cohabitation (*qv*) prior to entry into a formal civil or religious marriage (*qv*). The practice was advocated in the 1920s by a Denver judge, Benjamin B. Lindsey, who used the term *companionate marriage*. Lindsey's model allowed divorce (*qv*) by mutual consent provided there were no children. In the event of children, a divorce would be granted only when the children's welfare was assured.

This idea of a two-step marriage, a trial marriage that might be followed by a parental marriage, was later advocated by Margaret Mead (*qv*), Havelock Ellis (*qv*), Bertrand Russell, James Hemming, and Virginia Satir. Satir also advocated avoiding lifelong commitments in favor of a renewable marriage contract. Russell and Hemming avoid the use of the term *marriage* for the first stage because of its connotation of commitment. Russell and Ellis suggested that even full commitment should not be viewed as necessarily giving the legal right of sexual exclusivity. Trial marriages became more common starting in the 1960s. A major purpose of cohabitation or "living together" is to test compatibility before marrying. *See also* POSSLQ; sexually open marriage; comarital relations; satellite relations.

tribade *See* tribadism.

tribadism A sexual (*qv*) activity in which two women lie together, one on top of the other, with their genitals (*qv*) touching, and stimulate each other by rubbing. While lesbians describe tribadism in positive terms as lovemaking, the *Oxford English Dictionary* describes a "tribade" as "a woman who practices unnatural vice with other women."

TRIC agent An acronym for *tr*achoma and *i*nclusion *c*onjunctivitis, The TRIC agent is one of several strains of pathogenic *Chlamydia trachomatis* (*qv*) responsible for a variety of sexually transmitted diseases (*qv*), including lymphogranuloma venereum (*qv*), nongonococcal urethritis (*qv*), pelvic inflammatory disease (*qv*), Reiter's disease (*qv*), and conjunctivitis.

trichomoniasis A vaginal infection with burning, itching, and a frothy, thin, foul-smelling, yellowish-green or gray discharge produced by the protozoan parasite *Trichomonas vaginalis* (*qv*). In the male, trichomoniasis is usually asymptomatic (*qv*), although urethritis (*qv*) may follow an infection. The infection is transmitted by sexual intimacy and rarely by moist washcloths or during delivery (*qv*) from mother to newborn. The parasite does not invade the uterus (*qv*) because of the latter's unsuitable pH.

Trichomonas vaginalis (L.) A motile parasitic protozoan that causes vaginitis (*qv*) with a copious foul-smelling discharge and itching. *See also* trichomoniasis.

Tri Ess Acronym for the Society for the Second Self, a nationwide sorority for crossdressers (*qv*) established by Virginia Prince, grande dame of crossdressers and transgenderist (*qv*). Publisher of a quarterly magazine, *Femme Mirror*. Address: Box 194, Tulare, CA 93275.

trimester A three-month period; commonly used in reference to a stage in pregnancy (*qv*), (i.e., first, second, or third trimester).

triolism *See* troilism; threesome.

triorchidism Having three testicles (*qv*).

triphasic contraceptive pill A low-dosage combination birth control pill (*qv*) in which the amount of estrogen (*qv*) and progesterone (*qv*) varies during each third of the menstrual cycle (*qv*). The estrogen dosage increases at midcycle, and progesterone slowly increases throughout the cycle. This pill appears to have fewer side effects than other contraceptive pills because of its lower dosages of estrogen and progesterone. *See also* combination contraceptive pill; progestin-only contraceptive pill. As of 1990, available only in Europe.

triplet One of three offspring born of the same gestation (*qv*) period during a single pregnancy (*qv*).

triple X syndrome *See* XXX; X trisomy.

trisomy A chromosomal anomaly in which one of the 23 pairs of homologous (*qv*) chromosomes (*qv*) is represented by three instead of the normal two chromosomes. *See also* Klinefelter syndrome; XXX syndrome.

troilism A psychological condition in which a person depends on being sexually involved simultaneously with two other persons, or on fantasizing (*qv*) being in a threesome (*qv*) in order to obtain sexual arousal (*qv*) or satisfaction.

trophoblast cells The invasive cells of the placenta (*qv*) that facilitate implantation (*qv*) into the uterine mucosa. These cells secrete human chorionic gonadotropin (*qv*).

true birthrate The ratio of total births (*qv*) to the total female population of childbearing age (between the ages of 15 and 45). *See also* birthrate; crude birthrate; refined birthrate.

true twin A monozygotic twin (*qv*).

TSR The acronym for a testosterone (*qv*) sterilized (*qv*) (female) rat that exhibits a persistent estrous (*qv*) syndrome. Since a TSR lacks an ovulatory estrous cycle, it is sterile. Lifelong TSR is induced by an injection of testosterone prior to the age of 11 days. If the injection is given within five days after birth, a smaller dose is needed to achieve a lifelong effect.

TSS *See* toxic shock syndrome.

tubal abortion A tubal pregnancy (*qv*) in which an ectopically (*qv*) implanted (*qv*) embryo (*qv*) is expelled from the fallopian tube (*qv*) into the peritoneal cavity. When expulsion occurs, significant internal bleeding may lead to acute abdominal and pelvic pain. The condition may be asymptomatic, with the products of conception (*qv*) being reabsorbed. Tubal abortions rarely result in an abdominal implantation and pregnancy. A tubal pregnancy may also result in a life-threatening rupture of the tube as the embryo grows. This outcome can be avoided by surgical removal of both the embryo and the tube before rupture.

tubal abscess An abscess in a fallopian tube (*qv*) resulting from an infection. Symptoms may include menstrual (*qv*) irregularities, abdominal discomfort, colicky pain, and fever.

tubal insufflation A procedure designed to detect a blockage in the lumen of the fallopian tubes (*qv*) and commonly used as one of several tests to ascertain the possible cause of infertility (*qv*). Tubal blockage is tested by injecting a gas, such as carbon dioxide, into the uterus (*qv*). If the tubes are open, the gas escaping through the tubes into the abdominal cavity will register as a wavy pattern on a pressure gauge attached to the tubes. If the tube is blocked, gas does not escape, and the pattern is flat. Occasionally the test has a desirable side effect in opening a closed tube.

tubal ligation Female surgical sterilization (*qv*) involving cutting, cauterizing, or tying the fallopian tubes (*qv*), usually with an abdominal incision. Also known as salpingectomy (*qv*). In the *Irving procedure*, the tubes are severed after being tied off or ligated, with one end buried in the uterine wall (*qv*) and the other in the nearby ligament. In the *Madlener procedure*, the tube is tied with a non-absorbable suture material. In the *Pomeroy procedure*, the tube is tied off with an absorbable material and then severed. In the *Kroener procedure*, the tubal fimbriae are removed and the tubal os (*qv*) sealed. The tubes can also be closed by a mild electrical discharge that destroys the tubal tissue. Transabdominal approaches are rapidly being replaced by less invasive and simpler transvaginal approaches or by transabdominal approach using a laparoscope (*qv*).

tubal pregnancy An ectopic (*qv*) pregnancy (*qv*) in which the conceptus (*qv*) or embryo (*qv*) implants in the fallopian tube (*qv*). Approximately 2 percent of all pregnancies are ectopic. Of these, 90 percent are tubal. Tubal pregnancies rarely occur in first pregnancies. Prior tubal injury, usually due to a past infection. is the most important predisposing factor. Some tubal implants apparently die and are reabsorbed, but those that continue developing are difficult to diagnose and are potentially lethal to the woman. Treatment is a laparotomy (*qv*) and surgical removal of the conceptus and tube.

tubectomy The surgical removal of a fallopian tube. Also known as salpingectomy (*qv*).

tubercle A nodule, small eminence, or projection, as in a genital tubercle (*qv*).

tuberculosis prostatitis A tubercular infection that has spread from the lungs to the prostate gland (*qv*), resulting in fibrous growth and calcification of the prostate. Also known as tuberculous endosalpingitis. *See also* salpingo-oophoritis.

tuberculous salpingo-oophoritis An insidious form of tubercular infection involving the fallopian tubes (*qv*) and/or ovaries (*qv*), usually diagnosed only after a thorough diagnosis for infertility (*qv*). The symptoms are usually mild and not pathognomonic (*qv*), consisting of menstrual (*qv*) difficulty and a dull, unspecified pelvic pain. These symptoms result from a tubal infection or salpingitis (*qv*) that produces a cheeselike pus. Previously known as tuberculous endosalpingitis.

tubular pregnancy *See* ectopic pregnancy; tubal pregnancy.

tubular testicular (or ovarian) adenoma A benign tumor of the ovarian (*qv*) or testicular (*qv*) epithelium (*qv*) in which the tumor cells are arranged in a recognizable glandular structure. This form of adenoma, similar to that observed in masculinizing tumors of the adrenal glands, may be found in the gonads of hermaphrodites (*qv*), in the undescended testicle(s) (*qv*) of otherwise normal males, and in the ovaries of amenorrheic (*qv*) females.

tufting A medical complication associated with salpingitis (*qv*) involving an involution of the fimbriae (*qv*) at the ovarian opening of the fallopian tube (*qv*) that leaves only a small tuft of fimbriae and results in infertility (*qv*).

tumescence Literally, a ''swelling''; the erection (*qv*) and enlargement of the sexual organs (*qv*), particularly the clitoris (*qv*), orgasmic platform (*qv*), and the penis (*qv*), resulting from the vasocongestion (*qv*) accompanying sexual stimulation. In tumescence, blood flow increases into the cavernous tissue of the penis, clitoris, vestibular bulb (*qv*), and labia (*qv*) while blood outflow decreases. *See also* detumesence. Havelock Ellis (*qv*) proposed tumescence as the first stage of sexual response cycle (*qv*).

tunica albuginea (L.) The white collagenous fibrous covering surrounding the testicle (*qv*); derived from the vaginal process, an outpocketing of the pelvic cavity.

tunica dartos (L.) The inner layer of involuntary muscles of the scrotal (*qv*) sac that contract during sexual stimulation, touch, strenuous exercise, and exposure to cold. *See also* dartos.

TUR *See* TURP.

Turner-Ombredanne orchidopexy A surgical procedure for correcting an undescended testicle (*qv*) in which the undescended testicle is sutured into a space on the other side of the scrotum (*qv*) between the normal descended testicle and the septum or middle wall of the scrotum.

Turner syndrome A sex chromosome abnormality (*qv*) caused by nondisjunction leading to a missing X chromosome (*qv*), giving a karyotype (*qv*) of 45,XO and a female body type with congenital ovarian agenesis (*qv*), persistent juvenile genitalia (*qv*), and other symptoms. Also known as ovarian agenesis. The incidence of Turner syndrome is 1 in 3,000 to 1 in 5,000 births, lower than expected because many result in miscarriage (*qv*). Although the second X chromosome in a normal 46,XX female is partially inactivated in the Barr body (*qv*), this second X chromosome is essential for normal embryonic ovarian development. Although females with Turner syndrome lack the second X chromosome, they may appear reasonably normal anatomically until puberty (*qv*), when a lack of estrogenic hormone production in the nonfunctional streak ovaries (*qv*) results in a lack of sexual maturation and secondary sex characteristics (*qv*).

Symptoms may include webbed skin on the back of the neck, low nape hairline, retarded growth, persistence of juvenile sexual organs (*qv*), obesity, spinal deformities, triangular-shaped face, prominent ears, small jaw, hearing defects, and myopia. Lymphedema affects four out of five, and dwarfism is common. Symptoms may differ in variant forms in which a second X is present but has a partial deletion, or the individual is a chromosomal mosaic (*qv*) with two strains of cells, one normal 46,XX and the other 45,X. Rarely is an individual with Turner syndrome fertile (*qv*).

Language, motor, and learning deficits are reported in this condition along with retarded spatial-nonverbal IQ. Right brain hemisphere impairment may result in low self-esteem, reduced self-confidence, and lack of social adeptness. Reduced spatial and face-interpreting skills may cause adolescent emotional and social problems.

Etiology. The most common chromosomal pattern resulting in Turner syndrome is a chromatin-negative (*qv*) genetic female with only one sex chromosome—45,X0. Mosaic forms of Turner syndrome occur in which the affected person has one cell line with 45 chromosomes and only one X—the classic Turner chromosome complement—and a second cell line with a normal female chromosome complement. In mosaic Turner syndrome, the severity of symptoms depends on the proportion and distribution of the 45,XO cells. Moreover, when the Y chromosome (*qv*) is partially or fully inactivated in a chromatin-negative (*qv*) 46,XY individual, the result may be a sterile but otherwise normal female or a short male with classic Turner symptoms.

Turnock v. Ragsdale An Illinois law requiring that abortion (*qv*) clinics meet standards similar to those in hospital operating rooms, which the U.S. Supreme Court agreed to hear following its 1989 ruling in *Webster v. Reproductive Health Services* (*qv*).

TURP Abbreviation for transurethral resection of the prostate (*qv*), a surgical procedure in which a portion of an overgrown prostate is removed. This procedure is performed using an endoscope (*qv*) inserted through the urethra (*qv*) to the interior of the prostate to direct the physician in excising the prostate tissue. A transurethral approach is preferred to a transabdominal or transrectal approach since it does not result in nerve damage, which may affect sexual functioning and/or micturition.

TV Abbreviation for transvestite (*qv*).

21:7 oral contraceptive program One of several regimens for administering a hormonal oral contraceptive (*qv*), with a daily pill combining estrogens (*qv*) and/ or progesterone (*qv*) taken for 21 days followed by a placebo (*qv*) or no pill for 7 days.

twin One of the two offspring born of the same pregnancy (*qv*). *Dizygotic* or *fraternal twins* (*qv*) result when two separate ova (*qv*) are fertilized (*qv*) by two separate sperm (*qv*). By contrast, *monozygotic* or *identical twins* (*qv*) result from fertilization of a single ovum by one sperm. The developing embryonic mass or blastocyst then divides into two embryonic masses. The most common form of monozygotic twins separates at the inner cell mass stage, shares a common placenta (*qv*) but has separate amnions (*qv*), and develops within a single chorionic cavity. A second type separates at the embryonic disc stage and shares both a common placenta and a common amnion. The rarest form separates at the blastomere stage and develops fully separate amnions and chorions. The tendency to twin is inherited, and the use of some fertility drugs (*qv*), such as Clomid (*qv*), increases its possibility. Twins occur in roughly 1 in 80 pregnancies. *See also* conjoined twins; vanishing twin.

twin transfusion syndrome The connection of the placental circulation systems in some twins (*qv*) by vascular anastomoses. In some twins, placental fusion allows blood to be shunted from one fetus (*qv*) to the other, with the fetal donor becoming anemic and the recipient becoming polycythemic (too many red blood cells). Such transfusions occur in about 15 percent of all twin births.

two-digit classification A shorthand classification system using O, i, ii, iii, to indicate live births (*qv*) and pregnancies (*qv*). The first digit indicates the number of live births a woman has had, and the second number indicates the number of pregnancies with a virgule (/) separating the two codes (O/i indicates a woman who has had one pregnancy but it did not result in a live birth; ii/iii indicates a woman who had two live births out of three pregnancies).

Tyson's glands Several small glands located on the inner surface of the foreskin (*qv*) and under the penile corona (*qv*) on either side of the frenulum (*qv*) that contribute to a cheesy-like substance known as smegma (*qv*). Also known as preputial glands.

Tzanck test A diagnostic test for herpes (*qv*) and other diseases based on microscopic examination of cellular material obtained from skin lesions.

U

UCR *See* unconditioned response.

ultraertia An excess in the intensity or multiplicity of sexuoerotic (*qv*) responsiveness during the proceptive phase (*qv*). This excess may or may not extend into the acceptive phase (*qv*) of mating behavior. Ultraertia is subjectively experienced as strength, urgency, or incessancy of sexual desire or libido (*qv*).

ultrasonography The process of representing deep structures of the body by measuring and recording the reflection of pulsed or continuous sound waves in the ultrasonic frequency range. Applications include fetal monitoring and diagnosis of fetal abnormalities and length of fetal gestation (*qv*).

Ulysses A 1918–1920 novel by the Irish author James Joyce about a day in the life of Leopold Bloom, his wife Molly, and his friend Stephen Daedalus, a young Irish writer and teacher. Serial publication started in 1918 in France, resulting in numerous seizures by U.S. Customs officials because its many explicit sexual passages were deemed obscene (*qv*). In the early 1930s, Bennett Cerf of Random House signed a contract with Joyce and apparently engineered a customs seizure to force a test of the obscenity ruling and importation ban in court. In 1933, in a landmark decision, New York District Court Judge John M. Woolsey ruled that the ban was illegal because explicit sexual descriptions in the genuine service of art do not render a work obscene. *See also* Miller v. United States; Roth v. United States; pornography. Resource: W. Kendrick, *The Secret Museum: Pornography in Modern Culture* (New York: Viking, 1987).

umbilical cord The flexible tubular connection between the fetal navel (*qv*) or umbilicus (*qv*) and the placenta (*qv*) that allows nutrient transfer from the maternal to the fetal side of the placenta and transfer of fetal waste products to the maternal circulation system for excretion. The umbilical cord contains two umbilical arteries, one umbilical vein, and a gelatinous material called Wharton's jelly (*qv*), which prevents kinking of the blood vessels. The umbilical cord begins to develop in the fifth week of pregnancy (*qv*), reaching a length of about 2 feet and a diameter of 1/2 inch in the newborn (*qv*). After delivery (*qv*), the cord is clamped or ligated and severed. Within a week to 10 days, the cord remnant atrophies, leaving the navel, or belly button.

umbilicus (L.) The point on the abdomen where the umbilical cord (*qv*) joined the fetal abdomen, usually marked by a depression after birth although it may also protrude. Also called navel (*qv*); belly button.

unchaste The opposite of chastity (*qv*).

unconditional love Eric Fromm's term for a type of love (*qv*) that is absolute and given without conditions.

unconditioned response (UCR) An instinctive or unlearned reaction to a stimulus, such as the suckling reflex of an infant (*qv*); a response evoked by a certain stimulus situation at the beginning of any given learning or conditioning period. An unconditioned response theoretically occurs naturally and is not acquired by association and training. Also variously known as an inborn, instinctive, or unconditioned reflex. A reflexogenic erection (*qv*) triggered by touching the genitals (*qv*) is an unconditioned response; a psychogenic erection mediated by conscious processing of sensory input to the brain is a conditioned or learned response dependent on conditioned learning of the erotic nature of sensory input.

undersexed *See* desire phase dysfunction; inhibited sexual desire; hyposexuality; hypoactive sexual desire.

undescended testes *See* cryptorchidism.

undinism Undine or Ondine being a fabled Francogermanic female water spirit, undinism refers to a sexual-erotic response to urination. Urophilia (*qv*) and urolagnia (*qv*) are the more common and preferred terms.

unengaged head The head of a near-term fetus (*qv*) is not engaged in the cervical (*qv*) region of the mother's uterus (*qv*) in preparation for delivery (*qv*).

unequal twins Two nonjoined, fraternal fetal twins (*qv*) born in the same delivery (*qv*), but with one twin fully developed and the other underdeveloped. *See also* superfetation.

unilateral sexual precocity Premature development of the genitalia (*qv*), accessory organs, and sexual characteristics on one side of the body with normal development on the other side.

uniovular twin *See* monozygotic twin.

uniparous A single birth (*qv*); a woman who has had one delivery.

unisex Any behavior, characteristic, accessory, career, or life-style shared by or participated in by both men and women; androgynous. *See also* androgyny.

unitypic Differentiation of homologous (*qv*) male and female anatomical structures from the same embryonic primordium (*qv*) or anlagen (*qv*), such as the clitoris (*qv*) and penis (*qv*), which arise from the genital tubercle. Also applied to development of the brain and behaviors.

universal, social A principle of social life claimed to hold true for all societies, such as the idea that sexuality is always shaped by the individual culture (*qv*) in which it is expressed.

unlust *See* unpleasure.

unnatural act, sex, or sin Sexual acts considered illegal and/or sinful and immoral because they are performed by people who are not married to each other and do not lead to procreation (*qv*). In contrast, natural sex acts (*qv*) involve marital, penis-in-vagina intercourse (*qv*), and ejaculation (*qv*) and are therefore procreative. Thus, oral sex (*qv*), contraceptive coitus (*qv*), masturbation (*qv*), and anal intercourse (*qv*) are considered by some to be unnatural sexual acts. Rape (*qv*), incest (*qv*), adultery (*qv*), and fornication (*qv*), being coital but engaged in by an unmarried couple, are immoral but natural. This ethical distinction is commonly used in conservative, fundamentalist, and some Catholic traditions, although the phrase also persists in legal terminology. *See also* natural law.

unpleasure A psychoanalytic (*qv*) term for feelings of tension, discomfort, and frustration that follow when the pleasure drive of the id (*qv*) is denied gratification, particularly in the areas of food and sex. Some psychiatrists use the synonym *unlust*.

unsexed by failure The loss of sexual desire often experienced by males who find their masculine identity threatened by loss of employment, a divorce, or midlife crisis. This phenomenon was originally described by Margaret Mead, who coined the phrase. Its existence has been clinically confirmed by Masters and Johnson and others who have documented the suppression of testosterone production in males under stress which, in turn, allegedly results in decreased sexual interest and desire. Psychological factors may also exist in this type of sexual dysfunction.

unwell A euphemism for premenstrual syndrome (*qv*) or menstruation (*qv*).

uranism Karl Heinrich Ulrichs' term for a man who is, like a woman, sexually repelled by women and attracted to men because he has the mind of a woman within the body of a man. The term has been used as a synonym for homosexuality (*qv*). Ulrich devised two related terms, also derived from Aphrodite Urania, the Greek goddess of love: *urning*, referring to the male or female partner who assumes the passive or female role in a homosexual relation or to a passive male homosexual, and *urninde*, referring to a passive lesbian (*qv*). Ulrich's original usage in *Argonauticus* (1869) is also applicable to transsexualism (*qv*). Resource: J. Money, *Gay, Straight, and In-Between: The Sexology of Erotic Orientation* (New York: Oxford University Press, 1988), p. 88.

Ureaplasma urealyticum (L.) A member of the bacterial group Mycoplasma; a major cause of nongonococcal urethritis (*qv*) in both men and women. This organism is found in the urogenital tract of 50 percent of all asymptomatic people and is therefore indigenous and nonathogenic in most people. When this organism infects the chorionic surface of the placenta (*qv*), fetal prematurity (*qv*), neonatal (*qv*) death, and perinatal disease may follow.

ureter The normally collapsed tube that carries urine (*qv*) from the kidney to the urinary bladder. *See also* urethra.

urethra The tube through which urine (*qv*) leaves the bladder and passes out of the body. Urine passes from the kidneys through the ureters to the bladder and then is excreted through the urethra. In the female, the urethra averages 3 centimeters in length and opens between the labia minora (*qv*) and between the clitoris (*qv*) and vaginal (*qv*) opening. In the male, the urethra averages 20 centimeters and extends through the penis (*qv*), with three major divisions: the *prostatic urethra* inside the prostate gland (*qv*), an inch-long *membranous urethra* between the prostate and bulb of the penis, and the *penile urethra* enclosed by the corpus spongiosum (*qv*) in the shaft of the penis. The female urethra carries only urine; in the male it can carry semen (*qv*) or urine.

urethral abscess A cavity containing pus in the submucosal tissue lining the penile urethra (*qv*), resulting from an infection. *See also* Littre's glands.

urethral bulb The prostatic portion of the urethra (*qv*). The urethral bulb expands like a balloon during the first or emission phase (*qv*) of ejaculation (*qv*) when semen (*qv*) is ejected into the prostatic urethra while the internal and external urethral sphincters (*qv*) are closed.

urethral character A psychoanalytic (*qv*) term for a personality characterized by chronic bedwetting and by being overly ambitious and boastful to compensate for the self-esteem lost in incontinence.

urethral eroticism A psychoanalytic (*qv*) term for sexual pleasure (*qv*) associated with urination. *See also* urolagnia.

urethral groove The lower surface of the undifferentiated fetal genital tubercle (*qv*); a shallow groove that closes over and forms the penile urethra (*qv*) in males and remains open as part of the female vulva (*qv*).

urethral meatus The external opening of the urethra. *See also* hypospadia; hyperspadia.

urethral stage In psychoanalytic theory (*qv*), the phase of psychosexual development (*qv*) between the anal (*qv*) and the phallic stages (*qv*) when the urethra (*qv*) is the primary erogenous area (*qv*) and urination results in sexual pleasure.

urethral stricture A contraction or closure of the urethra (*qv*) by scar tissue or following faulty surgery.

urethritis Any infection of the urethra (*qv*), gonococcal or nongonococcal in origin. *See also* nongonococcal urethritis; nonspecific urethritis (NSU).

urethrocele Protrusion of the female urethra (*qv*) through the fascia of the anterior vaginal wall; a type of hernia.

urethroplasty Plastic surgery to construct an artificial urinary canal or urethra (*qv*) in a penis (*qv*) in order to correct a birth defect (*qv*) or injury.

urinary fistula An abnormally positioned opening of the urinary passage, or urethra (*qv*). A urinary fistula may result from the failure of a penile surgical suture to repair along its full length. *See also* hypospadia.

urinary responses The urge to urinate following vaginal intercourse (*qv*) due to internal stimulation of the urinary bladder by coital thrusting (*qv*); also an initial response to stimulation of the Grafenberg spot (*qv*) in the female.

urine The fluid extracted from the renal blood and excreted from the kidneys into the urinary bladder where it is stored before being released. Urine passes from the kidneys through the ureters for storage in the bladder and is eventually voided through the urethra (*qv*). Normally clear and straw-colored, urine is usually slightly acidic and marked by the characteristic odor of ammonia. Its normal constituents are: water, urea, sodium chloride, potassium chloride, phosphates, uric acid, organic salts, and the pigment urobilin. Its abnormal constituents may include blood, steroid metabolites, ketone bodies, protein, bacteria, glucose, and pus.

urine test A general term for pregnancy tests (*qv*) that detect pregnancy by identifying human chorionic gonadotropin (*qv*) or a metabolite of this hormone in urine (*qv*).

urinism *See* urolagnia.

urning *See* uranism.

urninde *See* uranism.

urogenital floor muscles A group of five muscles covering the floor of the pelvic cavity. In the male, these muscles facilitate the rhythmic contractions that produce ejaculation (*qv*): the bulbocavernosus, sphincter urethrae, erector penis, transversus perinei profundus, and transversus perinei superficialis. In the female, the bulbocavernosus is known as the sphincter vaginae and the ischiocavernosus as the erector clitoridis.

urogenital folds Paired embryonic folds on either side of the vulva (*qv*), beginning just in front of the genital tubercle (*qv*) and extending dorsally to the perineal region (*qv*). In the male, they fuse to form part of the penile (*qv*) shaft. In the female, they remain separate and form the medial or inner labia minora (*qv*). *See also* urogenital swellings.

urogenital sinus An elongated shallow cavity formed by the division of the cloaca (*qv*) in early embryonic development, containing the openings of the ureters (*qv*) and mesonephric ducts (*qv*) and giving rise to the vestibule or vulva (*qv*), the urethra (*qv*) and, in the female, part of the vagina (*qv*) and, in the male, part of the urethra (*qv*). In some types of hermaphroditism (*qv*), differentiation of the sinus is incomplete and results in a birth defect (*qv*) of the external genital orifices.

urogenital swellings Paired embryonic folds on the outer edges of the fetal vulva (*qv*) extending from the genital tubercle (*qv*) dorsally to the perineum (*qv*). In the male, the urogenital swellings fuse to form the scrotum (*qv*). In the female, they remain separate and form the lateral or outer labia majora (*qv*). *See also* urogenital folds.

urogenital system (UG system) The urinary and genital (*qv*) or reproductive organs and associated structures. In the male, the components of the urogenital system are two kidneys, two ureters, the bladder, and the urethra (*qv*) of the urinary system with the male genitalia—testes (*qv*), seminal vesicles (*qv*), seminal ducts (*qv*), prostate (*qv*), and penis (*qv*). In the female, the components are two kidneys, two ureters, the bladder, and the urethra with the ovaries (*qv*), uterine tubes (*qv*), uterus (*qv*), vagina (*qv*), and clitoris (*qv*).

urolagnia The condition of responding sexuoerotically to or depending on the scent, taste, or sight of urine (*qv*) or urination to obtain sexual arousal (*qv*) and facilitate or achieve orgasm (*qv*). Urolagnia may be expressed in the desire to watch one's partner urinate, by smelling urine or soiled underclothing, by urinating on one's partner, by being urinated on, or by drinking urine. *See also* undinism; urophilia.

urology, urologist The branch of medicine and its practitioners concerned with the anatomy, functioning, disorders, and care of the male urogenital (*qv*) tract and the female urinary tract. A gynecologist (*qv*) specializes in the female genital system.

urophilia *See* undinism; urolagnia.

urorectal septum A mesodermal (*qv*) ridge covered with endoderm (*qv*) that divides the embryonic cloaca (*qv*) into the urogenital sinus and rectum; the perineum (*qv*).

uterine Pertaining to the uterus (*qv*).

uterine angle That portion of the uterine wall surrounding the fallopian tube (*qv*).

uterine cavity The hollow portion of the uterus (*qv*) including the cervical canal (*qv*).

uterine cycle In humans, the monthly or near-monthly cycle of proliferation and shedding of the uterine endometrium (*qv*), regulated by ovarian estrogens (*qv*) and progesterone (*qv*). Following the end of the menstrual flow, estrogens from the theca interna of the ovarian follicle (*qv*) cause proliferation of the uterine mucosa with a doubling or tripling in its thickness. Uterine glands increase in number and length, and the arteries elongate in preparation for implantation (*qv*). The proliferative phase of the cycle varies in length and depends on the length of the follicular phase of the ovarian cycle (*qv*). Following ovulation (*qv*) and development of the corpus luteum (*qv*), mucosal proliferation continues but with a shift toward synthesis and storage of glycogen and accelerated vascular congestion and edema. This secretory phase, regulated by progesterone and estrogens secreted by the corpus luteum (qv), lasts 14 days unless the ovum is fertilized and embeds in the uterine mucosa. If fertilization (*qv*) and implantation do not occur, a drop in the ovarian hormones triggers a sloughing of the spongy, engorged uterine mucosa in a menstrual flow (*qv*) that lasts 3 to 6 days. Following the end of menstruation (*qv*), the cycle is repeated.

uterine displacement Any shift of the uterus (*qv*) from a position arched over the urinary bladder in the mid-axis of the body. *See also* wandering uterus.

uterine hernial syndrome A congenital (*qv*) deformity in which an otherwise normal, fertile (*qv*) male is found to possess a partially developed uterus (*qv*) with fallopian tubes (*qv*), due to the failure of Mullerian ducts (*qv*) to degenerate in the third month of gestation (*qv*).

uterine orgasm *See* A-frame orgasm.

uterine perforation An accidental tearing or puncturing of the uterine wall; a common consequence of botched abortions (*qv*).

uterine tube *See* fallopian tube.

uteroplacental insufficiency Any placental disorder that prevents normal fetal development to term (*qv*).

uterosacral ligaments Fibrous cords connecting the cervix (*qv*) with the bony sacrum of the pelvis at the lower end of the spinal cord and supporting the uterus (*qv*).

uterovaginal canal The fused middle and distal portion of the paired Mullerian ducts (*qv*) in a female fetus (*qv*) of 8 to 12 weeks age that will develop into a single uterus (*qv*) and vagina (*qv*). In the male fetus, this structure degenerates under the influence of the Mullerian inhibiting substance (*qv*), leaving only functionless vestiges like the uterus masculinus (*qv*).

uterus The womb; a hollow, pear-shaped internal muscular organ in women, located between the fallopian tubes and vagina, whose inner lining shows cyclical changes (*see* estrus; menses; menstrual cycle), and in which the fertilized ovum (*qv*) normally implants (*see* implantation) and the resulting embryo (*qv*) and fetus (*qv*) develops during pregnancy (*qv*). Anatomically the uterus is retroperitoneal and located above and behind the bladder and in front of the sigmoid colon. It consists of three layers: endometrium (*qv*), myometrium, and parametrium. The inner endometrial lining is subject to the menstrual cycle (*qv*) and produces the menstrual decidua (decidua functionalis). Beneath this layer is the decidua basalis, which does not degenerate, giving rise each month to a new functional layer. The muscles of the myometrium wrap around the uterus obliquely, laterally, and longitudinally, providing the contractions of labor (*qv*) and delivery (*qv*). Constriction of these muscles also reduces blood flow to the placenta (*qv*) to prevent hemorrhaging in childbirth. The canal of the cervix (*qv*) provides an entry for the sperm (*qv*) and an exit for the menstrual flow (*qv*) and newborn (*qv*). The fallopian tubes (*qv*) at the cephalic end provide a passage between the superior cavity of the uterus and the ovaries (*qv*), where fertilization usually occurs. The uterus is covered by the serosa, which is a continuation of the peritoneal membrane. A variety of ligaments suspend the uterus in the pelvic cavity. *See also* A-frame orgasm; tenting.

Sexist biases that focus on the reproductive function and value of women frequently use the womb as a symbol of woman's fertility (*qv*) and nurturance, representing the source of life. Many social and poetic symbols of fertility and femininity (*qv*) have been associated with the womb; for example, hysteria was allegedly caused by a wandering uterus (*qv*), a condition supposedly cured by hysterectomy (*qv*). Even today many believe that the removal of the uterus destroys a woman's sexual interests and capacities. Menstruation has been referred to by traditional gynecologists (*qv*) as the "weeping of a disappointed womb."

uterus, bicervical bicornis (L.) A congenital (*qv*) anomaly in which the paired Mullerian tubes (*qv*) fail to fuse fully, resulting in a single vagina (*qv*) with two cervixes (*qv*) leading to two uterine cavities.

uterus, bicornis unicollis (L.) A congenital (*qv*) anomaly in which one of the paired Mullerian tubes (*qv*) fails to develop so that a single vagina (*qv*) leads through a single cervix (*qv*) to a uterine cavity with one fallopian tube (*qv*), the other tube ending in a separate but undeveloped uterine cavity; a form of uterine atresia.

uterus, bilocular A congenital (*qv*) anomaly in which the middle portion of the paired Mullerian tubes (*qv*) fails to fuse. Specific forms include a bicervical type with a double cervix (*qv*) and a divided uterine cavity just inside the cervix and a single main uterine cavity above; a complete type with a double cervix and two distinct uterine cavities, each with its own single fallopian tube (*qv*); a unicervical type with a single cervix and a partially divided uterine cavity.

uterus, didelphys A congenital (*qv*) anomaly in which the distal and midportion of the paired Mullerian tubes (*qv*) fail to fuse, resulting in a double vagina (*qv*) and double uterus (*qv*).

uterus, unicervical bicornis A congenital (*qv*) anomaly in which the midportion of the paired Mullerian tubes (*qv*) fails to fuse completely, leaving a single vagina (*qv*) and a single cervix (*qv*) leading to two uterine cavities.

uterus, wandering *See* wandering uterus.

uterus masculinus (L.) An alternate name for the utricus prostraticus or utricle, a vestigial remnant of the Mullerian (*qv*) ducts in the male, the male homologue (*qv*) of the vagina (*qv*) and uterus (*qv*) in the female.

uterus with cervical atresia A congenital (*qv*) anomaly in which the cervical canal (*qv*) from the uterine cavity (*qv*) to the vagina (*qv*) does not open.

uterus with cervical/vaginal atresia A congenital (*qv*) anomaly in which the distal portion of the paired Mullerian tubes (*qv*) fuses but fails to develop, leaving a normal uterus (*qv*) with no cervical canal (*qv*) or vagina (*qv*).

UTI Any urinary tract infection.

utricle *See* uterus masculinus.

utricus prostraticus (L.) *See* uterus masculinus.

uxorilocal *See* matrilocal.

V

vacuum aspiration The method of abortion (*qv*) that is most commonly used in the first trimester (*qv*). Vacuum aspiration is performed under local or light general anesthesia to allow dilation (*qv*) of the cervix (*qv*). The contents of the uterus (*qv*) are sucked out (aspirated) through a plastic tube connected to a vacuum pump.

vacuum curettage A variation of vacuum aspiration (*qv*) abortion (*qv*) in which the uterine wall is scraped with a curette. *See also* dilation and curettage.

vagina The collapsed, highly expandable, tubular structure leading from the uterus (*qv*) to the vulva (*qv*). This traditional dictionary definition of vagina reveals an interesting psychology in dealing only with anatomy and not mentioning the vagina's function as the "organ of copulation" (*qv*) as standard definitions of penis (*qv*) always do. The vagina has three functions: it receives the penis (*qv*) during sexual intercourse (*qv*), serves as an exit channel for the monthly menstrual flow (*qv*), and is the birth canal (*qv*). In many women the vagina is also a seat of sexual pleasure when distended through penetration by the penis, fingers, or a dildo (*qv*), or through stimulation of the Grafenberg spot (*qv*).

The vagina lies behind and below the bladder and in front of the rectum (*qv*). In the adult woman, the anterior wall is about 7 centimeters long and the posterior wall about 9 centimeters. It widens from the vulva upward and narrows at the uterus, forming a curved vault around the cervix (*qv*). The mucosal lining covers erectile tissue and highly vascularized layers of longitudinal and circular muscle. The anterior wall contains the Grafenberg spot (*qv*). The vaginal wall lacks nerves for superficial touch but contains sensors for deep pressure. Lubrication (*qv*) occurs as a result of filtration of blood under pressure in the underlying submucosal layer. The transudate reaches the surface by filtering through the stratified squamosal epithelium of the mucosa. *See also* orgasmic platform; vaginal orgasm. *See also* vagina (*Addendum*).

vagina, atrophic *See* atrophic vaginalis.

vaginal adhesions The development of firm, fibrous growths in the upper vagina (*qv*) of a postmenopausal (*qv*) woman, which then descend and form attachments obstructing the external vaginal opening.

vaginal agenesis or atresia A congenital (*qv*) defect in which the vagina (*qv*) is malformed or does not develop.

vaginal atrophy *See* atrophic vaginalis.

vaginal axis An imaginary line from the vaginal opening to the posterior side of the vaginal cul-de-sac.

vaginal ballottement A technique of palpating the fetus (*qv*) through the vaginal wall by bouncing the fetus gently as it floats in the amniotic fluid (*qv*). The technique is used to detect a pregnancy (*qv*), and to ascertain cervical engagement of the fetal head or a floating fetus.

vaginal balls *See* Ben-Wa balls.

vaginal barrel The vagina (*qv*).

vaginal canal The collapsed tubular cavity formed by the vaginal walls. *See also* vagina.

vaginal contraceptive film *See* contraceptive film.

vaginal creams Medicated ointments containing estrogens (*qv*) and used for symptomatic treatment of vaginal atrophy (*qv*) and lack of the normal vaginal lubrication (*qv*) that leads to dyspareunia (*qv*). *See also* vaginal dryness; vaginal jelly.

vagina dentata (L.) In psychoanalytic theory (*qv*), the unconscious fantasy (*qv*) that the vagina (*qv*) has teeth that can castrate (*qv*) a male during coitus (*qv*). In males, this fantasy may be rooted in the castration anxiety (*qv*), while in females the basis may be penis envy (*qv*) and a desire to castrate males out of a subconscious revenge for the woman's supposed loss of a penis as a child. This fantasy is also encountered as misinformation picked up by sexually inexperienced teenagers from peers. The image of a toothed vagina may also represent a classic symbol of men's fear of sex and women.

vaginal discharge Any flow of fluid from the vagina (*qv*), excluding menstrual flow. A clear or pearly-white discharge is normal during the reproductive years, with less discharge before menarche (*qv*) and after menopause (*qv*). This normal discharge is produced by secretions of the endocervical glands. Vaginal or cervical inflammation or infections can cause increased discharge, which may have a foul odor or color and may be accompanied by irritation of the vulva (*qv*).

vaginal dryness Insufficient vaginal lubrication (*qv*) following sexual stimulation or premature cessation of vaginal lubrication during intercourse (*qv*). Vaginal dryness may have physiological or psychological origins. When it arises naturally from the reduced estrogen (*qv*) levels of menopause (*qv*), it can be treated with topical estrogens. When psychogenic in origin, normal sexual response may be achieved by counseling for anxiety, fears, or negative feelings that inhibit sexual arousal (*qv*) and the lubrication. Vaginal dryness can be symptomatically relieved with a water-soluble lubricant. It may also be relieved by masturbation (*qv*).

vaginalectomy Removal of a portion of the tunica vaginalis (*qv*) of the testis (*qv*).

vaginal envy A form of envy experienced by male-to-female transsexuals (*qv*) who not only desire to be rid of their male genitalia (*qv*) but also to obtain female sexual organs (*qv*) through plastic surgery.

vaginal epithelioma An invasive, metastatic, rapidly spreading malignancy of the epithelial lining of the vagina (*qv*).

vaginal father In psychoanalytic theory (*qv*), a male who fantasizes or dreams that he has a vagina (*qv*). This belief appears to originate from overidentification with one's mother. The belief is usually associated with a predilection for motherly roles in homemaking and child rearing and in unaggressive behavior coupled with an intense rivalry with women.

vaginal fistula An abnormal congenital (*qv*) or trauma-induced passage between the vagina (*qv*) and rectum (*qv*), urinary bladder, or urethra (*qv*).

vaginal fluid *See* transudation; vaginal lubrication.

vaginal foam A contraceptive (*qv*) containing a spermicide (*qv*) in an aerosol foam medium. Use of a vaginal foam is recommended in conjunction with a condom (*qv*), contraceptive diaphragm (*qv*), or cervical cap (*qv*). Directions usually recommend shaking the container vigorously at least 20 times to mix spermicide and carrier. The applicator is inserted deep into the vagina (*qv*) and then withdrawn 1/2 inch before plunger is pressed. One or two applications are recommended depending on brand. The foam should be applied no more than

15 minutes prior to intercourse (*qv*) and left undisturbed for at least 6 hours. Subsequent applications should be made before each additional act of coitus (*qv*). Allergic reactions may be avoided by changing brands and avoiding scented or flavored foams. Actual failure rate (*qv*) when used alone is 22 pregnancies in 100 women in a year. Use with a condom or diaphragm increases effectiveness to protection of 95 out of 100 women. Vaginal foam containing nonoxynol-9 (*qv*) also provides some protection against certain bacterial sexually transmitted diseases (*qv*), and possibly herpes (*qv*) and acquired immune deficiency syndrome (*qv*).

vaginal hypoesthesia A form of partial sexual anesthesia in which a woman self-reports no erotosexual (*qv*) sensitivity in the vaginal (*qv*) area although clitoral (*qv*) response may be experienced. *See also* vulval anesthesia.

vaginal jelly A contraceptive (*qv*) containing a spermicide (*qv*) in a jelly medium and designed for use with a contraceptive diaphragm (*qv*) or cervical cap (*qv*).

vaginal lubricant A water-soluble gel or cream used when the lubrication produced by the vagina (*qv*) itself is not sufficient to allow pleasurable stimulation of the clitoris (*qv*) or penetration of the vagina. *See also* vaginal dryness.

vaginal lubrication The transudation (*qv*) of plasma fluids from the blood vessels in the deep vaginal wall that lubricate the vaginal canal (*qv*), thereby facilitating stimulation and penetration of the vagina. The plasma fluids work their way between the cells of the vaginal wall into the vaginal cavity, where they provide lubrication. This is the first physiological response to sexual stimulation in the female, usually occurring within a few seconds of any effective stimulation. It is a normal outcome of vasocongestion (*qv*) and sexual arousal (*qv*). Recent research suggests that frequent use of cocaine may reduce vaginal lubrication. *See also* vagina.

vaginal melanoma An extremely dangerous, often lethal, molelike malignancy of the pigmented cells of the vaginal wall that develops from a prior melanoma elsewhere in the body.

vaginal orgasm An orgasm (*qv*) experienced and perceived as resulting from stimulation of the vagina (*qv*) alone, without any clitoral stimulation. Sigmund Freud (*qv*) first theorized a distinction between an "immature" orgasm (*qv*) triggered by clitoral stimulation and a "mature" orgasm resulting from vaginal intercourse. Clinical studies by W. Masters and V. Johnson refuted this distinction when they found that all orgasms depend directly or indirectly on clitoral stimulation. More recent studies of the Grafenberg spot (*qv*) suggest that there may be three general types of female orgasm: clitoral, vaginal, and blended. *See also* A-frame orgasm; tenting; blended orgasm.

vaginal plethysmograph A device for measuring and recording changes in the size and volume of the vaginal canal (*qv*); it allows the degree of vasocongestion (*qv*) and sexual arousal (*qv*) to be quantified. *See also* plethysmograph.

vaginal sarcoma A malignant growth in the muscular and subcutaneous layers of the vaginal wall. Although the growths may be shed because their rapid growth outstrips the blood supply, metastasizing cells may spread to other organs of the body, particularly the lungs.

vaginal secretion *See* vaginal lubrication.

vaginal spasms Recurrent and intermittent contractions of the perineal (*qv*) and paravaginal muscles surrounding the vaginal entrance that prevent vaginal penetration (*qv*) and intercourse (*qv*). Vaginal spasms occur before or during the acceptive phase (*qv*) of a sexual episode and are often due to earlier unresolved sexual traumas, fears, or anxieties. Psychological and behavioral therapies (*qv*) using graduated vaginal dilators or finger insertion exercises are helpful. Vaginal spasms are an uncommon hypophilic (*qv*) condition usually associated with gender identity conflict (*qv*), a history of rape (*qv*) or incest trauma (*qv*), or intense childhood suppression of sex. Also known as vaginismus.

vaginal sponge *See* contraceptive sponge.

vaginal suppository A small mass shaped for easy insertion into the vagina (*qv*) containing spermicidal (*qv*) chemicals that melts when inserted, thereby providing contraceptive (*qv*) protection similar to the contraceptive vaginal foams (*qv*). The suppository is inserted at least 10 minutes before intercourse (*qv*) to allow melting. It provides protection for up to 2 hours after insertion and should be left undisturbed for 6 to 8 hours after intercourse.

vaginal sweating *See* transudation; vaginal dryness; vaginal lubrication.

vaginectomy Excision of all or part of the vagina (*qv*).

vaginicoline Refering to microorganisms that normally reside in the vagina (*qv*).

vaginismus (L.) (**vaginism**) *See* vaginal spasms.

vaginitis A general term for any vaginal infection. Vaginitis may result from a variety of infections, usually gonococcal, yeast, or fungal. *See also Hemophilus vaginalis; Candida albicans; Trichomonas vaginalis.* Vaginitis can also result from chemical irritation or from allergic reactions to latex condoms (*qv*) or scented and flavored vaginal foams (*qv*) or jellies (*qv*). Vaginitis due to atrophy of the vaginal wall occurs in some women following menopause (*qv*).

vaginocele A hernia or tumor that projects into the vagina (*qv*); a colopocele.

vaginoplasty Surgical construction or reconstruction of the vagina (*qv*) to remedy a birth defect (*qv*), as part of a sex reassignment operation (*qv*) for a male-to-female transsexual (*qv*), or to remedy an accidental trauma to the vagina.

value In general, a behavior, attitude, or belief that is seen as desirable, useful, important, or worthy of esteem. In the sociology of T. Parsons, social order depends on the existence of a system of shared values, including sexual values and taboos (*qv*). When values are internalized (*qv*) as legitimate and binding, they serve as a link between individuals and their group. However, societies exist despite considerable disagreement over values. An excellent example is the wide divergence in the United States of values on abortion (*qv*), pornography (*qv*), sex education (*qv*), and homosexuality (*qv*). *See also* informal value; formal value; sexual values. Resources: T. Parsons, *Social Systems and the Evolution of Action Theory* (New York: Free Press, 1977); T. Parsons, *Sociological Theory and Modern Society* (New York: Free Press, 1967).

vampirism The belief in preternatural creatures who, like the fabled Count Dracula, suck blood from sleeping victims as a means of achieving immortality and sexual gratification (*qv*). Some psychologists include biting and scratching during loveplay and intercourse (*qv*) as a form of vampirism.

vandalized lovemap The diversion of a normophilic (*qv*) psychosexual development (*qv*) into a paraphilic (*qv*) path by an early traumatic sexual experience. *See also* lovemap; sex play; sexual rehearsal play.

van de Velde *See* Velde, Theodore H. van de.

vanilla sex A colloquial expression referring to sexual activities typically associated with bland heterosexuality (*qv*) (e.g., penile-vaginal intercourse followed by male ejaculation [*qv*]), in contrast with other forms of heterosexual (*qv*) or homosexual (*qv*) activity that may produce far greater sexual arousal (*qv*) in both (or all) partners. Although there appears to be no generic term for the latter sort of behavior, the expression vanilla sex is often used with amused disdain for boring or commonplace sexual preferences and habits.

vanishing testes A form of testicular dysgenesis (*qv*) in which the testes (*qv*) of a male fetus (*qv*) start to develop, producing sufficient androgens (*qv*) to trigger normal male anatomical development, but then degenerate and disappear.

vanishing twin A recent finding suggests that 10 to 20 percent of all twin pregnancies (*qv*) and seven of every ten early diagnosed twin pregnancies end in a single birth; the missing fetus is termed the vanishing twin. The increased use of fetal monitoring with ultrasound (*qv*) for a variety of fertility (*qv*) and gestational (*qv*) problems has resulted in the increased diagnosis of early twin (*qv*) pregnancies. However, in a significant percentage of such multiple pregnancies, one fetus dies and is reabsorbed, while the other goes to term (*qv*) and live birth (*qv*). However, since the mother of an early diagnosed twin pregnancy is told to expect twins, she often needs follow-up counseling when she in fact gives birth to only one child. In the past, twin pregnancies were usually diagnosed in the second or third trimester (*qv*) when miscarriage (*qv*) is much less likely.

variable In scientific research, a factor or concept that is defined in such a way that its magnitude can be measured. A *dependent variable* (*qv*) is the factor or concept the researcher chooses to control or explain. An *independent variable* (*qv*) is a factor that the researcher does not control or manipulate. In sociological usage, a dependent variable is the phenomenon explained or caused by something else; the causal or explanatory variable is the independent variable.

variant sexual behavior The preferred, nonjudgmental, contemporary term for sexual behaviors (*qv*) that in previous times were known as unnatural (*qv*), deviant (*qv*), or perverted.

varicocele An enlarged, twisted varicosity (*qv*) of the veins in the spermatic cord (*qv*) that supplies the epididymis (*qv*) and testes (*qv*). A varicocele is a soft, sometimes painful, swelling, most common in men ages 15 to 25, which more often affects the left spermatic cord than the right. Varicoceles cause about 40 percent of all cases of male sterility (*qv*). *See also* ovarian varicocele.

varicose, varicosity An abnormal condition usually involving a vein, characterized by swelling or convoluted, tortuous twists in a small area.

vas deferens (pl. vasa deferentia) (L.) Paired tubes that carry the mature spermatozoa (*qv*) from the epididymis (*qv*) above the testes (*qv*) out of the scrotum (*qv*), through the pelvic and abdominal cavities, over the urinary bladder, to the seminal vesicles (*qv*) where they mix with seminal secretions from these glands. Each vas leads into a short ejaculatory duct, which then enters the wall of the prostate gland (*qv*) and joins the urethra (*qv*). Surgical cutting, tying, or clamping the vasa is a common method of permanent male contraception (*qv*). Also known as ductus deferens. *See also* vasectomy.

vas efferens (pl. vasa efferentia) (L.) Several short ducts that connect the hundreds of seminiferous tubules (*qv*) in the testes (*qv*) with the rete testes (*qv*). The vasa efferentia convey the sperm (*qv*) from the rete testis into the epididymis (*qv*), which connects to the vas deferens (*qv*).

vasectomy A surgical form of male sterilization (*qv*) in which the paired vasa deferentia (*qv*) are cut and tied or clamped within the scrotal sac (*qv*). This operation does not stop sperm (*qv*) production, only their release during ejaculation (*qv*). The sperm are reabsorbed in the epididymis (*qv*). This process may trigger an autoimmune response (*qv*) and antibody formation (*qv*). Sexual potency—the ability to have an erection (*qv*)—and the ejaculation of seminal fluid (*qv*) are unaffected by the surgery, although the ejaculate contains no sperm. Following surgery, two semen checks with a zero sperm count establish the success of the operation. The permanent sterility resulting from vasectomy can sometimes be reversed with new microsurgery reconstruction. *See also* vasovasostomy.

vasoactive intestinal peptide (VIP) A co-neurotransmitter along with acetycholine or as a neurotransmitter in its own right, VIP is both a powerful relaxer of smooth muscle and a dilator of peripheral blood vessels. First isolated from the human intestine, this protein composed of 28 amino acids, has been idenified in the central and peripheral nervous systems, the retina, lungs, and both male and female genitalia (*qv*). Preliminary studies have shown that the degree of erection (*qv*) increases in proportion with the amount of VIP. Other actions of VIP include keeping the air passages of the lungs open and free during breathing. Asthma, a bronchial disorder involving constriction of the airways, is associated with a deficiency of VIP, resulting from the development of autoantibodies that break down VIP. This suggests that research of erectile dysfunction (*qv*) in healthy and asthmatic males might produce new information on the role of VIP in erectile dysfunctions.

vasocongestion A normal increase in the amount of blood concentrated in certain body issues, especially in the female breasts (*qv*), the labia minora (*qv*), and the cavernous (*qv*) and spongy bodies (*qv*) of the penis (*qv*) and clitoris (*qv*). The primary physiological response to sexual stimulation, vasocongestion results from dilation of arterial vessels combined with constriction of venous vessels in response to sexual erotosexual (*qv*) stimuli. The result is erection (*qv*) of the clitoris or penis, enlargement of breasts and labia from edema, and transudation (*qv*) of fluids in the vagina, and sex flush (*qv*). *See also* myotonia.

vasoconstriction A narrowing of blood vessels that results in decreased blood supply to a structure or organ. *Antonym*: vasodilation. *See also* vasocongestion.

vasodilator centers Erection centers located in the spinal cord that cause dilation of blood vessels in the corpora cavernosa (*qv*) and corpus spongiosum (*qv*). One center is part of the parasympathetic nervous system (*qv*) and is located in the sacral portion of the spinal cord. This system is generally activated by tactile stimulation of the penis (*qv*) and other erogenous (*qv*) areas. A second center is part of the sympathetic nervous system (*qv*) and is located in the thoracic portion of the cord. It is activated by impulses from the brain that are the result of erotic thoughts, fantasies (*qv*), or auditory, visual, or olfactory stimuli. This second system augments the parasympathetic erection center but may also inhibit it.

vasodistention *See* vasodilator centers.

vasovasostomy Surgical reversal of a vasectomy (*qv*). Although the vasa deferentia (*qv*) may be reopened, in many cases fertility (*qv*) is not restored, perhaps because circulating autoantibodies disrupt sperm production (*qv*).

VD An abbreviation for venereal disease (*qv*). *See also* sexually transmitted diseases.

VDRL test The abbreviation for Venereal Disease Research Laboratory test, a blood test for syphilis (*qv*) that depends on flocculation (*qv*) of the patient's serum with the specific antigen (*qv*) of the syphilis bacterium. Since both false positives (*qv*) and false negatives (*qv*) may result with this test, a positive finding should be confirmed by more definitive procedures.

veiling In the Arab world, the *mousaharabieh* is a veil that covers a woman's face whenever she is in public or in the presence of unrelated males; a small slit allows the woman to see while passing unnoticed and unrecognized in the men's world. *See also* chador.

Velde, Theodore H. van de (1873–1937) A Dutch physician and author of the revolutionary sex manual *Ideal Marriage: Its Physiology and Technique* (1926, 1930), Velde broke away from the moralizing discussion of the standard missionary position (*qv*) and sexual behavior in general. He described 10 different positions for intercourse and dared to advocate the ''genital kiss'' as an acceptable part of foreplay. Considered unsensational and overly sentimental today, it was in its time judged risque and placed on the Index of Forbidden Books by the Catholic Church. Resource: D. Wallechinsky and I. Wallace, *The People's Almanac #2* (New York: Bantam Books, 1978), p. 921.

vellus hair *See* lanugo hair.

vena cava syndrome A condition of near-term (*qv*) pregnancy (*qv*) in which the inferior vena cava, which returns blood from the lower body to the heart, is compressed against the spine by the gravid (*qv*) uterus (*qv*) when the woman lies down on her back; the result is falling maternal blood pressure, reduced blood supply to the placenta (*qv*), and fetal distress (*qv*).

venereal A general term referring to anything associated with or caused by genital contact, sexual intimacy (*qv*), or coitus (*qv*).

venereal disease (VD) Any contagious disease transmitted by genital contact, sexual intimacy (*qv*), or oral (*qv*), anal (*qv*), and vaginal intercourse (*qv*). The preferred term is sexually transmitted disease (STD). *See also* acquired immune deficiency syndrome; candida; chancroid; condyloma; gonorrhea; granuloma; hemophilus; herpes; lymphogranuloma; nongonococcal urethritis; pubic lice; scabies; syphilis; trichomonas.

venereal disease phobia *See* cypridophobia.

Venereal Disease Research Laboratory test *See* VDLR.

venereal sore *See* chancre.

venereal warts *See Condyloma acuminata.*

venereology The study of venereal diseases (*qv*).

venery An obsolete term for sexual indulgence. *See also* licentiousness; prominuous

venous Pertaining to the veins in the circulatory system and the blood they generally return to the heart.

ventromedial nucleus of the hypothalamus The frontal (ventral) of two groups of nerve-cell bodies in the middle, tuberal region of the hypothalamus (*qv*) associated with food intake and sexual behavior.

Venus In Roman mythology, the goddess of spring and beauty; later equated with Aphrodite (*qv*), the Greek goddess of love. The legendary birth of Venus from the sea led to the belief in the aphrodisiac (*qv*) qualities of seafood, such as oysters, and in consequence the prohibition of some seafoods by some religious groups because of this connection.

Venus, mound of *See* mons veneris.

Venus of Willendorf The most famous of more than 60 paleolithic sculptures of the female form, found in Willendorf, Austria. Most Venus figurines are 4 to 5 inches high and have been found in eastern Central Europe with a few in France, the Ukraine, and Siberia. Carved more than 20,000 years ago from mammoth ivory, soft stone, or baked clay, the statues show no attempt to portray a face but have luxuriant contours of the torso. Current scholarly opinion is mixed about their meaning and use, ranging from "undeniably sexual" to "never did sexuality play such a small part in the representation of a female figure," from "a magical invocation of fertility" to "no fertility symbol, but a matron deformed by childbearing,'' from ''fundamentally religious'' to ''it is safe to reject any belief that they have religious significance.'' Resource: M. Gimbutas, *The Language of the Goddess* (New York: Harper & Row, 1989).

vernix caseosa (L.) A greasy, cheeselike substance that protects the skin of the fetus (*qv*) from the watery amniotic fluid (*qv*) and insulates it from thermal loss. The vernix caseosa forms in the sixth month and consists of secretions of sebaceous glands (*qv*), fetal lanugo hair (*qv*), and desquamated epithelial cells.

version, fetal Alteration of the position of the fetus (*qv*) in the uterus (*qv*). Fetal version can occur naturally or be induced to facilitate delivery of a breech-presenting fetus. The basic types of fetal version are internal cephalic, external podalic, and combination version. In an external cephalic version, a fetus presenting in the breech position (*qv*) is manipulated by external pressures so that it rotates in the uterus and its head can enter the cervical canal (*qv*) first. In an internal podalic version, the manipulations are done internally by maneuvering the fetus manually through the cervical canal. A combined version uses both external and internal manipulations of the fetus. Improved fetal monitoring with external manipulation and/or Caesarean section (*qv*) are preferred today, with podalic and combined version seldom utilized.

verumonanitis An inflammation of that portion of the prostate gland (*qv*) surrounding the opening of the prostatic ducts, caused by an infection of the urethra (*qv*), prostate gland (*qv*), seminal vesicles (*qv*), and/or excessive sexual activity. *See also* verumontanum.

verumontanum (L.) A prominent portion of the male urethral crest—an elevated portion on the rear wall of the prostatic urethra (*qv*) contains the openings of the ejaculatory ducts (*qv*) and utricle (*qv*).

vertex presentation In childbirth (*qv*), the head-first entry of the fetus (*qv*) into the cervical (*qv*) opening of the vagina (*qv*). This is the most common and normal positioning of the fetus for delivery (*qv*). *See also* version, fetal.

vestal virgin In ancient Roman society, the six virgin (*qv*) priestesses who served for 30 years in the temple of Vesta, the Roman goddess of the hearth. The sexual status of these priestesses combined that of a virgin with elements of a bride, matron, and even a man.

vestibular glands The paired Bartholin's glands (*qv*) or greater vestibular glands (*qv*) lie on either side of the vaginal entrance into which they secrete a mucoid lubricating fluid.

vestibule The space or cavity at the opening of a canal or duct, for example, the vulva (*qv*) into which the urethra (*qv*) and vagina (*qv*) open.

vestibulovaginal bulb An elongated mass of erectile tissue on both sides of the outer opening of the vagina (*qv*). During erection (*qv*), this mass becomes vasocongested and aids in gripping the penis (*qv*) during coitus (*qv*).

viability A medical determination that a fetus (*qv*) can survive outside the uterus (*qv*). In the 1973 *Roe v. Wade* (*qv*) Supreme Court decision legalizing abortion (*qv*), the rights of the pregnant (*qv*) woman were given priority until the fetus is viable. In 1973, the fetus was considered to have reached viability at 1,000 grams somewhere in the seventh month. Hence, the mother's rights prevailed through the second trimester (*qv*). While recent medical advances in perinatal intensive care have allowed some fetuses in the 24 to 28 week range and as small as 500 grams to survive, their long-term prognosis is poor, and few live to leave the hospital. It is virtually unknown for a fetus less than 23 weeks old to survive even with the best life support systems available.

The issue of personhood (*qv*) is often cited in the question of viability, although it is tangential to the ability of the fetus to survive on its own. Neocortical cell development does not achieve a level of integration capable of supporting human thought until after 28 weeks of gestation. In reality, the outer limit of fetal viability depends on two biological factors, which appear unchangeable. Prior to 24 weeks, kidney development is insufficient to support life outside the uterus. Prior to 24 weeks, fetal lung development is at the glandular stage and without the capillary connections that allow respiration. Also, the lungs are too stiff to expand and contract effectively.

In the first 12 weeks of gestation, ultrasound scans (*qv*) are accurate, plus or minus 3 days, in estimating fetal age. By 20 weeks, ultrasound dating is accurate within 7 to 10 days. By the third trimester, the accuracy is plus or minus 21 days. There is no direct way to test lung maturity before 32 weeks when detergent-like phospholipids are present in sufficient amount to keep the air sacs of the lungs from collapsing and when the circulation and structure of the lungs are sufficient to allow unassisted life outside the uterus. Amniocentesis (*qv*) can be used to ascertain fetal viability but not before the thirty-fourth week of gestation. *See also* Webster v. Reproductive Health Services. Resource: E. Doerr and J. W. Prescott, eds., *Abortion Rights and Fetal "Personhood"* (Long Beach, CA: Centerline Press, 1989).

viable infant A newborn (*qv*) who weighs at least 1,000 grams or is 28 weeks or more in gestational age (*qv*). Infants as small as 500 grams can survive with the aid of intensive hospital perinatal care, though the smaller the newborn, the lower its survival chances and the more risk of physical and mental retardation. *See also* low birth weight; viability.

vibrator A battery-powered or electrical plug-in hand-held device that can provide intense sexual stimulation to the erogenous areas (*qv*) of the body and the genitalia (*qv*) by way of high-speed vibrations.

vicarious menstruation An abnormal condition in which unusually fragile blood vessels in the nasal passages or eyes are more susceptible to hemorrhage during the time of menstruation (*qv*).

vice Any behavior or practice that a particular group or society judges to be immoral, unnatural, or depraved and therefore socially unacceptable. Vice typically is used to refer to unacceptable sexual behavior, as in vice squad. The term *secret vice* was common in Victorian (*qv*) society as a euphemism for masturbation (*qv*). *See also* Acton, William.

victimless crime An unlawful act that harms no one and is performed alone or with a consenting adult partner.

victim precipitation The belief that a rape (*qv*) or incest (*qv*) victim is at least partially responsible for the attack, either inviting or precipitating it. While a victim of sexual assault or rape may do something stupid, such as walk alone down a deserted street in an unsafe neighborhood late at night, this does not transfer the blame of a rape from the perpetrator to the victim. However, the public, law enforcement officials, and family members often assume victim precipitation when dealing with an assault victim. Another example of victim precipitation is the common suggestion that the ''seductive behavior'' of an incest victim makes the victim and not the assailant responsible for the incestuous relation.

Victorianism An undefined but broad set of conservative, even antisexual, social values prevailing in northern European countries and the United States in the last half of the nineteenth century and early twentieth century. Named for Victoria, queen of Great Britain between 1837 and 1901, Victorian values held that sex is an animalistic behavior unmentionable in proper society.

Ironically, Victoria herself apparently greatly enjoyed the marital sex she shared with her consort Prince Albert—the royal pair produced nine children in addition to enjoying privately numerous works of semi-erotic art—although she disapproved of sex outside of marriage (*qv*) and in particular the many affairs of her son, the future Edward VII.

Although the middle class had adopted some ideas of the romantic movement, the attacks of some romantics on long-cherished institutions made romantic views of sex (*qv*) and marriage (*qv*) unpopular with bourgeois Victorians. Premarital virginity (*qv*) was strictly imposed on women, who were supposed to learn about the physical aspect of marriage from their husbands. Sex was tolerated by proper wives because it was essential for procreation (*qv*). Simultaneously, Victorian hypocrisy allowed a rampant pornography (*qv*), prostitution (*qv*), and sexual exploitation of lower-class women by middle- and upper-class men.

The fear of the health effects of masturbation (*qv*) and excessive sexual activity became a major social obsession. The Victorian value system started to weaken in the short but much freer reign of Edward VII, with the teachings of Sigmund Freud (*qv*), and especially the social turmoil of World War I. Resources: B. Murstein, *Love, Sex and Marriage through the Ages* (New York: Springer, 1974). pp. 248–278; G. J. Barker-Benfield, *The Horrors of the Half-Known Life* (New York: Harper & Row, 1976). *See also* degeneracy theory; Acton, William; Graham, Sylvester; Kellogg, John; clitorectomy; Comstock law; double moral standard.

Vindication of the Rights of Woman *See* Wollstonecraft, Mary.

VIP *See* vasoactive intestinal peptide.

virago (viraginity) An old term for a shrewish, scolding, and vituperative woman.

virgin A man or woman who has never had sexual intercourse (*qv*). *See also* celibacy; demi-vierge; hymen; technical virgin; vestal virgin; virginity.

virginal anxiety A state of apprehension and uncertainty experienced by a man or woman during his or her first sexual encounter.

virginal tribute *See* droit du seigneur.

virgin birth In biology, a pregnancy (*qv*) resulting when an unfertilized ovum (*qv*) develops so that the resulting offspring has a genetic mother but no genetic father. In many religious traditions, the belief that a prophet or god/man was conceived without sexual intercourse (*qv*) and through the intervention of a god. Spontaneous virgin birth or parthenogenesis is common among some insect species, where females reproduce without mating (*qv*). Among higher animals, virgin birth occurs in some fish and reptiles, but is rare in mammals (*qv*). In ancient Greek and Roman mythologies, demigods were regularly conceived as the result of the union of a god with a mortal female. In Christianity, the conception of Jesus is believed to have been conceived by the Virgin Mary under the influence of the Holy Spirit. A pregnancy resulting from artificial insemination (*qv*) rather than natural coitus (*qv*) with penile/vaginal penetration (*qv*) may be considered a type of virgin birth.

virginity The state of being a virgin (*qv*). Males in many cultures have traditionally placed a high value on female virginity for a variety of socioeconomic and psychological reasons, including concern over the legitimacy of one's heirs, flattering the feeling of male superiority, an expectation of more pleasure during defloration (*qv*) of a virgin, the absence of previous experience that could become the basis for unfavorable comparisons, and the demand for "undamaged property" in a purchase marriage (*qv*).

An intact hymen (*qv*), a tight vagina (*qv*), and bleeding during defloration (*qv*) are commonly said to be signs of virginity although none of these signs guarantees that the female has not had vaginal intercourse (*qv*). Likewise, their absence is not proof that she has had coitus. In industrialized nations, the hymen is commonly ruptured or stretched by use of vaginal tampons (*qv*) and exercise. As recently as the 1950s, American medical authorities recommended medical defloration or dilating the hymen of older women and women with thick hymens. *See also* celibacy; demi-vierge; vestal virgin.

virginity complex *See* hymenolatry; madonna complex.

virginity taboo A social prohibition against the defloration (*qv*) of a virgin (*qv*) prior to her marriage (*qv*). The social value of premarital virginity has changed radically in the United States since the days of Victorianism (*qv*) when virginity was an absolute priority for any proper young lady. In the 1948 Kinsey study (*qv*), over 95 percent of American women reported adhering to this taboo (*qv*). Since the sexual revolution (*qv*) of the 1960s and 1970s, the incidence of premarital virginity has decreased below 50 percent nationwide. In most countries that extol premarital virginity for women; sexist biases dictate that men are not expected to be virgins when they marry.

virile Having the qualities a culture attributes to men (*qv*) and manhood; capable of reproduction. *See also* masculine.

virilescence *See* virilization.

virilization The gradual appearance of some secondary sexual characteristics (*qv*) in the male (e.g., facial hair); in females, the deepening of the voice, usually after menopause (*qv*). In younger women virilization can be caused by androgen (*qv*)-producing tumors, resulting in premature puberty (*qv*).

virilism Development of male secondary sexual characteristics (*qv*) in a woman. *See also* hirsutism; virilization.

virility The capacity and ability to function sexually as a male.

virilocal *See* patrilocal.

vital fluids, strength The not-uncommon belief that the loss of seminal fluid (*qv*) in ejaculation (*qv*) drains vital fluids from the body and/or brain, thereby depriving a man of his strength. *See also* semen myths.

vital statistics *See* biostatistics.

vitelline Associated with the yolk material (*qv*), a nutrient containing protein and lecithin for the very young embryo (*qv*); part of or associated with the primitive yolk sac (*qv*). The vitelline membrane encloses the ovum (*qv*).

viviparous The capacity of bearing live offspring rather than eggs; occurs in all mammals (*qv*), and in some fish and reptiles. *See also* oviparous; ovoviviparous.

voice change The testosterone (*qv*)-induced enlargement of the larynx or voice box, resulting in a deepening of the voice; one of the more noticeable secondary sex characteristics (*qv*) accompanying male puberty (*qv*). Castration (*qv*), particularly when performed before puberty, can prevent the deepening of the male voice. *See also* castrati.

voluntary state One of the states in the United States where abortion (*qv*) laws do not limit second- and third-trimester (*qv*) abortions, for example, by requiring a court order or medical documentation that the abortion is needed to save the mother's life. *See also* life-only standard.

voluptas sexualis or veneris (L.) A nineteenth-century term for sexual pleasure.

von Baer, Karl Ernst *See* Baer, Karl Ernst von.

von Fernwald's sign A bulge developing on the outer surface of the uterus (*qv*) marking the location of implantation (*qv*) of the developing fetus (*qv*).

Voronoff, Serge A Russian physician who was one of several experimenters in the 1920s attempting to rejuvenate older men by implanting testes (*qv*) of various animals, especially primates; also known to contemporaries as the monkey gland treatment.

voyeur (voyeurism) A paraphilic (*qv*) individual sexually aroused (*qv*) and achieving orgasm (*qv*) by secretly watching another person, almost always a stranger, undressing or engaging in sexual behavior. Arousal can be enhanced by the risk of apprehension. *Slang:* peeping tom. *See also* scoptophilia.

voyeuse (Fr.) A female voyeur (*qv*).

vulcanization A process for treating crude rubber with heat and sulphur compounds to produce a resilient, elastic, and flexible product. The process was discovered in 1839 by Charles Goodyear, making possible the manufacture of rubber condoms (*qv*) and diaphragms (*qv*). Before vulcanization, condoms were made from the lining of animal intestines, linen, and other equally unattractive and/or ineffective materials. The first condoms were made from crepe rubber with a lengthwise seam. Seamless rubber condoms and vulcanized rubber diaphragms became available and popular after 1870.

vulva A collective term for the external female sexual structures: the mons veneris (*qv*), labia majora and minora (*qv*), clitoris (*qv*), Bartholin's glands (*qv*), and urethral and vaginal orifices. Vulva was the name of a powerful Scandinavian goddess. *See also* pudendum; vestibule.

vulval orgasm *See* tenting.

vulvar dystrophy A new term for leukoplakia (*qv*) of the vulva (*qv*)—white patches of the vulva that may, over years, progress to carcinoma.

vulvectomy Surgical removal of part or all of the vulvar tissue, most frequently as a treatment for malignant or premalignant neoplastic disease. *Simple vulvectomy* involves only the skin; *radical vulvectomy* entails removing underlying tissue and lymph nodes.

vulvovaginal glands *See* Bartholin's glands; vestibular glands.

W

wandering uterus An outdated medical or pseudomedical term for a uterus (*qv*) that is not in the midline position above the urinary bladder and at a right angle to the vagina (*qv*); this allegedly abnormal position was thought to be the cause of dysmenorrhea (*qv*), pelvic congestion, and lower backache, as well as painful intercourse (*qv*) or dyspareunia (*qv*). Hippocrates believed this alleged disorder to occur in women whose uterus wanders to different parts of the body in search of a child. The folklore of a wandering uterus may be traced to Plato's *Timaeus*, the origin of the myth that links the uterus with the psychological condition of hysteria (*qv*). *See also* testeria.

Wandervogel movement A 1920s German youth movement, similar to the Boy Scouts of America, except that nudism (*qv*) was practiced, leading to charges of sexual promiscuity (*qv*) and homosexuality (*qv*). *See also* naturism.

warts, venereal *See Condyloma acuminata*.

Wasserman test An obsolete diagnostic blood test for syphilis (*qv*) based on detecting blood antibodies to the syphilis bacterium. States began requiring the Wasserman test for marriage licenses in 1938. Because the Wasserman test gives false positives (*qv*) and negatives (*qv*), it has been replaced by more accurate tests like the VDRL (*qv*).

waters (water sac) An informal term for amniotic fluid (*qv*); ''breaking of waters'' refers to rupture of the amniotic sac (*qv*) and flow of the amniotic fluid out of the vaginal canal during labor (*qv*) and delivery (*qv*).

W chromosome The sex-determining chromosome (*qv*) in certain insects, birds, and fishes, comparable to the Y chromosome (*qv*) in mammals (*qv*). Normal males in these species are homogametic (*qv*) and have two Z chromosomes (*qv*), whereas the females are heterogametic (*qv*) and have one Z and one W chromosome.

wean, to To induce a child to give up breast-feeding (*qv*) and accept other food in place of breast milk; usually between ages 6 and 12 months.

weanling A recently weaned (*qv*) infant.

Webster v. Reproductive Health Services A 1989 five-to-four decision of the U.S. Supreme Court upholding a Missouri law and opening the door for individual states to test the limits of restrictions they can place on the legalization of abortion (*qv*) in *Roe v. Wade* (*qv*). The Court ruled that it is constitutional for a state (1) to prohibit the use of public hospitals or other taxpayer-supported facilities for abortions not necessary to save the life of the woman, even if no public funds are spent; (2) to prohibit public employees, including doctors, nurses and other health care providers, from performing or assisting in an abortion not necessary to save a woman's life; and (3) to require that medical tests must be performed on any fetus (*qv*) thought to be at least 20 weeks old to determine its viability (*qv*). *See also* Turnock v. Ragsdale; Ohio v. Akron Center for Reproductive Health; Hodgson v. Minnesota.

wedding The marriage (*qv*) ceremony, civil or religious. An enormous variety of ceremonies have been used historically and cross-culturally to structure and make licit the reproductive union of men and women.

wedding ring A ring given or exchanged in the marriage (*qv*) ceremony by bride and groom to symbolize their promise of fidelity (*qv*) and commitment; worn on the fourth finger of the left hand. The ring(s) exchanged at an engagement have the same symbolism since originally the engagement was equivalent to marriage in northern Europe.

wedlock The married state. *See also* marriage.

weeping In medical usage, oozing or exuding of plasma fluid through the vaginal wall resulting in lubrication (*qv*) of the vaginal canal (*qv*) in preparation for intercourse (*qv*). *See also* transudation, vaginal sweating.

Weinberg and Williams Survey A 1970s sociological study of over 1,000 male homosexuals (*qv*) in the United States and Europe, sponsored by the Kinsey Institute (*qv*). Conducted by Martin S. Weinberg and Colin J. Williams, the study drew on male homosexuals on the mailing lists of the Mattachine Societies (*qv*) of New York and San Francisco and homosexuals interviewed in Amsterdam and Copenhagen. The results were published in *Male Homosexuals: Their Problems and Adaptations* (New York: Oxford University Press, 1974).

welbrutin An antidepressant drug produced by Burroughs-Wellcome, claimed to be a major new aphrodisiac (*qv*). It was withdrawn by the manufacturer in 1988 for further study because of seizures in bulemics who used the drug.

Western Blot test A highly specific test for the presence of several specific antibodies against the HIV-I virus (*qv*), which is responsible for acquired immune deficiency syndrome (*qv*). It is used to confirm positive findings from the mass screening results of the ELISA test (*qv*), which detects only one HIV-I antibody. Because that antibody is also present with other antigens (*qv*), the ELISA test often gives false positives (*qv*), which can be eliminated with the Western Blot test.

Westphal's sign The loss of the patellar or knee-jerk reflex, a diagnostic sign of late syphilis (*qv*) and neurosyphilis (*qv*), associated with tabes dorsalis (*qv*) or the progressive degeneration of peripheral neuromuscular control and coordination.

wet day That day in the menstrual cycle (*qv*) when secretion of cervical mucus (*qv*) increases and becomes more opaque and less sticky than on previous days. These changes in cervical mucus mark the approach of ovulation (*qv*) and the increased risk of conception. *See also* Billings' contraceptive method; Spinnbarkheit.

wet dream A dream with sexuoerotic (*qv*) content that ends in a seminal discharge (*qv*) for a male. Wet dreams occur with greatest frequency in pubertal (*qv*) and adolescent (*qv*) boys. The content of the dream may be forgotten entirely, and the individual may only be aware of the resulting ejaculation (*qv*). Also known as nocturnal emission (*qv*).

wet nurse A woman who breast-feeds and cares for another woman's infant (*qv*).

Wharton's jelly A gelatinous connective tissue in the mature umbilical cord (*qv*). Its main function is to prevent kinking of the umbilical arteries and vein.

whipping A common component in sadomasochism (*qv*), whipping includes beating or lashing another person with a whip, belt, thong, or similar long, flexible instrument, especially when engaged in for purposes of sexual stimulation and gratification. *See also* dippoldism; flagellantism; flagellant.

whites A colloquial term for leukorrhea (*qv*).

white slave A legal and colloquial term for a woman who has been forced into prostitution (*qv*). Following the abolition of slavery in the British Empire in 1833 and in the United States in 1865, an analogy was made between black slavery and white female prostitution. Abolition of white slavery became a major focus of social reformers and feminists in the late nineteenth and early twentieth centuries. *See also* White Slave Act.

White Slave Act Technically known as the Mann Act, this law, passed by the U.S. Congress in 1910, defined as a felon any person who transports or aids in the transportation across state lines of any female for the purpose of prostitution (*qv*), debauchery (*qv*), or "any other immoral purpose." The penalty was set at a $5,000, five years in prison, or both. The law was enacted in response to a paranoid fear of a massive, nationwide conspiracy called the "white slave trade," supposedly controlled by criminal organizations, consisting mostly of illegal Chinese immigrants. The term *white slave* is derived from a popular nineteenth century drama, entitled *The White Slave*, about a kidnapped young woman who is forced into prostitution. Stories of rampant white slavery were common in the popular press of the late 1800s, especially in sensationalist publications like the *Police Gazette*.

white tunic The tunica albuginea (*qv*), a sheath of white collagenous fibers enclosing the testis (*qv*).

whore (v. and n.) A prostitute (*qv*), typically a woman who sells sexual favors for money. To *whore* means to act as a whore, and is more often said of women than men. To *whore around*, when said of a woman, means to have promiscuous sexual relations with a variety of partners, not always for money. When said of a man, the verb means to frequent whores, whorehouses, or brothels (*qv*). The word whore is Old English in origin, *hore*, with the same meaning as the modern term. The Old English derives from the Proto Indo-European *ka-*, meaning "to desire," so that in Old Germanic languages, an adulterer is a *horaz*, a man who desires a woman (*k* to *h* is a known sound shift in the history of these languages). By extension, the desired woman linguistically became in Old English the *hore*, or in modern English, the *whore*.

Colloquially, by extension, a whore can be a man or woman who sells non-sexual services, skills, or talents under emotionally unsatisfying conditions. Often the term is said of oneself or one's colleagues in a self-amused but self-derogatory manner: "We're all whores in this business," meaning that the customer's needs are placed before all other considerations, or that demands of marketing, often questionable or unethical, are seen as primary in the performance of one's job.

whoredom The state of being a whore (*qv*).

whorehouse A brothel (*qv*) or other place where prostitutes (*qv*) work.

whoremaster An old-fashioned term for a man who consorts with whores (*qv*). A man or woman who pimps for whores or otherwise assists in selling their services.

whoremonger An old-fashioned term for a man who consorts with whores (*qv*). A man or woman who pimps for whores or otherwise assists in selling their services.

whoreson An old-fashioned and Shakespearean insult accusing a man of being the offspring of a whore (*qv*); an extremely serious insult; *see also* sexual insults.

whorish Having the attributes of a whore (*qv*); accused of being promiscuous (*qv*), sluttish, or slatternly.

whory *See* whorish.

widow, widowhood A woman whose husband (*qv*) has died and who has not remarried; the state of being a widow; colloquially, a woman whose husband is inattentive to her because he has other, but nonsexual, activities that claim his emotional interests; for example, a golf widow.

Different societies treat widowhood in different ways. In some, there are religiously mandated periods of mourning following the man's death, after which the woman is free to remarry if she chooses. In other societies, such as modern America, the initial stages of widowhood are primarily a psychological period of bereavement and grieving, associated with adjustments made by the woman in her financial affairs, with no restriction concerning when she may remarry. In still other societies, like those of Hinduism that follow the now illegal custom of suttee (*qv*), widowhood is necessarily followed by the woman's immolation on her late husband's funeral pyre. Overall, however, traditions like suttee are rare, and it can generally be said that widowhood involves a complex and often painful series of social, psychological, and economic readjustments for the woman and her immediate family (*qv*).

The likelihood of a woman being widowed has changed with history. Demographically, one consequence of war is to increase the risk and incidence of widowhood for women in certain age cohorts with the concurrent lack of socially appropriate or psychologically available men, making it unlikely that most of such widows will remarry. In modern North American and European societies, where the life expectancy of women is greater than that of men, it is likely that older married women will be widowed and, given the deficit of older unmarried men, unlikely that they will remarry. This was not always true in America. In colonial and pioneer times, when women frequently died in childbirth, it was more likely for a man to outlive his wife, or perhaps more than one wife, than it was for wives in general to outlive their husbands. Advances in medicine and limitations on warfare have altered the experience of adulthood, so that in many retirement communities today there are far more widowed women than women with living husbands or widowers.

None of these processes or facts is historically novel, as is shown by the history of the word widow itself. It derives from Old English *widuwe*, with exactly the same meaning as the modern word. Furthermore, the Old English word derives from a still earlier word in Proto Indo-European, the rootstock language from which the Germanic languages, including English, the Romance languages including Latin, the Slavic languages, Greek, Sanskrit, and Hittite, all derived many thousands of years ago. That root word has been reconstructed by historical linguists as *widhewo*, meaning a woman separated from her husband by his death. The root *widh-* appears in later Classic Latin words like *dividere*, meaning "to separate." The point achieves some importance because certain feminist (*qv*) critics of what they perceive to be sexist language have argued that *widow* derives from an ancient Sanskrit word meaning "to be empty," with the implication that calling a woman a widow is saying that women without men are empty and of no importance. Such critics then reject the word widow as sexist (*see* sexism). However, the Sanskrit word in question itself appears to derive from the older Proto Indo-European word just mentioned as a specialization of its meaning of "sundering" or "separation." Furthermore, other Indo-European languages do not resemble Sanskrit in their usages of words derived from *widh-*. Accordingly, it seems that the Sanskrit word was an offshoot of the branching of Indo-European languages, with the majority of these languages, including English, retaining a meaning for *widh-* that is closer to the rootstock of "bereft," "sundered," "separated," or "divided" from someone. Accordingly, it seems that for many thousands of years, it has been sufficiently common for men to die before their wives that there has been a need for a word to describe a woman separated from her husband by death.

widower A man whose wife (*qv*) has died and who has not remarried; *see* widow. Also, any device or mechanism that kills men in battle. The expression, "The Gatling Gun was a real widower," meaning it made widows of men's wives, is an example of the latter usage and of male oblique discourse in which an offhand word usage describes something genuinely gruesome, often with laughter that comes from an internal despair.

widow's inheritance A custom in some polygamous (*qv*) African societies in which a man inherits all his father's wives, except his own mother, so as to continue the family line.

wife (wives) A woman (*qv*) married to a man (*qv*); a woman generally, as in words like fishwife, meaning a woman who sells fish (this usage is now rare). The word wife is relational rather than categorical. Thus, one would be far more likely to say "Mary is John's wife," to describe Mary's relationship to John, than to say "Mary is a wife," and thereby place her in a category of human beings called "wives." The word husband (*qv*) is also used relationally, so that the two words, wife and husband (*qv*), are correlatives of each other.

In modern America and Europe, being a wife is defined legally, socially, emotionally, and financially. The legal definition depends on the family (*qv*) and marital law of a jurisdiction, but generally, the marriage (*qv*) ceremony legally makes the woman the man's wife regardless of other aspects of being married (e.g., being in love [*qv*], being sexually intimate, or sharing the same domicile). Socially, the word wife refers to a status and points to the woman's involvement in the full range of matters that custom associated with the woman's role in marriage. Accordingly, the social and cultural meanings of the word have changed, and are continuing to change, as the status of women changes generally in society. For example, in the traditional concepts of family and marriage, the wife's role was helpmate and mother (*qv*), with duties associated primarily with the domestic sphere of life. Newer concepts of equality and the experience of dual-career marriages have brought the wife into the world outside the home and the husband into sharing household and parental responsibilities. New meanings of the word wife can combine notions of sexual lover, best or dearest friend, and source of emotional support. Many of these changes have arisen following feminist (*qv*) criticisms of the traditional role of the wife, which critics have seen as little more than being an unpaid, overworked, and neglected housekeeper, sexual servant, and full-time caretaker of children. Other factors involved in the changing definition of *wife* include shifts in women's employment patterns, with over half of married women and mothers working outside the home and contributing significantly to the family income, and the increasing numbers of women in higher education, which stresses the intellectual and ideological needs for gender (*qv*) and sexual equality as essential for a happy marriage.

In non-Western societies, the concept of *wife* varies considerably depending on the kinship (*qv*) system of the society. Cultures that permit polygyny (*qv*) often have detailed social codes of behavior and custom regulating the rights, privileges, and duties of the husband's several wives, according to the age, maternal status, and marriage order of the different women. For example, the oldest wife may have most of the domestic authority, including authority over younger wives, whereas the younger wife or wives may be the husband's sexual favorite(s). In other societies, a group of wives and possibly concubines (*qv*) may live separated from the society of men except for occasional interactions with the husband; *see also* harem. In still other societies, which superficially resemble modern America in having monogamy (*qv*), the wife may be primarily the mother of the man's children but have her primary emotional and social connections to her own kin and her blood relatives. Many other, culturally distinct, definitions of *wife* exist, and have been studied extensively by anthropologists.

The origin of the word wife is obscure. It appears first in Old English, as *wyf* or *wif*, and in cognate forms in Old High German, meaning "a woman," especially a woman of non-noble lineage. The German word *Weib*, meaning "wife," is cognate to the English *wife*. In Gothic, which is a Germanic language considerably predating both Old English and Old High German, there is no word cognate to *wife*. Instead, Gothic has two words, possibly related to each other by origin and certainly by sound. The first is *qinð*, the cognate of *muliere* in

Latin. The *Oxford English Dictionary* does not translate *muliere* in this context. Normally, in classic Latin, *muliere* means "woman," although a slang usage of *muliere* meant an anal-receptive male. The second Gothic term is *qens*, meaning "wife" in the sense of a woman to whom a man is married. This term is cognate to the modern English *queen*, meaning a woman of royal birth who rules a country, nation, or people. It is also cognate to Old English *cewen*, meaning "wife," again in the sense of a woman to whom a man is married. However, modern English no longer retains words based on the *k/n* sounds, such as *queen* or *cewen*, for the word wife. Instead, it appears that somewhere between the period of Gothic, during the fourth and fifth centuries C.E., and Old English and Old High German, some four or more centuries later, a pair of words, *qind* and *qens*, were replaced with another word, of unknown origin, spelled *wif* or *wyf* in Old English, and meaning "woman." In turn, the *wif/wyf* word became specialized to mean a married woman; in other words, a wife in the modern sense.

Although the *Oxford English Dictionary* says that the origin of the Gothic *qens* and *qinð* are unknown, one can speculate from sound alone that they may be cognate with one of the most tabooed words in modern English, the word *cunt* for a woman's genitalia (*qv*), and, by insulting and pejorative extension, for a woman herself. In turn, these Gothic words remind one of Greek-derived words based on the prefix *gyno-*, meaning "of or pertaining to women," as in *gynecology* (compare Greek *konnos*, cited in Grose's 1811 dictionary of English slang under *cunt*). Indeed, historical linguists interested in reconstructing the most ancient root language upon which English, German, Greek, Latin, and Russian, among other languages, are all based—called Proto-Indo-European— have suggested that the *gyno-* and *g/n-* based words derive from the Proto-Indo-European *gwen-*, meaning "woman." However, one is also reminded of Latin *cunnus*, literally, a "wedge" (as in *cuneiform* or wedge-shaped letters). In classic Latin, *cunnus* has a figurative or metaphorical meaning identical to the tabooed word cunt, which appears in the formal *cunnilingus*, meaning stimulation of the *cunnus*, the female genitalia, with the tongue (*lingus* in Latin). This derivation of the word cunt is made more probable by the use of *queynt* by the wife of Bath in referring to her own genitals in Chaucer's *Canterbury Tales*.

Accordingly, one can speculate that there once existed a series of words that contained the *k/n* sounds, and the closely related hard-*g/n* sounds, that were used to refer to women, to the female genitalia, and to men who enacted the anal-receptive role in male-male activities. These, one may further suggest, were replaced with a variety of other words, including *wife*, leaving only the now rare *quean* for a male homosexual (*qv*) and possibly the heavily tabooed *cunt* for the woman's genitalia, in the company of *queen*, meaning a woman of royal family who rules a people or nation. It is completely unknown what historical and cultural processes caused these dramatic and far-reaching changes in the usage and acceptance of the different words, but they are among the basic factors shaping the language of sexuality (*qv*) for a millennium and a half. *See also* concubine; conjugal duties; husband; mistress; adultery; polygamy; polygyny.

wife (battering) beating *See* battered wife syndrome; marital rape.

wife inheritance A custom in some polygamous (*qv*) African societies in which a man is the principal heir of his maternal uncle, including the uncle's wife or wives.

wife lending *See* sexual hospitality.

Wilde, Oscar (1854–1900) Born in Dublin, Ireland, Wilde gained fame as a dramatist, poet, and author of witty paradoxes and epigrams but more notoriety as England's most blatant and famous homosexual (*qv*) of the Victorian (*qv*) era. One of Ireland's best-known expatriates, Wilde's first fame came as a student of John Ruskin at Magdalen College, Oxford, and later for his prize-winning poem *Ravenna* (1878). When he married in 1884, there was little evidence of his homosexuality. His love affair (*qv*) with Lord Alfred Douglas led to a libel suit against Lord Alfred's father, a scandalous trial in Old Bailey, and a two-year sentence served in Reading Gaol (1895–1897) commemorated by his *Ballad of Reading Gaol* written under the pseudonym "C•3•3," which was Wilde's cell number.

wimmin A spelling adopted by some feminists for "woman/women" to avoid the "-man/-men" endings of these words. *See also* woman; womon, womyn.

window courting *See* fensternl.

wish fulfillment In psychoanalysis (*qv*), the realization of one's desires and goals in dreams and fantasies (*qv*); also the relief of tensions resulting from instinctual needs, libido (*qv*), and aggression.

Witches' Hammer The English title of *Malleus maleficarum*, a Latin manual on witchcraft written in 1486 by two German Dominican priests, Jakob Sprenger and Heinrick Kramer. With 30 editions in 250 years, this manual became a guide for civil and religious authorities for examining and persecuting women suspected or accused of all forms of "evil behavior," particularly a supposed insatiable lust (*qv*) and having sexual relations (*qv*) with the devil. *See also* incubus; succubus. *Malleus maleficarum* asserts the existence of witches and then states that any woman who rejects the reality of witches is herself a witch. Rules are spelled out for identifying, trying, and executing witches. Two typical statements are: "all witchcraft comes from carnal lust which in women is insatiable" and "among ambitious women [those] are more deeply infected who are more hot to satisfy their filthy lusts."

witch's milk A colloquial term for a milklike substance secreted from the breast (*qv*) of the newborn (*qv*); caused by circulating maternal lactating hormone (*qv*). Also known as hexenmilch (*qv*).

withdrawal Removal of the penis (*qv*) from the vagina (*qv*) before ejaculation (*qv*) occurs. As a contraceptive (*qv*) method, it has a very high failure rate due to preejaculatory penile leakage of fluid from the Cowpers' glands (*qv*), which may contain viable sperm (*qv*). Also known as coitus interruptus (*qv*).

withdrawal bleeding The passage of blood from the uterus (*qv*), associated with the shedding of uterine endometrium (*qv*) that has been stimulated and maintained by hormonal medication. The occurrence of withdrawal bleeding when hormonal medication is stopped indicates that amenorrhea (*qv*) is not due to uterine factors but to hormonal or ovarian causes.

withdrawal contraceptive method *See* withdrawal.

Wolfenden Report (England) A 1957 report issued by the blue-ribbon Committee on Homosexual Offenses and Prostitution in England. The committee was established by the British Parliament in 1954, mainly at the instigation of the Moral Welfare Council of the Church of England. The main conclusions and recommendations of the report were that "homosexual behavior between consenting adults in private be no longer a criminal offense" and that prostitution (*qv*) should be decriminalized, leaving only those laws affecting public nuisances. J. F. Wolfenden was the committee chairman, hence the report's common name.

Wolff, Kaspar Friedrich (1733–1794) Born and educated in Germany and professor of anatomy and physiology in Russia, Wolff is considered the cofounder of modern embryology (*qv*), together with Karl Ernst von Baer (*qv*). In 1759, Wolff first described the mesonephros or Wolffian body (*qv*) and the mesonephric tubules in 1759, the lateral thickening of the urogenital or Wolffian ridge. In 1768, he demonstrated epigenesis (*qv*) by showing how a blastoderm layer forms the chick's intestine. He outlined a layer theory of development to replace the embryonic preformation theory (*qv*), leading to the primary germ-layer theory (*qv*) developed by Heinrich C. Pander and Karl Ernst von Baer.

Wolffian body *See* mesonephros; Wolffian ducts.

Wolffian ducts Paired embryonic ducts found in both male and female fetuses (*qv*) in the first trimester (*qv*) and associated with the transitory mesonephric kidneys (*qv*). In the male fetus, the Wolffian ducts develop into the internal vasa deferentia (*qv*) and associated structures, the epididymis (*qv*), seminal vesicles (*qv*), and prostate (*qv*). This male differentiation is controlled by fetal testosterone (*qv*). In the third through eighth week, these ducts drain the mesonephric kidneys. As the mesonephric kidneys degenerate and their function is taken over by the metanephric or definitive kidneys, the Wolffian ducts attach to the testes (*qv*). In the absence of sufficient testosterone and in females, the Wolffian ducts degenerate. The ducts were named for Kaspar F. Wolff (*qv*). *See also* Mullerian ducts.

Wollstonecraft, Mary (1759–1797) An English writer, Wollstonecraft published *A Vindication of the Rights of Woman*, the original feminist (*qv*) manifesto, in 1792. Having observed the French Revolution and being a great admirer of both Rousseau and Talleyrand, Wollstonecraft was incensed by the civil status of women, which was about equal to that of American slaves, and by the education of women, which was limited to making them pleasing and useful to men. Although she did not challenge the traditional place of women in the home, she did urge opening new employment opportunities. Her failure to sense the need to organize women in support of her manifesto, coupled with her scandalous life—a career in journalism, two lovers, an illegitimate child, and a suicide attempt—allowed the public to ignore her writing. Quickly forgotten after her untimely death in childbirth (*qv*), her work was ignored until John Stuart Mill published *On the Subjugation of Women* (1869). She was the mother of Mary Wollstonecraft Shelley, the author of *Frankenstein*.

woman, women An adult female (*qv*) human being, either singly, plural, or collectively, as in the words womankind and womenkind; female nature, as in "the woman in her"; a female servant or hired domestic worker, as in the phrase "cleaning woman"; a heterosexual (*qv*) mistress (*qv*), paramour (*qv*), lover, or wife (*qv*), as in "Bess, you is my woman now," from George Gershwin's operetta *Porgy and Bess*; male heterosexual activity or preoccupation, as in "He has women on his mind," or in the word "womanizing," meaning a male effort to find many female sexual partners; in political discourse, both main-line and radical, a group of people seen as having common political and economic interests, as in the phrase "women voters" and the organization the League of Women Voters; in radical, especially feminist (*qv*), discourse, women seen as potentially radical or even revolutionary, as opposed to political forces and alliances, often seen as male-dominated and patriarchal (*see* patriarchy), that uphold the status quo, particularly in matters of women's rights and gender equality.

As implied by these capsule definitions, the word woman has a variety of meanings that shift from nuance to nuance depending on the context of usage, the speaker's intentions, and the hearer's understanding. Moreover, in 1909, Cicely Hamilton noted that the word "is apt to convey two distinct and different impressions, according to the sex of the *hearer*" (C. Kramarae and P. A. Treichler, eds., *A Feminist Dictionary* [London: Pandora Press, 1985], page 489, italics added). Additional complexities of definition arise because the word woman is close in meaning to other words like *lady* and *girl* that have other meanings and nuances to different speakers and hearers. An alien learning English would find it difficult to judge when to use the word woman as opposed to lady, girl, or even female—and to judge what these terms mean when the native speaker utters or writes them. Currently, the meanings and usages of all these terms are in flux, making the task of composing definitions even more difficult.

Until relatively recently, few speakers, and in particular few men, used the term woman in casual speech for an adult female human being, the first sense given in the capsule definitions above. In ordinary discourse, as opposed to literary, legal, or official language, the commonly used terms were lady and girl. Today, some speakers avoid the latter two words and instead use either the more generic *woman* or gender-neutral expressions. Even so, the words lady and girl remain in the vocabulary, together with slang and colloquial expressions that have overlapping nuances of meaning emphasizing different perceived aspects of femaleness. These are illustrated below.

The word lady was used primarily as a formal or semi-formal term for any adult female whom the speaker did not know well, particularly when emotional or social distance was intended or when a polite or genteel tone was desired. These usages still occur today in sentences such as, "There's a lady waiting for you," "Ladies first," or "Watch your mouth—there's a lady present." In this usage, the correlative (but rarely used) term for males is "gentlemen," as in the formal address, "Ladies and gentlemen, it is my honor to present . . . ." The same correlative pair occurs in the labels attached to toilet facilities in public places: "Ladies" and "Gentlemen" (or sometimes "Gents"), where the effort is made to avoid possible offense to anyone. A female child might once have been chided by being told, "Young ladies don't do *that*," where "that" referred to anything the adult (usually female) speaker did not like.

Thus, the term lady had, and still often has, a formal ring to it, a characteristic associated with its use as a formal title for women members of the British Peerage (e.g., "Lady Bracknell," "Lady-in-Waiting," to the Queen). In America, where no peerage exists, the term lady has connoted gentility, propriety (especially in matters of language, manners, and dress), and good breeding, all synonymous with the behavior and appearance of a person belonging to certain socioeconomic groups or strata of society. Accordingly, the word lady had, and still can have, a deferential tone. In some dialects of American English (e.g., in the South), it remains the only formal term one can use with a woman one does not know or does not know well.

By contrast, if early American speakers used the word lady with someone they did not know well, they said "girl" for adult females in their own social circle, for females in lower status groups, for females younger than the speaker, and for females of any age judged physically or sexually attractive. Thus, a female domestic worker could have been called a "cleaning girl" regardless of her age (the word maid has virtually an identical meaning for a domestic worker); a female employee a "working girl"; and an unmarried young female a "bachelor girl," in analogy with the male term bachelor.

In early American English, the terms lady and girl took on additional, often less polite, meanings that came increasingly to dominate the semantic fields later occupied by these words. Thus, the word lady took on a slightly sardonic tinge— "She's playing the fancy lady," meaning she was putting on airs; or "Lady Bountiful," an appelative referring to a female who saw herself as supporting charitable causes but who did so in a superior or condescending way. In these usages, attributes of ladyhood—gentility, propriety, and good breeding—took on humorous or even embittered qualities for the speaker who lampooned the pretense of being a *lady* by overstressing the word.

Simultaneously, a trend developed in American English to use the word lady, often as a suffix, to elevate the status of people who had hitherto been called girls, maids, or servants. Thus, "cleaning lady," a replacement for "cleaning girl" or "housemaid," is a linguistic effort to treat the domestic worker not as an inferior but rather as inherently or intrinsically having all the attributes of any other person, including the "lady of the house." In this usage, the word lady is a substitute or euphemism for a term deemed insulting or derogatory.

However, the word lady, particularly when used as a suffix, also became a genteelism, an expression used by anyone hoping to sound more refined or better educated than he or she otherwise might appear to be. Once again, such efforts evoked sardonic or satirical responses, and an overly genteel speaker could be parodied as someone who called a mare a "lady horse." In this, the target was anyone who used overly genteel or hypercorrect forms in an effort to appear fair or "democratic" in his or her treatment of other people, especially when a belief in one's own superiority underlay the effort.

As a formal or proper term of address, the word lady is a correlative of the male *lord*, usages that remain alive as titles in the British peerage. These terms arose from Old English *hlefdige* and *hlaford*, where the root *hlef-* and *hlaf-* mean "-loaf," as in a loaf of bread, and the suffixes *-dige* and *-ord* mean respectively "knead" as in "to knead a loaf of bread" and "keeper" or "warder" as in "keeper of the loaves." Thus, the word lady originally denoted the woman who made the bread for the house; in other words, who fed everyone, whereas the word lord originally denoted the man who kept or protected the bread. With time, these came to refer to those who oversaw the making of all food and the protecting of the manor; the holders of the manor or, in brief, nobility. Quite in keeping with this lineage of meaning, in past American usage, the word lady meant a female of good birth or family, well-bred, refined, genteel, and proper; in congruence with Victorian sexual views, a lady was not considered openly sexual. As the usage developed further, the word lady became a genteelism that led to the parody of a lady as someone over-refined, overly proper, and overly genteel, especially in sexual matters. The term is still used, however, as a form of address to a female unknown to the speaker and as a polite term—"Excuse me, lady, is that your car?" The overall consequence is that the word lady is layered with a variety of meanings that are sometimes contradictory and often convey a complexity of meaning and nuance that can be difficult to decipher.

An excellent illustration of these complexities is the apparently Victorian joke in which one man asks another, "Who was that lady I saw you with last night?" and the other man answers indignantly, "That was no lady, that was my wife!" In an effort to deny one meaning of the word lady (i.e., "lady of the night," a euphemism for a prostitute [*qv*]), the second man inadvertently insults his own wife by denying her the status implicit in another meaning of the word. Given these complexities, euphemistic meanings, genteelisms, and other obscurities, the word lady as a synonym for modern woman is losing linguistic ground in the speech of many Americans.

Likewise, the word girl has had a complex history, with many layers of meaning and nuance. The word first appears in Middle English, and no origin is known for it. However, its meanings have consistently centered around relative youthfulness, with strong overtones of sexual attractiveness and perhaps availability, as well as non-elite birth or family origin. In the first sense, the correlative is *boy*, as in "boys and girls," and the word is still widely used and considered proper for any female below the age of puberty (*qv*). The sense of sexual attractiveness appears in the phrase, "She's a pretty girl," which could once have been said of a female of any age, though increasingly such colloquial uses describe younger females. However, the central example of this use is the word girlfriend, meaning someone to whom a male is attached socially, emotionally, and sexually; the correlative is boyfriend. In the combined sense of youthfulness and sexual attractiveness, the word girl is almost the only term used casually on college campuses or in lower schools, where it is apparently felt that the word woman denotes maturity, age, or status, and where the word lady is often used sardonically or caustically.

When used by women, the word girl can mean any group of women, as in the phrase, "The girls in the office are giving Sally a birthday party." If said by a woman, this phrase connotes equality and camaraderie, which levels or reduces differences in age, status, or wealth. It is a casual expression denoting a non-casual thought, that there are commonalities among women transcending accidents of status or age. When spoken by a man in this context, however, the word girl often has contemptuous or derogatory meanings. When said by a male supervisor (e.g., "I'll ask my girl to make coffee"), it connotes both the gender superiority and the superior status of the individual man. This use is cognate to the use mentioned above of the word girl in phrases like "cleaning girl" for a woman domestic worker. In this example, the word girl implies inferiority, incompetence, submission, and/or stupidity. Accordingly, some speakers of both sexes today avoid the word girl completely, usually substituting either the word woman or a gender-neutral term. However, in contrast to male speech, the word girl rarely implies incompetence or submission when used by women.

The term girl in particular has been vigorously criticized by women writers and feminists (*qv*) in recent decades. Pointing to its pejorative and insulting meanings, these critics have added considerable power to an existing trend of subsuming a variety of different meanings under the single term woman. At present, this usage of *woman* as a generic is correct and proper, and has not become a genteelism or a hypercorrect form. Simultaneously, a trend exists to eliminate the word or suffix *-woman* when it appears in terms for which gender-neutral expressions exist: "policewoman" has become "police officer," and "cleaning woman" has become "domestic worker" or "domestic." The underlying process appears to be the sense, shared by many speakers of American

English, that the word woman should not be used casually where insult or inaccuracy might result. This trend is illustrated by the occurrence of labels for toilet facilities: ''Men'' and ''Women.''

A second sense of the word woman contrasts it to the correlative term girl. This form is often used in writing, not speech, generally to connote a sexually mature female with reproductive potential, or a mother (qv). No particular social status is implied, and neither is any particular degree of sexual attractiveness. In technical discourse, including some definitions in this *Dictionary*, the synonym is *female*, used as a noun. As currently used, both words denote a sexually mature female human being—a *woman*—without imputing social or other meanings.

In this generic usage, the word appears in phrases like ''women's fashions'' and ''woman workers.'' Used in this sense, the word lady is largely outdated and seems condescending, except in special cases, such as the International Ladies' Garment Workers' Union (ILGWU), where ''workers'' are often women but the expression ''ladies' garments'' is an older genteelism for women's foundation garments as well as outerwear.

There are other examples of how a complex history reverses the meanings associated with the words woman and lady. One is ''woman driver,'' a highly insulting expression for someone thought to be careless, nervous, ignorant of traffic rules, and indifferent to the road welfare of others. By contrast, ''lady driver'' is either neutral, hypercorrect, or suggestive of someone who is overly careful, overly anxious, and overly concerned with traffic legalities. The neutral term, ''woman who drives,'' illustrates nicely how linguistic context shapes the specific meaning of the words woman and lady.

In general, the principle appears to be that *woman, lady,* and *girl* all take on different nuances when paired with specific adjectives or other modifying expressions. A full discussion would fill a book in itself, but the adjectives *old* and *sales* illustrate the point. The phrase ''old woman'' implies physical unattractiveness and low financial/social status, especially when coupled with additional phrases. ''She's just an old woman'' implies that the person is nothing more than an ''old woman,'' and therefore considered as nothing at all. When said to a man, the phrase ''Don't be an old woman'' implies that the speaker thinks the man addressed is weak, timid, and unmanly. In this expression, the word woman carries a strong pejorative sense. However, the term saleswoman is neutral, as opposed to the genteel term saleslady (which is still widely used by many speakers, especially if the salesperson sells women's clothing, cosmetics, or health products; if she works in an upscale boutique; or if the speaker wishes to be polite). In this context, the term salesgirl implies social and service distance. If, when speaking of office personnel and middle management in particular, one says ''woman manager,'' the term is neutral despite its gender reference, whereas ''lady manager'' is openly insulting. By contrast, affection and alliance are expressed, clearly if colloquially, when a male refers to his wife (qv) in the phrase, ''She's my old lady.'' On the other hand, a teenage boy intends and readily conveys a degree of disdain and contempt when he says, ''She's my old lady'' in referring to his mother. Furthermore, a woman can say of herself, ''There's life in the old girl yet,'' meaning that she has not yet succumbed to the expectations of passivity, age, weakness, or frailty that folklore attribute to older women. Finally, the terms woman, lady, and girl can have equivalent meanings even though they are surrounded by different adjectives, as in ''fallen woman,'' ''loose woman,'' ''woman of easy virtue,'' ''bad girl,'' ''call girl,'' ''lady of the night,'' and ''lady of the evening.''

These examples show that the meanings of *woman*, *lady*, and *girl* have all shifted rapidly and drastically, and that their precise meanings depend on the speaker's intentions, the hearer's understandings, and on the exact linguistic and social environment in which they are used. One and the same phrase or word may have dramatically different meanings according to the gender (*qv*) and ages of the speaker and hearer. In consequence, it can be concluded that although the word woman, as well as its near synonyms, may center on the meaning ''adult female human being,'' its meanings are variable and in flux as woman's status and history shift and change.

Usage of the word woman to mean a romantic or sexual partner (as in Gershwin's ''Bess, you is my woman now'') is relatively rare in so-called educated speech, and appears to be either a regionalism, a form of dialectal speech, or a conscious imitation of such speech, as in Gershwin's usage. The term girl, however, remained alive in this usage (e.g., in the word girlfriend). The difference between the words woman and lady in this context can be illustrated by comparing the phrase ''Hey, lady, move your car,'' as uttered by a man to convey impatience restrained by a felt need for politeness, to the phrase, ''Hey, woman, move your car,'' which carries either an openly insulting or an earthy tone, depending on the relationship of the speaker and the woman addressed.

Woman or women meaning male sexual activity with females—when considered inappropriate or excessive—has been in common use, both literary and verbal, and continues. In Brecht's *Threepenny Opera* (Blitzstein translation), Mrs. Peachum sings: ''Now there's a man, the living tool of Satan/He charges forth while others are debating'/Conniving cocky knave with all the trimmin'/I know one thing will trim him down—women.'' ''Trim down'' here implies both the psychological sense of deflating his ego and the sexual sense of bringing down his ''cocky'' erection (*qv*) through sexual activity. Another common use is ''You gotta fix up my buddy here with a date—he needs a woman real bad.'' Here, the buddy does not need a woman to cook him dinner, but to ''trim him down'' sexually. Neither *girl* nor *lady* is usually used in this sense; ''girls on his mind'' implies that the man is young and may not yet be sexually active, although he might like to be.

Two additional factors have altered the recent meanings of the word woman: first, the extensive criticisms by feminist writers of the sexism (*qv*) implicit in the many uses of the word, and second, the employment of large numbers of women in jobs, professions, and careers that previously had primarily employed men. It seems likely that the decrease in use of the word girl, except among young people, is due to feminist criticisms. However, feminist writers have been less successful in replacing the word woman with alternatives spelled *wimmin* (*qv*), womon (*qv*), or womyn, created with the aim of eliminating the suffix -*man* from the word; *see* man. Language reform movements have not been famous for their success over the centuries. Perhaps the greatest linguistic impact of feminist critiques has been to shift definitions of woman toward senses connoting greater respect, higher prestige, and increased value.

However, shifts in employment patterns and their attendant bureaucratic consequences (e.g., on tax forms) have had considerable linguistic effect. Gender-neutral terms are now quite common (e.g., fire fighter, police officer), and governmental agencies, like the Internal Revenue Service, routinely use gender-neutral terms to describe job categories (e.g., sanitation worker), as do many popular publications, particularly women's magazines. The substitution of the suffix -*person* for -*man* in corporate and academic language has assisted this trend (e.g., chairperson instead of chairwoman or chairman). Nonetheless, a trend can be detected in which the -*person* suffix has come to denote a woman specifically, as in a speaker who says that "she is chairperson" but "he is chairman." (This shift has occurred before in the English language.)

This substitution of gender-neutral terms for describing professions or job categories illustrates a significant aspect of the English language itself. The suffix -*man* can mean either "a male human being" or "a person generally" (*see* discussion under man). In the first sense, it is a contradiction to speak of a woman police officer as a policeman, although the second sense might allow this use. When confronted by this contradiction, speakers of English appear to give a gender meaning to the suffix -*man* before they give it a generic or gender-neutral meaning, so that the word policeman has as its primary sense the meaning "a male who is a police officer." In other words, gender identification precedes job identification. To resolve the contradiction between the two meanings of -*man*, speakers of English seem quite willing to employ gender-neutral expressions, like fire fighter, flight attendant, or police officer, when both men and women occupy these professions, while retaining the -*man* suffix for occupations that still primarily employ males, such as the word fisherman.

Bewildered users of the words woman, lady, girl, and other near-synonyms may take some comfort in knowing that these complexities are not recent. In Proto-Indo-European (PIE)—the root language from which developed English, German, French, Latin, Greek, and the Slavic languages, among others—the rootstock word for "female human being" has been reconstructed by historical linguists as *gwen-*. With time, and as different languages evolved from the original PIE, *gwen-* gave rise to other words also meaning "female human beings," notably, words derived from ancient Greek *gyn(o)-* and their relatives in other languages, such as *zhenshchina*, meaning "woman" in Russian. Similar words also occurred in Gothic, a very old Germanic language (ca. 350 C.E.; basically, English is a Germanic language): *qens*, meaning a woman ruler, and *ginð*, meaning woman and possibly an anal-receptive homosexual man. These words are the historical precursors of the modern English terms *queen*, meaning a female ruler, and *quean*, a male anal-receptive homosexual (the word queer, a pejorative colloquial for such a person, is not related to the word *quean*); *see* wife. In Old English, one word for female human being was *cewen*, derived directly from the *gwen-/gyn(o)-qinð* system of words in the older languages. It can also be argued that the now heavily tabooed word *cunt* for female genitalia (*qv*) and, insultingly, for a woman, also derives from this family of words.

However, for unknown reasons, in Old English and in Old High German, words based on the *c, k, g/n-t* sounds disappeared, except for specialized terms like *queen* and the tabooed *cunt*, and speakers of these languages began to use a new term, *wip/wyf/wif*, for female human being. This set of words is of unknown origin, and is not found in PIE nor in other Indo-European languages. It gave rise to the modern English *wife*, even though in old English *wip/wyf/wif* meant not a married woman but any woman or women in general. Modern English retains a few usages of *wife* meaning "female human being," as in *fishwife* for a woman who sells fish, and very possibly *housewife* in the sense of "woman of the house" rather than a married woman who lives at home and is caretaker of the house. In modern English, "the Wife of Bath" in Chaucer's *Canterbury Tales* would be "the Woman of Bath."

Nonetheless, it appears that speakers of Old English were not fully satisfied with this new word *wyf/wif*, because they added to it a suffix that means "person" in Old English and PIE: the ending *-man*. The new compound was *wifman* or *wyfman* (plural, *wifmen*), meaning a "female human being person." It rather sounds as if these speakers of Old English were not too clear about the meaning of the then newly coined word *wif/wyf* and had to make sure it applied to people by adding *-man* to it. With time, the word *wyfman* softened its pronunciation to become *women* of modern English.

In summary, the Proto-Indo-European for "female human being" is *gwen-*, which gave rise to *gyno-*, *qinð*, and *qens*, from which modern English obtained *queen* and *quean*, and, very likely, *cunt*. This system of words was replaced in Old English and Old High German with another word, of obscure origin, *wyf/wif/wip*, also meaning "female human being," which, in turn, came to mean "a married woman" in modern English. With time, speakers attached the suffix *-man*, meaning person, to *wyf/wif* to obtain *wyfman* or *wifman*. This word softened in sound to become the modern English *woman*.

Consequently, if today we are not quite sure whether to use *woman*, *lady*, *girl*, *female*, or some other term for "female human being," we are not alone. This word has one of the most complex histories of any word in modern English. Resources: C. Kramarae and P. A. Treichler, eds., *A Feminist Dictionary* (London: Pandora Press, 1985); Robin Lakoff, Language and woman's place, *Language in Society* 2(a)(973): 45–80; *The Oxford English Dictionary*.

womanish When said of man, having qualities not normatively associated with being manly (*qv*). Usually, these qualities are frailness, indecisiveness, emotionality, and lack of strength of purpose and character. It is among the most sexist (*see* sexism) terms in English, for it implies unpleasant characteristics to women and then attacks men who are thought to possess those characteristics. Modern male liberationist (*qv*) writers would speak of sensitivity, gentleness, thoughtfulness, and emotionality for these traits in either men or women, and consider them as valuable and desirable. Such is the power of words to reverse meanings.

womankind Women (*see* woman) in general. Formed in parallel with mankind, in that word's sense of meaning male human beings, womankind is a fairly recent coinage created to reduce the disparity or injustice seemingly present in including women anonymously in terms such as humankind or even mankind in the sense of humanity in general. The word connotes a sense of honor and importance felt by some writers to be absent in expressions like "women in general" or "females."

womanly Having attributes normatively attributed to women (*see* woman). Traditionally, these qualities center on nurturance, maturity of body and sensuality (*see* sensual), and related aspects of femininity (*qv*). The term is often used to mean full, rounded breasts (*qv*) and body, as in "a womanly figure." It is applied only to women and never to men; *see also* womanish.

woman with penis The psychoanalytic (*qv*) concept that some children between ages 2 and 5 believe that all women at one time possessed a penis (*qv*) like men or will later grow one. *See also* castration anxiety; penis envy.

woman-year A statistical measure for comparing the effectiveness of various methods of contraception (*qv*); a woman-year represents 12 months of exposure to the risk of pregnancy (*qv*) for a sexually active woman between menarche (*qv*) and menopause (*qv*).

womb *See* uterus.

womb envy A form of male envy of women's ability to become pregnant (*qv*) and bear children. Male-to-female transsexuals (*qv*), as well as heterosexual (*qv*) males, may experience womb envy.

womb fantasy In Freudian dream analysis, the wish to return to the security of fetal life and escape from the pressures and anxieties of everyday life. This fantasy may be expressed in images of being in a cave, on an island, or in an empty room.

women at risk Women who are at a higher than average risk for pregnancy (*qv*) because their status in a low-income family, limited education, or teenage status reduces their access to and use of contraceptives (*qv*).

women's lib Strictly, an abbreviation for the women's liberation (*qv*) movement; the shortening of the full expression is often to trivialize the goals of women's liberation and feminism (*qv*).

women's liberation A title given by women to feminism (*qv*) and to feminist (*qv*) groups in the United States in the late 1960s. The phrase came from activists in the Student Non-Violent Coordinating Committee at a 1964 meeting in Mississippi when women members challenged the demeaning positions they were assigned in the organization. *See also The Feminine Mystique.*

women's movement Although the term is often used as a synonym for feminist movement (*qv*) and women's liberation (*qv*) movement, women's movement is a more generic term for women's struggle for equality with men; the term does not carry the theoretical orientation of liberation and feminist philosophy that emerged from 1960s leftist politics.

women's studies *See* sociology of gender.

womon, womyn Spellings adopted by some feminists for "woman/women" to avoid the "-man/-men" endings of these words. *See also* wimmin, woman.

Woodstock The common reference to one of America's most famous rock festivals, held in August 1968, when 400,000 young people gathered at Woodstock, New York, and established the temporary "Woodstock Nation." Nudity (*qv*), marijuana, hard drug use, and open sexual displays were part of the "happening," which was quickly imitated at other rock festivals across the nation. Woodstock became symbolic of the sexual revolution (*qv*) of the 1960s and 1970s.

wrongful birth A newly emerging legal and medical concept applied to parents or to medical professionals who knowingly allow the conception (*qv*) and/or birth (*qv*) of a seriously handicapped infant. The concept of wrongful birth is premised on the culpability of individuals who conceive a handicapped child although they know that they are carriers for some serious genetic defect (*qv*) and are at risk of passing this defect on to any offspring. The term may also be applied to a malpractice suit against a physician because of a failed tubal ligation (*qv*) or vasectomy (*qv*), or because of the physician's failure to inform fully the pregnant woman of the known risk of genetic defects associated with her age, ethnic or genetic background. Some have claimed that the recent discovery of causal connections between the maternal use of alcohol and cocaine and fetal defects and newborn handicaps should be used to bring legal charges of fetal abuse and wrongful birth. Lawsuits based on wrongful birth are usually initiated to seek financial compensation for medical expenses, child support, and/or pain and suffering. *See also* wrongful life action.

wrongful life action A civil lawsuit brought against a physician or health facility to obtain financial compensation for professional negligence that resulted in the birth (*qv*) of an unwanted or handicapped child. Such lawsuits have been based on failed tubal ligations (*qv*), vasectomies (*qv*), and abortions (*qv*) coupled with a negligent failure on the part of the physician to confirm the success of the treatment, on the failure to confirm a pregnancy (*qv*) in time to allow an abortion, or on incomplete or inaccurate medical supervision or advice about a pregnancy that results in the birth of a handicapped child.

X

xanith An Arabic term usually translated as male homosexual (*qv*), although it is applied only to men who partially impersonate women in their clothing, manner, life-style, and sexuoerotic role with other men. *See also* transvestite; he-she.

X chromosome The larger of the two sex chromosomes (*qv*) in the karyotype (*qv*) of humans and other species. Human males have one X (*qv*) and one Y (*qv*) chromosome in addition to 44 autosomal chromosomes. The male gamete (*qv*), the sperm (*qv*), carries either an X or a Y plus 22 autosomes (*qv*). Females have two X chromosomes and 44 autosomes. The normal ovum (*qv*) has 22 autosomes and a single X. The X chromosome contains many X-linked (*qv*) genes associated with clinically significant disorders such as hemophilia, Duchenne muscular dystrophy, and color-blindness. *See also* Barr body.

Xenon-washout blood flow test Injection of xenon, a heavy, inert, colorless gas, into the blood supply of the male genitalia (*qv*) to diagnose possible causes of erectile dysfunction (*qv*). *See also* infusion cavernosography.

X-linked trait An inherited trait controlled by a gene (*qv*) carried on the X chromosome (*qv*). X-linked recessive traits are expressed in males because the male has only one X chromosome while an X-linked recessive gene is not expressed in females unless both X chromosomes carry the same recessive gene. Hemophilia, color-blindness, and Duchenne muscular dystrophy are produced by recessive genes (*qv*) and typical of X-linked traits. In the rare X-linked dominant trait, all affected individuals have at least one affected parent, and all daughters of an affected male are affected but none of his sons. *See also* sex-limited trait; sex-linked trait; sex-influenced trait.

XO The genetic notation for Turner syndrome (*qv*); more commonly written 45,XO to indicate 44 autosomes (*qv*) plus a single X chromosome (*qv*). The XO karyotype (*qv*) is in contrast with the XX (*qv*) karyotype normally found in a female.

X polysomy *See* XXX; XXXX.

XX The genetic notation for normal female; also written 46,XX to indicate a total of 46 chromosomes (*qv*) in the body cells—44 autosomes (*qv*) and two X (*qv*) sex chromosomes.

XXX, or X trisomy A human chromosomal aberration characterized by the presence of three X chromosomes (*qv*) and two Barr bodies (*qv*) instead of the normal complement of XX (*qv*) and a single Barr body. X trisomy occurs approximately once in every 1,000 live female births. There is no significant clinical symptom of X trisomy, although some degree of mental retardation is common. The offspring of a 47,XXX female is usually normal because of selective migration of XX into the polar body instead of the ovum (*qv*) during meiosis (*qv*). Also written 47,XXX.

XXXX, XXXXX, or X polysomy The genetic designation of an abnormal sex chromosome (*qv*) complement in which the female has four or five X chromosomes (*qv*) instead of the normal XX (*qv*) in somatic cells. Although there is no consistent clinical manifestation of X polysomies, the risk of congenital anomalies and mental retardation increases significantly with the increase in the number of X chromosomes.

XXY, XXXY, XXXXY, XXYY Genetic anomalies resulting in Klinefelter syndrome (*qv*).

XY The genetic notation for a normal human male; also written 46,XY to indicate a total of 46 chromosomes (*qv*) in body cells including 44 autosomes (*qv*) and one X (*qv*) and one Y (*qv*) sex chromosome.

XY female *See* testicular feminization syndrome; androgen insensitivity syndrome.

XYY syndrome This syndrome, characterized by a chromosome (*qv*) complement of 47, XYY, results in a male with a lag in physical development, leading to a slightly lower intelligence, a tendency to lower academic performance, and subsequent poor social adjustment. Small, late-descending testes (*qv*) and low sperm count (*qv*) are also common. In the early 1970s, this syndrome was diagnosed in an unusually high percentage of violent criminals, suggesting the extra Y chromosome (*qv*) might cause excessive aggression and antisocial behavior in males. However, in 1976, a definitive study concluded that the poor social adjustment and aggression were due more to the slower physical and mental development than directly to the extra Y chromosome. In matched comparisons of 47,XXY and 47,XYY, John Money and colleagues reported an increase in homosexual (*qv*) and bisexual (*qv*) orientations and an increased incidence of paraphilias (*qv*) in XYY men. Resource: J. Money, *Gay, Straight, and In-Between: The Sexology of Erotic Orientation* (New York: Oxford University Press, 1988), p. 47.

Y

Yab-Yum (Tib.) A Tibetan term for the mystical oneness and wholeness achieved by sexual intercourse (*qv*); the combined male and female principles viewed as the ideal cosmic oneness that resolves all dualities.

yang In ancient Chinese philosophy, the yang is the masculine, active, sun, and heaven side of a duality of fundamental forces that pervade the universe and control human life. The yang force determines the outward shape of the male sex organ (*qv*), the penis (*qv*). With the yin (*qv*), the yang forms a duality of complementary polarity of forces at work in all nature rather than a dichotomous dualism (*qv*), as is common in Western philosophies where male and female, active and passive, heaven and earth, matter and spirit, body and soul are seen as exclusionary pairs. *See also* Yab-Yum.

yang fluid Semen (*qv*); in the Taoist tradition portrayed as a celestial dragon.

yantra In Hindu philosophy, a yantra represents the harmonious balance of the mind, the five senses of touch, sight, hearing, smell, and taste, and the male and female functions of the universe. This mystical symbol, composed of two superimposed triangles, is used in meditation to help create a harmony of emotions, in rituals, and as a protective amulet. *See also* yin; yang.

Y chromosome One of two sex chromosomes (*qv*) in humans and higher mammals, present only in the male. Morphologically, the Y chromosome (*qv*) is much smaller than the X chromosome (*qv*) and has fewer genes. The H-Y antigen gene (*qv*) and testicular-determining factor gene (TDF) (*qv*) are found on the Y chromosome and may be involved in differentiation of the primordial gonads (*qv*) in the male fetus (*qv*) to form the testes (*qv*). There are no known medically significant conditions associated with the Y chromosome as there are with the X chromosome.

yeast infection *See* Candida albicans.

yellow body *See* corpus luteum.

yin In ancient Chinese philosophy, the feminine, passive, moon, and earth side of a duality of fundamental forces that pervade the universe and control human life. The yin force determines the inward shape of the female sex organ (*qv*), the vagina (*qv*). With the yang (*qv*), the yin forms a duality of complementary polarity of forces at work in all nature rather than a dichotomous dualism (*qv*) as is common in Western philosophies where male and female, active and passive, heaven and earth, matter and spirit are seen as exclusionary pairs. According to the teachings of Tao (*qv*), the power of the yin is stronger than any male power. Thus men need to learn how to take feminine fluids into themselves to gain wisdom and health.

Y-linked trait A trait controlled by a gene (*qv*) carried on the Y chromosome (*qv*). Such traits are expressed only in males and are inherited from father to son. Females cannot carry the gene or show its effects. Hairy ear (stiff bristles in the outer ear) is one of the few such traits known. Such traits are also called holandric, meaning "fully male."

yoga In Hindu and Buddhist philosophy, a mystic and ascetic practice involving intense and complete concentration, especially upon a deity, in order to establish an identity of consciousness with the object of concentration. Yoga usually involves the discipline of prescribed postures and controlled breathing. It advocates eight stages of discipline and exercise designed to liberate its practitioners from nature and return them to the original changeless state, beyond time and space. Yoga has strong similarities to the eightfold path of Buddhism.

Some teachers of yoga stress a physiology in which a great vein runs from the lowest part of the spine, where the serpent power, or kundalini (*qv*), rests, to the highest and most powerful psychic center symbolized by the lotus (*qv*). By arousing the serpent power and channeling it upward, the yogi hopes to gain spiritual energy and salvation when the kundalini is united with the highest lotus. Other yoga techniques involve a ritual path to the spiritual (karma-yoga); a devotional path (bhakti-yoga); an intellectual path (jnana-yoga); and a meditational path (dhyana-yoga). Yoga and bhoga (*qv*) (physical pleasure) are two alternative paths to liberation and the union of the individual with the universal. *See also* Tantra; Tantric sexual rituals.

yohimbine An alleged aphrodisiac (*qv*) derived from the bark of the west central African yohimbine tree, *Pausinystalia yohimba*.

yolk The nutritive material, rich in fats and proteins, contained in the ovum (*qv*) as nourishment for the developing embryo (*qv*). The amount of yolk depends on the species-specific type of reproduction. Thus eggs of externally fertilized species and those that lay eggs that develop outside the mother must contain sufficient yolk to carry the embryo through to hatching. The internally fertilized ovum of the mammal contains very little yolk.

yolk membrane *See* vitelline membrane.

yolk sac One of four extraembryonic membranes in the vertebrate embryo (*qv*), the yolk sac serves nutritive and respiratory functions in the fetuses (*qv*) of lower vertebrates and other functions in mammals (*qv*) since the placenta (*qv*) develops very early to provide nutrition. The other three embryonic membranes are the amnion (*qv*), chorion (*qv*), and allantois (*qv*). The allantois and the yolk sac give rise to the primordial germ cells (*qv*) which migrate to the primordial germinal ridges (*qv*), where they participate in formation of the ovaries (*qv*) or testes (*qv*). The yolk sac is also the site of primitive blood cell formation.

yolk stalk The narrow duct connecting the yolk sac (*qv*) with the midgut of the embryo (*qv*) during early embryonic development. It is obliterated by development of the umbilical cord (*qv*).

yoni (Skt.) The Hindu name for the vagina (*qv*). In the Tantric rites (*qv*) and Hindu temples, the yoni and lingam (*qv*) are frequently portrayed in stone and wood sculptures and worshipped. The yoni is variously symbolized by a triangle, fish, double-pointed oval, horseshoe, egg, and fruits. Likenesses of the yoni and lingam are also worn as sexual amulets.

youth A young person; the period of psychosexual development (*qv*) between puberty (*qv*) and adulthood or maturity; adolescence (*qv*).

Z

Z chromosome The sex-determining chromosome (*qv*) in certain insects, birds, and fishes equivalent to the X chromosome (*qv*) in humans. Normal females of some species have a single Z chromosome and one W chromosome (*qv*). The males are homogametic and have two Z chromosomes. This sex determination mechanism is the opposite of that found in mammals (*qv*), where the female is homogametic XX and the male heterogametic XY.

ZIG *See* zoster immune globulin.

zipper ring An intrauterine contraceptive device (*qv*) made of coiled nylon thread.

zona fasciculata (L.) The inner layer of the adrenal gland cortex (*qv*), which secretes small amounts of steroid sex hormones (*qv*), particularly testosterone (*qv*). Functional tumors of this layer result in virilization (*qv*) in affected females and premature puberty (*qv*) in affected males.

zona pellucida (L.) The thick, transparent, noncellular gelatinous membrane enclosing the mammalian ovum (*qv*). It is secreted by the ovum when it develops in the ovarian follicle. From fertilization (*qv*) to implantation (*qv*), it helps hold together the dividing blastocyst (*qv*) cells.

zona radiata (L.) A zona pellucida (*qv*) that has a striated appearance caused by radiating canals within the membrane.

zooerastia, zooerasty Sexual excitement or orgasm (*qv*) achieved through contact with an animal. *See also* bestiality; zoophilia.

zoolagnia *See* zoophilia.

zoomania A psychopathological state characterized by excessive fondness for and preoccupation with animals. *See also* zoophilia; zoosadism.

zoophilia A paraphilic (*qv*) disorder in which sexuoerotic (*qv*) response and gratification are derived from fondling animals or from the fantasy or act of engaging in sexual activity with an animal. Zoophilia may occur sporadically as oral or genital contact with an animal as a component of adolescent (*qv*) sexual exploration without leading to a long-term zoophilia. Also known as bestiality.

zoosadism A paraphilic (qv) dependence on inflicting pain on animals in order to facilitate sexual arousal (*qv*) and orgasm (*qv*). *See also* zoophilia.

zoosperm A spermatozoon (*qv*).

zoster *See* herpes zoster.

zoster immune globulin (ZIG) A passive immunizing agent used in preventing or attenuating herpes zoster (*qv*) viral infection in immunologically compromised individuals; in limited experimental use as of 1990.

Zovirax *See* Acyclovir.

zygogenesis The formation of a zygote (*qv*); reproduction (*qv*) by the union of gametes (*qv*).

zygosis A form of sexual reproduction (*qv*) achieved by the union of two similar reproductive cells and fusion of their nuclei rather than by union of dimorphic ovum (*qv*) and sperm (*qv*).

zygote In embryology (*qv*), the developing ovum (*qv*) after it is fertilized (*qv*), through early cleavage (*qv*), until as a blastocyst (*qv*) it embeds in the uterine mucosal lining.

Appendix A: An Abstract of Philias and Paraphilias

General Classification of Sexual Responses

Sexual responses can be classified in terms of the degree or intensity of response, ranging from hypophilic, to normophilic, hyperphilic, and paraphilic.

Hypophilia refers to a proceptive and/or acceptive response below the normal range. Several sexual dysfunctions are in this category—desire phase dysfunctions, inhibited arousal and orgasm.

Normophilia indicates a response that conforms erotosexually with the norms dictated by custom, religious, or civil authorities. It is the opposite of paraphilia.

Hyperphilia refers to a proceptive and/or acceptive response above the normal range. Premature ejaculation, Don Juanism, satyriasis, and nymphomania fit in this category.

Paraphilia refers to recurrent responsiveness to and obsessive dependence on an unusual or socially unacceptable stimulus in order to experience sexual arousal and achieve orgasm.

A List of Paraphilias

PHILIA	SEXUALLY ATTRACTED TO OR AROUSED BY
Acrotomophilia	An amputee partner
Adolescentilism	Imitating an adolescent although older
Algophilia	*See* masochism
Amphiphilia	A bisexual orientation
Amputation fetish	*See* acrotomophilia, apotemnophilia
Androgynophilia	A bisexual orientation
Andromimetophilia	An andromimetic female or preoperative female-to-male transexual
Androphilia	A male

Apodysophilia	Exhibitionism
Apotemnophilia	Being or fantasizing being an amputee
Asphixophilia	Erotic self-strangulation
Autoagonistophilia	Being observed or on stage while engaged in sexual activity
Autoassassinatophilia	Staging one's own masochistic death
Autoflagellation	Self-inflicted whipping
Automasochism	Self-inflicted pain
Automutilation	Self-inflicted mutilation
Autonecrophilia	Imagining oneself as a corpse
Autonepiophilia	Impersonating an infant and being treated as a baby; infantilism
Autopedophilia	Impersonating an infant and being treated as a baby
Autophilia	Sexual love of self
Autoscopophilia	Looking at one's own body and genitalia
Biastophilia	Surprise attack and violent assault on a nonconsenting stranger
Chrematisophilia	Being charged or forced to pay for sexual services
Coprography	Creating graffiti about excrement
Coprolagnia	Thinking about, seeing, smelling, or handling feces
Coprophagia	Eating feces
Coprophilia	Smell or taste of feces, seeing someone defecate
Diaperism	*See* autonepiophilia, nepiophilia
Ecouteurism	Listening to accounts of sexual encounters or a couple making love
Eonism	Male cross-dressing as a female
Ephebophilia	A postpubertal or adolescent partner
Erotic pyromania	Arson
Erotic self-strangulation	*See* asphixophilia
Erotolalia	Obscene talk
Erotomania	Morbid exaggeration or preoccupation with sexual matters
Erotophonophilia	Lust murder
Exhibitionism	Publicly exposing one's genitals
Fetishism	Any nonsexual inanimate object or a nongenital body part

Formicophilia	Small creatures, ants, insects, or snails crawling on the genitalia
Frottage	Rubbing against a stranger in a public place
Gerontophilia	Having a much older sexual partner
Gynemimetophilia	Having a sexual partner who is a transvestite, gynemimetic, or preoperative male-to-female transexual
Gynephilia	*See* gynophilia
Gynophilia	A woman as a sexual partner
Heterophilia	A partner of the opposite sex
Homocidophilia	Lust murder, erotophonophilia
Homophilia	A partner of the same sex
Hybristophilia	A sexual partner who is a criminal
Hyphenophilia	Touching or feeling skin, fur, hair, leather, or fabric
Hypoxyphilia	*See* asphixophilia
Infantilism	Impersonating an infant and being treated as a baby; autonepiophilia
Juvenilism	Impersonating a juvenile and being treated as such by a sexual partner
Kleptomania	*See* kleptophilia
Kleptophilia	Compulsive stealing
Klismophilia	Being given an enema
Masochism	Being the recipient of punishment, discipline, humiliation, and forced servitude
Mixoscopia	Watching a loved one have sex with another person
Mixoscopia bestialis	Watching a loved one have sex with an animal
Monopediomania	A partner who is one-legged
Morphophilia	A partner whose body characteristics are selectively particularized, prominent, or different from one's own
Multiphilia	Recurrent short-term limerance or falling in love and pairbonding with new partners
Mysophilia	Something soiled or filthy (e.g., sweaty or soiled underwear, used menstrual pads)
Narratophilia	Using or hearing dirty or obscene words or reading or listening to erotic narratives in the presence of one's partner
Necromania	Corpses and anything to do with death

Necrophilia	Sexual activity with a corpse
Nepiophilia	Playing the role of a parent with an infant
Olfactophilia	Smells and odors emanating from parts of the body, especially the sexual areas
Osmolagnia	Smells and odors emanating from parts of the body, especially the sexual areas
Pedomania	*See* pedophilia
Pedophilia	A prepubertal or early pubertal boy or girl
Peodeiktophilia	Evoking surprise, dismay, shock, or panic from a stranger by exhibiting the flaccid or erect penis
Pictophilia	Viewing erotic pictures, films, or videotapes alone or in the presence of a partner
Polyiterophilia	Repetition of the same activity—manual, oral, anal, vaginal, or penile—many times with many partners
Pornographomania	Writing sexually obscene material, graffiti, and letters
Pornolagnia	Prostitutes
Rapism	The terrified resistance of a nonconsenting victim to a sexual assault and degradation
Raptophilia	*See* rapism
Renifleurism	Particular smells
Retifism	Women's shoes
Sadism	Humiliating, punishing, torturing, and inflicting pain on a partner
Sadomasochism	The reciprocal interaction of a sadistic authority figure with a masochistic victim, with or without mutual consent of the victim
Saliromania	Filth, ugliness, or deformity
Scatophilia	Talking about sexual or obscene matters to an unknown person
Scoptophilia, passive	Having other persons view one's genitalia
Scoptophilia, active	Viewing sexual acts and/or the sexual
Somnophilia	Intruding on and fondling a stranger who is asleep
Spectophilia	Spiritual beings, or having sex with such
Stigmatophilia	One's partner or self being tattooed, scarified, or pierced for the wearing of gold jewelry, especially in the genital region

Symphorophilia	Stage-managing the possibility of a disaster, such as a traffic accident, fire, or flood, and then watching it happen
Taphophilia	Cemeteries
Telephone scatophilia	Talking about sexual or obscene matters over the telephone to an unknown listener
Telephonicophilia	*See* telephone scatophilia
Toucherism	Surreptitiously touching a stranger on an erotic body part
Transvestism	Cross-dressing
Transvestophilia	*See* transvestism
Undinism	Urine and urination
Urolagnia	The smell or taste of urine
Urophilia	Urine and urination
Voyeurism	Secretly watching another person undressing or engaging in sexual behavior
Zoolagnia	Oral contact with animals, or the smell of animals
Zoophilia	Animals
Zoosadism	Inflicting pain on animals

A Classification of Paraphilias

The most comprehensive classification of paraphilias has been devised by John Money, *The Destroying Angel* (Buffalo NY: Prometheus Books, 1985).

Sacrificial Paraphilias

One or both of the partners must atone for the wicked or degenerate act of defiling the saint with ecstatic lust. The atonement is accomplished when one or both persons undergoes an act of penance, suffering, or sacrifice. Sacrificial paraphilias vary in degree of consent or force and in playfulness and pain.

Masochism (*qv*) or self-sacrifice and sadism (*qv*) or partner sacrifice are the most common type of this paraphilia. Other forms are symphorophilia (*qv*), or being turned on by disasters, asphyxiophilia, or self-strangulation (*qv*), and erotophonophilia, or lust murder (*qv*).

Predatory Paraphilias

The sinful act of lust is so defiling it can be indulged in only if it is stolen or taken from an innocent person by force or stealth. The stimulation may come from being the predator or the prey.

The most notorious predatory paraphilia is biastophilia (*qv*), rapism (*qv*), or raptophilia (*qv*). Other forms include somonophilia, or the "sleeping princess syndrome" (*qv*), kleptophilia (*qv*), in which stealing results in sexual arousal, and the Stockholm syndrome, in which the victim of terrorism identifies with the terrorist.

Merchantile Paraphilias

The sexual stimulation comes from the saintly person's assuming the role of a sinner or whore, as in troilism (*qv*) and narratophilia (*qv*).

Fetish Paraphilias

A compromise is made with the saintliness of chastity and abstinence by including in the sexual act a token that symbolizes the wickedness and degeneracy of the sinful, lustful act. The fetish or token permits the sexual partner to remain pure and undefiled because the fetish (*qv*) object is the sinful agent of erotic excitement and sexual satisfaction.

This category includes autonepiophilia or diaperism (*qv*), coprophilia (feces) (*qv*), hyphephilia (fabrics, especially rubber and leather) (*qv*), mysophilia (filth) (*qv*), klismaphilia (enemas) (*qv*), urophilia or undinism (urine) (*qv*), olfactophilia (smell) (*qv*), and foot fetish.

Eligibility Paraphilias

Self-abandonment to the lustful act can be achieved only if the partner has some quality that places him or her beyond the protection privileges and limits of being saintly and undefiled. The partner's entire physique may be involved as when there is a paraphilic dependence on the partner or self being fat or skinny.

In stigmatophilia (tattooing) (*qv*), apotemnophilia (*qv*), and acrotomophilia (*qv*) only a part of one's own or the partner's body is deformed or crippled. The distancing of lust in an extramarital affair and seeking partners from socially unacceptable classes are common forms of this paraphilic type. Zoophilia (*qv*) in which the sexual partner is an animal, and necrophilia (*qv*), in which the partner must be dead, are the extremes of erotic eligibility distancing. Age-discrepancy paraphilias (*qv*)—gerontophilia (*qv*), ephebophilia (*qv*), pedophilia (*qv*), and infantophilia (*qv*)—are another form of eligibility paraphilias.

Allurement Paraphilias

Some part of the preparatory or courtship phase is pushed into the center, where it replaces the main event of intercourse and orgasm. The distancing of lust of the person who can then remain innocent.

In this category, John Money includes exhibitionism (*qv*), voyeurism, frottage (*qv*), telephone scatophilia (*qv*) or obscene phone calls (*qv*), autoagonistophilia (*qv*), pictophilia (*qv*), and scoptophilia (*qv*).

Appendix B: An Abstract of Phobias and Sexual Anxieties

PHOBIA	FEAR OF
Anal-castration anxiety	Toilets, defecation
Androphobia	Men
Anuptaphobia	Remaining unmarried
Aulophobia	Penislike musical instruments
Automysophobia	Being unclean, dirty; "messy" sex
Bromidrosiphobia	Body smells
Coitophobia	Sexual intercourse
Coital aninsertia	Sexual intercourse
Coprophobia	Defecation and excrement
Cypridophobia	Contracting a venereal disease
Enosiophobia	Sinning, especially in a sexual way
Erotophobia	One's sexual nature and responses
Erythrophobia	Color red; blushing, sex flush
Eurotophobia	Female genitalia
Gamophobia	Marriage
Genital penetration phobia	Sexual intercourse
Genophobia	Sex
Gymnophobia	Naked body
Gynophobia	Women
Hamartophobia	Sex, especially in a sexual way
Haptephobia	Being touched
Hedenophobia	Experiencing sexual pleasure
Heterophobia	Heterosexual persons

Homoerotophobia	Homosexual persons
Homophobia	Homosexual persons
Maieusiophobia	Childbirth
Ophidiophobia	Fear of snakes as a symbol of sex
Parthenophobia	Virgins, young girls
Patriphobia	Inherited genetic defect, disease
Peccatophobia	Sinning in a sexual way
Penetration phobia	Vaginal, oral, or anal penile penetration
Phallophobia	Penis, especially when erect
Proctophobia	Enemas, rectal exams, anal sex
Scatophobia	Defecation and excrement
Scoptophobia	Being looked at or seen naked
Sexophobia	Anything to do with sex
Snake phobia	Snakes as a penis symbol
Spermatophobia	Semen
Teratophobia	Monsters, giving birth to defective or deformed infant
Tocophobia	Childbirth

Appendix C: Biographical Sketches in This Dictionary

Abelard, Pierre (1079–1142)

Acton, William (1813–1875)

Adler, Alfred (1870–1937)

Aquinas, Thomas (1225–1274)

Aretino, Pietro (1492–1557)

Aristotle (384–322 BC)

Augustine of Hippo (354–430)

Baer, Karl Ernst von (1792–1876)

Benjamin, Harry (1885–1986)

Block, Iwan (1872–1922)

Brown-Séquard, Edouard (1817?–1894)

Carile, Richard (1790–1843)

Casanova, Giovanni (1725–1798)

Comstock, Anthony (1844–1915)

De Sade, Marquis (1740–1814)

Dickinson, Robert Latou (1861–1950)

Dick-Read, Grantly (1890–1959)

Ellis, Havelock (1859–1939)

Fallopius, Gabriello (1523–1562)

Freud, Sigmund (1856–1939)

Graaf, Regnier de (1641–1673)

Grafenberg, Ernst

Graham, Sylvester (1794–1851)

Hall, G. Stanley (1884–1924)

Hamm, Stephen

Hirschfeld, Magnus (1868–1935)

Jorgensen, Christian (1927–1989)

Jung, Carl (1875–1962)

Kellogg, John (1852–1943)

Kinsey, Alfred Charles (1894–1956)

Krafft-Ebing, Baron Richard von (1840–1902)

Leeuwenhoek, Anton van (1632–1723)

Malinowski, Bronislaw (1884–1942)

Malpighi, Marcello (1628–1694)

Malthus, Thomas Robert (1766–1834)

Marquis de Sade *See* de Sade, Marquis

Maslow, Abraham H. (1908–1970)

Mead, George Herbert (1863–1931)

Mead, Margaret (1901–1978)

Moll, Albert (1862–1939)

Muller, Johannes Peter (1801–1848)

Noyes, John Humphrey (1811–1886)

Piaget, Jean (1896–1980)

Rank, Otto (1884–1939)

Reich, Wilhelm (1897–1957)

Sacher-Masoch, Leopold von (1836–1895)

Saint-Hilaire, Etienne Geoffroy (1772–1844)

Sanger, Margaret (1883–1966)

Soranus of Ephesus (98–138)

Spallanzani, Lazzaro (1729–1799)

Steinach, Eugen (1861–1944)

Stopes, Marie Carmichael (1880–1958)

Tissot, Simon André (1728–1797)

Velde, Theodore H. van de (1873–1937)

von Baer, Karl Ernst *See* Baer, Karl Ernst vonVoronoff, Serge

Wilde, Oscar (1854–1900)

Wolff, Kaspar Friedrich (1733–1794)

Wollstonecraft, Mary (1759–1797)

Appendix D: Decisions of the U.S. Supreme Court Related to Sexual Behaviors

Beal v. Doe, 1977: abortion

Bellotti v. Baird, 1979: parental consent in abortion

Bolger v. Youngs Drug Products Corp, 1982: contraceptive information

Bowers v. Hardwick, 1986: homosexual behavior

Colautti v. Franklin, 1979: physician's discretion on viability

Doe v. Bolton, 1973: abortion

Doe v. Bridgeton Hospital Association, 1977: abortion. *See* Poelker v. Doe

Doe v. Commonwealth Attorney for Richmond, 1976: antisodomy law

Eisenstadt v. Baird, 1972: sale of contraceptives

Gaylord v. Tacoma School District, 1977: employment rights of homosexuals

Griswold v. Connecticut, 1965: sale of contraceptives

Harris v. McRae, 1980: abortion funding

Hartigan v. Zbaraz, 1987: restricted access for teenage abortion

H.L. v. Matheson, 1981: informing parents of minor's abortion

Hodgson v. Minnesota, 1990: parental consent for minor's abortion

Maher v. Roe, 1977: abortion funding

Miller v. United States, 1973: pornography

Ohio v. Akron Center for Reproductive Health, 1990: informing parents of a minor prior to abortion

Planned Parenthood Association of Kansas City v. Ashcroft, 1983: second-trimester abortions and parental consent for abortion

Planned Parenthood of Central Missouri v. Danforth, 1976: parental consent for abortions

Poelker v. Doe, 1977: elective abortions

Roe v. Wade, 1973: legalization of abortion

Roth v. United States, 1957: pornography—three legal criteria for obscenity

Simopolous v. Virginia, 1983: abortions in clinics and restrictions on abortion

Singer v. U.S. Civil Service Commission, 1977: employment rights of homosexuals

Thornburgh v. American College of Obstetricians and Gynecologists, 1986: requirements on physician to inform patient of abortion risks

Turnock v. Ragsdale, 1990: abortion clinic facilities

Webster v. Reproductive Health Services, 1989: abortion, Roe v. Wade

Appendix E: An Atlas of Human Sexuality

Note: Figures 2, 7, 9, 11 through 14, and 19 are reproduced with permission from the second edition of Robert T. Francoeur's text *Becoming a Sexual Person*, published by Macmillan Publishing Company, 1991. Computer graphic designs for the remaining illustrations were provided by Danielle A. Francoeur.

Figure 1
A Summary Roadmap of Psychosexual Development

Processes and Elements

Critical
Periods

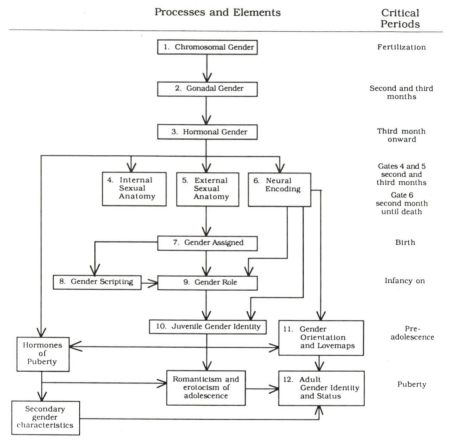

The lifelong process of psychosexual development has been compared to a roadmap with a dozen gates. Some gates, or windows, are one-dimensional, either/or, and irreversible, in the sense that once a fertilized egg has either XX or XY chromosomes, or once a fetus develops testes or ovaries, or a penis or clitoris, it has passed through a one-dimensional gate and cannot return to take the other path. Other gates involving hormones, social scripting, and neural encoding are two-dimensional, with masculinizing and femininizing components. These two-dimensional gates remain more or less flexible throughout one's life. This figure shows a 12-gate model in which the authors have expanded the original suggestion of John Money and Patricia Tucker in *Sexual Signatures: On Being a Man or a Woman* (Boston: Little, Brown, 1975). For a detailed explanation of the developmental gates illustrated in Figures 1 through 10, see entry under *sex variables*.

748

Figure 2
The Genetics of Egg and Sperm Production

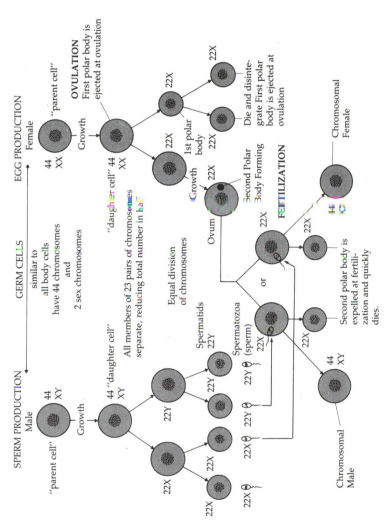

Spermatogenesis, production of the sperm, is detailed on the left side of this figure while oogenesis or production of the egg is shown on the right side. The results of fertilization, the union of egg and sperm, are shown at the bottom of the figure. For a detailed explanation of the developmental gates illustrated in Figures 1 through 10, see entry under *sex variables*.

Figure 3
Gate 1: Chromosomal/Genetic Gender

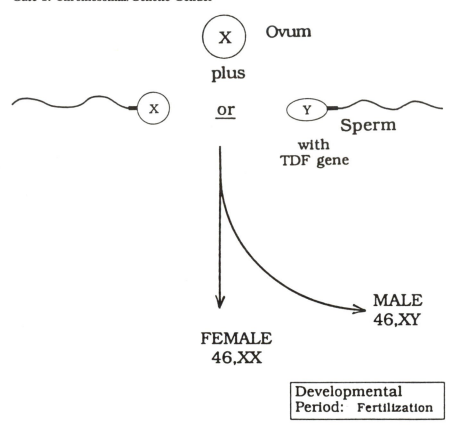

Developmental
Period: Fertilization

Fertilization marks a passage through a one-dimensional gate or developmental window that establishes an individual's chromosomal character for life. One is then either a genetic male 46,XY or a genetic female with 46,XX. Alternatively, some individuals may have an abnormal chromosome makeup, e.g., Turner syndrome (45,XO), Klinefelter syndrome (47,XXY), or other anomalies. For a detailed explanation of the developmental gates illustrated in Figures 1 through 10, see entry under *sex variables*.

Figure 4
Gate 2: Gonadal Gender

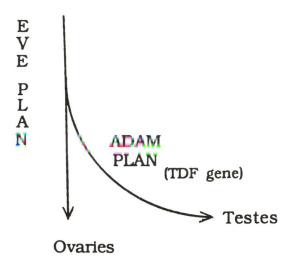

Undifferentiated Gonads

E
V
E

P
L
A
N

ADAM
PLAN
(TDF gene)

→ Testes

Ovaries

Developmental
Period:

Male: 6th week

Female: 12th week

The fetus passes through a second one-dimensional gate between weeks 6 and 12 when undifferentiated fetal gonads become either testes or ovaries. Very rarely does a fetus develop a combination of ovariotesticular tissues, making it a true hermaphrodite. For a detailed explanation of the developmental gates illustrated in figures 1 through 10, see entry under *sex variables*.

Figure 5
Gate 3: Hormonal Gender

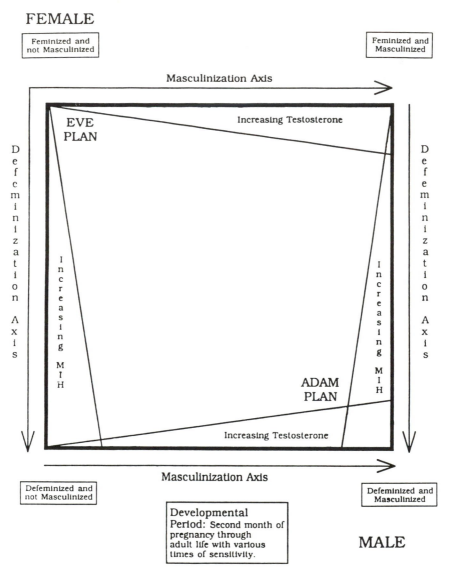

FEMALE

| Feminized and not Masculinized | Feminized and Masculinized |

Masculinization Axis

EVE PLAN

Increasing Testosterone

Defeminization Axis (left side)

Increasing MIH

Defeminization Axis (right side)

Increasing MIH

ADAM PLAN

Increasing Testosterone

Masculinization Axis

| Defeminized and not Masculinized | Defeminized and Masculinized |

Developmental Period: Second month of pregnancy through adult life with various times of sensitivity.

MALE

Hormone production by the testes or ovaries begins in the second month of pregnancy and continues throughout life. The prenatal masculinizing action of androgens and defeminizing Mullerian inhibiting hormone result in a complex two-dimensional balance illustrated in this figure. After birth, the feminizing action of estrogens adds to the complexity of this gate. For a detailed explanation of the developmental gates illustrated in Figures 1 through 10, see entry under *sex variables*.

Figure 6
Gate 4: Internal Sexual Anatomy

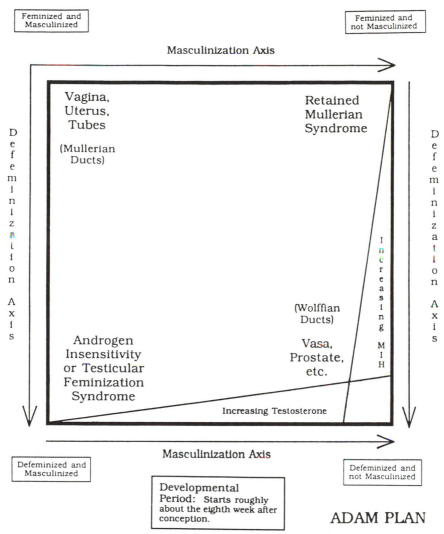

EVE PLAN

Feminized and Masculinized

Feminized and not Masculinized

Masculinization Axis

Vagina, Uterus, Tubes

(Mullerian Ducts)

Retained Mullerian Syndrome

D e f e m i n i z a t i o n A x i s

D e f e m i n i z a t i o n A x i s

Increasing MIH

(Wolffian Ducts)

Androgen Insensitivity or Testicular Feminization Syndrome

Vasa, Prostate, etc.

Increasing Testosterone

Masculinization Axis

Defeminized and Masculinized

Defeminized and not Masculinized

Developmental Period: Starts roughly about the eighth week after conception.

ADAM PLAN

This two-dimensional model illustrates one consequence of the two-dimensional hormonal diagram shown in Figure 5. Figure 7 applies this diagram to the anatomical differentiation of internal sexual anatomy. For a detailed explanation of the developmental gates illustrated in Figures 1 through 10, see entry under *sex variables*.

753

Figure 7
Gate 4: Development of Internal Fetal Sexual Anatomy

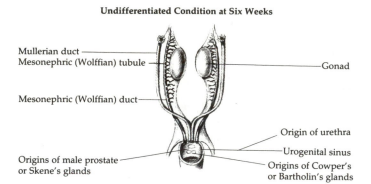

Undifferentiated Condition at Six Weeks

Mullerian duct
Mesonephric (Wolffian) tubule
Gonad
Mesonephric (Wolffian) duct
Origin of urethra
Urogenital sinus
Origins of male prostate
or Skene's glands
Origins of Cowper's
or Bartholin's glands

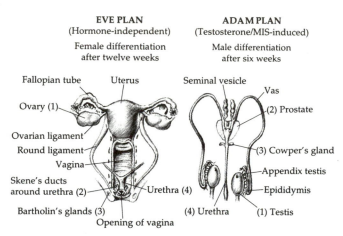

EVE PLAN
(Hormone-independent)
Female differentiation
after twelve weeks

ADAM PLAN
(Testosterone/MIS-induced)
Male differentiation
after six weeks

Fallopian tube   Uterus   Seminal vesicle
Ovary (1)   Vas
                                          (2) Prostate
Ovarian ligament
Round ligament   (3) Cowper's gland
Vagina   Appendix testis
Skene's ducts
around urethra (2)   Urethra (4)   Epididymis
Bartholin's glands (3)   (4) Urethra   (1) Testis
Opening of vagina

Note: The numbers in parentheses indicate organs that are homologous
in the male and female; organs with the same number in parentheses
differentiate from the same embryonic origins.

Differentiation of our internal sexual anatomy begins in the third month of pregnancy, controlled by the absence or balance of critical amounts of testosterone and Mullerian inhibiting hormone. This anatomical description complements Figure 6.

When the TDF gene triggers the development of testes, these glands begin producing two androgenic hormones, testosterone and Mullerian inhibiting substance (MIS). Testosterone helps the Wolffian ducts become the internal male duct system while MIS causes degeneration of the Mullerian ducts. *See* Adam Plan.

In the absence of the TDF gene, testosterone and MIS, the development of the primordia follow the Eve Plan (*qv*). The Mullerian ducts differentiate and the Wolffian ducts degenerate.

See Figure 9 for the parallel development of the external sexual anatomy. For a detailed explanation of the developmental gates illustrated in Figures 1 through 10, see entry under *sex variables*.

Figure 8
Gate 5: External Sexual Anatomy

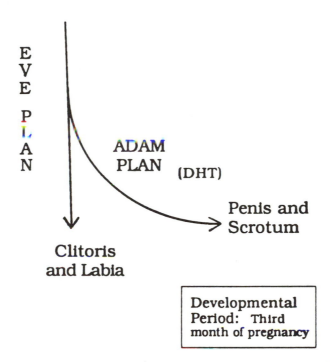

Undifferentiated
Genital Tubercle,
Folds, and Swellings

EVE PLAN

ADAM PLAN (DHT)

Clitoris and Labia

Penis and Scrotum

Developmental
Period: Third
month of pregnancy

The primordia of the external genitals are limited to an either/or development. Either they become female, developing into a clitoris and major and minor labia, or they become a penis with scrotum. This development can be ambiguous, as occurs in an intersex. The anatomical implications of this diagram are shown in Figure 9. For a detailed explanation of the developmental gates illustrated in Figures 1 through 10, see entry under *sex variables*.

Figure 9
Gate 5: Development of External Fetal Sexual Anatomy

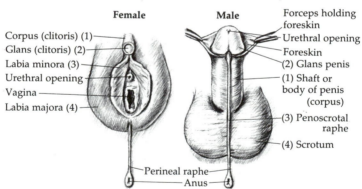

a. Undifferentiated Condition before Six Weeks

Glans area
Urethral fold
Urethral groove

Anal tubercle

Genital
tubercle

Tail (cut away)

EVE PLAN
(Hormone-independent)

b. Six to Eight Weeks

ADAM PLAN
(DHT-induced)

Glans
Coronal groove
Site of future origin of foreskin
Urethral fold
Urogenital groove
Labioscrotal swelling
Urethral folds partly
fused
Anus

c. Full Development Twelve Weeks after Conception

Female   Male

Corpus (clitoris) (1)
Glans (clitoris) (2)
Labia minora (3)
Urethral opening
Vagina
Labia majora (4)

Forceps holding
foreskin
Urethral opening
Foreskin
(2) Glans penis
(1) Shaft or
body of penis
(corpus)
(3) Penoscrotal
raphe
(4) Scrotum

Perineal raphe
Anus

Note: Homologous structures in the male and female are indicated
by similar numbers in parentheses.

During the first six weeks of embryonic life the sexual anatomy is still undifferentiated. Its development can go in either direction of female or male development, depending on the presence or absence of the TDF gene, Y chromosome, and the male or androgenic hormones produced by the testes if these develop.

In the seventh and eighth weeks, the external sexual anatomy begins to develop rapidly, but it is still impossible to ascertain the sex of the fetus by the external form. By the end of the first trimester, the fetus is clearly male or female in its sexual anatomy.

See Figure 8 for a diagrammatic presentation of this gate; see Figures 6 and 7 for the parallel development of the internal sexual anatomy. For a detailed explanation of the developmental gates illustrated in Figures 1 through 10, see entry under *sex variables.*

Figure 10
Gate 6: Biobehavioral Neural Templates

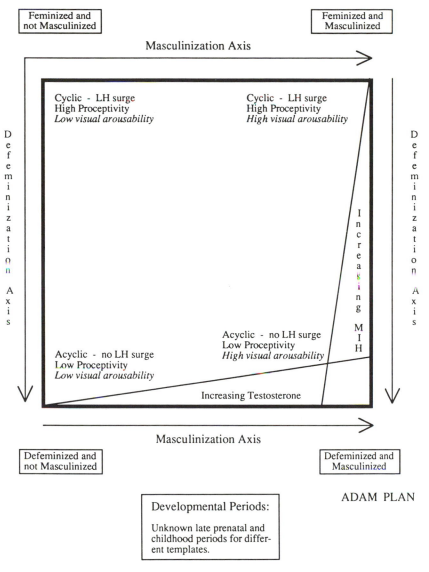

In addition to directing and channeling the development of the internal and external sexual anatomies, genes and gonadal hormones influence the gender-differentiated development of different pathways, tendencies, and neural templates in the cells and systems of the brain. The nature, extent, and factors involved in masculinizing and defeminizing various tendencies and patterns in the brain are highly controversial and hotly disputed. For a detailed explanation of the developmental gates illustrated in Figures 1 through 10, see entry under *sex variables*.

Figure 11
External Female Sexual Anatomy

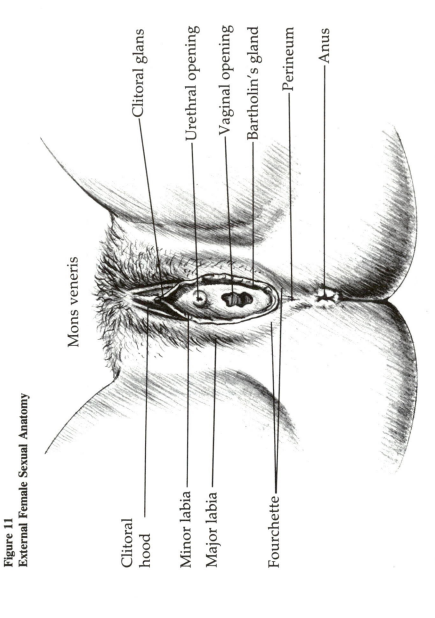

Mons veneris

Clitoral glans

Urethral opening

Vaginal opening

Bartholin's gland

Perineum

Anus

Clitoral hood

Minor labia

Major labia

Fourchette

This sketch shows the position and relationships of the structures that make up the vulva of the female. The three major pelvic muscles indicated are internal and lie beneath the skin and in the floor of the pelvic cavity.

Figure 12
Internal Female Sexual Anatomy

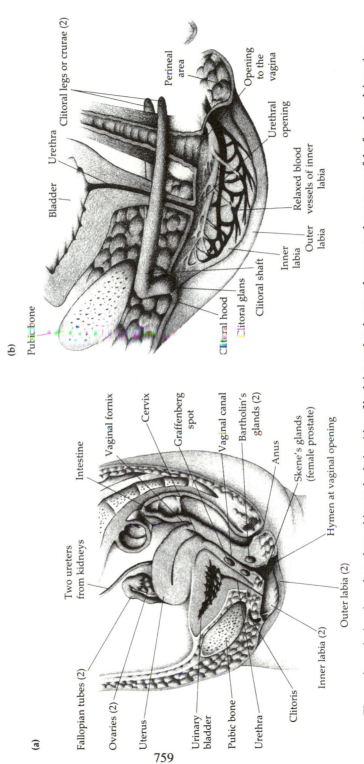

(a)

Fallopian tubes (2)

Ovaries (2)

Uterus

Urinary bladder

Pubic bone

Urethra

Clitoris

Inner labia (2)

Outer labia (2)

Two ureters from kidneys

Intestine

Vaginal fornix

Cervix

Graffenberg spot

Vaginal canal

Bartholin's glands (2)

Anus

Skene's glands (female prostate)

Hymen at vaginal opening

(b)

Pubic bone

Bladder

Urethra

Clitoral legs or crurae (2)

Perineal area

Opening to the vagina

Urethral opening

Relaxed blood vessels of inner labia

Inner labia

Outer labia

Clitoral shaft

Clitoral glans

Clitoral hood

These schematic drawings show the position and relationships of both internal and external organs and structures of the female pelvic region (a), with detail of the clitoris shown in (b). Compare with Figure 11.

759

Figure 13
Male Sexual Anatomy

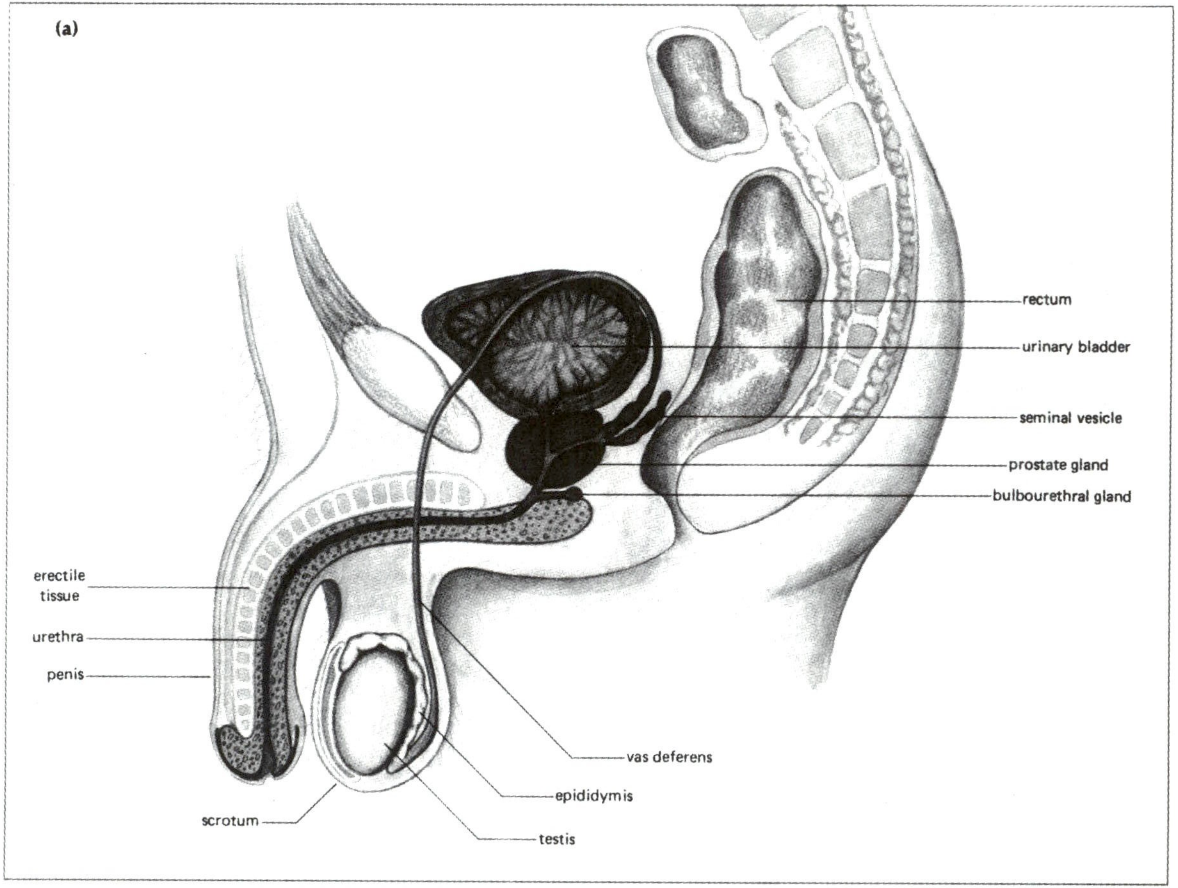

(a)

rectum

urinary bladder

seminal vesicle

prostate gland

bulbourethral gland

vas deferens

epididymis

testis

scrotum

erectile tissue

urethra

penis

Figure 14
Neural Pathways in Sexual Responses

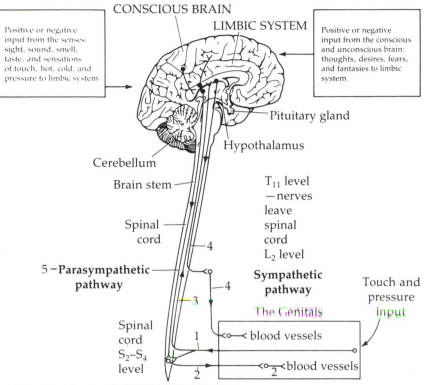

Positive or negative input from the senses: sight, sound, smell, taste, and sensations of touch, hot, cold, and pressure to limbic system

CONSCIOUS BRAIN

LIMBIC SYSTEM

Positive or negative input from the conscious and unconscious brain: thoughts, desires, fears, and fantasies to limbic system

Pituitary gland

Hypothalamus

Cerebellum

Brain stem

Spinal cord

T_{11} level —nerves leave spinal cord L_2 level

5 —Parasympathetic pathway

Sympathetic pathway

Touch and pressure input

The Genitals

Spinal cord S_2–S_4 level

blood vessels

blood vessels

Neurons 1 and 2 produce REFLEXOGENIC AROUSAL

a. A reflex arc occurs between the sensory neuron (1) and a motor neuron (2) of the-parasympathetic pathway.

b. The parasympathetic impulses (2) cause blood vessels in the genitals to dilate—vasocongestion.

PSYCHOGENIC AROUSAL

Neuron 3. The sensory pathway transmits neural impulses to the limbic system and cerebral cortex. (If processed as pleasurable, this impulse will increase vasocongestion via the sympathetic and parasympathetic pathways.)

Neuron 4. The sympathetic pathway causes vasoconstriction and reduces vasocongestion. This pathway is probably always firing to some degree (tonic activity). When signals entering the limbic system are pleasurable, activity in this pathway decreases, lessening vasoconstriction and increasing vasocongestion. If input to the limbic system is unpleasurable, sympathetic activity increases, reducing vasocongestion.

Neuron 5. Parasympathetic impulses are activated by pleasurable input from the limbic system, increasing vasocongestion.

Summary:

Psychogenic erection and lubrication probably arise from inhibition of the sympathetic and facilitation of the parasympathetic pathway.

Reflexogenic erection and lubrication involve a reflex arc independent of the limbic system.

Under normal circumstances, all three pathways may be operating and the relative activity of each determines the final outcome, vasocongestion or no vasocongestion.

Source: Norman A. Scherzer, Ph.D., Essex County College, Department of Biology.

Figure 15
The Psychophysical Sexual Response Cycle

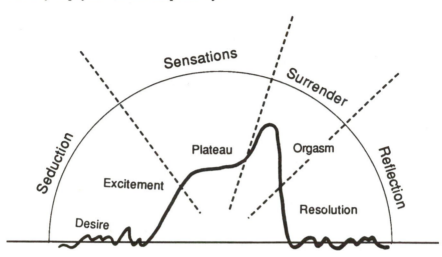

This diagram combines the standard physiological sexual response cycle described by Wilhelm Reich, William Masters, and Virginia Johnson Masters, with the desire phase described by Helen Singer Kaplan and the psychological model proposed by David Reed.

Figure 16
Gender Components

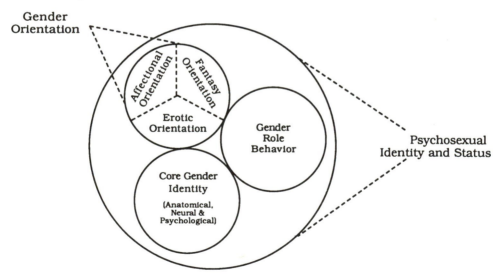

This model illustrates one way of integrating the components of psychosexual development.

762

Figure 17
The Kinsey Six Scale

HETEROSEXUAL AND HOMOSEXUAL BEHAVIOR AND FANTASIES

0	1	2	3	4	5	6
Exclusively heterosexual behavior	Incidental homosexual behavior	More than incidental homosexual behavior	Equal amount of heterosexual and homosexual behavior	More than incidental heterosexual behavior	Incidental heterosexual behavior	Exclusively homosexual behavior

Ambisexual behavior

To present the results of their surveys of the sexual behaviors of American men and women, Alfred Kinsey and his colleagues devised a continuum scale, running from 0 for a person who has been exclusively heterosexual in his or her behavior and sexual fantasies to 6 for a person whose sexual behavior and fantasies have always focused on persons of their own gender.

Figure 18
Stayton's Panerotic Potential Model

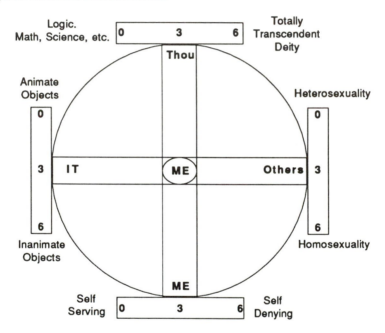

William Stayton has suggested a model of gender and sexual orientations that broadens the focus of the Kinsey Sexual Orientation Scale and Fred Klein's Sexual Orientation Grid, by acknowledging the possibility that individuals can find erotic nurturance and intimacy in almost anything in the universe.

Figure 19
The First Week of Pregnancy

(b) Detail of egg production in one ovary, fertilization, and implantation

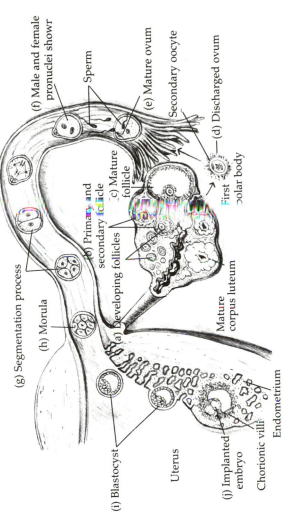

(g) Segmentation process

(h) Morula

(f) Male and female pronuclei shown

Sperm

(e) Mature ovum

Secondary oocyte

(d) Discharged ovum

First polar body

(c) Mature follicle

(b) Primary and secondary follicles

(a) Developing follicles

Mature corpus luteum

(i) Blastocyst

Uterus

(j) Implanted embryo

Chorionic villi

Endometrium

Primordial germ cells, egg nests on the surface of the ovary, begin developing, on average, two weeks before ovulation. A few follicles start but usually only one matures and ovulates. Check Chapter 4 and Figures 4.4 and 6.7 for genetic details of this development. If the egg is fertilized, it continues down the fallopian tube, hopefully to implanting 5 to 7 days later in the uterine lining.

Several primordial germ cells, egg nests just below the surface of the ovary, begin development on average two weeks before ovulation. As this cluster of primordial germ cells matures, all but one is reabsorbed. A single egg follicle matures and one egg is ovulated. If the egg is fertilized in the fallopian tube, it begins cell division and passes down the fallopian tube, possibly implanting in the uterine wall five or six days later.

765

Addendum for the New Expanded Edition

ablatio penis Surgical removal of the penis (*qv*). This surgery is one component in the treatment of a male-to-female transsexual (*qv*); some transsexuals who cannot afford or otherwise qualify for professional sex reassignment surgery may attempt self-castration. This surgery is also used in treatment of cancer of the penis. The term may also refer to accidental damage to the penis that results in its loss.

ABP *See* androgen-binding protein.

ACT UP (AIDS Coalition to Unleash Power) A decentralized, activist group founded in New York in 1987 in response to the urging of Larry Kramer. ACT UP seeks to influence government policy on the AIDS epidemic through use of the media and confrontational direct action strategies, including civil disobedience. Chapters can be located through the gay press (*qv*), gay groups, and HIV/AIDS service organizations.

adrenarche A term increasing used to indicate the onset of early pubertal secondary sex characteristics (*qv*) stimulated by hormones (*qv*) from the adrenal glands (*qv*).

AFP *See* alpha fetoprotein.

AIDS Coalition to Unleash Power *See* ACT UP.

aliphatic acids Aromatic chemicals, produced by sexually mature primate (*qv*) females including women, that have a pheromone (*qv*) effect as a sexual attractant for males.

alpha fetoprotein (AFP) A protein normally produced by a fetus and not found in adults, which is often produced by males with testicular cancer. Assay of AFP can be used to monitor the effectiveness of therapy. A high AFP titer in a fetus may indicate a spinal cord anomaly.

androgen-binding protein (ABP) A protein produced by the sustentacular cells (*qv*) of the testes (*qv*) under the stimulation of FSH. ABP binds testosterone (*qv*) and the ABP-testosterone complex stimulates sperm production.

androgen disorders in women A relatively new health concern focusing on the role and assumed importance of maintaining a low, normal cycle of androgenic hormones in both pre- and postmenopausal women. Between menarche (*qv*) and menopause (*qv*), a woman's adrenal glands produce a steady low amount of androgens (*qv*) at the same time the ovaries secrete androgens in a cycle that matches the estrogen cycle. In women with normally high levels of testosterone (*qv*), the spike of estrogen (*qv*) and testosterone may bring them into the androgen ranges of low-testosterone males. While the effects of androgens in males are well documented, research on their effects on women before and after menopause is just beginning. In Europe, post menopausal women are often given concurrent estrogen and androgen. The contraceptive hormone pill, anti-androgen drugs, and synthetic steroid hormones that suppress adrenal (*qv*) activity are used to treat women with abnormal high androgen levels. *See also* congenital virilizing adrenal hyperplasia.

anovulatory bleeding Dysfunctional uterine bleeding due to failure of an ovarian follicle (*qv*) to develop to the point of ovulation (*qv*) and corpus luteum (*qv*) formation. This arrested development subjects the endometrium (*qv*) to continuous estrogen (*qv*) stimulation causing it to shed in an irregular pattern instead of shedding over a 4 to 7 day period. This often occurs at the start of puberty (*qv*) or near menopause (*qv*) when ovarian function is starting up or diminishing. Rarely, this condition is caused by a corpus luteum which fails to degenerate, prolonging the secretory phase of the endometrium. Treatment involves hormonal manipulation.

anterior commissure A bundle of neuronal fibers that connects the right and left hemispheres of the cerebral cortex, primarily the two temporal lobes, in the mammalian brain; reported by Allen and Gorski to be smaller in homosexual men than in heterosexual men, and 12 percent larger in females than in males. Based on tentative but growing evidence, on average, homosexual men differ from heterosexual men in their visuospatial abilities, verbal fluency, and patterns of lateralization—the assignment of behavioral and cognitive functions to right and left hemispheres. The anterior commissure is not known to be associated with sexual behaviors or activities, and experts doubt that its fiber tracts would be responsive to adult hormonal changes. Resources: L. S. Allen and R. A. Gorski. 1991. Sexual dimorphism of the anterior commissure and massa intermedia of the human brain. *Journal of comparative neurology.* 312:97–104. C. Hooper. 1992 (October). Biology, brain architecture, and human sexuality. *Journal of N.I.H. Research.* 4:53–59.

azidothymidine (AZT) (Addition) Recent research indicates it may be ineffective in delaying the onset of AIDS for those already infected with HIV. AZT has been shown to be very effective in reducing the transmission of HIV infection from a pregnant HIV positive woman to her fetus.

baculum *See* os penis.

blastocyst cell cloning or twining Separation of eight or more cells in a morula (*qv*), followed by transfer to the uteruses of surrogate mothers (*qv*) to produce clones or genetically identical multiple offspring. This technique is used in breeding endangered animal species. The term *blastocyst* is a misnomer in this context.

blastocyst cell sampling Micromanipulation of an eight cell morula (*qv*) growing in tissue culture following in vitro fertilization (*qv*) to remove a single cell which is then grown in tissue culture to produce sufficient cells to allow genetic testing. Meanwhile, the remaining cells are temporarily frozen until the health status can be ascertained. If the embryonic mass has no known genetic defects, it can be transferred to a uterine cavity that has been made receptive to implantation (*qv*) and gestation (*qv*) by hormone manipulation. The term *blastocyst* is a misnomer in this context.

blighted twin A fetus (*qv*) in a multiple pregnancy which fails to develop, dies early, and is retained within the uterus until the surviving fetus is delivered. *See also* fetus papyraeus.

bottom/top Terms used primarily in the gay/lesbian community and by sadomasochism (*qv*) practitioners to indicate polarity of sexual dominance within relationships. While "bottom" generally corresponds to "M" and "top" to "S," the terms do not always imply S/M activities. Among lesbians, bottoms are not necessarily femmes, nor are tops butches. *See also* butch/femme.

bride A woman at her marriage, or just about to be married or very recently married. The word is most frequently applied during the wedding day and during the honeymoon. It comes from Old and Middle English, with a related but obsolete meaning of daughter-in-law. The word is remarkably specific, having no other uses in English, although it has attained extended metaphoric meanings, as in "The Church is the bride of Christ."

bridegroom *See* groom.

butch/femme A style of lesbian (*qv*) loving and self-presentation, characterized by complementarity of sexual, emotional, and social identities both within and outside relationships. To the outsider, "butch" women appear more stereotypically masculine, while "femme" women appear more feminine and able to pass as heterosexual. However, perceptions, experiences, and definitions of butch/femme among lesbians are far more diverse and complex. Resource: Joan Nestle, "Butch-Fem (Lesbian) Relationships," *Encyclopedia of Homosexuality,* ed. by Wayne R. Dynes, vol. 1, pp. 177–79 (New York: Garland, 1990). Butch is also sometimes used to designate macho or hypermasculine qualities in males.

Cathar, Catharism *See* Manicheanism.

child bride A prepubescent girl who is married at her parents' and others' behest, often for dynastic or economic reasons. *See* child marriage.

Clomid Trade name for clomiphene citrate.

clomiphene citrate (Clomid) A fertility drug which acts by combining with estrogen (*qv*) receptors and blocking them. This prevents negative feedback by estrogen to the hypothalamus (*qv*) and pituitary (*qv*) which results in the release of FSH (*qv*) and LH (*qv*) by the pituitary. FSH and LH then stimulate follicle (*qv*) development, ovulation (*qv*), and corpus luteum (*qv*) development.

cloning See blastocyst cell cloning or twining.

CMV See cytomegalovirus.

cohabitarche A term recently proposed by some Scandinavian sexologists to designate the beginning of cohabitation (*qv*) in a dyadic relationship.

computer sex *See* cybersex.

corpus callosum A claw-shaped thick bridge of millions of neural fibers that connect the right and left hemispheres of the mammalian brain. Gender dimorphic differences have been reported in the corpus callosum, especially in the splenium at the posterior of the corpus and in the anterior commissure (*qv*).

In terms of the onset of puberty (*qv*) and brain development, genes and sex hormones, often influenced by odors, are the controlling factor. In the early teen years, genes program the neuron fibers of corpus callosum to decrease in number. The onset of puberty stops this process. Because males enter puberty on average two years later than girls, the genes have two more years to reduce the males pathways. As a result, girls commonly end up with a larger corpus callosum and an enhanced communications between their cerebral hemispheres and more integrated patterns of thought. Males, on the other hand, have an increased ability to separate the functions of right and left cerebral hemispheres. Dimorphism in the corpus callosum is also connected with handed-ness, with the corpus callosum 11 percent larger in left handed and ambidex-trous persons.

Resources: C. M. McCormick and S. F. Witelson. 1991. A cognitive profile of homosexual men compared to heterosexual men and women. *Psychoneuro-endocrinology*. 16:459. C. M. McCormick, S. F. Wittelson, and E. Kingstone. 1990. Left-handedness in homosexual men and women: neuroendocrine impli-cations. *Psychoneuroendocrinology*. 15:69. M. Hines, *et al.* 1992. Cognition and the corpus callosum: Verbal fluency, visuospatial ability, and language lateralization related to midsaggital areas of the callosal subregions. *Behavioral Neuroscience*. 106:3.

cybersex A general term referring to sex-related services and products involv-ing personal computers. May include erotic computer games and visuals, sex-information and sex-talk computer bulletin boards, and virtual sex. Resource: P. Robinson and N. Tamosaitis. *The Joy of CyberSex: The Underground Guide to Electronic Erotica* (New York: Brady/Prentice-Hall, 1993).

cystitis (Addition) A bladder (*qv*) infection which is more common in women that men because of a shorter urethra (*qv*). Young sexually active females are more predisposed because of the transfer of bacteria during intercourse. Also common in older males who have difficulty emptying their bladder due to an enlarged prostate (*qv*). Symptoms include burning pain on urination and a fre-quent desire to urinate. The condition usually responds well to antibiotics.

cytomegalovirus (CMV) A member of the herpes (*qv*) family of viruses (*qv*) which produces marked enlargement of the cells it infects. CMV infection is common with over 50% of the U.S. population seropositive. The virus is a risk to the fetus if the pregnant woman has a reactivation and the virus is present in cervical and vaginal fluids at the time of delivery. The virus also crosses the placenta (*qv*). Damage to the fetus includes blindness, underdevelopment of the brain, and mental retardation. The virus is a major cause of blindness in immunocompromised individuals, i.e., AIDS patients.

D and C *See* dilation and curretage.

ddC *See* reverse transcriptase inhibitors.

ddI *See* reverse transcriptase inhibitors.

d4T *See* reverse transcriptase inhibitors.

dial-a-porn Services providing sexual stimulation through the telephone lines, for a fee. Upon dialing a particular number, callers may listen to prerecorded talk designed to be arousing. Other services provide direct contact with an individual who talks to the caller and simulates various fantasies, depending on the caller's preference. Dial-a-porn services are usually designed for gay or heterosexual men.

DNA probe Use of artificially copied radioactive labelled marker segments of genetic material to test for presence of specific defective genes in fetal chromosomal material obtained by amniocentesis (*qv*) or chorionic villi biopsy (*qv*).

doula Spanish term for a woman who assists a pregnant woman to prepare for childbirth and adjust in the two or three weeks after birth. A doula does not assist in the delivery as a midwife (*qv*) does.

drag A colloquial and sometimes humorous term for cross-dressing (*qv*), especially by male homosexuals as part of flamboyant display or a theatrical performance (a "drag show"). *See also* female impersonator, transvestism.

drag queen A female impersonator (*qv*) or a male homosexual (*qv*) who frequently wears women's clothes.

ecto-hormone An early, now obsolete term for pheromone (*qv*). The term, meaning "external hormone" (*qv*), was based on the similarities between hormones as chemical messengers secreted and circulated within the body of an animal and pheromones as chemical messengers secreted by an organism that then circulate between individuals. Since both hormones and pheromones affect physical and mental development, physiological processes, and behavior, the analogy is logical despite the obvious differences.

egg donation Implantation of donor ova (*qv*) with sperm (*qv*), or *in vitro* fertilized ova from another female. The donor may be a friend, relative, an anonymous female, or surplus zygotes (*qv*) left over from induced multiple ovulation (*qv*) of a woman undergoing IVF herself.

ejacularche A recently coined term used by Israeli and Scandinavian sexologists to designate the onset of ejaculation (*qv*) capacity in pubertal (*qv*) males; the male counterpart for menarche (*qv*) in a pubertal female. *See also* nocturnal emission.

emasculate To castrate (*qv*) a male; to deprive a man of his manly strength, potency, or vigor.

enterocele A protrusion of a herniated sac containing a loop of the small intestine into an area between the uterosacral ligaments; can be congenital or caused by trauma.

erotology The scholarly study of the erotic (*qv*), including erotica (*qv*) and pornography (*qv*).

essentialism The view that a person's sexual identity, gender orientation, and preferences are innate and intrinsic to a person's nature either as an individual or as a human being. The essentialist view also holds that human sexuality differs little, if at all, across history and among cultures, except where personal idiosyncrasy causes minor variations in a person's habits. In gay and lesbian writing, essentialism refers specifically to the view that homosexuality is identical or virtually the same in different cultures and throughout history. *See* constructionism.

estrogens, environmental Chemicals and pollutants that disrupt biological processes and emasculate (*qv*) or feminize males of a variety of species by mimicking the effects of naturally produced estrogens (*qv*). Among 50 some such agents are: DDT and its even more toxic metabolite DDE, kepone, heptachlor, dieldrin, mirex, tocophene, some polychlorinated biphenyls (PCBs), ingredients in common plastics, and breakdown products of common detergents. Resource: J. Raloff. 1994 (January 8 and 22). The gender benders; That feminine touch. *Science News*. 145:24–27, 56–59.

femme *See* butch/femme.

ferm An abbreviation proposed by biologist Anne Fausto-Sterling for a female pseudohermaphrodite (*qv*) with ovaries (*qv*) and male sex organs, penile-like clitoris (*qv*), and/or scrotal-like labia (*qv*). A ferm may result from some congenital (*qv*) malformation involving virilization (*qv*) or masculinization (*qv*) of a female fetus (*qv*) by endogenous male hormones, as occurs with a fetal adrenal (*qv*) tumor or congenital virilizing adrenal hyperplasia (*qv*), or by exogenous androgens administered to a miscarriage-prone mother. Fausto-Sterling advocates a minimum of medical intervention and social acceptance of ferms as one of at least five sexes. See also: herm, merm. Resource: A. Fausto-Sterling. The five sexes: Why male and female are not enough. *The Sciences*. 1993 (March/April), pages 20–25.

fisting, "fistfucking," "handballing" Insertion of fingers and hand into the rectum or vagina of a sexual partner. Several well-lubricated fingers outstretched and held together are inserted first, then the remaining fingers followed by the whole hand. When fully inside, the hand may be made into a fist. As with anal intercourse (*qv*), caution, mutual desire, and lubrication are required. Latex gloves should be used for protection against roughness and STDs. Fisting is rare, but practiced by men and women, heterosexual and homosexual.

gamete in fallopian tube transfer *See* GIFT.

gay press Journals, magazines, and newspapers published by, for, and about homosexuals and the gay/lesbian community. Sometimes also includes book publishing houses with gay or lesbian management and serving gay and lesbian readers.

gender bender A popular term for an environmental estrogen (*qv*) that more or less feminize male anatomical development and render males sterile. This phenomenon, well documented among reptiles and other endangered animal species, is complex and largely unexamined in humans. Another usage refers to any phenomenon that causes the viewer/listener/observer to doubt their perceptions of gender, as in the reference *"Mrs. Doubtfire* (or *Tootsie*) is a real gender bender of a movie."

genomic imprinting A phenotypic (*qv*) expression of some trait or disease that depends on maternal or paternal inheritance. A deletion on the proximal long arm of chromosome 15 produces Angelman syndrome when the deletion occurs in the maternal chromosome and Prader-Willi syndrome when it occurs on the chromosome 15 inherited from the father.

GIFT Acronym for gamete (*qv*) in fallopian tube (*qv*) transfer. A technique for resolving infertility in which sperm (*qv*) and ovum (*qv*) are introduced into the lumen of a fallopian tube where *in vivo* fertilization can occur. Often used when a laboratory is not available for *in vitro* fertilization and growth of the zygote (*qv*) prior to uterine transfer. *See also* ZIFT.

GnRH pump A mechanical pump used clinically to deliver 90 minute pulses of gonadotropin releasing hormone (GnRH) (*qv*) to stimulate release of FSH (*qv*) and LH (*qv*) by the pituitary (*qv*); used in the treatment of certain types of infertility in women.

gonadotropin-releasing hormone agonists (GnRH-Ag) Any one of several synthetic peptides which mimic the activity of GnRH (*qv*). When injected intramuscularly the level of the GnRH agonist remains elevated in the blood thereby obliterating the 90 minute pulse cycle of GnRH needed to stimulate the anterior pituitary. Without stimulation of the anterior pituitary (*qv*) there is no release of FSH (*qv*) and LH (*qv*), and no ovulation (*qv*). GnRH agonists are used to treat breast cancers which require estrogen for their growth. GnRH agonists are also administered to women who are being given fertility drugs in order to prevent interference from endogenous FSH and LH and thereby facilitate production of multiple ova.

graffiti (graffito, singular) Anonymously authored statements, sayings, poems, invitations, jokes, etc., written on publicly viewed surfaces, particularly walls and stalls of public toilets. Graffiti can be traced from ancient times and were found on the walls in Pompeii. Obscene themes are common, e.g., "Here I sit all broken hearted/Came to shit but only farted"; "Necrophilia is a dying art." Resource: Allen Walker Read, *Classic American Graffiti* (Waukesha, WI: Maledicta Press, 1977, orig. printed 1935).

groom A man newly married or about to be married. The word is most often applied only during the wedding. The older form is *bridegroom,* which combines Anglo-Saxon *bryd* with *guma,* "man" (which is cognate with Latin, *homin-,* also meaning *man*). The second *r* in *bridegroom* is due to confusion with or substitution of *groom,* which derives from an Old French word meaning servant. So *bridegroom* does not mean "servant of the bride" or "one who prepares or grooms her," but means "the bride's man." It is one of the rare examples in English where the male role is linguistically secondary to the female.

herm In classical studies, a herm is a stone phallus veneration of male generative principle and male domination over women. Also, an abbreviation proposed by biologist Anne Fausto Sterling for a true hermaphrodite (*qv*), an individual with gonadal tissue of both sexes in ovotestes (*qv*) or one ovary (*qv*) and one testes (*qv*), with resultant male, female, or intersex (*qv*) sexual anatomy. Most herms have 46,XX karyotype (*qv*), are chromatin positive (*qv*), and best raised as females. Fausto-Sterling advocates a minimum of medical intervention and social acceptance of herms as one of at least five sexes. See also: merm, ferm. Resource: A. Fausto-Sterling. 1993 (March/April). The five sexes: Why male and female are not enough. *The Sciences* (New York Academy of Sciences). 20–25.

homosexuality and the brain See INAH-3; anterior commissure; suprachiasmatic nucleus.

homosexuality, biology of Neuroanatomical studies of the structural differences in the INAH-3 (*qv*) center of the hypothalamus, the anterior commissure (*qv*), the suprachiasmatic nucleus (*qv*), and massa intermedia (*qv*), suggest that biological forces, including hormones (*qv*), genetically controlled hormone receptors, neurotransmitters (*qv*), and their neuroreceptors, act early in fetal life and globally to establish a brain architecture that differs among women and homosexual and heterosexual men. Several family history studies and research on the twins and siblings of male homosexuals also suggest that there is a significant familial or genetic component in some male homosexuality and that for some homosexual men, a marker gene inherited on the X chromosome through the maternal line is linked with their sexual orientation; see Xq28.

Implicit in the results of studies linking biological factors, homosexual orientations with genes, familial tendencies, neuroanatomical differences, neural cross-coding, and prenatal hormones is the conclusion that these factors may well operate in all sexual orientations, be they homosexualities, heterosexualities, or bisexualities. Resources: R. C. Pillard, J. Poumadere, and R. A. Carretta. 1992. A familial study of sexual orientation. *Archives of Sexual Behavior*. 11(6):511–17. D. H. Hamer, *et al*. A linkage between DNA markers on the X chromosome and male sexual orientation. *Science*. 1993 (July 16). 261:321–27. J. M. Bailey and R. C. Pillard. 1991 (December). A genetic study of male sexual orientation. *Archives of General Psychiatry*. 48:1089–96. J. M. Bailey, R. C. Pillard, M. C. Neale, and Y. Agyei. 1993 (March). *Archives of General Psychiatry*. 50:217–23. Pillard, R. C., and J. D. Weinrich. 1986 (August). Evidence of familial nature of male homosexuality. *Archives of General Psychiatry*. 43:808–12. W. Byne and B. Parsons. 1993 (March). Human sexual orientation: The biologic theories reappraised. *Archives of General psychiatry*. 50:228–39. F. I. Whitam, M. Diamond, and J. Martin. (1993). Homosexual orientation in twins: A report on 61 pairs and three triplet sets. *Archives of Sexual Behavior*. 22(3):187–205. LeVay and D. H. Hamer. Evidence for a biological influence in male homosexuality. *Scientific American*. 1994 (May). 44–49. W. Byne. The biological evidence challenged. *Scientific American*. 1994 (May). 50–55.

homosexuality, genetics of *See* homosexuality, biology of.

HPG axis *See* hypothalamic-pituitary-gondotropic axis.

hypothalamic-pituitary-gonadotropic (or **gonadal**) **(HPG) axis** The cycle of sex hormone production, both stimulatory and inhibitory, that involves the hypothalamus (*qv*), anterior pituitary (*qv*), and gonads (*qv*) and affects all sexual development, differentiation, and behavior in mammals. At puberty, genetic and environmental factors start the physiological sequence with cyclic or tonic production of gonadotropin-releasing hormone (GnRH) (*qv*) in the hypothalamus and extrahypothalamic neural centers. GnRH activates production of follicle stimulating (FSH) (*qv*) and luteinizing (LH) hormones (*qv*), in the anterior pituitary.

In women, FSH and LH are responsible for ovarian follicle (*qv*) growth, secretion of estrogens (*qv*) and progesterone (*qv*) during the ovarian cycle, and for ovulation (*qv*). Negative feedback by estrogen and progesterone shuts down the production of FSH and LH as well as the release of GnRH. In men, FSH and LH stimulate respectively production of androgen binding protein (*qv*) and testosterone (*qv*), both of which are needed for sperm production. Rising levels of sperm cause the sustentacular cells of the testes to release inhibin which blocks the release of FSH. Testosterone level is maintained by negative feedback inhibiting the release of GnRH and LH. Sex hormones from the ovaries, testes, and adrenal glands affect all sexual development, differentiation, and behaviors.

Also known as brain-testicular, brain-ovarian, or brain-gonadal axis.

idiopathic hypogonadotropic hypogonadism (IHH) A rare syndrome in males that suppresses puberty. Males with this syndrome develop normally during pregnancy, apparently because the mother supplies enough gonadotropic hormones (*qv*) to stimulate the fetal gonads and masculinize their sex organs. After birth the lack of gonadotropins leaves their testes inactive. Affected males appear normal at birth, with no obvious physical or mental defects. Their childhood development is also normal, except that without the surge of testosterone (*qv*), puberty never starts. Males with IHH score significantly lower than control males on the spatial relations subtest of the Wechsler Adult Intelligence test and on the block design subtests of the Differential Aptitude test. Results were more severe in males with the least amount of testosterone. Males with an acquired form of this syndrome show no differences from control males if their loss of testosterone onsets after puberty.

IHH *See* idiopathic hypogonadotropic hypogonadism.

INAH-3 The third of four minute circuits found in the interstitial nucleus of the anterior hypothalamic region (*qv*) of the hypothalamus (*qv*) which appears to be involved in sexual attraction to women, being well-developed in heterosexual males and poorly developed in heterosexual women. The lack of development of the INAH-3 region in homosexual males approximates that of heterosexual women.

Resources: S. LeVay. A difference in hypothalamic structure between heterosexual and homosexual men. *Science*. 1991 (August 30). 253:1034–37. S. LeVay. *The Sexual Brain*. Cambridge: MIT Press, 1993. S. LeVay and D. H. Hamer. Evidence for a biological influence in male homosexuality. *Scientific American*. 1994 (May). 44–49. W. Byne. The biological evidence challenged. *Scientific American*. 1994 (May). 50–55. See also: L. S. Allen and R. A. Gorski. 1992 (August). Sexual orientation and the size of the anterior commissure in the human brain. *Proceedings of the National Academy of Science, USA. Neurobiology*. 89:7199–7202.

Institute for the Advanced Study of Human Sexuality An educational institution accredited by the State of California to offer several graduate degrees exclusively in sexology (*qv*). Incorporated as a private nonsectarian graduate school in 1976, the Institute includes a comprehensive collection of sexological and erotological materials in various media, housed in 11 specialty libraries. Address: 1523 Franklin Street, San Francisco, CA 94109. A precursor of the Institute, known as the National Sex Forum, developed the Sexual Attitude Restructuring Workshop (*qv*).

interstitial nuclei of the anterior hypothalamic (INAH) region Four minute neural circuits, each about the size of a grain of sand, in the anterior hypothalamic region. Allen, Gorski and others have reported the second and third INAH are gender dimorphic; LeVay has reported that gender orientation-related differences in the INAH-3 (*qv*) center. See also: sexually dimorphic region; suprachi-asmatic nucleus; anterior commissure; corpus callosum.

life-style *See* sexual life-style.

Lolita A prepubescent female judged especially heterosexually or erotically attractive by an older person. From the novel by Vladimir Nabokov.

Lolita complex Persistent sexual attraction in an older male for pubescent or prepubescent females.

lymphotrophic Any agent that either stimulates or inhibits the activity of lymphoid cells.

Manicheanism A religion of third century AD and later that spiritualized the struggle between good and evil on this earth as a eternal battle between the god of light and the god of dark. Based on older Persian doctrines of Zoroastri-anism, Manicheanism spread through the Roman Mediterranean, and was early declared a heresy by the Catholic Church. St. Augustine of Hippo was a youth-ful adherent to Manicheanism, and scholars detect signs of its influence in his later Christian writings.

Although it did not flourish after the fifth century, Manicheanism survived in Europe in medieval sects of the Bogomils, Cathars, and Albigensians, among others. Of notable importance in medieval Manicheanism, to which the generic term Catharism is often given, is the doctrine that human beings were created not by God the Father, but by the demiurge Ialdabaoth who formed humankind from dirt and filth and therefore inescapably tainted with his own evil. In Provençal Catharism of the first centuries of this millennium, procre-ative and reproductive sexuality were believed merely to propagate an intrinsi-cally evil status quo from which no grace nor salvation is ever possible. Ac-cordingly, the Cathar spiritual elect forswore all forms of sexuality, fertile heterosexual intercourse in particular. Accused of heresy and sodomy, Catha-rism was destroyed as an organized sect in the Albigensian crusades of 1208. Relics of Catharism remained scattered in Europe and can be found at a dis-tance today in various modern churches of Satan, the Ordo Templi Orientis, and Crowleyism.

For the orthodox, Manicheanism, Catharism, and modern Satanism are per-versions of Christian, especially Roman Catholic, rites and rituals that blas-pheme and traduce true faith. For their adherents, Manicheanist religions pro-vide a dualist explanation for Good and Evil that sees a cosmic war between coequal deities of Good and of Evil for whom the soul of humankind is a central prize. Some practitioners hold that Good cannot lodge in meek, passive acceptance of Earthly evil, especially evils propagated by organized Christian churches, and so adore symbols of Eternal Opposition to Christianity. Other practitioners hold that sexuality is a primal spiritual good, whose repression by organized Christianity represents only one face of clerical evil. Catharist rejection of all forms of sexual intercourse has reappeared in writings by some modern anti-sex feminists.

massa intermedia The massa intermedia, a neuronal fiber structure that crosses the third ventricle between the two thalami, was found in 78 percent of the females and 68 percent of the males examined by Allen and Gorski. Among subjects with a massa intermedia, the structure was an average of 53 percent larger in females than in males. Inclusive of all subjects studied and allowing for overall male-female differences in brain size, the massa was a mean of 76 percent larger in females than in males. Resource: L. S. Allen and R. A. Gorski. 1991. Sexual dimorphism of the anterior commissure and massa intermedia of the human brain. *Journal Comparative Neurology.* 312:97–104.

mate As a noun, *mate* refers to a person's committed sexual and social partner without reference to the partner's gender. By extension, the word also means good friend, buddy, or co-worker (e.g., shipmate). In biology and animal husbandry, the term means copulatory partner, whether self-selected by the animals or provided by the breeder, without necessary reference to the relationship's duration. Sometimes it is used in anthropomorphic parallel for long-term animal bonding. The verb *to mate* is typically restricted to more or less sexual coupling for both humans and animals. *See* mating.

menotropins (Perganol) An ovarian stimulant used to induce fertility, consisting of a mixture of FSH (*qv*) and LH (*qv*). HCG (*qv*) is given the day before menotropins. In females it is used to correct anovulatory (*qv*) cycles which are not due to primary ovarian failure. In males with primary or secondary hypogonadotropic hypogonadism (*qv*) it is used in combination with HCG to stimulate spermatogenesis. It is used to induce the production of multiple ova, when administered for a week or more, which can then be harvested for IVF (*qv*).

menstrual suppression Inhibition of the normal menstrual cycle (*qv*) in a female resulting from exposure to subliminal chemical messengers or pheromones (*v*) contained in the urine of a strange male. Production of gonadotropic releasing hormone (GnRH) (*qv*) by the hypothalamus is apparently inhibited by the subliminal odor of a pheromone contained in the male's urine. Inhibition of GnRH production results in a failure of the pituitary to produce follicle stimulating (*qv*) and luteinizing hormones (*qv*), which in turn results in inhibition of the menstrual cycle. No human parallel has been observed.

merm An abbreviation proposed by biologist Anne Fausto-Sterling for a male pseudohermaphrodite (*qv*) with testes and female sex organs. A mild insufficiency of androgens (*qv*) from testes (*qv*) may result in a small penis (*qv*), hypospadia (*qv*), vulviform scrotum (*qv*); severe testicular androgen (*qv*) deficiency allows persistence of the Mullerian or paramesonephric ducts (*qv*), hence a vagina (*qv*) and uterus (*qv*) develop with external female anatomy. In cryptorchid hypospadia hermaphroditism (*qv*), the testes are undescended and the penis has an open urinary sinus instead of an enclosed urethral tube, which gives ambiguous or intersexual (*qv*) external genitalia. Fausto-Sterling advocates a minimum of medical intervention and social acceptance of merms as one of at least five sexes. See also: ferm, herm. Resource: A. Fausto-Sterling, "The Five Sexes: Why Male and Female Are Not Enough," *The Sciences*. 1993 (March/April), pages 20–25.

Metrodin Trade name for urofollitropin.

microinsemination A form of *in vitro* artificial insemination (*qv*) using micromanipulation to insert a single sperm (*qv*) through the zona pellucida (*qv*) into an ovum (*qv*) in cases when the male's sperm are not capable of penetrating the zona pellucida and membrane of the ovum to fertilize it. The resulting zygote (*qv*) is allowed to divide and then is transplanted into either the fallopian tube or uterus. See GIFT, ZIFT

mixoscopic zoophilia Sexual pleasure or stimulation experienced while watching animals copulate. *See also* bestiality.

musk The noblest perfume of venery, musk has been valued as a perfume and sexual attractant since ancient times. Musk is not a very scientific or specific term; it covers many similar aromatic secretions and end-products of hormone breakdown. The main male hormone, testosterone (*qv*), has a musky scent. Smegma (*qv*), the waxy secretion of sebaceous (*qv*) glands around the rim of the glans of the penis (*qv*) and clitoris (*qv*), starts off colorless and odorless. Only when bacteria go to work on it under the foreskin (*qv*), does it develop a cheesy consistency and begins to smell musky.

    Sweat from the arm pit, saliva, and urine contain several pheromones derived from the breakdown of androgens (*qv*) that are often described as "musky," although some women describe their aromas as "flowery." The "musky" scent of male semen probably comes from the prostatic fluid that makes up a third of semen (*qv*) and contains testosterone and its metabolic products. Human urine also contains delta-2-androsterone-one-17, a "musky" male hormone metabolite. In the late 1970s, George Dodd isolated, purified, and synthesized one of the compounds in human sweat, alpha-androstenol. A relative of musks and androstenone, this scent smells almost exactly like sandalwood, an ancient and still popular sexy perfume.

    Women also produce musky secretions derived from their armpit sweat, and similar secretions from the Bartholin's glands (*qv*) in the moist inner labia and vulva, from the Skene's glands (*qv*) along the urethra, and in aliphatic acid (*qv*) secretions of the vagina. Women also produce "musky" smegma around the glans of the clitoris and minor labia. In addition, progesterone (*qv*), a hormone that increases in the two weeks between release of the egg and the menstrual flow, contributes another characteristic odor.

Many different animals and plants produce musky scents as part of their reproductive processes. Originally harvested from the musk glands of the musk deer in the Himalayan Mountains, musk is widely used as a base in expensive perfumes, and mimicked by chemists who synthesize similar aromatic products.

nerve sparing operation A form of radical prostatectomy (*qv*) that does not sever or damage the ejaculatory (*qv*) and erectile (*qv*) nerves to the penis (*qv*); developed in the early 1980s. *See also* transurethral resection of the prostate.

Nonoxynol-9 A spermicide (*qv*); when used vaginally it reduces the risk of HIV infection as well as other STDs (*qv*), such as gonorrhea (*qv*) and chlamydia (*qv*). However, excessive dosage may cause vaginal ulcers and thus increase the risk of infection.

oligohydraminos A marked reduction in amniotic fluid (*qv*) often due to fetal renal failure or blockage of the fetal urethra (*qv*). Amniotic fluid is made in large part by the fetal kidneys and excreted into the amniotic cavity (*qv*).

Perganol Trade name for menotropins.

polyhydraminos A condition in which there is an excess of amniotic fluid (*qv*); often due to either inability of the fetus (*qv*) to swallow secondary to anencephaly, or to a congenital blockage of the upper gastrointestinal tract. The fetus normally swallows and eliminates several hundred milliliters of fluid per day.

postmenopausal pregnancy The use of estrogen and progesterone hormones (*qv*) to facilitate implantation and maintain pregnancy of a transplanted embryonic mass in the uterus of a postmenopausal (*qv*) woman. The *in vitro* fertilized (*qv*) donated ovum (*qv*) is transplanted to the uterine (*qv*) cavity or fallopian tube (*qv*) in hopes of normal gestation. *See* GIFT, ZIFT.

prostate disease See prostate cancer; benign prostatic enlargement.

prostate specific antigen (PSA) A protein produced in large quantities by a carcinogenic or hypertrophied prostate (*qv*); used in the diagnosis of prostatic cancer (*qv*) and as a marker to determine the effectiveness of treatment.

prostatectomy, radical The complete removal of the prostate (*qv*) and surrounding tissue. This operation often results in both erectile (*qv*) and ejaculatory (*qv*) failure. New surgical procedures have been somewhat successful in reducing or eliminating such failures.

PSA See prostate specific antigen.

pubertal development, Tanner's stages of The process of physical sexual maturation, known as puberty (*qv*), involves more than a dozen different secondary sex characteristics (*qv*) developing over a period of 10 years.

Body size on average is taller and heavier in males than in females, with the age of onset between 10.5 and 16 years. Thinning and balding of head hair is more common in males than in females. Development of facial hair coincides with puberty in males and is only noticeable in females in their later years. The neck of males is on average thicker and longer with a larynx that is one-third larger; the female neck is rounder and shorter.

Development of the gonads (*qv*), whose hormones control many secondary sex characteristics, is a major landmark of puberty. Growth of the testes (*qv*) and scrotum (*qv*) usually extends from age 10 to 13.5, with growth of the penis (*qv*) about a year behind. The ovaries (*qv*) become functional somewhere between age 10 and 16.5, with the onset of menstruation (*qv*) a major landmark. The body hair of males is genetically controlled and more evident on chest and arms. Development of pubic hair (*qv*) is triangular in pattern, with the apex pointing upward; onset is between ages 10 and 15. Development of female public hair shows a straight line across the top with onset between ages 8 and 14. There is no gender difference in the axillary (underarm) hair which develops on average about two years after pubic hair.

Male breasts (*qv*) are rudimentary with development of female breasts starting between ages 8 and 13. During puberty the male chest enlarges in every dimension while the female chest becomes smaller and narrower. The male shoulders become broader and squarer; the female shoulders, rounder and sloping. Muscle mass in males becomes more obvious; in females, it is largely hidden beneath fatty tissue. The arms in males become longer, thicker and have a straight "carrying angle;" the female arms are bent somewhat out at the elbows. Male legs are straight from hip to foot; female legs bent slightly at the knees.

rare male advantage (or effect) A technical term from animal genetics referring to enhanced reproduction by those males whose phenotype (*qv*) and genotype (*qv*) are statistically rare in a population. The effect is partly a result of the rare male attracting more females than more commonplace males. Well documented in *Drosophila,* the laboratory fruit fly, this phenomenon is not known to have a human equivalent.

reverse transcriptase inhibitors Any agent that prevents the enzyme reverse transcriptase (RT) from converting RNA (*qv*) into DNA (*qv*). It is the primary target for most drugs directed against the HIV virus (*qv*) responsible for AIDS. The primary drug of choice is AZT (*qv*). As of this printing, three other inhibitors of RT have been approved for patients who cannot tolerate AZT, or who are infected with AZT resistant strains of HIV. These drugs are ddI, ddC, and d4T. *See also* AZT.

sexarche A recently coined term used by Scandinavian and Israeli sexologists to designate the onset of sexual intercourse (*qv*) or coitus (*qv*).

sex differences in the brain Anatomical and physiological differences between brains and related neural structures in men and women. In their gross anatomy, male and female brains are virtually identical, but laboratory medical and biochemical studies show that sex differences may exist in small, functionally defined regions of the brain. These include differences in neural centers specifically controlling the release of luteinizing hormone (*qv*), which occurs cyclically in the female, but not male, mammalian brain. Some, but not all, observers report neural dissimilarities pertaining to visualization ability and language skills. *See also* corpus callosum, INAH-3, massa intermedia, suprachiasmic nucleus. Resources: D. Kimura. Sex differences in the brain. *Scientific American*. 1992 (September). 267(3): 118–25. C. Tavris. *The Mismeasure of Woman*. New York: Simon and Schuster, 1992.

sex industry A neutral, nonjudgmental term used to cover businesses that provide erotic stimulation for money. Generally includes: prostitution (*qv*), writing and production of erotica/pornography (*qv*), massage parlors (*qv*), erotic performances of various types, and dial-a-porn (*qv*) telephone services.

sexually dimorphic nucleus An alternate term for the INAH-3 region (*qv*) in the hypothalamus (*qv*), as used by Allen and Gorski; the term is also used to refer to several different nuclei or circuits in the brain which differ in size and/or structure between men and women. Resource: C. Hooper. 1992 (October). Biology, brain architecture, and human sexuality. *Journal of N.I.H. Research*. 4:53–59.

sexually dimorphic region In general, any region of the brain or other organ that develops with gender-specific differences. The INAH-3 (*qv*) circuit in the hypothalamus (*qv*), the anterior commissure (*qv*), the suprachiasmatic nucleus (*qv*), corpus callosum (*qv*), and massa intermedia (*qv*) appear to develop differently in males and females, although the functional significance of these differences in size and shape remains to be ascertained. Resource: L. S. Allen and R. A. Gorski. 1992 (August). Sexual orientation and the size of the anterior commissure in the human brain. *Proceedings National Academy of Science, USA. Neurobiology*. 89:7199–202.

sex work(er) A neutral, nonjudgmental term used to cover a variety of sexually stimulating services provided for money. Generally includes: prostitution (*qv*), striptease (*qv*), modeling or acting for erotica/pornography (*qv*), erotic dancing or other performance, massage parlor (*qv*) work, and staffing dial-a-porn (*qv*) telephone lines. *See also* sex industry.

stew An Old English term, still in use today, for a brothel (*qv*) or house of prostitution (*qv*).

suprachiasm(at)ic nucleus This region of the hypothalamus (*qv*), which controls circadian rhythms (*qv*), has been reported larger, on average, in homosexual men than in heterosexual men. Resources: D. F. Swaab and M. A. Hoffman. 1990. An enlarged suprachiasmatic nucleus in homosexual men. *Brain Research*. 537:141. D. F. Swaab and M. A. Hoffman. 1988. Sexual differentiation of the human hypothalamus: Ontogeny of the sexually dimorphic nucleus of the preoptic area. *Developmental Brain Research*. 44:314.

sustenticular cells *See* Sertoli cells.

Tanner's stages of pubertal development *See* pubertal development, Tanner's stages of.

telephone sex *See* dial-a-porn.

transgene Replacement of a defective gene (*qv*) with a normal gene from another species of animal or plant using gene splicing techniques.

transurentral resection of the prostate (TURP) A technique used to treat an obstructed prostatic urethra (*qv*) due to benign prostatic hyperplasia (*qv*). A hollow tube is inserted into the penile urethra. Within the tube are fiber optics for visualization of the prostate and a snake-like cutting instrument for shaving off pieces of the prostate, and a suction device for removal of the prostatic tissue. A new epithelial lining will regenerate soon after surgery. This technique does not damage nerve tissue and normal sexual function is not affected.

tunica vaginalis The scrotal end of the vaginal process (*qv*) which becomes the outer covering of the testes (*qv*).

TURP *See* transurethral resection of the prostate.

urofollitropin (Metrodin) A gonadotropin (*qv*), pure FSH (*qv*), isolated from the urine of postmenopausal (*qv*) women; used to stimulate follicular growth and maturation in women with secondary ovarian failure.

uterine prolapse The bulging of the uterus (*qv*) into the vagina (*qv*) when the cardinal ligaments, which support the uterus, weaken. Often a pessary (*qv*) ring is inserted into the vagina to hold the uterus in place; surgery is another option.

vagina (Addition) In educated American speech, vagina is often used as a synonym for any or all of the female genitalia, particularly the vulva (*qv*), so that the medical and anatomical term has achieved additional meanings. The word is sometimes also used as a polite substitute for terms deemed vulgar or obscene, such as *cunt* or *pussy* and even the medical term *vulva*. The term joins a host of others that refer to women's sexual and reproductive anatomy, like *pudendum muliebre,* that derive from classical Latin and are euphemisms in the service of delicacy.

From its classical Latin derivation, *vagina* means sheath, husk, hull, or scabbard for a sword. Its use for the female reproductive channel links it to the entire metaphoric family of men's words that assimilate female sexual anatomy to receptive cavities, in this case, for a weapon housed in it. English slang possesses very close equivalents for the Latin original, such as *slit, box,* and *gash,* but the original colloquial meaning of *vagina* has long been forgotten through its adoption by modern medicine, science, and genteel English speech. Likewise, Latin *pudendum* translates as English *shameful* or *scandalous* (*muliebre,* of the woman) but considerable linguistic distance separates modern English from the anti-female and moralizing Latin meanings. Because today we no longer understand Latin, Latinisms can serve us today as neutral, polite, or technical words, even though the original Latin meant exactly the same as the English slang term it is replacing. Resource: Mildred Ash. The vulva: A psycholinguistic problem. *Maledicta.* 1980. 4(2): 213–19.

velamentous insertion of the umbilical cord Abnormal placement of the umbilical (*qv*) arteries and veins within the fetal membrances as opposed to traveling together within the umbilical cord. This may be lethal to the fetus (*qv*) if the velamentous vessels are within the portion of the fetal membranes extending over the cervix (*qv*), since they can be compressed or ruptured during labor (*qv*).

ventromedial nuclei of the hypothalamus (VMN) A sexually dimorphic (*qv*) region of the hypothalamus (*qv*) containing as small group of neurons, influenced by estrogen, progesterone, serotonin, norepinephrin, oxytocin and other neurotransmitters, that regulates the induction of lordosis (*qv*).

virtual sex Erotic experience delivered through sophisticated electronic simulation. Currently not state of the art, but envisioned in the foreseeable future. To experience virtual sex, an individual would don special goggles, earphones, and gloves or—in the most sophisticated designs—a bodysuit, all wired to a nearby computer, where software would supply interactive electronic stimuli. Three-dimensional images would give the illusion of being with another person (say), while audio would provide background sounds and voices, and the body coverings supply electronically the illusion of tactile sensations. Resource: Phillip Robinson and Nancy Tamosaitis, *The Joy of CyberSex: The Underground*

Guide to Electronic Erotica (New York: Brady/Prentice-Hall, 1993). *See also* cybersex.

virus Small infectious agents consisting of a strand of DNA or RNA (retrovirus) (*qv*) surrounded by a protein shell called a capsid. Subunits of capsids called capsomeres are geometrically arranged. Some viruses have their capsid covered by an outer lipid and protein envelope. Viruses cannot reproduce on their own; they require the use of their hosts organelles for the production of new viral proteins.

See cytomegalovirus, Epstein-Barr virus; herpes simplex I and II; herpes zoster; human immunodeficiency virus; human T-lymphotrophic virus (I, II, III, and IV); simian T-cell lymphotrophic virus-I.

VMN *See* ventromedial nuclei of the hypothalamus.

VNO *See* volmeronasal organ.

volmeronasal organ (VNO) The VNO system, which sits in the roof of the vertebrate mouth below the more advanced *main* olfactory system in the upper reaches of the nose, is part of the *accessory* or secondary olfactory system. Discovered by the Danish anatomist Ludwig Levin Jacobson in mammals in 1811 and in newborn humans by Potiquet in 1891, the paired VNO are elongated narrow sacs located at base of the nasal septum and immediately above the roof of the mouth. In the VNO sacs, a sensory epithelium similar to that of the olfactory neurons on the upper reaches of the nasal passages begins decoding the pheromone (*qv*) messages and converting this information into electrical impulses.

Pheromone messages from the VNO are fed through a maze of neurons directly to a tiny organ called the accessory olfactory bulb (AOB) buried just below the frontal lobes of the brain. After some additional decoding here, the messages go directly to the amygdala, an area in the limbic system (*qv*) concerned with a variety of behavioral mechanisms and emotional responses. From the amygdala (*qv*), the signals are fed to the hypothalamic circuits that regulate hormones and control the body's basic Four F's—feeding, fighting, fleeing, and sex.

The VNO is essential to reproduction in lower mammals and especially reptiles. Without its response to odors, production of key sex hormones would be disrupted. Without trigger signals from the VNO the hypothalamus (*qv*) would not start, stop, and cycle the production of a releasing hormone that regulates production of several hormones in the pituitary gland (*qv*).

Xq28 A genetic marker region at the end of the long arm of the X chromosome (*qv*) associated in preliminary research in 1993 with homosexual orientation in some males. While the pioneering research by Dean Hammer and associates at the National Cancer Institute awaits confirming studies, the early research suggests that the Xq28 genetic region is inherited through the maternal line and shared by male homosexuals within the maternal line. The nature of the effects of genes in the Xq28 region and the role of these genes in contributing to the biological tendencies associated with male homosexuality remains to be determined. See also: homosexuality, biology of. Resource: D. H. Hamer, *et al.* A linkage between DNA markers on the X chromosome and male sexual orientation. *Science.* 1993 (July 16). 261:321–27.

ZIFT Acronym for zygote in fallopian tube transfer, a reproductive technology that involves in vitro fertilization (*qv*) of an ovum (*qv*) with frozen or fresh semen (*qv*), followed by transfer of the resulting zygote (*qv*) to the fallopian tube (*qv*) whence it passes into the uterine cavity and hopefully implants in the uterine endometrium (*qv*). *See also* GIFT.

zona drilling A reproductive technology in which a microscopic hole is drilled in the zona pellucida (*qv*) surrounding the unfertilized ovum (*qv*) to allow a single sperm (*qv*) to enter and fertilize the ovum. See microinsemination.

zoophilia *See* bestiality.

zygote in fallopian tube transfer *See* ZIFT.

About the Contributors

ROBERT T. FRANCOEUR, Ph.D., has authored or edited over twenty books on human sexuality and evolution, including *Utopian Motherhood: New Trends in Human Reproduction* (1970), *Eve's New Rib: Twenty Faces of Sex, Marriage and Family* (1972), *Hot and Cool Sex: Cultures in Conflict* (1974), and *The Future of Sexual Relations* (1974). In recent years, he has focused his synoptic and synthesizing skills on writing college textbooks: *Becoming a Sexual Person* (1982, 1984, 1991) and *Taking Sides: Clashing Views on Controversial Issues in Human Sexuality* (1987, 1989, 1991). He has contributed chapters to reference works such as *The Handbook of Marriage and the Family, Contemporary Families and Alternative Lifestyles: Handbook on Research and Theory,* and the multi-volume *Handbook of Sexology,* as well as chapters in over fifty other books. Francoeur has taught human sexuality, human embryology, and human genetics since 1965 at Fairleigh Dickinson University, served as President of the Eastern Region of the Society for the Scientific Study of Sex from 1988 to 1990, and as an editorial consultant for the *Journal of Sex Research.* He was a 1974 SUNOCO Science Lecturer for the National Science Teachers Association, recipient of the 1974 annual award of the Educational Foundation for Human Sexuality, and is a fellow of the Society for the Scientific Study of Sex. An adjunct professor in the graduate Program in Human Sexuality at New York University, Francoeur has also taught in that university's Sexuality in Two Cultures program in Copenhagen. His most recent project is *The International Encyclopedia of Sexuality,* scheduled for publication by Continuum in 1995.

MARTHA CORNOG, M.A., M.S., a linguist and librarian, is an active member and past national secretary of the Society for the Scientific Study of Sex. She has served as an editorial assistant for the *Journal of Sex Research,* and authored technical papers and reports in information science and sexual linguistics. For several years she coordinated an adjunct training program for teaching pelvic exams at Hahnemann University. She has worked as special projects coordinator for an information industry trade association and is currently employed at the American College of Physicians. Cornog is coauthor of the reference and resource manual *For Sex Information: See Librarian* (Greenwood, 1995), and contributing editor to *Human Sexuality: An Encyclopedia* (Bullough and Bullough, eds. Garland, 1994) including a major appendix on sexological research.

TIMOTHY PERPER, Ph.D., is a Philadelphia-based independent sex researcher and writer. Originally trained as a biologist, with his doctorate from City University of New York, he has been studying human courtship and flirtation for over a decade, assisted in part by full support grants from The Harry Frank Guggenheim Foundation. He is author of *Sex Signals: The Biology of Love* (1985) and numerous articles on human and animal sexual behavior. He served as associate editor (1985–1988) and book review editor (1984–1988) for the *Journal of Sex Research,* and is currently chair of the Scientific Committee of the Eastern Region of the Society for the Scientific Study of Sex. He is a longtime member of the Society for the Scientific Study of Sex and an elected fellow of the American Anthropological Association. His work on courtship and flirtation has received extensive national and international media coverage and he is recognized as an expert on the ethology and ethnography of human courtship behavior and symbolism. Perper is coauthor of the reference and resource manual *For Sex Information: See Librarian* (Greenwood, 1995), and a Contributing Editor to *Human Sexuality: An Encyclopedia* (Bullough and Bullough, eds. Garland, 1994).

NORMAN A. SCHERZER, Ph.D., has taught human sexuality, human anatomy and physiology, and related subjects at Essex Community College and at Rutgers, the State University (Newark) for over twenty years. He has lectured widely on AIDS and has been a longtime active member of the Society for the Scientific Study of Sex. He has served as a consultant for several textbooks in human sexuality and presented papers at national and regional meetings of the Society for the Scientific Study of Sex, the American Association of Sex Educators, Counselors, and Therapists, and at the International Congress of Sexology in Heidelburg in 1988. Scherzer also teaches as an adjunct professor in the Master's and Doctoral Program in Human Sexuality at New York University and is Clinical Associate Professor at the University of Medicine and Dentistry of New Jersey.

Of related interest from Continuum

Rob Baker
The Art of AIDS: From Stigma to Conscience

The first comprehensive exploration of the aesthetic dimensions of the AIDS epidemic. "Rob Baker was one of the first—and one of the very best—to write seriously about pop culture in the Sixties. Now he gives us an essential, remarkably concise, analytic yet personal, and constantly readable overview of plague art."—LINDA WINER, *New York Newsday*

252 pages 0-8264-0653-X $24.95

Sigmund Freud
Psychological Writings and Letters
Edited by Sander L. Gilman

The classic works on sexuality, infant sexuality, dreams, psychological procedure, telepathy, jokes, and the uncanny—also featuring a selection of Freud's correspondence.

324 pages 0-8264-0723-4 $14.95 paperback; 0-8264-0722-6 $29.50 hardcover

James Vaughn Kohl and Robert T. Francoeur
The Scent of Eros: Mysteries of Odor in Human Sexuality
Foreword by William E. Hartman and Marilyn A. Fithian

This is the first book to look into the fascinating new discoveries about the odors that control human sexual behavior. "This is science at its best, with adventure, ideas, and lots of facts."—HELEN FISHER

"On the trail of the wild pheromone, Kohl and Francoeur lead us on a treasure hunt through history, literature, and scientific data."—GINA OGDEN

276 pages 0-8264-0677-7 $24.95

Donald McCormick
Erotic Literature: A Connoisseur's Guide

"Truly a connoisseur's guide, *Erotic Literature* serves as both a reminder of the centrality of sexuality to human experience and a guide to its artistic celebration in world literature."—*Wilson Library Bulletin*

288 pages 0-8264-0594-0 $14.95 paperback

John Money
Reinterpreting the Unspeakable: Human Sexuality 2000

A ground-breaking and essential manual for the complete interviewer in clinical practice. "Dr. John Money was one of my principal influences when I was writing *Sexual Personae*. He is the leading sexologist in the world today."
—CAMILLE PAGLIA

252 pages 0-8264-0651-3 $29.95

Dr. Ruth Westheimer
Dr. Ruth's Encyclopedia of Sex

An authoritative work on all facets of sexuality, for home or school library, edited by the internationally famous sex educator.

"Entries address all aspects of sexuality—from mechanics and biology to cultural, legal, and religious concerns. The range of material covered in this volume is impressive."—*Publishers Weekly*

312 pages 7″ x 10″ 0-8264-0625-4 $29.50

Available at your bookstore or from the publisher: **The Continuum Publishing Company, 370 Lexington Avenue, New York, NY 10017 1-800-937-5557**